LEXICON UNIVERSAL ENCYCLOPEDIA

Lexicon Publications, Inc.
New York, N.Y.

ISBN 0-7172-2021-4

Library of Congress Catalog Card Number 87-17594

PHOENICIAN		ETRUSCAN
EARLY HEBREW	Qq	EARLY LATIN
EARLY ARAMAIC		CLASSICAL LATIN
EARLY GREEK	MODERN LATIN	GERMAN-GOTHIC

Q

Q/q is the 17th letter of the English alphabet. Both the letter and its position in the alphabet were derived from the Latin alphabet, which in turn derived it from the Greek by way of the Etruscan. The Greeks took the letter, which they called *koppa,* from the Semitic sign *qoph,* but it had disappeared by the time of the classical Greek alphabet. The Etruscans, however, used *Q/q* for the sound of *k* before *u,* a usage that was perpetuated in early Latin. In Latin the combination *qu* developed into a single sound, *kw.* As a result, in modern English, *Q/q* is always followed by *u* and is usually pronounced *kw* as in *quake, quick,* and *equal.* However, in some words, mostly taken from French, *qu* has the sound of *k,* as in *grotesque, oblique,* and *queue.*   I. J. GELB AND R. M. WHITING

Q fever

Q fever, caused by *Coxiella burnetti,* is different from other rickettsial diseases of humans in that it is commonly acquired by inhalation of contaminated aerosols rather than from an insect bite. Ticks may also transmit the disease. The usual reservoir of infection is livestock—cattle, sheep, and goats. The disease normally begins abruptly about 9 to 20 days after respiratory exposure and is characterized by headache, fever, chills, cough, aching muscles, severe malaise, and, in about half the cases, pneumonia. Its duration ranges from a few days in young persons to one to three weeks in older persons. Fatalities are rare; antibiotics provide effective therapy.
    PETER L. PETRAKIS

Qaddafi, Muammar al-   [kah-dah'-fee, moo-ahm-mahr' ahl]

After coming to power in 1969, Libyan leader Muammar al-Qaddafi negotiated the removal of U.S. and British military bases and took control of the Libyan assets of foreign oil companies. In 1973 he introduced a so-called cultural revolution in Libya and created workers' committees to supervise all aspects of economic and social life. A militant pan-Arab nationalist, Qaddafi supports Palestinian guerrilla groups and has attempted to merge Libya with Egypt, Syria, Tunisia, Chad, and Morocco.

Muammar al-Qaddafi, b. June 1942, became head of state of Libya after leading a bloodless coup that overthrew the Libyan monarchy on Sept. 1, 1969. Since coming to power, he has led his country on a course of radical revolution at home and abroad, drawing international attention during the 1980s for his lavish support of radical causes.

Qaddafi, a devout Muslim, was born into a nomadic desert family and attended a religious primary school. Before being expelled from a Fazzan secondary school for pan-Arab political activity he made several friends who later joined him in toppling King IDRIS I. His only travel abroad before the coup was the 9 months he spent in a training course in England after graduating (1965) from the Libyan Military Academy.

The Qaddafi regime was popular in its early years, as it undertook serious efforts to distribute the country's large oil revenues equitably and to assert Libya's independence and nonalignment. By the mid-1970s, however, signs of disaffection appeared as Qaddafi embarked on a radical revolution abroad and at home, imposing the utopian socialist dictates of his Green Book, which outlines his revolutionary philosophy. Although Qaddafi formally resigned his government positions, the revolutionary system of popular authority proved to be little more than a facade for his growing personal power. His commitment to unifying the Arab world, his opposition to Israel and the United States, and his efforts to export his idiosyncratic revolution met with little success, but he was accused of meddling in the internal affairs of other African nations, supporting various terrorist groups, and ordering the assassination of Libyan dissidents abroad. Qaddafi's alleged support of international terrorism led the United States, on Apr. 15, 1986, to launch air attacks against Libyan targets it linked to terrorist activities.   LISA ANDERSON

Bibliography: Bianco, M., *Gadafi,* trans. by M. Lyle (1975); First, R., *Libya: The Elusive Revolution* (1974); Wright, J., *Libya* (1982).

Qashqai   [kahsh'-ky]

The Qashqai are a Turkish-speaking tribe of pastoral nomads in southern Iran. They migrate between winter pastures near the Persian Gulf and summer pastures on the Iranian Plateau. Their origins are unclear. First mentioned in the 18th century, the Qashqai were possibly formed by a union of groups of TURKMEN and perhaps of KURDS and Lurs.

Like other Iranian tribes, the Qashqai have three structural levels: families formed into a section; sections formed into a clan; and the whole tribe, traditionally headed by an ilkhan, who in the past was appointed by the shah. The Qashqai have shown greater cohesion than most Iranian tribes. In World War I they were defeated by the British, and in 1930 they were disarmed by the shah. In 1943 they refused to surrender German agents to the British because their tribal code forbade it. Their numbers were greatly reduced during a 1962–63 rebellion against the Iranian land-reform law. At last count they numbered about 500,000.   BRIAN SPOONER

Bibliography: Allgrove, Joan, *The Qashqā'i of Iran* (1976); Oberling, Pierre, *The Qashqā'i Nomads of Fars* (1974).

Qatar   [kah'-tahr]

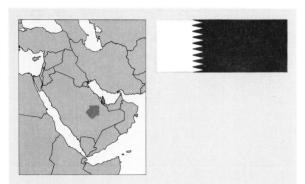

Wealth from the petroleum industry has transformed Doha from a center of pearling and piracy to the capital and busy port city of the sheikhdom of Qatar. New buildings, such as the clock tower (left) and Government House (right), have been built along the waterfront.

STATE OF QATAR

LAND. Area: 11,000 km² (4,247 mi²). Capital and largest city: Doha (1983 est. pop., 190,000).

PEOPLE. Population (1985 est.): 301,000. Density (1985 est.): 27 persons per km² (71 per mi²). Distribution (1985): 90% urban, 20% rural. Annual growth (1975–80): 5.2%. Official language: Arabic. Major religion: Islam.

EDUCATION AND HEALTH. Literacy (1980): 40% of adult population. Universities (1986): 1. Hospital beds (1980): 1,862. Physicians (1980): 307. Life expectancy (1975–80): women—58.3; men—54.8. Infant mortality (1985): 38 per 1,000 live births.

ECONOMY. GNP (1983): $7.6 billion; $27,000 per capita. Labor distribution (1980): agriculture and fishing—10%; industry, services, and commerce—70%; government—20%. Foreign trade (1983): imports—$1.5 billion; exports—$3.3 billion; principal trade partners—Japan, France, West Germany, Italy, United States, Spain, United Kingdom. Currency: 1 Qatar riyal = 100 dirhams.

GOVERNMENT. Type: emirate. Legislature: none. Political subdivisions: none.

COMMUNICATIONS. Railroads (1986): none. Roads (1982): 1,287 km (800 mi). Major ports: 2. Airfields (international, 1986): 1.

The sheikhdom of Qatar occupies a peninsula that juts into the PERSIAN GULF from the Arabian Peninsula (see ARABIA). On the south it shares an undemarcated border with Saudi Arabia and the United Arab Emirates (UAE). A former British protectorate, Qatar became independent on Sept. 1, 1971.

LAND, PEOPLE, AND ECONOMY

Qatar's terrain is barren, with low, sandy hills reaching a high point of only 105 m (345 ft) at Aba Al-Bawl Hill, in the south.

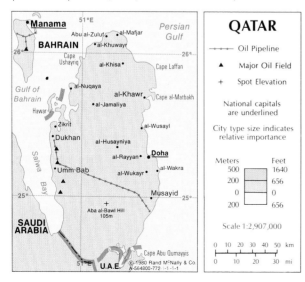

Rainfall averages less than 127 mm (5 in) per year, and the average annual temperature range is about 21°–27° C (70°–80° F). The principal natural resource is petroleum.

About 70% of Qatar's inhabitants live in DOHA, the capital. Less than 30% of the population are indigenous to Qatar, although the majority are Arabs. The expatriot population includes Palestinians, Indians, Pakistanis, and Iranians. Almost all Qataris are orthodox Sunni Muslims of the Wahhabi sect (see WAHHABISM). Petroleum wealth has financed the expansion of health and education services. The University of Doha was founded in 1973.

Qatar, a member of the ORGANIZATION OF PETROLEUM EXPORTING COUNTRIES, derives 90% of its income from petroleum. Despite a decline in oil revenues in the 1980s due to a drop in world oil prices and the Iran-Iraq war, the value of petroleum exports still exceeds that of imports. Oil wealth has been used to establish fertilizer, flour, and cement industries. Natural gas, limestone, and clay are also exploited. Some 80% of all jobs in the private sector are held by foreign nationals. Although only 1% of the land is cultivated, due to the lack of water, Qatar grows most of its own vegetables. It is largely self-sufficient in fish and exports small quantities of food to other Persian Gulf states.

GOVERNMENT AND HISTORY

Qatar is a traditional monarchy, ruled by Emir Khalifa bin Hamad al-Thani. The Basic Law of 1970 allows for a council of ministers, led by an appointed prime minister who is currently the sheikh himself, and a 30-member advisory council. When it became independent in 1971, Qatar elected not to join the United Arab Emirates. No legal political parties exist in the country, although some clandestine opposition groups are active.

Originally dominated by the nearby island of Bahrain in the Persian Gulf, Qatar fell under the rule of the Ottoman Turks from 1872 until World War I. It became a British protectorate in 1916, during the war, and began exporting petroleum in 1949. In 1971, Qatar became independent under Sheikh Ahmad bin Ali al-Thani. Five months later he was deposed in a bloodless coup by his cousin, Sheikh Khalifa bin Hamad al-Thani. In 1976 all petroleum interests were nationalized. Qatar is an active member of the Gulf Cooperation Council. It signed a bilateral defense agreement with Saudi Arabia in 1982 and has supported Iraq in the Iran-Iraq war.

IRA M. SHESKIN

Bibliography: Anthony, J. D., *Arab States of the Gulf* (1975); Long, D., *The Persian Gulf* (1976); Mallakh, R. E., *Qatar: Energy and Development* (1985); Nafi, Z. A., *Economic and Social Development in Qatar* (1983); Zahlan, R. S., *The Creation of Qatar* (1979).

Qattara Depression   [kah-tah'-ruh]

The Qattara Depression, an arid, sandy basin in the LIBYAN DESERT in northern Egypt, drops to Africa's second lowest point, 133 m (435 ft) below sea level. The eastern tip of the basin lies 56 km (35 mi) south of El Alamein on the Mediterranean coast. About 275 km (170 mi) long and 110 km (70 mi) wide, the basin has an area of about 19,500 km² (7,500 mi²). It receives less than 50 mm (2 in) of rain annually, but any precipitation creates marshy conditions. In 1942 the British Eighth Army, under Gen. Bernard Montgomery, stopped the German advance into Egypt in the Qattara Depression during the Battle of El ALAMEIN.

quadrant

The quadrant has been used from medieval times to measure the altitude of the Sun or a star and for surveying. In its simplest form the quadrant is a flat plate in the shape of a quarter circle marked with a degree scale along the curved side; two sights are attached to one of the radial sides and a plumb bob hangs from the apex. Many sophisticated variants were developed by Arabic and medieval astronomers. On some the time could be read directly from the position of the Sun or specified stars.

Observatories used large wall-mounted quadrants for precise astronomical measurements from Ptolemaic times through the 1700s. The seaman's reflecting quadrant, invented by John Hadley (1682–1744) of England, was the precursor of the modern sextant (see NAVIGATION). The quadrant was brought to its greatest accuracy by London instrument maker John Bird about 1750–70.   R. S. AND M. K. WEBSTER

quadratic function

An algebraic expression of the second degree is called a quadratic expression or function. It is a POLYNOMIAL in which the highest-power term is quadratic; that is, the exponent of this term is two. If the quadratic expression is set equal to zero it is called a quadratic equation. In standard form this is given as $ax^2 + bx + c = 0$. The solutions, or roots, of this equation are given by the quadratic formula

$$x = \frac{-b \pm \sqrt{b^2 - 4ac}}{2a}$$

The expression $b^2 - 4ac$ is called the DISCRIMINANT of the equation.

quadrilateral

A quadrilateral is a plane figure formed by four intersecting line segments. The points of intersection of the segments are called vertices. A line segment connecting either pair of nonadjacent vertices is called a diagonal of the quadrilateral. The most general quadrilateral—in which no sides are parallel—is called a trapezium. Specific types include the PARALLELOGRAM, the RECTANGLE, the SQUARE, and the TRAPEZOID.

Quadruple Alliance

Quadruple Alliance is the name of three European alliances formed in the 18th and 19th centuries. The first was formed (Aug. 2, 1718) by Austria, France, Britain, and the Dutch Republic to oppose Spain after the Spanish king PHILIP V seized Sardinia and Sicily, violating settlements concluded (1713–14) at the end of the War of the Spanish Succession (see UTRECHT, PEACE OF). The allies occupied Sicily and northern Spain and forced Spain to renounce all claim to Sicily and Sardinia. By the Treaty of The Hague (Feb. 17, 1720), Savoy surrendered Sicily to Austria in exchange for Sardinia.

The second Quadruple Alliance was formed toward the end of the NAPOLEONIC WARS by Britain, Prussia, Austria, and Russia, each of which pledged (Mar. 9, 1814) not to conclude a separate peace with Napoleon. The alliance was renewed at the Congress of Vienna (1814–15; see VIENNA, CONGRESS OF) after the final defeat of Napoleon. The parties then agreed to hold regular congresses to ensure the maintenance of the political status quo. The CONGRESS SYSTEM collapsed after Britain withdrew from the alliance in 1822.

The last Quadruple Alliance was established in 1834 when Britain and France went to the aid of ISABELLA II of Spain and MARIA II of Portugal, monarchs facing challenges from more conservative claimants to their thrones. The alliance defeated the pretenders in both countries.

quagga   [kwag'-uh]

The quagga, E. quagga, is an extinct zebra that once inhabited the steppes of southern Africa. Its stripes faded toward the rear of the body, so that the back was a solid yellowish brown. The last surviving quagga died in the Artis Zoo, Amsterdam, in 1883.

The quagga, Equus quagga, a type of ZEBRA once numerous in southern Africa, became extinct by 1883 because of a high demand for its hide. A member of the HORSE family, Equidae, it had typical zebra striping that was confined to the head, neck, and forequarters. Studies of protein and DNA fragments in quagga hides indicate that the animal was actually a variant of the plains zebra.   EVERETT SENTMAN

quail   [kwayl]

The California quail, Lophortyx californicus (male, foreground, and female, background), ranges from Baja California to British Columbia.

The name *quail* designates birds belonging to two divisions of the pheasant family, Phasianidae: the New World quail, subfamily Odontophorinae; and the Old World quail, subfamily Phasianinae, which also includes partridges.

Most New World quail are brightly marked and crested, and the two sexes are distinct in color. They lack spurs on their tarsi and have stronger bills than Old World quail. About 30 species are distributed from southern Canada to northern Argentina, ranging from deserts (for example, the scaled quail, *Callipepla squamata*) to cloud forests (the bearded tree quail, *Dendrortyx barbatus*). None is migratory and most are considered game birds.

The bobwhite, *Colinus virginianus*, a North American game bird, measures up to 28 cm (11 in) in length; the male has a white throat and bands across each side of the head. It is considered beneficial to farmers because its diet includes a wide variety of agricultural pests.

The Old World common quail, *Coturnix coturnix*, domesticated in Japan and other countries, often migrates in dense flocks. The sparrow-sized Chinese painted quail, *Excalfactoria chinensis*, is the smallest known gallinaceous bird—that is, a bird related to the domestic fowl.   GARY D. SCHNELL

Bibliography: Johnsgard, Paul A., *Grouse and Quails of North America* (1973); Rosene, Walter, *The Bobwhite Quail* (1969).

Quakers: see FRIENDS, SOCIETY OF.

qualitative chemical analysis

Qualitative analysis is the branch of chemistry concerned with the identification of the components of chemical substances, either pure or present in a mixture. Qualitative analysis answers the question "what?," whereas QUANTITATIVE CHEMICAL ANALYSIS answers the question "how much?"

Methodology. The methodology of qualitative analysis involves tests, which should be simple and direct and easily performed with readily available equipment, chemicals, and instruments. The results of the tests should be clear, reproducible, and easily interpreted.

Qualitative analysis frequently is used to identify (establish the chemical identity of) a pure substance, usually an organic chemical. This procedure requires the determination of several chemical and physical properties of the "unknown," followed by a search of published chemical and physical properties of known compounds. Identification of the unknown is accomplished when a "known" is found with identical chemical and physical properties. If such a "known" is not found, the unknown must be a newly identified substance.

Test results may be a reading from a particular instrument, an observation of some physical property (for example, the temperature at which the substance melts), or a chemical reaction. Such reactions attempt to cause the appearance or disappearance of a characteristic color or precipitate, the evolution or absorption of a gas, or the formation of a characteristic odor. If the test indicates the presence of a substance, it is called a positive test; if it indicates that the substance is absent, it is a negative test. The tests must be specific (giving a positive test for the substance in a mixture of chemical compounds), sensitive (able to detect a small quantity of the substance in a mixture), and free from interference from related species.

Sample Size. The amount of the material to be identified is an important consideration in qualitative analysis. The chemical methods listed below usually require milliliters (ml) of samples, and spot tests (described below) require less than 0.1 ml. Some of the instrumental techniques listed below operate with considerably smaller sample sizes; for example, excellent mass spectra (see MASS SPECTROMETRY) of an unknown sample may be obtained using less than 10^{-6} (one millionth) grams of material.

Systematic Inorganic Qualitative Analysis. Frequently, "qualitative analysis" is used in a limited sense to refer to a process for determining the presence or absence of about 25 metal cations in aqueous solution. Because of the complexity of identifying each of the metal cations with individual tests, the process of systematic inorganic qualitative analysis begins with tests for major groups of cations using group reagents.

The cation analysis scheme most frequently used today is based on the procedures developed by the German chemists Heinrich Rose (1795–1864) and Carl Remigius Fresenius (1818–97). The scheme involves the analysis of a solution that may contain 21 different metals, all in positive oxidation states (usually as positive ions, although some may appear in more than one oxidation state), plus the ammonium ion, NH_4^+. The qualitative analysis of anions (such as SO_4^{2-}, PO_4^{3-}, and $C1^-$) is carried out by a similar scheme but relies more often on specific individual tests.

Organic Qualitative Analysis. Because of the almost infinite number of possible organic compounds, a systematic approach that would end in a characteristic test for each is impossible. The process of organic qualitative analysis involves determining if the sample is a single, pure compound; determining its physical constants (including melting point, boiling point, and index of refraction); analysis for the presence of various elements; solubility tests; determination of the presence of functional groups (see ORGANIC CHEMISTRY); and, finally, the preparation and analysis of derivatives.

Spot Tests. A spot test is a procedure used to determine the presence or absence of a substance, organic or inorganic, by the use of a simple procedure—frequently a single step using a single reagent. In most cases, 0.5 milliliters or a few milligrams of a sample is required. The test is usually carried out on a porcelain (spot) plate or on a piece of filter paper. This procedure is useful for pure substances or simple mixtures when the presence of specific substances is in question.

Chromatography. Various types of CHROMATOGRAPHY enable the analyst to separate complex organic and inorganic mixtures by exploiting differences in adsorption and solubility. The methods used in chromatography range from the simple visual interpretation of paper chromatography to the complex instrumental analysis of high-pressure liquid chromatography (HPLC). These and other methods (column, thin-layer, gel, gas) of chromatography can provide both qualitative and quantitative data.

Physical Methods and Modern Instrumentation. Many inorganic and organic compounds may be identified by determining their physical properties without resorting to the chemical methodology of the inorganic and organic qualitative analysis schemes. The observation of some physical properties is simple (for example, color, odor, and solubility) whereas others (the results of the interaction with electromagnetic radiation of various energies—see SPECTROSCOPY) require complex instrumentation. Several of these methods are listed below.

sodium   strontium   potassium   barium   selenium   copper

The occurrence of certain metallic elements in a material can be determined easily and quickly by means of a flame test. The flame test simply involves dipping a clean platinum wire loop into a solution of the material to be tested and then holding the loop in the nearly colorless upper portion of the flame of a Bunsen burner. A color is imparted to the flame that is characteristic for a given element and serves as a qualitative test for its presence. Typical colors obtained in flame tests of various elements are shown.

Emission of Light. This area of spectroscopy examines the light emitted by atoms and molecules when excited under various conditions. Regardless of its chemical form, each element emits a characteristic set of spectral lines (light of certain wavelengths) when excited (see SPECTRUM and QUANTUM MECHANICS).

Absorption of Light. All substances absorb electromagnetic radiation (light) of certain energies or wavelengths. Colored substances absorb some visible light. Organic compounds absorb infrared light at wavelengths that are characteristic of the compound and its functional groups. Valuable information concerning the identity of a compound is obtained by the careful determination of its absorption of light at various wavelengths. Included in this area are ultraviolet, visible, and infrared spectroscopy.

Other Optical Methods. Pure liquids can be characterized on the basis of their refractive index (see INDEX OF REFRACTION) using a refractometer. Many other substances, frequently organic liquids or solutions, rotate the vibrational plane of POLARIZED LIGHT. With the use of the POLARIMETER the analyst may determine that the compound exhibits this property and the magnitude of the effect.

Interactions with Electricity. The voltage at which a substance in solution is reduced (gains electrons) is an important identifying characteristic. The instrument most frequently used to determine this property is called a POLAROGRAPHIC ANALYZER.

X-Ray Emission and Diffraction. Many substances emit X rays of characteristic wavelengths when they are bombarded with X rays of shorter wavelengths or by high-energy electrons. By analyzing the emitted X rays, the substance may be identified. The structure of many compounds in the solid state may be determined by the characteristic diffraction patterns that result upon exposure to X rays (see X-RAY DIFFRACTION).

Radiochemical Instrumental Techniques. Radioactive elements emit radiation of characteristic energies (see RADIOACTIVITY and RADIOCHEMISTRY). Other elements may be made radioactive by bombarding them with neutrons or other high-energy particles (activation analysis). These are among the most sensitive of all methods for the determination of the presence of individual elements.

Mass Spectrometry. Many pure organic compounds may be identified by the use of mass spectrometry. This instrumental technique most frequently involves ionizing the molecule in a vacuum and analyzing the resulting fragments using a combination of electrical and magnetic fields. This method alone may enable the analyst to determine the molecular weight and structure of the unknown.   NORMAN V. DUFFY

Bibliography: Hahn, Richard B., and Welcher, Frank J., *Inorganic Qualitative Analysis,* 2d ed. (1968); Kolthoff, I. M., and Elving, P. J., eds., *Treatise on Analytical Chemistry,* 17 vols. (1975–85); Nebergall, William H., et al., *College Chemistry with Qualitative Analysis,* 6th ed. (1980); Sorum, H., and Lagowski, J., *Introduction to Semimicro Qualitative Analysis* (1983); Szabadvary, Ferenc, *History of Analytical Chemistry* (1966).

Quanah: see PARKER, QUANAH.

quantitative chemical analysis

Quantitative analysis is that part of analytical chemistry which deals with determining relative amounts of one or more chemical constituents of a sample. In principle the analysis is simple; one measures the amount of each analyte (constituent of interest) in a known amount of sample. In practice, however, the analysis is often complicated by interferences among sample constituents, and chemical separations are necessary to isolate the analyte or remove the interfering constituents.

Quantitative analyses are carried out on small samples that are representative of larger amounts of the same material. Care must be taken to ensure that the small sample is representative of (identical in composition to) the larger amount.

A most demanding step in many analytical procedures is isolating the analyte, or separating from it those sample constituents which otherwise would interfere with its measurement. Some common separation methods are precipitation,

distillation, extraction into an immiscible solvent, and various chromatographic procedures. Loss of analyte during separation procedures must be guarded against. The purpose of all earlier steps in an analysis is to make the final measurement a true indication of the quantity of analyte in the sample. Many types of final measurement are possible, including gravimetric analysis, volumetric analysis, and the use of sophisticated instruments to measure a wide variety of optical, electrochemical, and other physical properties of the analyte.

GRAVIMETRIC ANALYSIS

Gravimetric analysis is one of the classical methods of quantitative analysis. In gravimetric analysis, determinations are made from weight measurements; the other classical method, volumetric analysis, involves adding a carefully measured volume of a reagent. Modern analysis also makes extensive use of instrumentation.

General Methods. A vital step in gravimetric analysis is the separation of the analyte from the rest of the sample as a pure substance—either the analyte itself or a chemical derivative of it. Separation may be accomplished by precipitation or volatilization. In precipitation methods a reagent (precipitant) is added that reacts chemically with the analyte to yield an insoluble product of known composition; this precipitate is isolated by filtration, then washed, dried or ignited, and weighed. In volatilization methods the analyte is quantitatively converted to a gas of known composition; the analysis is based on either the weight of the volatilized substance or the weight of the remaining residue. Most gravimetric methods are of the precipitation type.

After a representative sample has been weighed, dissolved, and, in some cases, treated to remove interferences, a gravimetric analysis usually proceeds by the following steps:

Addition of the Precipitant. Both purity and filterability (particle size) often depend on the conditions during precipitation, and a compromise may be necessary if conditions conducive to high purity result in a precipitate of poor filtration characteristics or vice versa. Ordinarily, a dilute solution of the precipitant is added slowly, with efficient mixing, to a hot solution of the sample until an excess is present.

Digestion of the Precipitate. After the precipitate is formed, it is allowed to "digest"—that is, to stand in contact with the hot mother liquor for an hour or longer. During digestion the precipitate undergoes a variety of aging processes, such as partial recrystallization, that result in larger particles and improved purity.

Filtration and Washing of the Precipitate. To reduce solubility loss, the solution is ordinarily cooled to room temperature before filtration. The choice of the proper porosity of filter paper or filter crucible depends on the nature of the precipitate, which may be crystalline, gelatinous, or a flocculated colloid, as well as on its particle size. Filtration and washing are performed together.

Drying, Igniting, and Weighing the Residue. A precipitate collected on paper must be ignited to destroy the paper before weighing. A precipitate collected on a filter crucible is simply dried or ignited at an appropriate temperature before weighing. Besides removing volatile wash liquid, heating often converts the precipitate to a more stable product of known composition, or better "weighing form."

Calculation of Results. Calculating the result of a gravimetric analysis requires only two measured weights, that of the sample and that of the final product derived from the sample. Usually, the final product is not the analyte itself but a species that contains the analyte or is chemically related to it. In either case, the weight of the analyte is obtained by multiplying the weight of the final product by a conversion factor.

VOLUMETRIC ANALYSIS

In volumetric analysis the analyte is determined by TITRATION. Unlike gravimetric analysis, in which an unmeasured excess of reagent is added to completely precipitate the analyte, a titration requires the accurately measured addition of reagent (titrant) needed to exactly react with all of the analyte. The titrant is added drop by drop until all the analyte has reacted. This step is the endpoint. Knowing the exact amount of titrant used allows the determination of the amount of analyte.

Volumetric methods are much more widely used than gravimetric methods because they are often as accurate, and usually more rapid and convenient; except for the analytical balance, only simple volumetric glassware (accurately calibrated burets, pipets, and volumetric flasks) is required.

A chemical reaction must meet the following criteria to serve as the basis of a titration: (1) The reaction must occur rapidly; otherwise, premature and uncertain indication of the endpoint occurs. Sometimes difficulties associated with slow reactions can be overcome by adding a catalyst to speed the reaction, or by adding a measured excess of the titrant and back-titrating with a suitable second titrant after the first reaction is complete. (2) The reaction must be both quantitative and stoichiometric; that is, the reaction must proceed to completion and no side reactions should occur. (3) Other substances in the sample solution should not react with the titrant or interfere with the titration reaction. (4) A method should exist to locate the endpoint, either by use of a suitable chemical INDICATOR or some instrumental method.

Calculating the result of a volumetric analysis is simple and based on the knowledge that, at the endpoint, the amount of titrant equals the amount of analyte. The units used are equivalents (see EQUIVALENT WEIGHT).   LAURANCE A. KNECHT

Bibliography: Brumblay, Ray, *First Course in Quantitative Analysis* (1970); Day, R. A., and Underwood, A. L., *Quantitative Analysis,* 5th ed. (1986); Wilson, Larry, *Introductory Quantitative Analysis* (1974).

Quantrill, William C.   [kwahn'-tril]

William Clarke Quantrill, b. Canal Dover, Ohio, July 31, 1837, d. June 6, 1865, was a Confederate guerrilla leader during the U.S. Civil War. His guerrilla bands burned and looted Union strongholds in Kansas and Missouri, diverting thousands of Union troops. On Aug. 21, 1863, Quantrill's Raiders pillaged Lawrence, Kans., killing more than 150 civilians. Mortally wounded by Union troops in May 1865, Quantrill died in prison in Louisville, Ky.

Bibliography: Castel, A. E., *William Clarke Quantrill* (1962).

quantum chromodynamics

In physics, quantum chromodynamics (QCD) is a theory that explains the strong nuclear force in terms of force carriers called GLUONS, acting between subatomic particles called QUARKS. Protons, neutrons, and other particles of the HADRON class are composed of quarks. In theory, there are six types, or ''flavors,'' of quarks, further characterized by three indistinguishable qualities referred to as ''colors.'' Color changes and quark grouping are manifestations of the strong nuclear force (see FUNDAMENTAL PARTICLES).

quantum electrodynamics

In physics, quantum electrodynamics (QED) is the theory that explains the electromagnetic force of electrons and other charged particles in terms of force carriers called photons. QED was developed in the 1920s and 1930s, based upon principles of electromagnetism, relativity, and quantum mechanics (see ELECTROMAGNETIC RADIATION).

quantum mechanics   [kwahn'-tuhm]

Quantum mechanics is the fundamental theory used by 20th-century physicists to describe atomic and subatomic phenomena. It has proven very successful in tying together a wide range of observations into a coherent picture of the universe.

While quantum mechanics uses some of the concepts of Newtonian mechanics, the previous description of physical phenomena, it differs fundamentally from the Newtonian description. For example, in Newtonian physics, quantities were believed to be continuously variable, able to take on any value in some range. An example is angular momentum, which, for a particle revolving in a circular orbit about some center of attraction, is proportional to the speed multiplied by the distance from the center. Because that distance could have any value in Newtonian mechanics, so could the angular mo-

mentum. In quantum mechanics, on the other hand, angular momentum is always restricted to certain discrete values, whose ratios are simple rational numbers.

An even more fundamental difference between quantum mechanics and previous physical theories is that probability enters in a basic way into how quantum mechanics describes the world. This is made evident by the ways that quantum mechanics and Newtonian mechanics deal with predictions of the future. For something described by Newtonian mechanics, such as the solar system, it is possible, if sufficiently accurate measurements are made at one time, to predict the future behavior of the system to arbitrarily great accuracy. For systems described by quantum mechanics, even one as simple as an atom with a single electron, precise prediction of future behavior is usually impossible. Instead, only predictions of the probability of various behaviors can be made. This can be illustrated by the description of an unstable radioactive nucleus. Quantum mechanics does not predict when the individual nucleus will decay, although if many similar nuclei are surveyed, one can predict what fraction will decay in any time interval. This novel feature of quantum mechanics, known as indeterminism, has been one of the things that has led some prominent physicists, such as Albert EINSTEIN, to resist it. Nevertheless, it appears to be an unavoidable feature of physics at the atomic and subatomic levels.

EARLY HISTORICAL DEVELOPMENT

Planck's Work. Quantum mechanics was developed over a period of thirty years, during which it was successively applied to several physical phenomena. The first use of quantum ideas was made in the analysis of how electromagnetic radiation is produced. This was done by the German physicist Max PLANCK in 1900. Planck was trying to account for the distribution, among different frequencies, of the radiation emitted by a hot object, such as the surface of the Sun. He found that to obtain results in agreement with observation, he had to assume that the radiation was not emitted continuously, as was previously believed. Instead, it was emitted in discrete amounts, which he called quanta. For these quanta, there was always a relation between the frequency f, and the amount of energy emitted E, of the form $E = hf$. Here h is a universal constant introduced by Planck, and now named after him. Planck's constant has the units of energy multiplied by time, known as action. Its numerical value is approximately 6.63×10^{-34} joule-seconds. The specific result of Planck's analysis was a formula expressing the amount of energy radiated at any frequency as a function of the temperature of the emitting object. This relation, the blackbody distribution, agrees accurately with observation (see BLACKBODY RADIATION).

Photons. In Planck's work, the nature of the quanta was rather mysterious. It was clarified by the work of Einstein, who in 1905 proposed that light itself was composed of individual packages of energy, which later came to be known as photons. Einstein also proposed that the frequency of the light is related to the energy of the photons composing it by Planck's formula. Einstein's theory of light quanta, which was rejected by many of his contemporaries, including Planck, was verified both by Robert Millikan's work on the PHOTOELECTRIC EFFECT, and by the discovery by Arthur Compton of the COMPTON EFFECT, or the scattering of photons by electrons.

Bohr's Theory. Another significant early use of quantum ideas was by Niels BOHR, who in 1913 showed that by assuming that the angular momentum of electrons in a hydrogen atom could only take on values that are an integer multiple of Planck's constant divided by 2π, he could derive accurate expressions for the frequencies of light emitted by the atom. Bohr's analysis implied that only certain energy values are possible for the electron in the atom, that there is a minimum value, and that in this minimum energy state, the electron cannot radiate energy. This result helped explain how the atom could be stable, and how all atoms of one element have the same chemical properties. However, it proved impossible to extend Bohr's ideas directly to atoms more complex than hydrogen. Also, the strange blend of Newtonian and quantum ideas left physicists uneasy about the supposedly basic principles of their science.

FORMS OF QUANTUM MECHANICS

The development of actual quantum mechanics—the mathematical theory—took place in the years 1924–27. Initially there were two seemingly different approaches: matrix mechanics, invented by Werner HEISENBERG, and wave mechanics, invented by Erwin SCHRÖDINGER. However, it was soon shown that these were distinct aspects of a single theory, which came to be known as quantum mechanics. This unified version was invented by Paul DIRAC. In matrix mechanics, physical quantities such as the position of a particle, are represented not by numbers, but by mathematical quantities known as matrices (see MATRIX). Matrix mechanics is most useful in dealing with situations in which there is a small number of relevant energy levels, such as a particle with definite angular momentum in a magnetic field.

Wave Mechanics. Wave mechanics is more useful in a situation where the number of energy levels is infinite, as with an electron in an atom. It is based on the idea originally suggested by Louis deBROGLIE, that particles such as electrons have waves associated with them. The wavelength, λ, of the wave is related to the mass, m, and speed, v, of the particle by the relation $\lambda = h/mv$. This implies that for electrons moving at 10% the speed of light, such as those produced by some television tubes, the wavelengths are about 10^{-10} meters, or about the distance between atoms in a crystalline solid. This prediction of deBroglie was verified by Clinton Davisson and by George Thomson, who were able to pass the electron waves through metallic crystals, and so produce diffraction patterns similar to those produced by X rays.

The Schrödinger Equation. In 1925, Erwin Schrödinger developed an equation, now bearing his name, which describes how a wave associated with an electron or other subatomic particle varies in space and time as the particle moves under the influence of various forces. This equation has many types of solutions, and Schrödinger imposed the condition that for a particle bound in an atom, the solution should be mathematically well defined everywhere. When applied to the case of an electron in a hydrogen atom, Schrödinger's equation immediately gave the correct energy levels previously calculated by Bohr. However, the equation could also be applied to more complicated atoms, and even to particles not bound in atoms at all. It was soon found that in every case, Schrödinger's equation gave a correct description of a particle's behavior, provided that the particle was not moving at a speed near that of light.

In spite of this success, the meaning of the waves remained unclear. Schrödinger believed that the intensity of the wave at a point in space represented the ''amount'' of the electron that was present at that point. In other words, the electron was spread out, rather than concentrated at a point. However, it was soon found that this interpretation was untenable, because even if a particle was originally concentrated on a small region, in most cases it would soon spread over an increasingly larger region, in contradiction to the observed behavior of particles.

Born's Probability Interpretation. The correct interpretation of the waves was discovered by Max BORN. While studying how quantum mechanics describes collisions between particles, he realized that the intensity of the deBroglie-Schrödinger wave was a measure of the probability of finding the particle at each point in space. In other words, a measurement would always find a whole particle, rather than a fraction of one, but in regions where the wave intensity was low, the particle would rarely be found, whereas in regions of high intensity, the particle would often be found.

Heisenberg's Uncertainty Relation. An important contribution to the interpretation of quantum mechanics was given in 1927 by Heisenberg. He analyzed various ''thought experiments'' that were designed to suggest information about the location and velocity of a particle. An example would be the use of a microscope to image an electron. It is known that, because of the wave properties of light, a precise electron image requires the use of light of very short wavelength, and therefore high frequency. However, the Planck-Einstein relation implies that for such light, the photons must carry a large amount of energy and momentum. In the collisions between such photons and electrons, the electron momentum will be changed uncontrollably from what it was before the collision. As a result, the increased precision with which the electron's position is known is unavoidably accompanied by a loss of accuracy in the knowledge of its momentum. On the basis of this and related analyses, Heisenberg was led to formulate his UNCERTAINTY PRINCIPLE, which in its simplest form, states a reciprocal relation between the uncertainty Δx, with which we can know the position of any object, and simultaneously, the uncertainty Δp, with which we can know its momentum. The mathematical statement of the uncertainty relation is given by $\Delta x \Delta p > h/4\pi$. For an object of everyday size this limitation on simultaneous measurements is very unimportant, when compared to ordinary experimental uncertainties. For this reason, there is rarely any significant difference between the predictions of Newtonian and quantum mechanics for such objects. However, for an electron in an atom, the uncertainty restrictions are so significant that they essentially determine the atom's size and minimum energy.

The Copenhagen Interpretation. With Born's probability interpretation of the wave intensity and Heisenberg's uncertainty principle, the elements of the standard indeterministic interpretation of quantum mechanics were in place by 1930. This interpretation is often known as the Copenhagen interpretation, because Niels Bohr, who made important contributions to its formulation, ran an influential physics institute there during this period. However, many physicists, including Einstein and Schrödinger, who accepted the mathematical formulation of quantum mechanics, were uncomfortable with the Copenhagen interpretation, and criticized it. The question of the correct interpretation of the mathematical formalism has remained something of a problem up to the present, and is discussed further below.

APPLICATIONS OF QUANTUM MECHANICS

Directly after its discovery, quantum mechanics was applied to many problems in atomic physics and chemistry, such as the structure of many-electron atoms and of molecules. These applications were generally successful in explaining old observations and in predicting newer ones. An example of the latter case was the successful prediction that hydrogen molecules could exist in two types, depending on the relative orientation of the angular momentum of the nucleus. This type of success led Paul Dirac, in 1928, to describe quantum mechanics as ''including all of chemistry and most of physics.'' Although the second half of this statement has not proven to be perfectly accurate, extensions of quantum mechanics have been successful in explaining an ever-growing number of physical phenomena. For example, in the 1930s and 1940s, George GAMOW used quantum mechanics to explain radioactive alpha decay of atomic nuclei.

For some applications to atomic nuclei, and for accurate calculations in atomic physics, it became necessary to extend the original form of quantum mechanics to make it consistent with Einstein's special theory of RELATIVITY. This was first done by Dirac in 1927, with an equation bearing his name. Dirac's equation proved immediately successful in accounting for a property of electrons known as spin. Spin is angular momentum of rotation about an axis through the electron, somewhat like that of the Earth rotating about its own axis. It was previously known that all electrons carry a spin of $h/4\pi$, but the reason was not clear. The Dirac equation explained this and accurately accounted for some magnetic properties of spinning electrons. It also made a novel prediction of the existence of particles similar in mass and spin to electrons, but with opposite electric charge. These particles, which have come to be known as positrons, were discovered by Carl Anderson in 1932. There were the first example of antiparticles, whose existence is predicted by any theory that satisfies the requirements both of quantum mechanics and special relativity (see ANTIMATTER).

QUANTUM FIELD THEORY

The study of antiparticles and their properties highlighted a new aspect of relativistic quantum theories, the creation and annihilation of matter. Dirac had predicted, and it was soon observed, that electrons and positrons could be created together in pairs, when high-energy photons passed through matter. Furthermore, a positron that comes near to an electron quickly disappears together with the electron, converting into several photons. In order to describe transformations in which the number of particles changes, it was necessary to apply quantum mechanics to a new area, that of fields.

In Newtonian physics, a field represents a physical quantity, such as electric force, which varies from point to point in space and time according to precise mathematical equations. Such classical fields can have any numerical value at any point. The general version of quantum theory was first applied to the electromagnetic field by Dirac, who showed that this combination automatically implied the existence of photons with the properties assumed by Planck and Einstein. Furthermore, Dirac was able to use this quantum field theory formalism, which came to be known as QED, or QUANTUM ELECTRO-DYNAMICS, to describe how photons are emitted and absorbed by charged particles, as when an electron in an atom radiates. An important practical application of QED in the late 1950s was the invention of the laser.

A number of physicists applied similar ideas to other, previously unknown fields in order to describe processes in which the numbers of other types of particles change. For example, Enrico Fermi, in 1933, used quantum field theory to explain the emission of electrons from a nucleus, the process known as BETA DECAY. The general lesson learned from this is that fields satisfying the laws of quantum mechanics and relativity

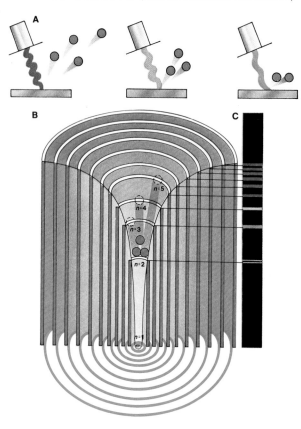

According to the quantum theory, light is emitted and absorbed by matter in quanta, or discrete amounts of energy that are related to the frequency of the light. In the photoelectric effect (A), electrons are ejected when light quanta fall on certain metals. More electrons are expelled as the light intensity increases because the number of quanta increase, but the electron velocities depend only on the light's frequency and decrease from a high value for violet light to a lower value for red light. When the electrons in an excited atom (B) drop from an orbit of high energy to one of lower energy, they emit light and produce the bright lines in the element's spectrum (C).

automatically describe particles that can be created or destroyed.

Virtual Particles. Quantum field theory had some unforeseen consequences. One aspect of Heisenberg's uncertainty principle is that the law of conservation of energy is not strictly observed for short periods of time. Because of this, a particle such as an electron can briefly emit and then reabsorb other particles, such as photons. These transients, called virtual particles, influence the properties that we measure for the electron. In particular, they change its mass from what it would have been if they did not exist. The extra mass due to virtual particles is called the self mass. Unfortunately, when physicists in the 1930s tried to calculate the self mass due to virtual photons, they got an infinite result. For some time, this result paralyzed progress in quantum field theory. However, in the 1940s, a method was found for dealing with infinite self mass, and certain related infinities. This procedure, known as renormalization, has dominated quantum field theory since.

Renormalization. The idea behind renormalization is that the self mass is not directly measurable. Only the combination of self mass and any intrinsic mass that the electron might have can be observed. It was suggested, first by Hendrik Kramers, that an infinite self mass might combine with an infinite intrinsic mass to give the finite observed mass. It should then be possible to express all other observable quantities in terms of this sum, avoiding the problem of infinities. Calculations involving this procedure, known as mass renormalization, are quite delicate to carry out. Indeed, they were only done successfully after new techniques were introduced in the late 1940s by Julian SCHWINGER and Richard FEYNMAN. These methods are designed to be consistent with relativity theory at all stages, unlike earlier methods, which made sharp distinctions between space and time. Feynman's methods involve the use of suggestive pictures, now called Feynman diagrams, which are correlated with any process to be calculated. For example, the emission of a photon by an electron is pictured as a solid line of indefinite length, representing the electron, with a wavy line, representing the photon, originating in the middle of the electron line. Feynman described a set of rules by which the probability of occurrence of any process could be calculated directly from the associated diagram.

In the late 1940s, using the methods of Feynman and Schwinger, scientists calculated small corrections, due to emission and absorption of virtual photons, for the energies of electrons in hydrogen atoms, and for the magnetic properties of electrons. These calculations, which have continued to ever higher levels of accuracy, in some cases agree with observation to the incredible accuracy of one part in a billion. This is probably the greatest triumph that theoretical physics has yet achieved.

Gauge Field Theories. The success of QED led many physicists to believe that other renormalizable quantum field theories could be found to describe properties of subatomic particles that are not included in QED, such as the strong forces that bind neutrons and protons into nuclei, and the weak forces responsible for beta decay. For many years this hope was not realized, because not enough was known either about types of renormalizable theories or about the particles to which such theories should be applied. This situation changed in the 1960s and 1970s, following the invention, by Chen-Ning Yang and Robert Mills, of a particular kind of renormalizable quantum field theory known as a gauge field theory. It was shown that one type of gauge field theory, named QUANTUM CHROMODYNAMICS, or QCD, was capable of describing the strong interactions provided that it was applied not to protons and neutrons, but to quarks, hypothetical particles that compose protons and neutrons and other particles affected by strong interactions. A second gauge field theory was shown by Sheldon GLASHOW, Steven WEINBERG, and Abdus Salam, to be capable of describing electromagnetic and weak interactions together, thus unifying in a single theory, two important aspects of nature.

In spite of the success of renormalizable quantum field theories, some prominent theoretical physicists, such as Dirac, have expressed misgivings about them. Although observable quantities are finite in these theories, this is achieved through manipulations with infinite quantities that are mathematically suspect and aesthetically unpleasant.

THE INTERPRETATION OF QUANTUM MECHANICS

Although quantum mechanics is now over 60 years old, and has been very successful in providing explanations for physical phenomena, there remains a dissatisfaction among some physicists both with the theory itself and with the prevailing Copenhagen interpretation. Much of this criticism derives from the radical change from earlier theories that quantum mechanics represents, but some of it involves problems that arise within quantum mechanics itself.

Hidden Variable Theories. One criticism of quantum mechanics relates to its indeterminacy. This was Einstein's original objection, although he later developed others. Because an individual radioactive nucleus will eventually decay at a specific time, Einstein and others believed that a complete physical theory should allow this time to be predicted exactly, rather than just statistically. While Einstein did not specify what type of theory he had in mind to replace quantum mechanics, others have suggested that the solution be sought in some type of "hidden variable" theory. In hidden variable theories, physical properties other than those we can measure would determine those events about which quantum mechanics can only make probability predictions. The mathematician John von Neumann proved long ago that no hidden variable theory can agree exactly with the predictions of quantum mechanics, but the predictions have not all been examined, so there exists some possibility that a hidden variable theory could be formulated which agrees with all observations that have been made. However, none has yet been produced which physicists find satisfactory.

Reduction of the Wave Function. A second problem with the interpretation of quantum mechanics, which troubles even those who accept the theory, involves the idea of measurement. Schrödinger's wave equation can be used to describe how any system changes from one time to another. If the wave is known everywhere in space at one time, it can be predicted everywhere at a later time. However, knowing the wave intensity only allows for probability predictions of the results of measurements. When a measurement is actually made, the observer suddenly obtains exact information about at least one property of the system, such as its energy. This change from probabilistic to exact information has come to be called the reduction of the wave function. It has been proven that even if the interaction between the measuring instrument and the system being observed is taken into account, this reduction cannot be properly described by the Schrödinger equation. Various scientists have taken different attitudes toward this result. Some have championed the view that the consciousness of an observer plays a fundamental role in reduction of the wave function. Others have argued that because quantum mechanics cannot account for reduction, it is incomplete. Perhaps the most widely accepted view is that reduction of the wave function always involves the interaction of a microscopic object, such as an electron, with a macroscopic system, the measuring instrument. When this interaction takes place, there is an irreversible change in the macroscopic measuring instrument, and it is this change that results in the reduction of the electron's wave function. While there may be some truth to this view, it only solves part of the problem, because irreversibility itself is not completely understood.

The Einstein-Podolsky-Rosen Paradox. Another problem concerning the interpretation of quantum mechanics derives from work by Einstein with Boris Podolsky and Nathan Rosen. In an article published in 1935, they pointed out that the predictions of quantum mechanics—in particular, the idea of indeterminacy—in some cases were in conflict with what they considered to be a plausible criterion for reality. The situation envisaged was one in which a physical system that is originally a whole, splits into two parts that eventually become widely separated. The reality condition they imposed was that measurements done on one part of the separated system should not affect the other part of the system. An example of

their analysis is an atom containing an electron and proton, each with spin angular momentum of $h/4\pi$, but with total spin zero, which breaks apart so that the electron goes in one direction and the proton in another. Because of the conservation of angular momentum, the total angular momentum of the electron and proton remains zero even when they are widely separated. If a physicist determines that the electron spin lies along some direction, he can immediately infer that the proton spin points in the opposite direction. The reality condition would then imply that the proton spin was already determined to have this value before the measurement was made on the electron.

Bell's Theorem. An argument given by John Bell, in 1964, dealt with the fact that Einstein's conclusion contradicts quantum mechanics. His finding, known as BELL'S THEOREM, derives from statistical measurements of spin values of many correlated electrons and protons. It states that any theory satisfying Einstein's reality condition—that reality is a localized phenomenon, and particles have determined properties—necessarily implies a relation among the results of a series of measurements. A series of experiments to test Einstein's reality condition, and Bell's theorem, have been carried out. The results do not support Einstein's reality condition, but instead support quantum mechanics.

QUANTUM MECHANICS TODAY

Research that employs quantum mechanics remains at the center of contemporary physics. One aspect of this research involves the search for approximate methods that can be applied with the basic principles of quantum mechanics in studies of situations that are so complex that they cannot be dealt with exactly. Much of the research in condensed-matter physics is of this nature. An important discovery in this area is that in some situations, the discreteness of physical quantities that usually occurs on the subatomic level can also occur on the macroscopic level. The quantized HALL EFFECT, a property of electrical resistance of certain substances under the influence of electric and magnetic forces, is a recently discovered example of this.

Another important area of research involves the attempt to include gravity among the phenomena that can be described by quantum mechanics. Although there are no observations yet which require the use of a quantum theory of gravity, physicists believe that such phenomena may occur inside black holes, and may have occurred everywhere in the earliest moments of the universe. It has not yet been possible to formulate a consistent quantum theory of gravity, either by beginning with Einstein's non-quantum general theory of relativity, or by applying the usual ideas of quantum field theory. Currently, some physicists are pursuing an approach based on a quantum theory of strings, objects extended in one spatial dimension, as opposed to conventional particles, which are extensionless points (see SUPERSTRING THEORY). String theories may succeed in uniting gravity with the other forces of nature in a unified quantum-mechanical description of nature. Meanwhile, there is no doubt that quantum mechanics is the most successful theory of physical phenomena yet invented by the human mind.   GERALD FEINBERG

Bibliography: Dirac, Paul A., *Quantum Mechanics* (1958); Feinberg, Gerald, *What Is the World Made of?* (1977); Herbert, Nick, *Quantum Reality* (1985); Itzykson, Claude, and Zuber, Jean B., *Quantum Field Theory* (1980); Jammer, Max, *The Conceptual Development of Quantum Mechanics* (1966); Pagels, Heinz R., *The Cosmic Code* (1982); Sakurai, Jon, *Modern Quantum Mechanics* (1985); Schilpp, Paul A., *Albert Einstein, Philosopher Scientist* (1973); van der Waerden, Bartel, *Sources of Quantum Mechanics* (1967); Wheeler, John, and Woyciech, Zurek, *Quantum Theory and Measurement* (1983).

Quantz, Johann Joachim   [kvahnts]

Johann Joachim Quantz, b. Jan. 30, 1697, d. July 12, 1773, was a leading composer of the "Berlin school" of the mid-18th century and one of the outstanding flutists of his time. He was in the Dresden orchestra when discovered by Crown Prince Frederick (later known as Frederick the Great), whose flute instructor he became in 1728. After Frederick assumed the throne, Quantz was appointed (1741) composer to the courts in Berlin and Potsdam, where he performed regularly with the emperor and supplied him with new flute music—about 300 flute concertos and 200 other flute pieces. His most durable work, however, is the *Essay on the Method of Playing the Transverse Flute* (1752; Eng. trans., 1966), a major source of information about 18th-century performing practices.

Bibliography: Reilly, E. R., *Quantz and His "Versuch"* (1971).

Quapaw   [kwah'-paw]

The Quapaw, or Arkansas, are a tribe of North American Indians who originated in the Ohio Valley. They separated from the OSAGE and OMAHA at the confluence of the Ohio and Mississippi (Quapaw means "downstream") to go downstream to the Arkansas River. They spoke a Siouan language closely related to Osage and Omaha. Their bark-covered earth lodges were located in fortified villages; they cultivated maize and beans and occasionally hunted bison. Hernando DE SOTO made contact with them about 1540, and Jacques MARQUETTE and Louis JOLLIET visited them in the next century.

Before 1720 smallpox killed many of the Quapaw. Only 1,000 remained in 1818, when they ceded 30 million acres (12 million ha) to the United States for $4,000 and annuities. A remaining million acres (0.4 million ha) for a reservation were ceded in 1824. The following year the Quapaw moved to the Caddo Reservation in Louisiana, where diseases and floods struck them. A treaty of 1833 gave them land in northeast Oklahoma. They scattered during the Civil War, but in the late 1800s survivors gathered on the reservation to reestablish tribal life. Zinc was discovered on the reservation in the 1920s, and the Quapaw prospered. Reduced to a population of 400 in 1900, the Quapaw on or near the reservation increased to 1,193 (1981 est.), including Osage and Ottawa who have entered the tribe through intermarriage. Despite their history of forced migrations and dispersals, some Quapaw still maintain features of their traditional life.   ERNEST L. SCHUSKY

quarantine

A quarantine is the detention or isolation of persons or animals suspected of having been exposed to a communicable disease. Although quarantine literally means "a period of forty days," the detention period is determined by the longest usual incubation period of the disease in question; the quarantine is lifted if symptoms of the disease do not appear during that time. Quarantine also refers to the refusal to allow ships to discharge passengers or cargo when they are suspected of carrying infectious disease.   PETER L. PETRAKIS

Quarenghi, Giacomo   [kwah-reng'-gee]

The Italian architect Giacomo Quarenghi, b. Sept. 20, 1744, d. Feb. 18, 1817, went to Russia about 1780 at the request of Catherine the Great and was among the most distinguished and influential architects who worked there. A master of the neoclassical style, he thoroughly understood classical architectural styles as well as the designs of Andrea Palladio. His architecture was dignified, severe, and impressive. His projects in and around Saint Petersburg included the English Palace at Peterhof (1781–91), the Academy of Sciences (1783–89), the State Bank (1783–90), the Hermitage Theater (1783–87), and the Alexander Palace at Tsarkoe Selo (1792–96). Quarenghi also worked for Catherine's successor, Paul I, but Alexander I, who came to the throne in 1801, was unsympathetic to him. Thus, his design for a church in Moscow, meant to be a war memorial, was never realized.   ANN FARKAS

Bibliography: Hamilton, G. H., *The Art and Architecture of Russia*, rev. ed. (1983).

quark   [kwahrk]

In nuclear physics, a quark is a hypothetical entity representing a basic constituent of matter—even more fundamental than the proton and neutron, which were once thought to be "elementary" particles. Quarks have not been observed, and it is conjectured that they have properties that render them unobservable. Even so, there is sufficient indirect evidence for

PROPERTIES OF QUARKS

Quark	Mass (GeV)*	Charge	Charm	Strangeness
Up	0.378	+⅔	0	0
Down	0.336	−⅓	0	0
Strange	0.540	−⅓	0	−1
Charmed	1.5	+⅔	+1	0
Bottom	4.72	−⅓	0	0
Top	30–50	+⅔	0	0

*GeV = Gigaelectron volts.

most scientists to accept their existence.

The quark theory was independently proposed in 1963 by two physicists, Murray GELL-MANN and George Zweig of the California Institute of Technology. The theory was advanced in an attempt to establish order from the bewildering array of known subatomic particles (about 200) and to find some underlying simplicity. Noting that all of the hadronic (strongly interacting) particles could be grouped into families according to formal mathematical principles, Gell-Mann and Zweig showed that all of the properties of the particles could be understood if it were assumed that these particles were built up from other, more elementary, particles. These new entities have come to be known as "quarks," the name originating from an arcane line in James Joyce's *Finnegan's Wake:* "Three quarks for Muster Mark."

Not all particles are affected by quark theory. The LEPTONS, a class of particles that includes the electron, muon, and neutrino, do not participate in the strong nuclear interaction and are thought not to be composed of quarks. Quarks combine to form HADRONS. A large subgroup of the hadrons is the BARYONS, a class that includes the proton and all heavier particles that ultimately decay into a proton and something else. Baryons are assumed to be made of three quarks. Another subgroup, the MESONS, are assumed to be made of one quark and one antiquark. Each quark has an antiquark analogue that differs only in the sign of its electrical charge (see ANTIMATTER). The differences among the various mesons and baryons are explained by the fact that they are composed of different types and combinations of quarks.

The original quark theory called for three types, or "flavors," of quarks called up, down, and strange (u, d, and s). All ordinary matter can be constructed from just the up and down quarks. The s quark is needed to explain certain particles created by high-energy events that have the "strangeness" property of existing for longer periods of time (10^{-12} sec) than predicted (10^{-24} sec). One of the remarkable features of quarks is that they carry an electric charge that is a fraction of e, the charge of the electron, which was considered the fundamental unit of charge. The u quark bears a charge of $+\frac{2}{3}$ and the d quark a charge of $-\frac{1}{3}$. The proton is made of two u quarks and one d quark; its total charge is $\frac{2}{3} + \frac{2}{3} - \frac{1}{3} = 1$. Similarly, the uncharged neutron is composed of one u quark and two d quarks. An additional nuclear property given the whimsical name "charm" was experimentally verified in 1974 when Burton Richter and Samuel Ting simultaneously discovered the J/psi particle. This required the postulation of a fourth quark, the "charmed," or c, quark. In 1977 the "bottom," or b, quark was detected, and, in 1984, the "top," or t, quark. These last two quarks are also referred to as "beauty" and "truth," respectively.

As if this proliferation of quarks were not enough, theorists assume that each "flavor" of quark is actually three quarks, indistinguishable to an observer but appearing different to each other, so that the Pauli exclusion principle is not violated. This property is called "color," and it is believed that the strong interaction may be an indirect manifestation of a more basic "color force," which is carried by GLUONS and is responsible for the permanent entrapment of quarks. Each of the six postulated quarks can have any one of three colors, usually called red, blue, and green. It is thought that quarks can exist only in certain color groupings (of 2 or 3 quarks) that produce a so-called color-neutral state. The theory behind the color force is called QUANTUM CHROMODYNAMICS (QCD).

No experiment has yet detected a single, isolated quark. Most attempts have involved searching for a particle with a charge that is a fraction of the electron charge. No matter how hard nuclear physicists collide hadrons, though, they only succeed in creating quark-antiquark pairs. The difficulty of separating quarks may be due to an increase in the nuclear force at larger (on a nuclear scale) distances. The inability to isolate a quark represents the unsolved problem of ''quark confinement.''   STEPHEN FLEISHMAN

Bibliography: Close, F. E., *Introduction to Quarks and Partons* (1980); Fritzsch, Harald, *Quarks: The Stuff of Matter* (1983); Huang, K., *Quarks, Leptons and Gauge Fields* (1982); Okun, L. B., *Leptons and Quarks* (1983).

See also: FUNDAMENTAL INTERACTIONS; FUNDAMENTAL PARTICLES.

quarter horse

The quarter horse is capable of extremely fast starts and can often beat the Thoroughbred over short distances. An American light horse with great endurance, it is used as a cattle horse and a polo pony.

The quarter horse is thought to have originated in the mid- to late 1600s in the American colonies of Virginia and the Carolinas. It was used for racing on straight quarter-mile (400-m) tracks, from which it derives its name. At such a short distance, equal to 2 furlongs, fast starts and the ability to reach top speed quickly are of great advantage, and the first quarter horses were bred with these points in mind. Bred probably from local native stock, and Thoroughbred as well, the quarter horse was developed with a relatively short body, broad, muscular hindquarters, strong, sloping shoulders, and sturdy feet. The breed or breed type appeared in the southwestern United States on the frontier cattle ranches, where its quick starting, stopping, and turning made it valuable as a working cow pony. The quarter horse is used in rodeo in various competitions and stunts.

Quarter horses may be any solid color, as well as buckskin, smoky, and palomino, but paints or pintos are not permissible. Quarter horses generally range in size from 14-2 to 15-2 hands high (58 to 62 in/147 to 157 cm), but may reach 16-1 hands (65 in/165 cm).

The American Quarter Horse Association was founded in 1940 to promote the breed and to maintain a registry of quarter horses.

Bibliography: Denhardt, Robert M., *Quarter Horses: A History of Two Centuries* (1967); Nye, Nelson, C., *The Complete Book of the Quarter Horse* (1964); Osborne, Walter, *The Quarter Horse* (1977).

quarry   [kwohrts]

Quartz, which is the most abundant SILICA MINERAL and which occurs in most igneous and practically all metamorphic and sedimentary rocks, is nearly pure silicon dioxide (SiO_2). It has also been found in some lunar rocks and meteorites. The name *quartz* is believed to have originated in the early 1500s from the Saxon word *querklufterz* (cross-vein ore), which was corrupted to *quererz* and then to *quartz*. Quartz was well known to the ancients, who called it crystal or rock crystal.

Quartz is colorless and transparent when pure. It is diamagnetic but does not conduct electricity. Its hardness is 7 on the Mohs scale, and its specific gravity is 2.651. Quartz has no cleavage and fails by brittle fracture; the fracture surfaces have vitreous luster.

Crystallography. Quartz occurs in a wide range of crystal sizes, from single crystals weighing many tons to cryptocrystalline varieties whose crystallinity may be seen only with the aid of an electron microscope. Quartz crystallizes in the trigonal trapezohedral class of the rhombohedral subsystem of hexagonal symmetry. The quartz symmetry class lacks a center of symmetry or planes of symmetry. The *c* crystallographic axis is perpendicular to three polar axes (*a*) separated by 120° in a plane. Because the polar axes differ on each end, the application of mechanical stress to such an axis produces electrical charges of opposite sign at each end (piezoelectricity); conversely, applied electrical fields produce mechanical stresses. The piezoelectric property makes quartz valuable in pressure gauges, electronic frequency-control devices, radios, and other applications. Because no symmetry planes are parallel to the *c* axis, crystals may develop either a left-handed or right-handed configuration (enantiomorphism); in nature, the characteristics of left- and right-handedness occur approximately equally. The structure consists of spirals of tetrahedra linked at their corners, each tetrahedron consisting of a silicon atom at the center and four oxygen atoms at the corners. The silicon-oxygen distance is 0.161 nanometers (1 nm = 10^{-9} m), and the axial dimensions are *a* = 0.4913 nm and *c* = 0.5405 nm at 25° C (77° F). Most quartz crystals are twinned, although this may not be visible to the eye. The polar axes and enantiomorphism permit complex twinning.

Varieties. Although coarsely crystalline quartz occurs in colorless or white (milky) masses, colored varieties are numerous and popular. AMETHYST (violet); smoky quartz; cairngorm, or morion (black); citrine (yellow); and rose quartz are common and arise by the incorporation of a tiny fraction of elements that substitute for silicon atoms, such as iron, aluminum, manganese, and titanium. The entry of such elements requires the concomitant entry of small atoms such as hydrogen, lithium, or sodium to preserve charge balance. Inclusions of other minerals, in some instances oriented, can occur throughout quartz crystals. The included minerals can be RUTILE (sagenite or rutilated quartz); fibrous amphiboles (CAT'S-EYE is grayish green; TIGER'S-EYE is yellow brown; hawk's-eye is blue); and platy minerals, such as mica, iron oxides, or chlorite (aventurine).

Very-fine-grained and cryptocrystalline varieties of quartz are numerous. Collectively called chalcedonic quartz, these

Quartz, the most abundant mineral on Earth, is found in a variety of forms and colors in nearly all rock types. Rock crystal, normally a colorless, transparent, long, prismatic crystalline form, shown embedded in marble, is sometimes colored by impurities.

varieties form slowly from evaporating or cooling solutions as crusts and fillings of veins and open spaces. When color banding is conspicuous, the variety is called AGATE. Agate with numerous flat bands of white, black, or dark brown is called ONYX. Translucent red or brown chalcedonic quartz colored by iron oxides; green varieties colored by chlorite, amphiboles, or nickel minerals; and mottled moss agates are used as semiprecious stones. BLOODSTONE is a green variety of chalcedonic quartz with red spots. Chalcedonic quartz is often colored by chemical processes. Finely crystallized quartz called CHERT AND FLINT occurs within calcareous or silty sedimentary rock as gray or black layers or nodules. JASPER is very-fine-grained quartz with abundant iron oxides—it may be red, brown, yellow, dark gray, or black.

When heated above 573° C (1,063° F) at 1 bar (14.50 lb/in²) of pressure, quartz assumes higher symmetry as the threefold *c* axis becomes sixfold. This hexagonal form is known as high quartz or β-quartz. The transformation temperature is pressure-dependent, increasing by approximately 25 C degrees (45 F degrees) per kilobar. When high quartz is cooled below the inversion temperature, inversion to low quartz occurs rapidly. The first mild heating of quartz commonly will be accompanied by the emission of light (thermoluminescence), and irreversible color changes may occur in colored varieties. For example, amethyst may be transformed to citrine at 250° C (482° F) or higher. Vigorous rubbing of one quartz crystal by another may also produce visible light (triboluminescence).

Formation. Quartz forms in rocks of igneous origin only after other silicates have incorporated the other available cations. Thus only compositions that are more than approximately 47 percent (by weight) SiO_2 contain quartz. As the content of SiO_2 in the bulk composition of magma increases, increasing amounts of free SiO_2 appear as quartz or other silica minerals. Quartz can be dissolved in hot water or steam and is thus transported from place to place in the Earth, being deposited by cooling of the transporting fluid or by release of pressure. Because quartz is relatively resistant to mechanical abrasion, it is abundant in stream sediments, on beaches, and in wind-blown sands. QUARTZITE and SANDSTONE are mostly quartz, and many other sedimentary and metamorphic rocks contain substantial proportions of quartz.

Uses. Quartz is used as a component of glass, ceramics, refractories, cements, and mortar; as an abrasive; as a chemical raw material for the manufacture of sodium silicate, silicon carbide, silicon metals, organic silicates, and silicones; and as a component in numerous other industrial materials.

DAVID B. STEWART

Bibliography: Dake, Henry C., et al., *Quartz Family Minerals: A Handbook for the Mineral Collector* (1938); Deer, W. A., et al., *Rock-Forming Minerals*, vol. 4 (1963); Frondel, Clifford, *The System of Mineralogy of James Dwight Dana and Edward Salisbury Dana*, vol. 3: *Silica Minerals*, 11th ed. (1962); Quick, Lelande, *The Book of Agates and Other Quartz Gems* (1963); Sosman, R. B., *The Phases of Silica* (1965).

quartz monzonite   [mahn'-zuh-nyt]

Quartz monzonite, or adamellite, is a light-colored plutonic rock intermediate between GRANITE and GRANODIORITE. It comprises coarse crystals of quartz and about equal amounts of plagioclase and potassium feldspar. Dark minerals include biotite and hornblende. Accessories are apatite, magnetite, and zircon. Quartz monzonite forms large plutons in the root zones of mountain complexes and fold belts. It probably forms from the melting of sandy and clayey sedimentary rocks or from metamorphic transformation.

WILLIAM D. ROMEY

quartzite   [kwohrt'-syt]

The metamorphic rock quartzite consists mainly of interlocking quartz grains recrystallized to such an extent that the rock can break across the individual grains as easily as around them. Quartzite is formed from sandstone or chert during regional and contact metamorphism. Relict textures and structures of the original rocks, such as shape and size of the

grains and type of bedding, help in identifying the original rock. In quartzite derived from sandstone, dustlike inclusions may show outlines of original rounded sand grains. Micaceous quartzites are formed from impure sandstone and may grade into schist or gneiss, depending on the amount of mica or feldspar, respectively, that is present. A mosaic of small grains is typical of quartzite derived from chert. A thin-bedded structure of cherts composed of alternate siliceous and shaly layers is typically preserved during the metamorphisms. Recrystallization under directed pressure or stress results in elongation and parallelism of the quartz grains, or in a preferred orientation of crystallographic axes of quartz grains of any shape. Geologists making detailed studies of rock deformation analyze statistically the preferred orientation. Quartzites are resistant to weathering and commonly project as high hills and ridges.

ANNA HIETANEN

quasar

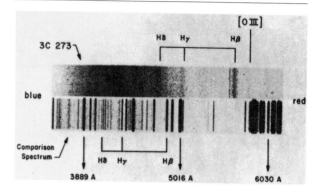

Comparison of the H_δ, H_γ, and H_β emission lines of the quasar 3C 273 (top) with those of a standard laboratory spectrum (bottom) reveals that the quasar's lines have been greatly shifted to the red end of the spectrum. The amount of shift indicates that 3C 273 is receding from Earth at 15% of the speed of light. If Hubble's distance-velocity law applies, the quasar must be nearly 3 billion light-years away.

Quasars are the most luminous known objects in the universe, some of them having luminosities more than 100 times greater than that of the brightest known galaxy. Some quasars are markedly and erratically variable in their light in a period of minutes; their diameters must therefore be less than 100 light-minutes across, or about the size of the solar system. These small sizes have been roughly corroborated by special radio techniques involving two widely separated radio telescopes operating together as a very long baseline interferometer. Thus more than 100 times the luminosity of the entire Galaxy is emitted from a volume 10^{17} times smaller than that of the Galaxy—an incredible outpouring of energy from a relatively small volume of space.

Quasars detected as radio sources are called radio quasars, quasi-stellar radio sources, or quasi-stellar sources (QSSs); radio-quiet quasars detected by other means are called quasi-stellar objects (QSOs) or quasi-stellar galaxies (QSGs).

DISCOVERY

Up to 1960, astronomers had made a handful of optical identifications with radio sources (see RADIO ASTRONOMY). In 1960, for the first time and thanks to vastly improved radio techniques for pinpointing the positions of radio sources, a 16th-magnitude starlike, or quasi-stellar, object, 3C 48, was positively identified with a radio source. Completely puzzling, however, was its optical spectrum—a continuous one on which were superposed a few unidentified faint, broad emission lines. By 1963 a number of other similar quasi-stellar objects, or quasars, including the 13th-magnitude object 3C 273, were identified with radio sources. They had somewhat similar spectra to 3C 48, but the unidentified emission lines were at entirely different wavelengths. The great breakthrough came in 1963 when the astronomer Maarten SCHMIDT perceived that three of the six broad emission lines of 3C 273 had wavelengths corresponding to the well-known Balmer lines of hydrogen (H_β, H_γ, and H_δ) all shifted to the red end of the spectrum by 15.8% of their normal, or rest, wavelengths. Infrared observations by J. B. Oke showed that the strong red H_α line was also shifted to the expected infrared wavelength. The remaining two lines were identified with well-known strong lines of O III and Mg II, with a similar shift in wavelength.

With this key clue to guide him, Schmidt identified these and other lines in other quasars, fitting together the bits of information like pieces in a jigsaw puzzle. He was guided by the knowledge of what lines might be expected to appear and by the fact that even for very large values of z (z is the RED SHIFT, calculated by the formula $z = \Delta\lambda/\lambda_0$, where $\Delta\lambda$ is the charge in wavelength and λ_0 is the normal wavelength), the ratios of the shifted wavelengths of two or more lines were identical with the ratios of the normal wavelengths. More than 250 quasar red shifts have now been determined.

Some quasars discovered since the mid-1980s have a z of more than 4, making them the most distant objects yet found in the universe. A z of more than 4 means that spectral lines are shifted to wavelengths more than 4 times greater than normal, implying that the objects are moving away from Earth at 93 percent of the velocity of light or higher.

A few quasars, observed spectroscopically at high dispersion, show sharp absorption lines as well as broad emission lines; in some cases these absorption lines come in patterns corresponding to several discrete values of z. Occasionally, an absorption z is larger than the emission z. The origin of the absorption lines is still mysterious, as is the mechanism that produces the emission lines.

INTERPRETATION

If the quasar red shifts obey the same red-shift–distance law as do the galaxies (see EXTRAGALACTIC SYSTEMS), their distances can be immediately calculated. Such distances, called cosmological distances, are calculated from their red-shift recessional velocities by the equation $v = H_0 d$, where H_0 is a constant of proportionality, known as HUBBLE'S CONSTANT, that is currently estimated to be 55 ± 7 km/sec/megaparsec, and d is the distance of the object. If this interpretation is correct, most of the quasars are more distant than any known galaxy and hence are the most distant known objects in the universe. Even the smallest observed z (0.036) for a quasar implies a distance of about 700 million light-years; if such distances are correct, these objects are clearly not stars.

Strenuous efforts are under way to find distances to quasars independently of their red shifts. Some quasars appear to be located within clusters of galaxies and show the same red shift as the galaxies. These quasar distances are almost certainly cosmological and presumably correct. Some conflicting observations have been made, however, of quasars that lie almost in the same line of sight with galaxies having different red shifts, marginal evidence being claimed for interactions between the quasars and these galaxies. Should such interactions exist, they would imply that the quasars in question are not actually as far away as had been thought. Such cases remain few and are highly disputed. For example, the claim by astronomer Halton Arp to have found a link between quasar Markarian 205 and spiral galaxy NGC 4319 in 1971 was finally disproved by further observations in 1984.

The conservative explanation of quasars, accepted by the majority of astronomers, is that they do lie at their apparent cosmological distances and that they are violently active nuclei of very distant galaxies. The general assumption has come to be that quasars are a relatively temporary phase in the early evolution of most larger galaxies, and that the phenomenon of quasars is closely related to that of the massive BLACK HOLES widely thought to lie at the centers of the larger galaxies. JOHN B. IRWIN

Bibliography: Davies, Paul, *The Edge of Infinity* (1981); Ferris, Timothy, *The Red Limit* (1977); Finkbeiner, Ann, "The Farthest Thing Ever Seen," *Sky & Telescope*, October 1986; Golden, Frederic, *Quasars, Pulsars, and Black Holes* (1977); Kaufmann, W. J., III, *Universe* (1985); Maran, S. P., "The Quasar Controversy Continues," *Natural History*, January 1982; Shaffer, D. B., and Shields, G. A., "Why All the Fuss about Quasars?" *Astronomy*, October 1980; Shipman, H. L., *Black Holes, Quasars and the Universe*, 2d ed. (1980); Trimble, Virginia, and Woltjer, Lodewijk, "Quasars at 25," *Science*, Oct. 10, 1986; Turner, E. L., "Quasars and Gravitational Lenses," *Science*, Mar. 23, 1984; Weedman, Daniel W., *Quasar Astronomy* (1986).

quasi-stellar objects: see QUASAR.

Quasimodo, Salvatore [kwah-zee-moh'-doh]

Salvatore Quasimodo, b. Aug. 20, 1901, d. June 14, 1968, was a prominent Italian poet whose verse ranged from lyrical celebrations of his native Sicily reminiscent of the Greek classics to moving poems about human suffering and the ravages of war. His poems are remarkable for the beauty of their lyricism and their profound, often obscure, hermetic imagery. Major collections of his work include *Ed è subito sera* (And It Is Suddenly Evening, 1942), *Il falso e vero verde* (The False and the True Green, 1956), and *La terra impareggiabile* (The Incomparable Land, 1958). Also a fine translator of the Greek and Latin classics, Quasimodo was awarded the Nobel Prize for literature in 1959.

Bibliography: Mandelbaum, Allen, ed. and trans., *The Selected Writings of Salvatore Quasimodo* (1960; repr. 1969).

Quaternary Period [kwuh-tur'-nuh-ree]

The Quaternary is the current period (2.5 million years ago to the present) of geologic time. As originally defined (1829) by Jules Pierre François, the term embraced a heterogeneous assemblage of rocks and essentially corresponded to the Miocene, Pliocene, Pleistocene, and Recent epochs of modern usage. It subsequently came to connote deposits of the most recent ice age, but this definition has been shown to be superfluous, inasmuch as glacial deposits date well back into the preceding Tertiary Period, at least on the continent of Antarctica. The Quaternary is now customarily subdivided into a PLEISTOCENE EPOCH and a postglacial Holocene or RECENT EPOCH, the boundary between which lies at approximately 10,000 (radiocarbon) years ago.

During the Quaternary Period the Earth has experienced numerous glacial-interglacial cycles (see ICE AGES) and witnessed the evolution of modern *Homo sapiens* from protohuman hominid ancestors (see PREHISTORIC HUMANS), as well as the relatively recent extinction of a large number of mammal species. Some geologists equate the Quaternary Period with the Pleistocene Epoch and interpret the Recent Epoch as the most recent interglacial stage of the Pleistocene.

Quebec (city) [kwi-bek']

Quebec, at the confluence of the St. Lawrence and Saint Charles rivers in southeastern Canada, is the capital of the province of Quebec, the oldest city in Canada, and one of the most distinctive and picturesque of all North American metropolises. The name is thought to be derived from an Algonquian Indian word that means "abrupt narrowing of the river," a reference to Quebec's location at the head of the St. Lawrence River estuary. The population of the city is 164,580, and that of the metropolitan area, 603,267 (1986). Most of Quebec's population is Canadian born, French-speaking, and Roman Catholic. January temperatures in the city average $-16°$ C ($3°$ F), and the July average is $19°$ C ($67°$ F). The annual precipitation averages 848 mm (33 in).

Contemporary City. The city contains two major sections— Upper Town and Lower Town. The smaller Upper Town is clustered on the tableland west of Cape Diamond, the 101-m-high (333-ft) promontory overlooking the St. Lawrence. A completely walled section is the core of the Upper Town. It is primarily a governmental and cultural center of narrow, cobbled streets reminiscent of European cities. Upper Town is also the site of the once-fortified Citadel and a castlelike hotel, the Château Frontenac, which is the city's dominant skyline feature. Lower Town, at the base of Cape Diamond,

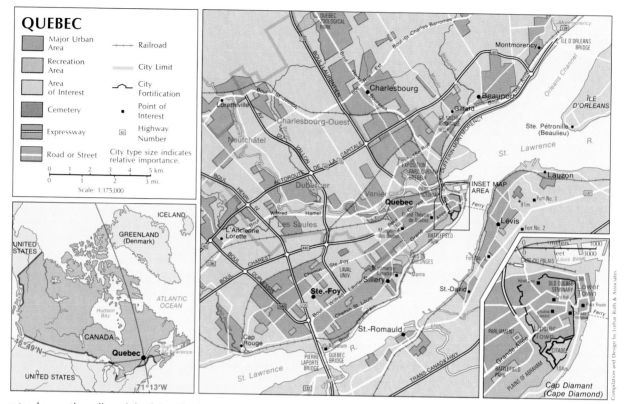

QUEBEC

■	Major Urban Area	┼──┼──	Railroad
■	Recreation Area	∙∙∙∙∙	City Limit
■	Area of Interest	⌐_⌐	City Fortification
■	Cemetery	∙	Point of Interest
■	Expressway	40	Highway Number
■	Road or Street	City type size indicates relative importance.	

Scale: 1:175,000

extends over the valley of the Saint Charles River to the north and into the Laurentian foothills beyond. It encompasses residential sections as well as commercial and industrial districts.

Quebec is a busy seaport and industrial center, manufacturing newsprint, grain, cigarettes, and garments. Its major functions, however, are administrative, commercial, and ecclesiastical. Tourism is another important segment of the economy. Quebec is the seat of Laval University (1852). Historic landmarks include the Church of Notre Dame des Victoires (1688) and the Anglican cathedral (1810).

Dufferin Terrace, a broad, wooden promenade in Quebec City, overlooks the St. Lawrence River. Situated on the river's north bank, Quebec City is a seaport and the provincial capital. The immense Château Frontenac, a hotel, is in the background.

History. The initial settlement of Quebec was established in 1608 by Samuel de CHAMPLAIN as a combined fort and trading post. Quebec was the scene of frequent battles between British and French forces until finally captured by the British under James WOLFE in 1759 in the Battle of the Plains of Abraham. When the Province of Lower Canada (now Quebec) was created in 1791, Quebec was chosen its capital.

TOM McKNIGHT

Quebec   (province)

Quebec (French: Québec) is the largest of the Canadian provinces, with an area of 1,540,680 km² (594,860 mi²). It stretches from the U.S. border and the Gulf of St. Lawrence north to Hudson Strait and from Hudson Bay east to Labrador and the Atlantic coast. It is bounded on the west and southwest by the province of Ontario. Quebec is nicknamed *la belle province* ("the beautiful province") because of its variety of lakes, forests, and open country, its commercial centers, and its French culture.

Quebec was first settled in 1608 by the French. Today 80% of the province's population is French-speaking; it is the only such province in Canada. The demand for greater provincial autonomy has increased, and since the 1960s more political, economic, and social controls have passed from federal to provincial jurisdiction. Some Quebecers advocate complete independence from Canada, but the separatist movement was dealt a blow by the defeat of a proposal for sovereignty in a 1980 referendum. Quebec nevertheless remains a major focus of the Canadian debate on federal-provincial relations.

LAND AND RESOURCES

More than 80% of the entire province is made up of the CANADIAN SHIELD, a vast, lake-studded plateau extending from the far north to the LAURENTIAN MOUNTAINS in the south and sloping westward to Hudson Bay. Deep valleys dissect the plateau edge. An extension of the APPALACHIAN MOUNTAINS, including the Shickshock Mountains, reaches from the east coast of the United States to the GASPÉ Peninsula of southeastern Quebec. In a fault zone between the Canadian Shield and the Appalachians lie the St. Lawrence lowlands formed by the St. Lawrence River. Near Montreal this lowland region is punctuated by the Monteregians, a line of isolated hills.

Soils. In the warmer southern part of the shield, podzol soils have developed, whereas in the colder north immature tundra soils are underlain by permanently frozen ground called permafrost. Bog soils are extensive around James Bay. The Appalachians have shallow, brown podzols, and the St. Lawrence lowlands have gray brown podzols, the best agricultural soils in the province.

Climate. Temperatures range from a January average of −9° C (16° F) at Montreal to −25° C (−13° F) at Inoucdjouac (formerly Port Harrison) in the Arctic zone. July temperatures average 22° C (71° F) at Montreal and 11° C (52° F) at Port Hamson. Precipitation ranges from an annual average of about 1,000 mm (40 in) at Montreal to 356 mm (14 in) in the Arctic; at least one-third of the precipitation is snow.

Rivers and Lakes. Quebec contains approximately 183,890 km² (71,000 mi²) of fresh water. Of the two major drainage systems, one flows eastward to the Atlantic by way of the ST. LAWRENCE RIVER, and another drains north and westward to Hudson and James bays. The major lakes include Mistassini, Gouin Reservoir, Manicouagan Reservoir, Eau Claire, Bienville, and Saint Jean.

Vegetation and Animal Life. Low shrubs and lichens dominate the tundra in the north. The subarctic climate of the central and southern shield supports coniferous forests. Hardwoods predominate in the St. Lawrence lowlands. A mixture of hardwoods and fir, spruce, and pine cover the Appalachians. Wildlife is varied: polar bear, seal, arctic fox, and hare in the far north; wolf, black bear, caribou, deer, and moose in the coniferous forests. Partridge, ducks, and geese and trout, pike, pickerel, bass, and salmon attract sports enthusiasts.

Resources. Mineral resources form the basis of much of Quebec's economy: iron ore, gold, copper, and zinc from the Canadian Shield; asbestos and copper from the Appalachians; and limestone from the Montreal plain. Quebec imports all of its petroleum, gas, and coal, but many of its rivers have been harnessed for water power. Productive forests cover one-third of Quebec. Increased public awareness of environmental problems has led to legislation to further regulate mining and forest exploitation and to reduce water and air pollution.

PEOPLE

The population of Quebec is distributed unevenly. Although much of the total area is unsettled, nearly 80% of the population are urban and are concentrated in the southwest. Approximately 45% of the population live in the MONTREAL census metropolitan area. Other major cities are TROIS-RIVIÈRES, Quebec City, Chicoutimi, and Sherbrooke. About 45,000 Indians and Eskimo (Inuit) live in widely scattered fishing and hunting villages. Quebec's population increased by 1.6% during 1981–

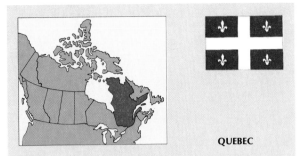

QUEBEC

LAND. Area: 1,540,680 km² (594,860 mi²); rank: 1st. Capital: Quebec (1986 pop., 164,580). Largest city: Montreal (1986 pop., 1,015,420). Municipalities: 1,614. Elevations: highest—1,652 m (5,420 ft), at Mont D'Iberville; lowest—sea level, along the Atlantic coast.

PEOPLE. Population (1986): 6,540,276; rank: 2d; density: 4.25 persons per km² (11 per mi²). Distrib. (1981): 77.6% urban, 22.4% rural. Average annual change (1981–86): +0.32%.

EDUCATION. Enrollment (1986–87 est.): elementary and secondary—1,157,700; higher—278,700. Institutions of higher education (1986): 91.

ECONOMY (monetary figures in Canadian dollars). Total personal income (1985): $98.5 billion; rank: 2d. Median family income (1985): $31,690. Labor force distribution (1985): manufacturing—548,000 persons; agriculture—85,000; other primary industries—45,000; trade—491,000; public administration—195,000; services—937,000; transportation, communications, and other utilities—221,000; finance, insurance, and real estate—156,000; construction—126,000. Agriculture: net income (1982 prelim.)—$663 million. Fishing: value (1981)—$46.8 million. Forestry: lumber production (1984)—3,752 million board feet. Mineral production: value (1982 prelim.)—$2.0 billion. Manufacturing: value added (1984)—$23.6 billion.

GOVERNMENT (1987). Lieutenant Governor: Gilles Lamontagne. Premier: Robert Bourassa, Liberal. Parliament: Senate—24 members; House of Commons—17 Liberals; 58 Progressive Conservatives. Provincial legislature: 122 members. Admitted to Confederation: July 1, 1867, one of four original provinces.

86. The birthrate, once the highest in Canada, has dropped to one of the lowest, about 15 per 1,000 (1981). The population is 82% French-speaking and 11% English-speaking. Roman Catholics account for 87% of the population; 7% are Protestant, 2% are Jewish, and 4% practice other religions.

Education and Cultural Activity. Education was originally the responsibility of the Roman Catholic church. After the British

The fairgrounds of Expo '67, which occupy two islands in the St. Lawrence River, are marked by the enormous geodesic dome covering the U.S. pavilion. Expo '67, an international exposition hosted by Montreal in 1967, celebrated the centennial of Canada's confederation.

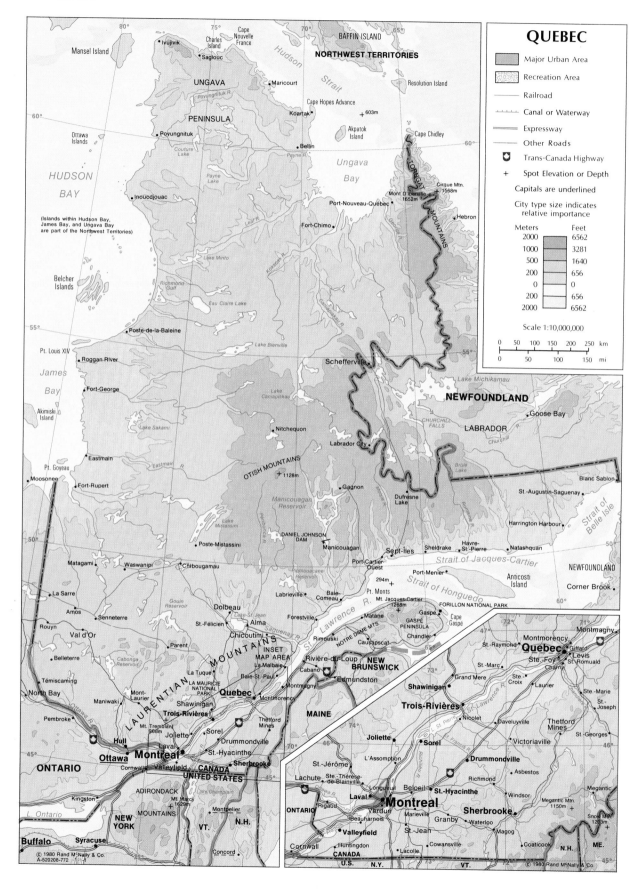

QUEBEC

Major Urban Area

Recreation Area

Railroad

Canal or Waterway

Expressway

Other Roads

Trans-Canada Highway

Spot Elevation or Depth

Capitals are underlined

City type size indicates
relative importance

Meters	Feet
2000	6562
1000	3281
500	1640
200	656
0	0
200	656
2000	6562

Scale 1:10,000,000

| 0 | 50 | 100 | 150 | 200 | 250 km |

| 0 | 50 | 100 | 150 mi |

© 1980 Rand McNally & Co.
A-520208-772

© 1980 Rand McNally & Co.

(Left) *Percé, a county seat located on the coast of the Gaspé Peninsula in southeastern Quebec, is a fishing port and a summer resort. The Gaspé Peninsula, which extends into the Gulf of St. Lawrence, is an important mining and dairy-farming region.*

(Below) *Logs float past a covered bridge on the Gatineau River near Grand Remous, in south central Quebec. Quebec possesses the most forest area of any Canadian province and is a national leader in the production of pulp and paper products.*

conquest (1759) and Confederation (1867), two parallel but independent systems of education evolved: French Catholic and English Protestant, reflecting the dual nature of the population. The Ministry of Education was established (1964) to provide more uniform standards for the whole province. The province's seven universities include McGILL UNIVERSITY (English language), LAVAL UNIVERSITY and the University of QUEBEC (both French language), and the University of Montreal.

The many small regional museums, art and music centers, and performing groups play as important a cultural role as those in the major cities. The latter include the Montreal and Quebec symphony orchestras; the Montreal opera; the Museum of Fine Arts, the Place des Arts (Concert Hall), and the National Library, all in Montreal; and, in Quebec City, the National Archives and Museum of Quebec. The province has a number of permanent theatrical or dance groups and a major film agency for creative documentary and feature films.

Historic Sites and Recreation. Among the preserved historic sites in Quebec City are the Plains of Abraham battlefield, where the English under James WOLFE defeated the French under the marquis de MONTCALM; the fortified French city; and several Catholic churches, including Notre Dame (1688), and seminaries. In the Montreal area are the Saint Sulpice Seminary; the old Lachine canals; Notre Dame Church (begun 1820); and restored fur-trading posts.

Federal and provincial parks offer year-round outdoor recreational opportunities and attract several million visitors annually. Quebec City's winter carnival (in February before the Lenten season) and Montreal's Expo '67 World's Fair site are popular attractions. Professional hockey, baseball, and football teams from Montreal compete in North American leagues.

Communications. Numerous radio and television stations broadcast in Quebec, the majority of them in French. Montreal has English- and French-language daily newspapers. *Le Journal de Montreal* has the largest daily circulation in the province. Quebec City's major daily newspapers are in the French language.

ECONOMIC ACTIVITY

Fur trading and fishing were early economic endeavors in Quebec, and by 1860, the province also had an adequately developing manufacturing sector. Mining began to develop in the early 20th century. Today, the services sector contributes the greatest part of Quebec's gross domestic product.

Forestry and Mining. Forest products—wood pulp, paper (especially newsprint), lumber, and plywood—are important to the economy. More than 40% of Canada's pulp and paper come from Quebec.

Quebec's greatest source of mining income is from iron-ore production, followed by gold. The province has about 40% of Canada's iron-ore reserves and nearly a quarter of the gold reserves. Other valuable metals are copper and zinc. Quebec also provides about 90% of Canada's asbestos. Many ores, notably iron and asbestos, are exported with little processing, mainly to the United States.

Manufacturing and Energy. Quebec ranks second among Canadian provinces in the value of manufacturing shipments. The province's mineral wealth is the basis for much smelting and refining and for heavy manufacturing of automobiles, aircraft, and machinery. Food and beverages processing is the leading industry in Quebec. Industries based on timber and pulp are also of major importance, with most pulp and paper mills located in the cities of the St. Maurice River Valley. Brass and copper products, electrical machinery and equipment, chemicals, and petroleum products are also valuable. Textiles and apparel are still significant but are suffering from foreign competition.

Major energy sources in Quebec are petroleum, coal, natural gas, and hydropower. The province is a leading producer of hydroelectric power in North America, and because of its abundant water resources, the hydropower produced in Quebec is cheaper than in most other regions of the continent. Since 1963, Quebec's hydroelectric plants have been under the control of the provincial government. Major hydroelectric plants are located near James Bay and on the Bersimis, La Grande, Manicouagan, Outardes, St. Lawrence, and St. Maurice rivers. Quebec also has nuclear power resources.

A freighter cruises past the cliffs of Quebec City, the capital of Quebec and an important Canadian port. Located in the southeastern portion of the province, Quebec City was established as a European settlement in 1608 by the French explorer Samuel de Champlain.

Agriculture and Fishing. Dairy farming is Quebec's predominant agricultural activity. Principal field crops are fodder, corn, mixed grains, barley, oats, tobacco, and wheat. Potatoes are the major vegetable grown in Quebec, and apples are the province's most important fruit. Quebec is also the world's foremost producer of maple sugar and syrup.

The Gulf of St. Lawrence and the estuary of the St. Lawrence River are the centers of the fishing industry. Cod and lobster provide about half of the value of the fish catch.

Tourism and Transportation. Because of the beauty of the natural landscape and the unique French history and culture, Quebec has a thriving tourist industry, supported by thousands of kilometers of roads and operating rail tracks. Main routes connect Ontario, Quebec City, New Brunswick, and New York. Montreal, one of the hubs of the Canadian and U.S. transportation network, has two international airports and serves as an ocean and inland port.

GOVERNMENT

Constitutional government is based on the BRITISH NORTH AMERICA ACT (1867), which at Confederation in 1867 divided powers between the federal and provincial governments. Quebec retained, as well, many of the administrative and civil judiciary traditions of the old French regime. The province exercises more control and seeks more autonomy than most other provinces over many socioeconomic and cultural affairs. The parliamentary system provides, by universal suffrage from age 18, an elected provincial assembly consisting of 122 members from 122 constituencies. A federally appointed lieutenant governor has no real powers; most power rests with the premier, the leader of the majority provincial party. The Court of Appeals is Quebec's highest court. It and the Superior Court are made up of federally appointed judges.

HISTORY

The territory around the Gulf of St. Lawrence and the lands drained by the St. Lawrence River were claimed by Jacques CARTIER for France after his expeditions in 1534 to the Gaspé Peninsula and in 1535 to present-day Montreal. He encountered native Algonquian peoples and Eskimo. European settlement followed with the establishment of the first habitation in 1608 by Samuel de CHAMPLAIN at Quebec City. The colony of NEW FRANCE grew slowly. Encouraged by King Louis XIV of France, and welcomed by such administrators as Jean TALON and the comte de FRONTENAC (governor from 1672 to 1682), more than 10,000 immigrants arrived in the 150 years of the French regime, 7,000 of whom stayed. They cleared the land, established schools, churches, and industries, explored westward, and extended the fur trade. A modified feudal system developed for the colony's administration in which the Roman Catholic church played a major role.

By about 1750 the population, aided by a high birthrate,

had reached 65,000. British-French rivalries in Europe led to conflicts over hegemony in America, resulting in the FRENCH AND INDIAN WARS. In 1759 the British general James Wolfe captured Quebec City, ending the hostilities. In the 1763 Treaty of Paris (see PARIS, TREATIES OF) France ceded all of New France to Britain.

Contact with and further immigration from France ceased. New colonists arrived from Britain, and, after the American Declaration of Independence in 1776, Loyalists from America arrived and settled in the foothills of the Laurentians and the Appalachians, in the Maritimes, and in the new area of Upper Canada (Ontario). Through the QUEBEC ACT of 1774, the Constitutional Act of 1791, and the British North America Act of 1867 (when Quebec joined Ontario, Nova Scotia, and New Brunswick to form the Confederation of Canada), the French-speaking inhabitants were allowed to retain their language and religious and civil administrative systems.

The French remained dominant in agriculture, and they continued to outnumber English-speakers. In the early 1800s the English-speaking inhabitants had begun to develop lumber, paper, mining, textile, and other industries and to establish commercial, financial, and trading companies, many centered in Montreal, which grew rapidly. Thus the English controlled the economic structures of the province, although the French, who formed 80% of the population, dominated the political scene. French Quebecers resented their position, and Louis PAPINEAU led (1837) an unsuccessful revolt (see REBELLIONS OF 1837).

Industrialization and urbanization, accelerated by World War I, continued, and by 1921, 56% of Quebec's population lived in urban areas. As Canada expanded westward and northward, and as world economic structures and trading patterns evolved, more of the economic control of Quebec passed out of the province to Ontario, Great Britain, and the United States, especially that over the mineral and forest resources.

Provincial rights and autonomy became stronger political objectives. World War II hastened the modernization process and the questioning of traditional patterns, including the role of the church in society and government. Successive Quebec governments enacted legislation to achieve greater provincial control of socioeconomic policies. Most sought to do this within the existing Canadian Confederation, but they encountered rising sentiment in favor of the complete independence of Quebec from the rest of Canada. In 1976 the Parti Québécois, led by René LÉVESQUE, which advocated the formation of a separate sovereign state, was elected. In 1980, Quebec voters soundly defeated a referendum proposal that would have mandated federal-provincial negotiations of terms of sovereignty. Lévesque resigned as party leader and premier in 1985, and his party subsequently lost the provincial election to the Liberal party. The separatist issue officially was ended in 1987 when the Quebec government signed the 1982 CONSTITUTION ACT, following agreement regarding an addition to the constitution that acknowledged Quebec as a "distinct society" within Canada. R. NORMAN DRUMMOND

Bibliography: Coleman, William D., *The Independence Movement in Quebec* (1984); Dion, Leon, *Quebec: The Unfinished Revolution*, rev. ed. (1976); Fitzmaurice, John, *Quebec and Canada: Past, Present, and Future* (1985); Neatby, Hilda M., *Quebec: The Revolutionary Age, 1760–1791* (1966); Nish, C. C., ed., *Quebec in the Duplessis Era, 1935–1959* (1970); Stanley, G. F., *New France: The Last Phase, 1744–1760* (1968); Trudel, Marcel, *The Beginning of New France* (1972); Wade, Mason, *The French Canadians, 1760–1967*, 2 vols. (1968).

Quebec, University of

Established in 1968, the University of Quebec is a coeducational, francophone, public institution in Sainte-Foy. The six constituent colleges each have separate facilities and faculties. The colleges at Chicoutimi (enrollment: 6,800; library: 41,000 volumes), Montreal (enrollment: 26,550; library: 250,000 volumes), Rimouski (enrollment: 4,218; library: 24,500 volumes), and Trois-Rivières (enrollment: 8,628; library: 541,000 volumes) were founded in 1969. The colleges at Hull (enrollment: 5,000; library: 50,000 volumes) and at Abitibi-Témiscamingue (enrollment: 2,190; library: 100,000 volumes) were established in 1981.

Quebec Act

The Quebec Act, passed by the British Parliament in 1774, created a government for the French Roman Catholic colony of Quebec, which had been ceded to Great Britain by the Treaty of Paris (1763). Quebec's governor, Guy CARLETON, was largely responsible for the terms, which officially recognized the Roman Catholic church, French civil law, and the seigneurial land-tenure system in Canada. The act also set up an appointed council to assist the governor and extended Quebec's boundaries south to the Ohio River and west to the Mississippi. Some historians argue that the act was inspired by the spirit of liberalism; others say that it was designed to preserve the loyalty of the French Canadians in the event of an American revolt. Many Americans in the 13 colonies to the south of Quebec regarded the act as one of the INTOLERABLE ACTS. GEORGE F. G. STANLEY

Bibliography: Coupland, Reginald, *The Quebec Act: A Study in Statesmanship* (1925); Neatby, Hilda M., *Quebec: The Revolutionary Age, 1760–1791* (1966) and *The Quebec Act* (1972).

Quechua [kech'-oo-uh]

The Quechua are a South American Indian people who from earliest times have occupied the central Andean highlands of Peru and Bolivia. Like the INCA who occupied the highlands from the 11th to the 15th century, they speak the Quechua language, a branch of the Andean-Equatorial stock. They also show other remnants of an Inca heritage in their pre-Columbian-style stone houses, pan-pipe music, a religion embodying pagan rites and costumes beneath a Roman Catholic surface, and a mythology rooted in an obscure past.

Together with the AYMARA, the Quechua constitute most of the rural population of highland Peru. Using traditional agricultural techniques, they grow crops of potatoes and maize in addition to keeping herds of llamas, alpacas, and sheep and raising pigs. Villages consist of kin groups, and marriage partners are chosen from within the village. Until the agrarian reform in the 1960s most Quechua were sharecroppers and wage laborers on the big inland plantations, although some lived on the coast in slums near large cities. Quechuan, which Peru has named an official language, was spoken by about 11 million Indians in the late 1980s. LOUIS C. FARON

Bibliography: Arguedas, Jose M., *The Singing Mountaineers: Songs and Tales of the Quechua People*, ed. by Ruth Stephan (1957; repr. 1971); Osborne, Harold, *Indians of the Andes: Incas, Aymaras and Quechuas* (1952; repr. 1972); Steward, Julian H., ed., *The Andean Civilizations, Handbook of South American Indians*, vol. 2 (1946).

queen

A queen is a woman ruler of a monarchy. The title may also be held by the wife of a king. A woman who occupies the throne in her own right is known as a queen regnant; the wife and widow of a king are known, respectively, as a queen consort and a dowager queen. Marriage to a king does not automatically make a woman a queen, although becoming one in this manner is more common than the awarding of a kingship to the husband (prince consort) of a queen regnant. The right of a woman to succeed to the throne is a relatively modern phenomenon in European history. In the 16th century, Mary Tudor, who ruled as Mary I, was the first accepted woman on the English throne. In France and several other European countries, the so-called SALIC LAW prohibited a woman from inheriting the crown. Three contemporary queens regnant are Elizabeth II of Great Britain, Beatrice of the Netherlands, and Margaret II of Denmark.

Queen, Ellery

Writing under the pseudonym of Ellery Queen, two cousins, Frederic Dannay, b. New York City, Jan. 11, 1905, d. Sept. 3, 1982, and Manfred Bennington Lee, b. New York City, Oct. 20, 1905, d. Apr. 3, 1971, coauthored a popular mystery series featuring a likable, intelligent detective. Among the best of the Queen novels are *Calamity Town* (1942) and *And on the Eighth Day* (1964). Dannay and Lee wrote scripts for the long-running Ellery Queen radio show that began in 1939, and in 1941 they founded *Ellery Queen's Mystery Magazine*. Ellery Queen has inspired several films and television series.

Bibliography: Nevins, F. M., Jr., *Royal Bloodline: Ellery Queen, Author and Detective* (1973).

Queen Anne style

Regarded as quintessentially English, the style of decorative arts named for Queen Anne developed from the assimilation of Dutch influence brought to England in the reign (1689–1702) of William III. By the time Queen Anne (r. 1702–14) came to the throne, a marked trend toward simplicity of form had emerged. In domestic architecture the Queen Anne style was plain and unassuming, often characterized by the use of red brick, sash windows, and hipped roofs. (The international baroque, practiced by Sir Christopher Wren and Sir John Vanbrugh during Anne's reign, has never been regarded as "Queen Anne style.") Furniture, generally of walnut and sometimes inlaid with marquetry, was also unassuming in form and often graced by the cabriole leg. The unadorned perfection of Queen Anne silver is famous. Even gilt gesso tables, such as those designed by James Moore, preserve this understated character. The style persisted well into the 18th century, and a Queen Anne revival occurred in late-19th-century England, associated with the applied arts and with the architecture of Richard Norman SHAW. JOHN MORLEY

Bibliography: Allen, B. S., *Tides in English Taste, 1619–1800* (1937); Summerson, J., *Architecture in Britain: 1530–1830*, 6th rev. ed. (1977).

Queen Anne's lace

Queen Anne's lace, *Daucus carota*, of the carrot family, Umbelliferae, is a widely distributed herb native to Eurasia. Also called the wild carrot, it grows to about 1 m (3 ft) high and has hairy stems and usually flat-topped, circular flower clusters (umbels), which are white or pink. At one time it was used as a stimulant and a diuretic.

Queen Anne's War: see FRENCH AND INDIAN WARS.

Queen Charlotte Islands

The Queen Charlotte Islands are a group of about 150 islands paralleling the western coast of Canada about 160 km (100 mi) from the mainland. The islands have an area of about

9,583 km² (3,700 mi²), and the population of 5,621 (1981) is mostly HAIDA Indians. Graham and Moresby are the two largest islands, with mountain ranges that rise to nearly 1,220 m (4,000 ft). The main towns are Masset, Skidegate, and Rose Harbour. The economy depends on the mining of copper, coal, and iron ore as well as lumbering and fishing. Discovered by the Spaniard Juan Pérez in 1774, the islands were named by the Englishman Capt. George Dixon in 1787.

Queen Elizabeth

The QE II, Britain's largest ocean liner since its launching in 1967, is 294 m (963 ft) long and offers luxury accommodations for as many as 1,700 passengers.

The *Queen Elizabeth* was a British OCEAN LINER. It was driven by steam turbines and, weighing 83,675 U.S. tons and having a length of 312 m (1,031 ft), was slightly larger than its sister ship, the *Queen Mary*. The *Queen Elizabeth* was launched in 1938 and along with the *Queen Mary* operated as a troop ship during World War II. The *Queen Elizabeth* went into commercial transatlantic service in 1946. In 1969 the ship was sold to American investors, who planned to have it anchored and used as a tourist attraction; in 1972, however, the liner was destroyed by fire while anchored in Hong Kong. The *Queen Elizabeth II*, a replacement for the ship, made its maiden voyage in 1969. The new liner weighs 68,863 U.S. tons and is 294 m (963 ft) long.   ARTHUR BIDERMAN

Bibliography: Lacey, Robert, *Queens of the North Atlantic* (1976).

Queen Mary

The *Queen Mary*, a famous British OCEAN LINER, was launched in 1934 and was the sister ship of the *Queen Elizabeth*. The *Queen Mary* weighed 81,235 U.S. tons and was 309 m (1,020 ft) in length; it carried more than 2,000 passengers and a crew of 1,100. The ship had four screw propellers and was one of the first merchant vessels to be fitted with antiroll stabilizers. In 1938 the *Queen Mary* won the *Blue Riband*—a trophy awarded for the passenger ship making the fastest North Atlantic crossing—with an average speed of 31.69 knots (58.69 km/h). The liner was withdrawn from service in 1967 and is anchored at Long Beach, Calif., where it serves as a museum and conference center.   ARTHUR BIDERMAN

Bibliography: Potter, Neil, and Frost, Jack, *The Queen Mary* (1971).

Queens

The largest borough of NEW YORK CITY in area, Queens lies at the western end of Long Island and is coextensive with Queens County. The population is 1,891,325 (1980). The borough is primarily residential, but industries located there process foods and cut lumber. Kennedy and La Guardia airports are located there. Settled by the Dutch in 1635, Queens became a borough of New York City in 1898. The 1939 and 1964 WORLD'S FAIRS were held in Queens.

Queens College: see NEW YORK, CITY UNIVERSITY OF.

Queen's University at Kingston

Established in 1841 by the Presbyterian Church of Canada on the model of the University of Edinburgh, Queen's University at Kingston (enrollment: 10,500; library: 1,370,950 volumes) is a coeducational, private, nondenominational institution in Kingston, Ontario, Canada. It has faculties of arts and sciences, education, business, law, medicine, and nursing, all with undergraduate and graduate programs. Its affiliated school is Queen's Theological College (1912, United Church of Canada). The library houses collections of Canadiana.

Queensland

Queensland, Australia's giant northeastern state, covers 1,727,200 km² (666,900 mi²), almost one-quarter of the continent. Four times the size of California, it is the country's third most populous state, with a population of 2,275,700 (1980 est.). BRISBANE is the capital.

Dividing the eastern third of the state from the western portion is the GREAT DIVIDING RANGE. A vast plain with occasional subdued ranges characterizes the western two-thirds. Generally, summer temperatures are hot, averaging 31° C (88° F) in January; winters are mild with a July average of 11° C (52° F). Most rain falls during the summer. Precipitation averages between 1,000 and 1,300 mm (40 and 50 in) along the east coast but decreases rapidly toward the arid interior. Statewide, grass is the dominant vegetation, but dense rain forests predominate along the coasts.

Queensland's Caucasian population is largely of British ancestry and is about 80% urban. Almost half of all city dwellers live in Brisbane. A string of secondary cities, stretching along the coast, includes Townsville, Gold Coast, Rockhampton, and Cairns. Queensland has the largest aboriginal population in Australia, with the majority living in rural areas.

Although most Queenslanders are employed in cities, rural industries produce the leading export products. Sheep are of historic importance, but in recent years the beef industry has grown more rapidly. Major crops include sugarcane, cotton, and wheat. Mining has been the glamour industry since the 1960s; bauxite, copper, lead, zinc, silver, and coal are most important. Tourism is increasing.

Originally part of New South Wales, Queensland became a separate colony in 1859. The western migration of many farmers in the 1860s and '70s quickly populated the interior, but droughts brought economic failure to many of these pioneers. Queensland became a state of the Commonwealth of Australia in 1901. Since 1922 the state has had a unicameral legislature, the only one in Australia.

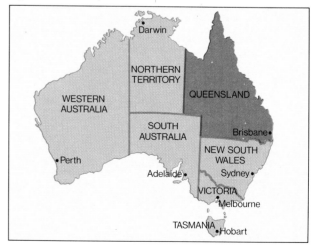

quelea   [kwee'-lee-uh]

Queleas are three species of African birds in the genus *Quelea* in the weaver family, Ploceidae, and are related to the common house sparrow. The best-known is the red-billed quelea, *Quelea quelea,* also called the red-billed dioch or the black-faced dioch, which is widely distributed south of the Sahara. It grows to 12 cm (4.75 in) long and has a short tail and a thick, stubby bill. It is grayish above, lightly tinged with pink below, and black on the forehead, chin, and cheek, with a pink bill. It is tremendously abundant and may aggregate into enormous flocks. The nests, usually built in trees, are woven of grasses and are rounded in shape, with an entrance on the side. The eggs are incubated for only 10 days, and the young remain in the nest for about 16 days more. The red-billed quelea undertakes mass migrations correlated with the rains and seed production. Because of their abundance, these birds are extremely destructive to grainfields.

Quellinus, Artus [kvel-ee'-nuhs, ahr'-tuhs]

Artus Quellinus (or Quellin) the Elder, b. 1609, d. Aug. 23, 1668, was a major representative of Flemish baroque sculpture who combined originality with an ability to translate Peter Paul Rubens's painting style into stonework. Quellinus studied in Rome with François Duquesnoy, and by 1647 he was in Amsterdam, where he spent 14 years decorating the Town Hall (now the Royal Palace) with allegorical figures; the crowning achievement of the project was the judge's bench in the Hall of Justice. Many of his sketches and studies for the project are preserved in the Rijksmuseum in Amsterdam. Quellinus also sculpted portrait busts, which reveal his preference for physical likenesses as opposed to psychological insights.   ROBERT F. CHIRICO

Bibliography: Rosenberg, Jakob, et al., *Dutch Art and Architecture 1600–1800* (1977).

Quemoy [ki-moy']

Quemoy (or Chinmen) is a small island group off the Chinese coast in the Taiwan Strait. Both Quemoy and the neighboring Matsu island group served as fortified outposts for the Nationalist government on Taiwan. The Quemoy group consists of 1 main and 11 smaller islands with a total area of 147 km² (57 mi²) and a population of 50,272 (1982 est.). The Matsu group lies 211 km (131 mi) to the north and consists of 19 islets with a total area of 28.8 km² (11.1 mi²) and a population of 8,199 (1982 est.). Heavy bombardment of the islands by the mainland Chinese in 1958 forced a diplomatic confrontation between the United States and China.

Queneau, Raymond [ken-oh']

Raymond Queneau, b. Feb. 21, 1903, d. Oct. 25, 1976, was a French poet and novelist, best known as a humorist and experimenter in literary forms. Rejecting traditional differences between prose and poetry, Queneau, in such fanciful novels as *The Bark Tree* (1933; Eng. trans., 1968) and *Zazie* (1959; Eng. trans., 1960), combined popular speech, unorthodox spelling and syntax, and enigmatic subject matter to create what he termed "natural" works. His novels *Pierrot* (1942; Eng. trans., 1950) and *The Sunday of Life* (1952; Eng. trans., 1976) showed the influence of surrealism. A master of parody and irony and the possessor of an enormous vocabulary, Queneau produced a tour de force in *Exercises in Style* (1947; Eng. trans., 1958), in which the same story was recounted in 99 different styles. Queneau was also editor of the *Encyclopédie de la Pléiade.* His verbal inventiveness and bold experimentations with fiction made Queneau one of the most innovative writers of the 20th century.

Bibliography: Guicharnaud, Jacques, *Raymond Queneau,* trans. by June Guicharnaud (1965); Shorley, Christopher, *Queneau's Fiction* (1985); Thiher, Allen, *Raymond Queneau* (1985).

Quercia, Jacopo della [kwer'-chah]

The Sienese sculptor Jacopo della Quercia, b. c.1371, d. Oct. 20, 1438, was one of the major Italian artists of the transition from the Middle Ages to the Renaissance. His earliest masterpiece is the graceful marble Tomb of Ilaria del Carretto (c.1406) in the Cathedral of Lucca. Quercia's roots in the late

Gothic style are evident in Ilaria's fluent, linear draperies, but the *putti* with garlands around the base of the sarcophagus, derived from ancient Roman models, are emphatically classical. A curious combination of elegant Gothic rhythms and massive classical form characterizes Quercia's three overlapping projects of the next decades: the marble reliefs in the Trenta Chapel at San Frediano in Lucca (c.1413–22); the marble reliefs and statues of the Fonte Gaia (1414–19), much-damaged fragments of which are now in the Palazzo Pubblico of Siena; and the bronze relief and marble statues on the baptismal font in the Sienese Baptistery (1417–34).

Quercia's greatest work is the decoration of the main portal of San Petronio (1425–38; Cathedral of Bologna); the ten marble panels that flank the doorway, depicting stories from the Book of Genesis, are among the most impressive sculptures of the 15th century. The treatment of space in these reliefs is rather conservative, but the weighty, monumental figures and the muscular, idealized nudes testify eloquently to Quercia's powerful conception of the human body.   MARK J. ZUCKER

Bibliography: Hanson, Anne Coffin, *Jacopo della Quercia's Fonte Gaia* (1965); Pope-Hennessy, John, *Italian Gothic Sculpture,* 2d ed. (1972); Seymour, Charles, Jr., *Jacopo della Quercia, Sculptor* (1973).

Querétaro (city) [kay-ray'-tah-roh]

Querétaro, the capital of the state of Querétaro in central Mexico, lies about 175 km (110 mi) northwest of Mexico City. The city has a population of 293,586 (1982 est.), and its economy is based on cotton textile manufacturing and food processing. Querétaro came under Spanish control in 1531. The 1810 revolt of Hildalgo y Costilla was planned there, and Emperor Maximilian surrendered there in 1867.

Querétaro (state)

Querétaro, a state of Mexico, is located on the central plain. It has an area of 11,449 km² (4,420 mi²) and a population of 872,000 (1984 est.). Most of the inhabitants are descendants of Otomí-Chichimec Indians. The capital is Querétaro. Agriculture, mining, and livestock account for the balanced economy in this area of high mountains and fertile valleys. Rich in mercury, silver, and gold, Querétaro is also known for its opals. Conquered by the Spanish in 1531 and colonized from 1550, Querétaro became a state of independent Mexico in 1824.
                                                               LEON YACHER

Quételet, Lambert Adolphe [kay-tuh-lay']

The Belgian mathematician, astronomer, and statistician Lambert Adolphe (Jacques) Quételet, b. Feb. 22, 1796, d. Feb. 17, 1874, laid the foundation for modern-day statistics and social physics with his paper "Sur l'homme et le développement de ses facultés, essai d'une physique sociale" (On Man and the Development of His Faculties; an Essay in Social Physics; 1835). Influenced by Pierre Laplace and Joseph Fourier, Quételet discovered the NORMAL DISTRIBUTION and developed methods for the computation of probabilities, which he applied to population statistics. At the observatory he established (1833) in Brussels at the request of the Belgian government, he worked on statistical, geophysical, and meteorological data; studied meteoric showers; and established methods for the comparison and evaluation of such information.

Bibliography: Hankins, Frank H., *Adolphe Quételet as Statistician* (1908; repr. 1968).

quetzal [ket-sahl']

One of the most beautiful birds in the world, the quetzal, *Pharomachrus mocino,* lives in humid mountain forests of southern Mexico and Central America. It is a member of the trogon family, Trogonidae.

The male is bright metallic green with golden highlights above and scarlet below, with the underside of the tail being white. He measures about 38 cm (15 in) in length, and beyond the end of his tail he has a magnificent train of long

(Left) *The quetzal, P. mocino, a Central American bird of great beauty, is the national bird of Guatemala. Aztecs and Mayans regarded the quetzal as sacred, plucking tail plumes from living male birds for ceremonial purposes.*

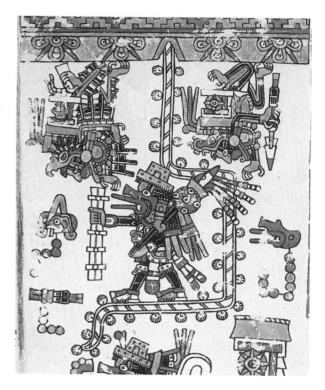

(Right) *Quetzalcóatl, one of the oldest and most prominent deities of the ancient Mexican pantheon, is portrayed in this Aztec codex in his aspect as the wind god, Ehecatl. Revered as the god of learning, Quetzalcóatl is most commonly depicted as a plumed serpent.*

green feathers that extends another 38 to 76 cm (15 to 30 in). These are not tail feathers; rather, they are elongated upper tail coverts. In the duller-colored female, this train of feathers is short. The quetzal figured prominently in the art and mythology of cultures of the region.   ROBERT J. RAIKOW

Quetzalcóatl   [ket-sahl-koh-aht'-ul]

The feathered serpent god, Quetzalcóatl, is one of the oldest and most important deities of ancient Mesoamerica. He is known to have been worshiped as early as AD 300 in highland Mexico and perhaps much earlier on the Gulf coast. At the time of the Spanish conquest (16th century) he was worshiped all over AZTEC and MAYA territory.

Quetzalcóatl was a creator god, and in one story he journeyed to the underworld to collect the bones from which he fashioned the human race after he sprinkled them with his own blood. In this aspect he was the god of self-sacrifice, wisdom, and science. As Ehecatl, he was god of the wind. He

was also god of the planet Venus, which is both morning and evening star—the morning aspect represented by the feathered serpent, the evening aspect by Xolotl, a dog-headed monster. This duality made him the patron deity of twins, the god to whom barren women prayed for children.

The title *Quetzalcóatl* was taken by several historical rulers and heroes from Mexico to Guatemala so that confusion often arises between historical and mythological events. The story of the exile of Quetzalcóatl, for example, probably refers to a real event, the driving out of King Topiltzin Quetzalcóatl from the city of TULA in the 12th century, to which have been added mythological stories about the deification of the god-man and his promise to return and claim his earthly kingdom. This prophecy was still current in the day of MONTEZUMA II. Montezuma II thought that Hernán Cortés was a deity because the latter landed (1519) in Mexico on the day One Reed, the calendar day of Quetzalcóatl's birth.

WARWICK BRAY

Bibliography: Davies, Nigel, *The Toltecs, until the Fall of Tula* (1977); Lafaye, Jacques, *Quetzalcóatl and Guadalupe,* trans. by B. Keen (1976).

queuing theory   [kue'-ing]

Queuing theory is the branch of probability theory that studies the behavior of queues, or waiting lines. Queues typically arise in arrival-service-departure settings, such as automobiles at a toll plaza, telephone calls coming into an exchange, customers awaiting a bank teller, computer programs awaiting processing in a computer, and repair jobs submitted to a central repair shop. If the capacity to service the arrivals is not adequate, the waiting time will be long. On the other hand, extra service capacity is expensive. Queuing theory seeks to predict the behavior of the waiting lines so that informed decisions can be made regarding how much service capacity should be made available.

The first element of a queuing model is an "input process," which describes the pattern of arrivals over time. The arrivals are not regular, but rather are random, so that the input process is a STOCHASTIC PROCESS. The second element is a description of the service mechanism. Are there one or several servers? Do all arrivals wait in a single line, or does each server have a separate waiting line? These are nonrandom aspects of the service mechanism, which can be changed to cut costs or reduce the waiting times. The service mechanism also has random aspects. The service time varies from case to case, so that the probability distribution of service times must be specified in the model.

Once a model is given, the behavior of the waiting line can be studied. Interest usually centers on the length of the waiting line (or lines) and the length of time between arrival and service. These quantities are RANDOM VARIABLES rather than fixed quantities. Answers are sought to such questions as "What is the probability that a customer must wait five minutes or more before being served?" or "What is the average waiting time between a repair request and service by the central maintenance shop?"   DAVID S. MOORE

Bibliography: Cooper, R. B., *Introduction to Queuing Theory*, 2d ed. (1981); Gorney, Len, *Queuing Theory: A Solving Approach* (1981); Gross, Donald, and Harris, Carl M., *Fundamentals of Queuing Theory* (1974); Saaty, Thomas L., *Elements of Queuing Theory with Applications* (1983).

See also: OPERATIONS RESEARCH; PROBABILITY.

Quevedo y Villegas, Francisco Gómez de
[kay-vay'-doh ee veel-yay'-gahs]

The Spanish social critic, essayist, novelist, and poet, Francisco Gómez de Quevedo y Villegas, b. Sept. 17, 1580, d. Sept. 8, 1645, was the foremost representative of the Stoic and Senecan outlook in Golden Age Spain.

Although highly regarded by his contemporaries for his moral and religious treatises and translations of ancient philosophers, Quevedo is remembered today chiefly for his satirical fiction, in which he bitterly attacks human weaknesses and corruption. His picaresque novel *La Vida del Buscón* (1626; trans. as *The Swindler*, 1972) and the episodic burlesque *Sueños* (1627; trans. as *Visions*, 1696) are nevertheless marked by humor and liveliness. Quevedo was also a prolific writer of satirical verse.   DANIEL EISENBERG

Bibliography: Baum, D. L., *Traditionalism in the Works of Francisco de Quevedo y Villegas* (1970); Bleznick, D. W., *Quevedo* (1972); Ettinghausen, H., *Francisco de Quevedo and the Neostoic Movement* (1972).

Quezon, Manuel Luis   [kay'-sohn]

A leading Philippine nationalist and statesman, Manuel Luis Quezon, b. Aug. 19, 1878, d. Aug. 4, 1944, helped pave the way for Philippine independence during the final period of U.S. colonial rule. He was president of the commonwealth from 1935 to 1944.

Quezon fought in the 1901 insurrection against U.S. rule, but after its failure he cooperated with the U.S. territorial government. He became majority leader of the first Philippine assembly under U.S. rule in 1907 and served as Filipino resident commissioner in Washington from 1909 to 1916. Subsequently, he was president of the senate in the bicameral Philippine national legislature. Quezon led the successful protest against

Manuel Luis Quezon, president of the Philippines from 1935 until 1944, actively sought his homeland's independence from U.S. control. The Japanese invasion (1941–42) forced him to leave for the United States, where he headed the government in exile until his death.

the Hare-Hawes-Cutting Act (passed by the U.S. Congress in 1933), because, although it promised independence, it also allowed U.S. military bases to remain in the Philippines after independence. After the act was rejected by the Filipinos, he worked for passage of the Tydings-McDuffie Act of 1934, which pledged complete Filipino independence on July 4, 1946. Elected president of the resulting new Philippine Commonwealth, he displayed an increasing tendency toward authoritarian rule, and his Nationalist party became in effect the only political force in the islands.

Following the overrunning of the Philippines by the Japanese late in 1941, Quezon was evacuated by submarine; he governed in exile until his death.   RICHARD BUTWELL

Bibliography: Gwekoh, Sol H., *Manuel L. Quezon* (1948).

Quezon City

Quezon City, the former capital and the second largest city of the Philippines, is located on Luzon Island, adjacent to Manila. The population is 1,165,865 (1980). Quezon City is mostly residential but has a major textile industry. Planned in 1937 as the new capital of the Philippines, Quezon City officially replaced Manila in 1948. New government buildings were constructed, and the transfer was still in progress when the seat of government was returned to Manila in 1976.

quick clay

Quick clay is a natural aggregate made up of very fine mineral particles—more than half of them less than 2 micrometers in diameter—and water. It may change suddenly from a solid to a rapidly flowing liquid because of jolting actions such as an earthquake, an explosion, or the jarring of a pile driver, and can slide over land with a slope of less than 1°, carrying along heavy structures in its path. Quick clays, loosely consolidated and usually dark blue gray when wet, were formed during the most recent advance of the continental glaciers. Their water content is more than 50%, and their salt content is low.   HAYDN H. MURRAY

Bibliography: Grim, R. E., *Applied Clay Mineralogy*, 2d ed. (1968).

quicksand

Quicksand, contrary to popular belief, is not a type of sand, but rather a flow condition within the sand. A saturated sand becomes quick—quick meaning alive—when upward flow of water through the sand applies seepage forces equal to or exceeding the buoyant weight of the sand. Hence, any sand and even gravels can be made quick provided sufficient quantities of water are made to flow upward through the soil. Because the rate of flow required to make sands quick decreases with particle size, quick conditions in nature occur most commonly in fine sands.

The laws of physics disprove the existence of any forces that would tend to suck a human or animal into quicksand. A human is just able to float in freshwater, which has a unit weight of 1.00 g/cm^3 (62.4 lb/ft^3). In salt water, which has a unit weight of 1.02 g/cm^3 (64 lb/ft^3), floating is relatively easy. Quicksands, by comparison, have a unit weight of 1.60 g/cm^3 (100 lb/ft^3) or more; thus a human can easily float in such a material.   T. LESLIE YOUD

Bibliography: Hillel, D., *Fundamentals of Soil Physics* (1980).

Quidor, John   [ki-dohr']

Little known in his lifetime, the American painter John Quidor, b. Tappan, N.Y., Jan. 26, 1801, d. Dec. 13, 1881, has been recognized in the 20th century as a major figure in American art. The subjects of many of his paintings were taken from the novels and stories of Washington Irving and James Fenimore Cooper. Quidor added his own fanciful details to produce pictures of marked originality, strong color, masterful composition, and richly comic invention. In the 1840s he painted a series of biblical subjects, now lost.   DAVID TATHAM

Bibliography: Baur, John I. H., *John Quidor* (1966).

quietism [kwy'-et-izm]

Quietism is the name usually given to a form of late-17th-century Christian mysticism whose chief proponent was the Spanish priest Miguel de MOLINOS. The quietists believed that the soul could have direct communion with God without any active religious practices and that this communion was best attainable through a state of absolute passivity and annihilation of the will. In 1687, Molinos was imprisoned in Rome, and 68 of his propositions were condemned by the pope. Later quietism achieved brief influence at the French court of Louis XIV through the activities of Madame de Guyon (1648–1717), a friend of Madame de Maintenon, and the cautious sympathy of Archbishop FÉNELON. It virtually disappeared, however, after the movement was condemned in the Conference of Issy (1695), and Fénelon was censored by the pope (1699).   T. TACKETT

Bibliography: Backhouse, W., comp., *Guide to True Peace* (1946; repr. 1979).

Quileute-Hoh and Chemakum [kwil'-uh-yoot, chem'-uh-kuhm]

The Quileute-Hoh and Chemakum are tribes of North American Indians of the Pacific Northwest. The Quileute and Hoh are divisions of one group, traditionally residing on the Soleduck and Hoh rivers on the west coast of Washington State. They and the Chemakum, on the west shores of Admiralty Inlet below Hood Canal, are the only speakers of Chemakuan languages, which are not demonstrably related to any other Indian tongue although remote relationships to Wakashan and Salishan have been suggested (see INDIAN LANGUAGES, AMERICAN). The Chemakum, reputedly warlike at one time but outnumbered by equally warlike Coast SALISH neighbors, were dwindling in numbers during historic times and early in this century became extinct. Little is known of their lifeway except that it was similar to that of their Salishan-speaking neighbors. The Quileute-Hoh, in earlier times whalers and sea-hunters like their Makah neighbors, also exploited the salmon-runs in their rivers and the fish and mollusks of their shores. Their houses were large multifamily structures of cedar planks, partitioned by planks or storage boxes. Most descendants of the Quileute and Hoh live on their reservation at La Push, Wash.; their population was estimated at more than 350 in 1981.
                                                    PHILIP DRUCKER

Bibliography: Owen, R., et al., *The North American Indians* (1967).

quillwort [kwil'-wurt]

Quillworts are about 60 species of aquatic or wetland perennial herbs constituting the genus *Isoetes* in the quillwort family, Isoetaceae. Like the ferns, quillworts are primitive, spore-bearing, nonflowering plants with fluid-conducting (vascular) tissues and are classified with the club mosses as one of the fern allies, Lycopodiophyta. The quillwort has a minute, fleshy, flat-topped rootstock from which arises a tuft of grasslike leaves up to 50 cm (20 in) high. Spores are produced in the enlarged, spoon-shaped bases of the leaves.

quilting

Quilting is a needlework technique used to hold a layer of insulating or padding material between two outer layers of fabric. To prevent the interior layer from shifting, numerous runs of stitches are worked across the sandwiched layers. Long ago, people in China, Egypt, and elsewhere wore quilted garments for warmth and for protection in battle. Quilting is still used for making garments and bedcovers because quilted materials retain warmth better than do single-layers.

There are several types of quilting. Wadded quilting is evenly filled with thick padding, whereas flat quilting has little or no padding. In trapunto, parts of the design are raised by being heavily padded; in corded, or Italian, quilting, heavy yarn is threaded between double rows of stitching. The making of pieced, or patchwork, quilts was an especially popular form of FOLK ART in preindustrial America. The top of a pieced quilt consists of small scraps of fabric pieced together to create a complicated pattern; the quilting stitches follow the seams between the elements of the design. Although hand quilting has survived in the United States and elsewhere as a decorative art, most commercial quilting is now done by machine.   MARK DITTRICK

Bibliography: Colby, A., *Quilting* (1971; repr. 1979); Haders, P., *The Warner Collector's Guide to American Quilts* (1981); Kihn, Y. M., *The Collector's Dictionary of Quilt Names and Patterns* (1980); Safford, C. L., and Bishop, R., *America's Quilts and Coverlets* (1972).

Quimby, Phineas Parkhurst

Phineas Parkhurst Quimby, b. Lebanon, N.H., Feb. 16, 1802, d. Jan. 16, 1866, developed a philosophy of mental healing that laid the foundation for NEW THOUGHT. At first a hypnotist, he turned to mental healing in the belief that he had rediscovered the secret of Jesus' healing ministry. He held that all disease is an error of the mind and could be cured by a proper understanding of the relation between the divine and the human. One of Quimby's patients was Mary Baker EDDY, who may have derived from him the inspiration for CHRISTIAN SCIENCE; she denied this, however. The New Thought movement grew out of the "mental science" of another Quimby patient, Warren Felt Evans.

Bibliography: Dresser, H. W., ed., *The Quimby Manuscripts* (1921); Hawkins, Ann B., *Phineas Parkhurst Quimby* (1970).

quince [kwins]

The quince C. oblonga, a small tree of the rose family, has been cultivated since ancient times for its fragrant fruit. It is inedible when raw, but when thoroughly cooked it makes excellent preserves.

Quince is the common name for various shrubs and small trees in the rose family, Rosaceae. The common quince, *Cydonia oblonga,* is a slow-growing, wide-spreading shrub or small tree that yields greenish yellow or golden yellow fruit. The fruit is bitter and not palatable when raw; it is eaten cooked in fruit compotes, preserves, and jams. Of little commercial importance in the United States, the common quince is more widely cultivated in the temperate zones of Europe and Argentina. The flowering, or Japanese, quince, *Chaenomeles speciosa,* bears flowers in shades ranging from creamy white to scarlet and is a favorite ornamental in home gardens. Pear trees are often dwarfed by grafting them onto quince rootstocks.

Quincy [kwin'-zee]

Quincy is a city in eastern Massachusetts, about 13 km (8 mi) south of Boston on Quincy Bay, an arm of Boston Bay. Its population is 84,743 (1980). A commercial and major ship-building center within the Boston metropolitan area, Quincy has industries that manufacture electronic and soap products. Quincy was the birthplace of two U.S. presidents, John Adams and John Quincy Adams, and of John Hancock. The Adams National Historic Site includes the Adams family house (1685–18th century), birthplaces of both Adamses, and their burial sites at United First Parish Church (1828). Settled in 1625 by Thomas Morton, the town was originally the northern part of Braintree. It was incorporated in 1792 and named for Col. John Quincy, a local resident. Quincy was a farming community until the development of granite quarries in 1750. The shipbuilding industry developed after 1894.

Quincy, Josiah

Josiah Quincy, b. Boston, Feb. 4, 1772, d. July 1, 1864, was a member of the U.S. House of Representatives, a reform mayor of Boston, and president of Harvard University. Representing Boston in Congress from 1805 to 1813, he was an ardent Federalist and a die-hard opponent of the War of 1812. As mayor of Boston in the 1820s, he did much to modernize the city. As president of Harvard (1829–45) he professionalized the Law School and wrote a two-volume history of the university. He also wrote a biography of his father, Josiah Quincy (1744–75), a political leader prior to the American Revolution.

Bibliography: McCaughey, Robert A., *Josiah Quincy, 1772–1864: The Last Federalist* (1974).

Quine, Willard Van Orman   [kwyn]

Willard Van Orman Quine, b. Akron, Ohio, June 25, 1908, is an American philosopher and logician. He was educated at Oberlin College and Harvard University and has been on the faculty at Harvard since 1936. His work is mainly in symbolic logic and the logic of ordinary language, but he also writes on ontology. Quine was influenced by such positivists as Rudolf Carnap, but his denial of the distinction between analytic and synthetic statements marks a major deviation from positivism, as does his view on the logical status of the problem of what exists. The pragmatism of Clarence Irving Lewis is evident in Quine's view that logic and language evolve as tools of inquiry. His books include *From a Logical Point of View* (1953), *Word and Object* (1960), *Philosophy of Logic* (1970), and *Theories and Things* (1981).   E. DARNELL RUCKER

Bibliography: Davidson, Donald, and Hintikka, Jaakko, eds., *Words and Objections: Essays on the Work of W. V. Quine* (1969); Orenstein, Alex, *Willard Van Orman Quine* (1977); Shahan, Robert W., and Swoyer, Chris, eds., *Essays on the Philosophy of W. V. Quine* (1979).

quinidine   [kwin'-uh-deen]

Quinidine is the generic name for an ALKALOID drug derived from CINCHONA bark. It has antimalarial and fever-reducing effects similar to the related drug quinine; its main importance, however, is its antiarrhythmic effect in the treatment of such disorders of heart function as fibrillation and heart block.

quinine   [kwy'-nyn]

Quinine is an alkaloid drug obtained by extraction of the bark of the cinchona tree of South America and Indonesia. The drug was once the only one available for MALARIA treatment, and it is still used as a muscle relaxant. It has largely been replaced by synthetic drugs, however, because of the serious hypersensitivity reactions it can produce.

quinone   [kwi-nohn']

The quinone group of organic compounds are present in many plants and in some animals. Cyclic hydrocarbons with one or more ring structures, quinones exist in two isometric forms. They are usually high colored—yellow, orange, or red—and most are toxic. Widely distributed in nature, they play diverse roles—as pigments in plants, growth factors, antibiotics, catalysts, and respiratory inhibitors. Vitamin K, which promotes blood clotting, is a natural quinone.

The name *quinone* comes from the first preparation—in 1838—of *p*-benzoquinone by a complicated oxidation of quinic acid. Today there are many synthetic quinones, usually prepared by the oxidation of the corresponding HYDROQUINONE, a reaction that is a key step in the silver-based photographic process. Synthetic quinones are used in medicine, in dyes and fungicides, and as antioxidants and stabilizers in varnishes, paints, fats, and oils.   K. THOMAS FINLEY

Quintana Roo   [keen-tah'-nah roh'-oh]

Quintana Roo, a state in southeastern Mexico on the Yucatán Peninsula, has an area of 50,212 km^2 (19,387 mi^2) and a population of 209,858 (1980). The capital is CHETUMAL. The state is dominated by tropical lowlands inhabited by scattered communities of MAYA. Henequen, chicle, and cotton are the main agricultural products. Fish, sponges, and turtles are taken from offshore waters. Three islands off the coast—Cancún, Cozumel, and Isla Mujeres—are centers of tourism. The Spanish landed in Quintana Roo in 1517; it became a Mexican territory in 1902 and a state in 1974.   LEON YACHER

Quintilian   [kwin-til'-ee-uhn]

Quintilian is the anglicized name of Marcus Fabius Quintilianus, AD c.35–c.100, a Roman of Spanish origin whose *Institutio Oratoria* (c.95) is the most thorough textbook on the art of oratory that has come down from ancient times. A 12-book work that shows the influence of Cicero, the *Institutio Oratoria* touches on all aspects of Roman education and public speaking, including the organization of a speech, the use of argument, stylistic devices, the technique of memorization, and the art of delivery. Quintilian also stresses the importance to the speaker of a good character, some knowledge of philosophy, and a thorough familiarity with literature. A noted professor in Rome, Quintilian put forth educational theories that remained influential through the Renaissance.

Bibliography: Kennedy, George, *The Art of Rhetoric in the Roman World* (1972) and *Quintilian* (1969); Gwynn, Aubrey, *Roman Education from Cicero to Quintillian* (1966); Quintilian, *Institutio Oratoria*, ed. and trans. by H. E. Butler, 4 vols. (1920–22).

Quiriguá   [kee-ree-gwah']

Quiriguá, a lowland MAYA center on the Motagua River in eastern Guatemala, is best known for its large stelae, upright stone shafts carved with hieroglyphic texts and rulers' portraits. Quiriguá flourished as a civic-ceremonial center during the Classic period (AD 250–950). During most of its history, it was politically subordinate to COPÁN, 50 km (31 mi) to the south. The stelae of Quiriguá, the tallest in the Maya world, are in the style of Copán, as is its architecture.

The Carnegie Institution of Washington sponsored small-scale excavation and restoration at Quiriguá early in the 20th century. A new project was begun there in the 1970s by the University of Pennsylvania.   JOHN S. HENDERSON

Bibliography: Ashmore, Wendy, et al., *Quiriguá Reports*, vol. 1 (1979); Morley, G. G., *Guide Book to the Ruins of Quiriguá* (1935).

Quirino, Elpidio   [kee-ree'-noh, el-pee'-dee-oh]

Elpidio Quirino, b. Nov. 16, 1890, d. Feb. 29, 1956, was the second president (1948–53) of the Republic of the Philippines. In 1946, following Philippine independence, Quirino, who had been elected on the ticket of Manuel Roxas y Acuna, became his country's first vice-president. Succeeding to the presidency at the death of Roxas in 1948, he was elected to the office in 1949. Quirino broke with the Roxas policy of crushing the insurgent Communist Hukbalahaps (Huks), and he persuaded the Huk leader, Luis Taruc, to accept an amnesty. A renewed Huk uprising in August 1948, however, forced Quirino's defense minister, Ramón MAGSAYSAY, to put down the rebellion. Magsaysay ran against and defeated Quirino in the 1953 presidential election.   RICHARD BUTWELL

Bibliography: Gwekoh, Sol H., *Elpidio Quirino* (1949); Smith, Robert A., *Philippine Freedom 1946–1958* (1958).

Quirinus [kwir'-in-uhs]

In early Roman mythology Quirinus was an important deity who was ranked in a trinity with JUPITER and MARS. Of Sabine origin, he was a god of war and was sometimes identified with Mars. Later, he became identified with ROMULUS, the legendary founder of Rome, and gave his name to the Quirinal Hill, one of the seven hills of Rome.

Quiroga, Juan Facundo [kee-roh'-gah]

Juan Facundo Quiroga, b. 1788, d. Feb. 16, 1835, was an Argentine caudillo of the postindependence era who was virtually the absolute ruler of the Andean provinces. Quiroga, known as the "tiger of the plains," was a staunch believer in federalism; he led the successful armed opposition to the unitary constitution of 1826 (which had centralized government power at the expense of the regional caudillos). Quiroga subsequently pressed unsuccessfully for the adoption of a federal constitution. He was assassinated in 1835, presumably by order of Juan Manuel de Rosas, his chief political rival.

Quisling, Vidkun [kvis'-ling, vid'-kuhn]

Vidkun Abraham Lauritz Jonsson Quisling, b. July 18, 1887, d. Oct. 24, 1945, was a Norwegian fascist in World War II whose name became a synonym for traitor. A military attaché in Petrograd (now Leningrad) during the Russian Revolution, he worked with Fridtjof Nansen distributing famine relief in the USSR from 1922 to 1926, leaving that country in 1929. Norwegian minister of defense from 1931 to 1933, he founded (1933) the National Unity party, modeled on the German Nazi party. In 1940 he aided the Germans in their conquest of Norway and was their puppet ruler throughout the war. After the war the Norwegians convicted him of high treason and shot him.

Bibliography: Hayes, Paul M., *Quisling: The Career and Political Ideas of Vidkun Quisling, 1887–1945* (1972).

quiteron [kwit'-uh-rahn]

The quiteron is an electronic device under study for its power-dissipation advantages over the transistors now used for digital switching in computers and other integrated-circuit arrays. Its name derives from "heavy-quasiparticle-injection tunneling effect" (see TUNNEL EFFECT). Developed in the early 1980s by Sadeg M. Faris of IBM, the quiteron employs the phenomenon of SUPERCONDUCTIVITY. It contains three layers of superconducting material separated by insulation. When it is not operating, the layers are in thermal equilibrium; but when a voltage is applied to one of its junctions, many quasiparticles are produced in the middle layer. (A quasiparticle is an electron, under superconducting conditions, that has a smaller effective charge than an ordinary electron.) Thermal equilibrium is lost, and quasiparticles can tunnel through to the second junction. This change in resistance, which takes place in less than a billionth of a second, is equivalent to the "on-off" switching function of an ordinary transistor.

Quito [kee'-toh]

Quito, the capital and second largest city of Ecuador, has a population of 866,472 persons (1982). Located in the Andean highlands, 24 km (15 mi) south of the equator, it lies on a fertile plateau, 2,850 m (9,350 ft) above sea level. The nearby volcano Pichincha is dormant, but the city is subject to earthquakes. Leather goods, cotton and woolen fabrics, and jewelry are manufactured in Quito. The city retains much 16th-century Spanish architecture and has 86 churches and two major universities—Central University (1586) and Catholic University of Ecuador (1946). Inhabited by Quitu Indians before the 11th century, the city became the northern capital of the Inca Empire in 1487 and was taken by Sebastián de Benalcazar in 1536. A local uprising against Spanish rule was defeated in 1809, but Ecuadorian independence was won after the Battle of Pichincha in 1822.

Qum

Qum (also Qom or Kum) is a city in northwestern Iran located about 120 km (75 mi) southwest of Tehran. The population is 424,408 (1982 est.). A trade and rail center for the surrounding agricultural region, Qum also has textile factories. The city is best known, however, as a pilgrimage site for Shiite Muslims. The principal landmark is the gold-domed Shrine of Fatimah; more than 400 other saints and kings, including Shah Abbas II, are interred in Qum.

Established during the 9th century AD, the city was sacked (1380s) by Timur, revived under the Safavids during the 16th century, and destroyed (1722) by Afghans. Following Iran's Islamic revolution of 1979, Ayatollah Ruhollah KHOMEINI ruled the country from Qum, his native city.

Qumran [koom-rahn']

Khirbet Qumran, meaning the ruin of Qumran, stands on a rocky projection of the high cliffs overlooking the northwest corner of the Dead Sea, in the Israeli-occupied West Bank region. A few foundations date from the 8th to the 7th century BC. Most of the ruins are a walled complex of buildings built by a community of ESSENES who had withdrawn from Jerusalem and who produced the DEAD SEA SCROLLS, which were found in caves nearby. Rooms include a meeting room, scriptorium, laundry, potter's shop, kitchen, pantry, workshop, and, most important, a system of cisterns, fed by canals leading down from cliffs above, used to store water in this arid region. Building began about 150 BC, and flourished from late in that century until an earthquake in 31 BC. The site was subsequently rebuilt but was later destroyed in AD 68 by the Romans, who left a garrison there.   ANTHONY J. SALDARINI

Bibliography: Davies, Philip, *Qumran* (1982); Fritsch, Charles T., *The Qumran Community: Its History and Scrolls* (1956; repr. 1973); Milik, Jozef T., *Ten Years of Discovery in the Wilderness of Judaea* (1959); Ploeg, J. P. M. van der, *The Excavations at Qumran* (1958); Schubert, Kurt, *The Dead Sea Community*, trans. by John Doberstein (1959; repr. 1974); Vaux, Roland de, *Archaeology and the Dead Sea Scrolls* (1973); Vermes, Geza, *The Dead Sea Scrolls* (1978; repr. 1981).

quota [kwoh'-tuh]

A quota, in international trade, is a type of trade barrier that nations place on the physical amount of imports or exports of specific kinds of goods. A quota differs from a TARIFF, which is a schedule of taxes or duties placed on imports that does not categorically place limitations on the amount of the goods that may be imported. Both tariffs and quotas are regarded as detrimental to the concept of FREE TRADE, and the GENERAL AGREEMENT ON TARIFFS AND TRADE (GATT) works to reduce such trade barriers.

A government may use a quota on imports to protect some of its own industries from foreign competition. In order to encourage the sale of American-made cars, for example, in 1981 the United States placed a quota—originally intended to last for only three years—on the number of cars imported from Japan. The quota was still in place in the late 1980s, and its effect was higher U.S. prices for both U.S.-made and Japanese cars. Developing nations often impose quotas to protect their infant industries. Governments may impose export quotas in order to conserve a material in short supply. Quotas may also be set on exports to maintain a certain overseas price level. The Organization of Petroleum Exporting Countries (OPEC) in effect establishes quotas on the foreign oil sales of its members in order to maintain its established prices.

J. DONALD WEINRAUCH

Bibliography: Canto, V. A., *The Determinants and Consequences of Trade Restrictions in the U.S. Economy* (1985).

Qutb Minar [kuh'-tuhb mee'-nahr]

One of the earliest examples of Mogul architecture in India is the Qutb Minar, a MINARET located near New Delhi. It was erected about 1230 to commemorate the military triumph of Qutb-ud-Din Aybak of the Delhi Sultanate. The tower, which is decorated with relief work, stands 73 m (240 ft) high.

PHOENICIAN
EARLY HEBREW
EARLY ARAMAIC
EARLY GREEK
P CLASSICAL GREEK

Rr
MODERN LATIN

ETRUSCAN
EARLY LATIN R
CLASSICAL LATIN R
RUSSIAN-CYRILLIC Р
GERMAN-GOTHIC ℜ

R

R/r is the 18th letter of the English alphabet. Both the letter and its position in the alphabet were derived from the Latin, which in turn derived it from the Greek by way of the Etruscan. The Greeks took the letter, which they called *rho,* from the Semitic sign *resh.* Both the Greek and Etruscan alphabets used a sign similar to modern *P/p* for *r;* when the Latin alphabet began using the modern form of *p,* however, a variant of the Etruscan *p* with a tail under the loop was used for *r.* The modern *R* developed from this form.

R/r is a liquid consonant in the same manner as *L/l.* It is made with the tip of the tongue raised while allowing the voiced breath to vibrate it. The sound heard is a combination of the voicing and the tongue vibrations. The position of the tip of the tongue and the amount of vibration allowed determine the exact nature of the *r* sound. Before a vowel, *R/r* is normally pronounced as in *rise, rapid, forest;* before a consonant, except *h* or in final position, however, it is often much attenuated or dropped completely, especially in the dialects of certain geographical areas. I. J. GELB AND R. M. WHITING

R-34 and R-101

The British had a program for developing rigid airships during and after World War I. Of particular importance were the R-34 and R-101. The R-34 was built in Scotland in 1917–19; its first flight was March 14, 1919. It was 165 m (543 ft) long and 24 m (78.7 ft) at maximum diameter and was rendered airborne by 55,259 m^3 (1,950,000 ft^3) of hydrogen. Its five 250-hp engines provided a top speed of 37.5 km/h (60 mph). In July 1919 the R-34 flew from Scotland to Mineola, N.Y., the first westward crossing of the Atlantic by air. It returned to England a few days later, completing the first round-trip crossing by an aircraft. In January 1921 the R-34 was wrecked in a bad landing at Howden, England, and was subsequently scrapped.

The R-101 was designed and built in the period 1924–29 for commercial service to India and Australia. It was originally 223 m (732 ft) long and 40.2 m (132 ft) at maximum diameter and was rendered airborne by 141,546 m^3 (4,998,000 ft^3) of hydrogen gas in 16 cells. Five 585-hp diesels gave a top speed of 120 km/h (75 mph). The R-101 made its first flight on Oct. 14, 1929. Its structure was later enlarged, increasing its capacity. The ship crashed and burned near Beauvais, France, on Oct. 4, 1930; of the 54 men on board, only 6 survived. This disaster marked the end of the British interest in the rigid airship.

RICHARD K. SMITH

Ra: see AMON-RE.

Ra expeditions [rah]

The Ra expeditions of 1969 and 1970 were two attempts by international crews led by Thor HEYERDAHL to cross the Atlantic Ocean in reed boats, to demonstrate that mariners from ancient Egypt could have reached the New World. The boats were named *Ra,* after the sun-god of ancient Egypt. Two years of research and $200,000 were invested to make the voyages authentically Egyptian.

The first boat, made by African boat-builders from Chad, consisted of 280,000 papyrus reeds and weighed more than 12 tons. It was about 15 m (50 ft) long, with the typically Egyptian upcurved bow and stern, a large trapezoidal sail, and five oars. On May 25, 1969, the *Ra* and its seven-member crew were towed out to sea from the ancient port of Safi in Morocco. The craft followed the Canary current and then the North Equatorial current westward across the Atlantic. Mishaps occurred, but the boat did not immediately capsize or sink, as critics had predicted. After eight weeks at sea, however, a severe storm in the Caribbean damaged the *Ra* beyond repair. Heyerdahl attributed this to his failure to follow the ancient design exactly. On July 16, 1969, the crew was rescued.

Heyerdahl had a second craft constructed in Morocco by Bolivian Indians from Lake Titicaca. The *Ra II* was shorter, thinner, rounder, and more rigid than its predecessor and carried eight men. The design created by the Bolivian boat-builders proved to be perfect. On May 17, 1970, the *Ra II* left the harbor of Safi. On the evening of July 12 the *Ra II* sailed into Bridgetown harbor in Barbados, 5,260 km (3,270 mi) from Safi. Heyerdahl's successful voyage, however, has not convinced most archaeologists that trans-Atlantic migrations were made from ancient Egypt to the New World.

Bibliography: Heyerdahl, Thor, *The Ra Expeditions* (1970; English trans., 1971).

Ra II, *a papyrus boat designed by Norwegian anthropologist Thor Heyerdahl, crossed the Atlantic from Morocco to Barbados in 1970. The expedition's goal was to prove Heyerdahl's hypothesis of cultural contact between the ancient Egyptians and the New World.*

Raabe, Wilhelm [rah'-be]

Wilhelm Karl Raabe, b. Sept. 8, 1831, d. Nov. 15, 1910, was a prolific German novelist who wrote under the pen name Jakob Corvinus. His early, historical novels, written during a period of great social change in Germany, are rooted in the Romantic tradition of the previous age. These were followed by grim, starkly realistic novels influenced by the pessimism of Arthur Schopenhauer. Raabe's novels written after 1870 are brighter in outlook and filled with engaging humor. His notable works include *The Hungry Pastor* (1864; Eng. trans., 1885) and *Abu Telfan's Return from the Mountains of the Moon* (1867; Eng. trans., 1885).   CARL R. MUELLER

Bibliography: Daemmrich, H., *Wilhelm Raabe* (1981); Fairley, Barker, *Wilhelm Raabe: An Introduction to His Novels* (1961).

Rabanus Maurus [ruh-bay'-nuhs maw'-ruhs]

Rabanus (also Hrabanus or Rhabanus) Maurus, c.780–c.856, was a Frankish churchman and scholar who is known as the preceptor of Germany for his advancement of learning there. Having studied under ALCUIN, he was appointed (803) master of the monastic school at Fulda. As abbot of Fulda from 822 to 842, he developed the abbey into one of Europe's leading intellectual centers. In 847 he became archbishop of Mainz. Rabanus wrote a number of works including *De arte grammatica, De institutione clericorum,* and biblical commentaries and poetry. Although never officially canonized, Rabanus has been honored as a saint. Feast day: Feb. 4.

Rabat [rah-baht']

Rabat, the capital of Morocco, is located at the mouth of the Bou Regreg on the northwestern coast. Its population is 518,616 (1982). Rabat has textile, food-processing, and asbestos industries. The site of the king's main residence and an administrative and cultural center, it has been the capital since 1913.

In addition to its modern section, Rabat has an old Arab town containing the ancient Muslim and Jewish quarters. The Kasbah des Oudaïa, a 17th-century fortress, is nearby. Rabat is the home of Muhammad V University (1957).

The city was founded in the 10th century as a military camp and was taken by the Almoravids in 1140 and by the Almohads in 1146. The settlement at Rabat was soon eclipsed by neighboring Salé.

The arrival of the French in 1912 gave Rabat new importance, and now Salé is a suburb of Rabat, linked to it by the Hassan II Bridge.

rabbi

Rabbi (Hebrew for "my master") is the title given recognized Jewish religious teachers, sages, and leaders. Originally a form of respectful address, it became a formal title in the 1st century AD for those authorized by their teachers—after an examination on Scripture and the law—to interpret and expound the Jewish law. This "ordination" (in Hebrew, *simichah,* literally "laying on of hands") did not confer sacramental power, for laymen may perform all religious rites of the SYNAGOGUE.

Originally the rabbi served without compensation, in accordance with Mishnaic law prohibiting financial benefits derived from the Torah; only in the late 14th century was a salaried rabbinate established. The rabbi functioned as a judge in civil cases, gave direction in matters of religious observance, supervised education and taught advanced students, and, in general, served as community leader. In the 19th century, rabbinical seminaries were established in Europe and North America; the seminary increasingly took over responsibility for conferring ordination.

In modern times the rabbi in Western countries has tended to become less of a scholar and more of a congregational minister in the Protestant style. The rabbinate was traditionally restricted to men, but Reform, Reconstructionist, and Conservative seminaries now ordain both men and women.

BERNARD J. BAMBERGER

rabbit

Rabbits are members of the order Lagomorpha, which also contains the HARES and the short-legged pikas. They were once considered rodents but differ from them in many ways. For example, they have two pairs of upper incisors (front teeth), one small pair immediately behind a larger; rodents have only one. Rabbits can be distinguished from hares by their young, which are born hairless, blind, and helpless; young hares are born furred, with the eyes open, and can hop minutes after birth. Such distinctions, however, are not always followed in popular names: jackrabbits, for example, are actually hares, and the domestic breed known as the Belgian hare is a rabbit.

The rabbit and hare family, Leporidae, contains 18 species of rabbits grouped into six or seven genera, the best known being the cottontails, *Sylvilagus,* and the Old World rabbit, *Oryctolagus.* Coat colors are usually uniform shades of browns or grays, but the Sumatran short-eared rabbit, *Nesolagus netscheri,* has a striped pattern of brown on gray, and a reddish rump. Female rabbits, or does, are generally larger than the males, or bucks. The smallest species are the North

chinchilla rabbit   **angora rabbit**   **eastern cottontail rabbit**

Cottontail rabbits are named for their white tails, which resemble balls of cotton. The eastern cottontail, S. Floridanus, has the widest distribution, ranging from southern Canada to the northern tip of South America. All domestic rabbits are descended from the Old World rabbit, O. cuniculus. Some, like the angora and chinchilla breeds, are raised for their fur or meat. Others are bred for use as laboratory animals.

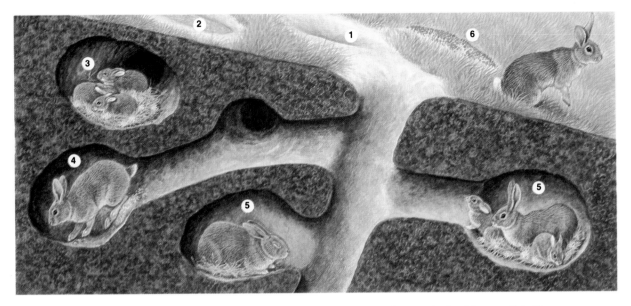

The Old World rabbit, O. cuniculus, *digs the burrow in which it lives. A warren consists of a network of such burrows, linked by passages to a central chamber. Main entrances (1) usually remain open, whereas smaller entrances (2), which often lead directly to young rabbits in a nest of straw and rabbit fur (3), can be closed while the mother is away. Here young females dig new burrows (4) on the outer edges of the warren, while older, dominant females (5) have burrows nearer to the main chamber. Specific areas set aside for defecation (6) are used over and over.*

American pygmy rabbit, *S. idahoensis*—sometimes placed in a separate genus, *Brachylagus*—which may be as small as 25 cm (10 in) long and 400 g (14 oz) in weight; and the similar-sized dwarf Old World rabbit found on the Madeiran island of Santo Porto, near the northwest coast of Africa. The largest is the North American swamp rabbit, *S. aquaticus*, which may be 53 cm (21 in) long and 2.7 kg (6 lb) in weight. Some of the 60 or more domestic varieties developed from the Old World rabbit may be considerably larger; the Flemish giant may exceed 7 kg (15 lb).

Rabbits are generally nocturnal or twilight-active and are native to all the continents except Antarctica and Australia; introduced into Australia, they increased to great numbers and destroyed much grazing land. The Old World rabbit, *O. cuniculus*, is gregarious, living in large colonial burrows, or warrens, which it digs itself. Its breeding season varies with locality; in central Europe it runs from February to July. Gestation lasts 28 to 31 days, with mostly four to six young to a litter, and females may have as many as seven litters per year. The young become sexually mature at 4 or 5 months and can continue breeding until about 6 years of age. Life span is about 9 years.

The North American eastern cottontail, *S. floridanus*, does not dig its own burrows but uses surface resting places, or forms, or the burrows of other animals. Eastern cottontails tend to be solitary, although they may gather into groups when feeding or mating. The breeding season runs from about the end of February into September. Gestation is 28 days, and litter size is usually 1 to 8 young. The young are fully furred within a week; their eyes open in 6 to 9 days. A female may have 5 litters per year.   EDWIN E. ROSENBLUM

Bibliography: Arrington, Lewis R., and Kelley, Kathleen C., *Domestic Rabbit Biology and Production* (1976); Hirschhorn, Howard, *All about Rabbits* (1974); Sheail, John, *Rabbits and Their History* (1971).

rabbit fever: see TULAREMIA.

Rabe, David   [rayb]

An American playwright, David Rabe, b. Dubuque, Iowa, Mar. 10, 1940, is the author of *The Basic Training of Pavlo Hummel* (1971) and *Sticks and Bones* (1971), dramas about the aftereffects of war. Drawn from his own experience in Vietnam, these works are notable for their brutal realism and moving characterizations. Rabe received an Obie Award in 1971 and a Tony Award in 1972. His other plays include *In the Boom Boom Room* (1973), *Streamers* (1976; film, 1983), and the highly acclaimed *Hurlyburly* (1984).

Rabelais, François   [rahb-lay']

François Rabelais painted a satiric portrait of 16th-century French society in his five-volume comic masterpiece, Gargantua and Pantagruel *(1532–64), an earthy and erudite collection of tales about a family of giants. Rabelais used the tales to lampoon the church, to affirm humanism, and to discuss the moral and intellectual issues agitating Renaissance France.*

Reflecting in his life and works the humanistic concerns of the French Renaissance, François Rabelais, born in Chinon, Touraine, 1483 or 1494, d. Apr. 9, 1553, was a French scholar and cleric who is remembered today for his satirical prose masterpiece *Gargantua and Pantagruel* (1532–64; Eng. trans., 1653–94). A vast, rambling compendium of adventure stories and learning of every kind, this work gave currency to the adjectives "gargantuan" and "Rabelaisian"; the excesses of the body celebrated here together with the exercise of the intellect are a joyous affirmation of life.

Comparatively little is known of Rabelais's career. In 1520 he was studying Greek in the Franciscan monastery at Fontenay-le-Comte. Five years later he was authorized by the pope to transfer to the Benedictine order. Subsequently he qualified as a doctor (1530) and practiced medicine in Lyon, where he is credited with performing one of the first public dissections in France; he published several scientific treatises in Latin. Mainly with his patrons Geoffroy d'Estissac and Cardinal Jean du Bellay and his brother Guillaume du Bellay, Governor of Piedmont, Rabelais traveled widely, on several occasions visiting Rome. He had at least two illegitimate children.

The first book of his great work, *Pantagruel* (1532), is a humanist's attack on prejudice and old-fashioned scholastic learning. Rabelais makes fun of linguistic affectation and legal jargon and proselytizes on behalf of humanist education and the Reformers' religious views: the Catholic church should be purified and simplified until it again resembles the church of the early Christians. In *Gargantua* (1534) the emphasis is more positive; Rabelais illustrates the content of an ideal education, the behavior of an ideal humanist prince, especially in war, and reveals a Utopia in the abbey of Thélème. Both these books were condemned by the Sorbonne on grounds of obscenity.

The bulk of the third book (1546) concerns the dilemma of Pantagruel's companion Panurge: should he or should he not get married? He consults a wide variety of specialists and nonspecialists, most of whom tell him that he will be cuckolded. In large part an intellectual encyclopedia, this book reflects the contemporary debate on the status of women known as the *Querelle des Femmes* and the religious issue of marriage versus celibacy; Rabelais's bias toward the Reformation viewpoint is discreetly implied.

In the fourth book (1552), in search of an answer to Panurge's question, the companions set sail for the Oracle of the Divine Bottle. They visit strange islands inhabited by extraordinary people and things and are caught in a storm and in a battle with an army of sausages. The book contains some ferocious antipapal satire and many statements on intellectual issues. The oracle is finally reached only at the end of the fifth book (1564), which is of doubtful authenticity and is generally less lively and original than its predecessors.

Rabelais is a difficult author for modern readers because of the dense intellectual content of nearly everything he wrote. The grotesque adventures of his giants, the comic and often obscene anecdotes, and the author's verbal exuberance can still delight despite the fact that no English translation can quite capture the unique flavor of the original. Chief among the many later novelists influenced by Rabelais are Laurence Sterne, Honoré de Balzac, James Joyce, and the contemporary American John Barth.   BARBARA C. BOWEN

Bibliography: Bakhtin, Mikhail M., *Rabelais and His World*, trans. by Helen Iswolsky (1971; repr. 1984); Berrong, R. M., *Every Man for Himself: Rabelais' Study of Social Order and Its Dissolution* (1985); Bowen, Barbara C., *Age of Bluff: Paradox and Ambiguity in Rabelais and Montaigne* (1972); Coleman, Dorothy G., *Rabelais: A Critical Study in Prose Fiction* (1971); Frame, D. M., *François Rabelais* (1977); Plattard, Jean, *The Life of François Rabelais*, trans. by L. D. Roache (1930; repr. 1968); Putnam, Samuel, ed., *The Portable Rabelais* (1977).

Rabi, Isidor Isaac

The American physicist Isidor Isaac Rabi, b. Rymanov, Austria (now in the Ukrainian SSR), July 29, 1898, received the 1944 Nobel Prize for physics for developing (1937) the molecular-beam magnetic-resonance method. Rabi discovered that observations of the behavior of a molecular or atomic beam in the presence of two inhomogeneous magnetic fields will reveal the magnetic moments of atoms and atomic nuclei.

Rabi received his Ph.D. from Columbia University in 1927 and has taught there since 1929. From 1940 to 1945 he served as associate director of the Radiation Laboratory at the Massachusetts Institute of Technology and investigated microwave radar for the military. He served (1946–56) on the General Advisory Committee of the Atomic Energy Commission.

Bibliography: Bernstein, Jeremy, "Physicist," *The New Yorker*, Oct. 13 and 20, 1975; Rabi, Isidor, *My Life and Times as a Physicist* (1960).

rabies

Rabies is a viral disease of humans and other mammals, especially carnivores. The virus is transmitted in saliva, either by the bite of an infected animal or by contact through the mucous membranes or breaks in the skin. Once within the body, the virus attacks the central nervous system. Symptoms develop 10 to 50 days after exposure; in humans they usually begin with depression, restlessness, fatigue, and fever. These are soon followed by a period of great excitability, excessive salivation, and convulsions, especially in the form of throat spasms. As a result the victim is unable to drink even though extremely thirsty—hence the old name for the disease, hydrophobia, meaning "fear of water." Death from paralysis and suffocation generally follows within 10 days. Once the symptoms of rabies appear, no treatment of the disease is possible.

A vaccine against rabies was first developed in France in the 1880s by Louis PASTEUR. Since then, human rabies cases have become rare in the United States and other developed countries because of effective vaccination programs for domestic animals. (People in high-risk occupations, such as veterinarians, forestry service agents, and health workers in developing countries, are also often immunized against the disease.) The few U.S. cases reported each year are mostly from contact with wild animals, the species most frequently associated with the spread of rabies being skunks, foxes, coyotes, raccoons, rabbits, and squirrels and other rodents. If a person is bitten by an animal that cannot be found, most physicians prefer to begin treatment for rabies rather than risk the person's life. This is especially true if the animal behaved abnormally—as, for example, a normally nocturnal animal that was active during the day. If the animal can be found and appears rabid, it is destroyed and its brain tissue examined to make a diagnosis; if it appears healthy, it is confined and watched for signs of the disease. Treatment, which is painful but essential, consists of an injection of rabies immune globulin, followed by a series of five injections of antirabies serum over the following month.   WILLIAM A. CHECK

Bibliography: Kaplan, Colin, ed., *Rabies: The Facts* (1977); Kaplan, Martin M., and Kaprowski, Hilary, "Rabies," *Scientific American*, January 1980; MacDonald, D. W., *Rabies and Wildlife* (1980).

Rabin, Yitzhak   [rah-been', yit-shahk']

Yitzhak Rabin, b. Mar. 1, 1922, Israel's prime minister from 1974 to 1977, was named defense minister in the national unity cabinet headed by Shimon PERES in 1984. He previously served as Israel's ambassador to the United States (1968–73) and as chief of staff of the armed forces (1964–68) and planned the 1967 Israeli victory in the Six-Day War. Rabin resigned as prime minister after he was found to have violated Israeli currency regulations by depositing $21,000 in a U.S. bank.

Bibliography: Rabin, Yitzhak, *The Rabin Memoirs* (1979).

raccoon

The North American raccoon, P. lotor, uses its hands to hold food while eating. In captivity a raccoon will often "wash" its food in water, behavior related to catching aquatic prey in the wild.

Raccoons are stocky-bodied, usually solitary, and nocturnal mammals of the genus *Procyon* in the family Procyonidae. They are generally regarded as consisting of seven species: the North American raccoon, *P. lotor;* the South American crab-eating raccoon, *P. cancrivorus;* and five other species, each confined to one or more small islands off Florida and Mexico and in the West Indies. The North American species, which is divided into about 25 geographic varieties, or subspecies, is from 23 to 30 cm (9 to 12 in) high at the shoulders and from 40 to 60 cm (15.5 to 23 in) long, plus a 24- to 26.5-cm (9.5- to 10.5-in) tail. Its weight is usually between 5.5 and 7.25 kg (12 and 16 lb), but very fat specimens may exceed 18 kg (40 lb). The long, coarse fur of the North American raccoon is commonly yellowish gray to grayish brown, with markings of four to ten (usually five or six) dark rings on the tail and a black mask across the face.

Raccoons prefer swampy areas or woods near water and are absent from very high elevations, very arid regions, and purely coniferous forests. Found throughout the United States except for large parts of some of the western states, they are omnivorous. Contrary to popular belief, raccoons do not wash their food before eating it; this habit, seen only when the animal is in captivity, is believed to be an outlet for the frustrated behavior of searching for small prey in water. In the north, if the temperature drops consistently below −4° C (25° F), or if the snows are heavy, the raccoon may spend weeks in a deep sleep but not in true hibernation. The breeding season for the North American raccoon is from February to early March in the north but begins as early as December in the south. Gestation averages 63 days, and a litter commonly contains 1 to 7 young. Although raccoons may live 14 years or more in captivity, they seldom survive beyond 7 years in the wild.

Bibliography: Johnson, Albert S., *Biology of the Raccoon* (1970); Paradise, Paul R., *All about Raccoons* (1976); Rue, Leonard Lee, *The World of the Raccoon* (1964).

race

A race is a population group or subspecies within the living human species, *Homo sapiens,* set apart from other subspecies on the basis of arbitrarily selected, commonly visible, or phenotypic criteria. The criteria most often selected are skin color, hair quantity and form, and the shape and form of the body, head, and facial features. A problem is presented, however, by the high variability of such characteristics within any group. Not all genes that transmit all phenotypic characteristics ascribed to a subspecies are transmitted in a cluster (see GENETIC CODE). As a result only some members of a particular "race" will have all the criteria for that race, although every member will probably have at least one.

The species *Homo sapiens* is not difficult for specialists to identify, nor is there difficulty in determining its constituent populations, those groups of human beings who inhabit the various areas of the earth. No such clear-cut agreement is possible in determining the nature of subspecies, or races, and many scientists today reject the concept of race. Other scientists use the race concept as an expedient shorthand expression for variants in anatomical traits exhibited by the populations of broad geographic homelands—zoographic regions with characteristic resident animals that shared the terrain with developing human populations.

Even in this geographic sense, however, the term *race* must be understood to have value only as a general term without precise definition, because it does not take into account hybridization and movement of populations with the consequent "gene flow" from one area to another, nor does it allow for continuing evolution. Human beings do, however, partially reflect their geographic origin in the physical traits that have been mentioned, and in some physiological characteristics such as tolerance of cold, heat, and altitude. The idea of geographic races was explored by scientists as early as the 18th

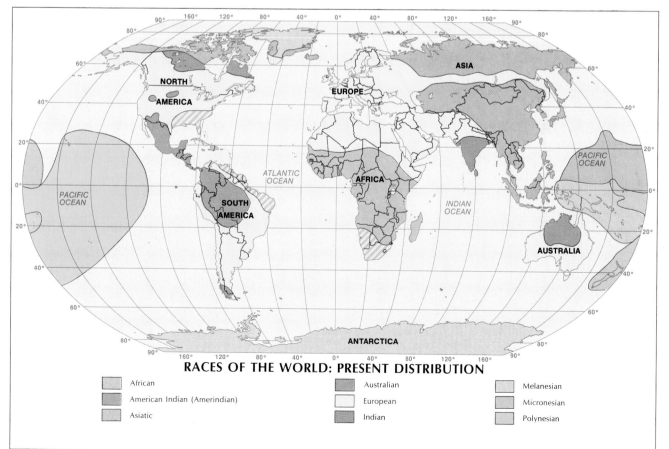

RACES OF THE WORLD: PRESENT DISTRIBUTION

African

American Indian (Amerindian)

Asiatic

Australian

European

Indian

Melanesian

Micronesian

Polynesian

century, notably by Johann BLUMENBACH, who distinguished five divisions of humankind, and from whose classification later ones developed. The identification of zoographic ancestral regions has been elaborated by the American anthropologist Carleton COON, among others.

Geographic Races. Classifying races by geographic regions can result in distinguishing more than 30 subdivisions of lands and peoples across the world; or, homeland regions in the Old World can be combined and reduced to three—the Ethiopian, the Palaearctic, and the Oriental.

The Ethiopian region includes the southern third of Arabia and sub-Saharan Africa. Before the end of the PLEISTOCENE EPOCH the Ethiopian region probably included the whole of Africa, but when the Sahara developed and divided the continent, Palaearctic forms invaded North Africa. The Ethiopian region gave rise to the African subspecies, with these distinguishing characteristics: yellow brown to brown or black skin; dark and tightly spiraled hair on head and body; moderately abundant body hair; generally heavy bones; teeth of medium to large size; noses broad with flaring nostrils; turned-out lips; and prominent buttocks.

The Palaearctic region comprises Africa north of the Sahara, Europe, and Asia except southern Arabia, India, Southeast Asia, and southern China. The western Palaearctic was probably the homeland of the Caucasoid, or Caucasian, subspecies, and the eastern Palaearctic was the homeland of the Mongoloid, or Mongolian, subspecies. Caucasian physical traits are the following: ivory to medium-brown skin; variable hair and eye color; wavy or curly hair; plentiful body hair; small teeth; prominent noses; and bones of medium weight. Mongolian physical traits are as follows: ivory to medium-brown skin; dark eyes and dark, straight hair; large front teeth; prominent cheek bones; and short limbs and long trunks, with lightweight bones.

The Oriental region encompasses India, southern China, Southeast Asia, and the northerly islands of Indonesia. It was probably the homeland of the Australoid, or Australasian race, although few live there today. Australasian people tend

to have medium-brown to black skin; wavy to tightly spiraled hair of variable color; moderate to abundant body hair; large teeth; broad noses; and heavy bones.

As is evident from these descriptions, a significant similarity exists in many of these traits in all three regions. The original racial homelands in Eurasia and Africa probably were never wholly isolated from each other. Instead, human groups migrated and interbred enough so that physically intermediate populations may have existed for thousands of years in the spaces between the homelands. This gene flow has probably maintained the genus *Homo* as a succession of single species in the Old World for several hundred thousand years. The fossil evidence suggests that in the Pleistocene Epoch, smaller-brained species of *Homo* gave rise to the large-brained *Homo sapiens* (see PREHISTORIC HUMANS). Gene flow among the homelands was great enough to preserve an essential biochemical and intellectual equality between the emerging human races, and evolutionary improvements such as speech, intelligence, and manual dexterity were spread throughout the species. This gene flow has been so pervasive that our species has never developed "pure" races in any meaningful genetic sense.

Migration and Gene Flow. The human species has migrated and hybridized dramatically in the past 40,000 years. As a result, some of the human subspecies have been drastically relocated. Late in the Pleistocene the Caucasians probably moved into northern Africa along with animals from the Palaearctic zone. From that time, if not earlier, a zone of racial intermediates has extended from the Sahara to Somalia. A similar zone of racial mixture is found in India between the more northerly Caucasians and the more southerly Australasians. Since the 16th century, Caucasians have spread into Siberia, the Americas, Australia, New Zealand, and southern Africa. Black Africans at the same time displaced the SAN (Bushmen) in South Africa, and millions of black Africans entered the New World as slaves.

The Australasian population group very early began movements south and east from their southern Asian homeland.

Australia was occupied more than 30,000 years ago. At present, the Australasian subspecies is represented by the Australian ABORIGINES, the peoples of MELANESIA and NEW GUINEA in the Pacific, and remnants nearer Asia. Aboriginal tribes of Australasian appearance are found in the ANDAMAN ISLANDS in the Bay of Bengal, SRI LANKA, parts of southern India, Malaysia, and the Philippines. Most of the Australasian homeland, however, is now occupied by racially Mongolian invaders from the north.

The Mongolians moved into the Americas about 30,000 years ago (see NORTH AMERICAN ARCHAEOLOGY). After the end of the Pleistocene, they probably displaced and hybridized with the Australasians in Southeast Asia. These mixed groups became master seafarers and spread the Austronesian languages into Melanesia, MICRONESIA, and POLYNESIA. Speakers of one of these languages even reached Madagascar and peopled it with tribes descended from Mongolians, Australasians, and black Africans.

Both gene flow and reproductive isolation have been at work in the formation of the human races. The human species has split into innumerable, often temporary, populations, undergoing local microevolution and subject to the pressures of NATURAL SELECTION by disease, nutrition, and climate. Recent evidence indicates how far apart these populations have become in their genetic endowments. One way to measure this evolutionary trend is by means of ''marker genes,'' which define the biochemical structure of certain molecules in the blood, such as the familiar A, B, and O blood types (see BLOOD). Blood groups show a striking split into eastern and western branches. The western group includes nearly all of the Africans and the Caucasians. Australasians and Mongolians, including the aboriginal peoples of the Americas and the Pacific Islands, comprise the eastern group.

Environmental Factors. In terms of physiological and genetic adaptations, all human beings are fundamentally tropical animals. Nevertheless, the peoples with the least exposure to severe climates, the Australasians and Africans, are dark skinned. This kind of skin is resistant to sunburn and skin cancer, but it is susceptible to frostbite.

Not all population groups seem to be equally well adapted to high altitudes. Most of the really successful populations in this respect are racially Mongolian; they thrive and reproduce quite well in such regions as Tibet, and in the high Andes, where the American Indians seem to be more successful than Caucasian groups.

Migration of early human groups to temperate climates seems to have led to lighter skins, less massive bones, and straighter hair. The skeleton, especially in Caucasians, matures slowly. Light skin is better protected than dark skin against frostbite. Also, the lighter-weight skeletons of this race may make fewer demands on Vitamin D, to the point where Caucasians may be less susceptible to rickets (a severe developmental disorder of the skeleton).

Another Caucasian peculiarity, shared elsewhere mainly by cattle-raising and milk-drinking tribes in Africa, is the ability to digest milk sugar (lactose) as adults. All other young mammals digest lactose before weaning but lose this capacity at older ages. The ability to digest this carbohydrate throughout life provides the calories of milk sugar in cold climates; also, the minerals in milk, coupled with efficient Vitamin D production by the skin, may protect young Caucasians against rickets.

Recent work on microevolution has repeatedly uncovered evidence of local inherited resistance to disease. MALARIA has been a major killer of exposed populations, mainly through parasitization and destruction of the red blood cells. Genetic resistance implies changes in the chemistry of these cells, which inconvenience the parasite at stages in its life cycle.

Eastern and Western peoples in the Old World have developed somewhat different genetic adaptations to malaria. Most typical of the Africans is the sickle-cell gene. Those who have one normal hemoglobin gene and one sickle-cell gene are less likely to acquire malaria. Africans who inherit abnormal sickle cells from both parents suffer serious health impairment (see SICKLE-CELL ANEMIA). Western populations in malarial re-

gions often show another gene, which gives rise to an ineffective or deficient ENZYME in the red cells, a feature believed to inhibit increase of the malaria parasite. Another such Western gene, beta thalassemia, produces benefits if inherited from only one parent but produces a severe ANEMIA if inherited from both parents. The Australasian and Southeast Asian adaptations to malaria are genetically different. Groups in Southeast Asia and New Guinea lack the sickle-cell gene and show a different thalassemia system. Therefore, malaria resistance—and also blood groups—divide the human species into East and West. (See GENETIC DISEASES.)

Work is being done today on certain genes present throughout the world in many populations, rather than in only one population, to investigate genetic adaptation to the conditions and requirements of various environments. Such studies show race as a constantly evolving process, rather than as static, immutable division of *Homo sapiens* into rigidly bounded groups.   EDWARD E. HUNT, JR.

Bibliography: Barzun, Jacques, *Race: A Study in Modern Superstition* (1937; repr. 1979); Brues, A. M., *People and Races* (1977); Budmer, W. F., and Cavalli-Sforza, L. L., *Genetics, Evolution, and Man* (1976); Coon, C. S., *The Origin of Races* (1962); Eveleth, P. B., and Tanner, J. M., *Worldwide Variation in Human Growth* (1976); Garn, S. M., *Human Races*, 3d ed. (1970); King, James C., *The Biology of Race*, rev. ed. (1982); Montagu, Ashley, ed., *The Concept of Race* (1964; repr. 1980); Osborne, R. H., *The Biological and Social Meaning of Race* (1971).

race riots   (in U.S. history)

Throughout most of U.S. history race riots have been outbreaks of mob action in which groups of different racial and ethnic backgrounds fight each other. In most instances these riots have been between blacks and whites; the few exceptions include the riots between Mexican–Americans and whites in Los Angeles during World War II.

Mob action against blacks occurred as early as the 18th century when whites attacked black enclaves in the cities of the North, burning and plundering homes and assaulting blacks. During the Civil War, white workers who feared job competition attacked freed black workers in northern cities. In the New York City DRAFT RIOTS of 1863, working-class whites, subject to a new conscription law, turned their hostility toward blacks, many of whom were murdered. In the early 20th century, race riots usually represented white reaction against the influx of Southern blacks into Northern cities, particularly during World War I. In East Saint Louis, Ill., violence erupted in 1917 over the issue of the employment of blacks in a factory that held government contracts. Reflecting a new militancy, newly urbanized blacks responded aggressively to white assaults.

By the 1960s a new kind of racial violence had evolved. These outbreaks usually occurred in black neighborhoods where black citizens took to the streets in what began as social protest but often degenerated into rioting, looting, and arson. Although much of the plundering was directed at white merchants and landlords, black owners of buildings and businesses were also victimized. These disorders differed from earlier race riots in that few whites—except for police officers and fire fighters—were directly involved. Newark, N.J., Watts (Los Angeles), and Detroit are examples of cities that experienced rioting in the mid-1960s. Rioting in black neighborhoods reached its height in 1968 when, after the assassination of Martin Luther KING, Jr., rioting occurred in approximately 150 cities. Later that year a special advisory commission established by President Lyndon B. Johnson—called the Kerner Commission after its first chairperson, Otto Kerner—issued a report placing much of the blame for the unrest on chronic high unemployment in black neighborhoods. In 1980 social unrest in Miami's black community gave way to three days of severe rioting.   RONALD L. LEWIS

Bibliography: Graham, Hugh Davis, and Gurr, Ted Robert, eds., *Violence in America* (1969); Grimshaw, Allen D., ed., *Racial Violence in the United States* (1969); Henri, Florette, *Black Migration: Movement North: 1900–1920* (1975); Knopf, Terry Ann, *Rumors, Race and Riots* (1975).

race runner

The six-lined race runner, C. sexlineatus, *a lizard of North America, moves quickly through open country, its most common habitat.*

At least three species of lizards in the genus *Cnemidophorus,* of the family Teiidae, are called race runners for their great speed, clocked at 29 km/hr (18 mph). (The other 18 to 42 species in the genus are more commonly called whiptails.) They are slender and long-tailed, with large scales on the head, small granular scales on the back, and a pattern of stripes or spots. The six-lined race runner, *C. sexlineatus,* found mostly in open, dry areas of the southern and central United States, reaches 8.6 cm (3⅜ in) in length plus an 18-cm (7-in) tail and has 6 (sometimes 7 or 8) light-colored stripes of white, yellow, gray, or blue.

Rachel

In the Bible, Rachel was the second wife of JACOB and the mother of JOSEPH and Benjamin (Genesis 29–35). When she died, Jacob erected a monument over her tomb at Ephrath, traditionally identified with Bethlehem. She is regarded as one of the four Jewish matriarchs.

Rachmaninoff, Sergei   [rahk-mah'-neen-awf, sir-gay']

The composer, pianist, and conductor Sergei Vasilievich Rachmaninoff is considered the last in the great tradition of Russian romantic composers. He was born Apr. 1 (N.S.), 1873, at his family's estate, Semyonovo, in the Russian province of Novgorod. At about the age of 5, he began piano studies with his mother. In 1882 he entered the Saint Petersburg Conservatory, but he transferred 3 years later to the Moscow Conservatory. There he studied under the rigorous supervision of Nikolai Zverev, through whom he met many of the most important Russian composers of the time. Tchaikovsky, especially exercised a major influence on him. He graduated in pi-

The Russian virtuoso pianist, conductor, and composer Sergei Rachmaninoff made his home in Europe and the United States after the Russian Revolution of 1917. As both performer and composer he excelled in a romantic style characterized by flowing melody and massive chords used for stirring dramatic effect.

ano in 1891 and in composition with the Great Gold Medal in 1892. At just 19 years of age, he sold some pieces outright to a publisher who failed to secure an international copyright. Among them was the C-sharp Minor Prelude (1892), which would bring publishers a fortune and the composer world fame. The failure of his First Symphony in 1897 stifled his inspiration for 3 years. Following treatment by hypnosis he produced the Second Piano Concerto in 1901. It inspired a period of creativeness that lasted until 1917, yielding 22 of his total production of 45 opus numbers. Apprehensive about the Bolshevik Revolution, he left Russia, making the United States his base of operations and, after 1939, his home. At first he composed nothing. Then between 1926 and 1940, five final works appeared, including the *Rhapsody on a Theme of Paganini* (1934) and the Third Symphony (1936). His international concert career intensified in exile. He toured until a month before his death on Mar. 28, 1943, in Beverly Hills, Calif.

Rachmaninoff's music often recalls distinctively Russian sounds. Russian bell sonorities are imitated, as in the cantata *The Bells* (1913), or reformulated into abstract ideas, as in the C-sharp Minor Prelude, the opening of the Second Piano Concerto, or the main theme of the finale of the Third Piano Concerto (1909). The modality, formulaic melody, and intonational rhythms of many themes recall melody types found both in Russian Orthodox chant and the folk-ballad song, as in the opening of the Third Piano Concerto and the first theme of the First Symphony.   MALCOLM HAMRICK BROWN

Bibliography: Bertensson, Sergei, and Leyda, Jay, *Sergei Rachmaninoff,* with the assistance of Sophia Satina (1965); Norris, Geoffrey, *Rakhmaninov* (1976); Riesemann, Oskar von, *Rachmaninoff's Recollections* (1934); Seroff, Victor, *Rachmaninoff* (1950; repr. 1970); Walker, Robert, *Rachmaninoff: His Life and Times* (1979; repr. 1981).

Racine   [ruh-seen']

Racine, a city in southeastern Wisconsin on Lake Michigan at the mouth of the Root River, is the seat of Racine County. The city's population is 85,725 (1980). Racine is an industrial city and a port of entry; its diversified manufactures include wax products and machinery. In 1834 settlers occupied a site on the river claimed by Capt. Gilbert Knapp, and they named the settlement Port Gilbert in his honor; the present name was adopted in 1837. Harbor improvements and the construction of a bridge across the Root in the 1840s, followed by the railroad's arrival (1855), brought rapid growth.

Racine, Jean   [rah-seen']

The rival of Pierre Corneille for the title of the greatest French tragic dramatist, Jean Racine, b. Dec. 22, 1639, d. Apr. 21, 1699, infused the high style of neoclassicism with the tension of human passion. Often set in ancient times, his plays combine the Greek concept of inexorable fate with a 17th-century metaphysics and an acute sense of human nature. Racine's tightly structured dramas of obsessive love, particularly in women, remain among the masterpieces of world drama.

Orphaned in early childhood, Racine was raised by a grandmother who subscribed to the extreme doctrine of original sin as taught by JANSENISM, a Reform movement within Roman Catholicism. Sent (1655) to the Jansenist school at Port-Royal, Racine was profoundly influenced by their tenets while receiving a thorough classical education; his fusion of the Greek idea of fate with the Jansenist belief in man's helplessness later produced unique tragedies of the struggle of the will against the passions.

When, in 1658, Racine left Port-Royal to pursue the study of philosophy in Paris, he subordinated his spiritual interests to the intellectual delights and ambitions of the secular world. Having already composed religious and pastoral poetry, he now adopted the contemporary custom of dedicating poems to potential patrons, and his marriage ode for King Louis XIV, *La Nymphe de la Seine* (The Nymph of the Seine, 1660), gained him recognition. After a brief absence (1661) from Paris during which he placated his family by feigning interest in a clerical life, he returned to the city, where he published more poems and cultivated the friendship of his great

Jean Racine, one of the outstanding dramatists of the 17th-century French theater, proved himself the master of classical tragedy in such plays as Andromache *(1667)*, Britannicus *(1669)*, and Phèdre *(1677)*. In these and other works Racine's heroes and heroines fall victim to their own uncontrollable passions and are forced to accept the weakness of the human condition.

contemporaries Boileau, La Fontaine, and Molière. Molière, already a noted man of the theater, produced Racine's first plays, *The Thebiad* (1664; Eng. trans., 1723) and *Alexander the Great* (1665; Eng. trans., 1714). Confirmed in his theatrical vocation by the reception accorded these plays, Racine broke with the Jansenists and devoted himself entirely to his art.

Beginning with *Andromache* (1667; Eng. trans., 1675) and ending with his masterpiece, *Phèdre* (1677; Eng. trans., 1707), the plays of this decade of Racine's life established him as the peer of the long-renowned Corneille and, in the opinion of many, as France's leading dramatist. Elaborating on the aftermath of the Trojan war, *Andromache* shows Hector's widow caught in the crosscurrents of passion among her captors as King Pyrrhus abandons her for his fiancée, Hermione, who, desperate, instigates his assassination at the hands of her love-maddened suitor, Oreste. In its portrayal of foredoomed love, the play revives classical fatalism; in its analysis of motivation, it foreshadows modern psychology. As great a success as Corneille's *The Cid* had been three decades earlier, *Andromache* occasioned a great rivalry between the two dramatists that was intensified by Racine's treatment of the Corneillean theme of political strife in *Britannicus* (1669; Eng. trans., 1714) and came to a climax with *Bérénice* (1670; Eng. trans., 1922). Appearing at virtually the same time as a tragedy on the identical subject by Corneille, the latter play established Racine's preeminence. Encouraged by his triumph, Racine experimented with a contemporary setting in *Bajazet* (1672; Eng. trans., 1855) and with an almost exclusively inner, psychological action in *Mithridates* (1673; Eng. trans., 1926). Although his success, symbolized by his election (1672) to the Académie Française, continued, Racine came under increasing attack from other playwrights. His *Iphigenie* (1674; Eng. trans., 1861), a return to Greek material, prevailed over a rival version; but the savagery of partisan attacks on *Phèdre*, combined with a personal moral crisis, led Racine to retire from theatrical activity in 1677. Marrying the same year, he reconciled his differences with Port-Royal and, devoting himself to his new duties as royal historiographer, abandoned secular drama. His last two plays, *Esther* (1689; Eng. trans., 1715) and *Athalie* (1691; Eng. trans., 1722), were on biblical themes, written for performance by students at a school for the sacred and secular education of young women.

Exemplified by *Phèdre*'s analysis of the passion of Theseus's wife for her stepson, Racine's characters are a classical construction, expressive dramatic verse, and moving and accurate analysis of human motivation and passion. Unlike Corneille's characters, who are moral giants endowed with indomitable will, Racine's are intensely human. Corneille, as La Bruyère remarked, "paints human beings as they ought to be"; Racine "paints them as they are."

Bibliography: Abraham, Claude Kurt, *Jean Racine* (1977); Barthes, Roland, *On Racine*, trans. by Richard Howard (1964); Brereton, Geoffrey, *Jean Racine: A Critical Biography*, 2d ed. (1973); Cloonan, William, *Racine's Theatre: The Politics of Love* (1972); Lapp, John C., *Aspects of Racinian Tragedy* (1955); Mourges, Odette de, *Racine, or the Triumph of Relevance* (1967); Racine, Jean, *Complete Plays*, trans. by Samuel Solomon, 2 vols. (1968); Turnell, Martin, *Jean Racine—Dramatist* (1972); Weinberg, Bernard, *The Art of Jean Racine* (1963).

racism

Racism refers to any theory or doctrine stating that inherited physical characteristics, such as skin color, facial features, hair texture, and the like, determine behavior patterns, personality traits, or intellectual abilities. In practice, racism typically takes the form of a claim that some human races are superior to others. An abuse of the concept of differences among peoples, it has contributed to the practices of PREJUDICE and DISCRIMINATION among groups in many parts of the world.

Racism was a prevalent ideology in Europe and America in the late 19th and early 20th centuries. Racist theories about supposed physical or intellectual superiority were advanced by Arthur de GOBINEAU and Houston Stewart CHAMBERLAIN, both of whom insisted that supreme among the races were members of the mythical Nordic, or Aryan, race. Nazi Germany under Adolf Hitler based its extermination of millions of Jews and other "non-Aryans" on this theory of race supremacy and the corollary concept of racial purity.

As an ideology, racism has been on the wane since the 1940s, although in a few countries, such as South Africa (see APARTHEID), it has had the support of the political leadership. In other countries it lingers on as a folk mythology. The overwhelming bulk of scientific opinion in both the social and the biological sciences, however, now rejects the notion that large human populations, such as the so-called white, black, and yellow races, behave differently because of their physical appearance, or that they can be said to be genetically superior or inferior to one another. Genetic differences between population groups do exist, of course. None of these group differences, however, has yet been shown to affect personality, intelligence, or, indeed, any ability that significantly relates to social behavior.

Race Defined. The concept of race as representing separate subspecies of *Homo sapiens* has little if any biological significance, and today many scientists reject the use of the term in the human context (see RACE). In common usage, *race* is a socially defined term, and the definition differs from society to society. For example, many people who are socially defined as blacks in the United States, because they have one or more black ancestors, would be called whites in Brazil. The social significance of race, then, is limited to what people make of it: a society is racist to the extent that its members draw unwarranted conclusions from the physical differences between peoples.

In recent years the term *racism* has been at times misapplied to various related but distinct social attitudes and occurrences. For example, feelings of cultural superiority based on language, religion, morality, manners, or some other aspect of culture are sometimes labeled *racist,* but the proper term for such feelings is ETHNOCENTRISM. Another loose usage of the term is the notion of institutional racism—meaning any practice that results, intentionally or otherwise, in differential representation of different human groups. For example, a college entrance examination is sometimes said to be institutionally racist if it results in a low admission rate of certain minority groups, irrespective of its intention. A more appropriate usage would be to say that such a test is discriminatory in its results.

Causes of Racism. The causes of racism are complex and cannot be reduced to a single factor. Its rise and fall are often linked with real conflicts of interest and competition for scarce resources. Historically, racism has commonly accompanied slavery, colonialism, and other forms of exploitation and gross inequality. In other cases relatively powerless groups that have felt threatened by social and economic instability have blamed other powerless groups for their predicament. The insecure white working class and lower middle class of industrial societies, for example, have often expressed racist attitudes toward defenseless minorities, such as blacks in the

United States or Commonwealth immigrants in Great Britain.

Rapid social change often fosters racism. Examples are the sudden immigration of highly visible groups of foreigners, quick changes in the racial composition of a neighborhood, or the threat of political change brought on by a nationalist movement. Racism, in short, is frequently an irrational reaction to a real or perceived threat to the status quo. It can therefore suddenly flare up, as with ANTI-SEMITISM in Germany in the 1930s and '40s, or remain dormant, depending on such external circumstances as economic depression and the willingness of organized groups to exploit racism for political ends.   PIERRE L. VAN DEN BERGHE

Bibliography: Allport, Gordon W., *The Nature of Prejudice* (1954); Banton, Michael, *Race Relations* (1967); Hofstadter, Richard, *Social Darwinism in American Thought* (1959); Leone, Bruno, ed., *Racism: Opposing Viewpoints* (1978); Mason, Philip, *Race Relations* (1970); Montagu, Ashley, *Man's Most Dangerous Myth: The Fallacy of Race,* 5th ed. (1974); Poliakov, Leon, *The Aryan Myth* (1974); Rex, John, *Race Relations in Sociological Theory* (1970); van den Berghe, Pierre L., *Race and Racism: A Comparative Perspective,* 2d ed. (1978).

Rackham, Arthur [rak'-uhm]

Arthur Rackham's illustration of the Pool of Tears, a scene from the 1907 edition of Lewis Carroll's Alice's Adventures in Wonderland, displays the sensitive, fanciful characterization and sinuous line typical of his work. Rackham, one of the leading illustrators of the late 19th and the early 20th century, was greatly influenced by the Art Nouveau movement.

Arthur Rackham, b. Sept. 19, 1867, d. Sept. 6, 1939, was a British illustrator noted for his imaginative and fantastic drawings. He first achieved fame with his illustrations for Grimm's *Fairy Tales* (1900); thereafter he illustrated many kinds of books, such as special Christmas volumes and sumptuous limited editions of Germanic legends. His works included Washington Irving's *Rip Van Winkle* (1905), R. H. Barham's *Ingoldsby Legends* (1907), Charles Dickens's *A Christmas Carol* (1915), Izaak Walton's *The Compleat Angler* (1931), and Edgar Allan Poe's *Tales of Mystery* (1935).

Rackham's work reflects the tortured imagery of Northern folklore. His trees have nightmarish anthropomorphic forms, although realized with great sensitivity and delicacy; conversely, his human figures are often gnarled and twisted like the bark and twigs of trees, giving them the quality of pagan elemental beings. Original drawings by Rackham may be seen in many galleries, including the Tate Gallery, London, and the Musée du Luxembourg, Paris.   RAYMOND LISTER

Bibliography: Gettings, Fred, *Arthur Rackham* (1976); Hudson, Derek, *Arthur Rackham: His Life and Work* (1960; repr. 1974).

racquetball

Racquetball is a relatively new racquet-and-ball sport that is played indoors by either 2 or 4 players on a standard 4-wall handball court 20 ft high, 20 ft wide, and 40 ft long (6.1, 6.1, and 12.2 m). Certain aspects of the game resemble squash, paddleball, and handball, but the origins of the sport are ob-

scure. Joe Sobek, a former squash and tennis teacher from Greenwich, Conn., is unofficially recognized as the inventor of racquetball. In 1950 he started working on a game that would be less intricate than squash but more interesting than paddleball. Rules and regulations were first codified in North America in 1968. Racquetball is played with basically the same rules that govern HANDBALL except that balls can be played off the ceiling. Points can be scored only by the server and are registered when the opponent fails to strike the ball after the first bounce or if a shot fails to carry to the front wall. Points are also awarded if a player is guilty of intentional blocking. The first to score 21 points in a game wins; 2 victories out of 3 games decide a match. The short racquet, lively ball—it may reach speeds of 265 km/h (165 mph)—and enclosed court add to the game's tremendous popularity in North America. A standard racquet is 18 in (45.7 cm) long and has a wrist strap at the end of the handle. Racquet frames are made of wood, steel, aluminum, or fiberglass (which top players prefer). The racquets are strung with nylon filament.   GERALD S. COUZENS

Bibliography: Leve, Charles, *Inside Racquetball* (1973); Shay, Arthur, and Leve, Charles, *Winning Racquetball* (1976).

radar

Radar was the name given during World War II to an electronic system by which radio waves were bounced off an aircraft in order to detect its presence and locate its position. The term is an acronym made from the fuller term *radio detection and ranging*. A large number of researchers helped to develop the devices and techniques of radar, but the development of the earliest practical radar system is usually credited to Sir Robert WATSON-WATT.

OPERATION

A radio TRANSMITTER generates radio waves, which are then radiated from an ANTENNA, "illuminating" the airspace with radio waves. A target, such as an aircraft, that enters this space scatters a small portion of this radio energy back to a receiving antenna. This weak signal is amplified by an electronic AMPLIFIER and displayed on a CATHODE-RAY TUBE (CRT),

This radar screen is one of many at the Kansas City Air Route Traffic Control Center, responsible for maintaining safe distances between aircraft flights over a multistate area. Electronic signals that the craft emit are picked up by radar antennas and relayed to the center.

where it can be studied by a radar operator. Thus the presence of the aircraft has been detected, but to determine its position the aircraft's distance (range) and bearing must be measured. Because radio waves travel at a known constant velocity—the speed of light, which is 300,000 km/sec, or 186,000 mi/sec—the range may be found by measuring the time taken for a radio wave to travel from transmitter to aircraft and back to the receiver. For example, if the range were 186 miles, the time for the round trip would be $(2 \times 186) \div 186,000 =$ two-thousandths of a second, or 2,000 microseconds. In pulse radar the radiation is not continuous but is emitted as a succession of short bursts, each lasting a few microseconds. This radio-frequency pulse is emitted on receipt of a firing signal from a trigger unit that simultaneously initiates the time-base sweep on the CRT. Thus the electronic clock is started, and when the echo signal is seen on the tube the time delay can be measured, giving the range; the pulses are emitted at the rate of a few hundred per second so that the operator sees a steady signal.

HISTORY

The long-wave radar systems that were used to defend Britain from German aircraft during 1940–41 measured range accurately but were much less accurate in measuring direction, because the radiated beams were very wide. By reducing the wavelength of radio waves it became possible to build antennas to form narrow beams that could be rotated like a lighthouse beam. Only when the aircraft lay within the beam would a radar echo be received; thus with such a narrow-beam system the bearing could be observed directly. Another advance in radar was duplexing—switching methods that allowed the same antenna to be used for both transmission and reception. In addition, the echo signals were now displayed on a CRT that used a radial time-base that rotated in synchronism with the aerial; therefore, the scattering targets appeared in their correct plan positions relative to the radar station, and this form of display was named the plan position indicator (PPI). The most important advance made during this phase of radar development, however, was the invention of the cavity MAGNETRON, a device for generating high-power microwave pulses, by Sir John T. Randal and Henry A. Boot in 1940. Pulse powers of 500 kW in the S band (10 cm) and 150 kW in the X band (3 cm) were quickly made available, and compact radars having beam widths of 1° or less were soon deployed for early-warning purposes, for use in aircraft against other aircraft (AI = aircraft interception), or for aircraft patrolling over the sea to detect enemy warships and surfaced submarines (ASV = aircraft to surface vessel). Radar in the S and X bands was also used as an aid in blind bombing missions to delineate the ground beneath the aircraft, functioning as a navigational aid as well as a target identifier. Microwave radars were also important to the antiaircraft artillery units of the army, providing target detection and automatic firing of the guns. Similarly, radar became an indispensable aid to naval operations.

The great operational advantage of microwave radars during World War II was that they were relatively free from electronic counter measures (ECM) by the enemy. Electronic warfare has now become a major threat to military radar systems, and modern radars have to be designed to reduce the effects of ECM. For example, antennas have been developed with increased resolving power but with very low side lobes so that active jamming cannot penetrate into the receiver as readily as with earlier systems. Simultaneously, the effect of passive jamming is reduced: the observation of false targets because of backscatter from "chaff"—falling clouds of scattered tinfoil strips—is reduced.

ADVANCES IN RADAR

Modern radar also provides excellent moving-target indication (MTI) by use of the Doppler shift in frequency that a radio wave undergoes when it is reflected from a moving target (see DOPPLER EFFECT). Target detection is hindered by "clutter" echoes arising from backscatter from the ground or raindrops. The modern radar, with its higher transmitter power and more sensitive receiver, causes clutter to be even more pronounced so that even flocks of birds may show up on the screen. Antenna design can reduce these effects, and the use of circularly polarized waves reduces rain echoes.

The wartime radar operator interpreted the mass of data displayed on his PPI. The tracing of the histories of many targets simultaneously, however, which is what is needed in modern civil or military air-traffic control, requires that the incoming radar data be electronically processed to make it more accessible to the controller for the task of airspace management (see TRAFFIC CONTROL). Progress toward satisfying this need had to await the arrival of large-scale integrated circuits and charge-coupled devices and the development of the technology for processing digital signals. Another important advance has been the development of computerized handling of video data, as in automatic plot extraction and track formation.

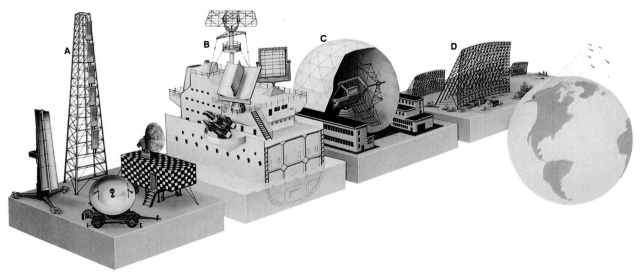

A radar device emits radio waves and analyzes the echoes returned when these waves encounter an object. Mathematical interpretation of the returned radio signal yields information on the location, distance, direction, and speed of the object. Originally developed in the 1930s, radar was first applied on a wide scale during World War II. German radar equipment (A), in use from 1942, was designed for accurate targeting of antiaircraft fire. Shipborne missile-tracking systems (B) were a later development. Interference caused by rain could be minimized by enclosing the radio antenna under a rigid ray dome (C). Radar is utilized in early-warning surveillance systems for intercontinental ballistic missiles (D). Nonmilitary uses for radar now include storm tracking, air-traffic flow, satellite and rocket guidance, and surveying.

Radar engineers recognize that detection of a target still remains a matter of statistical probability, rather than certainty, in spite of all the great advances in components made since World War II.

APPLICATIONS

Although radar was first developed as a military aid, it has proved to be a very effective sensing and measuring device for use in many civil systems and in many fields of scientific research. It is employed for the blind landing of aircraft and for airport surface surveillance, and it is used in aircraft for cloud and collision warning. Other civil uses include merchant-ship navigation and docking radar, highway traffic control, and security systems. Scientific applications include lunar and planetary studies; METEOROLOGICAL INSTRUMENTATION for studying clouds and precipitation; measurement of the thickness of ice sheets from aircraft; satellite surveys of the Earth's surface; and ionospheric and magnetospheric investigations. Radar is now also making a major contribution to certain behavioral studies in biology, for example, the migration and flight behavior of birds, observations of the swarming of insects, crop protection, and investigations relating to the acoustic ECHOLOCATION system of bats.   E. EASTWOOD

Bibliography: Battan, Louis J., *Radar Observation of the Atmosphere*, rev. ed. (1981); Carpentier, Michael, *Radar—New Concepts*, rev. ed. (1968); Skolnik, Merill I., *Introduction to Radar Systems*, 2d ed. (1980) and *Radar Handbook* (1970); Toomay, J. C., *Radar Principles for the Non-Specialist* (1982).

radar astronomy

Radar astronomy is a relatively short-range astronomical technique limited to the study of objects in the solar system. It has had a key role in establishing exact distances and orbital dimensions for the planets and the rotation rates of Venus and Mercury and in determining the nature of the surfaces of the Moon and the planets.

In radar astronomy a powerful radio transmission is emitted in the direction of the object of interest. This transmission has a precise frequency that is generally controlled by an

The altitudes and velocities of meteors entering the Earth's atmosphere (A) are determined from measurements of radar signals reflected back from the ionized gas trails produced by the meteors. The density of ionized gas in interplanetary space (B) can be determined from measurements of the time required for radio waves of different wavelengths to be reflected from the Moon. The speed and signal strength of the reflected waves are changed by passage through the gas. Long-wavelength radio waves are affected most.

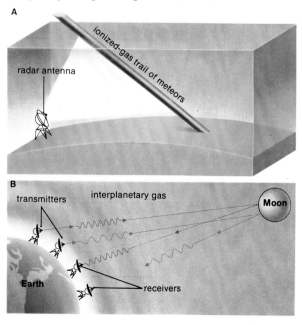

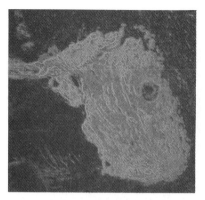

This radar image of the mountainous area of Venus known as Maxwell Montes was obtained at Arecibo Observatory, Puerto Rico. False colors provide a clear view of its folds and faults. The range is about 620 mi (1000 km) long.

atomic clock and adjusted continuously to compensate for the changing DOPPLER EFFECT caused by the Earth's rotation and orbital motion. The transmission is in the form of pulses or is otherwise "modulated" (time scales are sometimes of the order of millionths of a second) to allow precise timing of the time-of-flight of the signal to the object of interest and back to Earth. A small fraction of the transmitted power is reflected back to Earth, where some small part of this power is captured by the radar telescope and received and analyzed by the radar receiver and its associated electronics. Typically, the signal is reflected from a large number of different places on the Moon, satellite, or planet. The radar echoes from the various places arrive at the telescope at different times. The echoes have a radio frequency different from the transmitted signal because of the Doppler effect introduced by the motion and rotation of both the echoing object and the Earth. The precise time-of-flight of an echo and its Doppler-shifted frequency may be used to establish where on a planet or satellite the echo came from, thus allowing the mapping of echoing regions on the object and the determination of its rotation. It has been possible to make radar pictures of planets by using the time-of-flight and Doppler information.

The most powerful radar observatories have been the Haystack Observatory of the Lincoln Laboratory near Chelmsford, Mass. (no longer used as a radar observatory); the GOLDSTONE TRACKING STATION of the Jet Propulsion Laboratory in Pasadena, Calif., sponsored by NASA, which has an antenna 64 m (210 ft) in diameter and a transmitter with an output power of almost ½ million watts; and the ARECIBO OBSERVATORY, which has an antenna 305 m (1,000 ft) in diameter and a transmitter with an output power of nearly ½ million watts. Sometimes at these observatories a second telescope is used to receive the radar echoes, in addition to the main telescope, in order to determine more precisely the location of the echoing places. At Arecibo, for example, the second antenna is 30 m (100 ft) in diameter and is located 10 km (6 mi) from the main telescope.

Radar astronomy established the exact dimensions of the solar system, making precise navigation of spacecraft possible. It revealed certain portions of the Moon to be very rough and dangerous for the landing of spacecraft. It served in a similar way for the first Viking lander mission to Mars, where radar revealed which portions of that planet were safe for landing. Radar astronomy first showed that Venus rotated in a retrograde sense (backward with respect to most of the other planets) and with the very long period of 243 days, and radar devices are continuing to probe beneath the thick clouds of Venus to map its surface. Radar astronomy also revealed that Mercury, rather than presenting one hemisphere continuously to the Sun, as the Moon does to the Earth, has a rotational period precisely ⅔ its orbital period, causing the planet to present alternate hemispheres to the Sun at successive close approaches.   FRANK D. DRAKE

Bibliography: Beatty, J. K., "Radar Views of Venus," *Sky & Telescope*, February 1984; Evans, John V., and Hagsfors, Tor, eds., *Radar Astronomy* (1968); Kobrick, Michael, "Topology of the Terrestrial Planets," *Astronomy*, May 1982.

radar meteorology

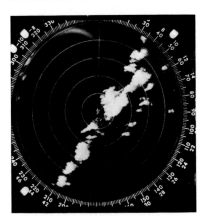

Radar echoes, or reflected radio waves, have been used to study thunderstorms and hurricanes and have led to a better understanding of their internal structure. The radio waves used in these studies are reflected from large raindrops, hailstones, and ice crystals. Such waves are used to locate and follow the precipitation regions moving within clouds.

In World War II radars operating in centimeter wavelengths were discovered to be detecting echoes from rain and other types of precipitation. This discovery has led to the development of the science of radar meteorology. Basically, radar is used operationally in two main areas: mapping the amount and intensity of precipitation and identifying severe storms. Radar does not miss a shower completely, as standard rain-gauge networks can, and it gives a reliable estimate of the duration of the rainfall.

Mapping. Pulses in the 3-cm (X-band) to 10-cm (S-band) wavelength range are most efficient in detecting water and ice particles of raindrop size. Even very light precipitation can be detected to a range of about 320 km (200 mi), but at this distance, even at 0° elevation, the beam is at a height of 8 km (5 mi) and is detecting precipitation there, rather than at the ground. During the past 10 years attempts have been made to use radar as a means of obtaining the total rainfall over a specified area, such as a watershed, especially when conditions are showery and the sparse rain-guage networks are inadequate to make reliable assessments. The radar must be calibrated by comparing the volume and intensity of the radar echoes with the rainfall measured by a dense network of rain gauges. Because the radar reflectivity factor is related to the sixth power of the raindrop diameter, certain assumptions must be made about the droplet size distribution. Generally good correspondence exists between the estimates from the radar and the gauge isohyets (the line of points receiving equal rainfall), but a number of factors limit the accuracy of the correspondence.

Storm Identification. Squall lines and thunderstorms are very obvious on radarscopes. Severe local storms can thus be detected and followed by radar quite readily. The extensive network of weather radar stations in the United States reduces the chance that a severe storm pattern can creep up unnoticed on a large community, although the system is by no means infallible. A radar with antenna sweeping the horizon can receive echo patterns that allow the recognition of the tornado cyclone. Tornado alerts or watches are issued when large squall systems, identified on the radarscopes, so warrant. From the thunderstorm echo, radar operators often observe a hook-shaped protuberance, which occasionally alters shape to a figure 6 and then to a doughnut. Hailstorms, identified by maximum echo height and echo intensity, can be detected with a great degree of accuracy.

Other Radar Systems. If 1.8-cm wavelength (K-band) radar, which detects very small cloud droplets, is aimed vertically, it returns echoes only from any part of the atmosphere occupied by clouds and thus allows the determination of the base and the top of thick, low-lying cloud layers. Special airborne sensors can be calibrated to relate the development of electric fields to the growth and shape of radar echoes.

Weather radar has the capability to make resolutions in both time and space, but quantitative data are not easily obtained. The digital radar system, which uses electronics, over-comes this deficiency. In this technique, echo-intensity information, for example, in a small area (dependent upon the instrument's resolution capabilities) is integrated over a selected period and printed out in grid form as a single digit (operationally a scale of six is generally used) related to the summed intensity. These computer-radar systems (digitized radar) are particularly useful in identifying areas with extreme precipitation intensities. Such data assist in local forecasting and especially in issuing flash-flood warnings.

Another radar system, the Doppler radar, detects and interprets the Doppler effect in terms of the radial velocity of the target. The system uses the fact that the signal received from a moving target differs slightly in frequency from the transmitted wave. In recent times, electronic devices have color-enhanced the radar image, a technique that opens exciting new possibilities for better resolution and detection of important phenomena, such as tornado cyclones and the movements of hurricanes, and of the results of cloud seeding.

Bibliography: Battan, Louis J., *Radar Observation of the Atmosphere* (1973) and *Radar Observes the Weather* (1962); Williams, Aaron, *The Use of Radar Imagery in Climatological Research* (1973).

Radcliffe, Ann   [rad'-klif]

An English writer of GOTHIC ROMANCE, Ann Ward Radcliffe, b. July 9, 1764, d. Feb. 7, 1823, gained an international reputation from her variations on one successful formula—tales of terror and suspense in which apparently supernatural occurrences are explained in the last chapters by natural and rational causes. *A Sicilian Romance* (1790), *The Romance of the Forest* (1791), and her most famous work, *The Mysteries of Udolpho* (1794), demonstrate her talent for picturesque descriptions of romantic locales and her ability to create psychological atmospheres of horror. Mary Shelley in England and Edgar Allan Poe in the United States worked in the tradition she established, and later Gothic and Byronic heroes show the influence of Schedoni, a villainous character in *The Italian* (1797).

PHILIP FLYNN

Bibliography: Grant, Aline, *Ann Radcliffe, a Biography* (1951); Murray, Eugene B., *Ann Radcliffe* (1972); Ware, Malcolm, *Sublimity in the Novels of Ann Radcliffe* (1963).

Radcliffe-Brown, Sir Alfred R.

Alfred Reginald Radcliffe-Brown, b. Jan. 17, 1881, d. Oct. 24, 1955, was a leading British social anthropologist. His effect on ethnological studies of the indigenous societies of Africa, Australia, and North America was profound and lasting. Trained at Cambridge University, he did important ethnographic fieldwork among the people of the ANDAMAN ISLANDS in 1906–08. Thereafter he concentrated on theoretical work and teaching. A follower of the French sociologist Émile DURKHEIM, Radcliffe-Brown believed that behavior patterns and institutions should be examined in terms of how they functioned as part of the entire social system. His goal was a science of society that would formulate laws explaining how these systems operated. He taught for many years in Cape Town, South Africa (1921–25), in Sydney, Australia (1925–31), and at the University of Chicago (1931–37) before returning to Oxford (1937–46). Among his works are *The Andaman Islanders* (1922) and *A Natural Science of Society* (1948).

STEVEN KOWALEWSKI

Bibliography: Fortes, Meyer, *Kinship and the Social Order* (1969).

Radcliffe College

Established in 1879, Radcliffe College (enrollment: 2,325; library: 173,000 volumes), a private 4-year liberal arts school for women, is coordinated with Harvard University in Cambridge, Mass. Although Radcliffe has its own administration, it shares classes, faculty, and facilities with Harvard College. Radcliffe graduates receive Harvard degrees.

Raddall, Thomas H.   [rad'-awl]

The English-born Canadian writer of historical novels and short stories, Thomas Head Raddall, b. Nov. 13, 1903, first won the Governor General's Award for the best Canadian book of the year with his collection of stories *The Pied Piper of Dipper Creek* (1939). He won the award again in 1943, 1948, and 1957. In 1949 he was elected to the Royal Society of Canada, receiving its gold medal for literature in 1956.

Radek, Karl   [rah'-dyik]

Karl Radek, b. Austrian Poland (in present Lvov, USSR), 1885, d. 1939?, was a leading international Communist publicist in the early part of the 20th century. He was originally named Karl Sobelsohn. While a student at the universities of Kraków and Bern he joined the Polish Social Democratic party and began publishing highly polemical writings in left-wing magazines. After the March revolution of 1917 in Russia he accompanied V. I. Lenin as far as Sweden in the famous sealed train that carried Lenin back to Russia. After the Bolshevik revolution of November 1917, Radek joined the Russian Bolshevik party and took part in the Brest-Litovsk peace talks that took Russia out of World War I. In 1919 he was arrested in Berlin after being sent there to reorganize the German Communist party. Released that December, he returned to Russia, where he was elected to the executive committee of Comintern. In 1927 he was expelled from the party as a Trotskyite but was readmitted three years later. An editor of *Izvestia* from 1931 to 1936, he fell victim to the GREAT PURGE in 1937; he was convicted of treason and died in prison.   K. M. SMOGORZEWSKI

Bibliography: Lerner, Warren, *Karl Radek* (1970).

Radhakrishnan, Sir Sarvepalli   [rah-duh-krish'-nuhn, sur-vuh-puhl'-lee]

One of modern India's most respected scholars and statesmen, Sir Sarvepalli Radhakrishnan, b. Sept. 5, 1888, d. Apr. 17, 1975, served as president of India from 1962 to 1967. In the course of his academic career he taught philosophy at the universities of Andhra, Mysore, and Calcutta, was Spaulding professor at Oxford University (1936–39), vice-chancellor of Benares Hindu University (1938–48), and chancellor of Delhi University (1953–62). His many influential books and articles on Indian philosophy and religion include *Indian Philosophy* (2 vols., 1923–27), *An Idealist View of Life* (1932), and *Eastern Religions and Western Thought* (1939). Radhakrishnan also led the Indian UNESCO delegation (1946–52), was ambassador to the USSR (1949–52), and served as vice-president of India (1952–62) before becoming president.   KARL H. POTTER

Bibliography: Harris, Ishwar C., *Radhakrishnan* (1982); Schilpp, Paul A., ed., *The Philosophy of Sarvepalli Radhakrishnan* (1952).

radial keratotomy: see EYE DISEASES.

radian

A radian, a unit of angular measure, is the central angle of a CIRCLE that intercepts an arc equal in length to the radius of the circle. Thus the radian measure of an ANGLE is determined by the number of times the radius of a circle for which it is a central angle is contained in the arc that it intercepts on that circle. The relation between the degree and radian measures of an angle is given by the formula 2π radians $= 360° = 1$ revolution. Therefore, 1 rad $= 57.2958° = 57°17'45''$.

F. JOE CROSSWHITE

radiation

Radiation is energy transmitted in the form of waves, particularly as ELECTROMAGNETIC RADIATION. Radiation is also the means by which such transmission takes place and is one of the three distinct processes by which heat can be distributed (see HEAT AND HEAT TRANSFER).

Electromagnetic radiation comprises a variety of wave phenomena, including visible light, gamma rays, X rays, ultraviolet and infrared radiation, and radio waves. All forms of electromagnetic radiation obey the same fundamental physical laws (see MAXWELL'S EQUATIONS; WAVES AND WAVE MOTION). For example, all are able to radiate through a vacuum and all do

Highly radioactive substances, too dangerous to be handled directly, are manipulated by a worker using a hydraulic rod and lever device. Thick lead or concrete walls and lead-treated windows absorb the radioactive emissions and protect the worker from contamination.

so at the same rate, the speed of light. Unless the radiation interacts with matter, each form can be distinguished only by its wavelength, frequency, or energy. Interaction with matter causes certain effects that are characteristic of all waves, as well as other effects that depend on the wavelength.

Radioactive substances emit three kinds of invisible emanations, originally called radiation because it was believed each was some kind of ray or energy. It is now known that two of them are actually streams of particles—alpha radiation is helium nuclei and beta radiation is electrons. The third, gamma radiation, is indeed a form of electromagnetic radiation.

STEPHEN FLEISHMAN

See also: BLACKBODY RADIATION; RADIOACTIVITY.

radiation injury

Radiation is a form of physical energy and as such can react with any material that it encounters. If a plant or animal cell is irradiated, the chemical changes induced can cause damage to the cell nucleus and its chromosomes. A cell system can repair a portion of this damage, but certain cells may survive that retain some form of injury, which decreases their capacity to function normally. This article deals with the injury caused by ionizing radiation, or radiation that can break molecular bonds; for the possible hazards of nonionizing radiation, see MICROWAVES.

In mammals exposed to ionizing radiations such as X rays, gamma rays, neutrons, or charged particles, such radiation injuries as mutations, cancers, reduction in life span, sterility, and damage to the eye lens resulting in cataracts can occur. If cells are killed by radiation, certain tissues (such as of the bone marrow, the intestinal lining, or the skin) may be able to replace the dead cells within a few days; the graying of hair by high doses of radiation, however, is permanent, providing evidence that above a certain dose level, pigment-producing cells are not replaced. Other tissues may develop scar tissue at the site of irradiation.

At high dose levels, the percentage of cells killed is large and the disruption of physiological function may be fatal. Deaths in mammals caused by high doses of radiation are separated into four syndromes that take into account such factors as total dose, damage to critical organs or tissues, and the time between irradiation and death. These syndromes are classified according to whether damage occurs to the central nervous system (CNS), gastrointestinal tract, or bone marrow, or whether changes occur up to many years after the irradiation (as in the case of many cancers). The degree of injury and the time of expression after irradiation are influenced by the total radiation dose, the duration of time over which the dose is received, and the amount of tissue irradiated. If the period between exposures to radiation is lengthened and the dose rate is decreased, radiation injury is usually minimized. A brief dose of high-level radiation, however, given over a few minutes to one hour, is 50% fatal in humans within a few months as a result of bone-marrow damage. If the same dose were spread out evenly over one month, death would not occur within a few months, but the life span of the exposed person would be shortened by several years. If the amount or volume of tissue irradiated is small, the relatively large amount of uninjured adjacent tissue usually permits a continuation of normal physiological function. The risk of a late effect, such as cancer, still is increased, but the chance that the individual will manifest any of the syndromes described is low. Such localized irradiations are given to patients in the form of cancer therapy, in which repeated doses are administered over a 4- to 6-week period, depending on individual circumstances, to kill the cancer cells.　　　E. J. AINSWORTH

Bibliography: Coggle, J. E., *Biological Effects of Radiation,* 2d ed. (1983); Gofman, J. W., *Radiation and Human Health* (1981); Selman, Joseph, *Elements of Radiobiology* (1983).

radiation pollution:　　see POLLUTION, ENVIRONMENTAL.

radiation pressure

Radiation falling on a surface exerts a pressure; its value is proportional to the net flux of energy divided by the speed of light. If a particle is traveling in an orbit around the Sun, solar radiation will appear to come from a position slightly shifted toward the direction in which the particle is moving, just as to a moving pedestrian raindrops appear to fall from a direction tilted toward the direction in which the person walks. This displacement is an aberration of light (see ABERRATION, STELLAR) and causes a net retarding force to act on the particle (Poynting-Robertson effect) that will ultimately cause the particle to fall into the Sun.　　　LAWRENCE H. ALLER

radiation therapy

Radiation therapy, or radiotherapy, is a standard treatment for CANCER. It involves exposing a patient to ionizing radiation in doses designed to kill the malignancy (see NUCLEAR MEDICINE). Ionizing radiation affects both normal and malignant tissues; the latter, however, are more sensitive to exposure and can be treated if they have not metastasized too extensively throughout the body and are not surrounded by normal tissue that is especially sensitive to radiation, such as bone marrow or lymphocytes.

A radiation therapist carefully defines the known and the probable extent of a tumor and selects the best type of radiation for the situation. Because the response to radiation by a specific tumor depends on the duration of exposure and the distance between the radiation source and the tumor, the therapist develops a treatment plan that permits the absorption of a fatal amount of radiation by all tumor cells but causes relatively minor damage to normal tissue surrounding the tumor. Computers are often used to determine the doses necessary for treatment of specific tumors.

Sophisticated physical and biological techniques are used for radiation therapy, often accompanied by computer analyses. The usual mode of therapy is an external high-energy beam directed at the tumor site; X RAYS, gamma rays, and such isotopes as cobalt-60 and iodine-131 are often used. The patient is carefully shielded except for the site of therapy, which remains exposed. The beam of radiation is administered for a few minutes a day for 2 to 6 weeks. Normal tis-

sues lying in the exposed area and blood are monitored to ensure that irradiation is limited to the tumor cells.

If tumors are small, localized, and superficial or easily accessible, then radioactive sources can be placed around or within the malignancy. For instance, interstitial therapy involves implanting radioactive needles or isotopes into tumors usually located on the skin or inside the mouth. Intracavitary and mold therapy involve inserting the radioactive source near the tumor site, such as in the uterus or near lymph glands or bone. The radioactive sources are then removed after several hours or a few days of treatment.

Radiation therapy differs from RADIOGRAPHY in that the former is used in the treatment or control of disease and the latter is an X-ray technique—used to diagnose malignancies (see also RADIOLOGY).　　　MELVIN L. REED, M.D.

Bibliography: Fletcher, G. H., ed., *Textbook of Radiotherapy* (1980); Hendee, W. R., *Radiation Therapy Physics* (1981); Order, S. E., et al., *Principles of Successful Radiation Therapy* (1979); Pizzarello, D. J., ed., *Radiation Biology* (1982).

radiator, automobile:　　see COOLING SYSTEM, ENGINE.

radical　(chemistry)

In chemistry, a radical is an ionized (electrically charged) group of atoms that behaves as a single unit; the group is derived from the dissociation of organic compounds. Some of the more common radicals are ammonium (NH_4^+), carbonate (CO_3^{2-}), hydroxyl (OH^-), nitrate (NO_3^-), and sulfate (SO_4^{2-}). The term is also used, but less correctly, in organic chemistry to designate certain uncharged units, such as alkyl and aryl groups. A specialized meaning is extended to active molecular fragments known as FREE RADICALS.

radical　(mathematics)

A radical is the indicated ROOT of a quantity. (The root, when it is multiplied by itself a specified number of times, yields the given quantity.) The symbolic notation $\sqrt[n]{x}$ includes the radical sign $\sqrt{\ }$, an index number n, and a radicand x. The radical sign is derived from the letter r. The index number specifies which root is desired, and the radicand identifies the quantity whose root is being sought. The bar of the radical sign should extend over the entire radicand, for example, $\sqrt[2]{2x}$, $\sqrt[3]{(x + y)^2}$, $\sqrt[5]{16}$. It is also common to omit the index number for the second root, or SQUARE ROOT, writing $\sqrt{4}$ instead of $\sqrt[2]{4}$.　　　F. JOE CROSSWHITE

radicalism

Radicalism is a political stance advocating fundamental changes in the existing political, economic, and social order. The radical posture tends to be rooted in what are perceived to be fundamental values, and its driving purpose is to force the status quo to conform to those principles. Radicals tend to regard any gestures toward compromise with the existing order as heresy. Often their principles are based on tenets laid down by an authoritative philosopher or political leader.

Modern radicalism originated in the challenge to established privilege, whether such privilege was based on alleged divine authority, nobility of birth, or entrenched wealth. It expressed itself in a long series of events and movements ranging from the peasant revolts of 16th-century Germany to the radical labor movements of the late 19th century. The word *radicalism* was first used to describe the movement toward parliamentary reform in Great Britain in the late 18th century. The particular radical contribution of the French Revolution was Jacobinism, a political style that combined fervent dogmatism with evangelistic appeals to the dispossessed masses. During the American Revolution Thomas PAINE's radical writings ridiculed the institution of monarchy and asserted the rights of all people. In the United States in the 1830s the Jacksonian populist reforms were looked upon as radical by conservatives; in fact, when these reforms are compared with the European radical movements of the early 19th century, they were quite moderate. In Britain the LUDDITES and CHARTISM were true radical movements. On the Continent a wide array of radical movements sprang up. The REVOLUTIONS OF 1848 were instigated by both radical and moderate factions.

Although traditionally radicalism has been primarily a movement of the left, not surprisingly the passionate appeals of the left produced various forms of radicalism of the right. Thus, while the doctrines of the radical left were based on notions of equality, the radicalism of the right espoused elitism. NAZISM acclaimed the superiority of the German nation and the so-called Aryan race. FASCISM in general was a rightist reaction to the fears of Marxist communism, the 20th century's most potent radicalism of the left. In the United States radicalism of the right expressed itself particularly through the resurgent KU KLUX KLAN of the 1920s and the McCarthyism of the cold-war era.

Radicalism of the left, having only temporarily gained momentum during the Great Depression, underwent a vigorous, worldwide resurgence in the 1960s. In particular, many young people were shocked into fervent radicalism upon their discovery of the extensive reality of racial and economic discrimination; of the apparent mismanagement of the environment; and, in the United States especially, of the agonies of the VIETNAM WAR. By the late 1970s much of the "New Left" movement had lost its vigor; elements of the movement, however—such as the Baader-Meinhof gang in West Germany and the Red Brigades in Italy—frustrated by the apparent durability of the political and social status quo, turned to terrorism. In developing countries radicalism remained a potent force with nationalist and religious manifestations.

TON DeVOS

Bibliography: Alinsky, Saul David, *Rules for Radicals* (1971); Bacciocco, Edward J., *The New Left in America* (1974); Greig, Ian, *Today's Revolutionaries* (1970); Hampden-Turner, Charles, *Radical Man: The Process of Psycho-Social Development* (1970); Marcuse, Herbert, *Counterrevolution and Revolt* (1972).

radio

Radio is a form of communication in which intelligence is transmitted without wires from one point to another by means of electromagnetic waves. Early forms of communication over great distances were the telephone and the telegraph. They required wires between the sender and receiver. Radio, on the other hand, requires no such physical connection. It relies on the radiation of energy from a transmitting antenna in the form of radio waves. These radio waves, traveling at the speed of light (300,000 km/sec; 186,000 mi/sec), carry the information. When the waves arrive at a receiving antenna, a small electrical voltage is produced. After this voltage has been suitably amplified, the original information contained in the radio waves is retrieved and presented in an understandable form. This form may be sound from a loudspeaker, a picture on a television, or a printed page from a teletype machine.

HISTORY

Early Experimenters. The principles of radio had been demonstrated in the early 1800s by such scientists as Michael FARADAY and Joseph HENRY. They had individually developed the theory that a current flowing in one wire could induce (produce) a current in another wire that was not physically connected to the first.

Hans Christian OERSTED had shown in 1820 that a current flowing in a wire sets up a magnetic field around the wire. If the current is made to change and, in particular, made to alternate (flow back and forth), the building up and collapsing of the associated magnetic field induces a current in another conductor placed in this changing magnetic field. This principle of ELECTROMAGNETIC INDUCTION is well known in the application of TRANSFORMERS, where an iron core is used to link the magnetic field of the first wire or coil with a secondary coil. By this means voltages can be stepped up or down in value. This process is usually carried out at low frequencies of 50 or 60 Hz (Hertz, or cycles per second). Radio waves, on the other hand, consist of frequencies between 30 kHz and 300 GHz (1 GHz = 1 × 10⁹ Hz).

In 1864, James Clerk Maxwell published his first paper that showed by theoretical reasoning that an electrical disturbance that results from a change in an electrical quantity such as voltage or current should propagate (travel) through space at the speed of light. He postulated that light waves were electromagnetic waves consisting of electric and magnetic fields. In fact, scientists now know that visible light is just a small portion of what is called the electromagnetic spectrum, which includes radio waves, X rays, and gamma rays (see ELECTROMAGNETIC RADIATION).

Heinrich Hertz, in the late 1880s, actually produced electromagnetic waves. He used oscillating circuits (combinations of capacitors and inductors) to transmit and receive radio waves. By measuring the wavelength (λ) of the waves and knowing the frequency of oscillation (f), he was able to calculate the velocity (v) of the waves using the equation $v = f\lambda$. He thus verified Maxwell's theoretical prediction that electromagnetic waves travel at the speed of light.

Marconi's Contribution. It apparently did not occur to Hertz, however, to use electromagnetic waves for long-distance communication. This application was pursued by Guglielmo MARCONI; in 1895, he produced the first practical wireless telegraph system. In 1896 he received from the British government the first wireless patent. In part, it was based on the theory that the communication range increases substantially, as the height of the aerial (antenna) is increased.

The first wireless telegraph message across the English Channel was sent by Marconi in March 1899. The use of radio for emergencies at sea was demonstrated soon after by Marconi's wireless company. (Wireless sets had been installed in lighthouses along the English coast, permitting communication with radios aboard nearby ships.) The first transatlantic communication, which involved sending the Morse-code sig-

(Above) *Guglielmo Marconi, a pioneer of radio, in 1895 produced the first practical wireless telegraph.*

(Left) *Lee De Forest invented the triode in 1907, which helped to introduce the use of electronic devices for radio amplification.*

nal for the letter *s*, was sent, on Dec. 12, 1901, from Cornwall, England, to Saint John's, Newfoundland, where Marconi had set up receiving equipment.

The Electron Tube. Further advancement of radio was made possible by the development of the ELECTRON TUBE. The DIODE, or valve, produced by Sir Ambrose FLEMING in 1905, permitted the detection of high-frequency radio waves. In 1907, Lee DE FOREST invented the audion, or TRIODE, which was able to amplify radio and sound waves.

Radiotelephone and Radiotelegraph. Up through this time, radio communication was in the form of radio telegraphy; that is, individual letters in a message were sent by a dash-dot system called MORSE CODE. (The International Morse Code is still used to send messages by shortwave radio.) Communication of human speech first took place in 1906. Reginald Aubrey FESSENDEN, a physicist, spoke by radio from Brant Rock, Mass., to ships in the Atlantic Ocean.

Armstrong's Contributions. Much of the improvement of radio receivers is the result of work done by the American inventor Edwin ARMSTRONG. In 1918 he developed the superheterodyne circuit. Prior to this time, each stage of amplification in the receiver had to be adjusted to the frequency of the desired broadcast station. This was an awkward operation, and it was difficult to achieve perfect tuning over a wide range of frequencies. Using the HETERODYNE PRINCIPLE, the incoming signal is mixed with a frequency that varies in such a way that a fixed frequency is always produced when the two signals are mixed. This fixed frequency contains the information of the particular station to which the receiver is tuned and is amplified hundreds of times before being heard at the loudspeaker. This type of receiver is much more stable than its predecessor, the tuned-radio-frequency (TRF) receiver.

In order to transmit speech the radio waves had to be

(Left) *Another leader in the growth of radio, Edwin H. Armstrong invented the feedback circuit in 1912 and the superheterodyne circuit in 1918, later developing frequency modulation.*

(Below) *Users of the first radio sets had to listen in on headphones.*

modulated by audio sound waves (see MODULATION). Prior to 1937 this modulation was done by changing the amplitude, or magnitude, of the radio waves, a process known as AMPLITUDE MODULATION (AM). In 1933, Armstrong discovered how to convey the sound on the radio waves by changing or modulating the frequency of the carrier radio waves, a process known as FREQUENCY MODULATION (FM). This system reduces the effects of artificial NOISE and natural interference caused by atmospheric disturbances such as lightning.

Radiobroadcasting. (This subject is treated in more detail under RADIO AND TELEVISION BROADCASTING.) The first regular commercial radio broadcasts began in 1920, but the golden age of broadcasting is generally considered to be from 1925 to 1950. NBC was the first permanent national network; it was set up by the Radio Corporation of America (RCA). Radio was also being used in the 1930s by airplane pilots, police, and military personnel.

Significant changes in radio occurred in the 1950s. Television displaced the dramas and variety shows on radio; they were replaced on radio by music, talk shows, and all-news stations. The development of the TRANSISTOR increased the availability of portable radios, and the number of car radios soared. Stereophonic broadcasts (see STEREOPHONIC SOUND) were initiated in the early 1960s, and large numbers of stereo FM receivers were sold in the 1970s. A recent development is stereo AM, which may lead to a similar boom for this type of receiver in the 1980s.

OPERATION

Frequency Allocations. In the United States the FEDERAL COMMUNICATIONS COMMISSION (FCC) allocates the frequencies of the radio spectrum that may be used by various segments of society (see FREQUENCY ALLOCATION). Although each user is assigned a specific frequency in any particular area, general categories are identified. Some representative allocations are indicated in the accompanying table.

FREQUENCY ALLOCATIONS

Frequency Range	Frequency Category	Use
30–535 kHz	Low to medium (LF–MF)	Maritime and aeronautical navigation and communication
535–1605 kHz	Medium (MF)	Standard AM broadcast
27 MHz	High (HF)	Citizens band (CB) radio
30–50 MHz	Very high (VHF)	Police, fire, forestry
50–54 MHz	Very high	Amateur 6-meter band
54–216 MHz	Very high	Includes television channels 2 through 13
88–108 MHz	Very high	Standard FM broadcast
470–890 MHz	Ultrahigh (UHF)	UHF television channels 14 to 83
1.3–1.6 GHz	Ultrahigh	Radar
4–8.5 GHz	Superhigh (SHF)	Satellite communication
30–300 GHz	Extrahigh (EHF)	Experimental and amateur radio

The Transmitter. The heart of every TRANSMITTER is an OSCILLATOR. The oscillator is used to produce an electrical signal having a frequency equal to that assigned to the user. In many cases the frequency of oscillation is accurately controlled by a quartz crystal, which is a crystalline substance that vibrates at a natural resonant frequency when it is supplied with energy. This resonant frequency depends on its thickness and the manner in which it is cut. By means of the piezoelectric effect (see PIEZOELECTRICITY), the vibrations are transformed into a small alternating voltage having the same frequency. After being amplified several thousand times, this voltage becomes the radio-frequency carrier. The manner in which this carrier is used depends upon the type of transmitter.

Continuous Wave. If applied directly to the antenna, the energy of the carrier is radiated in the form of radio waves. In early radiotelegraph communications the transmitter was keyed on and off in a coded fashion using a telegraph key or switch. The intelligence was transmitted by short and long bursts of radio waves that represented letters of the alphabet by the Morse code's dots and dashes. This system, also known as interrupted continuous wave (ICW) or, simply, continuous wave, is used in modified form today in high-speed teletype, facsimile, missile-guidance telemetry, and space-satellite communication. In these cases, the carrier is not switched off but shifted slightly in frequency by amounts between 400 and 2,000 Hz. These shifts in frequency are made in a coded fashion and are decoded in the receiver. This method keeps the receiver quiet between the dots and dashes and produces an audible sound in the receiver corresponding to the coded information.

Amplitude Modulation. In radio-telephone communication or standard broadcast transmissions the speech and music are used to modulate the carrier. This process means that the intelligence to be transmitted is used to vary some property of the carrier. One method is to superimpose the intelligence on the carrier by varying the amplitude of the carrier, hence the term *amplitude modulation* (AM). The modulating audio signal (speech or music) is applied to a MICROPHONE. This produces electrical signals that alternate, positively and negatively. After amplification, these signals are applied to a modulator. When the audio signals go positive, they increase the amplitude of the carrier; when they go negative, they decrease the amplitude of the carrier. The amplitude of the carrier now has superimposed on it the variation of the audio signal, with peaks and valleys dependent on the volume of the audio input to the microphone. The carrier has been modulated and, after further amplification, is sent by means of a transmission line to the transmitting antenna.

The maximum modulating frequency permitted by AM broadcast stations is 5 kHz at carrier frequencies between 535 and 1,605 kHz. The strongest AM stations have a power output of 50,000 watts.

Frequency Modulation. Another method of modulating the carrier is to vary its frequency. In frequency modulation (FM), on the positive half-cycle of the audio signal the frequency of the carrier gradually increases. On the negative half-cycle the carrier frequency is decreased. The louder the sound being used for modulation, the higher will be the change in frequency. A maximum deviation of 75 kHz above and below the carrier frequency is permitted at maximum volume in FM broadcasts. The rate at which the carrier frequency is varied is determined by the frequency of the audio signal. The maximum modulating frequency permitted by FM broadcast stations is 15 kHz at carrier frequencies between 88 and 108 MHz. This wider carrier frequency (15 kHz for FM as opposed to 5 kHz for standard AM broadcasts) accounts for the high fidelity of FM receivers. FM stations range in power from 100 watts to 100,000 watts. They cover distances of 24–105 km (15–65 mi), because FM relies upon line-of-sight transmission.

It should be noted that television transmitters use both AM and FM. The video, or picture, signals are transmitted by AM and the sound by FM.

The Antenna. An ANTENNA is a wire or metal conductor used either to radiate energy from a transmitter or to pick up energy at a receiver. It is insulated from the ground and may be situated vertically or horizontally.

The radio waves emitted from an antenna consist of electric and magnetic fields, mutually perpendicular to each other and to the direction of propagation. A vertical antenna is said to be vertically polarized because its electric field has a vertical orientation. An AM broadcast antenna is vertically polarized, requiring the receiving antenna to be located vertically also, as in an automobile installation. Television and FM broadcast transmitters use a horizontal polarization antenna.

For efficient radiation the required length of a transmitting (and receiving) dipole antenna must be half a wavelength or some multiple of a half-wavelength. Thus an FM station that broadcasts at 100 MHz, which has a wavelength of 3 m (9.8 ft), should have a horizontally polarized antenna 1½ m (4.9 ft) in length. Receiving antennas (sometimes in the form of "rabbit ears") should be approximately the same length and placed horizontally.

For an AM station broadcasting at 1,000 kHz, the length

should be 150 m (492 ft). This is an impractical length, especially when it must be mounted vertically. In this case, a quarter-wavelength Marconi antenna is often used, with the ground (earth), serving as the other quarter wavelength.

The Receiver. When the modulated carrier reaches the receiving antenna, a small voltage is induced. This may be as small as 0.1 μV (microvolt) in some commercial communication receivers but is typically 50 μV in a standard AM broadcast receiver. This voltage is coupled to a tunable circuit, which consists of a coil and a variable capacitor. The capacitor has a set of fixed metal plates and a set of movable plates. When one set of plates is moved with respect to the other, the capacitance is changed, making the circuit sensitive to a different, narrow frequency range. The listener thus selects which transmitted signal the receiver should reproduce.

The Crystal Receiver. One of the earliest methods of detecting radio waves was the crystal receiver. A crystal of galena or carborundum along with a movable pointed wire called a cat whisker provided a simple RECTIFIER. This component allows current to flow in one direction only, so that only the upper half of the modulated wave is allowed to pass. A capacitor is then used to filter out the unwanted high-frequency carrier, leaving the audio to operate the earphones. Since no external electrical power or amplifiers are used, the only source of power in the earphones is the incoming signal. Only strong signals are audible, but with a long antenna and a good ground, reception of a signal from 1,600 km (1,000 mi) away is sometimes possible.

The TRF Receiver. Following the development of the triode, increasing selectivity, sensitivity, and audio output power in tuned-radio-frequency (TRF) receivers was possible. This process involved a number of stages of radio-frequency amplification prior to the detection stage. In early receivers each of these stages had to be separately tuned to the incoming frequency—a difficult task. Even after single-dial tuning was achieved by ganging together the stages, the TRF was susceptible to breaking into oscillation and was not suitable for tuning over a wide range of frequencies. The principle is still used, however, in some modern shipboard emergency receivers and fixed-frequency microwave receivers.

The Superheterodyne Receiver. Practically all modern radio receivers use the heterodyne principle. The incoming modulated signal is combined with the output of a tunable local oscillator whose frequency is always a fixed amount above the incoming signal. This process, called frequency conversion or heterodyning, takes place in a mixer circuit. The output of the mixer is a radio frequency that contains the original information at the antenna. This frequency, called the intermediate frequency (IF), is typically 455 kHz in AM broadcast receivers. No matter what the frequency that the receiver is tuned to, the intermediate frequency is always the same; it contains the information of the desired station. As a result, all further stages of radio-frequency amplification can be designed to operate at this fixed intermediate frequency.

After detection, audio amplifiers boost the signal to a level capable of driving a loudspeaker.

Comparison of AM and FM. Although the method of detection differs in AM and FM receivers, the same heterodyne principle is used in each. An FM receiver, however, generally includes automatic frequency control (AFC). If the frequency of the local oscillator drifts from its correct value the station will fade. To avoid this problem, a DC voltage is developed at the detector and fed back to the local oscillator. This voltage is used to change automatically the frequency output of the local oscillator to maintain the proper intermediate frequency. Both AM and FM receivers incorporate automatic gain control (AGC), sometimes called automatic volume control (AVC). If a strong station is tuned in, the volume of the sound would tend to be overwhelming if the volume control had previously been set for a weak station. This drawback is overcome by the use of negative feedback—a DC voltage is developed at the detector and used to reduce automatically the gain, or amplification, of the IF amplifiers.

The prime advantage of FM, in addition to its fidelity, is its immunity to electrical noise. Lightning storms superimpose noise on an AM signal by increasing the amplitude of the signal. This effect shows up in a receiver as a crackling noise. An FM receiver, because it decodes only the frequency variations, has a limiter circuit that restricts any amplitude variations that may result from added noise.

Single Sideband Systems. When an audio signal of 5 kHz is used to amplitude-modulate a carrier, the output of the transmitter contains sideband frequencies in addition to the carrier frequency. The upper sideband frequencies extend to 5 kHz higher than the carrier, and the lower sideband frequencies extend to 5 kHz lower than the carrier. In normal AM broadcasts both sidebands are transmitted, requiring a bandwidth in the frequency spectrum of 10 kHz, centered on the carrier frequency. The audio signal, however, is contained in and may be retrieved from either the upper or lower sideband. Furthermore, the carrier itself contains no useful information. Therefore, the only part that needs to be transmitted is one of the sidebands. A system designed to do this is called a single sideband suppressed carrier (abbreviated SSBSC, or SSB for short). This is an important system because it requires only half of the bandwidth needed for ordinary AM, thus allowing more channels to be assigned in any given portion of the frequency spectrum. Also, because of the reduced power requirements, a 110-watt SSB transmitter may have a range as great as that of a 1,000-watt conventional AM transmitter. Almost all HAM RADIOS, commercial radiotelephones, and marine-band radios, as well as CITIZENS BAND RADIOS, use SSB systems. Receivers for such systems are more complex, however, than those for other systems. The receiver must reinsert the nontransmitted carrier before successful heterodyning can take place.

Radio has become a sophisticated and complex area of electrical engineering, especially when compared to its elementary origin. Every day new radio applications are being found; these range from digital radio-controlled garage-door openers to weather satellites and from tracking systems for polar bear migrations to radio telescope investigations of the universe. This wide range of uses demonstrates the important part radio plays in the world today.   ALLEN MOTTERSHEAD

Bibliography: Aitken, Hugh G., *Syntony and Spark: The Origins of Radio* (1976); American Radio Relay League, *Radio Amateur's Handbook* (annual); Arnheim, Rudolf, *Radio* (1936; repr. 1971); Carr, Joseph J., *Elements of Electronic Communications* (1978); DeFrance, J. J., *Communications Electronics Circuits*, 2d ed. (1972); Hawks, Ellison, *Pioneers of Wireless* (1927; repr. 1974); Hilbrink, W. R., *Who Really Invented Radio?* (1972); Marcus, Abraham and William, *Elements of Radio*, 6th ed. (1972); Schwartz, Martin, *Radio Electronics Made Simple* (1982); Shrader, R. L., *Electronic Communication*, 4th rev. ed. (1980).

radio astronomy

Radio astronomy is the study of the universe through observations of the radio waves emitted by cosmic objects. Everything in the universe radiates radio waves, and modern radio telescopes are capable of detecting these waves from almost all known objects.

Because the physical processes giving rise to radio emission are sometimes different from or more powerful than the processes giving rise to other types of radiations, objects can often be detected more easily by radio observations. In addition, important aspects of objects, such as the strength of magnetic fields, can often be determined only by radio observations. As a result, radio astronomy complements optical, X-ray, gamma-ray, infrared, and ultraviolet astronomy. All of these studies combine to reveal the true nature of celestial objects. (See ASTRONOMY AND ASTROPHYSICS; GAMMA-RAY ASTRONOMY; INFRARED ASTRONOMY; ULTRAVIOLET ASTRONOMY; X-RAY ASTRONOMY.)

Radio astronomy was born in 1931 with the discovery by Karl JANSKY at the Bell Telephone Laboratories in New Jersey that radio waves were coming from the sky. His discovery was followed by the work of Grote Reber, a radio engineer at Wheaton, Ill., who in 1937 constructed a steerable parabola radio telescope and used it to map the distribution of radio emission in the sky. This study was followed by work in many

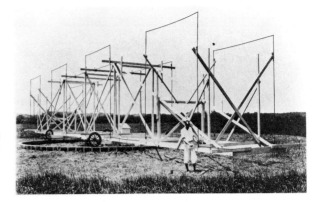

The first detection of extraterrestrial radio waves was made in 1931 by Karl Guthe Jansky, a physicist on the staff of the Bell Telephone Laboratories in Holmdel, N.J. Jansky is seen adjusting the 30 × 4-m (98 × 13-ft) rotatable aerial array with which he made his discovery.

countries during and immediately after World War II; radar technology, originally developed for military purposes, was used for pioneering radio astronomy observations as well as for making radar observations of neighboring planets (see RADAR ASTRONOMY). The radio emission from the Sun was discovered in this way, and radio telescopes in Australia established the existence of discrete sources of radio emission.

These discoveries led to the construction throughout the world of ever bigger and more sensitive radio telescopes during the 1950s and 1960s. Particularly active countries were England, Australia, the Netherlands, and the United States. By the mid-1960s radio astronomy had become the cutting edge of modern astronomy, leading the way to the majority of major new discoveries, such as the existence of RADIO GALAXIES, QUASARS, PULSARS, BACKGROUND RADIATION from the primordial fireball, and a host of complex molecules in interstellar space (see ASTROCHEMISTRY).

CAUSES OF RADIO EMISSION

As late as 1950 some astronomers thought that radio observations would play no important role in the study of the universe. They believed that the only significant source of radio waves was thermal radiation caused by the heat of a body. Calculations indicated that the thermal radiation at radio wavelengths would be so faint that no useful radio measurements could be made of anything except perhaps the Sun and planets. The radio intensities observed by Jansky and Reber were, however, approximately 10 million million times brighter than might have been expected from the thermal emission of the stars and galaxies. This result implied that far more powerful mechanisms for the production of radio waves existed in the universe.

Nonthermal Radiation. The only important nonthermal mechanism of radio emission, and the one that almost always produces the observed radiation, is known as SYNCHROTRON RADIATION. This is radio emission from very energetic nuclear particles orbiting in a magnetic field. Scientists believe that these are, in every case, electrons orbiting in the magnetic field of, for example, a galaxy. To produce synchrotron radiation these electrons must have a total energy much higher than the energy associated with their mass (m), which is mc^2, or 0.5 million electron volts. In space, electrons have energies as great as 100 billion billion electron volts, which means that magnetic fields must be accelerating them far beyond the energies produced in manufactured nuclear accelerators. In the interstellar magnetic field, which may be only one-millionth as strong as the magnetic field of the Earth, the electrons may complete only a few orbits a second. With their very high energies, however, the synchrotron mechanism causes the electrons to radiate primarily at radio frequencies and with very great intensity.

Because of the large release of energy, the overall radiation from celestial objects is likely to be relatively great, allowing

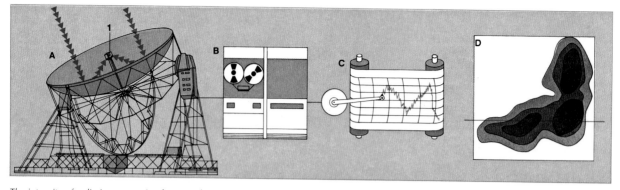

The intensity of radiation emanating from a radio source such as Centaurus A is mapped through use of a steerable dish reflector (A). The radio waves from a narrow region of the sky are focused onto the centrally mounted antenna (1), which transmits the signals to amplifying and recording equipment (B). As the telescope sweeps across the sky, the signal-intensity output is graphed on a pen recorder (C). After several sweeps a contour map (D) is built up, with the areas of more-intense radio flux represented by a darker shade.

astronomers to detect and study many of the objects and to observe them at very great distances. Thus radio astronomy has given the astronomer a means to trace the history of the universe, even perhaps back to the creation of the universe.

Thermal Radiation. Although the nonthermal radio emission and the objects associated with it have been of the greatest interest, thermal radiation has also turned out to be a valuable source of information. With it astronomers have studied the gas clouds of our galaxy (see GALAXY, THE) and other galaxies (see EXTRAGALACTIC SYSTEMS), the emission nebulae, and the PLANETS.

RADIO SOURCES WITHIN THE GALAXY

When the sky is scanned with a radio telescope, a very bright band of radio emission is found that coincides with the Milky Way. The brightness of this band relative to the other cosmic sources of radio emission is much greater than the relative brightness of the Milky Way as compared to the ordinary stars as seen with the unaided eye. This radiation from the disk of our galaxy is, at most radio frequencies, synchrotron radiation from cosmic-ray electrons spiraling in the magnetic fields of our galaxy (see COSMIC RAYS).

In addition to the bright radiation of the Milky Way, the sky is filled with distinct sources of radio emission. Some of these come from solar system objects, while others arise in more distant parts of the galaxy or outside of the galaxy. None of the bright radio sources is associated with any of the bright, well-known optical stars; instead, these sources of radio emission are associated with objects that in all cases are rather faint optically but radiate large amounts of radio energy due to synchrotron radiation or very high temperature. Aside from the solar system, the most prominent sources of radio emission within the galaxy are supernova remnants, pulsars, most ionized emission nebulae, and interstellar atoms and molecules (see INTERSTELLAR MATTER).

The Solar System. The SUN is an interesting and complex source of radio waves. It radiates a steady level of thermal radio emission because of its high temperature. When observed at long radio wavelengths, however, the radio emission observed is very intense and is typical of a hot object whose temperature is 1,000,000 K rather than the 5,800 K temperature of the solar surface. This high-temperature radiation comes from the solar CORONA, which becomes the visible "surface" of the Sun when observed at long radio wavelengths. In addition to this steady emission, the Sun exhibits at least six other kinds of complicated, time-variable radio emissions. All of these seem to be associated with SUNSPOT activity and the SOLAR FLARES that accompany this activity. One type of radio emission varies slowly as the Sun rotates. Another is noise storms, which last hours to days. Also occurring are at least four different types of solar radio bursts—large increases in radio emission from a small region of the Sun, usually near a sunspot. One type of burst may last only a few seconds, while another type may persist for minutes or hours. Often the radio emission making up a burst occurs only at a very limited

range of frequencies, a range that changes as time goes on, usually to lower frequencies. This occurrence provides evidence that the burst is caused by material ejected from the Sun that moves up in the solar atmosphere to less dense regions where the typical frequencies for radio emission are lower.

Radio observations of Venus have shown that the temperature of its surface is much higher than once imagined, about 480° C (900° F), a result since confirmed by spacecraft. This high temperature is maintained by a GREENHOUSE EFFECT caused primarily by the dense carbon dioxide atmosphere and the clouds of Venus.

Radio observations of Mercury have shown that temperature on its surface rises as high as 425° C (800° F). Observations of the Moon have shown that the mean temperature of the lunar surface is only slightly less than that of the Earth, but that the temperature of the surface plunges to about −100° C (−150° F) at night. Similarly, the temperature on the Martian surface, which barely reaches the freezing point of water during the day, approaches −100° C (−150° F) at night.

The biggest surprises in solar-system research have been provided by Jupiter, which exhibits three different types of radio emission. First, radio emissions are caused by thermal emission from the body of the planet. Higher and higher temperatures are observed as observations are made at longer and longer wavelengths for two reasons: because of the greenhouse effect and because the radio telescope looks deeper into the Jovian atmosphere at the longer wavelengths, a consequence of the fact that the atmosphere is made partially opaque by ammonia gas, with the amount of obscuration less at long wavelengths. Indeed, temperatures little different from terrestrial temperatures are found deep in the Jovian atmosphere. A second type of radio emission, called decimeter emission, is synchrotron emission from a vast system of radiation belts that are held within the magnetic field of the planet. These belts are like the Van Allen radiation belts of the Earth but contain many more energetic particles whose origins are not understood. The third type of radio emission, called decameter emission, is a sporadic, very intense radio emission that is observed only at low frequencies of about 20 MHz. It consists of groups of short bursts of radio emission usually lasting only fractions of a second, with a group of bursts lasting sometimes tens of minutes. The probability of such emission is very dependent on the position of the satellite Io, suggesting that Io causes energetic electrons from the radiation belts of Jupiter to travel down the magnetic lines of force to the ionosphere of the planet, where they radiate the decameter emission.

Although Saturn is similar to Jupiter it possesses a much weaker radiation belt, because the rings of the planet destroy energetic electrons. Relatively high temperatures, approaching terrestrial temperatures, are observed at long wavelengths. Radio emissions of Uranus and Neptune indicate lower temperatures; the presence of a greenhouse effect and almost terrestrial temperatures low in the atmosphere are indicated here also. The asteroids, comets, and Pluto emit too little radio emission for detection by contemporary radio telescopes, except for faint radio emission from several comet molecules.

Supernova Remnants and Pulsars. Supernova remnants are the clouds of gas that have been expelled in the violent nuclear explosion of a star known as a SUPERNOVA. These clouds, which often appear as hollow spherical shells, contain large quantities of electrons of relativistic energy, that is, electrons moving at speeds approaching the speed of light. Radiating through the synchrotron process, the electrons were evidently created in the supernova explosion; in some cases, however, this explosion has left behind a spinning NEUTRON STAR, which is both a pulsar and a continuous producer of new relativistic electrons and cosmic rays.

The pulsars are radio sources in the Milky Way that are very unusual because, rather than producing a continuous radio intensity at the Earth, they produce short, regularly spaced bursts of radio emission. These bursts typically last about 1/20th of a second and occur at intervals of about one second. The time between pulses is extremely regular, except that a slow increase in the period between pulses is detected if a pulsar is studied for many months. Astronomers have deduced from such data that the objects are spinning neutron

stars, the products of supernova explosions. They are made of bulk nuclear matter, primarily neutrons, and their density is about 10^{15} times the density of water. They have very strong magnetic fields, about 10^{12} times stronger than the Earth's field. This field, spinning with the neutron star, acts as a super powerful electric generator capable of accelerating electrically charged particles to relativistic energies that exceed the highest energies produced in terrestrial nuclear accelerators. The particles accelerated in this way radiate synchrotron radiation in well-defined beams that spin with the pulsar. As these beams sweep across the Earth, the pulse of the pulsar radiation can be observed.

The most important example of a pulsar is in the CRAB NEBULA, the remains of a star that exploded on July 4, 1054, and was so bright that it was visible for three weeks in the daytime and for almost two years at night. This remnant is about 6,000 light-years from the Earth, and is still expanding outward at a speed of about 1,000 km/sec (6 mi/sec). At most frequencies it is the third brightest cosmic radio source and is a shell filled with relativistic electrons that radiate synchrotron radiation at X-ray and optical frequencies as well as radio. The total power radiated is equal to about 100,000 times the total power radiated by the Sun. The source of this power is particles accelerated and expelled from the most rapidly spinning pulsar discovered so far, a pulsar that is in the center of the object and that spins about 30 times per second.

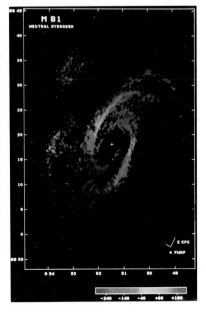

(Left) *In this radio contour map, here superimposed over an optical photograph, of M 51 (the Whirlpool Galaxy) and its companion galaxy NGC 5195, the white lines are lines of constant radio intensity. These lines converge rapidly at such regions of maximal radio intensity as the nuclei of both galaxies and the spiral arms of M 51. The other sources seen are probably more-distant radio systems.*

(Below) *The distribution and velocity of neutral hydrogen in M 81 is revealed in this false-color image of the 21-cm (8.3-in) radiation emanating from that nearby spiral galaxy. The brightness indicates the intensity, whereas the colors represent the velocities, or Doppler shift: red to yellow, recession; green, no shift; blue to violet, approach (see the inset strip at lower right). The rotation of this galaxy is clearly evident.*

Ionized Emission Nebulae. The other bright sources of radiation in the Milky Way are the ionized emission NEBULAE. In these objects, a very hot star has produced ultraviolet radiation that has ionized and heated the interstellar gas around it. This hot, charged gas is an excellent emitter of radio waves produced by thermal processes. These sources of radio emission—one of the brightest is the Great Nebula in Orion—are more prominent at the higher radio frequencies because the spectrum of synchrotron radiation is most intense at low frequencies, even though thermal emission has about the same intensity over a broad frequency range.

Stars. Several dozen normal stars have been detected as faint radio sources in our galaxy. The detectable radiation appears to come from hot shells or coronae, like that of the Sun, surrounding these stars.

Interstellar Atoms and Molecules. A very important feature of the galactic radio emission is the strong radiation on specific wavelengths, or so-called spectral lines, that are emitted by atoms and molecules in the interstellar gas. The most prominent of these is the radiation of neutral atomic hydrogen, the most abundant element in the universe, at the wavelength of 21 cm. The atoms in this case and others radiate at a specific frequency but may arrive at Earth at a different frequency due to the Doppler effect associated with the motion of the atoms toward or away from the Earth. By studying this Doppler shift in the frequencies of the observed spectral lines, the astronomer can deduce the temperatures and motions of the gas clouds that the radiation comes from. In this way the velocities and arrangements of gas clouds in our galaxy and others have been determined.

In addition to atomic hydrogen, spectral lines have been discovered, surprisingly, from more than 40 different molecules. Those found so far are primarily organic molecules. The largest contain as many as 13 atoms and have molecular weights of more than 100. Carbon monoxide is found to be very abundant in space, as is formaldehyde. The molecules that are most effective in producing molecules important to biology in laboratory experiments are also abundant in space. This discovery suggests that interstellar chemistry perhaps played a role in the development of life on Earth and elsewhere, or else that the process was mimicked here.

Extraterrestrial Civilizations. At several observatories in the United States, Canada, and the Soviet Union, astronomers are searching for radio signals from other civilizations. Much more elaborate coverage over long time periods is called for, however, before such searches could in any way be considered statistically meaningful (see LIFE, EXTRATERRESTRIAL).

EXTRAGALACTIC RADIO SOURCES
Most of the bright objects in the radio sky are outside our galaxy. At least two distinct classes of objects exist—radio galaxies and quasars—but radio surveys of the sky also reveal a variety of less classifiable objects.

Radio Galaxies. Although all galaxies, including the Milky Way, emit some radio waves because they contain energetic electrons and magnetic field, some galaxies emit from a thousand to ten million times more radio energy than normal galaxies. These radio galaxies are very often peculiar in their optical appearance. A common type has a bright central region; other cases are elliptical galaxies with dust clouds. In a majority of cases the intense radio emission comes not from the optical body of the galaxy but from two very large regions placed symmetrically about the center of the galaxy, several galactic diameters away from the center. An important example is the radio galaxy NGC 5128, also known as Centaurus A, which has two radio lobes extending 10° across the sky, or 20 times the diameter of the full moon. These lobes span a distance of 3 million light-years, or 30 galactic diameters.

In other cases a radio galaxy may have a very intense region of radio emission near the center of the galaxy, sometimes accompanied by a halo of bright radio emission extending throughout the galaxy. Many hundreds of such galaxies are known. The radio emission from radio galaxies is very highly polarized, indicating that its origin is the radio radiation of very energetic electrons moving at nearly the speed of light and spiraling in the weak magnetic field of the galaxy.

These energetic electrons are the result of some very violent event, still not understood, in which an amount of energy equivalent to the total annihilation of up to ten million stars is released. Calculations indicate that the typical radio galaxy will be a brilliant radio emitter for anywhere from 100 million to 1 billion years.

Quasars. Quasars are far more extreme examples of radio galaxies and are the brightest objects in the universe. Even if situated near the bounds of the observable universe, they are easily detected by small radio telescopes. Their radio emission is typically 1 million to 100 million times greater than that of a normal galaxy, and they are as bright as or brighter than the brightest radio galaxies. In every case a quasar appears to be a galaxy with a very bright small region in its center, as seen optically. Because they create optical images that are indistinguishable from stars, they are called "quasi-stellar radio sources," or "quasars" for short. Spectral analysis of the objects, however, shows that they are indeed distant galaxies, in many cases receding from the Earth with a velocity that is a large fraction of the velocity of light. Their radio and optical emission changes with time, sometimes increasing or decreasing substantially in only a few months. This rapid change indicates that the main source of their energy is at most only a few light-months in size.

In about ten cases astronomers have found that small regions of radio emission are moving outward from the nucleus of these galaxies with enormous speeds; the deduced velocities actually may be as much as ten times the velocity of light. It is believed that the true velocities of the emitting regions do not exceed light velocity; if they do exceed light-speed, some new and remarkable laws of physics are required. Instead, astronomers believe that the superlight velocities are an illusion created by projection effects. Otherwise the radio appearance of quasars is much like that of radio galaxies. Accounting for the source of the energy in quasars is one of the most interesting of astronomical problems. Perhaps the energy is the result of a chain of explosions of supernovas or the result of a tremendous number of collisions between stars in a very dense cluster of stars at the center of the galaxy. However, the favored theory at present is that the energy is released from matter falling into a massive BLACK HOLE at the center of the galaxies.

BL Lacertae Objects. A class of objects very similar to quasars are the objects known as BL LACERTAE OBJECTS, named for the first of these to be recognized, the variable "star" BL Lacertae. Long known as a starlike object that varied in its light, BL Lacertae is actually a galaxy. Many such objects are now known. They are distinguished rather arbitrarily from quasars on the basis that their light and radio variations occur in much shorter times—sometimes in days—than the variations in quasars, and their optical spectra do not show the atomic emission spectral lines characteristic of quasars. They are probably a special variety of quasars.

Background Radiation. A profound aspect of the radio sky is the uniform glow of radio emission found in all parts of the sky. Careful study shows that it has the same spectra as a thermally radiating body whose temperature is only 2.7 K. Surprisingly, such a spectrum is the same as the spectrum that has been predicted theoretically (see BLACKBODY RADIATION) to result from the big-bang cosmology (see BIG BANG THEORY). In this cosmology, the universe in its early phases consisted of a primordial fireball, an expanding sphere of high-energy photons that eventually was largely converted into matter. However, as astronomers look back in time with a radio telescope, they observe this fireball receding at nearly the speed of light. This recession, with its accompanying redshift, causes the apparent temperature of the fireball, 2.7 K, to be far less than what would have been measured at the fireball. All tests of this blackbody radiation so far have been consistent with the idea that in this radiation astronomers are observing the earliest periods in the development of the universe. This interpretation is supported by studies of the numbers of radio sources of different brightness, which suggest that the density of objects was much higher long ago, consistent with the big bang theory.

usually a circular region whose angular size is approximately 57° times the ratio of the observed wavelength to the diameter of the telescope. The largest single paraboloidal telescopes have a beamwidth, or resolution, of about one arc-minute—about the same as that of the human eye. Much greater resolution can be obtained with INTERFEROMETERS in which two or more radio telescopes are connected together to simulate the performance of a much larger telescope. In this case the resolution is 57° times the ratio of the wavelength to the maximum separation of the telescopes used in the interferometer. This separation may be thousands of meters or even an intercontinental distance, leading to resolutions as small as a few ten-thousandths of an arc-second.

The sensitivity of a radio telescope refers to the faintness of the signals that can be detected. It depends on both the energy-collecting area of the telescope and on the radio noise added to the incoming radio signals, primarily by the radio receiver but also to a lesser extent by the antenna itself. Special circuits have been constructed to minimize the effects of this noise, but physical laws prevent its complete elimination. In a

Among the world's major radio telescopes are (above) the 91.4-m-diameter (300-ft) meridional transit dish located at the National Radio Astronomy Observatory in Green Bank, W.Va.; (right) the fourteen 25-m-diameter (82-ft) parabolic dishes that constitute the Synthesis Radio Telescope at Westerbork Radio Observatory in the Netherlands; and (below) the 305-m-diameter (1,000-ft) spherical reflecting dish set in a natural basin near the town of Arecibo in western Puerto Rico.

high-quality receiver the minimum detectable signal becomes fainter in proportion to the reciprocal of the square root of the bandwidth used and in proportion to the reciprocal of the square root of the time over which the received signal is averaged. Both these qualities are utilized in modern radio telescopes to improve sensitivity. In some cases bandwidths of hundreds of Megahertz are used. In such cases, signal averaging times may be as much as 30 hours.

Astronomers prefer to build their radio telescopes on as large an area as possible, in order to capture the maximum amount of energy, and with energy-collecting elements that are constructed to precise geometric configurations that allow operation at higher radio frequencies and provide better resolution. They have found that it is particularly important to design structures that preserve their precise geometry in the presence of the changing force of gravity as the structure moves, the force of the wind, and the thermal deflections due to uneven heating of the telescope structure.

Steerable Paraboloid. In 1937, Grote Reber built the first steerable paraboloid antenna as an amateur project at Wheaton, Ill. This antenna became the prototype of most modern large radio telescopes. During and immediately after World War II the large radar instruments built for military purposes were used as radio telescopes. In the 1950s the main thrust of radio telescope construction was to build ever larger steerable paraboloids, a process that culminated in the 91.4-m (300-ft) paraboloid at Green Bank, W.Va., built in 1963, and the 100-m (328-ft) telescope near Bonn, West Germany, constructed in the late 1960s. The development of more precise antennas allowed operation at higher radio frequencies, which is important to the study of interstellar molecules. The most powerful for the study of such molecules is the 11-m (36-ft) radio telescope operated by the National Radio Astronomy Observatory at Kitt Peak, Ariz. An important variation of the paraboloidal antenna is the use of a fixed spherical antenna, as in

RADIO TELESCOPES

The first radio telescope, built by Karl Jansky in 1929, was originally intended for the purpose of studying the causes of short-wave interference. It was an ensemble of simple dipole antennas that could be rotated on a track. Most modern instruments are large parabolic reflector radio antennas that focus the radio emission from a small region of the sky to a focal point, where a small antenna captures the radio energy and delivers it to a very sensitive radio receiver. Other types of radio telescopes include the Mills Cross and the Very Large Array (see NATIONAL RADIO ASTRONOMY OBSERVATORY).

Resolution Sensitivity. The resolution of a radio telescope is the size of the region in the sky from which the telescope collects radiation. Sometimes called the beamwidth, the area is the world's largest radio telescope, 305 m (1,000 ft) in diameter, constructed in 1963 near Arecibo, Puerto Rico. Another such antenna is the Soviet RATAN-600—an acronym for Radio Astronomy Telescope of the Academy of Sciences (Nauk)—in the northwestern Caucasus; it has about ¼ the reflecting area of the Arecibo antenna.

The operation of the paraboloid radio telescope is identical in concept to that of large optical telescopes. A reflector consisting of a paraboloid is oriented so that its axis is pointed at the place in the sky whose radio emission is to be measured. An excellent reflector surface at radio wavelengths need be smooth only to an accuracy of about ¼₀ wavelength or better, or typically about 1 millimeter. Thus ordinary sheet metal is usually used. The paraboloid reflects all rays coming to it from the place of interest to the focus of the paraboloid. At that point a radio antenna is located to capture the focused radio waves and convert them into an electrical signal of the same frequency as the incoming waves. This antenna is often a microwave horn or a simple dipole antenna. In the Arecibo telescope the reflector is spherical and focuses the radio emission to a long line, some 29 m (96 ft) long, rather than to a point. An ensemble of antennas must be placed all along this line to capture the focused radiation.

The electrical signal is carried from the antenna through a waveguide or wires to a high-sensitivity radio receiver. This receiver has electronic or waveguide filters that allow only those radio frequencies to pass that the astronomer wishes to observe. The signals, which may be at a very low power level such as 10^{-20} watt, are then amplified in a special amplifier. The amplifiers used are low noise, meaning that they themselves add a minimum of radio noise to the weak incoming signals. The most commonly used amplifiers are the parametric amplifier, often cooled to a very low temperature with liquid air to give low noise performance, or the MASER, a special form of amplifier using atomic processes to give exceptionally low noise performance. These must usually be cooled to a temperature of 4 C degrees above absolute zero or lower, usually by immersing them in liquid helium, a procedure that leads to practical difficulties and high expense.

Following amplification, a circuit detects the signal, meaning that it establishes the average power of the rapidly oscillating signal. This average radio power, which often changes many times in a second and may even change in less than a millionth of a second in some pulsar radiation, is then recorded. At present the most common recording method is an electronic digital voltmeter that provides a digital value of the radio emission; a computer is then used to record these digital values on magnetic tape. Later, the scientist involved will take these raw values and subject them to further mathematical manipulations in order to take into account such things as the amplifier gain and telescope size to lead to a value that is relevant to the physics taking place in the source observed.

A common application of radio telescopes is in the observation of radio spectral lines of such things as atomic hydrogen, carbon monoxide, or formaldehyde. To do this expeditiously a radio receiver is preferred that receives a large number of adjacent frequency bands, or channels, simultaneously. This reception can be achieved by incorporating the appropriate number of selective filters in the radio receiver and providing each one with its own detector and data recorder; the latter may be a single computer time-shared by all the channels. This procedure is technically demanding and inflexible, however, because it calls for an entire new set of filters whenever channel bandwidth must be changed. One way to overcome these difficulties is to use an electronic device called an autocorrelator to analyze the radio signals. This device utilizes digital electronic circuitry to calculate the function describing the waveform of the amplified signal developed in the receiver. A simple mathematical treatment of this function in a computer, called a Fourier transformation, can recover the spectrum of the radio emission. Most radio spectrum analyzers now use this approach; in some systems more than 4,000 channels are observed simultaneously.

The computer has come to play a wide range of roles in the radio telescope. It converts the signals to digital values for recording, records the signals, and performs mathematical manipulations on the recorded signals to convert them into physically meaningful data. In some cases computers automatically steer telescopes, control receiver frequencies, bandwidths, and observing times, and perform other functions.

Mills Cross. The quest for good resolution and large energy-collecting area has led to the development of several ingenious radio telescope systems. One of the earliest was the Mills Cross, invented in 1953 by Bernard Mills of the University of Sydney, Australia. In the Mills Cross two antennas are used, each long and thin and fixed to the ground. Because of their shapes each antenna has good resolution in one direction, the direction parallel to its long dimension, and poor resolution in the other direction. In a Mills Cross, the two antennas are arranged at right angles to one another, usually so that they look like a cross from above (hence the name), and the signals from the two antennas are multiplied together. The result is an overall response that gives good resolution in both directions. The largest Mills Cross is at Molonglo, Australia, where the antennas are each one mile long. Other large Mills Crosses are at Bologna, Italy, and Penticton, British Columbia. The configuration of a Mills Cross makes pointing the telescope's response pattern difficult and following objects as the Earth moves impossible; the telescope is also difficult to operate at different radio frequencies. As a result new Mills Crosses are not being built.

Radio Interferometers. A very important development of the early 1960s and subsequent years was the application of groups of radio antennas as radio interferometers. In this approach, several antennas are connected together simultaneously, usually by an ordinary electrical cable connection but sometimes via radio links over distances of more than 80 km (50 mi). Alternatively, the signals received at various antennas can be tape-recorded and subsequently played into a common radio receiver simultaneously. The radio interferometer permits extremely high resolution and a very large equivalent antenna collecting area at much less cost than would be called for if these were achieved with a single large antenna. This procedure is the basis of most of the major instruments recently constructed or planned.

One of the most important developments to grow out of the successful application of interferometers was the process of aperture synthesis, pioneered by Sir Martin RYLE. When two parabolic antennas are connected together as an interferometer, the pair gives the same information to the radio receiver as two points on a much larger paraboloid. Research showed mathematically that if a pair of antennas was moved so that the many lengths and orientations of the line connecting them duplicated all the lines that occur in a paraboloid, then the information from the antennas could be combined to give exactly the same performance as the larger paraboloid would have achieved. This method made it feasible to duplicate the performance of a large paraboloidal radio telescope, for example, 1.6 km (1.0 mi) in diameter, by moving two antennas to a large number of positions within a circle on the Earth 1.6 km (1.0 mi) in diameter.

In aperture synthesis the signals received at the antennas must be recorded precisely. When all the moves of the antennas have been achieved, the recorded signals can be combined to construct a picture of a small portion of the sky that would have the same clarity as though a 1.6-km (1.0-mi) telescope, in this example, had been built. This approach has proven effective. In existing aperture synthesis systems, large numbers of antennas are used, with each antenna connected to every other antenna; this procedure allows observance of a large number of antenna spacings and orientations at a given instant. The antennas themselves are physically moved to change the length of the lines connecting the antennas, and the rotation of the Earth is utilized to achieve an effective rotation with respect to the sky.

One large operating aperture synthesis is located at Westerbork, the Netherlands, where antennas are spaced along a line one kilometer long. Another powerful system is operated by Cambridge University. The largest system now in existence is the Very Large Array, which the National Radio Astronomy

Observatory has built on the Plains of San Augustin near Socorro, N.Mex. This system, which was finished in 1981, possesses 27 steerable paraboloids, each 25 m (82 ft) in diameter, arranged along three railroad tracks. The three rail lines form an equiangular "Y" shape, and each is 20 km (12 mi) long. All the antennas are connected to the other antennas, giving 351 interferometer pairs at any given time. The resolution that is achieved by this instrument is a few tenths of an arc-second, about the same as that of the largest optical telescopes under the best atmospheric conditions. The entire array provides astronomers with the equivalent performance of a fully steerable radio dish 27 km (17 mi) in diameter; while it was under construction, the array already produced magnificent results.

Another powerful application of interferometry is called Very Long Baseline Interferometry. In this technique, two or more radio telescopes at different locations observe the same region simultaneously. Atomic clocks are used at each telescope to control the radio telescope electronics and to synchronize the observations to accuracies that are better than one-thousandth of a second. At each station video tape recorders are used, with atomic clock synchronization, to record the signals received. The tapes are then brought to a processing location where they are played simultaneously into a device that mimics the electronic operation of the interferometer electronics that would have been used if the telescopes had been connected together in the conventional way. The output is a normal output from an interferometer but with the telescopes widely separated. This procedure is commonly used with a group of four or more telescopes spread all across the United States. It is also sometimes used with intercontinental baselines utilizing telescopes in the United States and in Australia, England, or the Soviet Union. Resolutions far better than optical resolutions are obtained, which are comparable to those which could be obtained by a fully steerable radio dish nearly the size of the Earth.

FUTURE OF RADIO ASTRONOMY

Radio astronomy is pursued at a large number of institutions, including many universities and at two U.S. centers sponsored by the National Science Foundation: the National Astronomy and Ionosphere Center, which operates the Arecibo Observatory, and the National Radio Astronomy Observatory, which operates telescopes at Green Bank, W.Va., Kitt Peak, Ariz., and the Very Large Array, near Socorro, N.Mex.

Work began in the mid-1980s on the construction of a radio installation that is to stretch across the United States and its territories. Called the Very Long Baseline Array, it will consist of ten parabolic antennas, each 25 m (82 ft) in diameter. The dishes are to be located in the states of Hawaii, Washington, California, Arizona, New Mexico (two antennas), Texas, Iowa, and Massachusetts and on St. Croix in the Virgin Islands; its operations center will be in Socorro, N.Mex. Scheduled to be completed in the early 1990s, the Very Long Baseline Array will have a resolution 1,000 times that of any currently existing optical or radio telescope. Canada is planning a similar array, called the Canadian Long-Baseline Array, which will consist of eight telescopes, each 32 m (105 ft) in diameter, arranged in a line across the southern part of the country. In the Southern Hemisphere, Australia is also planning a continent-wide array of radio telescopes. Another promising idea being explored is the development of an interferometer using one radio telescope aboard an orbiting spacecraft to observe simultaneously with another telescope on Earth or also in orbit.

Radio telescopes are also being constructed to explore the last remaining untapped region of the electromagnetic spectrum: the submillimeter region that lies between the very shortest radio wavelengths and the very longest wavelengths of infrared radiation. Because waves in this region of the spectrum are strongly absorbed by atmospheric water vapor, the submillimeter radio antennas to receive them must be built in arid regions, preferably at high altitudes. Such installations exist or are being planned by British, Dutch, West German, U.S., and other radio astronomers at sites such as Mauna Kea in Hawaii.   FRANK D. DRAKE

Bibliography: Abell, G. O., *Drama of the Universe* (1978); Chown, Marcus, "A Radio Telescope Bigger than the Earth," *New Scientist,* Jan. 31, 1985; Ferris, Timothy, *The Red Limit* (1977); Field, G. B., and Chaisson, E. J., *The Invisible Universe* (1985); Gordon, M. A., "VLBA—A Continent-Size Radio Telescope," *Sky & Telescope,* June 1985; Heiserman, D. L., *Radio Astronomy for the Amateur* (1975); Hey, J. S., *The Radio Universe,* 3d ed. (1984); Hjellming, R. M., and Bignell, R. C., "Radio Astronomy with the Very Large Array," *Science,* June 18, 1982; Smith, D. H., "The Submillimeter Giants," *Sky & Telescope,* August 1985; Spitzer, Lyman, Jr., *Searching between the Stars* (1982); Verschuur, G. L., and Kellerman, K. I., *Galactic and Extra-Galactic Radio Astronomy* (1974).

See also: OBSERVATORY, ASTRONOMICAL.

Radio City Music Hall

Radio City Music Hall, the world's largest indoor theater (6,000 seats), opened in 1932 in New York City's ROCKEFELLER CENTER. The theater was designed by Donald Deskey in collaboration with the center's architectural team. Its immense stage (44 × 21 m/144 × 69 ft) is equipped with almost every known technical device; its semicircular proscenium arch is repeated in the ever-widening gilded arches that roof the enormous auditorium. Leading to the theater and its three balconies is the resplendent six-story grand foyer, perhaps the finest surviving ART DECO room in the world. Its two gigantic cylindrical chandeliers of Lalique glass are reflected in the floor-to-ceiling mirrors of the side walls. A majestic grand staircase fills the end wall. The smoking lounge beneath the foyer is decorated in black glass and silver trim.

Bibliography: Karp, Walter, *The Center: A History and Guide to Rockefeller Center* (1983); Krinsky, Carol, *Rockefeller Center* (1978).

Radio Free Europe and Radio Liberty

Radio Free Europe and Radio Liberty, a U.S.-government–financed nonprofit corporation with headquarters in Munich, West Germany, broadcasts more than 1,000 hours of programming weekly from 46 transmitters into Eastern Europe and the Soviet Union. These two radio stations were founded in 1950 and 1951, respectively, as separate stations and were merged into one corporation, RFE/RL, Inc., in 1976.

RFE broadcasts to five East European countries (Bulgaria, Czechoslovakia, Hungary, Poland, and Romania) in six languages; RL broadcasts into the Soviet Union in 15 languages. The stations provide their listeners with information that their own media do not provide. Programming includes news, commentary, sports, music, and religion.

Until 1971 the two stations were financed by U.S. government funds covertly channeled through the Central Intelligence Agency. In 1973 a semiautonomous agency, the Board for International Broadcasting, was created to oversee the operations of RFE/RL and to act as the conduit and auditor of the funds.

Bibliography: Board for International Broadcasting, *Annual Report;* Tyson, J. L., *U.S. International Broadcasting and National Security* (1983); U.S. Government Printing Office, *The Right to Know—Report of the Presidential Study Commission on International Radio Broadcasting* (1973).

radio galaxies: see RADIO ASTRONOMY.

radio journalism: see JOURNALISM.

radio telescope: see OBSERVATORY, ASTRONOMICAL; RADIO ASTRONOMY.

radio and television broadcasting

Radio and television broadcasting is a firmly established element of American life. The A. C. Nielsen Company, which measures audience size, reported in 1985 that 98.1% of U.S. homes contained at least one television set and that the average set is turned on for seven hours per day. More than 60% of television viewers receive their news from their sets rather than from newspapers, and over half that number trust television more than newspapers. According to the Radio Advertising Bureau, in 1985 only 1% of U.S. homes had no radio, and the average household owned at least five radios.

Since its inception in the 1920s, broadcasting has provoked a variety of responses from institutions affected by it. Business sees it as the most important contemporary advertising medium. Many educators, however, regard television as a foe of literacy and serious thought. Whatever its failings, television is capable of exerting an influence that no other medium of communication can match. In 1960, for example, the 70 million people watching the debates between presidential candidates Richard M. Nixon and John F. Kennedy formed new impressions of the candidates that led to Kennedy's election. During the Depression President Franklin D. Roosevelt used radio to broadcast his fireside chats to the anxious nation. In its coverage of the U.S. space program, of the Watergate scandals, and of unfolding crises, such as terrorist hijackings, television has been responsible for shaping public opinion.

Numerous critics have pointed out broadcasting's tendency toward escapism. In 1927, H. G. Wells condemned radio as useful only to "very sedentary persons living in badly lighted houses or otherwise unable to read. . .and who have no capacity for thought or conversation." Edward R. Murrow said in 1958: "Television in the main insulates us from the realities of the world in which we live. If this state of affairs continues, we may alter an advertising slogan to read, 'Look now, pay later.'"

THE ORIGINS OF BROADCASTING—RADIO

Early Years: 1920–26. Broadcasting spread rapidly across the country during the early 1920s on a primarily amateur basis. Before World War I the inventors Guglielmo MARCONI, Lee DEFOREST, Reginald Aubrey FESSENDEN, and Edwin ARMSTRONG had laid the technological foundations of RADIO, but a wartime ban on nonmilitary broadcasting delayed radio's acceptance until the ban was lifted in 1919. Thereafter, hundreds of amateur stations sprang up. In 1922 more than 500 stations were licensed by the government. Most listeners employed homemade sets built around a galena or silicon crystal to receive signals from the "ether."

Lack of government regulation abetted radio's growth and rapid commercialization. The U.S. Department of Commerce was in charge of regulating stations on the basis of the Radio Act of 1912 and assigned three- and then four-letter codes to stations. The act also confined most domestic broadcasting to the same wavelength, 360 m, thus creating an aerial traffic jam of overlapping signals. In 1922 the Commerce Department permitted more-powerful stations to use the 400-m wavelength on condition that they play only live music. This two-tier structure encouraged large and small broadcasting

On July 2, 1921, one of the first radio broadcasts, a ringside commentary on Jack Dempsey's heavyweight title defense against Georges Carpentier, was transmitted by RCA from New Jersey. These people on the Atlantic City boardwalk could listen to the broadcast at a radio-equipped cart for a fee of 25 cents per round.

systems to form associations to share costs and bring popular entertainment from cities to rural areas.

Both the Westinghouse Corporation and American Telephone and Telegraph (AT&T) made early efforts to capitalize on the broadcasting boom by establishing stations. In 1920 the Westinghouse engineer Frank Conrad received a license for what is regarded as the nation's first true radio station, KDKA in Pittsburgh, Pa. KDKA broadcast scheduled music programs, sports, and the 1920 presidential election. During the following year Westinghouse began to sell radio sets. The least expensive model cost $25. By 1924 the radio-listening audience numbered 20 million.

AT&T inaugurated its radio station, WEAF, in New York City in 1922. Soon after, WEAF broadcast the first paid commercial announcement, a 10-minute speech on behalf of the Queensborough Corporation, a real-estate concern. The advertisement cost $50. AT&T then licensed out-of-town stations to carry its programs, which included the Browning King Orchestra, the Ipana Troubadors, commentary by H. V. Kaltenborn, and congressional debates. On the strength of its "toll," or sponsored approach to broadcasting, WEAF made a $150,000 profit in 1923, to the dismay of amateur enthusiasts who decried the commercialization of the airwaves. Herbert Hoover, then Commerce Department secretary, said: "It is inconceivable that we should allow so great a possibility for service to be drowned in advertising chatter."

American Marconi, the U.S. subsidiary of Marconi's highly successful British company, was bought by a newly formed Radio Corporation of America (RCA) in 1919, in large part to keep some of the new technology of radio in American hands. In 1920, Westinghouse, General Electric, and AT&T agreed to share the important broadcasting patents each had developed. RCA entered the patent pool in 1921. In return, the three original patent holders acquired an interest in the new company.

David Sarnoff and the Founding of NBC. American Marconi's primary commitment had been to transoceanic telegraphy, and the establishment of RCA was also intended to advance U.S. interests in that field. The notion that radio itself might become a "household utility" was advanced by David SARNOFF, a onetime telegraph operator and American Marconi employee. As early as 1916, Sarnoff had suggested that music could be brought into American households via "a simple Radio Music Box," or wireless receiver. As commercial manager of RCA, Sarnoff began to manufacture radios, and their sale became the chief source of RCA profits.

With those profits, Sarnoff hoped to establish a national broadcasting network, whose principal elements were to be "entertainment, information, and education, with emphasis on the first feature—entertainment." In 1926, RCA purchased WEAF from AT&T for $1 million as the nucleus of a broadcasting network. AT&T retained a financial interest in broadcasting by supplying land lines to link the network's stations. During the same year, RCA established its broadcasting subsidiary, the National Broadcasting Company.

Guglielmo Marconi, the inventor of the wireless radio, and David Sarnoff, president of the Radio Corporation of America (RCA), are seen in this photograph taken in 1933 at the RCA transmitting center in Riverhead, Long Island. The Marconi Wireless Company was taken over by RCA in 1919, using Marconi's pioneering work to develop Sarnoff's idea of marketing radios for the home.

William S. Paley bought a network of radio stations in 1928 and from it built the vast Columbia Broadcasting System. He served as president of CBS until 1946 and as chairman of the board until 1983. In 1986, when CBS suffered a crisis involving finances, ratings, and morale, he was brought back as temporary chairman.

In 1927, Congress passed the Radio Act, which created a Federal Radio Commission empowered to license and regulate stations. Networks, whose influence was largely unforeseen, were free from direct FRC regulation.

William Paley and the Founding of CBS. The Columbia Broadcasting System, organized as a rival network to NBC, was founded in 1927, and rapidly passed through a number of owners—including the Columbia Phonograph Company, which gave the network its name. In 1928, William S. PALEY, scion of a wealthy cigar manufacturing family, bought the network, and bolstered the financially weak firm by selling shares, borrowing money, and moving the network headquarters to Madison Avenue, New York City, not far from NBC's on Fifth Avenue. Paley also negotiated new affiliate contracts. Whereas NBC charged affiliates to carry sustaining (nonsponsored) programs, CBS supplied them free in return for 5 hours of affiliates' time. The favorable terms helped CBS attract 47 stations to its roster by the end of 1929. Paley's entrepreneurial acumen now offered a significant challenge to NBC's dominance of domestic broadcasting.

The Depression also affected RCA, which no longer earned profits on the sale of radios. Thus NBC was forced to adopt a fully commercial policy much like that of CBS. In 1931, NBC made its first profit: $2,300,000. The following year, during a complex reorganization inspired by a threatened monopoly suit, RCA head Owen D. Young resigned, and Sarnoff took his place. In 1933 he moved RCA-NBC to its current headquarters in Rockefeller Plaza, New York City.

Programming and Advertising. Although live music served as the staple of most early radio programming, networks soon realized that vaudeville-trained comedians lured larger audiences and served as effective on-the-air speakers for sponsors' products. Two white men, Freeman Gosden and Charles Correll, created a daily 15-minute-long comedy sketch based on the hard times of two black characters. AMOS 'N' ANDY, made its NBC debut in 1929 and eventually attracted an audience estimated at 40 million. Other popular comedians of the Depression era included Fred ALLEN, Jack Benny, BURNS AND ALLEN, Ed WYNN, and Jane Ace and Goodman Ace. The comedians adopted a light tone, offering respite from economic problems at home and mounting political tension in Europe. Networks did not produce these popular, sponsored programs themselves. They leased facilities to advertising agencies who in turn hired the performers.

Because advertising time was sold according to the estimated popularity of a given program, networks and sponsors relied on ratings as the arbiter of a performer's success. In 1930, Crossley, Inc., tabulated the first formal ratings, showing that NBC's "Amos 'n' Andy" was four times more popular than any CBS show. To fill hours dominated by popular NBC programming, CBS turned to prestigious but inexpensive dramas broadcast on a sustaining basis. Under the direction of William B. Lewis, the "Columbia Workshop" introduced the writers Archibald MacLeish and Norman Corwin, the actor-di-

rector Orson WELLES, and the composer Bernard Hermann to radio audiences. Their work often had a political undertone. Welles's adaptation of H. G. Wells's science-fiction story The WAR OF THE WORLDS, broadcast on Oct. 30, 1938, and intended as a Halloween joke, created panic in many areas with its convincing account of an alien landing at Grover's Mills, N.J. In response to the CBS sustaining programming, NBC broadcast adaptations of Shakespeare starring John Barrymore and scored a significant coup by inducing Arturo Toscanini to leave Italy and take up the direction of the newly formed NBC Symphony Orchestra, beginning in late 1937.

Radio and World War II: 1938–45. The threat of world war spurred the development of network news departments. The coverage offered by a young CBS correspondent, Edward R. MURROW, of Hitler's march to Vienna in 1938 brought a new sophistication and immediacy to radio reporting. CBS that year inaugurated the world news roundup, and Murrow helped recruit for CBS such outstanding correspondents as Walter CRONKITE, Winston Burdett, Richard C. Hottelet, Larry Le Sueur, Eric Sevareid, William L. Shirer, and Howard K. Smith. Murrow's live reports of the Battle of Britain brought the far-off war into American living rooms in 1940. From within the United States the radio commentators Elmer Davis, Quincy Howe, H. V. Kaltenborn, and Raymond Swing offered analyses of world events. The "Columbia Workshop" also joined the war effort as it became part of the Office of War Information, and CBS dramatists turned to propaganda. Corwin's verse oratorio On a Note of Triumph, broadcast May 8, 1945, celebrated the Allied victory.

THE COMING OF TELEVISION

Early Years: 1935–44. In 1929, David Sarnoff had learned of the television experiments of Vladimir Kosma ZWORYKIN, a Soviet immigrant then working at Westinghouse. Whereas many other television inventors relied on mechanical devices to re-

Orson Welles's famous adaptation of H. G. Wells's classic War of the Worlds became a landmark in radio history when it was presented (1938) as part of his "Mercury Theatre" drama series. Welles's realistic broadcast convinced millions of U.S. listeners that a Martian invasion was actually occurring and precipitated widespread panic. Adventure and mystery shows were popular forms of entertainment during the heyday of radio.

Edward R. Murrow, regarded as the finest of all radio and television journalists, broadcast from London during World War II and was primarily responsible for discrediting the anti-Communist propaganda of Sen. Joseph McCarthy in 1954.

produce visual images, Zworykin emphasized the importance of an all-electronic system. Sarnoff eventually invested $50 million in Zworykin's inventions, and in 1939 demonstrated a television system at the New York World's Fair. Franklin D. Roosevelt spoke before the camera, becoming the first president to appear on television.

Despite Sarnoff's bold moves, several factors converged to delay the coming of television. The war forced RCA to suspend television development in favor of military production. A struggle over wavelength allocations, combined with a running battle over government regulation, further slowed television's progress. In 1933 the inventor Edwin Armstrong demonstrated a new static-free method of transmission, FREQUENCY MODULATION (FM), far superior to the AMPLITUDE MODULATION (AM) then in use. Armstrong's advocacy of FM, which caught the ear of the government, threatened to block the introduction of Sarnoff's television, which required some of the same hotly contested frequencies. In order to make peace, Sarnoff offered Armstrong $1 million for the FM patent rights, but Armstrong, by then operating his own FM radio station, W2XMN, refused. In 1940 the FEDERAL COMMUNICATIONS COMMISSION, successor to the FRC, approved FM for radio broadcasting, but, by allowing FM stations to duplicate AM programming, it dampened much of the promise of an alternative system. The FCC, however, ensured FM's survival by requiring that it also be used for television transmission. In 1944 the FCC determined frequencies for both FM and television: 12 very high frequency (VHF) and 70 ultra-high frequency (UHF) television channels, with FM broadcasting located just above channel 6 on the VHF spectrum.

The Birth of ABC: 1941–55. The FCC, created by the Communications Act of 1934, was meant to regulate broadcasting largely through its power to license stations. Drawing on Section 303 of the act, which specified that the FCC exercise its authority as "public convenience, interest, or necessity requires," the commission decided to dismantle the RCA-NBC monopoly. In 1941 the FCC issued its *Report on Chain Broadcasting,* which in effect ordered NBC to sell one of the two networks it operated. The report noted that RCA exercised a "practical monopoly of network broadcasting" since 25% of all radio stations were affiliated with NBC. A Supreme Court decision of 1943 confirmed the FCC's right to force NBC to divest itself of one of its networks.

That year, NBC sold the Blue network to Edward J. Noble, a businessman who had made his fortune as a candy manufacturer. Renamed the American Broadcasting Company (ABC), the new network, after experimenting with inexpensive public-affairs programming, discovered that it would have to em-

phasize commercial programming if it were to survive in the marketplace. An FCC moratorium on construction of new television stations between 1948 and 1953 further hampered ABC's ability to enter new markets. Most existing television stations were affiliates of the better established CBS and NBC. In 1951, Noble agreed to sell his interest in ABC to Leonard Goldenson, head of United Paramount Theatres, and the FCC approved the ABC-UPT merger in 1953. With a background in movie promotion, Goldenson led ABC into thoroughly commercial programming designed to appeal to a youthful audience. Two early ABC successes, "Disneyland" (1954) and "The Mickey Mouse Club" (1955), gave the network its first profit, $6 million. ABC was also the first to buy the products of Hollywood film studios, which had initially competed with television as their greatest rival for audiences. Soon television became the studios' biggest customer.

McCarthyism and the Golden Age of Television: 1953–60. In 1947 the House Un-American Activities Committee began an investigation of the film industry, and Joseph McCARTHY soon began to inveigh against what he claimed was Communist infiltration of the government. Broadcasting, too, felt the impact of this shift of the national mood. Three former members of the FBI published "Counterattack: The Newsletter of Facts on Communism," and in 1950 a *Counterattack* pamphlet, "Red Channels," listed the supposedly Communist associations of 151 performing artists, including Corwin and Welles. Artists thus blacklisted found it nearly impossible to get work. CBS instituted a loyalty oath for its employees. When anti-Communist vigilantes applied pressure to advertisers—the source of network profits—it became imperative that the industry defend itself. The task fell to the man considered by many the industry's moral leader, Edward R. Murrow.

In partnership with the news producer Fred Friendly, Murrow began "See It Now," a television documentary series, in 1950. "See It Now" occasionally explored examples of McCarthy-inspired intimidation. On Mar. 9, 1954, Murrow narrated a report on McCarthy himself, exposing the senator's shoddy tactics. Murrow observed: "His mistake has been to confuse dissent with disloyalty." Offered free time by CBS, McCarthy replied on April 6, calling Murrow "the leader and the cleverest of the jackal pack which is always found at the throat of anyone who dares to expose Communist traitors." In this TV appearance McCarthy proved to be his own worst enemy, and it became apparent that Murrow had helped to break McCarthy's reign of fear. In 1954 the U.S. Senate censured McCarthy, and CBS's "security" office was closed down.

That the McCarthy denouement occurred on television rather than on radio indicated the new medium's importance. The number of television sets in use had risen from 6,000 in 1946 to some 12 million by 1951. As viewers shifted from radio to television, radio's popularity and profit declined. Jack Benny's New York-area rating fell from 26.5% in 1948 to less than 5% in 1951. "Amos 'n' Andy" fell from 13% to 6%. In 1952, CBS's radio network showed a deficit for the first time since 1928.

Ambitious network programmers with a taste for the experimental scheduled unorthodox series, especially between 1953 and 1955. NBC television president Sylvester Weaver devised the "spectacular," a notable example of which was "Peter Pan" (1955), starring Mary Martin, which attracted 60 million viewers. Weaver also developed the magazine-format programs "Today," which made its debut in 1952 with Dave Garroway as host, and "Tonight," which began in 1953 with Steve ALLEN as host. NBC had been known since 1948 as the home of Milton BERLE on "The Texaco Star Theater." Weaver scheduled other comedy revues, including "Your Show of Shows," starring Sid Caesar and Imogene Coca.

Both NBC and CBS presented such noteworthy dramatic anthologies as "Kraft Television Theater," "Studio One," "Playhouse 90," and "The U.S. Steel Hour." Memorable television dramas of the era—many of them transmitted as live shows—included Paddy Chayefsky's "Marty," starring Rod Steiger, and Reginald Rose's "12 Angry Men" and "Thunder on Sycamore Street." The Radio-Television Workshop of the Ford

The comedian Milton Berle, a master of slapstick farce and outrageously bad jokes, was popular between 1948 and 1956, when he was known as "Uncle Miltie." He is shown here in pie face with guest stars Buffalo Bob, Howdy Doody, and Clarabell the clown in a characteristic skit from NBC's "Texaco Star Theater."

(Left) *Lucille Ball and Desi Arnaz star in a scene from "I Love Lucy," which ran from 1951 to 1957 and won enormous and enduring popularity, continuing into reruns.*

(Right) *In 1960, John F. Kennedy and Richard M. Nixon engaged in a series of four debates. These, the first televised debates between presidential candidates, influenced the results of the 1960 election as well as the conduct of subsequent presidential races.*

Foundation added cultural variety to early television programming with "Omnibus." "Omnibus," (1952–59), explored almost every form of artistic endeavor.

The golden age of television programming came to an ignominious end with the sudden popularity of the game show. "The $64,000 Question" and "Twenty-One" shot to the top of the ratings in the mid-1950s, indirectly contributing to the demise of "See It Now" and the climate of serious television. In 1959, however, the creator of "The $64,000 Question," Louis G. Cowan, by that time president of CBS television, was forced to resign from the network amid revelations of widespread fixing of game shows.

Filmed and Videotaped Television: 1960–80. Cowan's successor at CBS, James Aubrey, doubled that company's profits between 1960 and 1965 by canceling costly, unpredictable live anthologies and scheduling filmed situation comedies, such as "The Beverly Hillbillies" and "Petticoat Junction." CBS's situation comedy "I Love Lucy" had been a favorite since the early 1950s, and the fact that it was on film allowed the network to rerun episodes at low cost. These developments were assisted by the introduction of videotape in 1956, which made it possible to record television signals on magnetic tape for later replaying. By 1980 recorded programming had virtually replaced "live" television, except for sporting events.

In 1964 broadcasting began in color on prime-time television. The FCC initially had approved a CBS color system developed by Peter Goldmark, then swung in RCA's favor after Sarnoff had swamped the marketplace with black-and-white sets compatible with RCA color. (The CBS color system was not compatible with black-and-white sets, and its introduction would have required the public to purchase new sets.) The development of color television cost RCA $130 million, further intensifying the commercial atmosphere.

On Jan. 12, 1971, CBS introduced a new situation comedy, "All in the Family," that explored prejudice and family strife through its portrayal of a likable bigot, Archie Bunker, played by Carroll O'Connor. The series, the most influential of the 1970s, marked a trend toward programming that, while continuing to fit traditional genres, reflected widespread social mores rather than avoiding them. Other socially conscious series of the era included "The Mary Tyler Moore Show" and "Maude," but daytime television continued to rely heavily on soap operas and quiz shows.

In 1975, ABC, traditionally regarded as a poor third in terms of popularity and prestige, suddenly rose to the top of the ratings, largely because of shrewd scheduling by the chief of its entertainment division, Fred Silverman. He scheduled the miniseries "Roots," seen on successive winter nights in 1977 by an estimated 80 million viewers, as well as such popular nostalgic series as "Happy Days." CBS regained its high ratings in 1980 with the hugely successful series "Dallas," and NBC entered two top-quality shows in the ratings race: "Hill Street Blues" (1980) and "St. Elsewhere" (1982).

By 1985, however, as the networks competed for more advertising money and against the attractions of CABLE TV and videocassette recorders, NBC replaced CBS at the top by featuring such popular entertainments as "The Cosby Show," a program about a middle-class black family.

The Growth of PBS. Prompted by the three commercial networks' abandoning of sustaining or public-service programming, a Carnegie Commission report (1967) recommended the creation of a fourth, noncommercial, public television network built around the educational nonprofit stations already in operation throughout the United States (see TELEVISION, NONCOMMERCIAL). Congress created the Public Broadcasting System that year. Unlike commercial networks, which

Ed Sullivan (left, center), with his Sunday night variety show, and Walter Cronkite (right), anchor (1962–81) of CBS Evening News, both left their mark on U.S. society. Here, Sullivan introduces the young Beatles to his vast audience. Cronkite, with his reputation for integrity and trustworthiness, established the habit of watching TV news for millions.

Reputedly television's highest-paid performer, Johnny Carson is known for his urbane, mildly indecent monologues and for the sharp repartée with guests on his long-running program, "The Tonight Show."

The Public Broadcasting System has attracted enthusiastic audiences with "Masterpiece Theatre," a group of British TV productions. Shown here is a scene from the popular series "Upstairs, Downstairs" (1974).

are centered in New York City, PBS's key stations—all of which produce programs that are shown throughout the network—are spread across the country. PBS today comprises more than 300 stations, more than any commercial network.

Early PBS anti–Vietnam War programming incurred the wrath of the Nixon administration, but nonpolitical imports from British television proved extremely popular. In 1969, PBS broadcast the 26-part British Broadcasting Corporation adaptation of John Galsworthy's *The Forsyte Saga* and followed with such other British series as "Upstairs, Downstairs," "The Pallisers," "Brideshead Revisited," and "The Jewel in the Crown." Well-received PBS programming produced in the United States includes SESAME STREET, "Bill Moyers' Journal," "The MacNeil-Lehrer Report," and "Nova." PBS funds come from three major sources: congressional appropriations—which suffered substantial cuts in 1982—viewer donations, and private corporate underwriters.

Social Concerns and Television. Newton Minow, then chairman of the FCC, in 1961 described "the vast wasteland" of TV as "game shows, violence. . .sadism, murder, western badmen, western good men, private eyes, gangsters, more violence, and cartoons." Most current television criticism echoes the themes that Minow sounded.

The 1972 report of the surgeon general and the National Institute of Mental Health claimed that exposure to television violence encouraged aggression in children. The industry responded in 1975 by instituting "family viewing time" between 7 and 9 PM, when the programs shown were to be suitable for all ages. At the same time, however, commercial television's offerings designed specifically for small children dwindled and eventually disappeared, replaced by still more of the standard cartoon fare, with its heroes and its violence.

TV's "docudramas" are also frequently a subject of controversy. They often portray historical personages (Robert Kennedy, J. Robert Oppenheimer, Mussolini, Gen. George S. Patton, among many others) in dramatic situations that are essentially fictitious. On the other hand, the networks have attempted to confront such major social issues as drug abuse, AIDS, battered wives, rape, and homosexuality by presenting dramas that honestly elucidate the problems involved.

BROADCASTING—PRESENT AND FUTURE
The changes that have occurred in broadcasting over the past decade result in large part from the rapid growth of communications technology, which has caused a burgeoning of new techniques for sending, receiving, and preserving TV signals (see VIDEO). Cable TV and satellite transmission, along with the increasing use of videocassette recorders, have transformed the operations of the industry, as have deregulation and a financial climate that has encouraged mergers and takeovers of some of the oldest and most powerful broadcasting entities. In 1985–86 alone, Capital Cities Communication took

over ABC; General Electric bought RCA; Time, Inc., bought Group W Cable; press mogul Rupert MURDOCH bought the six stations owned by Metromedia; and WOR-TV (New York) was purchased by MCA, Inc.; smaller radio stations and cable companies have also changed ownership.

The attempt of broadcaster Ted Turner to buy CBS forced the network deeply into debt. To prevent Turner's purchase bid, CBS had to buy back a quantity of its stock, issuing new stock to finance the buy-out. Turner's takeover threat may have weakened the network to the point where, in mid-1986, it brought 85-year-old William S. Paley back as chairman, hoping to rebuild morale, reshape the network, and recapture some of its past profitability.

Radio Broadcasting. When television became the major electronic entertainment in the 1950s, the demise of radio was predicted by many experts. Instead, the medium flourishes as strongly now as in its heyday. According to the FCC, in the mid-1980s there were over 3,800 FM stations and 4,800 AM stations—an increase of more than 1,500 in one decade.

There are no more national commercial networks, however. Even the stations controlled by what were once the major networks now have only a local reach. Each station narrowly targets its potential listeners, hoping to attract a specific type of audience. FM stations, for the most part, each specialize in a particular type of music: hard rock, soft rock, jazz, classical, nostalgia pop, and so forth. AM carries more talk shows, news, and information programming.

The advent of satellite transmission has produced a new type of network, however. Radio producers now sell shows, via satellite link, to any station with the equipment to receive them. Many of these network shows are among the most popular on radio and feature such well-known personalities as late-night conversationalist Larry King, news commentator Paul Harvey, and sex therapist Dr. Ruth Westheimer.

Radio's most unexpected success story is the rise in popularity of the two public radio networks, National Public Radio and American Public Radio. Both supply programming to public radio stations across the country. NPR specializes in news and information shows, and its two lengthy news programs, "Morning Edition" and "All Things Considered," attract an audience that grows larger every year. APR produces primarily cultural and music programming. Its most notable success is the two-hour combination of nostalgia, old-time music, and parody, "The Prairie Home Companion," with its now famous creator, Garrison Keillor.

The Changing Structure of the Television Industry. From the early days of TV until the coming of cable and satellite broadcasting, the structure of the industry mirrored that of its predecessor, radio. There were the three big national networks, ABC, CBS, and NBC, with headquarters in New York City, and affiliated stations across the country who were fed programming by their networks. Smaller networks existed, but they were shut out of the nationally broadcast programs that the big networks either produced themselves or bought from a small group of independent producers. Advertising rates were based on the size of the national audience for each show, as estimated by a rating system devised by the A. C. Nielsen Co. Long-running shows would eventually go into syndication—that is, they were sold as a package to both network and independent stations, so that a rerun episode of "Leave It to Beaver" or "I Love Lucy" was shown somewhere in the United States almost around the clock.

The three networks still exercise power in the world of television, but their influence is challenged by a growing system of smaller networks, like Murdoch's 6-station Fox group, or the Taft 12-station network. Over the last decade the number of independent stations—those with no network affiliation—has quadrupled to 300. Programming now originates from the smaller network groups as well as from the three New York networks, in addition to a large group of independent programmers, many of whom sell their material—game shows and cartoons as well as "sit coms" and specials—on a syndicated basis to any station that will buy. Some of television's most successful programs are made by producer/syndicators.

Cable TV carries not only the major networks, but their competition as well, and makes movies available to cable subscribers long before they are shown on the networks.

The rating system is fundamental to the operation of television because its results determine audience size and, therefore, the fees stations can charge advertisers. Nielsen long monopolized the system, using 1,700 households as his sample audience, with "Audimeters" attached to their TV sets as well as diaries listing who watched what. As television channels grew in number, as the number of television sets per household multiplied, and as specialized programming such as the Music Television Cable channel (MTV) attracted audiences that were outside Nielsen's sample, his statistics began to be questioned. New systems, such as the "people meter," claim to measure TV watching more accurately. But, as advertising rates escalate, advertising agencies and advertisers have grown suspicious of the accuracy of any ratings system as the basis for measuring audience size.

Cable and Satellite Transmission. In the mid 1980s almost half of all American TV households were wired for CABLE TV, subscribing to one of the 7,000 cable systems that span the country (see also TELEVISION TRANSMISSION).

In 1975, RCA orbited the first COMMUNICATION SATELLITE designed for the relaying of TV signals, allowing producers and sellers of TV programs to market their product to any cable company with a satellite receiving dish. Today, almost 50 satellite-transmitted programmers offer an enormous range of program types, from an all-sports system (ESPN) to religious programs (see RELIGIOUS BROADCASTING), to programs designed

Typical of the new, syndicated breed of animated programs, "The Transformers," a cartoon show for children, is based on a real toy. Such shows are no longer confined to Saturday mornings, but now appear—usually on independent stations—every weekday.

for special audiences and various language groups. The range of channels available to subscribers is determined by the individual cable companies, most of whom offer as their basic minimal-price service the three network stations within a metropolitan area, along with a few local, independent stations. Special entertainment channels—also called premium channels—such as Home Box Office (HBO) and Showtime require additional payment.

Because of the initial heavy expense of wiring a community with cable—an expense the cable company itself undertakes—cable systems operate under exclusive franchises made with each municipality. Congress's Cable Communications Policy Act of 1984 allows cable companies for the first time to raise their fees after two years of a franchise agreement, whether or not a municipal council agrees; beginning in 1987, cable systems will become almost completely rate-deregulated. Today, however, the major point of contention with municipalities continues to be their demand for access both to community programming and to a pubic channel for community use.

Cable systems were also required to obey the "must carry" rule that forced them to carry all local broadcast signals within a certain radius of their transmitter. In 1986 the ruling was declared unconstitutional, but the FCC must still resolve the problem of local stations, which—if the cable operators have their way—might vanish from cable offerings. One possible

"Miami Vice," a popular cops-and-crime program, sparked a new look in men's fashions in the 1980s and derived much of its style from music videos, with quick cuts, high-tech effects, and pulsing music.

The mid-1980s renaissance of the game show may have been caused by the great success of "Wheel of Fortune," once (1975) a modest morning program, now the most popular syndicated show ever.

solution is the use of an "A/B" switch, which allows subscribers to switch between cable and broadcast signals. The switch is available now on some new television sets, but it would have to be installed on older sets.

To avoid paying the monthly subscription fee (or to gain signal reception in remote areas where cable had not penetrated), many people chose to buy backyard dish antennas, smaller versions of the "earth stations" used by cable operators to capture satellite signals. Some television programmers considered the use of home dishes a theft of their product. In 1986 several satellite programmers began to scramble their signals so that only cable earth stations could receive them. Others needed decoders, which were expensive and often unavailable. Many home-dish owners have joined in suits against the channels that have scrambled their programs, and Congress has been petitioned to forbid the practice.

On the other hand, some programmers see the home dishes as a positive omen, a sign of the time when every house will own a small receiving dish and, for a fee, receive programs directly off a satellite. Direct Broadcast Satellite systems (DBS) have the advantage—to the programmer—of cutting out the need for cable. All the fees involved would go directly to the broadcaster, increasing profits by at least 50%. DBS has been tried in the United States, but at a time when the most appropriate technology did not exist. Japan will soon have a four-channel DBS service, however, and British media tycoon Robert Maxwell will offer DBS throughout Europe, via two French communications satellites.

Broadcasting Deregulation. The FCC was created in 1934 not only to assign frequencies to radio and, later, television stations, but also to carry out the decision of Congress that—in return for giving broadcasters a license to profit from the use of the radio spectrum ("the public domain")—stations were required to provide some programs that served the public. In essence, they were to act as trustees of the public interest, and every three years television stations appeared before the FCC to receive their license renewals, with logbooks of their daily programming to prove that they were carrying out their trusteeship. The number of stations any one firm or individual could own was limited to 5 on VHF (the stations with the strongest signals, channels 2 through 13), along with 7 AM and 7 FM stations.

Within the past few years, however, the FCC has chosen to treat broadcasters not as trustees of a public resource, but as businessmen whose primary duty is to maintain or increase their stations' share of the TV audience. The rules that cut into stations' profitability have been weakened or eliminated. Broadcasters are no longer required to devote a small portion of their broadcasting day to public affairs and children's shows. In addition, the number of commercials a station may use per hour has been raised. A television station may now keep its license for five years (seven for a radio station) before it need apply for renewal, and it is no longer required to keep a logbook to prove that it has served the public in the ways outlined by Congress. One person or firm may now own up to 12 FM stations, 12 AM stations, and 12 TV stations.

In 1987 the FCC abolished the Fairness Doctrine, a rule that required radio and television stations to offer opposing views on issues of public interest. The FCC agreed with broadcasters, who claimed that, rather than adding to public knowledge, the doctrine discouraged issue-oriented programming. Partisans of the doctrine in Congress, however, hope to restore it through legislation. Congressional debate will inquire into how the public interest can best be served, and whether—as the FCC holds—the large number of stations now competing for audiences offer a "free market" in ideas.

Internationalization via Satellite. Until recently, television in Europe was a government monopoly, and although there were a few spectacularly successful stations—notably Britain's two BBC channels—by and large, European TV was a fairly dull affair, enlivened now and then by made-for-TV movies by such directors as Federico Fellini and Ingmar Bergman or by American imports. Advertising in most countries was either banned or strictly limited. Stations were maintained by taxes and licensing fees paid by television set owners.

In 1954, Britain created the Independent TV Authority, whose stations may accept advertising, and later allowed another commercial station, the Fourth Channel, to go into operation. In 1986, France privatized TFI, one of the three government-controlled channels, although it limits the amount of advertising TFI may carry.

Satellite broadcasting, the videocassette recorder, and cable—although it has been slow in coming—are beginning to challenge the monopoly European governments still hold over TV. Media moguls like Rupert Murdoch see Europe as a golden opportunity for television investment. Murdoch's Sky Channel broadcasts 18 hours a day by satellite to 5 million cabled European homes. Other hopeful international TV entrepreneurs include Silvio Berlusconi, who owns 3 Italian networks and production facilities in Spain and Italy, and Ted Turner, owner of the all-news CNN channel that reaches more than 40 countries.

The scarcity of cable-wired homes is a major obstacle to plans for international satellite programming. In some European countries the governments have plans to invest in cable systems themselves. France, for example, intends to cable 1 million homes a year; West Germany plans to spend almost $400 million annually to bring cable to its citizens.

LAURENCE BERGREEN

Bibliography: Barnouw, E., *A History of Broadcasting in the U.S.*, 3 vols. (1966–70); Bergreen, L., *Look Now, Pay Later: The Rise of Network Broadcasting* (1980); Brown, L., *Encyclopedia of TV* (1982); Gitlin, T., *Inside Prime Time* (1983); Halberstam, D., *The Powers That Be* (1979); Kaminsky, S., and Mahan, J. H., *American TV Genres* (1985); Newcomb, H., and Alley, R., *The Producer's Medium: Conversations with Creators of American TV* (1983); *A Public Trust: The Report of the Carnegie Commission on the Future of Public Broadcasting* (1979); Williams, M., *TV: The Casual Art* (1982).

radioactive fallout: see FALLOUT.

radioactive tracer: see NUCLEAR MEDICINE.

radioactivity

Radioactivity is the spontaneous emission of energy in the form of particles or waves (electromagnetic radiation), or both, from the atomic nucleus of certain elements.

Research into the radioactivity of pitchblende, an ore of uranium, led Marie and Pierre Curie to discover the radioactive elements polonium and radium in 1898. The Curies and Antoine Becquerel shared the 1903 Nobel Prize for physics for their discovery of radioactivity.

HISTORY

The discovery of radioactivity occurred in 1896 when Antoine Henri Becquerel observed that uranium emitted penetrating rays continuously and without initiation. The term *radioactivity* was coined by Pierre and Marie Curie to designate this phenomenon. They proved that the radioactivity of uranium was an atomic property and not a chemical one. Marie Curie later discovered the radioactive elements polonium and radium in uranium ore. These elements possess shorter HALF-LIVES (the time it takes for the radioactive decay of one-half of a radioactive sample) and are more highly radioactive than uranium.

Ernest Rutherford showed that one of the components of this radiation was deflected upon passage through a thin sheet of metal. He concluded that this phenomenon was due to positive electric charge repulsion between the metal ions of the lattice and a positively charged particle emitted by the radioactive sample and later shown to be a helium ion (an alpha particle). This led to the postulation of the nucleus and was one of the foundations for the formulation of the structure of the ATOM.

ATOMIC STRUCTURE AND NUCLEAR TRANSFORMATIONS

An atom is composed of two major components, a positively charged nucleus surrounded by a cloud of negatively charged particles (electrons). The nucleus is composed of protons and neutrons, which are collectively called nucleons. Protons are positively charged nucleons, whereas neutrons are uncharged nucleons. The sum of protons and neutrons is the atom's mass number.

An atom is neutral with respect to charge, with the number of protons equaling the number of electrons. The number of protons is equivalent to the atomic number, whereas the number of neutrons may vary for a given atomic number; each variation is called an ISOTOPE. Therefore, isotopes of a given atomic number will vary in their mass numbers. Usually, the lighter elements have fewer isotopes than the heavier elements.

An isotope of a given element may be designated with the atomic symbol for the element either preceded or followed by a superscript number representing the mass number, as in ^{14}C or C^{14}. Another accepted designation is the element name followed by a hyphen and the mass number of the isotope, as in nitrogen-15.

Stable and Unstable Nuclei. In general, the proton-neutron ratio as well as their total number determines the stability of the nucleus. Unstable nuclei tend to adjust their proton-neutron ratio to a more stable form by means of the spontaneous disintegration via expulsion of one or more of the nucleons, that is, radioactivity.

Stable isotopes vary in number from element to element, with the naturally occurring element uranium having no stable isotopes. It is not clear why certain combinations of protons and neutrons are stable while others are not.

Unstable nuclei, or radioisotopes, undergo radioactive decay resulting in particle or electromagnetic radiation. Radioisotopes may occur naturally or be produced artificially (see ISOTOPE; RADIOCHEMISTRY).

The vast majority of radioisotopes are artificially produced, since the only naturally occurring radionuclides (radioisotopes) surviving from the time of the creation of matter are those that decay very slowly, and members of a decay series (naturally produced continuously) are very scarce. Some radioisotopes are produced continually by COSMIC RAY bombardment of atmospheric atoms. Carbon-14 and hydrogen-3 are formed from nitrogen-14 in this manner.

Artificially produced radioisotopes were first synthesized more than 40 years ago when Curie and Joliot transformed aluminum-27 to phosphorus-30. Bombardment of stable nuclei with either charged or uncharged particles is the usual method for radioisotope production. This result may be achieved by nuclear reactors, which are the primary source of radioisotopes for biological purposes, by particle accelerators such as the cyclotron and linear accelerator, or by other neutron sources such as a neutron generator.

Types of Nuclear Transformations. In undergoing spontane-

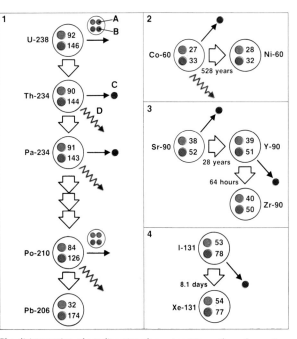

The disintegration of a radioactive element continues through a series of different radioactive species until a stable, nonradioactive atom results. Thus, the natural radioactive element uranium-238 (1) decays by ejecting an alpha particle, or helium ion. Because the helium nucleus consists of two protons (A) and two neutrons (B), the remaining nucleus of thorium-234 is left with 90 protons and 144 neutrons. The thorium then ejects an electron (C) and a gamma ray (D) and changes to proactinium-234. The process goes on until stable lead-206 is obtained. The artificial radioisotopes—cobalt-60 (2), strontium-90 (3), and iodine-131 (4)—similarly decay to stable atoms.

ous nuclear changes, radioisotopes decay to more stable forms while giving off one or more of three types of emissions: alpha particles, beta particles, and gamma rays. The emission of alpha or beta particles converts one element into another via a nuclear charge change. Gamma radiation is a form of nuclear energy dissipation.

Alpha particle emission occurs only in elements of high atomic weight. An alpha particle is a helium nucleus consisting of two protons and two neutrons. Emission of an alpha particle from a radioisotope results in the formation of another element four mass units lighter and two atomic numbers lower. Examples of this type of radioactive decay include $^{226}Ra \rightarrow ^{222}Rn + \alpha$ and $^{209}Po \rightarrow ^{205}Pb + \alpha$.

Beta particles are of two types, negatrons (electrons) and positrons. Radioisotopes with excess neutrons may decay into a more stable form by the conversion of a neutron into a proton, with the concurrent emission of a negative beta particle (negatron, β^-). Negatron emission results in an increase in atomic number of one unit. Any excess energy in the nucleus is dissipated as gamma rays. Examples of negatron radioactive decay include $^{32}P \rightarrow ^{32}S + \beta^-$ and $^{60}Co \rightarrow ^{60}Ni + \beta^-$.

Radioisotopes with excess protons may become more energetically stable by positive beta particle (positron, β^+) emission. A nuclear proton is converted to a neutron with the concurrent emission of a positron. The atomic number decreases by one unit and any excess energy is emitted as gamma radiation. Examples of positron radioactive decay include $^{13}N \rightarrow ^{13}C + \beta^+$ and $^{15}O \rightarrow ^{15}N + \beta^+$. (See BETA DECAY.)

Gamma radiation, the emission of energetic PHOTONS, most often results in concurrence with beta emission; however, some nuclides decay by gamma ray emission alone. This means of decay does not change the mass number or the atomic number but provides a delayed means of disposing of excess energy from an energetic nucleus. Examples of gamma ray radioactive decay include $^{131}I \rightarrow ^{131}I + \gamma$.

A unique decay mode is demonstrated by radium-223, which expels a carbon isotope nucleus (^{14}C), and becomes lead-206.

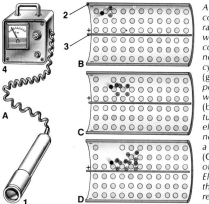

A Geiger Müller counter (A) detects radioactive particles with a tube (1) containing (B) a negatively charged cylinder (2), neon gas (gray), and a positively charged wire (3). A particle (black) entering the tube knocks out an electron (blue) from a neon atom and forms a positive ion (red). (C) These collide with other atoms. (D) Electrons collect on the wire. A meter (4) records them as a pulse of current.

Other modes of radioactive decay are electron capture and internal conversion.

UNITS AND STANDARDS

The rates of emission of radiation for different radioisotopes vary considerably. Each individual radioisotope, however, has its own intrinsic decay rate. The decay constant is defined as the given fraction of atoms disintegrating in a specific unit of time. A more useful way of expressing the decay constant is the half-life ($t_{1/2}$). The half-life of a radioisotope is the time it takes for its radioactivity to decrease by one-half. Half-lives vary from fractions of seconds to billions of years.

The standard unit of radioactivity is the curie, which is defined as the number of disintegrations occurring in one gram of radium per second. Radium was chosen because it was available in pure form and has a long half-life, 1,600 years. The curie is equivalent to 3.7×10^{10} disintegrations per second (dps). The curie is a rather large unit, so several fractions of this unit have found wide use. The millicurie (mC) is equal to one-thousandth of a curie, or 3.7×10^7 dps, while the microcurie (μC) is equal to one-millionth of a curie, or 3.7×10^4 dps, or 2.22×10^6 disintegrations per minute (dpm).

The usual state of a radioisotope is as a mixture with a large amount of the stable isotopes of the same element. Specific activity, defined as the amount of radioactivity per given weight or weight equivalent of a sample, expresses the relative abundance of a radioisotope in a sample. Specific activity is often expressed as dps or dpm, counting rates (counts per minute, cpm), or curies, mC, or μC per unit weight.

MEASUREMENT OF RADIOACTIVITY

Radioactivity is quantitated in several ways. Absolute counting measures every disintegration occurring in the sample (dps or dpm), whereas relative counting measures a given detected fraction of the true disintegrations occurring (cps or cpm). Relative counting is much easier and is the more frequently used approach. Several different methods of relative counting are used successfully. These include gas ionization, scintillation, and autoradiography.

Gas ionization techniques use the principle of ion pairs formed in gases upon exposure to radiation. An electric potential is applied between two electrodes in a gas-filled ion chamber. The negatively charged ions move to the anode while the positively charged ions move to the cathode. This creates a pulse, which is amplified and recorded. Gas ioniza-

tion without gas amplification may be achieved using ionization chambers equipped with Lauritsen electroscopes or with a vibrating reed electrometer. Gas-ionization counting with gas amplification may be achieved using proportional counters or the well-known Geiger-Müller counter.

Scintillation in a solid fluor is a counting technique in which a fraction of the ionizing radiation is transferred to solid compounds that fluoresce. The absorbed energy in the fluor gives rise to visible or near ultraviolet energy emissions (scintillations) that are detected and amplified by a photomultiplier tube and recorded. Scintillation in a liquid fluor is a similar technique, except that the radioisotope and the fluor are dissolved in a liquid medium. Energy transfer goes through the solvent to the fluor and is finally detected as scintillations. Detection, amplification, and recording are similar.

Autoradiography is a photochemical detection method in which a radioactive sample is placed on a photographic emulsion on film. Radiation from the sample interacts with the silver halide in the emulsion. The resulting development of the film allows an estimate of the radioactivity in the sample to be taken.

USES AND APPLICATIONS

A general classification of the uses and applications of radioisotopes in industrial processes or in scientific research based on the radioisotopic properties results in five major divisions:

1. Uses based on the effect of ionizing radiation on matter;
2. Uses based on the effect of matter on ionizing radiation;
3. Age-dating based on the decay rates of specific naturally occurring radioisotopes;
4. Direct energy transformation;
5. Physical and biological radiotracer applications.

The interaction of radiation with matter has many practical applications. Gamma radiation has been used in food sterilization, polymer manufacture, and cancer therapy; cobalt-60 and radium-226 are commonly used for these purposes. Other uses include thickness gauging and tool-wear estimation. A number of products are manufactured in a roll or continuous sheet that needs to be of uniform and known thickness. The amount of radiation passing through a sheet of material depends upon its thickness. Thus, with proper calibration, radioactivity can be used to monitor the thickness of these types of products.

In age-dating, the half-life of the radioisotope is critical. Isotopes such as carbon-14, potassium-40, uranium-238, tritium (hydrogen-3), and others are used to determine the age of specific items or events. For instance, the carbon-14 content of living matter is in equilibrium with the carbon-14 content of the atmospheric carbon dioxide. Upon death, the carbon-14 in the dead material would no longer be exchangeable with carbon dioxide in the air, so the carbon-14 would diminish as dictated by its half-life, without replenishment from atmospheric carbon-14 dioxide. Comparison of the carbon-14 content of the dead material with the carbon-14 content of the air, which is assumed to have remained approximately the same since creation, allows the calculation of the age of the material (see RADIOMETRIC AGE-DATING).

Conversion of the energy (heat) from selected radioisotopes—such as plutonium-238 or strontium-90—to electrical energy can be achieved by an array of thermocouples and provides an ideal energy source for satellites or remote automated weather stations.

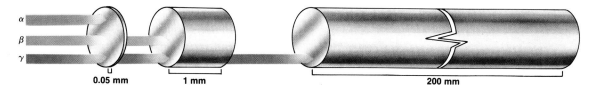

The three types of rays (alpha, beta, and gamma) emitted by radioactive elements can be distinguished by their penetrating power. Alpha rays are unable to pass through a film of aluminum that is only 0.05 mm (0.002 in) thick, whereas a 1-mm-thick (0.039-in) aluminum foil is needed to stop beta rays. The thickness of material required to stop these rays depends on their energy and on the material. Gamma rays are scarcely affected by a 200-mm-thick (7.87-in) aluminum sheet. The best shielding for gamma rays is an element of high atomic number, such as lead.

The use of radioisotopes in biological research is widespread because of the extreme sensitivity of radioactive assays and the fact that the metabolic rate of a compound may be traced in living systems. A typical radiotracer experiment may result in a detection level of 10^{-8} with respect to the detection level of the unlabeled compound. Carbon-14, tritium, phosphorus-32, sulfur-35, and others are used in this way.

HAZARDS AND SAFETY

The effect of radiation on living matter can be quite devastating (see RADIATION INJURY). Therefore, radiation safety and monitoring is particularly important. Radiation safety problems fall into three categories: personnel protection, contamination control, and waste disposal (see NUCLEAR ENERGY).

Energy dissipation must be quantified to determine exposure levels. Biological effects of radiation are determined by the amount of energy absorbed. Therefore the time of exposure and rate of exposure must be defined. The roentgen (R) was defined as the quantity of gamma or X radiation required to produce one electrostatic unit of electricity of either sign per cubic centimeter of dry air. However, the roentgen is valid only for photon interaction with air and does not relate to tissue absorption or particulate radiation. Normally, exposure is expressed in roentgens/hour or milliroentgens/hour. A unit based on the energy dissipation of radiation in biological tissue was devised in 1953 and called the rad. It was defined as 100 ergs of energy imparted by any ionizing radiation that is dissipated in one gram of irradiated material. The rad is the unit of choice when tissue irradiation is concerned.

Monitoring of radiation is essential to determining exposure. Area monitoring is usually accomplished with portable monitors such as Geiger-Müller survey meters or portable ionization chambers (see GEIGER COUNTER). Personnel monitoring is often achieved by film badges, which develop upon exposure to certain levels or total quantities of radiation.

Disposal of radioactive wastes may be accomplished by maximum dilution or maximum concentration. Dilution usually means dumping into the sewer, release into the air, or incineration. Disposal by concentration and storage is necessary for high levels of radioactivity. RONALD D. JOHNSON

Bibliography: Jenkins, E. N., and Lewis, I., *Radioactivity: A Science in Its Historical and Social Context* (1979); Mann, W. B., and Ayres, R. L., eds., *Radioactivity and Its Measurement,* 2d ed. (1980); Miller, D. G., *Radioactivity and Radiation Detection* (1972); Pizzarello, D. J., ed., *Radiation Biology* (1982); Stewart, D. C., *Handling Radioactivity* (1981).

radiocarbon dating: see RADIOMETRIC AGE-DATING.

radiochemistry

Radiochemistry is the subdiscipline of chemistry that deals with those ISOTOPES of chemical elements which are radioactive, and with the utilization of those isotopes to further the understanding of chemical and biochemical systems. This area of chemistry is closely allied to NUCLEAR PHYSICS, which concentrates on the forces that act within the nucleus of the atom and the exact nature (charge, mass, energy, for example) of the RADIOACTIVITY of an unstable nucleus.

There are two classes of radioactive isotopes: natural and artificial. Most of the radioactive isotopes found in nature are members of a radioactive disintegration series that begins with a radioactive isotope of uranium, actinium, thorium, or neptunium. Many radioactive isotopes that do not occur naturally may be artificially created by bombarding the nucleus of a stable isotope with high-speed particles, resulting in a transmutation. Thus either natural or artificial radioisotopes exist for every known element. The chemical applications of radioactive isotopes are based on the assumption that, up to the moment of its disintegration, the isotope has chemical and physical properties (except for normal mass differences) identical to the stable isotopes of the same element. The inclusion of a radioactive isotope, therefore, would cause no chemical variation in a reaction or system.

Radiochemistry is used frequently in both quantitative and qualitative analysis. Radioactive isotopes, called tracers, are used in isotope dilution experiments in which a known

amount of a pure compound that contains a radioactive isotope of known activity is added to a sample containing an unknown amount of the same compound, which is usually not radioactive. On separation of any size fraction of this compound, the amount of the compound in the original sample may be determined from the amount of radioactivity in the recovered portion. Radioactive isotopes are also used to determine the rates and mechanisms of chemical reactions. This method frequently involves reacting a compound containing a radioactive isotope of an element with a second compound and determining the rate at which radioactivity appears in the product. Carbon-14 is a useful radioactive isotope for tracer studies in organic and biochemical systems, including the determination of the age of materials that were once alive (see RADIOMETRIC AGE-DATING).

The identity and amounts of many elements present in trace amounts in mixtures may be determined by neutron activation analysis. This procedure involves the conversion of nonradioactive isotopes of chemical elements into radioactive isotopes, and the determination of the type and intensity of the radioactivity that results. NORMAN V. DUFFY

Bibliography: Friedlander, Gerhart, et al., *Nuclear and Radiochemistry,* 3d ed. (1981); Malcombe-Lawes, David J., *Introduction to Radiochemistry* (1980).

radiography

The technique known as radiography, in which X RAYS are passed through objects to produce photographic images, is used for medical and industrial purposes. Because X rays have a short wavelength and high energy, they can easily penetrate most matter; their degree of absorption depends on the density, thickness, and chemical composition of the object. A radiograph is the picture made by the X rays that have passed through an object; the photographic film used is treated with certain chemicals so that it becomes sensitive to X rays.

Radiography is used medically to diagnose such disorders as tumors and bone fractures. Industries use similar techniques to examine manufactured goods for internal flaws without damaging the product. WILLIAM M. GREEN, M.D.

Bibliography: Hiss, Stephen S., *Understanding Radiography,* 2d ed. (1983).

See also: NUCLEAR MEDICINE; RADIATION THERAPY; RADIOLOGY.

radioimmunoassay [ray'-dee-oh-im-yoo'-noh-as'-ay]

Radioimmunoassay, an extremely sensitive medical technique, is used to measure the concentration of antigenic substances in the body. The antigen to be measured is injected into an animal, causing the animal to produce antibodies against it. The animal serum containing the antibodies is then treated with a radioactive sample of the same antigen. The reaction between the radioactive antigen molecules and those of their specific antibodies causes radioactive antigen-antibody complexes to be formed. When a solution containing an unknown concentration of the same antigen in nonradioactive form is then added to the solution, competition between the radioactive and nonradioactive forms of the antigen for the same binding sites on the antibodies causes some previously bound radioactive antigen to be displaced from the antibodies and go into solution. The amount displaced is determined by separating the antigen-antibody complexes and measuring the radioactivity remaining in the solution; this amount is proportional to the amount of nonradioactive antigen present in the unknown solution. The measurement of radioactivity can be made with great sensitivity and accuracy in an instrument called a scintillation counter.

Any substance capable of provoking antibody formation in an animal can be assayed by this technique. It is frequently used to measure hormones that are in such low concentration in body fluids that they cannot be measured by chemical methods. Before radioimmunoassay was invented, hormones had to be measured by bioassay, a laborious and inexact method that involved injecting a hormone into animals and measuring its biological effects. PETER L. PETRAKIS

radioisotope: see ISOTOPE; RADIOCHEMISTRY.

radiolarian   [ray-dee-uh-lair'-ee-uhn]

Radiolarians represent a group of strikingly beautiful amoeba-like shelled microorganisms in the protozoan class Sarcodina. Although the strong, opal, siliceous skeleton of many radiolarians appears heavy, for example, genus *Hexacontium*, these protozoans are highly adapted for floating. The many fine skeletal spines and thin capsules surrounded by living cytoplasm give a high ratio of surface to volume that retards sinking in the sea, where radiolarians are found exclusively. In addition, vacuoles containing fluid with a low specific gravity give the outer cytoplasm a frothy appearance and increase buoyancy. The siliceous skeleton is secreted by nearly all radiolarians, and needlelike pseudopods—extensions of the body mass for trapping food—project through the shell. The skeletons vary widely, depending on the species, and many exhibit complex geometric designs. Some radiolarians are among the largest protozoans, measuring several mm in diameter.

Radiolarians reproduce by multiple division of cell nuclei, but the life cycle is poorly known. In some the preexisting skeleton breaks apart, and each daughter nucleus controls a portion and regenerates the rest to form an entire skeleton. (The outer cytoplasm lacks nuclei but may contain symbiotic smaller protozoans, which may possess chlorophyll, giving the entire radiolarian a greenish appearance.) After death the skeletons of radiolarians sink to the sea bottom. In the central ocean basins, where water depth exceeds 4,500 m (14,800 ft) and calcareous shells of other planktonic organisms dissolve, radiolarian skeletons constitute the primary sedimentary material of the deep sea.   ALAN KOHN

Bibliography: Farmer, J. N., *The Protozoa* (1980).

radiology

Radiology is the branch of medicine specializing in the use of X rays, various radioactive materials, and other imaging procedures to diagnose and treat disease. A radiologist is a physician, and in the United States is required to take a minimum of 4 years of radiology specialty training following graduation from medical school before becoming eligible to take the specialty examination. Radiology can be divided into two large clinical fields: diagnostic radiology and radiation therapy. The radiologist may elect to practice in one or both, depending on his or her qualifications. In recent years individuals usually chose one clinical field or the other.

X Rays. Radiology became an integral part of medical diagnosis shortly after the discovery in 1895 by Wilhelm Konrad ROENTGEN of a new form of electromagnetic energy called X rays. Because of their short wavelength they have the ability to penetrate matter. Absorption of X rays varies according to the density of the material through which they pass. Because body structures vary in density, they can be distinguished by passing the X rays through them and onto a suitable optical receptor, usually a radiograph or fluoroscopic screen. Photographic film is affected by X rays in the same way as it is by visible light. Thus a radiograph (see RADIOGRAPHY) can be formed by passing the X ray through a body part onto photographic film. Most radiographs, however, and all fluoroscopy use another property of X rays: the ability to cause fluorescence of certain crystalline substances such as zinc, cadmium sulfide, and calcium tungstate. These markedly reduce patient radiation exposure because a screen formed by a layer of these substances produces visible light by X-ray fluorescence, which can be used to form an image on film. In a routine radiograph exposed using fluorescent screens, less than 5 percent of the energy necessary to expose the film emulsion comes from the X rays directly; the remainder is from the visible light emitted by the screens.

In addition to radiographs of osseous structures (bones), the chest, and trunk, radiopaque contrast materials can be placed in internal organs to demonstrate their structure and function. The upper gastrointestinal series and barium enema are uti-

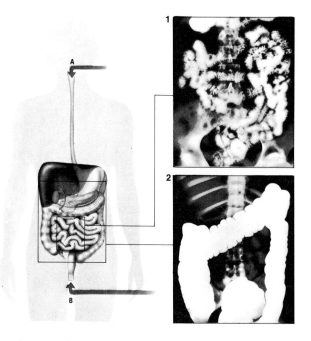

To photograph the organs of the gastrointestinal tract, barium sulfate, a radiopaque fluid, is introduced into the mouth (A) or rectum (B). X rays are absorbed by the fluid, producing a white image on treated film. A trained radiographer can follow the progress of the fluid through the small intestine (1) or large intestine (2), noting the presence of abnormalities. Other forms of radiated energy used in diagnosis are sound waves (echography) and heat (thermography).

lized to show the esophagus, stomach, small intestine, and colon (large intestine). An intravenous urogram (or pyelogram) enables evaluation of the kidneys and urinary tract. Special techniques permit definition of individual internal parts. One of the most sophisticated radiologic procedures, in terms of both technical skill and specialized equipment, is angiography. With this the radiologist is able to place a very thin plastic tube into almost every artery and vein and opacify it with contrast material. This enables sharp depiction of the internal anatomic structure and pathology of an organ.

One of the most significant recent advances in diagnostic imagery has been achieved through the merger of computers and X-ray systems. It is called computerized axial tomography (CAT, or CT)—the computer-assisted formation of an image of a slice or layer of the body. It has made it possible to diagnose previously inaccessible areas rapidly, safely, and painlessly. It has replaced procedures that formerly entailed significant risk and required hospitalization, and has thus reduced diagnostic costs. CT scanning has especially revolutionized neurologic diagnosis.

Other Imaging Techniques. Besides X rays, radiologic imaging uses modalities such as ultrasonography (see ULTRASONICS), positron emission tomography (see PETT), and NUCLEAR MAGNETIC RESONANCE IMAGING, or NMR. In ultrasonography, when high-frequency sound waves come into contact with structures deep within the body, part of the sound energy is reflected back to the body surface, where it can be converted electronically into a picture. The images frequently reveal information that cannot be obtained on conventional X-ray films. The eye and the heart (echocardiography) can also be investigated without surgery. No significant deleterious effects have been identified from diagnostic ultrasound, and it is widely used—especially to solve problems of high-risk or complicated pregnancies. Because risk studies are incomplete, however, the National Institutes of Health and the Food and Drug Administration recommended in 1984 that it not be used routinely during normal pregnancies.

Positron emission tomography is a nuclear medical technique that makes use of the unique properties of POSITRON de-

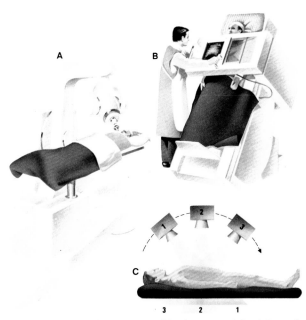

X rays are used both for diagnosis and for therapy. High-level doses of radiation can be focused on cancer cells to prevent their reproduction, leaving healthy cells intact (A). Radiographs of the chest (B) may reveal evidence of tuberculosis and other lung or heart diseases. In a tomograph (C) the X-ray tube is moved along an arc (1, 2, 3) to obtain an image of all internal structures within a selected plane. Computerized tomography, also known as CT scanning, enables the radiographer to view the plane from different angles.

cay to obtain excellent spatial resolution and quantification of common metabolic reactions in the body. Because of the short half-life of most positron-emitting isotopes, however, and because high-energy gamma rays are emitted, an on-site cyclotron and a tomographic scintillation camera are required. Current uses include assessments of brain function, blood flow, and metabolism.

The latest radiologic imaging modality is NMR—or, preferably, MRI (magnetic resonance imaging)—which, like CT X-ray machines, uses computers to construct high-contrast, two-dimensional tomographic images of the body. MRI, however, can do this in any body plane. These devices use magnetic fields and low-level electromagnetic radiation rather than ionizing radiation; on the basis of current knowledge, these fields and radiation levels are biologically safe. MRI holds the promise of yielding entirely new diagnostic information, including that of the metabolic activities of various tissues and tumors.

Radiology also includes much of the subspecialty of NUCLEAR MEDICINE, which uses radioactive substances for diagnosis and treatment. There is more emphasis on evaluation of organ function than on structure with this technique. Small amounts of radioactive substances are introduced into the body and circulate to the organ of interest. These are imaged by sophisticated detection systems that permit evaluation of biologic processes. WILLIAM M. GREEN, M.D.

Bibliography: Prasad, Kedar M., *Human Radiation Biology* (1974); Simon, George, and Wightman, A. J. A., *Clinical Radiology*, 4th ed. (1982); Squire, Lucy F., *Fundamentals of Radiology*, 3d ed. (1982).

radiometer

The radiometer is a device invented by Sir William CROOKES to demonstrate the mechanical effect of light radiation. It consists of four equally spaced vanes, silvered on one side, black on the other, attached to a vertical-axis rotor. The rotor is mounted in an evacuated glass enclosure. When a beam of sunlight is directed at the assembly, the vanes rotate about the axis. The effect is caused by the greater absorption of radia-

tion by the blackened side of the vanes. Residual air molecules in the enclosure strike both the black and the silver sides equally, but they absorb more heat from the black sides and rebound with greater energy. The differential force causes the vanes to spin, the black faces moving away from the sunlight.

The microwave radiometer, developed in 1946 by R. H. Dicke, an astronomer and physicist, is a much more complex apparatus used for measurement of radiation from the Sun, Moon, and stars, and recently for terrestrial measurement of microwave electrical "noise." The microwave radiometer is in effect a microwave radio receiver that detects noiselike energy radiated by a heated body. There is no theoretical upper temperature limit, and low-temperature measurements have been made to within 0.4 Centigrade degrees above absolute zero. FRANK J. OLIVER

Bibliography: Laverghetta, Thomas, *Microwave Measurements and Techniques* (1976).

radiometric age-dating

Age determinations of rocks, minerals, and other geological samples are based on RADIOACTIVITY and provide important information about the geologic history of the Earth and the Moon. Most rocks and minerals contain radioactive atoms of certain chemical ELEMENTS, which exist in nature for one of three reasons: (1) these elements formed during nucleosynthesis prior to the formation of the solar system and have not yet decayed completely because their decay rates are slow; (2) they are the unstable products of the decay of other, longer-lived radioactive elements; and (3) they are continually produced by nuclear reactions caused by the interaction of cosmic rays with molecules in the atmosphere.

HALF-LIVES OF SOME RADIOACTIVE ATOMS OCCURRING IN NATURE

Parent	Daughter	Half-Life of Parent* (Years)
Long-lived Parents		
$^{40}_{19}K$	$\rightarrow ^{40}_{18}Ar$	11.93×10^9
	$\rightarrow ^{40}_{20}Ca$	1.396×10^9
	$\rightarrow ^{40}_{18}Ar + ^{40}_{20}Ca$	12.50×10^9
$^{87}_{37}Rb$	$\rightarrow ^{87}_{38}Sr$	48.81×10^9
$^{238}_{92}U$	$\rightarrow ^{206}_{82}Pb$	4.468×10^9
$^{235}_{92}U$	$\rightarrow ^{207}_{82}Pb$	0.7038×10^9
$^{232}_{90}Th$	$\rightarrow ^{208}_{82}Pb$	14.01×10^9
Short-lived Daughters of $^{238}_{92}U$		
$^{234}_{92}U$	$\rightarrow ^{230}_{90}Th$	2.48×10^5
$^{230}_{90}Th$	$\rightarrow ^{226}_{88}Ra$	7.52×10^4
$^{210}_{82}Pb$	$\rightarrow ^{206}_{80}Hg$	22.26
Products of Nuclear Reactions by Cosmic Rays		
$^{3}_{1}H$	$\rightarrow ^{3}_{2}He$	12.33
$^{10}_{4}Be$	$\rightarrow ^{10}_{5}B$	1.6×10^6
$^{14}_{6}C$	$\rightarrow ^{14}_{7}N$	5,730

*The half-life ($t^{1/2}$) of a radioactive atom is the time required for half of a given number of these atoms to decay. It is related to the decay constant by $t^{1/2} = \ln 2/\lambda$.

Law of Radioactivity. The decay of radioactive atoms and the resulting formation of their stable daughters is described by the law of radioactivity. If all the daughter atoms that form by decay of a radioactive parent (such as $^{40}_{19}K$ or $^{87}_{37}Rb$) in a mineral are allowed to accumulate, then the relationship between the number of parent atoms that remain (P) and the number of daughter atoms (D) per unit weight of mineral or rock is given by $D = D_0 + P(e^{\lambda t} - 1)$. In this equation λ is the decay constant of the parent, D_0 is the number of daughter atoms per unit weight incorporated into a mineral at the time of its formation, and t is the time elapsed since formation of the mineral. Therefore, t is the age of the mineral, provided it remained "closed" to the parent and its daughter. The equation is used for dating rocks or minerals by a variety of methods, including the K-Ar, Rb-Sr and the U, Th-Pb methods. In general the concentrations of the chemical elements of the parent and daughter must be measured as well as the isotopic composition of the element containing the daughter. The isotopic composition, that is, the relative abundances of all naturally occurring atomic varieties (isotopes) of an element, is measured by a MASS SPECTROMETRY.

Potassium-Argon Method. Naturally occurring radioactive $^{40}_{19}K$ decays by electron capture to $^{40}_{18}Ar$. If none of the radiogenic $^{40}_{18}Ar$ atoms escape from the mineral or rock in which they were formed, they satisfy the equation $^{40}_{18}Ar = (\lambda_e/\lambda)^{40}_{19}K (e^{\lambda t} - 1)$, where $\lambda_e/\lambda = 0.1048$ is the fraction of $^{40}_{19}K$ atoms that decay to $^{40}_{18}Ar$ (the remainder form $^{40}_{20}Ca$), $\lambda = 5.543 \times 10^{-10}$/year is the decay constant of $^{40}_{19}K$, and $^{40}_{18}Ar$ and $^{40}_{19}K$ are given as numbers of atoms per unit weight of the sample. The minerals that are datable by the K-Ar method include the micas (biotite and muscovite) and hornblende in igneous and metamorphic rocks, certain kinds of feldspar and unaltered glass in volcanic rocks, and the clay mineral glauconite in sedimentary rocks. The $^{40}Ar/^{39}Ar$ method of dating is an important extension of the K-Ar method; the concentration of $^{40}_{19}K$ is measured as $^{39}_{18}Ar$ produced by a neutron irradiation of the sample. K-Ar dates have been used to construct the geologic time scale, to paleogeologically map structural provinces in North America and other continents, and to establish a chronology for reversals of the Earth's magnetic field.

Rubidium-Strontium Method. Approximately one-third of all rubidium atoms are $^{87}_{37}Rb$, which is radioactive and decays to stable $^{87}_{38}Sr$ by emission of a beta particle. The abundance of this isotope in rubidium-bearing minerals therefore increases as a function of time according to the equation:

$$\left(\frac{^{87}Sr}{^{86}Sr}\right) = \frac{^{87}Sr}{^{86}Sr_0} + \frac{^{87}Rb}{^{86}Sr}(e^{\lambda t}) - 1$$

where $^{87}Sr/^{86}Sr$ and $^{87}Rb/^{86}Sr$ are ratios of these atoms in the rock or mineral at the present time, $(^{87}Sr/^{86}Sr)_0$ is the value of this ratio in the rock or mineral at the time of its formation, $\lambda = 1.42 \times 10^{-11}$/year is the decay constant of $^{87}_{37}Rb$, and e is the base of natural logarithms (see e). Most rubidium-bearing minerals, such as the micas, feldspars, and glauconite, can be dated by this method, based on reasonable assumptions regarding the initial $^{87}Sr/^{86}Sr$ ratio. The Rb-Sr method is especially effective when used to date suites of whole-rock samples by the isochron method. The slope of the isochron formed by samples having the same age and the same initial $^{87}Sr/^{86}Sr$ ratio, in coordinates of $^{87}Sr/^{86}Sr$ and $^{87}Rb/^{86}Sr$, is proportional to the age of the rocks. This procedure has been used to date the oldest known terrestrial rocks, from Greenland, which are about 3.7 billion years old, as well as lunar rocks. Stony meteorites have yielded a Rb-Sr isochron date of 4.6 ± 0.1 billion years that is accepted as a reliable estimate of the age of the Earth.

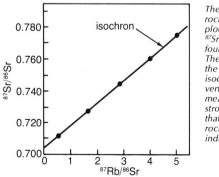

The age of many rocks is found from a plot of the ratios of ^{87}Sr, ^{86}Sr, and ^{87}Rb found within them. The intersection of the straight line, or isochron, with the vertical axis is a measure of the two strontium isotopes that existed when the rock was formed and indicates its age.

Uranium or Thorium and Lead Methods. All the isotopes of uranium and thorium are radioactive and decay to stable isotopes of lead by sequential emission of alpha and beta particles. Because uranium and thorium commonly occur together, such minerals can be dated by three independent methods based on the decay of $^{238}_{92}U$ to $^{206}_{82}Pb$, $^{235}_{92}U$ to $^{207}_{82}Pb$, and $^{232}_{90}Th$ to

$^{208}_{82}Pb$. The relevant decay constants are: $\lambda(^{238}_{92}U) = 1.55125 \times 10^{-10}$/year, $\lambda(^{235}_{92}U) = 9.8485 \times 10^{-10}$/year, and $\lambda(^{232}_{90}Th) = 4.9475 \times 10^{-11}$/year. Most minerals containing uranium and thorium are not suitable for dating, either because they lose radiogenic lead or are too rare to be useful. Instead, the minerals zircon, monazite, sphene, and apatite, in which uranium and thorium occur as trace elements, are primarily used for dating. However, the dates obtained from the three decay schemes are commonly discordant. This difficulty can be overcome by means of the concordia diagram. Concordia is the locus of all U-Pb systems yielding concordant dates. Discordant samples plot along straight-line chords below or above concordia. By extrapolating discordia lines, the correct age can be obtained from the point of intersection with concordia. The U, Th-Pb method has been widely used to date the granitic gneisses of Precambrian age that occur on all of the continents.

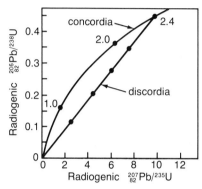

Concordia plots are based on the decay of ^{235}U to ^{206}Pb and ^{238}U to ^{207}Pb. Two curves are obtained. Concordia curves occur if the two uranium isotopes give the same age for a mineral in a rock. Discordia curves result if the ages differ. The rock's correct age is given by the intersection of the two curves.

The Fission-Track Method. When an atom of $^{238}_{92}U$ undergoes spontaneous fission ($\lambda = 8.46 \times 10^{-17}$/year), the fragments leave damage trails in crystals that can be made visible under the microscope by etching. The number of such tracks per unit area on a polished and etched surface of a mineral is related to its uranium concentration and its age. The observed density of fission tracks is used to date uranium-bearing minerals and glasses. This method is sensitive to the temperature history of minerals because of the fading of fission tracks at elevated temperatures.

The Common-Lead Method. The isotopic composition of lead in its principal ore mineral, galena, can be treated as a mixture of primordial lead (inherited by the Earth from the solar nebula) and varying amounts of radiogenic lead, depending on the age of the ore deposit. Young ore deposits contain more radiogenic lead than do older ones because they have had less time for their uranium and thorium to decay. The common-lead method of dating is important because it can be used to date lead-bearing ore deposits, and because under certain circumstances it may reveal the age of the granitic basement rocks that form the continental crust.

The Ionium-Thorium Method. Ionium ($^{230}_{90}Th$) is a radioactive daughter of $^{238}_{92}U$. It enters the oceans by the discharge of rivers or by decay of $^{234}_{92}U$, which is its immediate parent. All the isotopes of thorium in the oceans are rapidly removed to the sediment, whereas uranium tends to remain in solution. This process separates ionium from its parent, and its radioactivity in the sediment therefore decreases with time as it decays to $^{226}_{88}Ra$. The radioactivity contributed by the common thorium isotope $^{232}_{90}Th$ remains practically constant because of this isotope's slow rate of decay. Therefore, the activity ratio of $^{230}_{90}Th/^{232}_{90}Th$ (R) of the sediment decreases with time, that is, with depth in ocean-floor sediments, according to $R = R_0 e^{-\lambda t}$, where $\lambda = 9.217 \times 10^{-6}$/year is the decay constant of ionium and R_0 is the value of the activity ratio of the thorium isotopes in the sediment at the time of deposition. The ionium method has been used to date sediment recovered in piston cores from the bottom of the ocean and to determine the rate of sediment accumulation. The method is suitable for dating sediment deposited during the past 150,000 years, which includes the time of the last ice age. Other radioactive daughters of $^{238}_{92}$U that have been used for dating are $^{234}_{92}$U and $^{210}_{82}$Pb.

Carbon-14 Method. Carbon-14 is a relatively short-lived radioactive atom of carbon that is produced in the upper levels of the atmosphere by the interaction of energetic neutrons, produced by cosmic rays, with the nuclei of stable $^{14}_{7}$N. The $^{14}_{6}$C atoms are rapidly incorporated into molecules of carbon dioxide, which is taken up by green plants in the course of photosynthesis. Therefore, the tissues of living plants and animals are radioactive because of the decay of the $^{14}_{6}$C they contain. As long as the plant or animal is alive, the level of radioactivity is constant, because the loss by decay is compensated by addition of $^{14}_{6}$C from the atmosphere. When the plant or animal dies, however, the radioactivity of $^{14}_{6}$C (A) decreases with time according to the equation $A = A_0 e^{-\lambda t}$, where $\lambda = 1.2096 \times 10^{-4}$/year is the decay constant of $^{14}_{6}$C, A_0 is the radioactivity at the time of death, and t is the time elapsed since then. Dating by the $^{14}_{6}$C method thus requires a measurement of the residual radioactivity of $^{14}_{6}$C and is applicable primarily to biological materials, such as wood, seeds, and bones. The method was developed by W. F. LIBBY and has been widely used by archaeologists, anthropologists, and geologists to date samples as old as 35,000 years, although 10,000 years has been the more practical limit. Using accelerator-augmented techniques, however, scientists hope to push this limit back toward 100,000 years.

Tritium Method. Tritium is a naturally occurring radioactive isotope of hydrogen that is produced in the upper atmosphere by nuclear reactions involving cosmic rays. The natural tritium content of water on the Earth's surface is very low, but significant increases have occurred as a result of the testing of nuclear weapons in the atmosphere. The episodic input of tritium from the atmosphere into the oceans and groundwater has been used to measure the rate of movement of water masses.   GUNTER FAURE

Bibliography: Bandy, Orville L., ed., *Radiometric Dating and Paleontologic Zonation* (1970); Berger, Rainer, and Suess, H. E., eds., *Radiocarbon Dating* (1979); Chippindale, Christopher, "Radiocarbon Comes of Age at Oxford," *New Scientist,* July 21, 1983; Currie, L. A., ed., *Nuclear and Chemical Dating Techniques* (1982); Harbaugh, J. W., *Stratigraphy and the Geologic Time Scale,* 2d ed. (1974); Stokes, William L., *Essentials of Earth History,* 4th ed. (1982).

radiosonde   [ray'-dee-oh-sahnd]

A radiosonde is an instrument, carried by an unpiloted balloon, that measures temperature, pressure, and humidity of the atmosphere and transmits the information by radio. Radiosondes were developed independently in France, the USSR, and Germany in the 1920s. Early versions were equipped with a clock or windmill, both of which had a horizontal axis to sequence data into the radio signal for instant recording on the ground. Later types had aneroid barometers, whose motion in response to atmospheric pressure allowed the temperature and humidity data to be sequenced into the radio signal; thermometers; and hygrometers. A giant balloon usually carries many different radiosondes so that they can be calibrated against each other. The United States has a network of about 70 radiosonde stations, and other countries have about 400 more; data from these stations are compiled twice daily (noon and midnight, Greenwich mean time) to provide maps of weather conditions worldwide. Balloons can climb to 50 km (30 mi), but the air is so rare there that thermometers will no longer function. Rocketsondes are used to measure pressure at higher altitudes, and temperature is measured by radar tracking.   WILLEM VAN DER BIJL

Bibliography: Neiburger, Morris, et al., *Understanding Our Atmospheric Environment,* 2d ed. (1982).

radiotherapy: see RADIATION THERAPY.

radish

The radish, *Raphanus sativus*, is an annual herb that belongs to the mustard family, Crucifereae. It is grown for its fleshy roots, which vary in size from the few grams of the popular

The edible root of the radish, R. sativus, *ranges in color from red to red and white to the pure white of the daikon* (upper right).

red American and European varieties to the one or more kilograms of the Japanese white radish, or daikon. The radish was developed from a wild plant that grew in the cooler regions of Asia; it spread to the Mediterranean region before the Greek era and was introduced into the New World early in the 16th century. There are three broad categories of radish roots: small, round, spring varieties that mature in 3 to 5 weeks; somewhat larger and more slender varieties that grow into summer; and larger, "winter" varieties that are grown in cooler weather. Some winter types may reach 60 cm (2 ft) in length and are used like turnips. The first two radish categories are generally eaten raw; the winter varieties are cooked.

Radishchev, Aleksandr Nikolayevich   [ruh-deesh'-chif]

Aleksandr Nikolayevich Radishchev, b. Aug. 31 (N.S.), 1749, d. Sept. 24 (N.S.), 1802, was a major voice of European-influenced liberalism against oppression in 18th-century Russia. He is remembered primarily for his powerful indictment of serfdom in *A Journey from St. Petersburg to Moscow* (1790; Eng. trans., 1858), written in the manner of Laurence Sterne's *Sentimental Journey*. Published privately after being refused by the printer, Radishchev's work so enraged Catherine the Great that she exiled its author to Siberia. Although pardoned at the accession of Alexander I in 1801, Radishchev became despondent over his inability to promote liberal reforms and committed suicide.

Bibliography: Lang, D. M., *The First Russian Radical* (1959; repr. 1977).

Radisson, Pierre Esprit   [rah-dee-sohn']

Pierre Esprit Radisson, c.1640–1710, a French fur trader and explorer, played an important role in establishing trade in the Hudson Bay drainage basin of Canada. He went to Canada during childhood and spent more than two years as a captive of Mohawk Indians. In 1659–60 he traded furs and explored in the area west of Lake Superior with his brother-in-law, Médard Chouart des Groseilliers. The French authorities prosecuted them for illegal trading, however, and the partners persuaded the British to establish posts at the mouths of rivers flowing into Hudson Bay. The explorations of Radisson and Groseilliers in 1668–69 encouraged the British to form (1670) the HUDSON'S BAY COMPANY; the partners worked for the new company until 1675.

In 1681, Radisson began work for the Compagnie du Nord, a French rival of the Hudson's Bay Company that traded on the bay at the mouth of the Nelson River. When the French court disowned his plundering activities against the British, Radisson returned (1684) to the Hudson's Bay Company and resumed trade on its behalf.   F. J. THORPE

Bibliography: Nute, G. L., *Caesars of the Wilderness* (1943; repr. 1969); Rich, E. E., *The Hudson's Bay Company, 1670–1870*, 3 vols. (1960).

radium [ray'-dee-uhm]

Radium is a radioactive metallic chemical element, the sixth and final member of the ALKALINE EARTH METALS of the periodic table. Its chemical symbol is Ra, its atomic number is 88, and its atomic weight is 226.025. The name is derived from the Latin word *radius*, meaning "ray."

Discovery. In 1896 the French physicist Antoine Henri Becquerel discovered radioactivity in the form of penetrating radiation given off by the element uranium. Polish physicist Marie Curie continued Becquerel's work. She discovered that the mineral pitchblende showed considerably more activity than could be ascribed to its uranium content. Marie and Pierre Curie carried out laborious and painstaking fractionations of several tons of uranium residues. In the course of these separations they isolated a new element, radium, in the form of the salt, radium chloride.

Occurrence. Radium is present in all uranium minerals, because it is a member of the radioactive disintegration series initiated by the decay of uranium. Pitchblende is the most important of these uranium minerals. It was originally mined in Czechoslovakia, but extensive deposits were later found in Zaire and near Great Bear Lake and Beaverlodge Lake in Canada. About 1 gram of radium can be isolated from about 7 tons of pitchblende. The second most important radium-bearing uranium ore is carnotite, found as a yellowish impregnation of sandstone in the western United States.

Radioactivity. The radioactive disintegration of uranium gives rise to the following series, where the half-lives of the isotopes are shown in parentheses: ^{238}U (4.5 billion years) → ^{234}U (248,000 years) → ^{230}Th (80,000 years) → ^{226}Ra (1,620 years) → ^{208}Pb (stable). The very short-lived elements of the series have been omitted. In such a system the components are in a steady state, so that each element, apart from the first and last, disintegrates at a rate equal to that at which it is formed. This means that any undisturbed sample of uranium contains a quantity of radium in proportion to the uranium content. The observed ratio is about 1:3,000,000.

Sixteen isotopes of radium are known. The most abundant is ^{226}Ra, which has a half-life of 1,620 years. Alpha, beta, and gamma radiation (see RADIOACTIVITY) is emitted from the various radioisotopes, and when the element is mixed with beryllium it also emits neutrons. One gram of the isotope ^{226}Ra undergoes 37 billion disintegrations per second, producing about 0.0001 cm^3 of radon gas per day. The unit of radioactivity, the *curie*, is defined as that amount of radioactivity which has the same rate of disintegration as 1 g of ^{226}Ra.

Physical and Chemical Properties. The element was first isolated as a pure metal in 1911 by Marie Curie and André Debierne by the electrolysis of a solution of pure radium chloride using a mercury cathode. The resulting amalgam yielded metallic radium upon distillation in an atmosphere of hydrogen. The metal is brilliant white when freshly prepared but blackens upon exposure to air, presumably owing to the formation of the nitride. The metal and its salts are luminescent, and the element imparts a carmine red color to a flame. Radium metal has a melting point of 700° C, an estimated boiling point of 1,700° C, and a density of 5.5 g/cm^3 at 20° C.

The chemical properties of radium are similar to those of other members of the alkaline earth metals, particularly barium. All radium compounds are isomorphous with (have crystal structures similar to) the corresponding barium compounds, and consequently the elements are difficult to separate. The outer electron configuration of radium is $6s^26p^67s^2$; consequently radium exhibits a valency of +2 exclusively.

Compounds. Radium sulfate, $RaSO_4$, is the least soluble of all known sulfates and is important in the separation of the element from its ores. The nitrate, $Ra(NO_3)_2$, the chloride, $RaCl_2$, and the bromide, $RaBr_2$, are soluble in water but not in con-

centrated solutions of the corresponding acids. Again, this insolubility is used in the purification of the element, especially in the separation of the last traces of barium. Radium carbonate, $RaCO_3$, is insoluble in water but dissolves in acids, and the sulfide, RaS_s, is insoluble in water. Radium hydroxide, $Ra(OH)_2$, is the most soluble of the alkaline earth hydroxides.

Uses. There is no recent chemistry of radium, and the element is only of historic interest. All of its original medical and technological uses have now been supplanted by other, more readily accessible, sources. At one time radium was extensively used in the treatment of cancer. Radium has been used on a large scale in industrial radiography for testing metal castings. Radium salts, when mixed with zinc sulfide, form a paste that has been used in luminescent paints for watch and meter dials. This process was discontinued when the radiation hazard was realized.   J. ALISTAIR KERR

Bibliography: Cotton, F. A., and Wilkinson, G., *Basic Inorganic Chemistry* (1976); Selman, Joseph, *Fundamentals of X-ray and Radium Physics*, 7th ed. (1985).

Radnorshire: see POWYS.

Radom [rah'-dawm]

Radom, a city in central Poland about 90 km (55 mi) south of Warsaw, is an administrative, transportation, and industrial center. It has a population of 213,500 (1984 est.). Known for its tanning industry, Radom also produces tobacco products, glass, and chemicals. Landmarks include 14th- and 16th-century churches. First mentioned in 1187, Radom was the seat of the Polish diet from the 14th to the 16th century. The city was taken by Austria in 1795 and came under Russian control in 1815. After World War I it became part of reconstituted Poland.

radon [ray'-dahn]

Radon is the sixth and last member of the INERT GAS series, Group O of the periodic table. Discovered in 1900 by F. E. Dorn, this element was called radium emanation, but when isolated by William Ramsay and Robert Whytlaw-Gray in 1908 the name was changed to niton, from the Latin *nitens*, meaning "shining." It has been known as radon (from radium) since 1923 and is given the symbol Rn. The atomic weight of radon is about 222 and the atomic number is 86. An approximate calculation indicates that every 2.6 km^2 (1 mi^2) of soil to a depth of 15 cm (6 in) contains about 1 gram of radium, which exists radon in trace amounts to the atmosphere.

Radon is a radioactive gas of which 20 isotopes are known, including radon-222 from radium, with a half-life of 3.823 days, and radon-220, also called *thoron*, from thorium, with a half-life of 54.5 seconds. Both isotopes emit alpha particles. The melting point of the element is −71° C, the boiling point is −61.8° C, and the gas density is 9.73 g/l at 0° C. Recent reports have indicated a reaction may occur between radon and fluorine, forming radon fluoride. At room temperature radon is a colorless gas, but when cooled below its freezing point the solid exhibits a brilliant phosphorescence that becomes yellow as the temperature is lowered, and orange red at cryogenic temperatures. Radon has been used therapeutically as an alpha-particle source in the treatment of cancer.

Unsafe levels of radon gas have been discovered in a number of homes throughout the United States. Apparently, radon-222, produced by natural radium in the ground, can enter a house through small fissures or in well water, and remain in the air if unventilated. The radon then decays to radioactive products, particularly isotopes of polonium, which can be absorbed in the lungs and can lead, over a long period of time and exposure, to lung cancer.

No rigorous study of the extent of indoor radon pollution has been made, although the U.S. Environmental Protection Agency set out to make such a study in 1986. A rough, early estimate was that radon in U.S. homes contributes to about 10,000 cases of lung cancer per year. Although initial discoveries pointed to particular areas susceptible to radon pollution, such as Maryland and eastern Pennsylvania, scientists now feel that high concentrations may exist in any part of the country—and indeed, a number of European countries are addressing the problem. So far, proposed remedies for indoor radon pollution, from ventilating houses to releasing air pressure in soil with suction, are extremely expensive.

J. ALISTAIR KERR

Bibliography: Holloway, J. H., *Noble Gas Chemistry* (1968); Nero, Anthony V., "The Indoor Radon Story," *Technology Review*, January 1986.

Raeburn, Sir Henry   [ray'-burn]

The painter Sir Henry Raeburn, b. Mar. 4, 1756, d. July 8, 1823, was one of Scotland's celebrated masters of portraiture. Having begun to paint miniatures in his youth, Raeburn later restricted himself to full-scale portraits. On the advice of Sir Joshua Reynolds, he spent two years studying in Rome. Upon his return to Edinburgh in 1787, Raeburn's portraits quickly became fashionable, remaining in great demand for about 30 years. His works, painted broadly and rapidly in strong, pleasing colors, have an unmistakable romantic quality, an effect heightened by the often spacious and atmospheric backgrounds. Among Raeburn's approximately 600 canvases are portraits of many famous contemporary Scots. One of the finest collections of his works is in the National Gallery of Scotland, Edinburgh.   RAYMOND LISTER

Bibliography: Baxandall, David, *Catalogue of the Raeburn Centenary Exhibition* (1956); Dibdin, E. Rimbault, *Raeburn* (1925).

Raffles, Sir Thomas Stamford   [raf'-ulz]

Sir Thomas Stamford Raffles, known as Raffles of Singapore, b. at sea, July 6, 1781, d. July 5, 1826, played a key role in the founding of Britain's East Asian empire. He became an employee of the British East India Company at an early age. During the British rule of Java (in present-day Indonesia) while Holland was under Napoleon's rule, Raffles served (1811–16) as the island's lieutenant governor-general. He introduced major administrative reforms and replaced traditional tribute in kind with a cash land tax.

After Java returned to Dutch control in 1816, Raffles, seeking a British alternative to Java, cast his eye on the small island of Singapore, located at the southern tip of the Malay Peninsula. Raffles directed the acquisition of the island for the East India Company in 1819 and founded the modern city of Singapore. Pursuing the liberal economic policies proposed by Raffles, Singapore became a thriving free port in the heart of colonial Southeast Asia, which was increasing in economic importance. In 1824 he returned to London, subsequently helping to found the London Zoo and serving as first president of the London Zoological Society. Raffles, who was knighted in 1817, was the author of *History of Java* (1817).

RICHARD BUTWELL

Bibliography: Collis, Maurice, *Raffles* (1966).

rafflesia   [ruh-flee'-zhee-uh]

Rafflesias are about 12 species of parasitic plants constituting the genus *Rafflesia* in the family Rafflesiaceae. Native to the Malaysian archipelago, the plants are parasitic on the roots and stems of plants of the grape family, Vitaceae, particularly shrubs of the genus *Cissus*. Rafflesias produce huge, fleshy flowers but no stems or leaves; the plant body consists almost wholly of fine, funguslike filaments buried within the tissues of the host plant. The flowers are pollinated by flies attracted to their rotting-meat smell. *R. arnoldii* produces the largest flowers in the world, reputed to reach 1 m (3 ft) across and up to 11 kg (24 lb) in weight.

rag worm

Rag worm is a common name for polychaete annelid worms of the genus *Nereis*. They are also known as mussel worms, pile worms, and sand worms and are found primarily in marine environments, burrowing in mud or sand. Rag worms range from 2.5 to 90 cm (1 to 35 in) in length. The initial head

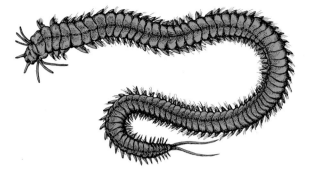

The rag worm N. diversicolor *is a primitive annelid worm. Its body comprises a long series of segments, unspecialized in form or function, that bear fleshy extensions (parapodia) for locomotion.*

segments bear two palps, four eyes, several tentacles, and sharp retractable jaws. These annelids feed on other worms and small marine organisms.   STEPHEN C. REINGOLD

raga   [rah'-guh]

Raga is the most characteristic element of Indian classical music, to which it bears the same relation as did modality to medieval plainsong. The province of raga is the structure and organization of melody. Like scales in Western music, ragas can be defined by the tones they contain, although the distribution of semitones in some ragas is incompatible with Western practice. Ragas need not have a full complement of seven scale steps; gaps are common (as in the pattern CDEGAC'). The ascending scale pattern (*arohana*) may differ from the descending pattern (*avarohana*).

Ragas are more than mere scale patterns. Knowledgeable listeners can recognize a raga from as little as a single phrase. The contour of the phrase, the notes emphasized, vocal inflection, and subtle variations of intonation all serve to identify a raga. These characteristics are considered precious and are transmitted from master to pupil. Nevertheless, all ragas are in constant if imperceptible evolution. Many ragas celebrated in ancient times are extinct; others persist under new names; still others are quite unlike modern ragas identically named. The ragas used in north and south India differ considerably in practice. Ragas are said to possess extramusical qualities and may be associated with deities, localities, seasons, times of day, and emotions.   DAVID SCHONFELD

Bibliography: Kaufmann, Walter, *The Ragas of North India* (1968) and *The Ragas of South India* (1976); Shankar, Ravi, *My Music, My Life* (1968); Wade, Bonnie, *Music in India: The Classical Tradition* (1979).

ragfish

The ragfish is a blunt-snouted, highly compressed marine fish of the family Icosteidae whose limp body is partly the result of its flexible skeleton, which is composed largely of cartilage. The ragfish ranges from southern California to Alaska and west to Japan. There are two species—the fantail ragfish, *Icosteus aenigmaticus,* and the larger brown ragfish, *Acrotus willoughbyi,* which attains a length of 2.1 m (7 ft) and a weight of 154 kg (340 lb). Adult ragfish live at depths of 82 to 366 m (270 to 1,200 ft).

Ragnarok   [rag'-nuh-rahk]

In Norse mythology Ragnarok is the final destruction of the world, when the gods and the giants will slaughter one another and in the process destroy all creation. According to the Icelandic Eddas, the giants will be led by the traitor-god LOKI and will attack ASGARD, the dwelling place of ODIN and the other major divinities. Their coming will be signaled by HEIMDALL, who will sound a mighty blast on his horn. After the destruction, however, a new Earth will appear and the creative process will begin anew.   C. SCOTT LITTLETON

Bibliography: Martin, John S., *Ragnarok* (1972).

ragtime

Ragtime was the most popular music idiom in the United States from 1896 to 1917. The style originated on the blackface minstrel stage (see MUSIC HALL, VAUDEVILLE, AND BURLESQUE), and the term means "ragged time," referring to the music's syncopated, off-beat rhythm. The most popular rags were such songs as "Hello! Ma Baby" (1899), "Under the Bamboo Tree" (1902), and "Alexander's Ragtime Band" (1911); of the many thousands of instrumental rags, the most famous was Scott JOPLIN's "Maple Leaf Rag" (1899). Thousands of rags reached the public in the form of sheet music, piano rolls, and recordings, but ragtime was also an improvised art and in this latter practice was a direct predecessor of JAZZ. Rags were designed both for listening and for dancing the cakewalk, two-step, one-step, and fox- and turkey-trots.

Current interest in ragtime is focused primarily on the piano music, especially the "classic rags" of Joplin, James Scott, Joseph F. Lamb, and Eubie BLAKE. During the early 1970s, republication of Joplin's music and a succession of recordings stimulated new interest in ragtime. Joplin's rag "The Entertainer" (1902) was used in the award-winning film *The Sting* (1973) and created an even broader public for ragtime.

EDWARD A. BERLIN

Bibliography: Berlin, Edward A., *Ragtime: A Musical and Cultural History* (1980); Blesh, Rudi, and Janis, Harriet, *They All Played Ragtime*, rev. ed. (1971); Waldo, Terry, *This Is Ragtime* (1976).

ragweed

Ragweed is any of about 35 species of widely distributed, annual or perennial plants of the genus *Ambrosia* in the daisy family, Compositae. The common ragweed, *A. artemisiifolia*, is a coarse, typically hairy-stemmed annual growing to about 1.5 m (5 ft) high, with usually deeply divided leaves. Its minute, greenish flowers with yellow stamens are borne in tiny clusters spaced along a slender, erect stalk. The giant ragweed, *A. trifida*, an annual with three-lobed leaves, reaches a height of 4.5 m (15 ft). Ragweed pollen is the most prevalent cause of autumn hay fever in the United States. The seedlike fruits form an important part of the winter diet of birds.

Rahner, Karl [rah'-nur]

Karl Rahner, b. Freiburg im Breisgau, Germany, Mar. 5, 1904, d. Mar. 30, 1984, is regarded by many as the foremost Roman Catholic theologian of the 20th century. He entered the Society of Jesus in 1922 and early on manifested a profound interest in philosophy, particularly the work of Immanuel Kant. Rahner subsequently came under the influence of existentialist philosopher Martin Heidegger.

For most of his career, Rahner taught systematic theology at Innsbruck and later at Munich. The range of his writings is wide, but he is perhaps best known for the work he has done on the fundamental relationship between the order of nature and the order of grace, specifically on the possibility of self-transcendence. Although not avoiding controversial questions, he has always stressed the continuity between modern interpretations of Catholic doctrine and their original formulations. Rahner's writings include his multivolume *Theological Investigations*.

RICHARD P. McBRIEN

Bibliography: Kress, Robert, *A Rahner Handbook* (1982); McCool, Gerald, *The Theology of Karl Rahner* (1969); Vorgrimler, Herbert, *Karl Rahner: His Life, Thought and Works*, trans. by Edward Quinn (1966).

rail

Birds of the family Rallidae are called rails. The birds' bodies are usually narrow enough to enable them to slip through dense vegetation, such as that found in the marshes they typically inhabit. Rails ordinarily remain on the ground and are difficult to flush, secretive, and sometimes nocturnal in habit. Some rails forage at dawn and dusk. Commonly heard rather than seen, they emit certain calls, often clicking or

The king rail *Rallus elegans* (above), *a chicken-sized bird, usually inhabits freshwater marshes. The smaller Virginia rail,* R. limicola (right), *lives in fresh and brackish water. The sparrow-sized black rail,* Laterallus jamaicensis (below), *prefers coastal salt marshes.*

ticking sounds, characteristic of the species.

These small- to medium-sized birds have moderate to long legs and long toes, which are advantageous for walking or running over soft ground. They are usually but not always gray, brown, and dull red; the plumage usually has a loose texture, and the sexes look alike. Bills range from stubby to elongate, depending on the species. Rails are omnivorous, but many species predominantly eat small animals. Their nests generally are well hidden and well separated. Clutches generally contain 6 to 12 eggs, and both sexes usually participate in incubating them. At the time of hatching, the precocious young are covered by a black or brownish down in most species and leave the nest immediately thereafter.

Rails are distributed throughout the world except in polar regions. About 132 species are recognized, some of which are important game birds. Two such game species of North America are the clapper rail, *Rallus longirostris*, and the Virginia rail, *R. limicola*. Despite the fact that they have stubby wings, a high ratio of weight to wing area, and apparently weak flight when flushed, some species migrate long distances, often flying at night. Species of various islands have independently evolved flightlessness. Rails on islands have proved vulnerable to human-caused disturbances, and at least 12 species and subspecies have become extinct within the past 300 years. The flightless rail of Wake Island in the Pacific Ocean is the only species of bird whose extinction is directly attributable to human warfare, being exterminated during World War II.

The rail family also includes gallinules and coots. Gallinules typically are marsh dwellers, and some have brightly colored bony shields covering the forehead and iridescent plumage. The coots have lobed toes specialized for swimming and diving.

GEORGE A. CLARK, JR.

Bibliography: Ripley, S. D., *Rails of the World* (1977).

railgun

A railgun is a device that uses electromagnetic forces to accelerate projectiles to high velocities. A strong pulse of electricity is sent through a pair of parallel rails, generating a magnetic field that accelerates a conducting projectile to

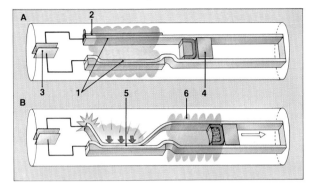

(A) *One type of railgun consists of a pair of electrically conducting rails (1), one of which is lined with explosive (2), a large capacitor (3), and a projectile (4) with a metal backing. (B) The railgun is fired by sending an electric pulse from the capacitor into the rails. The explosive then detonates, squeezing the rails together (5) and creating a powerful magnetic field (6) that acts on the current in the metal backing to accelerate the projectile.*

speeds that have reached 10 km/sec (6.2 mi/sec) in tests. Possible applications include inexpensive launching of payloads into space and creation of thermonuclear fusion reactions by collisions between high-speed projectiles.

railroad

A railroad, called railway in Great Britain, is a form of land transportation in which a permanent roadway with parallel rails provides a track for cars drawn by locomotives or for self-propelled motor units. Even before locomotives were perfected, such cars were pulled by horses and other animals. The principle of the flanged wheel (one having a projecting rim to guide it along a track) rolling on iron or steel rails furnishes a low-cost, high-volume, reliable mode of transport for both freight and passengers.

When railroads appeared in the early 19th century, they soon gained a major role in the Industrial Revolution, and the first successful lines were those built in such developing industrial nations as England, France, and the United States. By the mid-19th century railroads had proven superior in several ways to earlier forms of transportation, such as turnpikes, canals, and steamboats. (See the article TRANSPORTATION for a discussion of the various modes of transport.) Later, as industrial development reached Asia, Africa, South America, and Australia, railroads appeared on those continents. By the early decades of the 20th century, nearly 1,440,000 km (900,000 mi) of railroad had been built in the world, with some mileage in nearly every nation. By the 1970s this total had declined to about 1,240,000 km (775,000 mi), divided roughly as follows: North America, 36%; Europe, 34%; Asia, 12%; South America,

8%; Africa, 6%; and Australasia, 4%.

RAILROAD HISTORY

As early as the 16th century, crude railways—horse-drawn wagons with wooden wheels and rails—were used in mining operations in England and western Europe. By the 18th century their use was improved with the introduction of cast-iron wheels and rails.

In England horse power began to be replaced by the power of the STEAM ENGINE when Richard TREVITHICK, John Blenkinsop, and William Hedley successfully invented, built, and operated several steam locomotives between 1797 and 1813. George STEPHENSON built and equipped the Stockton & Darlington Railway between 1823 and 1825. This English line, 32 km (20 mi) long, was the first public railway in the world to be powered by a steam locomotive.

Railroads in the United States. Following the pioneer work of British inventor-engineers, the first railroads appeared in the United States during the late 1820s. In 1827 the merchants of Baltimore, Md., chartered the Baltimore & Ohio Railroad, hoping to increase their share of the trade with western states; it opened in 1830. The Delaware & Hudson Canal and Railroad Company in 1829 purchased a British-built locomotive, the STOURBRIDGE LION, but found it too rigid and heavy for track in the U.S. On Christmas Day, 1830, the South Carolina Railroad began passenger service on a 9.6-km (6-mi) stretch of track with the U.S.-built BEST FRIEND OF CHARLESTON, becoming the first railroad in the nation to use steam power in regular service.

In the 1830s the new form of transport gained acceptance, although there was some opposition, especially from canal owners and stagecoach operators worried about the competition to their businesses. The great bulk of the public, however, welcomed the railroad. Five of the six New England states had some rail mileage by 1838, and even such western states as Kentucky and Indiana were projecting new lines.

In 1840 more than 4,480 km (2,800 mi) of railroad were in operation, most near the Atlantic seacoast. The novelty of rail travel, the relatively high speed possible, and the advantage of year-round service combined to make passenger traffic revenue larger than freight on many early lines.

In 1850, 60% of the nation's rail mileage was located in New England and mid-Atlantic states, and the 14,400 km (9,000 mi) of road represented a total railroad investment of more than $300 million. By that time, U.S. railroads were clearly superior to turnpikes, canals, and steamboats. Shippers welcomed rail service, which was dependable throughout the year, cheaper than the Conestoga wagon, faster than the canal packet, and more direct in route than the river steamboat.

Perhaps no decade of rail growth in the United States was more important than the years following 1850. What had been a scattering of short lines from Maine to Georgia then grew into a rail network serving all the states east of the Mississippi River. By 1860 the total mileage was more than 48,000 km (30,000 mi), with much of the new construction in

A locomotive of the Canadian Pacific Railway, one of Canada's two largest railroad companies, winds through the Rocky Mountains of western Canada. Today this privately owned railroad is increasingly used for efficient overland freight transportation.

the West, especially in Ohio, Indiana, and Illinois. Many of the new lines in these states were extensions of such eastern lines as the New York Central, the Pennsylvania, the Erie, and the Baltimore & Ohio. This rapid western construction caused a shift in the total traffic flow from the north–south axis of the Ohio and Mississippi rivers to an east–west axis of trunk line railroads serving eastern seaports. Construction was so rapid that by the late 1850s rail mileage in the United States was nearly equal to that in the rest of the world. When the Civil War erupted in 1861, it was the first U.S. conflict in which railroads had an important role. Both sides made massive troop and supply movements by rail during the war, and basic weaknesses in southern railroads contributed to the ultimate defeat of the Confederacy.

The period between the Civil War and World War I was a golden age for U.S. railroads. For nearly 50 years after 1865 no new modes of transport seriously challenged this developing mode of transportation. A great expansion in mileage occurred in the same years that many new technical advances made possible major improvements in the operating efficiency of railroads. During those five decades, the rail network increased from 56,000 km (35,000 mi) in 1865 to 406,400 km (254,000 mi) in 1916. The completion (May 10, 1869) of the Union Pacific–Central Pacific line, which covered 2,848 km (1,780 mi) from the Missouri River to the Pacific Ocean, was one of the first major building efforts after the Civil War. In the next 25 years four other TRANSCONTINENTAL RAILROAD lines were built.

Four of the five Pacific railroads, along with dozens of other western lines, were aided in these years by land grants from the federal government. This aid program was started when land was given to the Illinois Central-Mobile & Ohio route in 1850. All of the land grant roads—which between 1850 and the 1870s received 53 million ha (131 million acres) of public land—were required to give the federal government reduced transportation rates of about 50%.

During the decades after the Civil War, a host of technical advances made possible a new integration and uniformity of railroad service. These innovations included the introduction of more powerful locomotives, the use of larger and more varied types of cars, the general adoption of a track gauge

(the distance between the inside faces of the rails) known as standard track gauge (1.44 m/4 ft 8½ in), and the general acceptance of the air BRAKE invented by George WESTINGHOUSE, improved couplers, and standard TIME ZONES. These contributions permitted a more economical rail service, which brought a major reduction in freight rates—from more than 2 cents a ton-mile at the end of the Civil War to less than 1 cent a ton-mile in the early 20th century. In these years railroad freight revenue became increasingly greater than passenger revenue. The reduction in freight rates and the improved service promoted industrialization, the expansion of urban population, the shift from regional to national markets, and the growth of the nation's modern interdependent economy.

The decades prior to World War I were also years of corruption and various forms of discrimination. False-front construction companies used in building western lines gave extra profits to builders such as Thomas Clark DURANT, who helped organize the CRÉDIT MOBILIER OF AMERICA for building the Union Pacific. Cornelius Vanderbilt (see VANDERBILT family), James FISK, and Jay GOULD were all masters at inflating and manipulating the securities of their lines. The evils of railroad pools, rebates, discriminatory freight rates, and charging "all the traffic will bear" contributed to agitation by western farmers for Granger laws, which regulated railroads and their freight rates in the 1870s (see GRANGER MOVEMENT). After the U.S. Supreme Court ruled that interstate commerce could be regulated only by the federal government, the U.S. Congress in 1887 approved federal regulation of railroads with the Interstate Commerce Act, which provided for establishment of the INTERSTATE COMMERCE COMMISSION (ICC). Much more stringent regulations were imposed in later federal laws.

Early in the 20th century the monopoly that had so long been held by railroads was challenged by a number of new modes of transport: electric interurbans (lines that connected neighboring towns); thousands and soon millions of private automobiles; intercity buses; larger and larger trucks; airplanes carrying mail, passengers, and high-priority freight; and a growing network of pipelines. As a result, railroads in the United States went into decline after World War I, with substantial losses in mileage, employment, and traffic.

Officials of the Union Pacific and Central Pacific railroads shake hands to mark the completion of the transcontinental railroad. As part of the ceremonies, a golden spike was driven in place to join the two rail lines on May 10, 1869, at Promontory Point, Utah.

The heavy wartime traffic from 1941 through 1945 helped the railways recover from the hard times of the Depression of the 1930s and to retire a major portion of their debt. Even this, however, did not create large profits for the industry. Following World War II the railroads replaced the steam locomotive with more efficient DIESEL-electric locomotives and introduced new, more efficient freight services. Nevertheless, by the mid-1970s, ten railroads in the Northeast and Midwest were in bankruptcy.

During the years since World War II, the federal government has tended to favor competing modes of transport with more generous subsidy programs and with less stringent regulation than that covering railroads. The 1971 introduction of the federally subsidized passenger service known as AMTRAK helped to relieve railroads of the annual passenger-service deficits they had known for many years. The Railroad Revitalization and Regulatory Reform Act of 1976 established the Consolidated Rail Corp. (ConRail), which, with federal assistance, has successfully renovated portions of six bankrupt Northeast railroads into a single viable freight system.

The Staggers Rail Act of 1980 substantially reduced the Interstate Commerce Commission's jurisdiction over railroads, permitting rail operators greater freedom to set rates, abandon or sell unprofitable lines, and offer service innovations designed to attract business and reduce costs. The new competitive environment afforded by Staggers has also sparked a restructuring of the industry through mergers and consolidations, and has stimulated unprecedented advances in new technology.

Railroads in the United States are classified according to certain annual operating-revenue minimums determined by the Interstate Commerce Commission. In 1985 the minimum for Class I carriers was $87.9 million; for Class II, it was $17.6 million. In 1985, the 25 Class I freight railroads accounted for more than 95% of all freight moved by rail. Amtrak, also a Class I railroad, moved virtually all intercity passengers.

Other Railroads in the Western Hemisphere. The total rail mileage in Canada, Mexico, and Central America amounts to about a third of that in the United States. In Canada the first rail service started in 1836, and by 1880 the network had expanded to about 11,200 km (6,960 mi). The CANADIAN PACIFIC RAILWAY was completed across the Rockies to the Pacific by 1885. The current mileage in Canada, nearly all built with standard gauge, is almost 100,000 km (62,000 mi). Two freight railroads, the federally owned CANADIAN NATIONAL RAILWAYS and the privately owned Canadian Pacific, constitute most of the nation's rail mileage. VIA Rail Canada, a government-funded corporation, operates Canada's passenger trains. In Mexico, the majority of the 20,200 km (12,550 mi) of track is built in standard gauge, and the government-owned National Railways of Mexico operates nearly two-thirds of the total mileage. Most of the limited mileage in Central America is of light construction narrow gauge.

More than 96,000 km (59,065 mi) of railway are in operation in South America, with much built in narrow gauge. Argentina, Brazil, Chile, Paraguay, and Peru all built their first lines during the 1850s, but some other countries did not construct their first roads until the 1870s. Today the major mileage in the continent is located in three countries: Argentina (34,800 km/21,600 mi), Brazil (24,000 km/14,900 mi), and Chile (7,400 km/4,600 mi). Most lines started as private ventures, but today the great bulk of the mileage is state owned.

The Railroads of Europe. After the United States, the greatest concentration of rail mileage is found in Europe. As noted earlier the first railroads were those developed and built in England in the second and third decades of the 19th century. After the success of the Stockton & Darlington Railway, others quickly followed. The Liverpool & Manchester, which opened in 1830, used steam power for both passenger and freight service and soon was taking traffic away from turnpike and canal competitors. Most British railways were fairly prosperous, inasmuch as their traffic expanded with the industrial growth in Britain. Quite early the government insisted upon the uniform use of standard (1.44 m/4 ft 8½ in) gauge and later passed laws concerning the use of improved brakes and higher safety

standards. During World War I the government took control, but not ownership, of all the lines, and in 1948 all the railroads in Great Britain were nationalized and reorganized as British Railways. Increased competition from highway transport has resulted in the abandonment of many branch lines. Thus, the 1984 rail mileage in the country was 17,200 km (10,690 mi), compared with 28,800 km (17,000 mi) in 1900, the heyday of the British rail system.

France had its first railway line by 1828, and Belgium, Germany, Italy, the Netherlands, and Russia all had some railroads in operation by the 1830s. Countries that were slower to industrialize were building railways by 1850. Most of the European countries followed the English in using standard gauge, but Spain and Portugal both adopted a gauge of 1.66 m (5 ft 6 in), whereas Russian roads were all built with a gauge of 1.5 m (5 ft). European railroads, like those of Great Britain, are generally state owned and operated. Russian lines were all nationalized with the revolution, and both German and French roads were state owned before World War II. Aside from the USSR, the European nations with the greatest mileage today are Germany (East and West), 42,700 km (26,500 mi), and France, 37,100 km (23,050 mi).

Unlike some industrial states, the USSR has continued to build railroads in recent years and in 1984 had a total mileage (Europe and Asia) of about 144,000 km (89,500 mi), second only to the United States. In 1891, Russia started the TRANS-SIBERIAN RAILROAD, and when the line from Moscow to Vladivostok was completed in 1916, it was the longest continuous rail line in the world (9,259 km/5,787 mi). A second Trans-Siberian railroad, the Baikal-Amur Mainline, was completed in 1984. Because of the great size of the USSR today, its large population, and its limited highway transport, the railroads of the Soviet Union lead the world in freight service (ton-miles per year).

Railroads of Asia, Africa, and Australia. Other than the Soviet Union, the major Asiatic nations with extensive railroad systems are India, China, and Japan. India's first railroads were built in the 1850s and followed English patterns, except in gauge. Indian lines were built extensively in the 1.66 m (5 ft 6 in) gauge and also in the meter (3 ft 3 in) gauge. More than 59,200 km (37,000 mi) of railroad are in operation in India today. Nearly the entire Indian system has been state owned since 1947. China built its first lines in the 1870s, but only 12,000 km (7,500 mi) were in operation by 1920. Much additional mileage has been built since the People's Republic of China came to power in 1949, and the present state-owned rail system operates nearly 52,500 km (32,600 mi) of lines.

Japan built its first lines in the 1870s and today has nearly 27,200 km (17,000 mi) in operation, most of it in 1.05 m (3 ft 6 in) gauge; three-quarters of it is owned by the state. Japanese lines are built to very high standards and carry a heavy passenger traffic. The development of railroads in Africa accompanied the European colonization of the 19th century. The Republic of South Africa has the most mileage, with a state-owned system of about 23,700 km (14,700 mi). The first railroad in Australia was opened in 1854. Most of the present 40,000-km (25,000-mi) rail system is state owned.

RAILROAD OPERATIONS

The three essential elements of a railroad are: (1) the roadbed and track, including necessary fills, cuts, bridges, and tunnels, (2) the LOCOMOTIVE, which may be steam, electric, or diesel-electric, and (3) the rolling stock, including passenger cars of various types and a variety of freight cars.

Roadbed and Track. In the planning and construction of a new railroad, the first step is for surveyors and civil engineers to seek out and survey a route, then establish standards relative to grade (inclination of a track), curvature, gauge, and quality of construction. Builders of railroads must make an early decision concerning track gauge. Because the English were the pioneer builders of railroads and locomotives, their adoption of a standard gauge of 1.44 m (4 ft 8½ in) was to be widely followed. It is probable that this gauge was adopted in England because it was the wheel spacing used on the wagons and tramways of prerailroad England. The railroads of the world have used a variety of gauges ranging from under 0.6 m

(2 ft) to as much as 2.1 m (7 ft). There are some economies of construction that result from using narrow gauge in mountain or frontier lines. Today standard gauge is universally used in North America and Europe and is found on about 60% of the world's total mileage.

Once the roadbed is fully graded, wooden ties, or sleepers, are distributed, and the rails are laid and spiked. Later a ballast of crushed rock or slag is applied, the track is aligned, and the ballast is tamped, or compacted, around the ties. The earliest rails were made of wood; later track often consisted of iron-strap rails fastened to long wooden stringers. In the 1830s, Robert L. Stevens of the Camden & Amboy Railroad designed the iron T-rail, which was fastened to ties with spikes. This type of rail soon became standard. Early rail often weighed no more than 20–25 kg/m (40–50 lb/yd), but heavier trains required heavier rail, and today's main lines are laid with rail weighing 50–70 kg/m (100–140 lb/yd). By the 1860s and 1870s, steel rail was beginning to replace iron on most heavily used lines. The standard rail length in the United States is 11.9 m (39 ft), while in Europe it is 30 m (98 ft 5 in). Welded rail, in lengths of 0.8 km (0.5 mi) or more, is used on most U.S. mainline track today. Successful experiments with concrete ties have been made in the United States and in Europe.

Alfred de Glehn's compound, four-cylinder steam engine was invented in the 1890s for the Northern Railway of France. It could exceed 120 km/h (75 mph), although such high speeds were prohibited in France until the introduction of color signals in 1930.

The Dunalastair class of locomotive, used by the Caledonian Railway, was one of the most successful engines in Scottish railway history.

The giant Beyer-Garratt articulated steam locomotive has drawn freight trains in South and East Africa since the early 1900s.

The Flying Hamburger of the German State Railways, introduced in 1932, was the first high-speed diesel-electric locomotive.

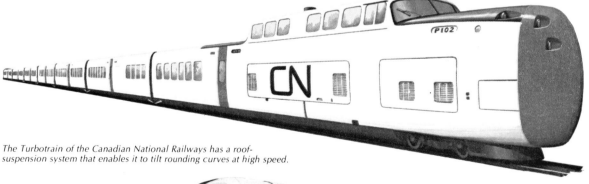

The Turbotrain of the Canadian National Railways has a roof-suspension system that enables it to tilt rounding curves at high speed.

British Railways' High Speed Train broke the world record for diesel trains at 230 km/h (143 mph) when it was introduced in 1973. Railway companies are now investigating new designs, including magnetic levitation trains and linear electric motors, which may reach speeds of up to 480 km/h (300 mph).

Locomotives. The first motive power on many railroads was horses or mules, but most lines quickly adopted steam locomotives. As trains grew longer and heavier during the 19th century, so did the locomotives. Peter Cooper's tiny TOM THUMB in 1830 developed perhaps one horsepower, while the Union Pacific ''Big Boys'' built in the 1940s weighed about 400 tons and developed 7,000 horsepower. In the early 20th century, electric locomotives were adopted in many countries, but by the 1950s most railroads were shifting to diesel-electric motive power. In 1985, 23,000 mainline locomotives were in use in the United States.

Cars and Rolling Stock. The early railroad passenger and freight cars were little more than stagecoaches and wagons fitted with flanged wheels. In the United States it did not take long for passenger cars and freight cars to be lengthened, with rigid axles being replaced by four-wheel swivel, or bogie, trucks at each end to improve the turning characteristics. European cars generally were shorter and frequently had only four wheels instead of the eight common in the United States. The two-truck passenger coach became common in England and Europe only in the last two decades of the 19th century. By World War I, wooden cars, both passenger and freight, were giving way to those made of steel.

By the late 1830s, Americans were riding in elongated cars with double seats on either side of a central aisle. With a capacity of from 40 to 50 persons, they were similar in basic design to those of the mid-20th century. In contrast, many British and European passenger cars consisted of several six- to eight-seat compartments with a corridor at one side of the coach. Sleeping cars were introduced in the United States by the time of the Civil War, or before, but they appeared in England only after 1870. In the late 1860s, George M. PULLMAN was building dining cars and sleeping cars for some American lines. Within the next 25 years electric lighting, steam heat, and vestibules (a flexible covered passageway between cars) were being added to much first-class passenger equipment. In the mid-20th century, streamlining, lightweight cars, domed observation cars, and economy slumber coaches were introduced by some U.S. lines as they sought to halt a decline in railroad passenger traffic. Since taking over the management of intercity rail passenger services in 1971, Amtrak has totally revitalized the American passenger car fleet. Nearly 900 new passenger cars have been put into service, and more than 600 cars from the 1940s and '50s have been completely rebuilt.

Changes in both size and type have appeared in freight equipment. In the mid-19th century, U.S. freight cars tended to be of three types: the open-top car, the boxcar, and the flatcar, each having a capacity of no more than 10 tons. European freight cars have increased only modestly in size, while the capacity of American cars has expanded greatly. The average capacity of freight cars in the United States in 1985 was 76 metric tons (84 U.S. tons). Among the types of freight cars most commonly used in the United States are open hopper cars (primarily used for hauling coal), covered hopper cars (for grain and other bulk commodities), tank cars used for hauling chemicals and other liquids, and flat cars, which can carry containers (see CONTAINERIZATION) or highway truck-trailers ''piggyback,'' or on which can be mounted multi-level racks for carrying automobiles. Piggyback freight traffic is the fastest-growing segment of the U.S. rail industry, with improved car designs—including articulated, skeletonized flat cars that offer greater fuel efficiency and cars that can carry double-stacked containers.

Traffic Control. As railroads expanded and developed, one area of high priority was internal communication and the necessary control and direction of all train movement. Because the telegraph was invented at about the same time that railroads were appearing in the United States and western Europe, this new mode of communication was soon adopted and widely used by most railroads. By the turn of the century the telephone began to supplement the telegraph. Various types of trackside signals and SEMAPHORES were improved in the 1860s when a manual block signal system was introduced. Later a system of manual (and then electrical) interlocking made it impossible for a signalman to line up signals and

Freight cars of varying functions used by railroads around the world include a flatcar (A) bearing storage containers used by Coras Lompair Eireann of Ireland, a car carrier (B) of the French National Railways, a tank car (C) used by the Austrian Federal Railway to haul liquid gas, box cars of the Canadian Pacific (D) and Western Pacific (E) railways, a coal-hopper car (F) of the New Zealand Railways, an open gondola car (G) of the Penn Central Railway, a grain-hopper car (H) of the South Australian Railway, a flatcar (I) of the Finnish State Railway, a refrigerated car (J) of the Italian State Railway, a cement car (K) used by British Rail, and a hopper car (L) of Indian Railways.

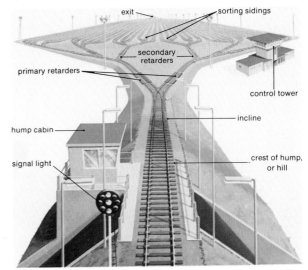

Modern hump yards, or switchyards, are automated and computerized for sorting and coupling freight trains. The yardmaster, in the tower, guides each car to the proper siding by remote-control.

switches in conflict with each other. Soon after World War I, a system of automatic train control was introduced.

Today, centralized traffic control permits a single operator to control all train movements over distances up to several hundred kilometers. Computers reach into virtually all aspects of railroad operations, from yard control and dispatching to information about car movements and inventory control. Microprocessors allow the use of computers on board locomotives. In the mid-1980s, work began on the development of an advanced train control system, which will use electronics and telecommunications to control the flow of traffic across entire railroad systems.

Labor. The diversity of railroad occupations is indicated by an ICC report (1976) of the then 496,000 employees working for Class I railroads. The report listed 128 different occupational groups. Aside from the executive staff, these groups are almost totally unionized. The first railroad laborers to organize were the operating personnel: engineers established their union in 1863, conductors in 1868, firemen and enginemen in 1873, and trainmen in 1883.

Figures for employment in 1985 indicate a job decline of about 38% in the previous decade. Class I railroads in 1985 employed about 324,000; classes II and III, an additional 30,000. The largest railroad union, the United Transportation Union, has about 123,000 active members (1986). Altogether, there are 17 railroad unions, several of them dating from their original 19th-century years of founding.

Over the past decades, the unions have found themselves forced to change work rules (see FEATHERBEDDING) and to offer labor concessions that had required years of struggle to put into place. In part these concessions have been granted because new technologies have made it possible to run railroads more efficiently and safely with smaller crews of operators and maintenance personnel. But the unions also face a future where their numbers are certain to decline still further, and their power to negotiate will inevitably become weaker.

PROBLEMS FOR TODAY'S RAILROADS
Almost all railroads today face serious and continuing financial problems. Unlike most industrial concerns, the rail industry requires a very large investment to produce modest annual revenues. Furthermore, the constant low rate of return makes it difficult for the industry to attract new capital.

The United States has heavily subsidized a highway system and in effect subsidizes the trucks that use it. Water and air carriers are also subsidized. Most of the world's railways are now state owned because they do, in fact, require heavy subsidies to keep operating. Today the only substantial rail mileage still privately owned is in Canada and the United States. Although large railway systems like those in France, Italy, West Germany, and Great Britain have a volume of rail travel at least twice that of the United States (and Japan's is 15 times as large), none of these nationalized rail systems is profitable.

In the United States, however, the Staggers Rail Act of 1980, which partially deregulated many aspects of rail freight operations, has allowed U.S. railroads to compete more effectively for traffic. New technology has allowed employment levels to be reduced. Mergers, consolidations, and reorganizations have resulted in fewer but larger Class I systems, and less total mileage. Concurrently, hundreds of regional and local short-line railroads have sprung up as major systems have sold off trackage they could not operate profitably. The smaller companies, with more labor flexibility and the ability to develop local traffic, are often able to run a line profitably while generating traffic for the larger systems with which they connect. Today, railroads move nearly as much freight as trucks, barges, and airlines combined, and do it with an improved technology that has allowed them to use fewer miles of track, fewer employees, fewer locomotives, and fewer cars.

HIGH-SPEED TRAINS
In 1964 the Japanese began to operate their famous "bullet" train, the Shinkansen, which runs from Tokyo to Nagoya, a 338-km (210-mi) trip that the train is capable of completing in 1⅓ hours, or at a speed of 258 km/h (160 mph). In many respects, the Shinkansen represents the high-speed train of the future. It runs on a specially constructed "dedicated" track. Each car is separately powered by four electric motors. Each Shinkansen consists of 16 permanently linked cars.

The French completed their *train à grand vitesse* (TGV) in 1981. It makes the Paris-Lyon trip—much of which requires climbing extremely steep gradients—at speeds of up to 274 km/h (170 mph). It, too, uses "dedicated track" over much of its route, and has permanently linked cars. Unlike the Shinkansen, however, it employs electric-powered locomotives.

British High Speed Trains roll on rehabilitated track, which is also shared by freight trains. "Tilt" trains, used successfully by Canada, travel at high speeds on conventional tracks, but compensate for the sharp curves that freight trains travel at low speed by using coaches that tilt, or "bank," as they negotiate the turns.

The most revolutionary new train design, the Maglev (Magnetic Levitation train), eliminates steel track and steel wheels altogether. Instead, it glides silently over a raised track, or guideway, lifted a few inches above the guideway surface by a magnetic field. Both West Germany and Japan have worked on Maglev prototypes for several years. The Japanese are experimenting with a system whereby the train is raised up off the track by repulsive magnets within the guideway. The West Germans' attractive system uses electromagnets set on the bottom of the train's undercarriage wings that encircle the edges of the guideway. When current flows through the magnets they are drawn toward a steel rail on the underside of the guideway, and the train lifts. Various other magnetic systems guide the train within the guideway walls, and brake or add speed.

A Japanese high-speed, or "bullet," train travels along an elevated track as it passes through Tokyo. This train has been successful in Japan, where rail-passenger volume is the heaviest in the world.

The German-designed Maglev (Magnetic Levitation Train) rides 1.27 cm (0.5 in) above its track, lifted and guided by powerful magnets in its undercarriage and propelled by motor elements in the guideway.

In West Germany, a prototype Maglev speeds around a 25-km (15.5-mi) track at 300 km/h (186 mph). Other experimental Maglevs have been built, and although inherent design problems are slowing their development (for example, the attractive Maglev must maintain a precise gap of 1.3 cm/0.5 in between the magnets and the steel rail, or the train will stop), Maglev enthusiasts see their invention as the solution to comfortable, economic, almost maintenance-free rapid travel, especially within urban areas.   JOHN F. STOVER

Bibliography: Allen, Cecil J., *Modern Railways* (1959; repr. 1973); Ball, Don, *America's Railroads: The Second Generation* (1979); Barwell, F. T., *Automation and Control in Transport* (1983); Course, Edwin, *Railways Then and Now* (1979); De Fontgalland, Bernard, *World Railway Systems* (1984); Hastings, Paul, *Railroads: An International History* (1972); Freeman, Allen G., *Railways: Past, Present, and Future* (1982); Jensen, Oliver, *The American Heritage History of Railroads in America* (1975); Nock, Oswald S., ed., *The Encyclopedia of Railroads* (1977); MacAvoy, Paul W., and Snow, John W., eds., *Railroad Revitalization and Regulatory Reform* (1977); Mercer, Lloyd, *Railroads and Land Grant Policy* (1982); Ransom, P. J., *Archaeology of Railways* (1981); Saunders, Richard, *The Railroad Mergers and the Coming of Conrail* (1978); Stover, John F., *The Life and Decline of the American Railroad* (1970).

Railway Brotherhoods

Railway Brotherhoods is a collective term for the several railroad labor organizations; most of them were founded as brotherhoods or orders rather than unions because they were originally conceived of as mutual-benefit insurance associations and professional or fraternal societies.

When these organizations were founded (the first in 1863) in the second half of the 19th century, railroad operating employees (engineers or engine-drivers, firemen, brakemen, conductors and, to a lesser extent, telegraphers and clerks) were something of an elite among industrial workers. Highly trained and skilled, they commanded and usually received good wages for their relatively hazardous work; because the work was dangerous—fatal or maiming crashes, fires, and yard accidents were much more common then than now—strong feelings of professional kinship developed, as did a common inability to buy expensive life and burial insurance. These factors, plus the fact that trade unionism was young in the United States and suspect in some eyes, led to the creation of the first brotherhoods as fraternal organizations.

All brotherhoods were pushed from their original fraternalism toward trade-union militancy and then toward industrial unionism. By the 1920s all were functioning as trade unions as well as brotherhoods. The term *the Brotherhoods* eventually came to mean all railroad labor unions, although one, the Switchmen's Union of North America (SUNA; founded 1894), does not trace itself back to an actual brotherhood.

Rail employment has declined since World War II and so has brotherhood membership. In 1969 the principal brotherhoods—the Brotherhood of Railway Trainmen, the Brotherhood of Locomotive Firemen and Engineers, the Order of Railway Conductors, and the SUNA—merged into the United Transportation Union. In 1986 the union had 123,000 members.   THOMAS K. WAGNER

Bibliography: Fink, Gary M., ed., *Labor Unions* (1977); Petersen, Florence, *American Labor Unions*, 2d ed. (1963).

rain: see PRECIPITATION   (weather).

rain forest: see JUNGLE AND RAIN FOREST.

rain shadow effect

The rain shadow effect, created by mountain barriers, results in lower amounts of precipitation on the mountain side away from the wind (leeward) than on the side from which the wind is coming (windward).

The effect is most evident in regions where prominent mountain ranges lie roughly perpendicular to the direction of prevailing winds and storm tracks. Air rising up the windward slopes of mountains (orographic lifting) expands and cools; these characteristics help to induce cloud formation and ORO-GRAPHIC PRECIPITATION. Consequently, air reaching the leeward side is drier and becomes warmer as it descends. Cloudiness and rainfall are reduced for some distance from the mountains on the leeward side, in the rain shadow.

rainbow

A rainbow is a colored arc in the sky, occurring when the Sun's rays shine upon falling rain. Every rainbow is a full circle; the full circle of arc cannot be seen from the ground but may be observed from an airplane. The center of the circle is always at a point in the sky opposite the Sun. The size of the visible portion of the rainbow depends on the altitude of the Sun, being largest when the Sun is at the horizon. Because the radius of a rainbow is 42°, it cannot be seen when the altitude of the Sun is greater than 42°; no part of the rainbow would be above the horizon. A rainbow exhibits the colors of the spectrum—the inner part is always violet and the outer red. Occasionally a second, larger arc (50° radius) is seen with the colors reversed.

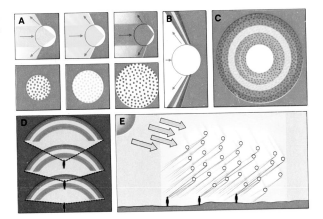

A rainbow is created when rays of sunlight are bent by atmospheric water particles acting as prisms. Each color within the ray of white light is refracted at a different angle, forming successively wider bands of color (A). Together these bands produce a full spectrum (B). Spectra from many raindrops combine to form a circular pattern, the rainbow (C). Only a short segment of the circle is visible to an earthbound observer. The position of this arc in the sky varies according to the viewer's position, but its angular size is always the same (D). A cross section (E) shows that all bands of a given color refract in the same direction relative to the source of light, the Sun.

A rainbow is a result of internal reflections of the Sun's rays by the individual drops of water. The second rainbow is caused by rays that undergo a second internal reflection. The coloring of the rainbow is a result of the dispersion of the Sun's rays into its component colors by the water drops.   J. W. BLAKER

Bibliography: Graham, F. Lanier, ed., *The Rainbow Book*, rev. ed. (1979); Greenler, Robert, *Rainbows, Halos and Glories* (1980); Klika, Thom, *Rainbows* (1979); Nussenzveig, H. M., "Theory of the Rainbow," *Scientific American*, April 1977.

See also: DISPERSION, PHYSICS; REFRACTION.

Rainbow, The

One of D. H. LAWRENCE's greatest novels, *The Rainbow* (1915) describes the lives of three generations of the Brangwen family, concentrating on the marriages of various Brangwens. Throughout the novel, the image of the rainbow symbolizes the characters' search for self-fulfillment. The novel was originally withdrawn by the publisher in response to objections to its frank treatment of sexuality.   R. M. FORD

Bibliography: Clark, Colin, *D. H. Lawrence, The Rainbow, and Women in Love* (1969).

Rainer, Yvonne

Yvonne Rainer, b. San Francisco, 1934, is one of the most important innovators in MODERN DANCE. After composition studies with Ann Halprin and Robert Dunn, she helped found the Judson Dance Theater in 1962, where she performed many works using nontechnical movement and organized on principles of chance. Rainer's *Trio A* (1966) defined a new dance genre of unaccented, tasklike phrases presented in simple geometric floor patterns. Later works combined film, props, and spoken texts with both old and recent dances; *Continuous Project—Altered Daily* (1970) was an inclusive study of the process of dance making rather than a finished dance product. Rainer has adapted her materials to narrative cinema by writing and directing several feature-length films, including *Film about a Woman Who . . .* (1974).   JOHN HOWELL

Bibliography: Rainer, Yvonne, *Work 1961–73* (1974).

Rainier, Mount   [ruh-neer']

Mount Rainier (4,392 m/14,410 ft) forms the heart of Mount Rainier National Park, Washington. A dormant volcano in the Cascade Range, it has been carved by many glaciers. George Vancouver sighted the mountain in 1792 and named it for fellow navigator Peter Rainier.

Rainier III, Prince of Monaco   [ren-yay']

Prince Rainier, b. May 31, 1923, succeeded his grandfather, Prince Louis II Goyon de Matignon-Grimaldi, as ruler of Monaco on May 5, 1949. On Apr. 18, 1956, he married Grace KELLY, the U.S. film actress. She died in 1982.

rainmaking: see WEATHER MODIFICATION.

Rainwater, James

Leo James Rainwater, b. Council, Idaho, Dec. 9, 1917, d. May 31, 1986, shared the 1975 Nobel Prize for physics for his 1950 explanation of the structure of a distorted nucleus, a model that forms the basis of present-day nuclear theory. A 1939 graduate of the California Institute of Technology, Rainwater worked on the Manhattan Project, received his Ph.D. from Columbia University in 1946—where he was a professor of physics from 1952 to 1986—and served as director of the Nevis Laboratory between 1957 and 1961.   MICHAEL MEO

raisin

Raisins are grapes that have been dried, usually in sunlight. Grapes used for raisins must be densely fleshed and have a high sugar content. The most important varieties are Thompson seedless, a white grape that produces the raisin known as Sultanina and Oval Kishmish; the ancient grape variety Muscat of Alexandria, a white, seeded grape producing raisins that are large and meaty and are often sold in clusters; and Black Corinth, which yields the small raisins that are marketed as Zante Currants. Among the world's largest producers of raisins are Turkey, the United States (particularly the state of California), Greece, Australia, and Iran.

In California raisin grapes are harvested and spread evenly in clusters on paper trays laid between the vine rows. When the grapes are brown and shriveled, they are put through a mechanical shaker that removes sand and other debris and separates the berries from the clusters. Raisins are dried to 13 to 15 percent moisture before being packed. To produce golden-bleached raisins, Thompson seedless grapes are dipped in a hot lye solution to crack the skins; then washed and exposed to the fumes of burning sulfur for 2 to 4 hours; and, finally, dehydrated. This process produces a yellow raisin that is used primarily in baked foods. In Spain and Australia Muscat raisins are dipped in a caustic solution to which olive oil has been added. In California, Black Corinth is often sun-dried on the vine and then machine harvested.

Approximately 4 to 4½ tons of grapes are required to produce 1 ton of raisins. An excellent concentrated food, raisins are rich in sugar and iron.   ROBERT J. WEAVER

Bibliography: Weaver, Robert J., *Grape Growing* (1976); Winkler, A. J., et al., *General Viticulture* (1974).

Raisin in the Sun, A

The best-known play by the black American playwright Lorraine HANSBERRY, *A Raisin in the Sun* (1959) depicts the dreams, frustrations, and ultimate spiritual triumph of a black family, the Youngers, who attempt to move into a white-dominated Chicago suburb after World War II. The first commercially successful drama to depict black family life sympathetically and the first play by a black woman to be produced on Broadway, it won the New York Drama Critics' Circle Award in 1959 and was made into a film (1961) and a musical (1973). The film received a special award at the Cannes Film Festival.

rajah

Rajah, or raj (from the Sanskrit *rajan*, "king"), is a Hindu title once given to Indian kings and princes but also used later by lesser rulers and by tribal chiefs. The appellation is frequently assumed by rulers and chiefs in Malaysia. The title *maharajah* ("great king") was often taken by Indian princes under the British rule.

Rajasthan   [rah'-juh-stahn]

Rajasthan, a state in northwestern India, covers an area of 342,214 km^2 (132,130 mi^2). The state has a population of 34,261,862 (1981). The capital is JAIPUR. The Aravalli Hills cross Rajasthan from southwest to northeast, and the THAR DESERT covers most of the northwest. Rajasthan's principal rivers are the Chambal, the Banas, and the Luni. Cotton, grains, and vegetables are grown in the southeast. Industry is based on petroleum, wool, minerals, chemicals, and handicrafts.

Most of the state consists of the former historic region of Rajputana. The Rajputs ruled the area from the 7th century until it came under Mogul control in the 16th century. After 1817, Rajputana gradually came under British protection. In 1947 it was reorganized as the independent Union of Rajasthan, which became part of India in 1950.

Bibliography: Hallissey, Robert C., *The Rajput Rebellion Against Aurangzeb: A Study of the Mughal Empire in Seventeenth-Century India* (1977); Matheson, Sylvia, *Rajasthan: Land Of Kings* (1984).

Rajput   [rahj'-poot]

The Rajputs are one of the largest CASTES in northwest India, mostly concentrated in the state of Rajasthan, with lesser numbers in Madhya Pradesh and Gujarat. They claim *Kshatriya* or warrior status—a claim reflected in their style of life, for unlike other high caste groups, the Rajputs freely indulge in meat-eating and the consumption of alcohol. Historically, the Rajputs came to the fore during the 8th century, when they founded a number of princely states. Later, the Rajputs came under the control of the MARATHAS, and after 1818 under British rule.

Despite their claims to warrior status, most Rajputs are peasant cultivators today. Rajputs are organized in status-ranked groups that trace ancestry through the male line. Most marriages are between women from lower-status groups and higher-status men. Status claims of Rajputs are made clear through marriage alliances, and therefore marriages involve large dowries and heavy expenditures on ceremonials. Although most Rajputs are Hindus, some are Muslim. In the 1980s the Rajputs numbered more than 14 million.

HILARY STANDING AND R. L. STIRRAT

Bibliography: Lewis, Oscar, *Village Life in Northern India* (1958); Hitchcock, J., and Minturn, L., *The Rajputs of Khalapur* (1966); Sharma, Dasharatha, *Lectures on Rajput History and Culture* (1971).

Rajput painting: see INDIAN ART AND ARCHITECTURE.

Rákosi, Mátyás   [rah'-koh-shee, maht'-yahs]

Mátyás Rákosi, b. Mar. 14, 1892, d. Feb. 5, 1971, dominated the Communist regime of Hungary after World War II. A Stalinist, Rákosi was exiled in the USSR during World War II. He returned to Hungary in 1944 with the victorious Soviet troops. Becoming secretary of the Communist party and controlling the security police, Rákosi gained complete control of Hungary by 1949 and was premier from 1952 to 1953. His regime was characterized by police terror, collectivization of agriculture, and nationalization of the economy. After the death of Joseph Stalin, Rákosi was replaced as premier by the reformer Imre NAGY. Rákosi ousted Nagy from power in 1955 but was quickly stripped of all political offices by Moscow. When the Hungarian Revolution broke out in 1956, Rákosi fled to the USSR.

Raleigh   [rah'-lee]

Raleigh is the capital of North Carolina and the seat of Wake County. Located in the east central part of the state, it has a population of 150,255 (1980). The city's industries manufacture food products, textiles, and electrical machinery. Raleigh is part of the Research Triangle complex, devoted to cultural, scientific, and educational research. Notable historical buildings include the Greek Revival-style capitol and U.S. president Andrew Johnson's birthplace, now a national historic shrine. The city is the seat of North Carolina State University (1887), Shaw University, and several other colleges. The North Carolina Museum of Art is also located there.

Raleigh was named for Sir Walter Raleigh. The area was chosen as the site of the state capital in 1788, and a town was laid out in 1792. The first capitol (1792–94) burned in 1831, and the present building was completed in 1840. During the Civil War the city was occupied by Gen. William Tecumseh Sherman's Union troops on Apr. 14, 1865.

Raleigh, Sir Walter   [raw'-lee]

Sir Walter Raleigh, English courtier, military adventurer, and poet, was a favorite of Queen Elizabeth I. He organized the first English colonizing venture in the New World, the ill-fated settlement on Roanoke Island, Va. Imprisoned by James I in 1603, Raleigh was finally released (1616) to lead an expedition, his second, to find gold in South America. He returned without gold and was executed, ostensibly for attacking a Spanish settlement.

Sir Walter Raleigh, or Ralegh, b. c.1552, English military commander, writer, and favorite of Queen ELIZABETH I, organized an early and unsuccessful attempt to found a settlement in North America—the so-called lost colony of Roanoke. The son of a country gentleman, Raleigh was educated at Oxford and took part in military operations in France as early as 1569. In 1578 he sailed on a voyage of exploration under command of his half brother, Sir Humphrey Gilbert.

Raleigh was a favorite courtier of Elizabeth from about 1581 until her death in 1603; she knighted him in 1584 and awarded him large estates and lucrative patents. The story that he once spread his cloak on the ground for the queen to walk on so that she would not muddy her feet is a legend but may be true. In 1584, Raleigh obtained a patent authorizing

colonization of lands in North America; he christened these lands Virginia in honor of the Virgin Queen. Raleigh never visited Virginia himself, and the attempt at settlement on Roanoke Island (in present North Carolina) failed. He was unsuccessful, too, in an attempt to plant a Protestant colony in southern Ireland.

Raleigh was out of Elizabeth's favor for a time in the 1590s because of her displeasure over his marriage to one of her maids of honor, Elizabeth Throckmorton. He was imprisoned briefly in 1592 but was later restored to the queen's good graces. He distinguished himself as a naval commander in expeditions to the Guiana coast of northeastern South America (1595), Spain (1596), and the Azores (1597). He was governor of the Isle of Jersey (1600–03).

Raleigh fell into serious disfavor when JAMES I succeeded to the throne; his political enemies had convinced the new king that Raleigh had conspired against James's succession. Raleigh was deprived of his offices and found guilty of conspiracy in 1603, then imprisoned in the Tower of London for 13 years. In 1616 he persuaded James to allow him to undertake another expedition to search for gold in South America. When this expedition failed, he was sent back to the Tower, partly because Spain demanded his punishment for sacking a Spanish settlement in Guiana. He was then executed, under the original sentence, on Oct. 29, 1618.

Raleigh was active as a member of Parliament under Elizabeth and was a great patron of writers, especially Edmund Spenser. He wrote poetry and prose, particularly during the period of his imprisonment. His most famous work is probably his unfinished *History of the World* (1614).

STANFORD E. LEHMBERG

Bibliography: Adamson, Jack H., and Folland, H. F., *The Shepherd of the Ocean* (1969); Lacey, Robert, *Sir Walter Raleigh* (1974); Rowse, A. L., *Sir Walter Raleigh: His Family and Private Life* (1962; repr. 1975); Winton, John, *Sir Walter Raleigh* (1975).

Ramadan   [rah-mah-dahn']

The 9th month of the Muslim year, Ramadan is a period during which all the faithful must fast between dawn and dusk. Observance of the fast is one of the five "pillars" of ISLAM. Because a lunar calendar is used, Ramadan falls at different times each year. It is sacred as the month in which the Koran was revealed to Muhammad.

Ramakrishna   [rah-mah-krish'-nuh]

Ramakrishna, or Paramahansa Sri Ramakrishna, b. Feb. 20, 1836, d. Aug. 16, 1886, is perhaps the most famous Indian holy man of recent times. A Bengali Brahmin originally named Gadadhar Chatterji, he experienced ecstatic mystic visions as a child. He became a priest at the temple of Kali in Dakshineswar near Calcutta and experimented with many different religious practices, including Tantra, Vedanta, Vaishnava cults, Islam, and Christianity. He pronounced that all religions were directed toward the same God along different paths.

Although Ramakrishna was not a scholar, he was praised by his pupils for illuminating old truths, and his influence on those who visited him was profound. His wife, Sarada-devi, and other pupils, such as VIVEKANANDA and Keshab Chandra Sen, spread his ideas. Vivekananda founded (1897) the Ramakrishna Mission, which is committed to social service in India and the teaching of Ramakrishna's ideas in its many centers abroad.

KARL H. POTTER

Bibliography: Diwakar, R. R., *Paramahansa Sri Ramakrishna* (1956); Isherwood, Christopher, *Ramakrishna and His Disciples* (1965).

Raman, Sir Chandrasekhara Venkata   [rah'-muhn, chuhn'-druh-sek-ah-ruh veng'-kuh-tuh]

The Indian physicist Sir Chandrasekhara Venkata Raman, b. Nov. 7, 1888, d. Nov. 21, 1970, worked mainly in optics and acoustics, fields to which he was drawn by a deep, almost mystical fascination for everything related to sight and sound. His most memorable achievement, honored by the 1930 Nobel Prize for physics, was the discovery (1928) that when visible light is scattered, the scattered light undergoes shifts in wavelength. The Raman effect lent support to the photon theory of light and furnished a valuable tool for probing the nature of matter.

ROBERT SILLIMAN

Ramanujan, Srinivasa   [rah-mah'-nuh-juhn]

Srinivasa Aaiyangar Ramanujan, b. Dec. 22, 1887, d. Apr. 26, 1920, was one of India's greatest mathematical geniuses. He made substantial contributions to the analytical theory of numbers and to work on elliptic functions, continued fractions, and infinite series. Basically self-taught in mathematics, Ramanujan was given a fellowship at the University of Madras after publication (1911) of a brilliant research paper on Bernoulli's numbers. In 1914 he went to Trinity College, Cambridge, to collaborate with an English mathematician, G. H. Hardy (1877–1947), producing some of his most important work there. In ill health, he returned to India in 1919 and died there the following year. He left a number of unpublished notebooks filled with theorems that have continued to be mined by mathematicians thereafter.

Bibliography: Berndt, B. C., *Ramanujan's Notebooks, Part 1* (1985); Hardy, G. H., *Ramanujan*, 3d ed. (1978).

Ramapithecus   [rah-muh-pith'-uh-kuhs]

In 1934 the American geologist G. E. Lewis discovered in the Siwalik Hills of north India fragmentary jaws and teeth of an extinct apelike creature that he named *Ramapithecus.* Lewis considered this find to represent the earliest fossil genus of the hominid (humanlike) line after its divergence from the pongid family of the apes (see PREHISTORIC HUMANS). In the 1960s, Elwyn SIMONS identified several additional *Ramapithecus* specimens discovered in the Siwaliks earlier in the century. In reanalyzing the material recovered by Lewis, Simons also noted the hominidlike features of the fossils, such as the shortened snout and the reduced size of the front teeth.

Today *Ramapithecus* fossils are known from sites in China, Turkey, Pakistan, and Kenya, as well as in the area of the original discoveries in north India. Fossils discovered (1975) in northeast Hungary and closely resembling those of *Ramapithecus* have been assigned to a new category, *Rudapithecus.* At the Fort Ternan site in Kenya absolute dating methods have indicated the age of the *Ramapithecus* fossils to be about 14 million years. Elsewhere, *Ramapithecus* fossils appear to date from between 12 and 8 million years ago. Because of the poor quality and limited range of the fossils (only jaws and teeth have been recovered), many paleoanthropologists continue to dispute the exact classification of *Ramapithecus.*

ALAN MANN AND NANCY MINUGH

Bibliography: Wood, B. A., et al., eds., *Major Topics in Primate and Human Evolution* (1986).

Ramayana   [rah-mah'-yuh-nuh]

Unlike the *Mahabharata,* the other great Sanskrit epic of India, the *Ramayana* appears to be the work of one person—the legendary sage Valmiki, who probably composed it in the 3d century BC. Its best-known recension (the work of Tulsi Das, 1532–1623) consists of 24,000 rhymed couplets of 16-syllable lines, organized into 7 books. The poem incorporates many ancient legends and draws on the sacred books of the Vedas. It describes the efforts of Kosala's heir, Rama, to regain his throne and rescue his wife, Sita, from the demon King of Lanka.

SCOTT FISCHER

Rambert, Dame Marie   [rahm-bair']

Dame Marie Rambert, originally Cyvia Rambam, b. Warsaw, Feb. 20, 1888, d. June 12, 1982, was, with Dame Ninette de VALOIS, the chief pioneering force in British ballet. Starting in modern dance, she studied with Emile Jaques DALCROZE and was recommended to Serge Diaghilev as an assistant to Vaslav NIJINSKY. Becoming interested in classical ballet, she later joined the Ballets Russes de Serge Diaghilev. In 1920 she founded a ballet school in London, followed in 1930 by the

Ballet Rambert, a ballet company. Among the choreographers who began under Rambert were Frederick Ashton, Antony Tudor, and Andrée Howard. In 1966 the company abandoned virtually all of its existing repertory and devoted itself thereafter to modern dance. Rambert's autobiography was published in 1972.

Bibliography: Bradley, Lionel, *Sixteen Years of Ballet Rambert, 1930–1946* (1946); Clarke, Mary, *Dancers of Mercury* (1962).

Rambouillet, Marquise de   [rahm-boo-ee-ay']

Founder of the most respected literary salon in Paris, Catherine de Vivonne, marquise de Rambouillet, b. 1588, d. Dec. 27, 1665, greatly influenced the development of French literature. Married at the age of 12 to Charles d'Angennes (later the marquis de Rambouillet), she found the court of Henry IV too coarse and began to invite prominent persons in society and the arts to her Paris home, which came to be known as the Hôtel de Rambouillet. Her circle included Racan, Madame de Sévigné, François de Malherbe, François de La Rochefoucauld, Madame de La Fayette, Cardinal Richelieu, and many others. Similar salons sprang up elsewhere and gave French writing in its classical period greater homogeneity than it could otherwise have had. The pretensions of the salons and their devotees became subjects of satire, as in Molière's *The Affected Young Ladies* (1659; Eng. trans., 1915).

Rameau, Jean Philippe   [rah-moh']

The most important French composer and theorist of the 18th century, Jean Philippe Rameau, baptized Sept. 25, 1683, d. Sept. 12, 1764, is best known for his stage works and keyboard music. After studying under his father and, briefly, in Milan, Rameau returned to France in 1701 and held several important posts as organist before settling permanently in Paris in 1722. During his last six years, Rameau engaged in bitter polemics about musical style with the philosophers D'Alembert and Rousseau.

Rameau's preeminence as a music theorist is based on 12 treatises and many articles written from 1722 (the year of his ground-breaking *Treatise on Harmony*) to 1762. From 1733 to 1757, Rameau composed his most important stage works. Chief among these compositions are the tragic operas *Hippolyte et Aricie* (1733), *Castor et Pollux* (1737), *Dardanus* (1739), and *Zoroastre* (1749); the opera-ballets *Les Indes galantes* (1735) and *Les Fêtes d'Hébé* (1739); and the lyric comedy *Platée* (1745). Although Rameau's dramatic music was modeled on that of his predecessors, such as Lully, its more complex harmony and the expanded role of the orchestra point directly to high-classic opera. Rameau also composed harpsichord pieces comprising three collections (1706, 1724, c.1728), four motets, six cantatas, and a set of chamber works.

JAMES R. ANTHONY

Bibliography: Anthony, James R., *French Baroque Music,* rev. ed. (1978); Girdlestone, Cuthbert, *Jean-Philippe Rameau,* rev. ed. (1969); Rameau, J. P., *Complete Theoretical Writings,* 6 vols., ed. by E. R. Jacobi (1967–72), and *Treatise on Harmony* (1971).

Ramée, Marie Louise de la: see OUIDA.

ramie   [ram'-ee]

Ramie is a strong, soft fiber from the bark of a nettlelike plant indigenous to East India and China. The plant, *Bohmeria nivea* of the nettle, or Uticaceae, family is grown in semitropical climates with abundant rainfall. The fiber is used for twine, thread, and packing. Cloth made of ramie, often mixed with other fibers, is used for tapestries, upholstery, trimmings, and toweling. The fiber is stripped from the bark by hand in the Far East, and by machine elsewhere. Stronger than cotton or linen, it does not shrink and takes dyes well but lacks elasticity and resistance to abrasion.

ISABEL B. WINGATE

ramjet

Also called the stato-reactor or athodyd (a shortened form of aerothermodynamic duct), the ramjet is in principle one of

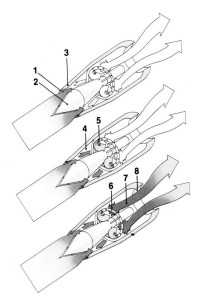

A ramjet contains a specially shaped duct with apertures at both ends. Air enters the intake aperture (1) at supersonic velocities. A cone (2) deflects the resulting shock waves onto the intake lips (3) and channels the air into the body of the duct (4). Here the air is slowed down to subsonic velocities, compressed, mixed with fuel from a spray bar (5), and ignited (6). The combustion produces exhaust gases (7), which exit through the nozzle at the rear of the duct (8) in a propulsive jet, boosting the engine forward and causing it to take in more air.

the simplest possible propulsion units. It is essentially a duct open at front and rear (an early nickname was "the flying stovepipe"). At high speed, air is rammed into the front of the duct and is highly compressed by the varying profile of the interior, the profile depending on whether the airflow is to be subsonic or supersonic. At the region of peak pressure and minimum velocity, the fuel is injected into the airflow in a combustion section, where it is ignited. Temperatures can be higher than in gas-turbine engines because there is no turbine to impose such a limitation. The intensely hot gas then expands to highly supersonic speed through the divergent propelling nozzle. Unlike gas-turbine jet engines, the ramjet can be used only to propel moving atmospheric vehicles; its main drawbacks are that it cannot start from rest by itself and that its efficiency is poor except at supersonic speeds.

Although its promise seemed great at the end of World War II, the ramjet has been used in few aircraft. Some of the fastest planes, however, such as the Lockheed SR-71A, cruise with afterburning turbojets behaving virtually as ramjets; the turbojet portion upstream reduces performance at speeds greater than Mach 3, but without it the airplane could not take off. Up to the mid-1980s ramjet missiles have been rare, examples being the U.S. Air Force Bomarc and the R.A.F. Bloodhound. Various types, especially combined with solid-fuel rockets in so-called ram-rockets, are under development for missile propulsion.   BILL GUNSTON

Ramón y Cajal, Santiago [rah-mohn' ee kah-hahl']

The Spanish physician and histologist Santiago Ramón y Cajal, b. May 1, 1852, d. Oct. 17, 1934, made many important contributions to knowledge of the brain and nervous system. By refining the method of staining nervous tissue developed by Camillo GOLGI, he was able to study the detailed structure of the brain's cerebrum and cerebellum and to establish that individual nerve cells (neurons) are the basic structure of the nervous system. He also established the relationship between nerve cell body and nerve fibers and described the morphology and connective processes of nerve fibers in the brain's gray matter. Ramón y Cajal shared the 1906 Nobel Prize for physiology or medicine with Golgi.

Bibliography: Ramón y Cajal, Santiago, *Recollections of My Life,* trans. by E. H. Craigie (1937; repr. 1966).

Rampal, Jean Pierre

The French flutist and musicologist Jean Pierre Rampal, b. Jan. 7, 1922, whose delicate phrasing and powerful breathing produce luscious and sonorous tones, is equally at ease inter-preting the 18th- and 19th-century romantics and the moderns. After stints as solo flutist first with the Vichy (1946–50) and Paris (1956–62) Operas, Rampal's later career has combined concert performances, recitals, and a vigorous recording schedule.

Ramsay, Allan (painter) [ram'-zee]

Allan Ramsay, b. Oct. 13, 1713, d. Aug. 10, 1784, was a Scottish portrait painter and the son of Allan Ramsay, the poet. After visiting (1736–38) Italy, Ramsay settled in London but also kept a studio in Edinburgh. He was immediately successful; his fine draftsmanship and charming coloring ensured portraits of great elegance and refinement. Later on, most of the work done in his studios was executed by assistants while Ramsay devoted himself to scholarship and to correspondence. As official painter to George III, Ramsay was responsible for the production of many replicas of royal portraits; these paintings were generally done by assistants. His masterpieces include *The Painter's Wife* (1755–60), *Jean Jacques Rousseau* (1766; both in the National Gallery of Scotland, Edinburgh), and *Lord Chesterfield* (1765; National Portrait Gallery, London). Ramsay dislocated his arm in 1778, forcing him to abandon painting; existing commissions were completed by Philip Reinagle, his pupil.   RAYMOND LISTER

Bibliography: Smart, Alastair, *The Life and Art of Allan Ramsay* (1952).

Ramsay, Allan (poet)

The Scottish poet Allan Ramsay, b. Oct. 15, 1686, d. Jan. 7, 1758, was the author of a pastoral drama, *The Gentle Shepherd* (1725), and an anthologist who helped to reawaken interest in early Scottish literature. A bookseller, he opened the first circulating library in Scotland. His collection of poetry written by Scots before 1600, *The Ever Green* (1724), included works by Robert Henryson and William Dunbar. It helped to inspire later works, notably the poetry of Robert Burns.

Bibliography: Martin, Burns, *Allan Ramsay* (1931; repr. 1972).

Ramsay, Sir William

The British physical chemist Sir William Ramsay, b. Oct. 2, 1852, d. July 23, 1916, received the 1904 Nobel Prize for chemistry for his discovery of the INERT GASES. From a conversation with Lord RAYLEIGH in 1894, Ramsay learned that nitrogen prepared chemically is always lighter than nitrogen prepared from air. Ramsay hypothesized that this results from the existence of some heavier gas in atmospheric nitrogen, and he isolated this new gas, argon, at the same time as Rayleigh. A lighter inert gas, helium, had been observed earlier in the Sun, but in 1895, Ramsay announced the existence of terrestrial helium. Beginning in April 1895, Ramsay worked with Morris W. Travers in a search for other inert gases. By evaporating liquid air and removing oxygen and nitrogen, they found krypton in 1898. From liquid argon they separated a fraction in which they observed spectroscopically the red presence of neon. Later in 1898 they obtained another inert gas, xenon, from the krypton residue. When F. E. Dorn discovered the last inert gas, radon, its atomic weight was determined by Ramsay (1904).   ROBERT J. PARADOWSKI

Bibliography: Travers, Morris W., *A Life of Sir William Ramsay* (1956).

Ramses I, King of Egypt [ram'-seez]

Ramses I, founder of the 19th dynasty of Egyptian kings, reigned between 1320 and 1318 BC. Apparently chosen to succeed by the last pharaoh of the 18th dynasty, Horemheb, in whose army he had been a commander, Ramses planned and started to build the colonnaded hall in the temple at Karnak.

Ramses II, King of Egypt

An Egyptian king (pharaoh) of the 19th dynasty, Ramses II (r. 1304–1237 BC) is remembered for his military campaigns and his extensive building program, the remains of which are still conspicuous. Succeeding his father, SETI I, Ramses pursued a

Ramses II, the third king of the Egyptian 19th dynasty, is depicted in this stone sculpture. His 67-year reign was a time of great prosperity and marked the height of Egyptian military power, culminating in a peace treaty (1283 BC) with the neighboring Hittites.

vigorous foreign policy by attacking the Hittites, the chief opponents of the Egyptian empire in the East. His first campaigns against them (1300–1299 BC) ended in an Egyptian retreat after a violent battle at Kadesh in Syria, during which Ramses narrowly escaped capture. The consequent loss of prestige sparked revolts within the empire, and Ramses could not resume direct hostilities against the Hittites until 1294; the conflicts were finally concluded by a peace treaty in 1283. He also fought in Trans-Jordan and Nubia and fortified the western coast road of Egypt against Libyan invaders.

Ramses was responsible for building many large temples, most notably that at ABU SIMBEL in Nubia. He also founded a new royal capital at Per-Ramesse ("the house of Ramses") in the Nile's eastern delta, where Israelites may have labored before the Exodus. During his long reign, Ramses had more than 100 children, and by his death in 1237, he had outlived 11 sons. He was succeeded by the 12th, Merneptah.

DAVID O'CONNOR

Bibliography: Gardiner, A. H., *Egypt of the Pharaohs* (1961); MacQuitty, William, *Ramesses the Great* (1978).

Ramses III, King of Egypt

Ramses III, a pharaoh of the 20th dynasty, saved Egypt from foreign invasion but failed to solve internal problems—political conspiracies and weakened social structure—that led to the collapse of the Egyptian state 80 years after his death. Succeeding his father, Sethnakhte, in c.1198 BC, Ramses fought off Libyan invasions in 1194 and 1188. In 1191 he also held back a horde of invading SEA PEOPLES of Aegean and west Anatolian origins who had been sweeping down the eastern Mediterranean coast toward Egypt. Despite external successes, royal power declined. The temples became richer and Ramses poorer; he attempted building only one major structure. Government was corrupt and inefficient, and Ramses himself was nearly assassinated before being succeeded by his son Ramses IV about 1166 BC. He was buried in the Valley of the Kings.   DAVID O'CONNOR

Bibliography: Gardiner, A. H., *Egypt of the Pharaohs* (1961).

Ramsey, Michael   [ram'-zee]

The English churchman Arthur Michael Ramsey, b. Nov. 14, 1904, was archbishop of Canterbury from 1961 to 1974. Before becoming primate of the Church of England, he was Regius professor of divinity at Cambridge (1950–52) and archbishop of York (1956–61). Ramsey fostered the ecumenical relations of the Church of England, although a scheme for union with the Methodists was rejected during his primacy. His writings include *God, Christ and the World* (1969).

Ramus, Petrus   [ray'-muhs]

Petrus Ramus (Pierre de la Ramée), b. 1515, d. Aug. 26, 1576, was an influential French anti-Aristotelian logician. His master of arts thesis (1536) was entitled *Quaecumque ab Aristotele dicta essent commentitia esse* (Whatever Aristotle Has Said Is a Fabrication). After receiving his degree from the Collège de Navarre, Paris, he taught at the Collège du Mans, Paris, and continued attacking Aristotle and his modern disciples. In his *Dialecticae partitiones* (Structures of Dialectic, 1543), he created a new two-part logic to replace Aristotle's *Organon*. The orthodox Aristotelians at the University of Paris responded by securing a royal decree (1544) that suppressed Ramus's books and forbade him to teach logic. In 1547 this ban was lifted, and Ramus was appointed (1551) professor of rhetoric and philosophy at the Collège Royal. In 1562 he embraced Calvinism. Leaving France in 1568, he taught successively at Geneva, Lausanne, and Heidelberg. He returned (1570) to Paris, where he was killed during the Saint Bartholomew's Day Massacre.

JOHN P. DOYLE

Bibliography: Ong, Walter J., *Ramus and Talon Inventory* (1958) and *Ramus, Method, the Decay of Dialogue* (1958).

Rand, Ayn   [rand, yn]

A Russian-born American writer who originated a philosophy known as Objectivism, Ayn Rand, b. Feb. 2, 1905, d. Mar. 6, 1982, advocated capitalism in economics and individualism in ethics. Two novels, *The Fountainhead* (1943) and *Atlas Shrugged* (1957), contain the heart of her philosophy: that rational self-interest should be the basis of action and that self-fulfillment is an individual's moral responsibility, with productive achievement the noblest activity. She saw altruism as both a personal and a political weakness. Rand's first work was a popular mystery drama, *The Night of January 16th* (1935). She collected her philosophical writings in *For the New Intellectual* (1961) and from 1962 on, edited a newsletter called *The Ayn Rand Letter*.

Bibliography: Greenberg, Sidney, *Ayn Rand and Alienation* (1977); O'Neill, William F., *With Charity toward None* (1971); Tuccille, Jerome, *It Usually Begins with Ayn Rand: A Libertarian Odyssey* (1972).

Randolph   (family)

The Randolphs rank among the most eminent and influential families in the history of Virginia. The founder of the Virginia Randolphs, **William Randolph**, b. c.1651, d. Apr. 11, 1711, went to the colony of Virginia from Warwickshire, England, about 1673. There he amassed large landholdings and was twice Speaker of the House of Burgesses (1696 and 1698). Through the marriages of his children, the Randolphs became allied with most of the other notable families of Virginia. Both Thomas Jefferson and John Marshall were related, through their mothers, to the Randolphs.

Sir John Randolph, b. Henrico County, Va., 1693, d. Mar. 2, 1737, son of William, continued the Randolph preeminence in politics, serving as king's attorney in Virginia, diplomat, and Speaker of the House of Burgesses (1734–37). His son, **Peyton Randolph**, b. Williamsburg, Va., September 1721, d. Oct. 22, 1775, also served as Speaker of the House of Burgesses—during most of the crucial years prior to the American Revolution. He was the first president of the Continental Congress and chairman of the Virginia Committee of Correspondence. His nephew, **Edmund Randolph**, b. Williamsburg, Va., Aug. 10, 1753, d. Sept. 12, 1813, was appointed aide-de-camp to Gen. George Washington in 1775. After the American Revolution he was prominent in Virginia politics and was the state's governor (1786–88). In 1787 he attended the CON-

Edmund Randolph was the first U.S. attorney-general and later succeeded Thomas Jefferson as secretary of state. Earlier in his career, as governor of Virginia and a delegate to the Constitutional Convention in Philadelphia, Randolph had played an important role in drafting the new U.S. Constitution.

STITUTIONAL CONVENTION and introduced the influential Virginia Plan—also called the Randolph Plan—upon which the final version of the federal Constitution was largely based. He later served (1789–94) as first attorney-general in the new federal government and then as secretary of state (1794–95). **John Randolph of Roanoke**, b. Prince George County, Va., June 2, 1773, d. May 24, 1833, served in the U.S. House of Representatives most of the time between 1799 and 1829 and also served briefly (1825–27) in the U.S. Senate. A fiery orator, he was a champion of individual liberty and state rights.

RICHARD R. BEEMAN

Bibliography: Daniels, Jonathan, *The Randolphs of Virginia* (1972); Eckenrode, Hamilton J., *The Randolphs: The Story of a Virginia Family* (1946); Kirk, Russell, *John Randolph of Roanoke* (1964); Reardon, John J., *Edmund Randolph: A Biography* (1974).

Randolph, A. Philip

Labor leader Asa Philip Randolph, b. Crescent City, Fla., Apr. 15, 1889, d. May 16, 1979, organized (1925) the Brotherhood of Sleeping Car Porters, which helped carry American blacks into the mainstream of the U.S. labor movement. As a student in New York City, he became involved in labor and socialist movements. He began (1917) a monthly magazine, *The Messenger,* which was later an important source of communications for the railway union and which encouraged greater black militancy. Randolph also worked for civil rights and influenced the organizing of President Franklin D. Roosevelt's Fair Employment Practices Committee to protect blacks in industry and government. In 1955, Randolph became vice-pres-

A. Philip Randolph organized the Brotherhood of Sleeping Car Porters in an era when black workers were often excluded from unions. He became a leader in the U.S. labor movement and a spokesman for civil rights, lobbying for an end to racial bias in employment.

ident of the newly merged AFL-CIO. He directed the 1963 March on Washington for Jobs and Freedom.

Bibliography: Anderson, Jervis, *A. Philip Randolph* (1973); Davis, Daniel S., *Mr. Black Labor: The Story of A. Philip Randolph* (1972); Harris, William H., *Keeping the Faith: A. Philip Randolph, Milton P. Webster, and the Brotherhood of Sleeping Car Porters, 1925–37* (1977).

Randolph, Edward

Edward Randolph, b. 1632, d. April 1703, was a controversial and unpopular British colonial official in America. Sent (1676) by the Lords of Trade to investigate Massachusetts, he submitted a critical report of the colony's government that led to the revocation (1684) of its charter. Appointed (1678) surveyor of customs for New England, Randolph antagonized the colonies by his attempts to enforce the British trade laws. In 1685 he was named secretary of the newly created Dominion of New England, a union that incensed many colonists. After the GLORIOUS REVOLUTION (1688–89), which deposed James II in England, the Dominion was overthrown, and Randolph was jailed and returned to England. He soon gained favor there, however, and served (1691–1703) as surveyor-general of all the American colonies.

OSCAR ZEICHNER

Bibliography: Hall, Michael G., *Edward Randolph and the American Colonies, 1676–1703* (1960).

random variable

A random variable is a numerical quantity associated with a chance-influenced experiment or phenomenon. The value it takes is not known with certainty before the experiment is performed or the phenomenon is observed, although the probabilities of all its possible values or outcomes are assumed to be fixed by some PROBABILITY law, which may or may not be known to the experimenter. Thus, if an experiment involved tossing a coin six times, the number of heads observed would be a random variable; it would not be known in advance exactly how many heads would be observed, but the probability of, for example, four heads being observed would be a known quantity.

Often, the underlying probability law that describes the distribution of a random variable is not known beforehand; in such a case, the observed value of the random variable can be used to give information about the underlying distribution. This is the problem dealt with in statistical INFERENCE.

GEOFFREY S. WATSON

Bibliography: Feller, William, *An Introduction to Probability Theory and Its Applications,* 2 vols. (1968, 1971).

random walk

The random walk is the simplest example of a STOCHASTIC PROCESS. Consider a particle that can occupy positions at distances $0, \pm 1, \pm 2, \ldots$ from some starting point. Suppose that at each instant of a sequence of times, the particle is moved one step to the right or left, with probabilities p and $q = 1 - p$, respectively; the sequence of positions is called a random walk. The random walk has been used as a discrete approximation of BROWNIAN MOTION and as a model for risk-taking situations—many economists currently assume that the stock market behaves as a random walk—and it has diverse applications.

A classic problem that represents many interesting questions is called the gambler's ruin problem. Suppose that two gamblers begin with fortunes a and b, respectively. They make a sequence of bets, each gambling a unit of money, such that at each bet the first gambler has probability p of winning. The probability that the first gambler finishes with all the money may be calculated; if $p = q = \frac{1}{2}$, the probability is $a/(a + b)$.

GEOFFREY S. WATSON

Bibliography: Feller, William, *An Introduction to Probability Theory and Its Applications,* 2 vols. (1968, 1971).

range: see FUNCTION.

range finder

A range finder, often used in military and photographic equipment, is an instrument that determines the distance from a home reference point to a distant object by optical and trigonometric means. Light from the object passes directly through a fixed, semitransparent mirror so that a person can see and keep the image of the object in view. Light from the object also travels to another mirror, which reflects the image to the semitransparent mirror. The viewer sees two images superimposed on one another, and the angle of the second mirror is adjusted until the direct image and the indirect one coincide. The distance between the two mirrors is fixed by the equipment so that the angle to which the second mirror is adjusted can be determined. The distance between the object and the instrument is then calculated by dividing the distance between the two mirrors by the tangent of that angle.

The accuracy of the measurement is limited mainly by how well the viewer can get the images to coincide and also by the distance between the mirrors, which must be maximized within practical limits of the equipment.

In more complex range finders, the mirrors may be replaced by penta prisms, which reduce problems of alignment. Telescopes may be built into the system to provide magnification, and a coincidence prism may be used to split the field of view into a top and a bottom half that the viewer must bring into coincidence. RADAR is a nonoptical range finder, using high-frequency radio waves instead of light to determine the distance of an object.   DOUGLAS M. CONSIDINE

Ranger

Ranger was a series of U.S. spacecraft that were designed to provide, in the 20 minutes before impact on the Moon, about 300 close-up photos per minute of the lunar surface that could be used for increased accuracy in mapping, for studies of small-scale structure, and for the initial stage of selecting landing sites (see also LUNAR ORBITER; SURVEYOR) for the manned APOLLO PROGRAM missions to follow. The best Earth-based photos of the Moon up to 1963, taken with the 120-in (305-cm) telescope at the Lick Observatory, had a resolution

In 1964, Ranger 7 transmitted close-up pictures of the Moon for about 13 minutes before striking the lunar surface at a speed of more than 9,000 km/h (5,600 mph). Numbers indicate: omnidirectional antenna (1); aperture (2), 33 cm (13 in), for camera lenses; solar panel latches (3); solar panels (4), capable of supplying 200 watts of power; battery (5); attitude-control gas storage (6); high-gain dish antenna (7); attitude-control electronics (8); conical camera shroud (9), 1.5 m (5 ft) high, housing six television cameras.

of about 270 m (890 ft). By comparison, the best Ranger photos, taken by *Ranger 9* just before impact, had a resolution of approximately 0.25 m (10 in).

The Spacecraft. The prime contractor for the Ranger program was the Jet Propulsion Laboratory of the California Institute of Technology. The spacecraft, which weighed about 365 kg (810 lb), had a hexagonal base about 1.5 m (5 ft) in diameter. A 2.5-m-high (8.25-ft) telescopelike cone structure, which contained 6 television cameras and an omnidirectional antenna, extended above this base. Two panels, containing 9,800 solar cells that provided 200 W of electricity, unfolded in flight and gave the spacecraft a wingspan of 4.6 m (15 ft).

All of the Ranger spacecraft were launched by an Atlas-Agena rocket from Kennedy Space Center. After Earth orbit was attained, the Agena second stage was briefly restarted (prior to separation from the spacecraft) in order to inject Ranger into a lunar trajectory. After midcourse corrections, the spacecraft crashed into the Moon at approximately 9,700 km/h (6,000 mph) about 66 hours after launch.

The Missions. The early missions failed to meet their objectives. *Rangers 1* and *2* (launched Aug. 23 and Nov. 18, 1961) were engineering test models, designed to test the parking-orbit mode of launching; in both cases the Agena engine failed to restart. The Atlas engine overaccelerated *Ranger 3* (launched Jan. 26, 1962), causing it to miss the Moon by 36,785 km (22,862 mi) and enter solar orbit. The failure of a control-system sequencer rendered *Ranger 4* (launched Apr. 23, 1962) inert; it curved around the Moon and crashed on the far side—the first U.S. spacecraft to hit the Moon. The failure of the spacecraft power system shortly after lunar-trajectory injection caused *Ranger 5* (launched Oct. 18, 1962) to miss the Moon by 724 km (450 mi) and enter solar orbit. *Ranger 6* (launched Jan. 30, 1964) impacted on the Moon in the crater Julius Caesar, but the television system burned out shortly after launch.

Ranger 7 was launched on July 28, 1964, and impacted 3 days later at 10.7° S, 20.7° W in the northwestern portion of the Moon's Mare Nubium, or Sea of Clouds. It sent back 4,316 photos, the best of which had a resolution of 0.41 m (16 in). The photos provided details of the impact area, which is crossed by rays of material ejected from the craters Copernicus and Tycho.

Ranger 8 left the Earth on Feb. 17, 1965, striking the Moon at 2.7° N, 24.8° E in Mare Tranquillitatis, or Sea of Tranquility. It took 7,137 photos, and unlike *Rangers 7* and *9*, which came in nearly vertically, it approached at an angle that permitted its cameras to sweep across a large portion of the lunar surface. This yielded pictures of a wide variety of features, including the first close-up views of the lunar highlands and a relatively low-level view of the mare's border, clearly showing some of the then-little-known lunar rilles. The best photo resolution was about 1.5 m (5 ft).

Ranger 9, last of its line, was launched on Mar. 21, 1965, and impacted on the Moon at 12.9° S, 2.4° W inside the crater Alphonsus. The 5,814 photos provided the first close-up views of a lunar-crater interior.

Other Results. The improved resolution of the Ranger photos over their Earth-based counterparts revealed several previously unknown aspects of the Moon, such as the small-scale topography. The photos showed striking similarities between mare and crater floors, a smoothed appearance in numerous shallow depressions, and a relative absence of rubble over substantial portions of the surface. *Ranger 9*'s target, the crater Alphonsus, gave signs of a complex history influenced by both internal and external forces. The mare in the photos showed an absence of large mountain ranges as well as of impact-saturated areas containing numerous overlapping craters. This discovery influenced the selection of mare regions as preferred sites for the Surveyor and Apollo landings.

JONATHAN EBERHART

Bibliography: Jet Propulsion Laboratory, *The View from Ranger* (NASA EP-38; 1966); Lewis, Richard S., *Appointment on the Moon*, rev. ed. (1969); Ley, Willy, *Ranger to the Moon* (1965).

See also: SPACE EXPLORATION.

rangers

Rangers are members of an infantry unit who are trained in irregular or guerrilla warfare tactics for the purpose of rapidly attacking enemy troops and raiding behind enemy lines. Partisan bands and commando groups have often been referred to as rangers. Groups of rangers—Rogers' Rangers, for example—were first used (1754–63) during the French and Indian War. In the American Revolution rangers on both sides served to scout and to harass the enemy. In the 19th century, mounted rangers such as the TEXAS RANGERS saw service in the Mexican War, the Indian Wars, and on both sides during the Civil War.

Rangers were reintroduced into the U.S. Army during World War II. The exploits of such groups as Darby's Rangers, Merrill's Marauders, and Wingate's Chindits were so successful that ranger companies became a regular part of infantry divisions. Following the Korean War, ranger companies were disbanded, and ranger personnel were deployed throughout regular infantry units. Specially trained guerrilla and long-range patrol forces, however, like the SPECIAL FORCES, are still an active part of the U.S. Army and were used (1961–73) in the Vietnam War.

Bibliography: Altieu, James J., *Darby's Rangers* (1945); Mahon, John K., and Danysh, Romana M., *Infantry*, rev. ed. (1972); Stillman, Richard J., *The U.S. Infantry: Queen of Battle* (1965).

Rangoon   [rang-goon']

The graceful Sule Pagoda, surrounded by smaller, similarly shaped stupas, rises from the central business district of Rangoon near Independence Square (left). Long a center of the Buddhist religion, Rangoon is today the political and economic capital of Burma.

Rangoon, the capital and largest city of Burma, is located on the Rangoon River in southern Burma, approximately 40 km (25 mi) inland from the Gulf of Martaban at the center of a rice-growing region. The city has a population of 2,458,712 (1983 est.). Rangoon experiences a tropical, summer monsoon climate.

The vast majority of the population is Burman (the dominant lowland peoples of the nation); other Burmese groups, Chinese, and Indians follow in number. The city's focal point—the ancient Buddhist Shwe Dagon Pagoda—is the center of Burmese religious life. Rangoon is the industrial center of Burma, and the major industries are textiles, rice milling, and sawmilling. River, road, and rail facilities connect the city with the rest of the country; a canal links Rangoon with the Irrawaddy River. The city's international airport was built in 1952. The port handles most of the country's exports and imports. Rangoon has a number of specialized institutes; the University of Rangoon was established in 1920.

During the mid-18th century the founder of the last Burman royal dynasty, Alaungpaya, established a port at the small coastal town of Dagon and renamed it Yangon (Rangoon), meaning "end of strife." The city became the capital of Lower Burma. The British first occupied the city between 1824 and 1826 and returned in 1852 following a second Anglo-Burmese War. Rangoon became the capital of all Burma following British annexation of the entire territory. With independence in 1948, Rangoon became the nation's capital.   RICHARD ULACK

rank, military

Military rank is the system of titles that forms the hierarchy of the armed services.

Army Rank. Modern army rank traces its origins to the mercenary companies of Renaissance Italy, at the time when professional soldiers began to replace part-time feudal warriors. At the head of the company stood the headman (Latin *caput,* "head"), from which is derived the title captain, or later, in Germany, *Hauptmann.* The captain was assisted by a deputy, or lieutenant (Latin, *locum tenens,* "place holder"). Both depended on a number of trustworthy soldiers who carried the title of sergeant, which was derived from that of the feudal warrior's personal attendants (Latin, *servientem,* "serving"). All modern ranks, with minor exceptions, are derived from these three. As armies grew larger, companies were organized into columns. The modern rank of colonel is derived from the head of each column (Old Italian, *colonnello*). When armies grew larger still in the 17th century, superior officers were generally appointed to command the whole army; for them general was added to the original company titles. In this way evolved the ranks of lieutenant general, captain general, and colonel general. At the same time the title major was attached to some of the lower ranks to indicate special responsibility. The ranks of captain major (now major) and sergeant major developed in this way. The latter could also be a general rank (sergeant major general), but that title was found to be cumbersome and was abbreviated to major general. This abbreviation explains why a (sergeant) major general in modern armies is subordinate to a lieutenant general.

The rank of marshal is derived from two Old High German words, *Marah,* "horse," and *Scalc,* "caretaker" or "servant." In the Teutonic tribes that overran the Roman Empire, the tribal chief's principal servant was his horse master (*Marah Scalc*). When the chiefs became kings of their conquered territories, the master of horse became a high court officer and, in wartime, the head of the cavalry. Later, in some countries, the courtly and military offices were divided; in Britain, for example, the earl marshal became, effectively, a civilian, and field marshals were appointed to command armies in the field.

When armies became permanent state organizations during the 17th century, the grant of rank became a royal prerogative, usually conferred by a commission from the king to a trusted subject. These commissioned officers in turn appointed suitable soldiers in their regiments to hold the minor ranks, which thus became known as noncommissioned. In Britain the commissioned ranks were salable until 1870, a practice that survived from mercenary days. General rank was, however, by official appointment, as was all rank in most other armies. During the 19th century armies everywhere began to apply tests of efficiency for promotion or to require officers to complete a course of training for the next rank. Officers of outstanding ability for whom a superior rank could not be immediately found were sometimes awarded a brevet to the next rank, which guaranteed them promotion when a vacancy occurred. It also became common practice to issue a warrant to the most senior of the noncommissioned officers, henceforth called warrant officers, which ensured that they could not arbitrarily be demoted. In most countries warrant officers now constitute an intermediate rank between commissioned and noncommissioned officers.

By 1900 the system of officer ranks was standard throughout

TABLE 1: MILITARY RANK IN U.S. ARMED FORCES*

Army	Navy	Air Force	Marine Corps
Officers			
General of the Army	Fleet Admiral	General of the Air Force	
General	Admiral	General	General
Lieutenant General	Vice Admiral	Lieutenant General	Lieutenant General
Major General	Rear Admiral (upper half)	Major General	Major General
Brigadier General	Commodore (wartime only)	Brigadier General	Brigadier General
	Rear Admiral (lower half)		
Colonel	Captain	Colonel	Colonel
Lieutenant Colonel	Commander	Lieutenant Colonel	Lieutenant Colonel
Major	Lieutenant Commander	Major	Major
Captain	Lieutenant	Captain	Captain
First Lieutenant	Lieutenant (junior grade)	First Lieutenant	First Lieutenant
Second Lieutenant	Ensign	Second Lieutenant	Second Lieutenant
Warrant Officers			
Chief Warrant Officer (W-4)	Same as Army	Same as Army	Same as Army
Chief Warrant Officer (W-3)	Same as Army	Same as Army	Same as Army
Chief Warrant Officer (W-2)	Same as Army	Same as Army	Same as Army
Warrant Officer (W-1)	Same as Army	Same as Army	Same as Army
Enlisted Personnel			
Sergeant Major of the Army (only one)	Master Chief Petty Officer of the Navy (only one)	Chief Master Sergeant of the Air Force (only one)	Sergeant Major of the Marine Corps (only one)
Command Sergeant Major or Sergeant Major	Master Chief Petty Officer	Chief Master Sergeant	Sergeant Major or Master Gunnery Sergeant
First Sergeant or Master Sergeant	Senior Chief Petty Officer	Senior Master Sergeant	First Sergeant or Master Sergeant
Sergeant First Class	Chief Petty Officer	Master Sergeant	Gunnery Sergeant
Staff Sergeant/Specialist 6	Petty Officer First Class	Technical Sergeant	Staff Sergeant
Sergeant/Specialist 5	Petty Officer Second Class	Staff Sergeant	Sergeant
Corporal/Specialist 4	Petty Officer Third Class	Sergeant or Senior Airman	Corporal
Private First Class	Seaman	Airman First Class	Lance Corporal
Private	Seaman Apprentice	Airman	Private First Class
	Seaman Recruit	Airman Basic	Private

* Coast Guard rank is the same as the Navy.

the major armies, although some national variations existed. In the French army, for example, the major is known as commandant. General's titles in the French army and in those of most other Latin countries followed the Napoleonic pattern of conforming to that of the appropriate formation commanded—general of brigade, for example. Few changes have been made in the system since 1900. The U.S. Army created for World War I hero Gen. John J. Pershing the field-marshal equivalent of general of the armies (subsequently army), whereas the USSR, which originally scorned rank titles, now has a more elaborate hierarchy than does any other country. Air force titles in most countries are similar to army ranks.

Navy Rank. Naval rank was slower to formalize than army rank because permanent navies came into being some time after permanent armies. The first title to acquire general currency was that of admiral, which was derived from the Arabic *amir-al-bahr*, "prince of the sea," by which the leader of the Muslim fleet in the Mediterranean was known as early as the 12th century. The term was brought back to Europe by the Crusaders, who spelled it by analogy with the Latin *admirabilis*, "admirable." As late as the 16th century, however, the word was applied as often to the commander's ship as to the man, who was more often called general, captain, or captain general. For this reason establishing a distinctive title for the ship's commander was delayed. In the British Royal Navy of the 17th century a man held title only while in post and on a ship of the line. He therefore came to be called a post captain, and vessels smaller than a sixth-rate ship were com-

TABLE 2: ARMY RANK IN SELECTED COUNTRIES

British Army	French Army	Soviet Army	British Army	French Army	Soviet Army
Officers					
Field Marshal	Maréchal de France*	Generalissimo of the Soviet Union	Captain	Capitaine	Captain
		Marshal of the Soviet Union	Lieutenant	Lieutenant	Senior Lieutenant
		Chief Marshal	Second Lieutenant	Sous Lieutenant	Lieutenant
		Marshal			Junior Lieutenant
General	Général d'Armée	General of the Army			
		Colonel General	**Enlisted Personnel**		
Lieutenant General	Général de Corps d'Armée	Lieutenant General	Warrant Officer I	Adjutant-Chef	Praporshchik
			Warrant Officer II	Adjutant	Glav Starshina
Major General	Général de Division	Major General	Staff Sergeant	Sergent-major	Starshina
Brigadier	Général de Brigade		Sergeant	Sergent	Senior Sergeant
Colonel	Colonel	Colonel	Corporal	Caporal-chef	Sergeant
Lieutenant Colonel	Lieutenant Colonel	Lieutenant Colonel	Lance-Corporal	Caporal	Corporal
Major	Commandant†	Major		Soldat, 1ere Classe	
			Private	Soldat, 2eme Classe	Private

* The title is technically not a rank but a "state dignity."

† It should be noted that the Commandant is called chef de bataillon in the infantry, chef d'escadrons in cavalry/armour, and chef d'escadron in the artillery.

TABLE 3: NAVAL OFFICER RANK IN SELECTED COUNTRIES

British Navy	French Navy	Soviet Navy
		Admiral of the Fleet of the Soviet Union
		Admiral of the Fleet
Admiral of the Fleet		
Admiral	Amiral	Admiral
Vice-Admiral	Vice-amiral	Vice-Admiral
Rear-Admiral	Contre-amiral	Rear-Admiral
Commodore	Chef d'escadre	
Captain	Capitaine de vaisseau	Captain 1st Class
Commander	Capitaine de frégate	Captain 2d Class
Lieutenant Commander	Capitaine de corvette	Captain 3d Class
Lieutenant	Lieutenant de vaisseau	Captain Lieutenant
		Senior Lieutenant
Sub-Lieutenant	Enseigne de vaisseau	Lieutenant
Midshipman	Aspirant	Junior Lieutenant

Leopold von Ranke, a 19th-century German historian, appears in a portrait by Julius Schrader. Ranke applied analytic methods to the study of history, particularly to the evaluation of source materials. In his teaching at the University of Berlin, he instructed students to discard the works of classical historians in favor of original documentary evidence.

manded by a master and commander, the common merchant title (abbreviated in 1794 to commander). Not until 1860 did Britain officially accord titles of rank to naval officers who were not actually in post. Custom, however, had long done so—to include also the captain's deputy, the lieutenant, and the apprentice officers, the midshipmen. During the 19th century the extra rank of lieutenant commander was invented to distinguish senior lieutenants in larger ships. In 1861 the rank sublieutenant was added. These additions recognized that the steam navy required on the same ship a considerable hierarchy of officers to perform a variety of functions unknown in simple sailing-ship days. In the French and German navies the names of types of ships were attached to officers' ranks. *Capitaine de frégate,* for example, outranked *capitaine de corvette.*

In the higher naval ranks, the old divisions of the line of battle—rear and van, the latter always commanded by the admiral's deputy, or vice admiral—had become attached to flag (admiral's) rank to give the titles in use today. In the Royal Navy the most senior officer had also long been known as admiral of the fleet, a title that became a rank in 1863. Its equivalent was *Grossadmiral* in the German Navy, which also used the unusual next rank of *Generaladmiral.* The U.S. Navy, which had generally followed British usage in these forms, adopted the title of fleet admiral in World War II.

JOHN KEEGAN

Bibliography: McDonald, Archie P., and Calahan, James E., eds., *Fighting Men; The Western Military Heritage* (1970); U.S. Joint Chiefs of Staff, *A Dictionary of United States Military Terms* (1963).

Rank, Otto

Otto Rank, b. Apr. 22, 1884, d. Oct. 31, 1939, was an Austrian psychoanalyst and associate of Sigmund Freud's. He was adept at applying analytical concepts to mythology and the arts. In stressing birth trauma—separation anxiety at birth—as the prototype of all subsequent anxiety, Rank both made his main contribution to psychoanalytic theory and necessitated his separation from Freud.

Bibliography: Alexander, Franz, et al., eds., *Psychoanalytic Pioneers* (1966); Karpf, Fay B., *The Psychology and Psychotherapy of Otto Rank* (1953).

Ranke, Leopold von   [rahn'-ke]

The German historian Leopold von Ranke, b. Dec. 21, 1795, d. May 23, 1886, is considered a pioneer in the development of critical historical scholarship. Trained as a classical philologist, Ranke applied critical methods of text analysis to the study of modern history. Ranke insisted that history be written on the basis of the careful examination of primary sources, a view he propounded in *Zur Kritik neuerer Geschichtsschreiber* (On the Criticism of New Historians), a treatise appended to his *History of the Latin and Teutonic Nations from 1494 to 1514* (1824; Eng. trans., 1846). Teaching at the University of Berlin from 1825, he organized research seminars in which he

trained several generations of historians in historical method. These seminars, devoted to the investigation of historical problems on the basis of the systematic, critical examination of documents, represented an innovation in the education of professional historians.

Ranke's way of conducting historical research and, to an extent, his manner of writing history became models for scholarly historians in the 19th century. At times misunderstood abroad as a fact-oriented positivist, Ranke was actually an idealist who was convinced that great moral forces manifested themselves in history. In his great works, *The History of the Popes* (3 vols., 1834–36; Eng. trans., 1908), *History of the Reformation in Germany* (6 vols., 1839–47; Eng. trans., 3 vols., 1845–47), *Civil Wars and Monarchy in France in the Sixteenth and Seventeenth Centuries* (5 vols., 1852–61; incomplete Eng. trans., 1852), and *A History of England, Principally in the Seventeenth Century* (7 vols., 1859–69; Eng. trans., 6 vols., 1875), Ranke traced the development of the modern European world. His heavy reliance on documents contributed to a history that focused on the foreign affairs of the great powers and on military events and gave considerable emphasis to religious ideas; it largely neglected the economic, social, and cultural aspects of modern European history, however.

GEORG G. IGGERS

Bibliography: Gay, Peter, *Style in History* (1976); Gooch, G. P., *History and Historians in the 19th Century* (1949); Krieger, Leonard, *Ranke: The Meaning of History* (1977); Von Laue, T. H., *Leopold Ranke: The Formative Years* (1950; repr. 1970).

Rankin, Jeannette   [rang'-kin]

Jeannette Rankin, b. Missoula, Mont., June 11, 1880, d. May 18, 1973, was an American feminist and pacifist and the first

Jeannette Rankin, American legislator and social reformer, met with other antiwar activists in 1936 to organize opposition to increased U.S. military involvement abroad. Rankin, the first woman elected to Congress, remained politically active into her 80s, working for feminist and pacifist causes.

female member of the U.S. House of Representatives. She was elected to the House in 1916 as a Republican from Montana and served one term, during which she voted against U.S. entry into World War I. Elected to a second term in 1940, Rankin was the only representative to vote against war with Japan the following year. In the late 1960s she was active in opposing the Vietnam War.

Bibliography: Josephson, H. G., *Jeannette Rankin: First Lady in Congress* (1979).

Rankine, William John Macquorn   [rang'-kin]

The Scottish engineer William John Macquorn Rankine, b. July 5, 1820, d. Dec. 24, 1872, was a major contributor to the science of thermodynamics during the 19th century and the author of a number of classic engineering textbooks. In 1838, Rankine dropped out of the University of Edinburgh to pursue a career in civil engineering. Several years later he began to publish papers on a wide variety of subjects, including railroad engineering, naval architecture, and heat engines. Rankine is best remembered for the latter work, which he discussed within the general context of his ''molecular vortex'' theory of heat.

DAVID A. HOUNSHELL

Ransom, John Crowe   [ran'-suhm]

John Crowe Ransom, b. Pulaski, Tenn., Apr. 30, 1888, d. July 3, 1974, promoted the term NEW CRITICISM in a book of that title (1941). One of the group of Vanderbilt University poets known as The Fugitives, Ransom contributed to their magazine and to their agrarian manifesto *I'll Take My Stand* (1930). After leaving the Vanderbilt faculty in 1937, he taught at Kenyon College until 1958, and for 21 years he edited the *Kenyon Review*. One of his best-known poems is ''Bells for John Whiteside's Daughter,'' a graceful, deeply ironic lament for a child's death. Ransom's revised and enlarged *Selected Poems* (1963) won the 1964 National Book Award for poetry.

Bibliography: Parsons, Thornton H., *John Crowe Ransom* (1969); Williams, Miller, *The Poetry of John Crowe Ransom* (1972); Young, Thomas D., *Gentleman in a Dustcoat: A Biography of John Crowe Ransom*, ed. by Louis Rubin (1977).

Rao, Raja   [row, rah'-juh]

Raja Rao, born in Hassan (Mysore), India, Nov. 5, 1908, and educated in India and France, is known for novels and short stories in which he has explored the meeting of East and West and the meaning of Indian experience. His first novel, *Kanthapura* (1938), has a key place in the development of Indian fiction written in English. No less important are his short stories in *The Cow of the Barricades* (1947) and his novels *The Serpent and the Rope* (1960), *The Cat and Shakespeare* (1965), and *Comrade Kirillov* (1976).

S. C. HARREX

Bibliography: Harrex, S. C., *The Fire and the Offering: The English-language Novel of India 1935–1970*, vol. 2 (1978); Mukherjee, Meenakshi, *The Twice-Born Fiction* (1971); Naik, M. K., *Raja Rao* (1972); Narasimhaiah, C. D., *Raja Rao* (1973).

rape

Rape is usually defined as the act of forcing sexual intercourse upon an unwilling victim. In the United States, rape was traditionally considered an act that occurred only against females and only outside marriage. In recent decades, however, some states have broadened the legal definition to include other forms of sexual contact and to include spouses and males as possible victims.

Legally, there are two kinds of rape, forcible and statutory, and both are treated as felonies in the United States. Forcible rape is defined as sexual intercourse with a nonconsenting victim through the use or the threat of force. Statutory rape is defined as sexual intercourse with a person under a specified age. This age varies from state to state and country to country but usually ranges from 12 to 18 years. Sexual intercourse with a person who is mentally deficient or unconscious and therefore incapable of giving consent is also sometimes considered statutory rape.

Rape and Criminal Justice. The origin of rape laws can be traced to the widespread belief that women were the property of men. A female was first considered the property of her father, to be bartered for in marriage. Because her virginity was valued as the principal asset, rape was considered a theft. Once a woman was married, she belonged to her husband. Rape then was treated as a crime against the husband's exclusive sexual rights to her. Because marriage gave these rights to the husband, legally, it was not possible for him to rape his own wife.

Because penalties for rape were severe, rape laws came to include elements that protected men against false accusation. The consent of the victim was often at issue, and the defense frequently argued that the woman had not resisted her alleged attacker. By the 20th century it had become increasingly difficult in U.S. courts for the victim to legally prove that she had been raped. She had to establish, often with a corroborating eyewitness, that intercourse had taken place, that it had not been provoked, and that violence had been threatened.

Rape is considered the most underreported of the violent crimes. It has been variously estimated that 50 to 90 percent of rapes occurring in the United States are not reported—because of shame, threat of retribution, or the victim's fear that she will not be believed. Convictions are difficult to obtain, and, even when convicted, the average rapist spends less than four years in jail for the offense. Between the early 1970s and early 1980s, there was a 74-percent increase in the number of reported forcible rapes, compared to a 58-percent increase in all violent crimes.

Impact of the Women's Movement. During the 1970s the women's movement helped to redefine rape as a crime of violence. In many Western countries legal definitions of rape have been expanded to differentiate degrees of sexual assault and to adjust the penalty according to the extent to which aggressive force is used. The aim of such changes is to allow more active prosecution.

Women's groups have developed rape-crisis and counseling centers to help victims and to inform both professionals and the public. These centers aid victims in coping with their feelings after a rape and support them as necessary in dealing with the medical, police, and legal systems. Additionally, some hospitals and police departments have implemented similar programs to help the victim. Preventive measures taken to deter the incidence of rape, particularly on college campuses in the United States, include improved street and corridor lighting, escort services, and self-defense training.

MARY ANNE SEDNEY

Bibliography: Brownmiller, Susan, *Against Our Will: Men, Women, and Rape* (1975); Groth, A. N., and Birnbaum, H. J., *Men Who Rape: The Psychology of the Offender* (1979); Hilberman, E., *The Rape Victim* (1976); Holmstrom, L. K., and Burgess, A. W., *The Victim of Rape: Institutional Reactions* (1978); McCombie, S. L., ed., *The Rape Crisis Intervention Handbook* (1980).

Rape of the Lock, The

Probably the finest MOCK EPIC poem in English, Alexander POPE's *The Rape of the Lock* (1712; revised and expanded in 1714) was written to reconcile two families then feuding over the trivial incident related by the poem. To describe the theft of a lock of the heroine's hair, Pope used the apparatus and elevated diction of epic poetry, offering a commentary on upper-class English society that is both mocking and admiring.

Bibliography: Brooks, Cleanth, *The Well-Wrought Urn* (1947).

Rape of Lucrece, The

The Rape of Lucrece (1594), William SHAKESPEARE's second published work, is a poem in 7-line stanzas recounting the legend of Lucretia, a Roman woman who is raped by the son of King Tarquin and commits suicide. The ultimate sources of this well-known story are Ovid's *Fasti* and Livy's *History of Rome*. Unlike Shakespeare's previous work, the erotic and sensuous *Venus and Adonis* (1593), this poem is a sober treatment of the virtues of chastity and honor.

Raphael   [rah-fah-el']

Raphael's splendid portrait (c.1515) of Baldassare Castiglione, author of The Book of the Courtier, *not only conveys the sitter's subtle personality but also makes him, appropriately, the personification of the ideal High Renaissance scholar and gentleman. (Louvre, Paris.)*

Son of the minor painter and chronicler Giovanni Santi, Raphael (Raffaello Sanzio, or Santi), b. Urbino, Italy, Apr. 6, 1483, was one of the greatest painters of the High Renaissance in Rome. It is generally believed that Raphael's father apprenticed him, probably no later than 1494, to the painter PERUGINO. Influence of the latter is clear in the young artist's early works, many of them painted for churches in or near Perugia. These early works include a *Crucifixion* (1503; National Gallery, London) and a *Coronation of the Virgin* (1502; Pinacoteca Vaticana, Rome). Raphael appears to have spent the years between 1504 and 1508 mainly in Florence, where he learned much from the art of the most advanced Florentine masters, especially Leonardo da Vinci. Early in this phase, Raphael painted *Saint George and the Dragon* (1506; National Gallery of Art, Washington, D.C.), as a gift from Duke Guidobaldo of Urbino to King Henry VII of England. The most impressive result of Raphael's Florentine period, however, is a large group of Madonnas and Holy Families, many still extant, among them the *Madonna of the Goldfinch* (1505–06; Uffizi, Florence) and the *Belle Jardinière* (1507; Louvre, Paris).

Around 1508–09, Raphael, although only 25 years old, was called to Rome by Pope Julius II to direct the decoration of the state rooms (Stanze) in the VATICAN PALACE. Here the painter found an opportunity to apply his classical vocabulary on a grand scale. A major impetus toward both classicism and monumentality was the art of Michelangelo, who was painting the ceiling of the Sistine Chapel, also in the Vatican Palace, at the very time of Raphael's arrival. On the four walls of the first room he decorated—the Stanza della Segnatura, completed in 1511—Raphael celebrated four aspects of human, and especially papal, accomplishment: theology (*Disputation over the Sacrament* or *Disputà*), philosophy (*School of Athens,* in which Raphael included portraits of both himself and Michelangelo among the philosophers), the arts (*Parnassus*), and law (*Cardinal Virtues* and *Giving of the Law*). Raphael next frescoed the Stanza d'Eliodoro, completed by mid-1514, where he depicted four historical events illustrating salvation of the church through divine intervention. In three of these frescoes, Raphael portrayed either Julius II or his successor, Leo X, who became Pope in 1513. The fourth fresco represents the miraculous liberation of Saint Peter (the first pope) from prison. About 1515, Raphael painted part of a third room, the Stanza dell'Incendio, named after its main fresco, the *Fire in the Borgo.*

While in Rome, Raphael was employed not only by the popes but also by a number of private patrons, particularly the Sienese banker, Agostino Chigi. In Chigi's suburban residence, now known as the Villa Farnesina, Raphael produced two works classical in theme as well as style: a wall fresco of the sea nymph Galatea (1513) and an entire ceiling with sto-

ries of Cupid and Psyche (1518–19). Around 1515, Raphael painted a portrait of the courtier and author Baldassare Castiglione (Louvre, Paris). A famous papal portrait of this period is Raphael's *Pope Leo X with Cardinals Giulio de'Medici and Luigi de'Rossi* (Uffizi, Florence).

Among the great religious works painted by Raphael on canvas or panel during his Roman years are the *Alba Madonna* (National Gallery, Washington, D.C.), the *Sistine Madonna* (Gemäldegalerie, Dresden), the *Madonna of the Chair* (Pitti Palace, Florence), and the *Transfiguration* (Pinacoteca Vaticana, Rome), the last executed in part by Giulio Romano, one of the most gifted of Raphael's numerous assistants and pupils.

In 1515–16, Raphael painted ten large watercolor cartoons (see CARTOON, art) illustrating the Acts of the Apostles as designs for tapestries to be hung in the Sistine Chapel. Seven cartoons survive in the Victoria and Albert Museum, London; the surviving tapestries are in the Vatican Museum. His own drawings, and engravings of his work by Marcantonio RAIMONDI, added further to Raphael's fame.

In 1514, Raphael succeeded Donato Bramante as chief architect of SAINT PETER'S BASILICA. At Saint Peter's, Raphael seems to have accomplished the substitution of a longitudinal for a central design, but nothing on his plan was actually built. Some of his other architectural designs were, however, carried out. These include a chapel for Agostino Chigi in Santa Maria del Popolo, Rome; the Vidoni-Caffarelli Palace (now much enlarged) and the Villa Madama (incomplete),

Raphael painted The Marriage of the Virgin *(1504) shortly after completing an apprenticeship with Perugino, whose tender simplicity of style he emulated in this serene work. (Brera, Milan.)*

both also in Rome; and the Pandolfini Palace in Florence. Raphael also became (1515) the first Superintendent of Antiquities in Rome. Raphael died in Rome at the age of 37. He was buried in the Pantheon amid universal mourning and acclaim.

EDITH W. KIRSCH

Bibliography: Beck, James, *Raphael* (1976); Camesasca, Ettore, *All the Frescoes of Raphael,* trans. by Paul Calocicchi, 2 vols. (1963), and *All the Paintings of Raphael,* trans. by Luigi Grosso, 2 vols. (1963); Crowe, Joseph A., and Cavalcaselle, Giovanni B., *Raphael: His Life and Works,* 2 vols. (1882–85); De Quincy, A. C., *History of the Life and Works of Rafaello,* ed. by S. J. Freedberg (1980); Fischel, Oskar, *Raphael,* trans. by Bernard Rackham, 2 vols. (1948); Middeldorf, Ulrich A., *Raphael's Drawings* (1945); Pope-Hennessey, John W., *Raphael* (1970); Suida, William E., *Raphael: Paintings and Drawings,* rev. ed. (1943).

Rapid City

Rapid City is the seat of Pennington County in southwestern South Dakota, on Rapid Creek at the eastern edge of the Black Hills. It has a population of 46,492 (1980). Rapid City is a gold, silver, and uranium mining center. The South Dakota School of Mines and Technology is there (1885). The city also serves the trade and industrial needs of the farming and lumbering enterprises in the area. Rapid City is a tourist mecca, as the gateway to nearby Mount Rushmore National Memorial, Crazy Horse Mountain, and Custer State Park. It is also the site of Ellsworth Air Force Base, a Strategic Air Command complex. Rapid City was settled in 1876 after the discovery of gold in the Black Hills.

rapid eye movement sleep: see SLEEP.

rapid transit: see SUBWAY.

Rappahannock River   [rap-uh-han'-uhk]

The Rappahannock River, in Virginia, rises in the Blue Ridge Mountains east of Front Royal and flows generally southeast for about 320 km (200 mi), passing Fredericksburg and finally emptying into Chesapeake Bay. Its main tributary is the Rapidan River. Several important Civil War battles were fought in the vicinity of the Rappahannock, notably the Fredericksburg and Chancellorsville campaigns.

rare earths: see LANTHANIDE SERIES.

Ras Shamra: see UGARIT.

Rashi   [rah'-shee]

Rabbi Solomon ben Isaac (or Yitzhaki, abbreviated as Rashi), b. 1040, d. July 13, 1105, a famed scholar who wrote definitive commentaries on the Hebrew Bible and most of the Babylonian Talmud, is considered one of the greatest authorities on Jewish Law. Rashi, who had studied at Mainz and Worms, established a Talmudic academy at Troyes and was a much-sought-after teacher and religious guide.

A master of brevity, he applied the method of utter simplicity, avoiding dialectics and unnecessary complications, stressing grammar and rational exposition; occasionally he used vernacular French or German words to clarify an unusual biblical phrase. At the same time, he did justice to the homiletic traditions. In certain cases he modestly admitted, "I don't know the meaning," and he quoted other authorities whenever he found their work helpful. His biblical commentary, printed in Hebrew in 1475, was translated into Latin and studied by those preparing the first German translation of the Bible.

NAHUM N. GLATZER

Bibliography: Hailperin, Herman, *Rashi and the Christian Scholars* (1963); Pearl, Chaim, ed., *Rashi* (1970).

Rasmussen, Knud   [rahs'-mu-suhn]

Knud Johan Victor Rasmussen, b. June 7, 1879, d. Dec. 21, 1933, was an explorer of Danish and Eskimo descent who devoted his life to ethnological studies throughout Arctic North America and tried to visit every known Eskimo group. To

benefit local Eskimo and to serve as a base for explorations, he established station THULE in 1910. During his most famous trek (1921–24), he became the first to cross the NORTHWEST PASSAGE by dogsled. During his travels he collected Eskimo legends and songs.

Bibliography: Rasky, Frank, *Explorers of the North* (1977).

raspberry

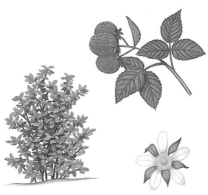

The red raspberry, R. idaeus, *is a biennial that bears fruit on canes. It is easily cultivated and is one of the hardiest of berries.*

The raspberry plant, a member of the genus *Rubus,* family Rosaceae, is widely cultivated for its fruit. Together with the BLACKBERRY, it comprises the group of plants commonly called brambles. The crowns and roots of brambles are perennial; the thorned canes, or fruiting portions of the plants, however, are biennial, bearing in their second year and then dying. Native to many parts of the world, the raspberry is exceptionally hardy and flourishes even in the northern United States and southern Canada. Varieties include red, purple, and black raspberries and "everbearing" cultivars that produce two crops in a season. Although the raspberry is a delicious fruit, commercial cultivation has been limited by the plant's vulnerability to virus diseases and by the high costs of harvesting by hand.

J. N. MOORE

Rasputin, Grigory Yefimovich   [ruhs-poo'-tin, gri-gohr'-ee yi-fee'-muh-vich]

The scandalous behavior of Grigory Yefimovich Rasputin, b. c.1865, d. Dec. 30 (N.S.), 1916, and the influence he wielded over the Russian imperial family served to erode its prestige and contributed directly to the collapse of the Romanov dynasty shortly after his own death. Originally surnamed Novykh, he was born into a peasant family in Siberia and spent much of his youth in debauchery, receiving the name

Rasputin was a Russian priest and faith healer who gained immense influence at the court of Nicholas II and Alexandra because of his apparent power to relieve the crown prince's sickness. His political influence and personal debauchery eventually provoked a group of nobles to murder him.

Rasputin ("debaucher"). He entered the church, however, and gained a reputation as a faith healer.

Appearing at the imperial court about 1907, Rasputin soon became a favorite of Empress ALEXANDRA FYODOROVNA and through her influenced NICHOLAS II. Rasputin's hold over Alexandra stemmed from his hypnotic power to alleviate the suffering of the hemophiliac crown prince, Aleksei, and from her belief that this rude priest was a genuine representative of the Russian people. Rasputin's conduct became increasingly licentious and shocking to the Russian public, however.

When Nicholas took personal command of Russian troops in 1915, Alexandra and Rasputin were virtually in charge of the government. Several conservative noblemen, recognizing Rasputin's destructive influence on an already deteriorating government, assassinated him. They first poisoned and then shot him; when these efforts failed, they drowned Rasputin in the Neva River.   FORRESTT A. MILLER

Bibliography: Purishkevich, V. M., *The Murder of Rasputin: First-Hand Account from the Diary of One of Rasputin's Murderers,* trans. by B. Costello (1985); Rasputin, Maria, and Barham, Patte, *Rasputin: The Man Behind the Myth, a Personal Memoir* (1977); Rodzianko, Mikhail V., *The Reign of Rasputin: An Empire's Collapse,* trans. by Catherine Zvegintzoff (1927; repr. 1973); Wilson, Colin, *Rasputin and the Fall of the Romanovs* (1964).

Rastafarians   [rah-stuh-far'-ee-uhnz]

Rastafarians are members of a Jamaican messianic movement dating back to the 1930s. According to Rastafarian belief the only true God is the late Ethiopian emperor HAILE SELASSIE (originally known as Ras Tafari), and Ethiopia is the true Zion. Rastafarians claim that white Christian preachers and missionaries have perverted the Scriptures to conceal the fact that Adam and Jesus were black. Their rituals include the use of marijuana and the chanting of revivalist hymns. REGGAE music is the popular music of the movement. The Rastafarians, who stress black separatism, have exercised some political influence in Jamaica.

Bibliography: Barrett, Leonard E., *The Rastafarians: Sounds of Cultural Dissonance* (1977); Myers, T. C., *The Essence of Rastafari Nationalism and Black Economic Development* (1986); Sparrow, Bill, and Nicholas, Tracy, *Rastafari: A Way of Life* (1979).

Rastrelli, Bartolommeo Francesco   [rahs-trel'-lee]

The favorite architect of Empress Elizabeth of Russia and the creator of the Russian rococo style, Bartolommeo Francesco Rastrelli, 1700–71, was an Italian whose architectural background was purely French. His buildings, mostly in and around Saint Petersburg (now Leningrad), included the Summer Palace (1741–44; destroyed), the Anichkov Palace (c.1744), the Peterhof (1747–52), and Smolny Cathedral (1748–55). His major projects were the Great Palace at Tsarskoe-Selo (1749–56; now Pushkin) and the Winter Palace (1754–62). Rastrelli's architecture was characterized by impressive scale, vivid exterior colors, and richness of baroque form. His royal palaces were suitable settings for the pleasure-loving empress and her court.   ANN FARKAS

Bibliography: Hamilton, George Heard, *The Art and Architecture of Russia,* 2d ed. (1975).

rat

Rat is the common name for about 1,000 species of rodents in 70 genera and eight families. These species include the kangaroo rats, *Dipodomys,* family Heteromyidae; wood rats, *Neotoma,* family Cricetidae; spiny rats, *Proechimys,* family Echimyidae; and the typical rats, *Rattus,* family Muridae. Most rodents called rats have an elongated body, a moderately pointed snout, approximately equal-length legs, and a long, sparsely haired or hairless tail. Rats are generally distinguished from mice by their larger size.

In the narrow sense, *rat* refers to members of the genus *Rattus,* which contains from 137 to 570 species, depending

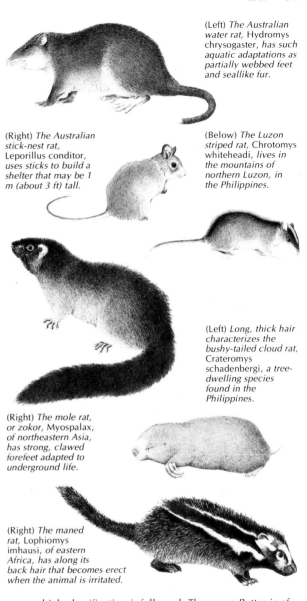

(Left) *The Australian water rat,* Hydromys chrysogaster, *has such aquatic adaptations as partially webbed feet and seallike fur.*

(Right) *The Australian stick-nest rat,* Leporillus conditor, *uses sticks to build a shelter that may be 1 m (about 3 ft) tall.*

(Below) *The Luzon striped rat,* Chrotomys whiteheadi, *lives in the mountains of northern Luzon, in the Philippines.*

(Left) *Long, thick hair characterizes the bushy-tailed cloud rat,* Crateromys schadenbergi, *a tree-dwelling species found in the Philippines.*

(Right) *The mole rat, or zokor,* Myospalax, *of northeastern Asia, has strong, clawed forefeet adapted to underground life.*

(Right) *The maned rat,* Lophiomys imhausi, *of eastern Africa, has along its back hair that becomes erect when the animal is irritated.*

upon which classification is followed. The genus *Rattus* is of special interest because two of its species, the black rat, *R. rattus,* and the Norway rat, *R. norvegicus,* have profoundly affected human history.

The black rat, also called the roof rat, is the primary host for bubonic plague, which is transmitted to humans by direct contact or through the bites of fleas that have fed on infected rats. The black rat is believed to have come originally from southern or southeastern Asia. Although the first written record of it in Europe was not until the 1200s, archaeological evidence places the black rat in Britain well before the plagues there of the 6th and 7th centuries. It was clearly the species that served as the major reservoir for the plague in those great epidemics, called the black death, that killed an estimated one-fourth of the population of Europe during the 1300s.

The black rat reached North and South America in the 1500s, and it is currently distributed in the United States in a narrow belt along both coasts and throughout most of the southeastern states. The black rat ranges from 16 to 22 cm (6.3 to 8.6 in) in length, plus a 17- to 24-cm (6.7- to 9.3-in) tail (always longer than the head and body combined), and from 115 to 350 g (4 to 12 oz) in weight. Black rats are usually grayish black with lighter gray underparts, but brown varieties are common. Breeding occurs throughout the year. Gestation is about 24 days; litter size usually ranges from 6 to 12 young.

The Norway rat, also called the brown rat, probably originated in eastern Asia, possibly northern China. The first record of its appearance in Europe was 1553, and it is now found throughout the United States. It is usually grayish brown above and pale gray or brown on its underparts, but blackish varieties also occur. Norway rats range from 22 to 26 cm (8.6 to 10.2 in) in length, plus an 18- to 22-cm (7- to 8.6-in) tail (always shorter than the head and body combined), and from 200 to 485 g (7 to 17 oz) in weight. Norway rats breed throughout the year. Gestation varies from 21 to 24 days, and litter size is usually between 6 and 12 young.

Their preference for different habitats usually keeps the black and Norway rats apart, but where they do meet, the larger and more aggressive Norway rat either forces the black rat to different portions of the habitat, such as the upper levels of buildings, or drives it completely out of the area. Both black and Norway rats will eat almost anything, but black rats show a preference for plant material and Norway rats for animal food. Norway rats even become predators, and they often associate in packs of 60 or more animals, usually all closely related and often all descended from a single pair. The rat pack is one reason that the Norway rat can survive in so many diverse environments. If a nursing female is killed, for example, other nursing females of the pack will raise her young.

With all its negative characteristics regarding human health and economics, the Norway rat, in the form of the usually albino laboratory rat, has enabled scientists and medical researchers to make significant contributions in studies of nutrition, genetics, and disease. Domestic rats also make excellent pets. CHARLES A. MCLAUGHLIN

Bibliography: Barnett, S. A., *The Rat, a Study in Behavior,* rev. ed. (1976); Chiasson, Robert B., *Laboratory Anatomy of the White Rat,* 4th ed. (1980); Greene, Eunice G., *Anatomy of the Rat* (1935; repr. 1971); Hirschhorn, Howard, *All About Rats* (1974); Zinsser, Hans, *Rats, Lice, and History* (1935).

ratel   [rayt'-ul]

A ratel, or honey badger, M. capensis, *follows the call of a bird, the African honey guide, to a beehive the bird has located. The ratel breaks open the hive and feeds on honey, while the bird searches among the remains for bee grubs and wax.*

The ratel, or honey badger, *Mellivora capensis,* in the weasel family, Mustelidae, is a carnivore that lives in brushlands and forests of Africa, India, and the Middle East. Its thick coat is gray above and black below. The skin is loose but very tough. The animal is about 60 cm (2 ft) long, excluding its tail, and is a good climber, living in trees as well as in burrows. It likes honey, and the HONEY GUIDE, or indicator bird, leads it to the nests of wild bees. The ratel also feeds on rodents and reptiles, even the cobra. EVERETT SENTMAN

Rathenau, Walther   [raht'-en-ow]

Walther Rathenau, b. Sept 29, 1867, d. June 24, 1922, a German industrialist and social theorist, served (1922) as foreign minister in the Weimar Republic. During World War I he had organized and directed Germany's War Raw Materials Department, and in 1921 he was minister of reconstruction. As foreign minister, Rathenau sought reconciliation with the victorious powers, taking steps toward meeting Germany's reparations obligations, and signed the Treaty of Rapallo between Germany and the USSR. This treaty cancelled Germany's war debt to the USSR, extended to the Soviet government its first diplomatic recognition, and enabled Germany to build and test new weapons secretly in the USSR. Nationalist elements in Germany detested Rathenau both as a Jew and as a representative of the Weimar government. He was assassinated by one such group in Berlin. An advocate of a decentralized form of social democracy, Rathenau wrote several books, including *The New Society* (Eng. trans., 1921). K. M. SMOGORZEWSKI

Bibliography: Felix, David, *Walther Rathenau and the Weimar Republic: The Politics of Reparations* (1971).

rational number

A rational number is defined to be the QUOTIENT of an INTEGER and a nonzero integer; that is, it is a number that can be written in the form of a FRACTION. For example, $3/2$, $-2/3$, and $1,072/83$ are all rational numbers, as are $0 = 0/1$, $1 = 1/1$, $2 = 2/1$, and so forth. Every integer n is equal to $n/1$ and so is a rational number. Given a rational number a/b, the integer a is called the numerator and b is called the denominator. Every rational number has many representations as a quotient of two integers: $2/3 = 6/9 = 8/12 = 18/27$. The fraction a/b is called reduced or in lowest terms if the integers a and b have no common factors (in the above example, $2/3$ is the reduced fraction). Two rational numbers a/b and c/d are equal provided $ad = bc$. All numerical calculations performed by people (or by computers) are actually done with rational numbers. All the IRRATIONAL NUMBERS that must be dealt with are in the end approximated by rational numbers for numerical computations. WILLIAM W. ADAMS

Bibliography: Niven, Ivan, *Numbers: Rational and Irrational* (1961; repr. 1975).

rationalism

Rationalism is a theory that contends that the most fundamental knowledge is based on reason and that truth is found by rational analysis of ideas independent of empirical data, emotive attitudes, or authoritative pronouncements. Rationalist beliefs, essentially philosophical, have significantly influenced science and religion as well.

Empiricists (see EMPIRICISM) claim that knowledge can be based only on information gained from the senses. Such information, the rationalists contend, is always open to question. They point to mathematics and logic as realms where unquestionable truths can be discovered by the use of reason alone. Baruch SPINOZA, perhaps the supreme rationalist of Western philosophy, presented his philosophical views in geometrical form and deduced theorems about the world based on axioms that he held to be rational truths.

The leading modern rationalists, the 17th-century philosophers Spinoza, René DESCARTES, and Gottfried Wilhelm von LEIBNIZ, sought to develop science in terms of basic concepts and the mathematical relationships between them. Empirical information, they conceded, might help in suggesting certain ideas, but the fundamental framework of science must be a mathematical schema of concepts and the laws logically deduced from them. (The empiricists, on the other hand, insisted that concepts that applied to the world had to be derived from experience, and they challenged whether any purely rational knowledge about the world existed.) The rationalist viewpoint led to applying mathematics in the sciences and to eliminating concepts—the notion of purpose, for example—that could not be expressed mathematically.

In religion, rationalism has been critical of accepted beliefs that cannot be logically justified. After the Reformation, rationalists questioned certain basic claims of Christianity (the Trinity, the incarnation, the resurrection, creation, the flood) because they did not meet rational standards. Some insisted that reason alone should be the only guide in interpreting Scripture. Religious rationalism—especially as embodied in the works of such 18th-century thinkers as VOLTAIRE, Jean Jacques ROUSSEAU, and the American Thomas PAINE—accompanied the development of DEISM and AGNOSTICISM and led to some modern forms of ATHEISM.

Rationalist philosophers have not necessarily been religious rationalists. Descartes and Leibniz, for example, accepted orthodox Christianity. On the other hand, many religious rationalists have been empiricists in their philosophy and have used empirical data to cast doubt on traditional religions.

RICHARD H. POPKIN

Bibliography: Aune, Bruce A., *Rationalism, Empiricism and Pragmaticism* (1970); Collins, A. W., *Thought and Nature* (1985); Heimann, Eduard, *Reason and Faith in Modern Society* (1961); Feyerabend, Paul K., *The Rise of Western Rationalism* (1978); Popkin, R. H., ed., *The Philosophy of the 16th and 17th Centuries* (1966).

rationing: see PRICE SYSTEM.

Rattigan, Terence   [rat'-uh-guhn]

A master of the well-made play, the British playwright Terence Mervyn Rattigan, b. June 10, 1911, d. Nov. 30, 1977, enjoyed enormous success with *The Winslow Boy* (1946), which appeals to the audience's sense of humanity. Rattigan later explored the themes of loneliness and misunderstanding in *The Deep Blue Sea* (1952) and *Separate Tables* (1954) and based *Ross* (1960) on the life of Lawrence of Arabia. Much of his work has been filmed. Rattigan was knighted in 1971.

ROBIN BUSS

rattlesnake

The timber, or prairie, or banded, rattlesnake, C. horridus, *is found from the eastern coast of the United States (as far north as New Hampshire) to Kansas and Oklahoma.*

Rattlesnakes are heavy-bodied, venomous snakes with movable front fangs, a heat-sensing pit on each side of the face, and, with rare exception, rattles on the tail. Venomous snakes with movable fangs make up the VIPER family, Viperidae. Rattlesnakes and other vipers with heat-sensing pits are placed in the subfamily Crotalinae of PIT VIPERS, although some classification systems instead place them in a separate snake family, the Crotalidae.

Rattlesnakes comprise two genera: *Crotalus,* which ranges from Canada into Argentina and contains about 28 species with many varieties, or subspecies; and *Sistrurus,* which includes the two species of pygmy rattlesnakes and the massasauga, found in the United States and Mexico. Rattlesnakes range in size from the eastern diamondback, *C. adamanteus,*

which averages between 0.9 and 1.8 m (3 and 6 ft) long but has attained a record length of 2.44 m (8 ft), to a number of small species, including the sidewinder, *C. cerastes,* the pygmy rattlesnake, *S. miliarius,* and the ridge-nosed rattlesnake, *C. willardi,* all of which are usually less than 60 cm (2 ft) long. Rattles are not included in such measurements.

The two pit organs, located between the nostril and eye on either side of the lower face, consist of an outer and inner chamber separated by a membrane, with a small, controllable opening leading from the inner chamber to the outside. Sensitive to infrared radiation and capable of detecting temperature differences of mere thousandths of a degree, the front-facing organs enable a snake to determine the location and size of a prey animal. Evidence further indicates that the nerve impulses from the organs cross to opposite sides of the brain, producing a stereoscoping heat image that precisely locates the prey and allows the snake to strike accurately in total darkness.

At the very front of the mouth on either side of the upper jaw is a short, deep bone called the maxilla; each bone bears a large, venom-injecting fang, normally carried folded back along the roof of the mouth. When pulled by a muscle, however, two bones called the pterygoid and the ectopterygoid push against the loosely attached maxilla, rotating it forward and erecting the fang. (The fangs are individually controlled and are not automatically erected whenever the mouth is opened.) Each maxilla has two fang sockets, and—normally two to four times a year—a fang is replaced by the first in a series of developing fangs directly behind it, moving into the empty socket. The old fang does not always drop out immediately, so a rattlesnake may have up to four working fangs in its mouth at one time. In general, the venom is largely blood-tissue-destroying (hemotoxic), but the tropical rattlesnake, or casabel, *C. durissus,* has venom that is largely nerve-destroying (neurotoxic). The hemotoxic-neurotoxic balance can vary greatly among other rattlesnake species and also, within a species, according to geographic location or the individual snake.

Rattlesnakes are generally characterized by the presence of rattles, but one species, the Santa Catalina rattlesnake, *C. catalinensis,* lacks them. Each rattle segment is a modified horny scale that once capped the tip of the tail. Unlike other snakes, which shed these caplike scales at each molt, the rattlesnake sheds it but once, at the first molt after birth. From then on the caps are retained. All of the retained terminal scales are thick and large and have one or more narrowed, or constricted, portions, giving them an hourglass or multilobed shape. When molting occurs, the terminal scale is loosened but held to the new terminal scale by the interlocking of their respective constricted portions. The new scale has at least one more constriction, and hence one more lobe, than the previous one and so projects in front of it. The end of the scale is reabsorbed, however, before the next molt. Rattlesnakes molt an average of three times a year and frequently break off and lose their end rattles, so the number of rattles is not an indication of a snake's age.

Rattlesnakes mate in the spring in warmer climates or in the fall in colder regions. Females may retain sperm within their oviducts for a considerable time and bear successive litters without additional matings. Gestation is generally between 140 and 200 days and is apparently greatly influenced by climate. All rattlesnakes are live-bearing, with females producing an average of 8 to 15 young at a time. Females may reproduce every year, but in colder regions they may bear young only once every two years. Rattlesnakes reach sexual maturity at about 3 years of age and have lived in captivity for over 20 years.

EDWIN E. ROSENBLUM

Bibliography: Glass, T. G., Jr., *Snakebite First Aid* (1981); Klauber, Lawrence M., *Rattlesnakes,* abr. ed. (1982); Shaw, Charles E., and Campbell, Sheldon, *Snakes of the American West* (1974).

Ratzel, Friedrich

Friedrich Ratzel, b. Aug. 30, 1844, d. Aug. 9, 1904, was a German geographer and ethnologist. Known as the founder of anthropogeography, he originated the concept of *Lebens-*

raum, meaning "living space" and concerning human groups in relation to spatial units. He taught at the University of Munich (1875–86) and was professor of geography at Leipzig (1886–1904). The concept of *Lebensraum* was later used by the National Socialists to rationalize German expansion.

GEOFFREY JOHN MARTIN

Ratzinger, Joseph

German churchman Joseph Alois Ratzinger, b. Apr. 16, 1927, is a prominent member of the Roman Curia. He was a professor of theology before becoming archbishop of Munich-Freising and a cardinal in 1977. In 1981 Cardinal Ratzinger was named by Pope John Paul II to head the Vatican's Congregation for the Doctrine of the Faith, a body charged with safeguarding Catholic orthodoxy. Known as an opponent of church progressives, he aroused controversy when, in a 1985 interview published as *The Ratzinger Report,* he expressed disillusion with the results of the Second Vatican Council.

Rauschenberg, Robert   [row'-shen-burg]

The American artist Robert Rauschenberg, b. Port Arthur, Tex., Oct. 22, 1925, has been a leading figure in pop art, "happenings," environmental art, and experimental theater. He studied in Paris, at Black Mountain College in North Carolina, and at the Art Students League, New York City. Rauschenberg's early works include the "combine" paintings of the late 1950s, which grew from modest collages of newspaper fragments and photographs into complex, three-dimensional creations. The most spectacular, *Monogram* (1959; Moderna Museet, Stockholm), consists of a stuffed ram encircled by an automobile tire; the base is splashed with paint and collage elements. Since the 1960s Rauschenberg has produced silk-

Reserve (1961) is one of the "combine" paintings that Robert Rauschenberg began to produce during the 1950s. Combine painting, like collage, incorporates mundane objects, but Rauschenberg extended the form by using the canvas as a mirror of the incoherent profusion of modern life. (National Gallery of Art, Washington, D.C.)

screened kaleidoscopic works based on media culture, including the transfer of photographs to silk screen. He has also experimented with motors, plexiglass, and sound. He won the grand prize at the 1964 Venice Biennale. In 1981 he published *Rauschenberg Photographs.*

Bibliography: Tomkins, Calvin, *Off the Wall: Robert Rauschenberg and the Art World of Our Time* (1981).

Rauschenbusch, Walter   [row'-shen-bush]

The Baptist clergyman and theologian Walter Rauschenbusch, b. Rochester, N.Y., Oct. 4, 1861, d. July 25, 1918, was a leading advocate of the SOCIAL GOSPEL movement. After studies in Rochester and Germany, Rauschenbusch graduated (1886) from Rochester Theological Seminary and was called as pastor to the Second German Baptist Church in New York City's notorious Hell's Kitchen. There, in the face of complex urban social problems, he came to believe that Jesus preached social as well as individual salvation and began to place new emphasis on the Kingdom of God. While in New York, he co-edited (1889–91) a workers' paper, *For the Right,* and helped found (1892) the Brotherhood of the Kingdom, a Baptist group dedicated to social action. In 1897 he began to teach in the German school of Rochester Theological Seminary, becoming professor of church history there in 1902. His writings include *Christianity and the Social Crisis* (1907) and *A Theology for the Social Gospel* (1917).

JOHN F. PIPER

Bibliography: Handy, Robert T., ed., *The Social Gospel in America: 1870–1920* (1966); Sharpe, Dores R., *Walter Rauschenbusch* (1942).

rauwolfia   [row-wul'-fee-uh]

Rauwolfia, or snakeroot, *Rauvolfia serpentina,* is a plant belonging to the DOGBANE family, Apocynaceae. Native to India, Sri Lanka, and the East Indies, it is a low-growing evergreen shrub that has snakelike roots. Rauwolfia has been used in folk medicine for centuries and, more recently, as a source of the medicinal alkaloid RESERPINE.

LARRY C. HIGGINS

Ravel, Maurice   [rah-vel']

Maurice Ravel, b. Mar. 7, 1875, was one of France's great composers and an important master of early-20th-century music. He began piano studies at the age of 7, and in 1889 he entered the Paris Conservatory, studied composition, and became identified with advanced movements. Never a virtuoso pianist, Ravel concentrated on composing. He interrupted his career to serve in the French army in World War I. A private person subject to fits of depression, he retired from Paris after the war to a villa at Montfort-l'Amaury, where he devoted himself to composing and to his hobby of collecting mechanical toys. Recognized as France's leading contemporary composer following the death of Debussy in 1918, Ravel made visits abroad, touring England and, in 1928, the United States. In his later years he apparently suffered from a neurological disorder diagnosed at the time as Pick's disease, and a serious auto accident in 1932 seemed to initiate a continuous deterioration of his condition. Brain surgery failed, and he died on Dec. 28, 1937.

Often named with Debussy as an impressionist, Ravel was essentially a classicist in the French tradition of clarity, polish, and disciplined craftsmanship. His imaginative piano music—such as the *Sonatine* (1905), *Miroirs* (1905), the stunning *Gaspard de la nuit* (1908), and *Le Tombeau de Couperin* (1917)—was particularly influential. His subtly crafted chamber works include his String Quartet (1902), the *Introduction and Allegro* for harp and ensemble (1905–06), the Trio for Piano and Strings (1914), the Sonata for Violin and Cello (1920–22), and the jazz-influenced Violin Sonata (1923–27). Jazz was also assimilated in his Piano Concerto in G (1930–31), composed simultaneously with his Piano Concerto for the Left Hand. Brilliant as a composer of songs, he showed great flair for the stage in his two operas, the witty *L'Heure espagnole* (The Spanish Hour, 1911) and the fantasmagoric *L'Enfant et les sortilèges* (The Child and the Spells, 1925). His ballet for Diaghilev, *Daphnis et Chloé* (1909–12), was followed by *Ma Mère*

Maurice Ravel, one of the greatest French composers of the early 20th century, was renowned for such compelling works as Gaspard de la nuit *(1908) for piano and the immensely popular* Boléro *(1928). His masterpiece, the ballet* Daphnis et Chloé *(1909–12), exhibits the strongly individual style, skillful orchestration, and superb craftsmanship that distinguish Ravel's composition.*

l'Oye (1915), *La Valse* (1919–20), and the popular *Boléro* (1928). These compositions, like his famous transcription (1922) of Mussorgsky's *Pictures at an Exhibition* and Ravel's other orchestral works, such as *Pavane for a Dead Infant* (1898), *Alborada del gracioso* (1905), *Rapsodie espagnole* (1907), and *Valses nobles et sentimentales* (1911), many of which originated as piano pieces, display both Ravel's wizardry as an orchestrator and his capacity to rethink the same music idiomatically in different media.   JOHN W. BARKER

Bibliography: Davies, Laurence, *Ravel Orchestral Music* (1970); Demuth, Norman, *Ravel* (1947; repr. 1979); Jankelevitch, Vladimir, *Ravel* (1959); Myers, R. H., *Ravel: Life and Works* (1960); Orenstein, Arbie, *Ravel* (1975); Roland-Manuel, *Maurice Ravel* (1947).

raven

The larger members of the bird genus *Corvus* in the crow family, Corvidae, are referred to as ravens. Their closest relatives are the crows, magpies, and jays. Among the ravens the common raven, *C. corax*, of the Northern Hemisphere and the white-necked raven, *C. cryptoleucus*, of the southwestern United States to central Mexico are typical.

The common raven, found in a wide range of habitats, is deep, glossy black, as are other ravens. The largest SONGBIRD (order Passeriformes), it weighs almost 1.25 kg (3 lb) and reaches up to 66 cm (26 in) in length. This raven has long wings, a strong bill and feet, a wedge-shaped tail, and nostrils shielded by stiff feathers. Nests are usually large, made of sticks and often placed on cliff ledges; sometimes the raven nests in trees. Common ravens eat a variety of animal and plant material, including carrion. The smaller white-necked raven, 48 cm (19 in) in length, confined to arid habitats, is

The common raven, C. corax, *which is generally regarded as a pest, is rarely seen outside of rural areas because it has been driven off by guns and poison. Its diet is quite varied; in addition to frequenting garbage dumps, it eats the eggs and young of other birds.*

often difficult to see because the white only occurs at the base of the neck feathers.   GARY D. SCHNELL

Bibliography: Wilmore, Sylvia B., *Crows, Jays, Ravens and Their Relatives* (1977).

Ravenna   [rah-ven'-nah]

Ravenna is a city located in the Emilia-Romagna region of northern Italy and connected to the Adriatic Sea, 8 km (5 mi) to the east, by canal. Ravenna has a population of 137,093 (1982 est.). The city is an agricultural market, railroad junction, and industrial center. Chief manufactures are fertilizers, furniture, cement, chemicals, and plastics. Ravenna is exceptionally rich in Roman and Byzantine artistic remains of the 5th and 6th centuries. These include the Byzantine Church of SAN VITALE, the mausoleum of Empress Galla Placidia (see GALLA PLACIDIA, MAUSOLEUM OF), the Church of Sant' Apollinare Nuovo, and the Church of Sant' Apollinare in Classe.

The city was probably occupied by northern Italic tribes as early as 1400 BC. It came under Rome in 191 BC. ODOACER of the Heruli and THEODORIC the Ostrogoth ruled Italy from Ravenna during the 5th and 6th centuries. The city served (c.585–751) as the capital of the Exarchate of Ravenna, the seat of Byzantine rule in Italy, before falling to the Lombards and later the Franks. A free commune during the 12th and 13th centuries, Ravenna was subsequently ruled by the Da Polenta family until Venice took control in 1441. The city was annexed to the Papal States in 1509 and joined the new unified kingdom of Italy in 1860.   DANIEL R. LESNICK

Rawalpindi   [rah-wul-pin'-dee]

Rawalpindi is a city in northeastern Pakistan 14 km (9 mi) southwest of the capital, Islamabad. An industrial center and important grain market, it has a poulation of 928,000 (1981). Industries include petroleum refining, textiles, and ironworks. Rawalpindi is the Pakistani Army headquarters, and from 1959 to 1960 it was the capital of Pakistan.

Settled around 1756 on the site of an old village inhabited by Rawals, Rawalpindi controlled the route into Kashmir. When the British arrived in the 19th century, they made the city headquarters of their northern army. Rawalpindi retains many evidences of British colonial rule.

Rawlings, Jerry   [raw'-lingz]

Jerry Rawlings, b. June 22, 1947, served as chief of state of Ghana in 1979 and again beginning in 1981. An almost unknown flight lieutenant before his May 1979 attempt to overthrow Lt.-Gen. Frederick W. K. Akuffo, he staged a successful coup in June. Akuffo and two other former heads of state were then charged with squandering public funds and executed. Although the popular Rawlings turned power over to an elected civilian regime in September, he staged another coup in December 1981, declaring that President Hilla Limann had failed to eliminate corruption. He instituted a variety of economic reforms and pledged to restore Ghana to prosperity.

Rawlings, Marjorie Kinnan

An American novelist and essayist, Marjorie Kinnan Rawlings, b. Washington, D.C., Aug. 8, 1896, d. Dec. 14, 1953, won the 1939 Pulitzer Prize for her best-selling novel *The Yearling* (1938). A classic story of growing up in the backwoods of Florida, it also achieved great popularity and critical success as a film (1946). Rawlings did her best work at her farm near Cross Creek, Fla., where she wrote six novels, a volume of short stories, and a collection of essays (1942). Her writing conveys the simplicity and beauty of the lives of the isolated farmers, hunters, and moonshiners who were her neighbors.

Bibliography: Bellman, Samuel I., *Marjorie Kinnan Rawlings* (1974); Bigelow, Gordon E., *Frontier Eden* (1966).

Rawlinson, Sir Henry Creswicke

The British army officer and Assyriologist Sir Henry Creswicke Rawlinson, b. Apr. 11, 1810, d. Mar. 5, 1895, provided the key to deciphering Mesopotamian CUNEIFORM by translating the Old Persian section of the trilingual cuneiform inscription of Darius I (r. 521–485 BC) at BEHISTUN, Iran. Through his work, knowledge of ancient Near Eastern and biblical history was greatly enhanced.

Posted to India in 1826, Rawlinson rapidly gained linguistic skills. In Persia (1833–39), he helped reorganize the shah's army and copied the Old Persian inscription on the cliff at Behistun. After distinguished service in Afghanistan, Rawlinson went (1843) to Beghdad, where he served (1851–55) as consul general. While in Mesopotamia he conducted archaeological excavations and completed his work on the Behistun inscription.

Rawlinson's publications (1837, 1846–53) revolutionized the study of Assyriology. He was knighted in 1856 and later sat in Parliament (1858, 1865–68) and was minister plenipotentiary to Persia (1859).   KATE FIELDEN

Bibliography: Budge, Sir E. A. W., *The Rise and Progress of Assyriology* (1925; repr. 1975); Rawlinson, G., *A Memoir of Sir Henry Creswicke Rawlinson* (1898).

Rawls, John   [rawlz]

John Rawls, b. Baltimore, Md., Feb. 21, 1921, is an American philosopher and educator. He has taught at Princeton and Cornell universities and at the Massachusetts Institute of Technology and, since 1959, at Harvard University. Rawls's *A Theory of Justice* (1971) develops a contract theory in opposition to intuitionism and utilitarianism and posits two principles: the individual's right to as much liberty as is compatible with the liberty of others, and that social and economic inequalities are to be set up for everyone's advantage and under conditions of equal opportunity.   E. DARNELL RUCKER

Bibliography: Daniels, Norman, ed., *Reading Rawls: Critical Studies on Rawls's A Theory of Justice* (1975); Wellbank, J. H., *John Rawls and His Critics* (1982); Wolff, Robert Paul, *Understanding Rawls: A Reconstruction and Critique of A Theory of Justice* (1977).

ray

Rays are cartilagenous fishes represented by several families in the order Rajiformes, which includes SKATES, GUITARFISHES, and SAWFISHES. Rays, like skates, have flattened bodies and enlarged pectoral fins that join the head; unlike skates, they usually lack caudal fins and are ovoviviparous. Most species are marine. The electric rays, family Torpedinidae, found in all temperate and tropical oceans, have electric organs (modified muscles) on each side of the head capable of delivering up to 200 volts. The Atlantic torpedo, *Torpedo nobiliana*, one of the larger species, grows up to 50 kg (110 lb) and about 1.8 m (6 ft). Stingrays, family Dasyatidae, have sawtoothed spines located at the base of the tail. Associated with the spine or spines is a venom gland, and the apparatus can cause severe injury. Some species are small; others may grow to 340 kg (750 lb) in weight and measure 2 m (7 ft) across the pectorals. The common North American genus is *Dasyatis*. Eagle rays, family Myliobatidae, are distinguished by having a distinct head region and a fleshy pad extending in front of the head; some also have a venomous spine. Most species are found in tropical seas, but some are temperate and a few are cold-water species. Of the cow-nose rays, family Rhinobatidae, *Rhinoptera bonasus* is a typical species found in temperate and subtropical waters. It averages slightly less than 1 m (3 ft) across the pectorals. The manta rays, family Mobulidae, are the largest and most pelagic of the rays. The Atlantic manta, *Manta borustris*, reaches 6.1 m (20 ft) across the pectorals and weighs more than 1,360 kg (3,000 lb). Mantas are harmless unless harpooned.   E. O. WILEY

Ray, John

John Ray, b. Nov. 29, 1627, d. Jan. 17, 1705, an English naturalist, laid the foundation for the systematics in taxonomy later developed by Carolus LINNAEUS. He used anatomy as the basic criterion for classifying plants and animals and established the species as the basic unit of classification.

Ray, Man

Man Ray juxtaposed his model, Kiki, with one of his masks in this eerie photograph (1926). Ray, also an acclaimed surrealist painter, sculptor, and filmmaker, was instrumental in the evolution of photography as a modern art form and devised many innovative techniques to further its development as an abstract art.

Man Ray, b. Philadelphia, Aug. 27, 1890, d. Nov. 18, 1976, was a pioneering painter and photographer in the Dada, surrealist, and abstract movements of the 1920s and '30s. After participating in radical art activities in New York, he moved (1921) to Paris, where he supported himself as a portrait photographer. In 1922 he published *Les Champs délicieux* (Delightful Fields), an album of abstract photographs made without use of a camera that he called rayographs. Later he experimented with solarization techniques and negative prints. He turned to filmmaking in 1923, producing *Le Retour à la Raison* (Return to Reason, 1923), *Anemic Cinema* (1925–26) with Marcel Duchamp, and *L'Étoile de Mer* (Star of the Sea, 1928). He exhibited his paintings and photographs frequently from the 1920s to the 1940s and later continued to synthesize painting and photography. He published *To Be Continued Unnoticed* (1948), *Alphabet for Adults* (1948), and *Self Portrait* (1963), an autobiography.   MELINDA BOYD PARSONS

Bibliography: Janus, *Man Ray* (1981); Los Angeles County Museum of Art, *Man Ray* (1966); Penrose, Roland, *Man Ray* (1975); Ray, Man, *12 Rayographs 1921–1928* (1963) and *Objects of My Affection* (1983); Schwarz, Arturo, *Man Ray: The Rigour of Imagination* (1977); State Gallery in Lenbachhaus, *New York Dada* (1973).

Ray, Satyajit   [ry, suht'-yuh-jit]

Satyajit Ray, b. May 2, 1922, is India's foremost film director. A versatile craftsman who has worked in several film genres, Ray is known best outside India for his moving depictions of Indian family life. His acknowledged masterpiece, the neorealist trilogy made up of *Pather Panchali* (1955), *Aparajito* (1956), and *The World of Apu* (1959), lyrically chronicles the day-to-day activities of a rural Bengali family and the coming of age of the boy Apu. Two other outstanding Ray films, *The Music Room* (1958) and *The Big City* (1963), deal with the changing nature of contemporary Indian life, whereas *Charulata* (1964) is a graceful adaptation of Rabindranath Tagore's classic portrait of the Indian middle classes in the Victorian era. In later films such as *Days and Nights in the Forest* (1970), *Company Ltd.* (1971), *Distant Thunder* (1973), and *The Chess Players* (1977), Ray focused on political and social themes without losing his humanistic perspective. He composed the music for many of his films, including *The Home and the World* (1984).

Bibliography: Seton, Marie, *Portrait of a Director: Satyajit Ray* (1971).

Rayburn, Sam

Samuel Taliaferro Rayburn, b. near Kingston, Tenn., Jan. 6, 1882, d. Nov. 16, 1961, served as Speaker of the U.S. House of

Representatives for 17 years, longer than any other person in history. Having moved to Texas as a child, Rayburn, a Democrat, served (1907–13) in the Texas legislature. Elected to the U.S. House of Representatives in 1912, he served there continuously for 48 years, a congressional record. A strong supporter of the New Deal, he became majority leader in 1937. Elected House Speaker in 1940, Rayburn held that post until his death, except for 4 years (1947–49, 1953-55) when the Republicans were in power. He was widely regarded as one of the most effective Speakers of the House in U.S. history.

Bibliography: Champagne, Anthony, *Congressman Sam Rayburn* (1984); Steinberg, Alfred, *Sam Rayburn: A Biography* (1975).

Rayleigh, Lord [ray'-lee]

The Englishman John William Strutt, 3d Baron Rayleigh, b. Nov. 12, 1842, d. June 30, 1919, made numerous contributions spanning every field of classical physics. His dramatic discovery—with Sir William Ramsay—of a new element, the inert gas argon, received much publicity, but his other achievements were more significant. Early in his career (1871) he solved the problem of the blue color of the sky by deriving the formula specifying how light scattering varies with the wavelength of the incident light. Drawn particularly to wave phenomena, he produced a classic two-volume work on sound and laid the foundations for the Rayleigh-Jeans law (1900), formulated to account for the distribution of energy in BLACK-BODY RADIATION. Lord Rayleigh was awarded the Nobel Prize for physics in 1904.   ROBERT SILLIMAN

Bibliography: Lindsay, R. Bruce, *Lord Rayleigh, the Man and His Work* (1970); Strutt, Robert John, *Life of John William Strutt, Third Baron Rayleigh, O. M. F. R. S.,* 2d ed. (1968).

Raymond, Henry Jarvis

The journalist Henry Jarvis Raymond, b. Lima, N.Y., Jan. 24, 1820, d. June 18, 1869, was with George Jones a cofounder (1851) of the *New York Times*. He opposed the sensationalism favored by Horace Greeley and other journalists of the period. During his 18 years as editor of the *Times*, Raymond established its reputation for political impartiality and accuracy and built it into one of the country's most respected dailies. Active politically throughout his career, Raymond was one of the early organizers of the Republican party. He served for several years on the New York State Assembly and from 1865 to 1867 as a U.S. congressman. He is also remembered for his important study *A History of the Administration of President Lincoln* (1864).

Bibliography: Brown, E., *Raymond of the "Times"* (1951); Maverick, Augustus H., *Raymond and the New York Press* (1870; repr. 1970).

Raynaud's disease [ray-nohz']

Raynaud's disease is a disorder of unknown cause (idiopathic) that is characterized by episodes of sudden spasms, or constriction, of small arteries in the hands and feet, resulting in greatly reduced blood supply. Raynaud's disease is more common in women than men, and its onset usually occurs in young adulthood. The affected areas will show a color change, going from pallor to blue or red. Intermittent constriction is triggered by cold or emotional upset. The right and left digits are affected simultaneously; in about half the cases, only the hands are involved. The disease may improve quickly, remain mild, or grow progressively worse. More rarely, blood clots and gangrene may complicate progressive cases. Pain is uncommon, but numbness and tingling sensations frequently occur. Drugs that dilate arteries may be used long term. Attacks may be terminated by keeping the hands and feet warm. The use of tobacco aggravates the problem, because it causes arteries to constrict.

When the condition is secondary to another disorder, it is called Raynaud's phenomenon. Treatment then depends on the cause of the disorders.   PETER L. PETRAKIS

rayon

The synthetic fiber known as rayon is produced from regenerated cellulose (wood pulp) that has been chemically treated. Fabrics made of rayon are strong, highly absorbent, and soft; they drape well and can be dyed in brilliant, long-lasting colors. Rayon fibers are also used as reinforcing cords in motor tires, and their excellent absorbency makes them useful in medical and surgical materials. Rayon can be used alone or blended with other synthetic or natural fibers. Today rayon accounts for about 6 percent of total synthetic fiber production in the United States. Rayon demand has remained fairly constant, despite the introduction of competitive noncellulose synthetic fibers, especially NYLON and polyester.

In 1664, Robert Hooke, a British scientist known for his observations of plant cells, speculated on the possibility of duplicating silk by synthetic means. Although fibers from nitrocellulose had been produced in 1855, the first successful commercial process was developed in 1884 by the French inventor Hilaire de CHARDONNET. Chardonnet demonstrated that cellulose nitrate could be dissolved in a mixture of ether and alcohol and extruded through a series of jets to form a continuous filament. He called the filament artificial silk. In 1924 producers agreed to call the fiber rayon.

Various methods are used to produce three types of regenerated cellulose fibers: viscose, cuprammonium, and cellulose acetate. Viscose rayon, used to make wearing apparel and heavy fabrics, involves treating cellulose—which is now derived from wood pulp—with caustic soda and carbon disulfide. A viscose solution is produced and is allowed to age for 2 to 4 days. It is then forced through metal nozzles that have fine holes (spinnerets), and filaments emerge from the other end into a bath of dilute sulfuric acid. Rayon can be prepared as a continuous filament yarn or cut into specified lengths and then spun like cotton or wool.

The cuprammonium process is used to make fine filaments to be used in silklike fabrics and sheer hosiery. The cellulose pulp, dissolved in caustic soda, is treated with copper oxide and ammonia. The filaments are forced out of the spinnerets into a spinning funnel and then stretched to the required fineness by the action of a jetstream of water.

In both the viscose and cuprammonium processes, cellulose is treated chemically and is then regenerated. Acetate and triacetate, however, are rayon fibers that are chemical derivatives (esters) of cellulose. They are considered a separate class

Cellulose, the major ingredient in both acetate and rayon fibers, is obtained from wood chips (1) by a sulfite process. Acetate fibers are formed from a diacetate reaction product of cellulose, mixed acid (2), and alkali (3). The diacetate is dissolved in acetone (4) and extruded through tiny holes in a spinneret into a hot-air tower. As acetone evaporates from the thin liquid streams, solid acetate filaments form and are wound on tubes (5). Viscose rayon is made from cellulose reacted (6) with aqueous alkali and carbon disulfide. A solution of viscose is produced that is pigmented (7) and pumped through holes into an acid bath (8). Rayon filaments are formed and wound up (9).

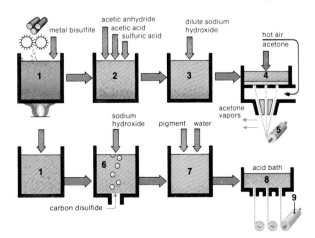

of fiber. Acetate fabrics are known for their brilliance of color and ability to drape well, properties that have made them particularly successful as apparel fabrics. Triacetate yarns have many of the same properties as acetate but are particularly well known for their ability to provide pleat retention in apparel. Short fibers of acetate are used as filling materials in pillows, mattress pads, and quilts and also as filtering agents in cigarettes.

See also: SYNTHETIC FIBERS; TEXTILE INDUSTRY.

Rayonnant style   [ray'-uh-nant]

In GOTHIC ART AND ARCHITECTURE the Rayonnant is an architectural style that evolved in the region of Paris during the reign of Louis IX (1226–70). Fostered by the king's patronage, it has also been called the Court Style. The word *Rayonnant* itself refers to the radiating spokes of the enormous rose windows. In contrast to the solid sculpturesque character of the previous High Gothic phase of French ecclesiastical architecture, the Rayonnant reduced the masonry structure of the churches to a tenuous skeletal system supporting vast expanses of traceried glass.

After 1250 the style spread from Paris to central and southern France, while in the Champagne it produced that perfect expression of the Rayonnant, the Church of Saint-Urbain, Troyes (begun 1262). In Alsace the astounding traceried curtain of the facade (begun 1277) of Strasbourg Cathedral was directly inspired by the Rayonnant transept facades (begun *c.*1247) of Notre-Dame de Paris, and the choir (begun 1355) of Aachen Cathedral, modeled on Louis IX's Sainte-Chapelle (1241–48), is only one of many German monuments influenced by the Rayonnant. The style even took hold in distant Prague, where the French architect Matthew of Arras began the new cathedral in 1344. In France, however, the impetus of the Rayonnant was already waning, soon to be extinguished in the dark days of the Hundred Years' War.

WILLIAM M. HINKLE

Bibliography: Branner, Robert, *St. Louis and the Court Style in Gothic Architecture* (1965); Grodecki, Louis, *Gothic Architecture,* trans. by I. Mark (1977); Stoddard, Whitney S., *Monastery and Cathedral in France* (1966).

Razin, Stenka   [rah'-zeen, steng'-kah]

Stenka Razin, actually Stephan Timofeyevich Razin, d. June 16 (N.S.), 1671, an ataman, or chief, of the DON COSSACKS, led a large-scale peasant revolt in Russia. During 1667–69 he raided and pillaged the lower Volga valley and trans-Caspian region with his Cossack band. In 1670 he organized peasants who had fled Moscow to the southern steppes to seek freedom with the Cossacks. Several non-Russian tribes also joined the revolt. The rebels, eventually some 20,000 strong, captured several cities before they were defeated by tsarist troops at Simbirsk (now Ulyanovsk). Razin was taken to Moscow and executed. He became a folk hero whose exploits are still celebrated in songs and legends.

RDX

RDX (Research Development Explosive), or cyclonite, [$CH_2N(NO_2)$]$_3$, a hard, white crystalline solid, is the base for many explosive compounds. It is called hexogen in Germany and T_4 in Italy. Discovered in 1899, it was a component of man, plastic explosives used during World War II. More brisant, or shatterable, than TNT, RDX's inability to be cast is overcome and its high sensitivity reduced when combined with other materials. RDX and a small amount of wax are combined to produce Composition A, which has been widely used as the explosive charge in armor-piercing shells. Composition B, a mixture of RDX, TNT, and wax, is slightly more sensitive than TNT but is nearly as brisant as RDX. Able to be cast, it is widely used in fragmentation bombs, artillery projectiles, and hand grenades. The various Composition Cs, popularly known as plastic explosives, are mixtures of RDX and plasticizers. They are about as sensitive as TNT but are more brisant. Because of their ability to be molded by hand,

Composition Cs are widely used in demolition and are standard military explosives.

DAVID N. BUCKNER

Re: see AMON-RE.

reactance

In electrical circuits, reactance is a property of the circuit that arises from the presence of capacitative and inductive elements. Reactance (X) depends on the applied frequency (f) and is measured in ohms. If inductance (L) is measured in henrys and capacitance (C), in farads, then

$$\text{inductive reactance } (X_L) = 2\pi fL$$

$$\text{capacitative reactance } (X_C) = \frac{1}{2\pi fC}$$

For a series circuit,

$$\text{impedance } (Z) = \sqrt{R^2 + X^2} = \sqrt{R^2 + (X_L - X_C)^2}$$

Because X_L increases and X_C decreases with an increase in frequency, at a certain frequency (the resonant frequency) inductive reactance will equal capacitative reactance and the two will cancel. Therefore at the resonant frequency the total impedance is only the resistance R of the circuit, and circuit current is at a maximum. The resonant frequency for a given L and C can be determined by setting $X_L = X_C$, and resonance will occur when $f = \frac{1}{2}\pi\sqrt{LC}$.

reaction, chemical

The reaction is the heart of the study of chemistry. All chemical reactions involve the breakage and reformation of CHEMICAL BONDS of molecules to form different substances. Chemistry, then, can be defined as the science of substances—their composition, structure, and properties and the reactions that change one substance into another.

A simple chemical reaction occurs when hydrogen gas combines with oxygen gas to form the compound water. On

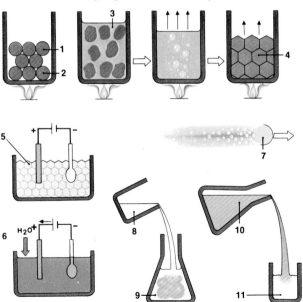

Reactions do not occur between heated solids such as aluminum sulfate (1) and potassium sulfate (2). If the solids are dissolved in water (3), however, and heating is continued until the water evaporates, the compounds combine to form alum (4). Dry copper sulfate crystals (5) will not conduct electricity, but when water is added (6) electrolysis occurs. Solids may react with liquids; sodium metal (7) reacts violently with water and liberates hydrogen. Reactions between liquids are common. Clear solutions of phenolphthalein (8) and alkali (9) produce a red solution (10), which is converted back to the colorless state by adding it to a colorless acid solution (11).

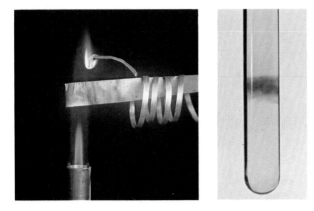

(Left) *The reaction rates of different materials vary considerably. Iron, for example, reacts so slowly with oxygen that it can be heated red hot without showing any appreciable change. A heated strip of magnesium, however, burns rapidly to form an oxide.* (Right) *The brown ring reaction is a simple method for detecting nitrate ions. A solution of potassium sulfate is carefully poured on top of an acidic nitrate solution so that the fluids do not mix. A characteristic brown color forms between the two layers if nitrate ion is present.*

the molecular level, two molecules of hydrogen (H_2) react with one molecule of oxygen (O_2) to produce two molecules of water (H_2O). The equation for this reaction is:

$$2H_2 + O_2 \rightarrow 2H_2O + \text{energy}$$

Chemical bonds actually are the result of the overlap of electron clouds, but for diagrammatic purposes they are represented by straight lines; the breaking and reforming of bonds in the above reaction can then be described as follows:

$$
\begin{array}{l}
\text{H—H} \qquad\qquad \text{H—O—H} \\
\qquad\quad + \text{ O}={O} \rightarrow \\
\text{H—H} \qquad\qquad \text{H—O—H}
\end{array}
$$

Chemical Reaction versus Physical Change. Care must be taken not to confuse a chemical reaction with a physical change, such as a change in state. Water, like all types of matter, can exist in either the solid, liquid, or gaseous state depending on the conditions of temperature and pressure. When the pressure is 1 atmosphere, the change from ice to water to steam occurs as shown:

$$H_2O \text{ (solid)} \xrightarrow[0°\text{ C}]{\text{energy}} H_2O \text{ (liquid)} \xrightarrow[100°\text{ C}]{\text{energy}} H_2O \text{ (gas)}$$

In these changes no chemical reaction is involved because no chemical bonds are broken and no new ones formed.

Energy. The reaction between hydrogen and oxygen releases a large quantity of energy, most of which is present as heat. Such an energy-releasing reaction is said to be exothermic, or exoergic. Once the water molecules are formed, however, they cannot again be converted to hydrogen or oxygen merely by cooling (withdrawing the energy from) the newly formed water. The reverse chemical reaction to convert water back to hydrogen and oxygen can be accomplished only if an equal quantity of energy (possibly in the form of electrical energy) is returned to the water molecules to break the bonds that hold the hydrogen and oxygen atoms together as water molecules. Such a reaction, which requires energy, is said to be endothermic, or endoergic (see CHEMICAL ENERGY; THERMOCHEMISTRY).

Chemical reactions are identified by the changes in the chemical properties of the substances during the course of the reaction. For example, table salt (sodium chloride, NaCl), when melted, can be decomposed to its elements by a passage of an electrical current through the melt. At the negative electrode the silvery molten metal sodium (Na) is formed, and at the positive electrode the poisonous, greenish yellow gas chlorine (Cl_2) is released. The above reaction can be represented by the following equation:

$$2NaCl \text{ (liquid)} \xrightarrow{\text{electrical current}} 2Na \text{ (liquid)} + Cl_2 \text{ (gas)}$$

In this equation the same number of sodium and chlorine atoms appear on both sides of the arrow because no atoms of matter can be destroyed during a chemical reaction; the only change can be in how they are bonded with each other. This type of reaction is called an electrical decomposition, or ELECTROLYSIS.

Oxidation and Reduction. Many common chemical reactions involve oxygen (O_2), which is present in the atmosphere. For example, the formation of rust (iron oxide, Fe_2O_3) is the result of the action of oxygen on iron (Fe) in the presence of moisture (see CORROSION):

$$4Fe + 3O_2 \xrightarrow{H_2O} 2Fe_2O_3$$

Gasoline, in the form of isooctane (C_8H_{18}), is burned with oxygen (see COMBUSTION) in engines to produce carbon dioxide (CO_2) and water plus the energy necessary to power the motor:

$$2C_8H_{18} + 25O_2 \rightarrow 16CO_2 + 18H_2O + \text{energy}$$

In animals, oxygen is combined with the hemoglobin of the blood in the lungs, where it is conveyed to the individual body cells. There it reacts, by a complicated series of events, to convert food into carbon dioxide, water, and energy.

These reactions, which all involve oxygen, are known as oxidation reactions. The opposite of oxidation is reduction. (For a more detailed explanation, see OXIDATION AND REDUCTION.) PHOTOSYNTHESIS is a reductive process, another complicated sequence of chemical reactions that enables plants to use energy from the Sun to produce glucose ($C_6H_{12}O_6$) and oxygen:

$$6CO_2 + 6H_2O \xrightarrow[\text{chlorophyll}]{\text{light}} C_6H_{12}O_6 + 6O_2$$

With the production of glucose, oxygen is also a product of the reaction and is again available to replenish the necessary oxygen of the atmosphere.

Catalysis. The decomposition of potassium chlorate ($KClO_3$) to produce oxygen at moderate temperatures will proceed if a CATALYST is employed to aid in the reaction. The catalyst is manganese dioxide (MnO_2), which survives the reaction unchanged:

$$2KClO_3 \xrightarrow[\text{heat}]{MnO_2} 2KCl + 3O_2\uparrow$$

A catalyst does not participate in a reaction; it merely speeds it up.

Reactions in the Environment. Although chemical reactions are responsible for life processes and are useful to a technological society, they can also lead to undesirable effects. One of the pollutants of modern day society is the sulfur dioxide produced when coal, which has sulfur impurities in it, is burned for energy.

$$S + O_2 \rightarrow SO_2$$

This oxide, in prolonged contact with oxygen, becomes sulfur trioxide (SO_3), which is then converted to sulfuric acid (H_2SO_4).

$$2SO_2 + O_2 \rightarrow 2SO_3$$
$$SO_3 + H_2O \rightarrow H_2SO_4$$

The resulting sulfuric acid is deposited in rainwater and can become a significant health problem because it can aggravate respiratory ailments in individuals. Sulfuric acid also causes serious deterioration of the marble or limestone used in many historic and artistic structures. This problem is of worldwide concern in preservation efforts. It is a result of the following reaction:

$$CaCO_3 + H_2SO_4 \rightarrow CaSO_4 + H_2O + CO_2\uparrow$$

The calcium sulfate ($CaSO_4$) that is formed eventually washes away, and the stone deteriorates.

One chemical reaction of constant concern in the home is

the action that hard water has on soap. The effective cause of hardness in water is the presence of calcium ions (Ca^{2+}) from the soluble calcium bicarbonate ($Ca[HCO_3]_2$) found in hard water. The reaction with soap and calcium ions is as follows:

$$Ca^{2+} + 2Na^+ (soap)^- \rightarrow Ca^{2+} (soap)^-_2 + 2Na^+$$

Soap, which is a sodium salt of a long-chain organic acid, undergoes an ionic reaction with the Ca^{2+} ion that results in the formation of an insoluble calcium soap that precipitates in the wash. This is the curd that produces the ring around the bathtub and results in the decreased effectiveness of the soap. In order to soften water, ION EXCHANGE units are employed in which the Ca^{2+} ion dissolved in the water is exchanged for two Na^+ ions on the zeolite of the softener unit.

DONALD J. COOK

Bibliography: Basolo, Fred, and Pearson, R. G., *Mechanisms of Inorganic Reactions*, 2d ed. (1967); Benfey, Otto T., *Introduction to Organic Reaction Mechanisms*, rev. ed. (1981); Campbell, J. Arthur, *Why Do Chemical Reactions Occur?* (1965); Pauling, Linus and Peter, *Chemistry* (1975).

reactor: see BREEDER REACTOR; NUCLEAR ENERGY.

Read, Sir Herbert

Sir Herbert Edward Read, b. Dec. 4, 1893, d. June 12, 1968, an English poet and critic, is remembered especially for his defense within England of modern art and culture. He was assistant keeper at the Victoria and Albert Museum, London (1922–31); professor of fine arts at the University of Edinburgh (1931–33); and editor of the *Burlington Magazine* (1933–38). As a writer, he was primarily a poet and a critic of poetry during the early years of his career, shifting his interests more toward the visual arts during the 1930s. Read concentrated his attention both on specific contemporary artists, whom he introduced to the British public, and on general questions concerning the philosophy of art. He developed theories that unite an understanding of art as an autonomous mode of knowledge and experience with a view of art as a response to, and expression of, the needs of society. His writings include *In Retreat* (1925), *Wordsworth* (1930), *The Meaning of Art* (rev. ed., 1931), *Art and Industry: The Principles of Industrial Design* (1934; rev. ed., 1945), *Art and Society* (1936), *Icon and Idea: The Function of Art in the Development of Human Consciousness* (1955), *The Art of Sculpture* (1956), and *Henry Moore* (1965).

JACQUELINE V. FALKENHEIM

Bibliography: Woodcock, George, *Herbert Read* (1925).

Reade, Charles [reed]

An English writer, Charles Reade, b. June 8, 1814, d. Apr. 11, 1884, was the author of a celebrated historical novel, *The Cloister and the Hearth* (1861). After studying law, he began to write for the theater. He then turned to carefully documented novels of contemporary life, dealing with such subjects as prisons and lunatic asylums. A similar concern for accuracy, but with greater detachment, characterized the depiction of the Middle Ages in his most famous novel.

Reading (England) [red'-ing]

Reading is the county town of Berkshire, England, on the River Kennet, 58 km (36 mi) west of London. The population of the city is 132,037 (1981). Reading, located on rail, highway, and air routes, is an industrial and market center, but its university (1892) has a strong agricultural bias. The site of a Danish settlement (871), Reading was chartered as a county borough in 1253 and made a city in 1639. It was virtually destroyed (1640s) during the English Civil War.

Reading (Pennsylvania)

Reading (1980 pop., 78,686), the seat of Berks County, is a city in southeastern Pennsylvania 72 km (45 mi) northwest of Philadelphia. Located in the center of the fertile Pennsylvania

Dutch region, Reading, a rail and manufacturing center, produces hosiery, textiles, steel, and metal products. Reading was settled in 1748 by Thomas Penn, the son of William Penn, the state's founder. During the late 18th century the city was a prosperous iron and steel center. Its growth was further stimulated by the construction (1820s) of canals on the Schuylkill and Susquehanna rivers and the arrival (1884) of the Philadelphia and Reading Railroad.

Reading, Rufus Daniel Isaacs, 1st Marquess of

Rufus Daniel Isaacs, 1st marquess of Reading, b. Oct. 10, 1860, d. Dec. 30, 1935, was a British statesman who served as ambassador (1918–19) to the United States and viceroy (1921–26) of India. A lawyer, he was a Liberal member (1904–13) of the House of Commons and attorney general (1910–13) before serving as lord chief justice of England (1913–21). As viceroy of India, Reading reacted strongly to the growing movement for independence. He imprisoned Mahatma Gandhi in 1922 and used force to put down Sikh and Muslim rebellions. He was made a marquess in 1926 and in 1931 was foreign secretary in Ramsay MacDonald's National government.

Bibliography: Hyde, H. M., *Lord Reading* (1967); Reading, Gerald Rufus Isaacs, 2d Marquess of, *Rufus Isaacs, First Marquess of Reading* (1940).

reading disability: see DYSLEXIA.

reading education

The ability to read enables a person to satisfy certain personal and functional needs and to participate fully in contemporary society. It is a basic skill necessary for success in other areas of study, and it can lead to a lifetime pursuit of learning, critical thinking, and enjoyment. The ability to read, therefore, is a fundamental goal of—as well as a significant tool in—education.

Beginning Reading. The first learning experiences in school should create a foundation for successful reading. Programs should stress activities that are enjoyable and that foster favorable early reading experiences. Programs should also accommodate children's varied stages of social and intellectual development. Such factors as familiar experiences and home and family environment influence children's reading abilities. Research has shown that children with rich experiential and language backgrounds are better prepared for beginning reading than children who lack such backgrounds.

As children become acquainted with the materials that prepare them for formal reading during the nursery school, prekindergarten, kindergarten, and early primary years, they are exposed to and begin to master auditory perception, visual discrimination, visual and auditory memory, and fine and gross motor skills that aid in reading development. Children should be able to discern likenesses and differences among sounds, letters, and words. Instructional programs should not, however, rely solely upon these skills. Speaking and writing skills as well as listening are integral parts of a total reading program and should be introduced early in a well-balanced curriculum.

Because primary language competence—the ability to understand, process, use, and enjoy language—is a crucial factor in learning that directly affects reading competence, it is important to provide young children with many and varied opportunities to develop facility with both oral and written language. Activities involving such communication skills as self-expression, reasoning, dramatic play, and the appreciation of art, music, and literature are aimed at extending children's vocabularies, improving their abilities to express themselves, and developing a concept of symbols as well as cultivating the child as a whole.

Learning to Read. It is during the primary-school years that most children actually learn to read—a complex activity involving all of the senses. The first step often consists of learning the alphabet and the letters and combinations of letters that symbolize distinctive sounds of the language. Special alphabets, such as the INITIAL TEACHING ALPHABET, are also used to familiarize students with sound-symbol relationships. Children learn sounds and then blend sounds to form words. Mere word-calling, however, is not reading, which is a form of communication in which meaning is derived from words written in a certain context.

Because no single approach to reading is better than another, it is best to expose children to many kinds of programs and then to incorporate appropriate aspects of each program into a comprehensive reading curriculum. Most schools use eclectic basal reading programs, which cover a wide range of reading skills through sequential instruction. In such programs learning materials usually progress from readiness books to preprimers, primers, first readers, and then to a series of books for each succeeding year. Supplementary materials include filmstrips and workbooks. Most of the reading materials deal with activities and experiences familiar to a typical child and incorporate language patterns, concepts, and interests that are appropriate to the student's age level.

In another method of instruction, which is based solely on language-experience activities or whole language patterns, vocabulary and sentence patterns build the foundation for reading. Students learn to relate their experiences through storytelling. Their stories are written down and become the source of reading material.

Individualized reading is another procedure. Students select their reading materials based on their own interests. Through self-selection and self-pacing, this program enables students to progress at their own rates. Frequent student-teacher conferences are required to monitor student progress.

Comprehension and Reading Rate. Reading comprehension, the ability to read for meaning, develops gradually, and comprehension skills should be taught at each stage of reading development. As the structural elements of written communication develop, children recognize relationships among ideas and patterns of organization. They follow words into sentences and sentences into paragraphs in various ways: by topic, details, sequence, classification, comparison and contrast, and cause and effect.

The three main strands of reading comprehension are literal, inferential, and critical. Literal reading captures the surface meaning of the information explicitly supplied by the author. Inferential reading is interpretive, requiring the reader to draw a conclusion or to predict an outcome based not only on the information explicitly provided but also on what the author implies. Critical reading involves evaluation and judgment—the reader may be asked to distinguish between fact and opinion or to question the accuracy of information.

The rate at which one reads depends in part on the nature of the material being read. Reading fiction for pleasure often requires less time and fewer comprehension skills than does reading, for example, technical information or subject matter in such areas as mathematics, science, and the arts.

Reading and Current Issues. LITERACY AND ILLITERACY, the ability and inability, respectively, to read and write, are important factors in contemporary society. Concern over functional illiteracy has contributed to recent proposals for higher educational standards and for competency testing in schools. The merits of BILINGUAL EDUCATION, one method of achieving literacy for language-minority groups, continue to be debated. Another debate concerns the effect of television on reading and reading ability. Although research has been inconclusive, it has shown that television, when properly used, can add to the teaching and learning process. Public television, through such shows as "Sesame Street" and "The Electric Company," has made significant contributions to reading education. Books related to television programs and entire scripts with teacher lesson plans have been used to coordinate reading education with television viewing.   MARIAN SOTSKY

Bibliography: Bettelheim, Bruno, and Zelan, Karen, *On Learning to Read* (1982); Chall, Jeanne S., *Learning to Read: The Great Debate*, 2d ed. (1983); Harris, Albert J., and Sipay, Edward R., *How to Increase Reading Ability*, 7th ed. (1980); Smith, Frank, *Reading without Nonsense* (1979); Stauffer, Russell G., *The Language-Experience Approach to the Teaching of Reading*, 2d ed. (1980).

Reagan, Ronald   [ray'-guhn]

Ronald Wilson Reagan was elected the 40th president of the United States on Nov. 4, 1980, and was inaugurated on Jan. 20, 1981. At the age of 69, he was the oldest man and the first movie actor ever sworn into that office. His previous executive experience included two terms as president of the Screen Actors Guild (1952, 1959–60) and as governor of the nation's most populous state, California (1966–74).

Early Life and Career. Born on Feb. 6, 1911, in Tampico, Ill., Reagan had strong roots in small-town, middle America. He worked his way through Eureka College (B.A., 1932), had some success as a sportscaster, and began an acting career with Warner Bros. in 1937. He was to appear in about 53 films, with an interlude (1942–45) in the U.S. Army. Reagan married the actress Jane Wyman in 1940 (divorced 1948) and in 1952 wed Nancy Davis. He moved into television in the 1950s and became the popular host of "Death Valley Days" (1962–65) and spokesman for the General Electric Company. Inheriting from his father a New Deal orientation in politics, Reagan shifted his views in the 1950s and spoke out against "big government" and communism. By the 1960s he was a favorite speaker on the conservative circuit, and it was natural that he should support Barry Goldwater in 1964.

With the shattering defeat of the Republicans that year, Reagan was widely regarded as an ex–movie actor with simplistic views, no constituency of any size, and no future. His big years lay ahead, however. In 1966 he easily defeated the incumbent governor of California, Democrat Edmund "Pat" Brown, and began two 4-year terms that made him a national figure. Reagan won the loyalty of conservatives by initially opposing state spending and tax increases, but he proved to be a pragmatist when California's growth required an expansion of government services. When he left Sacramento the state's budget showed a $550-million surplus.

Reagan had been mentioned as a presidential contender in every campaign since 1968, and he tirelessly traveled the lecture circuit, excoriating the evils of liberalism. Republican rivals thought him too old to be a force in 1980, but with well-financed, loyal support, he swept through the primaries to nomination. He selected George BUSH as his running mate.

Presidential Campaign. Democrats began the campaign by underestimating Reagan's strengths. His age was offset by robust health. His views, however, appeared to be farther to the right than majority opinion—a vulnerability that President Jimmy Carter expected to expose. But Reagan, the master of television, phrased his views with an air of reasonableness and geniality, promising prosperity by "getting the government off our backs." Burdened by his failure to free the Americans held hostage by Iran and by a deteriorating economy, Carter saw his thinly based support erode as the voters concluded that Reagan was a safe choice to replace an ineffective regime. Reagan's margin of victory was sizable, the Californian carrying 44 states against Carter's 6, the popular vote 43 million to 36 million.

The Reagan Presidency. Immediately after his inauguration, Reagan launched a bold program that, if carried to conclusion, would fundamentally alter the U.S. political economy. Regarding the economy as in a state of crisis, the Reagan program for economic "revitalization" had been incubated by conservative theorists around the new president. To call forth the allegedly pent-up energies of entrepreneurial capitalism and restore growth, the Reagan plan offered a triad of measures: sharp budget cutting to shrink the public sector; tax cutting, especially in the higher and business brackets, to unleash investment; and a broad retreat from business and social regulation. This policy was "supply-side economics," and Reagan promised a surge of noninflationary growth.

Despite many doubters, Reagan jammed his program through Congress in 1981—a major tax cut, $43 billion in budget cuts in domestic programs, and cutbacks in environmental and business regulation. House Democrats resisted this reversal in tax and spending policies, but Reagan's successful appeals to the public, combined with the assassination attempt in which he was wounded by shots fired by John W. Hinckley, Jr., on March 30, generated irresistible support.

RONALD WILSON REAGAN
40th President of the United States (1981–)
Born: Feb. 6, 1911, Tampico, Ill.
Education: Eureka College (graduated 1932)
Profession: Actor, Public Official
Religious Affiliation: Christian Church
Marriage: Jan. 25, 1940, to Jane Wyman (1914–)—
divorced, 1948; Mar. 4, 1952, to Nancy Davis (1923–)
Children: Maureen Elizabeth Reagan (1941–); Mi-
chael Edward Reagan (1945–); Patricia Ann Rea-
gan (1952–); Ronald Prescott Reagan (1958–)
Political Affiliation: Republican
Writings: *Where's the Rest of Me?* (1965)

Vice-President: George Bush
Secretary of State: Alexander Haig (1981–82);
George Shultz (1982–)
Treasury: D. Regan (1981–85); J. Baker (1985–)
Defense: Caspar Weinberger (1981–87); Frank
Carlucci (1987–)
Attorney General: William French Smith (1981–
85); Edwin Meese (1985–)
Interior: James Watt (1981–83); William Clark
(1983–85); Donald Hodel (1985–)
Agriculture: J. Block (1981–86); R. Lyng (1986–)
Commerce: M. Baldrige (1981–87); C. W. Verity
(1987–)
Labor: Raymond Donovan (1981–85); William
Brock (1985–87); Ann McLaughlin (1987–)
Health and Human Services: R. Schweiker (1981–
83); M. Heckler (1983–85); O. Bowen (1985–)
Housing and Urban Development: Samuel Pierce
Transportation: Andrew Lewis (1981–83); Eliz-
abeth Dole (1983–87); J. H. Burnley (1987–)
Energy: James Edwards (1981–82); Donald Hodel
(1982–85); John Herrington (1985–)
Education: Terrel Bell (1981–84); William
Bennett (1985–)

Reagan's economic policy was cast into serious doubt by
the fall, when economic recession deepened. Wall Street
agreed with Budget Director David Stockman's admission that
Reagan's massive defense increases dwarfed budget cuts elsewhere and insured large continuing deficits, while public-
opinion polls indicated a growing conviction that the tax cuts
had mainly benefited the rich. The promised prosperity did
not seem to be filtering down from the wealthy.

The "revolution" seemed to have stalled, and 1982 was
spent in budgetary wrangles, while all factions waited to see
if the Reagan program would end the recession. Inflation
dropped out of double figures, but interest rates remained

high until the fall, when a change in Federal Reserve policy
caused them to decline. Unemployment in 1982 was the highest in 40 years, however. The political future of the Reagan
administration clearly depended on the response of the economy to supply-side medicine.

Reagan's defense buildup commenced, while foreign relations saw a stronger anti-Soviet stance but no major depar-
tures. The administration appeared internally divided on
many matters, such as the Middle East and Central America,
and in July 1982, Alexander HAIG was replaced as secretary of
state by George P. SHULTZ. The Israeli invasion of Lebanon in
the summer of 1982 prompted the dispatch of U.S. and other
peacekeeping forces to that beleaguered country. In a September appeal to solve the Israeli-Arab dispute, Reagan laid
out a detailed proposal for Palestinian self-rule in association
with Jordan, which was flatly rejected by Israel. The congressional elections of November 1982 gave the Democrats a larg-
er-than-normal, 26-seat gain in the House, while the Senate
was unchanged in party totals.

Although the commitment of U.S. Marines to Lebanon had
seemed a minor step in late 1982, the events of 1983 suggested
a pattern that increasingly divided American opinion. Heavy
casualties suffered by the Marines in Beirut raised anxieties
about the administration's Lebanese intervention (and early in
1984 the Marines were withdrawn). In late October 1983 the
president ordered an invasion of the Caribbean island of Gre-
nada and overthrew the country's anti-American dictatorship.
U.S. troops were on extended maneuver in Central America,
and the CIA worked openly to overturn the Sandinista regime
in Nicaragua. Arms control talks with the Soviet Union were
frozen in mutual distrust as a new deployment of U.S. nuclear
missiles began in Europe in November 1983. In each of these
initiatives, the president's rationale was the necessity of coun-
tering Soviet advances, but this strategy worried many because of the lack of diplomatic results.

In 1983 the economic picture brightened, with a resurgent
stock market, low inflation, and rising production. Recovery
was menaced by enormous deficits, but the jobless rate continued to inch downward.

Early in 1984, Ronald Reagan announced his decision to run
for a second term. Strong support came primarily from conservatives who approved of the military buildup and probusiness
policies. Equally fervent, however, were his critics—environ-
mentalists, minorities, and those who feared that nuclear war
might come from the very arms race that Reagan proposed as
a path to "strength." The Democrats nominated former Vice-
President Walter F. MONDALE, who made history by selecting
N.Y. Rep. Geraldine FERRARO as his running mate.

Yet the campaign of 1984 developed no clear issues. Mondale charged that Reagan would cut social security benefits
and raise taxes after reelection and criticized the huge federal
deficits. Reagan, who said little of his program for a second
term (except that he would not raise taxes), spoke of America
"standing tall" again. The president's radiant optimism, plus
the continued economic recovery, produced a stunning victory. Reagan won 59% of the vote and carried 49 states.

Reagan and Bush were inaugurated for second terms in January 1985. In July Reagan underwent surgery to remove a cancerous intestinal polyp. The contrast between his upbeat
mood and underlying ailments was mirrored in the national
economy, where a moderate recovery overlay worrisome
trends: huge trade deficits, a shaky farm economy, a 1985
budget deficit of $211 billion. Reagan's domestic agenda in
1985 was limited chiefly to a tax-reform measure that congressional Democrats resisted, then altered. The sweeping reform
bill Reagan signed on Oct. 22, 1986, slashed rates for individuals but eliminated many deductions, and had bipartisan par-
entage. More clearly an administration policy—and finally
victorious in Congress (by summer 1986)—was Reagan's request for $100 million in aid to the "contra" rebels against the
Nicaraguan government.

A decisive moment in Reagan's second term appeared to
have come at the second summit meeting between Reagan
and Soviet leader Mikhail Gorbachev in Iceland in October
1986 (the first meeting had been in Geneva in November

1985). The leaders apparently came close to agreeing to drastic reductions in nuclear missiles, but Reagan resisted the Soviet demand that the U.S. STRATEGIC DEFENSE INITIATIVE ("Star Wars") be limited to laboratory research, and the meeting ended in bitter disappointment. Despite Reagan's vigorous campaigning for Republican candidates, the Democrats took control of the Senate in the 1986 elections by the unexpectedly wide margin of 55 to 45 seats.

Shortly after, Reagan and his aides faced a damaging internal crisis, the IRAN-CONTRA AFFAIR, involving secret arms sales to Iran and diversion of some of the profits to the Nicaraguan "contras." Reagan had apparently not known of the diversion, which exposed his "management style" as inept. On the defensive in these final months, he saw two Supreme Court nominations (Robert Bork and Douglas Ginsburg) fail, and a stock-market collapse late in 1987 raised questions about his economic policies. History's verdict, perhaps, would center more on the arms-control agreement, eliminating all medium- and short-range missiles in Europe, that Reagan signed with Gorbachev in Washington in December 1987.

OTIS L. GRAHAM, JR.

Bibliography: Cannon, Lou, *Reagan* (1982); Dallek, Robert, *Ronald Reagan* (1984); Greenstein, Fred, ed., *The Reagan Presidency* (1983); Reeves, Richard, *The Reagan Detour* (1985); Smith, Hedrick, et al., *Reagan* (1981); Wills, Garry, *Reagan's America* (1987).

real estate: see PROPERTY.

real number

The set of all RATIONAL NUMBERS together with the set of all IRRATIONAL NUMBERS forms the set of real numbers. Any rational number a/b, where a and b are integers and $b \neq 0$, can be written as either a terminating decimal or as a repeating decimal. For example, $2 = 2.0$, $-3 = -3.0$, $5/2 = 2.5$, and $-1/4 = -0.25$ are all rational numbers that can be written as terminating decimals. On the other hand, $1/3 = 0.333 \ldots$ and $2/7 = 0.285714285714 \ldots$ are examples of repeating decimals. It is also possible to describe decimals that are not terminating or repeating. Numbers that are represented by nonterminating, nonrepeating decimals are called irrational numbers; examples of such numbers are $\sqrt{2}$, $\sqrt[3]{5}$, and π. Thus the set of real numbers can be described as the set of all decimals—terminating, repeating, or nonrepeating. Not all numbers, however, are real numbers (see COMPLEX NUMBER).   ROY DUBISCH

Bibliography: Cohen, Leon W., and Ehrich, Gertrude, *The Structure of the Real Number System*, rev. ed. (1977); Targett, David, *Coping with Numbers* (1984).

realism   (art)

In relation to the fine arts the term *realism* has conveyed a number of different meanings. Until the end of the 19th century it most often connoted naturalism, or the representation of the external world as it is actually seen. Such an approach stresses perceptual experience as opposed to suggestive expression through metaphor or abstraction. In this sense, the term may be used to describe the naturalism of the Italian painter Michelangelo Merisi da CARAVAGGIO and his followers, which appeared at the end of the 16th century.

During recent decades of the 20th century the term *realism* has been used to describe the movement away from abstraction and toward representational art. The same word, however, is also used to describe abstract art that sees reality as inner truth and opposes "mere appearances."

The art historical definition of *realism* originated in the movement that was dominant primarily in France from about 1840 to 1870–80 and that is identified particularly with the work of Gustave COURBET. The main precedents for 19th-century French realism are found in the work of artists painting in the tradition of Caravaggio. Realism, however, was decidedly an outgrowth of its particular time—one of great political and social upheaval. This unrest stirred the realists to reject prevailing canons of academic and romantic art and to undertake instead a nonescapist, democratic, empirical investigation of life as it existed around them. They painted ordinary people leading their everyday lives. Although other artists had depicted similar subjects in earlier times, the realists took a fresh and unemotional view.

Realism was most emphatically proclaimed in 1855, when Courbet, having been rejected for the Paris Exposition, arranged a private showing of his paintings that centered on his huge *The Artist's Studio* (1855; Louvre, Paris). He also distributed a manifesto of realism outlining his program. Among the other realists were Honoré DAUMIER, most noted for his incisive mockery of the petty bourgeoisie, and Jean François MILLET, whose scenes of workers in the countryside are more low-keyed and reflective in tone than those of Courbet. The works of Edouard MANET and Edgar DEGAS during the 1860s and '70s are also realist, which demonstrates the connection between realism and impressionism. The work of the PRE-RAPHAELITES in England and of Adolf von MENZEL in Germany are also related to the realist movement.   BARBARA CAVALIERE

Bibliography: Nochlin, Linda, *Realism and Tradition in Art 1848–1900* (1966) and *Realism* (1971); Reff, Theodore, ed., *Exhibitions of Later Realist Art* (1981); Rubin, James H., *Realism and Social Vision in Courbet and Proudhon* (1981).

Gustave Courbet's The Artist's Studio (1855), subtitled A True Allegory Concerning Seven Years of My Artistic Life, *portrays the artist at work amid an inattentive assembly of undistinguished figures* (left) *and Parisian friends* (right). *A nude model replaces the traditional Muse, who may represent unadorned Nature or Truth. Courbet's emphasis on the familiar so offended accepted aesthetic precepts that he was forbidden to display his work at the Paris Exhibition of 1855. (Louvre, Paris.)*

realism (literature)

Realism in literature has two distinct but closely related meanings. More broadly, realism is the use of observed and familiar detail in any literary context. As such, it is present in varying degrees in almost all literary works to create a fictional realm whose nature is accessible to the reader. Thus while the heroic epic actions of the *Iliad* are larger than life, the poem's great realism of detail—descriptions of weapons, human emotions, natural phenomena—makes its world familiar as an aspect of reality.

More specifically, realism is a literary movement that began in the mid-19th century as a reaction against ROMANTICISM in literature. Whereas romanticism presented an idealized vision of life, compounded of personal hopes and feelings, realism aspired to be an accurate portrayal of life as it is, a mimetic depiction of the outer world based on careful observation. Realism was an embodiment of the changed view of the universe brought about by the development of the empirical sciences, substituting experimentation for essence, flawed material being for transcendental perfection.

The term *realism* as applied to a literary mode first appeared in France in the 1820s. By mid-century it was beginning to be used to denote a new kind of writing in France, Russia, and England. This new literary creed emerged primarily in the form of the NOVEL, which could closely approximate the speech and detail of everyday life better than poetry or even drama. In France, realism's first major exponent was Honoré de BALZAC. In a wide-ranging series of novels, entitled La COMÉDIE HUMAINE (1829–47), Balzac, who saw himself as "secretary to the 19th century," gave a complete and accurately detailed record of French society. Balzac was followed by Gustave FLAUBERT, whose *Madame Bovary* (1857) is considered the foremost French realist novel. Later in the century, Émile ZOLA formulated a branch of literary realism called naturalism, which carried realism to extremes in its emphasis on the grosser aspects of human behavior. (See NATURALISM, in literature, for an explication of its similarities to and differences from realism.) The French realist tradition presented objectively, without authorial intrusion, a cause-and-effect material universe that eschewed the far away and long ago of the romantics and repudiated exaggerated heroes in favor of ordinary people.

In Russia, realism's chief practitioners were Leo TOLSTOI, Fyodor DOSTOYEVSKY, and Anton CHEKHOV, who developed their own strain of realism. Many critics see the Russian form as more hopeful and compassionate than the French.

In England the realist movement was not so pervasive, for Victorian men of letters objected to its manner and moralists deplored its content. Nevertheless, realism attained new heights in England with George ELIOT, whose *Middlemarch* (1871–72) is often deemed the greatest 19th-century English novel. Fully conscious of her role as sociological reflector of English provincial life, Eliot extended realism into the complexities of the psychological, and her methods would find their extreme elaboration in the suprarealist novels and stories of the American Henry JAMES (whose favorite author was Balzac). George MOORE (Irish novelist, poet, and playwright), cited as a naturalist, and George GISSING (*New Grub Street*, 1891) were of lesser stature, although they too wrote about the common folk. Arnold BENNETT, a popular and prolific Edwardian novelist, depicted with dexterity the life of the Five Towns, a pottery-making district in the Midlands, about 1900.

In the United States the banner for realism was carried by William Dean HOWELLS as critic and for a time as novelist (*The Rise of Silas Lapham*, 1885). Although Sinclair LEWIS (*Main Street*, 1920) followed in that tradition, the battle was carried on more vigorously by the naturalists Frank NORRIS, Jack LONDON, Theodore DREISER, James T. FARRELL, and, in dramaturgy, Eugene O'NEILL.

For about a century realism was the vital and increasingly dominant literary mode in the entire Western world. When in the 20th century theoretical physicists began to discard, or at least to question, the realists' tightly causal model of the universe and to allow the random and the relative, realism as a literary doctrine lost some of its compelling force. Having spawned many of the world's finest novels, the movement still surfaces occasionally in contemporary literature, as in the novels of manners written by the American Louis AUCHINCLOSS.

Reviewed by LILIAN R. FURST

Bibliography: Becker, G. J., *Realism in Modern Literature* (1980) and, as ed., *Documents of Modern Literary Realism* (1963); Cady, E. H., *The Light of Common Day: Realism in American Fiction* (1971); Grant, Damian, *Realism* (1970); Howells, William Dean, *Criticism and Fiction* (1891); Kolb, H. H., *The Illusion of Life* (1969); Levin, Harry, *The Gates of Horn: A Study of Five French Realists* (1966); Pizer, David, *Realism and Naturalism in Nineteenth Century American Literature* (1966) and *Twentieth Century American Literary Naturalism* (1982); Williams, I. M., *The Realist Novel in England* (1974).

realism (philosophy)

Realism denotes two distinct sets of philosophical theories, one regarding the nature of universal concepts and the other dealing with knowledge of objects in the world.

In late-classical and medieval philosophy, realism was a development of the Platonic theory of Forms and held, generally, that universals such as "red" or "man" have an independent, objective existence, either in a realm of their own or in the mind of God. Medieval realism is usually contrasted with NOMINALISM, and the classic critiques from this viewpoint were provided by Peter Abelard and William of Occam.

In modern philosophy realism is a broad term, encompassing several movements whose unity lies in a common rejection of philosophical IDEALISM. In its most general form realism asserts that objects in the external world exist independently of what is thought about them. The most straightforward of such theories is usually known as naive realism. It contends that in perception humans are made directly aware of objects and their attributes and thus have immediate access to the external world. This view fails, however, to explain perceptual mistakes and illusions, and most realists argue that causal processes in the mind mediate, or interpret, directly perceived appearances. Thus the objects remain in essence independent, although the causal mechanism may distort, or falsify, the individual's knowledge of them.

Bibliography: Armstrong, D. M., *Universals and Scientific Realism*, Vol. 1 (1978); Leplin, Jarrett, ed., *Scientific Realism* (1985); Smith, Peter, *Realism and Progress of Science* (1982); Veatch, Henry, *Realism and Nominalism Revisited* (1954); Wild, John, *Introduction to Realistic Philosophy* (1984).

reaper

The reaper is a device or machine used for harvesting grains. It operates by means of revolving bars or teeth, which press the sheaves of grain against a cutting apparatus. Until the development of the reaper, harvesting was done with manual cutting tools such as the sickle and scythe, or a plank with jagged iron teeth placed on a wheeled box drawn by animals. The development of the mechanical reaper enabled farmers to grow crops on a large scale.

The first recorded English patent for a mechanical reaper was issued to Joseph Boyce in 1799. Soon after, many reapers were developed employing either revolving cutters or vibrating knives. None gained widespread use. Two Americans, Obed Hussey and Cyrus H. McCORMICK, are usually given credit for inventing the modern reaper. Hussey's reaper was patented in 1833, McCormick's in 1834. In 1850, McCormick purchased the patent rights to Hussey's cutting bar. The McCormick-Hussey reaper cut grain with a reciprocating cutting bar and had a reel that put the cut grain onto a conveyer, where it was manually bound. Through extensive advertising and mass production, as well as presentation at the Great Exhibition of London in 1851, this model gained widespread use throughout the United States and Europe. It dominated the farm-implement market until the advent, in the 1870s, of wire and then twine binders, which cut and bundled the sheaves of grain mechanically. In the 20th century the reaper was replaced by the COMBINE.

EDWARD L. SCHAPSMEIER

Bibliography: McCormick, Cyrus, *The Century of the Reaper* (1931; repr. 1971).

Reason, Age of: see ENLIGHTENMENT.

reasoning

Reasoning is thinking to some purpose according to a set of rules. The rules may be logical (including mathematical) or psychological.

Logical reasoning emphasizes the process of valid inference, using propositions, truth tables, and syllogisms. A simple proposition is a statement with events, subject and predicate—for instance, "All dogs bark." Truth tables are used to evaluate various hypothetical constructions of compound propositions or argument-chains, often of the form "If . . . then . . . ." or "Either . . . or . . . ." Syllogisms are limited forms of two premises and a conclusion: "All dogs bark; Spot is a dog; therefore Spot barks." The conclusion is valid, and it is true if the premises are true.

Although of limited import in logic, syllogisms are generally held in psychology as the model for mature thinking. Syllogisms have also been applied to attitude formation in social psychology; here the attitude corresponds to the conclusion—"Barking is bad; Spot barks; therefore Spot is bad."

Logicians also distinguish between deductive and inductive forms of reasoning. Deduction involves drawing out what is implicit in the premises or in a formal system. Therefore, it is reasoning from general rules to specific instances. Induction involves summarizing many observations to generalize to a conclusion. In psychology, deductive reasoning is the use of abstraction and analysis; inductive reasoning is the use of experience and observation.

Psychological reasoning is also called thinking, cognition, PROBLEM SOLVING, and concept formation. The many approaches to the study of psychological reasoning may be divided into four categories: clinical, learning, developmental, and information processing.

Clinical Approach. Sigmund Freud distinguished between two thought processes (see PSYCHOANALYSIS). The primary process responds to internal, biologically derived drives, serves the pleasure principle of tension reduction, and operates unconsciously and nonrationally. The secondary process responds to repeated social and environmental interactions, serves the reality principle of understanding the world and predicting events, and operates consciously and rationally. Other clinical theorists have developed different thought-classification schemes.

Learning Approach. BEHAVIORISM emphasizes overt behavior and stimulus-response connections. Thinking may be considered implicit muscle movement and speech. Problem solving involves gradual, continuous behavior change with the appearance of being automatic or rote. Much research has addressed this appearance, demonstrating that these processes may underlie intelligent and creative problem solving. GESTALT PSYCHOLOGY emphasizes the creative, intelligent, and organizational aspects of problem solving. Insight, for example, is interpreted as a sudden, correct solution to a problem that creatively combines previously unrelated ideas. The Gestalt approach to problem solving is more sympathetic to the newer development and information-processing approaches than is behaviorism.

Developmental Approach. DEVELOPMENTAL PSYCHOLOGY emphasizes active interactions between changing maturational systems and the physical and social environment. Jerome S. BRUNER distinguishes three strategies, or modes, for representing reality: enactive, representation by actions; iconic, representation by images; and symbolic, representation by linguistic symbols. Jean PIAGET specifies four developmental stages in which individuals construct an understanding of reality via internalized, reversible mental operations that act upon the world to produce a cognitive independence from physical appearance. Sensory-motor thought, the first stage, is characterized by physical interactions with objects and development of the concept of object permanence—the recognition that objects exist independently of one's perception of them or interaction with them. The second stage, preoperational thought, is characterized by internal representation involving symbols but limited mainly to the present and to self-centered interpretation. Concrete operational thought, the third developmental stage, is characterized by notable independence of thinking and reasoning from self and from physical appearance and early development of logical thinking. In formal operational thought, the final stage, complete independence from appearance, develops, and systematic, formal, deductive thinking is typical.

Information Processing Approach. Information processing analyzes thinking in computer terminology: input-output, storage or memory, and operators or processors. Operators represent strategies for generating solutions to a problem. These solutions are, most broadly, algorithms, known solutions with specific procedures to be followed, and heuristics, procedures of uncertain outcome but with a past history of useful problem solving.   FRED HEILIZER

Bibliography: Cederblom, Jerry, and Paulsen, David, *Critical Reasoning*, 2d ed. (1985); Evans, Jonathan, ed., *Thinking and Reasoning: Psychological Approaches* (1983); Geach, P. T., *Reason and Argument* (1977); Lindsay, Peter H., and Norman, Donald A., *Human Information Processing*, 2d ed. (1977); Passmore, John, *Philosophical Reasoning* (1969); Revlin, Russell, and Mayer, Richard E., *Human Reasoning* (1978); Toulmin, Stephen, et al., *An Introduction to Reasoning*, 2d ed. (1984); Wason, Peter C., and Johnson-Laird, P. N., *Psychology of Reasoning* (1972).

See also: ARTIFICIAL INTELLIGENCE; COGNITIVE PSYCHOLOGY; INTELLIGENCE; LEARNING THEORY; LOGIC.

Réaumur, René Antoine Ferchault de   [ray-oh-muer']

The French scientist René Antoine Ferchault de Réaumur, b. Feb. 28, 1683, d. Oct. 17, 1757, made outstanding contributions to physics, biology, natural history, and technology. His investigations (1722) of the production and treatment of steel proved invaluable to France's then-backward ferrous metal industry. Between 1734 and 1742, Réaumur published the six-volume *Mémoires pour servir à l'histoire des insects* (Memoirs for Following Insect Study), which emphasized insect behavior and function. He is perhaps best known for his invention of an improved thermometer and the introduction of the Réaumur scale.   STEPHEN FLEISHMAN

Réaumur scale

The Réaumur scale is a TEMPERATURE scale, once widely used in Europe and particularly in France, in which the normal melting point of ice is taken as 0 and the normal boiling point of water as 80. Its originator, René Antoine Ferchault de Réaumur (1683–1757), wrote that 80 is "a number convenient to divide into parts." Réaumur's scale is noteworthy for originally having been based, like the modern thermodynamic temperature scale, on a single fixed point: the freezing point of water. The remainder of Réaumur's thermometric scale was determined by the thermal expansion properties of the spirits of wine of such a dilution that "the volume is 1,000 when condensed by the freezing of water, and 1,080 when rarefied by boiling water." The Réaumur scale has been superseded by the Celsius scale.   HENRY A. BENT

Rebecca   [ree-bek'-uh]

In the Bible, Rebecca (or Rebekah) was the wife of the patriarch ISAAC and the mother of ESAU and JACOB. After years of childlessness, she finally conceived the twins, whose struggle in her womb was taken as a sign of their impending hostility. Rebecca sided with Jacob, the younger son, and helped him cheat Esau out of Isaac's final blessing (Gen. 24–27).

Rebellions of 1837

The Rebellions of 1837 in Upper and Lower Canada (now Ontario and Quebec) were spurred by Britain's refusal to grant greater home rule. The locally elected legislative assembly in each province was dominated by the crown-appointed governor, executive council, and legislative council. In Upper Canada the prevalence of Anglicans, a minority in the province, among the appointed officials increased discontent. In Lower Canada, exacerbating factors were an economic depression and the presence of a mostly English-speaking officialdom in a largely French-speaking province.

The rebellion in Upper Canada, led by William Lyon MacKENZIE, died almost before it began. In December a small group of rebels planning to attack Toronto were dispersed by militia north of that city. In Lower Canada, French Canadians led by Louis J. PAPINEAU staged a more substantial uprising in November–December 1837, mainly in the Richelieu River valley, east of Montreal. Papineau fled to New York State, and the rebellion was severely repressed.

In the wake of the rebellions, the British government sent Lord DURHAM to Canada. His report recommended a union of the two provinces—which was accomplished in 1841—and responsible government, that is, a cabinet type of executive accountable to an elected legislature. The latter suggestion was finally implemented in 1848.   P. B. WAITE

Bibliography: Kilbourn, William, *The Firebrand* (1956); Read, Colin, *The Rising in Western Upper Canada* (1982); Schull, Joseph, *Rebellion: The Rising in French Canada, 1837* (1971).

Reber, Grote   [ree'-bur]

The American radio engineer Grote Reber, b. Wheaton, Ill., Dec. 22, 1911, designed and constructed (1937) in his own backyard the first radio telescope, a 31-ft (9.4-m) bowl-shaped antenna, with which he discovered the first discrete radio sources in the sky. Reber alone did research in RADIO ASTRONOMY in the period before World War II. Reber worked at the National Bureau of Standards (1947–51) and the National Radio Astronomy Observatory (1957–61). He has also done radio-astronomy research atop the extinct volcano Haleakala in Hawaii and in Tasmania, Australia.   STEVEN J. DICK

Bibliography: Hey, J. S., *The Evolution of Radio Astronomy* (1973).

rebus   [ree'-buhs]

Rebuses, now primarily picture-and-word puzzles for children, were originally substitutes for difficult words and phrases in semiprimitive societies. They have occurred in almost all cultures at one time or another. A simple form of rebus might be the drawing of a heart or a doe, to represent a surname. A more complex rebus might be 👁️ will 🐝 at your 🏠 by 🌅, which translates as "I will be at your house by sundown." The term *rebus* comes from Picardy, France, where the Latin *res*, meaning "thing," was used to describe the way illegal political satires were expressed. Sam Loyd, a 19th-century American puzzlemaker, popularized rebuses in the United States.

recall

Recall is the procedure for removing public officials from office before the completion of their terms. It is initiated by petitioning for a special election to decide on the individual's retention in office. The number of signatures necessary varies among states and localities and according to the office involved. The usual requirement is 25 percent of the votes cast for that office at the last election. In some jurisdictions, voters decide between the challenged official and other candidates for that office. In other jurisdictions the issue of recall is decided first, and then—if the vote is in favor of recall—elections are held. Different jurisdictions authorize recall for different officials, but judges are often exempted.

Recall—which is believed to have originated in Switzerland—and REFERENDUM AND INITIATIVE were among the methods proposed by the reformers of the late 19th and early 20th centuries in the United States to increase popular control of government, to improve the quality and operations of local governments, to reduce the power and influence of political bosses and machines, and to guard against widespread corruption and graft. The first U.S. city to adopt (1903) recall procedures was Los Angeles; the first state was Oregon (1908). Recall is most frequent in local government. Only 13 states

provide for the removal of governors through recall, and recall does not operate at the national level.   RITA J. IMMERMAN

Bibliography: Wilcox, Delos F., *Government by All the People* (1932; repr. 1972).

receiver   (communications)

In wireless communication, such as radar, radio, and television, intelligence is transmitted through space in the form of radio waves by means of a TRANSMITTER. The equipment necessary to pick up, amplify, and convert these radio-frequency (rf) signals back into their original form, usually speech or music, is called a receiver. For brevity, only RADIO receivers will be discussed here. The basic receiver consists of six parts: (1) the receiving antenna, which accepts carrier frequencies from all stations within range of the receiver; (2) a tuning stage, or TUNER, which picks out the desired modulated carrier wave; (3) one or more amplification stages that increase the weakly received signal to usable levels (see AMPLIFIER); (4) a detector, or demodulator, that extracts the modulation signal from the carrier wave; (5) an audio amplifier that brings the still-weak signal up to a level that is powerful enough to operate the sound producer; and (6) the actual sound producer, which may be a LOUDSPEAKER, a headset, or some other device that converts the radio signal into sound.

The sensitivity of a radio receiver—its ability to pick up and use weak signals—is largely determined by the number of amplification states that precede the sound-production device. The signal-to-noise ratio indicates how much amplification of the signal the receiver can provide as compared to the amount of NOISE that it introduces during the process. Selectivity is the ability of a receiver to select only the desired signal, rejecting all other signals. This process is accomplished by use of tuned or resonant circuits; the quality of these circuits determines selectivity. The stability of a receiver is its ability to remain on a certain frequency once the receiver has been tuned to that frequency. The better radio receivers have circuits for automatic frequency control (AFC) to accomplish this. Fidelity refers to the ability of the set to reproduce faithfully the original signal (see HIGH FIDELITY).   HAL HELLMAN

Bibliography: Gosling, W., ed., *Radio Receiver* (1985).

Recent Epoch

The Recent, or Holocene, Epoch is the younger major subdivision of the Quaternary Period. After the last Pleistocene Epoch glaciation, an interglacial interval of warming followed, causing the glaciers to withdraw (see GLACIER AND GLACIATION; ICE AGES). This marked the beginning of the Recent Epoch. The rate of decay shown by radiocarbon (carbon 14) occurring in early Recent wood, peat, shells, and bones indicates that the Recent Epoch began approximately 10,000 years ago.

The Recent Epoch was one of five subdivisions of the Cenozoic defined (1833) by Sir Charles Lyell. He observed that the percentage of living marine invertebrate species recognizable in fossil faunas showed an increase in progressively younger strata. That epoch containing 100 percent living species and also thought at that time to contain the earliest evidence of humans was called Recent. It is now known that humans are much more ancient.

GEOLOGY AND TECTONICS

The Earth's surface is covered by more material of Recent times than of any other age. Marine sediments (see SEDIMENT, MARINE) are mostly confined to areas close to modern continental margins. Deep-sea coring indicates that a thin layer (10 to 30 cm/4 to 12 in) of post-Pleistocene sediment has accumulated. These consist of foraminiferan (*Globigerina*) or radiolarian OOZE (marine plankton) or fine red clay. In near-shore marine environments, various natural processes have reworked either sands and gravels of the Pleistocene or modern erosional sediments, or, in the restricted tropics of today, organic carbonate deposits such as coral reefs. Continental sediments reflect the varied depositional environments and processes: lakes, swamps, rivers, glaciers, and wind.

Volcanic activity has been extensive; over 500 eruptions are known in recorded history from volcanos such as HEKLA, PELÉE,

VESUVIUS, and Tamboro, but prehistoric eruptions elsewhere were very numerous. Island arcs, those volcanic islands found along continental margins, are the most active volcanoes. Such arcs are prevalent around the Pacific Ocean but are also found in the Caribbean and Atlantic.

Land subsidence and uplift, due to tectonics and to the aftermath of glaciation, have also occurred. The Rhine, Danube, Rhône, Nile, Amazon, Mississippi, and other great RIVER DELTAS exhibit subsidence due to sediment load. Meltwater from the glaciers has caused a relative eustatic sea-level rise of as much as 130 m (430 ft), and gentle, shelving coastal plains may occupy inland sites as much as 400 km (250 mi) from those occupied during the maximum glaciation. CORAL REEF growth in tropical regions reflects this Recent sea-level rise. In Scandinavia and eastern Canada melting of the Pleistocene glaciers has caused uplift of about 275 m (900 ft).

Soils, groundwater, and several nonmetallic minerals form the most important economic products of the Recent Epoch. The soils are often the product of both Pleistocene and Recent activity, for example, in the United States, the LOESS of the wheatlands of both the Northwest and the Mississippi River valley and the lime-rich cornbelt soils of the Midwest. The world's many rich alluvial soils are primarily the result of Recent processes. Many groundwater supplies are situated in Recent deposits. Nonmetallic minerals, such as various salts produced when large lakes evaporated, form important sources of borates, phosphates, and calcium chloride.

CLIMATE AND LIFE

The areas of the continents recently vacated by glaciers show much erosion. Warmer, dry regions have acquired SAND DUNES. Lakes (see LAKE, body of water; LAKE, GLACIAL) and bogs (see SWAMP, MARSH, AND BOG) developed as some areas received high levels of precipitation during the early Recent Epoch. Climatic fluctuations of both rainfall and temperature are recorded in pollen records, and sometimes in the migration of humans and animals. Many of the large interior lakes of the Pleistocene Epoch have dried up or become saline.

The spread of PREHISTORIC HUMANS to all habitable parts of the globe took place mostly during Recent times. The initial discovery by humans almost 10,000 years ago that they could exploit metallic mineral deposits, such as copper, and could make bronze (see BRONZE AGE) and later iron (see IRON AGE), was an important milestone in the development of civilization. Striking changes in the flora took place as successive types of vegetation established themselves in the wake of the melting ice or in response to climatic change. Such vegetative changes influenced human and animal migration as well.

Change in many mammal species also occurred during the Recent Epoch. The large and diverse mammal fauna of the southwestern United States during the Pleistocene Epoch consisted of numerous large animals—MAMMOTHS, MASTODONS, SABER-TOOTHED CATS, ground SLOTHS, camels, dire wolves, horses, and lions, among others—all of which disappeared in Recent times. Human activities have directly resulted in the extinction of such animals as the DODO BIRD and the passenger PIGEON, and many animals on the list of ENDANGERED SPECIES are threatened by agricultural, industrial, or other activities of humans.   V. STANDISH MALLORY

Bibliography: Bradley, R. S., *Quaternary Paleoclimatology* (1985); Douglas, Ian, and Spencer, eds., *Environment Change and Tropical Geomorphology* (1985); Flint, R. F., *Glacial and Quaternary Geology* (1971); Lowe, J. J., and Walker, J. C., *Reconstructing Quaternary Environments* (1985); Mahaney, W. C., *Quaternary Dating Methods* (1984); Vita-Finzi, Claudio, *Recent Earth History* (1973).

recession

Recession is a condition in which a nation's economic activity—the production and consumption of goods and services—declines. Recession is also defined as a period when the growth of a nation's economy slows to a halt or even declines slightly. It is the second phase of the classic BUSINESS CYCLE of expansion, or prosperity; recession; contraction, or depression; and recovery. Economists disagree about the cause of recessions; some think that they are set off by declines in consumer spending; others point to decreases in capital invest-

ment; still others blame government budget policy. In any event, both capital investment and consumer spending do decline during recessions, as do wholesale sales, employment, personal income, and construction.

Since World War II no recession in the United States (1945–46, 1949, 1954, 1956, 1960–61, 1970, 1973–75, 1980–83) has worsened into a depression—as did those in 1807, 1837, 1873, 1882, 1893, 1920, 1933, and 1937—perhaps because of the success of government economic intervention. In times of recession the federal government has usually acted to create jobs by increasing its spending (see FISCAL POLICY) and the supply of money in circulation (see MONETARY POLICY). As employment picks up, consumer spending increases and the economy is usually on the way to recovery. A factor complicating economic policy-making during the 1970s and early '80s, however, was continued high rates of inflation in times of recession (see STAGFLATION).

Bibliography: Anell, Lars, *Recession, the Western Economies, and the Changing World Order* (1981); Hansen, A. H., *Business Cycles and National Income* (1964); Heilbroner, R. L., *Beyond Boom and Crash* (1978).

Recife   [ray-see'-fay]

Recife (formerly Pernambuco), the capital of the Pernambuco state in northeastern Brazil, lies on the Atlantic coast. Many in the population of 1,183,391 (1980) are blacks, descendants of African slaves brought in colonial times to work on the region's sugarcane plantations. Sometimes called the "Venice of Brazil," Recife lies on the banks of the Capibaribe and Beberibe rivers and on an island near the mouths of the rivers; bridges link its three main sections.

Recife is an important industrial and agricultural center. It is also one of Brazil's leading ports and is connected by air, highway, and rail to the hinterland. Exports include cotton, sugar, rum, hides, and cereals. The city is the seat of SUDENE, a federal government agency responsible since 1959 for the economic development of northeastern Brazil. Recife has many fine public buildings, colonial churches, and museums, including the Sugar Museum. The state university (1946) and several other institutions of higher learning are located there. Carnival festivities draw many tourists.

The first settlers on the site were the Portuguese in the 1520s, who engaged in cutting and shipping brazilwood. The city was founded in 1548 and then occupied by the Dutch from 1630 until 1654. Brazil's first printing press was brought to Recife in 1706. South America's oldest daily newspaper, *Diário de Pernambuco*, has been published in Recife since 1825.   JAMES N. SNADEN

recitative   [res-i-tuh-teev']

Recitative is a manner of reciting or declaiming words in musical works, usually but not exclusively in Latin, Italian, German, French, or English, associated with sacred or secular texts. Such declamation, often functional rather than artistic, serves to carry forward a narrative in poetry or prose and generally leads to a balance between text and melody as, for example, in an ARIA. Most broadly, however, recitative is a complex style in its own right. As an aspect of PLAINSONG, it is used for the singing of psalms, lessons, tones for the Passions, and other parts of the liturgy calling for rapid and simple declamation. It also appears in liturgical music dramas and oratorios. Heinrich Schütz employed recitative either unaccompanied (the Passions), with continuo (*Christmas Oratorio*, 1664–65), or within a four-part instrumental frame (*Easter Oratorio*, 1623). This variety of types is found later in Bach's music: in his Cantata No. 28 (c.1736), for example, a recitative (subtitled "arioso") for voice and continuo leads to a more fully scored example for voice and strings. The arioso type came into favor during the 17th century and was described as a style "gracefully embellished with ornaments appropriate to the thought," which refers to the recitative soliloquy exploited in Italy by Monteverdi, Cavalli, and others, based on earlier experiments by Florentine composers. Choral (or "chordal") recitative had been successfully used by Giaches de Wert, Monteverdi, and others aiming at a recitative style in full five-part harmony.

On the operatic stage, recitative ranged from rapid speech-style declamation to a melodious arioso, which was sometimes in the form of an expressive lament. In the 18th century, the *secco* (continuo only) type was popular because of its speed of narrative; *stromentato* (with orchestra) tended to be more dramatic. Many later operas, including those by Wagner and Richard Strauss, lean heavily upon a modified recitative style. Instrumental recitatives are by no means uncommon and are found in works by Bach, Beethoven, Johann Kuhnau, Schoenberg, Ludwig Spohr, and others.

DENIS STEVENS

Bibliography: Conrad, Peter, *Romantic Opera and Literary Form* (1977); Drummond, John D., *Opera: A History* (1979).

recoilless rifle

A recoilless rifle is a lightweight portable gun with a rifled barrel. Such weapons do not have the sophisticated recoil system of conventional artillery, but offset recoil by allowing some of the propellant gases to escape through a nozzle at the back of the gun.

The simplest way to eliminate recoil would be to put two identical guns back to back and fire them at exactly the same time; the recoil of one would exactly balance the other. This principle was used by an American industrialist, Gregory Davison, to develop a system that became the forerunner of present-day recoilless rifles. In 1910, Davison merged two back-to-back guns into one with a central breech that was loaded by separating the two barrels. A single charge of propellant fired a shell out of one barrel and an equal quantity of lead shot out of the other. The lead shot that balanced shell momentum traveled only a short distance before it fell to the ground. This arrangement was not ideal, but it was tried on a few aircraft in World War I. Such aircraft were too flimsy to carry a large gun, and the recoil-free Davison gun placed no strain on the airframe when it was fired. The largest Davison fired a 4.5-kg (12-lb) shell. It was discontinued after 1918.

The concept was revived in Germany in the 1930s when a portable field gun was required. This weapon is the basis of systems in use today. The principle requires the velocity of the gas escaping to the rear to be increased so as to balance the weight of a heavy shell. To achieve this, however, the amount of propellant must be about five times the normal charge, and a much larger and heavier cartridge case is required. Another difficulty is the backblast, which limits the range of the gun and is difficult to conceal. Because of these limitations, recoilless guns are now used primarily for short-range antitank defense when the barrel can be pointed directly at the target.

A. J. BARKER

recombinant DNA: see GENETIC ENGINEERING.

Reconstruction

In U.S. history Reconstruction refers to the period (1865–77) following the Civil War and to the process by which the states of the Confederacy were readmitted to full membership in the Union. The period was marked by struggles between political parties about how Reconstruction should proceed and between the president and Congress over who should direct it.

Differing Views of Reconstruction. Reconstruction aroused violent controversy over the constitutional powers of the federal government to intervene in a state's affairs, over whether the victors should try to change the South fundamentally, and over the status of the black ex-slaves, or freedmen. Political affiliations were a key determinant of views on those issues. Northern Democrats believed the Constitution strictly limited federal power, anticipated that most Southern whites would vote Democratic, and had little sympathy for black aspirations. They favored a rapid Reconstruction that would make few demands on the ex-Confederates.

Republicans took a broader view of federal power. The more radical of them believed that the secessionist states had forfeited their status and could be treated by Congress as territories or conquered provinces. Republicans also thought that steps had to be taken to forestall future rebellions. In addition, most felt that blacks were entitled to fundamental human rights, and many hoped Southern Republicanism could be built with the help of black support.

Initial Plans of Reconstruction. During the war President Abraham LINCOLN hoped to set up loyal governments in the Southern states that were under Union control. He appointed provisional governors and instructed each to call a conven-

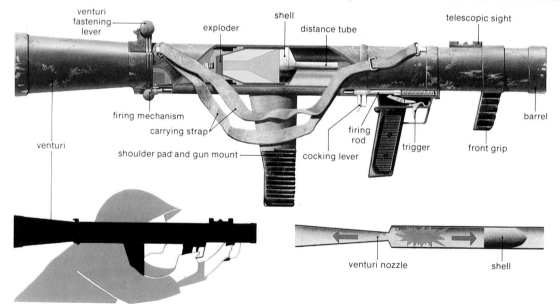

The *Carl-Gustav M2 recoilless gun, developed in Sweden, is a modern antitank weapon designed for use by the infantry. It fires an 84-mm (6.7-in) shell and has an effective range of 500 m (1,600 ft). The M2 employs the Krupp system (detail) to absorb recoil caused by firing. Gas from the burning propellant escapes through a venturi nozzle in the rear of the gun; the constriction increases the velocity of the gas to counterbalance the backward motion caused by the forward acceleration and weight of the shell. Part of the NATO arsenal, the 16-kg (36-lb) M2 is carried, aimed, and fired by one person, but an additional person must carry and load the ammunition.*

Thomas Nast's cartoon attacks Andrew Johnson's mild Reconstruction plan, seen as a betrayal of what the Union soldier fought for. Radical Republicans in Congress replaced Johnson's proposals with a more stringent plan, embodied initially in the 14th Amendment.

tion to create a new state government as soon as a group of the state's citizens equaling 10 percent of the voters in the 1860 presidential election had signed oaths of loyalty to the Union. Under this plan new governments were formed in Louisiana, Tennessee, and Arkansas, but Congress refused to recognize them. Republicans in Congress did not want a quick restoration, in part because it would bring Democratic representatives and senators to Washington, and in 1864 they passed the Wade-Davis Reconstruction Bill. This measure would have delayed the process of readmission until 50 percent of a state's 1860 voters had signed loyalty oaths, but Lincoln pocket vetoed the bill.

Presidential Reconstruction. Lincoln was assassinated just as the Confederates surrendered in April 1865, and Andrew JOHNSON inherited the problem of Reconstruction. Johnson adopted the Wade-Davis plan with some modifications. Allowing for few exceptions, he issued an amnesty to anyone who would take an oath to be loyal to the Union in the future. Acknowledging defeat, enough ex-Confederates signed these oaths to enable the immediate creation of new governments. Johnson required only that the new states ratify the 13th Amendment freeing the slaves, abolish slavery in their own constitutions, repudiate debts incurred while in rebellion, and declare secession null and void. By the end of 1865, all of the secessionist states but Texas had complied.

Congressional Reconstruction. Contending that it returned power to the same people who had just tried to destroy the Union, the Republican majority in Congress was unsatisfied with Johnson's program. It also noted that the program did nothing to protect the rights of the freedmen and that the Southern states were passing BLACK CODES to keep the former

slaves in a subservient position. In 1866, Congress passed the FREEDMEN'S BUREAU Act and the Civil Rights Act (see CIVIL RIGHTS ACTS) to help freedmen shift from slavery to freedom and to assure them equality before the law. Johnson vetoed these measures, allied himself with the Democrats, and insisted that the Southern states were now fully entitled to representation in Congress. The Republicans responded by refusing to recognize the legitimacy of the Southern states and by passing the laws over his veto. In June 1866, Republicans also proposed the 14TH AMENDMENT to the Constitution, which declared blacks to be citizens, prohibited states from discriminating against any class of citizens or denying any citizen fundamental rights, and banned Confederate leaders from holding federal or state office until Congress removed the disqualification.

The Southern state governments created under Johnson's plan refused to ratify this amendment, and in 1867, Congress passed a series of Reconstruction Acts. These laws placed the South under temporary military occupation. Reluctant to make the national government permanently responsible for the protection of the ex-slaves, Republicans decided to enfranchise blacks so that Southern politicians would have to treat them fairly to get their votes. Congress agreed to recognize new state governments only after they had guaranteed equal civil and political rights regardless of race and had ratified the 14th Amendment. Moreover, Confederate leaders were not allowed to vote in the process that created the new state governments. This program became known as Radical Reconstruction.

As commander in chief of the armed forces, Johnson was able to interfere with the enforcement of these laws. By 1868 he had been so successful in supporting Southern opposition that it seemed he might be able to sabotage the entire program. Several efforts to restrain him failed, but when he fired Secretary of War Edwin M. STANTON in an effort to gain complete control of the army, House Republicans claimed he had violated the TENURE OF OFFICE ACT (1867) and impeached him. In the trial that followed, the Senate narrowly acquitted Johnson (May 1868). By that summer all ex-Confederate states except Mississippi, Texas, and Virginia had accepted the terms of Radical Reconstruction. To round out their program, the Republicans in 1869 proposed the 15TH AMENDMENT to the Constitution forbidding racial discrimination in voting qualifications; it was ratified in 1870, and the recalcitrant states were also required to ratify it before being readmitted.

Radical Reconstruction in the South. The new governments in the South were the most progressive the region had ever seen. Supported by an almost unanimous black vote and, in some states, by a sizable minority of whites, Republicans were elected to office. The mostly white Republican leaders established the first state-supported free public school systems in the South, made labor laws fairer to employees, made tax laws more equitable, eliminated racially discriminatory laws and in some states outlawed discrimination by individuals, and tried to promote public improvements and economic development. In the process, the Republicans raised taxes much higher than Southerners were used to; fell prey to the corruption that plagued all the states in the 1870s; and alienated many Southern whites who resented a system of racial equality. These Southern whites charged the Republicans with misgovernment and called them corrupt CARPETBAGGERS (transplanted Northern Republicans) and SCALAWAGS (white Southerners who collaborated). Unable to erode black support for Republicans with promises, many white Southerners resorted to force through the KU KLUX KLAN and other organizations, and they refined their own political organization. By 1875 all but three Southern states—South Carolina, Louisiana, and Florida—were back in the hands of Southern Democrats, who discontinued most of the Republican reforms and began to circumscribe the freedom of blacks.

The Election of 1876 and the End of Reconstruction. During the early 1870s violence became so bad in the South that President Ulysses S. GRANT often sent troops there to protect Republicans during election campaigns. Northerners were tiring of the turmoil by the time of the 1876 presidential elec-

"The Solid South," which voted solidly for the Democratic party, emerged at the end of the Reconstruction period. The Republican party, identified here with Ulysses Grant, "Bayonet Rule", and carpetbag government, was long regarded as the oppressor.

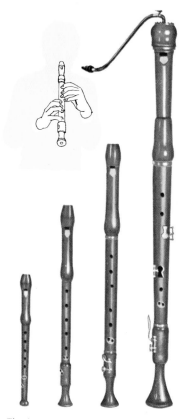

The four recorders commonly used today are (left to right) the soprano, alto, tenor, and bass, with the playing position shown (left). A simple recorder was known in 10th-century Europe, and by the 16th century a family of various-sized instruments had been developed. The recorder has remained a relatively simple, sweet-sounding instrument and is currently enjoying a widespread revival of popular interest.

tion and wanted a restoration of peace. The result of the 1876 presidential contest hinged on the disputed electoral votes of the three remaining Republican states in the South. Both sides agreed to send the votes to a special commission, which ruled Republican Rutherford B. HAYES the winner. Before the decision, Hayes had apparently let Southern Democrats know that he would not use federal troops to protect the Republicans in those states. Soon after taking office, he withdrew the troops to their barracks, and the last Southern Republican governments fell.

Reconstruction left a nasty legacy to future generations of Americans. White Southerners felt deeply wronged and for a hundred years perceived blacks as potentially dangerous political enemies. By failing to persevere in Reconstruction, Northerners permitted the creation of a caste system in the South that deprived black Americans of basic rights. The resulting racial hostilities persist to this day as do the effects of discrimination.   MICHAEL LES BENEDICT

Bibliography: Belz, Herman, *Emancipation and Equal Rights* (1978); Benedict, Michael Les, *A Compromise of Principle: Congressional Republicans and Reconstruction 1863-1869* (1975); Franklin, John Hope, *Reconstruction After the Civil War* (1961); Patrick, Rembert W., *The Reconstruction of the Nation* (1967); Perman, Michael, *Reunion without Compromise, the South and Reconstruction* (1973); Stampp, Kenneth M., *The Era of Reconstruction, 1865-1877* (1965); Trelease, Allen W., *Reconstruction: The Great Experiment* (1971).

record player: see PHONOGRAPH.

recorder

The principal type of European flute from the 16th to the mid-18th century was the end-blown fipple FLUTE called the recorder (German: *Blockflöte;* French: *flûte à bec*). It was usually built of wood and had eight finger holes. Its whistle mouthpiece made it easier to play than the transverse flute, for it required only good control of the breath to direct the air to a point that produced a soft, sweet tone. Eight sizes were described in Michael Praetorius's *Syntagma musicum* (1615), but the largest and smallest were rarely used. Recorders were played together in consorts, were used in chamber music and orchestras, and—treble recorders especially—were used in solo sonatas.

The instrument fell into disuse before the end of the 18th century, probably because its tone lacked sufficient strength to compete with other, newer instruments. Its 20th-century revival is due to the interest of amateurs and performers of old music. Four sizes are now in common use: soprano and alto (called descant and treble in England), tenor, and bass. The bass has a crook like a bassoon to bring the finger holes within reach. Some modern recorders are made of plastic, but serious performers prefer wooden instruments.

ELWYN A. WIENANDT

Bibliography: Hunt, Edgar, *The Recorder and its Music*, rev. ed. (1977).

recording: see SOUND RECORDING AND REPRODUCTION; VIDEO RECORDING.

rectangle

A rectangle is a four-sided plane figure (a QUADRILATERAL), all of whose angles are right angles. Alternatively, a rectangle may be defined as a PARALLELOGRAM having one right angle; this implies that all the angles are right angles. A line segment connecting opposite (nonadjacent) vertices of a rectangle is called a diagonal and divides the rectangle into two congruent triangles. If adjacent sides have lengths a and b, then the perimeter of the rectangle, that is, the distance around the sides, is given by $P = 2a + 2b$. The area of the rectangle is given by the product of two adjacent sides (area = ab). If adjacent sides of a rectangle have the same length ($a = b$), then the figure is a SQUARE and has perimeter $4a$ and area a^2.

Bibliography: Moise, Edwin E., *Elementary Geometry from an Advanced Standpoint* (1966); Schnell, Leroy, and Crawford, Mildred, *Plane Geometry* (1953).

rectifier

A rectifier is an electronic component that permits passage of only the positive or negative portion of an alternating electrical current. Modern rectifiers are usually made from a pn junction formed in a SEMICONDUCTOR. Most rectifiers are made from silicon, a semiconductor that is fairly readily available, inexpensive, and able to withstand high temperatures, although formerly, selenium was commonly used. Before the development of semiconductors, two-electrode electron tubes (see DIODE) were commonly used as rectifiers, and they still are used in certain special applications.

All rectifiers perform the same basic function of rectifying an electronic current, that is, transforming an alternating current (AC) containing both positive and negative components into a fluctuating current having only a positive or negative component—a direct current (DC). Their physical construction and operating specifications, however, are exceedingly diverse.

Rectifiers intended for low-power applications such as the detection of a modulated radio or microwave signal are generally small, often being composed of a small chip of an appropriate semiconductor such as silicon, germanium, or gallium arsenide installed in one end of a cylindrical package made from metal, glass, or ceramic. These low-power semiconductor diodes may be as small as a grain of rice and can be included among the microminiature components formed on the surface of an INTEGRATED CIRCUIT.

Medium-power rectifiers designed to rectify electrical current supplied to various kinds of electronic equipment are usually installed in a metal case to permit excess heat to be radiated into the surrounding air. Often they include a threaded stud so that they can be attached to a metal plate called a heat sink, which may include metal fins to encourage rapid radiation of excessive heat.

High-power rectifiers are used in applications such as the power supply of heavy-duty motors, battery chargers, and welding equipment. They are installed in metal packages and are almost always attached to a heat sink. Additional cooling may be supplied by a blower fan, and there are also water-cooled heat sinks.

Rectifiers may be designed to handle a wide range of voltages. For the rectification of high voltages, such as those found in television receivers, rectifiers composed of a stack of several individual semiconductor chips housed within a protective plastic package are employed. Rectifiers also may be interconnected in various ways to make more efficient use of the voltage being rectified. A single rectifier blocks half of an AC voltage applied to it while allowing the other half to pass; it is therefore referred to as a half-wave rectifier. Two or four separate rectifiers, however, can be arranged in a circuit in such a way that they will rectify both halves of an AC signal into direct currect. Such a circuit is called a full-wave rectifier. The output voltage has a ripple, but it can be smoothed by electronic filtering (see FILTER, ELECTRONIC).

Among the many applications for rectifiers are the suppression of arcs at the contacts of switches and relays, temperature sensing, voltage regulation, isolation of one component or circuit from another, and digital logic. Some of the specialized rectifiers in common use include various kinds of pn-junction diodes, such as the ZENER DIODE, a component with the ability to regulate a voltage at a specified level. The light-emitting diode (LED) is also a rectifier, although its principal application is the production of visible light for numeric displays and indicators, or infrared radiation for optical communications and object detection.   FORREST M. MIMS III

Bibliography: Hunten, Donald M., *Introduction to Electronics* (1964).

rectum: see DIGESTION, HUMAN; DIGESTIVE SYSTEM; INTESTINE.

recycling of materials

Recycling waste and used materials for some useful purpose is an effective means of conserving resources, of reducing waste disposal, and, often, of cutting costs. For economic reasons, industries reuse much of the scrap materials generated in their facilities. Some demolition materials and a larger amount of scrap metal from automobiles are recycled. A small but increasing amount of residential and commercial waste is currently recycled.

Three basic methods of recycling materials are in current use. First, residual wastes from industrial and agricultural processes can be utilized. For example, ashes can be used in concrete, organic wastes can be composted, and combustible wastes can be burned to produce steam or electricity. As the costs of producing energy and disposing of waste have increased, municipal projects have begun to use the energy potential of urban wastes (see WASTE DISPOSAL SYSTEMS).

Second, materials can be reused for their original purpose. The best example is the returnable beverage container. Whereas a nonreturnable can or bottle can be used only once, a returnable bottle averages about 15 to 20 fillings before breaking, and thus saves resources and money while reducing manufacturing pollution, litter, and solid waste. By 1984, nine states had passed laws restricting nonreturnable beverage containers, and other states were considering such laws. Oregon's law has been in effect since 1972. A 1975 report concluded that beverage container litter in Oregon had decreased by an estimated 66%.

A third means of recycling is to reuse industrial waste materials in the manufacture of new products. The recovery and reuse of paper pulp, glass, and metals are prominent examples of such recycling. Many projects for solid-waste energy recovery have facilities for the separation and recovery of heavier materials—glass and metals—prior to combustion of the lighter materials to produce power. The most effective form of recycling is by separating recyclable materials prior to their becoming part of the waste stream. (A 36-in stack of newspapers is the paper equivalent of one tree. Only about 16% of residential and commercial paper is recycled.)

Recycling of metals results in resource and energy savings. Whereas separation of metals prior to the aggregation of wastes is most effective, municipal wastes can be shredded, and iron and steel removed by magnets. Nonferrous metals—aluminum, copper, zinc, lead, and others—can be separated using a froth flotation method in which the aggregate of shredded metals is placed in a solution whose specific gravity can be changed. Since the metals have different specific gravities, each metal will be caused to float at different times and can thus be separated. This technique is often used in metals recovery from old automobiles, but only a few of the new municipal waste-handling systems employ it.

The energy used to reprocess waste materials may be far less than that required for making virgin materials. It takes only about 5% of the energy used to produce a ton of aluminum from ore to make usable aluminum from scrap; about 26% of the energy needed to make steel from iron ore, to produce a ton of steel from scrap; and about 30% of the energy used to produce a ton of paper from trees if the paper is made instead from recycled paper. As energy costs rise, the economic incentive for recycling increases. Recycling often involves other costs, however. Old newspapers, for example, must be deinked and repulped before they can be converted back to newsprint.

In the early 1970s the price for scrap materials increased in response to increasing industrial activity. As industrial activity slowed in 1974 and 1975, however, so did the demand for secondary materials, particularly paper, and prices dropped abruptly, causing the closing of many municipal recycling centers. As industrial activity increased in 1976, the prices recovered. A more stable market will result when industries are committed to using scrap on a day-to-day basis rather than only when virgin materials are costly or in short supply.

Adverse government policies—such as a depletion allowance for virgin materials, and freight rates that are much higher for scrap materials than for virgin materials—also affect the secondary-materials market. As a result, for example, much of the scrap steel available in the western United States is exported to Japan.   JOHN RANDOLPH

Bibliography: Barton, A. F., *Resource Recovery and Recycling* (1979); Bewick, M. W., ed., *Handbook of Organic Waste Conversion* (1980); Goldstein, J., *Recycling* (1979); Kut, David, and Hare, Gerard, *Waste Recycling for Energy Conservation* (1981); Martin, A. E., ed., *Small-Scale Resource Recovery Systems* (1982); Page, Talbot, *Conservation and Economic Efficiency* (1977); Rodale Press Editors, *Recycling* (1973).

Red Badge of Courage, The

Stephen CRANE's novel *The Red Badge of Courage* (1895), which appeared when the U.S. Civil War was still treated primarily as the subject for romance, was the first realistic fictional work on that subject to attain widespread popularity and critical acclaim. Its realism is all the more remarkable because Crane had no experience of war when he wrote the book. He was, however, able to describe it from the viewpoint of the protagonist, Henry Fleming—from his initial dreams of heroics through his internal struggle against cowardice, his acceptance of his place among the troops, and his first encounter with death.

red beds

Red beds are sedimentary rock formations, commonly shale and siltstone, characterized by reddish to red brown coloration. They were deposited on land and in lakes and deltas in continental environment subject to extended seasonal wet and dry periods. During the rainy seasons, silt and clay washed in by the rains were deposited over large flat expanses. During the dry seasons that followed, the shallow water cover evaporated, leaving mud flats to dry and bake in sunlight. The combined action of the Sun and the atmosphere oxidized whatever organic material was washed in. The same conditions caused iron (Fe) in the sediments to oxidize to its ferric state (Fe^{+3}). These two processes removed all organic material (only 5 percent is needed) that could color the sediment black and to provide a reddish coloring agent (ferric iron).

Successive years of alternating deposition and oxidation built layer upon layer of red sediments. With compaction and lithification, these sediments became the red beds revealed today in the geologic strata. The harsh environment in which red beds formed was not conducive to preservation of animal remains.

KENNETH W. KILMER

Red and the Black, The

A masterpiece of psychological realism, STENDHAL's *The Red and the Black* (1830) is often cited as being the first modern French novel. Setting Julien Sorel's quest for happiness and distinction against the background of France in 1830, which he brilliantly portrays and satirizes, Stendhal minutely analyzes his hero's actions and complex character. Intelligent, shrewd, and mercenary, Julien is also generous, passionate, and sensitive. Rising through wit and opportunism from his humble origins, Julien is ultimately betrayed as much by his own passion and sensitivity as by the crassness and mediocrity he both deplores and exploits.

JOSEPH A. REITER

red blood cell: see BLOOD.

Red Cloud

Red Cloud, or Makhpiya Luta, 1822–1909, head chief of the Oglala Lakota, a SIOUX Indian group, for years frustrated efforts of the U.S. government to open up the West. From 1859 on he and his band, living near Fort Laramie, Wyo., attacked white immigrants encroaching on Indian territory along the North Platte River. By 1865 he was effectively discouraging white intrusion by way of the BOZEMAN TRAIL. Red Cloud led the 1866 massacre of 80 troops from Fort Kearney, one of the posts built to protect the trail, an event that led to the abandonment of the trail by the whites in 1868. A peace treaty of that year, which Red Cloud signed, seems to have been a turning point for the war chief. After visiting Washington, D.C., where he perhaps was impressed by the numbers and power of white people, he agreed to settle down as a reservation chief. According to some of his contemporaries, such as SITTING BULL and CRAZY HORSE, he sold out to the whites, permitting corrupt and deplorable conditions on Sioux reservations. He lost his status as head chief in 1881. After the WOUNDED KNEE massacre (1890) he lived quietly on Pine Ridge Reservation.

BEATRICE MEDICINE

Bibliography: Hyde, George E., *Red Cloud's Folk* (1937; repr. 1976); Olson, James C., *Red Cloud and the Sioux Problem* (1965).

Red Cross

The Red Cross, officially known since 1986 as the International Movement of the Red Cross and Red Crescent, is an international humanitarian organization with independent affiliates in 137 countries and an estimated total membership of 250 million people. With the aim of voluntary service to others, the Red Cross was established to provide welfare service for victims of war and to help carry out the terms of the GENEVA CONVENTIONS of war. Its work has been extended to include such peacetime services as maintaining blood banks, offering training in first aid and water safety, and caring for victims of such disasters as floods, fires, and famines. It also aids refugees.

The Swiss humanitarian Jean Henri Dunant (1828–1910) established and brought recognition to the Red Cross. The first voluntary relief services that he proposed were organized in 1863. A second body, the League of Red Cross and Red Crescent Societies (founded 1919), promotes cooperation among the national societies. The International Red Cross comprises these two bodies. It has received the Nobel Peace Prize three times—in 1917, 1944, and 1963.

The American Red Cross, founded in 1881 by Clara BARTON, is authorized by congressional charter requiring the society to assist in wartime and to provide disaster relief. Local offices may also provide services needed in their communities. The Red Cross is funded privately. The national headquarters is in Washington, D.C. With 2,932 chapters, it had a staff of 20,796 in 1986.

Bibliography: Gilbo, Partick F., *The American Red Cross: The First Century* (1981); Peachment, Brian, *The Red Cross Story* (1978).

Red Data Book

The Red Data Book is a comprehensive, five-volume compilation of all plants and animals considered to be in danger of extinction. It lists the characteristics, population data, and protective measures for each endangered species. The book is published by the International Union for the Conservation of Nature and Natural Resources.

Red Jacket

Red Jacket, c.1758–1830, also known as Sagoyewatha, was a fiery SENECA chief known for his flamboyant personality, oratory, and political shrewdness. His ability to remain uncommitted even in such crises as John Sullivan's devastating raids on Iroquois settlements in 1779 has been interpreted as self-serving. Also, although he publicly opposed land sales to settlers in order to gain his people's support, he secretly yielded land to maintain esteem among whites.

After the Seneca were drawn into the Revolutionary War on the side of the British, Red Jacket reputedly proved to be an unenthusiastic warrior, although he wore the British uniform coat, which earned him his English name Red Jacket. After the war, he worked to maintain peace between his people and the United States. During the War of 1812 he fought on the American side against the British. He later became well known as an advocate of the maintenance of separate Iroquois jurisdiction and customs.

JAMES W. HERRICK

Bibliography: Hubbard, J. N., *An Account of Sa-Go-Ye-Wat-Ha, or Red Jacket and His People* (1886; repr. 1972); Wallace, A. F. C., *The Death and Rebirth of the Seneca* (1969).

red lauan [luh-wahn']

Red lauans, *Shorea negrosensis*, trees of the Philippine Islands that have been given the name "Philippine mahogany," are classified in the dipterocarp family, Dipterocarpaceae. Veneer wood from these trees is used extensively in house construction. Except for the names Philippine mahogany and African mahogany (referring to the genus *khaya*), the term *mahogany* is used by the U.S. Federal Trade Commission only for wood from trees of the genus *Swietenia*.

Red River (China): see YÜAN RIVER.

Red River   (United States)

The Red River (or Red River of the South) is a 1,639-km-long (1,018-mi) tributary of the Mississippi River. It rises in eastern New Mexico, follows part of the Texas-Oklahoma border, and flows southeast through Arkansas to Shreveport, La. About 11 km (7 mi) upstream of its Mississippi River confluence, the Red divides into the Old River, which continues to the Mississippi, and the Atchafalaya, which flows south to enter the Gulf of Mexico west of the Mississippi Delta. It drains an area of 236,700 km^2 (91,400 mi^2). Fulton, Ark., 632 km (455 mi) upstream, is at the head of navigation.

Flood-control and development projects include Denison Dam (1944), which impounds Lake Texoma. Cotton, cattle, and winter wheat are raised in the river valley; industries include lumbering and petroleum. The river was the site of a Confederate victory at Mansfield, La., during the Civil War.

Red River of the North

The Red River of the North is formed by the Bois de Sioux and Otter Tail rivers in western Minnesota and flows north for about 880 km (545 mi) along the North Dakota–Minnesota boundary to Lake Winnipeg in Manitoba. The river valley is a rich agricultural region. It was explored in 1732–33 by Pierre Gaultier de Varennes, sieur de La Vérendrye.

Red River Rebellion

The Red River Rebellion of 1869–70 was an armed rising of the métis (people of mixed French and Indian ancestry) of the Red River Settlement in what is now Manitoba, Canada. The HUDSON'S BAY COMPANY, its rule over the settlement having been lax, yielded its jurisdiction to the Dominion of Canada in 1870. Local residents, particularly the métis, feared disruption of their way of life by an onrush of Canadian settlers. Led by Louis RIEL, they seized Fort Garry (now Winnipeg) in November 1869 and set up a provisional government. Canada negotiated with the rebels, and the result was the admission of Manitoba as a province in July 1870.   P. B. WAITE

Bibliography: Flanagan, Thomas, *Louis David Riel* (1979); Stanley, G. F. G., *The Birth of Western Canada*, rev. ed. (1960).

Red River Settlement

The Red River Settlement was a colony located in the valley of the Red River of the North in present-day Manitoba, Canada. Its founder, Thomas Douglas, 5th earl of SELKIRK, obtained an extensive grant of land there from the HUDSON'S BAY COMPANY in 1811. The same year he sent a group of Scots to the area to establish an agricultural colony, and other settlers followed (1812–15). The colony, later known as Assiniboia, was opposed by the NORTH WEST COMPANY, a rival of the Hudson's Bay Company. The Nor'Westers believed that the colony was an attempt to interfere with its communication lines with Montreal. They tried to persuade the colonists to leave and then resorted to violence that culminated on June 19, 1816, in the massacre of Red River's governor and 19 of his men at Seven Oaks (near modern Winnipeg).

Lord Selkirk reestablished the colony in 1817, and it began to grow after the Hudson's Bay Company absorbed the North West Company in 1821. Many métis, buffalo hunters, and traders settled there. Originally administered by officials appointed by Lord Selkirk and his heirs, the colony was transferred to the Hudson's Bay Company in the 1830s. After 1850, when communications were opened with Minnesota and Canada, the weakness of company rule became apparent, and in 1869 the company surrendered to Canada its rights of jurisdiction. The following year, despite an insurrection (the Red River Rebellion), the area was admitted to the Canadian Confederation as the province of Manitoba.   GEORGE F. G. STANLEY

Bibliography: Morton, A. S., *A History of the Canadian West to 1870–71* (1939); Pritchett, J. P., *The Red River Valley 1811–1849* (1942); Ross, Alexander, *The Red River Settlement* (1857; repr. 1972).

Red Sea

The Red Sea, a long, narrow body of water between northeastern Africa and the Arabian Peninsula, serves as a connecting waterway between the Mediterranean Sea and the Indian Ocean. It covers an area of about 437,700 km^2 (169,000 mi^2) to a maximum depth of 2,190 m (7,200 ft). At its northern end the Red Sea forks into the Gulf of Aqaba (see AQABA, GULF OF) and the Gulf of Suez. The former leads through the Straits of Tiran to the ports of Elat (Israel) and al-Aqaba (Jordan). The Gulf of Suez leads to the Mediterranean Sea via the SUEZ CANAL. The strait of BAB EL-MANDEB at the southern end connects the Red Sea with the Gulf of Aden, the Arabian Sea, and the Indian Ocean. In addition to Elat and Aqaba, major ports on the sea include Jidda in Saudi Arabia, Port Sudan in Sudan, Suez in Egypt, Mesewa in Ethiopia, and al-Hudayda in Yemen (Sana).

The Red Sea became an important sea lane after the opening of the Suez Canal in 1869. Since that time it has been the focus of many political and diplomatic confrontations. The 1967 ARAB-ISRAELI WAR was precipitated by the closing of the Straits of Tiran by Egypt and Saudi Arabia.   PETER SCHWAB

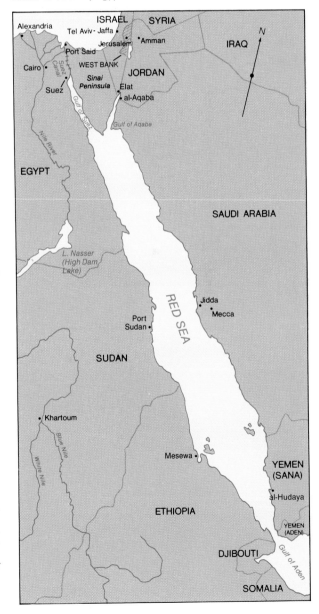

red shift

The phenomenon of the red shift is of central importance in modern COSMOLOGY, where it is commonly encountered. If the wavelength of light measured by a distant observer is longer than that which would be measured at the source of the light, the light is said to be red shifted—that is, shifted toward the red, or long-wavelength, end of the spectrum. Similarly, a blue shift is a displacement toward the blue, or short-wavelength, end of the spectrum. Red and blue shifts are most easily detected when the spectrum of a distant object contains identifiable features, such as absorption or emission lines of a particular element, and the positions of these lines are compared with those on a standard spectrum of the element obtained in a laboratory.

Two types of red shift are known. The first results from the line-of-sight relative motion between the source and the observer, explained by the DOPPLER EFFECT. If the shift z is small, the velocity v of the source relative to the observer may be obtained by the equation $z = \Delta\lambda/\lambda_0 = v/c$ where $\Delta\lambda$ is the change in wavelength, λ_0 is the rest wavelength (that which would be seen if the observer and the source were at rest relative to each other), and c is the velocity of light (300,000 km/sec, or 186,000 mi/sec). All stars in our Galaxy have slight Doppler red or blue shifts.

For larger Doppler shifts, the equation

$$z = \frac{\Delta\lambda}{\lambda_0} = \sqrt{\frac{c + v}{c - v}} - 1,$$

derived from the theory of special relativity, must be used to obtain the velocity of the object. All but the nearest galaxies (see EXTRAGALACTIC SYSTEMS) have substantial red shifts, indicating that nearly all galaxies are receding from our own. Such expansion of the universe confirms cosmological models based on the theory of general relativity.

In 1929, Edwin Hubble and Milton Humason discovered that the recessional velocity v and the distance d of galaxies are related linearly by the empirical relation $v = H_0 d$, where H_0 is a constant of proportionality now known as HUBBLE'S CONSTANT. Thus if galactic red shifts are interpreted as effects of recessional velocity (and most astronomers are confident of such an interpretation), then the red shift of a galaxy can be used to determine its distance.

The second type of red shift results from the presence of a gravitational field. According to the theory of general relativity, the spectrum of light from a source located at a distance R from a mass M will suffer a gravitational red shift z when de-

tected by a distant observer such that $z = GM/Rc^2$ where G is the gravitational constant.

In QUASARS a number of greatly red-shifted emission lines have been identified. Astronomers have not independently proven, however, that the red shifts of quasars obey Hubble's velocity-distance law. Most astronomers think quasars lie mainly toward the edge of the known universe, but some maintain that quasars actually are relatively nearby objects; the subject remains under debate. Another controversy has arisen from the work of American astronomer William Tifft, whose studies of galactic red shifts would seem to indicate that the red shifts are quantized. That is, galaxies seem to exist in preferred red-shift states, as elementary particles do in quantum theory. Most astronomers, however, do not accept this concept.

HONG-YEE CHIU

Bibliography: Gribbin, John, "Galaxy Red Shifts Come in Clumps," *New Scientist,* June 20, 1985; Helfland, David, "The Great Redshift Debate," *The Sciences,* October 1981; Zeilik, Michael, *Astronomy,* 4th ed. (1985).

red-spotted newt

The red-spotted newt, N. viridescens, *a small salamander adapted to cold habitats, can live in ice-covered ponds during winter.*

The red-spotted newt, *Notophthalmus viridescens,* family Salamandridae, is found in the eastern United States and southern Canada. Growing to about 10 cm (4 in) long, it is commonly greenish with a series of large red spots on each side. Mating occurs in the early spring, and females lay from 200 to 400 eggs, which hatch in 20 to 35 days. Within three months the larvae transform into a terrestrial, immature stage called the red eft, remaining so for up to three years before returning to the water as adults; in some cases the larvae change directly into adults. (See SALAMANDER.)

red tide

A red tide is typically a reddish but sometimes a brown or yellow discoloration of seawater caused by an enormous increase, or bloom, in the numbers of certain microscopic organisms. The discolored area may cover several square kilometers, and the density of occurrence of the microorganisms may reach many millions per liter, or quart, of seawater. A common example, *Mesodinium rubrum,* a ciliate protozoan, causes a bright red, but harmless, discoloration.

Toxic red tides, which vary in potency, generally occur in calm coastal waters during the summer months. Their appearance is often attributed to the coincidental occurrence of abundant food and optimal temperatures. Such tides are generally caused by several species of microorganisms called DINOFLAGELLATES, which are usually classified as algae. The most common of these toxic dinoflagellates are *Gonyaulax polyedra, G. catenella, G. tamarensis,* and *Gymnodinium breve.* Their neurotoxins cause extensive mortality among invertebrates, fish, and birds. Clams, mussels, oysters, and other shellfish that feed on the dinoflagellates, however, appear to be immune and may concentrate the poisons within their bodies for a considerable length of time. Thus if humans or other vertebrates eat appreciable quantities of shellfish containing the toxins, they are liable to suffer partial paralysis (paralytic shellfish poisoning) or, in some cases, death, because of paralysis of the heart and respiratory system.

TIMOTHY R. PARSONS

A normal spectrum (A) is for a star at rest with respect to the Earth. All spectral lines would be shifted (B) to the blue end of the spectrum if the star approached the Earth, whereas the lines would be moved (C) toward the red end if the star receded. The amount of blue or red shift depends on the star's relative speed.

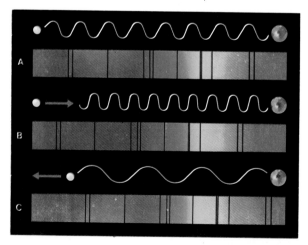

Bibliography: Arehart-Treichel, Joan, *Poisons and Toxins* (1976); Halstead, Bruce W., *Dangerous Marine Animals*, 2d ed. (1979), and *Poisonous and Venomous Marine Animals of the World*, rev. ed. (1978); Palmer, C. Mervin, *Algae and Water Pollution* (1977); Russell, Findlay E., and Saunders, Paul R., *Animal Toxins* (1967).

redbud

The eastern redbud tree, C. canadensis, *native to the northeastern United States and Canada, grows up to 7 m (15 ft) in height. It is used as a landscape tree because of its attractive leaves and spring flowers.*

Redbuds are seven species of small trees or shrubs of the genus *Cercis* in the pea family, Leguminosae, native to northern temperate regions. The eastern redbud, *C. canadensis,* of eastern North America, bears heart-shaped leaves and usually pinkish flowers. The western redbud, *C. occidentalis,* of the southwestern United States, commonly grows as a shrub with purplish flowers and rounded leaves. The Judas tree, *C. siliquastrum,* is native to Eurasia and grows to a height of 12 m (40 ft). Its name derives from the legend that Judas Iscariot hanged himself from a redbud.

Redding, Otis

Singer and songwriter Otis Redding, b. Georgia, Sept. 9, 1941, is considered one of the greatest exponents of SOUL MUSIC. He was killed in a plane crash on Dec. 10, 1967. Among his admirers were the Rolling Stones and Aretha Franklin, whose 1967 recording of his song ''Respect'' was an instant hit. Although he achieved considerable success during his lifetime, Redding's greatest fame came posthumously, with the 1968 release of his song ''Sittin' on the Dock of the Bay.''

Bibliography: Schiesel, Jane, *The Otis Redding Story* (1973).

Rederijkers   [ray'-dur-ay-kurs]

Members of literary associations known as Chambers of Rhetoric (Rederijkerskamers) and organized like trade guilds, the Rederijkers (from the French, meaning ''rhetoricians'') became prominent in the Netherlands during the 15th century, reaching the height of their importance in the 16th. Commissioned by towns to perform on ceremonial occasions, Rederijkers wrote and presented formal poetry, especially intricate refrains, as well as such allegorical plays as *Elcerlijc,* the probable original of *Everyman.* Prominent members of the Amsterdam Chambers included Gerbrand BREDERO, Pieter HOOFT, and Joost van den VONDEL.   R. P. MEIJER

Redfield, Robert

Robert Redfield, b. Dec. 4, 1897, d. Oct. 16, 1958, was an American cultural anthropologist noted for broadening the

scope of American anthropological study beyond its traditional orientation toward primitive tribal peoples. Originally trained in law, he earned his Ph.D. in anthropology at the University of Chicago in 1928 and began teaching there the same year. Redfield conducted extensive ethnographic fieldwork in Mexico. His best-known theoretical contribution is the folk-urban continuum, in which idealized lifeways in traditional peasant communities are contrasted with those in city communities. Among Redfield's publications are *Tepotzlan: A Mexican Village* (1930); *The Folk Culture of Yucatan* (1941); *The Primitive World and Its Transformation* (1953); and *The Little Community* (1955).   JAMES W. HERRICK

Redford, Robert

One of Hollywood's most popular leading men, Charles Robert Redford, Jr., b. Santa Monica, Calif., Aug. 18, 1937, had his first success on Broadway in Neil Simon's *Barefoot in the Park* (1963; film, 1967). Redford's reputation soared with the films *Butch Cassidy and the Sundance Kid* (1969) and *The Sting* (1973), in which he played roguish but lovable crooks opposite Paul Newman. His other notable films include *Downhill Racer* (1969), *Jeremiah Johnson* and *The Candidate* (both 1972), *The Way We Were* (1973), *The Great Gatsby* (1974), *All the President's Men* (1976), *The Natural* (1984), and *Out of Africa* (1985). Redford won an Oscar as best director for *Ordinary People* (1980). He has long been active in environmentalist causes.

Redgrave   (family)

The combined careers of the Redgrave family span more than four decades of British theater and films. **Sir Michael Redgrave**, b. Mar. 20, 1908, d. Mar. 21, 1985, was knighted in 1959 for his distinguished contributions to the British stage. By contrast, his screen career was oddly disappointing despite an amiable beginning with *The Lady Vanishes* (1938) and occasional peaks such as *Kipps* (1941), *Dead of Night* (1945), *The Browning Version* (1951), and *The Go-Between* (1971). His extreme height made him difficult to cast. His elder daughter, **Vanessa Redgrave**, b. Jan. 30, 1937, although gaining notoriety for her radical politics, is an accomplished actress, highly praised for her roles in *Morgan* (1966), *Blow-up* (1967), *Isadora* (1968), *Julia* (1977; Academy Award), the television movie *Playing for Time* (1980; Emmy), *The Bostonians* (1984), and *Wetherby* (1985). A younger daughter, **Lynn Redgrave**, b. Mar. 8, 1943, playing more often in comedies, made a touchingly awkward heroine in *Georgy Girl* (1966), and turned to television in the 1970s and 1980s.   LESLIE HALLIWELL

Bibliography: Findlater, Richard, *Michael Redgrave, Actor* (1956) and *Player Kings* (1971); Redgrave, Michael, *Mask or Face: Reflections in an Actor's Mirror* (1953).

Redlands, University of   [red'-luhnds]

Established in 1907 and affiliated with the American Baptist Convention, the University of Redlands (enrollment: 2,750; library: 270,000 volumes) is a coeducational liberal arts school in Redlands, Calif. It offers bachelor's and master's degrees.

redlining: see MORTGAGE.

Redmond, John   [red'-muhnd]

John Edward Redmond, b. Sept. 1, 1856, d. Mar. 6, 1918, led the Irish party in the British House of Commons for nearly two decades. He became leader of the Parnellite faction in 1891, after Charles Stewart PARNELL's disgrace and death, and in 1900 was elected chairman of the reunited Irish party. Between 1910 and 1914, Redmond was able to force enactment of the Third HOME RULE BILL, which was suspended, however, for the duration of World War I. Redmond's endorsement of the war effort and his reluctant agreement to the proposed partition of Ireland cost him support. By 1917 he was opposed by the revolutionary SINN FEIN.   DAVID W. MILLER

Bibliography: Gwynn, Denis, *The Life of John Redmond* (1932).

Redon, Odilon [ruh-dohn', oh-dee-lohn']

The French symbolist artist Odilon Redon, b. Apr. 20, 1840, d. July 6, 1916, isolated by frail health and parental indifference at an early age, peopled his loneliness with imaginary beings, as he was later to people his works. After studying painting in Paris, where he was encouraged by J. B. C. Corot, he made charcoal drawings and lithographs, such as *Death: "My Irony Surpasses All Others"* (1889), an illustration for Gustave Flaubert's *The Temptation of Saint Anthony*. Although death's words are embodied in a skull-headed figure emerging from writhing coils, their expression resides in the encroaching shadows. Like Rembrandt, whose art he studied in the Netherlands in 1878, Redon used chiaroscuro, strongly contrasted light and dark, to convey subjective values.

With the birth of a son in 1889, and the admiration of young independent painters, radiant color harmonies replaced the dominance of black in Redon's works. His drawings, Redon said, did not describe anything, but, like music, transported the spectator into the ambiguous world of the undetermined. *Evocation of Roussel* (1890; National Gallery of Art, Washington, D.C.) is not a traditional portrait of the composer. Instead the figure and the flowers emerge from amorphous colors symbolizing their evolution from the artist's imagination. The face, veiled with a brown tone, becomes a poetic mystery. In his *Cyclops* (c.1898; Kröller-Müller Museum, Otterlo, the Netherlands) the bizarre one-eyed creature depicted, and the improbable landscape, are underlined with a structural logic stemming from Redon's assiduous study of botany and osteology. The decorative effect provided by the large color shapes and variegated details associates Redon's pictorial attitude with the late-19th-century postimpressionist and Art Nouveau styles.

Redon's late bouquet paintings, like the *Vase of Flowers* (1914; Museum of Modern Art, New York City), may at first

Cyclops (c.1898), by Odilon Redon, a portrayal of the one-eyed giant of classical Greek legend, strikingly exemplifies this painter's ability to represent hallucinations, often based on literary inspiration. (Rijksmuseum Kröller-Müller, Otterlo, the Netherlands.)

seem naturalistic, but the vague, dreamlike backgrounds and the cold blues within the flowers' general warmth turn them into perverse suggestions. JOAN SIEGFRIED

Bibliography: Hobbs, Richard, *Odilon Redon* (1977); Selz, Jean, *Odilon Redon*, trans. by Eileen Hennessy (1971); Werner, Alfred, *Introduction to the Graphic Works of Odilon Redon* (1969).

redstart

The American redstart, S. ruticilla, is an accomplished flycatcher. The male's markings (left) are unlike those of any other warbler.

The redstart is a small Old World bird, *Phoenicurus phoenicurus*, of the thrush family, Turdidae, widely distributed throughout Europe and western Asia. It is about 13 cm (5.5 in) long and has a rusty red rump and tail and, in the male, an orange breast and black bib. The name *redstart* is also applied to a number of other birds in the thrush family including the closely related Eurasian black redstart, *P. ochruros*, and the more distantly related Asiatic plumbeous redstart, *Rhyacornis fuliginosus*. In the New World the name *redstart* refers to a number of species in the wood warbler family, Parulidae. The American redstart, *Setophaga ruticilla*, is about 13 cm (5.5 in) long; males are jet black with bright orange patches on the wings and tail; females and young have yellow patches on olive brown. The American redstart nests from the southeastern United States into northwestern Canada and winters from Mexico into South America. The genus *Myioborus* of the wood warbler family contains 11 species known as *redstarts*, including *M. picta*, the painted redstart, which ranges from the southwestern United States into Nicaragua.

Redstone

Redstone was the rocket used to launch the first U.S. manned suborbital flights during the MERCURY PROGRAM. It was originally developed by the Army Ballistic Missile Agency (ABMA) at Redstone Arsenal in Huntsville, Ala., to satisfy a requirement for a ballistic missile with a range of 322 km (200 mi) for use in the field by the U.S. Army. The original Redstone stood 21 m (69 ft) tall, had a diameter of 178 cm (70 in), and a liftoff weight of 28,123 kg (62,000 lb). Redstone used much of the technology of the German A-4 (V-2) rocket. The propellants were liquid oxygen and ethyl alcohol, and guidance was obtained by an inertial system acting upon graphite exhaust vanes and small aerodynamic rudders. The engine developed 346,900 newtons, or 35,400 kg (78,000 lb) of thrust, and was based on an engine built for the winged surface-to-surface missile Navaho.

Redstone was first test-launched at Cape Canaveral on Aug. 20, 1953, when it traveled just 7,315 m (24,000 ft). By the end of 1958, 36 more launchings had demonstrated the missile's great potential. Sixteen of them were built by Redstone Arsenal under the technical direction of Wernher von Braun; the others, by Chrysler Corporation. The weapon entered service with the U.S. Army in West Germany in June 1958.

The Redstone became the basis for the JUPITER and JUNO rockets, the first of which launched *Explorer 1*, the first U.S. satellite. With the motor and tank section lengthened and the 7.3-m (24-ft) Mercury capsule and escape tower substituted for the upper section and warhead, the Redstone used in the MERCURY PROGRAM had an overall height of 25 m (83 ft). The chimpanzee Ham survived a suborbital ballistic flight aboard *Mercury-Redstone 2* on Jan. 31, 1961. Alan B. Shepard, Jr., made the first manned suborbital flight on May 5, 1961, aboard *Mercury-Redstone 3*; the flight lasted just 15 min 22 sec from launch to splashdown. Virgil I. Grissom made a similar ballistic hop on July 21, 1961, aboard *Mercury-Redstone 4*.

KENNETH GATLAND

Bibliography: Emme, Eugene M., ed., *The History of Rocket Technology* (1964); Swenson, Loyd S., Jr., Grimwood, James M., and Alexander, Charles C., *This New Ocean: A History of Project Mercury* (NASA SP-4201; 1966).

See also: ROCKETS AND MISSILES.

reduction: see OXIDATION AND REDUCTION.

redwood

Once widespread in the Northern Hemisphere, the approximately 40 species of redwoods have dwindled to only 3: two in California and one in China. The redwoods, also called sequoias, are members of the family Taxodiaceae, variously called the redwood, bald-cypress, or swamp-cypress family. The coast redwood, *Sequoia sempervirens*, often referred to simply as the "redwood," is believed to be the tallest tree in the world. One specimen in Redwood Creek Valley, Calif., was reported to measure 117.3 m (385 ft) high. The coast redwood is a coniferous evergreen with a fibrous, deeply furrowed, reddish brown bark up to 25 cm (10 in) thick. It has flat needles and tiny cones of 2.5 cm (1 in) or less in length; the cones mature in one season. The coast redwood is restricted to areas in which recurrent ocean fogs provide the trees with the required high humidity. This area forms an irregular coastal strip about 725 km (450 mi) long and 8 to 56 km (5 to 35 mi) wide and varies in altitude from sea level to 900 m (3,000 ft). Coast redwoods are still extensively harvested for building lumber and other uses, particularly in applications where resistance to dampness is important. Concerted efforts are being made to extend protection to the remaining exploited groves.

The giant redwood, usually called the big tree, was for-

The redwood, S. sempervirens, a conifer that is native to the North American Pacific coast, is the tallest tree in the world.

merly classified in the same genus, *Sequoia,* as the coast redwood, but now it is generally placed in a genus of its own as *Sequoiadendron giganteum.* Although not as tall as the coast redwood nor with the extensive trunk diameter of some baobabs of tropical Africa, the big tree's combination of immense height and trunk diameter make it the most massive living thing. Heights of about 99 m (325 ft) and diameters of 9 m (30 ft) have been reported: such trees would weigh an estimated 5,500 metric tons (6,000 tons). Immense size implies considerable age, and the big trees are among the oldest living things, some being estimated as exceeding 3,500 years in age. The big tree has a fibrous, furrowed, reddish brown bark, which may exceed 50 cm (20 in) in thickness. Its small, blue green needles appear to clothe the shoots; its cones reach 9 cm (3.5 in) in length and take two seasons to mature. Big trees are confined to altitudes of 1,500 to 2,560 m (5,000 to 8,400 ft) on the western slopes of the Sierra Nevadas in central California. Their entire range is approximately 450 km (280 mi) long and 32 km (20 mi) wide. Once widely harvested for their wood, the big trees are now of insignificant commercial value because they are so few in number or are in protected areas.

The dawn redwood, *Metasequoia glyptostroboides,* native to south central China, was first known only from its fossil remains, which were scientifically described in 1941. It was not until several years later that botanists became aware that the tree still existed. The dawn redwood differs from the other redwoods in several ways, including the fact that it is deciduous and not evergreen.

Bibliography: Engbeck, J., *The Enduring Giants* (1973); Silverberg, R., *Vanishing Giants* (1969); Taylor, N., *The Ageless Relics* (1963).

Redwood National Park

Redwood National Park, authorized by Congress in 1968, lies along the Pacific coast in northwestern California near the Oregon border. It has an area of 441 km² (170 mi²). Contained within the park are three California state parks—Jedediah Smith Redwoods, Prairie Creek Redwoods, and Del Norte Coast Redwoods. Redwoods, the world's tallest trees, often grow to more than 90 m (300 ft); the Tall Tree stands 112 m (368 ft). Wildlife in the park includes moose, deer, cougars, and bears. Whales, sea lions, and seals can be seen offshore.

reed

Reed is the common name for a variety of large, perennial plants of the grass family, Gramineae. The common reed, *Phragmites australis,* usually classified as *P. communis* or sometimes as *P. maximus,* is found in wetlands, most commonly brackish-water environments, throughout most of the world. It rarely produces fully developed seeds and usually spreads by means of its vigorous interlocking rootstock (rhizome), which tends to crowd out all other kinds of vegetation. The rootstock of a single plant may extend for more than 10 m (33 ft). The common reed, *Arundo donax,* also called the giant reed, has jointed, pithy stems (culms) that may reach 5.8 m (19 ft) in height. The stems bear long, narrow, blue green to gray green leaves that measure up to 60 cm (2 ft) long. Graceful, featherlike flower clusters (panicles of spikelets) are produced at the top of the stems in late summer. The flower clusters are purplish red when young but later become a silvery white. The stalk (rachilla) within each spikelet in a cluster bears long, silky hairs that accentuate the cluster's plumelike appearance. Native to southern Europe, the common reed has been introduced into the southern United States and tropical America as an ornamental and for erosion control. Its woody stems are used to produce reeds for certain musical instruments.

Reed, Sir Carol

An accomplished British film director who was knighted in 1952, Sir Carol Reed, b. Dec. 30, 1906, d. Apr. 25, 1976, had his first outstanding success with *The Stars Look Down* (1939). Two excellent war films, *The Way Ahead* (1944) and a documentary, *The True Glory* (1945), followed. Reed's postwar international reputation derived largely from such taut, highly literate suspense dramas as *The Fallen Idol* (1948) and *The Third Man* (1949), both scripted by novelist Graham Greene, and *The Man Between* (1953). Reed further distinguished himself with *The Key* (1958), *Our Man in Havana* (1959), and the musical *Oliver!* (1968), for which he won an Academy Award.

Reed, Ishmael

The American writer Ishmael Reed, b. Chattanooga, Tenn., Feb. 22, 1938, is best known for his highly original fiction. Experimental in form, each of his novels is an exuberant, phantasmagoric satire on Western cultural values and a celebration of black survival against great odds. In *The Free-Lance Pallbearers* (1967), *Yellow Back Radio Broke-Down* (1969), *Mumbo-Jumbo* (1972), *The Last Days of Louisiana Red* (1974), and *Flight to Canada* (1976), Reed uses an array of cultural and historical references to rewrite history according to the values of "neo hoo-dooism," Reed's term for all that is culturally spontaneous and joyful. Neo hoo-dooism as an alternative to the traditions of whites also figures in his collection of poetry, *Conjure: Selected Poems 1963-70* (1972).

Bibliography: Bellamy, Joe David, ed., *The New Fiction: Interviews with Innovative American Writers* (1974).

Reed, John

John Reed, b. Portland, Oreg., Oct. 22, 1887, d. Oct. 19, 1920, American journalist, poet, and revolutionary, wrote the internationally famous *Ten Days That Shook the World* (1919), a sympathetic eyewitness account of the Bolshevik revolution of 1917. A graduate (1910) of Harvard University, Reed wrote poetry and began a career in journalism at *American Magazine*. Becoming interested in social problems, he joined the staff of Max Eastman's radical journal *Masses* in 1913. Reed's firsthand reports for the magazine *Metropolitan* on Pancho Villa's Mexican revolt in 1914 and on World War I in Eastern Europe in 1914-15 established his reputation as a war correspondent.

Visiting Petrograd (now Leningrad), Russia, in 1917 during the Bolshevik revolution, Reed became a supporter and friend of V. I. Lenin before returning home. In 1919 he was expelled from the U.S. Socialist party and became head of the Communist Labor party. Indicted for sedition, Reed fled to the USSR in late 1919.

Bibliography: O'Connor, Richard, and Walker, Dale L., *The Lost Revolutionary* (1967); Rosenstone, Robert A., *Romantic Revolutionary* (1975).

Reed, Thomas B.

Thomas Brackett Reed, b. Portland, Maine, Oct. 18, 1839, d. Dec. 7, 1902, was a U.S. legislator best known for formulating the "Reed Rules" of parliamentary procedure. Elected to Congress in 1876 as a Republican from Maine, he served until 1899, including two terms (1889-91, 1895-99) as Speaker of the House.

Called "czar" because of his arbitrary use of power, he brought the speakership to the peak of its political influence, notably by introducing (1890) rules designed to limit debate and facilitate the passage of legislation. "Czar" Reed wielded the Speaker's power of recognition, drastically curbing Democratic FILIBUSTERS. Under his leadership, the 51st Congress produced such a mass of legislation that it was dubbed the billion-dollar congress.

Bibliography: McCall, Samuel W., *Thomas B. Reed* (1914; repr. 1972).

Reed, Walter

The military surgeon Walter Reed, b. Belroi, Va., Sept. 13, 1851, d. Nov. 22, 1902, proved in 1901 that YELLOW FEVER is caused by a filterable virus transmitted by the bite of the *Aedes aegypti* mosquito. After working to improve sanitary conditions and prevent the spread of typhoid during the Spanish-American War, Reed was appointed (1900) to head a commission studying yellow fever in Cuba. In a series of experiments he and his commission disproved the theory that yellow fever was caused by bacteria and found that it did not spread by contact. The subsequent clearing of mosquito-breeding areas in the southeastern United States and Latin America halted the disease. The Walter Reed Medical Center outside Washington, D.C., founded in 1909, is named for Reed.

Bibliography: Kelly, Howard, *Walter Reed and Yellow Fever*, 3d ed. (1923); McGrady, Mike, *Jungle Doctors* (1962).

reed instruments: see WIND INSTRUMENTS.

reed organ

The reed-organ family includes the ACCORDION, CONCERTINA, HARMONICA (or mouth organ), harmonium, and American organ. Those instruments, descended from the Chinese SHENG, came into existence early in the 19th century. They all employ the principle of the free reed, which beats to and fro in a slot. The harmonium and American organ are similar in their uses of free reeds, a keyboard, drawstops to alter the tonal qualities, and pedals that supply air to the bellows.

The application of a keyboard to reeds dates from the first decade of the 19th century; the first patents on the harmonium were taken out by A. F. Debain in 1840. Other manufacturers soon added devices that changed the sound and capabilities of the instrument: the most important include "percussion," in which a hammer strikes the end of the reed as the air activates it; a prolongation attachment that permits certain keys to continue sounding after they are released; a device to emphasize the top or bottom notes; and knee swells to suddenly add the full force of the instrument. Several composers, including Dvořák, Sigfrid Karg-Elert, and César Franck, wrote for the harmonium as a concert instrument.

The American, or cottage, organ differs from the harmonium—it sucks air into the reeds rather than expelling it. It has a more balanced but less varied tone, closer in quality to the pipe organ. First developed at a French factory, the principle was brought to America and adopted by the Estey (1856) and Mason & Hamlin (1861) manufacturers. An automatic swell device and a fan-operated vox humana were later added. American organs were popular for home use and were often found in small churches before the days of the electric organ.   ELWYN A. WIENANDT

Bibliography: Gellerman, Robert F., *The American Reed Organ* (1973); Ochse, Orpha, *The History of the Organ in the United States* (1975).

reef: see CORAL REEF.

Reeve, Tapping

The American jurist Tapping Reeve, b. Brookhaven, N.Y., October 1744, d. Dec. 13, 1823, established one of the first law schools in the United States. A graduate of the College of New Jersey (now Princeton University), Reeve began to practice (1772) law in Litchfield, Conn., and opened (1784) Litchfield Law School. Reeve served (1798-1814) on the Connecticut superior court and was chief justice (1814-16) of the state supreme court of errors. He initiated the movement to permit married women to control their own property. Before Litchfield Law School closed in 1833, many later-eminent people studied there, including Aaron Burr, John C. Calhoun, and Horace Mann.

referendum and initiative

Referendum and initiative are related forms of direct legislative democracy that were used in ancient Greece and are practiced in various modern countries, especially Switzerland. Referendum is the referring of a bill or political question to the direct vote of the electorate. It may be an obligatory or optional supplement to the usual procedures of legislative passage.

Initiative is the proposal of a law or constitutional amendment proposed by a specified percentage of voter signatures on a popular petition. There are two types of initiative: direct and indirect. In the former, a proposed law is placed directly on the ballot for the approval of the state's voters; in the latter, a proposal is first sent to the state legislature. If the proposal is not enacted by the legislature, it is then placed on the ballot for consideration by the electorate. A referendum by petition provides an opportunity for voters to veto a legislative enactment. In states with this referendum procedure, a legislative bill takes effect only after a certain period of time during which the bill may be suspended by a voter petition. The bill is then submitted to a referendum.

Parts of Switzerland have used the referendum since the 1500s. Countries that now use types of referenda include Australia, France, Ireland, Italy, Sweden, and some new nations in Africa and Asia.

In the United States the use of referendum and initiative grew out of the movement for progressive reform at the beginning of the 20th century. Although referendum and initiative do not exist in all states (39 states had provisions for referenda in 1977, and only 21 provided for initiative), in many they are important instruments at the public's disposal to express public opinion and implement policy. California, where initiative and referendum procedures are particularly important, may, in a major election, present to its voters as many as 20 proposals for legislation. The celebrated proposal on property tax, Proposition 13, passed in 1978, is an outstanding example. Voters in nearly every state are given the opportunity to vote on bond issues and amendments to state constitutions in this manner.

Although citizens in some states with these procedures have the opportunity to participate more directly in state policy making, reformers have conceded that these procedures have their drawbacks. Not all eligible voters go to the polls. Many who do go ignore or fail to understand the importance of the referenda. Often the language of the proposed legislation is complicated. More importantly, direct legislation does not prevent powerful individuals and interest groups from manipulating policy issues behind the scenes, and carefully orchestrated advertising campaigns frequently characterize attempts to gain either approval or disapproval of various referenda issues.   MARTIN A. BIERBAUM

Bibliography: Butler, David, and Ranney, Austin, eds., *Referendums* (1978); Grimond, Joseph, and Neve, Brian, *The Referendum* (1975); Oberholtzer, Ellis P., *The Referendum in America* (1912; repr. 1971); Wilcox, Delos F., *Government by All the People* (1932; repr. 1972).

refinery: see PETROLEUM INDUSTRY.

refining, metal

Refining is a process through which oxides, gases, and other impurities are removed from a metal. This process is generally the final step in the production of metals from their ores. Several refining techniques are used. In fire refining, a metal is heated until it melts, after which air or an oxidizing slag is introduced to remove the impurities by precipitation from the molten metal. Distillation is used for refining low-boiling metals such as cadmium, mercury, and zinc. The metal is placed in a retort and heated to the boiling point; the vapors are then condensed and collected separately from the impurities. Metals such as gold and copper must be electrorefined. With this process, an electric current is sent through an electrolytic bath, resulting in pure metal being deposited at one of the electrodes and the impurities at the other electrode. In chemical refining, acids are used to dissolve impurities from metals. In general, purifications are achieved by any chemical treatment that has a preferential action on the metal.   PHILLIP W. MORTON AND JOHN F. KANE

reflection

Whenever light strikes the surface of any material substance, part of the light is turned backward, or reflected from the surface, the remainder being transmitted into the material. If the surface is rough or matted, the reflected light goes off in all different directions. This is called diffuse reflection. An example is the paper on which this printing appears. Diffuse reflection of light renders nonluminous objects visible. If the surface is very smooth, however, the reflected light goes in a definite direction determined by the direction of the incident light (see below). This phenomenon is known as regular, or specular, reflection.

The term *reflectance* is used to denote the fraction of light energy that is reflected by a material. Metals generally have high values of reflectance, silver being the best reflector with a reflectance of about 96%. The reflectance of a clean glass surface is about 6%.

Light is reflected from a plane surface at an angle equal to the angle made by the incoming (incident) light. The angles of incidence and reflection are customarily measured as the angles made by the light rays and the normal, a line drawn perpendicular to the surface at the point of incidence. Thus, the law of reflection states that the angle of incidence equals the angle of reflection.

If the surface is not plane but curved, it may still be considered to be made up of many very small, elementary plane surfaces. The path of any light ray striking a curved surface can still be determined from the law of reflection. This law is the basis for computing the image-forming characteristics of curved MIRRORS.   GRANT R. FOWLES

Bibliography: Born, Max M., and Wolf, Emil E., *Principles of Optics*, 5th ed. (1975); Jenkins, Francis A., and White, Harvey E., *Fundamentals of Optics*, 4th ed. (1976).

Reflections on the Revolution in France

Written by Edmund BURKE to combat the influence in England of those who supported the principles of the French Revolution, *Reflections on the Revolution in France* (1790) achieved an immense success in England and Europe and became a basic document for those who valued social stability. Burke, an Anglo-Irish statesman and orator regarded as the father of modern conservatism, condemned the revolution for its disregard of important social and political institutions and its attempts to bring about radical change. He had in fact favored the American Revolution because of its more moderate character, but he argued in *Reflections* for the values of tradition, religion, property, the family, the nobility, and the nation. Written during the moderate phase of the French Revolution, the book accurately predicted the rise of a dictator in France. It provoked strong criticisms, the most notable of which was Tom Paine's *The Rights of Man* (1791).   HERBERT M. LEVINE

Bibliography: Canavan, Francis P., *The Political Reason of Edmund Burke* (1960); Cobban, Alfred, *Edmund Burke and the Revolt against the Eighteenth Century* (1960); Cone, Carl B., *Burke and the Nature of Politics* (1957 and 1964).

reflector: see TELESCOPE.

reflex

The reflex, an involuntary act that represents the lowest level of nervous response to natural stimuli, underlies all animal behavior. This pattern of neuronal activity, which may or may not involve conscious thought, is conducted by three components of the NERVOUS SYSTEM—a sensory system, a neuronal center of integration, and a motor system—that are simple enough to ensure accurate, quick transmittal of impulses in response to stimuli. .

The sensory system consists of afferent nerve cells (neurons)—which relay sensory information to the central nervous system—and receptor cells. Receptor cells, located for the most part in the skin, eyes, tongue, nose, inner ear, muscles, and joints, convert the energy of a stimulus—usually chemical, mechanical, light, or heat energy—into electrochemical nerve impulses. In turn, the impulses are carried over specific pathways of the nervous system to the nerve centers located in the spinal cord, the medulla, the hypothalamus, and the cerebellum. A particular nerve center integrates sensory input from various afferent fibers as well as from other nerve centers. Finally, nerve centers discharge impulses as motor responses to muscles, organs, and glands. The motor output in-

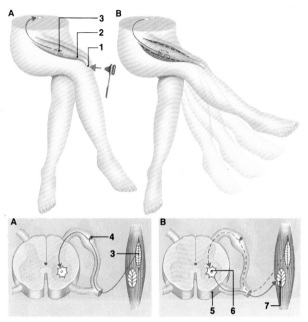

A reflex action is the involuntary response of a muscle or gland to a sensory stimulus. Once initiated, the reflex travels from the stimulated body part to the spinal cord and back again, along an arc made of connected neurons. A neuron is a nerve cell with long extensions, or axons, that branch out from a central cell body. In the first part of a typical reflex sequence (A), a light hammer tap on the patellar tendon, below the kneecap (1), stretches the quadriceps muscle (2) of the thigh. This action stimulates receptor cells called muscle spindles (3), which translate the pressure of the tap into an electrochemical message. A sensory neuron (4) conveys the message from the receptor cells to the spinal cord. In the second part of the reflex sequence (B), the spinal cord (5), having received the electrochemical message, immediately passes it on to a motor neuron (6), which conveys the message to nerve terminals, called endplates (7), in the quadriceps muscle, causing the muscle to contract. The entire sequence, from hammer tap to knee jerk, is accomplished in a fraction of a second. Such purely spinal reflexes as the tendon tap involve no action by the brain; their only contact with the central nervous system is in the spinal cord. Other examples of spinal reflexes are sneezing, coughing, yawning, and blinking. Reflex actions work so quickly that they are completed before the conscious mind has registered the stimulus.

volves efferent neurons known as motor neurons.

Synapse. The synapse, a functional connection between neurons, is the site at which integration or modification of reflex activity occurs (see NEUROPHYSIOLOGY). The transmission across synapses is mediated by a neurotransmitter, a chemical substance released from a nerve ending that has received an impulse. The neurotransmitter diffuses across the synaptic cleft between the neurons and activates receptors that either enhance or inhibit impulse transmission.

Reflex Threshold. The intensity and pattern of stimuli largely shape the strength and type of the reflex that is elicited. Increasing intensity and frequency of impulses to a nerve center will reach a threshold, at which point the response is triggered. Increments of the impulse after that threshold has been attained, however, do not elicit a corresponding increase in the reflex response. For this to happen, more motor units must be activated—a process known as recruitment. In general, reflexes involving only a few motor neurons are elicited first by a low-intensity efferent message and continue to respond for a relatively long time.

TYPES OF REFLEXES

Knee Jerk. Vertebrate postural reflexes primarily involve the spinal cord, the most familiar and simplest being the monosynaptic stretch, otherwise known as the knee jerk. The sensory receptors for this reflex arc are located in muscle spindles embedded in skeletal muscles. When the kneecap tendon is tapped the muscle is stretched and the muscle spindles in the thigh are excited. Because this reflex

response involves sensory neurons that directly synapse with motor neurons in the spinal cord, transmission time is brief, and the thigh muscle quickly contracts, extending the leg.

Withdrawal Reflex. The flexor withdrawal reflex, a spinal reflex, requires adequate noxious stimulation resulting in the withdrawal of a limb from the stimulus. If a person touches a hot object, the reflex to withdraw immediately from the object precedes the sensation of pain. The withdrawal reflex of one limb may be accompanied by the extension of other limbs in an attempt to maintain body support.

Cardiovascular and Respiratory Reflexes. The medulla oblongata, part of the brainstem, contains nerve centers for cardiovascular and respiratory reflexes, which are vital to life function. For instance, an increase in blood pressure activates special receptors in the carotid sinus and the aortic arch, which are large arterial blood vessels; impulses signaling this increase in pressure are carried by the vagus and glossopharyngeal nerves to the medullar reticular formation of the brainstem. The reflex response from this center slows down the heart rate, which returns blood pressure to normal.

A number of respiratory reflexes are controlled by spinal and brainstem nerve centers. These reflexes include coughing and gagging, as well as involuntary regulation of carbon dioxide and oxygen levels in circulating blood. Related reflexes are vomiting, yawning, sneezing, and hiccuping.

Balance and Posture. Important reflex nerve centers related to POSTURE, balance, and eye position also are located in the brainstem. Receptors for these reflexes are found in the vestibule of the inner ear. These reflexes serve two functions: to stabilize the position of the head and provide information about angular and linear acceleration of the head, and to maintain visual image by stabilizing the eyes during head movement. Individuals suffering from motion sickness generally experience disturbances of these vestibular receptors.

Eye Reflexes. Reflex nerve centers of the midbrain involve movement of the eyeball, constriction of the pupil in response to light, and adjustment of the lenses in order to focus on objects. The most familiar of these reflexes is the pupillary light reflex, in which the pupil constricts when light is flashed into the eye. When the eyes are directed to an object close at hand, several reflexes come into play: the eye muscles contract, drawing the eyes into alignment so that images in each eye focus on the same part of the retina; the lenses thicken in order to maintain a sharply focused image; and the pupils narrow to regulate the depth of focus. A visual fixation reflex also occurs, as demonstrated by the eye movement of a passenger in a moving vehicle who looks out the window at the passing scenery. The passenger's eyes turn slowly in the direction of the moving field, then jump back quickly to fix the visual gaze.

CONDITIONED REFLEXES

Perhaps most fascinating to physiologists and psychologists are the features of a reflex that may be modified by learning. Two model systems, one outlined by Edward L. THORNDIKE (1895) and another by Ivan P. PAVLOV (1906), have been used extensively by researchers to examine learning, or how behavior is modified. Thorndike found that animals modify their behavior if a reward is imminent, that is, learning occurred faster if the correct performance was rewarded. Pavlov found that dogs could be trained to salivate in response to an inappropriate stimulus (a bell ring) if the bell was previously associated with the appropriate stimulus (the presence of food).

JOHN T. HACKETT

Bibliography: Bullock, T. H., *Introduction to Nervous Systems* (1977); Gardner, E. D., *Fundamentals of Neurology*, 5th ed. (1968); Kandel, E. R., *Cellular Basis of Behavior* (1976); Nathan, P. W., *The Nervous System* (1969).

Reform Acts

The Reform Acts were a series of British legislative measures (1832, 1867–68, 1885) that broadened the parliamentary franchise and reduced disparities among constituencies. Electoral reform had been urged in the 1780s by William PITT the Younger as well as Charles James Fox, but the reaction against the French Revolution created a more conservative political climate. By the late 1820s the movement for reform was again strong, and the Whig government of the 2d Earl GREY overcame opposition to the first Reform Bill by threatening to create enough Whig peers to ensure its passage through the House of Lords. The bill was enacted in 1832.

The first Reform Act eliminated many "rotten boroughs" (depopulated constituencies) and "pocket boroughs" (constituencies controlled by the crown and other landowners), transferring their representation to such previously unrepresented large cities as Birmingham and Manchester and to the more populous counties. The vote was extended to males who occupied premises valued at £10 annually, bringing the middle class into the political arena, and the introduction of systematic registration procedures spurred the development of party organizations. Although the act expanded the franchise by 50 percent, still, only 1 out of 30 persons could vote, and the landowning class remained dominant.

Popular agitation spurred by John BRIGHT and others led to a further extension of the franchise in 1867. After the failure of the Liberals under Lord John Russell (later 1st Earl RUSSELL) to win passage of their Reform Bill, the Conservative Benjamin DISRAELI succeeded with more radical proposals. The act of 1867 extended the vote to most homeowners and renters and thus enfranchised many urban laborers. The final Reform Acts, which were passed in 1884 and 1885 under the Liberal government of William GLADSTONE, assimilated the county with the borough franchise and gave the vote to most agricultural workers.

The secret ballot (1872) and the Corrupt and Illegal Practices Act (1883) were other important 19th-century measures of electoral reform. The Representation of the People Acts of 1918 and 1928 extended the vote to women; the act of 1949 eliminated plural voting; and the 1969 act lowered the voting age from 21 to 18.   DONALD SOUTHGATE

Bibliography: Brock, Michael, *The Great Reform Act* (1973); Cowling, Maurice, *1867: Disraeli, Gladstone and Revolution* (1967); Smith, F. B., *The Making of the Second Reform Bill* (1966).

Reformation   [ref-ur-may'-shuhn]

The Reformation of the 16th century was a movement within Western Christendom to purge the church of medieval abuses and to restore the doctrines and practices that the reformers believed conformed with the Bible and the New Testament model of the church. This led to a breach between the ROMAN CATHOLIC CHURCH and the reformers whose beliefs and practices came to be called PROTESTANTISM.

CAUSES

The causal factors involved in the Reformation were complex and interdependent. Precursors of the Reformation proper included the movements founded by John WYCLIFFE (the LOLLARDS) and John HUSS (the HUSSITES) during the 14th and 15th centuries. These reform groups, however, were localized (in England and Bohemia) and were largely suppressed. Changes in the intellectual and political climate were among the factors that made the reform movement of the 16th century much more formidable.

The cultural RENAISSANCE that occurred during the preceding century and a half was a necessary preliminary, because it raised the level of education, reemphasized the ancient classics, contributed to thought and learning, and offered HUMANISM and rhetoric as an alternative to SCHOLASTICISM. Especially through its emphasis on the biblical languages and close attention to the literary texts, the Renaissance made possible the biblical exegesis that led to Martin LUTHER's doctrinal reinterpretation. Moreover, Christian humanists like Desiderius ERASMUS criticized ecclesiastical abuses and promoted the study of both the Bible and the church fathers. The invention of printing by Johann Gutenberg provided a powerful instrument for the spread of learning and Reformation ideas.

That grave ills were spreading through the church was already evident at the Fourth LATERAN COUNCIL in 1215, at which Pope INNOCENT III called for reform. The papacy itself was weakened by its move from Rome to Avignon (1309–77), by the Great SCHISM of the papacy, which lasted four decades thereafter, and by the doctrine that supreme authority in the

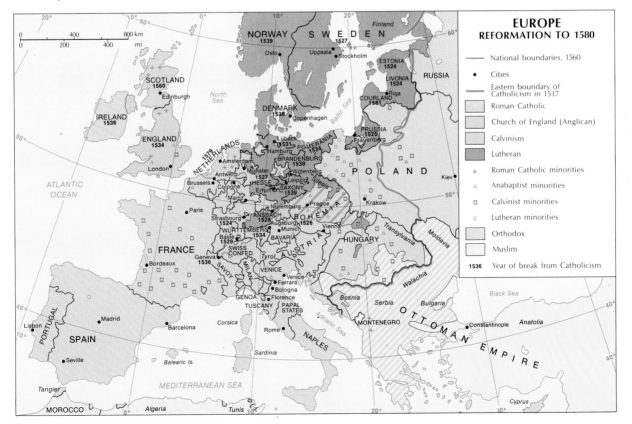

EUROPE
REFORMATION TO 1580

— National boundaries, 1560
• Cities
— Eastern boundary of Catholicism in 1517
  Roman Catholic
  Church of England (Anglican)
  Calvinism
  Lutheran
+ Roman Catholic minorities
△ Anabaptist minorities
□ Calvinist minorities
○ Lutheran minorities
  Orthodox
  Muslim
1536 Year of break from Catholicism

church belonged to general councils (CONCILIARISM). The Renaissance popes were notoriously worldly. Abuses such as simony, nepotism, and financial excesses increased. The church was riddled with venality and immorality. The sale of INDULGENCES was a particularly unfortunate practice because it impinged upon true spiritual repentance and improvement of life. At the same time a genuine upsurge of popular religiosity manifested itself and increased the disparity between the people's expectations and the church's ability to satisfy spiritual needs. Some turned to mysticism and inward religion, but the great mass of people were restless and dissatisfied.

A significant political change occurred during the later Middle Ages as well. The HOLY ROMAN EMPIRE, which had lost cohesion partly as a result of its struggle with the papacy in the INVESTITURE CONTROVERSY, was weakened by the growth of virtually independent territorial princedoms and free imperial cities. Externally the empire was weakened by the gradual evolution of the nation-states of modern western Europe. The monarchies in France, England, and, later, Spain were developing dynastic strength and unity that enabled them largely to control the church within their borders.

Economically, the rise of commerce and the shift to a moneyed economy had the effect of creating a stronger middle class in a more urban society. The church met financial difficulty during this time because it had become involved in the manorial economy, possessed landed wealth, and had trouble meeting its many obligations.

DEVELOPMENT

Luther. The Reformation began in Germany on Oct. 31, 1517, when Martin Luther, an Augustinian university professor at Wittenberg, posted 95 theses inviting debate over the legitimacy of the sale of indulgences. The papacy viewed this as a gesture of rebellion and proceeded to take steps against Luther as a heretic. The German humanists supported Luther's cause during the early years. The reformer's three famous treatises of 1520, *An Open Letter to the Christian Nobility of the German Nation Concerning the Reform of the Christian Estate, The Babylonian Captivity of the Church,* and *On the Freedom of a Christian,* also won him powerful popular support. He was excommunicated in 1521, but in April of that year at the Diet at Worms he stood before Holy Roman Emperor CHARLES V and the German princes and refused to recant unless proven wrong by the Bible or by clear reason. He believed that salvation was a free gift to persons through the forgiveness of sins by God's grace alone and received by them through faith in Christ.

Luther was protected by FREDERICK III, elector of Saxony, and other German princes—partly out of intellectual and religious conviction, partly out of the desire to seize church property, and partly to assert independence of imperial control. In 1530 many princes and cities signed the AUGSBURG CONFESSION presented at the Diet of Augsburg as an expression of the evangelical faith. After years of conflict the settlement reached in the Peace of Augsburg (1555; see AUGSBURG, PEACE OF) provided that each German prince would determine the religious affiliation (Roman Catholic or Lutheran) of the territory he ruled. LUTHERANISM also became the established religion of Denmark, Sweden, Norway, and Finland. Apart from the role of the princes, however, the Reformation spread rapidly as a popular movement. It penetrated Poland, Bohemia, Moravia, Hungary, and Transylvania.

Zwingli. The Reformation in Switzerland initially developed in Zurich under the leadership of the priest Ulrich ZWINGLI. Zwingli had been influenced by Erasmus and by Christian humanism. He arrived at an evangelical understanding of Christianity from his study of the Bible and from contacts with Lutherans. On Jan. 1, 1519, he began a 6-year series of sermons on the New Testament that moved the city council and the people of Zurich toward reform. The favorable response to *The Sixty-Seven Articles,* which he prepared for public disputation with a papal representative in 1523, proved the popularity of his program. He called for the abolition of the Mass (and its replacement by a symbolic Lord's Supper), independence from episcopal control, and a reform of the city-state in which both priests and Christian magistrates would conform

to the will of God. His influence spread to other Swiss cantons such as Basel, Saint Gall, and Bern.

Calvin. Through Lutheran tracts and merchant missionaries, the evangelical movement spread to France, where it won many converts, among whom was John CALVIN. In 1536, Calvin went to Geneva, where a reformation led by Guillaume FAREL was well under way. Calvin was persuaded to stay in Geneva and helped organize the second major surge of Protestantism. In his *Ordinances* of 1541, he gave a new organization to the church consisting of pastors, doctors, elders, and deacons. His *Institutes of the Christian Religion* (1536) had great influence in France, Scotland (where John KNOX carried the Calvinist reformation), and among the PURITANS in England. Geneva became the center of a great missionary enterprise that reached into France, where the HUGUENOTS became so powerful that a synod met in Paris in 1559 to organize a nationwide church of some 2,000 reformed congregations. As a result of the French Wars of Religion (see RELIGION, WARS OF), the Huguenot party was checked and the French monarchy kept the kingdom Catholic. (See also CALVINISM; PRESBYTERIANISM; REFORMED CHURCHES.)

England. Although England had a religious reform movement influenced by Lutheran ideas, the English Reformation oc-

(Right) *The German friar and scholar Martin Luther precipitated the Protestant Reformation when he nailed his 95 Theses to the door of the Wittenberg Church in 1517.*

(Below) *The worship service of an early Calvinist community is depicted in this 1564 painting showing the interior of a Huguenot church in Lyon, France.*

curred as a direct result of King HENRY VIII's efforts to divorce his first wife, CATHERINE OF ARAGON. The formal break with the papacy was masterminded by Thomas CROMWELL, the king's chief minister. Under Cromwell's direction Parliament passed the Act in Restraint of Appeals (to Rome; 1533), followed by the Act of Supremacy (1534) fully defining the royal headship over the church. As archbishop of Canterbury, Thomas CRANMER annulled Henry's marriage to Catherine, allowing the king to marry Anne BOLEYN. Although Henry himself wished to make no doctrinal changes, Cromwell and Cranmer authorized the translation of the Bible into English, and Cranmer was largely responsible for the BOOK OF COMMON PRAYER, adopted under Henry's successor, EDWARD VI. The gains that Protestantism made under Edward (r. 1547–53) were lost under his Catholic sister MARY I (r. 1553–58). The religious settlement (1559) under ELIZABETH I, however, guaranteed the Anglican establishment. (See also ENGLAND, CHURCH OF.)

The Radicals. The radicals consisted of a great variety of sectarian groups known as ANABAPTISTS because of their common opposition to infant baptism. The Anabaptist leader Thomas MÜNZER played a leading role in the PEASANTS' WAR (1524–26), which was suppressed with the support of Luther. In Münster, radical Anabaptists established (1533) a short-lived theocracy in which property was held communally. This too was harshly suppressed. The radicals also encompassed evangelical humanists and spiritualists who developed highly individualistic religious philosophies.

RESULTS
An obvious result of the Reformation was the division of Western Christendom into Protestant and Catholic areas. Another result was the development of national churches; these strengthened the growth of modern national states, just as, earlier, growing national consciousness had facilitated the development of the Reformation. The Catholic COUNTER-REFORMATION—including the founding of the JESUITS by IGNATIUS LOYOLA (sanctioned 1540), the Council of TRENT (1545–63), the INQUISITION, the INDEX, and reformed clergy like Charles BORROMEO—gave new life to the old church and was in part a result of the Reformation movement. Finally, the Reformation introduced much radical change in thought and in ecclesiastical and political organization and thus began many of the trends that are taken to characterize the modern world.

LEWIS W. SPITZ

Bibliography: Bainton, Roland H., *Women of the Reformation* (1977); Chadwick, Owen, *The Reformation* (1964); Cowen, Ian B., *The Scottish Reformation* (1982); Dickens, A. G., *The English Reformation* (1964) and *The German Nation and Martin Luther* (1974); Elton, G. R., *Reform and Reformation: England, 1509–1558* (1978); Grimm, Harold, *The Reformation Era 1500–1650* (1954); Hillerbrand, Hans. J., *Christendom Divided: The Protestant Reformation* (1971); McNeill, John T., *The History and Character of Calvinism* (1954); Olin, John, *Luther, Erasmus and the Reformation* (1970); Ozment, G. R., *The Reformation in the Cities* (1975); Smith, P., *The Age of Reformation*, 2 vols. (1962); Spitz, Lewis W., *The Renaissance and Reformation Movement* (1971).

Reformed Church in America

The Reformed Church in America is a Protestant denomination with roots in Dutch CALVINISM. In the mid-1980s it numbered nearly 346,000 members in more than 900 churches, with its greatest strength in the Middle Atlantic states, Michigan, and Iowa. By 1628, Dutch settlers had established a church in New Amsterdam (now New York City). This and other American churches were directed from Amsterdam until the 18th century when, under the influence of revivalist Theodore Jacob Frelinghuysen (1691–1747), an American body was formed (1748). Difficulties between this group and others loyal to the Dutch body were eventually resolved (1771) through the efforts of John Henry Livingston (1746–1825), an influential leader at Queens College (now Rutgers University), New Brunswick, N.J., which had been founded by the Dutch Reformed. The Reformed Protestant Dutch Church adopted a new constitution in 1792; in 1867 it changed its name to the Reformed Church in America.

The denomination's doctrinal standards are the Belgic Confession (1561), the Heidelberg Catechism (1563), and the can-

ons of the Synod of Dort (1619). Its organization is essentially Presbyterian. It is somewhat closer to mainline Protestant bodies than a sister denomination of Dutch Calvinists, the Christian Reformed Church.

MARK A. NOLL

Bibliography: Hood, Fred J., *Reformed America* (1980); Van Hoeven, James W., ed., *Piety and Patriotism: Bicentennial Studies of the Reformed Church in America, 1776–1976* (1976).

Reformed churches

The Reformed churches, which originally used this designation to distinguish themselves from the "unreformed" Roman Catholic church, are those denominations of Protestants which are Calvinistic in theology and usually Presbyterian in church organization (see CALVINISM; PRESBYTERIANISM). They trace their origin to the reforming work in Zurich of Ulrich ZWINGLI and in Geneva of John CALVIN. The Reformed perspective spread rapidly to Germany, France (see HUGUENOTS), Holland, Hungary, Bohemia, and elsewhere on the Continent. In the British Isles, its principles shaped the Church of Scotland (see SCOTLAND, CHURCH OF) and influenced the Church of England, especially through PURITANISM. The Presbyterians constitute the largest Reformed bodies in America. Since 1877 a World Alliance of Reformed Churches has provided a forum for discussion and consultation.

MARK A. NOLL

refraction

When a beam of light enters a medium in which its velocity is different from that in its original medium, the path of the beam changes. This bending of the beam, called refraction, is characteristic of all waves—sound, radio, and mechanical. Most experience with refraction, however, is with light. The principles of refraction are used in a variety of optical devices: eyeglasses, microscopes, cameras, and binoculars.

Snell's Law. The basic law of refraction, first proposed in 1621 by the Dutch scientist Willebrord Snell, relates the magnitude of refraction to the velocity of light in the two media (equivalent to the INDEX OF REFRACTION). If i is the angle the incident beam makes with the normal (in optics, all such angles are measured from the normal, a line perpendicular to the surface), and r the angle of the refracted beam, then $\sin i / \sin$

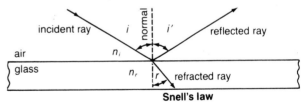

Snell's law

$r = n_r/n_i$, where n_r is the index of refraction of the medium containing the refracted beam and n_i the index of refraction of the medium with the incident beam. Thus, light entering a denser medium, from air into glass, for example, is bent toward the normal; on entering a less dense medium, light is bent away from the normal. If light goes through a substance with parallel surfaces, such as a window, the beam that emerges will be parallel to its incident beam but laterally displaced, or shifted.

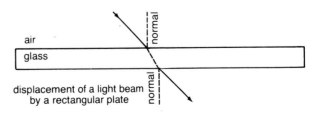

displacement of a light beam by a rectangular plate

Total Internal Reflection. Suppose a beam of light passes from glass to air. Air has a lower index of refraction, so the emerging beam is bent away from the normal. As the angle of incidence is increased, the beam in air moves farther from the normal until it makes a 90° angle with the normal and grazes the surface. The angle of incidence when this occurs is known as the critical angle. Increasing the angle incidence still further results in no light penetrating the glass-air boundary; instead, all the light is reflected back into the glass. This is known as total internal reflection, an effective way of reflecting light without using a mirror. (One disadvantage of mirrors is that they have two reflecting surfaces, resulting in a faint "ghost," or double image.) Total reflecting prisms are used in fine cameras, binoculars, and other optical instruments to change the direction of light. Light may be "transported" by transparent fibers and by glass or plastic rods; whether straight or curved, the light stays inside them because of successive internal reflections.

MARK S. VOGEL

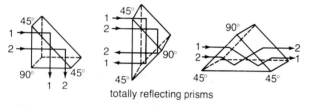

totally reflecting prisms

Bibliography: Born, Max, and Wolf, Emil, *Principles of Optics,* 5th ed. (1975); Mittleton, Thomas H., *Light Refractions* (1975); Reinecke, Robert, and Henry, Robert J., *Refraction,* 2d ed. (1976).

refractory materials

Refractory materials, or refractories, are materials that do not break down under great heat, have low thermal conductivity, and can withstand rapid changes in temperature. Most ordinary refractories are made from fireclays, naturally occurring clays containing aluminas and silicas. Fireclay is often formed into FIREBRICK, which is used to line furnaces, boilers, chimneys, and other structures that are operated at high temperatures. Refractories made from magnesite or dolomite offer greater heat resistance, and are used in smelters, open-hearth furnaces, and cement kilns. Other refractories are made from chrome ore, cement, zircon, silicon carbide, and graphite. In addition to brick, items made from refractories include crucibles, electric insulators, kilns, and rocket nose cones. In the 1960s, refractory plastics were developed for the electronic systems used in missiles.

Most refractories are classified as acid, basic, or neutral according to their chemical reactions at high temperatures. In the production of metals particularly, in order to prevent unwanted reactions between the metal and the refractory the choice of refractory will depend on its chemical nature.

Bibliography: Gilchrist, J. D., *Fuel, Furnaces, and Refractories* (1977); Hausner, Henry H., and Bowman, Melvin G., *Fundamentals of Refractory Compounds* (1968); Norton, Frederich H., *Refractories,* 4th ed. (1968).

refrigeration

Refrigeration is the cooling of a space or its content to a lower value than that of the surrounding space or of the ambient atmosphere. Until the advent of modern technology, natural ice was the only means of refrigeration. Ice acts as an efficient refrigerant because the temperature of melting ice remains at 0° C (32° F) until it is entirely melted. It absorbs heat from warmer surroundings, thereby cooling them while not itself becoming warmer until completely melted. Since the time of the Greeks and Romans, snow and ice were harvested in winter and stored in insulated pits for later use. Ice was a valuable cargo for 19th-century clipper ships, but it was difficult and expensive to ship. The demand for ice created a strong impetus for inventors to develop artificial cooling methods.

DEVELOPMENT OF ARTIFICIAL REFRIGERATION

A volatile liquid absorbs heat when it evaporates and can therefore be used to cool its surroundings. Moreover, the temperature at which evaporation occurs can be controlled by varying the pressure on the liquid. The first recorded instance

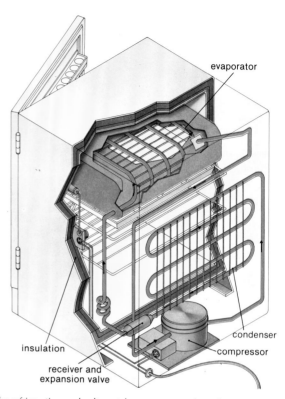

The refrigeration cycle alternately evaporates and condenses a refrigerant such as Freon-12. Liquid refrigerant stored at high pressure in the receiver is released through an expansion valve into the evaporator coils inside the refrigerator. With the pressure reduced, the refrigerant evaporates and absorbs heat from the interior. A compressor circulates the vaporized refrigerant to the exterior condenser coils, where it is condensed by pressure. Heat from the inside of the refrigerator is lost to the environment there. The cooled liquid then returns to the receiver.

of this phenomenon being used for cooling is credited to William Cullen at the University of Glasgow, who in 1748 evaporated ethyl ether under subatmospheric pressure to produce refrigeration. His process was successful but noncontinuous and never advanced much beyond the laboratory stage. Jacob Perkins, an American engineer living in London, patented (1834) the first practical ice-making machine, a volatile-liquid refrigerator using a compressor that operated in a closed cycle and conserved the fluid for reuse.

The first successful refrigeration machine in the United States was developed in 1844 by John Gorrie. His device did not use a volatile liquid but operated by the principle that air gets hot when compressed and cools when it expands. The air refrigerating principle was extensively used during the latter part of the 19th century and during the early years of the 20th century, although it is little used at the present time.

Another type of refrigeration unit, the absorption-type machine, was developed by Ferdinand Carré in France between 1850 and 1859. Such devices, which can operate exclusively by burning natural gas or other fuel, were commonly used prior to the widespread availability of electricity. The first machines of this type used water as a refrigerant and sulfuric acid as an absorbent, but in 1859, Carré switched to an ammonia-water system that is still in use. The public, however, resisted the use of artificial ice, fearing that it was unhealthful. Resistance declined after the American Civil War; during that war a number of Carré's machines had been slipped through the Union blockade and were able to provide much-needed ice to the southern states.

By 1860 the basic concepts underlying modern-day refrigeration had been developed, and the continuing problem to the present day has been mainly to develop and produce more efficient machines and better refrigerants and to adapt each to the refrigeration requirements of many new applications.

Ice manufacture was an early aspect of the fledgling refrigeration industry, followed closely by its introduction to cold-storage facilities, breweries, and refrigerated railway and ship transport. Starting in the early 1900s but more rapidly after 1910, air conditioning for comfort and for industrial use became significant. After World War I, particularly in the 1920s, the domestic refrigerator began to displace the icebox.

After World War II the use of air conditioning became widespread. Interest in this kind of refrigeration shows no sign of diminishing, and the market for its products is far from saturation. With the widespread dissemination of mechanical refrigeration in homes, the development of a frozen-food industry became possible, and this area also continues to grow at a rapid pace. Industrial uses of refrigeration are greatest in the areas of food storage and distribution. The chemical industry also uses refrigeration in enormous amounts in such areas as process control, separation of chemicals, petrochemical manufacture, and liquefaction of gases. Refrigeration at temperatures below $-150°$ C ($-240°$ F) is a special field called CRYOGENICS.

REFRIGERANTS
A satisfactory refrigerant for a vapor-compression machine should be a stable, incombustible, nontoxic, and nonirritating chemical that vaporizes and condenses at pressures and temperatures appropriate for its application. Unsatisfactory materials such as ethyl alcohol and sulfur dioxide were at first used. Ammonia, although irritating and somewhat toxic, represented a great improvement when it came into use after 1850. It is still widely used in industrial refrigeration. For air conditioning the need for a safe chemical was so great that an intensive search for a suitable refrigerant was undertaken. A team of researchers, led by Thomas Midgley, Jr., discovered in 1930 that by positioning chlorine and fluorine atoms in certain places in hydrocarbon compounds they could make suitable refrigerants. These halogenated hydrocarbons, or halocarbons, were developed under the trademark Freon. Since then other similar refrigerants have been developed. Freon-12 and similar refrigerants are now known as Refrigerants-12; the most widely used refrigerants, they are used in refrigerators for households and small units for retail stores and in air-conditioning systems. Freon-22 and other Refrigerants-22 are also widely used—in home freezers and small air-conditioning units. A search for new refrigerants is again in progress, however, because chlorine atoms released by halocarbons can have harmful environmental effects, damaging the OZONE LAYER of the atmosphere.

THE REFRIGERATION PROCESS
Refrigeration takes place when heat flows to a receiver colder than its surroundings. In the vapor-compression system the heat receiver is called an evaporator. Liquid refrigerant boils in it at a controlled temperature, absorbing heat to create the desired cooling. If the refrigerant were ammonia compressed to 290.9 kPa (42.2 psi) pressure, it would boil at $-10°$ C ($14°$ F) and absorb heat from any surrounding material at a higher temperature; about 1,290 kilojoules (1,223 Btu) would be absorbed for every kilogram evaporated. The warmed vapor from the evaporator is then compressed and pumped outside the refrigerated space. When the pressure is raised to 1350 kPa (195.8 psi), ammonia condenses at $35°$ C ($95°$ F) and cooling water or air carries away the excess heat. The liquid refrigerant then enters an expansion valve that causes the pressure to drop, and the cycle repeats itself when the refrigerant boils in the evaporator. Two basic pressures exist: a low one that sets the desired refrigerating temperature, and a high one that sets a condensation temperature sufficiently high to dissipate heat. By adjusting the volumetric capacity of the compressor to match the refrigeration needed in the evaporator, a wide range of evaporator pressures (temperatures) can be obtained. Using ammonia, a working range covering at least $-40°$ C ($-40°$ F) to $5°$ C ($41°$ F) can be obtained. Similar ranges are possible with other refrigerants.

Nearly all modern systems are of the vapor-compression type. Each system is tightly sealed, and if no leakage occurs the same refrigerant can serve for the life of the unit.

The use of absorption refrigeration has declined to the point that it is largely limited to air-conditioning applications in large-sized units. Because evaporator temperatures of air conditioners usually lie in a range of about $5°$ C ($41°$ F) to $12°$ C ($54°$ F), water can be used as a refrigerant, boiling under high vacuum conditions. The absorbent solution consists of lithium bromide dissolved in water. When a concentrated solution of this salt is sprayed in an absorber vessel, it can absorb the water that boils off in the evaporator. The diluted solution is then pumped into a vessel called the generator in which the absorbed water is boiled off, making the solution ready to return to the absorber to pick up another charge of water vapor.

BURGESS H. JENNINGS

Bibliography: Air Conditioning and Refrigeration Institute, *Refrigeration and Air Conditioning*, 2d ed. (1987); American Society of Heating, Refrigeration and Air-Conditioning Engineers, *ASHRAE Handbook of Refrigeration Systems and Applications* (1986); Gosney, W. B., *Principles of Refrigeration* (1982); Jones, J. C., Jr., *American Ice Boxes* (1981); Trott, A. R., *Refrigeration and Air Conditioning* (1981).

refugee

Refugees are persons who have fled their country or been expelled from it and who cannot or will not return because they fear persecution. A refugee is not quite the same as a displaced person; the latter term, which came into use during World War II, denotes someone displaced from his or her home as a result of war or disaster. In many cases, however, the distinction is hard to make.

Although refugees have existed throughout human history—the Spanish Jews in the 15th century and the aristocratic emigrés during the French Revolution, for example—the problem has assumed increasing importance in the 20th century. It is estimated that more than 40 million people have been uprooted since the outbreak of World War II. In 1986 there were more than 13 million refugees worldwide.

The majority of World War II refugees were Europeans; they included a large number of Jews who had escaped from German-occupied territories and other persons who had fled from advancing Soviet armies. In the postwar period the refugee problem has been most acute in Africa, the Middle East, Asia, and Central America. The dislocations were largely the result of ethnic and political strife, much of it attending the establishment of new governments and independent countries.

In Africa the emergence of new sovereign states generated power struggles and tribal animosities that produced several million refugees. The departure of European "colonials" and other minorities from the North African states exacerbated the refugee problem. In the Middle East the formation of the state of Israel and subsequent Arab-Israeli Wars led to the wholesale exodus of Palestinian Arabs and the creation of an enduring political problem.

In Asia huge numbers of people have been similarly displaced. After the establishment of a Communist government in China in 1949, about 2 million refugees settled on Taiwan; in addition, large numbers of Chinese escaped to the British crown colony of Hong Kong. The partition of the Indian subcontinent in 1947 resulted in what amounted to a population exchange between Hindu India and Muslim Pakistan. Indochina has also been the scene of population upheavals; the plight of the 2 million Vietnamese and Cambodians fleeing their countries between 1975 and 1980 presented a major new cause for international concern. Other groups of refugees have included about 203,000 Hungarians who fled Hungary in the wake of the 1956 revolution, about 850,000 Cubans who emigrated to the United States between the revolution in 1958 and the 1980 boatlift, between 2.5 and 3 million Afghans who fled to Pakistan after the Soviet invasion of 1979, and many thousands of people from war-torn El Salvador who have sought refuge in various Latin American countries and in the United States since.

The first attempts to deal with the refugee problem on an international level were made in 1921, when the League of Nations appointed Fridtjof NANSEN high commissioner for refugee work. Nansen's primary concerns were the large numbers of stateless Armenians and Greeks who had fled Turkey and the approximately 1.5 million Russians who had left their country after the 1917 revolution. To provide the refugees with some official standing, a travel document, the so-called Nansen Passport, was issued. Other international agencies established to work with refugees have included the United Nations Relief and Rehabilitation Administration (1943–47) and the International Refugee Organization (1947–51). In 1951 the UN High Commission for Refugees was established. Many nongovernmental agencies have also participated in refugee work. Although scores of millions of refugees have been resettled in new countries, many others still live in camps waiting for permanent homes.

The U.S. Refugee Act of 1980 provided for uniform admission of refugees, based on the UN definition of refugee. In practice, however, the U.S. RIGHT OF ASYLUM policy has favored refugees from Communist regimes and been less receptive to those from right-wing but "friendly" nations.

Bibliography: Ferris, Elizabeth, ed., *Refugees and World Politics* (1985); Holborn, Louise W., *Refugees: A Problem of Our Time: The Work of the United Nations High Commissioner for Refugees, 1951–1972*, 2 vols. (1975).

Refugees, Office of the United Nations High Commissioner for

After the International Refugee Organization (IRO) was abolished in 1951, the Office of the United Nations High Commissioner for Refugees (UNHCR) was established to carry on with providing legal and political aid to refugees. The primary responsibilities of the UNHCR include helping to return refugees to their homelands or to resettle them abroad, ensuring legal rights regarding employment and social benefits, and providing identity and travel documents. In promoting its goal, the UNHCR requires that governments accept refugees for at least a period of asylum. The UNHCR office was awarded the Nobel Peace Prize in 1954 and again in 1981.

Regan, Donald Thomas

Donald Thomas Regan, b. Cambridge, Mass., Dec. 21, 1918, served as U.S. secretary of the treasury under Ronald Reagan from 1981 to 1985, when he became the president's chief of staff. He previously spent 35 years with the brokerage firm Merrill Lynch and Company, rising through the ranks to the position of chairman. In Washington he earned a reputation as a Reagan loyalist with stronger executive than political skills. Criticized for White House "chaos" in reacting to the IRAN-CONTRA AFFAIR, Regan resigned in February 1987.

Regency

The last nine years (1811–20) of the reign of GEORGE III of Great Britain (r. 1760–1820) are known as the Regency. During this time, the king's son, the prince of Wales (later GEORGE IV), acted as regent because of his father's insanity. The period gave its name to a style of architecture and furniture design synthesizing the neoclassical and the exotic. In this era of considerable social and moral permissiveness, literary and artistic romanticism reached its climax.

During the Regency, the successful conclusion of the NAPOLEONIC WARS was followed by economic recession and the rise of early working-class movements. Ultraconservative Toryism, however, reigned supreme, and such movements were suppressed with force and legislation. The major events of the period included the WAR OF 1812 with the United States, the Congress of Vienna (1814–15; see VIENNA, CONGRESS OF), passage of the CORN LAW of 1815, and the Peterloo Massacre (1819) of workers in Manchester.   DON M. CREGIER

Bibliography: Bryant, Arthur, *The Age of Elegance* (1950); Priestley, J. B., *The Prince of Pleasure and His Regency 1811–1820* (1969).

Regency style

The Regency style flourished in England during the period of the Regency (1811–20) of George Augustus, prince of Wales. It was characterized by close adaptations of Greek, Roman, and Egyptian antiquities and was inspired to a certain degree

The Royal Pavilion at Brighton, a seaside villa remodeled (1815–23) by John Nash for the Prince Regent, exhibits the orientalizing style that became popular during the early 1800s. The revival of classical and exotic styles persisted until the mid-19th century.

by the contemporary French DIRECTOIRE and EMPIRE styles. The Regency tendency to adapt ancient forms may already be seen, for example, in the work of the architect and designer Henry HOLLAND and in the designs of the cabinetmaker Thomas SHERATON. In domestic architecture, GREEK REVIVAL forms predominated, with a lavish use of the Ionic and Corinthian orders. Regency architects include John NASH, Sir John SOANE, John Buonarotti Papworth, and George Basevi. Regency classical furniture—simple in outline and solidly constructed with large, uninterrupted surfaces—was based on designs by Thomas Hope, George Smith, and Richard Brown. Classical motifs also occur in Regency silver and plate, as made by the period's most important silversmith, Paul Storr, after the designs of John Flaxman, and by William Pitts and Benjamin Smith, Storr's contemporaries. Along with classical antique prototypes, Gothic, Chinese, and even rococo furniture and forms of decoration served as models during this period. The revival of the Chinese taste was initiated by the prince of Wales himself, who between 1815 and 1823 made extensive improvements to the ROYAL PAVILION AT BRIGHTON under the direction of John Nash, and had the interior decorated in the Chinese manner by Frederick Crace and Robert Jones.

Reviewed by KATHRYN B. HIESINGER

Bibliography: Musgrave, Clifford, *Regency Furniture* (1961); Pilcher, Donald, *The Regency Style 1800–1830* (1947); Reilly, Paul, *An Introduction to Regency Architecture* (1948).

regeneration

The term *regeneration* has been used to describe a variety of biological repair processes ranging from the continuous replacement of dying cells on the surface of a human cornea, for instance, to the regrowth of an amputated head of an earthworm. The ability to replace lost cells through mitosis (cell division) of those remaining cells is primary to all living systems. For example, a wound in the epithelial covering of most animals is quickly closed and the missing tissues are soon restored. Within 48 hours after removal of 68% of a rat's liver, the remaining 32% will double in mass. These are examples of regeneration after injury; in most living things there is also a continuous replacement of many cell types that have short lives.

The capacity to reconstruct body appendages is much less widespread than the ability to compensate for lost tissues. The complex anatomy of appendages requires more elaborate regeneration-control mechanisms than do the examples given above. This type of regeneration is dramatically illustrated in worms such as planaria and coelenterates such as the hydra, which can each grow a new head after losing the old one. Among the vertebrates, lizards, frog tadpoles, and salamanders are the best regenerators of appendages. All three can regenerate a tail, but only frog tadpoles and salamanders can produce new limbs. At metamorphosis frogs lose this capability, except for the South African clawed frog (genus *Xenopus*), which can regenerate in the adult stage.

The restoration of lost appendages best exemplifies the meaning of the term *regeneration*. In animals with an organized nervous system, that system is usually indispensable for regeneration to occur. If the nerves of supply are severed, salamanders can no longer replace an amputated limb. Removal of the spinal cord in the region of amputation renders salamanders and lizards unable to produce a new tail. Usually worms will not regenerate a head if the nerve cord is missing. Nerves seem to produce a trophic substance necessary for normal mitotic activity in the regenerate. Limbs that cannot regenerate usually have less neural tissue than those that can. Newborn opossums will regenerate their hind limbs if a piece of brain is implanted a few days before the time of amputation. The fact that induced regenerates are usually not well formed suggests that nonregenerators are also deficient in the mechanisms that control differentiation.

The controlling mechanisms may involve inhibitory substances. A tubularia, an organism similar to a hydra, has a head with tentacles attached to a stem containing a central cavity. If both ends of the stem are amputated, a head will usually form only on the end toward the original head. If, however, the stem is constricted with a string so that the central cavity is obliterated, a head will form on both ends. As the head develops on one end, inhibitory material normally passes to the other end and prevents head formation there. Constriction prevents the passage of this material, and thus a head forms on both ends. The information seems to move by the natural bioelectric fields generated by the organism. Nerves may promote salamander limb regeneration by organizing the bioelectric field so that information-containing molecules can pass in the correct direction.

An important feature of appendage regeneration in amphibians is the fact that the normal limb tissues seem to revert (dedifferentiate) to an embryonic type of cell in the region of amputation. These cells accumulate and produce a bump called the blastema. The lost structures are formed by cell division and differentiation of the blastema. Blastemas also occur in fish, annelids, arthropods, and planaria. In some cases, cells in the amphibian regenerate become something other than what they were previously. For example, if the limb bones are removed and the limb is amputated, the regenerated portion will contain a bone. Since the regenerate is produced from cells near the amputation surface, the bone must have come from cells that were not bone prior to amputation. This observation is extremely important because it shows that cells are not irreversibly committed to a particular life-style. The same mechanism probably operates in regeneration in lower forms such as worms, but some scientists believe that the cells involved here are a type of undifferentiated reserve cell called neoblasts. If cells do, in fact, dedifferentiate, scientists may eventually learn how to make any cell become another type on command and thus may be able to bring about the replacement of lost limbs in humans.

A wound epidermis is indispensable for limb regeneration. If a salamander limb is amputated and a flap of whole skin is grafted over the amputation surface, regeneration will not occur. It appears that the dermis intervening between the epidermis and the other stump tissues blocks regeneration. In animals that cannot regenerate, the dermis reappears prematurely. The wound epidermis promotes mitosis and somehow causes the distal accumulation of blastema cells. Human children below the age of about 11 have been observed to regenerate lost fingertips if the wounds are not prematurely covered.

Tumors seem to be rare in appendages capable of regeneration. In fact, injection of carcinogens into salamander limbs produces extra limbs rather than tumors. Some scientists think that regeneration-controlling mechanisms can pre-

If cut in two, both sections of a Hydra *polyp will regenerate. The top half will grow a new foot; the bottom half, a new head.*

Certain lizards break off their tails to escape from predators. The tail regenerates, but the original vertebrae are replaced by cartilage.

A single arm severed or torn from certain starfishes will regenerate a central body and new arms, producing an entire new individual.

vent carcinogen-activated cells from becoming tumorous and can guide them instead into structures compatible with life.

DONALD J. DONALDSON

Bibliography: Goss, R. J., *Principles of Regeneration* (1969); Hay, E. D., *Regeneration* (1966); Kingman, John F., *Regenerative Phenomena* (1972); McMinn, R. M., *Tissue Repair* (1969); Rose, S. M., *Regeneration: Key to Understanding Normal and Abnormal Growth and Development* (1970).

Regensburg   [ray'-gens-boork]

Regensburg (English: Ratisbon) is a Bavarian city in southeastern West Germany, at the confluence of the Danube and Regen rivers. Its population is 125,600 (1985 est.). Regensburg's location—at the point where the Danube narrows—promotes the city's transshipment industry, port, and railroad yards. Electronics, chemicals, textiles, cement, leather goods, ships, beer, and sausages are among the chief products of the city. Several regional governmental agencies and the seat of a Roman Catholic bishopric are located there. Regensburg University was founded in 1962.

Regensburg escaped severe damage during World War II. Many medieval buildings thus remain, including the Cathedral of Saint Peter (1275–1524), a famous stone bridge across the Danube (1135–46), and the Romanesque Saint Emmeram's Church, which was remodeled in the 18th century.

The site of the city was an early Roman camp (1st century AD) that was chosen (530) by the dukes of Bavaria as their seat until they were deposed by Charlemagne. Regensburg experienced great prosperity during the 12th and 13th centuries. Frequently a locus for diplomatic conferences, the city became the seat of the Imperial Diet of the Holy Roman Empire from 1663 to 1806. After the Napoleonic invasion, Regensburg was returned (1810) to Bavaria. It became part of the German Empire in 1871.

JONATHAN E. HELMREICH

regent

A regent governs during the absence, minority, or incapacity of a monarch. This position can be assumed by an individual or by a council, and the appointment may be made by the reigning monarch or by a governing body such as a parliament. Historically, periods of regency, especially when a minor heir was involved, were times of tension between those attempting to preserve centralized power for the crown and those—usually the nobility—seeking to augment their own power. In British history, the most famous regency was that assumed by the future George IV for his father, George III, in 1811 (see REGENCY).

Reger, Max   [ray'-gur]

Max Reger, German composer, organist, and pianist, b. Mar. 19, 1873, d. May 11, 1916, was a controversial figure who was welcomed by some as a successor to Brahms and dismissed by others as a pedantic technician. He was a pupil of his father, of the organist Adalbert Lindner, and of the eminent musicologist Hugo Riemann (1890–95). He taught at Wiesbaden, at Munich (where he also conducted a choral society), and, from 1907 until his death, at the Leipzig Conservatory.

Exceedingly prolific, Reger disdained program music and wrote nothing for the stage, but he left no other genre untouched. The pervading chromaticism of his music and the arbitrary modulations decried by his detractors are less in evidence in his numerous songs: these works, together with a few orchestral, chamber, keyboard, and choral compositions, comprise his contribution to the current repertoire.

Bibliography: Schonberg, Harold C., *Lives of the Great Composers* (1970); Stuckenschmidt, H. H., *Twentieth Century Composers: Germany and Central Europe* (1970).

reggae   [reg'-ay]

Reggae is a Jamaican musical style based on American soul music but with inverted rhythms and prominent bass lines. Rooted in Kingston's slums, reggae is the expression of Jamaica's poorest blacks. Many performers are RASTAFARIANS. The

themes of reggae lyrics include Rastafarianism, political protest, and the "rudie" (hooligan hero). Bob Marley (1945–81) and his group, the Wailers, were largely responsible for the widespread popularity of reggae. The film *The Harder They Come* (1973) brought the style to the United States. Reggae influenced a generation of white musicians—notably, Paul Simon ("Mother and Child Reunion," 1972) and Eric Clapton ("I Shot the Sheriff," 1974)—and reggae modes can often be detected in 1980s rock music. But—with the exception of a few bands (*Black Uhuru, Steel Pulse*) and the singer Linton Kwesi Johnson, a Jamaican poet living in England, where many reggae songs are now composed—the style itself has lost much of its old vitality.

JONATHAN KAMIN

Reggio di Calabria   [red'-joh dee kah-lah'-bree-ah]

Reggio di Calabria is a port city in the Calabria region of southern Italy, situated on the eastern shore of the Strait of Messina, which divides the mainland from Sicily. The population is 175,104 (1985 est.). Reggio is a seaport, tourist resort, and industrial center. A ferry operates across the strait to Messina, Sicily. The city has a major archaeological museum.

Greek colonists founded the city in the 8th century BC, and it was conquered by Rome in the 3d century BC. Alaric the Visigoth overran the city in AD 410, and during the following centuries it was captured and ruled successively by the Byzantines, Arabs, and Normans. During the 12th century the city became part of the kingdom of Sicily (later Sicily and Naples). Reggio was completely rebuilt after a devastating earthquake occurred in 1908.

DANIEL R. LESNICK

Reggio nell'Emilia   [red'-joh nel-lay-meel'-ee-ah]

Reggio nell'Emilia, the capital of Emilia-Romagna region in northern Italy, lies on the ancient Via Aemilia about 65 km (40 mi) northwest of Bologna. It has a population of 130,344 (1985 est.). The city is known for its cheese industry. Landmarks include a 13th-century cathedral and remains of the Canossa castle, 23 km (14 mi) to the south. At Canossa, Holy Roman Emperor HENRY IV did penance (1077) before Pope GREGORY VII. Founded by Romans in the 2d century BC, the city was ruled by the Este family from 1409 to 1796.

regiment

In traditional military organization, the regiment was the basic combat component of a nation's army. All three combat groups—infantry, cavalry, and artillery—were organized into regiments. Commanded by a colonel, the regiment consisted of battalions and service and administrative units. The term, which comes from the Latin *regimen* ("rule"), was first used in the 16th century to refer to French cavalry troops. In both Great Britain and the United States the regiment was often geographically based, and its colonel tended to be a leading political figure or landholder in the area. In the early 19th century Napoleon I created larger components than the regiment; they were (in ascending order) the brigade, the division, the corps, and the army. Other nations soon followed the French practice, and the regiment lost its status as an independent component. By the early 20th century 3 infantry regiments of about 3,000 soldiers each typically constituted an infantry division. Today most nations have reorganized their armies into battle groups, combat arms, and other such modern configurations.

Regina   [ruh-jy'-nuh]

Regina, a city of 175,064 (1986), is the capital and second largest city of Saskatchewan, Canada. It is located in the south central part of the province on Wascana Creek. With its excellent railroad and highway facilities, as well as an airport, Regina is the distribution center for the surrounding agricultural region. The city is the headquarters for the Saskatchewan Wheat Pool, the world's largest grain cooperative. Petroleum and natural-gas refining are also important to the local economy. Steel and wood products as well as automobiles, chemicals, cement, and fertilizers are manufactured there. The provincial government facilities and many of the city's cultural buildings are located in the parklike Wascana Center, built around artificial Wascana Lake.

Founded in 1882 and named Pile of Bones, the city was later renamed Regina to honor Queen Victoria. It was capital of the Northwest Territories from 1882 until 1905, when it became capital of the new province of Saskatchewan.

Regiomontanus   [ree-jee-oh-mahn'-tay-nuhs]

The German astronomer Regiomontanus (originally named Johann Müller), b. June 6, 1436, d. July 8?, 1476, played an important role in the revival of Renaissance astronomy. He was a student (graduated 1452) and later colleague (1457–61) of Georg von PEURBACH at the University of Vienna and completed (c.1461–63) Peurbach's translation (pub. 1496) of Ptolemy's *Almagest*. His reflection that Ptolemy's lunar theory required the apparent diameter of the Moon to vary in length much more than is actually observed caught Copernicus's attention. Regiomontanus also wrote an important work on trigonometry, published in 1533.   STEVEN J. DICK

Regnault, Henri Victor   [ren-yoh']

Henri Victor Regnault, a French chemist and physicist, b. July 21, 1810, d. Jan. 19, 1878, won acclaim in chemistry for his discovery (1835–39) of vinyl chloride, dichloroethylene, trichloroethylene, and carbon tetrachloride. In physics he is noted for his painstaking measurements showing that Dulong and Petit's law, Neumann's extension of the law from elements to compounds, and Boyle's law were merely approximate. In 1842 he was appointed by the French government to reexamine the physical constants involved in the operation of steam engines, a study that provided engineers with vital standard data.   JOHN T. BLACKMORE

regolith   [reg'-uh-lith]

Regolith is the layer of loose rock and mineral material that covers almost all land surfaces. Regolith, from the Greek for "blanket stone," includes all loose materials regardless of whether they were formed in place or were transported and then deposited. With the addition of water and organic materials, regolith is gradually transformed into soil.   PAUL A. KAY

regression: see CORRELATION AND REGRESSION.

regression, marine

Marine regression is a term that geologists use to describe a withdrawal of the sea and the resultant emergence of dry land. Regressions occur for various reasons: reduction in the volume of seawater because of the growth of polar ice masses (eustatic), upwarping of the land because of crustal stresses (tectonic), elevation of the land because of gravitational adjustment of crustal blocks of varying density (isostatic), or very rapid sedimentation.

See also: TRANSGRESSION, MARINE.

regulation, government: see GOVERNMENT REGULATION.

Regulators

The Regulator movements in North and South Carolina were the products of sectional and economic conflict on the eve of the American Revolution. Both movements were tied more closely to local discontent than they were to any widespread dissatisfaction with British rule. In fact, many of the Regulators later sided with the crown against the colonial ruling class that led the independence movement.

The conflict in North Carolina came to a head around 1768 when small farmers in the backcountry protested against the inequitable and inefficient system of local government prevailing in their area. Conflict between the Regulators and Governor William Tryon continued for several years, culmi-

nating in the defeat of the farmers at the Battle of Alamance on May 16, 1771. One of their leaders was executed on the battlefield, and six Regulators were hanged for treason following a court-martial.

The Regulators in South Carolina were also backcountry farmers. Upset by banditry and Indian attacks about which their local government did little, they formed associations in 1767; they refused to pay taxes and took vigilante action to impose their own form of law and order. In 1769, South Carolina set up a court system for the backcountry and conditions stabilized there.   RICHARD R. BEEMAN

Bibliography: Brown, R., *The South Carolina Regulators* (1963).

regulatory agencies: see GOVERNMENT, REGULATION.

Regulus, Marcus Atilius   [reg'-ue-luhs]

Marcus Atilius Regulus, d. c.250 BC, was a Roman general and statesman. As consul (267 BC) he captured Brundisium (now Brindisi). Again consul (256 BC) during the First PUNIC WAR, he defeated the Carthaginian army and navy. Regulus' demands for unconditional surrender backfired, however, and in 255 he was defeated by Carthage. Sent on parole to Rome to negotiate peace terms and an exchange of prisoners, he supposedly convinced the Romans to reject the Carthaginian terms and returned voluntarily to Carthage where he died in prison, possibly tortured to death.

rehabilitation medicine

Rehabilitation medicine is a medical speciality that deals with the diagnosis and treatment of neuromusculo-skeletal disorders and the restoration of the physically disabled to their highest possible levels of physical, psychological, social, vocational, and economic functions. The object of rehabilitation medicine is to eliminate or alleviate the disability or retrain the physically disabled to live as normal and productive a life as can be done within the limits of the impairment.

SERVICES OF REHABILITATION MEDICINE

Physicians throughout history have practiced rehabilitation to a greater or lesser extent. Modern rehabilitation medicine has developed primarily since World War II as an extension of physical medicine; both branches have merged as the speciality of physical medicine and rehabilitation, the specialist often being referred to as a physiatrist.

The number of physically disabled has increased, and public attitudes toward these people have radically changed, as reflected in the establishment of state and federal programs of vocational rehabilitation and other legislation recognizing the needs of the disabled. As a result, the speciality of rehabilitation medicine has expanded rapidly, and demands for its services have increased, often far beyond the capacity or the ability of the physician. Comprehensive rehabilitation therefore has been provided best by a multidisciplinary team of paramedical professionals, including physical therapists, occupational therapists, psychologists, rehabilitation nurses, social workers, speech pathologists, vocational counselors, teachers, recreational therapists, home economists, home planning consultants, orthotist-prosthetists, rehabilitation engineers, driver educators, and dietitians. All of these specialists work closely with the patient and the patient's family under the direction of the physiatrist.

The practice of rehabilitation medicine ranges from short-term management of various muscular skeletal ailments and pain syndromes to the long-term and complicated management of severe disabilities resulting from spinal-cord injuries, spina bifida, brain injuries, strokes, cerebral palsy, multiple sclerosis, muscular dystrophy, polyneuritis, amputations, arthritis, and major bone fractures, to mention a few. Minor disorders are treated by the primary physician and a small team of rehabilitation professionals employed by most hospitals and health-care facilities. The more complicated problems, however, are best managed in larger rehabilitation centers, which provide a wide range of services.

Before a detailed rehabilitation program is prescribed for a particular patient, a complete medical, functional, psychological, social, and vocational evaluation is undertaken. Then the patient's potential capacity for physical, functional, and economic improvement is assessed and realistic treatment goals are established. The prescribed program, including treatment, training, and counseling, is periodically reevaluated and modified as needed.

RECENT DEVELOPMENTS

The "whole person concept" of rehabilitation medicine has been successfully utilized in the management of disabilities other than neuromusculo-skeletal, such as those resulting from heart and lung diseases, cancer, and mental disorders. The increasing demand for electrodiagnostic procedures of nerves and muscles, such as nerve conduction studies and electromyography, is often met by the technical expertise of the physiatrist. The rehabilitation engineer, now becoming a more important team member, applies bioengineering to improve the quality of life for the physically disabled. Bioengineering includes improved artificial limbs and braces; equipment for training, work, and recreation; nursing supplies; modified vehicles; aids for mobility and driving; and elaborate electronic systems used for communication, education, and environmental control.

Perhaps the most significant development in rehabilitation medicine is the public recognition of the needs of the disabled and efforts made in the continuing fight for their human rights. Often a disabled person, who has been given full respect as a human individual when in the hospital and surrounded by the rehabilitation team, is greeted with misunderstanding and prejudice as a result of lack of information when living or working at home. Programs to heighten public awareness of the needs and abilities of these persons have become increasingly successful.   KRISTJAN T. RAGNARSSON

Bibliography: Kottke, F. J., et al., *Krusen's Handbook of Physical Medicine and Rehabilitation,* 3d ed. (1982); MacDonald, E. M., *Occupational Therapy in Rehabilitation,* 4th ed. (1976); Rusk, Howard A., ed., *Rehabilitation Medicine,* 4th ed. (1977).

Rehnquist, William   [ren'-kwist]

William Hubbs Rehnquist, b. Milwaukee, Wis., Oct. 1, 1924, was appointed to the U.S. Supreme Court by President Nixon in 1971; in 1986, President Reagan appointed him the 16th chief justice of the United States, succeeding Warren Burger, who retired. After graduating from Stanford Law School, Rehnquist served (1952–53) as law clerk to Supreme Court Justice Robert H. Jackson. He then established a private law practice in Phoenix, Ariz. Identified with the conservative wing of the Republican party, he was an assistant attorney general (1969–71) in the Nixon administration. Often standing in dissent on the Court, Rehnquist has taken strong positions generally on the side of law and order and against labor and civil rights advocates. His opinions have also reflected a flexible interpretation of the separation of church and state.

Rehoboam, King of Israel   [ree-uh-boh'-uhm]

Son and heir of King SOLOMON, Rehoboam was the last king of a united Israel and the first king of the southern Kingdom of JUDAH. His reluctance to temper his father's despotic rule precipitated (920 BC) the revolt of the ten northern tribes, which was followed by persistent warfare between the northern Kingdom of ISRAEL, united under JEROBOAM, and Judah.

Reich, Steve   [rysh]

The composer Steve Reich, b. New York City, Oct. 3, 1936, is closely identified with the concept of minimalism. Minimalist music uses the smallest possible amount of material to produce works that may evolve over long periods of time. In Reich's "phase music," instruments or voices begin together and gradually go out of phase. Chord progressions in his pieces shift gradually, one note at a time, within simple repeated patterns. The unfolding of this process in time is also known as "process music." Characteristic pieces by Reich are *Come Out* (1966; spoken-word tape loops) and *New York

Counterpoint (1985; 11 clarinets, 10 of which are taped). *Tehillim* (1981), a joyful setting of Hebrew Psalms, and *The Desert Music* (1983), a setting of the poetry of William Carlos Williams, are scored for large orchestras with voices.
DIKA NEWLIN

Bibliography: Battcock, Gregory, ed., *Breaking the Sound Barrier* (1981); Gagne, Cole, and Caras, Tracy, *Soundpieces* (1981).

Reich, Wilhelm   [ryk]

The Austrian psychoanalyst Wilhelm Reich, b. Mar. 24, 1897, d. Nov. 3, 1957, was perhaps the boldest figure in the history of modern psychiatry. While still in medical school in Vienna, he met Sigmund FREUD and became a psychoanalyst in 1920. Reich's most controversial psychiatric concept was that of orgastic potency—the full surrender of the organism to the emotions of love and the sensations of pleasure during the sexual embrace—as the basis of mental health.

Reich delineated the "character-muscular armor" as the main internal obstacle to healthy psychological functioning. The character armor consists of defensive character traits, like arrogance or apprehensiveness, that developed in childhood to ward off painful feelings. The muscular armor refers to chronic muscular spasms that represent the bodily expression of characterological rigidities. Thus, a stubborn, "stiff-necked" person might literally have a stiff neck.

Between 1927 and 1933 in Vienna and Berlin and under the aegis of leftist political parties, Reich brought sex education and counseling to large numbers of people in a way that connected emotional issues with social concerns. In the 1940s and 1950s in the United States, Reich investigated orgone energy, an energy that, he asserted, functioned as the life energy. Reich invented the orgone energy accumulator, which he believed had therapeutic properties. When he defied an injunction against this device, many of his publications were burned, and he was sentenced to a federal penitentiary where he died.

Reich's psychiatric contributions have profoundly influenced the practice of modern pyschotherapy, whereas his work on orgone energy has been dismissed by most scientists. His books include *Character Analysis* (1933; Eng. trans. 1945) and *The Mass Psychology of Fascism* (1933; Eng. trans. 1946).
MYRON SHARAF

Bibliography: Mann, W. Edward, and Hoffman, Edward, *The Man Who Dreamed of Tomorrow* (1980); Sharaf, Myron, *Fury on Earth* (1983); Wilson, Colin, *The Quest for Wilhelm Reich* (1981).

Reichstag   [ryks'-tahk]

The Reichstag was originally the parliament of the Holy Roman Empire, which was dissolved in 1806. The modern Reichstag, the German national legislature, first met in 1871, following the establishment of the unified German Empire under Otto von BISMARCK. Its powers were broadened during the Weimar Republic (1918–33). On Feb. 27, 1933, soon after Adolf HITLER became chancellor, the Reichstag building was destroyed by fire. Alleging that the fire was part of a Communist plot, the government immediately suspended civil rights and suppressed the opposition. In the elections of Mar. 5, 1933, Hitler's National Socialists fell short of the absolute majority they sought. Nevertheless, on Mar. 23, 1933, the new Reichstag, by more than the requisite two-thirds majority, voted Hitler the dictatorial powers he demanded, thereby relinquishing its authority.   DONALD S. DETWILER

Bibliography: Tobias, Fritz, *The Reichstag Fire,* trans. by A. J. Pomerans (1964).

Reid, Thomas

A Scottish philosopher of the common-sense school, Thomas Reid, b. Apr. 26, 1710, d. Oct. 7, 1796, was educated and later taught at King's College, Aberdeen, until he was appointed (1764) professor of moral philosophy at Glasgow. Reid was convinced that philosophy should reflect the ordinary, common-sense opinions of humankind. From this perspective he was strongly critical of David Hume's skepticism about the existence of cause and effect, the external world, and other common-sense beliefs. Reid's important writings include *An Inquiry into the Human Mind on the Principles of Common Sense* (1764), *Essays on the Intellectual Powers of Man* (1785), and *Essays on the Active Powers of Man* (1788). Reid's work had continuing influence through the writings of Dugald Stewart and Sir William Hamilton.   THOMAS K. HEARN, JR.

Bibliography: Barker, Stephen, and Beauchamp, Tom L., eds., *Thomas Reid: Critical Interpretations* (1976); Daniels, Norman, *Thomas Reid's Inquiry: The Geometry of Visibles and the Case for Realism* (1974).

Reid, Whitelaw

A noted journalist and diplomat, Whitelaw Reid, b. Xenia, Ohio, Oct. 27, 1837, d. Dec. 15, 1912, is best remembered for his brilliant eyewitness accounts of major Civil War battles. Reid established a reputation in journalism during the Civil War as war correspondent (1862–64) for the *Cincinnati Gazette.* He later joined the staff of the *New York Tribune,* and in 1872 he became its editor and publisher. Under his management, the *Tribune* became known for the accuracy of its reporting and grew into one of the city's leading dailies.

Reid's diplomatic career included 3 years as U.S. minister to France (1889–92) and tenure as the ambassador to the Court of Saint James (1905–12). He also mounted an unsuccessful candidacy for vice-president in 1892. A scholar of some note, Reid published important books on political, historical, and literary subjects, including *Ohio in the War* (1868), *Our New Interests* (1900), and *Problems of Expansion* (1900).

Reign of Terror: see FRENCH REVOLUTION.

Reimarus, Hermann Samuel   [ry-mah'-rus]

A German theologian and philosopher of the ENLIGHTENMENT, Hermann Samuel Reimarus, b. Dec. 22, 1694, d. Mar. 1, 1768, was a follower of Christian WOLFF in his philosophy; in theology Reimarus was an adherent of DEISM. He was one of the founders in Germany of the higher criticism—the attempt to examine the Bible from a purely scholarly point of view. Reimarus uncovered discrepancies between the Old and New Testaments. Among his contentions was the claim that the accounts of the resurrection and miracles were the product of conscious fraud on the part of the Apostles. Reimarus also did important work in the field of animal psychology.

NICHOLAS CAPALDI

Reims   [reemz or rans]

Reims (also Rheims) is a city in northeastern France on the Vesle River and the Aisne-Marne Canal, about 134 km (83 mi) northeast of Paris. It has a population of 194,656 (1982). Reims is the center of a major wine-growing region, specializing in champagne production. The city has been known for its textiles since the Middle Ages. Other important industries include the manufacture of chemicals, electrical and automotive equipment, bicycles, and food products. The city has port facilities on the Aisne-Marne Canal. The University of Reims was established in 1961.

Reims, named for the Remi, a Gallic tribe, was one of the principal urban centers of Gaul during Roman times. Later it was the coronation place of most of the French kings. The city suffered severe destruction during World War I when German forces captured and pillaged Reims for 10 days. The German army then occupied the heights overlooking the city for 4 years, and periodic bombing damaged or destroyed many of the buildings, including the important Gothic Cathedral of Notre Dame (13th century). Destruction also took place during World War II. The Germans surrendered unconditionally to the Allies on May 7, 1945, in a hall of the Collège Moderne in Reims, which had served as headquarters of the Allied command.   LAWRENCE M. SOMMERS

Reims Cathedral

Reims Cathedral, built (1211–1311) on the traditional coronation site of the kings of France, is one of the greatest monu-ments of GOTHIC ART AND ARCHITECTURE. Work on the cathedral commenced under the architect Jean d'Orbais and was completed under Robert de Coucy.

Reims Cathedral is a work of remarkable unity and harmony. The influence of CHARTRES CATHEDRAL is evident in Reims's quadripartite rib vaults, three-story elevation, and pier structure.

Reims's west front consists of three portals surrounded by sculptured arches, a rose window with superb 13th-century stained glass, and two matching towers. Gracing this facade is perhaps the richest body of sculpture of any Gothic church, one that shows an increasing realism and movement in contrast to the more rigid and formalized style of the 12th century. Part of the sculptural decoration, including the *Visitation* group, is executed in a classical vein, and part in a highly original style attributed to the so-called Joseph Master, whose elegant works presaged the 14th-century Gothic INTERNATIONAL STYLE in art. The cathedral, badly damaged during World War I, has been restored and stabilized (1918–37).

Bibliography: Frankl, Paul, *Gothic Architecture* (1962); Holbrook, Sabra, *Joy in Stone* (1973); Stoddard, Whitney S., *Monastery and Cathedral in France* (1966); Swaan, Wim, *The Gothic Cathedral* (1969).

reindeer

Reindeer, R. tarandus, a deer of Arctic regions of the world, migrate in herds across great distances between summer and winter grounds. The herds are usually followed by wolf packs, their primary enemies.

The reindeer of northern Europe and Asia and the caribou of North America were formerly considered different species. They are now classified as one, *Rangifer tarandus,* but the common names are still used to distinguish the two groups. Reindeer originally inhabited the tundra and northern woodlands of Eurasia, but it is believed that no truly wild reindeer still exist; all free-living reindeer are thought to be feral, that is, descended from escaped domestic stock. Reindeer husbandry is still practiced by the Lapps, Yakuts, and Tungus in northern Scandinavia and Siberia. Reindeer have been introduced into Alaska, Newfoundland, and other parts of North America with various degrees of success; caribou also occur across the Bering Strait in eastern Siberia. Reindeer are generally smaller than caribou, the larger males reaching 1.2 m (4 ft) high at the shoulders and 115 kg (250 lb) in weight. They (and caribou) are the only deer in which the females bear antlers. The antlers are long and slender, and the branching points, or tines, usually assume broad, or palmate, shape. The rutting, or mating, season extends from August to early November, and males may control a group of up to 10 or 12 females. Gestation is about 8 months, and usually a single young is born.

Bibliography: Banfield, A. W. F., *A Revision of the Reindeer and Caribou Genus Rangifer* (1961); Zhigunov, P. S., ed., *Reindeer Husbandry,* 2d ed., trans. by M. Fleischmann (1968).

reinforced concrete: see CEMENT AND CONCRETE.

Reinhardt, Ad   [ryn'-hahrt]

The painter and art theoretician Ad Reinhardt, b. Adolf Frederick Reinhardt in Buffalo, N.Y., Dec. 24, 1913, d. Aug. 30, 1967, is known for the extremely abstract paintings of his later career, particularly the "black paintings" of the 1960s. At Columbia University in New York City, Reinhardt studied art history; later, he taught at Brooklyn College (from 1947 until his death). His early works, which belong to the formative years of ABSTRACT EXPRESSIONISM, are composed of small rectilinear shapes painted in bright, contrasting colors. During the 1950s his canvases became increasingly monochromatic and symmetrical.   VALENTIN TATRANSKY

Bibliography: Lippard, Lucy R., *Ad Reinhardt: Paintings* (1966; repr. 1985); Reinhardt, Adolph Frederick, *Art as Art: The Selected Writings of Ad Reinhardt* (1975) and *25 Years of Abstract Painting* (1960).

Reinhardt, Django

Guitarist Jean Baptiste "Django" Reinhardt, b. Belgium, Jan. 23, 1910, d. May 16, 1953, had a substantial influence on contemporary jazz guitar style. Reinhardt, a gypsy, began with violin but turned to the guitar for rehabilitation of his left hand, which had been badly damaged in a caravan fire. This circumstance dictated his unusual two-fingered technique, which was most effective in slower tempos. Reinhardt cofounded (1934) the Quintet of Le Hot Club de France, which performed extensively and recorded until 1939. In 1946 he made his only U.S. tour, appearing with Duke Ellington's orchestra.

Bibliography: Collier, Graham, *Jazz* (1975); Delauney, Charles, *Django Reinhardt* (1961; repr. 1981).

Reinhardt, Max

Max Reinhardt, originally named Max Goldmann, b. Sept. 9, 1873, d. Oct. 31, 1943, was an Austrian stage director and producer who established himself as one of the most eclectic leaders of the modern experimental theater. Reinhardt was noted for his spectacular productions, which often involved unusual staging methods and elaborate special effects. In his early career Reinhardt headed several experimental theaters in Berlin before becoming director of the noted Deutsches Theater in 1905. During the decade that followed, he mounted a wide variety of productions in an equally wide range of styles, not only in Germany but throughout Europe. Celebrated Reinhardt presentations included Greek tragedy, the plays of Johann Wolfgang von Goethe and William Shakespeare, and the experimental drama of contemporaries such as Luigi Pirandello, George Bernard Shaw, and August Strindberg. Two of Reinhardt's most dazzling productions, *The Oresteia* (1919) and *Danton's Death* (1920), were performed before audiences of thousands in Berlin's massive Grosses Schauspeilhaus. The same year he founded the Salzburg Festival, for which he staged *Everyman*. Reinhardt emigrated to the United States when the Nazis came to power, becoming an American citizen in 1940. He continued his career in New York and Hollywood; his notable productions for the American stage include *A Midsummer Night's Dream* (1934), *Six Characters in Search of an Author* (1940), and *Rosalinda* (1942).

Bibliography: Carter, Huntley, *The Theatre of Max Reinhardt* (1914; repr. 1964); Reinhardt, Max, *The Genius: A Memoir of Max Reinhardt* (1979); Sayler, Oliver M., ed., *Max Reinhardt and His Theatre* (1924; repr. 1968); Styan, J. L., *Max Reinhardt* (1982); Wellwarth, G. E., and Brooks, A. G., *Max Reinhardt, 1873–1973* (1973).

relapsing fever

Relapsing fever is an INFECTIOUS DISEASE caused by a bacterial spirochete of the genus *Borrelia* and transmitted by human body lice or by ticks. The type spread by lice occurs under conditions of poor hygiene and famine; epidemics may take place during wartime. The type spread by ticks is transmitted to humans from such rodents as chipmunks and squirrels as well as from armadillos, opossums, and other small mammals. Symptoms manifest themselves after an incubation period of about 7 days and include a sudden onset of chills, followed by high fever, headache, muscle pain, cough, sore throat, and eye pain, all of which last from 3 to 6 days. The fever falls and then returns after about a week; relapses may continue 2 to 10 more times. Treatment includes the administration of tetracycline or chloramphenicol.   J. MICHAEL S. DIXON

relativity

Albert Einstein's theory of relativity is viewed as one of the greatest achievements in theoretical physics. It introduced to science the concept of "relativity"—the notion that there is no absolute motion in the universe, only relative motion—thus superseding the 200-year-old theory of mechanics of Isaac Newton. Einstein showed that we reside not in the flat, Euclidean space and uniform, absolute time of everyday experience, but in another environment: curved space-time. The theory played a role in advances in physics that led to the nuclear era, with its potential for benefit as well as for destruction, and that made possible an understanding of the microworld of elementary particles and their interactions. It has also revolutionized our view of COSMOLOGY, with its predictions of apparently bizarre astronomical phenomena such as the BIG BANG, NEUTRON STARS, BLACK HOLES, and gravitational waves (see GRAVITATION).

SCOPE OF RELATIVITY

The theory of relativity is a single, all-encompassing theory of space-time, gravitation, and mechanics. It is popularly viewed, however, as having two separate, independent theoretical parts—special relativity and general relativity. One reason for this division is that Einstein presented special relativity in 1905, while general relativity was not published in its final form until 1916. Another reason is the very different realms of applicability of the two parts of the theory: special relativity in the world of microscopic physics, general relativity in the world of astrophysics and cosmology.

A third reason is that physicists accepted and understood special relativity by the early 1920s. It quickly became a working tool for theorists and experimentalists in the then-burgeoning fields of atomic and nuclear physics and quantum mechanics. This rapid acceptance was not, however, the case for general relativity. The theory did not appear to have as much direct connection with experiment as the special theory; most of its applications were on astronomical scales, and it was apparently limited to adding miniscule corrections to the predictions of Newtonian gravitation theory; its cosmo-

Albert Einstein's theory of relativity profoundly altered the prevailing Newtonian view of the universe and made Einstein the preeminent physicist of the 20th century as well as its best-known image of a scientist. The special relativity theory has long since been confirmed in the subatomic world, and evidences of the validity of general relativity are being found in the far reaches of space.

logical impact would not be felt for another decade. In addition, the mathematics of the theory were thought to be extraordinarily difficult to comprehend. The British astronomer Sir Arthur Eddington, one of the first to fully understand the theory in detail, was once asked if it were true that only three people in the world understood general relativity. He is said to have replied, "Who is the third?"

This situation persisted for almost 40 years. General relativity was considered a respectable subject not for physicists, but for pure mathematicians and philosophers. Around 1960, however, a remarkable resurgence of interest in general relativity began that has made it an important and serious branch of physics and astronomy. (By 1977, Eddington's remark was recalled at a conference on general relativity attended by more than 800 researchers in the subject.) This growth has its roots, first, beginning around 1960, in the application of new mathematical techniques to the study of general relativity that significantly streamlined calculations and that allowed the physically significant concepts to be isolated from the mathematical complexity, and second, in the discovery of exotic astronomical phenomena in which general relativity could play an important role, including quasars (1963), the 3-kelvin microwave background radiation (1965), pulsars (1967), and the possible discovery of black holes (1971). In addition, the rapid technological advances since the 1960s have given experimenters new high-precision tools to test whether general relativity was the correct theory of gravitation.

The distinction between special relativity and the curved space-time of general relativity is largely a matter of degree. Special relativity is actually an approximation to curved space-time that is valid in sufficiently small regions of space-time, much as the overall surface of an apple is curved even though a small region of the surface is approximately flat. Special relativity thus may be used whenever the scale of the phenomena being studied is small compared to the scale on which space-time curvature (gravitation) begins to be noticed. For most applications in atomic or nuclear physics, this approximation is so accurate that relativity can be assumed to be exact; in other words, gravity is assumed to be completely absent. From this point of view, special relativity and all its consequences may be "derived" from a single simple postulate. In the presence of gravity, however, the approximate nature of special relativity may manifest itself, so the principle of equivalence is invoked to determine how matter responds to curved space-time. Finally, to learn the extent that space-time is curved by the presence of matter, general relativity is applied.

SPECIAL RELATIVITY

The two basic concepts of special relativity are the inertial frame and the principle of relativity. An inertial frame of reference is any region, such as a freely falling laboratory (see FREE FALL), in which all objects move in straight lines with uniform velocity. This region is free from gravitation and is called a Galilean system. The principle of relativity postulates that the result of any physical experiment performed inside a laboratory in an inertial frame is independent of the uniform velocity of the frame. In other words, the laws of physics must have the same form in every inertial frame. A corollary is that the speed of light must be the same in any inertial frame (because a speed-of-light measurement is a physical experiment) regardless of the speed of its source or that of the observer. Essentially all the laws and consequences of special relativity can be derived from these concepts.

The first important consequence is the relativity of simultaneity. Because any operational definition of simultaneous events at different locations involves the sending of light signals between them, then two events that are simultaneous in one inertial frame may not be simultaneous when viewed from a frame moving relative to the first. This conclusion helped abolish the Newtonian concept of an absolute, universal time.

Another consequence of relativity is that the transformation law, which permits the change from the coordinates x, y, z, t of one inertial frame to x', y', z', t' of another moving with velocity v relative to the first (in, say, the x direction), is no

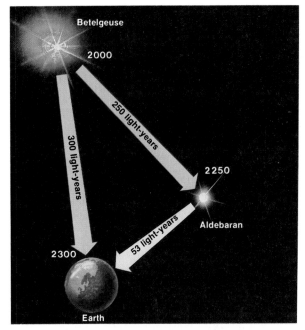

If Betelgeuse, a star in the constellation Orion, were to explode, and the explosion were noted on Earth in the year 2300, then, knowing that Betelgeuse lies 300 light-years distant, the event could be postdated as having occurred in the year 2000, Earth time. Similar dates could be assigned for the notice of that explosion elsewhere, as on the star Aldebaran. These would be simply Earth dates, however; the notion of absolute time must be abandoned in relativity because objects move in different inertial frames relative to one another.

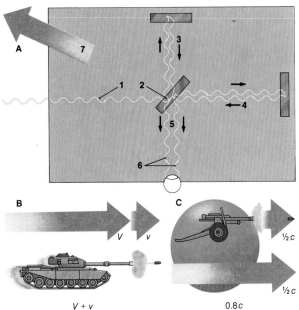

The Michelson-Morley experiment (A) was designed to detect the ether medium once thought to carry light waves. A light beam (1), split by a mirror (2), followed separate light paths (3, 4) and recombined (5), forming interference bands (6). If ether were present, light should take longer to make the round trip in the direction (7) of Earth's motion than at right angles to it. No time difference was observed, indicating no ether. Newton's laws of motion (B) predict that a shell fired with a velocity v from a tank moving at a speed V should have a velocity V+v relative to an outside observer. Einstein showed that the relative velocity should be $(v+V) \div (1+vV/c^2)$, where c is the velocity of light. Thus (C), if a shell is fired at $\frac{1}{2}c$ on a planet orbiting at $\frac{1}{2}c$, an outside observer will see the shell moving at 0.8c.

longer the Galilean transformation, given by $x' = x - vt$, $y' = y$, $z' = z$, $t' = t$. It becomes the Lorentz transformation: $x' = (x - vt)/\sqrt{1 - v^2/c^2}$, $y' = y$, $z' = z$, $t' = (t - vx/c^2)/\sqrt{1 - v^2/c^2}$, where c is the velocity of light (300,000 km/sec; 186,000 mi/sec). This transformation law was derived in 1895 by Hendrik A. Lorentz as a result of his work on electromagnetism and the theory of electrons. Einstein demonstrated that the law was a fundamental property of space-time. One effect predicted by the Lorentz transformation is the FITZGERALD-LORENTZ CONTRACTION, an apparent shortening by a factor $\sqrt{1 - v^2/c^2}$ of the length of a moving rod compared to an identical rod at rest. This effect was first proposed by George F. Fitzgerald in 1892 as a way to explain the failure of the 1887 MICHELSON-MORLEY EXPERIMENT to detect any dependence of the velocity of light on the Earth's motion through the so-called ETHER, the medium through which light was thought to propagate. Einstein pointed out that the principle of relativity made the ether concept superfluous, since the Michelson-Morley result could be accounted for using any inertial frame.

Another effect of special relativity is the apparent lengthening of time intervals measured by a moving clock by a factor $1/\sqrt{1 - v^2/c^2}$ compared to a clock at rest (see CLOCK PARADOX). This "time dilation" has been confirmed to high precision by numerous laboratory experiments, including one in 1966 in which unstable muons (μ-mesons) moving at velocities of $0.997c$ were found to live longer than muons at rest by exactly the correct factor of 12.

The law of composition of two velocities, given by $v_3 = v_1 + v_2$ in classical Newtonian mechanics, is now given by $v_3 = (v_1 + v_2)/(1 + v_1 v_2/c^2)$. Therefore no combination of velocities, each less than c, can ever produce a velocity in excess of c; furthermore, if one of the velocities is c, the combined velocity v_3 is automatically c, consistent with the postulate that the speed of light is the same in every inertial frame.

One consequence of modifying the Galilean-invariant mechanics of Newton to make it Lorentz-invariant is that the momentum of a particle of rest mass m is no longer mv, but $mv/\sqrt{1 - v^2/c^2}$, which means that the particle's mass increases as it moves faster. This relativistic increase of inertia prevents particles from being accelerated up to and beyond the speed of light and has been observed countless times in high-energy particle accelerators. Einstein also showed that what was energy in one inertial frame could be mass in another; therefore both are manifestations of the same entity and are related by the famous equation $E = mc^2$.

In some ways the most important consequences and confirmations of special relativity arise when it is merged with quantum mechanics, leading to many predictions in agreement with experiments, such as elementary particle spin, atomic fine structure, antimatter, and so on.

The mathematical foundations of special relativity were explored in 1908 by the German mathematician Hermann Minkowski, who developed the concept of a "four-dimensional space-time continuum," in which time is treated the same as the three spatial dimensions—the fourth dimension of Minkowski space-time.

THE PRINCIPLE OF EQUIVALENCE AND SPACE-TIME CURVATURE

The exact Minkowski space-time of special relativity is incompatible with the existence of gravity. A frame chosen to be inertial for a particle far from the Earth where the gravitational field is negligible will not be inertial for a particle near the Earth. An approximate compatibility between the two, however, can be achieved through a remarkable property of gravitation called the weak equivalence principle (WEP): all modest-sized bodies fall in a given external gravitational field with the same acceleration regardless of their mass, composition, or structure. The principle's validity has been checked experimentally by Galileo, Newton, and Friedrich Bessel, and in the early 20th century by Baron Roland von Eötvös (after whom such experiments are named). If an observer were to ride in an elevator falling freely in a gravitational field, then all bodies inside the elevator, because they are falling at the same rate, would consequently move uniformly in straight lines as if gravity had vanished. Conversely, in an accelerated elevator in free space, bodies would fall with the same accel-

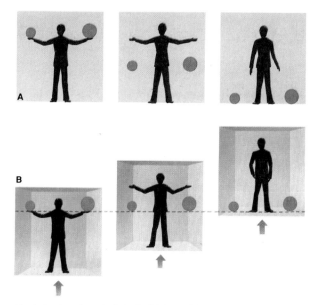

The behavior of two balls in Earth's inertial frame (A) and in that of an accelerating elevator in free space (B)—even if the balls differ in mass—is an example of Einstein's equivalence principle in special relativity. The balls in the elevator "drop" with the same uniform acceleration, just as if they dropped in Earth's gravitational field.

eration (because of their inertia), just as if there were a gravitational field.

Einstein's great insight was to postulate that this "vanishing" of gravity in free-fall applied not only to mechanical motion but to all the laws of physics, such as electromagnetism. In any freely falling frame, therefore, the laws of physics should (at least locally) take on their special relativistic forms. This postulate is called the Einstein equivalence principle (EEP). One consequence is the gravitational redshift, a shift in frequency f for a light ray that climbs through a height h in a gravitational field, given by $\Delta f/f = gh/c^2$ where g is the gravitational acceleration. (If the light ray descends, it is blue-shifted.) Equivalently, this effect can be viewed as a relative shift in the rates of identical clocks at two heights. A second consequence of EEP is that space-time must be curved. Although this is a highly technical issue, consider the example of two frames falling freely, but on opposite sides of the Earth. According to EEP, Minkowski space-time is valid locally in each frame; however, because the frames are accelerating toward each other, the two Minkowski space-times cannot be extended until they meet in an attempt to mesh them into one. In the presence of gravity, space-time is flat only locally but must be curved globally.

Any theory of gravity that fulfills EEP is called a "metric" theory (from the geometrical, curved-space-time view of gravity). Because the equivalence principle is a crucial foundation for this view, it has been well tested. Versions of the Eötvös experiment performed in Princeton in 1964 and in Moscow in 1971 verified EEP to 1 part in 10^{12}. Gravitational redshift measurements using gamma rays climbing a tower on the Harvard University campus (1965), using light emitted from the surface of the Sun (1965), and using atomic clocks flown in aircraft and rockets (1976) have verified that effect to precisions of better than 1 percent.

GENERAL RELATIVITY

The principle of equivalence and its experimental confirmation reveal that space-time is curved by the presence of matter, but they do not indicate how much space-time curvature matter actually produces. To determine this curvature requires a specific metric theory of gravity, such as general relativity, which provides a set of equations that allow computation of the space-time curvature from a given distribution of matter. These are called field equations. Einstein's aim was to find the simplest field equations that could be constructed in terms of the space-time curvature and that would have the matter distribution as source. The result was a set of 10 equations. This is not, however, the only possible metric theory. In 1960, C. H. Brans and Robert Dicke developed a metric theory (see GRAVITATION) that proposed, in addition to field equations for curvature, equations for an additional gravitational field whose role was to mediate and augment the way in which matter generated curvature. Between 1960 and 1976 it became a serious competitor to general relativity. Many other metric theories have also been invented since 1916.

An important issue, therefore, is whether general relativity is indeed the correct theory of gravity. The only way to answer this question is by means of experiment. In the past scientists customarily spoke of the three classical tests proposed by Einstein: gravitational redshift, light deflection, and the perihelion shift of Mercury. The redshift, however, is a test of the equivalence principle, not of general relativity itself, and two new important tests have been discovered since Einstein's time: the time-delay by I. I. Shapiro in 1964, and the Nordtvedt effect by K. Nordtvedt, Jr., in 1968.

The confirmation of the deflection of starlight by the Sun by the solar eclipse expedition of 1919 was one of the triumphant moments for general relativity and brought Einstein worldwide fame. According to the theory, a ray of light propagating through the curved space-time near the Sun should be deflected in direction by 1.75 seconds of arc if it grazes the solar surface. Unfortunately, measurements of the deflection of optical starlight are difficult (in part because of need for a solar eclipse to obscure the light of the Sun), and repeated measurements between 1919 and 1973 yielded inaccurate results. This method has been supplanted by measurements of the deflection of radio waves from distant quasars using radio-telescope interferometers, which can operate in broad daylight. Between 1969 and 1975, 12 such measurements ultimately yielded agreement, to 1 percent, with the predicted deflection of general relativity.

The time-delay effect is a small delay in the return of a light signal sent through the curved space-time near the Sun to a planet or spacecraft on the far side of the Sun and back to Earth. For a ray that grazes the solar surface, the delay amounts to 200 millionths of a second. Since 1964, a systematic program of radar ranging to the planets Mercury and Venus, to the spacecraft *Mariners 6, 7,* and *9,* and to the *Viking* orbiters and landers on Mars has been able to confirm this prediction to better than half of 1 percent.

Another of the early successes of general relativity was its ability to account for the puzzle of Mercury's orbit. After the perturbing effects of the other planets on Mercury's orbit were taken into account, an unexplained shift remained in the direction of its perihelion (point of closest approach to the Sun) of 43 seconds of arc per century; the shift had confounded astronomers of the late 19th century. General relativity explained it as a natural effect of the motion of Mercury in the curved space-time around the Sun. Recent radar measurements of Mercury's motion have confirmed this agreement to about half of 1 percent.

The Nordtvedt effect is one that does not occur in general relativity but is predicted by many alternative metric theories of gravity, including the Brans-Dicke theory. It is a possible violation of the equality of acceleration of massive bodies that are bound by gravitation, such as planets or stars. The existence of such an effect would not violate the weak equivalence principle that was used as a foundation for curved space-time, as that principle applies only to modest-sized objects whose internal gravitational binding is negligible. One of the remarkable properties of general relativity is that it satisfies EEP for all types of bodies. If the Nordtvedt effect were to occur, then the Earth and Moon would be attracted by the Sun with slightly different accelerations, resulting in a small perturbation in the lunar orbit that could be detected by lunar laser ranging, a technique of measuring the distance to the Moon using laser pulses reflected from arrays of mirrors deposited there by Apollo astronauts. In data taken between 1969 and 1976, no such perturbation was detected, down to a precision of 30 cm (1 ft), in complete agreement with the zero prediction of general relativity and in disagreement with the prediction of the Brans-Dicke theory.

A number of secondary tests of more subtle gravitational effects have also been performed during the last decade. General relativity has passed every one, while many of its

The concept of space-time requires time as a fourth dimension in order to specify location—because relative motion affects both space and time. An object's path in space-time is called a world line, *and a graph of a world line uses two space coordinates and time as a third. (A) In an airplane's flight from X to Y, the slope of its world line increases as its speed decreases, becoming vertical when the plane makes a fueling stop (times T1 to T3). A radio signal starting from X arrives at Y at time T2. In relativity theory, acceleration of an object as it passes near a massive body is viewed as a local distortion in space-time. (B) A comet passing the Sun is deflected (dc) in space-time, as is a ray of light (dl); a planet, slower, oscillates between extreme positions. (C) Space-time around the Sun is distorted differently for objects moving at different speeds, but each object, in its own version of space, appears to travel in a path of constant velocity.*

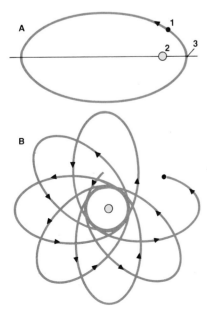

(A) *Mercury (1) moves around the Sun (2) in an elliptical orbit. The planet's perihelion (3)—the point closest to the Sun—also moves about the Sun, or precesses, so that Mercury follows a rosette-shaped orbital path (B). The gravitational pull of other planets accounts for nearly all of the precession, except for a small residual amount. This remaining amount is accounted for by Einstein's general theory of gravitation, which considers that part of the precession results from warping of space by the Sun's enormous mass.*

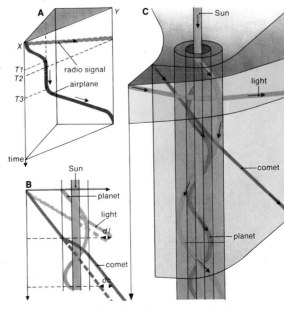

competitors have failed. Tests of gravitational radiation and inertial frame-dragging are now being devised. One experiment would involve placing spinning objects in Earth orbit and measuring expected relativistic effects.

COSMOLOGY

One of the first astronomical applications of general relativity was in the area of cosmology. The theory predicts that the universe could be expanding from an initially condensed state, a process known as the big bang. Despite many challenges (including the popularity during the 1950s of the steady-state theory), the big bang is now accepted as the standard model of the universe. Three important pieces of evidence, accumulated mainly since 1960, support this conclusion: (1) more precise measurements of the universe's expansion rate, first measured by Edwin Hubble in 1929, indicating that the big bang occurred between 10 and 20 billion years ago; (2) the discovery in 1965 of the 3K (3 degrees above absolute zero) microwave background radiation, a uniform "sea" of electromagnetic radiation left over from the earlier hot phase of the universe (700,000 years after the big bang); and (3) the realization that the observed cosmic abundance of helium (20 to 30 percent by weight) is necessarily produced in the conditions of the big bang. One aspect of the model that is still uncertain is whether the universe will continue to expand indefinitely or whether it will slow down and eventually recollapse to a "big crunch." Astronomical observations may yield an answer.

Another important application of general relativity is to the theory of neutron stars, bodies that have been so compressed by gravitational forces that their density is comparable to that within the atomic nucleus, and their composition is primarily neutrons. (A neutron star whose mass equals that of the Sun has a radius of only 10 km/6 mi.) They are thought to occur as a by-product of such violent events as supernovae and other gravitational implosions of stars. Pulsars, first discovered in 1967, are generally believed to be rapidly spinning neutron stars. Pulsars are objects that emit pulses of radio waves at

regular intervals, ranging from about 30 milliseconds to 3 seconds; as of 1979, 200 have been discovered. According to one model, the neutron star acts as a lighthouse, emitting a narrow beam from its surface that sweeps by an observer's telescope once each rotation period.

One of the most exotic predictions of general relativity is the black hole. Implosions of extremely massive stars can proceed beyond the neutron star configuration. As the matter continues to implode, it crosses an imaginary spherical surface known as the event horizon, located at a radius given by $2MG/c^2$, where M is the mass that has imploded and G is Newton's constant of gravitation; for one solar mass, this radius is about 3 km (1.9 mi). Once inside the event horizon, nothing—not even light—can escape. The exterior space-time geometry of the black hole is described by the Schwarzschild solution of the field equations if it has no rotation, and by the Kerr solution if it rotates (solutions discovered respectively in 1916 by Karl Schwarzschild and in 1963 by R. Kerr). Rather strong evidence now exists that the companion of the star denoted HDE 226868 in the constellation Cygnus is a black hole. According to the most favored model, gas from the atmosphere of HDE 226868 is stripped off by the gravitational field of the hole, heats up as it falls toward the hole, and emits copious amounts of X rays just before plunging across the event horizon. The X rays from this source, called Cygnus X-1, were detected in 1971 by a telescope on a satellite called *Uhuru*. Some theorists have speculated that supermassive black holes may exist at the centers of some clusters of stars (with masses of 10^3 solar masses) and of some galaxies (with masses of 10^6 to 10^9 solar masses), including perhaps our own.

One prediction of general relativity has not yet been verified: gravitational radiation, a wave of gravitational force that travels at the speed of light, transports energy, and induces relative motion between pairs of particles in its path or produces strains in bulk objects. Astrophysicists believe that it should be emitted by dynamic sources such as supernovae,

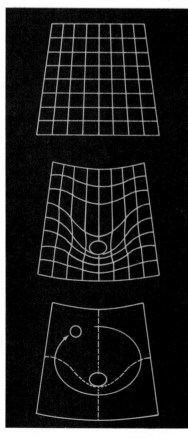

The curvature of space-time by the presence of matter is illustrated in this sequence of diagrams. Space is represented here as a flat rubber sheet that is covered with a grid of lines. A weight placed on the sheet depresses it and distorts the grid. In a similar manner the presence of a massive object, such as a star, distorts space-time. The area around the mass is now curved. Because the area of space-time around the star's mass is curved, a nearby mass, such as a planet, is held in orbit, like a bicycle on a banked racetrack, or else it falls in toward the star.

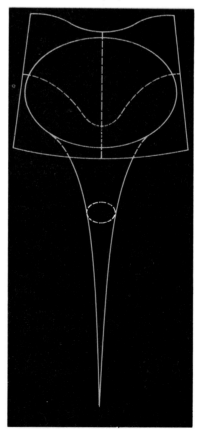

The preceding diagram is carried a drastic step further to show what happens near a black hole—a mass so great that it has collapsed inward upon itself. It has, in effect, gone out of existence, except for the extreme distortion of its neighborhood. A passing object that is pulled in toward the black hole cannot escape once it passes the event horizon, or Schwarzschild radius (small broken circle). Evidence is growing for the existence of black holes, predicted by general relativity.

Instruments for detecting gravitational radiation are being operated at Glasgow University, Scotland, among other sites, thus far without clear success. The existence of gravitational radiation, traveling at the speed of light, is one of the predictions of general relativity.

double-star systems, and black-hole formations and collisions. Although experiments around 1970 using 1.5-ton aluminum cylinders fitted with strain gauges were thought to have detected it, subsequent experiments by other groups did not confirm the detection. A worldwide effort is now in progress to build gravitational radiation antennas, not only to detect this phenomenon but also, ultimately, to make use of it as a new window on the universe.

Recently, indirect evidence for the existence of gravitational radiation has been discovered in a system known as a binary pulsar, a pulsar in orbit around a companion star. Careful measurements, by radio telescopes, of the motion of the pulsar have shown that the orbit is losing energy and is decaying at just the rate to be expected from the loss of energy by means of emission of gravitational waves by the system.   CLIFFORD M. WILL

Bibliography: Barnett, Lincoln, *The Universe and Dr. Einstein,* rev. ed. (1968); Born, Max, *Einstein's Theory of Relativity,* rev. ed. (1962); Einstein, Albert, *The Meaning of Relativity,* 5th ed. (1956); Gardner, Martin, *Relativity for the Millions* (1962); Reichenbach, Hans, *The Philosophy of Space and Time,* trans. by Maria Reichenbach (1958); Russell, Bertrand, *The A B C of Relativity,* 3d ed. (1969); Struble, Mitch, *The Web of Space-Time: A Step by Step Exploration of Relativity* (1973); Taylor, E. F., and Wheeler, J. A., *Spacetime Physics* (1966); Weinberg, Steven, *The First Three Minutes* (1977).

See also: CLOCK PARADOX; SPACE-TIME CONTINUUM; WORLD LINE.

Relay

Relay was an early experiment by NASA in the field of active-repeater COMMUNICATIONS SATELLITES. The two Relay satellites were designed to receive and retransmit a variety of television, telephone, and radio signals between the United States, Europe, Japan, and South America. *Relay 1* was launched from Cape Canaveral by a Delta rocket on Dec. 13, 1962, and entered an orbit with an apogee of 7,422 km (4,612 mi) and a perigee of 1,318 km (819 mi) at an angle of 47.5° to the equator, with a period of 186 minutes. *Relay 2* was similarly launched on Jan. 21, 1964. Its orbit was 7,412 km (4,606 mi) by 2,088 km (1,298 mi) at an angle of 46° to the equator and with a period of 195 minutes. The satellites were octagonal, made of aluminum, and 74 cm (29 in) wide and 84 cm (33 in) high. They weighed 77 kg (170 lb). The two transponders within the satellites were provided with 11 watts of power by 8,200 solar cells. Built by RCA, each satellite provided either a single television channel or 300 one-way voice channels. Alternatively, they could be switched to handle 12 simultaneous two-way telephone channels.

Because the orbit selected for the satellites passed through the Van Allen radiation belt, they carried special sensors to measure the flux of trapped protons in the belt. Additionally,

Relay 2 was used to locate a tracking station in Mojave, Calif., in an early experiment into the usefulness of satellites as aids in navigation. Both satellites continued to perform satisfactorily until they were shut off: *Relay 1* in February 1965, and *Relay 2* in September 1965.   MITCHELL SHARPE

relay

A relay is essentially an electrically controlled SWITCH that is used to open or close an electric circuit. The switch can be actuated by various means. Electromechanical operation is the most common and will be emphasized below, but other types of actuation are possible. An electromechanical device produces mechanical motion when it is energized by an electric current. A SOLENOID is such a device, and solenoids are often used in relays.

A standard type of relay consists of a coil with an enclosed, fixed iron core and a nearby movable armature. When the coil is energized, the armature is attracted to it; the resulting motion is then used to open or close the relay circuit. Such a relay requires a power of several watts for proper operation. The appearance of transistorized switching systems, which operate at powers of a few tenths of a watt, necessitated the design of relays that could function at these lower powers. The reed relay not only solved this problem but was also much smaller. It consists of two flat magnetic strips enclosed in a sealed capsule filled with an inert gas to prevent corrosion. The capsule is situated inside a coil; when the coil is energized, an electromagnetic field is created, causing the two contact strips, which are normally separated, to attract each other, make contact, and close the circuit. When the coil is deenergized, the field vanishes and the strips, because of their spring action, return to their normal separation. Reed relays are common in telephone switching equipment.

Many types of relays have been designed for various applications. They are used in CIRCUIT BREAKERS, COMPUTERS, IGNITION SYSTEMS, electric bells, telegraph systems, and electrical and electronic equipment.   ARTHUR BIDERMAN

Bibliography: Harper, Charles A., ed., *Handbook of Components for Electronics* (1977); Warrington, A. R., *Protective Relays: Their Theory and Practice,* vol. 1, 2d ed. (1969-73), and vol. 2, 3d ed. (1978).

religion

Religion is a complex phenomenon, defying definition or summary. Almost as many definitions and theories of religion exist as there are authors on the subject. In the broadest terms, three approaches are generally taken to the scholarly study of religion: the historical, the phenomenological, and the behavioral or social-scientific.

SCHOLARLY APPROACHES

The historical approach deals, of necessity, with texts, whether these be the doctrinal, devotional, or ritual texts that stem from the religious community per se or secular documents such as statistics through which the historian attempts to reconstruct the religious life of a community. The historians may weave both types of documents together to create a rich sense of the role of religion in the life of a people as a whole. A particularly fine recent example of this approach is Le Roy Ladurie's *Montaillou* (1975; Eng. trans., 1978), in which the social and economic life of a small medieval French village is seen against the backdrop of religious heterodoxy.

The phenomenological study of religion, although often starting with the results of the historian, is directed toward discovering the nature of religion—the fundamental characteristics that lie behind its historical manifestations. In this particular field the classic treatment remains Gerardus van der Leeuw's *Religion in Essence and Manifestation: A Study in Phenomenology* (1933; Eng. trans., 1938). Many scholars of comparative religion, such as Mircea ELIADE, may also be said to fall into this category, although their relations to the historical traditions are often complex. The phenomenological tradition has been criticized, both by the historians and the social scientists, for losing sight of the details of particular religions in overly general comparison and speculation, but contemporary scholars are attempting to overcome these

(Above) *Some Buddhist monks live solely on offerings from the laity, for possession of property is forbidden. Buddhism, one of the world's major religions, teaches that one of the paths to salvation, liberation from the suffering of existence, is renunciation of all material goods.*

(Right) *The monks at the monastery of Saint John the Evangelist on the Greek island of Patmos belong to the Byzantine rite of the Eastern churches. Monastic life, providing an opportunity for meditation and spiritual growth, is an integral part of many religions.*

problems by dissolving the artificial boundaries between the disciplines.

A clear example of this tendency may be seen in the rise of social scientific studies of religion in the last hundred years. Psychology, sociology, and especially anthropology have contributed great depth to the understanding of religious phenomena. In the psychology of religion, the two most important figures remain William JAMES and Sigmund FREUD. James's *Varieties of Religious Experience* (1902) established a set of topics and approaches to those topics that set the overall tone for much later work in the field. While James dealt primarily with conscious expressions of religious experience, Freud and the psychoanalytic tradition stemming from him attempted to fit the various forms of religious experience into the framework of a general theory of the unconscious. C. G. JUNG in particular has been influential among interpreters of religion, in part, no doubt, as the best-developed alternative to Freud himself.

One problem usually associated with the psychological approach is the difficulty of moving from the individual's experience to the structure and experience of the religious community. This problem has been confronted by the sociological and the anthropological traditions since the last third of the 19th century. William Robertson SMITH, Émile DURKHEIM, and Max WEBER were the leading figures in creating a sociological tradition in the analysis of religion.

The year 1922 is sometimes taken as marking the beginning of modern anthropology and with it the complex studies of existing cultures and their religions that have done much to illuminate contemporary thought about religion. In that year Bronislaw MALINOWSKI and A. R. RADCLIFFE-BROWN published

studies based on in-depth field work in foreign cultures. Their functionalist approach to the analysis of religion became a school, from which a steady flow of detailed studies of religion in cultural context continues unabated. Perhaps the most eminent figure in this tradition was Sir Edward EVANS-PRITCHARD, whose influential works continue to serve as points of departure for analysts of religion.

Meanwhile, a French tradition was developing out of the school of Durkheim that was in some ways analogous with and in others opposed to the British school. In this context structure has played a role akin to that of function. Claude LÉVI-STRAUSS has developed a complex theory of the way in which religious symbol and myth are transformed in the articulation by a culture of the cosmos in which it finds itself.

This brief treatment cannot do justice to the variety of approaches to the study of religion, but one thing should be made clear. Any approach taken in isolation from the others will lead to distortion and bias. The attempt to integrate a number of theories stemming from a wealth of traditions is necessary to grasp the character of the religions of the world.

CHARACTERISTICS OF RELIGION

Keeping in mind the dangers of general characterizations, what are the distinctive features of religion? Several concepts may be isolated that, even though not necessary or sufficient conditions if taken separately, may jointly be considered "symptomatic" of religions.

The Holy. Religious belief or experience is usually expressed in terms of the holy or the sacred. The holy is usually in opposition to the everyday and profane and carries with it a sense of supreme value and ultimate reality. The holy may be understood as a personal GOD, as a whole realm of gods and spirits, as a diffuse power, as an impersonal order, or in some other way. Although the holy may ultimately be nothing but the social order, a projection of the human mind, or some sort of illusion, it is nevertheless experienced in religion as an initiating power, coming to human life and touching it from beyond itself.

Religions frequently claim to have their origin in REVELATIONS, that is, in distinctive experiences of the holy coming into human life. Such revelations may take the form of visions (MOSES in the desert), inner voices (MUHAMMAD outside Mecca), or events (Israel's exodus from Egypt; the divine wind, or *kamikaze*, which destroyed the invading Mongol fleet off Japan; the death and RESURRECTION of JESUS CHRIST). Revelations may be similar to ordinary religious experience, but they have a creative originating power from which can flow an entire religious tradition.

Response. Response to the holy may take the form of participation in and acquiescence to the customs and rituals of a religious community or of a commitment of faith. Faith is not merely belief but an attitude of persons in which they commit themselves to the holy and acknowledge its claim upon them. In a deeply religious person, faith commitment tends to shape all of that person's life and character.

Beliefs. As religious traditions develop, they generate systems of belief with respect to both practice and doctrine. These systems serve to situate the members of the religious tradition in the world around them and to make intelligible this world in relation to the holy. In early or primitive traditions this practice and doctrine usually find expression in bodies of myth (see MYTHOLOGY) or in ritual law. In those traditions which develop an extensive literate class, THEOLOGY often comes to supplant myth as the vehicle for refining and elaborating belief. The more this happens, the more the belief system has to be evaluated. The importance attached to right belief ("orthodoxy") has varied from religion to religion and from period to period. It has loomed large in Christianity, as for example in the great Christological and Trinitarian controversies from the 3d century onward.

Rituals and Liturgy. Religious traditions almost invariably involve ritual and liturgical forms as well as systems of belief. These may take the form of SACRIFICE or SACRAMENT, PASSAGE

The reading of the Torah is a fundamental part of Jewish liturgical services. The Torah, or the first five books of the Bible, presents a system of moral and religious conduct and is revered as the essence of the divine revelation received by Moses on Mount Sinai.

RITES, or invocations of God or the gods. The most important cultic acts are in most cases those performed by the entire community or a significant portion of it, although in many traditions private devotional forms such as prayer, fasting, and pilgrimage are also practiced. A distinction is often made between religion and magic in this context. In magic, attempts are made to manipulate divine forces through human acts. In truly cultic acts such as prayer and sacrifice, the prevailing attitude is one of awe, worship, and thanksgiving.

Participation in communal rituals marks a person as a member of the community, as being inside and integral to the community that is articulated in the system of beliefs. That in many traditions the disfavor of the community is expressed in its barring a person from the important cultic acts is not surprising because these acts insure the proper standing of the individual and community in relation to the holy.

Ethical Codes. Connected with beliefs is yet another aspect of religion, the possession of an ethical code incumbent upon the members of the community. This is particularly evident in highly structured societies such as India, where the CASTE system is an integral part of traditional Hinduism. MARDUK in ancient Babylon and Yahweh in ancient Israel were believed to be the authors of the laws of those nations, thus giving these laws the weight and prestige of holiness. The PROPHETS of Israel were social critics who claimed that righteous acts rather than cultic acts are the true expression of religion. As religions develop, they come to place increasing stress on the ethical, and sometimes religion is almost totally absorbed into morality, with only a sense of the holiness of moral demands and a profound respect for them remaining.

Community. Although religious solitaries exist, most religion has a social aspect that leads its adherents to form a community, which may be more or less tightly organized. In earlier times the religious community could scarcely be distinguished from the community at large; all professed the same faith, and the ruler was both a political and a religious leader. In the course of time, however, religious and civil societies have become distinct and may even come into conflict. In modern secular states—India and the United States, for example—a plurality of religious communities coexist peacefully within a single political entity. Each religious community, whether in a pluralistic or homogeneous society, has its own organized structure. A common though by no means universal feature of these religious organizations is a priesthood (see PRIEST) charged with teaching and transmitting the faith and performing liturgical acts.

FORMS OF RELIGIOUS EXPERIENCE

The complex phenomenon described above constitutes what may be called the religious experience of humankind. In different religions and in different individuals, one or more of the characteristics mentioned may predominate, whereas others may be weak or almost nonexistent. This difference explains why religion is best treated as a polymorphous concept and why it is better to see religions as linked by variable family likenesses than by some constant but elusive essence.

Basic Forms. Even though many varieties of religious experience exist, they seem to occur in two basic forms. In the first, the sense of the holy is conjoined markedly with an awareness of human finitude. This conjunction is expressed in Friedrich SCHLEIERMACHER's characterization of religion as a "feeling of absolute dependence"; it might be called the negative approach to religious experience. The awareness of the holy is set against the foil of finitude, sinfulness, and meaninglessness. At an earlier stage in his career, however, Schleiermacher defined religion differently—as the "sense and taste for the Infinite." Here the awareness of the holy is conjoined with the human experience of transcendence, of going beyond every state of existence to a fuller existence that lures on the human being. This method may be called the affirmative approach.

Although one approach or another may dominate, both belong to the full range of religious experience. Both find their place in Rudolf OTTO's classic, *The Idea of the Holy* (1917; Eng. trans., 1923), as a person's encounter with the *mysterium tremendum et fascinans*. *Mysterium* points to the otherness

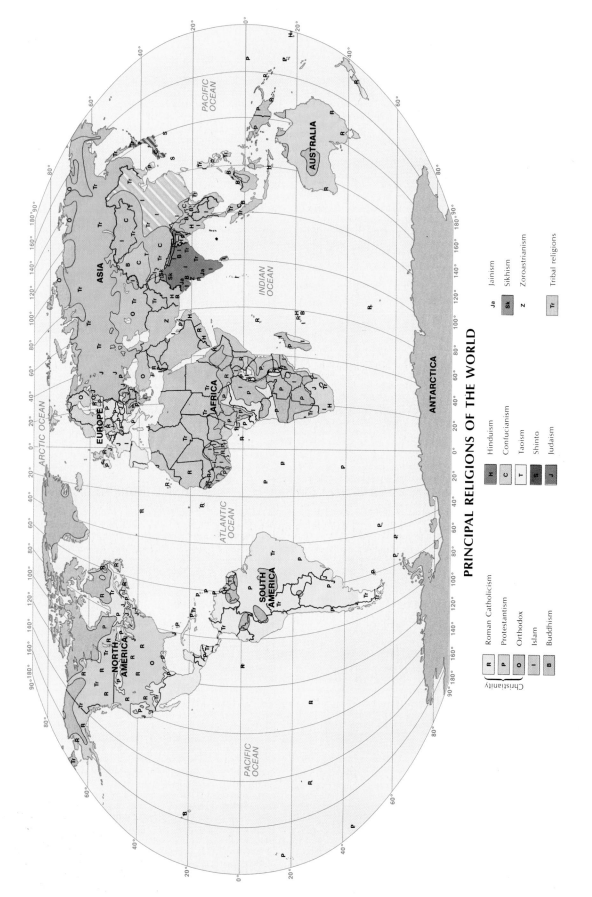

PRINCIPAL RELIGIONS OF THE WORLD

Christianity
- **R** Roman Catholicism
- **P** Protestantism
- **O** Orthodox
- **I** Islam
- **B** Buddhism

- **H** Hinduism
- **C** Confucianism
- **T** Taoism
- **S** Shinto
- **J** Judaism

- **Ja** Jainism
- **Sk** Sikhism
- **Z** Zoroastrianism
- **Tr** Tribal religions

of the holy; *tremendum* to its overwhelmingness in relation to human finitude; and *fascinans* to the lure that draws individuals out of and beyond themselves. Otto's work has been regarded as a masterly achievement in the phenomenology of religious experience.

Validity of Religious Experience. The question about the validity of religious experience must also be raised. Do religious people or worshiping communities encounter a holy reality that is outside of themselves and other than anything purely natural? Schleiermacher believed that the capacity for religious experience is universal in human beings. He therefore claimed that it could be accepted as self-authenticating and could take the place of the traditional proofs offered for the existence of God. Few people today would concede Schleiermacher's claim. Not only might they deny having the kinds of experiences he described; they might also suggest quite different interpretations for them. Many traditional revelations, which seemed to be miracles in a prescientific age, might now be judged as natural events or coincidences. Inner voices and private visions might be explained psychologically as subconscious mental processes. From Ludwig FEUERBACH to Freud, belief in God has been explained as a projection of the human mind; Karl MARX and other social analysts have seen religious belief as the product of socioeconomic forces. Each of these naturalistic explanations of religious belief has drawn attention to some element that enters into the religious complex, but it may be questioned whether such theories account exhaustively for the phenomenon of religion. The question about the validity of religious experience must ultimately be dealt with by returning to rational arguments for and against theism or, more broadly, for and against the existence of some holy reality, despite Schleiermacher's arguments to the contrary.

A Typology. Any typology that attempts an ordering of religions is the product of a particular tradition in which others are seen relatively to its own centrality. For instance, starting from the perspective of the Christian experience of the holy as both transcendent and immanent makes possible the construction of a series in which the various traditions are related more or less closely to CHRISTIANITY insofar as they emphasize one or the other. That is, Christian tradition strongly asserts the transcendence of God as an essential element in its Judaic heritage, but it just as strongly insists upon the immanence of God in the incarnation and in the sacraments. Roughly speaking, JUDAISM and ISLAM fall on the transcendent side of the series, whereas HINDUISM and BUDDHISM fall more on the immanent. A detailed analysis along these lines, taking into account the variety of traditions within Christianity, reveals illuminating affinities, as for example between CALVINISM and Islam and among the various mystical traditions. Thus the construction of a typology, despite the limitations of any given perspective, draws attention to both the unity and diversity of religions.

Conclusion. In a world where the status and future of religion is in so many ways uncertain, understanding of religious concepts is not likely to be reached with extreme views, whether this extremism takes the form of a dogmatic and isolationist claim to the superiority of an individual's own faith or a vague blurring of the genuine differences among the traditions. A middle ground must be established by those who accept the need for patient dialogue to uncover and explore both the agreements and disagreements among the religions. This third way aims at deepening the commitment and understanding of religious groups in their own traditions while at the same time making them more open to and ready to learn from other traditions.   JOHN MACQUARRIE

Bibliography: Banton, Michael, ed., *Anthropological Approaches to the Study of Religion* (1966); Bellah, R. N., *Beyond Belief: Essays on Religion in a Post-Traditional World* (1970); Bleeker, C. J., and Widengren, George, eds., *Historia Religionum: Handbook for the History of Religions*, 2 vols. (1969); Bowker, John, *The Sense of God* (1973); Budd, Susan, *Sociologists and Religion* (1973); de Vries, Jan, *Perspectives in the History of Religions* (1961; Eng. trans., 1977); Douglas, Mary, *Natural Symbols: Explorations in Cosmology*, rev. ed. (1973); Eliade, Mircea, *The Sacred and the Profane: The Nature of Religion* (1957; Eng. trans., 1959) and *A History of Religious Ideas*, 3 vols.

(1976– ; Eng. trans., 1978–); Eliade, Mircea, and Kitagawa, J. M., eds., *History of Religions: Essays in Methodology* (1959); Hill, Michael, *A Sociology of Religion* (1973); Kitagawa, J. M., ed., *The History of Religions: Essays on the Problem of Understanding* (1967); Pye, Michael, *Comparative Religion* (1972); Rosten, Leo, ed., *Religions of America* (1975); Sharpe, E. J., *Comparative Religion: A History* (1975); Shinn, L. D., *Two Sacred Worlds: Experience and Structure in the World's Religions* (1977); Smart, Ninian, *The Phenomenon of Religion* (1973) and *The Science of Religion and the Sociology of Knowledge* (1973); Smith, W. C., *The Meaning and End of Religion: A New Approach to the Religious Traditions of Mankind* (1963) and *Faith and Belief* (1979); Thouless, R. H., *An Introduction to the Psychology of Religion*, 3d ed. (1971); Waardenburg, J. D. J., *Classical Approaches to the Study of Religion*, 2 vols. (1973), and *Reflections on the Study of Religion* (1978); Wach, Joachim, *The Comparative Study of Religions* (1958); Werblowsky, R. J. Z., *Beyond Tradition and Modernity: Changing Religions in a Changing World* (1976); Zaehner, R. C., ed., *The Concise Encyclopedia of Living Faiths* (1959).

See also: PRIMITIVE RELIGION.

Religion, Wars of

The Wars of Religion were religious and political civil wars fought in France intermittently from 1562 to 1598, at a time when French Calvinists (HUGUENOTS) formed a strong and often aggressive minority. The wars were caused and prolonged by the alignment of rival aristocratic factions along opposing religious lines during the rule of two weak monarchs, Charles IX (r. 1560–74) and HENRY III (r. 1574–89). From 1562 to 1576, the Huguenots, led at first by Louis I de CONDÉ and Gaspard de COLIGNY, were supported only by external Protestant armies in their conflict with the Catholic crown. After 1572, when several thousand Huguenots were killed in the SAINT BARTHOLOMEW'S DAY MASSACRE, a third party of moderate Catholics, known as the Politiques, emerged under the family of Montmorency.

An ultra-Catholic party called the Holy League, led by the house of GUISE, was formed in 1576 to oppose a peace favorable to the Protestants accorded by Henry III. When the Bourbon Protestant leader, Henry of Navarre (later HENRY IV), became heir to the throne in 1584, the league grew more militant against both king and Huguenots. It procured the assassination of Henry III in 1589 and continued to fight against Henry IV (r. 1589–1610), even after his conversion to Catholicism in 1593. Henry IV eventually defeated the league, and in 1598 the Huguenots received a more stable form of toleration under the Edict of Nantes (see NANTES, EDICT OF).

During the period of the Wars of Religion, the French crown began to depend on ennobled lawyer-administrators, who held their offices almost as private property and alienated the warrior aristocracy. As the wars continued, however, the emergence of urban and peasant protest movements caused the higher orders to draw together and look to the crown for protection. The French social structure became less flexible, and the monarchy was able to initiate the system of absolutism that governed France for the next two centuries.

J. H. M. SALMON

Bibliography: Coudy, Julien, *The Huguenot Wars* (1969); Salmon, J. H. M., *Society in Crisis: France in the Sixteenth Century* (1975); Thompson, James W., *The Wars of Religion in France, 1559–1576* (1957).

religious broadcasting

Religious broadcasting in the United States dates back to the earliest days of radio; the first radio broadcast, on Christmas Eve 1906, was religious in content. Regularly scheduled religious broadcasting began with the establishment of continuous programming in 1920. When television superseded radio in the 1950s, Roman Catholic bishop Fulton J. SHEEN, with his program "Life Is Worth Living," was among the medium's first superstars. Typical religious programming of the 1940s and '50s, however, was of the public-service variety. Broadcasting stations distributed free air time to religious groups—usually on Sunday morning—dividing it between Protestants, Catholics, and Jews.

The big networks had a close relationship with the liberal "mainline" Protestant denominations represented by the National Council of Churches. Protestant fundamentalist and evangelical groups, which did not belong to the council, were effectively locked out of national broadcasting and found it difficult to buy time on local stations too. In 1960, however, the Federal Communications Commission ruled that stations might sell time for religious programs and still count it as part of the public-service broadcasting that was required of them. Evangelical groups then became major purchasers of air time, and by the mid-1970s they dominated religious broadcasting. Robert Schuller, a minister of the Reformed Church in America, is now the only major syndicated religious broadcaster in the mainline Protestant tradition, and even his program—"Hour of Power"—is not sponsored by his denomination.

The "electronic church" ministry of popular television evangelists such as Oral ROBERTS, Jim Bakker, Jerry FALWELL, M. G.."Pat" ROBERTSON, and Jimmy Swaggart has been widely criticized on a number of counts. TV evangelists support themselves by appealing to their audiences for donations. Premiums in the form of inexpensive jewelry, books and pamphlets, cassettes, or printed copies of sermons are offered to those who call or write. Respondents are then solicited further by direct-mail techniques. Mainline church leaders claim that such "commercializing" cheapens religion.

Others have charged that radio and TV preachers lure people from local pews with superior pulpit oratory. Those who elect to take their religion in the comfort of their living rooms, it is said, cease to contribute to local churches, giving their dollars to religious broadcasters instead. In 1984, however, the Gallup Organization released a study showing that regular consumers of religious broadcasting actually tend to be more involved in local congregations than nonviewers, and that their financial contributions to local churches are greater.

In 1987 scandal rocked the world of TV evangelism as Jim Bakker and his wife Tammy Faye were forced off the air amid charges of financial irregularities, drug abuse, and sexual misconduct; a "holy war" ensued in which Bakker, Jimmy Swaggart, and Jerry Falwell hurled accusations at one another in public.

Intensive advocacy of conservative political causes by TV evangelists such as Falwell, founder of the MORAL MAJORITY, has also been a source of controversy. Although some early religious broadcasters—notably Father Charles COUGHLIN, the "radio priest" of the 1930s—had been openly political, most people in the field had initially been reluctant to mix religion and politics.

During the first half of the 1980s the Arbitron rating service reported a weekly television audience of 20 to 24 million for religious programming; other estimates are higher. Radio audiences are more difficult to measure, but they are believed to be larger than television audiences. Up to now, the typical listener and viewer has been older, female, below the national median in education and income, and disproportionately Southern. Pat Robertson, founder and president of the Christian Broadcasting Network (CBN) and the most commercially successful of contemporary religious broadcasters, has also been the most successful in attracting a broader audience. CBN's flagship program, "The 700 Club," has a combination talk show and magazine format with conservative political and economic commentary.   JEFFREY K. HADDEN

Bibliography: Hadden, Jeffrey, and Swann, Charles, *Prime Time Preachers* (1981); Horsfield, Peter, *Religious Television: The Experience in America* (1984).

religious cults

There is no definition of cult that is universally accepted by sociologists and psychologists of religion. The term *cult* is popularly applied to groups characterized by some kind of faddish devotion to a person or practice that is significantly apart from the cultural mainstream. For example, certain kinds of activities may take on cultlike ritualistic characteristics (recent widespread interest in intense physical exercise has been termed the *physical fitness cult*). Movie stars, entertainers, and other public figures sometimes generate passionate bands of followers that are called cults (the Elvis Presley

The Hare Krishna sect, a cult based on Hindu religious beliefs, is one of the largest contemporary Hindu movements outside India. Over the last two decades the cult has flourished, especially in the United States, where renewed interest in Eastern religion and philosophy has raised many questions concerning traditional Western conventions and values.

cult, to cite one). Groups that form around a set of esoteric beliefs—not necessarily religious—may also be termed cults (for example, flying saucer cults). When applied to religious groups, *cult* retains much of this popular usage but takes on more specific meaning, especially when contrasted with other kinds of religious organizations.

Cults and Other Forms of Religious Organization. The most commonly used classification of religious organizations is as churches or sects.

Church refers to a religious organization claiming a monopoly on knowledge of the sacred, having a highly structured or formalized dogma and hierarchy, but also being flexible about membership requirements as the organization attempts to minister to the secular society of which it is a part.

Sects, on the other hand, are protests against church attempts to accommodate to secular society. A sect views itself as a defender of doctrinal purity, protesting what it interprets as ecclesiastical laxity and excesses. As protectors of the true faith, sects tend to withdraw from the mainstream of worldly activities, to stress strict behavior codes, and to demand proof of commitment.

Cults have some of the same characteristics as sects. In fact, some scholars prefer not to make a distinction. There are, however, some noteworthy differences. Cults do not, at least initially, view themselves as rebelling against established churches. Actually, the practices of cults are often considered to enrich the life of the parent church of which they may be a part. Cults do not ordinarily stress doctrinal issues or theologi-

More than 900 members of the California-based People's Temple, a cult led by the Rev. Jim Jones, died (1978) in a mass murder-suicide at the Temple's commune in Jonestown, Guyana. The deaths are appalling testimony to the power that Jones exercised over his followers.

Robert M. Klein/NYT Pictures

The Korean religious leader Sun Myung Moon founded his Unification church in 1954. Now headquartered in the United States, the church espouses Moon's own version of Christianity, emphasizing the power of communal activity and direct experience of the divine. Critics accuse the cult of brainwashing its members.

cal argument and refinement as much as they emphasize the individual's experience of a more personal and intense relationship with the divine. Most of these groups are ephemeral, seldom lasting beyond a single generation; transient; and with fluctuating membership.

MYSTICISM is frequently a strong element in cult groups. Religious orders such as the FRANCISCANS began as cults built around the presence of a charismatic leader who emphasized a life-style dedicated to attaining high levels of spirituality. MORMONISM began as a cult, became a sect, and eventually evolved into a church. All the great world religions followed this same pattern of development as they accumulated members and formalized hierarchy and dogma.

Contemporary Cults. Cults are as old as recorded history, but contemporary interest in cults became amplified during the late 1960s and early 1970s as numbers of educated middle-class youths abandoned traditional religions and embraced beliefs and practices that were either culturally unprecedented (Eastern religions) or seemed to be atavisms of days long past (Fundamentalist Christianity). During this period, young people were increasingly found living in various types of religious communes and engaging in unconventional behavior, such as speaking in tongues (glossolalia), faith healing, meditating (often under the tutelage of a spiritual leader or guru), and following leaders that conventional society tended to look upon with suspicion and distaste. Interest in cults turned to a combination of fascination and revulsion upon the mass suicide of the Jones cult in November 1978, when more than 900 followers of James Jones died in JONESTOWN after drinking a mixture of powdered fruit drink and cyanide.

Modern cults come in a bewildering variety of ideologies, practices, and forms of leadership. They range from those adhering to a sort of biblical Christianity to those seeking satori (sudden enlightenment) via the pursuits of Zen Buddhism. Some cults have a flexible, functional leadership, such as many groups in the CHARISMATIC MOVEMENT emanating from the mainline Christian religions, and others have mentors who control and orchestrate cult events, such as the Reverend Sun Myung MOON, leader of the Unification church. Some Hindu gurus, such as Bhagwan Shree Rajneesh of the Rajneeshee sect, are believed by their followers to be living embodiments of God. Regardless of their ideological and ritual differences, however, the common denominator of all the modern cults is an emphasis on community—as well as on direct experience of the divine. In a cult, participants often find a level of social support and acceptance that rivals that found in a nuclear family. Cult activity, which is often esoteric and defined as direct contact with the divine, generates a sense of belonging to something profound and of being a somebody. The modern cult may be viewed as a cultural island that gives adherents an identity and a sense of meaning in a world that has somehow failed to provide them these things.

Cults are challenges to conventional society. As such, they engender intense questions concerning their possible impact.

The modern cults have clearly raised anew the legal issue of how far a society is willing to go to guarantee religious freedom. Some of the cults have been accused of brainwashing members and thereby violating the 1st Amendment to the Constitution. Court cases involving young people who were forcefully removed from cults by parents are still being decided. Future court decisions could significantly modify traditional protection of religious diversity in the United States.

RICHARD J. BORD

Bibliography: Appel, Willa, *Cults in America* (1983); Bromley, D. G., and Shupe, A. D., *Strange Gods* (1982); Ellwood, Robert, *Alternative Altars* (1979); Glock, C. Y., and Bellah, R. N., eds., *The New Religious Consciousness* (1976); Pavlos, A. J., *The Cult Experience* (1982); Zaretsky, I. I., and Leone, M. P., eds., *Religious Movements in Contemporary America* (1974).

religious freedom: see FREEDOM OF RELIGION.

religious orders

In the Christian tradition, religious orders are associations of men or women who seek to lead a life of prayer and pious practices and who are devoted often to some specific form of service. Members usually bind themselves publicly, or sometimes privately, by vows of poverty, chastity, and obedience to lead a dedicated life.

In the Roman Catholic church these associations are of several types. The religious orders, narrowly defined, include monastic orders (of which the largest is the BENEDICTINES), mendicant orders or friars (such as the FRANCISCANS or DOMINICANS), and canons regular (priests living in a community attached to a specific church). All of these make solemn vows and say office in choir. In general they all have their origin in the Middle Ages. Clerks regular are societies of priests who make vows and are joined together for the purpose of priestly ministry; the JESUITS are a well-known example. Societies in which priests, brothers, or sisters, bound by vows, live in community to perform certain kinds of services are called religious congregations and include, among others, the Passionists, Redemptorists, and Vincentians. Religious institutes such as the Christian Brothers are usually composed of unordained persons who take vows and devote themselves to such tasks as teaching. Members of secular institutes are generally laypersons who do not live in community or wear a particular kind of garb but make promises of poverty, chastity, and obedience and live an ordinary life within conventional circumstances. Roman Catholic orders of nuns or sisters are generally smaller but more numerous than those of their male counterparts and are devoted primarily to teaching. Some monastic communities are enclosed—the monks or nuns rarely leaving their monastery or convent—and devoted to the contemplative life.

In the Eastern church, where MONASTICISM had its beginnings, religious orders are not differentiated as they are in the West, and most Eastern Orthodox religious are monastics.

Following the Reformation, monasticism disappeared in Protestant countries, but the influence of the OXFORD MOVEMENT in the 19th century brought about the reestablishment of religious orders among Anglicans (Episcopalians). A few other Protestant groups have also established religious orders, among which the best-known modern example is at Taizé, France. Among the Eastern religions, Buddhism has a strong monastic tradition.

CYPRIAN DAVIS, O.S.B.

Bibliography: Anson, Peter, *The Call of the Cloister: Religious Communities and Kindred Bodies in the Anglican Communion* (1955); Knowles, David, *Christian Monasticism* (1969) and *From Pachomius to Ignatius: A Study in the Constitutional History of the Religious Orders* (1966); Vicaire, Marie-Humbert, *The Apostolic Life*, trans. by William De Naple (1966).

reliquary [rel'-uh-kwair-ee]

A reliquary is a receptacle, usually richly decorated and made of precious materials, for the safekeeping or exhibition of a relic, an object venerated for its association with a holy person, often a martyr. Relics are often credited with curative or miraculous powers and are associated with various religions throughout the world. The cult of holy relics in the Christian church had its beginnings around the 7th century AD, and reliquaries were numerous by the 10th century. The Crusades were a stimulus to the traffic in relics, many being brought back to Europe by the Crusaders for presentation to churches, monasteries, and cathedrals, where they became the goals of pilgrimages.

Reliquaries took many forms: caskets, miniature church buildings such as the Eltenberg Reliquary (c.1170; Victoria and Albert Museum, London), and figural works. Examples of the latter kind include the reliquary busts of Saint Januarius (1304–06; Naples Cathedral) and Charlemagne (1215; Aachen Cathedral). Related to these are "anatomical" reliquaries in the form of the contained relic, such as those for the arm of Saint Magnus and the leg of Saint Theodore (both 11th century; Saint Mark's Church, Venice). A particular flat, rectangular form called *staurotheke* was devised during the 11th century to contain relics of the True Cross (the one on which Christ was crucified). Small reliquaries were also made to wear as amulets. The SAINTE-CHAPELLE in Paris was built (1248) in the form of a reliquary to house the Crown of Thorns.

BETTY ELZEA

Bibliography: Henderson, George, *Early Medieval* (1972) and *Gothic* (1967).

Remarque, Erich Maria   [ruh-mahrk']

Author of one of the most influential works of the 20th century, Erich Maria Remarque, b. Erich Paul Remark in Osnabrück, Germany, June 22, 1898, d. Sept. 25, 1970, became world-famous following the publication of his first novel, ALL QUIET ON THE WESTERN FRONT (1929; Eng. trans., 1929). Remarque drew on his experiences as a young soldier in World War I for the book whose title contrasts ironically with the

Erich Maria Remarque is best remembered as the author of one of the most highly regarded novels dealing with World War I, All Quiet on the Western Front (1929). Many of his subsequent works concern the plight of stateless refugees, a subject close to Remarque, for his own German citizenship was revoked by the Nazis in 1938.

naturalistically described horrors of a "quiet" day on the front. A sequel, *The Road Back* (1931; Eng. trans., 1931), and *Three Comrades* (1938; Eng. trans., 1937) had more limited success. With his books banned (1933) by the Nazis and his citizenship abrogated (1938), Remarque emigrated (1939) to the United States. Of his later novels, dealing mostly with war or exile, which include *Spark of Life* (1952; Eng. trans., 1951), *The Black Obelisk* (1956; Eng. trans., 1957), and *The Night in Lisbon* (1963; Eng. trans., 1964), only one, *Arc de Triomphe* (1946; Eng. trans., 1946), achieved widespread success.

G. W. FIELD

Rembrandt   [rem'-brant]

The Dutch artist Rembrandt Harmenszoon van Rijn, b. July 15?, 1606, d. Oct. 4, 1669, was one of the greatest masters of

(Above) *Rembrandt, whose ability to dramatize facial expression is unrivaled, painted several portraits of himself. In this Self Portrait (1658), done in his 52d year, he is transfixed by anxious introspection. (Kunsthistorisches Museum, Vienna.)*

(Left) *Commissioned to paint a philosopher, Rembrandt executed Aristotle Contemplating the Bust of Homer (1653), a work displaying the full force of his imagination. Aristotle, dressed as a man of Rembrandt's time, is surrounded by darkness but bathed in light that seems to emanate from the poet's image. (Metropolitan Museum of Art, New York City.)*

European art. His paintings, drawings, and etchings have been admired and avidly collected since the 17th century. They express a range of emotions and moods that convey Rembrandt's sensitivity to humanity and to nature. Above all, his works reveal a profound understanding of complex psychological interactions.

Rembrandt's early career as an artist sheds light on two aspects of his personality: his sympathetic awareness of individuals encountered in everyday life and his desire to become a history painter, that is, an artist who depicted scenes from classical mythology, Christian legend, and ancient history. Rembrandt grew up in humble circumstances in Leiden. He enrolled (1620) at the University of Leiden, which he left (1621) to begin his training as an artist. After studying with two obscure Leiden painters, Rembrandt went to Amsterdam (c.1624) to study with the history painter Pieter LASTMAN. He returned to Leiden six months later and worked there as an independent artist until 1631–32, when he once again went to Amsterdam.

During his Leiden period Rembrandt made many studies of peasants, the elderly, and members of his family in paintings, prints, and drawings. He also produced a number of self-portraits. In a series of etchings dating from the late 1620s, he experimented with different expressions and with CHIAROSCURO, or contrasting light and shadow effects, to determine how it could enhance the drama of a composition. In the *Presentation in the Temple* (1631; Mauritshuis, The Hague), Rembrandt's chiaroscuro effect focuses attention on the main figure group by shrouding the surrounding space in darkness.

Around 1633, Rembrandt received an important commission from Prince Frederick Henry of Orange (1584–1647) for a series of paintings depicting the Passion of Christ. The compositional source for one of these paintings, *Descent from the Cross* (1633; Alte Pinakothek, Munich), was Peter Paul Rubens's great altarpiece in Antwerp, which was known to Rembrandt through a print.

Rembrandt apparently moved to Amsterdam about 1632 because of the opportunities available there in PORTRAITURE. In his first major portrait commission, *The Anatomy Lesson of Dr. Tulp* (1632; Mauritshuis), he used strong chiaroscuro accents and expressive poses to transform a staid group portrait into an animated gathering. This facility with group portraits greatly enhanced Rembrandt's reputation, and for the remainder of the decade he was at the height of his fame.

In 1634 Rembrandt married Saskia van Uylenburgh, the daughter of a respected and wealthy family, who became his favorite model. In 1639 he purchased a large home in Amsterdam, now the Rembrandthuis Museum. He also attracted many students, more than 50 of whom are known by name, including Govert Flinck (1615–60), Nicolaes MAES, and Carel Fabritius (1622–54).

The culmination of Rembrandt's popular success as an artist was his largest work, *Night Watch* (1642; originally *Militia Company of Captain Frans Banning Cocq;* Rijksmuseum, Amsterdam). The drama and excitement of this painting, which depicts figures apparently readying themselves for a procession, provides yet another example of Rembrandt's ability to transform a traditional group portrait into a dramatic event.

The 1640s was a period of transition for Rembrandt. The exuberance of his earlier works gave way to more restrained treatment, especially after Saskia died (1642) shortly following the birth of Titus (d. 1668), Rembrandt's only surviving son. Rembrandt turned his attention to such quiet and reflective scenes as that depicted in his etching called *The Hundred Guilder Print* (c.mid-1640s), which represents Christ as a warm and understanding teacher preaching to the poor and infirm.

Rembrandt's paintings of the 1650s and 1660s gained in power and conviction through his ability to focus on the essential elements of the pictorial subject. One of the most impressive of his mature paintings is *Jacob Blessing the Sons of Joseph* (1656; Gemäldegalerie, Kassel). Leonardo da Vinci's *Last Supper,* known to Rembrandt through a 16th-century print, was the compositional basis for a number of his paintings, including the *Syndics* (1661–62; Rijksmuseum) and his

Conspiracy of Julius Civilis (1661 or 1662; Nationalmuseum, Stockholm).

Although Rembrandt was not a fashionable artist during his later years and had many financial difficulties, including a declaration of insolvency (1656), the myths surrounding his isolation from Dutch society are ill-founded, as he continued to receive important commissions until his death.

ARTHUR K. WHEELOCK, JR.

Bibliography: Benesch, Otto, *The Drawings of Rembrandt, a Critical and Chronological Catalogue,* 6 vols., rev. ed. (1973); Bredius, Abraham, *Rembrandt: The Complete Edition of the Paintings,* rev. ed. (1969); Clark, Kenneth M., *An Introduction to Rembrandt* (1978) and *Rembrandt and the Italian Renaissance* (1966); Gerson, Horst, *Rembrandt Paintings,* trans. by Heinz Norden (1968); Haak, Bob, *Rembrandt, His Life, Work, and Times,* trans. by Elizabeth Willems-Treeman (1969); Rosenberg, Jakob, *Rembrandt,* 2 vols., 2d rev. ed. (1964); Slive, Seymour, *Rembrandt and His Critics: 1630–1730* (1953) and *Drawings of Rembrandt with a Selection of Drawings by His Pupils and Followers,* 2 vols. (1965); White, Christopher, *Rembrandt and His World* (1964) and *Rembrandt as an Etcher: A Study of the Artist at Work* (1969); White, Christopher, and Boon, Karel G., *Rembrandt's Etchings: An Illustrated Catalogue,* 2 vols. (1970).

Remek, Vladimir   [re'-mek]

The Czech cosmonaut Vladimir Remek, b. Sept. 26, 1948, was the first person of neither U.S. nor Soviet citizenship to fly in space. Prior to being chosen (1976) in the first group of East European cosmonauts, Capt. Remek, the son of the deputy defense minister of Czechoslovakia, was a jet pilot who had attended aviation schools in Czechoslovakia and the USSR. Together with Commander Aleksei GUBAREV, he was launched into space on board SOYUZ 28, on Mar. 2, 1978. The spaceship docked with the SALYUT 6 space station with two cosmonauts already on board, for a week of joint space research. Gubarev and Remek returned to Earth on March 10.   JAMES OBERG

Bibliography: Hooper, Gordon R., "Missions to Salyut 6," *Spaceflight,* December 1978.

Remembrance of Things Past

A monumental, kaleidoscopic work that combines in its seven constituent novels characteristics of several different fictional forms, Marcel PROUST's *À la recherche du temps perdu* (1913–27; trans. as *Remembrance of Things Past,* 1931) is one of the most impressive novels of the 20th century. Simultaneously a document of fashionable French society during the *belle époque* and World War I, and an introspective journey "in search of lost time," the narrator follows his memory from early childhood through the loves and social aspirations of his youth to his perception in middle age that the past cannot be recaptured by an act of the will. Time, Marcel concludes, can be transcended only by art, and the work ends with his resolve to write, to fix in literature the world he has known.

The individual novels constituting the work include, in the translation by C. K. Scott Moncrieff, *Swann's Way* (1913), *Within a Budding Grove* (1918), *The Guermantes Way* (1920–21), *Cities of the Plain* (1921–22), *The Captive* (1923), *The Sweet Cheat Gone* (1925), and, in the translation of Andreas Mayor, *The Past Recaptured* (1927; Eng. trans., 1951).

Bibliography: Green, Frederick C., *The Mind of Proust: A Detailed Interpretation of A la Recherche du Temps Perdu* (1949); Moss, Howard, *The Magic Lantern of Marcel Proust* (1962); Spaulding, Philip A., *A Reader's Handbook to Remembrance of Things Past,* rev. ed. (1975).

Remington, Frederic

An American artist who recorded the rapidly disappearing Wild West, Frederic Sackrider Remington, b. Canton, N.Y., Oct. 1 or 4, 1861, d. Dec. 26, 1909, first made his reputation as an illustrator and painter. In 1881 he began wandering around the western United States, working for a time as a cowboy. After studying (1886) painting at the Art Student's League in New York with J. Alden Weir, Remington continued to visit the West, where he followed the campaigns of the U.S. cavalry. His first commission for *Harper's Weekly* illustrated an

Trooper of the Plains (1868), a small bronze sculpture by Frederic Remington, displays this 19th-century artist's fascination with the life of the American pioneer. Remington did much to create the legend of the Wild West. (Metropolitan Museum of Art, New York City.)

incident that occurred in the last great Indian war led by Geronimo.

By 1891, Remington settled in New Rochelle, N.Y., where he filled his studio with the western material that provided the specific details upon which he based his paintings. No matter how exciting the scenes, his literal definition of the blue-jacketed pony soldiers and Indians and the naturalistic relation of form and space save his work from the sensationalism common to contemporary dime novels.

Watching the sculptor Frederic Ruckstull at work during the summer of 1895 inspired Remington to model his cowboys, Indians, and troopers in clay. Although his bronze Bronco Buster (1895; one version in New-York Historical Society, New York City) contains all the details characteristic of his paintings, the form is sculptural in conception. The three-dimensional medium helped Remington heighten the vitality of the rearing horse.

During the Spanish-American War, Remington worked as an artist and correspondent in Cuba, supplying illustrations for periodicals. The Old West, however, remained his favorite subject. Comin' through the Rye (1902; Metropolitan Museum of Art, New York City) presents four uproarious cowboys riding out on ponies whose hooves barely touch the ground. The group rejects such traditional sculptural principles as the expression of weight and support and suspended action in favor of levitation and directed movement.

JOAN SIEGFRIED

Bibliography: Baigell, Matthew, The Western Art of Frederic Remington (1976); Hassrich, Peter, Frederic Remington: Paintings, Drawings, and Sculpture in the Amon Carter Museum and Sid W. Richardson Foundations Collections (1973); McCracken, Harold, Frederic Remington, Artist of the Old West (1947); Wear, Bruce, The Bronze World of Frederic Remington (1966).

Remizov, Aleksei Mikhailovich   [rem'-ee-zuhf]

Aleksei Mikhailovich Remizov, b. July 6 (N.S.), 1877, d. Nov. 28, 1957, became recognized before World War I as one of Russia's most original poets. An heir of the Symbolist movement, he restored to the literary language forgotten expressions and enriched it with many neologisms.

Remizov viewed the Communist takeover of 1917 as a calamity; this opinion was reflected in The Lay on the Destruction of the Russian Land (1918) and in Russia in Turmoil (1921), the latter a striking panorama of the Russian Revolution. Emigrating to Paris in 1921, Remizov continued to publish, although his difficult style has delayed widespread translation of his works.

MAURICE FRIEDBERG

Remojadas   [ray-moh-hah'-dahs]

The archaeological site of Remojadas, near the mouth of the Tecolutla River in Veracruz, Mexico, has given its name to a distinctive style of pre-Columbian American pottery found in the surrounding region. Remojadas pottery actually represents a wide variety of ceramic vessels and figurines, spanning 2,000 or more years. Lower Remojadas includes preclassic material of the 1st millennium BC. Ceramics of the Upper Remojadas, dating from the classic period (AD 250–950), show relationships with the styles of EL TAJÍN and TEOTIHUACÁN.

JOHN S. HENDERSON

Bibliography: Adams, R. E. W., Prehistoric Mesoamerica (1977).

Remonstrants   [rem-ahn'-struhnts]

The name Remonstrants was given to the followers of the Dutch Protestant reformer Jacobus Arminius (1560–1609; see ARMINIANISM) who in 1610 drew up a document known as the Remonstrance. This document, after asserting the primacy of Scripture over creeds, set forth a revision of CALVINISM: Christ died for all, not only for the elect; divine GRACE is not irresistible; Christians can fall from grace, through free will, and be lost. These affirmations constituted a rejection of the most extreme Calvinist interpretation of PREDESTINATION.

The Remonstrants were condemned by the Dutch Reformed Church at the Synod of Dort (1618–19). Fourteen years of persecution followed, during which their services were forbidden and their clergy silenced or exiled. Among the refugees arose a Remonstrant Reformed Brotherhood which, after the ban was lifted in 1623, became the Remonstrant Reformed Church Community. It continued as a small free church after 1795, when full toleration was established, and influenced evangelical theology in both the Netherlands and the United States. The present membership in the Netherlands is about 25,000.

FREDERICK A. NORWOOD

Bibliography: Harrison, A. W., Arminianism (1937).

remora   [rem'-uh-ruh]

The striped remora, Echeneis naucrates, which is up to 1 m (3.3 ft) long, is the largest of the species of remora. The prominent sucking disk on the remora's head acts by suction to hold the fish's host.

Remoras are about 9 species of long-bodied fishes, ranging from approximately 15 cm to 1 m (6 in to 3 ft) in length, that spend much of their lives attached to sharks, whales, and other large marine bodies. Attachment is by means of an oval disk on the top of the head. The disk is a modification of the spiny first dorsal fin, with the spines split in two and spread downward to form about 11 to 24 movable cross-ridges that divide the disk into many small, shallow chambers. To attach to an object, the remora presses the disk against it, sealing the chambers; the cross-ridges are then raised, forming a partial vacuum that holds the fish securely. Because the ridges are raised by pivoting forward, a force pushing the remora rearward (as would occur when attached to a swimming host) pivots the ridges higher, increasing the hold. A forward movement by the remora pushes the ridges back down, detaching the fish. Remoras are commonly thought to attach to feed on leftover scraps of their hosts' meals or on their external parasites, but instead it appears rather likely that the remoras have primarily evolved an almost energy-free method of travel. Remoras, constituting the family Echeneididae, are found worldwide in warm seas.

remote control: see AUTOMATION; FEEDBACK; SERVOMECHANISM.

remote sensing

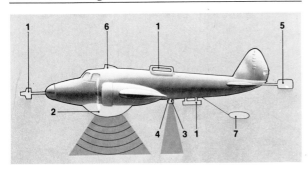

Remote-sensing equipment is often carried in aircraft to gather and record data about the Earth's surface and atmosphere. Types shown include nonimaging electromagnetic systems (1); microwave radar systems (2); photographic optical systems (3); television systems (4); systems for measuring gamma radiation (5); systems for sampling air (6); and systems for measuring the magnetic field (7).

Remote sensing is the science of detecting and measuring or analyzing a substance or object from a distance.

There are two broad classes of remote sensors: active and passive. Active remote sensors—for example, radar—transmit some form of energy such as an electromagnetic pulse and detect the energy reflected or otherwise returned from the subject. Passive remote sensors, such as cameras, depend on emissions or reflections of energy from natural sources.

History. The term *remote sensing* is relatively new, having come into general use in the 1960s, but the concept began in the 19th century. Cameras are one of the oldest forms of passive remote sensors, and X-ray devices, radar, and sonar have a considerable history as active remote sensors. Photography using near-infrared (radiation just beyond the visible spectrum) was first used during World War II to detect camouflage consisting of dead or artificial foliage. Since then it has been used to monitor the health of vegetation for agricultural and forestry applications. Thermal infrared heat-detection radiometers were also developed during World War II and their use greatly expanded thereafter. Microwave radiometers were developed from sensitive radar receivers toward the end of World War II. Many major advances in remote sensing occurred during the 1960s along with the development of laser systems and advances in the space program.

Applications. The first uses of remote sensing were primarily military, but environmental and energy-related applications are now the most promising. Some of these include: hydrological applications, such as precipitation measurement, monitoring snow depth and ice cover, flood control, hydroelectric generation, and water transport management; agricultural applications, such as monitoring crop types, acreage, stage of growth, soil moisture, blights or infestations, and expected yields; and forestry applications, such as monitoring types of trees, stage of growth, and lightning and fires.

Meteorological applications encompass monitoring severe storms, detecting and measuring precipitation, monitoring clouds and their movement, measuring winds and turbulence, and monitoring insolation (the daily influx of solar energy). Ecological and pollution applications consist of biological monitoring, thermal pollution (waste-heat) monitoring, and air- and water-pollution monitoring. Geographic and geologic applications include land-use and terrain mapping, geological mapping, and detection of mineral deposits. Oceanographic applications encompass monitoring of waves, currents, tem-

perature, salinity, turbidity, and other parameters and phenomena. Other diverse applications include air traffic control, probing other planets and deep space, and law enforcement.

Principles and Instrumentation. Most active and passive remote sensors employ a detecting or sensing system that scans or surveils the subject, a recording system that stores the information received, and an analysis or display system. Sometimes a combined analysis and display system is operated concurrently with the sensing system in order to aid in data gathering and to provide some preliminary information. In that case recordings are made and later analyzed in the typical manner. The displays are two-dimensional, usually composed of many scan lines from the sensor similar to aerial photographs or television pictures.

The term *signature* is applied in remote sensing to any identifying feature that appears in the analysis or display process through which a desired subject can be positively identified against what may be a complex background or surroundings. For example, it may be necessary to identify a particular mineral, crop blight, or type of air or water pollution. Signature, as applied to imagery, usually refers to visual characteristics that identify the subject and separate it from other similar objects. However, other types of signatures may be much more complex, requiring spectral analysis or other techniques.

Remote sensors may be surface-based, stationary or mobile, on land or sea; airborne in aircraft, helicopters, or balloons; or carried aboard spacecraft, such as satellites, a space shuttle, or a space station. These various bases are usually referred to as sensor platforms. The resolution, or detail with which a remote sensor can monitor a subject, generally depends on the distance from the sensor platform to the subject.

For a given platform, the remote sensors that employ the shortest wavelengths (highest frequencies) usually provide the best resolution of the subject. One reason for this is that the size of the sensor system required to obtain a given resolution increases as the sensor wavelength increases. Thus microwave sensors that operate at wavelengths longer than those of thermal infrared generally produce poorer resolution.

However, there is an important tradeoff for this requirement of larger equipment and generally poorer resolution as the sensor wavelength is increased. The longer wavelengths have the best penetration power. Microwaves, for example, can penetrate through clouds, whereas visible and infrared wavelengths do not. This is true for both active and passive sensors. Therefore, microwave radar systems can be used to penetrate and sense subjects that are not visible to optical-wavelength laser radar systems. Also, microwave systems can be used to penetrate vegetation for geologic mapping, to monitor snow depths, and to indicate soil moisture.

Microwave radars are used to measure and map the precipitation patterns and other parameters of hurricanes and other severe storms. Thermal infrared and microwave radiometers can monitor and measure urban "heat islands," waste-heat discharges in water, and natural warm and cold water currents. Outside the electromagnetic spectrum, acoustic sounders are used to detect and measure stratified thermal layers in the atmosphere for air-pollution and meteorological applications.

H. W. HISER

Bibliography: Barrett, E.C., and Curtis, L. R., *Introduction to Environmental Remote Sensing*, 2d ed. (1982); Crackneld, A. P., *Remote Sensing in Meteorology, Oceanography, and Hydrology* (1981); Lillesand, T. M., and Kiefer, R. W., *Remote Sensing and Image Interpretation* (1979); Mooradian, A., and Killinger, D. K., *Optical and Laser Remote Sensing* (1983); Sabins, F. F., Jr., *Remote Sensing: Principles and Interpretation* (1978); Veziroglu, T. N., ed., *Remote Sensing Energy-Related Studies* (1975).

Renaissance [ren'-uh-sahns]

The term Renaissance, describing the period of European history from the early 14th to the late 16th century, is derived from the French word for rebirth, and originally referred to the revival of the values and artistic styles of classical antiquity during that period, especially in Italy. To Giovanni BOCCACCIO in the 14th century, the concept applied to contemporary Italian efforts to imitate the poetic style of the ancient Romans. In 1550 the art historian Giorgio VASARI used the word *rinascita* (rebirth) to describe the return to the ancient Roman manner of painting by GIOTTO DI BONDONE about the beginning of the 14th century.

It was only later that the word *Renaissance* acquired a broader meaning. Voltaire in the 18th century classified the Renaissance in Italy as one of the great ages of human cultural achievement. In the 19th century, Jules MICHELET and Jakob BURCKHARDT popularized the idea of the Renaissance as a distinct historical period heralding the modern age, characterized by the rise of the individual, scientific inquiry and geographical exploration, and the growth of secular values. In the 20th century the term was broadened to include other revivals of classical culture, such as the Carolingian Renaissance of the 9th century or the Renaissance of the 12th century. Emphasis on medieval renaissances tended to undermine a belief in the unique and distinctive qualities of the Italian Renaissance, and some historians of science, technology, and economy even denied the validity of the term. Today the concept of the Renaissance is firmly secured as a cultural and intellectual movement; most scholars would agree that there is a distinctive Renaissance style in music, literature, and the arts.

The Renaissance as a Historical Period.   The new age began in Padua and other urban communes of northern Italy in the 14th century, where lawyers and notaries imitated ancient Latin style and studied Roman archaeology. The key figure in this study of the classical heritage was PETRARCH, who spent most of his life attempting to understand ancient culture and captured the enthusiasm of popes, princes, and emperors who wanted to learn more of Italy's past. Petrarch's success stirred countless others to follow literary careers hoping for positions in government and high society. In the next generations, students of Latin rhetoric and the classics, later known as humanists, became chancellors of Venice and Florence, secretaries at the papal court, and tutors and orators in the despotic courts of northern Italy. Renaissance HUMANISM became the major intellectual movement of the period, and its achievements became permanent.

By the 15th century intensive study of the Greek as well as Latin classics, ancient art and archaeology, and classical history, had given Renaissance scholars a more sophisticated view of antiquity. The ancient past was now viewed as past, to be admired and imitated, but not to be revived.

In many ways, the period of the Renaissance saw a decline from the prosperity of the High Middle Ages. The Black Death (bubonic and pneumonic plague), which devastated Europe in the mid-14th century, reduced its population by as much as one-third, creating chaotic economic conditions. Labor became scarce, industries contracted, and the economy stagnated, but agriculture was put on a sounder basis as unneeded marginal land went out of cultivation. Probably the actual per capita wealth of the survivors of the Black Death rose in the second half of the 14th century. In general, the 15th century saw a modest recovery with the construction of palaces for

This painting is probably a likeness of Petrarch, a primary force in the development of the humanism characteristic of Renaissance thought. Mediating between classical and Christian philosophy, Petrarch inaugurated the age in which the intellectual focus shifted from theology to the development and experience of the individual.

the urban elites, a boom in the decorative arts, and renewed long-distance trade headed by Venice in the Mediterranean and the HANSEATIC LEAGUE in the north of Europe.

The culture of Renaissance Italy was distinguished by many highly competitive and advanced urban areas. Unlike England and France, Italy possessed no dominating capital city, but developed a number of centers for regional states: Milan for Lombardy, Rome for the Papal States, Florence and Siena for Tuscany, and Venice for northeastern Italy. Smaller centers of Renaissance culture developed around the brilliant court life at Ferrara, Mantua, and Urbino. The chief patrons of Renaissance art and literature were the merchant classes of Florence and Venice, which created in the Renaissance palace their

(Above) Three of Florence's greatest 15th-century scholars (left to right), Pico della Mirandola, Marsilio Ficino, and Politian, are seen in a detail from Cosimo Rosselli's Miracle of the Sacrament *(c.1486; Sant' Ambrogio, Florence). (Left) Under the patronage of the Medici family, portrayed in Benozzo Gozzoli's* Procession of the Magi *(c.1459), Florence flourished as an intellectual and artistic center of the Italian Renaissance. (Palazzo Medici-Riccardi, Florence.)*

(Above) *Desiderius Erasmus, seen in a portrait by Hans Holbein the Younger, is considered the greatest classicist of the northern Renaissance. (Louvre, Paris.)*

(Below) *An ink sketch of Sir Thomas More and his family by Hans Holbein the Younger was found among Erasmus' papers. More, a Christian humanist closely associated with Erasmus, was one of the major figures of the English Renaissance. (Palazzo Ducale, Urbino, Italy.)*

own distinctive home and workplace, fitted for both business and rearing and nurture of the next generation of urban rulers. The later Renaissance was marked by a growth of bureaucracy, an increase in state authority in the areas of justice and taxation, and the creation of larger regional states. During the interval of relative peace from the mid-15th century until the French invasions of 1494, Italy experienced a great flowering of culture, especially in Florence and Tuscany under the MEDICI. The brilliant period of artistic achievement continued into the 16th century—the age of LEONARDO DA VINCI, RAPHAEL, TITIAN, and MICHELANGELO—but as Italy began to fall under foreign domination, the focus gradually shifted to other parts of Europe.

During the 15th century, students from many European nations had come to Italy to study the classics, philosophy, and the remains of antiquity, eventually spreading the Renaissance north of the Alps. Italian literature and art, even Italian clothing and furniture designs were imitated in France, Spain, England, the Netherlands, and Germany, but as Renaissance values came to the north, they were transformed. Northern humanists such as Desiderius ERASMUS of the Netherlands and John Colet (c.1467–1519) of England planted the first seeds of the Reformation when they endeavored to discover the original intent and meaning of the New Testament by applying to it the critical historical methods developed in Italy. The northern humanists—who, like their Italian counterparts, served as advisors to kings and princes—created a flexible, colloquial Latin style so that their writings would have a broad appeal. Through their efforts, knowledge of classical mythology, ancient history, and Greek and Latin literary forms became widespread and was soon absorbed into the vernacular literature.

Philosophy, Science, and Social Thought. No single philosophy or ideology dominated the intellectual life of the Renaissance. Early humanists had stressed a flexible approach to the problems of society and the active life in service of one's fellow human beings. In the second half of the 15th century, Renaissance thinkers such as Marsilio FICINO at the Platonic Academy in Florence turned to more metaphysical speculation. Though favored by the humanists, Plato did not replace Aristotle as the dominant philosopher in the universities. Rather there was an effort at philosophical syncretism, to combine apparently conflicting philosophies, and find common ground for agreement about the truth as did Giovanni PICO DELLA MIRANDOLA in his *Oration on the Dignity of Man* (1486). Renaissance science consisted mainly of the study of medicine, physics, and mathematics, depending on ancient

masters, such as Galen, Aristotle, and Euclid. Experimental science in anatomy and alchemy led to discoveries both within and outside university settings.

Under the veneer of magnificent works of art and the refined court life described in Baldassare CASTIGLIONE's *Book of the Courtier,* the Renaissance had a darker side. Warfare was common, and death by pestilence and violence was frequent. Interest in the occult, magic, and astrology was widespread, and the officially sanctioned persecution for witchcraft began during the Renaissance period. Many intellectuals felt a profound pessimism about the evils and corruptions of society as seen in the often savage humanist critiques of Poggio Bracciolini (1380–1459) and Desiderius Erasmus. Sir Thomas MORE, in his *Utopia,* prescribed the radical solution of a classless, communal society, bereft of Christianity and guided by the dictates of natural reason. The greatest Renaissance thinker, Nicolò MACHIAVELLI, in his *Prince* and *Discourses,* constructed a realistic science of human nature aiming at the reform of Italian society and the creation of a secure civil life. Machiavelli's republican principles informed by a pragmatic view of power politics and the necessity of violent change were the most original contribution of the Renaissance to the modern world.

Influence. The Renaissance lives on in established canons of taste and literature and in a distinctive Renaissance style in art, music, and architecture, the last often revived. It also provided the model of many-sided achievement of the creative genius, the "universal man," exemplified by Leonardo da Vinci or Leon Battista ALBERTI. Finally, the Renaissance spawned the great creative vernacular literature of the late 16th century: the earthy fantasies of RABELAIS, the worldly essays of MONTAIGNE, the probing analysis of the human condition in the plays of William SHAKESPEARE and in the work of Miguel de CERVANTES.   BENJAMIN G. KOHL

Bibliography: Baron, Hans, *Crisis of the Early Italian Renaissance,* rev. ed. (1966); Burckhardt, Jakob C., *The Civilization of the Renaissance in Italy* (1944); Ferguson, W. K., *The Renaissance in Historical Thought* (1948); Gilmore, Myron P., *The World of Humanism* (1952); Hale, J. R. (as ed.), *A Concise Encyclopaedia of the Italian Renaissance* (1981) and *Renaissance Europe, 1480–1520* (1971); Hay, Denys, *The Italian Renaissance in Its Historical Background,* 2d ed. (1977); Kristeller, Paul O., *Renaissance Thought and Its Sources* (1979); Miskimin, Harry A., *The Economy of the Early Renaissance* (1970).

Renaissance art and architecture

The term *Renaissance,* adopted from the French equivalent of the Italian word *rinascita,* meaning literally "rebirth," describes the radical and comprehensive changes that took place in European culture during the 15th and 16th centuries, bringing about the demise of the Middle Ages and embodying for the first time the values of the modern world. The consciousness of cultural rebirth was itself a characteristic of the Renaissance. Italian scholars and critics of this period proclaimed that their age had progressed beyond the barbarism of the past and had found its inspiration, and its closest parallel, in the civilizations of ancient Greece and Rome.

THE RENAISSANCE IN ITALY

The "rebirth" of art in Italy was connected with the rediscovery of ancient philosophy, literature, and science and the evolution of empirical methods of study in these fields. Increased awareness of classical knowledge created a new resolve to learn by direct observation and study of the natural world. Consequently, secular themes became increasingly important to artists, and with the revived interest in antiquity came a new repertoire of subjects drawn from Greek and Roman history and mythology. The models provided by ancient buildings and works of art also inspired the development of new artistic techniques and the desire to re-create the forms and styles of classical art.

The emergence of the artist as a creator, rather than a mere artisan, sought after by patrons and respected for his erudition and imagination, was both a result and a prime cause of

(Left) *Donatello's bronze* David *(c.1430–32), the first nude statue in the round to be made since ancient times, embodies the revitalized classicism that infused Italian art during the Early Renaissance. (Bargello, Florence.)

the development of Renaissance art. As the social role of the artist charged, so did attitudes toward art. Art was valued, not merely as a vehicle for religious and social didacticism, but as a mode of personal expression to be judged on aesthetic grounds.

Although the evolution of Italian Renaissance art was a continuous process, it is traditionally divided into three major phases: Early, High, and Late Renaissance. The last phase has been the subject in recent years of complex interpretations that recognize many competing and contrasting trends. Some scholars date the beginning of the Italian Renaissance from the appearance of GIOTTO DI BONDONE in the early 14th century; others regard his prodigious achievements in naturalistic art as an isolated phenomenon. According to the second view, the consistent development of Renaissance style began only with the generation of artists active in Florence at the beginning of the 15th century.

The Early Renaissance. The principal members of the first generation of Renaissance artists—DONATELLO in sculpture, Filippo BRUNELLESCHI in architecture, and MASACCIO in painting—shared many important characteristics. Central to their thinking was a faith in the theoretical foundations of art and the conviction that development and progress were not only possible but essential to the life and significance of the arts. Ancient art was revered, not only as an inspiring model but also as a record of trial and error that could reveal the successes of former great artists. Intending to retrace the creative process rather than to merely imitate the final achievements of antiquity, Early Renaissance artists sought to create art forms consistent with the appearance of the natural world and with their experience of human personality and behavior. The challenge of accurate representation as it concerned the mass, weight, and movement of sculptural form, or the pictorial considerations of measurable space and the effects of light and color, was addressed in the spirit of intense and methodical inquiry.

Rational inquiry was believed to be the key to success; therefore, efforts were made to discover the correct laws of proportion for architecture and for the representation of the human body and to systematize the rendering of pictorial space. Although these artists were keenly observant of natural phenomena, they also tended to extrapolate general rules from specific appearances. Similarly, they made an effort to go beyond straightforward transcription of nature, to instill the work of art with ideal, intangible qualities, endowing it with a beauty and significance greater and more permanent than that actually found in nature. These characteristics—the

(Below) *Florence Cathedral, also known as* Santa Maria del Fiore *and as the* Duomo, *was begun by Arnolfo di Cambio in 1295 and, after innumerable enlargements and delays, completed in 1462. The huge octagon supporting the dome was finished in 1414; in 1420, Filippo Brunelleschi, the first great architect and engineer of the Early Renaissance, began the vast dome, built with an inner shell of brick and a thinner double shell roof.*

Masaccio's The Tribute Money *(1425), a key work in the development of Renaissance painting, depicts three scenes from the Gospel of Matthew. The Apostles are grouped around Christ* (center), *who settles the dispute between Saint Peter* (left) *and the tax collector of Capernaum* (right). *At the far left, Peter finds a coin in a fish's mouth; at the far right, he pays the tax with the coin. (Brancacci Chapel, Santa Maria del Carmine, Florence.)*

rendering of ideal forms rather than literal appearance and the concept of the physical world as the vehicle or imperfect embodiment of monumental spiritual beauty—were to remain fundamental to the nature and development of Italian Renaissance art.

The term *Early Renaissance* characterizes virtually all the art of the 15th century. Florence, the cradle of Renaissance artistic thought, remained one of the undisputed centers of innovation. About 1450 a new generation of artists that included such masters as Pollaiuolo (see POLLAIUOLO family) and Sandro BOTTICELLI came to the fore in Florence. Other Italian cities—Milan, Urbino, Ferrara, Venice, Padua, Naples—be-

The High Renaissance. The art of the High Renaissance, however, sought a general, unified effect of pictorial representation or architectural composition, increasing the dramatic force and physical presence of a work of art and gathering its energies and forming a controlled equilibrium. Because the essential characteristic of High Renaissance art was its unity—a balance achieved as a matter of intuition, beyond the reach of rational knowledge or technical skill—the High Renaissance style was destined to break up as soon as emphasis was shifted to favor any one element in the composition.

The High Renaissance style endured for only a brief period (c.1495–1520) and was created by a few artists of genius,

(Left) *The erotic* Venus and Mars, *painted (c.1480) by Sandro Botticelli to ornament a bedroom, is imbued with the same fervor as his religious works. (National Gallery, London.) (Below) In* The Dead Christ *(c.1480), Andrea Mantegna transforms a virtuosic exercise in extreme foreshortening into an unforgettable expression of grief, suffering, and grim reality. (Brera, Milan.)*

came powerful rivals in the spreading wave of change. Leon Battista ALBERTI's work in Rimini and Mantua represented the most progressive architecture of the new HUMANISM; Andrea MANTEGNA's paintings in Padua displayed a personal formulation of linear perspective, antiquarianism, and realistic technique; and Giovanni Bellini's (see BELLINI family) poetic classicism exemplified the growing strength of the Venetian school.

By the late 15th century the novelty of the first explosive advances of Renaissance style had given way to a general acceptance of such basic notions as proportion, contraposto (twisted pose), and linear perspective; consequently many artists sought means of personal expression within this relatively well-established repertoire of style and technique. The Early Renaissance was not, as was once maintained, merely an imperfect but necessary preparation for the perfection of High Renaissance art but a period of great intrinsic merit. In retrospect, however, Early Renaissance painting seems to fall short of thoroughly convincing figural representation, and its expression of human emotion is stylized rather than real. Furthermore, the strength of individual features of a work of art is disproportionate to the whole composition.

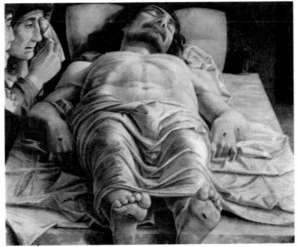

among them LEONARDO DA VINCI, Donato BRAMANTE, MICHELAN-GELO, RAPHAEL, and TITIAN. Leonardo da Vinci's unfinished *Adoration of the Magi* (1481; Uffizi Gallery, Florence) is regarded as a landmark of unified pictorial composition, later realized fully in his fresco *The Last Supper* (1495–97; Santa Maria delle Grazie, Milan). Leonardo is considered the paragon of Renaissance thinkers, engaged as he was in experiments of all kinds and having brought to his art a spirit of restless inquiry that sought to discover the laws governing diverse natural phenomena. In a different way, Michelangelo has come to typify the artist endowed with inexplicable, solitary genius. His universal talents are exemplified by the tomb of Julius II (c.1510–15), San Pietro in Vincoli, Rome; the Medici Chapel (1519–34), Florence; the SISTINE CHAPEL ceiling (1508–12) and *Last Judgment* (1536–41), Rome; and the cupola of SAINT PETER'S BASILICA (begun 1546)—works that represent major and inimitable accomplishments in the separate fields of sculpture, painting, and architecture. Raphael, a man of very different temperament, evoked, in paintings of Madonnas and in frescoes, not overwhelming forces but sublime harmony and lyric, graceful beauty.

The Late Renaissance. A major watershed in the development of Italian Renaissance art was the sack of Rome in 1527, which temporarily ended the city's role as a source of patronage and compelled artists to travel to other centers in Italy, France, and Spain. Even before the death of Raphael, in 1520, anticlassical tendencies had begun to manifest themselves in

Raphael's tender Madonna of the Chair *(1513–14) is perhaps the most intimate of his many versions of the subject. Intended for private devotion, the painting is in the tondo (circular) form fashionable in the High Renaissance; the exquisite facial features make the work among his most appealing. (Pitti Palace, Florence.)*

In The Virgin and Child with Saint Anne *(begun c.1501), all of the High Renaissance achievements in technique and approach are brought by Leonardo da Vinci to a familiar subject. The solidly modeled figures, bathed in serene light, are silhouetted against a spectral mountain landscape in deep perspective. (Louvre, Paris.)*

Roman art. Some early exponents of MANNERISM, including Jacopo Carucci PONTORMO, PARMIGIANINO, and ROSSO FIOREN-TINO, contributed to the development of a style that reached its most extreme expression in the work of Giorgio VASARI and Giovanni da BOLOGNA. Mannerism was an aesthetic movement that valued highly refined grace and elegance—the beautiful *maniera*, or style, from which Mannerism takes its name. Although the fundamental characteristics of Late Renaissance style were shared by many artists, this period, dominated by Mannerism, was marked by artistic individuality—a quality demonstrated to its fullest extent by the late works of Michelangelo. The display of individual virtuosity became an important criterion of artistic achievement, and rivalry often provoked competition based on brilliance of individual performance. The self-consciousness of Mannerist artists, and their efforts to match or surpass the great masters who had immediately preceded them, were the symptoms of a somewhat overripe development, far removed from the fresh dawn of discovery that first gave meaning to the concept of the Renaissance.

The Tempietto, built in 1502 by the High Renaissance architect Donato Bramante, stands in the courtyard of Rome's San Pietro in Montorio over the traditional site of Saint Peter's crucifixion. The design is based on the ancient Temple of the Sibyl at Tivoli, but Bramante's addition of a high drum and a tall ribbed dome gives the shrine a soaring verticality. The little temple was to be surrounded by a round 16-column peristyle.

(Left) The Entombment *(1526) is the central painting in a series executed for the Capponi Chapel in Florence's Church of Santa Felicità by the Mannerist artist Jacopo Carrucci, more commonly called Pontormo. The bizarre elements of the work—the theatrical asymmetry of the composition, the absence of a real setting, the tormented facial expressions, the strangely colored garments that cling and float around the contorted figures— make it an example of Mannerism in its most extreme form; it heralds the end of the Renaissance and the beginning of baroque art.*

(Above) *Michelangelo's marble* Pietà *was commissioned in 1497 and completed by 1500, when the great High Renaissance master was in his mid-20s. The seated Virgin supports the body of the dead Christ across her lap, and with her left hand she makes a gesture that signifies acceptance of divine will. The group is carved with extreme delicacy, and the entire surface is highly polished, in the Early Renaissance sculptural tradition that Michelangelo had learned in Florence. (Saint Peter's Basilica, Vatican city.)*

(Left) *Giovanni da Bologna's most famous bronze statue is his* Mercury *(1564), of which this is one of several castings. A technical and artistic tour de force, the figure of the winged messenger of the gods is meant to be viewed from all sides. The deliberate complexity of the spiraling pose is characteristic of Mannerism, the final phase of Renaissance art. (Bargello, Florence.)*

THE RENAISSANCE IN THE NORTH

The Netherlands. Debate continues as to whether the concept of the Renaissance considered valid for Italy may be properly applied to the art of northern Europe prior to the year 1500.

Fifteenth-century northern artists did not intensively cultivate classical sources, nor did they show the predeliction for abstract and theoretical systems of representation that characterized Italian art. Nonetheless, the radical transformation of northern artistic traditions that took place during the 15th and 16th centuries, although by no means parallel to Italian developments, can be appropriately described as a Renaissance.

Jan van EYCK, the supreme master of the Netherlandish school, is recognized as having been the first to exploit the full potential of the new medium of oil painting. In his masterwork, the *Ghent Altarpiece* (1432; Church of Saint Bavo, Ghent), and in portraits such as the wedding portrait of Giovanni Arnolfini and his wife (1534; National Gallery, London), this technique is used with the utmost refinement to render minute detail, delicate textures, and the luminous effects of light.

The enigmatic Master of Flémalle (see CAMPIN, Robert) made an equally important contribution to the vivid, miniaturizing realism of Netherlandish painting. In his two most famous works, the Dijon *Nativity* (c.1420; Musée des Beaux-Arts, Dijon) and the *Merode Altarpiece* (c.1426; The Cloisters, New York City), the Master of Flémalle, like van Eyck, combined his direct, fresh observation of nature with elaborate symbolic structures that lend a profound dimension to mundane objects within his religious scenes.

Rogier van der WEYDEN, famous for portraits and altarpieces such as the *Descent from the Cross* (1439–43; Prado, Madrid), worked in a more idealistic vein, instilling his compositions with unprecedented monumentality and emotional intensity. With the rising importance of new schools of painting in the cities of Brussels, Louvain, and Haarlem, which came to rival that of Bruges, painting continued to flourish in the Netherlands during the mid- and late 15th century. Van der Weyden, an intriguing and idiosyncratic genius, exercised a dominant influence on many later figures including Dirk BOUTS. Other notable artists were the short-lived painter GEERTGEN TOT SINT JANS, who specialized in tender, nocturnal scenes that demonstrate a superb feeling for light effects; Hans MEMLING, whose style is characterized by a languid, delicate air; and Gerard DAVID, whose works were more severe and monumental in quality.

The greatest painter of the late 15th century, Hugo van der GOES, was active in Ghent and Bruges. His *Portinari Altarpiece* (1474–76; Uffizi Gallery, Florence), depicting the Nativity, is a work of crucial importance because it was executed for the Florentine church of San Egidio and introduced many Italian artists to the earthy and lively realism of Netherlandish oil painting technique.

Germany. German art of the 15th century was dominated by many local, independent schools. Largely based on the Gothic INTERNATIONAL STYLE, German art received important influences from the Netherlands that intensified as the century progressed. The painter-sculptor Hans MULTSCHER displayed a typically German blend of Gothic conventions, naturalistic observation, and a strange fascination with brutal aspects of human behavior. In Basel the painter Konrad WITZ created a severe and impressive style indebted to van Eyck; whereas the reputed pupil of Rogier van der Weyden, the painter-engraver Martin SCHONGAUER, emerged, through his graphic work, as an incredibly refined draftsman, eventually to serve as a model for Albrecht DÜRER.

The Renaissance in Germany is dominated by the great genius of Dürer, both a painter and engraver. His astonishing and unequaled performances in woodcut and engraving permanently transformed the graphic arts and greatly enhanced their potential (see ENGRAVING). Dürer's fascination with the world, his curiosity about the fundamental principles and theories that governed nature, and his desire to express its various beauties in ideal, monumental form, were features shared with Italian artists. It was in fact through his two visits to Italy, and contact there with such figures as Giovanni Bellini, that Dürer was stimulated to develop his unique style.

The art of Dürer's contemporary Mathias GRÜNEWALD, most fully represented by the multipaneled *Isenheim Altarpiece* (1515; Musée d'Unterlinden, Colmar, France), is by contrast filled with high-pitched expressive power conveyed through agonized human forms, and brilliant, piercing color schemes. The visionary and irrational aspect of Grünewald's art, rooted in the medieval world, is one of many echoes of the past that were to repeat themselves many times in the subsequent development of German art. Both Dürer and Grünewald had to contend personally with the spiritual and intellectual foment caused by the Protestant Reformation, which, although of profound religious and social consequence, produced no characteristic form of artistic expression.

So personal had been Dürer's involvement with southern Renaissance ideals, that no established school or tradition developed in his wake. The DANUBE SCHOOL—whose principal members, Lucas CRANACH the Elder, Albrecht ALTDORFER, and Wolf HUBER, reflected an extraordinary awakening of interest in landscape painting—was a loose grouping of masters. Despite their fascinating diversity they shared a common sympathy for miniaturizing anticlassical tendencies derived from late Gothic art.

Hans HOLBEIN the Younger, a painter of great talent and insight, was originally a member of the Augsburg school, a rival in importance to that in Nuremberg. He later practiced in Basel, and finally in England as court painter to Henry VIII, developing in the process a psychologically penetrating precise style of portraiture that paralleled in many ways work being done simultaneously in Italy and France.

France. In the 15th century the art of France, like that of Germany, came increasingly under the influence of the Nether-

The Descent from the Cross *(1439–43), the central panel of a lost altarpiece, is perhaps Rogier van der Weyden's most impressive achievement. The Flemish master placed his monumental figures in a sepulcher rather than in the customary landscape. (Prado, Madrid.)*

The four central panels of Jan van Eyck's large Ghent Altarpiece *(1432) depict the enthroned God the Father flanked by the Virgin Mary and John the Baptist; below, throngs of Apostles, saints, martyrs, and prophets converge to worship at the altar on which stands Christ as the Lamb of God. (Church of Saint Bavo, Ghent, Belgium.)*

landish school. The painter Jean FOUQUET and the anonymous master responsible for the celebrated *Villeneauve Pietà* (c.1460; Louvre, Paris) were also aware of contemporary Italian art. By introducing elements of clarity and stability in their work, they achieved a unique combination of formal weight and factual and portraitlike design.

At the beginning of the 16th century Italian styles became extremely popular in France because artists such as Leonardo da Vinci, Benvenuto CELLINI, Francesco PRIMATICCIO, Rosso Fiorentino, and Niccolò dell'Abbate (c.1512–71) were employed there by Francis I. Features of Italian Renaissance style were adopted at first by French artists in a rather superficial manner, producing effects of fascinating disquiet alongside native forms of medieval origin, in such hybrid structures as the Château de BLOIS (1515–20), which incorporates Italian decorative architectural elements with the medieval-style architecture.

Architecture burgeoned with the construction of the massive and luxurious Château de Chambord and Château de FONTAINEBLEAU. The court workshop established at the Château de Fontainebleau became an important center, known as the school of Fontainebleau (see FONTAINEBLEAU, SCHOOL OF), that in its exaggerated elegance and complex fantasies combining sculpture, painting, and architecture, represented a high point in the development of Mannerism.

By the mid-16th century a number of highly talented French masters made their appearance, among them the architect Philibert DELORME, who reasserted a classical style based on measure and proportion. The painter François Clouet (see CLOUET family) developed a highly polished and sensuous style of court portraiture, and during the last decades of the century Germain PILON produced sculptures that represent the highest achievements of the French Renaissance.

Reviewed by ULRICH HIESINGER

(Above) *The Château de Fontainebleau, one of the largest palaces in France, was begun by Francis I in 1528. In the Fountain Court, seen here across the Carp Pond, the inner left wing and the Gallery of Francis I at its back are parts of the original Renaissance palace.*

(Right) *Francis I on Horseback (c.1539) is attributed to Jean Clouet, chief painter to the king. The monarch is depicted in his black-and-gold parade armor. (Uffizi, Florence.)*

(Above) *One of the most brilliant paintings of the German Renaissance is* The Resurrection *from the gigantic* Isenheim Altarpiece *(1515) by Matthias Grünewald. (Musée d'Unterlinden, Colmar, France.)*

(Right) *The Four Horsemen of the Apocalypse is one of a series of 15 woodcuts illustrating the biblical text, made (c.1497–98) by Albrecht Dürer, Germany's most versatile Renaissance master. (Graphische Sammlungen, Munich.)*

Bibliography: Baron, Hans, *The Crisis of the Early Italian Renaissance* (1966); Benesch, Otto, *The Art of the Renaissance in Northern Europe,* 2d ed. (1965); Blunt, Anthony, *Artistic Theory in Italy, 1450–1600* (1940) and *Art and Architecture in France, 1500–1700,* 2d ed. (1970); Burckhardt, Jakob C., *The Civilization of the Renaissance in Italy,* 4th ed. (1960); Freedberg, Sydney J., *Painting in Italy 1500–1600* (1970) and *Painting of the High Renaissance in Rome and Florence,* 2 vols. (1961); Friedlander, Max J., *Early Netherlandish Painting,* 14 vols., trans. by Heinz Norden (1967); Gilbert, Creighton, *History of Renaissance Art throughout Europe* (1973); Hartt, Frederick, *The History of Italian Renaissance Art* (1969); Meiss, Millard, *The Painter's Choice: Problems in the Interpretation of Renaissance Art* (1977); Panofsky, Erwin, *Early Netherlandish Painting,* 2 vols. (1954) and *Renaissance and Renascences in Western Art,* 2d ed. (1965); von der Osten, Gert, and Vey, Horst, *Painting and Sculpture in Germany and the Netherlands 1500–1600* (1969); Wittkower, Rudolph, *Architectural Principles in the Age of Humanism,* 3d ed. (1962).

See also: FLEMISH ART AND ARCHITECTURE; FRENCH ART AND ARCHITECTURE; GERMAN ART AND ARCHITECTURE; ITALIAN ART AND ARCHITECTURE.

Renaissance music

The Renaissance is characterized musically by a style of predominantly vocal POLYPHONY that prevailed roughly from 1420 to 1600. Until about 1500, however, this style had only a slight

This 15th-century painting by Ercole de'Roberti portrays Renaissance singers performing with lute accompaniment. During the Renaissance both church and secular music reached a high level of artistic excellence with the development of such musical forms as the canzone, mass, and motet and with the use of polyphony. The richly lyrical 16th-century madrigal was the major musical form originated by Renaissance composers.

relationship to Renaissance humanism; rather, it was differentiated from the late medieval style that preceded it by such purely musical features as its greater melodic and rhythmic integration, enlarged range and texture, and subjection to harmonic principles of order. After 1500 this integrated style developed into distinct vocal and instrumental idioms, and vocal music, under the influence of humanism, became increasingly devoted to the expression of texts. This development weakened the dominance of polyphony, which some musicians considered inimical to expression. By 1600 harmony had come to dominate polyphony, musical coherence was sometimes subordinated to expression, and instrumental music was liberated from the forms and styles of vocal music. At that point Renaissance musical style was eclipsed by a new style—the baroque.

THE 15TH CENTURY

The Renaissance style was foreshadowed about 1400 by English composers, led by John DUNSTABLE, who introduced a rich, consonant harmony based on intervals of the third and sixth. After about 1420 a new polyphonic style took root on the Continent; in this style all voices shared in melodic development and harmonic function. Practitioners of the new style in the 15th century included Gilles BINCHOIS, Guillaume DUFAY, Heinrich ISAAC, JOSQUIN DES PREZ, Jacob OBRECHT, Jean d'OKEGHEM, and Antoine Busnois (d. 1492). All these composers were Netherlanders or French, although most were also active in Italy. Musical forms cultivated by them were the CANZONE, CHANSON (especially *rondeau*), MASS, and MOTET. The theoretical formulation of the style was accomplished (*c*.1470–*c*.1550) in the writings of Johannes TINCTORIS, Pietro Aron (*c*.1490–1545), Franchino Gafori (1451–1522), and Heinrich Glareanus (1488–1563). Despite the importance of Italy as the fountainhead of the Renaissance, Italian contributions to the musical style appeared in quantity only at the end of the 15th century with *frottole* and *laude* by Marchetto Cara (d. 1527) and Bartolomeo Tromboncino (*c*.1470–*c*.1535).

THE 16TH CENTURY

The *frottole,* a light Italian part song, gave rise to the MADRIGAL, a humanist musical setting of neo-Petrarchan poetry usually for four or five voices, the most typical and at the same time most experimental of Renaissance musical forms. Many important madrigal composers up to the mid-16th century were Franco-Netherlanders, such as Adrian WILLAERT, Jacob Arcadelt (*c*.1514–68), Cipriano de Rore (1516–65), and Philippe Verdelot (d. 1567); but some were Italian, such as Costanzo Festa (*c*.1490–1545). Humanist works were composed to Latin texts, in a more severe style than the madrigal, by Josquin des Prez, Willaert, Rore, Paul Hofhaimer (1459–1537), and Ludwig Senfl (*c*.1490–1543). French lyric and narrative poetry received humanist musical settings by Clément JANEQUIN and Claudin de Sermisy (*c*.1490–1562). Later in the 16th century, French measured verse based on Greek models was set by Claude Lejeune (1528–*c*.1600).

Church Music. Classic Renaissance polyphony reached its height in the mass and the motet written in a style of smoothly flowing, balanced phrases of imitative counterpoint for four to six voices, carefully shaped to express the text. This style was established in the later works of Josquin des Prez and developed with some refinements but little essential change by William BYRD, Roland de LASSUS, Giovanni Pierluigi da PALESTRINA, Tomas Luis de VICTORIA, Nicholas Gambert (*c*.1500–*c*.1556), Cristóbal de Morales (*c*.1500–53), Jean Mouton (*c*.1475–1522), Philippe de Monte (1521–1603), Clemens non Papa (*c*.1510–*c*.1558), and Adrian Willaert. The principles of 16th-century composition achieved their most complete formulation in the writings of Gioseffo Zarlino (1517–90), a pupil of Willaert.

Alongside this sophisticated polyphony created to meet the needs of the Roman Catholic church, a simpler style arose to serve the Protestant churches established by the Reformation: German Lutheran chorales by Johann Walter (1496–1570), French Calvinist psalms by Louis Bourgeois (*c*.1510–*c*.1561) and Claude Goudimel (*c*.1505–72), and Anglican anthems by Orlando GIBBONS, Thomas TALLIS, and William Byrd. Counterreform in Roman Catholic church music was initiated by the Council of Trent (1545–63), which influenced late-16th-century sacred music by, among others, Jacobus de Kerle (*c*.1531–91), Vincenzo Ruffo (*c*.1520–87), and Palestrina.

Secular Music. Secular music in many countries attained an artistic level equal to that of church music. Late-16th-century madrigal composers had their most characteristic representatives in Luca MARENZIO and Giaches de Wert (1535–96); chanson composers were represented by Guillaume Costeley (*c*.1531–1606). The style of the madrigal was adopted for German and English songs by Hans Leo HASSLER, Thomas MORLEY, Thomas WEELKES, and John WILBYE. Solo songs (airs) with lute accompaniment became popular in Spain, France, and England, reaching their height in the works of John DOWLAND.

Idiomatic instrumental music appeared in solo works for lute and keyboard (organ, harpsichord) and in ensemble works for wind and stringed instruments. Notable achievements were the preludes and fantasias for the Spanish *vihuela* by Luis Milán (*c*.1500–*c*.1561); organ *ricercari* and *toccate* by Marco Antonio Cavazzoni (*c*.1490–*c*.1560) and Claudio Merulo (1533–1604); harpsichord dances and variations by John BULL, William Byrd, and Antonio de Cabezon (1510–66); ensemble dances in collections published by Pierre Attaingnant (d. *c*.1550) and Tilman Susato (d. *c*.1561); ensemble *canzone* and *ricercari* by Andrea GABRIELI (see GABRIELI family), Adrian Willaert, and Gabrieli's nephew Giovanni; and fantasias for viols by Byrd and Gibbons.

Printed books of polyphonic music first appeared in a chanson collection (*Harmonice musices Odhecaton A*) published at Venice by Ottaviano Petrucci in 1501. Music printing became a major industry by midcentury, revolutionizing the dissemination and social role of music, shifting emphasis from courtly and liturgical functions to those of popular entertainment and private devotion among the middle class.

Decline of Polyphony. Toward the end of the 16th century the norms of Renaissance style were subjected to strains arising within the humanism of the Renaissance itself, a development sometimes called Mannerism. The study of Greek musical theory promoted experimental chromaticism in works of Carlo GESUALDO, Rore, Lassus, and Nicolò Vicentino (*c*.1511–72), and Greek musical practice suggested the monodies of Giulio CACCINI and the invention of dramatic RECITATIVE by Jacopo PERI. Zarlino's theoretical system was attacked by Vicentino in the name of ancient music, and the concept of polyphony was questioned on the same grounds by Vincenzo Galilei (*c*.1520–91), father of the physicist Galileo. Solo song and recitative, obbligato instruments, and the *basso continuo* (see FIGURED BASS) supplanted the polyphonic texture of Renaissance music by about 1600. The last great madrigalist of the Renaissance, Claudio MONTEVERDI, was also the first great composer of baroque opera.

MARTIN PICKER

Bibliography: Blume, Friedrich, *Renaissance and Baroque Music* (1967); Brown, Howard M., *Music in the Renaissance* (1976); Grout, Donald J.,

A History of Western Music, 3d ed. (1980); Lowinsky, Edward E., "Music in the Culture of the Renaissance," in Renaissance Essays, ed. by Paul O. Kristeller and Philip Wiener (1968); Reese, Gustave, Music in the Renaissance, 2d ed. (1959).

Renan, Ernest   [ruh-nahn']

Ernest Renan, b. Feb. 28, 1823, d. Oct. 2, 1892, was a French scholar whose Life of Jesus (1863; Eng. trans., 1864) generated enormous controversy because it portrayed Jesus in purely human terms. Renan began training for the priesthood but lost his faith and took up independent biblical studies. He wrote Life of Jesus while traveling in Palestine on an archaeological expedition. After its publication he lost his position as professor of Hebrew at the Collège de France, although he was restored to the post in 1870 and was elected to the Académie Française in 1878. The Life of Jesus was the first volume of his History of the Origins of Christianity (1863–99; Eng. trans. in 7 vols., 1890). Renan's other works include The History of the People of Israel (5 vols., 1887–93; Eng. trans., 1888–96) and the popular Recollections of My Youth (1883; Eng. trans., 1883).   REGINALD H. FULLER

Bibliography: Chadbourne, R. M., Ernest Renan (1968; repr. 1978); Epinasse, F., Life of Ernest Renan (1895; repr. 1980); Schweitzer, A., The Quest of the Historical Jesus, trans. by W. Montgomery, 3d ed. (1963); Wardman, H. W., Ernest Renan: A Critical Biography (1964).

Renault, Mary   [ruh-nawlt']

The English writer Mary Renault, pseudonym of Mary Challans, b. Sept. 4, 1905, d. Dec. 13, 1983, was known for the high quality of her fictional re-creations of the ancient Greek world. Based on careful research and enlivened by credible characters and often exciting narratives, her historical novels achieved a rare authenticity. Among the best were The Last of the Wine (1956), set in the Athens of Plato and Socrates; The King Must Die (1958), an evocation of the legend of Theseus; and her trilogy on Alexander the Great—The Persian Boy (1972), The Nature of Alexander (1980), and Funeral Games (1981). Her earlier novels dealt with contemporary subjects; The Charioteer (1953), for instance, is a sympathetic treatment of homosexuality set during World War II. Renault, who moved to South Africa in 1948, was a critic of apartheid.

Bibliography: Dick, Bernard, The Hellenism of Mary Renault (1972); Wolfe, Peter, Mary Renault (1969).

René of Anjou, King of Naples   [ruh-nay' ahn-zhoo']

King of Naples (1435–42), René of Anjou, b. Jan. 6, 1409, d. July 10, 1480, occupies a place in both the political and the literary history of his time. René inherited (1434) from his brother Louis III of Anjou the French lands of Provence and Anjou, as well as a claim to the throne of Naples (see NAPLES, KINGDOM OF). In 1435 on the death of Joan II of Naples he became titular king but was driven out (1442) by a rival claimant, ALFONSO V of Aragon. He then turned his attention to his interests in France. He fought (1449–50) alongside CHARLES VII of France against the English in Normandy and in 1466 accepted the title king of Aragon from the Catalans rebelling against John II of Aragon. He was the author of two romances in prose and verse.   JAMES M. POWELL

Bibliography: Leary, F. W., The Golden Longing (1959).

Renfrew   [ren'-froo]

Renfrew is a former county in southwestern Scotland along the firth of Clyde, situated on fertile, undulating lowlands west of Glasgow. PAISLEY and Renfrew are the principal urban centers. One of the most heavily industrialized areas of Scotland, Renfrew produces ships, automobiles, and heavy machinery; livestock raising, dairy farming, and the cultivation of potatoes, wheat, and oats supplement industry. After the Romans left the region during the early 5th century, Renfrew became part of the kingdom of Strathclyde. Renfrew was made a separate county of the Scottish kingdom in 1404, at which time the title baron of Renfrew was conferred on the oldest son of the Scottish monarch. During the reorganization of Scotland's local government in 1975, Renfrew was incorporated into the administrative region of STRATHCLYDE.

Reni, Guido   [ray'-nee]

The Italian painter and engraver Guido Reni, b. Nov. 4, 1575, d. Aug. 18, 1642, was a leading master of the classical baroque style. Born in Bologna, Reni was originally trained by the Flemish Mannerist painter Denis Calvaert, but joined the Carracci family workshop about 1595. Reni went (c.1600) to Rome as an independent master, and there came in contact with the work of Caravaggio. Reni's early works show the influence of Caravaggio in color, composition, and lighting, as in the Crucifixion of Saint Peter (c.1604; Pinacoteca Vaticana, Rome). Thereafter, he was drawn to the art of classical antiquity and that of Raphael. One of his most famous works, the Aurora ceiling fresco (1613–14; Casino Rospigliosi, Rome), combines these influences, which also inspired the Deeds of Hercules series (1617–21; Louvre, Paris) and the Apollo Flaying Marsyas (c.1625; Musée des Augustins, Toulouse). As the dominant artist in Bologna from 1614, Reni inspired several contemporaries, such as Francesco Albani and Guercino, and younger masters, such as Guido Cagnacci and Carlo Maratti. His Immaculate Conception (1627; Metropolitan Museum of Art, New York City) was sent to Seville, where it influenced Bartolomé Esteban Murillo.   EDWARD J. SULLIVAN

Bibliography: Wittkower, Rudolf, Art and Architecture in Italy, 1600–1750, 3d ed. (1973; repr. 1980).

Rennes   [ren]

Rennes is a city in Brittany, northwestern France, located about 300 km (190 mi) southwest of Paris. The population is 234,000 (1982). Wide city streets and canals radiate from the central hub of the city, long a regional center rich in customs and historical monuments. Rennes is an agricultural market and industrial center producing railroad and farm equipment and automobiles. Historic landmarks include the Jardin du Thabor and the 17th-century Palais de Justice. The University of Rennes is there.

The principal town of the Celtic Redones tribe, Rennes was subsequently taken by the Romans and by the 10th century had emerged as the capital of Brittany. The city was almost completely destroyed by fire in 1720 and suffered heavy bombing during World War II.

Reno   [ree'-noh]

Reno, on the Truckee River in western Nevada, is the seat of Washoe County. It has a population of 100,756 (1980). A famous resort city, Reno is popular for its crisp climate, magnificent scenery, recreation in the Sierra Nevada, and its casinos and night entertainment. Reno's industries process potatoes and livestock and manufacture lumber products, chemicals, and mining machinery. Because of Nevada's Free Port Law, Reno is an important warehousing and distribution center. It is the location of the University of Nevada (1864), especially noted for the Mackay School of Mines Museum and the Desert Research Institute. The city is also the headquarters for the Toiyabe National Forest.

The site was settled in 1858 by pioneers en route to California via the Donner Pass. Arrival of the Central Pacific Railroad in 1868 ensured the town's development. First called Lake's Crossing, the town was renamed for the Union general Jesse Lee Reno, a Civil War hero.

Renoir, Jean   [ren-wahr']

One of the greatest and best-loved of all French filmmakers, Jean Renoir, b. Sept. 15, 1894, d. Feb. 13, 1979, the second son of the impressionist painter Auguste Renoir, exercised a major influence on French cinema for almost 50 years. From his beginnings in the silent era, aspects of his mature film style were apparent: a love of nature, rejection of class values, and

Jean Renoir's 1937 film Grand Illusion *starred Jean Gabin* (center) *and Pierre Fresnay* (right) *as French soldiers plotting their escape from a German prisoner-of-war camp during World War I. In the film Renoir explored the changing rules of combat and the conflict between patriotism and the more profound ties based on class solidarity.*

a mixture of joy and sorrow. Some of his earliest films were made with his wife Catherine Hessling as star, among them an interpretation of Zola's *Nana* (1926), and *The Little Match Girl* (1928).

During the 1930s Renoir was at the top of his form in two celebrations of anarchy, *La Chienne* (The Bitch, 1931) and *Boudu sauvé des eaux* (Boudu Saved from Drowning, 1932). A new social concern appeared in *Toni* (1935), *Le Crime de Monsieur Lange* (1936), and especially *La Vie est à nous* (People of France, 1936), made for the French Communist party during the heyday of the Popular Front. Renoir's reputation, however, rests mainly on *A Day in the Country* (1936, completed 1946), based on a bittersweet de Maupassant story; a free adaptation of Gorki's *The Lower Depths* (1936); and the widely acclaimed *Grand Illusion* (1937). Two very different masterpieces written and directed by Renoir, the tightly structured *The Human Beast* (1938) and the largely improvised *Rules of the Game* (1939)—which perfectly captured the mood of France before its collapse in 1940—crowned this prolific period.

Renoir spent the war years in Hollywood, but even the best of his films made in the United States, such as *The South-*

erner (1945) and *The Diary of a Chambermaid* (1946), lack the excitement of his prewar work. He found a new approach and a new philosophy in India, where he made his first color film, *The River* (1950), before returning to Europe to make the colorful and relaxed films of his maturity: *The Golden Coach* (1952), *French Can Can* (1954), and *Paris Does Strange Things* (1956). Always an innovator, Renoir used television techniques in the 1959 filming of *Le Testament du Docteur Cordelier* and *Picnic on the Grass,* the latter strongly evocative of the sun-filled landscapes beloved by his father. For his last film, *The Elusive Corporal* (1962), set in World War II, he returned to themes earlier explored in *Grand Illusion* and *The Lower Depths.* Renoir's considerable influence on the French New Wave directors of the late 1950s can be seen especially in the films of François Truffaut.   ROY ARMES

Bibliography: Bazin, André, *Jean Renoir,* ed. by François Truffaut (1973); Braudy, Leo, *Jean Renoir—The World of His Films* (1972); Durgnat, Raymond, *Jean Renoir* (1974); Gilliatt, Penelope, *Jean Renoir: Essays, Conversations, and Reviews* (1975); Renoir, Jean, *My Life and My Films* (1974).

Renoir, Pierre Auguste

The French painter Pierre Auguste Renoir, b. Limoges, France, Feb. 25, 1841, d. Dec. 17, 1919, was one of the founders of IMPRESSIONISM. Within the impressionist group his work stands out as the most traditional in outlook and technique, as well as the most sensual.

At the age of 13 he began painting flowers on dishware at a porcelain factory and later painted fans and screens. In 1862 he entered the studio of Charles Gleyre (1808–74) and became friends with Claude Monet and Alfred Sisley, who shared his inclination to take up painting outdoors. By the time (1869) that he and Monet worked together at La Grenouillère, on the Seine, Renoir had developed a delicate touch and vibrant brushwork that were distinctly his own.

In the early 1870s, Renoir and his friends joined with other avant-garde artists to form a loose-knit artistic circle now known as the impressionist movement. He participated in the first impressionist exhibition (1874) and throughout the 1870s

Pierre Auguste Renoir's The Luncheon of the Boating-Party *(1881) displays the qualities of French impressionism to their best advantage: intense color and brightly lit open-air subjects painted directly from nature. Festive social events were a favored subject for Renoir, who shared this penchant with Édouard Manet. (Phillips Collection, Washington, D.C.)*

remained committed to impressionist ideals. Renoir, however, continued to produce paintings of a more traditional sort, including portraits and scenes of leisure enjoyment, such as *Le Moulin de la Galette* (1876; Musée de l'Impressionnisme, Paris). In his portraits and society paintings, Renoir masterfully rendered the shimmering interplay of light and color on surfaces, the prime goal of impressionism, but he also retained an underlying sensuality.

Renoir's growing dissatisfaction with the formal restrictions of pure impressionism intensified during a visit (1881–82) to Algiers and Italy. In response, he made his figures larger and placed them closer to the picture-plane, with a setting treated like a simple backdrop. This friezelike treatment, best exemplified in his *Dance at Bougival* (1883; Museum of Fine Arts, Boston), led to his so-called "harsh manner" of the mid-1880s, in which he purified his contours and used frozen, static poses.

Beginning in the 1890s, Renoir concentrated almost exclusively on the female figure, using warmer flesh tones, more exotic colors, and a tapestried treatment of landscape. In 1905 he settled at Cagnes near Nice; its sun-drenched climate is reflected in the intense colors of his later works. In his last years (after 1913), he also executed sculpture with the aid of an Italian assistant.   MARK ROSKILL

Bibliography: Gaunt, William, *Renoir*, 2d ed. (1971); Pach, Walter, *Renoir* (1950); Photiadès, Vassily, *Renoir Nudes* (1964); Renoir, Jean, *Renoir, My Father* (1962); Rewald, John, *The History of Impressionism*, 4th rev. ed. (1973); Traz, George de, *Renoir: His Life and Work*, trans. by Mary I. Martin (1975); Wheldon, Keith, *Renoir and His Art* (1975).

Rensselaer Polytechnic Institute   [ren'-suh-leer]

Established in 1824 and the oldest engineering school in the United States, Rensselaer Polytechnic Institute (enrollment: 5,360; library: 270,000 volumes) is a private coeducational college in Troy, N.Y. The courses of study, leading to bachelor's, master's, and doctorate degrees, emphasize science and technology. The institute has cooperative engineering programs with many colleges and six-year medical and law programs with Albany Medical College and Albany Law School, both at Union College in Schenectady, N.Y.

rent control

Rent control is a legal restriction on rents that landlords can charge tenants. Its initial purpose was to stabilize rents and to curtail unnecessary evictions. Initiated in the United States during World War I, rent control was a temporary wartime response to rises in the cost of living and to housing shortages caused by the allocation of building materials and labor to defense industries. In 1921 the Supreme Court, in *Block* v. *Hirsch* and *Brown Holding Co.* v. *Feldman*, upheld the constitutionality of rent control. After the war, controls were extended in order to aid tenants, because, in many cities, the demand for residential housing far exceeded the supply.

During World War II rent control was instituted on a broader scale by the federal government with the enactment of the Emergency Price Controls Act of 1942. With the Housing and Rent Act of 1947, the termination of federal controls—allowing local municipalities to extend rent control—was begun, and in *Woods* v. *Miller* (1948), the Supreme Court ruled that the continuation of rent control by state and local statutes was constitutional.

By the mid-1950s, however, most states, except New York, had abolished rent control. Because of limited housing and the political power of tenants, New York City's rent-control laws today still cover more than 400,000 apartments, a cause, critics contend, of property deterioration and owner abandonment. The enactment of the Rent Stabilization Law of 1969, viewed as a compromise, affected more than 850,000 apartments constructed after 1947. It allowed periodic increases in rent on a more liberal basis than the stricter rent controls. The New·York State Emergency Tenant Protection Act of 1974 reinforced the rent-stabilization concept by including approximately 383,000 units under the 1969 stabilization law. Other cities and states have recently enacted similar rent-control legislation to prevent inordinate increases in rent while providing owners with reasonable increments to meet rising prices.   KENNETH P. NOLAN

Bibliography: Hayek, F. A., et al., *Verdict on Rent Control* (1973); Heilbrun, James, ed., *Rent Control: Its Effect on Housing Availability and Assessed Values* (1977); Lett, Monica, *Rent Control* (1976).

Renwick, James   [ren'-wik]

Saint Patrick's Cathedral (1858–88), New York City, a Gothic Revival structure designed by James Renwick, fuses elements of continental and English Gothic styles. Renwick's work did much to establish Gothic as a leading style of American ecclesiastical architecture.

The architect James Renwick, b. New York City, Nov. 18, 1818, d. June 23, 1895, is best known as the designer of New York City's SAINT PATRICK'S CATHEDRAL (begun 1858; dedicated 1879), a major monument of the American GOTHIC REVIVAL.

Renwick was graduated from Columbia in 1836. After serving as engineer and supervising architect on the city's Croton aqueduct and reservoir, he won first prize in a competition for the design of Grace Church in New York City, his first important commission and one of his most admired buildings. Completed in 1846, this English Gothic edifice led to other important church commissions, including that for Saint Patrick's.

Renwick's penchant for architectural styles with strongly romantic overtones was influenced by the writings of the English architect Augustus Pugin and his followers, known as the Ecclesiologists. In Washington, D.C., Renwick's picturesque composition of the original Smithsonian Institution, familiarly called "The Castle" (1844–55), in a Norman Romanesque style stands out in striking contrast to the neoclassical buildings that now surround it. His other important buildings include the first Corcoran Gallery (1859; Washington, D.C.), now named the Renwick Gallery, and the Main Hall at Vassar College (1860; Poughkeepsie, N.Y.).   RON WIEDENHOEFT

Bibliography: Anson, Peter F., *Fashions in Church Furnishings* (1960); Pierson, William H., *American Buildings and their Architects* (1978); Withey, Henry F. and Elsie R., *Biographical Dictionary of American Architects Deceased* (1956; repr. 1970).

reparations

Reparations is the term for money or other compensation that a defeated country pays to the victors or to individuals who have suffered in war. The word came into use after World War I. Germany was forced to pay reparations under the Versailles Treaty (see PARIS PEACE CONFERENCE), which blamed Germany for starting World War I and held it responsible for the resulting damage. Germans protested that the amount set by the interallied Reparations Commission in 1921, 132 billion gold marks, was unrealistically high and could not be paid. Many Americans sympathized with these German protests, and the United States waived most of its reparations claims.

When Germany defaulted on its reparations payments, France and Belgium moved (1923) troops into the Ruhr district in western Germany to force payment. The occupation ended (1924) after an international commission headed by American Charles G. DAWES formulated the Dawes Plan, which lowered German payments to one billion gold marks annually for five years and 2.5 billion thereafter. This schedule was replaced (1929) by the Young Plan, named after another American, Owen D. YOUNG, which lowered payments again. All payments ceased with the economic crisis of the 1930s.

After World War II reparations were imposed on Germany, Japan, and the other defeated powers, and the USSR enforced some claims against Germany. Victims of Nazi persecution, including the state of Israel, received about $2 billion from West Germany, but other reparation payments were modest.

DONALD S. BIRN

Bibliography: Bergman, Carl, *A History of Reparations* (1927); Kuklick, Bruce, *American Policy and the Division of Germany: The Clash with Russia over Reparations* (1972); Wheeler-Bennett, John, *The Wreck of Reparations* (1933; repr. 1972).

repertory theater

The permanent, professional, nonprofit stage organizations outside New York City, known as repertory, regional, and resident theater, have profoundly altered the presentation of drama in the United States since the mid-20th century. Prior to their emergence, Broadway was the dominant center for the production both of classics and of new plays that touring companies or commercial "stock" entrepreneurs later distributed across the country. Today Broadway is dependent upon resident theaters for some of its best productions. Several factors—particularly economic depression and such rival entertainment media as movies, radio, and television—eroded the old Broadway monopoly.

The earliest rebels included the still-active Cleveland Play House (begun in 1916), the Hedgerow Theater in Moylan, Pa., and the Barter Theater in Abingdon, Va. The experimental theater launched (1947) by Margo JONES in Dallas, Tex., how-

The Arena Stage repertory company of Washington, D.C., founded in 1950 by Zelda Fichandler, appears at the Kreeger Theater in a scene from their production of the popular comedy You Can't Take It with You *by George S. Kaufman and Moss Hart.*

ever, proved the most important seminal effort in the genesis of regional theater. Until her death (1955), Jones concentrated on finding new plays, encouraging fledgling authors, and preaching local self-reliance. One of her colleagues, Nina Vance, started (1947) the Alley Theater in Houston, Tex., but, unlike Jones, produced standard works in order to develop an audience.

Other early troupes were the Mummers Theater, founded in 1949 in Oklahoma City, Okla., and one of the most important and prestigious companies of all, the Arena Stage, started in 1950 by Zelda Fichandler in Washington, D.C. Boston, Memphis, Tenn., Milwaukee, Wis., and San Francisco also pioneered in the development of regional and repertory theaters.

The Ford and Rockefeller foundations contributed to the theater's greatest expansion when in the late 1950s they extended their philanthropic activities to the performing arts. For several years existing theater groups received large grants for new buildings and subsequently for other aspects of production. Further help for the campaign to decentralize theater activity—an objective repeatedly cited by sponsors—came when the federal government founded (1965) the National Endowment for the Arts and began providing additional help with educational funds.

A measure of the rapid growth of regional theater was that by 1965 it was employing more Actors Equity union members than Broadway itself. Some groups failed, but other companies, such as the Guthrie Theater in Minneapolis, Minn., the Mark Taper Forum in Los Angeles, the Trinity Square in Providence, R.I., the American Conservatory Theater in San Francisco, and the Long Wharf in New Haven, Conn., provided high-quality leadership. The Theater Communications Group, a privately financed service agency, reported (1978) that 167 resident professional theaters in 84 communities were accommodating an annual audience of more than 11 million, in contrast to 3 million a decade earlier.   WILLIAM GLOVER

Bibliography: Novick, Julius, *Beyond Broadway: The Quest for Permanent Theatres* (1968); Zeigler, Joseph W., *Regional Theatre: The Revolutionary Stage* (1973).

repetition: see FIGURES OF SPEECH.

Repin, Ilya Yefimovich   [rep'-in]

The leading Russian realist painter of the 19th century, Ilya Yefimovich Repin, b. Aug. 5 (N.S.), 1844, d. Sept. 29, 1930, belonged to the group known as the Peredvizhniki (Wanderers), who frequently addressed political and social issues in their art. His first major work was *The Volga Boatmen* (1870–73; State Russian Museum, Leningrad); he later achieved great popularity with his colorful historical canvases and large-scale genre paintings. *They Did Not Expect Him* (c.1884; Tretyakov Gallery, Moscow) depicts the return of an emaciated political exile to his startled family. Repin also produced portraits of his friend Leo Tolstoi and the composer-conductor Anton Rubinstein. He died in Kuokkala, Finland (now USSR), which was renamed Repino in his honor.

representation

Representation, in politics, is the process by which one person stands or acts for a large number of individuals in formulating the policies and operations of a GOVERNMENT. A monarch, a diplomat, or even a flag may represent. Modern representative government, however, is typically characterized by an elected LEGISLATURE. Legislative representation is usually based on numbers of or territorial groupings of the general population. Electoral districts may correspond to existing political subdivisions (for example, preexisting states, counties, cities, cantons, and so on) or may be specially drawn, usually on the basis of population. For example, U.S. senators are elected at large from each state, whereas members of the House of Representatives represent congressional districts, whose boundaries are altered as population shifts.

Some countries have used PROPORTIONAL REPRESENTATION, a system in which representatives are apportioned among political parties in proportion to the number of votes each party receives. Various other methods of representation exist; for example, the fascist governments of Italy, Germany, and Spain used corporative representation based on such economic groupings as farmers, trade unions, and business interests.

Origins of Representatives. Both institutionally and conceptually, representation largely originated during the Middle Ages. Ancient Greece had no concept of representation. Although political practices included selecting some officials by lot and sending delegates abroad, DEMOCRACY in the Greek city-states was direct rather than representative, with all citizens entitled to meet and act on each political issue personally. Rome used some political representatives and developed legal agency (see AGENT), but the Latin verb *repraesentare* meant only artistic representing, or literally making present an absent thing. Medieval monarchs consulted with feudal and church lords; later they sometimes summoned knights and burgesses (townsmen) to meet with them in council. This practice was initially a duty, not a right, and the function of the representatives was advisory. Nevertheless, such councils became increasingly powerful as periodic financial crises forced monarchs to summon representatives of lower estates to ask for more financial support. As these councils became more institutionalized, representative legislatures evolved, began to challenge monarchial power, and came to be regarded as representing the whole realm. During the 17th century, individual members came to be called representatives, and representation came to be considered a matter of right. During the 18th century, representation became a particularly explosive issue. The inadequacy of their representation in the British Parliament was a major complaint of the American colonists, and "No taxation without representation" became a rallying cry for the American Revolution. During the 19th and 20th centuries, representation was further institutionalized and democratized; executives were made responsible to elected legislature; POLITICAL PARTIES developed; SUFFRAGE was gradually extended; and various electoral systems were tried. Today the idea of representation is so widely accepted that every government in the world claims to be completely representative of those it governs.

Theories of Representation. A number of controversies arise in the theory of representation. First, there is dispute over what representation is or means. Thomas HOBBES defined representation as acting in the name of another, who has authorized the action, so that the representative's act is ascribed to and binds the represented. When people authorize a sovereign in the SOCIAL CONTRACT, they make the sovereign their unlimited representative; whatever the sovereign does is authorized and binds them, so that every effective government represents. Some modern theories of representative democracy stress the diametrically opposite view: a representative is someone ultimately held to account by the represented. Representation is defined not by initial authorization, as in Hobbes, but by final accountability. The representative has special obligations, and the represented, special rights and powers. For still other theorists, representation is "standing for" or "acting for" something or someone absent. Representatives may stand for others by resemblance so that the legislature is regarded as a miniature of the nation (for instance, in proportional representation), or the individual representative, as typical of his constituency. Representation may mean standing for others as a symbol (see FASCISM); here no resemblance is required. Finally, seen as "acting for" others, representation is not a merely passive "standing for" and goes beyond merely formal authorization or accountability: it is a substantive kind of activity.

A second controversy in the theory of representation concerns this substantive activity. It may be called the "mandate-independence controversy," usually formulated as a dichotomous choice: should a representative do what the constituents want or what the representative thinks best? Mandate theorists stress the representative's obligations to the constituents, arguing that the representative really represents

them only if the representative's actions reflect their opinions and wishes (as when a member of congress votes in accord with OPINION POLLS taken in his or her district). Independence theorists, such as Edmund BURKE, stress the representative's role in a national legislature and the representative's obligation to the public good; they say that the representation is not representing if he or she merely acts as a mechanical transmitter of decisions others have made.

A third controversy concerns the value and the very possibility of genuine representation. Jean Jacques ROUSSEAU argued that so-called representative institutions only substitute the will of a few for that of the whole community, with no likelihood that the two might coincide. He concluded that voters are free only at the moment of elections; as soon as they are represented, they are once more subject to an alien will. Since the 17th century, representation has been advocated on the grounds that a modern nation is too densely populated to govern itself directly. This view has repeatedly been challenged along Rousseauian or populist lines; that participation in self-government is intrinsically, not just instrumentally, valuable; that only a politically involved and active people is free; and that representative institutions have come to discourage active citizenship.   HANNA FENICHEL PITKIN

Bibliography: Birch, Anthony H., *Representation* (1972); Burke, Edmund, *Burke's Politics*, ed. by Ross J. S. Hoffman and Paul Levack (1949); Clarke, Maude V., *Medieval Representation and Consent* (1936; repr. 1964); De Grazia, Alfred, *Public and Republic* (1951); Hobbes, Thomas, *Leviathan* (1651; repr. 1953); Mill, John Stuart, *Considerations on Representative Government*, ed. by Currin Shields (1861; repr. 1958); Pennock, J. Roland, and Chapman, John W., eds., *Representation* (1968); Pitkin, Hanna F., *The Concept of Representation* (1967); Pole, J. R., *Political Representation in England and the Origins of the American Republic* (1966); Rousseau, Jean Jacques, *The Social Contract*, trans. by G. D. H. Cole (1762; repr. 1950).

repression: see DEFENSE MECHANISMS.

reproduction

Asexual or sexual reproduction is the mechanism by which cellular life perpetuates itself. In asexual reproduction, new individuals are produced by simple division of nonreproductive cells, by budding from a parent system, by formation of spores, which germinate directly into a new individual, or by other means; there is no requirement for cells or cell nuclei from one individual to fuse with those of another. Asexual generations are essentially identical, because a single parent transmits its exact set of genes to each descendant (see CLONING). In sexual reproduction, new generations arise after fusion between nuclei or cells from different parental lineages, producing genetic variety. Cells that fuse are usually sex cells, called gametes, such as SPERM and EGGS, called ova. The sex cells pair to produce a zygote, such as a fertilized egg, which then initiates the new generation.

Each kind of reproductive system provides some advantages, of either short- or long-term evolutionary importance. Asexual systems are prolific and quickly colonize new habitats. Many asexual descendants of similar genetic constitution and adaptiveness soon fill a habitat. Sexual species are variable, so that at least a few out of many genetic types often can adapt to different or fluctuating living conditions, thus providing more chance for continuation of the population. In general, sexual species are genetically adaptable to new and sometimes abruptly changing environments, whereas asexual species do best in static surroundings.

GAMETES

The two major events in a sexual cycle are gamete formation and gamete fusion. There are male and female sexes in most animals and plants, but there may be more than two sexes or mating types in various protozoa, algae, and fungi. Each sex produces one kind of gamete, and fusion occurs between different types of gametes. In mammals, hormones from the hypothalamus region of the brain stimulate pituitary hormone release, which in turn regulates synthesis of sex hormones in ovary and testis. Production, maturation, and release of gametes are regulated by such hormonal interactions.

Gametes usually fuse only with gametes of the opposite

type. In some protozoa, algae, and fungi, they may resemble ordinary growing (vegetative) cells, but most animals and the land plants produce specialized, large, nonmotile eggs and smaller, motile sperm. Sperm reach the egg by swimming or by muscular propulsion from female structures after insemination, or they may be taken to the egg during pollen tube growth within female structures of seed-bearing plants.

BACTERIA

Bacteria, as well as protozoa, generally reproduce asexually by a process called binary fission, in which the cell simply divides into two. Cell conjugation, however, can occur in the colon bacillus, *Escherichia coli*, during which some genetic material is exchanged between two individuals. In true sexual reproduction there is complete fusion between nuclei, and each parent therefore contributes a complete set of genes to the new generation.

ALGAE AND FUNGI

There are various reproductive patterns in algae, fungi, and plants, but the basic theme of nuclear or gamete formation and fusion occurs. Algae and fungi display quite varied patterns, including life cycles in which there is a predominant haploid (one set of chromosomes) phase, or a predominant diploid (two sets of chromosomes) phase, or an alternation between haploid and diploid phases (see ALTERNATION OF GENERATIONS), among others. Different species of unicellular green alga (genus *Chlamydomonas*) may produce similar or dissimilar gametes, but the zygote is the only diploid stage. The zygote undergoes a reduction division (see MEIOSIS) almost immediately, producing haploid vegetative cells that later may behave as gametes. In the branched, filamentous green alga (genus *Cladophora*), there are species that produce both haploid and diploid plants of similar appearance. The diploid plant produces haploid, motile vegetative cells by meiosis, and these develop into haploid plants capable of producing gametes. Gamete fusion then leads to new diploid plants of another cycle. Although the haploid and diploid plants look alike, there is an alternation of haploid and diploid plant phases in the life cycle. *Oedogonium* is another filamentous green alga, but it produces separate and dissimilar haploid male and female plants. Sperm from a dwarf male plant will fertilize eggs from the larger female plant to produce the diploid zygotes. Zygote meiosis leads to new haploid plants of the next generation. There is a predominant diploid phase in the life cycle of the brown alga *Laminaria,* a marine kelp. The large diploid plant is a sporophyte in which spores are produced by meiosis; these develop into small, haploid male and female gamete-producing plants, or gametophytes, which produce sperm and eggs, respectively. The fertilized egg develops into the large, familiar seaweed plant. Such an alternation of sporophyte and gametophyte phases in a life cycle is typical of mosses, ferns, and seed-bearing plants but is unusual among algae.

Various reproductive patterns occur among fungi, generally of a different nature than among algae. In species of sac fungi (class Ascomycetes), ascospores are produced by meiosis, and these germinate to become the mass of filaments forming the mycelium, or fungus body. Gamete-producing structures develop along these filaments, and after a complex series of events there is nuclear fusion that leads to diploid cells. Meiosis occurs in these cells, producing ascospores, and the cycle begins again. In mushrooms and related fungi (class Basidiomycetes), haploid basidiospores germinate to produce a mycelium consisting of uninucleate haploid cells. Cell fusion occurs between filaments from individuals of different mating types, producing binucleate cells, which eventually form the mushroom or another familiar structure. In locations such as the surface of "gills" on the underside of the mushroom cap, large numbers of terminal cells expand to become specialized bodies called basidia. Paired nuclei fuse within the basidium to form diploid nuclei, which then undergo meiosis. Haploid basidiospores are formed as protuberances of the basidia.

PLANTS

Among the land plants there has been an evolutionary trend toward decreasing size of the gametophyte and increasing size of sporophyte, as well as complete dependence of the gametophyte on the sporophyte plant. The evolutionary trend is from separate sexes to hermaphroditism, but various arrangements encourage or mandate cross-fertilization.

In mosses, the well-known plant is the gametophyte, and the small sporophyte grows from the zygote retained within the gametophyte, so that the sporophyte is dependent on the gametophyte for food and water. Meiosis occurs in sporophyte cells, producing spores that germinate into gametophytes. Sperms and eggs are produced within the leafy, green gametophytes.

Fern gametophytes are tiny, independent, green plants in which eggs and sperm are produced. Sperm require water in order to swim to the egg, where fertilization occurs. The fertilized egg develops into the large, familiar fern sporophyte. Spores are produced by meiosis on the underside of the fern leaf; these spores germinate and become gametophytes.

Alternation of sporophyte and gametophyte phases is less apparent in the gymnosperm and angiosperm life cycles, but it does occur. The prominent sporophyte produces two kinds of spores, each kind developing into an inconspicuous male or female gametophyte. The male gametophyte consists of two cells surrounded by protective cells of the pollen grain. Pollen is carried to the female sporophyte containing one or more female gametophytes which have developed from large spores; the egg is produced within the female gametophyte. Sperm do not require water for delivery to the egg, since germination of the pollen grain on receptive sporophyte structures leads to growth of the pollen tube; the pollen tube then carries the sperm down to the egg within the microscopic, protected gametophyte.

The fertilized egg develops into an embryo that remains in the protected confines of the female sporophyte. Certain maternal tissues develop into the layers of seed coat around the embryo, and stored foods are also present around the embryo. Naked seeds are released by gymnosperms, but seeds are enclosed by a fruit formed from sporophyte tissues of the flower in angiosperms. Seeds and the embryonic plants within are dispersed by various means (for example, wind, water, and insects) to different environments. Some of these environments prove suitable for seed germination and the eventual development of a new sporophyte plant, as the embryo matures into a seedling and finally to a reproductive stage. All these features are adaptations to successful life on the land. In conjugation no new individual is formed; the same number of individuals exists as before, and their numbers did not increase until binary fission takes place. Nevertheless, conjugation has the evolutionary advantage of introducing genetic variation.

ANIMALS

The predominant sexual mode in animals is separate male and female individuals. Some invertebrate species are hermaphroditic, consisting of individuals having both ovaries and testes, and self-fertilization can occur, as in some tapeworms. Cross-fertilization usually occurs between mating pairs such that each releases sperm, which fertilize the partner's eggs. Sex is determined in many animals (and some plants) according to a sex chromosome mechanism that leads to a 1:1 ratio of females and males. Some organisms have a gene-based mechanism of sex determination, whereas others have various means that lead to hermaphrodites or to males and females in unequal proportions.

Most fishes and amphibians release sperm and eggs directly into the water, where fertilization occurs and embryo development begins. Vertebrate land animals (reptiles, birds, and mammals) usually experience internal fertilization, which required evolutionary modifications in reproductive anatomy and physiology. Males deposit sperm within the female reproductive tract during cloacal contact or by insertion of a penis into the vagina or other reproductive duct. Water is not necessary to accomplish reproduction, so true land animals can occupy habitats not accessible to aquatic species. The seed-bearing plants are also independent of water for reproduction since sperm nuclei are delivered by pollinating agents, after which internal fertilization occurs within the female structures.

Evolutionary modifications for life on land also involve increased protection for the egg and developing embryo. The egg is retained after fertilization, and the embryo develops to a certain stage within the mother's body. In land vertebrates special embryonic membranes separate the embryo from its maternal surroundings. The embryo is nourished by foods stored in the yolk sac or other structures, and it continues to grow in warm and safe conditions. Embryonic development continues for a time after the egg is laid, until the foods are gone. In most mammals, the embryo can develop for a longer term within its mother, since nutrients and oxygen are provided from the mother's bloodstream to the embryo through the placenta. In birds and mammals there is continued parental care after hatching or birth. Such species can safely produce fewer eggs and fewer embryos since their survival is more likely.

Except for humans, mammals are reproductively active only when they are capable of breeding. This interval, called estrus in the female, is the time when the female ovulates and the male is prepared and able to inseminate her. There may be one or more estrous cycles in a breeding season, but the time of breeding coincides with the time when conception and pregnancy are possible. Most animals engage in courtship displays, produce vocalizations, or secrete chemical attractants that signal sexual and reproductive readiness. Most of these sexual behaviors are under hormonal control. Among primates, Old World monkeys and apes develop conspicuous changes in the sex skin around the genitalia, or otherwise signal sexual receptivity to the opposite sex. There is no particular correlation in human beings between sexual activity and the optimum time for conception and pregnancy. Sexually mature women ovulate once per monthly cycle throughout the year, unless they are pregnant, until menopause, when these menstrual cycles cease. Sexually mature men produce sperm every day and can inseminate the female and initiate pregnancy at any time. Menstruation indicates that conception has not occurred. There is overt blood flow only in various primates, and human females are unique in having a menstrual cycle instead of an estrous cycle (see REPRODUCTIVE SYSTEM, HUMAN). CHARLOTTE J. AVERS

Bibliography: Asdell, Sydney A., *Patterns of Mammalian Reproduction*, 2d ed. (1964); Austin, C. R., and Short, R. V., *The Evolution of Reproduction* (1975); Bold, Harold C., *The Plant Kingdom*, 4th ed. (1977); Cook, Stanton A., *Reproduction, Heredity and Sexuality* (1964); Finn, C. A., ed., *Oxford Reviews of Reproductive Biology*, vol. 1 (1979); Najarian, Haig H., *Sex Lives of Animals without Backbones* (1976); Sadleir, Richard M., *The Reproduction of Vertebrates* (1973); Stevenson, Forrest, *Plant Life Cycles* (1975); Street, P., *Animal Reproduction* (1974).

reproductive system, human

Male and female human reproductive systems develop from a similar set of embryological structures, and many structural

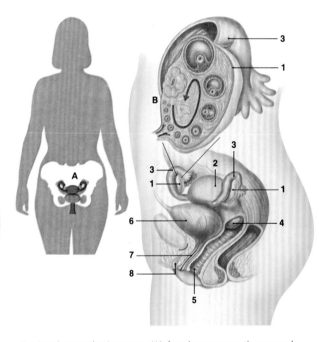

The male reproductive system (A) is designed to produce spermatozoa and to transmit them into the female reproductive system, where one of them may fertilize an egg. Sperm and eggs are both gamete cells, containing chromosomes, that join together to create new life. Millions of sperm are produced each day in the testicles (1). Because the temperature within the body is too high to permit sperm production, the testicles hang just outside the pelvic area in a pouch of skin called the scrotum. Mature sperm are stored in the epididymis (2). A cross section of a testicle (B) shows a system of conical lobules, each of which contains one or more coiled tubules in which sperm are made. Channels lead from the lobules to the epididymis and from there to the vas deferens, or sperm ducts (3). During sexual stimulation, sperm pass through the vas deferens into the urethra (4), where they mix with fluids from the seminal vesicles (5), prostate gland (6), and Cowper's gland (7) to form semen. Simultaneously, spongelike structures in the penis (8) become filled with blood, causing it to elongate and become erect. If stimulation continues, the muscles of the penis contract rhythmically, expelling the semen. The penis and urethra also function as parts of the urinary system, eliminating urine from the bladder (9). The bladder's entrance to the urethra is closed when sexual stimulation occurs.

The female reproductive system (A) functions on a continuous cycle of preparation for childbearing. Each month a mature egg (ovum) is released by one of the ovaries (1). The cross section of an ovary (B) shows, counterclockwise, the changes in an egg follicle as it develops (bottom), rises toward the surface (right), releases the mature egg (top), becomes an estrogen-producing "yellow body" (left), and disappears, leaving a temporary white scar (center). The ovum is transmitted to the uterus (2) through the oviducts, or Fallopian tubes (3), a journey that takes approximately 3 days. The uterus, also known as the womb, is a hollow, muscular organ about the size of a fist. Its lower end, the cervix (4), protrudes into the vagina (5), which is the sheath of soft skin that receives the penis during intercourse. During the first half of the ovulatory cycle, the inner lining of the uterus is enriched with blood and glandular fluids. If the egg is not fertilized in the oviduct by a male sperm cell, this lining is shed in a process called menstruation. If fertilization does occur, the egg attaches itself to the uterine lining and begins the 9-month period of growth that will culminate in the birth of a child. The bladder (6) and urethra (7) function separately from the female reproductive system. In front of the urethral opening is the clitoris (8), a sensory organ that fills with blood and rhythmically contracts during sexual stimulation.

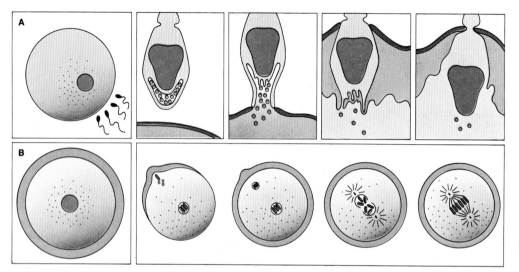

When fertilization occurs (A), a sperm cell fuses with an egg cell. As the two merge, the acrosome—a caplike vesicle in the head of the sperm—releases enzymes (orange) that enable the sperm to penetrate the egg. After the sperm nucleus enters the egg, a fertilization membrane forms (B), which prevents other sperm from entering. The sperm nuclei then migrate toward the egg nucleus; the two nuclei fuse; and the chomosomes align prior to cell division.

and functional parallels exist. Individual differences occur in the shape and structure of genitals, but without interfering with reproductive or sexual function. Also, the sexual anatomy of a young child differs from that of a mature adult and, in turn, adult sexual anatomy alters in the later years of life.

MALE REPRODUCTIVE SYSTEM

The male reproductive system basically is designed to produce and transport sperm cells. At the same time, the male genitals play an obvious role in sexual behavior, because reproduction cannot take place unless sperm cells are deposited in the female reproductive system. The major organs of the male reproductive system are the testes (testicles), the prostate, the seminal vesicles, the vas deferens, the epididymis, and the penis. Although the bladder empties through a duct that runs through the length of the penis, it is not considered part of the reproductive system.

Testes. The testes, which are contained in a pouch of skin called the scrotum, are located outside of the body because they require a lower temperature than the rest of the body in order to accomplish one of their main functions: the production of sperm cells (spermatogenesis). If the temperature of the scrotum rises by only a few degrees, the process of spermatogenesis may be seriously impaired. Each of the two testes are suspended from the body and held in place by a spermatic cord; the skin of the scrotum contains numerous sweat glands that assist in the cooling process.

Spermatogenesis. Within the scrotum, each testis is contained by a thick protective capsule, within which is a network of tightly coiled tubes called the seminiferous tubules; if uncoiled, these tubules would stretch to almost a mile in length. Spermatogenesis takes place within the seminiferous tubules. Sperm production fully occurs usually by the age of 16, even though it can begin before a boy reaches puberty. The male continues to produce sperm throughout his life but with a marked slowing of the process in the later years. A man often is able to father children when he is into his seventies or eighties, but the peak of his fertility is usually earlier in the life cycle. The testes also produce the male hormones, or androgens, in a number of large cells called the interstitial cells of Leydig, which are located between the seminiferous tubules. Like the production of sperm, the manufacture and secretion of these hormones begins about the time of puberty and continues throughout life. The hormones are manufactured in the testes and circulate throughout the body, affecting various organs.

Pathway of the Sperm. After sperm are produced in the seminiferous tubules, they move through the testes into another system of ducts called the epididymis. Although the epididymis is only about 3.8 cm (1.5 in) in length, it is so tightly coiled that it would measure about 12 m (20 ft) in length if extended. The sperm cells remain in this duct system and continue to mature for about 2 weeks and then pass into a longer transportation duct called the vas deferens. The male sterilization procedure, or vasectomy, is named for this duct because the operation involves cutting the vas deferens so that the sperm cells cannot travel from the testes to the penis.

Seminal Fluids. Before the sperm cells reach the penis, they travel through a number of internal organs: the prostate, the seminal vesicles, and Cowper's glands. The major function of these internal organs is to produce fluids that will provide the sperm cells with a nourishing and balanced environment. Only a very small proportion of the male ejaculate is actually made up of sperm cells; the remainder consists of the seminal fluids secreted by these internal organs. Because of this factor, a male who undergoes vasectomy will continue to ejaculate about the same volume of fluid as a fertile male. Although seminal fluids are not absolutely necessary in order for a man to be fertile, these fluids allow the sperm cells to live longer within the acidic environment of the vagina.

The Penis. In the final phase of their journey, the sperm cells pass through the urethral duct, which runs through the center of the penis. The penis contains a large number of arteries, veins, and small blood vessels as well as erectile tissue, the last of which consists of three hollow, spongelike cylinders of tissue. When a male has an erection, these spongy tissues fill with blood and become firm. Unlike a number of other mammals—for instance, the whale—no bones are located within the human penis. Erection is caused solely by the relaxation of the blood vessels within the penis. Thus, when a man is under emotional or physical stress, he may experience some difficulty achieving a firm erection because the blood vessels may not relax sufficiently.

FEMALE REPRODUCTIVE SYSTEM

The female reproductive organs are designed for conception, pregnancy, and childbirth. Like the male, female anatomy includes both internal and external sexual organs. The internal organs are more closely related to reproductive function and the external organs tend to be related to sexual function.

Function of the Female System. Just as the testes produce sperm, which are the basic reproductive material in men, ovaries produce eggs, or ova. The two ovaries are located to the right and the left of the uterus, to which they are connected by Fallopian tubes. During each menstrual cycle the ovaries mature and release an egg cell (see MENSTRUATION). When a female infant is born, she already has in her ovaries all the egg cells that will be released during her life. These egg cells, however, do not mature until the time of puberty, when the menstrual cycle begins under the influence of female hormones. This process continues until the MENOPAUSE, when the menstrual cycle ceases and hormone production diminishes.

The second major function of the ovaries is the production of the female hormones estrogen and progesterone. Like the

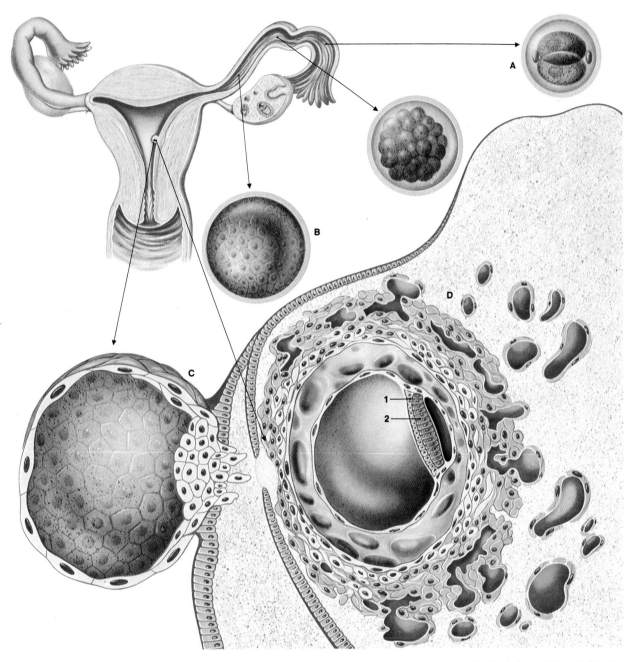

Within a few hours of conception, the fertilized egg, or zygote, still traveling through the oviduct, begins to divide (A). Each division doubles the number of cells, until the zygote is a rapidly expanding ball filled with fluid (B), a stage of the developing embryo that is known as the blastula. On approximately the sixth day after conception, the zygote reaches the uterus and implants itself in the uterine wall (C). Its outer layer of cells burrows into the lining (D) and develops into the placenta. Its inner layer splits into a layer of endoderm cells (1) and a layer of ectoderm cells (2), which enclose the amniotic and yolk sacs. These cells will later form the skin, nerves, and organs of the developing fetus.

male, the female produces hormones that circulate throughout the body and serve to keep the sexual system ready for reproduction. Unlike the male, however, the female secretes varying amounts of different hormones in a distinct, monthly cycle. During the first half of the cycle, hormones cause a single egg cell to mature; at midcycle, ovulation, or the release of the egg cell from the ovary, takes place. Also during the first half of the cycle, the lining of the uterus (endometrium) prepares to receive and nourish a fertilized egg. If fertilization and pregnancy have not occurred, hormone levels tend to decrease, the uterine lining is shed, and the cycle begins anew. The pattern of ovarian hormone release is regulated by

the pituitary gland, which is located in the brain; for this reason, physical or emotional stress can affect the length or regularity of the menstrual cycle.

Ovulation. In the adult woman each of the two ovaries is about the size and shape of an unshelled almond and is grayish in color. During ovulation the egg cell breaks through or ruptures the wall of the ovary, at which time a small amount of bleeding may occur. Within the ovary are a number of compartments called follicles, which contain egg cells at various stages of development. After the egg cell is released, the follicle, referred to in this instance as the corpus luteum, remains within the ovary and continues to secrete hormones. If no pregnancy develops, the corpus luteum shrinks and disappears by the next menstrual cycle; if pregnancy does occur, the corpus luteum continues to secrete hormones for about 6 months.

Pathway of the Egg. After the mature egg is released from the ovary, it must travel a short distance to the entrance of the Fallopian, or uterine, tubes, which work as a transport system, moving the egg from the ovary to the uterus, and at the same time, secreting substances that nourish the egg. If fertilization—the meeting of egg and sperm—is to occur, it must take place within the Fallopian tube. Generally, the egg takes about 3 days to make the short journey from ovary to uterus; however, fertilization can take place only within the first 24 hours of this passage.

The Uterus. The uterus, or womb, is about the size and shape of an inverted pear in women who have never borne children. During pregnancy, this muscular container increases enormously in size and weight. After childbirth the uterus tends to remain slightly larger in size but retains the same shape.

The bulk of the uterus is a network of dense muscular fibers interlaced in all directions; the contractions of childbirth begin when these muscles work to move the fetus towards the vagina.

At the bottom of the uterus is the cervix, a passageway between the uterus and vagina. It is normally very small and, at times, is blocked entirely by mucus that is secreted by the cervical glands. During birth, however, it opens wide enough to allow for passage of the fetus.

The Vagina. Like the uterus, the vagina is normally a small organ with little internal space: in the resting state, the walls of the vagina are touching one another. Also like the uterus, the muscles of the vagina are able to expand greatly during intercourse or childbirth, after which they return to their normal size. In shape, the vagina resembles an elongated "S" and is usually about 10 cm (4 in) long in the mature female. The vagina, in addition to muscular tissue, contains a rich network of blood vessels; when a woman is sexually aroused this network fills with blood in much the same way that the male's penis becomes erect due to increased blood flow. In turn, the pressure of this blood causes the mucous lining of the vagina to secrete drops of fluid; this lubrication response is a primary sign of female sexual arousal.

Female external sexual anatomy consists of the labia majora, labia minora, and clitoris. The labia majora, or outer lips, are two folds of skin that normally enclose the external genitals. The labia minora, or inner lips, are two smaller skin folds containing a rich network of blood vessels. They are normally pinkish in color but may show a variety of color changes when a woman is sexually stimulated.

The Clitoris. According to sex researchers William Masters and Virginia Johnson, the clitoris is a unique organ in human anatomy, having as its major purpose the sensation of sexual pleasure.

The clitoris, like the penis, to which it is homologous, is made up of erectile tissue—that is, when a woman is sexually stimulated, the clitoris fills with blood and becomes firm. Normally, the clitoral body is covered by a fold of skin called the clitoral hood.

In attempting to understand female sexuality, many people at one time thought that the size of the clitoris was related to the intensity of a woman's sexual response. Another theory suggested that the distance between the clitoris and the vaginal opening determined the ease of reaching orgasm during intercourse. Research, however, has shown that sexual arousal and orgasm may have little relationship with the size, shape, or position of the clitoris. LINDA ROSEN

Bibliography: Demarest, Robert J., and Sciarra, John J., *Conception, Birth and Contraception*, 2d ed. (1976); Knepp, Thomas H., *Human Reproduction: Health and Hygiene*, rev. ed. (1967); Navarra, J. G., et al., *From Generation to Generation: The Story of Reproduction* (1970); Swanson, Harold D., *Human Reproduction: Biology and Social Change* (1974).

See also: BIRTH CONTROL; DEVELOPMENT; FERTILITY, HUMAN; SEX; SEX HORMONES; SEXUAL DEVELOPMENT; SEXUAL INTERCOURSE.

reptile

Reptiles are vertebrate, or backboned, animals constituting the class Reptilia and are characterized by a combination of features, none of which alone could separate all reptiles from all other animals. Among the assemblage of identifying characteristics are (1) cold-bloodedness; (2) the presence of lungs; (3) direct development, without larval forms as in amphibians; (4) a dry skin with scales but not feathers (a characteristic of birds) or hair (a characteristic of mammals); (5) an amniote egg; (6) internal fertilization; (7) a three- or four-chambered heart; (8) two aortic arches (blood vessels) carrying blood from the heart to the body; mammals have only one aorta, the left; birds also have but one, the right; (9) a metanephric kidney; (10) twelve pairs of head (cranial) nerves; amphibians have ten; and (11) skeletal features such as (a) limbs with usually five clawed fingers or toes, (b) at least two spinal bones (sacral vertebrae) associated with the pelvis; amphibians have but one, (c) a single ball-and-socket connection (condyle) at the head-neck joint instead of two, as in advanced amphibians and mammals, and (d) an incomplete or complete partition (the secondary palate) along the roof of the mouth, separating the food and air passageways so that breathing can continue while food is being chewed.

These and other traditional defining characteristics of reptiles have been subjected to considerable modification in recent times. The extinct flying reptiles, called pterosaurs or PTERODACTYLS, are now thought to have been warm-blooded and covered with hair; and the DINOSAURS are also now considered by many authorities to have been warm-blooded. The earliest known bird, ARCHAEOPTERYX, is now regarded by many to have been a small dinosaur, despite its covering of feathers; and the extinct ancestors of the mammals, the therapsids, or mammallike reptiles, are also believed to have been warm-blooded and haired. Proposals have been made to reclassify the pterosaurs, dinosaurs, and certain other groups out of the class Reptilia into one or more classes of their own, and these issues are now receiving a great deal of attention from paleontologists and zoologists.

Cold-bloodedness. Reptiles are cold-blooded; that is, they lack the ability to regulate their metabolic heat (heat derived from the oxidation, or "burning," of food and from other processes) for the production of sustained body warmth and a constant body temperature. Cold-bloodedness, however, does not mean that a reptile is necessarily cold. A LIZARD basking in the sun may have a higher body temperature than a mammal. Because cold-bloodedness is a misleading term, biologists employ two others instead, describing reptiles as poikilothermic and ectothermic. *Poikilothermy* refers to the condition in which body temperature varies with the temperature of the environment; it is contrasted with homeothermy, a characteristic of birds and mammals, in which body temperature remains essentially the same through a wide range of environmental temperatures. *Ectothermy* refers to the condition in which an animal depends on an external source, such as the Sun, rather than its own metabolism, for body warmth. Birds and mammals, which use their internal metabolic heat for body warmth, are referred to as endothermic.

Respiration. All reptiles possess lungs, and none passes through an aquatic larval stage with gills, as do many of the amphibians. In SNAKES, presumably as an adaptation to their long, thin bodies, the left lung is reduced in size or entirely lacking. Although lungs are the primary means of respiration in all reptiles and the only means of respiration in most reptiles, a number of species are also able to utilize other parts of the body for the absorption of oxygen and the elimination of carbon dioxide. In aquatic TURTLES, for example, the tissues (mucous membranes) lining the insides of the mouth are capable of extracting oxygen from the water; some file snakes, family Acrochordidae, and SEA SNAKES, family Hydrophiidae, as well as the soft-shelled turtle, *Trionyx*, can use their skin for respiration when submerged.

Skin and Scales. Part of the ability of the amphibians' descendants, the reptiles, to invade dry-land environments was

Of the living orders of reptiles, two arose earlier than the Age of
Reptiles, when dinosaurs were dominant. Tuataras, of the order
Rhynchocephalia, are found only on New Zealand islands, whereas
the equally ancient turtles, order Chelonia, occur nearly worldwide;
shown is the chicken turtle, Deirochelys reticularia. The order
Crocodilia emerged along with the dinosaurs; shown is the East
Indian saltwater crocodile, Crocodylus porosus. Snakes and lizards,
order Squamata, are today the most numerous reptile species; shown
are the black-necked spitting cobra, Naja nigricollis; land iguana,
Conolphus subcristatus; and white-bellied worm lizard,
Amphisbaena alba.

saltwater crocodile

tuatara

land iguana

black-necked
spitting cobra

white-bellied
worm lizard

chicken turtle

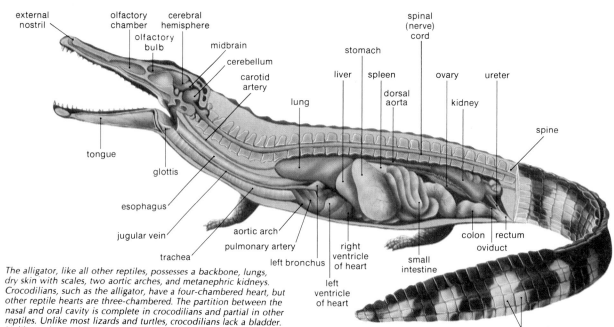

external nostril
olfactory chamber
cerebral hemisphere
olfactory bulb
midbrain
cerebellum
carotid artery
spinal (nerve) cord
stomach
liver
spleen
ovary
ureter
dorsal aorta
kidney
lung
spine
tongue
glottis
esophagus
jugular vein
trachea
aortic arch
pulmonary artery
left bronchus
right ventricle of heart
small intestine
colon
rectum
oviduct
left ventricle of heart
colon
epidermal scales

The alligator, like all other reptiles, possesses a backbone, lungs, dry skin with scales, two aortic arches, and metanephric kidneys. Crocodilians, such as the alligator, have a four-chambered heart, but other reptile hearts are three-chambered. The partition between the nasal and oral cavity is complete in crocodilians and partial in other reptiles. Unlike most lizards and turtles, crocodilians lack a bladder. Unlike snakes and lizards, crocodilians and turtles have a poorly developed Jacobson's organ for detecting tastes and odors.

the development of a dry skin that served as a barrier to moisture and greatly reduced the loss of body water. The reptile skin, like that of other vertebrate animals, consists of two main parts: an outer epidermis and an underlying dermis. The epidermis produces horny, or keratinized (like fingernails), scales on its upper surface. These scales are not the same as (that is, not homologous to) the scales of fishes, which are bony, are formed in the dermis, and lie beneath the epidermis. The reptile's scales increase the skin's resistance to water, further reducing moisture loss; some scales may be modified for specialized functions, such as protective spines. Reptile scales may be small and overlapping, as in many lizards, or large and adjoining, as in turtles, where they are commonly called scutes. Some reptiles also have bony plates or nodules formed and lying within the dermis. Called dermal scales or osteoderms, these bony plates are similar in origin to fish scales. When present in lizards and crocodilians (see CROCODILE), the dermal scales are separated from one another, with each usually lying beneath and supporting an epidermal scale above. In turtles the bony plates are fused together to form a bony shell beneath the epidermal scales.

In lizards and snakes the scales do not increase in size as the animal grows; consequently, the old scales must be periodically shed and replaced by a new set of somewhat larger scales. Shedding may also occur when the outer layer becomes worn or when much food is consumed, as well as for causes not yet fully understood. In the shedding, or molting, process, also called ecdysis, the older upper layer of the epidermis with its attached scales loosens and breaks away from a newer layer that has developed beneath it. In turtles and crocodilians the large epidermal scales, or scutes, are not molted but are retained and are enlarged and thickened by additional layers of keratin from beneath; the uppermost layers of the scutes, however, may be lost through wear or other factors.

The Amniote Egg. A necessary part of the invasion of dry-land environments by the early reptiles was the development of an egg that could be laid out of water without drying up and that could "breathe" air rather than water. This egg, developed by the first reptiles, was the amniote egg, so named because it contains a membrane called the amnion. The amniote egg is found not only in reptiles but also in birds and (ancestral) mammals, and all three groups are sometimes collectively referred to as amniotes.

The amniote egg is different from the fishlike egg of most amphibians. It is enclosed in a protective shell, which is either flexible and leathery or rigid and calcareous. Within the shell is the fertilized egg cell lying on top of a large mass of yolk. The yolk is surrounded by a membrane (the yolk sac) and provides nourishment for the developing embryo. As the fertilized egg cell divides and redivides, and the embryo begins to form and grow, a folded membranous tissue grows up around the embryo, enclosing it in a double-walled sac. The outer wall of the sac is called the chorion, the inner wall, the amnion. The embryo is surrounded by fluid held with the amnion. The fluid provides the embryo with the aquatic environment it obviously still requires but which in amphibians is supplied by the waters of a pond or stream.

Another sac, called the allantois, projects from the embryo's lower digestive tract (the hind gut) and acts as a bladder to receive the embryo's waste products. The allantois sac becomes quite large, expanding out until its wall joins that of the chorion to form the chorioallantoic membrane, which is pressed up against the inside of the shell. Not only does the allantois serve as a bladder, receiving and storing insoluble wastes, but it also acts as a sort of "lung," allowing oxygen and carbon dioxide to pass to and from the embryo through the slightly porous (permeable) egg shell.

Internal Fertilization. Because the egg cell reaches the outside environment surrounded by the shell of the egg, it is necessary that it be fertilized before it leaves the female's body; thus, in all reptiles fertilization is internal, with males depositing sperm within the females' genital tracts. In snakes and lizards the male organ, called the hemipenes, is actually a pair of structures, with one of the pair, or hemipenis, situated internally on each side of the male's vent. Each hemipenis, which itself may be forked, is a functional structure: either one may be protruded from the vent and used in mating, the choice usually depending upon the placement of the male's mate. In turtles and crocodilians there is a single penis, which serves only for the transmission of sperm and not also for the elimination of excretory products, as in mammals. In the lizardlike tuatara, *Sphenodon*, the only living species in its order, the male lacks a copulatory organ, and mating is accomplished by the pressing together of the male's and female's cloacae, as in most birds.

The Heart. Except for crocodilians, which have a four-chambered heart, all reptiles have a three-chambered heart consisting of two atria and one ventricle. The chamber called the right atrium receives deoxygenated, or "spent," blood return-

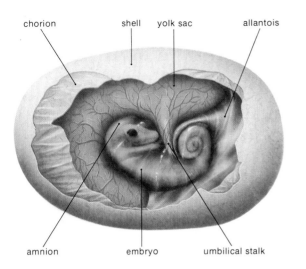

chorion   shell   yolk sac   allantois

amnion   embryo   umbilical stalk

Reptiles produce an amniote egg, rich in yolk and enclosed in a shell, that is adapted to development on land. The developing embryo is connected to the main food supply, the yolk, which is enclosed in a yolk sac. A fluid-filled sac, the amnion, surrounds the embryo and keeps it from drying out. Another sac, the allantois, stores the embryo's wastes and permits gas exchange through the shell. The chorion surrounds both the amnion and allantois. In crocodilians and turtles the egg white, or albumen, functions as a water reserve.

ing from the body tissues. It passes this blood into the ventricle, from where it is pumped to the lungs for oxygenation. The oxygenated blood from the lungs returns to the left atrium and once again enters the same ventricle, from which it is pumped to the body tissues.

Even in the three-chambered heart, however, as recent research has shown in contrast to earlier beliefs, there is little mixing of oxygenated and deoxygenated blood. This has been achieved by the development within the ventricle of interconnected "subchambers" within which a sequence of changes in blood pressure takes place. Several anatomical variations occur among the reptiles, but a simplified description of the lizard heart will serve to illustrate one way in which this circulatory efficiency was accomplished.

The ventricle of the lizard heart is incompletely partitioned into two subchambers by a muscular ridge that descends from the roof of the heart almost to the floor. The right subchamber is called the right ventricle, or cavum pulmonale; it leads to the lungs. The left subchamber is called the left ventricle, or cavum venosum; it receives blood from the right atrium and leads to the body. The two subchambers are connected not only beneath the partition but also across its incomplete rearward end.

A third subchamber, called the cavum arteriosum, is situated in the upper wall of the right ventricle; it receives blood from the left atrium and is connected through a valve-controlled opening to the left ventricle.

When the two atria contract, oxygenated blood from the left atrium enters the third subchamber, or cavum arteriosum, pressing against and shutting the valves controlling the opening into the left ventricle; this closes off the third subchamber and temporarily holds its contained blood in storage. At the same time the deoxygenated blood in the right atrium has been pumped into the left ventricle, filling it to overflowing, the excess blood moving across the open posterior end of the muscular partition into the right ventricle. The three ventricular subchambers are now filled with blood; oxygenated blood in the third subchamber (cavum arteriosum) and deoxygenated blood in the two ventricles.

Resistance to blood flow is lower in the pulmonary (heart-lung) circuit than in the systemic (heart-body) circuit, so that when the ventricles contract, the deoxygenated blood in the right ventricle follows the path of least resistance and proceeds through the pulmonary artery into the lungs. The emptying of the right ventricle causes more deoxygenated blood

from the left ventricle to move around the open end of the partition into the right ventricle and to continue on to the lungs. The contraction of the ventricle also brings the partitioning muscular ridge into full contact with the floor of the heart, sealing off any flow from the right ventricle back into the left ventricle.

As the ventricles continue their contraction, the pressure on the blood held within the third subchamber (cavum arteriosum) exerts a reverse force on the valves, opening the passageway between the third subchamber and the left ventricle. The oxygenated blood in the third subchamber now moves into the left ventricle and from there into the aortas leading to the body circulation.

Metanephric Kidney. Adult amphibians have an opisthonephric kidney, that is, one that was developed from the main mass (except for the foremost end) of kidney-forming tissue in the embryo; the collecting tubules of the amphibian's opisthonephric kidney are connected to a drainage tube called the archinephric, or Wolffian, duct. In contrast, the metanephric kidney of adult reptiles (and birds and mammals) arises from the rearmost part of the kidney-forming tissue of the embryo—the front and middle portions having given rise to the pronephric and mesonephric kidneys, which eventually degenerate. The collecting tubules of the metanephric kidney are connected to a "newly evolved" drainage tube, the ureter. The Wolffian duct, having lost its excretory function, becomes partly involved in the transmission of sperm in males but is a degenerate vestige in females. In mammals the ureter drains into the bladder, which empties to the outside through another tube called the urethra. Crocodilians and snakes lack bladders, but even where one is present, as in most lizards and turtles, it is formed simply by an outpocketing of the cloaca and has no connection with the ureter. The cloaca, whose name comes from the Latin word for sewer, is a body chamber leading to the outside and into which empty the excretory products of the kidneys, the waste products of the intestines, and the reproductive products of the testes and ovaries. The reptilian ureter empties into the cloaca, and if a bladder is present it receives and holds the urine overflow.

Skull. The reptilian skull ranges from the reduced, loosely joined, or kinetic, skull of snakes to the large, solid skull of crocodilians. On each side of the skull behind the eye sockets there may be one or two openings formed at the junctions of certain bones. The openings are believed to be an adaptation for more-efficient functioning of the jaw muscles, possibly by allowing them to bulge outward when the jaws are closed. Because the positions of the openings, as determined by the bones surrounding them, were considered critical in the classification of reptiles, skull types were designated by the row, or arch, of bones beneath each opening rather than by the openings themselves. The Greek root *apse,* meaning "arch," was used in the naming of the skull types. A reptile skull without any temporal openings, and hence without arches, was termed *anapsid* (an, "without"; apsid, "arches"). Anapsid skulls are characteristic of the extinct, primitive cotylosaurs and of the living turtles.

When openings are present, their positions are best described in relation to the two skull bones extending from behind the eye socket to the rear of the head: the postorbital and squamosal bones. In the euryapsid-type skull there is a single opening high on each side of the head situated in the upper part of the junction between the postorbital and squamosal bones, which form the opening's lower border, or arch. In the parapsid-type skull, considered by some to be only a variant of the euryapsid, there is also a single opening high on each side of the head, but it is located above the postorbital and squamosal bones; its lower border, or arch, is formed by the supratemporal and postfrontal bones. An euryapsid-type skull was present in the extinct plesiosaurs, a parapsid-type skull in the extinct icthyosaurs.

A skull with a single low opening on each side of the head, situated in the lower part of the junction between the postorbital and squamosal bones and bordered below by parts of the squamosal, quadratojugal, and jugal bones, is termed *synapsid.* The extinct mammallike reptiles, order Therapsida,

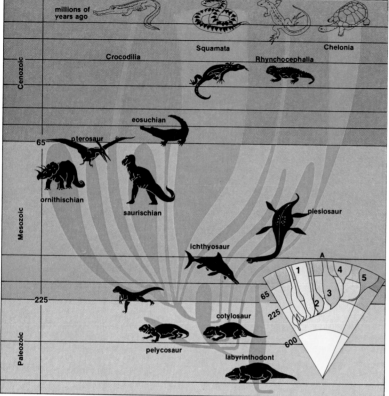

In the age of reptiles, 225 to 65 million years ago, the dominant life forms on land and in the sea and air were all reptilian. Pictured are the most familiar of these, the dinosaurs and such related forms as the sea-dwelling Plesiosaurus and winged Pteranodon. Not all of these animals were contemporaries of one another during the lengthy Mesozoic Era, and some of them may possibly have been warm-blooded. The dinosaurs ranged in size from the small Procompsognathus to the huge Brontosaurus, both of them saurischian, or lizard-hipped; the plated Stegosaurus was ornithischian, or bird-hipped. Both these lines of dinosaur evolution—saurischian and ornithischian—developed a great diversity of forms before they died out at the end of the Cretaceous Period, as did the pterosaurs, plesiosaurs, and fishlike ichthyosaurs. The evolutionary chart depicts the development of the class Reptilia as a whole, from the early ancestral labyrinthodonts to the surviving modern orders: Crocodilia (crocodiles and related animals), Squamata (lizards and snakes), Rhynchocephalia (tautaras), and Chelonia (turtles). Inset A on the chart uses a larger time scale to compare the origin, evolution, and prevalence of the different vertebrates—fish (1), amphibians (2), reptiles (3), birds (4), and mammals (5)—up to the present time.

from which the mammals evolved, had synapsid skulls.

If a reptile skull has two openings, one high and one low, on each side of the head, situated in both the upper and lower parts of the junction between the postorbital and squamosal bones, it is classified as diapsid. Diapsid skulls are characteristic of dinosaurs and of the living crocodilians. Modern lizards and snakes also have diapsid skulls, but in the lizards the arch of the lower opening has been lost during evolution, leaving only the single upper opening and its arch. In snakes both the lower and upper arches have been lost, leaving no openings and very little bone; the reduction of bone and the increase of space in this area contribute to the kinetic qualities, or movability, of the snake's skull.

Sense Organs. Vision is the most commonly employed reptilian sense for the detection of objects in the environment. The BLIND SNAKES, such as those of the family Typhlopidae, appear to lack eyes, but eyes are present beneath the scales of the head. The ability to see different colors rather than just shades of gray is definitely present in some daylight-active lizards and turtles, and it may be present in some snakes as well. The unblinking eyes of snakes and some lizards are said to result from the animal's inability to close its lidless eyes. Actually, the lower eyelid has become transparent and is raised and permanently fused to the vestigial remnant of the upper eyelid; thus, the eye is technically always closed rather than always open.

The reptile eye is normally "set" for distance vision and must be acted upon (accommodated) to focus on things near. In all reptiles but snakes, near vision is achieved by contractions of muscles in the ciliary body surrounding the lens, forcing the lens into a more rounded shape. In snakes the contraction of special muscles forces the lens forward in adjustments for near vision.

A functioning median, parietal, or third eye is present in the upper skull of some lizards. The median eye, which has the basic eye structure of cornea, lens, and retina, is not able to distinguish shapes but rather responds to light and dark; it is believed to be involved in the control of certain secretions and in certain adaptive behaviors.

The ear structure in most reptiles consists of (a) an eardrum, which lies close to or near the surface of the skin (there is no external ear); (b) a small bone, called the columella or stapes, which conducts the vibrations of the eardrum through the cavity of the middle ear; and (c) the inner ear, which receives and analyzes the vibrations being transmitted by the columella. Turtles have well-developed ear structures but usually give little evidence of hearing ability. Certain TORTOISES, however, appear especially sensitive to low sounds of about 100 Hz. Snakes lack both the eardrum and the middle-ear cavity but retain the columella, which is positioned against the lower part of the skull at the jaw hinge (the quadrate bone). Lacking eardrums, a snake cannot "hear" airborne sounds in the usual sense, but experiments have shown that the snake's inner ear does respond to low-frequency airborne sounds, or pressure vibrations, possibly by transmission of the vibrations through the skull bones. A snake can readily detect earthborne sounds, or vibrations.

The Jacobson's, or the vomeronasal, organ is a specialized chemical detector located in the roof of the mouth. It is present in rudimentary form in turtles and crocodilians but is highly developed in snakes and lizards. The rapid in-and-out flicking of a snake's tongue is to pick up tiny chemical particles, which adhere or dissolve in the moisture on the tongue and are then conveyed back to the two openings of the Jacobson's organ for identification.

Origin and Evolution. The first known reptiles appeared during the Pennsylvanian Period (or upper Carboniferous), about 300 million years ago. The oldest of these, *Hylonomus,* was about 70 cm (27 in) long and lizardlike in shape. It was discovered in the Coal Measures of Nova Scotia. The reptiles evolved from AMPHIBIANS known as anthracosaurs, which were part of the labyrinthodont group (amphibians with highly complex patterns in the surface of the teeth). The reptiles probably evolved during the Mississippian Period (or lower Carboniferous), about 40 million years earlier, but at present there is no fossil evidence to indicate this more precisely. Evidence for the transition from amphibian to reptile, however, does exist in related forms such as *Seymouria,* from the Permian Period, about 275 million years ago.

The reptiles expanded during the Permian, the last period of the Paleozoic Era, but it was during the following MESOZOIC ERA, from about 225 million to 65 million years ago, that they came to dominate not only the land but also the sea and air. During this era, known as "the age of reptiles," they radiated out into many diverse and sometimes bizarre forms and occupied a wide array of ecological niches. The dinosaur group, if still regarded as reptiles, included the largest land animals that ever lived. The age of reptiles came to a close at the end of the Cretaceous, the last period of the Mesozoic Era. The undetermined reasons for this decline have been the subject of intensive study for many years.

Classification and Types. The class Reptilia (living and extinct reptiles) is divided into 6 to 12 subclasses by different authorities. A number of these subclasses, such as the Synapsida, are completely extinct. The subclasses contain about 24 orders, but only 4 of these are still represented by living animals. The living reptiles comprise the turtles (about 250 species), the lizards (about 3,000 species), the TUATARA (one species), the amphisbaenians, or WORM LIZARDS (about 40 species, usually included with the lizards), the snakes (about 2,700 species), and the crocodilians (about 21 species). Of these, the reticulated python, *Python reticulatus,* is usually considered to be the longest reptile, reaching 10 m (33 ft) in length; however, the anaconda, *Eunectes murinus,* has been reported as exceeding 11 m (36 ft) in length. The heaviest living reptile is the leatherback turtle, *Dermochelys coriacea,* which has attained 725 kg (1,600 lb) in weight. The smallest reptile is possibly the dwarf gecko, *Sphaerodactylus elegans,* which reaches only about 34 mm (1.3 in) in length.

The following is a brief, acceptable classification of the living reptiles, class Reptilia:

Subclass Anapsida
  Order Chelonia (turtles)
    Suborder Cryptodira
    Suborder Pleurodira
Subclass Lepidosauria
  Order Rhynchocephalia (tuatara)
  Order Squamata
    Suborder Amphisbaenia (worm lizards)
    Suborder Sauria (lizards)
    Suborder Serpentes (snakes)
Subclass Archosauria
  Order Crocodylia (crocodilians)

EDWIN E. ROSENBLUM

Bibliography: Bellairs, Angus, *The World of Reptiles,* 2 vols. (1970); Cochran, Doris M., and Goin, Coleman J., *The New Book of Reptiles and Amphibians* (1970); Conant, Roger, *A Field Guide to Reptiles and Amphibians of Eastern and Central North America,* 2d ed. (1975); Ditmars, R. L., *Reptiles of the World* (1933); Goin, C. J., et al., *Introduction to Herpetology,* 3d ed. (1978); Harrison, Al H. *The World of the Snake* (1971); Leutscher, Alfred, *Keeping Reptiles and Amphibians* (1978); Minton, Sherman A. and Madge R., *Venomous Reptiles* (1969); Schmidt, Karl P., and Inger, Robert F., *Living Reptiles of the World* (1957; repr. 1970); Wright, Albert H. and Anna A., *Handbook of Snakes of the United States and Canada,* 2 vols. (1957).

Repton, Humphry   [rep'-tuhn]

Humphry Repton, b. May 2, 1752, d. Mar. 24, 1818, succeeded the distinguished Capability Brown to become the most prominent English landscape gardener of his day. The aim of the landscape gardener, according to Repton, should be to articulate and reinforce the natural beauty of the landscape, avoiding both the extreme of cultivated artificiality and that of excessive ruggedness. He also believed that the successful practice of his art required a knowledge of architecture as well as gardening. He collaborated with the architect John Nash for a time (c.1792–99) and later with his own architect sons. Also a landscape theorist, Repton published his ideas in several books, including *Sketches and Hints on Landscape Gardening* (1794), *Observations on the Theory and Practice of*

Landscape Gardening (1803), and An Inquiry into the Changes of Taste in Landscape Gardening (1806).

VALENTIN TATRANSKY

Bibliography: Hyams, Edward S., *Capability Brown and Humphry Repton* (1971); Stroud, Dorothy, *Humphry Repton* (1962); Pevsner, Nikolaus, *Studies in Art, Architecture, and Design*, vol. 1 (1968).

republic

A republic is a form of GOVERNMENT in which SOVEREIGNTY rests in those people entitled to elect, either directly or indirectly, representatives who hold office for limited periods of time. In a republic the head of state is a nonhereditary officer most often called the president. The president may also be the actual chief executive, or such power may reside with a prime minister or premier.

A republic may or may not be a democracy, depending on voting qualifications, the degree of suffrage, and the presence of real electoral alternatives. Some political systems are democratic but are not republics because they have a hereditary head of state, as, for example, Great Britain.

Republics can be classified in three types of government: (1) presidential systems, such as the United States and Mexico, in which the chief of state is the chief of government as well; (2) parliamentary systems, in which the chief of state holds a largely ceremonial function and executive authority resides in a prime minister or premier, such as in Italy or West Germany; and (3) a presidential-parliamentary hybrid, such as in France, where the president shares some executive powers with a premier.

RITA J. IMMERMAN

Bibliography: Blondel, Jean, *An Introduction to Comparative Government* (1969); Friedrich, Carl J., *Constitutional Governments and Democracy* (1969); Hermens, F., *The Representative Republic* (1958).

Republic, The

One of the major works of the Greek philosopher PLATO, *The Republic* (*c*.370 BC) advances many of Plato's principal ideas, notably those concerned with government and justice. Composed as a debate between Socrates and five other speakers, *The Republic* is best known for its description of the ideal state (based on Sparta), which Plato argues should be ruled by philosopher-kings. The principles of justice that govern the state correspond to those which rule the individual, and the philosopher is best suited to govern because he perceives this natural harmony. An important section, the allegory of the cave (book 7), presents Plato's concept of the ideal Forms. The cave is the world of illusion and ignorance; only the philosopher has ventured beyond the shadows of the cave to perceive the ideal models of justice.

Bibliography: Guthrie, W. K. C., *A History of Greek Philosophy*, vol. 4 (1975); Plato, *The Republic*, trans. by W. H. D. Rouse (1956).

Republican party

The Republican party is one of the two major political parties in the United States, the other being the Democratic party. From the time it ran its first presidential candidate, John C. FRÉMONT, in 1856, until 1980, Republican presidents were in the White House for 72 years, and another, Ronald REAGAN, was inaugurated in 1981. Traditionally, Republican support has come primarily from New England and the Midwest. After World War II, however, its strength greatly increased in the Sunbelt states and the West. Generally speaking, after World War I the Republican party became the more conservative of the two major parties, with its support coming from the middle class and from the corporate, financial, and farming interests. It has taken political stances generally in favor of free enterprise, fiscal responsibility, and laissez-faire and against the welfare state.

The Founding of the Party. Scholars agree that the origins of the party grew out of the sectional conflicts regarding the expansion of slavery into the new Western territories. The stimulus for political realignment was provided by the passage of the Kansas-Nebraska Act of 1854. That law repealed

The first national convention of the Republican party (1856) selected John C. Frémont as its presidential candidate and William Dayton as his running mate. Campaigning on an antislavery platform, Frémont lost the election but received a third of the popular vote.

earlier compromises that had excluded slavery from the territories. The passage of this act served as the unifying agent for abolitionists and split the Democrats and the Whig party. "Anti-Nebraska" protest meetings spread rapidly through the country. Two such meetings were held in Ripon, Wis., on Feb. 28 and Mar. 20, 1854, and were attended by a group of abolitionist Free Soilers, Democrats, and Whigs. They decided to call themselves Republicans—because they professed to be political descendants of Thomas Jefferson's Democratic-Republican party. The name was formally adopted by a state convention held in Jackson, Mich., on July 6, 1854.

The new party was a success from the beginning. In the 1854 congressional elections 44 Republicans were elected as a part of the anti-Nebraskan majority in the House of Representatives, and several Republicans were elected to the Senate and to various state houses. In 1856, at the first Republican national convention, Sen. John C. Frémont was nominated for the presidency but was defeated by Democrat James Buchanan. During the campaign the northern wing of the KNOW-NOTHING PARTY split off and endorsed the Republican ticket. That action helped to establish the Republicans as the principal antislavery party.

Two days after the inauguration of James Buchanan, the Supreme Court handed down the *Dred Scott* v. *Sandford* deci-

The Wide-Awakes, a Republican club that adopted the name of an earlier nativist organization, march through New York City in a torchlight parade supporting Abraham Lincoln in the 1860 election. Lincoln won by carrying every free state, with 180 electoral votes.

sion, which increased sectional dissension and was denounced by the Republicans. At this time the nation was also gripped by economic chaos. Business blamed tariff reductions, and Republican leaders called for greater tariff protection. The split in the Democratic party over the issue of slavery continued, and in 1858 the Republicans won control of the House of Representatives for the first time. One Republican who failed that year was Abraham LINCOLN, defeated in his bid for a U.S. Senate seat by Stephen A. Douglas.

Lincoln, the Civil War, and Reconstruction. At the second Republican national convention, in 1860, a hard-fought contest resulted in the presidential nomination of Abraham Lincoln. The Republican platform specifically pledged not to extend slavery and called for enactment of free-homestead legislation, prompt establishment of a daily overland mail service, a transcontinental railroad, and support of the protective tariff. Lincoln was opposed by three major candidates—Douglas (Northern Democrat), John Cabell Breckinridge (Southern Democrat), and John Bell (Constitutional Union party). Lincoln collected almost half a million votes more than Douglas, his nearest competitor, but he won the election with only 39.8 percent of the popular vote.

Shortly thereafter, the Civil War began. Reverses on the battlefield, disaffection over the draft and taxes, and the failures of army leadership brought Lincoln and the Republicans into the 1864 election with small hope for victory. Party leaders saw the need to broaden the base of the party, and accordingly, they adopted the name National Union party. Andrew JOHNSON of Tennessee, a "War" Democrat, was nominated as Lincoln's running mate. Significant military victories intervened before election day and contributed to Lincoln's overwhelming reelection. After Lincoln's assassination the Radical Republicans, led by Sen. Charles SUMNER and Rep. Thaddeus STEVENS, fought President Johnson's moderate RECONSTRUCTION policies. Ultimately, relations between Johnson and Congress deteriorated, culminating in impeachment of the president; he was acquitted by a single vote.

The Republican Era. The defeat of the South left the Democratic party—closely allied with the Confederacy—in shambles. The Republicans, on the other hand, were in the ascendancy. With the election of Ulysses S. GRANT, the Republicans began a period of national dominance that lasted for more than 70 years and was only occasionally breached by a Democratic victory. Between 1860 and 1932 the Democrats controlled the White House for only 16 years. Grant's administration, with its support from the northern industrialists who had made fortunes in the Civil War, became riddled with scandal and corruption—the worst in the nation's history. Grant was not personally involved, however, and was renominated in 1872. A split among the Republicans ensued: the more liberal elements, opposed to the harshness of the

The battered GOP elephant in Thomas Nast's cartoon symbolizes the damage sustained by the Republican party in the hotly disputed victory of its candidate, Rutherford B. Hayes, over Democrat Samuel Tilden in the 1876 presidential election. Although Tilden won a majority of the popular votes, a special commission awarded the disputed electoral votes of four states to Hayes.

Radical Republicans on the Reconstruction issue and the scandals of the administration, broke away and took the name LIBERAL REPUBLICAN PARTY. They, along with a faction of the Democratic party, nominated Horace GREELEY for president. Despite this opposition, Grant was reelected by a substantial margin. A continuation of the scandals along with the panic of 1873 caused the Republicans to lose control of the Congress in 1874 in one of the greatest turnovers in history. The Republicans did, however, emerge from that election with a new party symbol, the elephant, after it first appeared in a newspaper cartoon by Thomas NAST.

In 1876 the Republicans nominated a virtual unknown, Rutherford B. HAYES of Ohio. The warring factions of the party were reunited as Hayes promised to remove the federal troops from the South and urged civil service reform. The Democratic candidate, Samuel J. TILDEN of New York, received the greatest number of popular votes, but widespread charges of electoral irregularities led to the appointment of a congressional electoral commission to review the results and decide who should receive disputed votes in four states. The commission, controlled by Republicans, granted all the votes to Hayes, thereby giving him the election by an electoral-college margin of 185 to 184.

The Hayes administration was tarnished by the means in which it came to office but was generally efficient. Hayes ended Reconstruction, reformed the civil service, and espoused sound money policies. All these actions were unpopular with the old-guard Republicans led by Roscoe CONKLING, and Hayes did not seek a second term. Instead, James A. GARFIELD was nominated as the Republican candidate in 1880. Chester A. ARTHUR of New York was nominated for vice-president. After winning a close election, Garfield was assassinated and Arthur became president. In spite of a past record as a "spoilsman," one who placed the party faithful in government jobs, Arthur astonished many with his success in getting passed the Pendleton Act, creating a civil service based on the merit system. He was never able to gain control of his party, however, and was the only president denied renomination by his party's convention. James G. BLAINE of Maine received the nomination instead and faced Democrat Grover Cleveland of New York in the 1884 election. In a campaign that became infamous as one of the dirtiest in history, Cleveland, aided by the MUGWUMPS led by Carl SCHURZ, defeated Blaine by a narrow margin.

Much of Cleveland's presidency was dominated by debate over the protective tariff. In 1888, after Blaine declined to run, the Republicans chose Benjamin HARRISON of Indiana as their nominee. Campaigning strongly in favor of the protective tariff, Harrison defeated Cleveland by an electoral vote of 233 to 168, although he received 100,000 fewer popular votes. For the first time in years the Republicans also captured both houses of Congress. The Republicans passed the SHERMAN ANTI-TRUST ACT, admitted several new states to the Union, and passed the highly protective McKinley Tariff Act.

Drinking from a bottle marked "2d Term," President Grant and his cronies revel under the canopy of "Despotism" in this 1872 cartoon. Grant's scandal-ridden first term prompted many discontented Republicans to form the separate Liberal Republican party.

In The Pygmies Attack, *a political drawing by Joseph Keppler, Republican president William McKinley firmly upholds the banners of expansionism and adherence to the gold standard against the ineffectual challenge of antiimperialist and free-silver Democrats. In the election of 1900, McKinley defeated his Democratic opponent, William Jennings Bryan, by a comfortable margin.*

Youthful, charismatic Theodore Roosevelt was selected as William McKinley's running mate in 1900 by Republican party leaders who hoped that the activist governor of New York would be relegated to obscurity by the vice-presidency. Elevated to the chief executive's office by McKinley's assassination in 1901, the dynamic Roosevelt dominated the Republican party and national politics for the next decade.

In the congressional elections of 1890 the party suffered its worst defeat since 1874. President Harrison, although not popular within his party, was renominated in 1892 but lost the election to Grover Cleveland. This defeat was the worst the Republicans had suffered since the party's birth. A severe depression and the panic of 1893—and a generally lackluster Cleveland administration—provided hope for the Republicans. The advent of a surprisingly strong POPULIST PARTY in 1892 siphoned off votes from the Republicans in the border states and from the Democrats in the South. Even so, the Populist thrust was relatively short-lived. By tying themselves too closely to FREE SILVER as a major issue the Democrats weakened themselves.

In 1896, William McKINLEY of Ohio became the Republican candidate after a campaign orchestrated by Mark HANNA, a Cleveland politician-businessman who feared the rise of populism and a decline in business prosperity. In what many political historians believe was the most significant election since 1860, McKinley beat William Jennings BRYAN by a substantial margin. McKinley received support from the industrial Northeast and the business community. Bryan received his votes from agricultural areas, the South, the West, and from the laboring man. These alliances presaged those that were ultimately to shape the political coalitions of the first half of the 20th century. The Republicans had committed themselves to conservative economics—a stance that they consistently retained thereafter.

McKinley's first term was dominated by the 10-week-long SPANISH-AMERICAN WAR (1898) and the subsequent acquisition of Guam, Puerto Rico, the Philippines, and the annexation of Hawaii. These events increasingly thrust the United States into world politics. The only question regarding the Republican ticket in 1900 was who would replace Vice-President Garret HOBART who had died the previous year. Governor Theodore ROOSEVELT of New York was chosen. McKinley again defeated William Jennings Bryan but was assassinated in 1901. Theodore Roosevelt was sworn in as president, inaugurating a remarkable era in American political history.

Theodore Roosevelt and Progressivism. Under Theodore Roosevelt the country saw reforms in economic, political, and social life. Republicans took the lead in conservation efforts and, to the dismay of some old stalwarts, began implementing Roosevelt's trust-busting ideas. Roosevelt's overwhelming reelection in 1904 inaugurated a new era of regulatory legislation (see GOVERNMENT REGULATION) and conservation measures. As he had promised, he chose not to run in 1908 and urged the party to nominate William Howard TAFT of Ohio.

Taft defeated Bryan, who was running for the third time; Taft's style, however, and his conservatism alienated the liberals within the Republican party. Those liberals, led by Robert M. LA FOLLETTE of Wisconsin, organized (1911) the National Progressive Republican League as a means of wresting party control from the conservatives. At the Chicago convention in 1912, Roosevelt challenged Taft for the nomination. Failing to win, Roosevelt bolted the party and ran as the PROGRESSIVE PARTY candidate. Thus split, the Republicans decisively lost the presidency to Woodrow Wilson.

In 1916 the Republicans nominated Supreme Court Justice Charles Evans HUGHES, but Wilson's domestic record, his personal popularity, and his pledge to keep the United States out of the war in Europe were obstacles too great for Hughes to overcome. Despite Wilson's promises, the United States was drawn into World War I, and party politics gave way to bipartisan prosecution of the war. Republicans won control of the House of Representatives and the Senate in the 1918 elections and, at the end of the war, prevented the United States from joining the League of Nations by rejecting ratification of the Versailles Treaty.

The Republican ticket of Warren G. HARDING and Calvin COOLIDGE won the 1920 election by a landslide. Harding's administration was plagued by scandals (see TEAPOT DOME), which were inherited by Coolidge after Harding's death in 1923. In a politically astute move, Coolidge appointed two

Calvin Coolidge (left) accompanies president-elect Herbert Hoover before the latter's inauguration in 1929. Hoover, a former cabinet member, had become the Republican presidential nominee after the incumbent Coolidge had surprised the country by announcing: "I do not choose to run for President in 1928."

special prosecutors to deal with the scandals, one from each party. Nominated in his own right in 1924, Coolidge was re-elected by a large margin. In 1928, Coolidge declined to run again, and the Republicans turned to Herbert HOOVER of California. Hoover won by an unprecedented landslide against Alfred E. SMITH. Republicans also won control of both houses of Congress. Many believed that another era of Republican hegemony was dawning, but a rapidly escalating worldwide economic depression brought Hoover and his party to their knees. Although the Hoover administration took steps to stop the decline of the economy, its remedies were generally thought to be ineffectual and too late. Hoover was renominated in 1932 in the depths of the Depression of the 1930s, but Franklin D. Roosevelt defeated him in one of the great landslide victories in U.S. history. The 70-year era of Republicanism was at an end. One of Roosevelt's major accomplishments was wooing the black vote away from the Republicans.

The Republicans in the Minority: 1932–52. The Republicans were unable to find a candidate who could match Roosevelt's popular appeal. Alf LANDON and Wendell L. WILLKIE failed in 1936 and 1940, respectively. Mostly isolationist before World War II, the Republicans backed the war effort, a stance that was to lead to support—enunciated by Sen. Arthur H. VANDENBERG—for bipartisan foreign policy after the war. The 1944 elections came at a critical time in the midst of World War II, and New York governor Thomas E. DEWEY became the fourth Republican candidate to be overwhelmed by Roosevelt. In 1948, Dewey again was the Republican nominee, this time against Roosevelt's successor, Harry S. Truman. He conducted a lackluster campaign, lulled into complacency by polls and expert opinions that forecast a landslide Republican victory. Truman, however, defeated Dewey in a great upset.

The Eisenhower Era. In 1952 the Republican national convention nominated Gen. Dwight D. EISENHOWER to head its ticket. Although the party was split over the defeat of conservative senator Robert A. TAFT of Ohio for that nomination, its ticket went on to win a landslide victory, carrying 39 states. Eisenhower's running mate was California senator Richard M. NIXON. The 1956 ticket of Eisenhower and Nixon won another decisive victory, due in part to Eisenhower's moderate course in foreign policy, his successful ending of the Korean War, and his great personal popularity. Democratic control of both houses, however, won in 1954, was continued.

In 1960, Vice-President Nixon won an easy victory for nomination but lost the election to John F. Kennedy of Massachusetts by the smallest popular margin in the 20th century—a difference of only about 113,000 votes out of more than 68 million cast. After a bitter internal party struggle prior to the 1964 Republican convention, Sen. Barry M. GOLDWATER of Arizona wrested the presidential nomination and control of the Republican party away from the Eastern moderates and began an attempt to convert the party into an ideologically pure conservative party. His landslide defeat by Lyndon B. Johnson, however, left the party organization in shambles.

The Nixon-Ford Years. In 1968, Richard Nixon reappeared to win the party's nomination and selected Maryland governor Spiro T. AGNEW as his running mate. Nixon went on to win the election over Democrat Hubert H. Humphrey, who was unable to bring his party together after divisions brought on by U.S. involvement in the Vietnam War.

President Nixon's first term was marked by many successes, including improved relations with China, a more cooperative relationship with the USSR, an improved economy, and what appeared to be significant steps toward peace in Vietnam. In 1972 the Democrats nominated a prominent antiwar senator, George S. McGovern of South Dakota. Nixon was reelected by an enormous popular-vote margin, carrying every state except Massachusetts and the District of Columbia. Even so, the Democrats continued to control both houses of the Congress by considerable margins. The campaign, however, carried the seeds of the political destruction of Richard Nixon. A burglary of the Democratic National Committee headquarters in the WATERGATE office complex during the campaign led to revelations of widespread civil and criminal misconduct within the campaign organization, the administration, and the White House; impeachment hearings were held, and eventually Nixon resigned in 1974. An earlier scandal involved Vice-President Agnew, who was forced to resign in 1973 after being convicted of income-tax evasion.

Nixon was succeeded by Vice-President Gerald R. FORD of Michigan, who had been appointed to the office after the resignation of Agnew. Ford faced a serious economic situation beset by high unemployment, rising inflation, high interest rates, and huge budget deficits. He was criticized by the moderate wing of his party for doing too little to allay the nation's economic ills and just as roundly by conservatives for offering amnesty to Vietnam-era draft evaders and for appointing Nelson ROCKEFELLER to the vice-presidency. After a difficult primary contest against conservative Ronald REAGAN of California, Ford lost the election to Democrat Jimmy Carter by a narrow popular and electoral margin.

The Reagan Administrations. By 1980 the apparent inability of the Carter administration to control the serious economic situation, coupled with a perception of U.S. impotence abroad (exemplified by the Iranian seizure of U.S. hostages), favored a Republican resurgence. Reagan easily won the party's presidential nomination (his most liberal opponent, John ANDERSON, subsequently ran for the presidency as an independent) and went on to gain a landslide victory over Carter, taking 489 electoral votes (against Carter's 49) and 51 percent of the popular vote. At the same time, the Republicans won 12 additional seats in the U.S. Senate, taking control of that body

President Ronald Reagan, in a nationally televised press conference on Nov. 19, 1986, defended his authorization of secret arms sales to Iran. It was subsequently revealed that some of the profits from the arms sales had been diverted to Nicaraguan rebels. The tangled Iran-contra affair was the subject of congressional hearings in 1987.

(Left) *Arms raised in the victory sign, President Dwight D. Eisenhower accepts the Republican party's presidential renomination in 1956 as Vice-President Richard M. Nixon looks on. The Eisenhower-Nixon ticket won a second term in another landslide election. In 1968, Nixon headed the Republican ticket and was elected president over Hubert Humphrey by a very narrow margin.*

for the first time in 25 years. The swing toward conservative candidates, who were aided by the aggressive campaigning of such New Right organizations as the NATIONAL CONSERVATIVE POLITICAL ACTION COMMITTEE and MORAL MAJORITY, appeared to herald a new Republican era.

This Republican resurgence, however, was only partially confirmed in the 1984 elections. Although in his reelection bid Reagan routed Walter F. MONDALE, taking 59% of the popular vote and a record-breaking 525 electoral votes (to Mondale's 13), the Republicans lost two Senate seats, while retaining a majority. Democrats continued to control the House; the Republicans won back only about half of the 26 seats there that they had lost in 1982. In 1986 the Democrats won control of the Senate by 55 seats to 45; Republicans took some comfort in having lost only a few seats in the House. A Democratic Congress posed problems for Reagan—already vulnerable politically because of the IRAN-CONTRA AFFAIR—in his last years in office.   ROBERT J. HUCKSHORN

Bibliography: Abbott, Richard H., *The Republican Party and the South, 1855–1877* (1986); Burdette, Franklin L., *The Republican Party: A Short History,* 2d ed. (1972); Fairlie, Henry, *The Parties: Republicans and Democrats in This Century* (1978); Hess, Stephen, and Broder, David, *The Republican Establishment* (1967); Jones, Charles O., *The Republican Party in American Politics* (1965); Mayer, George H., *The Republican Party, 1854–1966,* 2d ed. (1967); Polakoff, Keith A., *Political Parties in American History* (1981); Reinhard, David W., *The Republican Right since Nineteen Forty-five* (1983).

requiem   [rek'-wee-uhm]

The Latin term *requiem* for the Roman Catholic Mass for the dead comes from the opening words of the service, *Requiem aeternam dona eis* (Grant them eternal rest). Originally set to plainchant, the requiem has existed in polyphonic settings at least since the 15th century. Its musical sections normally consist of Introit: *Requiem aeternam;* Kyrie (Lord, have mercy); Gradual: *Requiem aeternam;* Tract: *Absolve Domine* (Absolve, O Lord); Sequence: *Dies irae* (Day of wrath); Offertory: *Domine Jesu Christe;* Sanctus; Agnus Dei (Lamb of God); Communion: *Lux aeterna* (Light eternal shine upon them). In some early requiems, the texts for the Gradual and Tract differ from those listed, whereas most later settings, such as Verdi's, conclude with the *Libera me, Domine* (Deliver me, O Lord) from the Absolution, which begins the burial service. An overall historical view of the extant settings reveals instances of divergence despite the fixed forms of the liturgical Mass.

The earliest extant polyphonic setting of the requiem is that of Jean d'Okeghem. Thereafter the number increases rapidly and includes works by most of the great 16th-century masters of polyphony, including Roland de Lassus, Cristóbal Morales, Giovanni Pierluigi da Palestrina, Pierre de la Rue, and Tomás Luis de Victoria. Requiems in the baroque style were composed by, among others, Antonio Lotti, Alessandro Scarlatti, and Marc Antoine Charpentier. The classical requiem is exemplified by works of Michael Haydn, Mozart, and Antonio Salieri. The opulent orchestration of the 19th century added an almost nonliturgical splendor to the requiems of Berlioz, Cherubini, Dvořák, Schumann, and Verdi. Brahms's *German Requiem* (1869) is based on biblical texts chosen by the composer. Other later settings include those of Benjamin Britten, Maurice Duruflé, Fauré, and Stravinsky.   DENIS STEVENS

reserpine   [re-sur'-peen]

Reserpine, an alkaloid chemical, is found in roots of tropical *Rauvolfia* species of trees and shrubs. The drug reserpine, extracted from the snakeroot plant, *R. serpentina,* is used to treat high blood pressure; however, it should not be given to patients who have peptic ulcer or ulcerative colitis or who suffer from mental depression. Resperpine's mechanism of action involves the depletion of two neurotransmitters, the catecholamines and serotonin.   RICHARD H. RUNSER

Reserve Officers Training Corps

The Reserve Officers Training Corps (ROTC) system trains high school and college students to serve as officers in the U.S. armed forces. Established in 1916, the ROTC has roots in a much older citizen-soldier tradition embodied in the U.S. Constitution. The nation's founders opposed large standing armies and preferred to vest the country's security in a MILITIA system. The training of officers for the armed forces became primarily the responsibility of the civilian higher-education system. The antecedents of ROTC are found in such colleges as Norwich University, founded in 1819, by a former acting superintendent at West Point, as the American Literary, Scientific, and Military Academy.

During the early years of the Civil War, military training was institutionalized by the MORRILL ACT (1862), which in creating the land-grant colleges required that they provide a block of instruction on military tactics. In 1888 additional institutions were approved to receive federal assistance for military training.

In 1916 the National Defense Act created the ROTC to develop a reserve of trained officers, available for service in national emergencies, with senior units based in colleges and universities and junior units based in high schools and approved academies. The program was expanded with the additions of the Naval ROTC (NROTC) in 1926 and the Air Force ROTC (AFROTC) in 1946. Today the ROTC program is the primary source of officers for all of the armed forces. In 1985 nearly 100,000 men and women were enrolled in senior ROTC units and 216,000 in junior units. This represented a considerable increase over enrollments in the late 1960s and 1970s when the Vietnam War provoked student antipathy toward the military.

Programs conducted separately by the U.S. Army, Navy, and Air Force, offer a wide variety of opportunities. These include flight training, summer training on military installations and ships, and classroom training in leadership and management, communication skills, and the theory, history, and dynamics of military affairs. Full 4-year scholarships are available in all programs, and scholarship recipients accept a commitment to serve on active duty.   M. RICHARD ROSE

Bibliography: Collins, Arthur S., *Common Sense Training* (1978); Lyons, Gene M., and Masland, John W., *Education and Military Leadership: A Study of the R.O.T.C.* (1959; repr. 1975); MacCloskey, Monro, *Reserve Officers Training Corps* (1965).

reservoir: see DAM; HYDROELECTRIC POWER; WATER SUPPLY.

resin

Resins are natural or synthetic compounds that can form thin, continuous films, enabling them to be molded into solid objects or spun into thread. They have broad, diverse chemical composition and many applications. Many resins are thick, viscous fluids, and others are hard, brittle, noncrystalline solids. Their molecular structures may be complex, or they may be made of large numbers of relatively simple repeating units called monomers, which when combined form polymers. Few resins are directly soluble in water, accounting for their use in areas where water resistance is paramount. The vast majority of resins can be made soluble by hydrocarbon solvents.

Natural Resins. The name *resin* once referred only to naturally available compounds, for example, rosin, capal, dammar, amber, and mastic. All of these are derived from vegetable sources and are collected as exudates from living trees and plants or extracted from stumps and heartwood of forested or fossilized trees. In most nonarid regions of the world, trees are cultivated or cut for their resin content; resins from specific trees or localized sources, however, are often preferred. Dammar resin, for example, is derived from pines of the genus *Agathis,* native to Southeast Asia. It has been long favored as a hardener for high-quality VARNISHES.

Another natural resin of major importance is lac (see SHELLAC). This clear, yellow or orange resin is secreted from a scalelike insect that is encouraged to colonize trees in sections of India and Thailand. Other resins, such as myrrh, aloe, and labdanum, have achieved prominence for their use in perfumes, incense, and medicines.

Synthetic Resins. In the 20th century the chemical industry experienced a dramatic growth in both technology and volumes produced. Increases in world population, the success of the automobile, and insatiable demands helped spur widespread research to develop synthetic products as replacements of inadequate resources. In addition, the quality and performance requirements of newly produced goods overtaxed the abilities of existing resins.

CELLULOSE, nitrated heavily during World War I to produce smokeless gunpowder, was modified to provide a film-forming resin. Although highly flammable, it offered exceptional qualities, such as high gloss, durability, and fast drying in inks, paints, and wood coatings. Cellulose acetate, another modification, was the basis for the fiber rayon. Alkyd resins, the backbone of modern solvent-based paints and other varied products, were widely commercialized. These versatile resins essentially replaced the natural resin component in a varnish with esters of polycarboxylic acids and polyhydroxyl alcohols of excellent toughness and clarity.

Demands for synthetic RUBBER during World War II led to the development of styrene butadiene resins and latexes. Vinyl and acrylic resins, largely limited to military use, were later made available for general use. These resins offered unsurpassed stability and durability under most adverse climatic conditions and eventually totally supplanted other grades as paint binders and in exterior plastic displays, automobile coatings, and food packaging applications.

Numerous other chemical varieties have proliferated in recent years. Such resins as polystyrene, vinyl toluene, phenolics, epoxies, urethanes, polyethylene, and polyamides (nylon) are available. They all offer specific qualities as films, PLASTICS, or coatings.   JOHN J. OBERLE

Bibliography: Ash, M. and I., *Encyclopedia of Plastics, Polymers and Resins*, 3 vols. (1981–83); Davidson, R. L., *Handbook of Water-Soluble Resins* (1980); May, C. A., ed., *Resins for Aerospace* (1980); Mantell, Charles L., et al., *Technology of Natural Resins* (1942).

resistance, electrical

Electrical resistance is a property of an electrical circuit that opposes the flow of current. In circuits where the current (I) and voltage (V) are related by a simple proportionality constant, as in OHM'S LAW, $V = RI$, the proportionality constant R is the resistance of the circuit. Resistance is analogous to friction in hydraulic or mechanical systems and causes energy dissipation in the form of heat. A physical device that displays these properties is called a RESISTOR. The power (P) dissipated in a resistor is given by $P = VI = (RI)I = RI^2$ Watts (Joule's law).

The unit of resistance is the ohm (1 ohm = 1 volt/ampere) and is usually denoted by the Greek omega, Ω. The resistance of metals usually increases with temperature while that of semiconductors decreases. At very low temperatures, the resistance of some elements or alloys falls to zero (see SUPERCONDUCTIVITY).

Because electric charges give up energy in passing through a resistor, there is a voltage drop in the positive current direction, which establishes the usual sign convention. Ohm's law is sometimes written as $I = GV$, where $G = 1/R$ and is called the conductance and is measured in mhos (inverse ohms).

A. G. ENGELHARDT AND M. KRISTIANSEN

resistivity

The resistivity of a material is a measure of its ability to conduct current as a result of an applied electric potential or voltage. Resistivity and conductivity are complementary concepts. Resistivity is an inherent property of a substance, unrelated to its shape or size as is resistance. Its units of measure are ohm-meters. The resistivity of common materials varies over a tremendous range (more than a factor of 10^{20}) and in most (but not all) materials increases with temperature. A material with zero resistivity is called a superconductor. SUPERCONDUCTIVITY occurs in certain metals and alloys (for example, niobium-tin) at very low temperatures, usually below 20 K.

A. G. ENGELHARDT AND M. KRISTIANSEN

resistor

A resistor is an electrical component designed to oppose the flow of current in a CIRCUIT and to convert electrical energy into heat energy. In electronic circuits, resistors are introduced to limit current to a safe value, to drop voltage to some required value, to divide up voltage, or to discharge energy, as from a CAPACITOR.

Resistors may be described in terms of their resistance (in ohms), their ability to dissipate heat (in watts), their functional makeup (fixed or variable), their construction, or the percentage tolerance of their resistive value. Fixed-carbon-composition resistors are available from 2 ohms to 30 million ohms, in power ratings from 0.1 to 2 watts. Power-type resistors, consisting of an alloy ribbon wrapped around a ceramic support, can dissipate hundreds of watts. A film-type resistor, in which a film of carbon or metal is deposited on an insulating cylinder, has high-frequency and high-voltage uses. Variable resistors have a sliding contact for varying the resistance. Low-powered types called POTENTIOMETERS are used for volume controls in radios and amplifiers; high-powered types called RHEOSTATS may be used, for example, in light-dimming switches. (See THERMISTOR.)   ALLEN MOTTERSHEAD

Bibliography: Thomson, C. M., *Fundamentals of Electronics* (1979); Wellard, C. L., *Resistance and Resistors* (1960).

Resnais, Alain   [re-nay']

Known for his innovative literary approach to film, Alain Resnais, b. June 3, 1922, became one of the leading directors of French NEW WAVE cinema when it emerged in the late 1950s. Before his feature debut Resnais had spent 11 years making brilliant documentary films on subjects ranging from the painter Van Gogh (1948) and Picasso's *Guernica* (1950) to the celebrated *Night and Fog* (1955), an unforgettable description of the Nazi extermination-camp system.

Most of Resnais's full-length films were made in collaboration with a novelist or playwright of note (his early collaborators include Maguerite Duras on *Hiroshima Mon Amour* (1959), Alain Robbe-Grillet on *Last Year at Marienbad* (1961), Jean Cayrol on *Muriel* (1963), and the 1966 *La Guerre est finie* with Jorge Semprun); yet each film is characterized by Resnais's own distinctive approach to the exploration of time and memory, and by a totally novel structure.

After a long break from filmmaking in the early 1970s, Resnais returned with two exquisitely shot films, *Stavisky* (1974) and *Providence* (1977). *Mon Oncle d'Amerique* (1980), a sophisticated mixture of fiction and fact, natural science, philosophy, and comedy, won the New York Critics Circle Award for the year's best foreign film. The 1984 comedy *Life Is a Bed of Roses* was the first Resnais film received without critical enthusiasm.   ROY ARMES

Bibliography: Armes, Roy, *The Cinema of Alain Resnais* (1968); Monaco, James, *Alain Resnais* (1978); Sweet, Freddy, *The Film Narratives of Alain Resnais* (1981); Ward, John, *Alain Resnais or the Theme of Time* (1968).

Resnik, Judith A.

The American astronaut Judith Arlene Resnik Oldak, b. Akron, Ohio, Apr. 5, 1949, d. Jan. 28, 1986, was one of the seven crew members killed during the launch of the SPACE SHUTTLE *Challenger* from Cape Canaveral in 1986. Resnik obtained a Ph.D. in electrical engineering from the University of Maryland in 1977 while working for the Radio Corporation of America. She also did research at the National Institutes of Health's neurophysiology laboratory before her selection as an astronaut in 1978. She became the second woman astronaut to enter space when she flew the 12th Shuttle mission, Aug. 30–Sept. 5, 1984, aboard *Discovery*.

resonance   (chemistry)

In chemistry, resonance is a concept of molecular bonding in which the structure of a molecule can be represented by two or more different structures that differ only in the position of electrons. An example is sulfur dioxide, SO_2, shown as an electron-dot formula:

$$:\ddot{O}: \;\; :\ddot{S}: \;\; :\ddot{O}: \;\;\leftrightarrow\;\; :\ddot{O}: \;\; :\ddot{S}: \;\; :\ddot{O}:$$

The two-headed arrow is conventionally used to indicate resonant structures. The term is an unfortunate one because it creates the erroneous impression that a pair of electrons is sometimes a part of one bond and sometimes the other, or that the molecule resonates (flips back and forth) between the two structures. Sulfur dioxide and other resonant molecules have only one structure, which is not representable by the simplified methods of writing structures according to the octet rule.

In addition to explaining molecular structure, the concept of resonance is important because resonant molecules are more stable than predicted; that is, they are less reactive because more energy is required to break resonant chemical bonds than nonresonant bonds. Radicals such as nitrate (NO_3^-), sulfate (SO_4^{2-}), carbonate (CO_3^{2-}), and phosphate (PO_4^{3-}) tend to react as units rather than as individual atoms because they are stabilized by resonance. Resonance accounts for the unexpected reactions of some organic chemicals (see DIENE) and was the solution to the classic BENZENE problem.

STEPHEN FLEISHMAN

resonance (physics)

Resonance usually refers to the large absorption of energy and the resultant large amplitude of motion that occurs when a vibrating system is driven by an external force at its natural frequency of vibration. The principles of resonance are at work when a person pushes a child in a swing; the greatest effect will be achieved for the least effort if the force is applied at the natural frequency of the swing and in phase with the motion. In molecular, atomic, nuclear, and subnuclear systems, the concept of resonance is of considerable importance. The reason lies in the quantum-mechanical nature of these systems. Their energy can change only in discrete steps; only certain amounts of energy, and therefore only certain frequencies of radiation, are absorbed. Some subnuclear particles are so elusive that their existence is known only through a resonant absorption of energy.

STEPHEN V. LETCHER

Respighi, Ottorino [rays-peeg'-ee]

Ottorino Respighi, b. July 9, 1879, d. Apr. 18, 1936, was Italy's most important postromantic composer. Trained first in Bologna, he then studied with Rimsky-Korsakov in Saint Petersburg and with Max Bruch in Berlin. He was a professional violinist (1903–08) and taught composition (1913–25) at Rome's Santa Cecilia Academy. An unusually versatile composer, he wrote in diverse forms and styles; his love of medieval and Renaissance music inspired original scores and arrangements of delicacy and subtlety that contrast with the large-scale orchestral works at which he excelled. Respighi composed eight operas but rejected Italian operatic stereotypes; he also wrote much piano and chamber music. His most famous works are the tone poems, *The Fountains of Rome* (1917), *The Pines of Rome* (1924), and *Roman Festivals* (1929). Also popular are his three sets of *Ancient Airs and Dances* (1917, 1924, 1932) and the suite *The Birds* (1927).

JOHN W. BARKER

Bibliography: Respighi, Elsa, *Ottorino Respighi* (1962).

respiration, cellular: see METABOLISM.

respirator

The respirator is a mechanical device used to ventilate the lungs of patients who cannot readily breathe by themselves.

The "iron lung"—the first operative respirator—consisted of a long, metal cylinder in which a patient was placed, covering the body except for the head. The machine created external, positive pressure to help expand the lungs. The more recently designed portable, lightweight respirator device is generally attached to a surgically incised opening in a patient's trachea and pushes air into the lungs. Once the pressure is released the lungs relax, pushing the air back out.

respiratory system

An aerobic organism must abstract oxygen from environmental air or water in order to support its life functions. The process of obtaining oxygen (O_2) and releasing the cellular waste product, carbon dioxide (CO_2), into the environment is known as respiration. A tiny unicellular organism, with a diameter no greater than 1 mm (0.04 in), can obtain sufficient oxygen and simultaneously dispose of carbon dioxide by means of passive diffusion through its cell membrane. Multicellular organisms, however, had to evolve specialized respiratory systems for supplying O_2 to their tissues and removing excess CO_2. These systems are capable of functioning over a wide range of metabolic demands and within a minimum energy expenditure.

Invertebrate animals basically have rudimentary gas exchange systems; the simplest of these animals, such as sponges and flatworms, rely on gas exchange across the body surface to meet respiratory needs. Invertebrates having more complex body structures, such as the earthworm, have not only gas exchange across the body surface but also a simple circulatory system, which carries oxygenated blood to deeper regions of the body. Arthropods such as insects have a network of tracheal tubes that open at the body surface and connect with inner tissues. Tracheal tube systems of aquatic insects or larvae are specialized to obtain oxygen from water. Gas exchange in echinoderms such as starfish occurs across the surface of the tube feet. Many invertebrates have gills, ranging from a single layer of cells protruding from the body surface to stacked layers of highly vascular tissue. Book lungs of spiders consist of internal, leaflike plates of tissue; air enters through abdominal openings and circulates through these plates.

SKIN, GILLS, AND LUNGS

All successfully evolved respiratory systems have certain common characteristics. First, they have a large, thin, and highly vascular respiratory membrane that allows efficient gas diffusion to occur between the blood and the external medium. Second, the CIRCULATORY SYSTEM is capable of carrying sufficient oxygen to, and carbon dioxide from, the body tissues. Third, they have the ability to replenish the oxygen that is in immediate contact with the respiratory surface.

Within these constraints, three types of vertebrate respiratory systems have evolved: GILLS, LUNGS, and specialized areas of skin (integument). Because lungs and gills originate embryologically as outpockets of the gut, the respiratory membrane of these organs is well protected inside the body. The tiny distance across this membrane between the oxygen source and blood, 0.36 to 2.5 microns for lungs and 0.30 to 3.0 microns for gills, guarantees adequate gas exchange. Both lungs and gills have openings to the environment. The lungs are connected to bronchial tubes that in turn are attached to the trachea, leading to oral and nasal passages. Gas exchange takes place in terminal air sacs (alveoli) that are located within the lungs. Gills are located in the back of the mouth, and water passes through the mouth, past the gills, and out again by way of gill slits. Gas exchange occurs in the secondary lamellae of the gills. In amphibians and some fishes, specialized areas of skin function as a respiratory membrane.

Blood and Oxygen Transport. The blood flowing through a respiratory organ is able to load sufficient oxygen and deliver it to body tissues. It then loads carbon dioxide and carries it back to the respiratory organ. Blood transports oxygen by means of hemoglobin, a substance present in all vertebrate blood except for some Antarctic fishes. Hemoglobin contains ionized iron molecules to which oxygen temporarily bonds during transport to the tissues. Depending on the species, the

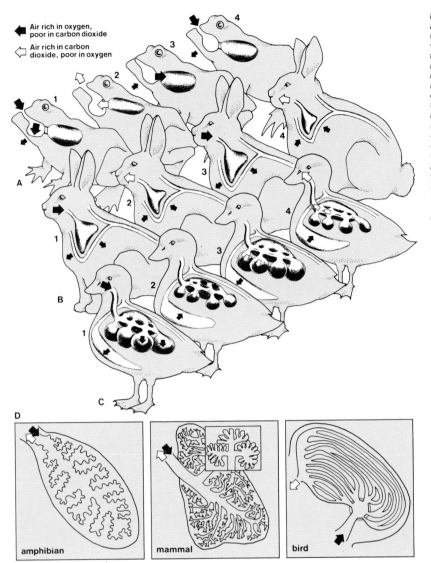

Air rich in oxygen, poor in carbon dioxide

Air rich in carbon dioxide, poor in oxygen

D

amphibian

mammal

bird

Lungs are the basic respiratory organs of air-breathing vertebrates. Diagrams of a frog (A), rabbit (B), and duck (C) represent various respiratory cycles; cross sections of their lungs (D) illustrate the structure of the respiratory surface in an amphibian, mammal, and bird. A frog's lungs are relatively simple, with a modest surface area of about 100 cm² (15.5 in²); by comparison, the gas-exchange surface of a pair of human lungs is about 70 m² (750 ft²). The frog depends on a positive pressure mechanism for ventilation. The floor of the mouth is lowered (A1), drawing air through the nostrils and into the mouth cavity. The previously inflated lungs then expel (A2) oxygen-poor air past the mouth cavity (with minimal mixing) and out through the nostrils. The nostrils close as the floor of the mouth contracts (A3), creating a positive pressure that pumps the "fresh" air into the lungs. The airway between the mouth cavity and lungs closes (A4), retaining air in the lungs, and the nostrils open; the cycle can then repeat. Mammalian lungs have a complex structure, with a large alveolar surface for gas exchange. Contraction of inspiratory muscles (B1) causes the diaphragm and rib cage to expand the chest cavity; the resulting negative pressure (suction) draws air through the nostrils, filling the lungs. When the muscles relax (B2), the diaphragm and rib cage cause air to be pushed out of the lungs. This inhalation-exhalation cycle repeats (B3–4). A paired set of air sacs characterizes a bird's respiratory system; the relatively inelastic lungs, which contain a system of air capillaries for gas exchange, constitute only 9 to 17 percent of the total respiratory air space. Contraction of inspiratory muscles expands the chest and abdominal cavities; the reduced pressure draws fresh air into the posterior air sacs (C1) and stale air from the lungs into the anterior sacs (C3). When expiratory muscles contract, fresh air is expelled from the posterior sacs (C2) through the lungs; stale air is expelled from the anterior sacs (C4) through the nostrils.

blood is capable of loading from 5 to 25 ml of oxygen for every 100 ml of blood. The carbon dioxide produced in the tissues during metabolism is carried away primarily in the form of bicarbonate ions (HCO_3^-), which are soluble in the blood plasma.

Respiratory Pump. Oxygen is continually replenished and carbon dioxide discarded at the air/water-blood interface by the action of a respiratory pump. This provides fresh air or water to the respiratory membrane, which is the process of inspiration, and expels water or air that is low in oxygen and high in carbon dioxide, the process of expiration. This cyclical process is known as ventilation. During the repetitions of this cycle, the quantity of inspired air or water that passes across the membrane in one minute is called the minute volume and is the product of the number of breaths in a minute (respiratory rate) and the amount of air or water that passes through with each breath (tidal volume). Alterations in respiratory rate and tidal volume, or both, adjust gas exchange in order to accommodate an animal's changing metabolic needs.

FISHES

Most fishes employ a double pumping system that provides an almost uninterrupted flow of water into the mouth and across the gills. During inspiration the floor of the mouth cavity depresses, forming a negative pressure that causes water to flow into the mouth. The gill flaps close, and the postgill cavity expands, causing an even greater negative pressure on

the postgill side. This creates a pressure gradient that permits water to flow across the lamellae. The mouth floor then raises, causing a more positive pressure in the mouth cavity, which maintains the pressure gradient and water flow. When pressure in the post-gill chamber exceeds that of the ambient water, the gill flaps open and stale water is expelled through them.

Many fishes also depend on air for respiration. A catfish, for example, relies on respiration through its skin during overland migrations. In stagnant waters, some fishes remain close to the air-water interface where oxygen is highly concentrated because of surface diffusion. Other species have developed lunglike accessory respiratory structures and have blood with a high oxygen capacity.

AMPHIBIANS

Amphibians utilize skin, lungs, and, in some forms, such as tadpoles and salamanders, gills. The system that predominates depends on a species' environment. For example, a primarily aquatic amphibian, such as the aquatic newt, breathes through its skin for 75% of its oxygen and through its lungs for the other 25%. A tree frog, on the other hand, breathes through its lungs for 75% of its oxygen and through the skin for the remaining 25%. The frog, which is the most abundant amphibian, depends on a positive pressure pump to inflate its lungs. The floor of the mouth depresses, and air is suctioned through the nostrils. The nostrils close and the mouth floor

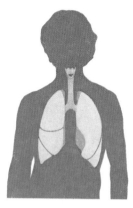

(Left) *In the human respiratory system, the organs of respiration, the lungs, are two roughly cone-shaped structures that nearly fill the chest cavity. Inhaled air passes through the trachea, or windpipe, and infiltrates the lungs by means of branching tubes that terminate in clusters of alveoli, or tiny air sacs. The alveoli are surrounded by networks of capillaries, or minute blood vessels, and the blood picks up oxygen from the inhaled air and releases its waste carbon dioxide gas, which is then exhaled. (Right) The breathing process is made possible by the diaphragm, a strong muscle (shown in orange) under the lungs. During inhalation (A) the diaphragm and rib cage expand the chest cavity; during exhalation (B) the diaphragm and the muscles of the rib cage relax, allowing the lungs to release their air.*

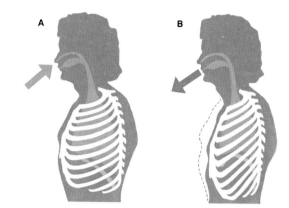

raises, causing air to flow into and inflate the lungs. Expiration is by means of passive elastic recoil of the lungs.

REPTILES
Reptiles depend primarily on lung respiration. Consequently their lungs have a large internal surface area available for gas exchange. Elastic and smooth muscle fibers facilitate lung inflation and deflation. Complex airways consist of a distinct trachea and bronchi. Instead of using the mouth cavity, a reptile's respiratory pump is powered by suction that is created by lowering the pressure in the lungs to below that of the atmosphere. This is accomplished by muscular expansion of the ribs and the thoracic cavity. A reptile's respiratory cycle has three phases: inspiration, apnea, and expiration. During inspiration the rib cage expands and the glottis opens, lowering the pressure in both the abdomen and the lungs in comparison to the pressure of the ambient air. This causes air to flow into the lungs. During the period of apnea, in which no respiratory movement occurs, the glottis closes and the respiratory muscles relax. Expiration is usually by passive elastic recoil of the lungs. However, turtles and tortoises have rigid shells that prevent elastic recoil, so they must utilize energy during both expiration and inspiration.

MAMMALS
Mammals have a highly developed respiratory system, containing a trachea, bronchi, and extensive branchings (bronchioles) that terminate at the alveoli. Mammalian alveoli are much smaller than those of lower vertebrates, resulting in a significantly larger relative surface area for gas exchange. Inflation of the lungs is accomplished by the contraction of inspiratory muscles, which, by enlarging the thoracic cavity, reduce the lung pressure and allow air to flow into them. The most important muscle used during mammalian inspiration is the diaphragm, a large, dome-shaped sheet of muscle that separates the abdominal and thoracic cavities. Quiet expiration occurs passively by means of the elastic recoil of the respiratory muscles and lungs. If rapid expiration is required, expiratory muscles must come into play.

BIRDS
The respiratory system of birds is uniquely adapted to a high metabolic rate, the high energy cost of flying, and the need for sufficient oxygen at high altitudes. This system, which provides virtually continuous gas exchange, is also important for thermoregulation and communication. It consists of two lungs and an extensive, paired series of air sacs that fill much of the chest and abdominal cavities and are connected to auxiliary air spaces, located in the bones, that are much larger in volume than the lungs.

The bird's trachea, which splits into two primary bronchi, carries fresh air through the lungs and delivers it to the two abdominal air sacs. Secondary bronchi carry air to the other air sacs. Air is then carried by tertiary bronchi that penetrate the lung tissue and terminate in air capillaries, a dense network of minute air channels with highly vascular walls. These air capillaries function like alveoli in mammals, both being the site of gas exchange. Stale air flows from the lungs to the anterior air sacs and is expelled through the trachea. Fresh air courses through the air capillaries during both inspiration and

expiration. During inspiration inspiratory muscles enlarge the thoracic-abdominal cavity, decreasing the pressure in all the air sacs. Fresh air flows into all the air sacs except the anterior sacs. Some air then enters the lungs, while stale air in the lungs flows into the anterior sacs. Expiration is accomplished by expiratory muscles, which increase pressure in the thoracic-abdominal cavity. Stale air is expelled into the environment, and fresh air from the air sacs is pushed into the lungs by way of the posterior air sacs. The entire process is facilitated by the action of the diaphragm, which in birds is a thin membrane of connective tissue instead of a sheet of muscle. It is connected to muscles that are attached to the body wall. Contraction of these muscles causes the diaphragm to flatten. The avian diaphragm diminishes the lung volume during inspiration and expands it during expiration.

The change in lung volume between inspiration and expiration is small because the avian lung is much stiffer than its mammalian counterpart. The air sacs, however, significantly inflate and deflate during respiration. In a bird during flight, inspiration occurs on the upstroke and expiration on the downstroke. The downward stroke of the wings compresses the ribcage, expelling the stale air from the anterior air sacs out through the trachea.   FRANÇOIS HAAS

Bibliography: Braun, Harold A., et al., *Introduction to Respiratory Physiology*, 2d ed. (1980); Gong, Henry, Jr., ed., *The Respiratory System* (1982); Jones, John D., *Comparative Physiology of Respiration* (1972); Randall, D. J., et al., *The Evolution of Air Breathing in Vertebrates* (1981); Widdicombe, John, and Davies, Andrew, *Respiratory Physiology* (1984).

respiratory system disorders

Respiratory diseases affect the RESPIRATORY SYSTEM, which includes the nose, mouth, throat, larynx, trachea, bronchial tubes, and lungs. These diseases may be acute or chronic and result from a variety of causes.

INFECTIONS
Viruses. Infections are the most common cause of respiratory diseases and may be produced by viruses, bacteria, fungi, protozoa, and microorganisms known as *Mycoplasmas, Legionellas,* and *Rickettsias.* Viruses are highly communicable from person to person and cause the common head cold (RHINITIS) and chest cold (tracheobronchitis; see COLD, COMMON). Other viruses cause different types of INFLUENZA and also cause PNEUMONIA and other illnesses, such as measles, polio, and chicken pox, that may be associated with respiratory tract complications.

Bacteria. A large number of bacteria, the most common being species of *Streptococcus, Staphylococcus,* and *Hemophilus,* may infect any part of the respiratory system, causing such diseases as SINUSITIS, BRONCHITIS, PHARYNGITIS, STREP THROAT, TONSILLITIS, WHOOPING COUGH, and pneumonia. A bacillus, *Mycobacterium tuberculosis,* causes TUBERCULOSIS, and other *Mycobacteria* cause diseases with almost identical symptoms. The latter live in soil and water and are not transmitted from person to person as is the tuberculosis bacillus.

Fungi. Pathogenic fungi can infect the lungs and cause pneumonialike illnesses such as HISTOPLASMOSIS, blastomycosis, and COCCIDIOIDOMYCOSIS. Fungi, which live primarily in the soil and are inhaled into the lungs, are not transmissible from person to person. Actinomycosis and nocardiosis are similar diseases caused by bacteria. FUNGUS DISEASES are treated with the antibiotic amphotericin B, whereas actinomycosis responds to penicillin and nocardiosis to sulfa drugs.

Protozoa and Worms. Protozoa and other parasites are rare causes of lung diseases in the United States, but an infection known as paragonimiasis, caused by a flatworm known as the lung fluke, is prevalent in the Orient. The hydatid disease, or echinococcosis, is prevalent in Australia, New Zealand, and Argentina and is caused by a cyst-forming tapeworm. A protozoan, *Pneumocystis carinii,* causes pneumonia in children and in recent years has become the most common cause of pneumonia in adults who are suffering from AIDS, or acquired immune deficiency syndrome (see AIDS).

Mycoplasmas, Legionellas, and Rickettsias. *Mycoplasma pneumoniae* is a tiny bacterialike organism that causes sinusitis, pharyngitis, bronchitis, and MYCOPLASMAL PNEUMONIA. Infection is spread by close and frequent contact. Another form of pneumonia, LEGIONNAIRE'S DISEASE, is caused by the tiny bacterium *Legionella pneumophila.* It is usually acquired from contaminated water in air-conditioning systems. RICKETTSIAS are very small microorganisms having some characteristics common to both bacteria and viruses. They cause Q FEVER, ROCKY MOUNTAIN SPOTTED FEVER, TYPHUS, and other diseases, most of which may have respiratory tract involvement. Infection is spread by fleas, lice, ticks, or mites.

CHRONIC OBSTRUCTIVE PULMONARY DISEASES
These conditions are also among the most common respiratory disorders. Characterized by narrowing of the bronchi (air passages) of the lungs, they include ASTHMA, chronic bronchitis, and EMPHYSEMA. The bronchial narrowing produces obstruction to the flow of air in and out of the lungs; the obstruction is most severe during the act of expiration. In the case of asthma, the size of the airways is reduced by spasm of the muscles in the bronchial walls; the condition can usually be reversed by proper treatment. Chronic bronchitis and emphysema are nearly always the result of long-term cigarette SMOKING, which causes swelling of the membrane lining the air passages. In the case of emphysema, actual destruction of lung tissue results in the formation of cystlike spaces in the lungs. Air is trapped in these structures during respiration and becomes useless.

ALLERGIES
Allergies are a common cause of respiratory diseases, producing hay fever, asthma, and certain forms of pneumonia. The individual suffering from these conditions has become oversensitive to contact with particular substances such as plant pollen and various types of organic dusts or chemicals. When these agents are inhaled, the body overreacts, producing the symptoms of the specific illness. Allergic pneumonia includes such disorders as farmer's lung, caused by exposure to bacteria in moldy hay; bagassosis, caused by exposure to stored sugarcane fibers with bacterial growth; air-conditioner or heating-system disease, caused by exposure to bacteria-contaminated mist from humidifiers (see DISEASE, OCCUPATIONAL); and other forms (see ALLERGY).

PNEUMOCONIOSES
Diseases due to inhalation of nonallergenic inorganic dusts are classified as pneumoconioses: silica causes silicosis; coal dust causes BLACK LUNG, or coal worker's pneumoconiosis; ASBESTOS fibers cause asbestosis; and beryllium causes berylliosis. These dusts injure the tissues of the lungs and often result in pulmonary fibrosis (scar formation) with resulting impairment of lung function and progressive disability.

TUMORS
Benign Tumors. TUMORS can be divided into two groups, benign (noncancerous) and malignant (cancerous). Benign tumors do not spread to other parts of the body, but they may cause damage by local growth and pressure on other structures, producing serious complications such as airway obstruction and bleeding. In addition, they may undergo malignant transformation. Examples of benign tumors are hamarto-

mas, lipomas, fibromas, and dermoid cysts. Adenomas, once classified as benign, are now considered low-grade malignancies.

Cancer. The most common form of malignant tumor of the respiratory tract is lung cancer, which began a rapid increase in frequency about 1940; in 1980 it was the leading cause of cancer deaths in American men and is also rapidly increasing in prevalence in women (see CANCER). Lung cancer has been attributed to cigarette smoking and environmental pollution: exposure to materials such as asbestos, chromium, and radioactive substances increases the probability of its development. The main types are carcinomas, lymphomas, and sarcomas. Bronchial carcinomas arise from the trachea or bronchi, and alveolar cell carcinomas arise from lung tissue. After developing a carcinoma of the lung, only 5 to 8 percent of individuals survive for 5 years or longer. Malignant tumors known as lymphomas arise in the lymph nodes related to the lungs and other body tissue. Sarcomas may originate in the lungs or in some other structure such as bone. Sarcomas have a poor prognosis, but recent advances in the treatment of lymphomas, particularly Hodgkin's disease, have increased the chance of cure or at least long-term survival.

DRUG-INDUCED PULMONARY DISEASES
Various drugs can cause either pulmonary fibrosis or edema (fluid in the lung). Such drugs include heroin, methadone, Darvon, and drugs used in the treatment of cancer (methotrexate and bleomycin), leukemia (busulfan), and infection (nitrofurantoin).

STRUCTURAL DISORDERS
Structural changes in the lungs or pleura result from a variety of causes, including pneumothorax and bronchiectasis. Pneumothorax is a condition characterized by collapse of the lung due to rupture of the membrane covering the lung and subsequent escape of air into the space between the lung and the chest wall. Pneumothorax may result from penetrating injury to the lung or as a complication of other diseases.

Bronchiectasis is the abnormal dilation of one or more bronchi, usually resulting from weakening of the bronchial wall by infection. This condition may follow pneumonia, whooping cough, or tuberculosis, or may be hereditary. Patients usually suffer from a chronic cough, copious sputum production, and occasionally expectoration of blood.

Pleural effusion, or fluid on the lung, is the accumulation of fluid in the pleural space; it can result as a complication of heart failure, pneumonia, lung cancer, tuberculosis, pulmonary infarction, and many other conditions. Atelectasis is a form of collapse of the lung due to occlusion of a bronchus by a benign or malignant tumor, by a foreign body such as a coin or peanut, or by the formation of plugs of thick mucus.

GENERALIZED DISEASES
A vast number of disorders, although not primarily respiratory, produce major or minor pulmonary manifestations. For instance, sarcoidosis, a tuberculosislike disease characterized by tumorous collections of cells, can involve the lungs. Blood clots originating in the veins or heart can break loose and travel to the lungs, creating a PULMONARY EMBOLISM by obstructing the lung arteries. This causes damage or death of the tissue supplied by the obstructed vessel. Heart failure may cause fluid to collect in the lungs, leading to shortness of breath (dyspnea) on exertion and attacks of breathlessness at night. Kidney failure may also be associated with collection of fluid and with other changes in the lung, referred to as uremic pneumonia. Other diseases that may be associated with pulmonary lesions are the autoimmune disorders that cause a person's immune defenses to attack the person's own body; these diseases include lupus erythematosis, periarteritis, systemic sclerosis (scleroderma), and rheumatoid arthritis.

CHILDREN'S DISEASES
CYSTIC FIBROSIS is a hereditary disease of children and young adults affecting the secretion of the glands that produce mucus, sweat, saliva, and digestive juices. The secretions become viscous, and an abnormally large amount of salt is present in the sweat. The disease affects the glands throughout the body, but pulmonary complications are very common.

WHOOPING COUGH caused by a bacteria, *Bordetella pertussis,* is a children's disease characterized by a high-pitched whooping sound accompanying frequent coughing. This disease may lead to pneumonia and death.

Respiratory distress syndrome (RDS), or HYALINE MEMBRANE DISEASE, is a disorder that occurs in newborn infants, most often in those born prematurely. It is an indication of incomplete development of the lungs; the infant suffers from difficulty in breathing and deficient transfer of oxygen into the blood. The disease is a leading cause of death in infants. A similar condition in adults, called ARDS (adult respiratory distress syndrome), has many causes, including severe infection, trauma, and the aspiration of stomach contents into the lungs.

HOWARD A. BUECHNER, M.D.

Bibliography: Burton, G. G., and Hodgkin, J. E., eds., *Respiratory Care*, 2d ed. (1984); Crofton, John, and Douglas, Andrew, *Respiratory Diseases*, 3d ed. (1981); Flenley, D. G., *Respiratory Diseases* (1981); Guenter, C. A., and Welch, M. H., *Pulmonary Medicine*, 2d ed. (1982); Kendig Edwin L., and Chernick, Victor, eds., *Disorders of the Respiratory Tract in Children*, 4th ed. (1983); Lee, Douglas H., *Environmental Factors in Respiratory Disease* (1972).

restaurant

The term *restaurant* refers to any of a wide variety of establishments in which people may buy and eat prepared meals. A restaurant may be full-service or self-service, and it may stand alone or be part of another facility, such as a factory, office, hotel, or club. The quality of food and service can range from that found in the ubiquitous "greasy spoon" to that of so-called "four-star" gourmet restaurants.

Public eating places have existed since ancient times, but the modern version of the restaurant (from the French *restaurer*, "to restore") did not appear until the 18th century. The word was first applied in its current usage by A. Boulanger when he opened an eating establishment in Paris in 1765. Others of this type followed in France, then in Great Britain, and most of them were expensive. In the 19th century, restaurants offering a wide choice of food increasingly replaced the older, limited-menu eating house. Rapid societal changes in 20th-century Europe and, especially, the United States—such as the growth of automobile transportation, of travel and leisure time, and of urban business and industry—created a demand for fast-food and self-service operations, as well as mass-production restaurants (pizza or steak houses, for example). The number of restaurant chains has also increased.

The restaurant industry is a substantial sector of the U.S. economy. In 1983 about 394,000 U.S. commercial eating establishments existed, up approximately 17% from 1972. In 1984 the industry employed about 8 million people, and Americans spent nearly $142 billion, or 6.1% of their disposable income, eating out. Fast-food places continue to proliferate: in 1970 they accounted for 17.8% of all restaurants, but in 1983, about 29%. (See also FOOD SERVICE SYSTEMS).

Bibliography: Emerson, Robert L., *Fast Food: The Endless Shakeout* (1979); Solomon, Kenneth L., and Katz, Norman, *Profitable Restaurant Management*, 2d ed. (1981); Stern, Jane and Michael, *Goodfood* (1983) and *Square Meals* (1984); Trillin, Calvin, *American Fried: Adventures of a Happy Eater* (1979).

Reston [res'-tuhn]

Reston (1980 pop., 36,407), a suburb of Washington, D.C., in northern Virginia, is a NEW TOWN—a planned community with its own commercial, industrial, and residential areas. Gulf Reston, Inc. financed the project from 1967 until 1978, when the Mobil Oil Corporation purchased about half the land and continued to develop it.

Reston, James Barrett

The American journalist James Barrett Reston, b. Scotland, Nov. 3, 1909, has covered numerous major events during a long and distinguished career—among them the Yalta Conference, the Robert Oppenheimer case, and the death of Stalin. He became known for his liberal views and for his influence on public opinion. Reston began his career with the *Springfield* (Ohio) *Daily News* (1932–33) and then became a report-

James Reston's career with the New York Times *spans more than four decades during which he has served as a war correspondent, bureau chief, executive editor, and vice-president of the paper. Reston, twice a recipient of the Pulitzer Prize, has written the Washington political column of the* Times *since 1974.*

Photo Jill Krementz © 1968

er for the Associated Press (1934–39). He achieved prominence with his fervently patriotic book *Prelude to Victory* (1942) and as London correspondent (1939–41) for the *New York Times*. In 1941 he joined the paper's Washington bureau and subsequently was chief Washington correspondent (1953–64), associate editor (1964–68), executive editor (1968–69), and vice-president (1969–74). Beginning in 1974 he wrote the Washington political column. Reston's numerous awards and honors include Pulitzer Prizes for national reporting in 1945 and 1957.

CALDER M. PICKETT

Bibliography: Talese, Gay, *The Kingdom and the Power* (1969).

Restoration

In English history, *Restoration* refers to the period after the fall (1660) of the republican Commonwealth and Protectorate, when the monarchy was restored in the person of CHARLES II. Early in 1660 the Convention Parliament invited Charles to return from exile on condition that he grant an amnesty to his former enemies (excepting those responsible for the execution of his father, Charles I) and guarantee religious toleration. Having met these conditions in the Declaration of Breda, Charles landed in England on May 25, 1660. The promise of religious toleration was broken when the royalist Cavalier Parliament adopted the CLARENDON CODE (1661–65).

In French history, *Restoration* means the period (1814–30) of the restored Bourbon monarchy, after the overthrow of Napoleon I.

Restoration drama

The reopening of London theaters by Charles II in 1660 began the 40-year period of Restoration drama, noted for its theatrical innovations, such as movable scenery, opera, and the introduction of actresses, and especially its satiric comedy and bombastic tragedy. The drama of the era had close ties to the court, an association reflected in the licentiousness and linguistic vitality of so-called wit comedy, or the comedy of manners.

Although criticized for its libertinism and narrow social focus, at its best Restoration comedy intelligently explores the social and sexual gamesmanship of fashionable society, whether as comic spectacle, as in the plays of Aphra BEHN, Sir George ETHEREGE, and George FARQUHAR; as questionings of personal and social morality, exemplified by the work of William CONGREVE and Thomas Otway; or as evidence of man's moral self-betrayal by hypocrisy and lust—an aspect of the drama of William WYCHERLEY. Restoration tragedy, however, is generally undistinguished. John DRYDEN championed the heroic, or rhymed, couplet as a tragic form early in his career but later abandoned it.

Bibliography: Harwood, John, *Critics, Values, and Restoration Comedy* (1982); Hume, Robert, *The Development of the English Drama in the Late Seventeenth Century* (1976); Lynch, Kathleen, *The Social Mode of Restoration Comedy* (1926); Nicoll, Allardyce, *A History of English Drama 1660–1900*, 4th ed., vol. 1 (1952); Wilson, John H., *A Preface to Restoration Drama* (1965).

resurrection

The concept of resurrection from the dead is found in several religions, although it is associated particularly with Christianity because of the central belief in the resurrection of Jesus Christ. Hope of a resurrection may have entered Judaism from Persian sources, although the idea has deeper roots in Old Testament Yahwism and the concept of God's covenant with Israel. The resurrection life was variously conceived, but the type of hope that passed into early Christian thought centered on the transformation of human life from the dead into a transcendental mode of existence. This was expressed poetically as "shining like the stars in heaven" (Dan. 12:3) or becoming "like the angels" (Mark 12:25).

After the EASTER experiences, earliest Christianity expressed its faith in what had happened to Jesus as resurrection in the transcendental sense. This concept is sharply distinguished from resuscitation, or a return to this-worldly existence, as narrated in the raisings of Lazarus and others attributed to Jesus. Saint Paul conceived the resurrection of Jesus as the first instance of an apocalyptic-type resurrection ("Christ the firstfruits," 1 Cor. 15:20, 23); as a result of Christ's resurrection, all believers may hope for resurrection at the SECOND COMING OF CHRIST. Paul indicates that the resurrection body will be new and "spiritual" (1 Cor. 15:35–54); most theologians interpret this to mean that it is the personality that is resurrected.

Islam also believes in the resurrection of the dead, as did traditional Judaism.   REGINALD H. FULLER

Bibliography: Fuller, Reginald H., *The Formation of the Resurrection Narratives* (1971); Hooke, S. H., *The Resurrection of Christ as History and Experience* (1967); Perkins, Pheme, *Resurrection: New Testament Witness and Contemporary Reflection* (1984); Perrin, Norman, *The Resurrection according to Matthew, Mark, and Luke* (1977).

See also: IMMORTALITY; JUDGMENT, LAST.

retailing

Retailing is the selling of finished goods and services to the consumer for personal or family consumption. It includes store retailing (for example, SUPERMARKETS, DEPARTMENT STORES, and RESTAURANTS), nonstore retailing (for example, door-to-door sales, VENDING MACHINES, and the MAIL-ORDER BUSINESS), and service retailing (for example, HOTELS and such personal services as dry cleaners). Approximately one out of eight employed persons in the United States works in retailing.

Types of Retail Establishments. Small, privately owned retail businesses may be either independent or franchised. Franchising, in which the retailer pays to adopt the name and sell the product of the firm selling the franchise, has grown in the United States in recent years, while the independents have declined. Franchisees and small independents account for about one-half of all retail sales in the United States and Canada, mainly in nonstore and service retailing and in selected store operations. In most other countries small independent merchants are more prevalent.

Department stores command large sales volumes by providing a wide variety of nonfood merchandise while offering extensive customer service. Their importance grew steadily from their inception during the mid-19th century until about 1930, when a decline set in that lasted until they more effectively met the challenge of chain stores and discount houses. Today department stores account for more than 10 percent of retail sales in the United States and Canada.

Supermarkets are large self-service food stores that dominate today's grocery-store business. They began as no-frills operations and first flourished in response to the economic pressures of the 1930s. The spread of household refrigeration enhanced their attraction by reducing the need for frequent purchases. Supermarkets now devote increased attention to nonfood merchandise, such as toys, hardware, and clothing.

Chain stores are groups of stores with similar characteristics and merchandise operating under central ownership. By buying in quantity and underselling their competitors, they expanded so successfully in the 1920s and '30s that many people feared the demise of the independent retailer. Attempts to limit chain stores in the United States included the Robinson-Patman Act, pricing laws, and license fees. Today chains account for more than one-third of all retail sales.

To compete with chain stores, many independents entered into cooperative arrangements called voluntary chains or cooperative wholesale warehouses. A voluntary chain is a group of independent retailers who contract with a wholesaler to obtain special prices and supervisory assistance in return for doing the bulk of their buying from that wholesaler. A cooperative wholesale warehouse is jointly owned by a group of retailers for the purpose of distribution efficiency. Consumer cooperatives are retail stores owned by consumers to take advantage of their collective buying power. They are far more prevalent in Europe than in the United States.

Shopping centers are planned clusters of complementary stores. Originally developed for the suburbs, today they are also found in urban areas. Shopping centers emerged as an important retail development after World War II, with the growth of the suburbs, increased use of the automobile, and traffic congestion in downtown areas. After years of phenomenal growth, their future development is expected to be moderate because of saturated markets, slower population growth, and tighter legal restrictions.

Mail-order retailers solicit purchases and accept orders by telephone or mail. Developed in the late 19th century to offer greater merchandise assortments at reasonable prices to rural customers, mail order is now used by urban retailers to supplement their regular sales. Vending machines, introduced in 1880, are important outlets for some merchandise, such as cigarettes and candy. They account for less than one percent of retail sales. Other nonstore retailing includes door-to-door sales and itinerant sales, as by mobile food vendors.

Aspects of Retailing. As the final link between producers and consumers, retailers must follow closely any changes in demand for the products they stock. They serve as buying agents for the public, locating and selecting merchandise and setting price levels. Retailers may carry some goods on consignment, not paying for them until they are sold to the consumer. More often, they buy goods outright and manage their inventories to avoid undue financial burden.

Store retailers must choose a site and plan store layout and decor, with the dual aims of attracting customers and controlling costs. They may make use of advertising and in-store merchandising. Retailers must also make decisions about the range of services they wish to provide for their customers. These may include deliveries, returns and allowances, and extensions of credit.   JACK J. KASULIS

Bibliography: Bluestone, B., et al., *The Retail Revolution* (1981); Duncan, D. J., et al., *Modern Retailing Management*, 10th ed. (1983); Hartley, R. F., *Retailing*, 3d ed. (1983); Hendrickson, R., *The Grand Emporiums* (1980); Mason, J. B., and Mayer, M. L., *Modern Retailing*, 3d ed. (1984); McNair, M. P., and May, E. G., *The Evolution of Retailing Institutions in the United States* (1976).

See also: MARKETING; WHOLESALING.

retardation, mental: see MENTAL RETARDATION.

retarded, education of the: see SPECIAL EDUCATION.

retrovirus

A retrovirus is a VIRUS that reproduces itself in a manner distinct from that of most other viruses. The core of any virus is a single molecule of NUCLEIC ACID, either DNA or RNA. When a virus invades a cell, this genetic material is usually replicated in its original form. A number of RNA viruses, however, make a copy of their genetic material in the form of DNA instead. In order to do so, they must be able to produce a particular enzyme that can construct a DNA molecule using an RNA template. This enzyme, called RNA-directed DNA polymerase, is also called reverse transcriptase because it reverses the normal cellular process of transcription (see GENETIC CODE; PROTEIN SYNTHESIS). An RNA virus whose life cycle involves the process of reverse transcription is called a retrovirus. The DNA molecules produced by this process are then inserted into the genetic material of the host cell, where they are replicated as DNA along with the DNA of the host's chromosomes; they are thereby distributed to all daughter cells during subsequent cell divisions. At some later time, in one or more of these daughter cells, the virus then produces RNA copies of its genetic material. These become covered with protein coats and leave the cell to repeat the life cycle.

Retroviruses have gained wide attention because they can cause severe diseases in organisms. If a retrovirus contains an ONCOGENE within its nucleic acid, the infected cell will be transformed into a CANCER cell. Retroviruses without oncogenes can also cause cancer, however, by inserting themselves into the host-cell DNA near certain genes that then become abnormally activated and make the cell malignant. In either case, the virus is often referred to as an RNA tumor virus. In humans, a number of related retroviruses, collectively called human T-cell lymphotropic viruses (HTLV), are involved in various diseases that affect the T-type of lymphocyte (see BLOOD; IMMUNITY). The first of these viruses to be studied, HTLV-I, causes adult T-cell LEUKEMIA, which occurs mainly in Japan, Africa, and the Caribbean region. The second, HTLV-II, is associated with a relatively benign T-cell variant of hairy-cell leukemia. Some researchers have labeled a third virus as HTLV-III, although the virus destroys its host T-cells in the course of multiplying within them, rather than causing them to become cancerous. This so-called HTLV-III retrovirus is the one associated with acquired immune deficiency syndrome (see AIDS). Other researchers have not grouped it with the HTLV viruses.   LOUIS LEVINE

Bibliography: Essex, M., et al., eds., *Viruses in Naturally Occurring Cancers* (1980); Lauffer, M. A., and Maramorsch, K., eds., *Advances in Virus Research* (1984); Matthews, R. E., ed., *Classification and Nomenclature of Viruses* (1982).

Return of the Native, The

Thomas HARDY's novel *The Return of the Native* (1878) achieves the intensity of classical Greek tragedy in its depiction of a pitiable human struggle against relentless fate. The author's somber view of human existence is expressed both in the superb opening description of Egdon Heath and in the tragic lives of Clym Yeobright, the returned native of the heath, his cousin Thomasin, Damon Wildeve, and Eustacia Vye. Nature is shown to be both beautiful and morally indifferent, and humankind is depicted as responsible to a great degree for its own tragedy.

Réunion   [ray-oon-yohn']

Réunion is an island in the western Indian Ocean located about 645 km (400 mi) east of Madagascar. The island covers an area of 2,512 km² (970 mi²) and has a population of 515,814 (1982). Saint-Denis is the capital.

A narrow coastal plain gives way inland to high plateaus and mountains, including several inactive volcanoes and one active one. From early spring until late summer, trade winds bring heavy rainfall to southern and eastern Réunion, supporting the cultivation of sugar. Tourism and the distillation of rum are also important to the island's economy.

Discovered by Portuguese explorers, Réunion was claimed in 1642 by the French, who established a permanent settlement in 1665. It was a French colony until 1946, when it became an overseas department of France.

Reuter, Paul Julius, Baron von   [roy'-tur]

Paul Julius Reuter, originally named Israel Beer Josaphat, b. Hesse, Germany, July 21, 1816, d. Feb. 25, 1899, founded the news agency that exists today as the London-based Reuters, Ltd. (see PRESS AGENCIES AND SYNDICATES). He began a banking career and moved to Berlin, where in 1844 he was baptized a Christian, changed his name, and married.

After moving to Paris in 1848, Reuter became a translator in the Havas news agency and in 1849 established his own service of commercial reports at Aachen, on the Belgian-Prussian border. In 1851, Reuter transferred his service to London, adding a general news report in 1858. He organized a worldwide exchange of news in 1870.

Reuter became a British subject in 1857. In 1871 the duke of Saxe-Coburg and Gotha, Germany, made him Baron Julius von Reuter, a title later recognized in England. After Reuter's retirement (1878), his son Herbert directed the agency, but the senior Reuter continued as an advisor until his death.
                                                        R. W. DESMOND

Bibliography: Storey, Graham, *Reuters: The Story of a Century of News Gathering* (1951).

Reuther, Walter P.   [roo'-thur]

Walter Reuther was a prominent U.S. labor leader from the 1930s until his death. As president of the United Auto Workers (UAW) and the Congress of Industrial Organizations (CIO), Reuther was instrumental in the 1955 merger of the American Federation of Labor (AFL) and the CIO. He then became vice-president of the AFL-CIO.

Walter Philip Reuther, b. Wheeling, W.Va., Sept. 1, 1907, d. May 9, 1970, was president of the United Auto Workers (UAW) from 1946 until his death, president of the Congress of Industrial Organizations (CIO) from 1952 to 1955, and vice-president of the AFL-CIO between 1955 and 1968. Reuther started factory work at the age of 16 and quickly became involved in union affairs. Prominent in the sit-down strikes of the late 1930s that accompanied the establishment of the UAW, Reuther won many benefits for his membership, including annual wage increases based on productivity, cost-of-living raises, and health and pension benefits. As president of the CIO, he helped to plan its merger with the American Federation of Labor (AFL) in 1955.

Bibliography: Barnard, John, *Walter Reuther and the Rise of the Auto Workers* (1983); Cormier, Frank, and Eaton, W. J., *Reuther* (1970); Reuther, V. G., *The Brothers Reuther and the Story of the UAW* (1976).

revelation

Revelation, in the religious sense, is an insight into divine reality usually claimed by the founder or original adherents of a religion. Revelations may take various forms. They may be visions, inner voices, or a combination of these (for example, Moses' experience at the burning bush, or Muhammad's revelations, which he said were like the ringing of a bell that later resolved itself into words). In the Judeo-Christian tradition, especially, revelations may be historical events that are understood to yield an interpretation of history as a whole (for example, Israel's deliverance from Egypt and the death and resurrection of Jesus Christ).

The Eastern religions stress the manifestation of the divine in all nature ("general revelation"). This concept is also present in Judaism, Christianity, and Islam, but these religions, which look on God as a personal force, focus on particular revelations, encounters in which God discloses truths that would otherwise be unknowable.

Muslims believe that the Koran was dictated verbatim to Muhammad. Judaism and Christianity also hold their holy book, the Bible, was divinely inspired, although most modern theologians interpret its propositions as deriving from, rather than constituting, revelation (the content of the latter being understood as a fundamental experience of the divine rather than as a series of verbal statements). Among Christians, Protestants believe that the Bible, with latitude of interpretation, is the sole source of revelation, whereas Roman Catholics and Orthodox find the authority of revelation in apostolic traditions as well.   JOHN MACQUARRIE

Bibliography: Abraham, W. J., *Divine Revelation and the Limits of Historical Criticism* (1982); Baillie, John, *The Idea of Revelation in Recent Thought* (1956); Brunner, Emil, *Revelation and Reason* (1984); Dulles, Avery, *Models of Revelation* (1983); Moran, Gabriel, *Theology of Revelation* (1966); Niebuhr, Richard, *The Meaning of Revelation* (1967; repr. 1983).

Revelation, Book of

The Book of Revelation is the last book of the New Testament of the Bible. Its title comes from the first verse of the text, "the revelation of Jesus Christ . . . to his servant John." The book is also called The Apocalypse, and it is the only piece of New Testament writing cast almost entirely in the apocalyptic mode (see APOCALYPTIC LITERATURE). Irenaeus states that Revelation was written during the reign of the Roman emperor Domitian, probably about AD 95. Tradition asserts that the apostle Saint JOHN wrote Revelation during his exile on Patmos. Some scholars do not accept this attribution because of the stylistic differences between Revelation and the other works attributed to John—the Gospel and Epistles.

After a prologue, the book comprises two main parts. The first (chapters 2–3) contains letters to the seven churches of Asia, warning them against false teachers and offering encouragement. The rest consists of a series of visions, replete with allegories, numbers, and other symbols, and a strong eschatological message. These features are characteristic of the apocalyptic writing then in vogue.

Interpretation of the Book of Revelation has been a source of much controversy. Some have held that it had a message only for the 1st-century world. Others maintain that the book is a prophecy to be fulfilled totally in the future (see MILLENARIANISM). Undoubtedly, John spoke to the situation of his day. The letters to the seven churches indicate a situation of crisis, probably brought on by Roman persecutions of the Christians. From his understanding of the revelation of God for his day, he painted a vision of God's final triumph over evil that has sustained many Christians in later eras.

In the Book of Revelation, John is interpreting the significance of the cross and resurrection for the future, be it near or distant. He declares their meaning for time and history until the end. God is on his throne (chapter 4); Christ has won the victory (chapter 5); God is at work in the midst of apparent chaos (seals, trumpets, and bowls). The true victors are those called out in Christ from every tongue, nation, and people (chapters 5, 20). Although God's work in history has been hidden except to eyes of faith, the final stanza will reveal that all history has truly been his story (chapters 17, 20). The victory won in history by the cross will be displayed in history by the return, and God will ultimately be revealed as all in all (chapters 21, 22).   DOUGLAS EZELL

Bibliography: Bullinger, E. W., *Commentary on Revelation* (1984); Ellul, Jacques, *Apocalypse* (1977); Heidt, W. G., *The Book of Apocalypse* (1962); Tickle, John, *The Book of Revelation* (1983).

Revels, Hiram R.   [rev'-ulz]

Hiram Rhoades Revels, b. Fayetteville, N.C., Sept. 1, 1822, d. Jan. 16, 1901, became the first black to serve in the U.S. Senate. The child of free black–Indian parents, he was educated in a seminary in Ohio and at Knox College in Illinois and was ordained (1845) a minister in the African Methodist Episcopal church. When the Civil War began Revels recruited blacks for the Union army and enlisted as chaplain of a black regiment. A Republican senator from Mississippi in 1870–71, he filled the seat once held by Jefferson Davis. Revels advocated the

Hiram Revels, the first black U.S. senator, appears (far left) with the black representatives in the 41st and 42d Congresses: (from the left) Benjamin S. Turner, Robert C. De Large, Josiah T. Walls, Jefferson F. Long, Joseph H. Rainey, and Robert B. Elliott.

restoration of civil and political rights to former Confederates. On leaving the Senate he became president of Alcorn Agricultural and Mechanical College in Mississippi.

Bibliography: Lawson, Elizabeth, *Gentleman from Mississippi* (1960).

revenue sharing

Revenue sharing is a program in which the federal government shares a set percentage of federal tax collections with local and state or provincial governments. The advocates of these plans emphasize two advantages: federal governments are more effective tax collectors than smaller governmental units, and local communities can best decide the allocation of federal moneys. Control of resources is a central issue in the Canadian and U.S. revenue-sharing debates.

The proponents believe that local governments are better able to decide which public services are most important to support financially. They contend that federal governments often spend money for such programs as welfare, health, training, and education without knowing local preferences. Opponents of the plans fear that unrestricted grants may lead to local tax cuts and less spending for domestic use.

In the United States the Nixon administration urged revenue sharing as a way to slow the growth of the federal bureaucracy and return important federal programs to localities. In 1972, Congress approved revenue sharing. This federal aid program provided no-strings-attached subsidies to more than 39,000 municipalities, townships, and counties. Because personal income was considered in allocating revenue-sharing funds, poor areas received more on a per-capita basis than wealthy ones. The program remained controversial—in part because some moneys went to communities with no demonstrable need. In 1981, President Reagan announced his intention to eliminate revenue sharing; it ended on Sept. 30, 1986. In the 14 years of its existence, the program had disbursed about $85 billion.   J. DONALD WEINRAUCH

Bibliography: Bahl, Roy, *Financing State and Local Government in the 1980's* (1984); Dommel, Paul R., *The Politics of Revenue Sharing* (1974); Juster, F. Thomas, ed., *The Economic and Political Impact of General Revenue Sharing* (1977).

Revere, Paul   [ruh-veer']

An American patriot and silversmith, Paul Revere, b. Boston, Jan. 1, 1735, d. May 10, 1818, became a legendary hero at the start of the American Revolution, when he rode from Charlestown to Lexington, Mass., on the night of Apr. 18, 1775, to warn the populace of approaching British troops. An official courier for the Massachusetts Committee of Correspondence, he arrived in Lexington shortly before another rider, William DAWES, and warned John HANCOCK and Samuel

Paul Revere, a Boston silversmith and patriot, appears in a portrait (1768) by John Singleton Copley. Revere provided many services to the American cause during the Revolution, including printing currency, casting weapons, and commanding a fort guarding Boston Harbor. He is principally remembered for riding across the Massachusetts countryside on the night of Apr. 18, 1775, to warn American patriots of a British advance on Lexington. (Boston Museum of Fine Arts.)

ADAMS to escape. Revere then started for Concord accompanied by Dawes and Samuel Prescott but was halted by a British patrol. Only Prescott reached Concord. Revere's exploit was celebrated in Henry Wadsworth Longfellow's famous but generally inaccurate poem, "Paul Revere's Ride" (1863).

A leader of the SONS OF LIBERTY, Revere had earlier been involved in numerous patriot activities including the BOSTON TEA PARTY (1773). In 1779 he participated in the Penobscot expedition in Maine; although Revere was accused of cowardice, a court-martial 2 years later cleared him.

Revere is remembered as much as a craftsman as he is as a patriot. His anti-British engravings of episodes such as the Boston Massacre were effective propaganda. He cast musket balls and cannon during the war and designed and printed the first Continental currency. After the war he became one of New England's leading silversmiths and a pioneer in the production of copper plating in America.

GEORGE ATHAN BILLIAS

Bibliography: Brigham, Clarence, *Paul Revere's Engraving* (rev. ed. 1969); Buhler, Kathryn C., *Paul Revere, Goldsmith* (1956); Forbes, Esther, *Paul Revere and the World He Lived In* (1942; repr. 1962); Goss, Elbridge, *The Life of Colonel Paul Revere* (1891; repr. 1972).

reversible and irreversible processes

All events or processes in nature may be considered reversible or irreversible according to whether the original state may be restored. The distinction between the two kinds of processes is vital to the understanding of THERMODYNAMICS, and the general properties of such processes have useful applications in physics, chemistry, biology, and engineering.
Reversibility. Precise definitions of reversible and irreversible processes depend on the type of system in which the process occurs. For a so-called macroscopic system, such as a machine or a collection of a large number of independent components of the type studied in thermodynamics, a process is considered reversible or irreversible depending on whether or not it is possible to return the system to its initial state by a slight (infinitesimal) change in the external conditions acting on the system. This condition for reversibility is very stringent; essentially all processes involving macroscopic systems

are irreversible, and the concept of a reversible process in those systems is an abstract idealization.

Any process that involves dissipation of energy, such as through friction, or which lets the system deviate from equilibrium, is irreversible. General examples are processes that occur spontaneously or those associated with the return of a system to equilibrium after some disturbance.

A specific example of a reversible process in a mechanical system is that of a ball rolling in a frictionless groove on a table that has a slight incline. By inclining the table in the other direction, the direction of the ball's roll may be reversed. If the ball rolls off the table, the process of falling would be irreversible, because a large change (lifting the ball) would be needed to restore the system to its initial state.

An example of a reversible process in a thermodynamic system is the slow compression of a gas with a frictionless piston in a well-insulated cylinder. If the external pressure on the piston is decreased by an infinitesimal amount, the gas may expand, returning to its initial state. If there is friction between the piston and cylinder, however, the process is irreversible, because the external pressure would have to be decreased by a noninfinitesimal amount before the gas would expand. Other examples of irreversible processes are the release of gas from a high-pressure container, heat flow from a hot to a cold body, striking of a match, and consuming food.
Entropy. An alternative definition of reversible and irreversible processes uses the concept of ENTROPY and the second law of thermodynamics. Entropy is a quantitative property of a system that may be changed by processes in the system and also by interactions of the system with its external environment. It may be thought of as a measurement of randomness, or disorder. According to the second law, the change in entropy because of processes in the system must be either positive or zero. For reversible processes the change in entropy is zero, and for irreversible processes it is always positive. Thus an irreversible process always leads to an increase in entropy, or amount of disorder. The system may be restored to its original state only by energy from outside the system. An example of a process that increases disorder is the shuffling of a deck of cards.

Many general results for irreversible processes may be proved in thermodynamics. For instance, engines that use heat energy to do work may use irreversible or (approximately) reversible processes. Those that use irreversible processes do less work for the same amount of energy than those that use reversible processes.
Time Reversal. For a so-called microscopic system, such as an atomic or subatomic system consisting of a small number of components, a more useful definition of reversibility is that a process is reversible if the time-reversed process, which would occur if time could run backwards, may also occur in the system. This type of reversibility is called TIME REVERSAL INVARIANCE. It holds for processes such as collisions of idealized billiard balls, where reversing time corresponds to reversing velocities so that the balls retrace their paths. Collisions of molecules and atoms appear to be time reversal invariant, so the fundamental laws governing the KINETIC THEORY OF MATTER are reversible in this sense. At the level of elementary particles, all but one class of interactions appear to be time reversal invariant. The exception involves weak interactions of neutral kaons (K-mesons).

ROBERT BUDNY

Bibliography: Feynman, Richard P., et al., *The Feynman Lectures on Physics* (1963); Prigogine, Ilya, *Introduction to Thermodynamics of Irreversible Processes*, 3d ed. (1967); Schlegel, Richard, *Time and the Physical World* (1968).

revivalism

Revivalism is a predominantly North American Protestant phenomenon in which itinerant preachers exhort their hearers to accept forgiveness of personal sin through faith in Jesus Christ and to commit themselves to spiritual self-discipline and religious exercises such as prayer, Bible reading, and church support.

Revivalism in America has been in reaction to a perceived

overemphasis by the major denominations on ritual, cultural accommodation, and doctrinal or ideological correctness at the expense of personal religious experience. Four specific periods of intense religious revival were: the GREAT AWAKENING (c.1720-70), in which Jonathan Edwards and George Whitefield played major roles; the Second Great Awakening and its aftermath (c.1787-1860); the period of Dwight L. MOODY, the Holiness Movement, and the reaction to liberalism (c.1870-1926); and the renewal of mass evangelism in the 1950s, characterized by Billy GRAHAM.   PAUL MERRITT BASSETT

Bibliography: McLoughlin, W. G., *Modern Revivalism* (1959); Smith, T., *Revivalism and Social Reform* (1957); Sweet, W. W., *Revivalism in America* (1944); Weisberger, B. A., *They Gathered at the River* (1958).

revolution

A political revolution involves fundamental changes in the structure of a society, its basic beliefs, and individual behavior. During the 20th century important revolutions have occurred in Russia (see RUSSIAN REVOLUTIONS OF 1917), China, Vietnam, and Cuba. Earlier revolutions include those in Puritan England (see ENGLISH CIVIL WAR), the AMERICAN REVOLUTION, and the FRENCH REVOLUTION. Revolutions, as distinguished from coups d'etat or rebellions, can best be understood by examining three aspects of the revolutionary process: the goals of the revolutionaries, the means they use to implement their goals, and the effects of their rule.

Revolutionary Goals. Revolutionaries seek to achieve extensive changes in the social and political system. In place of the old order, with its emphasis on status and privilege, for instance, they may seek a society that values social equality, individual achievement, and political participation based on mobilization and organization. In particular, revolutionaries may support greater equality of economic conditions; they may strive to mobilize such groups as youths, women, poor farmers, and factory workers. They may encourage equal social interaction among young and old, men and women, and members of different social classes. Revolutionaries also strive for basic structural changes. Many present-day revolutionaries believe that as government becomes more centralized and broadens its scope of activities, it can more easily engineer fundamental social changes. They aim to redistribute land, achieve rapid industrialization, secure economic independence from foreign powers, increase educational facilities, and improve health services. Revolutionaries in many cases also hope to create a new person in a new society. They stress the need to change people's behavior and attitudes. The values they seek in the new revolutionary citizen include austerity, discipline, hard work, altruism, and a concern for

the political order that transcends self-interest and group privileges. Revolutionaries try to instill such values and attitudes through mass political education in the school, army, political party, and work place.

How Revolutions Occur. Revolutionaries must begin by gaining control of the government. In order to win support, they must convince at least some groups in the country that change is both possible and desirable; their arguments about this goal comprise a systematic set of beliefs, or IDEOLOGY, postulating the feasibility and desirability of change. In addition, revolutionary leaders need an organization—a political party, a guerrilla band, an army, or a movement—to mobilize human and material resources. By bringing together those who support the revolutionary cause and scattering the supporters of the old regime, these organizations help destroy the established political order. In this connection, most revolutionaries are prepared to use coercion and violence to counter the physical force of leaders opposed to fundamental change.

The revolutions of the 20th century have occurred in societies dominated by rigid, repressive regimes that were facing disintegration. The most notable examples have been Russia in 1917, China and Vietnam after World War II, and Cuba during the late 1950s. In most instances war, demands for modernization, and internal conflicts cause institutional breakdowns. The established elites lose confidence in their abilities and rights to govern. Revolutionary leaders such as Vladimir Ilich LENIN and Leon TROTSKY in Russia, MAO TSE-TUNG and CHOU EN-LAI in China, HO CHI MINH in Vietnam, and Fidel CASTRO in Cuba have voiced programs that seem to promise a deliverance from the grievances felt by such groups as factory workers, poor farmers, and middle-class radicals (lower-ranking civil servants, teachers, students, intellectuals, and lawyers). In every successful revolutionary takeover, the leaders of the revolution manage to encourage defections from the police and army defending the old regime. By demobilizing segments of the armed forces, the revolutionaries deter the established authorities from using force to crush their opposition. After gaining political power, they organize a strong political party, army, and secret police to carry out their aims and maintain themselves in power.

In countries where revolutionaries did not win power or were unable to maintain it, they failed to mobilize enough sympathetic groups, encourage enough defections from the established armed forces, and organize a revolutionary army or guerrilla band sufficiently powerful to defeat the coercive force wielded by defenders of the old regime. This lack of organization and coercive power partly accounts for the failures of the revolutionary left in Germany during 1918-19, Béla

The storming of the Bastille by the Paris mob on July 14, 1789, marked the beginning of popular participation in the French Revolution. Parisians played a key role in the Revolution until the establishment (1795) of the Directory. The Revolution overthrew the absolutist monarchy and rigid social hierarchy of the ancien regime and eventually transferred power to the middle classes.

(Above) *Vladimir Ilich Lenin addresses a crowd of soldiers soon after the Russian Revolution of November 1917. The Bolsheviks found much of their support among the Russian armed forces.*

(Left) *Fidel Castro, who seized control of Cuba in January 1959 after a 2-year guerrilla campaign, sought to transform Cuba into a socialist state along Marxist-Leninist lines.*

KUN's Hungarian Soviet Republic (1919-20), Che GUEVARA's attempts to organize a revolution among the Bolivian Indians during the late 1960s, and the unsuccessful revolutions sponsored by the Movement for the Revolutionary Left (MIR) in Chile and the Tupamaros in Uruguay during the early 1970s.
Consequences of Revolution. Even when revolutionaries succeed in seizing political power and keeping it for a long period, they do not necessarily realize their long-term goals. The Puritan Revolution of the 1640s in England and the French Revolution of 1789 failed to establish the organizational bases needed to carry out comprehensive programs. The Marxist-Leninist revolutionaries of the 20th century have been more successful in developing strong political institutions, particularly in the USSR, China, Vietnam, and Cuba (see COMMUNISM). They have centralized political power, expanded resources through programs of industrialization, education, and health care, and repressed vestiges of the old regimes. In each instance a powerful political party controls and organizes society. Revolutionary attempts to create a new citizen, however, have for the most part not succeeded as desired. Although there have been great advances in industry and education, the attitudes and behavior patterns characteristic of the old society still remain. Party leaders have acquired privileges not available to the masses. Corruption is, in many instances, still widespread. Private enterprise has been replaced by a rigid, centralized bureaucracy. Finally, despite the revolutionary rhetoric, equality of economic opportunity has not been matched by equality in economic condition, social status, or access to political power. CHARLES F. ANDRAIN

Bibliography: Arendt, Hannah, *On Revolution* (1963); Brinton, Crane, *The Anatomy of Revolution*, rev. ed. (1965); Cohan, Al S., *Theories of Revolution: An Introduction* (1976); Dunn, John M., *Modern Revolutions* (1972); Greene, Thomas H., *Comparative Revolutionary Movements* (1974); Gurr, Ted R., *Why Men Rebel* (1970); Huntington, Samuel P., *Political Order in Changing Societies* (1968); Johnson, Chalmers,

Revolution and the Social System (1964) and *Revolutionary Change* (1966); Russell, D. E. H., *Rebellion, Revolution and Armed Force* (1974); Skocpol, Theda, *States and Social Revolutions* (1979).

Revolutions of 1848

During 1848 a series of revolutions broke out in rapid succession across Europe. The most general causes were the economic depression and crop failures of the preceding three years coupled with the political frustration felt by liberal middle-class and nationalistic groups.

The first outbreak occurred on Feb. 22 in Paris, driving LOUIS PHILIPPE from his throne and bringing in a provisional government dedicated to a democratic franchise and "national workshops" to reduce unemployment. The election of a French national assembly, however, brought to Paris provincial deputies who opposed the workshops. The result was a working-class uprising in June that was crushed with frightful bloodshed. The national assembly, dominated by the middle class, went on to establish the Second Republic with a democratically elected legislature and executive. In December Louis Napoléon (see NAPOLEON III) was elected president.

In Vienna, capital of the Austrian Empire, the news from Paris inspired popular demonstrations that drove the conservative minister Klemens von METTERNICH from office. A sequence of German liberal reform ministries followed, but the other nationalities within the Austrian Empire wished to control their own affairs. On March 5, Hungary gained autonomy and proceeded to draft a constitution; in turn the Croats organized at Zagreb to seek freedom from Hungary. In Italy, where the expulsion of Austria had long been the goal of the Italian unity movement called the RISORGIMENTO, a Venetian republic was proclaimed, and a revolution in Milan (March 18-22) was promptly supported by a new liberal regime in Sardinia-Piedmont. But the tide soon turned.

The French revolutionaries of February 1848, portrayed in this cartoon, came from both the impoverished working class and the politically alienated bourgeoisie. This unstable alliance proclaimed victory when Louis Philippe abdicated after only two days of fighting.

In March 1848, after hearing of the successful French uprising, Berliners mounted the barricades. Demanding constitutional government and the unification of Germany, the liberals won short-lived concessions from the Prussian king, Frederick William IV.

in August the Hungarians surrendered. That summer a Roman republic created by Giuseppe MAZZINI and Giuseppe GARIBALDI collapsed, and the Austrian forces recaptured Venice.

In Germany, too, the Paris revolution inspired unrest. A bloody confrontation in Berlin (March 15–21) forced the Prussian king FREDERICK WILLIAM IV to summon a constitutional assembly, an example followed in other German states. Above all, however, the liberals hoped to create a unified German empire, and to this end the FRANKFURT PARLIAMENT was elected and convened (May 18). It adopted a bill of rights and a moderately democratic form of government. When Schwarzenberg made clear his determination to centralize Austria, however, the Frankfurt Parliament decided to exclude the German-speaking provinces of Austria from the German empire and in March 1849 offered the crown of a constitutional Germany to the king of Prussia. He declined, and without Prussia the work of the parliament came to nothing. Meanwhile, in Prussia itself the king dissolved the constituent assembly and imposed his own constitution, which favored the wealthy classes but gave Prussia a measure of parliamentary government.

Despite a few lasting gains, the Revolutions of 1848 resulted in severe defeats for liberal nationalists seeking democratic reform. ENNO E. KRAEHE

Bibliography: Langer, W. L., *Political and Social Upheaval, 1832–1852* (1969); Robertson, Priscilla, *The Revolutions of 1848: A Social History* (1952); Stearns, P. N., *1848: The Revolutionary Tide in Europe* (1974).

revolver

A revolver is a FIREARM in which ammunition is fed to the firing mechanism by a revolving barrel. The weapon may be a pistol, a shoulder gun, or a machine gun, but most early models were pistols. Consequently, a revolver is generally assumed to be a particular type of repeating pistol.

Handguns working on the revolver principle first appeared in 16th-century Europe. The difficulty with early models was igniting the propellant, because matchlocks and flintlocks did not work well unless they were upright. The flintlock designed in 1818 by the American gunsmith Elisha Collier, which incorporated a clockwork mechanism to rotate the cylinder and a self-priming pan cover, was judged to be the best of its time. Not until the invention of the copper percussion cap (1815) could a reliable revolver be developed, and during the 19th century the first "pepperbox" revolvers (so called because their clusters of barrels resembled pepper shakers) made their debut. But pepperboxes were heavy and cumbersome; they also had an unfortunate tendency to act as a Roman candle: when one cap fired, it ignited the rest. And because the barrels were smoothbore, their accuracy was poor.

In 1836, the American inventor Samuel Colt began manufacturing a simple cocking mechanism that has since formed

In June, Czech leader František PALACKÝ organized a Pan-Slav Congress in Prague to demand equality with the Germans. On June 17, Austrian forces crushed this rebellion and a month later regained control in Milan. Then a constituent assembly convened in Vienna to draft a constitution for the empire. It succeeded in abolishing serfdom, but in October it was driven from Vienna by a working-class rebellion; its work was later repudiated by a new prime minister, Felix Schwarzenberg (see SCHWARZENBERG family). In December the young FRANCIS JOSEPH succeeded FERDINAND I as emperor of Austria and imposed a severely centralized administration. On Apr. 13, 1849, the Hungarians, under Lajos KOSSUTH, declared their independence. Schwarzenberg called in a Russian army, and

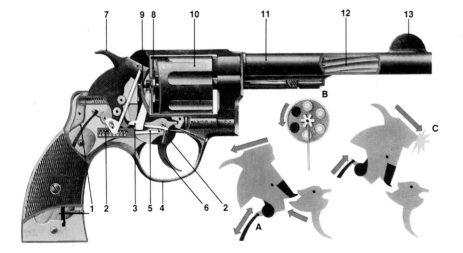

The main parts of a revolver are indicated in this cutaway view of a Smith and Wesson .38-caliber model. They include the main spring (1), trigger springs (2), cylinder stop (3), trigger guard (4), lever (5), trigger (6), hammer (7), bullet in chamber (8), ratchet (9), revolving cylinder (10), barrel (11), rifling (12), and sight (13). The firing sequence begins when the trigger is squeezed, forcing back the hammer and compressing the main spring (A). Rotating the cylinder brings a bullet into position (B). The final pull on the trigger releases the spring; the hammer drops forward and strikes a charge contained in the cartridge. The charge ignites (C), firing the bullet down the barrel.

the basis of almost every modern revolver. As the hammer cocking the trigger was pulled back, the cylinder rotated and locked in position. Colt's first models were fitted with percussion ignition. The Colt's light trigger pull was popular because it permitted accurate shooting, and rapid fire was accomplished by ''fanning'' (holding the trigger back while slapping the hammer).

Revolvers have a high rate of fire, but reloading is slow. Although devices have been invented to aid rapid reloading, they have never become popular. Several revolver rifles have seen action; the Gatling gun was a revolver. The revolver principle is employed in the modern Vulcan aircraft gun, which has a cyclic rate of fire of 600 rounds per minute, and whose barrels are rotated by one electric motor while the ammunition is fed by another.   ARTHUR JAMES BARKER

Bibliography: Akins, Charles, *American Pistols and Revolvers,* ed. by Ted Bryant and Bill Akins (1980); Hogg, I. V., *Revolvers* (1984); Myatt, Frederick, *The Illustrated Encyclopedia of Pistols and Revolvers* (1981).

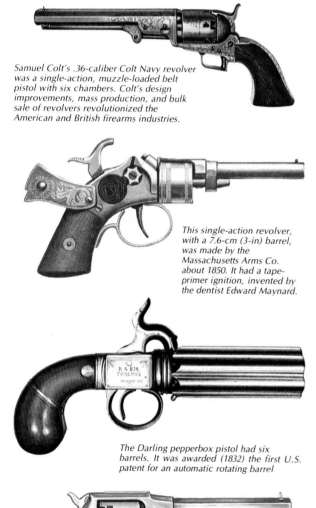

Samuel Colt's .36-caliber Colt Navy revolver was a single-action, muzzle-loaded belt pistol with six chambers. Colt's design improvements, mass production, and bulk sale of revolvers revolutionized the American and British firearms industries.

This single-action revolver, with a 7.6-cm (3-in) barrel, was made by the Massachusetts Arms Co. about 1850. It had a tape-primer ignition, invented by the dentist Edward Maynard.

The Darling pepperbox pistol had six barrels. It was awarded (1832) the first U.S. patent for an automatic rotating barrel

The muzzle-loaded, .36-caliber Remington revolver was manufactured by the Remington Arms Co. of Ilion, N.Y., in 1859. Like most percussion revolvers of the day, it was ''single action,'' requiring the shooter to cock the hammer before each firing.

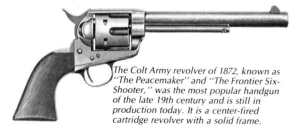

The Colt Army revolver of 1872, known as ''The Peacemaker'' and ''The Frontier Six-Shooter,'' was the most popular handgun of the late 19th century and is still in production today. It is a center-fired cartridge revolver with a solid frame.

Rexroth, Kenneth   [reks'-rawth]

In the early 1950s, American poet, critic, and painter Kenneth Rexroth, b. South Bend, Ind., Dec. 22, 1905, d. June 6, 1982, helped found the San Francisco Poetry Center with Allen Ginsberg and Lawrence Ferlinghetti. Rexroth made a crucial link between the modernism of Ezra Pound and William Carlos Williams and the more rambunctious experiments of the beat-generation poets, among whom he was often counted.

Largely self-educated, Rexroth worked at many jobs and described his bohemian life in *An Autobiographical Novel* (1966). As devoted to Oriental poetry as Pound, he published excellent translations in *One Hundred Poems from the Japanese* (1955) and other collections. His own poems combine a delicate imagism with strong social concerns and were published in numerous collections, among them *The Phoenix and the Tortoise* (1944), *In Defense of Earth* (1956), and *New Poems* (1974). Although Rexroth was sometimes considered cantankerous and idiosyncratic, his criticism helped to broaden the audience for contemporary poetry.   JOHN TYTELL

Bibliography: Gibson, Morgan, *Kenneth Rexroth* (1972).

Reye's syndrome   [rys]

Reye's syndrome is a rare, often serious, and sometimes fatal disease of children. It typically occurs after a viral infection such as influenza or chickenpox. Because the administration of salicylates such as ASPIRIN to children with these diseases has been strongly associated with onset of Reye's syndrome, people are warned against the practice. Onset is sudden and is marked by high fever, headache, vomiting, and disturbances of the central nervous system, sometimes followed by convulsions, coma, permanent brain damage, or death. The disease is named for an Australian pathologist, R. D. K. Reye, who first described it in 1963.

Bibliography: Kolata, G. B., ''Reye's Syndrome,'' *Science,* Mar. 28, 1980.

Reykjavik   [rayk'-yah-veek]

Reykjavik is the capital and largest city of Iceland, situated on Faxa Bay on the southwest coast. The population is 87,309 (1983). A transportation center with road and air connections, Reykjavik is also the main industrial and commercial city of Iceland. Industries include food and fish processing, metalworking, textile manufacturing, and shipbuilding. It is also a fishing port. This modern-looking city, constructed primarily of concrete, is heated by water obtained from nearby hot springs. It has a university (1911), a school of music (1930), a national library (1818), a national museum (1863), and a national theater. Landmarks include the parliament building, the cathedral, and the library.

Founded by Ingólfur Arnarson in 874, Reykjavik began as a small fishing village inhabited mostly by Danish settlers. A charter was granted in 1786, and the city became an episcopal see of the established Lutheran church in 1796. Since 1843, Reykjavik has been the seat of Iceland's parliament, the Althing, which has been in existence for more than 1,000 years. Reykjavik was made the capital of Iceland in 1918.

Reymont, Władysław Stanisław   [ray'-mohnt, vlahd-is'-lahf stahn-ees'-lahf]

The Polish novelist Władysław Stanisław Reymont, b. May 7, 1867, d. Dec. 5, 1925, received the Nobel Prize for literature in 1924. His epic novel, *The Peasants* (1904–09; Eng. trans.,

1924–25), in four volumes, documents the life and rituals of a small peasant village. The novel celebrates nature and the peasants, who are seen as elemental, close to the earth and the animals they tend. In this world, Christian and pagan themes contend, poetry and brutality coexist. Reymont frequently uses dramatic contrasts, such as a death during a wedding or a seduction during a high mass. His prose, impressionistic and sometimes operatic, includes dialect and fairy-tale stylization. In *The Peasants* and other works, such as *The Promised Land* (1899; Eng. trans., 1927), the author describes human misery and social injustice and obliquely suggests the need for political change.   MICHAEL KANDEL

Bibliography: Krzyżanowski, Jerzy Ryszand, *Władysław Stanisław Reymont* (1972).

Reynard the Fox   [ray'-nahrd]

A series of loosely connected beast fables in verse that became popular in medieval Europe, *Reynard the Fox* appears in French, Flemish, and German literature. The fables usually concern the struggle between the sly Reynard and the powerful wolf Isengrim. The story may be regarded as an allegory of social conflict, and by the 15th century it had assumed the didactic purpose of satirizing political power struggles. Versions include the French *Le Roman de Renart* (c.1175), William Caxton's English translation of the Flemish (1481), and T. J. Arnold's adaptation (1860) of Goethe's *Reinecke Fuchs*.

Reynolds, Sir Joshua

Joshua Reynolds, b. July 16, 1723, d. Feb. 23, 1792, was the leading English portrait painter of the 18th century and the author of the classic *Discourses* on the principles of art. At the age of 17 he went to London to study with the portrait painter Thomas Hudson and by 1743 was producing his own

Sir Joshua Reynolds's portrait Nelly O'Brien (1762–63), like other early works, evokes the sitter's character in a direct and sympathetic manner. Reynolds's later works employed classical devices in the "Grand Style" he actively promoted. (Wallace Collection, London.)

portraits. A stay (1750–52) in Italy introduced him to the great works of the Renaissance.

On his return to England he executed several portraits that brought him into prominence in London society, and soon he was inundated with commissions from fashionable and literary patrons. With his impeccable social and artistic credentials, Reynolds was the obvious choice as first president (1768) of the newly formed Royal Academy. At the Royal Academy he began (1769) to deliver the series of addresses that would eventually (1778) be compiled in the *Discourses*, whose exaltation of the so-called grand style of the Renaissance and baroque painters set the aesthetic standard of the day. His position as the supreme arbiter of English painting style was cemented further by his appointment (1784) as Painter-in-Ordinary to the king.

Reynolds's output was enormous, and his impact on contemporary artistic taste was strengthened greatly by the large number of replicas of his work produced with the aid of assistants. His ability to bring his sitters to life is brilliantly manifested in his portrait *Samuel Johnson* (1772; Tate Gallery, London). An equal facility with women's portraits is apparent in his delicate characterization of renowned society beauty *Nelly O'Brien* (1762–63; Wallace Collection, London).

The pictorial effects of the grand manner he espoused so ardently are most apparent in the "quotations" that dignify many of Reynolds's portraits. His *Sarah Siddons as the Tragic Muse* (1784; Huntington Art Gallery, San Marino, Calif.), for example, employs a gesture borrowed from Michelangelo's *Isaiah* in the Sistine Chapel. Homage to the great masters of the 16th and 17th centuries is also apparent in the baroque lighting effects he used so frequently. In *Self-Portrait* (1780; Royal Academy of Art, London), Reynolds acknowledged his debt to past artists by formulating a composition inspired by Rembrandt and by placing a bust of Michelangelo within the picture.   WILLIAM GAUNT

Bibliography: Hilles, Frederick W., *The Literary Career of Sir Joshua Reynolds* (1967); Hudson, Derek, *Sir Joshua Reynolds* (1959); Wark, Robert R., ed., *Sir Joshua Reynolds: Discourses on Art* (1975); Waterhouse, Ellis K., *Reynolds* (1941; repr. 1973).

Reynolds, Osborne

Osborne Reynolds, b. Aug. 23, 1842, d. Feb. 21, 1912, was an English scientist whose classical papers on fluid dynamics remain basic today to turbine operation, lubrication, fluid flow and streamlining, cavitation, and even tidal motion as it affects shores and estuaries. In both hydrodynamics and aerodynamics the Reynolds number is a dimensionless ratio related to the velocity at which smooth flow shifts to turbulent, as is the Reynolds stress to the drag between adjacent layers in counterflow. These quantities are particularly useful in experimental studies.   CARL A. ZAPFFE

Bibliography: Crowther, James G., *Scientific Types* (1970).

Reynolds v. Sims

In *Reynolds* v. *Sims* (1964) the U.S. Supreme Court expanded the doctrine of equitable and fair APPORTIONMENT of state legislatures first announced in BAKER V. CARR (1962). The plaintiff had challenged the apportionment of the Alabama legislature, to which roughly one-quarter of the population could elect a majority of state senators and representatives.

A federal district court ordered the state to reapportion but then nullified two plans that did not apportion the legislative districts solely on the basis of population. The state appealed to the Supreme Court, which held that the equal protection clause of the 14th Amendment requires that the seats in both houses of a state legislature be apportioned on a population basis. Chief Justice Warren's view was that if legislative districts were unequal in population, a citizen's vote would be diluted and to the extent that "a citizen's right to vote is debased, he is that much less a citizen." The Court rejected the notion that state government was analogous to the federal government, in which senators represent sovereign political subunits (the states). *Reynolds* sparked a revolutionary change in legislative reapportionment.   ROBERT S. STEAMER

Reza Shah Pahlavi   [ree'-zah shah pah'-luh-vee]

Reza Shah Pahlavi, b. Mar. 16, 1878, d. July 26, 1944, shah of Iran (1925–41), created the modern Iranian state and founded the Pahlavi dynasty. An army officer, he helped organize a nationalist coup in 1921 and became war minister. In 1923 he became prime minister. Having forged a modern army, he deposed the weak Qajar dynasty two years later and assumed the imperial crown. He stamped out tribal independence; forced the British and Soviet governments to give up their privileges in Iran; adopted a secular legal code; appropriated ecclesiastical income; built secular schools, roads, hospitals, and the Trans-Iranian Railroad; and promoted the emancipation of women.

Reza Shah antagonized the British and Soviet governments, however, and when their forces occupied Iran to ensure their supply lines in World War II, he abdicated (1941) in favor of his son, MUHAMMAD REZA SHAH PAHLAVI. Reza Shah died in South African exile.   ROBERT G. LANDEN

Bibliography: Avery, Peter, *Modern Iran*, 2d ed. (1967); Wilber, D. N., *Riza Shah Pahlavi: The Resurrection and Reconstruction of Iran, 1878-1944* (1975).

Rh factor

The Rh factor is an ANTIGEN whose name is derived from the rhesus monkey, on whose red BLOOD cells it was first discovered. Later found in humans, the Rh factor, along with other blood antigens, must be taken into account in blood transfusions. Blood from an Rh-positive donor will cause an Rh-negative recipient to produce antibodies against the Rh factor. The antibodies will cause a hemolytic transfusion reaction if the recipient again receives Rh-positive blood. The hemolytic reaction destroys the donated cells.

Erythroblastosis fetalis, or Rh hemolytic disease of the newborn, is caused by Rh factor incompatibility between a pregnant woman and her fetus. It can occur only when the mother is Rh-negative and the father is Rh-positive. Because the Rh factor is genetically dominant, the resulting fetus may be Rh-positive. The disease develops if fetal Rh factor enters the mother's circulatory system through a breach in the placenta, usually late in the pregnancy or during delivery. The mother's immune system treats the fetal Rh factor as a foreign protein and produces antibodies against it. The antibodies can pass through an intact placenta into the fetal circulation (usually in a later pregnancy) and cause a potentially fatal anemia by destroying the red blood cells. The life of an affected infant may be saved through a nearly complete transfusion of Rh-negative blood at birth. The injection of the mother with a special vaccine within 72 hours of the birth of each child prevents the antibody formation in most cases.
PETER L. PETRAKIS

Bibliography: Zimmerman, David R., *Rh: The Intimate History of a Disease and Its Conquest*, intro. by James Watson (1973).

Rhadamanthus   [rad-uh-man'-thuhs]

In Greek mythology, Rhadamanthus was the son of Zeus and Europa and one of the judges of the underworld (Hades).

Rhaeto-Romanic language: see ROMANCE LANGUAGES.

Rhamphorhynchus   [ram-for-rink'-uhs]

Rhamphorhynchus is one of the most common of the primitive flying reptiles (suborder Rhamphorhynchoidea, order Pterosauria). Known from dozens of European specimens, it was about 60 cm (2 ft) long and lived during the Late Jurassic Period, about 160 million years ago. Remarkably well-preserved examples from the famed lithographic Solnhofen Limestone of Bavaria, West Germany, show distinct impressions of long, narrow wing membranes that were supported by a single, extremely elongated fourth finger. A few specimens indicate that the wing membrane was reinforced by in-

Rhamphorhynchus, a prow-beaked flying lizard that lived about 160 million years ago, had a skin-web wing between its forelimbs and body. Its fourth digit extended about 0.5 m (1.6 ft) and supported the wing. At the end of its tail was a rudderlike appendage.

ternal fibers rather than by other bones of the hand, as in bats and birds. The body was relatively small, but the neck was very long and supported a large head bearing long, spikelike teeth. The hind legs were weakly developed and seemingly of poor design for active movement on land. The reptile's very long tail was reinforced by hair-sized, ossified tendons. At the end of the tail was a vertical kitelike vane that may have served as a rudder. *Rhamphorhynchus*'s association with marine deposits suggests that it lived like some of the modern seabirds.

Rhamphorhynchus and most other pterosaurs are usually described as gliders or poor fliers, but this description may be incorrect. Large extensions, or processes, on the upper arm bones and a large breastbone with a prominent keel for muscle attachment are clear indications that these creatures had very large flight muscles and were thus capable of active flight similar to that of most birds. In fact, several parts of the shoulder skeleton are remarkably similar to the same structures in some nonsoaring birds. *Rhamphorhynchus* and other pterosaurs probably spent little time on land, except for nesting, but probably rested like gulls on the water. Evidence in a few specimens of a hairlike covering suggests that they may have been warm-blooded, or endothermic, like mammals and birds.   JOHN H. OSTROM

Bibliography: Colbert, E. H., *Evolution of the Vertebrates* (1969); Romer, A. S., *Vertebrate Paleontology* (1966).

rhea   [ree'-uh]

Rheas, or pampas ostriches, are two species of large flightless birds in the family Rheidae, order Struthioniformes. The common rhea, *Rhea americana*, lives on pampas of southern Brazil and central Argentina, where it is hunted for sport and food by gauchos (cowboys) with bolas (leather slings weighted with stones).

It reaches 1.7 m (5.6 ft) in total height and 25 kg (55 lb) in weight. Males fight for a harem; 6 or more females may lay 12 to 18 eggs in one nest before the male drives them away, incubates the eggs for 6 weeks, and shepherds the young for another 6 weeks. The diet is mainly vegetable but includes insects and small animals. The slightly smaller Darwin's rhea, *Pterocnemia pennata*, occupies Andean foothills from Peru to Patagonia.   FRED E. LOHRER

The common, or greater, rhea, R. americana, is the largest New World bird. Although flightless, the rhea runs as fast as a horse can gallop.

ernment during the KOREAN WAR. Rhee was forced to resign in the midst of the April 1960 student uprising against his increasingly despotic rule.   ANDREW C. NAHM

Bibliography: Allen, Richard C., *Korea's Syngman Rhee* (1960).

Rheingold, Das: see RING OF THE NIBELUNG, THE.

rhenium   [ree'-nee-uhm]

Rhenium is a chemical element and one of the transition metals. Its symbol is Re, its atomic number 75, and its atomic weight 186.2. Two isotopes exist in nature: ^{185}Re is stable and ^{187}Re is radioactive. Rhenium is found in gadolinite, molybdenite, columbite, rare-earth minerals, and some sulfide ores. It was discovered by Walter Noddack, Ida Tacke, and O. C. Berg in 1925. Rhenium alloys are used in electron tubes, as semiconductors, and in thermocouples. The metal's usefulness is limited because of its expense.

rheostat   [ree'-uh-stat]

A rheostat, like a POTENTIOMETER, is a variable RESISTOR usually used to control the flow of electricity (current) through an electric circuit. A rheostat is commonly in the form of a tightly wound coil of wire over which a contact may be moved. The resistance of the device is determined by the length of coil through which the current must pass before entering the contact. A plate of resistant material—such as graphite—or a conducting liquid may be used as the resistive element instead of the coil. A light-dimming switch is a typical application of a rheostat.

rhesus monkey   [ree'-suhs]

Rhee, Syngman   [ree, sing'-muhn]

Syngman Rhee, an American-educated Korean nationalist, was elected as the first president of the Republic of (South) Korea in 1948. Although Rhee commanded the loyalty of his nation during the Korean War and the years of recovery, his rule became despotic and he was deposed in 1960.

Syngman Rhee, b. Apr. 26, 1875, d. July 19, 1965, led the Korean movement for independence from Japan and was the first president (1948-60) of the Republic of Korea (South Korea). After exposure to Western influence at a U.S. mission school in Seoul, Rhee joined (1896) the Independence Club, advocating progressive reform and opposing foreign domination. Beginning in 1898 he was imprisoned for 6 years; he then went to the United States, where he received (1910) a doctorate from Princeton University. Having converted to Christianity, he returned to Korea as a YMCA worker shortly before Japan annexed his country in 1910. Opposed to Japanese rule, he was forced to flee to the United States in 1912. There Rhee was elected (1919) president of the Korean provisional government in exile. Following World War II he returned to the U.S.-controlled area of Korea and in 1948 became the first president of South Korea. He was reelected in 1952, 1956, and 1960. A staunch anti-Communist, he worked vainly for the toppling of the Communist North Korean gov-

The rhesus monkey, M. mulatta, was extensively used in biological research until its export was banned by India, formerly the principal supplier of this important experimental animal. The rhesus was used in the development of the Salk poliomyelitis vaccine and was the first monkey carried into the stratosphere by rocket.

The rhesus monkey, *Macaca mulatta,* of the family Cercopithecidae, is more properly called a macaque, as are the other members of the genus *Macaca.* Native to southeastern Asia, rhesus monkeys are found in forests, on rocky hillsides, and in temples and villages. They live in troops averaging about 18 and typically consisting of 4 adult males, 8 adult females, and their young. Rhesus monkeys range in length from about 46 to 63 cm (18 to 25 in), plus a furry tail about half as long as the head and body; they weigh from 4.5 to about 10 kg (10 to 22 lb). Their silky coats are dull yellowish brown in color. The monkeys were extensively used in medical research—a use that seriously depleted the rhesus population. The Rh factor, a protein substance in red blood cells, was discovered in and named for the *Rh*esus in 1940.

Rheticus [ray'-tee-kus]

The German mathematician and astronomer Georg Joachim Rheticus, b. Feb. 16, 1514, d. Dec. 4, 1574, was the first to spread the knowledge of the Copernican heliocentric theory, through the publication of his *Narratio prima* (First Report, 1540; Eng. trans., 1939) three years before COPERNICUS's own work. Rheticus visited Copernicus from 1539 to 1541, may have helped persuade him to publish the *De Revolutionibus*, and supervised the early stages of its printing.

STEVEN J. DICK

Bibliography: Rosen, Edward, trans. and ed., *Three Copernican Treatises: The Commentariolus and the Letter Against Werner of Copernicus and the Narratio Prima of Rheticus* (1939; repr. 1971).

rhetoric and oratory

As defined by Aristotle, rhetoric is that branch of discourse which concerns persuasion. In Aristotle's time rhetoric was considered one of the two primary forms of expression—the other being poetry. The word is derived from the Greek *rhetor*, meaning "speaker in the assembly," and in ancient times rhetoric was concerned with the practice of oratory, or formal public speaking.

The art of rhetoric is said to have originated with Corax of Syracuse and his pupil Tisias in Greece during the first quarter of the 5th century BC in response to the citizens' need for help in pleading their own cases in court for the restoration of their property, which had been confiscated by the tyrant Thrasybulus. Aristotle's *Rhetoric* (c.330 BC), the oldest extant complete text on the subject, contains most of the concepts and principles that informed education in rhetoric and oratory for the next 2,000 years.

Aristotle's Classifications. Aristotle defined three kinds of persuasive oratory: forensic or judicial, the oratory of the courtroom, which is intended to prove the justice or injustice of a past action; deliberative, the oratory of the public forum, which is intended to move an audience to—or restrain an audience from—an action; and epideictic, the oratory of ceremony, which is intended to display sentiments appropriate for such occasions as funerals, inaugurations, and dedications. Aristotle then identified three means of persuasion: the appeal to reason (*logos*), the appeal to emotion (*pathos*), and the appeal of the speaker's character (*ethos*).

Under the influence of Aristotle's teachings, the study of rhetoric came to be divided into five parts: invention, the process of finding arguments for the speech; arrangement, the process of organizing the speech; style, the process of putting into words what has been discovered and arranged; memory, the techniques for memorizing the speech for oral presentation; and delivery, the techniques for managing voice and gesture in the act of presenting the speech.

For the process of invention, rhetoricians developed the elaborate system of the topics or general lines of argument. Arrangement concerned the number and order of the parts of an oration: the exordium, or introduction; the narration, or statement of the point at issue; the confirmation, or proof of one's case; the refutation, or undermining of the arguments of the opposition; and the peroration, or conclusion. The study of style was concerned mainly with the choice of words, the structure of sentences, and the use of rhythm and figures of speech.

Later Developments. The Romans Cicero and Quintilian greatly expanded Aristotle's account of rhetoric. They also insisted that to be successful the orator must acquire a broad liberal education. In the medieval period, when rhetoric, logic, and grammar became the trivium of the liberal arts in the schools, the province of rhetoric was extended to sermons and letter-writing. During the Renaissance, when rhetoric became the dominant discipline in the English grammar schools and universities, rhetoricians concentrated more on written prose and on such literary forms as drama and poetry than on speechmaking.

The long tradition of classical rhetoric begun by Aristotle is generally regarded as having ended with the publication of the rhetoric texts of George Campbell (1776), Hugh Blair (1783), and Richard Whately (1828). Today speech departments tend to study the history and theory of rhetoric for its own sake rather than its application to speechmaking.

EDWARD P. J. CORBETT

Bibliography: Corbett, Edward P. J., *Classical Rhetoric for the Modern Student* (1965); Howell, Wilbur S., *Logic and Rhetoric in England, 1500-1700* (1956) and *Eighteenth-Century British Logic and Rhetoric* (1971); Kennedy, George, *The Art of Persuasion in Greece* (1963) and *The Art of Rhetoric in the Roman World* (1972); Murphy, James J., *Rhetoric in the Middle Ages* (1974); Weaver, Richard, *The Ethics of Rhetoric* (1953).

Rhett, Robert Barnwell [ret]

Robert Barnwell Rhett, b. Beaufort, S.C., Dec. 21, 1800, d. Sept. 14, 1876, an American secessionist, was an early and unremitting proponent of an independent South. A state rights Democrat and disciple of John C. CALHOUN beginning in the 1820s, he was a U.S. representative (1837-49) and senator (1850-52). Convinced that the Democratic party would not protect Southern interests, he formed (1850) a secessionist movement in South Carolina. During the U.S. Civil War he used the *Charleston Mercury*, edited by his son, to denounce any tendency toward compromise on the part of the Confederate leadership and to attack the policies of President Jefferson Davis.

Bibliography: White, Laura A., *Robert Barnwell Rhett: Father of Secession* (1931; repr. 1965).

rheumatic fever

Rheumatic fever is an acute fever, generally of childhood, in which inflammation of the joints (arthritis) is often the most prominent symptom (hence the name) but which may leave the heart seriously damaged. It is a sequel to infection of the throat with a bacterium of streptococci, usually occurring 10 to 14 days earlier, although only a small percentage of persons with streptoccocal infection develop this complication. High fever of sudden onset is accompanied by arthritis, skin nodules, and rashes. Involuntary movements termed chorea may occur in conjunction with rheumatic fever. In some patients arthritis affects one joint after another, with the overlying skin becoming red and every movement causing pain; in others, however, the joint pain may be mild and thus regarded as "growing pains." In most cases the heart tissues become inflamed (carditis), and although this condition may be symptomless, permanent damage to the heart valves and muscles may result.

Treatment for rheumatic fever includes rest in bed and therapy with aspirin or steroids. After recovery patients with carditis are particularly susceptible to further attacks of rheumatic fever, which tend to cause progressive damage to the heart and especially deformity of the heart valves. Such subsequent attacks can be minimized by efforts to prevent the streptococcal infection that precedes and leads to rheumatic fever. Regular doses of antimicrobial drugs, such as penicillin, given throughout the childhood years or longer are effective in preventing recurrent attacks. The disease is most common in temperate climates and in overcrowded conditions. It is decreasing in incidence in many parts of the world, probably because of more effective treatment of streptococcal infections.

J. MICHAEL S. DIXON

Bibliography: Davis, Eli, and Thomas, Charles C., *Rheumatic Fever* (1969); Markowitz, Milton, and Gordis, Leon, *Rheumatic Fever*, 2d ed. (1972); Stollerman, Gene H., *Rheumatic Fever and Streptococcal Infection* (1975).

rheumatism

Rheumatism is a nonspecific term for several diseases that cause inflammation or degeneration of joints, muscles, ligaments, tendons, and bursae. The term includes rheumatoid ARTHRITIS and other degenerative diseases of the joints; BURSITIS; fibrositis; gout; lumbago; myositis; rheumatic fever; sciatica; and spondylitis.

Palindromic rheumatism is a disease that causes frequent and irregular attacks of joint pain, especially in the fingers, but leaves no permanent damage to the joints. Psychogenic rheumatism is common in women between the ages of 40 and 70, although men also contract this disease. Symptoms include complaints of pain in various parts of the musculoskeletal system that cannot be substantiated medically. This condition can be alleviated by psychotherapy.

One of the common forms of rheumatism is rheumatoid arthritis, a disease of unknown cause that affects 1 to 3 percent of the population. This disease causes joint deformities and impaired mobility as a consequence of chronic inflammation and thickening of the synovial membranes, which surround joints. As the disease progresses it produces ulceration of cartilage in the joints. Rheumatoid arthritis usually occurs between ages 35 and 40 but can occur at any age. It characteristically follows a course of spontaneous remissions and exacerbations, and in about 10 to 20 percent of patients the remission is permanent.   PETER L. PETRAKIS

Bibliography: Dixon, Allan, and Jayson, Malcolm I., *Understanding Arthritis and Rheumatism* (1976).

See also: JOINT AND JOINT ARTICULATION.

Rhine, J. B.   [ryn]

A pioneer of PARAPSYCHOLOGY, Joseph Banks Rhine, b. Juniata County, Pa., Sept. 29, 1895, d. Feb. 20, 1980, founded (1935) the Duke University Parapsychology Laboratory together with William McDougall. Rhine's statistical studies of extrasensory perception were fundamental to the development of parapsychology as a field for quantitative research. Rhine founded the *Journal of Parapsychology* in 1937.

Rhine River

The Rhine, the longest river in western Europe, flows across Switzerland, West Germany, and the Netherlands to the North Sea. Its watershed covers about 252,000 km² (97,300 mi²). The Vorderrhein and Hinterrhein rivers, which rise on the Saint Gotthard massif in the Alps, join at Tamins to form the Rhine. The river then flows northeast about 100 km (60 mi) between the mountains to Lake Constance (see CONSTANCE, LAKE). The Schaffhausen Falls near the western end of the lake set an absolute limit to navigation from the sea. The effective limit of navigation at Basel marks the downstream extent of the river's alpine section.

At Basel the Rhine's course turns northward and for about 320 km (200 mi) flows across a plain lying between the Vosges mountains and the BLACK FOREST. For much of this distance it follows the boundary between France and West Germany. HORST AND GRABEN topography dominates this segment of the Rhine valley. Near the river in this section of its course are the major port cities of Strasbourg, Karlsruhe, Mannheim,

RHINE RIVER

	Meters	Feet
▨ Major Urban Area	Above 4000	Above 13124
- - - Drainage Basin Outline	2000	6562
	1000	3281
⊥⊥⊥ Canal	500	1640
	200	656
+ Spot Elevation or Depth	0	Sea Level

National capitals are underlined

City type size indicates relative importance

Scale 1:8,000,000

0   50   100   150   km
0   50   100   mi

0	0
200	656

A barge moves past the village of Oberwesel, located along the left bank of the Rhine River. From the heights overlooking the village, the Schönburg (left)—a group of 3 castles with 18 watchtowers and a surrounding wall—once guarded this bend in the river.

and Mainz. The Rhine is joined by the MAIN RIVER at Mainz and the Neckar River at Mannheim.

Below Mainz the Rhine enters its gorge tract, one of the most scenic parts of its valley. The steep slopes are crowned with ruined castles—suggesting the name Heroic Rhine for this portion of the river's course. The valley walls are terraced for growing wine grapes. Within this tract the Rhine is joined from the west by the MOSELLE RIVER at Koblenz.

The river leaves the gorge at Remagen, and the riverbed widens and forms meanders across the plain of northwest Germany, passing Cologne, Düsseldorf, and Duisburg before entering the Netherlands. There it divides into three main streams: the Waal, the Lek, and the Ijssel, the last of which drains into the IJSSELMEER. The Waal and the Lek further divide to form the delta of the Rhine. Rotterdam lies on the Lek, 45 km (28 mi) from the sea. The Hook of Holland is located at the mouth of an artificial cut known as the New Waterway, which connects Rotterdam to the sea.

The upper Rhine is fed primarily by the melting snow of the Alps, with high water occurring in late spring and summer. Farther downstream the dominant source of water is the heavy rains in winter, when a secondary high level takes place.

Following extensive work on the river's bed, the Rhine became the most easily navigated and most-used river in Europe. Its middle course was straightened, its gorge section was deepened, and its lower course was protected by levees.

The Rhine is linked by canal with the Ruhr industrial region and with northern Germany; the Moselle provides access to France. The great volume of commerce carried on the river has made Rotterdam the foremost port in western Europe. The chief commodities transported are coal, iron ore, and petroleum. The Rhine-Main-Danube Waterway, when completed, will link the Rhine River with the Black Sea. A spill from a Swiss chemical plant badly polluted the river in 1986.

NORMAN J. G. POUNDS

Bibliography: Hills, C. A. R., *The Rhine* (1978).

Rhineland [ryn'-land]

The Rhineland—that part of Germany lying west of the Rhine River—consists of several regions: the Upper Rhine Valley, the Palatinate Upland, the Saar Basin, the Western Rhine Valley, the Lower Rhine Bay, and the Lower Rhine Plain. The major cities are COLOGNE, BONN, and AACHEN. The name *Rhineland* also refers to the demilitarized zone established by the Allies after World War I, which included an area east of the Rhine.

rhinitis [ry-ny'-tuhs]

Rhinitis is an inflammation of the nasal mucous membrane, usually caused by the common cold virus, as well as by irritants and ALLERGY to pollens and other agents. Chronic rhinitis may occur in disorders such as syphilis and leishmaniasis that are characterized by destruction of soft tissue and cartilage. Most cold viruses are members of a group called rhinoviruses, hence the name *rhinitis*. Rhinitis is the major symptom that occurs when the nose is the major focus of infection during a cold, although a cold can also settle in the pharynx, larynx, and chest. The main symptoms of rhinitis are sneezing, burning sensations, discharge of mucus, and obstruction from swelling of nasal membranes. The infection can spread to other parts of the respiratory system and to the sinuses and middle ear. The symptoms of rhinitis caused by a cold usually disappear in about a week. Allergic rhinitis (hay fever) produces symptoms similar to those of a cold, but it usually can be differentiated by a history of seasonal recurrence coinciding with periods of abundant airborne pollen, itching of the eyes, nose, and pharynx, and an abundance of cells called eosinophils in nasal secretions.   PETER L. PETRAKIS

rhinoceros

The once numerous rhinoceros family, Rhinocerotidae, in the order Perissodactyla, now contains only five living species. All are threatened with extinction, some imminently. Rhinoceroses are large mammals with large heads, small eyes, one or two horns on the snout, and three toes on each foot. All but the Sumatran rhino are virtually hairless except for the tip of the tail and a fringe on the ears. The Sumatran rhino is covered with a fairly dense coat of hair and is related to the extinct long-coated woolly rhino, *Coelodonta antiquitatis*, of Ice-Age Europe. The Indian and Javan rhinos are one-horned; the other three species are two-horned.

The rhino's horn is composed of keratin, as is the cow's horn, but unlike the cow's horn it is of a fused, fibrous construction and solid throughout, with no hollow for a core of

The Indian rhinoceros, Rhinoceros unicornis, *appears to have an armored hide, which is actually loose folds of skin.*

The square-lipped African white rhinoceros, Ceratotherium simum, *has a symbiotic relationship with oxpecker birds, which clean the rhino of ticks and make a warning cry if danger is near.*

bone. The fibers represent greatly modified hairs. The horn is attached to the skin and is supported by a raised, roughened area on the skull. Because many Asians, particularly the Chinese, believe the rhino horn has aphrodisiacal properties, the horns are widely sought after, and this demand accounts for much of the illegal killing of rhinos.

The three species of Asiatic rhinos include the Indian rhino, *Rhinoceros unicornis*, and the nearly extinct Javan rhino, *R. sondaicus*; the former, native to northeastern India, is now found in only a few protected areas; the Javan rhino, once distributed across southeastern Asia into the East Indies, now survives only in a small preserve at the tip of the island of Java. The Sumatran rhino, *Dicerorhinus sumatrensis*, is now confined to a few widely scattered areas in southeastern Asia and in the East Indies. The two species of African rhinos are the black rhino, *Diceros bicornis*, and the white rhino, *Ceratotherium simum*. The latter is believed to have received its name from a mistranslation of the Afrikaans word for ''wide,'' referring to its lips, rather than to its color, which varies from brown to gray. The living rhinoceroses range from 2 to 4.2 m (6.5 to 14 ft) long, from 1 to 2 m (40 to 80 in) high at the shoulders, and from 1 to more than 3 tons in weight. Extinct rhinoceroses include the largest land mammals that ever lived. *Baluchitherium*, which lived in Asia during the Oligocene and early Miocene (from about 37 million to 25 million years ago), reached 7 m (23 ft) in length—including a 1.2-m (4-ft) head—and 5.4 m (18 ft) in height at the shoulders.

EDWIN E. ROSENBLUM

Bibliography: Davis, J. G., *Operation Rhino* (1972); Guggisberg, C. A., *Rhino* (1967); United Nations, *Elephants and Rhinos in Africa: A Time for Decision* (1982).

Rhizobium [ry-zoh'-bee-uhm]

Rhizobium is a genus of soil bacteria often found living in small nodules on the roots of peas, soybeans, alfalfa, string beans, and other legumes. Inside the nodules the bacteria convert nitrogen from the air into a form that can be used by the plant. Carbohydrate produced by the plant is used in this process, called NITROGEN fixation.

Rhizopoda [ry-zah'-puh-duh]

Rhizopoda, or Sarcodina, is a class of PROTOZOA containing the amoeboid protozoa—those which move about and capture food by means of pseudopodia—and including the common *Amoeba proteus* and *Entamoeba histolytica*, the organism causing amoebic DYSENTERY. AMOEBA is a naked mass of

PROTOPLASM, but also included in the Rhizopoda are several groups of protozoans that secrete hard shells, or tests, around themselves. ARCELLA, for example, secretes a chitinous test; a FORAMINIFER secretes a shell of calcium carbonate; and a RADIOLARIAN secretes an outer shell usually containing siliceous substances. The shells of radiolarians and foraminifers have formed vast deposits in the Earth's crust, and the shells of the foraminifer *Globigerina* form a thick ooze covering vast areas of the ocean floor.

Bibliography: Kudo, Richard, *Protozoology*, 5th ed., rev. (1977).

Rhizopus   [ry'-zuh-puhs]

Rhizopus is a genus of FUNGI belonging to the class Zygomycetes. It includes *R. stolonifer,* which appears commonly on bread as a gray, webby mold spotted with black dots. Some species of *Rhizopus* are used industrially in manufacturing cortisone and fumaric acid.

Rhode Island

Rhode Island, one of the 13 original colonies and the smallest in area of the 50 states, is bounded on the north and east by Massachusetts, on the south by Rhode Island Sound, and on the west by Connecticut. The state is almost cut in two parts by NARRAGANSETT BAY, which penetrates 45 km (28 mi) to the state capital of Providence. Within the bay are 36 islands; Block Island lies 16 km (10 mi) offshore.

The official name, the State of Rhode Island and Providence Plantations, refers to early settlements on Aquidneck Island (later known as Rhode Island) and the Proprietors' Company for Providence Plantations on the mainland. Since settlement, Rhode Island has had a significant and varied history. It was the first colony to declare its independence from Great Britain and was a pioneer industrial state in the new nation. With increased competition from larger states with broader resource bases, Rhode Island has been forced to search for different paths leading to economic prosperity.

LAND AND RESOURCES

Rhode Island's two physiographic regions are the eastern lowlands and the western uplands. The eastern lowland, including the bay shores and islands, is gently rolling. Within Narragansett Bay the largest islands are Conanicut, Dutch, Prudence, and Rhode Island. The second region, the western

Providence, the largest city of Rhode Island, is located on the Providence River at the head of Narragansett Bay. One of the oldest cities in America, Providence was founded in 1636 by Roger Williams, a religious dissident who had been exiled from Massachusetts.

upland, occupies the western half of the mainland. It has steep slopes and rocky outcrops and encompasses about 20 hills exceeding 180 m (590 ft) in elevation. The effects of glaciation can be seen in the extensive areas of glacial outwash, disarranged drainage, swamps, and ponds.

Soils. Rhode Island has four major soil regions. The highest upland area has deep, poorly drained soils, whereas the largest portion of the mainland is covered by deep, well-drained podzols. Sandy and gravelly soils are found near Narragansett Bay and in scattered valley locations. Occasional marshes interrupt the well-drained soils of the lower west bay shores and the bay islands.

Drainage. The northern half of the state drains into Narragansett Bay via the Blackstone, Pawtuxet, Seekonk, and Woonasquatucket rivers. The Pawcatuck drains much of the south.

RHODE ISLAND

LAND. Area: 3,139 km² (1,212 mi²); rank: 50th. Capital and largest city: Providence (1984 est. pop., 154,148). Counties: 5. Elevations: highest—247 m (812 ft), at Jerimoth Hill; lowest—sea level, at the Atlantic coast.

PEOPLE. Population (1985 est.): 968,000; rank: 42d; density: 354.3 persons per km² (917.5 per mi²). Distribution (1984): 92.6% metropolitan, 7.4% nonmetropolitan. Average annual change (1980–84): +0.4%.

EDUCATION. Public enrollment (1984): elementary—89,372; secondary—44,662; higher (1985)—35,389. Nonpublic enrollment (1980): elementary—17,000; secondary—8,100; combined—3,800; higher (1985)—34,538. Institutions of higher education (1983): 13.

ECONOMY. State personal income (1984): $12.2 billion; rank: 41st. Median family income (1979): $19,448; rank: 28th. Nonagricultural labor distribution (1984): manufacturing—121,000 persons; wholesale and retail trade—88,000; government—57,000; services—97,000; transportation and utilities—14,000; finance, insurance, and real estate—23,000; construction—13,000. Agriculture: income (1984)—$62 million. Fishing: value (1984)—$70 million. Forestry: sawn timber volume (1977)—697 million board feet. Mining: value (1983)—$8 million. Manufacturing: value added (1982)—$3.8 billion. Services: value (1982)—$1.7 billion.

GOVERNMENT (1987). Governor: Edward D. DiPrete, Republican. U.S. Congress: Senate—1 Democrat, 1 Republican; House—1 Democrat, 1 Republican. Electoral college votes: 4. State legislature: 50 senators, 100 representatives.

STATE SYMBOLS. Statehood: May 29, 1790; the 13th state. Nicknames: Ocean State and Little Rhody; bird: Rhode Island Red; flower: violet; tree: red maple; motto: Hope; song: "Rhode Island."

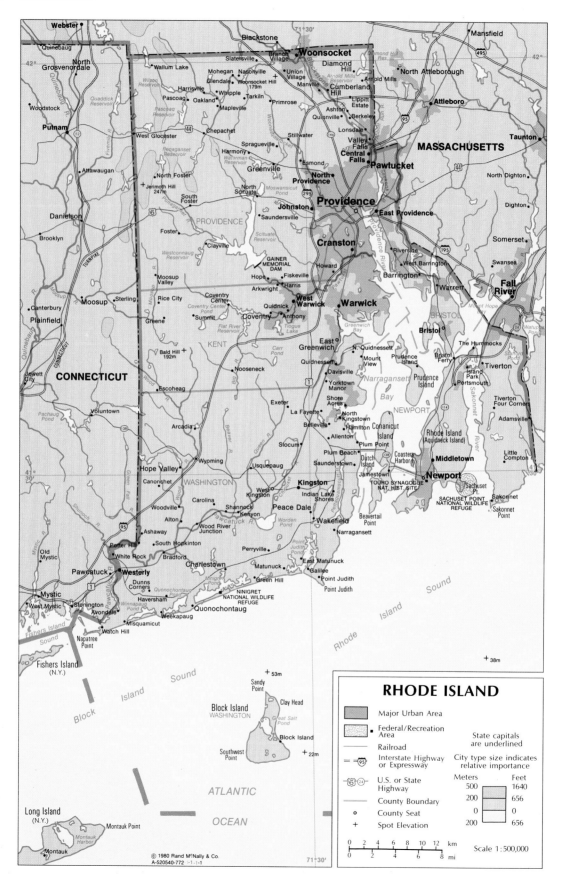

RHODE ISLAND

Major Urban Area

Federal/Recreation Area

Railroad

Interstate Highway or Expressway

U.S. or State Highway

County Boundary

County Seat

Spot Elevation

State capitals are underlined

City type size indicates relative importance

Meters	Feet
500	1640
200	656
0	0
200	656

Scale 1:500,000

(Left) *Many of Newport's opulent mansions, which front the Atlantic coast of Aquidneck Island, were built during the late 19th century, when the region became fashionable as a summer resort. Several mansions are maintained as museums and have been opened to the public.*

(Below) *A small farm on Conanicut Island appears in an aerial photograph taken above Narragansett Bay. Urban, industrial, and lacking space, Rhode Island ranks 49th among all states in the value of crops grown on its farms, with Alaska last.*

Climate. Rhode Island's basically humid continental climate is modified by the state's proximity to the ocean, but variability is the dominant characteristic. The average annual temperature is 10° C (50° F). The coldest months are January and February, with mean temperatures of −2° C (29° F); July, the hottest month, has a mean temperature of 23° C (73° F). The annual precipitation averages 1,016 mm (40 in).

Vegetation and Animal Life. About 60% of Rhode Island's land area is wooded. Because of the state's transitional location between northern and southern forests, hemlock, white pine, birch, maple, and several varieties of oak are present. In Rhode Island's highly urbanized environment, small animals survive in limited locations. Many mammal and bird species can be found within the state. Block Island, on the Atlantic flyway, is known for its diverse bird population. A wide variety of freshwater fish and amphibians inhabit inland waters in addition to the many finfish and shellfish found offshore.

Resources. Water is Rhode Island's major resource. Rivers furnished power for early mills and continue to supply water for homes and factories today. Potential supplies of ground and surface water are estimated to be about three times present use. The largest mineral deposits are those of sand and gravel. Westerly granite once was economically important, but now only limestone continues to be profitably mined.

Environmental Protection. Public and private groups are working to overcome environmental problems brought about by Rhode Island's dense population and long industrialization. Water pollution and flooding problems are the foremost concerns of this ocean-oriented state. The fragile environments of marsh and wetland areas are protected by law.

PEOPLE

The smallest of the 50 states has the second highest population density in the nation. In 1980 the 7 cities with more than 25,000 residents accounted for 54% of the total population. CRANSTON, PAWTUCKET, PROVIDENCE, EAST PROVIDENCE, and WARWICK had more than 50,000 people.

The 1980 census population was 87% urban, one of the highest percentages of all the states. The total number of inhabitants is actually declining; by 1980, Rhode Island had lost 0.3% of its 1970 census population.

The 1980 census enumeration counted 27,584 blacks, or 2.9% of the state's population. In 1910 the state had the highest percentage of foreign-born residents in the nation—30%. By 1980 about 9% were foreign born. Most of the recent immigrants are Hispanics. Although the early populations were

overwhelmingly Protestant, Roman Catholics now constitute the largest single religious denomination.

Education. Public education dates from the Henry Barnard School Law of 1845. Today the state board of regents for education and its subboards have policymaking power over all public schools.

In 1980 there were 154,000 students enrolled in grades 1 through 12 in the public schools. The elementary and secondary private-school enrollment in the state was 25,000 (1978). Enrollment in Rhode Island's public and private institutions of higher learning was 66,900 (1980). In addition to state-supported institutions, 8 private degree-granting schools operate within the state, including BROWN UNIVERSITY, BRYANT COLLEGE, and RHODE ISLAND SCHOOL OF DESIGN.

Cultural Activities and Historic Sites. Rhode Island's past is preserved in its many museums and historic sites. In NEWPORT, Touro Synagogue (1763), the oldest synagogue building in the United States, has been designated a national historic site. Of the state's many buildings dating from colonial times, a number have been named national historic structures. The AMERICA'S CUP competition was held in Newport from 1930 to 1983, the most famous of many yachting races held there. Among the state's theatrical companies, the Trinity Square Repertory Company in Providence is the most famous.

The American Eagle *competes in trials off Newport, R.I., to select a U.S. defender for the America's Cup. Beginning in 1851, this famous yacht race was always won by Americans until 1983, when the* Australia II *captured the cup. From 1930 to 1983 the race was held off Newport.*

Fishing boats and pleasure craft lie moored at the docks of a coastal community on Narragansett Bay near Rhode Island Sound. Although commercial fishing is of diminishing importance to the state economy, the value of the industry's annual catch exceeds $20 million.

Recreation. Many of Rhode Island's recreational opportunities are associated with its coastline, where boating, sailing, and fishing dominate. Inland, freshwater swimming and fishing from stocked streams are popular.

Communications. Rhode Island is served by 7 daily, 2 Sunday, and 16 weekly newspapers. Broadcasting facilities include 22 radio stations and 2 television stations.

ECONOMIC ACTIVITY

The economy of Rhode Island has developed around its skilled work force. About 60% of all employees are engaged in nonmanufacturing activities, particularly insurance, printing and publishing, wholesale and retail trade, education, and government. Growing tourism has provided opportunities for many service jobs. Per-capita income in 1977 was $6,775, less than the national average of $7,019.

AGRICULTURE, FORESTRY, AND FISHING

Agriculture has steadily declined in importance. In 1976 the state's 700 farms, covering 278 km² (107 mi²), employed less than 1% of the labor force. Specialty crops and produce for nearby urban markets are still grown. In 1978 farm products sales totaled $27.3 million. Dairy products, livestock, and poultry accounted for 43% of the total. Potatoes were the major field crop.

About 90% of the state's forestland is privately owned. Much is low-value growth, but oak and white pine are of commercial value. Unlike other New England areas, the

An artisan at a stonecutting shop in Newport, R.I., inscribes a stone memorial. In addition to its famous mansions, Newport's small shops, many of them housed in 18th-century restored structures, attract many visitors to the city's old downtown and shore areas.

state's fishing industry is prospering. The relatively new trawler fleet and the Point Judith Fisherman's Cooperative are significant to the industry's growth. Industrial fish rank first in weight of total catch, but a wide variety of table fish and shellfish are also caught.

Manufacturing. Rhode Island was among the first industrial states in the nation. Ships were its earliest products, but they have fallen in economic importance. In 1976 value added by manufacture reached almost $2.3 billion. The leading industries manufacture jewelry and silverware, textiles, machinery, fabricated metals, rubber, and plastics.

Tourism. The income from tourism in 1975 was estimated at $129 million. Once the playground of the rich, Newport has many mansions open to visitors. Increased investments have resulted in expanded accommodations and enlarged boating facilities. Camping and recreational areas have been developed inland.

Transportation. Interstate 95, linking New York and Boston, traverses Rhode Island and is an essential route for the state's industries and residents. More than 8,000 km (5,000 mi) of intrastate roads serve the people. The Newport Bridge (1969) replaced the last major ferry link in the lower bay. The main line of the Amtrak system is reached by independent feeder lines. Providence's deepwater port accommodates supertankers. The state operates seven airports, which in 1979 handled more than 1 million scheduled passengers and increasing amounts of freight.

Energy. Although Rhode Island produces little of its power, electrical power is available through participation in the New England Power Grid. Rhode Island is dependent on imported fuels; the port of Providence handles 13.6 million metric tons (15 million U.S. tons) of petroleum and gas each year. Offshore drilling for petroleum has been initiated.

GOVERNMENT AND POLITICS

The governor and four elected state officers—lieutenant governor, secretary of state, attorney general, and general treasurer—serve 2-year terms. The General Assembly consists of the 100-member House of Representatives and the 50-member Senate. The state's 5 counties serve only as judicial districts under the chief justice of the State Supreme Court. Superior, district, and family courts hold sessions in several locations. The state's municipalities consist of 8 cities and 31 towns comparable to townships outside of New England.

DORR'S REBELLION, protesting a legislative apportionment that favored rural areas and opposing suffrage for propertied men only, resulted in the Constitution of 1842. The document remains in effect.

From the Civil War period until the 1920s, Rhode Island favored the Republican party in U.S. presidential elections.

Since that time, however, the Democrats have won a good share of electoral victories—at the state as well as at the federal level.

HISTORY

At the time of the first white settlement in Rhode Island four Indian tribes lived in the area: the NARRAGANSETT, WAMPANOAG, Niantic, and Nipmuck—all members of the Algonquian linguistic group. In 1511, Miguel Corte Real, a Portuguese navigator, is believed to have sailed along Rhode Island's coast. Narragansett Bay was explored by Giovanni da Verrazano in 1524, and at the beginning of the 17th century Dutch traders—including Adriaen Block—sailed through the offshore waters.

Colonial Period. In 1636 the first permanent white settlement was founded by Roger WILLIAMS. He had left Boston and traveled overland, settling at present-day East Providence. In 1638 he and 12 other settlers on the mainland formed the Proprietors' Company for Providence Plantations.

In that same year William CODDINGTON and John Clarke were ordered to leave Massachusetts because of their support for the religious leader Anne HUTCHINSON. The two obtained an Indian deed to Aquidneck Island in Narragansett Bay and settled the northern end of the island at present-day Portsmouth. Because of a 1639 dispute between Coddington and Hutchinson, the former moved south and established Newport. In 1644, Aquidneck was renamed Rhode Island. Williams returned from England that same year with a charter for the colony that united the three settlements into "The Incorporation of Providence Plantations in the Narragansett Bay in New England." The colony's first legislative session was held in May 1647, at which time the Warwick colony of Samuel GORTON was included with the larger incorporation. In 1663 a royal charter recognizing Rhode Island's religious freedom and self-government was granted by the English king CHARLES II; the document remained in effect until the state constitution was drawn up in 1842.

Rhode Islanders maintained good relations with the Indians, but they were forced to flee to Newport when colonists in Connecticut and Massachusetts instigated KING PHILIP'S WAR (1675–76).

The maritime era arrived when surplus agricultural products enabled farmers to take to the seas. Large plantations on Rhode Island and in the southern part of the mainland grew corn, practiced animal husbandry, and processed wool, meat, and cheese for export. Foreign trade developed with the West Indies, the ports of Europe, and the Pacific via South America or Africa. Maritime activities included privateering against the enemies of Britain, slave trading, and whaling. Newport and several other towns were the main beneficiaries of trade. Disputes with Britain over trade and British determination to collect taxes resulted in the assignment of a fleet of armed revenue ships to Narragansett Bay. Increased hostility and violence resulted, including the burning (1772) of the GASPEE.

On May 4, 1776, Rhode Island became the first colony to declare independence, and Rhode Islanders fought in every Revolutionary War battle. Gen. Nathanael GREENE of Coventry, R.I., was second in command to George Washington. Newport was occupied by the British from December 1776 to October 1779, during which time 5,000 patriots fled and 500 houses were destroyed. The town did not recover quickly. Activity shifted to Providence, where maritime ventures initiated trade with China in 1787. Rhode Island was the last of the 13 colonies to ratify (1790) the constitution, a delay brought about by its citizens' apprehensions at yielding power to the federal government.

The Era of Manufacturing. The factory system in America was introduced when Samuel SLATER and Moses Brown established (1793) the first cotton textile mill in Pawtucket. The skills developed in colonial forges were used in making machinery. The gold-plating technique of Nehemiah Dodge (1794) and the establishment (1831) of a silver factory by Jabez Gorham were milestones in jewelry-silverware production. As foreign commerce decreased in the 1840s, rubber manufacture began. By 1890 the Providence area had become the largest producer of woolen goods in the United States. Many villages developed around the textile mills, which were located at waterpower sites. The tide of immigrants supplied the necessary laborers for the factories. Whaling, once an important part of Rhode Island's economy, declined after the mid-19th century when whale oil for illumination was supplanted by other fuels.

Beginning in the 1920s the textile industry began to move to the South, lured by cheaper labor and modern equipment. Local prosperity increased, however, with the development of defense-related industries. In World War I the Torpedo Station at Newport was a major employer. From World War II until its closing in 1973, the Naval Air Station at Quonset Point remained the largest civilian employer in the state. Also in 1973 the U.S. Navy moved 5,000 families from the Newport area because of ship reassignments. Electrical machinery, fabricated metals, and plastics manufacturing have strengthened the postwar economy.

Another factor that enabled Rhode Island to rebound strongly from the national recession of the early 1980s is diversification of economic activity. Increasing numbers of Rhode Islanders work in the fields of insurance, printing and publishing, wholesale and retail trade, and government. The expanding tourist industry, with perennial attractions such as Newport, provides jobs in a variety of service positions.

MARION I. WRIGHT

Bibliography: Bates, Frank G., *Rhode Island and the Formation of the Union* (1898; repr. 1967); Coleman, P. J., *Transformation of Rhode Island, 1790–1860* (1963; repr. 1985); Federal Writers' Project, *Rhode Island: A Guide to the Smallest State* (1937); James, Sydney V., *Colonial Rhode Island: A History* (1975); Lovejoy, David S., *Rhode Island Politics and the American Revolution, 1760–1776* (1958; repr. 1969); McLoughlin, William G., *Rhode Island: A Bicentennial History* (1978); Wright, Marion I., and Sullivan, Robert J., *The Rhode Island Atlas* (1983).

Rhode Island, state university and college of

The **State University of Rhode Island** (1892; enrollment: 13,616; library: 750,000 volumes) is a coeducational land-grant and sea-grant institution in Kingston with an extension division in Providence. It grants bachelor's, master's, and doctorate degrees and has a graduate school of library science and, at Narragansett Bay, one of oceanography. **Rhode Island College** (enrollment: 8,574; library: 270,000 volumes), established in 1854 as the Rhode Island State Normal School and given its present name in 1960, is a coeducational liberal arts college in Providence. It grants bachelor's and master's degrees.

Rhode Island School of Design

Established in 1877, Rhode Island School of Design (enrollment: 1,792; library: 69,000 volumes) is a private coeducational college in Providence, R.I. It offers bachelor's and master's degrees in fine and applied arts, photography, architecture, and landscape architecture. The school has a distinguished art museum where research may be conducted. A cooperative program with Brown University enables students to take supplementary courses at either institution.

Rhodes

Rhodes (Greek: Ródhos), the largest island of the Greek Dodecanese group, lies in the Aegean Sea off the southwestern coast of Turkey. The total area is 1,404 km² (542 mi²), and the population is 87,831 (1981). The city of Rhodes is the capital. A mountain range extending the length of the island reaches a height of 1,215 m (3,986 ft) in Mount Atláviros. Agriculture is the economic mainstay; olive oil, red wine, fruit, grain, and cotton are exported. Sponges are taken from offshore waters. Tourism is an important supplement to the economy. The city of Rhodes, the site of the ancient Colossus of Rhodes (one of the SEVEN WONDERS OF THE WORLD), has many medieval buildings erected by the Knights HOSPITALERS. Important ancient remains are at Ialysos, Kamiros, and Lindos.

Occupied in Minoan times, Rhodes was invaded (c.1000 BC) by the Dorians. The cities of Ialysos, Kamiros, and Lindos became major commercial centers. They founded colonies in the western Mediterranean (including Gela on Sicily). Dominated by Persia from the late 6th century BC, the Rhodian cities joined (c.470) Athens in the DELIAN LEAGUE but aligned with Sparta in the Peloponnesian War. During the war the city of Rhodes was founded as the capital of the Rhodian federation. It became a leading commercial and cultural center, retaining its preeminence into the Roman period.

In 1310 the island was granted to the Knights Hospitalers, who rebuilt the city of Rhodes and ruled until expelled by the Ottoman Turks in 1522. From 1912 to 1947, Rhodes was occupied by the Italians, who made capital improvements (paved roads, new buildings) and conducted extensive archaeological excavations.

Rhodes, Cecil John

Cecil Rhodes, British entrepreneur and statesman, amassed a fortune in diamonds and gold in South Africa during the late 19th century. He died in 1902 and left funds for the scholarship program in his name at Oxford University.

A British imperialist and statesman, Cecil John Rhodes, b. July 5, 1853, d. Mar. 26, 1902, helped establish British rule in southern Africa. Rhodes went to southern Africa in 1870 to join his brother Herbert on a cotton farm. Subsequently he went to the newly discovered diamond fields at Kimberley, where between 1871 and 1888 he became a rich man; he formed the De Beers Mining Company and eventually controlled 90 percent of the world's diamond production. Rhodes also acquired a substantial stake in the gold fields of the Transvaal and became prominent in politics.

In 1890 he took office as prime minister of Cape Colony, resolving to work for an understanding between British and Afrikaners and for a policy guaranteeing them both equality under the British flag. Rhodes meanwhile used his influence and wealth to create a new British foothold north of the Transvaal, to reduce Afrikaner political influence in southern Africa, and to promote the dream of a British empire from the "Cape to Cairo." In 1889 he received from the British government a charter setting up the British South Africa Company, a commercial concern with vast administrative powers. The company occupied Mashonaland in 1890, and three years later its forces defeated the powerful kingdom of the NDEBELE. By the end of the century Rhodes's company controlled a huge area, including Southern Rhodesia (now Zimbabwe) and Northern Rhodesia (now Zambia) which were named for him.

In 1896, Rhodes's premiership was brought to an end by the Jameson Raid (see JAMESON, SIR LEANDER STARR), which unsuccessfully sought to topple the Afrikaner government of Paul KRUGER in the Transvaal. Rhodes, however, continued to exercise vast power in the affairs of the two Rhodesias. He bequeathed part of his fortune to found the Rhodes scholarships at Oxford.   L. H. GANN

Bibliography: Flint, John, *Cecil Rhodes* (1974); Galbraith, John S., *Crown and Charter* (1974); Lockhart, John Gilbert, and Woodhouse, C. M., *Cecil Rhodes* (1963); Marlowe, John, *Cecil Rhodes* (1972); Michell, Lewis, *The Life and Times of the Right Honourable Cecil John Rhodes, 1853-1902*, ed. by Mira Wilkins, 2 vols. (1910; repr. 1977); Millin, Sarah G., *Rhodes*, rev. ed. (1952; repr. 1969).

Rhodes scholarships

Rhodes scholarships are awards established in the will (1899) of Cecil Rhodes to bring to Oxford University young men from the British Commonwealth and the United States. They were first awarded in 1903. Rhodes hoped to establish close ties among an Anglo-Saxon elite to "secure the peace of the world." The scholarships, which are for graduate work and cover tuition and living expenses for 2 years, may be extended for a third. They are now also open to women and are awarded by competition in the United States, where 32 scholarships are awarded, and in former British colonies in Asia, Africa, the Caribbean, Canada, Australia, and New Zealand. West German students also receive Rhodes scholarships. About 71 scholarships are awarded annually.

Bibliography: Aydelotte, Frank, *The American Rhodes Scholarships: A Review of the First Forty Years* (1946).

Rhodesia: see ZIMBABWE.

Rhodesian man: see BROKEN HILL MAN.

Rhodesian ridgeback

The Rhodesian ridgeback is a hound with a ridge of reverse-pointing hair along the midline of its back. According to reports as early as 1505, the first European settlers in South Africa had found dogs with ridges of hair along their backs among the Hottentots, or Khoikhoin. Over the years these native dogs interbred with European-type dogs brought to Africa by the settlers. The attributes of the modern breed were developed by the Boers of South Africa, who sought a hunter, watch dog, and companion that would be tolerant of the African climate and hunting conditions. Toward the end of the 19th century, ridgebacks were brought into Rhodesia, where they achieved considerable popularity and presumably their name. A breed standard was established in Bulawayo in 1922. Rhodesian ridgebacks measure usually between 63.5 and 68.5 cm (25 and 27 in) high at the shoulders and from 29.5 to almost 40 kg (65 to almost 90 lb) in weight. Their short, dense, smooth, glossy coats vary in color from wheaten yellow to deep yellowish red.

The Rhodesian ridgeback is a large hound developed in South Africa to hunt large game and to protect farms from predators. A cross of European and African breeds, the distinctive ridge of hair running along its back is inherited from a native African hunting dog.

rhodium

Rhodium is a chemical element, hard, white metallic of the platinum group. Its symbol is Rh, its atomic number 45, and its atomic weight 102.906. Rhodium was discovered in 1803 by William H. Wollaston. It is used primarily as an alloying agent for platinum and iridium; these alloys have greater mechanical strength and ability to withstand higher temperatures than do the pure metals.

rhodochrosite   [roh-duh-kroh'-syt]

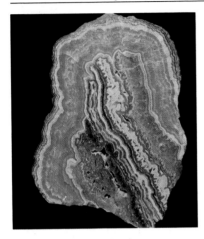

Rhodochrosite, a comparatively rare ore of manganese, is most often used for ornamental and decorative purposes. It is usually found as translucent, glassy, compact to granular cleavable masses in red, brown, or yellow gray shades. It also is often found with banded patterns.

The manganese carbonate mineral rhodochrosite ($MnCO_3$) is a minor ore of manganese used mainly as a decorative stone and gemstone. Typically displaying shiny rose-red, intricately banded surfaces, it forms granular to compact cleavable masses, crusts, or columns. Hardness is 3½ to 4, streak is white, and specific gravity is 3.7. Rhodochrosite occurs in moderate- to low-temperature hydrothermal ore veins, particularly of silver, lead, zinc, and copper, as well as in high-temperature metamorphic deposits.

Bibliography: Varentsov, I. M., *Sedimentary Manganese Ores* (1964).

rhododendron   [roh-duh-den'-druhn]

Rhododendron is the generic and common name of approximately 600 species of flowering shrubs or trees, usually ever-

The royal rhododendron, R. schlippenbachii, has pink, freckled flowers that bloom in spring. Its leaves turn a variety of colors in fall. Some species of rhododendron grow up to 12 m (40 ft) tall.

green, in the heath family, Ericaceae. Approximately 10,000 named varieties are listed in the International Register and about 2,000 of these are available. Azaleas are also included in the genus *Rhododendron,* but they are generally excluded from the "true rhododendrons." The name *rhododendron* comes from the Greek and means "red tree." The plant's large, beautiful blooms appear in the spring in a variety of colors including red, lilac purple, white, light rose, apple-blossom pink, rosy lilac, and deep rose. The flowers are usually produced in trusses. Rhododendrons range from 12-m (40-ft) flowering trees to matlike ground cover.

rhodolite: see GARNET.

rhodonite   [roh'-duh-nyt]

The manganese, iron, and calcium SILICATE MINERAL rhodonite [$(Mn,Fe,Ca)SiO_3$] is valued not only as a rose-red ornamental stone but also as a major ore of manganese in India. Usually associated with RHODOCHROSITE and other manganese minerals, it forms large, rounded, tabular crystals (triclinic system) or cleavable, compact masses. Hardness is 5½ to 6½, luster is vitreous, streak is white, and specific gravity is 3.4 to 3.7.

rhombohedral system: see HEXAGONAL SYSTEM.

Rhône River   [rohn]

The Rhône River, one of Europe's longest rivers, rises in Switzerland, flows southward through eastern France, and empties into the Mediterranean Sea after a course of about 800 km (500 mi). Its source is the Rhône glacier in the Swiss Alps at an altitude of about 1,830 m (6,000 ft). For about 160 km (100 mi) it flows through deep Alpine valleys before entering Lake Geneva. The city of Geneva lies at the river's outflow from the lake. Flowing into France, the Rhône is joined at Lyon by the SAÔNE, its principal tributary. Its course then turns southward through a turbulent trough between the Alps and the Massif Central. It empties into the Mediterranean by a large delta. In addition to the Saône, important tributaries include the Arve, Ardèche, Isère, and Durance. The Rhône is fed chiefly by the melting snows of the Alps. Its most rapid flow occurs in spring and early summer. In its lower course it enters the Mediterranean region of winter rains and consequently reaches a secondary high level in November and December.

The Rhône is turbulent and has been little used for navigation. In recent years, however, its course from Lyon to the sea has been improved by the construction of dams to regulate flow and generate hydroelectric power. River craft now use the river upstream to Lyon, although the traffic remains small. Agricultural improvements in the Rhône Valley have resulted in prosperous farms, orchards, and vineyards.

Although little used for transport, the Rhône has guided transportation. It is paralleled by heavily used roads and railroads from Lyon to the delta. The chief cities on its banks are Lyon, Vienne, Valence, Avignon (where the immense 14th-century papal palace overlooks the river), and Arles. The delta has no ports; a canal links the lower river with Marseille 40 km (25 mi) to the east.   NORMAN J. G. POUNDS

rhubarb

Rhubarb is a perennial herb, *Rheum rhabarbarum,* commonly but incorrectly known as *R. rhaponticum,* and is one of the few vegetables cultivated for the leaf stalks, or petioles. The broad, leafy portions and the roots contain poisonous substances, including oxalic acid, and should not be eaten. Rhubarb is a member of the buckwheat family, Polygonaceae, and is believed to be native to the region of Turkey. It was introduced into the United States in the late 1700s. A number of other closely related plants, including *R. officinale,* are also called rhubarbs and are raised as garden foliage plants or for their roots, which are the source of pharmaceutical compounds sometimes employed as laxatives. Several of the docks, or sorrels, in the genus *Rumex* of the same family but

The rhubarb plant, R. rhabarbarum, produces reddish stalks used in pies and sauces. The roots and large leaves are poisonous. Rhubarb, which probably originated in Asia, grows best in cool climates.

with edible leaves are also often called rhubarbs, including spinach rhubarb, *Rumex abyssinicus,* and monk's rhubarb, both *R. alpinus* and *R. patientia.*

Rhubarb is best adapted to cool climates and is usually grown from crown and roots rather than from seed. The plants should be located where small children do not have access to the poisonous parts.

rhyme

The practice in poetry of using words that end with similar sounds is called rhyme. In English verse, rhyme usually occurs at the end of a line (end rhyme), but it may also be used within lines. A so-called perfect rhyme, also called a masculine rhyme, is produced when differing consonants are followed by identical, stressed (accented) vowel sounds (boat/float). This type of rhyme is more common in English VERSIFICATION than two-syllable, or feminine, rhymes composed of an accented and an unaccented syllable (clever/never). The triple rhyme, with an accented syllable followed by two unaccented syllables (hauntingly/flauntingly), is even less frequent.

Rhyme did not exist in English poetry until the 14th century, although it did appear in the sacred Latin poetry of the early Christian church and in songs of the 4th century AD. The suitability of rhyme for serious subjects was questioned during the Renaissance by advocates of classical syllabic verse and again during the 20th century with the emergence of free verse. Rhyme remains, however, an essential musical device in light verse such as the LIMERICK and in songs; it is also a mnemonic technique used in children's poetry.

Bibliography: Lang, Henry, *The Physical Basis of Rime: An Essay on the Aesthetics of Sound* (1931; repr. 1969).

rhyolite

Rhyolite is a light-colored, fine-grained volcanic rock (see IGNEOUS ROCK) with a very high (more than 70%) silica content. It often contains phenocrysts of quartz and feldspar in a glassy matrix. Iron and magnesium minerals are rare or absent. Similar to the coarser grained granites in mineralogy and chemistry, rhyolite tends to be very viscous because of its high silica content, and upon eruption it generally forms steep-sided domes and plugs. Gas-rich rhyolite, however, erupts violently to form welded tuffs, or ignimbrites, and may spread out over great distances.   JAMES A. WHITNEY

Rhys, Jean   [rees]

A highly acclaimed British novelist of the 1920s and '30s who had fallen into obscurity, Jean Rhys, b. Aug. 24, 1894, d. May 14, 1979, was recognized afresh in the 1970s as much for her enduring modernity as for the feminist implications of her work. Her unrelentingly pessimistic early novels all deal with vulnerable, middle-class women cast adrift in large cities both by circumstances and by the men they have failed to keep. Rhys describes their precarious psychological state with rigorous objectivity and an admirably spare style in *Quartet* (1928), *After Leaving Mr. MacKenzie* (1931), *Voyage in the Dark* (1934), and *Good Morning, Midnight* (1939).

After World War II, Rhys published the *Wide Sargasso Sea* (1966), about the first, mad wife of Mr. Rochester, hero of Charlotte Bronte's *Jane Eyre,* and two collections of short stories, *Tigers Are Better Looking* (1968) and *Sleep It Off, Lady* (1976).

rhythm

Rhythm is the temporal element of music, the pattern of musical notes with regard to their duration and accentuation. (In a broader sense, rhythm is not restricted to music: speech, certain machines, and many natural processes may be described as rhythmic.) In most Western music rhythm occurs within a framework of regular pulsation, or METER; all time-values are multiples or fractions of a metrical unit. (In *isometric* music, prevalent from the 17th to the 19th century and associated with the classical dance, the units are grouped in measures of equal length, with the first beat of each measure accented; in *multimetric* music, prevalent during the Middle Ages and the Renaissance and revived during the 20th century, the measures are unequal and the accents, consequently, irregular.) Meter is not, however, a prerequisite of rhythm: much non-Western music and some early European folk music is essentially *ametric.*

The masterpieces of the Western tradition have immensely complex rhythmic structures, and it is largely the capacity for sensitive realization of these structures that distinguishes the great from the merely competent performer. Despite this, and despite the obvious ubiquity of rhythm in music, the subject has been widely neglected by educators and theorists, with the notable exception of Émile JAQUES-DALCROZE.

LAWRENCE FUCHSBERG

Bibliography: Cooper, Grosvenor, and Meyer, Leonard B., *The Rhythmic Structure of Music* (1960); Read, Gardner, *Modern Rhythmic Notation* (1978); Sachs, Curt, *Rhythm and Tempo* (1953); Yeston, Maury, *The Stratification of Musical Rhythm* (1976).

rhythm and blues

The term *rhythm and blues* (R & B) began as a music industry designation for records by black musicians for black audiences. Beginning as a replacement for the industry term *race*

B. B. King, the "king of the Blues," is one of the most influential contemporary blues artists. During the 1960s, as rock musicians such as Mike Bloomfield developed a style derivative of King's, King became a major force in the popularization of rhythm and blues.

records, it eventually came to denote the styles of music created by black, urban musicians since the 1940s.

In the late 1940s, when many jazz musicians began to play the rhythmically complex style known as BEBOP, black dancers turned to big bands playing a blues-derived, saxophone-dominated music with a heavy beat. It was louder, larger-scaled, and less subtle than the older blues and jazz styles, and it was soon supplemented by other styles: small sax-and-piano "jump bands" using boogie-woogie rhythms; country-blues bands featuring electric guitars and harmonicas; and black teenage vocal groups.

ROCK MUSIC, in its beginnings a white-produced music, borrowed the form, the beat, and the sound of rhythm and blues. While many black R & B performers became rock musicians, many others expanded their R & B styles. In the mid-1950s, Ray CHARLES and James BROWN combined the emotional, vocally complex style derived from GOSPEL MUSIC with R & B, creating what came to be known as SOUL MUSIC. R & B, recorded with strings and adolescent lyrics by such groups as the Supremes, became "uptown" or MOTOWN R & B. Aretha FRANKLIN sang in an R & B style that was closer to blues roots. In the 1970s, musical modes like SALSA were added, producing new complexities of rhythm and instrumentation. Much of the DISCO music of the 1970s was formularized R & B. Modified by rock sound and production values, the style continued into the 1980s, performed by Smokey Robinson, L. L. Kool J., Dionne Warwick, and many others.   JONATHAN KAMIN

Bibliography: Broven, J., *Rhythm and Blues in New Orleans* (1978); Fox, T., *Showtime at the Apollo* (1983); McCutcheon, L. E., *Rhythm and Blues* (1971); Shaw, A., *Honkers and Shouters: The Rhythm and Blues Years* (1978).

Riabouchinska, Tatiana   [ree-ah-boo-chin'-skah]

Tatiana Riabouchinska, b. Moscow, May 23 (N.S.), 1917, was known as one of the "baby ballerinas" of the 1930s, along with Irina Baronova and Tamara Toumanova. Trained in Paris by the émigré ballerina Mathilde Kshessinska, Riabouchinska made her debut at the age of 15 in the *Chauve-Souris* revue. In 1932 she was chosen by choreographer George Balanchine for Col. W. de Basil's Ballet Russe de Monte Carlo. She remained with that company for a decade, creating roles in numerous ballets by Balanchine, Leonid Massine, and David Lichine, whom she married in 1943. She appeared subsequently as guest artist in other internationally recognized companies and later taught in California.   TOBI TOBIAS

Ribaut, Jean   [ree-boh']

Jean Ribaut, b. c.1520, d. Oct. 12, 1565, French navigator and colonizer, founded a Huguenot colony in North America in 1562. Sent by Admiral Gaspard de COLIGNY, he explored the northern Florida coast and then established a settlement called Charlesfort at the present Port Royal, S.C. Ribaut returned to France in July 1562. He was unable to bring back assistance because of the religious war in France, and the colonists abandoned Charlesfort. In 1565, Ribaut sailed with reinforcements for the Huguenot colony of Fort Caroline that had been established a year earlier on Florida's Saint John's River by René Goulaine de LAUDONNIÈRE. After arriving there he sailed south to attack Pedro MENÉNDEZ DE AVILÉS, sent by the Spanish to drive the French from Florida. But Menéndez's forces, moving by land, destroyed Fort Caroline. They then killed Ribaut and his men, who had been shipwrecked.

Bibliography: Connor, Jeanette T., *Jean Ribault* (1927); Parkman, Francis, *Pioneers of France in the New World* (1865; repr. 1965).

Ribbentrop, Joachim von   [rib'-en-trohp, yoh'-ah-keem fuhn]

Joachim von Ribbentrop, b. Apr. 30, 1893, d. Oct. 16, 1946, was German foreign minister (1938–45) under the National Socialist (Nazi) regime. He joined the Nazi party in 1932 and became Adolf Hitler's leading foreign policy advisor in 1933, serving as ambassador (1936–38) to Great Britain before becoming foreign minister. An ardently loyal follower of Hitler,

he implemented major Nazi foreign policy initiatives, including the Anglo-German naval agreement (1935) and the NAZI-SOVIET PACT (1939). His influence declined during World War II. Found guilty of war crimes at the NUREMBERG TRIALS after the war, he was hanged.   K. M. SMOGORZEWSKI

ribbon worm

Ribbon worms, or proboscis worms, are slender, soft-bodied, flat, and unsegmented animals that constitute the phylum Rhynchocoela. The digestive tract is one-way, with a mouth and anus. The ribbon worms are characterized by a long, retractable, slime-covered proboscis (tube), often with a barb, which wraps itself around prey and draws them into the mouth. The body may be only 10 cm (2.5 in) long; however, it may stretch to 30 m (100 ft) in some species. Most ribbon worms can be found along shallow sea coasts.

LORUS J. AND MARGERY MILNE

ribbonfish

Ribbonfishes are long, ribbonlike deep-sea fishes with short, tapering tails and high foreheads or crests on top of the head. They live usually 100–300 m (about 300–1,000 ft) deep or more and are only occasionally seen. Some ribbonfishes reach 150–200 cm (about 60–80 in) in length. They have small mouths and eat crustaceans. About 10 species occur worldwide, and 3 families have been recognized in the suborder Trachipteroidei. The dealfish, in the family Trachipteridae, are scaled but lack an anal fin. Giant OARFISH, in the family Regalecidae, are often grouped with the dealfish and have elongated pelvic fins. Scaleless ribbonlike fish, or chest fish, with an anal fin are grouped in the family Lophotidae.

CAMM SWIFT

Ribeiro, Aquilino   [ree-by'-roo]

Aquilino Ribeiro, one of Portugal's finest modern novelists, b. Sept. 13, 1885, d. May 27, 1963, was the creator of regional fiction imbued with a pagan love of life and nature. In *Estrada de Santiago* (1922) and *When the Wolves Howl* (1954; Eng. trans., 1963) he was also a forceful social critic and a fine stylist. A man of wide intellectual interests, he also wrote biographies and essays on literary history and folklore.

Ribeiro, Bernardim

Bernardim Ribeiro, c.1482–c.1552, a Portuguese poet and novelist, is important chiefly for his sentimental, feminist novel *Menina e Moça* (Young Girl and Maiden, 1554), based on interrelated episodes narrated by a young woman. As an analysis of amorous passion from a woman's point of view, it was unique in its time, and it may be considered a forerunner of the modern psychological novel.   NORWOOD ANDREWS, JR.

Ribera, Jusepe de   [ree-bay'-rah]

The Spanish painter and etcher Jusepe (or José) de Ribera, baptized Feb. 17, 1591, d. Sept. 2, 1652, combined the mysticism and religious intensity of his native country with the naturalism of Caravaggio. During his lifetime his popularity was immense, and his influence persisted long after his death.

In 1616, after working in various parts of Spain and Italy, Ribera settled in Naples, where Caravaggio's influence was still strong and helped shape Ribera's early style. This influence is distinguished by sharp lighting and pronounced shadows constructed with dense pigment, mainly in strong earth colors. His tenebrism was in the tradition of Caravaggio, as were his single-figure compositions, usually in half or three-quarter length, against a dark background. Ribera, however, retained a distinctive Spanish sensuality in all his work. An example is *The Sense of Touch* (c.1615; Norton Simon Museum of Art, Pasadena, Calif.).

The Martyrdom of Saint Bartholomew (1639; Prado, Madrid) shows the more even illumination, lighter colors, and more vigorous, looser brushstrokes characteristic of his later style, which placed less emphasis on mass and volume. The works of his later years—such as the sensitive and graceful *Holy*

Jusepe de Ribera's The Clubfooted Boy (1652) demonstrates the affinity of the Spanish baroque for the striking naturalism of Caravaggio. Like Diego Velázquez, Ribera combined this characteristic with a peculiarly Spanish mysticism, giving the deformed peasant boy an air of tragicomic dignity and pathos. (Louvre, Paris.)

David Ricardo was a leading 19th-century British economist who, like Adam Smith before him, advocated a free-market system. Influenced by Thomas Malthus, Ricardo also believed that a population will increase faster than its means of support unless its growth rate is restrained in some fashion.

Family with Saint Catherine (1648; Metropolitan Museum of Art, New York City)—tend to be calmer and more radiant than his earlier paintings.

Ribera's paintings were favored by the viceroys who governed Naples for the Spanish crown, as well as by other prominent Spaniards living there. Taken to Spain, these pictures made Ribera an important influence in Spanish art, although he spent most of his life in Italy. His accomplished etchings, mostly done in the 1620s and of which only 16 can be attributed to him with certainty, also played a part in spreading his fame.

In Italy, Ribera acquired the nickname "Lo Spagnoletto" ("the little Spaniard"); he stressed his nationality by signing his paintings and etchings "Jusepe de Ribera español."

MADLYN MILLNER KAHR

Bibliography: Brown, Jonathan, *Jusepe de Ribera, Prints and Drawings* (1973); Felton, Craig, and Jordan, W. B., *Jusepe de Ribera* (1982); Trapier, Elizabeth du Gué, *Ribera* (1952).

ribosome   [ry'-buh-sohm]

Ribosomes, which are beadlike cellular organelles, are the site of protein synthesis in all cells. Ribosomes of procaryotic organisms are dispersed throughout the cytoplasm. They can be dissociated into a large and a small subunit, each of which can be further broken down into proteins and ribonucleic acid (RNA) molecules. Eucaryotic ribosomes are found in the cytoplasm—either free or bound to the endoplasmic reticulum—the nucleus, mitochondria, and chloroplasts. Although larger in size, they resemble procaryotic ribosomes in structural organization and properties.

During protein synthesis, many ribosomes simultaneously attach to a single messenger RNA molecule (mRNA) and translate the information of the genetic code into amino acids, which are used to build specific proteins.

See also: CELL; GENETIC CODE; PROTEIN SYNTHESIS.

Ricardo, David   [ri-kahr'-doh]

David Ricardo, b. Apr. 19, 1772, d. Sept. 11, 1823, was a leader of the British classical school of economists. He systematized the economic theory of his day and strongly influenced its subsequent development. Like Adam Smith before him, Ri-

cardo believed in limiting state intervention in economic life. His early publication *An Essay on the Influence of a Low Price of Corn on the Profits of Stock* (1815) argued against high tariffs on grain imports, and his theory of comparative advantage showed how the unimpeded flow of commodities among nations could be of mutual benefit to all parties (see FREE TRADE).

The Ricardian world, however, was not particularly harmonious, nor was its outlook very optimistic. Ricardo shared the population doctrine of his friend Thomas Robert MALTHUS and believed that population pressure would tend to keep wages near the subsistence level. Further, he saw the future progress of society as marked by conflicts among economic classes. His theory of rent held that, as population growth caused the cultivation of new acreage, landowners' incomes would rise. This rise would intensify the squeeze on the incomes of capitalists (profits) and laborers (wages) and would ultimately bring further progress to a halt. In trying to prove this theory in his *Principles of Political Economy and Taxation* (1817), he argued that commodities, with some exceptions, exchange in proportion to the labor embodied in their production. This "labor theory of value," though rejected by later Western economists, had great impact on the thinking of Karl MARX and his followers.

Noted for his theoretical rigor, Ricardo actually was a practicing economist only briefly. He came to it late from a business career and died at the age of 51, a scant 13 years after his first publication. He was very successful on the stock exchange and, in the last years of his life, served in Parliament.

RICHARD T. GILL

Bibliography: Blaug, Mark, *Ricardian Economics: An Historical Study* (1958; repr. 1973); Gootzeit, Michael J., *David Ricardo* (1975); Heilbroner, Robert L., *The Worldly Philosophers*, 5th ed. (1980); Hollander, Samuel, *The Economics of David Ricardo* (1979); Ricardo, David, *Works and Correspondence*, 10 vols., ed. by P. Straffa and M. H. Dobb (1951–55).

Ricci   (family)   [ree'-chee]

The Italian baroque painters Sebastiano Ricci, b. 1659, d. May 16, 1734, and his nephew Marco Ricci, b. 1676, d. c.1729, reinterpreted 16th-century Venetian art in a style that foreshadows the rococo. **Sebastiano Ricci**'s work, which is indebted to Paolo Veronese, is characterized by fluid brushstrokes, bold foreshortenings, and theatrical effects. His masterpiece is the *Madonna and Child with Saints* (1708; Church of San Giorgio Maggiore, Venice). Sebastiano's later work in London (1711–12) represents the finest decorative work in England of that time. **Marco Ricci**, the initiator of the 18th-century Venetian school of landscape, began by painting backgrounds for his uncle. In England his scenic paintings based on the late Titian were greatly admired.

ROSA MARIA LETTS

Bibliography: Daniels, Jeffery, *Sebastiano Ricci* (1976); Milkovich, Michael, *Sebastiano and Marco Ricci in America* (1965).

Ricci, Matteo

An Italian Jesuit missionary and scientist, Matteo Ricci, b. Oct. 6, 1552, d. May 11, 1610, was a founder of the Christian church in China and an originator of cultural and scientific interchange between Europe and China. Ricci joined the Jesuits in 1571 and received an education in mathematics and geography. In 1577 he was sent to India, where he was ordained. In 1582, Ricci joined another Jesuit, Michele Ruggieri, in Macao, and from there they entered China. Together they made a radical break with traditional missionary methods. In order to reach the cultured society of China, the missionaries confronted this educated elite on its own level by demonstrating comparable scholarship, culture, and talent. Their goal was to convert China as an entire culture.

Ricci's major contributions were not only his method of evangelization but also his numerous works, written in Chinese, on scientific, apologetic, catechetical, literary, and mathematical topics. From 1601 until his death, Ricci was an established and respected figure in Peking. His method of adapting Chinese ceremonies to the performance of Christian rites caused a prolonged controversy in the Roman Catholic church and was finally condemned by the pope in 1704 and 1715. Modern missionary methods have repealed this judgment and vindicated Ricci's foresight.

THOMAS E. MORRISSEY

Bibliography: Bernard, Henri, *Matteo Ricci's Scientific Contribution to China* (1935; Eng. trans., 1973); Spence, Jonathan D., *The Memory Palace of Matteo Ricci* (1984).

rice

Since ancient times, rice has been the most commonly used food grain for a majority of the people of the world. A member of the grass family, Gramineae, rice, *Oryza sativa*, can be grown successfully under climatic conditions ranging from tropical to temperate. Properly cultivated, rice produces higher yields than any other grain with the exception of corn; and although the total area planted in rice is far smaller than that devoted to wheat—the world total is about one-third less—the rice crop feeds a far greater proportion of the world's population.

Records of rice cultivation indicate that it was grown in China and India centuries before the Christian era. It became an important crop in Africa, around the Mediterranean, and in the Middle East and was widely grown during the period of the Greek and Roman empires. Later it became a prominent food crop in Italy, Spain, and Portugal. Rice was introduced in the United States in 1685 and was grown successfully in South Carolina and in other areas in the South. Later, the main production areas shifted toward the Southwest, and commercial production at the turn of the century was located in California, Arkansas, Louisiana, Texas, and Mississippi.

Rice Cultivation. Rice plants require a steady supply of water, and therefore, fields are often flooded by irrigation or planted during periods of excessive rainfall. Rice is planted with drills on dry land; on wet land, the seed is broadcast by hand and sometimes by airplane. Much rice is grown in nurseries, and the young plants are transplanted by hand into swampy soil. Rice fields are kept flooded until just before harvest. Water control retards weed growth, but chemical controls are also often necessary. Weeding is sometimes done by hand, but both ground and airplane spraying of pesticides and herbicides are practiced.

Rice plants start from a single shoot and then develop many tillers and pointed, flat leaves; the plants grow from 2 to 6 feet tall. The plant is commonly self-pollinating. The kernel, with its rough outer hull, consists of bran or aleurone layers, germ, and endosperm. More than 7,000 botanically different varieties have been identified, and most of these have been exchanged among production areas throughout the world for testing purposes. Yield has steadily increased in response to better soil preparation, water control, and the development of improved and disease-resistant varieties. Crop rotation systems have effectively produced better crops. The rice plant responds well to fertilizers, especially nitrogen.

Rice varieties are classified as short, medium, or long kerneled. Long-grain rice is often preferred over short or medium grains because it has less tendency to stick together when cooked. Rice varieties are also classified according to how early they mature, an important property because the harvest must be handled during dry weather. When rice is harvested the kernels possess about 20% moisture, and the crop cannot be processed or stored safely until the moisture content is reduced to approximately 12%. In large operations rice is taken directly from the combine to dryers, where moisture is reduced gradually to avoid cracking, which would make processing more difficult. When dry, the rice can be taken to the mill or stored in warehouses.

Harvesting. Throughout much of the world rice is harvested by hand, using knives or sickles. The stalks are cut, tied in bundles, and left in the sun to dry. All sorts of means are used to thresh the grain, ranging from using the weight of animals or tractors to threshing with various types of machines. On large farms, rice is harvested by self-propelled combines. Whole kernels of rice are desirable; therefore, threshing with a minimum of breakage is necessary, and usually breakage is related to moisture content. Harvesting and threshing usually involve breakage losses of approximately 5%. Small rice producers sell their paddy (the unhulled, or brown, rice) before storage becomes necessary. Large producers must provide adequate storage facilities that may be constructed of wood, metal, or concrete.

Where Rice is Grown. Mainland China, India, Indonesia, Bangladesh, Thailand, Vietnam, and Japan are the leading rice-growing countries. World rice production totaled almost 500 million metric tons (551 U.S. tons) annually in the late 1980s. In the United States, the leading states in rice production are Arkansas, Texas, California, Louisiana, Mississippi, and Missouri. A separate genus, WILD RICE (*Zizania aquatica*), is native to North America and is not cultivated.

In contrast to wheat and corn, only a small percentage of the total rice crop enters international trade. Not quite 3% of the total worldwide production becomes an export commod-

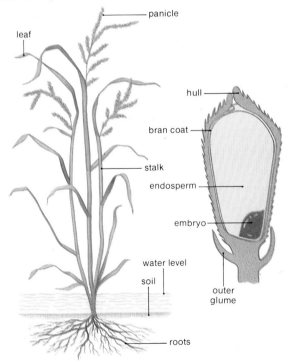

Rice, O. sativa, is one of the world's most important cultivated grains. The kernel (right) consists of a hull and a bran coat—both of which are removed in polishing "white" rice—and the endosperm and embryo, which constitute the edible portion of the rice grain.

Labels on figure: panicle, leaf, stalk, water level, soil, roots, hull, bran coat, endosperm, embryo, outer glume

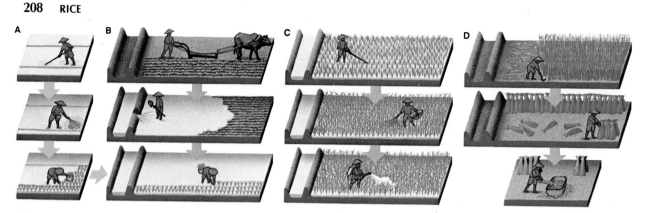

The process of rice cultivation has changed little since its earliest production, centuries ago. Rice seedlings are grown in nurseries (A) and transplanted to irrigated paddies (B) after 25-50 days. The plants must be carefully weeded despite their covering of 5-10 cm (2-4 in) of water (C). High-yield strains require the use of fertilizers and insecticidal sprays. Rice is commonly harvested using simple instruments, tied in bundles to dry, and threshed when moisture has been reduced to approximately 20% (D).

ity, although the United States exports approximately 40% of its total production. Limited international trade in rice has prevented the establishment of large, active trading centers like those for marketing other cereal grains, and formulation of official grain standards for rice has been slow to develop.

Rice Breeding. During the past quarter-century, rice breeding programs have been initiated in several countries. Resistance to diseases and insects was the major objective of the earlier research, but hybrid programs have dominated recently. High-yielding dwarf plants that can withstand water depths and that respond to fertilizers have been developed. Improved grain quality and higher protein levels have been added objectives of new programs designed to improve nutrition. New varieties can, under good cultural conditions such as soil fertility and water control, increase yields as much as 100% compared with conventional varieties.

The proximate analysis of rough rice is: protein, 7-11%; starch, 62-66%; lipids, 1-2½%; and minerals, 4½-6%. The protein content of rice is lower than that of wheat and other major cereal grains, although the new strains are somewhat higher in protein content. The whole (unhulled) rice kernel contains vitamins, thiamine, niacin, and riboflavin.

Uses. Rice is usually eaten as milled whole grain. Parboiling rice before it is milled—a centuries-old technique—is now a potential industrial procedure. Parboiled rice can be stored for long periods because cooking hardens the kernel, sterilizes, and controls moisture content. Quick-cooking rice is made by procedures that produce porosity of the kernel, permitting rapid water penetration and thus shortening cooking

time. Cooked rice can be flaked or puffed for breakfast food and is used in prepared baby foods. Rice flour, prepared from broken grain, is used in the baking and confectionery industries. Rice flour does not contain gluten and therefore cannot be used for baking bread. Flour from waxy-type rice has wider use as a thickening agent because of its more glutinous starch.

Rice bran, rich in lipids that can be refined into a high-grade edible oil, has long been a standard ingredient of livestock feed. Laundry starch and a powder used for cosmetics are made from rice starch. Rice hulls are used as polishing material, as cattle feed, and as fertilizer, and can also be converted to furfural, an industrial solvent. Fermented beverages are also produced from rice (see SAKE).

Because the milling process removes vitamins, an enriched rice, whose kernels are coated with vitamins and mineral supplements, is now available. As much as 20% of paddy rice is hull, 13% bran, and 3% polishings, all products that are removed when rice is milled. Unmilled, or brown, rice retains the outer bran layer and much of the nutrient value of whole rice. It is rarely eaten, however, in part because of problems relating to its storage.

J. A. SHELLENBERGER

Bibliography: Grist, Donald H., *Rice*, 5th ed. (1975); Houston, D. F., ed., *Rice: Chemistry and Technology* (1972).

Rice, Elmer

Elmer Rice, b. Leopold Reizenstein, New York City, Sept. 28, 1892, d. May 8, 1967, was a lawyer turned dramatist who be-

Rice paddies cover these terraced hillsides in Sri Lanka, producing large quantities of the grain, the staple of the national diet. Like many Asian nations, Sri Lanka retains this principal crop for domestic consumption.

gan his writing career with the courtroom drama *On Trial* (1914). Rice is best remembered for *The Adding Machine* (1923), an experimental play about mechanization, and *Street Scene* (1929), which depicts New York tenement life. His later dramas focus on the depression years and fascism. *The Living Theatre* (1959) is a collection of his essays.

Bibliography: Durham, Frank, *Elmer Rice* (1970); Hogan, Robert Goode, *The Independence of Elmer Rice* (1965).

Rice, Grantland

Henry Grantland Rice, b. Murfreesboro, Tenn., Nov. 1, 1880, d. July 13, 1954, was considered the dean of sportswriters in the United States. Rice entertained fans for nearly 50 years with his colorful turn of phrase ("Four Horsemen," "Galloping Ghost," "Manassa Mauler"), accurate judgment, and high moral standards ("It's not whether you won or lost but how you played the game"). His widely syndicated column was called "The Sportlight." His autobiography, *The Tumult and the Shouting: My Life in Sport* (1954), appeared shortly after his death.

Rice University

Established in 1891 and adopting the full name of its founder, William Marsh Rice, in 1960, Rice University (enrollment: 3,800; library: 1,200,000 volumes) is a private coeducational institution in Houston, Tex. It offers a full range of undergraduate and graduate degree programs.

ricebird

Ricebird is a name given to several species of Southeast Asian waxbills, family Estrilidae, considered destructive pests of cultivated rice crops. The name applies especially to the Java sparrow, *Padda oryzivora*, of Malaysia and to various species of mannikins, genus *Lonchura*. In the New World the bobolink, *Dolichonyx oryzivorus*, is also sometimes called a ricebird for similar reasons.

Rich, Adrienne

Adrienne Rich, a feminist poet and author, received the 1974 National Book Award for her collection of poems Diving into the Wreck (1973). Her poetry, precise and elegant, has evolved into a continuing chronicle of her spiritual and political growth, as demonstrated in The Fact of a Doorframe: Poems 1950–1984 (1984).

Photo Jill Krementz © 1973

The work of the American poet and feminist Adrienne Cecile Rich, b. Baltimore, Md., May 6, 1929, has evolved from the formal elegance of *A Change of World* (1951) to engagement of the issues of oppression and feminism in *Diving into the Wreck* (1973), a 1974 National Book Award winner, and *A Wild Patience Has Taken Me This Far: Poems 1978–81* (1981). She began to describe women's sensibilities in *The Diamond Cutter and Other Poems* (1955) and *Snapshots of a Daughter-in-law: Poems, 1954–62* (1963). Also an essayist and polemicist, Rich describes motherhood with candor in the prose study *Of Woman Born: Motherhood as Experience and Institution* (1976).

Richard, Gabriel [ree-shahr']

Gabriel Richard, b. Oct. 15, 1767, d. Sept. 13, 1832, a French Roman Catholic priest, made many contributions to early Michigan society. Ordained in 1791, he left France because of revolutionary anticlericalism. In the United States, he was initially assigned to Illinois Territory and, in 1798, was transferred to Detroit, where he established a seminary and other schools. He published the *Michigan Essay or Impartial Observer*, the first paper in Michigan, and helped to found (1817) the University of Michigan, where he served as vice-president, professor, and trustee. In 1823 he was elected to Congress—the only Catholic priest, until recently, to hold such a distinction. Richard was named first bishop of Detroit in 1827, but for some reason the nomination was suppressed until after his death.   HENRY WARNER BOWDEN

Bibliography: Woodford, Frank, and Hyma, Albert, *Gabriel Richard: Frontier Ambassador* (1958).

Richard, Maurice

Joseph Henri Maurice "Rocket" Richard, b. Montreal, Aug. 4, 1921, was an aggressive professional ice hockey player and the first National Hockey League (NHL) player to score 50 goals in a season (1944–45). Richard, who played his entire career with the Montreal Canadiens, was an extremely fast skater—hence his nickname. For years the offensive backbone of the Canadiens, he added to their tradition of greatness. In his 18-season career (1942–60) he scored 544 goals; he was selected for 8 all-star teams, led the NHL in goal scoring 5 times, and won (1947) the MVP award once. Richard was elected to the Hockey Hall of Fame in 1961.

Richard II (play)

With *The Tragedy of King Richard II* (written c.1595), William SHAKESPEARE began a history tetralogy that continues in *Henry IV*, Parts 1 and 2, and *Henry V*. Richard II exiles Henry Bolingbroke and confiscates his lands to finance his war in Ireland. Bolingbroke returns and, with the Percy family's aid, forces Richard to abdicate and proclaims himself Henry IV. After instigating Richard's murder, Henry expresses remorse and vows a pilgrimage to expiate his crime. The play constitutes an eloquent dramatic debate on the nature of kingship.

Richard III (play)

The Tragedy of King Richard III (written c.1592), one of William SHAKESPEARE's most popular history plays, owes its success to the portrait of the villainous Richard, duke of Gloucester. On the death of his brother Edward IV, Richard usurps the crown by murdering Edward's two sons, the so-called "Princes in the Tower." These and his other crimes are avenged by Henry, duke of Richmond, who kills Richard at the Battle of Bosworth Field and becomes Henry VII, the first Tudor king. Richard's hunchbacked body matches the perversion of his mind, but his disarming frankness and comic ingenuity compensate for the play's relative crudity.

Richard I, King of England

Richard I, the Lion-Hearted, b. Sept. 8, 1157, d. Apr. 6, 1199, king of England (1189–99), was the third son of HENRY II and ELEANOR OF AQUITAINE. Renowned as a Crusader and gallant knight, Richard neglected his kingdom, allowing his ministers to rule in his stead. Immature and petulant, he excelled only in fighting. Before becoming king, Richard was often at war with his father and brothers, and he spent all but six months of his reign outside of England campaigning or in captivity. Battle leader of the Third CRUSADE, Richard was shipwrecked near Venice on his return in 1192 and imprisoned by Duke Leopold of Austria. Leopold turned Richard over to Holy Roman Emperor HENRY VI, who released him in February 1194 only after a huge ransom had been pledged.

For the English, probably the most significant event of the crusade was Richard's assent to the Treaty of Messina (1191) with PHILIP II of France, an ally early in the Crusade; by that

Richard I, king of England, earned the title "Coeur de Lion," or "Lion Heart," for his boldness in combat. He used his kingdom as a source of money to finance his overseas expeditions, including the Third Crusade, returning from which he was captured and held for ransom by the Holy Roman emperor.

treaty the English king formally acknowledged his continental holdings as Philip's fief. Philip later used his position as overlord of the English king for his French dominions to justify his attack against Richard's brother and successor, King JOHN. Richard spent the last five years of his reign warring with Philip. Although he was later romanticized by Sir Walter Scott and others, Richard did little more than contribute to the financial exhaustion of his realm through the expenses of the Crusade and other wars, the king's ransom, and subsidies to his continental allies. Heavy taxation under Richard and his absence from England created dissatisfaction and initiated a decline in the power of the crown.   JAMES W. ALEXANDER

Bibliography: Appleby, John, England without Richard 1189–1199 (1965); Brundage, James, Richard Lion Heart (1974); Gillingham, John, Richard the Lionheart (1979); Norgate, Kate, Richard the Lion Heart (1924; repr. 1969).

Richard II, King of England

Richard II, b. Jan. 6, 1367, d. February 1400, king of England (1377–99), son of EDWARD, THE BLACK PRINCE, succeeded his grandfather EDWARD III. Precocious, clever, and ruthless, Richard had exalted notions of royal power but proved unable to implement them. Richard's uncle, JOHN OF GAUNT, duke of Lancaster, was effective ruler of England during the young king's minority. The minority council was disrupted, however, by internal rivalries and by the continuing Hundred Years' War (1337–1453) with France. When an oppressive poll tax

Richard II, last of the Angevin kings of England, was 10 years old at his coronation and 14 when he outwitted the rebellious peasants led by Wat Tyler. A reckless and ineffectual ruler, Richard was deposed by his cousin Henry Bolingbroke, who began the Lancastrian line of kings.

sparked the PEASANTS' REVOLT in 1381, Richard himself negotiated a truce with the rebels. After the death (1385) of his mother, Joan of Kent, Richard began to take control. He offended much of the English populace with his high-handed style of government, lack of interest in the French war, and reliance on a few young friends, especially Robert de Vere, earl of Oxford, and Michael de la Pole, earl of Suffolk, the chancellor. After Gaunt left for Spain in 1386, Suffolk was impeached in Parliament and a council was imposed on the king, despite Richard's charges of treason. The Merciless Parliament of 1388 met under the threat of rebellion by the king's five leading opponents, known as the Lords Appellant—the king's uncle, the duke of Gloucester; Gaunt's son, Henry Bolingbroke; the earl of Arundel; the earl of Warwick; and the earl of Nottingham (later duke of Norfolk)—who forced the exile or execution of several royal favorites.

Determined to exact revenge, Richard gradually built up a royalist faction. In 1397, Gloucester was murdered and Warwick and Arundel were condemned in Parliament. Ruling arbitrarily and without check, Richard alienated nearly all magnates. In 1398 he exiled Bolingbroke, who, taking advantage of Richard's temporary absence in Ireland, invaded England the following year. Richard quickly returned but was forced to abdicate and died in prison, perhaps murdered. Soon after, Bolingbroke became HENRY IV.   GEORGE HOLMES

Bibliography: McKisack, May, The Fourteenth Century (1959); Tuck, A., Richard II and the English Nobility (1973).

Richard III, King of England

Richard III was the last English king of the House of York. Although he was an effective administrator, his ruthlessness in securing the throne (which required the deposition and murder of his nephew Edward V) and in eliminating potential opposition brought large-scale revolt. After a brief reign (1483–85) Richard was killed in battle by the future Henry VII.

Richard III, b. Oct. 2, 1452, d. Aug. 22, 1485, king of England (1483–85), the last ruler of the House of York (see YORK family), seized power during the last years of the Wars of the Roses (see ROSES, WARS OF THE). He was the youngest son of Richard, duke of York. After his eldest brother, EDWARD IV, deposed the Lancastrian monarch HENRY VI and became king in 1461, Richard was made duke of Gloucester. In March 1471, Richard's troops played a decisive role in English victories against the Lancastrians at Barnet and Tewkesbury. Two months later Henry VI and his son were murdered, an act in which Richard is believed to have participated. Sent to rule northern England as the king's representative during the last years of Edward's reign, Richard pacified the unruly region, gaining the respect of its inhabitants.

On the succession of the boy king EDWARD V in April 1483, Richard established himself as protector in London, supported by William, Lord Hastings, and Henry Stafford, 2d duke of Buckingham. In the ensuing struggle for power, many of Richard's opponents—and his one-time ally, Hastings—were executed, and Edward was declared illegitimate. Richard was crowned on July 26. His position as king was weakened by his lack of a son; by reports, probably true, that he was responsible for the murders of Edward and his brother in August; and by the disaffection of supporters, including Buckingham, who rebelled in October 1483. After the successful invasion of Henry Tudor in August 1485, Richard was killed at Bosworth Field and Henry was crowned HENRY VII. A controversial figure, Richard was portrayed as a villain by writers under the Tudor monarchs, most notably by William Shakespeare in his play *Richard III*.   GEORGE HOLMES

Bibliography: Kendall, Paul M., *Richard the Third* (1955; repr. 1975); Ross, Charles, *Richard III* (1982); Seward, Desmond, *Richard III: England's Black Legend* (1984); Tudor-Craig, Pamela, *Richard III*, 2d ed. (1977).

Richards, Bob

Robert E. Richards, b. Champaign, Ill., Feb. 20, 1926, began his pole-vaulting career at the age of 12, but he did not reach stardom until after he had graduated from Bridgewater College and the University of Illinois. Although Richards divided his time between athletics and the ministry, in 1948 he won a bronze medal in the 1948 Olympic Games. After winning (1951) the Sullivan Award, Richards went on to win the Olympic gold medal in pole vaulting in 1952 and again in 1956. He won or tied for the national Amateur Athletic Union (AAU) outdoor title 9 times (1948–52, 1954–57) and the indoor title 8 times (1948, 1950–52, 1954–57).   HOWARD LISS

Richards, Dickinson Woodruff

The American physician Dickinson Woodruff Richards, b. Orange, N.J., Oct. 30, 1895, d. Feb. 23, 1973, shared the 1956 Nobel Prize for physiology or medicine with André COURNAND and Werner Forssmann for their "discoveries concerning heart catheterization and pathological changes in the circulatory system." Using a heart catheterization technique pioneered by Forssmann, Richards and Cournand were able to measure gas pressures in the lung and pulmonary artery and to improve the diagnoses of certain heart diseases and the surgical correction of certain heart defects, including the one responsible for so-called blue babies.

Richards, Gordon

Sir Gordon Richards, b. May 5, 1904, d. Nov. 10, 1986, was considered England's leading jockey during his racing career. Twenty-six times, between 1925 and 1953, he was England's top jockey. He won such leading stakes races as the Derby, the King George VI, the Queen Elizabeth Stakes, the Oaks, and the One Thousand and the Two Thousand Guineas. In 1933, Richards set a record by riding 259 winners, improved on with 269 victories in 1947. Richards rode 4,870 winners out of 21,828 mounts during his career. He was knighted by Queen Elizabeth II in 1953.   HOWARD LISS

Richards, I. A.

The English literary critic Ivor Armstrong Richards, b. Feb. 26, 1893, d. Sept. 7, 1979, laid the groundwork for the later development of the NEW CRITICISM in America. Richards's important books include his study of semantics, *The Meaning of Meaning* (with C. K. Ogden, 1923); *Principles of Literary Criticism* (1924), an exploration of the connections between art and science; and the influential *Practical Criticism* (1929). His research into the functions of language led him to work with the much-publicized learning system called Basic English. Among his collections of poetry are *Goodbye Earth and Other Poems* (1958) and *Beyond* (1974).

Bibliography: Hotopf, W. H. N., *Language, Thought and Comprehension: A Case Study of the Writings of I. A. Richards* (1965); Schiller, Jerome P., *I. A. Richards' Theory of Literature* (1969).

Richards, Theodore William

The American chemist Theodore William Richards, b. Germantown, Pa., Jan. 31, 1868, d. Apr. 2, 1928, was recognized during his lifetime as the leading authority in atomic-weight determinations. A Harvard University graduate, he served as full professor at Harvard from 1901 to 1928. Using superior gravimetric methods and applying physicochemical principles, he determined the atomic weights of a large number of elements with an accuracy never surpassed. His detection of the varying atomic weight of lead in 1913 coincided with the discovery of ISOTOPES by Frederick Soddy. Richards was awarded the 1914 Nobel Prize for chemistry for his work.

                        HUGO ZAHND

Bibliography: Ihde, Aaron J., *Great Chemists* (1961); Nobel Foundation, ed., *Nobel Lectures: Chemistry, 1901–1921* (1966).

Richards, Sir William Buell

Sir William Buell Richards, b. Brockville, Ontario, May 2, 1815, d. Jan. 26, 1889, was the first chief justice of the Canadian Supreme Court (1875–79). In 1851 he was appointed attorney general for Upper Canada (Ontario), a post that he held until 1853 when he was appointed to the Court of Common Pleas. In 1868 he became chief justice of the Queen's Bench in Ontario.

Richardson, Dorothy M.

An early experimenter in the stream-of-consciousness technique who was overshadowed by James Joyce and Virginia Woolf, British novelist Dorothy Miller Richardson, b. May 17, 1873, d. June 17, 1957, is best known for the novels collectively titled *Pilgrimage* (1938). Started in 1915, these chronicle the inner life of an intelligent, middle-class Englishwoman and her search for identity.   JEROME KLINKOWITZ

Richardson, Elliot L.

Elliot Richardson has pursued a multifaceted governmental career since 1959. After serving in Richard Nixon's cabinet as secretary of health, education, and welfare, secretary of defense, and attorney general, he resigned (1973) the last position rather than follow the president's orders to fire Archibald Cox, the special prosecutor investigating the Watergate scandal.

Elliot Lee Richardson, b. Boston, July 20, 1920, has held a number of top governmental and diplomatic posts, including three cabinet positions during the administration of President Richard Nixon: secretary of health, education and welfare (1970–72), secretary of defense (1972–73), and attorney general (1973). Under President Gerald Ford, he served as ambassador to Great Britain (1975–76) and as secretary of commerce (1976–77). President Jimmy Carter appointed him ambassador-at-large and special representative for the Law of the Sea Conference (1977–80).

Richardson received a law degree from Harvard University after a distinguished army career during World War II. He was appointed (1959) U.S. attorney for Massachusetts and served (1965–67) as lieutenant governor of Massachusetts. A moderate Republican, Richardson became well known for having resigned as attorney general after refusing to fire Archibald Cox, the special prosecutor during the WATERGATE scandal.

Richardson, Henry Handel

Henry Handel Richardson was the pseudonym of the Australian novelist Ethel Lindesay Robertson, b. Jan. 3, 1870, d. Mar.

24, 1946. Robertson left Australia for England in 1887 and returned only once for a brief visit. Her major work was a trilogy collected under the title *The Fortunes of Richard Mahony* (1930). It included *Australia Felix* (1917), *The Way Home* (1925), and *Ultima Thule* (1929). The story of an Irish doctor in 19th-century Australia, it explores the tensions between established colonials and new immigrants.   LEON CANTRELL

Bibliography: Elliott, W. D., *Henry Handel Richardson: A Critical Study* (1975); Green, Dorothy, *Ulysses Bound: Henry Handel Richardson and Her Fiction* (1973); Richardson, H. H., *Myself When Young* (1948).

Richardson, Henry Hobson

The Marshall Field Wholesale Store (1885–87), in Chicago, designed by Henry Hobson Richardson, exhibits the simple rhythmic and textural variation and the massive proportions typical of Richardson's style. The structure was demolished in 1930 and replaced by a parking lot.

The American architect Henry Hobson Richardson, b. Saint James Parish, La., Sept. 29, 1838, d. Apr. 27, 1886, became the most innovative and influential designer in his field during the latter part of the 19th century. Raised in New Orleans and educated at Harvard College, Richardson entered the École des Beaux-Arts in Paris in 1860. When the Civil War cut off his funds, he worked with Théodore Labrouste, the brother of the architect Henri Labrouste, acquiring a discipline that served to temper his taste for architectural exotica.

This restraint can be seen in some of Richardson's early designs in the United States. While Grace Church (1867; West Medford, Mass.) derives from English Victorian models, its pyramidal massing and use of rough-faced granite point toward his mature works. His own house (1868; Staten Island, N.Y.) combines high-pitched French mansard roofs with the fussy, shedlike forms of 19th-century American wood construction. Such conflicting tendencies are more marked in the State Asylum for the Insane (1871–81; Buffalo, N.Y.).

In later projects Richardson introduced the massive and simple masonry architecture, inspired by the Romanesque, for which he is famous. For example, Trinity Church (consecrated 1877; Boston), his most elegant religious structure, was built on a cruciform plan in yellow-gray granite and brownstone. Its crossing is capped by a massive lantern, the dominant element in a clearly pyramidal composition modeled on Salamanca Cathedral in Spain. Harvard University's rectangular Sever Hall (1878; Cambridge, Mass.) takes this process a step further. Its blocklike plan constitutes Richardson's urban mode; his suburban buildings are often asymmetrical. All tend to avoid the extremes of picturesqueness then popular. Although many of Richardson's designs were based on European sources, they are thoroughly American in materials and character.

Richardson's last buildings achieve a monumentality unequaled in American architecture. For example, in the huge Marshall Field Wholesale Store (1885–87; Chicago), his demolished masterpiece, Richardson emphasized the structure's blocklike function in the urban environment; it became the model for Louis SULLIVAN's massive AUDITORIUM BUILDING nearby.   LEON SATKOWSKI

Bibliography: Hitchcock, Henry-Russell, *The Architecture of H. H. Richardson and His Times* (1936); O'Gorman, James F., *H. H. Richardson and His Office, Selected Drawings* (1974); Van Rensselaer, Mariana Griswold, *Henry Hobson Richardson and His Works* (1888; repr. 1963).

Richardson, John

The soldier-journalist John Richardson, b. Oct. 4, 1796, d. May 12, 1852, is called Canada's first novelist. He fought the Americans in the War of 1812 and campaigned in the West Indies. Richardson published a newspaper and wrote poetry, history, autobiography, and several historical novels—among them *Wacousta* (1832), the tale of an Indian uprising.

Richardson, Sir Owen Willans

The British physicist Sir Owen Willans Richardson, b. Apr. 26, 1879, d. Feb. 15, 1959, won the 1928 Nobel Prize for physics for his work in thermionics—the emission of electrons by heated electrical conductors—and for his discovery of Richardson's law, a formula that describes the effect of heat on the interaction between electricity and matter. He taught at Princeton (1906–13) and King's College, London (1914–44).

Richardson, Sir Ralph

The English actor Ralph David Richardson, b. Dec. 19, 1902, d. Oct. 10, 1983, was one of the best-loved actors of the English-speaking stage. He also appeared in many films. Leaving art school to become an actor, Richardson made his debut in London in 1926. During the 1930s he acted in many Old Vic and Sadler's Wells productions with Laurence Olivier, and the two were appointed directors of the Old Vic in 1944. That same year he played the title role in *Peer Gynt*, which became one of his most memorable performances, along with that of Falstaff in *Henry IV*. As willing to perform in cameo roles as in major ones, Richardson invested the most ordinary characters with qualities that he drew from his own somewhat eccentric and mischievous nature. He often toured the United States, and he appeared on Broadway with John Gielgud in *Home* (1970) and in Harold Pinter's *No Man's Land* (1975).

Richardson, Samuel

Samuel Richardson, b. 1689, d. July 4, 1761, often described as the first major English novelist, exercised a profound influence on the development of the NOVEL. His three novels, PA-

Samuel Richardson, an 18th-century English novelist, secured an enthusiastic following with Pamela; or Virtue Rewarded *(1740). Although Richardson's work is criticized for its moralizing tone, his protagonists are regarded as the first realistic, emotionally complex characters in the English novel.*

MELA, CLARISSA, and *Sir Charles Grandison* (1753), all written in epistolary form, greatly influenced European fiction in the 18th century, and such diverse writers as Jane Austen, Jean Jacques Rousseau, and the Marquis de Sade paid tribute to his art. Born to a "Family of middling Note," he received an elementary education and was apprenticed (1706) to a London printer. Early in life he acquired a passion for writing letters, which he composed on his own and others' behalf. At the age of 50, well established as a printer, he was asked by two London booksellers to write a series of letters that might be used as models by less-educated people. *Letters Written to and for Particular Friends* (1751) contained a letter from a pious father to his daughter who, as the servant in a wealthy man's house, defends her virtue against a libidinous master.

From this correspondence grew Richardson's first epistolary novel, *Pamela; or, Virtue Rewarded* (1740). Both acclaimed and reviled, the book led to a host of imitations and burlesques, among them *Shamela* and *Joseph Andrews* (1742), which launched Henry Fielding on his career as a novelist. In 1747–48 appeared the enormously long and powerful *Clarissa; or The History of a Young Lady*, arguably the greatest fictional work of the 18th century. Also written as a series of letters, allowing shifting perspectives and minute analysis of psychological traits, the novel tells the tragic story of the contest between the saintly Clarissa and the libertine Lovelace, who obsessively pursues her into madness and death. Its chief characters became types, constantly referred to in the writings of the age. Richardson's final novel, *The History of Sir Charles Grandison*, was published in 1753–54. Whereas *Clarissa* had presented an exemplary woman, this novel tries to provide the ideal man, a corrective to the seductive Lovelace who, the author feared, was all too attractive to the reader. After publishing his last novel, Richardson worked as a printer, enjoyed the attentions of literary women, and continued writing letters.

Richardson turned the epistolary novel into serious art. Although verbose and mawkish at times, he overpowers the reader with the intensity and warmth of his sympathy, especially with women. Combining sentiment and realism, he tells stories that are unsurpassed for their probing of the darker reaches of the mind and their depiction of the claustrophobia of human relationships.   JANET M. TODD

Bibliography: Doody, Margaret A., *A Natural Passion: A Study of the Novels of Samuel Richardson* (1974); Eaves, T. C. Duncan, and Kimpel, Ben D., *Samuel Richardson: A Biography* (1971); Kinkead-Weekes, Mark, *Samuel Richardson* (1973); Wolff, Cynthia G., *Samuel Richardson and the Eighteenth-Century Puritan Character* (1973).

Richardson, Tony

Film director Tony Richardson, b. Jan. 5, 1928, has been a key figure in the development of the modern British cinema and theater. Richardson directed the first production of John Osborne's *Look Back in Anger* (1956) and later made a film of the play (1959). He has since worked primarily as a film director, producing *Saturday Night and Sunday Morning* (1960) and directing the film version of Henry Fielding's *Tom Jones* (1963). His many memorable films include *The Entertainer* (1960), *A Taste of Honey* (1961), *The Loneliness of the Long Distance Runner* (1962), *The Charge of the Light Brigade* (1968), and *Joseph Andrews* (1977).   ROY ARMES

Richelieu, Armand Jean du Plessis, Cardinal et Duc de   [ree-shel-yu']

Armand Jean du Plessis, Cardinal Richelieu, b. Sept. 9, 1585, d. Dec. 4, 1642, ruled France as the principal minister of LOUIS XIII from 1624 to 1642. He helped to establish the basis of royal absolutism in France and of French preeminence in Europe. Richelieu became bishop of Luçon in 1607. He was named a spokesman for the clergy in the States-General and so won the favor of the regent and queen mother, MARIE DE MÉDICIS, that he became secretary of state for foreign affairs in 1616. Expelled from office when King Louis XIII overthrew (1617) his mother's authority, Richelieu then acquired importance as a peacemaker in the continuing disputes between

Cardinal Richelieu, first minister of France under King Louis XIII, guided France to a position of power in Europe by an alliance with Protestant nations against the Habsburgs in the Thirty Years' War. The founder of the Académie Française, he reorganized internal French politics and established the supreme authority of the crown.

Marie and her son, gaining a cardinalate in 1622 and becoming chief of the royal council in 1624. His title was changed to first minister in 1628.

Richelieu's policy was to develop the absolute authority of the crown and to crush the independent power of the HUGUENOTS (French Protestants) while thwarting the European hegemony of the Spanish and Austrian Habsburgs by allying France with Protestant states in the THIRTY YEARS' WAR. He captured La Rochelle from the Huguenots and in 1629 deprived them of their military capacity while continuing to tolerate their religion. Although he took pains to justify his actions, for Richelieu the interests of the state overrode religion, ordinary morality, and constitutional procedures. As a result he alienated the devout Catholic party, the nobility, and the judicial hierarchy. Several noble conspiracies were raised against him, all of which he frustrated; they were usually supported by the king's brother, Gaston d'Orléans (see ORLÉANS family). Among the lower classes heavy taxation to support war caused an endemic state of revolt in the provinces. To control local privilege and disorder, Richelieu employed commissioners sent by the royal council, known as INTENDANTS. He also took an interest in literary and theological matters and founded the ACADÉMIE FRANÇAISE in 1635.

In the Thirty Years' War the cardinal supported the Dutch, the Danes, and the Swedes in the struggle against the Habsburgs. He also checked Spanish pretensions in Mantua and tried to block Spanish communications through eastern Switzerland. After the defeat of his Swedish and Protestant German allies, he declared war against Spain in 1635. In 1640, Richelieu backed anti-Spanish revolts in Catalonia and Portugal. His actions led to a sharp decline of Spanish power.

J. H. M. SALMON

Bibliography: Church, William F., *Richelieu and Reason of State* (1972); O'Connell, D. P., *Richelieu* (1968); Treasure, G. R. R., *Cardinal Richelieu and the Development of Absolutism* (1972); Wedgwood, C. V., *Richelieu and the French Monarchy*, rev. ed. (1962).

Richier, Germaine   [ree-shee-ay']

The French sculptor Germaine Richier, b. Sept. 16, 1904, d. July 31, 1959, devoted herself to expressing the most somber aspects of human emotion in sculptural form. She studied in Montpellier and Paris, for a time with Émile Antoine Bourdelle. After a stay in Switzerland during World War II, she began to dwell on images of terror and the fear of death. Using open structural forms (such as the skeleton and the web) that suggest incompleteness, Richier conveyed the horrors of a ravaged, lacerated world. Continually decomposing the human figure into symbolic forms, she pushed her technique to the limits of fragility, creating an image of humanity torn by the mental and physical anguish of war.   HARRY RAND

Bibliography: Cassou, Jean, *Germaine Richier* (1961); Seuphor, Michael, *The Sculpture of This Century* (1960); Tufts, Eleanor, *Our Hidden Heritage: Five Centuries of Women Artists* (1974).

Richler, Mordecai [rich'-lur]

The Canadian author Mordecai Richler writes from his background as a Montreal Jew in his sharply satiric and boisterous novels. Also an acclaimed scenarist, writing screenplays for such films as Life at the Top *(1965), Richler is best known as the author of* The Apprenticeship of Duddy Kravitz *(1959), which he adapted for the 1974 film of the same name.*

The characteristic subject of the Canadian novelist Mordecai Richler, b. Jan. 27, 1931, is Jewish life in the working-class districts of Montreal. Duddy Kravitz, the determined young schemer of *The Apprenticeship of Duddy Kravitz* (1959; film, 1974), Richler's most popular novel, lives in the Saint Urbain Street area of Montreal, where Richler himself was brought up. *Saint Urbain's Horseman* (1971) is a complex meditation on the problems of being Jewish in contemporary society. Other works by Richler include *The Acrobats* (1954), the collection of essays *Notes on an Endangered Species* (1974), and *Joshua Then and Now* (1980).

Bibliography: Sheps, G. David, ed., *Mordecai Richler* (1971); Woodcock, George, *Mordecai Richler* (1970).

Richmond [rich'-muhnd]

Richmond is the capital and one of the largest cities of Virginia. Located in the eastern part of the state on the James River near the Atlantic Ocean, it is the seat of Henrico County and has a population of 219,214 (1980). The 6-county metropolitan area has a population of 623,234. With its deepwater port, extensive rail facilities, and dense highway network, Richmond is a regional distribution, commercial, and finance center. Tobacco processing and chemical manufacturing are among its diversified industries. The city's historic sites include Saint John's Church (1741), where Patrick Henry made his "Liberty or Death" speech; the state capitol (1785), designed by Thomas Jefferson; the Confederate White House; and nearby Richmond National Battlefield Park (1944). U.S. presidents John Tyler and James Monroe and Confederate president Jefferson Davis are buried in the city's Hollywood Cemetery. Richmond is the home of several educational institutions, including the University of Richmond (1830) and Virginia Commonwealth University (1838).

The area was first explored in 1607 by members of the Jamestown colony. Permanently settled in 1637 by Thomas Stegg, who established a trading post, Richmond was laid out in 1737 by Maj. William Mayo and was named for Richmond on Thames, England. It was made state capital in 1779, replacing Williamsburg. It was attacked by the British in 1781. Major Civil War battles raged around Richmond, which replaced (1861) Montgomery, Ala., as capital of the Confederacy. Gen. Ulysses S. Grant took the city on Apr. 3, 1865, after much of it was burned.

Richter, Adrian Ludwig [rik'-tur]

The rural landscapes of the German romantic painter and illustrator Adrian Ludwig Richter, b. Sept. 28, 1803, d. June 19, 1884, are idyllic, meditative, naively charming scenes. Usually depicting peasants, shepherds, and animals, Richter's works are executed with meticulous detail and finish; they represent a combination of the romantic (Nazarene) tradition and the neoclassical. In 1820, Richter and his father, Karl (an engraver), published 100 etched plates entitled *Mahlerische An- und Aussichten;* both father and son served on the faculty of the Dresden Academy. As an illustrator, Richter is best known for his more than 2,000 wood engravings of fairy tales, tracts, and legends.   BARBARA CAVALIERE

Richter, Burton

The American physicist Burton Richter, b. New York City, Mar. 22, 1931, shared the 1976 Nobel Prize for physics with S. C. Ting. Richter received a Ph.D. from the Massachusetts Institute of Technology in 1956 and became a professor of physics at Stanford University in 1967. In 1974 he discovered a new subatomic particle, which he called a psi particle in view of the appearance of the track it left in the detector. This particle was actually identical with the J particle named by Ting and discovered simultaneously by him in a different experiment. The J/psi particle is believed to be made up of a QUARK with "charm" (a new quality of matter) combined with an antiquark with "anticharm."   RAYMOND J. SEEGER

Richter, Conrad

The American writer Conrad Michael Richter, b. Pine Grove, Pa., Oct. 13, 1890, d. Oct. 30, 1968, became known during the 1930s for his short stories and his first novel, *The Sea of Grass* (1937), about the settlement of the Southwest. His reputation, however, rests mainly on his "Ohio trilogy"—*The Trees* (1940), *The Fields* (1946), and *The Town* (1950), for which he won the 1951 Pulitzer Prize for fiction.   WARREN FRENCH

Bibliography: Gaston, Edwin W., Jr., *Conrad Richter* (1965); LaHood, Marvin J., *Conrad Richter's America* (1975).

Richter, Hans

A painter who was drawn to kinetic abstraction, Hans Richter, b. Berlin, Apr. 16, 1888, d. Feb. 1, 1976, is best known for his contributions to avant-garde cinema. In 1918—having been associated with De Stijl, constructivism, and Dadaism—Richter and the Swedish painter Viking Eggeling began producing abstractions on scrolls, which led them to conceive the idea of the first abstract motion picture, *Rhythmus 21* (1921). In 1932, Richter's anti-Nazi sentiments forced him to flee to Switzerland; he emigrated to the United States in 1941, becoming a professor at City College in New York City. Working with Marcel Duchamp, Max Ernst, Fernand Léger, and Alexander Calder, he explored the fantasies of a group of psychiatric patients in the film *Dreams That Money Can Buy* (1944–47).   BARBARA CAVALIERE

Bibliography: Gray, Cleve, ed., *Hans Richter* (1971); Jaffe, Hans L. C., ed., *De Stijl,* trans. by Mary Whitall (1971); Richter, Hans, *Dada: Art and Anti-Art,* trans. by David Britt (1965).

Richter, Johann Paul Friedrich

The German writer Johann Paul Friedrich Richter, b. Mar. 21, 1763, d. Nov. 14, 1825, helped establish the 19th-century German novel as a literary form. Richter signed his works using the pen name Jean Paul, the French form of his given name. An admirer of Jean Jacques Rousseau, he achieved literary recognition with *The Invisible Lodge* (1793; Eng. trans., 1833), an educational novel influenced by Rousseau's thought. Richter's major work, *Titan* (1800–03; Eng. trans., 1862), is a four-volume novel that idealizes the life of the poor and contrasts the dreamer with the man of action. In 1808, Richter was granted a lifetime pension by Prince Dalberg, and he continued to enjoy great literary success throughout his career. Although his works have since declined in popularity, his importance as a precursor of romanticism and as a pioneer in developing the psychological novel ensure him a lasting place in literature. His other works include satirical essays and treatises on education and poetic theory.

Bibliography: Berger, Dorothea, *Jean Paul Friedrich Richter* (1972); Harich, Walther, *Jean Paul* (1971); Smeed, John W., *Jean Paul's Dreams* (1966).

Richter, Sviatoslav   [svee-ah'-toh-slahf]

The Soviet pianist Sviatoslav Teofilovich Richter, b. Mar. 20 (N.S.), 1915, is one of the great keyboard virtuosos in the romantic tradition. He was trained principally in Odessa, where he worked as an accompanist at the opera, and made his official debut in 1935. In 1937 he enrolled in the Moscow Conservatory, studying with H. Neuhaus until 1947. He was awarded the Stalin Prize in 1949 and subsequently was declared "People's Artist of the USSR." His U.S. debut (1960) brought him great renown and was followed by similar triumphs in Western Europe. He has recorded extensively, with concentration on the standard repertory, including Johann Sebastian Bach, Franz Schubert, Robert Schumann, and the Russian masters.

KAREN MONSON

Richter scale

The Richter scale, named for the American seismologist Charles Richter (1900–85), is used to measure the magnitude of an EARTHQUAKE. Magnitude is a measure of an earthquake's size, but rather than being a direct measure of the intensity of ground shaking, it is a reflection of the strength of the seismic sound waves emitted by the earthquake, phenomena that can be detected at great distances from the earthquake's epicenter. Because an earthquake's magnitude can be determined solely from routine measurements made with SEISMOMETERS (instruments used to detect seismic waves), magnitude has become an important and commonly made measurement (see SEISMOGRAM).

The Richter scale is logarithmic. This means that a factor-of-ten difference in actual earthquake energy corresponds to a difference of one whole number on the scale. Earthquakes having magnitudes in excess of 6.0 are considered dangerous. The most powerful earthquake recorded in North America, the Alaska quake of 1964, reached 8.5 on the Richter scale; the quake that struck the western coast of Mexico and devastated Mexico City in 1985 registered 8.1 on the scale.

WILLIAM MENKE

Richthofen, Ferdinand von   [rikt'-hoh-fen]

Ferdinand von Richthofen, b. May 5, 1833, d. Oct. 6, 1905, was a pioneering German geographer and geologist whose major work on China gave direction to the development of modern geography. After a 12-year trip to eastern Asia, China, and the western United States, Richthofen, beginning in 1879, served as professor at the universities of Bonn, Leipzig, and Berlin. He wrote *China, the Results of My Travels and the Studies Based Thereon,* published (in part posthumously) from 1877 to 1912.

Richthofen, Manfred, Freiherr von

Manfred Richthofen, a World War I German fighter pilot, became known as the Red Baron. After 2 years of combat flying, Richthofen was killed when his famous red triplane was shot down in 1918.

Manfred Richthofen, b. May 2, 1892, d. Apr. 21, 1918, was a German flying ace in World War I who became famous as the Red Baron because he flew a red Fokker triplane. A fighter pilot from 1916, he was credited with shooting down 80 Allied planes in dogfights. He died when he was shot down.

Bibliography: Burrows, William E., *Richthofen: A True History of the Red Baron* (1969).

Rickenbacker, Eddie   [rik'-en-bak-ur]

Eddie Rickenbacker was the most decorated American combat pilot of World War I. He was later president of Eastern Airlines, which he developed into one of the nation's major passenger carriers.

Captain Edward Vernon Rickenbacker, b. Columbus, Ohio, Oct. 8, 1890, d. July 23, 1973, was an American flying ace in World War I and later an airline executive. After an early career as an automobile racer, Rickenbacker volunteered in the army flying service during World War I. He was accepted as a fighter pilot in March 1918 and shot down 22 enemy planes and 4 balloons, making him the top U.S. flying ace. Reentering the aviation field after an unsuccessful attempt at running an automobile company, he eventually became president (1938–53) and chairman of the board (1954–63) of Eastern Airlines. He wrote *Fighting the Flying Circus* (1919), *Seven Came Through* (1943), and an autobiography, *Rickenbacker* (1967).

Bibliography: Farr, Finis, *Rickenbacker's Luck: An American Life* (1979).

rickets

Rickets, a childhood disease of the bone, results from a diet deficient in vitamin D and inadequate exposure to sunlight. Lack of vitamin D interferes with the proper mineralization of bone and causes bone softness. This leads to such deformities as extreme bowlegs and spinal curvature, as well as general body tenderness. It has been estimated that at the turn of the 20th century about 90 percent of the children who died before the age of 4 years in northern European cities had rickets. Improved nutrition, however, has made the disease rare in North America and Europe (see NUTRITIONAL-DEFICIENCY DISEASES).

PETER L. PETRAKIS

rickettsia   [rik-et'-see-uh]

Rickettsia are a group of small, often disease-causing, rod-shaped bacteria with two genera, *Rickettsia* and *Coxiella,* in the family Rickett siaceae. At one time they were believed to be midway between the larger viruses and smaller bacteria in size and structure. It is clear now that these submicroscopic organisms are true bacteria, possessing typical bacterial cell walls and membranes and the biochemical means for protein synthesis and enzymatic activities. They differ from bacteria in that they are obligate intracellular parasites dependent on a host, usually a bloodsucking insect, for part of their life processes. Like viruses, rickettsia cannot be cultivated outside a living host; in laboratories, they are usually cultivated in fertile chicken eggs or appropriate tissue cultures, and maintained in this manner.

The life cycle of the majority of rickettsia involves an insect as the vector (carrier) and an animal as the alternate host. The infection of humans is not essential for maintaining the cycle. Rickettsia, however, can cause many serious human diseases that are usually transmitted by the bite of various animals: epidemic TYPHUS by the body louse; tsutsugamushi fever (scrub typhus) by the mite; and ROCKY MOUNTAIN SPOTTED FEVER by the tick. The exception is Q FEVER, which humans contract by drinking infected milk from cattle or by inhaling dust containing infected material. All rickettsial diseases respond to drug treatment with chloramphenicol and tetracyclines.

Bibliography: Burgdorfer, Willy, and Anacker, Robert, *Rickettsiae and Rickettsial Diseases* (1981); Marchette, N. J., ed., *Ecological Relationships and Evolution of the Rickettsiae*, 2 vols. (1982).

Rickey, Branch

Wesley Branch Rickey, b. Stockdale, Ohio, Dec. 20, 1881, d. Dec. 9, 1965, was one of baseball's foremost executives. His own baseball career as a catcher for the St. Louis Browns and the New York Yankees and later as a coach for the Browns was undistinguished. In 1917 he became president of the St. Louis Cardinals organization, and 3 years later he initiated the now-familiar baseball farm system. His innovation produced the talented ball players who later won five pennants for the Cardinals. Rickey became general manager (1942–50) of the Brooklyn Dodgers and built them into a championship team. He broke the color barrier in baseball by signing (1947) Jackie ROBINSON, who became the first black player in the major leagues. Rickey later served (1950–55) as general manager of the Pittsburgh Pirates. He was voted into the Baseball Hall of Fame in 1967.   HOWARD LISS

Bibliography: Polner, Murray, *Branch Rickey* (1982).

Rickey, George

The American sculptor George Warren Rickey, b. South Bend, Ind., June 6, 1907, is a leading exponent of KINETIC ART. Rickey studied in Paris during the late 1920s, where he met such modernist masters as André Lhote and Fernand Léger. Returning to the United States in 1930, he supported himself chiefly as an art teacher. In the 1940s, Rickey began to develop his mature style, a distinctive variation on constructivist precedents (see CONSTRUCTIVISM). He combines severely geometrical metal elements in sculptures that change form in response to currents of air. Rickey has also been active as a theoretician and as an organizer of constructivist exhibits.
                              CARTER RATCLIFF

Bibliography: Rosenthal, Nan, *George Rickey* (1977); Seltz, Peter, *George Rickey* (1966).

Rickover, Hyman   [rik'-oh-vur]

An admiral in the U.S. Navy, Hyman George Rickover, b. Russia, Jan. 27 (N.S.), 1900, d. July 8, 1986, was a leader in the development of nuclear propulsion for submarines and other naval ships and a critic of the U.S. educational system. He was raised in Chicago and educated at the U.S. Naval Academy and at Columbia University. During World War II he was head of the electrical section of the navy's Bureau of Ships. Rickover became convinced of the feasibility of nuclear-powered naval vessels, and in 1947 he was put in charge of the navy's nuclear-power program and appointed head of the Atomic Energy Commission's naval reactor branch. He directed the planning and construction of the world's first nuclear-powered submarine, the U.S.S. NAUTILUS, launched in 1954. In 1982, Rickover was forced to retire from active duty. His criticisms of U.S. education are contained in *Education and Freedom* (1959), *Swiss Schools and Ours: Why Theirs Are Better* (1962), and *American Education: A National Failure* (1963).

Bibliography: Blair, Clay, *The Atomic Submarine and Admiral Rickover* (1954); Polmar, Norman, and Allen, T. B., *Rickover* (1982); Tyler, Patrick, *Running Critical* (1986).

Ricoeur, Paul   [ree-kur']

Paul Ricoeur, b. Feb. 27, 1913, is a French philosopher who has taught at the universities of Paris and Chicago. He has tried to ground hermeneutics (the theory of interpretation) in phenomenology (a philosophic method stressing the description of experience), focusing on problems of language. Ricoeur's writings cover a wide range—psychoanalysis, religion, language, symbolism, and political and social thought. His three-part *Philosophy of the Will* (1950–60) is influential among philosophers and theologians.

riddles

A riddle is a question or a statement of a problem worded so that it has a double, or hidden, meaning. Riddles are of ancient origin. Oracles and soothsayers often couched knowledge in riddle form, believing that knowledge was a precious commodity not to be freely given to those of inferior intellect. Aristotle saw riddles as metaphorical statements of the symbolic meaning of natural phenomena.

Riddles are found in the Bible and the Koran and form a central part of Zen Buddhism (see KOAN). One famous riddle, found in Greek mythology, was solved by Oedipus. The Sphinx of Thebes asked him: "What animal is it that in the morning goes on four feet, at noon on two, and in the evening upon three?" Oedipus replied, "Man, who in childhood creeps on hands and knees, in manhood walks erect, and in old age goes with the aid of a staff."

Bibliography: Taylor, Archer, *The Literary Riddle before 1600* (1948; repr. 1976); Pepicello, W. J., and Green, Thomas A., *The Language of Riddles* (1984).

Ride, Sally

Sally Kirsten Ride, b. Encino, Calif., May 26, 1951, the first woman U.S. astronaut and third woman in space, received a Ph.D. in physics from Stanford University in 1977 and was selected as an astronaut in 1978. She flew on SPACE SHUTTLE missions on June 18–24, 1983, and Oct. 5–13, 1984. In 1986, Ride served on the presidential commission appointed to investigate the Shuttle *Challenger* disaster in January of that year. She was then appointed a special assistant to the administrator of NASA, heading a 10-member study team designed to guide U.S. space planning into the 21st century. Their 1987 report, which she wrote, called for a strong earth sciences program and establishment of a lunar base. Ride left NASA in 1987 to join the Stanford University Center for International Security and Arms Control.

Ridgway, Matthew B.

Matthew Bunker Ridgway, b. Fort Monroe, Va., Mar. 3, 1895, a U.S. commander in World War II, became commander of the United Nations forces during the KOREAN WAR. He graduated from West Point in 1917 and served in routine assignments between the two world wars. Named commander of the 82d Airborne Division in March 1942, Ridgway planned and led the first important airborne attack in American military history in the assault on Sicily (July 1943). He jumped with his troops into Normandy in June 1944 and later led the 18th Airborne Corps in important campaigns in Europe in the closing months of World War II.

Ridgway assumed command of the U.S. Eighth Army in December 1950 and halted the Chinese Communist invasion of South Korea. Becoming a full general and succeeding Douglas MacArthur as U.N. commander in April 1951, he drove the enemy out of most of South Korea and penetrated into North Korea. Ridgway was named NATO supreme commander in Europe in 1952 and U.S. Army chief of staff a year later. He retired in 1955. He wrote his memoirs, *Soldier* (1956), and *The Korean War* (1967).   WARREN W. HASSLER, JR.

riding

Riding and the equestrian arts comprise the techniques used to control a horse in its direction, gait, and speed; the knowledge of equine equipment (known as tack) and how it functions; and the ability to train and groom a horse. Riding styles, as well as apparel and tack, were developed out of specific historical requirements that were then modified to suit contemporary sporting needs.

Whatever the riding style or activity, riders communicate to their horses by means of aids, or cues. Leg, hand (by means of reins), body weight, and voice are the natural aids, while whip and spurs are the so-called artificial aids. After learning to mount, dismount, and attain proper body position, the novice rider must undertake to coordinate the aids, an important step in becoming proficient. To make the transition from the halt to the walk, for example, the rider squeezes his or her lower legs against the horse's sides at the girth to generate forward impetus while simultaneously relaxing the hands to allow the horse to begin moving. If necessary, a call or gentle application of crop (whip) or spurs will reinforce the command. To achieve the walk from a faster gait, the rider's hands restrain the mount while the legs, kept at the girth, prevent it from coming to a complete halt.

Various styles of riding require different techniques on the part of the rider, as well as specialized tack and apparel. Basic to each style is the "seat," or the rider's position in the saddle.

English-style riding is characterized by relatively lightweight, flat saddles. Posting to the trot, a continuous up-and-down body movement, is common to this style.

Hunter-seat riding takes its name from the sport of fox hunting. Until the end of the 19th century, fox hunters leaned backwards when jumping. The introduction of the forward seat, however, shifted the rider's weight to a point over the horse's center of gravity, in front of the saddle. The result was greater safety and control. In hunter-seat equitation the rider's upper body inclines forward at the trot and canter and especially over fences. Hands follow the horse's head and neck motion, particularly when jumping. Short stirrups enable the rider to clear the saddle, which has a slightly elevated cantle, or rear, designed to facilitate the proper jumping position. Breeches and leather boots extending almost to the knee provide support for the legs. A hard peaked hunt cap protects the head in case of falls.

In HORSE SHOWS, hunter-seat events include equitation classes; hunter classes, in which horses are judged on style, pace, and manners; and jumper classes, in which they are scored on their ability to clear high fences. Most of the horses so used are Thoroughbreds. Training a hunter or jumper begins by teaching the animal to negotiate low obstacles athletically and responsively. To maintain the horse's confidence, the heights and widths of fences are increased gradually.

Jessica Ransehousen and her mount canter about an earthen enclosure. The canter—along with the walk, trot, and gallop—is one of the natural gaits assumed by pleasure horses. For a brief moment during the canter, all four legs of the horse are raised off the ground.

The rider Klaus J. Jacobs and his horse demonstrate the extended trot at a show of precision riding in Switzerland. During the trot, which is considered the easiest gait for a horse to maintain, each diagonal pair of the animal's legs move alternately.

Saddle-Horse breeds and types originally provided comfortable mounts on which Southern plantation owners inspected their vast holdings. In saddle-seat riding the rider's legs are extended farther down than in hunter-seat riding and are not held against the horse's sides; hands are held high and somewhat apart; and the upper body is maintained at the vertical in all gaits. Thin, flat saddles interfere as little as possible with Saddle Horses' rapid and elevated leg movements, and double bridles, with both snaffle and curb bits, afford maximum control. Low boots, jodhpurs, and derby hats are proper apparel for showing in equitation, three-gaited classes (walk, trot, and canter), and five-gaited classes (plus slow gait and rack).

Cattle roping and other such ranch chores required cowboys to have secure yet maneuverable seats. In stock-seat riding the rider sits erect with legs extending almost straight down. Both reins are held in one hand above the high pommel, or saddle horn, of the heavy Western stock saddle. Western-trained horses are taught to neck rein (change direction in response to pressure on their necks) and to make sliding, rapid halts at the touch of the long-shanked curb bits. Riders wear broad-brimmed, tall hats, jeans or frontier pants under wide, protective leather chaps, and high-heeled boots. Stock-seat riding is seen primarily at rodeos, although some horse shows include equitation, parade (where tack and apparel are judged), and reining classes. Breeds so used include Quarter Horses, pintos, Appaloosas, and Arabians.

In dressage (a French word for "systematic training") competition, horses and riders are scored on how well they perform prescribed tests of patterns that vary in difficulty according to proficiency and experience. More advanced levels call for collection and extension (shortening and lengthening stride) and lateral movements. Dressage saddles are similar to saddle-seat tack, although with slightly more padding. Riders wear hunter-seat apparel or, at higher levels, tailcoats and top hats.

STEVEN D. PRICE

Bibliography: Burn, Barbara, *The Horseless Rider* (1979); Crabtree, Helen, *Saddle-Seat Equitation* (1970); Morris, George H., *Hunter-Seat Equitation* (1979); Prince, Eleanor F., and Collier, Gaydell M., *Basic Horsemanship: English and Western* (1974); Steinkraus, William C., *Riding and Jumping* (1969).

Ridley, Nicholas [rid'-lee]

Nicholas Ridley, b. c.1500, d. Oct. 16, 1555, was an English reformer and bishop who was martyred under Queen Mary I. Following studies at Cambridge and in France, he returned (1530) to Cambridge as a fellow of Pembroke College. Ridley served as chaplain to Archbishop Thomas Cranmer, whom he later helped compile (1549) the Book of Common Prayer, as bishop of Rochester, and from 1550 as bishop of London. Deprived of his see under the Catholic Queen Mary, he was convicted of heresy and burned at the stake in Oxford with Hugh LATIMER.

Bibliography: Ridley, Jasper G., *Nicholas Ridley* (1957).

ridley turtle

Two species of sea turtles in the family Cheloniidae are called ridley turtles. Both may attain a length of about 700 mm (27.5 in) and commonly weigh between 30 and 36 kg (65 and 80 lb). The Indo-Pacific ridley, *Lepidochelys olivacea*, occurs in parts of the Indian, the Pacific, and possibly the Atlantic oceans. It is almost uniformly olive colored and has at least six or seven large scales (pleural scutes) on each side of the midline of the upper shell (carapace). This turtle is mainly vegetarian, but shellfish and sea urchins are reported to be in its diet. Population of this overexploited species is becoming seriously depleted. The Atlantic ridley, *L. kempi*, the smallest of the Atlantic sea turtles and an endangered species, is found from the Gulf of Mexico northward along the Atlantic coast to Massachusetts. It has a gray coloration and only five pleural scutes on each side of the carapace. It nests from Texas to Veracruz, Mexico, but its main nesting site is a beach in Tamaulipas, Mexico.   JONATHAN CAMPBELL

The Indo-Pacific ridley, L. olivacea, a sea turtle, has been exploited for leather and oil in such areas as the Pacific coast of Mexico.

Riefenstahl, Leni   [ree'-fen-shtahl]

Adolf Hitler's favorite film director, Leni Riefenstahl, b. Berlin, Aug. 22, 1902, achieved an international reputation on the basis of two extraordinary documentaries. Her first film, the mystical *Blue Light* (1932), excited Hitler's imagination, and following her short documentary of the Nazi party's 1933 Nuremberg rally, *Victory of Faith* (1934), he commissioned her to give feature-length treatment to the same event in 1934. The result, *Triumph of the Will* (1935), was an impressive spectacle of Germany's adherence to Hitler and to National Socialist ideals, and a masterpiece of romanticized propaganda. Equally famous, and far less controversial, was her coverage of the 1936 Olympic Games in Berlin, the four-hour epic *Olympia* (1938). Blacklisting by the Allies (1945–52) and postwar ostracism ended Riefenstahl's career as a filmmaker. She was subsequently acclaimed for *The Last of the Nuba* (1974), a superb volume of photographs of Nuba tribal life in southern Sudan.   ROGER MANVELL

Bibliography: Infield, Glenn B., *Leni Riefenstahl* (1976); Sarris, Andrew, *Interviews with Film Directors* (1967).

Riel, Louis   [ree-el']

Louis Riel, b. Saint Boniface (now in Manitoba), Oct. 23, 1844, d. Nov. 16, 1885, Canadian rebel, led the métis—persons of mixed French and Indian background—in western Canada. Of métis origin, he began but did not complete studies for the priesthood in Montreal. Returning to the RED RIVER SETTLE-

Louis Riel, a 19th-century Canadian insurrectionist, exhorted Indians and métis, those of French-Indian extraction, to rise up against the transfer of their land in the Red River Settlement to Canadian authority in 1869. In 1884–85 he led a similar uprising in Saskatchewan but was captured and hanged.

MENT, where he had been born, he assumed (1869) leadership of the métis there who feared that their land rights and other interests were jeopardized by the transfer of HUDSON'S BAY COMPANY territories to Canada (see RED RIVER REBELLION). Riel was chosen president of a provisional government, and he and his representatives negotiated the admission of the settlement (1870) into the Canadian Confederation as the province of Manitoba. Soon after, however, Canadian troops suppressed his government, and Riel fled to the United States. After a period of wandering and confinement (1876–78) in asylums in Quebec, he settled in Montana as a teacher in 1879.

Called to Saskatchewan in 1884 to lead métis and whites in protests against Canada's western policies, Riel at first employed peaceful methods, but he soon (1885) set up a rebel government with the backing of the métis and Indians. On the defeat of his forces, he was captured and executed for high treason despite evidence of insanity. His execution intensified latent ethnic animosity in Canada.   ANDRÉE DÉSILETS

Bibliography: Flanagan, Thomas, *Louis David Riel: "Prophet of the New World"* (1979); Stanley, G. F. G., *Louis Riel* (1963) and *The Birth of Western Canada* (1961); Walsh, Frederick G., *The Trial of Louis Riel* (1965).

Riemann, Georg Friedrich Bernhard   [ree'-mahn]

Georg Friedrich Bernhard Riemann, b. Sept. 17, 1826, d. July 20, 1866, was one of the most influential 19th-century German mathematicians. He developed the subjects of partial differential equations, complex variable theory, differential geometry, and analytic number theory and laid the foundations for modern topology. His paper "Über die Hypothesen, welche der Geometrie zu Grunde liegen" (On the Hypotheses Which Lie at the Foundation of Geometry), presented in 1854, became a classic of mathematics, and its results were incorporated into Albert EINSTEIN's relativistic theory of gravitation.

Bibliography: Bell, Eric T., *Men of Mathematics* (1973).

See also: NON-EUCLIDEAN GEOMETRY.

Riemenschneider, Tilman   [ree'-men-shny'-dur]

Perhaps the greatest German sculptor of the late Gothic period, Tilman Riemenschneider, c.1460–1531, spent most of his life in Würzburg, where he was a leading citizen, held government office, and taught numerous pupils who promulgated his style.

In addition to many statues in stone and wood, particularly several versions of the Madonna and Child theme, all of Riemenschneider's major works were either stone tombs or large wooden altarpieces. The delicately carved *Altarpiece of Mary Magdalen* for the parish church of Münnerstadt (1490–92; now dispersed), based largely on engravings by Martin Schongauer, was his earliest masterpiece. His finest later works include the *Altar of the Holy Blood* in the Jakobskirche at Rothenburg (1501–05) and the *Altar of the Virgin* in the Herrgottskirche at Creglingen (c.1505–10). The architectural structures of these works are characteristically late Gothic in their extravagance and complexity, but the compositions of the individual scenes are remarkable for their balance and restraint. The figures show extraordinary insight and sensitivity.

Riemenschneider's tombs are among the most important monuments of their kind. The outstanding examples are the monuments of Prince Bishop Rudolf von Scherenberg in the Cathedral of Würzburg (1496–99); of Marshal Konrad von Schaumberg in the Marienkapelle at Würzburg (c.1499–1502); and of Emperor Henry II and his wife, Kunigunde, in the Cathedral of Bamberg (1499–1513). MARK J. ZUCKER

Bibliography: Müller, Theodor, *Sculpture in the Netherlands, Germany, France, and Spain, 1400–1500* (1966).

Rienzo, Cola di   [ree-ent'-soh]

Cola di Rienzo (or Rienzi), b. 1313, d. Oct. 8, 1354, Roman demagogue and revolutionary, tried to restore the Roman republic with himself at its head. A notary, he became (1344) the representative in Rome of Pope CLEMENT VI, who was in Avignon. Using this office he exiled local nobles and proclaimed himself tribune in 1347. He briefly won the support of the Roman people by lowering taxes and claiming Rome as capital of Italy but was soon forced into exile. After imprisonment in Prague and Avignon, Rienzo returned to Rome in 1354 as envoy of Pope Innocent VI. Popular discontent with his oppressive government led to a revolt during which Rienzo was killed. BENJAMIN G. KOHL

Bibliography: Fleischer, V. R., *The Rise and Fall of a Dictator* (1948; repr. 1970).

Riesener, Jean Henri   [ree-zuhn-air']

Jean Henri Riesener, 1734–1806, the most celebrated FURNITURE maker of the Louis XVI period, was a German by birth. He served an apprenticeship in Paris at the atelier of Jean François OEBEN, whom he succeeded upon Oeben's death in 1763. In 1768, Riesener married Oeben's widow and was made a master. Appointed *ébéniste du Roi* (royal cabinetmaker) in 1774, Riesener provided luxurious furniture for the French royal palaces during the following decade. His rich and extravagant pieces of this period are characterized by elaborate pictorial marquetry (wood inlay) with ormolu (gilt bronze) mounts. By the mid-1780s, however, serious attempts were made to curtail royal expenditures, and Riesener turned to veneers of plain woods and simple latticework patterns. No neat stylistic progression marks his output, however: the curvilinear complexities of Oeben's earlier rococo style remained as congenial to Riesener as the rectilinear simplicities of the emerging neoclassical style. Surviving the French Revolution and continuing in business until 1806, Riesener repurchased many of his earlier pieces. During the Directory period (see DIRECTOIRE STYLE) his workshops were busy cleansing earlier furniture—including his own—of feudal insignia.

Bibliography: Boger, Louise A., *The Complete Guide to Furniture Styles,* rev. ed. (1969).

See also: STYLES OF LOUIS XIII–XVI.

Riesman, David, Jr.   [rees'-muhn]

David Riesman, Jr., b. Philadelphia, Sept. 22, 1909, collaborated with Nathan Glazer and Reuel Denney on *The Lonely Crowd: A Study of the Changing American Character* (1950). Riesman made the famous distinction between "tradition-directed," "inner-directed," and "other-directed" societies; the first type uses tradition, the second a person's internal values, and the third other people's expectations to develop con-

formity in its members. Riesman has also made numerous contributions to the study of education in the United States and since 1967 has been a member of the Carnegie Commission on Higher Education.

Rietveld, Gerrit Thomas   [reet'-felt]

A leading member of the Dutch art movement called neoplasticism, or DE STIJL, and a contributor to its magazine, *De Stijl* (The Style), Gerrit Rietveld, b. June 24, 1888, d. July 25, 1964, devoted his early career to the design of furniture. His renowned red blue armchair (1918), entirely of wood, was an attempt to distinguish, by differences in color and scale, between the surfaces supporting the body and the structure maintaining these surfaces above the ground, which helped to open the way for the famous furniture designs of the Bauhaus. In 1924, Rietveld designed his principal work of architecture, the Schröder House in Utrecht, whose interpenetrating white, gray, and colored planes form a virtual three-dimensional translation of the paintings of Piet Mondrian, the leading neoplasticist painter. Following the revival of interest in *de Stijl* after World War II, Rietveld received a number of important commissions, including one for a large home (1951) for crippled children in Curaçao, and the Soonsbeek sculpture pavilion (1954), now part of the Kröller-Müller Museum at Otterlo, the Netherlands. ANN VAN ZANTEN

Bibliography: Baroni, Daniele, *The Furniture of Gerrit Thomas Rietveld* (1978); Brown, T. M., *Gerrit Rietveld, Architect* (1970).

Rif   [reef]

The Rif is a mountain range in northwestern Africa, which extends 270 km (180 mi) from Tangier along the Mediterranean coast of Morocco. It is a rugged region of difficult access inhabited by BERBERS. Of its many minerals, only iron ore is mined on a large scale. The highest peak is Tidiquin (2,455 m/8,054 ft).

rifampin: see ANTIBIOTICS.

rifle

A rifle is a small firearm that is braced against the shoulder when it is discharged. Its name is derived from the rifling, the shallow spiral grooves within the barrel that impart a spin to the bullet in order to give it greater accuracy. The term *rifle* may therefore be applied to any gun with a rifled barrel.

Rifled barrels were made and fitted to muzzle-loading muskets as early as the 15th century. Cutting the rifling was a slow, laborious process because each spiral groove had to be cut separately. Nevertheless, some excellent barrels were produced by manual methods. As early as 1732, German-American gunsmiths produced the forerunners of the extremely accurate, long-barreled Kentucky rifle, which took its name from its use by Kentucky sharpshooters in the Battle of New Orleans (1815).

The conversion from muzzle-loading smoothbore muskets to muzzle-loading rifles of the Kentucky type was the first stage in progression toward the modern rifle. The next development was the breech-loading rifle, loaded at the rear of the barrel, which was first issued in quantity in 1819. In Great Britain the first breech-loaders were conversions of muzzle-loaders, which the British army had in quantity. Fifty different systems were tested and examined at Woolwich Arsenal before the one designed by Jacob Snider of New York was selected as the simplest and most effective.

The next development, the magazine rifle, came in response to a military demand for increased firepower. Such weapons had magazines that stored several rounds of ammunition and had a means of transferring the rounds to the firing chamber. A reduction in the caliber size and better propellants permitted a smaller charge to be used and consequently reduced the size and weight of the ammunition. Improvements in manufacturing techniques also facilitated the production of interchangeable components.

The bolt-action magazine rifle was perfected by about 1890,

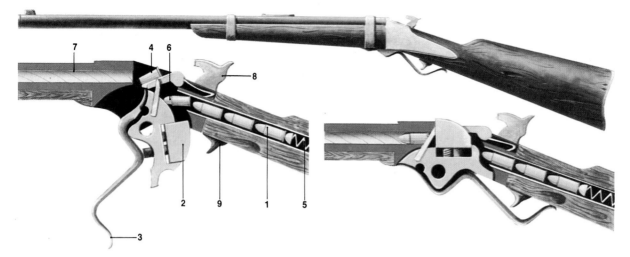

The Spencer Carbine (top) *uses the action of a lever to load and eject cartridges; its operation is seen in the cutaway drawing (above left). Cartridges are stored in a tubular magazine (1) in the butt of the gun, where they are held in place by the breech block (2). Depressing the lever (3) ejects the spent cartridge (4) and, by lowering the breech block, allows the spring (5) to push a fresh cartridge into the breech (6). Raising the lever brings the breech block into contact with the fresh cartridge, pushes it into the barrel (7), and closes the breech. The gun is fired by cocking the hammer (8) and then pulling the trigger (9). (Above right)* The Spencer Carbine, hammer cocked, is ready for firing.

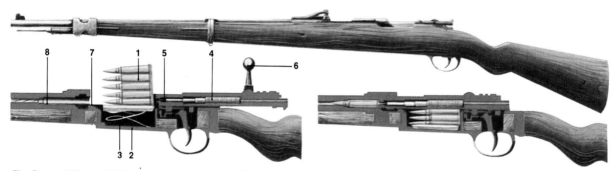

The German 7.92-mm (0.31-in) Mauser (top) *is a typical bolt-action rifle; the cutaway drawing (above left) illustrates its operation. The Mauser is loaded by inserting a five-round clip of ammunition (1) into a magazine (2) containing a spring (3). The cartridges are held in place by the bolt mechanism (4)—a metal cylinder containing the firing pin (5)—which is moved back and forth over the magazine using the bolt handle (6). When the bolt mechanism is retracted, the spring pushes a cartridge into the breech (7); when pushed forward, the bolt mechanism slides a cartridge into the firing chamber (8), closes the breech, and cocks the rifle. (Above right)* The loaded Mauser is ready for firing.

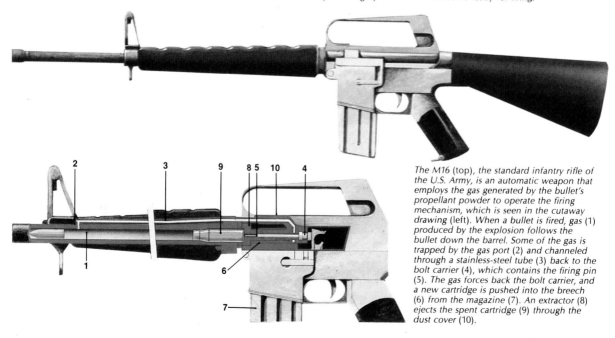

The M16 (top), *the standard infantry rifle of the U.S. Army, is an automatic weapon that employs the gas generated by the bullet's propellant powder to operate the firing mechanism, which is seen in the cutaway drawing (left). When a bullet is fired, gas (1) produced by the explosion follows the bullet down the barrel. Some of the gas is trapped by the gas port (2) and channeled through a stainless-steel tube (3) back to the bolt carrier (4), which contains the firing pin (5). The gas forces back the bolt carrier, and a new cartridge is pushed into the breech (6) from the magazine (7). An extractor (8) ejects the spent cartridge (9) through the dust cover (10).*

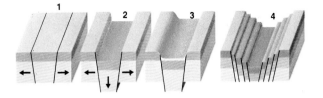

and within 10 years the armies of all the major nations were equipped with a version of it. These rifles weighed 3.5–4 kg (8–9 lb) and were sighted to a distance of about 2,000 m (6,600 ft).

Since its introduction the magazine rifle has undergone little design change. Minor refinements have been made, better ammunition has been developed, and smokeless powder has replaced black powder. The only concessions to modernity have been in the simplification of the sights, reductions in barrel and overall length, and the adaptation of designs suitable for mass-production techniques.

The final stage in the development of the rifle—automatic rifles—came recently. During the later 19th century, inventors strove to design rifles that used some of the energy developed by the combustion of the charge to reload the weapon automatically. Their efforts to produce semiautomatic and fully automatic rifles were hampered by the inconsistent quality of the available ammunition and by the lack of metal components. Some gas-operated semiautomatic rifles were produced. Those which were field-tested in the trenches during World War I, however, failed to gain favor because mud quickly clogged their mechanisms.

During the interwar years new designs of semiautomatic and fully automatic rifles were tested in several countries, but by 1939 only the United States and the USSR had issued self-loading weapons to their troops. The U.S. M1 Garand rifle, despite its failings, was the outstanding weapon of its class in the early years of World War II, and the production by the Germans of a 7.92-mm (0.31-in) intermediate round (a lighter-weight bullet than had been standard) and of the MP43 *Sturmgewehr* during the war influenced further development. The design of automatic rifles has probably now reached its zenith in such weapons as the Soviet AKM (Kalashnikov), the U.S. M16, the Swiss SG510, and the various U.S.-made Stoner and Armalite guns.   A. J. BARKER

Bibliography: Archer, D., *Jane's Pocket Book of Rifles and Light Machine Guns* (1977); Ezell, E. C., *The AK47 Story* (1986) and *The Great Rifle Controversy* (1984); Hogg, I. V., and Weeks, J., *Military Small Arms of the Twentieth Century* (1973); McNaugher, T. L., *The M-16 Controversies* (1984); Myatt, F., *An Illustrated Guide to Rifles and Automatic Weapons* (1985); Taylor, C., *The Fighting Rifle* (1986).

Rift Valley fever: see VIRUS.

rift valleys

Rift valleys are characteristically long, nearly linear valleys with steep, straight valley walls and often flat bottoms. They are formed by faulting along one or both valley walls; the floor of the valley is downdropped relative to the surrounding regions in response to extension of the crust. Rift-valley development is often considered to mark the site of the initial rifting apart of a continent prior to its separation by SEAFLOOR SPREADING, but not all rift valleys result in complete continental separation. The floor of the Gulf of Suez, for example, is a rift valley forming where Arabia is moving apart from Africa; seafloor spreading has not yet commenced, however, because the floor of the gulf is entirely continental. If the process continues, magma will eventually be injected into the center of the rift, forming new seafloor and marking the inception of seafloor spreading and the formation of a new ocean basin, as in the RED SEA. Alternatively, extension may cease, leaving a fully continental rift valley as a scar.

When active extension is taking place, rift valleys are sites of earthquake activity and, if extension is sufficient, volcanic activity. The most spectacular rift valleys are those of the EAST AFRICAN RIFT SYSTEM, a series of rift valleys extending more than 4,000 km (2,500 mi) through eastern Africa from Ethiopia to Mozambique. This rift system is the site of active volcanism and seismic activity, and although it has been active for the past 50 million years, it is still a continental rift.

Other active rift valleys include the MID-OCEANIC RIDGE, the DEAD SEA rift in the Middle East, the Baikal rift in central USSR, and the Shanshi graben in China. *Graben* (see HORST AND GRABEN) is a term sometimes used synonymously with rift

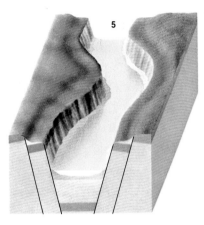

A rift valley is formed when tensional forces pull apart (1) the Earth's crust. An elongated, steep-sided trench (2) results when a graben, or crustal block, drops between two faults created by the tension. The sharp edges eventually are rounded (3) by erosion. A number of parallel faults (4) may allow the graben to sink in steps and form a step-faulted rift valley (5).

valley. Rifts in which extension ceased at an early stage and that are no longer active include the Rhine graben, which comprises most of the valleys of the Rhine and Rhône rivers of northern Europe, and the Connecticut River valley and Newark basin of the eastern United States. Just as both margins of the Red Sea were originally rift-valley margins, much of the continental slopes of continental margins are also of extensional origin. The east coasts of North and South America and the west coasts of Africa and Europe were formed by rift-valley development.   CHRISTOPHER H. SCHOLZ

Bibliography: Courtillot, Vincent, and Vink, G. E., "How Continents Break Up," *Scientific American*, July 1983; Quennell, Albert M., ed., *Rift Valley: Afro-Arabian* (1982) and *Continental Rifts* (1985); Selby, M. J., *Earth's Changing Surface* (1985).

Riga   [ree'-guh]

Riga is the capital of the Latvian republic of the USSR. Riga is situated along the Western Dvina River near its mouth on the Gulf of Riga of the Baltic Sea. The city's population is 875,000 (1984 est.), making Riga the largest city in the Baltic republics. The population is mixed, with 45% Russians, 40% Latvians, and 4% each Jews, Belorussians, and Ukrainians.

Riga consists of an old medieval city center, with narrow, winding streets and distinctive Gothic architecture, and a newer section with a grid street plan and modern buildings. The city has a cool, maritime climate, with a mean January temperature just below freezing and a mean July temperature of 17° C (62° F). Precipitation totals approximately 610 mm (24 in) annually. An attractive seacoast of sand dunes to the west of the city has given rise to one of the USSR's leading beach resorts, the city of Jurmala (1984 est. pop., 63,000).

Riga is a major Soviet seaport and manufacturing center, specializing in telephone equipment, radios, electrical equipment, transport equipment (electric rail cars and streetcars), and machine tools. The port carries on an active commercial cargo trade with Western Europe and serves as the base for an Atlantic deep-sea fishing fleet. As the cultural center of Latvia, the city is the seat of Latvian University (1919) and of the Latvian Academy of Sciences.

Founded in 1201 by the Teutonic Knights, Riga developed as a trading center between Russia and the Baltic Sea. It was a member of the Hanseatic League. It passed to Russia in 1721 and became one of that country's major seaports; manufacturing began in the later 19th century. Riga was the capital of independent Latvia from 1918 to 1940 and has remained the republic's capital under Soviet rule.   THEODORE SHABAD

Rigaud, Hyacinthe   [ree-goh', ee-ah-sant']

The French painter Hyacinthe Rigaud, b. July 18, 1659, d. Dec. 29, 1743, became the chief portraitist of the French royal court and one of Europe's most celebrated masters of portraiture. After serving apprenticeships in Montpellier and Lyons, Rigaud entered the École de l'Académie Royale in Paris in 1681. Rigaud was attracted by the robustness of the Flemish baroque style, especially as seen in the work of Sir Anthony van Dyck. His own paintings were often opulent, indulging his patrons' taste for extravagance, but Rigaud could also capture his sitter's personality. His most famous portrait is that of Louis XIV (1701; Louvre, Paris).   F. LANIER GRAHAM

Bibliography: Kalnein, Wend Graf, and Levey, Michael, *Art and Architecture of the 18th Century in France* (1972); Thuillier, Jacques, and Châtelet, Albert, *French Painting from Le Nain to Fragonard* (1964).

right of asylum

The right of asylum is the right to receive sanctuary or refuge in a foreign state, granted by that state to an individual who has been forced to flee his or her native country. The right most often pertains to political refugees, who are prevented from returning to their own countries because of a "well-founded fear of being persecuted for reasons of race, religion, nationality, or political opinion"—to quote from the United Nations Convention of 1951, which first established a definition of these refugees and outlined their rights to work, education, social security, and access to the courts in their country of asylum. Ninety-six nations, including the United States, had signed the Convention by the mid-1980s.

The notion of asylum is an ancient one. For many centuries, fugitives from the law, war, or private disputes could often find asylum in churches. As the authority of the church declined in Europe, these once-inviolable shelters became less secure (see SANCTUARY). It has always been the prerogative of a state, however, to choose whether or not to grant asylum to a refugee. Diplomatic asylum, based on EXTRATERRITORIALITY—that is, the principle that a nation's embassies and consulates are an extension of its territory—has sometimes been granted to political fugitives. (For example, Jozsef, Cardinal MINDSZENTY, lived as a refugee in the U.S. Embassy in Budapest from 1956 to 1971.)

After World War II, many thousands of European refugees were allowed to settle in the United States. From 1952, however, with the passage of the restrictive McCarren-Walter Immigration Act, the U.S. recognized as political refugees only those who had fled from Communist countries. The law was liberalized in 1980, using the language of the UN Convention. Nevertheless, the U.S. Immigration and Naturalization Service rarely grants the status of "political" refugee, labeling many of those who would claim it as "economic" refugees who seek a more comfortable life rather than political asylum.

Bibliography: Bau, I., *This Ground Is Holy: Church Sanctuary and Central American Refugees* (1985); Rubin, G. E., *The Asylum Challenge to Western Nations* (1984); Sinha, S. P., *Asylum and International Law* (1971).

right to bear arms

The right to bear arms is stated in the 2D AMENDMENT to the U.S. Constitution: "A well regulated militia being necessary to the security of a free State, the right of the people to keep and bear arms shall not be infringed." Opponents of gun-control laws cite the 2d Amendment as authority to declare all such laws unconstitutional. The Supreme Court (in *United States v. Cruikshank*, 1876, and *United States v. Miller*, 1939), however, has consistently ruled that the 2d Amendment protects only the states' rights to maintain a MILITIA and does not apply to the private ownership of guns.

right-handedness: see HANDEDNESS.

right to life movement: see ABORTION.

right of search

The right of search, in international law, permits a country at war to stop and search vessels on the high seas to prevent CONTRABAND of war from reaching the enemy. The right extends to private vessels from neutral countries. It is often used in conjunction with a BLOCKADE of the enemy's ports. During the Napoleonic Wars, British warships seized the cargoes of U.S. merchant ships trading with France and sometimes impressed American sailors into the Royal Navy. The United States, insisting on its neutral right (see NEUTRALITY) to trade with any nation, argued that the only contraband of war subject to seizure was munitions. The British replied that almost any product could aid the French war effort. This wrangle over neutral rights poisoned Anglo-American relations and was a precipitating factor of the WAR OF 1812. Today the British position prevails (except for impressment), and nations at war have a wide leeway in defining contraband.

right-to-work laws

Right-to-work laws are state laws that prohibit union-management agreements requiring a worker to join a union in order to obtain or hold a job. Most of these laws prohibit the CLOSED SHOP, in which employers hire only union members; the UNION SHOP, in which workers must join the union within a certain period of time after being hired; and agreements that require workers to maintain union membership in order to keep their jobs.

The "right to work" was originally a socialist slogan, formulated (1808) by Charles FOURIER, that became associated with trade unionism. It is a guaranteed right in the constitutions of many Communist countries, including Bulgaria and the USSR.

In the United States the phrase has become associated with management's efforts to put a brake on the growth of union membership. Aid was given to right-to-work advocates by the Taft-Hartley Act (1947; see LABOR-MANAGEMENT RELATIONS ACT), which banned the closed shop. It did permit the union shop under certain conditions but allowed state laws to take precedence. In the mid-1980s 21 states had right-to-work laws.

Bibliography: Anderson, N., *The Right to Work* (1938; repr. 1973); Dempsey, J. R., *The Operation of the Right-to-Work Laws* (1961); Hanson, C., et al., *The Closed Shop: A Comparative Study of Public Policy and Trade Union Security in Britain, the U.S.A., and West Germany* (1982).

Riis, Jacob August   [rees]

A journalist, photographer, and reformer, Jacob August Riis, b. May 3, 1849, d. May 26, 1914, publicized the plight of immi-

Jacob Riis's 1890s portrait of the Talmud School on Hester Street starkly records the material poverty of immigrants to New York's Lower East Side. His work inspired photographers who documented the Depression of the 1930s. (Museum of the City of New York.)

grants in New York City slum tenements. Born in Denmark, he moved to the United States at the age of 21, drifted into newspaper work, and worked as a police reporter for the *New York Tribune*. His photographs, articles, and books focused on the squalid living conditions of the city's poor and spurred legislation to improve those conditions. Among his books, *How the Other Half Lives* (1890) was most effective in this regard. Also celebrated is Riis's autobiography, *The Making of an American* (1901; repr. 1983). After retiring from newspaper work, Riis continued to campaign for improvements in urban living, such as better housing, parks, and playgrounds.

DONALD H. JOHNSTON

Bibliography: Lane, James B., ed., *Jacob A. Riis and the American City* (1974); Meyer, Edith P., *Not Charity, but Justice: The Story of Jacob Riis* (1974); Ware, Louis, *Jacob A. Riis: Police Reporter, Reformer, Useful Citizen* (1938; repr. 1975).

Rijeka   [ree-ek'-ah]

Rijeka, or Fiume, is a major port and naval base of Yugoslavia. The population is 193,044 (1981). Rijeka is located in the republic of Croatia on the Kvarner Gulf of the Adriatic Sea, about 60 km (40 mi) southeast of Trieste. The Julian Alps separate the city from the interior. Fishing, building and repairing ships, petroleum refining, and the production of machinery, paper, and leather goods are the mainstays of the economy. Lumber, sugar, and flour are exported, and petroleum, grains, phosphates, and coal are imported. Railroad connections link Rijeka with other Yugoslavian cities. Among its ancient landmarks are a Roman arch (1st century AD) and a 17th-century cathedral.

A fishing settlement before the Christian era, Rijeka was occupied by the Romans and named Tarsatica. Slavs settled the area during the 6th–7th century. In 1471 the city fell to Austria. Rijeka gained importance as a free port early in the 18th century, but its main growth came after Hungary took control in 1779. The city was held by Austria-Hungary for most of the 19th century. At the end of World War I, Rijeka was disputed between Italy and Yugoslavia, and in September 1919 the Italian nationalist poet Gabriele D'ANNUNZIO led an Italian free corps in seizing the city. He withdrew after the Treaty of Rapallo (1920) established Rijeka as a free port. In 1924, Rijeka was incorporated into Mussolini's Italy. Taken by the Yugoslavs in 1945, the city became part of Yugoslavia in 1947.

Rijksmuseum   [ryks'-moo-zay-uhm]

The Rijksmuseum, situated in Amsterdam, is the Dutch national museum. Its collection of approximately 5,000 paintings represents the variety of Dutch art from the 15th to the 19th century and includes major works from other countries.

The first step toward the creation of a national gallery was taken in 1808 when Louis Napoleon, then king of Holland, created the Great Royal Museum by taking over the collection of the National Art Gallery (opened 1800). In 1815 the collection was moved to the Trippenhuis and in 1885 to the present location, an eclectic Gothic-Renaissance structure designed by P. J. H. CUYPERS. It opened officially as the Rijksmuseum on July 13, 1885.

The Rijksmuseum originally incorporated five older collections (and their combined libraries): the National Painting Museum, the National Collection of Modern Art, the Netherlands Museum of History and Art, a collection of plaster casts of statuary that was disposed of after 1925, and the National Print and Drawing collection. In the 1920s a department of foreign art opened. Since 1952 the museum has housed the Collection of the Society of the Friends of the Arts of Asia, and in 1965 the department of Asiatic art was founded.

The major strength of the collection lies in the representation of 17th-century Dutch painting, including works by Frans Hals, Jan Steen, Jan Vermeer, and Rembrandt. Also well represented are the 15th-century masters from the northern Low Countries and 16th-century artists whose works exemplify the transition from late Gothic realism and stylization to baroque realism of the 17th century. Works of the Dutch landscapists,

such as Jacob van Ruisdael and Meindert Hobbema, form another major component of the collection, as does 19th-century painting.

The other parts of the museum, covering European sculpture and the applied arts, include Dutch sculpture from the 15th to the 17th century and some Italian and French sculptures, along with delftware, silverwork, glassware, furniture, and tapestries. The collection of prints and drawings, one of the world's finest, contains about 1,000 Rembrandt etchings and 100 of his drawings.

MAGDALENA DABROWSKI

Bibliography: *All the Paintings of the Rijksmuseum in Amsterdam* (1976); Meijer, Emile, *Rijksmuseum, Amsterdam* (1985); Newsweek, eds., *Great Museums of the World: Rijksmuseum, Amsterdam* (1969).

Riley, James Whitcomb

The American author James Whitcomb Riley, b. Greenfield, Ind., Oct. 7, 1849, d. July 22, 1916, was a Hoosier poet whose book *The Old Swimmin' Hole and 'Leven More Poems* (1883) made him one of the highest-paid poets of his time. His popularity had much to do with his humorous use of dialect and his sentimental celebration of the homely virtues. "Little Orphan Annie" and "When the Frost Is on the Punkin" are two of his best-known poems.

PAULA HART

Bibliography: Dickey, Marcus, *The Youth of James Whitcomb Riley* (1919; repr. 1973); Manlove, Donald C., ed., *The Best of James Whitcomb Riley* (1982); Revell, Peter, *James Whitcomb Riley* (1970).

Rilke, Rainer Maria   [ril'-ke, ry'-nur]

Rainer Maria Rilke was one of the foremost German poets of his time and one of the most influential of the 20th century. His search for objective lyric expression and mystical vision was manifested in works that convey a sense of sublime tragedy by using subtle and highly refined language complemented by soaring rhythm. Rilke expounded his theories of life and art in Letters to a Young Poet *(1929).*

The most influential German poet of the 20th century, Rainer Maria Rilke, b. Prague, Dec. 4, 1875, d. Dec. 29, 1926, produced a body of verse that is characterized by a succession of new beginnings, a result of his continuous attempt to define the task of the poet and of his struggle to find the value of life. He is considered one of the guiding spirits of modern poetry.

As a youth Rilke was subjected to a military education and to business school. These experiences, which were completely unsuitable to his temperament, undoubtedly strengthened his resolve thereafter to live purely as a poet. After abandoning his university education, he met (1897) Lou Andreas-Salomé, who remained influential in the poet's life even after she ceased being his mistress. Rilke traveled widely—to Munich, Berlin, Italy, Russia—consorting with literary people wherever he went, and after a marriage of one year to the sculptor Clara Westhoff, he moved to Paris in 1902. During World War I he served briefly in the Austrian militia. From 1919 until his death, from blood poisoning and leukemia, he lived mainly in Switzerland.

His early poetry—rich, sentimental, mellifluous, with its fluid texture achieved through the abundant use of run-on lines—cultivated the themes and aesthetic poses of fin-de-siècle romanticism. The hymnic *Book of Hours* (1905; Eng.

trans., 1941) is his best-known work from this period. *New Poems* (2 vols., 1907–08; Eng. trans., 1964) bears the imprint of his friendship with the sculptor Rodin, from whom he sought to learn how to conquer his subjectivity so that he could create continuously, without depending on inspiration. The term *Ding-Gedicht* ("thing-poem")—which has become associated with these meticulously crafted poems—describes the re-creation of the essence of external objects. In Rilke's protoexistentialist novel *The Notebook of Malte Laurids Brigge* (1910; Eng. trans., 1930), the young protagonist, a poor Danish poet in Paris, tries unsuccessfully to turn his wretchedness into beatitude. The longing for transcendence is also a theme of the celebrated *Duino Elegies* (1911–22; Eng. trans., 1930, 1939), in which the poet pits the highest possible order of intensity against his tragic sense of life's brevity. With these and *Sonnets to Orpheus* (1923; Eng. trans., 1936), Rilke arrived at a mystical sense of the unity of life and death, proclaiming his monistic cosmology in bold, mythopoeic, expressive metaphors. *Late Poems* (published posthumously in 1934) along with the two earlier works constitute a major achievement.   PETER HELLER

Bibliography: Bauer, Arnold, *Rainer Maria Rilke*, trans. by Ursula Lamm (1972); Butler, Eliza M., *Rainer Maria Rilke* (1941; repr. 1973); Fuerst, Norbert, *Phases of Rilke* (1958; repr. 1972); Peters, H. F., *Rainer Maria Rilke* (1960; repr. 1977); Prater, D., *A Ringing Glass* (1986).

rille   [ril]

The lunar mare surfaces possess many rilles, or sharp, narrow trenches, at least 20 of which are more than 100 km (60 mi) long. Hadley Rille, the landing site for *Apollo 15* in 1971, has a depth of more than 300 m (1,000 ft). Straight rilles are thought to result from faults or cracks in the lunar surface. Some sinuous, or snakelike, rilles are believed to result from lava tunnels that hardened at the surface and collapsed following the outflow of the molten lava, leaving channels on the lunar surface; others may have been produced through channel erosion by water or ash clouds. Some rilles radiate outward from craters.   JOSEPH S. WEISBERG

Bibliography: Mutch, T. A., *Geology of the Moon*, rev. ed. (1973).

Rimbaud, Arthur   [ram-boh']

Arthur Rimbaud, b. Oct. 20, 1854, the precocious boy-poet of French symbolism, wrote some of the most remarkable poetry and prose of the 19th century. His highly suggestive, subtle work drew on subconscious sources, and its form was correspondingly supple and novel. Rimbaud has been identified as one of the creators of free verse because of the rhythmic experiments in his prose poems *Illuminations* (1886; Eng. trans., 1957). His *Sonnet of the Vowels* (1871; Eng. trans., 1966), in which each vowel is assigned a color, helped popularize synesthesia (the description of one sense experience in terms of another), a device widely exploited by the symbolists. The hallucinatory images in *The Drunken Boat* (1871; Eng. trans., 1952) and Rimbaud's urging, in *Letter from the Seer* (1871; Eng. trans., 1966), that poets become seers by undergoing a complete derangement of the senses also reveal Rimbaud as a precursor of surrealism. Following his own dictum, Rimbaud lived an inordinately intense, tortured existence that he described in *A Season in Hell* (1873; Eng. trans., 1939).

The poet who came to symbolize alienated genius for French letters was a brilliant model student at a provincial school until the age of 15, when he turned rebel and fled to Paris. His homosexual relationship with Paul VERLAINE formed part of his spiritual disillusionment. Soon after it ended in 1873, Rimbaud abandoned his writing; he had not yet attained the age of 20. In another dramatic transformation he became a trader and gunrunner in Africa; 18 years later he died in Marseille on Nov. 10, 1891, following the amputation of his tumor-ridden right leg.   ALFRED ENGSTROM

Bibliography: Ahearn, Edward J., *Rimbaud* (1983); Frohock, Wilbur M., *Rimbaud's Poetic Practice* (1963); Hackett, C. A., *Rimbaud* (1981); Houston, J. P., *The Design of Rimbaud's Poetry* (1963); St. Aubyn, Frederic Chase, *Arthur Rimbaud* (1975); Starkie, Enid, *Arthur Rimbaud*, 3d ed. (1961; repr. 1978).

Rime of the Ancient Mariner, The

Written by Samuel Taylor COLERIDGE and first published in The LYRICAL BALLADS (1798), *The Rime of the Ancient Mariner* is a narrative poem that uses the narrative and prosodic technique of old ballads. It was planned with William Wordsworth, who contributed several lines and ideas. The narrator of the tale is an ancient mariner who commits a motiveless crime by killing a friendly albatross. Thereafter he is pursued relentlessly and condemned to a life in death. Only after he repents do supernatural powers carry his ship back home; but ever afterward he must do further penance by teaching others the lesson he has learned: to love and revere all things that God has made and loves.

Rimini   [ree'-mee-nee]

Rimini is a port city in the Emilia-Romagna region of north central Italy. The city is situated at the foot of the Apennines on the Adriatic coast. The population is 129,506 (1983 est.). The city serves as an agricultural market, railroad junction, important tourist resort, and industrial center for shipbuilding, railroad repairs, brick and tile making, and flour milling. Fishing is an important industry. Rimini's Roman remains include the Arch of Augustus and a bridge built by Tiberius. Other landmarks are the 15th-century Malatesta Castle, the Malatesta Temple (designed by Leon Battista Alberti in the 15th century), and several medieval and Renaissance churches.

Founded by Umbrians, the city came under the control of Rome in 268 BC. It was a free commune in the Middle Ages but was ruled by the MALATESTA family from 1239 to 1509, at which time it was annexed by the PAPAL STATES. The city joined Italy at unification in 1860. Rimini suffered severe Allied bombing in World War II.   DANIEL R. LESNICK

Rimmer, William   [rim'-ur]

The American visionary sculptor William Rimmer, b. Liverpool, England, Feb. 20, 1816, d. Aug. 20, 1879, learned stone carving as a boy. He held various jobs until, as a self-taught doctor, he began (1855) to practice medicine, subsequently earning his medical degree. The violent anguish of his *Falling Gladiator* (1861; bronze replica in the Boston Museum of Fine Arts) is expressed in the figure's powerful musculature. Rimmer's contemporaries found his forceful expression by means of sculptural form (rather than traditional literary values) unacceptable; thus much of his time and energy were absorbed by his popular lectures on anatomy for the artist.

JOAN C. SIEGFRIED

Bibliography: Gardner, Albert, "Hiram Powers and William Rimmer—Two Nineteenth-Century Sculptors," *Magazine of Art* 36 (February 1943); Whitney Museum of American Art and Museum of Fine Arts, Boston, *William Rimmer, 1816–1879*, text by Lincoln Kirstein (1946).

Rimsky-Korsakov, Nikolai Andreyevich   [rim'-skee-kohr'-suh-kawf]

Nikolai Andreyevich Rimsky-Korsakov, b. Tikhvin, Novgorod province, Russia, Mar. 18 (N.S.), 1844, d. June 21 (N.S.), 1908, is best known for his operas and orchestral works. Both parents, cultured members of the nobility, were amateur musicians. Nikolai started to play the piano at the age of six and soon tried composing. Music remained his avocation when in 1856 he entered the Imperial Naval Academy. In 1861 he joined the group of amateur composers taught by Balakirev, whom the critic Stasov, their intellectual mentor, would dub "the mighty handful"—Balakirev, Borodin, Cui, Mussorgsky, and Rimsky. Sea duty (1862–65) interrupted his composition of a symphony, but later he finished it with Balakirev's help. The FIVE (or "mighty five") vaunted their amateurism and aggressively launched their nationalist music against the professional establishment (primarily Anton Rubinstein). Rimsky's general strategy appeared in his symphonic sketch *Sadko* (1867), in which folkloric elements are couched in coloristic harmony and orchestration. In 1871 he resigned his commis-

Nikolai Rimsky-Korsakov, portrayed here by V. A. Serov, was a great Russian composer of the late 19th century. He challenged the musical tastes of his time by adopting elements of folk music in such works as The Snow Maiden (1882), containing echoes of traditional Slavonic melodies. Scheherazade (1888) evokes an Oriental atmosphere.

sion and accepted a teaching post at the Saint Petersburg Conservatory. Already a recognized composer, he had to teach himself the traditional musical disciplines and techniques before he could teach his students. An unfortunate academicism then tinctured his music, disappearing only in the 1880s with the appearance of such works as the opera *The Snow Maiden* (1882) and *Scheherazade* (1888), a symphonic suite. He directed the Free Music School and conducted its concerts (1874–81), assisted at the Imperial Chapel Choir (1883–94), conducted Beliaev's "Russian Symphony Concerts" (1886–1900), and undertook the controversial task of editing the works of his deceased friends Mussorgsky and Borodin. Eleven of Rimsky's 15 operas appeared between 1895 and 1907, beginning with *Christmas Eve* (1895) and ending with *The Golden Cockerel* (1907).

The folk music of Russia, including that of the Caucasus and Trans-Caucasus peoples, permeates Rimsky's music. Striking instances of asymmetrical rhythms are also derived from this source, foreshadowing the radical experiments of Stravinsky, his most famous student. Further, he discovered new possibilities of timbre and resonance in the late-romantic orchestra. His students also included Arensky, Nikolai Tcherepnin, Glazunov, Grechaninov, Ippolitov-Ivanov, Liadov, Miaskovsky, and Prokofiev.　　　MALCOLM HAMRICK BROWN

Bibliography: Abraham, Gerald E., *Rimsky-Korsakov* (1945; repr. 1976); Rimsky-Korsakov, Nikolai A., *My Musical Life*, trans. by Judah A. Joffe, 5th ed. (1972); Schonberg, Harold C., *Lives of the Great Composers* (1970); Zetlin, M., *The Five: The Evolution of the Russian School of Music*, ed. and trans. by George Panin (1959; repr. 1975).

Rinfret, Thibaudeau　　[rin'-fret]

Thibaudeau Rinfret, b. Montreal, June 22, 1879, d. July 25, 1962, a graduate of McGill University Law School, served as chief justice of the Canadian Supreme Court from 1944 to 1954. His knowledge of both English common law and the Napoleonic Code enabled him to reconcile differences between the two systems to the mutual benefit of English- and French-speaking Canadians.

ring

In mathematics, a ring is a mathematical system that consists of a set of elements that have certain properties. Any two elements of the set can be combined by means of a binary operation, and in a ring two binary operations are defined. They are called addition and multiplication but do not necessarily correspond to these ordinary operations. In general, for any two elements a and b in the ring R, elements $a + b$ and ab

are uniquely defined such that for all a, b, and c in R the following six axioms hold: (1) $a + (b + c) = (a + b) + c$; (2) there exists an element 0 (called the zero element) in R such that $0 + a = a + 0 = a$; (3) for each a, there exists an element $-a$ (called the inverse) in R such that $a + (-a) = (-a) + a = 0$; (4) $a + b = b + a$; (5) $a(bc) = (ab)c$; and (6) $a(b + c) = ab + ac$ and $(b + c)a = ba + ca$.

There are various classes of rings. A commutative ring is one in which $xy = yx$ for every x and y in the ring. An important commutative ring is the set of all polynomials with integral coefficients. If there exists an element 1 in the ring R so that $1x = x1 = x$ for every x in R, then the ring R is called a ring with unit. If the product of two nonzero elements is always nonzero, R is called an integral domain. A ring may be infinite or finite.　　　AVNER ASH

Bibliography: Adler, Irving, *The New Mathematics*, rev. ed. (1972); Bhattacharya, P. B., and Jain, S. K., *First Course in Rings, Fields and Vector Spaces* (1977); MacDuffee, Cyrus C., *An Introduction to Abstract Algebra* (1940; repr. 1966).

Ring of Fire

Ring of Fire is the popular name for a narrow zone of active volcanoes that nearly encircles the Pacific Ocean basin. It is composed of a series of ISLAND ARCS, some of which are connected and some isolated. Its northern section is the ALEUTIAN ISLANDS, extending from the Gulf of Alaska to Kamchatka. From Kamchatka, an arc continues southwest through the KURIL ISLANDS and JAPAN. From there the Ring of Fire splits into the RYUKYU and BONIN islands, which meet again in the Philippines. It then extends easterly in a complex series of arcs to Tonga and from there, south to New Zealand. The eastern margin is composed of the Andean arc (see ANDES), extending from southern Chile to central Mexico, and of the CASCADE RANGE in the northwestern United States.

CHRISTOPHER H. SCHOLZ

Ring of the Nibelung, The　　[nib'-uh-lung]

The Ring of the Nibelung (*Der Ring des Nibelungen*), a cycle of four operas—*Das Rheingold, Die Walküre, Siegfried,* and *Götterdämmerung*—was conceived by Richard WAGNER in 1848 and completed a quarter-century later. Wagner began with the intention of writing—the libretto is by the composer—a single opera drawn from several myths about the race of the Volsungs and the Nibelung's treasure; it was to be called *Siegfried's Death*, and its content corresponded generally to that of the present *Götterdämmerung* (Twilight of the Gods). Between 1848 and 1853, before composing any of the music, he wrote first *Young Siegfried* (corresponding to the present *Siegfried*) and then *Die Walküre* (The Valkyrie) and *Das Rheingold* (The Rhinegold) in an attempt to flesh out early parts of the story that were to have been narrated in *Siegfried's Death*. He began the musical composition of the cycle with *Das Rheingold* in 1853. By 1857 he had completed *Die Walküre* and two acts of *Siegfried*, at which point he interrupted the *Ring* for 12 years to compose *Tristan und Isolde* and *Die Meistersinger*. In 1869 he resumed work on *Siegfried*, and *Götterdämmerung* was completed in 1874. The complete cycle was first produced in Bayreuth, West Germany, in 1876.

DOUGLAS JOHNSON

Bibliography: Cooke, Deryck, *I Saw the World End* (1979); Culshaw, John, *Reflections on Wagner's Ring* (1976); DeGaetani, J. L., ed., *Penetrating Wagner's Ring* (1978); Donington, Robert, *Wagner's "Ring" and Its Symbols* (1963); Newman, Ernest, *The Wagner Operas* (1949); Wagner, Richard, *The Ring of the Nibelung*, trans. by Andrew Porter (1976); Westernhagen, Curt von, *The Forging of the "Ring"* (1976).

Ringling　　(family)

The Ringlings, an American family of circus proprietors, founded the world-famous Ringling Brothers and Barnum and Bailey Circus. Their circus empire was founded by five Ringling brothers, Albert, Otto, Alfred, Charles, and John, who set out in 1884 from Baraboo, Wis., with a modest, well-run wagon show. Within a few years the Ringling circus was traveling by railroad, covering most of the United States and Canada, and offering formidable competition to its rivals, which it bought up one by one. In 1907 the Ringlings acquired the renowned Barnum and Bailey Circus, which continued to tour separately until 1919, when the two shows were combined. Following the death of John, the last of the original Ringling brothers, John Ringling North, a nephew, took control of the circus. The Ringling Brothers and Barnum and Bailey Circus eventually gave up touring under a big top and since 1957 has limited its appearances to indoor arenas. The Ringling control finally came to an end in 1967, when the show was sold to a group of businessmen.   A. H. SAXON

Bibliography: Harlow, Alvin F., *The Ringlings* (1951); Matthews, K., and McDevitt, R., *Unlikely Legacy: The Story of John Ringling, the Circus, and Sarasota* (1979); North, Henry Ringling, and Hatch, Alden, *The Circus Kings: Our Ringling Family Story* (1960).

ringtail monkey: see CAPUCHIN.

ringworm

Ringworm is a skin infection, characterized by circular or ringed lesions whose infectious agent is a fungus. The most common sites of infection are the scalp and the groin. Scalp ringworm, occurring almost exclusively in children, is highly contagious and sometimes epidemic. Ringworm of the groin is also often called "jock itch." (See also FUNGUS DISEASES.)
                                                  PETER L. PETRAKIS

Rio de Janeiro   [ree'-oh day zhah-nay'-roh]

Rio de Janeiro, until 1960 the capital of Brazil, is a major port, the country's second largest city, and capital of the state of Rio de Janeiro. The city proper has a population of 5,091,000 (1980), and the metropolitan area has 9,014,000 residents. Rio has an area of about 450 km² (175 mi²). Located in southeastern Brazil, the city is bounded on the east by the 24-km-long (15-mi) Bay of Guanabara, on the south by a 35-km-long (22-mi) Atlantic coastline with many beautiful beaches, and on the west and north by rounded, forested mountains. The

inhabitants of this cosmopolitan city, located in one of the world's most beautiful settings, are called Cariocas.

Contemporary City. Recreation and tourism are among the leading sources of income. Sugarloaf Mountain rises 395 m (1,296 ft) at the entrance to the Bay of Guanabara, and a 40-m (131-ft) statue of Christ the Redeemer, sculptured in 1931, stands on Mount Corcovado (704 m/2,310 ft). In addition to the beaches, a major tourist attraction is Carnival, a colorful celebration held just prior to Lent.

Rio de Janeiro is a major financial center, with many banks. It is also a focal point for business and domestic commerce—many corporate headquarters are located there. The outstanding harbor has long made the city the nation's leading receiver of imports and the second most important general cargo port. Coffee, sugar, hides, lumber, tobacco, and iron ore are the main exports. Industries include food and tobacco processing; garment, shoe, glass, tire, chemical, and pharmaceutical manufacturing; publishing and printing; and shipbuilding and repairing.

The city has an international airport, Galeão, located on Governador Island. Travel throughout the metropolitan area has been facilitated by the 14-km (8.7-mi) Costa e Silva bridge, opened in 1974 to link the city with its suburb Niterói on the eastern side of the Guanabara Bay. A subway system opened in 1979.

Among the 200 churches, the most noteworthy is the Candelaria (begun 1755), now serving as the cathedral. Other landmarks include the National Museum of Art, the Municipal Theater, and the National Library (1810), the largest library in Latin America. Maracaña Stadium (capacity: 200,000) is the world's largest. The Federal University of Rio de Janeiro (1920) and several other educational and academic institutions are located there. Most buildings in Rio, a city with broad avenues, skyscrapers, and beautiful squares, were built during the 20th century. Three world-famous architects, Oscar NIEMEYER, Affonso REIDY, and Lúcio COSTA, designed many of Rio's buildings. As in most cities, there are also slums, called *favelas*, on the surrounding hillsides.

History. According to tradition, Guanabara Bay was discovered by the Portuguese Gonçalo Coelho, who entered it on

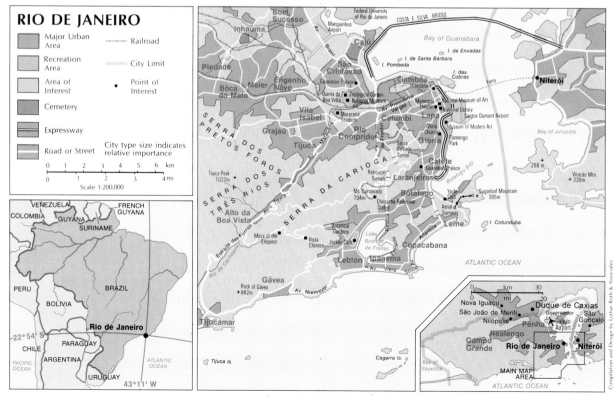

RIO DE JANEIRO

Major Urban Area	Railroad
Recreation Area	City Limit
Area of Interest	Point of Interest
Cemetery	
Expressway	
Road or Street	City type size indicates relative importance

Scale 1:200,000

Compilation and Design by Lothar Roth & Associates

Rio de Janeiro, a major port and one of South America's largest cities, is situated along Guanabara Bay in southeastern Brazil. The city, now a state capital, was the nation's capital from 1763 to 1960, when Brazil's administrative offices were transferred to Brasília.

Jan. 1, 1502, and, thinking that it was a river, named it Rio de Janeiro ("river of January"). The first settlers, however, were not Portuguese but French Huguenots, who settled there from 1555 to 1567, when the Portuguese forced them out.

The city's early growth followed the discovery of gold in the nearby state of Minas Gerais in 1698. Rio was selected as the only port through which the gold could be exported. In 1763, Rio became the seat of the governor general of Brazil, and by the end of the 18th century it was the largest city in the colony, with a population of 43,000.

The Portuguese court, fleeing from the invading French armies of Napoleon I, established its residence in Rio in 1808 and remained until 1821, making the city the capital of the Portuguese empire. When Brazil declared its independence in 1822, Rio became the capital.

In 1960 the seat of the federal government was moved to the newly built city of Brasília, and the former federal district that included Rio became the state of Guanabara. On Mar. 15, 1975, Rio was made the capital of the new state of Rio de Janeiro, which incorporates the former states of Rio de Janeiro and Guanabara.　JAMES N. SNADEN

Bibliography: Botting, Douglas, *Rio de Janeiro* (1978); Gautherst, Marcel, *Rio de Janeiro* (1965).

Río de la Plata　[ree'-oh day lah plah'-tah]

The Río de la Plata is the estuary formed by the confluence of the PARANÁ RIVER and URUGUAY RIVER in southeastern South America. About 275 km (170 mi) long and 225 km (140 mi) wide at the mouth, the Río de la Plata covers an area of 35,000 km² (13,500 mi²). The shores—Uruguay to the north and Argentina to the south and west—are densely populated. Because of 57 million m³ (2,000 million ft³) of silt deposited each year, the estuary must be dredged frequently. The principal ports are Buenos Aires in Argentina and Montevideo in Uruguay. Although probably entered by the Portuguese in 1501, the estuary is known to have been discovered by the Spaniard Juan Díaz de Solís in c.1515.

Rio Grande　[ree'-oh grand]

The Rio Grande, rising in the Rocky Mountains of western Colorado, is the fifth longest river of North America. From an elevation of more than 3,660 m (12,000 ft), it flows generally southeast through the high valleys of Colorado and New Mexico to Texas, where it follows the border between that state and Mexico. It empties into the Gulf of Mexico at Brownsville, Tex. The Rio Grande is about 3,025 km (1,880 mi) long and drains about 445,000 km² (172,000 mi²). The mean annual temperature at its source is 6° C (42° F) and at its mouth ranges from 21° to 27° C (70° to 80° F). Rainfall along its course averages 200–750 mm (8–30 in). Major tributaries are the Pecos, Devils, Chama, and Puerco rivers in the United States and the Salado, San Juan, and Conchos in Mexico.

Much of the drainage area is arid and barren, suitable only for grazing, but large irrigated sections produce grains, vegetables, cotton, and citrus fruits. Irrigation projects provide flood control as well as hydroelectric power. Tourism and mining of petroleum, gas, coal, silver, gypsum, and potash are also economically important. The Rio Grande is not navigable for commerce. Major cities along its course are Albuquerque, Brownsville, and El Paso in the United States and Ciudad Juárez, Matamoros, Nuevo Laredo, and Reinosa in Mexico.

The river was discovered and explored by the Spanish in the early 1500s, and mining and settlement began in the late 16th century. U.S. exploration began in the early 19th century.　STANLEY W. TRIMBLE

Rio Muni:　see MBINI.

Riopelle, Jean Paul　[ree-oh-pel']

Jean Paul Riopelle, b. Montreal, 1923, is the first Canadian painter to have established an international reputation. In 1947 he settled permanently in Paris, where he participated in the surrealist movement. During the 1950s he moved toward pure abstraction, creating mosaic patterns of brilliant color applied with a palette knife, as in his triptych *Pavane* (1954; National Gallery of Canada, Ottawa). Riopelle employs a vari-

In Pavane (1954), Jean Paul Riopelle created an intricate mosaic of rich, glowing color using small, regular strokes of his palette knife. The leading Canadian abstract painter, Riopelle was strongly influenced by the work of the American abstract expressionist Jackson Pollock. (National Gallery of Canada, Ottawa.)

ety of media, from colored ink and gouache to pastel and watercolor. In 1962 he was awarded the coveted UNESCO prize at the Venice Biennale.   DAVID WISTOW

riot

A riot is a violent offense against public order by three or more assembled persons. Legally it is a misdemeanor, punishable by fine or imprisonment; inciting to riot carries the same penalty. A 1715 English statute, the Riot Act, provided that 12 or more assembled persons who disturbed the peace and refused to disperse when read the Riot Act were guilty of a felony.

Rip Van Winkle

The central character of a short story by Washington IRVING, first published in *The Sketch Book of Geoffrey Crayon, Gent.* (1819), Rip Van Winkle was a ne'er-do-well in a village in the Hudson River Valley who slept for 20 years. Chased from home by his shrewish wife, Rip drank from a keg belonging to a band of little men who were playing ninepins. The brew caused his long sleep, and Rip awoke to find that his wife was dead, that no one in the village recognized him, and that he had slept through the American Revolution.

riparian rights   [ruh-pair'-ee-uhn]

Riparian rights are those privileges enjoyed by a person who owns land on a river or other body of water concerning use of the water and the bed under the water. The water in a river is not the person's property, but the person does own the bank and generally half the riverbed. Under common law, the owner can use unlimited amounts of water for domestic needs (household, animals, garden) but is usually limited to a so-called reasonable share for artificial needs, such as irrigation. The question of what is reasonable use in relation to the needs of other riparian landowners is one of fact and must be decided by a court. In the case of navigable streams, the riparian rights are considerably reduced.

Ripley, George   [rip'-lee]

The religious thinker, writer, and philosopher George Ripley, b. Greenfield, Mass., Oct. 3, 1802, d. July 4, 1880, began his career as a Unitarian minister after graduating from the Harvard Divinity School. He resigned from the ministry in 1841 because he wished to apply the principles of transcendentalism to human society and considered Unitarianism too conservative. With Ralph Waldo Emerson and Margaret Fuller he cofounded the DIAL, a transcendental publication. Ripley established BROOK FARM, an experimental cooperative community, and was its president from 1841 to 1847. There he edited *The Harbinger,* an influential journal of social reform. When Brook Farm failed, Ripley continued to edit *The Harbinger* in New York City until 1849. A popular book reviewer for the New York *Tribune* from 1849 to 1880, Ripley edited with Bayard Taylor *A Handbook on Literature and the Fine Arts* (1852). With Charles A. Dana he produced and edited a reference work, the *New American Cyclopedia* (1858–63).

Bibliography: Crowe, Charles, *George Ripley* (1967); Golemba, Henry L., *George Ripley* (1977).

Risorgimento   [ree-sohr-jee-men'-toh]

The Italian Risorgimento (resurgence) was the liberal, nationalist movement for unification (1796–1870). Its origins lay in a nationalistic reaction against the invasion and occupation of Italy by Napoléon Bonaparte (later NAPOLEON I), and it culminated with the annexation of Rome in 1870.

The Risorgimento was not an irresistible forward movement of liberal nationalism but a process occurring in fits and starts, and one interrupted by many internal conflicts. With the majority of Italians remaining on the sidelines through most of the struggle, Italy was unified in large measure by an opportunistic intellectual elite and with considerable foreign assistance, especially from NAPOLEON III's France.

In 1815 the Congress of Vienna (see VIENNA, CONGRESS OF)

Members of the Carbonari, a ritualistic, nationalist society active in Italy during the early 19th century, hold a clandestine meeting. Uprisings organized by the Carbonari in 1820 and 1821 stimulated the larger movement for Italian unification called the Risorgimento.

restored the old European order, bringing back most of the rulers who had been ousted during the Napoleonic era. Prince METTERNICH's Austria regained Lombardy, annexed Venetia, and indirectly dominated most of the rest of the Italian peninsula. The pope recovered the Papal States embracing Rome and the central region. The Kingdom of Naples and Sicily reverted to the Bourbons. Only the Kingdom of Sardinia-Piedmont (see SARDINIA, KINGDOM OF) was free of foreign control, but its ruling SAVOY dynasty, despite a reputation as a military power, did not become interested in unification until 1848.

The first Risorgimento movement was sparked by the CARBONARI, a secret organization that fomented unsuccessful popular uprisings in the 1820s. More important was Giuseppe MAZZINI's republican Young Italy movement, founded in 1831, which called for liberation through grass-roots revolts. Mazzini wanted to replace the existing states with a single, unitary republic with Rome as its capital. His influence peaked during the REVOLUTIONS OF 1848.

Mazzini's republicanism frightened the more moderate Italian leaders into offering competing programs. Vincenzo Gioberti's Catholic neo-Guelph group hoped to enlist the papacy in the national cause, but PIUS IX repudiated the Risorgimento in 1848. More significantly, the conte di CAVOUR, prime minister of Sardinia-Piedmont (1852–59, 1860–61), took steps to unite Italy as a liberal parliamentary monarchy under the house of Savoy. Realizing that he needed foreign help, Cavour skillfully enlisted the support of Napoleon III in a joint war against Austria in 1859, thereby acquiring Lombardy. The next year Romagna, Parma, Modena, and Tuscany voted for union with Sardinia-Piedmont. In exchange for recognizing this arrangement, France received Savoy and Nice.

In 1860, Giuseppe GARIBALDI conquered Sicily and Naples with his Red Shirts. The Kingdom of Italy, headed by Sardinian king VICTOR EMMANUEL II, was proclaimed in March 1861 after Sardinia absorbed Umbria and the Marches and the Two Sicilies chose union with Sardinia. Venetia was acquired as a result of Italy's alliance with Prussia in the SEVEN WEEKS' WAR (1866). Rome, which was seized when a French garrison was withdrawn during the Franco-Prussian War (1870), soon became the capital of Italy.   CHARLES F. DELZELL

Bibliography: Holt, Edgar, *Risorgimento: The Making of Italy, 1815–1870* (1970); Mack Smith, Denis, ed., *The Making of Italy, 1796–1870* (1968); Martin, George, *The Red Shirt and the Cross of Savoy: The Story of Italy's Risorgimento, 1748–1871* (1969); Salvatorelli, Luigi, *The Risorgimento: Thought and Action* (1970).

ristocetin: see ANTIBIOTICS.

Ritchie (family) [rich'-ee]

Several generations of the Ritchie family of Kentucky have achieved renown for their huge repertoire of folk songs, many of them handed down from the first American member of the family, **James Ritchie**, who came from England in 1768. By the early 1900s the family's fame had spread well beyond its native Cumberland mountains, and as academic interest in the American folk song grew, the Ritchies became a primary source for musicologists. John and Alan Lomax (see LOMAX family) recorded the Ritchies for the Archives of American Folk Song in the 1930s. A Ritchie daughter, **Jean** (b. Viper, Ky., Dec. 8, 1922), is a prolific writer, a singer, and an expert performer on the dulcimer.

Bibliography: Ritchie, Jean, *Singing Family of the Cumberlands* (1955), *The Dulcimer Book* (1963), and *Jean Ritchie's Dulcimer People* (1975).

Discography: *The Appalachian Dulcimer; Jean Ritchie, Singing Traditional Songs of Her Kentucky Mountain Family.*

Ritchie, Sir William Johnstone

Sir William Johnstone Ritchie, b. Annapolis, Nova Scotia, Oct. 28, 1813, d. Sept. 25, 1892, was the second chief justice of Canada. Although he initially opposed the creation of the Canadian Supreme Court, Ritchie accepted an appointment to it in 1875. He was made chief justice in 1879 and served with distinction until his death in 1892.

rites of passage: see PASSAGE RITES.

Ritschl, Albrecht [rich'-ul]

German theologian Albrecht Ritschl, b. Mar. 25, 1822, d. Mar. 20, 1889, influenced a generation of Protestant theologians. After pursuing studies at the universities of Bonn, Halle, Heidelberg, and Tübingen, he taught at Bonn (1846–64) and, until his death, at Göttingen. His early work followed the Tübingen school of New Testament interpretation, but by the mid-1850s he rejected the view that placed the Apostles and Saint Paul in antithesis. His most influential work was *The Christian Doctrine of Justification and Reconciliation* (3 vols., 1870–74; Eng. trans., 1872–1900).

Ritschl stressed that religious knowledge comes not from reason but from faith, in the form of value judgments. He emphasized the church as the community of faith that has received the gospel and for which Christ died. Individuals experience forgiveness and redemption personally—but in the church, not in individual mystical experience. He also placed a strong ethical emphasis on the Kingdom of God as the goal and result of the moral reformation of human beings.

The Ritschlian School, with its concerns for the community and ethics, included such famous names as Adolf von Harnack, Friedrich Loofs, and Ernst Troeltsch.

FREDERICK A. NORWOOD

Bibliography: Barth, Karl, *Protestant Thought: From Rousseau to Ritschl* (1959); Lotz, D. W., *Ritschl and Luther* (1974); Mueller, David L., *An Introduction to the Theology of Albrecht Ritschl* (1969).

Ritsos, Yannis [reet'-saws]

Yannis Ritsos, b. May 1, 1909, is one of the most celebrated poets of modern Greece. His popular poems *Epitaphios* (1936) and *Romiosini* (1958) have been set to music by Mikis Theodorakis, and his work has long been associated with left-wing political movements. He was twice imprisoned (1948–52; 1967) by right-wing governments that banned his books. *Romiosini* is a tribute to the Greek resistance fighters of World War II, and some of Ritsos's dramatic monologues are based on Greek myths.

Rittenhouse, David [rit'-en-hows]

The American astronomer and mathematician David Rittenhouse, b. Paper Mill Run, near Germantown, Pa., Apr. 8, 1732, d. June 26, 1796, made finely crafted clocks and mathematical instruments, including two large orreries that were recognized for their beauty and high degree of precision. He built what may have been the first American-made telescope. During the American Revolution, Rittenhouse served on the Board of War, making special contributions in the field of army munitions. He served as treasurer (1777–89) of Pennsylvania and as the first director (1792–95) of the U.S. Mint. Rittenhouse was president of the American Philosophical Society from 1791 until his death.

Bibliography: Ford, Edward, *David Rittenhouse* (1946); Hindle, Brooke, *The Pursuit of Science in Revolutionary America, 1735–1789* (1956) and *David Rittenhouse* (1964); Rice, Howard C., Jr., *The Rittenhouse Orrery* (1954).

Rivals, The

A play by Richard Brinsley SHERIDAN, *The Rivals* (1775) is a frequently performed comedy notable for its wit, sentimentality, and gallery of comic characters. Foremost among these is Mrs. Malaprop, whose constant misuse of words gave the word *malapropism* to the English language. The plot concerns the rivalry of Captain Jack Absolute and Bob Acres, a country squire, for the hand of Lydia Languish. For romantic reasons, Lydia will marry Jack only if his father, the ever-angry Sir Anthony, and her aunt, Mrs. Malaprop, oppose the marriage. Many misunderstandings and turns of the plot finally result in Lydia's agreement to the match.   MYRON MATLAW.

river and stream

Rivers convey excess water—precipitation minus evaporation and transpiration—from the continents to the oceans. Collectively, they represent the world's WATER RESOURCES, as they carry virtually all the water that is available for human management and use.

The four great civilizations of early human history developed in close dependence on rivers and the fertile, easily worked soils of their FLOODPLAINS: the Sumerians on the TIGRIS and EUPHRATES rivers in Iraq, the Harrapans on the INDUS in Pakistan, the Chinese on the HWANG HO ("Yellow River") and the YANGTZE RIVER in central China, and the Egyptians on the NILE RIVER in Egypt. Rivers and their valleys have continued to play important roles in the course of history; the exploration of much of North America was via river routes, and most of its major settlements are adjacent to rivers.

In addition to providing direct sources of water for domestic, agricultural, and industrial uses, rivers produce energy directly through hydropower generation (see HYDROELECTRIC POWER); they also provide the cooling water for many fossil- and nuclear-fueled power plants. They serve as transportation routes, as carriers and natural "treatment plants" for human wastes, and as the habitats of ecologically, economically, and recreationally valuable fish and wildlife. The continually changing nature of rivers and their often spectacular scenic features make them a source of inspiration for many writers and artists, as well as for more casual observers.

RIVER DISCHARGE, NETWORKS, AND DRAINAGE BASINS

On a global basis, the significance of rivers as a water resource lies not in the amount of water they contain at a given time (only about 0.14% of the Earth's liquid freshwater and about 0.01% of all water), but in their average discharge, which is the total volume carried in a given time period. Worldwide, this amounts to about 39,000 km³ per year, or, expressed differently, 28 trillion gallons per day. The flow of the Amazon is about five times greater than that of the second largest river, the Congo, and amounts to more than 17% of the world's total river flow. In practice, the discharge of a river at a point is determined by multiplying the surface width by the average depth by the average velocity. In the United States, river discharges are measured and reported for about 16,000 stations by the U.S. Geological Survey.

Terms such as *river*, *stream*, and *brook* have been applied historically; the hydrologic distinction between them is negligible. Although a river is commonly considered a linear fea-

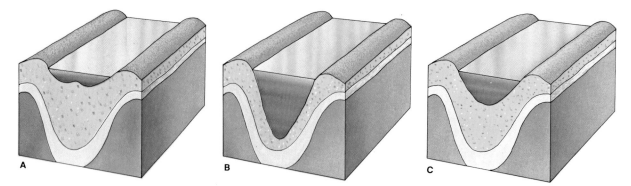

Except in mountainous regions, a river normally runs in a shallow channel cut into the sediments that fill a much deeper bedrock channel (A). During floods (B), streamflow increases, and the river deepens its bed by scouring sediment from the river bottom; it may cut down to bedrock in exceptionally powerful floods. As the flood weakens, the river redeposits excess sediment in the bedrock channel (C).

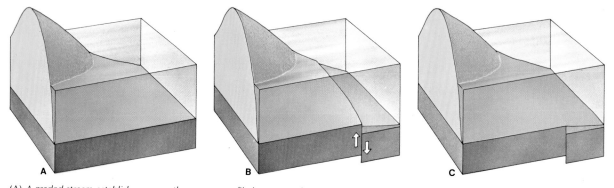

(A) A graded stream establishes a smooth, concave profile by means of erosion and deposition over a long period of time. If the streambed is subsequently dislocated by, for example, an earthquake that creates a fault scarp (B), the stream rapidly erodes the scarp and deposits the erosional debris downstream, building up the slope in that region. (C) Eventually, a new profile is established. Any change in the stream's controlling factors, such as a rise in baselevel or an increase in sediment load, will result in a similar adjustment of the longitudinal profile.

ture, in reality it is a treelike branching network. The smallest branches, which do not have tributaries, are designated as first-order streams. Where two first-order streams join, they form a second-order stream; the junction of two second-order streams forms a third-order stream, and so forth. If streams of about 1 mi (1.6 km) in length are considered as first order, the Mississippi River is a tenth-order stream; if smaller brooks and gullies are considered first order, the order of the Mississippi is much higher. A number of studies have shown that in a given region there tend to be three to five times as many streams of one order as of the next highest order. Also, the average lengths of streams and the average size of their drainage basins tend to increase regularly from one order to the next. Surprisingly, these regular relationships have been shown to be the result of random processes operating in the geologic evolution of river networks.

The area of land that contributes water to a river network upstream of a given point on a river is called the drainage basin, or watershed, of the river at that point. Such an area is generally defined on the basis of topography, by tracing drainage divides—ridge lines that separate the area contributing to one river network from that contributing to another—on a topographic map.

In a given region, the average volume of discharge at a given point on a river is directly proportional to the area of the drainage basin above that point. If this discharge is divided by the drainage area, and appropriate conversions of measurement units are made, the discharge can be expressed as a depth per unit time (for example, cm/yr or in/yr). When expressed this way, the average flow of streams of different sizes can be compared, and streamflow can be directly compared with precipitation (rainfall or melted snow), which is the ultimate source of all river water. For the United States as a whole, the average streamflow rate is about 23 cm/yr (9 in/yr), which is about 30% of the average precipitation of

76 cm/yr (30 in/yr). Average streamflows usually exceed 25 cm/yr (10 in/yr) east of the Mississippi River and rise to 100 cm/yr (40 in/yr) in mountainous areas. The rate for most of the region between the Mississippi and the mountains of the Far West is about 2.5 cm/yr (1 in/yr) but reaches 50 cm/yr (20 in/yr) in higher parts of the Rocky Mountains. In the Pacific Northwest, rates can be as high as 200 cm/yr (80 in/yr).

Water can enter the river network by falling directly onto a water surface, by traveling as overland flow from the surface of the drainage basin, or by moving as subsurface flow beneath the basin. About one-third of the discharge of the world's rivers comes from subsurface flow, which is of critical importance in maintaining streamflow between periods of rain and snowmelt. Virtually all of the remaining two-thirds comes from overland flow. In arid regions and urbanized areas, almost the entire drainage basin may contribute to this flow, whereas in humid regions generally only the low areas adjacent to stream channels supply it. In these areas, the GROUNDWATER level is typically close to the ground surface and rises due to infiltrating rain or snowmelt. When it reaches the surface, no further infiltration can take place, and subsequent rain or snowmelt on these areas runs off quickly to the stream as overland flow. In the remainder of the drainage basin, particularly if it is forested, the soil is so permeable and the groundwater so far beneath the surface that virtually all the precipitation infiltrates.

RIVER CHANNELS
In general, a river shapes its own channel. Most of the time, however, streamflow is considerably less than the discharge required to fill the channel, and it only occasionally exceeds the channel's capacity. This general disparity between streamflow and channel capacity arises because the channel size is determined by moderately large flows, capable of significant erosional work, that occur relatively frequently (every 2 to 3

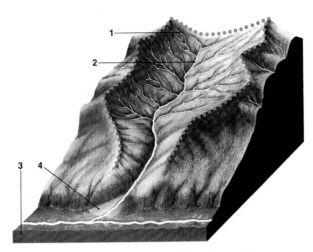

In mountain regions slopes often fit together to form drainage areas bounded by ridges, or divides (red dots), which separate different stream systems. Melted snow or rainwater initially flows down the slopes in sheets and along small channels, or rills (1). A number of rills meet at the bases of converging slopes and form a larger and deeper channel, or gully (2), which eventually widens into a stream channel. When a stream reaches the main valley floor (3), its velocity decreases and its load is deposited in the form of an alluvial fan (4).

and adjustment of the level of the water surface. The second largest adjustment to a change in discharge is in velocity, and the smallest is in width. As one proceeds downstream in a river network, however, the increase in discharge almost always accompanying the increase in drainage area is accommodated mostly by an increase in width, with a smaller rate of increase in depth. Thus rivers become relatively as well as absolutely wider as one proceeds downstream. Average velocity also usually increases downstream in a river system, but at a slow rate. Exceptions to the downstream increase in discharge that characterizes most stream networks occur in arid regions. Channels there remain dry for most of the year. During rainstorms runoff is rapid, sometimes causing FLASH FLOODS. As the water proceeds along the previously dry channel, it gradually infiltrates, causing discharge to decrease downstream.

The slope of a river channel decreases between its source and its mouth, and the longitudinal profile of a well-established stream is thus a smooth curve, concave upward. The slope also changes with time, in response to changes in the river's discharge, sediment load, and BASELEVEL (the level at which it enters a large body of standing water, such as an ocean). During a flood, for example, a river has a high velocity and is capable of carrying more sediment than normal. It therefore cuts down into the river bottom, picking up more sediment and decreasing its slope until its velocity matches its sediment load. When the flood ends and the discharge returns to normal, the river rids itself of the excess sediment by redepositing it in the channel, building up its slope until velocity and sediment load are once more in balance. The river thus constantly tends toward the ideal of a graded stream—one in which slope and velocity are perfectly adjusted to carry the sediment load. Because baselevel, discharge, and sediment load are all highly variable, this process is never complete.

River channels display a variety of patterns when viewed from the air or on a map. BRAIDED STREAMS consist of a network of interconnected channels, with numerous bars and islands between. Generally streams with relatively steep slopes,

years); very large floods do much erosional work but are too infrequent to have a long-term effect on channel size, whereas the small flows present most of the time do little work. Because the channel capacity is determined by flows that occur every few years, most rivers naturally overflow their banks every 2 to 3 years.

When the rate at which water is delivered to a channel changes, the river will adjust its discharge by changing its velocity, its depth, and its width. The greatest change is usually in depth, because of both scouring of the channel bottom

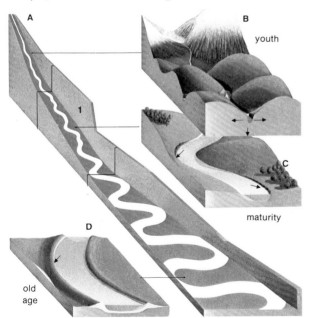

A longitudinal profile of a river (A) reveals its changing width and bed slope from source to mouth, which results from erosion of the original land surface (1) and from deposition of debris. Cross-profiles illustrate three erosion stages. (B) Vertical erosion in the steep-sloped upper section results in a V-shaped youthful valley. (C) Lateral erosion during the maturity stage leads to shallow valleys and gentle slopes. (D) During the old stage, lateral erosion and stream debris deposition eventually reduce the valley floor to an almost flat plain.

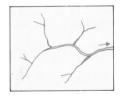

The direction in which rivers flow depends on the nature and structure of the underlying rock layers. In an area of uniform rock erosion a branching, treelike drainage pattern results (A) in which all tributaries flow toward the main stream. In regions with alternating weak and strong rock strata, tributary streams form along bands of easily eroded rock, resulting in a trellislike flow pattern (B). The slope of an area also affects the stream pattern. Thus rivers flow down all sides of a dome, or uplifted area, in a radial flow pattern (C).

TABLE 1: TEN LARGEST RIVERS OF THE WORLD

River	Country	Average Discharge	
		m³/sec	ft³/sec
Amazon	Brazil	180,000	6,350,000
Congo	Zaire	40,000	1,400,000
Yangtze	China	34,000	1,200,000
Paraná	Argentina	22,000	777,000
Orinoco	Venezuela	20,000	706,000
Brahmaputra	Tibet, India, Bangladesh	20,000	706,000
Ganges	India	19,000	670,000
Yenesei	USSR	19,000	670,000
Mississippi	USA	18,300	645,000
Lena	USSR	15,500	547,000

TABLE 2: TEN LONGEST RIVERS OF THE WORLD

River	Location of Mouth	Approximate Length	
		km	mi
Nile	Mediterranean Sea	6,650	4,150
Amazon	Atlantic Ocean	6,450	4,000
Yangtze	East China Sea	5,950	3,700
Hwang Ho	Yellow Sea	4,850	3,000
Congo	Atlantic Ocean	4,650	2,900
Missouri	Mississippi River	4,350	2,700
Lena	Laptev Sea	4,250	2,650
Niger	Gulf of Guinea	4,200	2,600
Yenisei	Arctic Ocean	4,100	2,550
Mississippi	Gulf of Mexico	3,800	2,350

they carry a considerable load of sand or gravel or both. Meanders (see MEANDER, RIVER) are series of rather regularly spaced symmetrical bends that tend to appear in streams with low slopes and channels made of silt and clay. The ratio of the radius of curvature of the bends and of the "wavelength" of the bends to the stream width remains quite constant from stream to stream. The exact mechanism that produces meanders is unknown, but they are a common feature of many types of flows, including meltwater streams on glaciers and the Gulf Stream, and are probably due to the action of corkscrewlike currents that exist even in straight flows. Irregularly curved river channels also occur.

SOLID CONCENTRATIONS
Rivers also carry dissolved and suspended solids. In the United States the average concentration of dissolved solids in unpolluted river water ranges from about 50 mg/l (0.06 oz/gal) in the humid western mountains and the Appalachians up to 1,000 mg/l (1.3 oz/gal) in the arid nonmountainous regions of the West. The average concentration of suspended solids is 100 mg/l (0.13 oz/gal) or less in humid forests but up to 100,000 mg/l (133 oz/gal) in desert areas.

For a given stream, dissolved-solids concentrations generally decrease as discharge increases, whereas the reverse is true for suspended-solids concentrations. Rivers thus play an important geologic role as the carriers of the products of rock weathering and mechanical erosion.　　S. LAWRENCE DINGMAN

Bibliography: Czaya, E., *Rivers of the World* (1983); Gregory, K. J., and Walling, D. E., *Drainage Basin Form and Process* (1973); Leopold, Luna B., et al., *Fluvial Processes in Geomorphology* (1964); Morisawa, Marie, *Rivers* (1981); Richards, Keith, *Rivers: Form and Process in Alluvial Channels* (1982); Russell, R. J., *River Plains and Sea Coasts* (1967); Schumm, Stanley A., *The Fluvial System* (1977) and, as ed., *River Morphology* (1972); Seeden, M., ed., *Great Rivers of the World* (1984).

See also: HABITAT; ICE, RIVER AND LAKE; RIVER DELTA; WATERFALL.

river blindness

River blindness, or onchocerciasis, is an infection of the skin by a threadlike worm, *Onchocerca volvulus*. It is one of the FILARIASIS diseases, a group of infections caused by various roundworms that are spread by a genus of blackflies, *Simulium,* which thrive near fast-running rivers. Prevalent in parts of Africa, Central America, and South America, it is characterized by skin irritation, skin nodules, and eye damage. The adult worms, which lie within the skin nodules, mate and produce larval forms called microfilariae, which invade the surrounding tissues and cause inflammation. The metabolic products of the microfilariae can cause hypersensitivity in various eye parts and may lead to blindness. The World Health Organization reports that in some tropical African villages more than 15 percent of the adult population has been blinded by onchocerciasis. Treatment consists of surgically removing as many nodules as possible; drugs such as diethylcarbamazine and suramin are administered to kill remaining adult worms, but they may have potentially fatal side effects. Another drug, ivermectin, was introduced in 1981 and shows promise of killing the roundworms without such side effects.
　　　　　　　　　　　　　　　　　　PETER L. PETRAKIS

river delta

Much of the detritus produced by continental erosion is carried away as sediment by rivers (see RIVER AND STREAM) and is subsequently deposited either in lakes or in oceans. These deposits may accumulate to form deltas. The term *delta* (from the Greek letter Δ) was first used (*c.*450 BC) by the Greek historian Herodotus in referring to the triangular alluvial deposits at the mouth of the Nile River.

Most large deltas form in relatively quiet bodies of water characterized by weak coastal currents, low tidal range, and low wave energy. Conversely, strong coastal currents and high wave energy on exposed coasts disperse sediment and militate against delta formation. Small deltas found in quiet freshwater lakes are generally simple in structure and lobate in shape. They are layered horizontally near the shore and farther out along the lake bottom; rapid deposition of the river's BED LOAD caused by the abrupt halting of its current produces inclined layers along the delta's sloping face.

Large deltas formed in the ocean are complex from both a process and a structural point of view. Depending on the density of the sediment-laden river water, the river flow may spread over the ocean water, disperse through it, or slide down the face of the delta as a density underflow. Continued sedimentation results in the building of a low-lying delta plain fringed seaward by a shallow marine platform. Branching distributary channels, bordered by partly submerged levees, may cross the delta surface, and swamps and marshes may cover it. Growth of a bar at the mouth of a main distributary channel has been suggested as one of the main causes of the branching of a river. During floods the bar acts as an obstruction; floodwaters are thus diverted to form an-

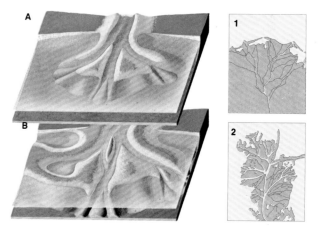

A river discharging into a quiet sea deposits a load of sediment at its mouth (A). The deposits eventually build up above sea level, extend the shoreline, and form a delta through which the river cuts radially branching channels, or distributaries (B). Deltas vary in shape. The Nile Delta (1) has a broadly curving, triangular-shaped shoreline, whereas the Mississippi Delta (2) has long, fingerlike land areas projecting out into the water along its distributaries.

other channel. The classic delta formed in this way has a "birds-foot" pattern of distributaries.

The overall morphology and internal structure of a large marine delta are controlled by the dynamics of the river system and by its interaction with the waves, tides, and currents of the coastal environment. The continued accumulation of sediment may result in the slow subsidence of the delta area, and rapid changes of sea level may initiate the development of new deltas (see TRANSGRESSION, MARINE). Although many deltaic areas are thickly populated, their proximity to sea level makes them vulnerable to flooding. Deltas are an important geological location for petroleum.   ALAN V. JOPLING

Bibliography: Coleman, James M., *Deltas: Processes of Deposition and Models for Exploration* (1976); Russell, Richard J., *River Plains and Sea Coasts* (1967).

Rivera, Diego   [ree-vay'-rah]

A fresco from the Ministry of Education Building in Mexico City, painted (1923–28) by Diego Rivera, depicts industrial workers showing support for Marx's Communist Manifesto. *Rivera's bold narratives constitute an effort to develop a Mexican art with popular appeal.*

Diego Rivera, b. Dec. 8, 1886, d. Nov. 24, 1957, was the most prominent painter of the modern Mexican mural movement. After attending the Academy of San Carlos, where one of his teachers was the landscapist José Maria Velasco, he became influenced by the caricaturist José Guadalupe Posada and other popular Mexican artists. During two trips (1907–10 and 1911–21) to Europe, he was profoundly influenced by the art of Giotto and Francisco Goya as well as by modern masters, notably Paul Cézanne, Pablo Picasso, and Pierre Auguste Renoir. Rivera executed some cubist works but soon discarded European avant-garde aesthetics in favor of an approach that reflected his view of the struggle between social classes. By the time he returned (1921) to Mexico, he was committed to a new popular art movement based on large mural works depicting contemporary Mexican life.

In his early mural projects, such as those at the National

Preparatory School (1922) and the Ministry of Education Building (1923–28) in Mexico City, he concentrated on social and political themes expressed in bold, dramatic forms. After a visit to Russia (1927–28), where his Marxist views were reinforced, he painted more ideologically oriented and realistically rendered murals, as at the National Palace (1929–55) and at Cuernavaca's Palace of Cortés (1929–30). His growing reputation led to invitations to paint frescoes at the San Francisco Stock Exchange (1931), the Detroit Institute of Art (1932), and Rockefeller Center (1933) in New York City—although the last-named work was destroyed by its sponsors because it contained a portrait of Lenin.

Rivera's murals are rich in archaeological detail and painted in a sharply outlined, linear style. Most of them have clear, three-dimensional figures in a shallow space, although a deep spatial extension of landscape appears at the top of some works. Rivera also executed many easel paintings and portraits and designed and built his Mexico City house, the Anahuacalli, which is now a museum housing the extensive collection of pre-Columbian art that he left to the Mexican people.   DONALD AND MARTHA ROBERTSON

Bibliography: Arquin, Florence, *Diego Rivera* (1971); Paine, Francis F., *Diego Rivera* (1931; repr. 1972); Reed, A. M., *The Mexican Muralists* (1960); Rivera, Diego, with Gladys March, *My Art, My Life* (1960); Wolfe, Bertram D., *The Fabulous Life of Diego Rivera* (1968).

Rivera, Fructuoso

Fructuoso Rivera, b. c.1785, d. Jan. 13, 1854, was a Uruguayan independence leader and president (1830–34, 1839–42) of Uruguay. One of the Thirty-three Immortals, the revolutionary group that won Uruguay's independence from Brazil, Rivera became the first president with the support of Juan Antonio LAVALLEJA, the leader of the Immortals. Rivera supported Manuel Oribe as his successor in 1834, but the two soon split. Rivera's faction, the Colorados (reds), forced Oribe and the Blancos (whites) out of office in 1838. In the ensuing civil war (1840–51), Oribe, backed by Juan Manuel de ROSAS of Argentina, drove Rivera into exile. Rivera returned in 1853 to help direct the provisional government of Uruguay.

Rivers, Larry

The well-known painter and draftsman Larry Rivers, b. New York City, Aug. 17, 1923, began his career as a jazz saxophonist. After study (1947–48) with Hans Hofmann, he devoted himself completely to art. The strongest influence on Rivers's early work was the action painting that dominated New York painting in the late 1940s and early 1950s, particularly the

Larry Rivers's Wedding Photograph *(1961) is a parody of the traditional commemorative portrait of bride and groom. The painting exhibits Rivers's characteristic tension between representational elements and a loose, expressionistic style. (Private collection.)*

work of Willem de Kooning. Rivers adapted action painting, mainly an abstract style, to the representation of several types of subject matter—intimate portraits (*Double Portrait of Birdie*, 1955), historical themes (*Washington Crossing the Delaware*, 1953), and the everyday details of urban life, including late-model cars, bank notes, clothes, and cigarette packages. Although much of his imagery anticipates pop art, Rivers's highly distinctive draftsmanship has its roots in the expressionism of New York art in the immediate post–World War II era. Rivers has also compiled *Drawings and Digressions* (1979), a commentary on his own work.   CARTER RATCLIFF

Bibliography: Harrison, Helen A., *Larry Rivers* (1984); Hunter, Sam, *Larry Rivers* (1972).

Riverside

Riverside, the seat of Riverside County in southern California, lies beside the Santa Ana River 85 km (53 mi) east of Los Angeles. The population is 170,876 (1980). The city is the hub of a large citrus-fruit and vegetable-growing region. Aircraft parts, paints, and air conditioners are manufactured in Riverside. The University of California at Riverside (1961) is located there. Originally part of the Rancho Jurupa, the town was laid out in 1870 and was first known as Jurupa.

Riviera   [riv-ee-air'-uh]

The Riviera is the strip of Mediterranean coast generally considered to extend from Cannes, France, to La Spezia, Italy. In France the limestone Maritime Alps descend abruptly to the sea to create the dazzling white cliffs and beaches of the CÔTE D'AZUR between Cannes and Menton. In Italy, where the Maritime Alps are joined by the limestone Ligurian Apennines, the Riviera is divided at Genoa into the Riviera di Ponente (west) and the Riviera di Levante (east). The Corniches, a network of roads on three levels between Nice and Menton, provide transportation between the coastal communities. The interior hills of PROVENCE to the north provide magnificent scenery and protect the French Riviera from the mistral, a cold wind that sweeps down the Rhône Valley.

Because of its picturesque scenery, mild, sunny climate, and subtropical vegetation, the Riviera is one of Europe's primary centers for tourism. The principal resorts of the western section include Saint-Raphaël, Saint-Tropez, and Fréjus. The Côte d'Azur has an almost continuous line of resorts—CANNES, Antibes, NICE, MONTE CARLO (Monaco), and Menton. The Italian Riviera features SAN REMO, Alassio, Santa Margherita, Rapallo, and LA SPEZIA.

Rapid urbanization has led to a decline in traditional occupations—fishing and the cultivation of olives, grapes, and citrus fruits. Grasse, 13 km (8 mi) northwest of Cannes, remains a center of the perfume industry, but many of the flowers used to make perfume there are now imported rather than grown locally. Nice is the regional center of the French Riviera; GENOA is the chief port of the industrial Po River valley of northern Italy.   TIMOTHY J. RICKARD

Riyadh   [ree-ahd']

Riyadh, the royal capital and largest city of Saudi Arabia, is located in the east central part of the Arabian Peninsula about 390 km (240 mi) from the Persian Gulf. Riyadh has a population of 1,308,000 (1981 est.). The country's immense wealth, accumulated since the discovery of vast petroleum deposits in the 1930s, is reflected in the city's modern appearance. Riyadh is also the nation's commercial and transportation center. Petroleum refining and cement manufacturing are the major industries. Riyadh University (now King Saud University) was founded in 1957.

Riyadh was a center of Wahhabism and the capital of the powerful Saud family from the early 19th century. The city was under the power of the rival Rashids from 1891 until 1902, when the Sauds regained control. In 1932, when the unified Kingdom of Saudi Arabia was proclaimed, Riyadh became the capital.

Riza-i-Abbasi   [ree-zah' ee ahb-bah-see']

Riza-i-Abbasi (active 1610–35) was an accomplished painter at the court of Shah Abbas Safavi of Iran. Riza's father, Maulana Ali Asghar Kashani, was an expert portrait painter on the staff of the imperial library, where the disciples of the miniaturist BIHZAD were among his colleagues. Entering the court of Shah Abbas in 1600, he gained a lofty reputation as a draftsman within a decade. His expressive brushwork gives his portraits, such as *Shah Abbas and the Indian Ambassador Khan Alam* (1633; State Library, Leningrad), an abstract appearance that resembles one large calligraphic stroke.   S. A. A. RIZVI

Bibliography: Gray, Basil, *Persian Painting* (1961).

RNA: see NUCLEIC ACID.

roach: see COCKROACH.

Roach, Max

Drummer, composer, and teacher Maxwell Lemuel Roach, b. Elizabeth City, N.C., Jan. 19, 1924, is a leading figure in modern jazz. Roach was drummer in Charlie Parker's quintet in the 1940s and played with all the seminal figures of the BEBOP movement, developing a drum style—the use of cymbals to create a sustained, legato rhythmic backup—that jazz drum-

The picturesque French Riviera town of Saint-Tropez is located along a sheltered Mediterranean bay, making it a popular harbor for both fishing and pleasure vessels. Overlooking the town, which is a fashionable summer resort, is the Massif des Maures.

mers have since almost universally adopted. He led his own small group in the 1970s, experimenting with unconventional percussion instruments. As a teacher, Roach has developed courses in jazz and jazz history and since 1973 has taught at the University of Massachusetts in Amherst.

roadrunner

The roadrunner, *Geococcyx californianus,* a large ground bird native to arid scrublands of the southwestern United States and Mexico, belongs to the cuckoo family, Cuculidae. It measures about 58 cm (23 in) and has brown plumage streaked with white above and on the throat, and white plumage below. It also has a bushy crest, blue and red eye rings, long, spindly legs, and a long tail.

The roadrunner seldom flies, preferring to depend on its swiftness afoot to reach safety when surprised. It preys on small snakes as well as insects, lizards, and, occasionally, the young of ground-nesting birds.

The roadrunner, G. californianus, is a fast-running ground bird native to the southwestern United States and northern Mexico. Also called the chaparral cock, it can attain speeds up to 40 km/h (15 mph).

roads and highways

A road or highway may be defined as an overland route between two points. To clarify some terminology, a road is generally a narrow route in a rural area; a street is an urban route; and a highway is a wide road that can carry more traffic at higher speeds. In the United States, a major highway—a multilane divided roadway with limited access (relatively infrequent entrances and exits)—is called an expressway, a freeway (if it has no tolls), or a turnpike (if it has tolls). Other names are used elsewhere: motorway (Great Britain), autobahn (Germany), and autostrada (Italy).

HISTORY

Modern roads are usually thought of as being mainly for wheeled traffic, but the Incas in South America, who never discovered the wheel, had a well-maintained road system stretching from modern Ecuador about 3,680 km (2,300 mi) southward.

Perhaps as early as 3000 BC, the civilizations of Egypt, Mesopotamia, and the Indus Valley developed roads, first for pack animals and then for wheeled vehicles. The Persians, beginning from the 6th century BC, linked up existing highways to form the "Royal Road" from Ephesus to Susa, and in the 3d century BC the Ch'in dynasty in China established a country-wide network of roads.

Roman Empire. The greatest road builders of the ancient world were the Romans who, in the three centuries before

Christ, made themselves rulers of all the countries bordering the Mediterranean and far beyond. As they developed from a city-state by conquering other small states, they built roads into the conquered regions to help consolidate their gains. They built the Via Latina after they had conquered Latium in 340 BC to connect Rome with Capua. At the instigation of Appius Claudius Caecus, who paid for part of the work himself, the most famous of ROMAN ROADS, the Via Appia (the Appian Way), was built on an alternative route to Capua starting in 312 BC; by 244 BC the road had reached Brundisium on the heel of Italy.

By the time of Hannibal's invasion, the Roman road system was well established in central and southern Italy. The revolutionary feature of the Appian Way was that it was paved, partly with stone and partly with lava. After that time roadbuilding formed an important function of Roman government, and before the end of the empire, good roads extended from the Forth River to the Euphrates, from the mouth of the Rhine to the Pillars of Hercules, and along the whole length of the North African coast. A remarkable network of roads was also built in the granary of Rome (now Tunisia).

A postal service was organized for transmitting government messages. The confidence with which Saint Paul wrote to the early Christians in various parts of the empire indicates that the service was soon used for private letters as well. Most of the road users traveled on horseback or on foot; high officials and the wealthy, however, used two- and four-wheeled carriages (see COACH AND CARRIAGE). Posting stations where horses could be changed and attended to were placed about every 16 km (10 mi) along the roads for government use; inns were also placed at reasonably frequent intervals to provide facilities for private travelers.

The Roman achievement is all the more remarkable because the surveyors had to plan the line of a new road and to make it as straight as possible without modern instruments (not even a compass) and often in wild and wooded country. A major reason why their roads lasted was their insistence on adequate drainage. A ditch was excavated a few feet from each side of a road, and the earth from this was used in forming a bank called the agger, which was constructed on foundations of broken stone, bricks, and pottery cemented with lime. Large polygonal blocks of hard stone or of lava (where available) were carefully fitted together to form the top surface of the road. The Latin word for this surface was *pavimentum*—the root of the modern term *pavement.*

The barbarian tribes, which broke into the Western Empire from the 4th century AD onward and finally destroyed it, were not concerned with centralized power; rather, they preferred the opposite. They disliked cities and in their settlements tended to avoid the Roman roads, which gradually decayed. Centuries passed before any real attempt was made to reconstruct the road system.

Middle Ages. As national states began to form in Europe, major routes became necessary to provide for the itinerant royal courts to move about. Beginning in the 11th century, the urge to go on pilgrimages to sacred shrines accelerated the development of international trade and made the roads busier than they had been since the collapse of the Roman Empire. Although road surfaces were poor by modern standards, the roads were well provided with inns and smithies. Wheeled vehicles were rare; both goods and people were carried on horseback.

Great Britain. The development of centralized government was not accompanied by centralized responsibility for road maintenance. In England the responsibility lay with the parishes, which each year elected a highway surveyor who could call on the able-bodied men of the parishes for a specified number of hours annually to repair the roads. Not until 1555 did the surveyors have statutory backing to enforce labor on the roads; in practice, however, the statute was practically unenforceable.

Next came the era of the TURNPIKE trusts. A number of people would join together to obtain parliamentary powers under which they would take over a length of road for 21 years or build a new one and pay for its maintenance by collecting

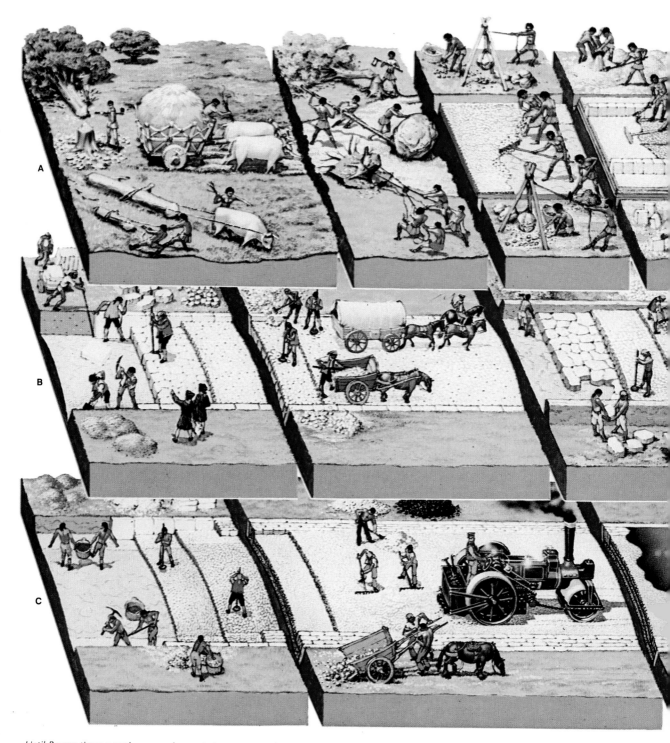

Until Roman times a road was merely a route between two places, marked by footprints and wheel tracks and lack of vegetation. The Romans constructed more permanent roads (A) that were generally straight and did not follow the contour of the surrounding land. They first removed trees, large boulders, and other obstacles and then laid a foundation of crushed stone, brick, and pottery held together with lime. The road was then surfaced with large polygonal blocks of stone or lava carefully fitted together, and drainage ditches were constructed on each side—a major reason for Roman roads lasting so long. Most of the traffic moved by foot or on horseback. By the end of the Roman Empire a remarkable network of roads covered approximately 85,000 km (53,000 mi). Eighteenth-century roads (B) were built on a foundation of large blocks. Several layers of gravel were added to the foundation and tamped down by hand; some roads had an additional surface of beaten earth. Much of the traffic comprised horse-drawn wheeled vehicles. Nineteenth-century roads (C) were similar to those of the 18th century, but some were raised and had a top surface of gravel that was first tamped down by hand and then by horse-drawn rollers (and later steamrollers). Twentieth-century roads (D) were built to handle the frequency and weight of motorized vehicular traffic. The foundation, instead of being constructed with crushed rocks, is provided by grading and stabilizing the subsoil itself. Additives, such as cement, lime, or bitumen, are mixed with the subsoil to stabilize it. Above the foundation is a base course of concrete and then a top surface of asphalt or concrete.

carrying relatively high-speed wheeled traffic. His method was to put down three layers of small stones, each stone weighing up to about 170 g (6 oz); each layer, about 10 cm (4 in) thick, was first rammed down by hand and then by horse-drawn rollers. First the ramming and then the weight of passing traffic ground the edges off the stones, making a watertight surface. Macadamized, or macadam, roads were almost standard in Britain until the onset of the motor age. The rubber tires of high-speed automobiles tended to loosen the stone surface, adding to the dust raised by vehicles. This problem led to a search for better road surfaces, such as asphalt (see TAR, PITCH, AND ASPHALT). Thomas TELFORD was another Scot who gained worldwide fame as an engineer. His method was to make the roads strong enough to take the maximum likely weight of traffic, so he gave more attention to the foundations than McAdam did. Heavy blocks of stone were put down with layers of smaller stones on top of them, and then the road was surfaced with gravel.

France. To the strongly centralized government of 18th-century France must be given the credit of making the first determined effort to evolve an adequately funded national system of roads. A department of bridges and roads (Corps des Ponts et Chaussées) was set up in 1716, and specifications were laid down for various types of road. Road engineering was recognized as a profession, largely because of the achievements of Pierre Tresaguet, who became inspector general of roads in 1775. His method of construction differed from those of McAdam and Telford because, although he also used layers of stones decreasing in size toward the top, he made each layer slightly cambered (curved from side to side, higher in the middle, and sloping downward toward both edges) for better drainage. The road had a stone curb at each edge to prevent the small stones from rolling off the road. He also made greater use of the subsoil to support the road. Napoleon had French road engineers make great improvements in the roads in many parts of Western Europe regardless of the cost in money or lives. The new roads over the SIMPLON PASS and Mont Cenis Pass were outstanding examples. Before Napoleon's time, the divided state of Germany had militated against the provision of more than short lengths of all-weather roads (roads of high enough quality to be passable even in poor weather, such as heavy rain).

United States. In the United States the old Indian trails served to mark the way for modern roads. The Mohawk Trail and the Natchez Trace are familiar names. Santa Fe, a missionary station receiving supplies from Mexico, gradually became an important trading post and attracted pioneers from the United States. As early as 1825, Congress voted $30,000 to survey and mark a trail to Santa Fe from Independence, Mo. The great westward migrations of the 1840s produced the Overland Trail with its branches to Oregon and eventually to California.

The coming of the first TRANSCONTINENTAL RAILROAD in the 1860s reduced the importance of the trails, until the development of the internal-combustion engine and automobile gave roads renewed importance. The British general Edward BRADDOCK in 1755 built a road out from Cumberland, Md. (the Cumberland Road) to assist in his march on the French at Fort Duquesne; little was done, however, to provide the settled states with all-weather roads until, as in England, turnpike trusts were established. Virginia built a turnpike in 1785 with public funds, but private enterprise provided the greater part of the network that developed and served the eastern states before the railroads came.

The states were often reluctant to finance the building of roads, and the federal government was even more so, although it did make a start in 1811 by contracting for the construction of the NATIONAL ROAD, virtually a reconstruction and extension of the Cumberland Road. After many years the National Road reached Saint Louis. After 1838 responsibility for the road was turned over to the individual states. The proliferation of RAILROADS in the United States in the second half of the 19th century and electric interurbans (high-speed intercity trolley lines) in the East and Midwest from about 1900 to 1920 somewhat reduced the need for all-weather roads even after the automobile had become a practical vehicle.

tolls. Road engineering, however, was still rudimentary, and many trusts did not know how to preserve the roads.

Real and lasting improvement came through the work of three engineers. John Metcalf (1717–1810) worked mainly in the north of England and, despite the fact that he was blind from the age of 6, devised a method of carrying roads across marshy ground on rafts of ling or heather tied in bundles. John Loudon McAdam (see MACADAM), a Scot, became a commissioner for highways. He devoted himself to studying methods of road improvement and, after settling in Bristol, became famous for his success in building roads capable of

Not until after World War I was a determined attempt made to improve the road system, but the new construction of this period was virtually confined to roads serving expanding communities.

The development of special-purpose roads in the United States actually dates from a concept that came from environmental considerations and not from a desire to allow motor traffic to travel without hindrance. William White Niles, a prominent member of the New York Zoological Society, persuaded the city in 1907 to buy sufficient land on both banks of the Bronx River to stop pollution of its water, and, as a part of the scheme, a four-lane road was constructed with limited access and no crossings on the road level. This small beginning led to the widespread system of scenic parkways.

During the Depression, Pennsylvania sponsored road improvements among other public works, creating the Pennsylvania Turnpike Commission, which, by the sale of bonds plus a direct state loan, raised enough money to build a 256-km (159-mi) motorway between Harrisburg and Pittsburgh. This toll road, opened in 1940, is generally considered the first superhighway, and many others soon followed.

New roads, it was discovered, can generate substantial business in the localities they serve, sometimes, however, with disastrous effects on the environment. In developing the complete highway, American engineers learned that the attainment of high speeds could not be the sole consideration. A road designed to avoid monotony for the driver is a contribution to safety (see SAFETY, AUTOMOTIVE). One difficulty facing all highway planners is how to connect highways with central cities without destroying part of the city itself. Tunnels and viaducts both have environmental drawbacks, and clover-leaf junctions with up to four levels of roadway consume a large amount of land.

Serious thought about the growth of long-distance road traffic led to a proposal in 1944 for a National System of Interstate and Defense Highways. Under the Federal Aid Highway Act (1956), the Federal Highway Trust Fund was established. Supported by certain federal taxes, it contributes 90% of the cost for roads in the INTERSTATE HIGHWAY SYSTEM.

Canada. In Canada, even though roads are a provincial responsibility, the government of the Dominion paid much of the cost of the TRANS-CANADA HIGHWAY, a 7,820-km (4,859-

mi) stretch of highway constructed in 1950-62, and has contributed to the ALASKA HIGHWAY and the Mackenzie Highway, which runs north from Edmonton. The Alaska Highway, which runs 2,451 km (1,523 mi) from Dawson Creek, British Columbia, to Fairbanks, Alaska, is maintained by both Canada and the United States. This highway, originally built in 1942 for U.S. military purposes, has contributed enormously to the development of the area.

International. In 1936 the International Association of Automobile Clubs proposed an international road system for Europe, but World War II stopped any serious discussion. Since World War II, however, individual countries have done much to develop a more adequate system.

Schemes were put forward in Britain in the 1920s for special motor roads; because these were to be built by private bodies that would recoup their expenditure by collecting tolls, however, the plans were not popular. The first advances were made by the Italian and German dictatorships, mainly for military reasons. Mussolini encouraged private firms to construct the autostrada; the first one opened in 1924. Although the pre-1939 roads were poor by today's standards, these early motor roads did incorporate the essential features of limited access and the absence of grade crossings (crossings on the same level as the road). Hitler grasped the value of an adequate road network and, in 1933, Fritz Todd was appointed inspector general of roads with orders to build 4,023 km (2,500 mi) of autobahnen (singular, AUTOBAHN). By 1942 he had constructed 2,108 km (1,310 mi) of roadway. Tremendous damage was done to the roads during the war, but this damage has been repaired and the roads improved since the war. The Netherlands was the only other country that had a program of highway construction before 1939.

Britain set out to build special motor roads (motorways) in 1956 and opened its first in 1959, linking London and Birmingham. Work went on steadily until the late 1970s, when lack of money virtually put a stop to new construction in favor of improving existing roads and bypassing towns.

In 1965, Japan opened its first special motor road—the Meishin Expressway from Kobe to Nagoya (193 km/120 mi), continued in 1970 by the Tomei Expressway from Nagoya to Tokyo (354 km/220 mi).

Organizations seeking to improve roads exist in most developed countries. The International Road Federation, which has offices in Washington, D.C., and Geneva, promotes the building of intercontinental highways or the improvement and linking of existing roads. Perhaps the most well-known highway project is the PAN AMERICAN HIGHWAY, which when complete will link the capitals of all the American nations. North of Panama the traveler can now drive through to Canada, but the Darien Gap on the isthmus of Panama has so far proved to be an impassable obstacle.

The I.R.F. also compiles annual statistics on road mileage in all the countries of the world except the USSR, East Germany, Kampuchea, Laos, and Vietnam; its 1979 figures show the United States with the greatest length of motorways—3,235,292 km (2,010,317 mi). In proportion to area, however, mileage in Belgium (with 12,359 km/7,680 mi of roads) and in the Netherlands (90,600 km/56,296 mi) head the list.

ROAD CONSTRUCTION

France is generally credited with the first successful laying of pavements of asphalt mastic in the early 19th century. In the middle of the century both France and England used compressed rock asphalt for city streets, and in the United States, bitumen (a natural asphalt) was used. The rapid growth of motoring in the early 20th century encouraged the use of asphalt because it produced a dustproof surface, but all the forms then in existence were apt to become slippery and

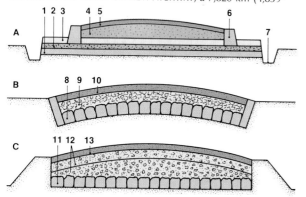

(Above) *Roman roads (A) consisted of a footing (1) of compacted earth, a base of stones (2), a concrete layer (3), filling material (4), and the road surface (5). They often had retaining stones (6) and drainage ditches (7). Roads built by Tresaguet (B) used a cambered layer of heavy stone (8) followed by a base course of large stones (9) and the road surface (10). Roads designed by Telford (C) called for a layer of flat, heavy stones (11) laid over level earth, followed by two cambered layers of small stones (12) and a gravel surface (13).*

(Right) *A cross section of an American highway demonstrates dramatic improvements in modern road construction. Laid over a footing (1) of compacted earth, the base course (2) is composed of sand, gravel, and minerals, to which asphalt is added. The road surface (3) is formed of asphaltic concrete, a mixture of sandstone, sand, gravel, and asphalt.*

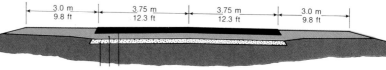

(Below) *The increasing use of automobiles in large urban areas has led to complex highway-interchange systems, such as that seen in an aerial photograph of downtown Chicago. Interchanges are generally located at main crossroads and connect city streets to major highways by means of curved, sloping roads, or ramps. They provide controlled safe and easy access to highways without interrupting the smooth flow of heavy traffic.*

(Above) *The construction of modern roads for automotive vehicles requires the use of many highly specialized machines. A foundation of sand and crushed rock is first laid down on a roadbed that has been scraped and leveled. Concrete is then poured by a spreader, running on tracks that also act as side supports, and compacted by vibrator to a firm surface.*

cause skidding when wet. From about 1929, while a surface was being constructed and the material was still hot, a dressing of bituminous-coated chippings was added, which gave the asphalt road a rough surface.

A great asset to the modern highway engineer has been the development of AERIAL PHOTOGRAPHY, which greatly assists the preliminary ground surveys for new roads and the planning of routes on the map (see SURVEYING). Before construction of a road begins, estimates are made of the likely cost of possible alternatives, taking into account the geological features, economic needs of the area, and possible damage to the environment. The expensive stage of earth moving must be kept to the minimum, and in areas where a road necessarily has an undulating course, the aim is to balance the cut (the excavations) against the fill (the embankments; see EARTH-MOVING MACHINERY). Detouring around natural obstacles, such as difficult strata or unstable subsoil conditions, is sometimes preferable to constructing a straight road.

Large numbers of laborers built the railroads; in road construction, however, much of the work is done by sophisticated machinery. The process starts with the loosening of the topsoil by a scraper; next, a bulldozer pushes the loosened earth to one side, so that the line of the road is clear. At this point the road is discernible from the air, even though it is nowhere near its final form. Excavations may have to be made, embankments constructed, and sharp curves straightened out. Once the road has its predetermined line and gradients, excavation can begin for the foundations, which must be capable of bearing the expected weight of traffic on the road. Within the last 30 years it has become possible in some situations to stabilize the subsoil itself rather than create a foundation of crushed rocks or concrete, provided that the subsoil is fairly uniformly graded. Cement, lime, or bitumen are used as additives. After the subsoil has been loosened, a binding agent is added, and the mixture is watered, tamped down, rolled, and, when hard, covered with a waterproof surface.

Above the foundation, or stabilized soil, comes a base course, usually of concrete, and then the top surface, or pavement, of asphalt or concrete. Shuttering—the use of wooden forms for support—is usually needed to hold concrete in position until it sets, but machines are now available that make this step unnecessary by producing firmly compacted concrete. Concrete can be laid by a spreader that runs on tracks; this step can be followed with the laying of a

steel-mesh reinforcement by a crane. Another spreader then puts on the top surface, and a vibrator compacts the surface. Another machine roughens the surface and checks that the camber—which is the slight arch upward in the middle of the road—is proper for good drainage.   CHARLES S. DUNBAR

Bibliography: Albert, William, *The Turnpike Road System, 1663-1840* (1972); Hindley, Geoffrey, *A History of Roads* (1977); Leavitt, Helen, *Superhighway—Superhoax* (1970); Overman, Michael, *Roads, Bridges and Tunnels* (1968); Rae, John B., *The Road and the Car in American Life* (1971); Robinson, John, *Highways and Our Environment* (1971); Shank, W. H., *Indian Trails to Superhighways* (1975); Wright, P H., and Poquette, R. J., *Highway Engineering*, 4th ed. (1979).

Roanoke [roh'-uh-nohk]

Roanoke (1980 pop., 100,427) is an independent city in Virginia between the Blue Ridge and Allegheny mountains. Situated on both the Sky Line Drive and the Blue Ridge Parkway, Roanoke is the area's commercial, industrial, and transportation center. Electrical equipment, furniture, apparel, and chemicals are manufactured there. Roanoke is headquarters for Jefferson National Forest, and the Booker T. Washington National Monument is located 32 km (20 mi) southeast of the city. Settled about 1740, Roanoke flourished as a transportation center for the region's coal mines after 1882, when the Shenandoah Valley Railroad connected with the Norfolk and Western Railroad.

Roanoke Colony

Roanoke Colony was an English settlement established on Roanoke Island, off modern North Carolina, in the 1580s. In 1584, Sir Walter RALEIGH, authorized to colonize in North America, sent out two ships, which landed on Roanoke. In 1585–86 a group led by Sir Richard GRENVILLE made an abortive attempt at settlement. Raleigh then dispatched three ships and 117 people (including women and children) to Roanoke in 1587. Their leader, John White, sailed back to England for supplies, but when he returned in 1590 the settlers had vanished without trace. Their fate remains a mystery.

Bibliography: Durant, David N., *Raleigh's Lost Colony* (1981).

Rob Roy

Rob Roy, actually Robert MacGregor, b. 1671, d. Dec. 28, 1734, was a Highland freebooter known as the Scottish Robin

Hood. Nominally a cattle dealer, he became a cattle thief who sold his neighbors protection against other rustlers. When the protection business failed, Rob Roy was accused of fraud and declared an outlaw. After his principal creditor, James Graham, 1st duke of Montrose, seized his lands, Rob Roy warred with the duke until 1722, when Rob Roy was forced to surrender. Later imprisoned, he was finally pardoned in 1727. His memory has been perpetuated and romanticized by Sir Walter Scott in the novel *Rob Roy* (1818).

CHARLES H. HAWS

Bibliography: Frewin, L. R., *Legends of Rob Roy* (1954).

Robbe-Grillet, Alain   [rohb-gree-ay']

Alain Robbe-Grillet, a French novelist and screenwriter, emerged as a major theoretician of the art of the "new novel" (nouveau roman). Feeling limited by the traditional novelist's dependence on subjective narrative and characterization, he developed a literary style claiming precise objectivity.

Photo Jill Krementz © 1973

The French author Alain Robbe-Grillet, b. Aug. 18, 1922, pioneered in the development of the NEW NOVEL, a form of fiction he explained and defended in his influential *Toward a New Novel: Essays on Fiction* (1964; Eng. trans., 1964). Beginning with his first work, *The Erasers* (1953; Eng. trans., 1964), Robbe-Grillet has consistently produced novels that avoid conventional renditions of plot and character, but focus on an "objective" world, composed of visual images and of objects that seem to exist without reference to anything beyond themselves. His novels include *The Voyeur* (1955; Eng. trans., 1958), *In the Labyrinth* (1959; Eng. trans., 1960), *(Topology of a Phantom City* (1976; Eng. trans., 1977), and *Djinn* (1981; Eng. trans., 1982). In the screenplays for such films as *Last Year in Marienbad* (1961), he attempts to visualize his fictional techniques.

Bibliography: Armes, Roy, *The Films of Alain Robbe-Grillet* (1981); Fraizer, Dale W., *Alain Robbe-Grillet* (1973); Morrisette, Bruce, *The Novels of Robbe-Grillet* (1975).

robbery

Robbery, in law, is LARCENY with force. It involves the unlawful and forcible taking of property or money from another against that person's will by using violence or intimidation. Robbery is generally regarded as a FELONY offense that is punishable by a term in a federal or state prison. If A picks B's pocket, then A is guilty of larceny, not robbery; if A strikes B and takes B's wallet, A has committed robbery. If the assailant threatens the victim with a gun, the assailant is liable to prosecution for the more serious offense of armed robbery.

Bibliography: Samaha, Joel, *Criminal Law* (1982).

Robbins, Frederick Chapman

American virologist Frederick Chapman Robbins, b. Auburn, Ala., Aug. 25, 1916, shared the 1954 Nobel Prize for physiology or medicine with John F. ENDERS and Thomas Weller for their development of methods for growing disease viruses in cultures of various types of body cells, enabling researchers to develop many later vaccines. Robbins obtained his M.D. from Harvard University in 1940 and worked with Enders's research team at Boston's Children's Hospital from 1948 to 1952. Thereafter he served on the staffs of Cleveland's Metropolitan General Hospital (1952–66) and of Case Western Reserve University School of Medicine (1952–80).

Robbins, Harold

Although his novels are consistently derided by critics as sensationalist and slipshod, writer Harold Robbins, b. New York City, May 21, 1916, is among the most widely read authors of modern times. Since his first novel, *Never Love a Stranger* (1948), he has written a string of successes, including *The Carpetbaggers* (1961; film, 1963), *The Adventurers* (1966; film, 1969), *The Betsy* (1971; film, 1977), *Spellbinder* (1982), and *Descent from Xanadu* (1984).

Robbins, Jerome

Jerome Robbins, b. New York City, Oct. 11, 1918, is America's most distinguished native-born choreographer of ballet and musical theater. Robbins performed as a dancer in Broadway shows (1938–40) and as a soloist (1940) with American Ballet Theatre (ABT). His initial choreography demonstrated his interest in theatrical ballets and technically complex "show" dancing: the ballet *Fancy Free* (1944) and the musical *On the Town* (1944), an elaboration of that ballet, were the first of many collaborations with composer Leonard Bernstein.

In 1949, Robbins became associate artistic director of NEW YORK CITY BALLET (NYCB) and created such noted ballets as *Afternoon of a Faun* (1953), *The Cage* (1951), and *The Concert* (1956). At the same time, he choreographed several musicals, including *Gypsy* (1959), *The King and I* (1951), and *Peter Pan* (1954). For *West Side Story* (1957), Robbins served as director-choreographer and created a new form of musical by integrating dancing with the narrative action. Robbins's dual activities continued with the musical *Fiddler on the Roof* (1964) and the ballet *Les Noces* (1965) for ABT.

In 1966, Robbins founded American Theater Laboratory, a 2-year experimental project; one of the results was the ballet *Watermill* (1972) for NYCB. Since 1969, Robbins has worked exclusively in ballet, returning to NYCB as ballet master in that year. Significant among his later creations are *Goldberg Variations* (1971), *The Four Seasons* (1979), *Glass Pieces* (1983), and *In Memory of . . .* (1985).

JOHN HOWELL

Bibliography: Kirstein, Lincoln, *The New York City Ballet* (1973).

Jerome Robbins is one of the most acclaimed and versatile American choreographers of the 20th century. Robbins integrates distinctly American themes and music into his classical and modern works, created primarily for the New York City Ballet, and uses these elements in musical theater. West Side Story (1957), which Robbins choreographed for both Broadway and Hollywood, receiving (1962) an Academy Award for the latter version, is one of his most popular works.

Robert, Hubert   [roh-bair']

The French landscape architect and painter Hubert Robert, b. May 22, 1733, d. Apr. 15, 1808, was particularly noted for his romantic paintings of ancient Roman ruins. Typical of these elegant, stylized views are the *Pont du Gard* (1787; Louvre, Paris) and *The Terrace* (1794; Baltimore Museum of Art). After studying in Rome for 11 years with Giovanni Paolo Pannini and Giovanni Battista Piranesi, Robert returned (1765) to France, where his work became enormously fashionable. He and his better-known contemporary Jean Honoré Fragonard borrowed much from each other's styles. Robert was a member of the Académie Royale and one of the first curators at the Louvre. As a landscape architect he helped to design the gardens at the Petit Trianon (1778), installing grottoes and ruins much like those in his paintings.

Bibliography: Kalnein, Wend Graf, and Levey, Michael, *Art and Architecture of the Eighteenth Century in France* (1972); Thuillier, Jacques, *French Painting from Le Nain to Fragonard*, trans. by J. Emmons (1964); Wiebenson, Dora, *The Picturesque Garden in France* (1978).

Robert Guiscard   [gees-kahr']

Robert Guiscard, b. *c.*1015, d. July 17, 1085, son of Tancred of Hauteville, was the leading Norman conqueror of southern Italy. In 1046 he joined his three brothers and other Norman adventurers who were aiding the Lombard princes in their rebellion against the Byzantine Empire. Robert, however, soon set out to conquer Calabria and Apulia on his own and in 1059 was recognized by Pope Nicholas II as duke of Calabria, Apulia, and Sicily. Aided by his brother Roger, who took (1061–91) Sicily from its Muslim rulers, Robert conquered Calabria (1060), Bari (1071), and Palermo (1072). Robert helped deposed Byzantine Emperor Michael VII regain his crown in 1082. His plans to usurp Michael's throne were interrupted when he was summoned (1083) by Pope Gregory VII to expel Holy Roman Emperor Henry IV from Rome. Guiscard died after returning to the Byzantine campaign.   James M. Powell

Bibliography: Douglas, David C., *The Norman Achievement* (1969); Norwich, J. J., *The Normans in the South* (1967).

Robert Wood Johnson Foundation

The Robert Wood Johnson Foundation, located in Princeton, N.J., is a private foundation whose purpose is to improve health care in the United States. Established by General Johnson in 1936 to support projects in New Brunswick, N.J., the foundation expanded its scope upon receiving the bulk of his estate in 1971. Its focus is improvement in access to health care and in the quality of health care services, and development of mechanisms for the analysis of public health policies. A typical grant is for training rural nurse practitioners—nurses who can perform some functions formerly reserved for physicians. In 1984 the foundation's assets were $1,173,836,335; 208 grants totaling $57.7 million were made.

Robert I, King of Scotland   (Robert the Bruce)

Robert the Bruce, crowned king of Scotland as Robert I in 1306, restored his country's freedom from English rule by his victory in the Battle of Bannockburn in 1314. Robert's legendary determination and courage have made his name a byword for Scottish nationalism.

Robert I, known as Robert the Bruce, b. July 11, 1274, d. June 7, 1329, king of Scotland, restored Scottish independence from England. In 1292, Bruce's grandfather lost his claim to the Scottish throne to John de Baliol in a succession suit decided by English King Edward I. During the next decade Bruce, then 8th earl of Carrick, switched his allegiance back and forth between Edward and the independence of Scotland.

After the execution (1305) of Sir William Wallace, a national hero, Bruce, not fully trusted by either side, murdered his old enemy John Comyn. This act committed him to the Scottish patriots, because Comyn had inherited Baliol's claim to the throne and was supported by Edward. On Mar. 27, 1306, Bruce was crowned at Scone. Following major setbacks in 1306–07, he rallied from an apparently hopeless situation and began systematically winning back his kingdom from the English. On June 24, 1314, at the Battle of Bannockburn, Bruce defeated Edward II, who had succeeded Edward I in 1307. This great victory established independence for Scotland and confirmed Bruce's claim to the throne. Robert I spent the remainder of his life fighting the English in Ireland and along the Scottish borders. In 1328, England formally recognized Scottish independence. Robert was succeeded by his son, David II.   Charles H. Haws

Bibliography: Barrow, G. W. S., *Robert Bruce* (1965); Mackenzie, A. M., *Robert Bruce, King of Scots* (1934).

Roberts, Sir Charles G. D.

A leader among Canadian poets, Sir Charles George Douglas Roberts, b. New Brunswick, Canada, Jan. 10, 1860, d. Nov. 26, 1943, published 12 volumes of poetry, consisting mostly of patriotic odes and nature poems. Roberts, who was knighted in 1935, was a leader of the Canadian poets known collectively as "The Group of the Sixties" and was also the author of books about nature, historical novels, and a *History of Canada* (1897).

Roberts, Elizabeth Madox

The American novelist Elizabeth Madox Roberts, b. Perryville, Ky., Oct. 30, 1881, d. Mar. 13, 1941, wrote movingly of Kentucky life before and during the Depression. She began her career as a writer with several volumes of verse, such as *Great Steep's Garden* (1915), but is remembered principally for her prose. Her first novel, *The Time of Man* (1923), and later works, among them *The Great Meadow* (1930) and *Black Is My Truelove's Hair* (1938), have been critically acclaimed. Robert's stories, sometimes interpretations of myth, portrayed Kentucky women struggling to overcome poverty and other hardships. Her characters' love of the land was lyrically suggested, and their sufferings, realistically described, took on a broad significance.

Bibliography: Campbell, Harry M., and Foster, Ruel E., *Elizabeth Madox Roberts: American Novelist* (1956); McDowell, Frederick P., *Elizabeth Madox Roberts* (1963).

Roberts, Frederick Sleigh, 1st Earl Roberts of Kandahar

A British field marshal, Frederick Sleigh Roberts, b. Sept. 30, 1832, d. Nov. 14, 1914, was the last commander in chief of the British army. He helped suppress the Indian Mutiny (1857–58) and distinguished himself in the Second Afghan War (1878–80), defeating the Afghan army near Kandahar. He was commander in chief in India (1885–93). Roberts became a field marshal in 1895, and from December 1899 to November 1900 he was commander in chief in the South African War, defeating the Boer forces in several key battles. In 1901 he was made an earl and became commander in chief of the British army. After 1904, when that post was abolished, Roberts campaigned vigorously for compulsory military service. He wrote *Forty-one Years in India* (1897).

Bibliography: Hannah, W. H., *Bobs, Kipling's General: The Life of Field-Marshal Earl Roberts of Kandahar* (1972); James, David, *Lord Roberts* (1954).

Roberts, Oral

Granville Oral Roberts, b. Ada, Okla., Jan. 24, 1918, is one of America's leading evangelists and faith healers. In the 1930s and '40s Roberts was pastor of several Pentecostal Holiness churches; in 1947 he began traveling extensively as a healing evangelist. He founded the Oral Roberts Evangelistic Association in 1948 and Oral Roberts University in Tulsa, Okla., in 1963. After 1968 he preached mainly on television and was associated with the United Methodist church. During the 1980s Roberts, increasingly occupied with raising funds for his financially troubled City of Faith medical center in Tulsa (opened in 1981), began sharing his ministry with his son, Richard Roberts.   JOHN F. PIPER

Roberts, Owen J.

Owen Josephus Roberts, b. Philadelphia, May 2, 1875, d. May 17, 1955, was an associate justice of the U.S. Supreme Court from 1930 to 1945. Appointed to the court by President Herbert Hoover, Roberts at first opposed the New Deal measures of Hoover's successor, Franklin D. Roosevelt, but became a New Deal supporter in the late 1930s. In 1942 he headed an investigation that blamed the U.S. military for being unprepared when the Japanese attacked Pearl Harbor.

Bibliography: Leonard, Charles A., *A Search for a Judicial Philosophy: Mr. Justice Roberts and the Constitutional Revolution of 1937* (1971).

Robert's Rules of Order

Originally entitled *Pocket Manual of Rules of Order for Deliberative Assemblies* (1876), *Robert's Rules of Order* is regarded in the United States as the authoritative statement of the parliamentary rules (see PARLIAMENTARY PROCEDURE) governing public meetings. The first edition, written by Henry Martyn Robert, an army engineer, was essentially an adaptation of the practice of the U.S. House of Representatives and was designed to enable civic-minded people to conduct organized debate in several different organizations without having to learn different parliamentary rules. Subsequently, the book has been revised many times and extensively enlarged.
                                                HERBERT M. LEVINE

Robertson, James

The American pioneer James Robertson, b. Brunswick County, Va., June 28, 1742, d. Sept. 1, 1814, was the founder and a leader of frontier settlements in present-day Tennessee. In 1771 he established the Watauga Colony on the Doe River in eastern Tennessee and helped organize a government under the WATAUGA ASSOCIATION. He also founded a community at the site of Nashville in 1780, headed the settlers' government, and led the region's defense against the Spanish-backed Creek Indians during the late 1780s.

Robertson, Oscar

Oscar Robertson, b. Charlotte, Tenn., Nov. 24, 1938, was one of the greatest guards ever to play basketball. After leading Crispus Attucks High School in Indianapolis, Ind., to two state championships, he played at the University of Cincinnati, where he was an All-American for three seasons (1958–60).
    As a member of the Cincinnati Royals and later the Milwaukee Bucks, both professional basketball teams, "Big O," as he was nicknamed, averaged 25.7 points and 9.5 assists per game over his 14-year career. The 1-m 95-cm (6-ft 5-in) star was selected to the National Basketball Association (NBA) all-star team nine times and was named the Most Valuable Player in the NBA for his play during the 1963–64 season.
                                                HOWARD LISS

Bibliography: Berkow, Ira, *Oscar Robertson: The Golden Year, 1964* (1971).

Robertson, Pat

Marion Gordon "Pat" Robertson, b. Lexington, Va., Mar. 22, 1930, is a U.S. Baptist minister, religious broadcaster, and po-

litical figure. The son of U.S. senator A. Willis Robertson (1887–1971), he is the founder (1960) of the Christian Broadcasting Network, and since 1968 has been the host of "The 700 Club," a television talk show with a conservative religious and political message. Robertson is a contender for the 1988 Republican presidential nomination.

Robeson, Paul   [rohb'-suhn]

The son of a former slave, American black actor and bass-baritone Paul Robeson, b. Princeton, N.J., Apr. 9, 1898, d. Jan. 23, 1976, was one of the most distinguished Americans of the 20th century. After graduating with Phi Beta Kappa honors from Rutgers University, where he twice received All-American football awards, he attended Columbia Law School and practiced law briefly before turning to the theater.
    Robeson's performances in Eugene O'Neill's plays during the early 1920s established him as a brilliant actor, and for two decades he was hailed as one of the greatest bass-baritones in the world. In the course of his many travels abroad, he learned numerous foreign languages and was greatly lionized. He played the title role in the 1943 Broadway production of *Othello*, which ran a record 296 performances. His acting in that play earned him, in 1944, the Academy of Arts and Letters' Gold Medal for best diction in the American theater and the Donaldson Award for best actor.
    Robeson championed the cause of the oppressed throughout his life, insisting that as an artist he had no choice but to do so. A trip to the Soviet Union early in his career had made him a lifelong friend of the USSR, which in 1952 awarded him the Stalin Peace Prize. Following World War II, when he took an uncompromising stand against segregation and lynching in the United States and advocated friendship with the Soviet Union, a long, intense campaign was mounted against him. Thereafter he was unable to earn a living as an artist in the United States and was also denied a passport. Finally in 1958 he was allowed to leave the country for Great Britain. He returned in 1963 in ill health and spent the last 13 years of his life in self-imposed seclusion.   STERLING STUCKEY

Bibliography: Gilliam, Dorothy Butler, *Paul Robeson: All American* (1976); Hoyt, Edwin P., *Paul Robeson, the American Othello* (1967); Robeson, Susan, *The Whole World in His Hands* (1981).

Paul Robeson became a controversial figure during the 1950s when his outspoken stance on civil rights and admiration for Soviet Communism culminated in the U.S. State Department's revocation of his passport. As a singer, Robeson is best known for his powerful rendition of "Ole Man River" in Jerome Kern's Showboat (play, 1928; film, 1936).

Robespierre, Maximilien   [roh-bes-pee-air']

Maximilien Marie Isidore Robespierre, b. Arras, May 6, 1758, d. July 28, 1794, is regarded by many historians as the most significant figure in the FRENCH REVOLUTION. A small man with a weak voice, fiercely concerned with first principles, he only gradually won recognition in the National Assembly (1789–91). Although later labeled an atrocious tyrant, he then advocated humanitarian reforms such as the abolition of capital punishment. An uncompromising democrat, he opposed the restriction of the franchise because he believed that goodness and good sense were to be found only in the common people. After King LOUIS XVI fled in 1791, Robespierre showed superb political skill; eschewing both premature republicanism and

Maximilien Robespierre, a leader of the French Revolution, believed that those who govern must possess absolute moral virtue. Convinced of his own rectitude, he came to regard all opposition as endangering the community and thus justified the use of Terror to impose the popular will.

The American robin, T. migratorius, commonly eats earthworms and insects. It ranges from Guatemala to the tree line in Alaska.

conservative reaction, he recreated the fragmented JACOBIN Society, which became his stronghold. There, excluded from the Legislative Assembly (1791–92) by his own decree against reelections, he continued to speak out. He condemned the frenzy for war with Austria.

Justified by events when the French army suffered reverses in the war and concluding that the king and the GIRONDISTS were betraying the Revolution, Robespierre promoted the republican revolution of Aug. 10, 1792; in September he was named a deputy for Paris to the National Convention. Although relentlessly attacked as a potential dictator, he justified the September Massacres of imprisoned nobles and clergy as inevitable and demanded the execution of the king as a political necessity. Believing unanimity to be imperative, he prompted the proscription of the Girondists in June 1793.

Robespierre's election to the Committee of Public Safety in July 1793 heralded a new era of repression; after September he became the principal spokesman for Terror. Believing that ruthless revolutionary government is legitimate when the community is endangered, he eliminated the factions of Jacques René HÉBERT and Georges Jacques DANTON in 1794, centralized political justice in Paris, and by the notorious Law of 22 Prairial expedited the work of the revolutionary tribunal. He also sought to promote social unity by accepting price controls and inaugurating the cult of the Supreme Being to check attacks upon Christianity and to stimulate patriotic virtue. When French military victories made this regime seem superfluous, Robespierre was overthrown; arrested on July 27, (9 Thermidor), 1794, he attempted suicide but was guillotined on the next day.

Always inclined to identify personal and political opposition as counterrevolutionary conspiracy, Robespierre had an uncompromising vision of political and social democracy. For him that vision was inseparable from patriotism, and the question of whether the Terror he upheld was becoming a means to a moral end remains unanswered.   M. J. SYDENHAM

Bibliography: Hampson, Norman, *Life and Opinions of Maximilien Robespierre* (1974); Jordan, David, *The Revolutionary Career of Maximilien Robespierre* (1985); Rudé, G. E., *Robespierre: Portrait of a Revolutionary Dictator* (1975); Thompson, J. M., *Robespierre*, 2 vols. (1935), and *Robespierre and the French Revolution* (1952).

robin

Robin is the common name for a number of songbirds, notably the American robin, *Turdus migratorius*, and the European robin, *Erithacus rubecula*, in the thrush family, Turdidae. American colonists named the medium-sized (25 cm/10 in), slate-backed, russet-breasted bird they found abundant in their new land for the much smaller (14 cm/5 in), friendly robin so popular in Europe, which has a brown back and orange breast. Depending on the severity of the local winter, the robin is either a resident or a migrant. Several other thrushes and some Old World flycatchers (family Muscicapidae) also are called robins.   WILLIAM F. SANDFORD

Robin Hood

Robin Hood is a legendary hero of medieval England who stole from the rich to give to the poor, thus showing his love for the common people. He is the subject of nearly 40 English and Scottish ballads and numerous tales, plays, and films. Robin Hood and his band, including Little John, Maid Marian, and Friar Tuck, are supposed to have lived in Sherwood Forest near Nottingham.   JAMES J. WILHELM

Robinson, Brooks

The Hall of Fame baseball player Brooks Calbert Robinson, b. Little Rock, Ark., May 18, 1937, is considered the greatest 3d baseman in major league history. Playing (1958–77) for the Baltimore Orioles, Robinson had a .971 lifetime fielding average and won a record 16 consecutive Gold Gloves (1960–75). He appeared in 18 straight All Star games and was the American League's MVP in 1964. He won the Hickok Belt—as the nation's best professional athlete—in 1970.

Robinson, Charles

Charles Robinson, b. Hardwick, Mass., July 18, 1818, d. Aug. 17, 1894, was a U.S. politician. Educated at Amherst, he practiced medicine before going to Kansas in 1854 as an agent of the New England EMIGRANT AID COMPANY, which was formed to assist free-soil partisans in Kansas. He helped lead the FREE-SOIL PARTY and was elected (1856) governor of Kansas under the free-state constitution adopted by a convention at Topeka. Because he ignored laws passed by the proslavery territorial legislature, members of the proslavery party arrested him on charges of treason and usurpation of office. Acquitted by a federal grand jury, Robinson was reelected (1859) under Kansas's new Wyandotte constitution. He assumed office in 1861, when Kansas was admitted to the Union, serving until 1863. He wrote *The Kansas Conflict* (1892).

Robinson, Eddie

Grambling State University football coach Edward Gay Robinson, b. Baker, La., Feb. 13, 1919, has won more games than anyone else in collegiate history, breaking Bear BRYANT's record in 1985. After graduating from Leland College (La.), Robinson began at Grambling in 1941 and has coached over 200 eventual professional players—more than anyone else—in accumulating, through 1985, a record 329 wins, 109 losses, and 15 ties.

Edward G. Robinson clutches his wounded arm in this scene from one of the first talking gangster films, Little Caesar (1930), a classic of the genre. In it Robinson portrayed mobster Rico Bandello, a character patterned loosely after the Chicago crime lord Al Capone.

Robinson, Edward G.

Edward G. Robinson, stage name of Emanuel Goldenberg, b. Romania, Dec. 12, 1893, d. Jan. 26, 1973, became one of the major figures of Hollywood films of the 1930s. Short and dynamic, with a distinctive voice, he specialized in gangster parts but later proved equally adept at comedy or in benevolent character roles. His most important films include *Little Caesar* (1930), *Dr. Ehrlich's Magic Bullet* (1940), *Double Indemnity* and *The Woman in the Window* (both 1944), and *Key Largo* (1948). LESLIE HALLIWELL

Bibliography: Robinson, Edward G., and Spiegelgass, Leonard, *All My Yesterdays* (1975).

Robinson, Edwin Arlington

Edwin Arlington Robinson, b. Head Tide, Maine, Dec. 22, 1869, d. Apr. 6, 1935, was a major American poet who is admired for his moving poetic vision and for his superb mastery of verse forms. Robinson grew up in Gardiner, Maine, which he immortalized in his poetry as Tilbury Town. His early short poems, such as "Richard Cory" and "Miniver Cheevy," about unhappy and disappointed individuals, remain the most widely read portion of his work. Character studies modeled on townspeople and members of Robinson's own family, these verses display his gift for ironic detachment and his shrewd awareness of the hidden aspects of human nature.

Although Robinson would eventually receive three Pulitzer Prizes for his poetry, he remained virtually destitute for many years of his career. In 1905, President Theodore Roosevelt, an early admirer of Robinson's work, secured him a clerkship in the New York Custom House. Wider recognition came with the publication of *The Town down the River* (1910). Thereafter, Robinson was able to support himself on his writings and to spend most of his summers in the company of other artists at the MacDowell Colony in Peterborough, N.H. "The Man against the Sky," published in 1916, is typical of his later poetry in its somber outlook and transcendental overtones. Other later works of importance include *Merlin* (1917), the first of three Arthurian tales dealing with the modern world, and the narratives *Amaranth* (1934) and *King Jasper* (1935). Robinson also wrote several plays. JAMES HART

Bibliography: Anderson, Wallace L., *Edwin Arlington Robinson: A Critical Introduction* (1967); Cary, Richard, ed., *Appreciation of Edwin Arlington Robinson* (1969); Coxe, Louise, *Edwin Arlington Robinson: The Life of Poetry* (1969).

Robinson, Frank

Baseball Hall of Fame member Frank Robinson, b. Beaumont, Tex., Aug. 31, 1935, is noted not only for his outstanding playing career but also for becoming the first black manager in the major leagues (Cleveland Indians, 1975–77; San Francisco Giants, 1981–84). Robinson joined the National League's Cincinnati Reds in 1956 and was Rookie of the Year. Five years later he was named NL Most Valuable Player (MVP). In 1966, after being traded to the Baltimore Orioles, he won the Triple Crown—leading the American League in batting (.316), home runs (49), and runs batted in (122)—and was voted that league's MVP, the only man ever to be MVP in both leagues. HOWARD LISS

Bibliography: Robinson, Frank, and Silverman, Al, *My Life Is Baseball* (1968); Schneider, Russell J., *Frank Robinson: The Making of a Manager* (1976).

Robinson, Henry Peach

The British photographer Henry Peach Robinson's photographs, such as Fading Away (1858), emulated the sentimental genre paintings popular during the mid-19th century. This photograph, a skillful composite of five different negatives, reflects the symmetrical composition and dramatic lighting characteristic of Robinson's work.

The English photographer Henry Peach Robinson, b. July 9, 1830, d. Feb. 21, 1901, was a pioneering exponent of pictorialist photography. He crystallized 19th-century photographic aesthetics through his prolific writings and the publication of his photographs, which resemble the large narrative paintings popular in the Victorian era. In his influential *Pictorial Effect in Photography* (1869), he applied the academic rules governing composition in painting to the newer medium, advocating contrived artificial compositions in photography. To produce prints like his famous *Fading Away* (1858), for example, he combined as many as five negatives. Until Peter Henry EMERSON's *Naturalistic Photography* (1889) appeared, Robinson's theories held sway in photographic circles.

ELIZABETH POLLOCK

Edwin Arlington Robinson was one of the most acclaimed poets in America during the first quarter of the 20th century. Today he is remembered for short, psychologically penetrating poems, such as "Miniver Cheevy," written in a terse, colloquial style. Robinson also achieved critical recognition for long narrative poems, such as Tristram (1927), for which he received his third Pulitzer Prize.

Robinson, Jackie

Jackie Robinson, an American baseball player, became the first black athlete to play in the major leagues when he debuted (1947) with the Brooklyn Dodgers. During his first year Robinson helped his team win the National League pennant and was voted Rookie of the Year. Robinson played for 10 seasons (1947-56) with the Dodgers, winning the Most Valuable Player award in 1949 and leading the team to its only world championship (1955) during the span of Robinson's career.

The American Jack Roosevelt Robinson, b. Cairo, Ga., Jan. 31, 1919, d. Oct. 24, 1972, major league baseball's first black player in modern times, was an athlete who combined outstanding physical skills with a burning, single-minded desire for victory. One of the game's most aggressive competitors, Robinson joined the Brooklyn Dodgers of the National League in 1947 at the age of 28 and helped lead the team to 6 World Series appearances in 10 years. A versatile athlete, he also starred in football and track while in college at the University of California in Los Angeles. While playing with the Kansas City Monarchs of the Negro National League he was signed to a major league baseball contract by Branch Rickey and assigned (1946) to the Dodgers' Montreal farm team of the International League. Robinson was brought to Brooklyn the next year, where he hit .297, scored 125 runs, and led the league in stolen bases (29) as the Dodgers won their first pennant since 1941. He was named Rookie of the Year. Primarily a second baseman, he also played at third and first base and in the outfield. In 1949 he was named the league's Most Valuable Player, leading the league in batting (.342) and stolen bases (37) in addition to scoring 122 runs and batting in 124 runs while reaching a career high of 203 hits. He was an outstanding fielder as well, leading the league in fielding average three times at his position. He was elected to the Baseball Hall of Fame in 1962.

Bibliography: Olsen, James T., *Jackie Robinson* (1974); Robinson, Jackie, with Duckett, Alfred, *I Never Had It Made* (1972); Rowan, Carl T., *Wait Till Next Year: The Life Story of Jackie Robinson* (1960).

Robinson, John

John Robinson, b. c.1576, d. Mar. 1, 1625, was the pastor in Leiden of the PILGRIMS before they sailed to America on the Mayflower. After graduating from Cambridge University, he served as an Anglican priest, probably at Norwich. About 1607 he joined a separatist congregation at Scrooby. Its members believed that the English church was not strict enough to maintain proper standards of godly living and, therefore, serious Christians should separate from it and form exclusive churches where true faith and strict morals would be characteristic of all members.

Within a year the unpopular dissenters fled to Holland and organized (1609) a church at Leiden with Robinson as their pastor. When some of his flock wanted to leave Holland, Robinson supported their plans to relocate in the New World, but he did not travel with them to establish the Plym-

outh Colony. He sent them letters of pastoral advice and hoped to join them eventually, but he died in Leiden.

HENRY WARNER BOWDEN

Robinson, Lennox

A leading figure in the IRISH LITERARY RENAISSANCE, Lennox Robinson, b. Oct. 4, 1886, d. Oct. 14, 1958, was manager and later director of Dublin's ABBEY THEATRE. Robinson's anthologies of Irish verse fostered new interest in Irish poetry. His own writings include the play *The Lost Leader* (1918) and the autobiographical *Curtain Up* (1942).

ROBIN BUSS

Robinson, Sir Robert

The English chemist Sir Robert Robinson, b. Sept. 13, 1886, d. Feb. 8, 1975, received the Nobel Prize for chemistry in 1947 in recognition of his investigations of the chemical structures of plant products, especially the ALKALOIDS morphine (1925) and strychnine (1946). He also completed structural studies and syntheses of anthocyan dyes, sex hormones, cholesterol, vitamin D_3, and antimalarials. From the 1930s he was influential, along with Sir Christopher Ingold, in the development of electronic theories in mechanistic organic chemistry, especially concerning the behavior of reactants as nucleophiles and electrophiles.

O. BERTRAND RAMSAY

Robinson, Sugar Ray

Walker Smith, b. Detroit, May 3, 1920, was an American professional boxer whom many boxing experts consider to have been the best pugilist of modern times. He acquired his ring-name when he borrowed the birth certificate of a friend named Ray Robinson so he could fight while he was yet below the minimum age. Sugar Ray won his first world title in the welterweight class on Dec. 20, 1946, when he defeated Tommy Bell. He then went on to win the middleweight title five times. The first time was on Feb. 14, 1951, when he knocked out Jake La Motta. He soon lost the title to Randy Turpin but regained it 2 months later. Robinson attempted to wrest the light-heavyweight title from Joey Maxim in 1952, but he collapsed from heat exhaustion (Robinson was ahead on points but failed to start the 14th round). He then announced his retirement. Robinson returned, however, in 1955 and recaptured the middleweight title from Carl Olson. Following a successful defense of his title against Olson, he lost to Gene Fuller (Jan. 2, 1957). His revenge was quick, and on May 1, 1957, Robinson beat Fuller. Robinson again lost the title, this time to Carmen Basilio on Sept. 23, 1957, but won it back May 25, 1958. He lost the title for good to Paul Pender on Jan. 22, 1960, and in three subsequent title bouts was unable to win it back. Robinson possessed balance, quickness, and devastating combination punches. In 202 professional

Sugar Ray Robinson was the first professional fighter to win the championship of a single weight division five times. After capturing the welterweight title in 1946, Robinson moved into the middleweight class, first winning its title in 1951. Although he lost that title in the ring three times and once relinquished it because of a premature retirement, Robinson was able to regain his title four times before finally retiring in 1965.

fights he posted 109 knockouts, won 66 decisions on points, had 6 draws, lost 18 decisions, was knocked out once, and had 1 no decision and 1 no contest.

Bibliography: Carpenter, Harry, *Masters of Boxing* (1964); Robinson, Ray, with Dave Anderson, *Sugar Ray* (1970).

Robinson Crusoe

Daniel DEFOE's famous novel, fully titled *The Life and Strange Surprising Adventures of Robinson Crusoe of York, Mariner* (1719), was based on the experiences of Alexander Selkirk, who, after quarreling with his captain, asked to be put ashore on a desert island and was rescued 4 years later. It is written in the style of a factual report. The primary external events are Crusoe's discovery of a footprint and his rescue of the man Friday from cannibals. It is also the spiritual autobiography of Crusoe, exploring in minute detail one man's struggle to understand and maintain his personal integrity during years of solitude.   JANET M. TODD

Bibliography: Ellis, F. N., *Twentieth Century Interpretations of Robinson Crusoe* (1969); Novak, M., *Defoe and the Nature of Man* (1963).

Robinson-Patman Act

The Robinson-Patman Act, passed in 1936 to protect small businesses against discriminatory practices that favor large chain stores, supplemented the CLAYTON ANTI-TRUST ACT of 1914. The Robinson-Patman Act prohibits a businessperson from discriminating in price between purchasers of commodities of equal grade and quality if this results in less competition or monopoly. The seller may discriminate if it can be proved that differences exist in the cost of supplying the customer or that the action was made in good faith to meet a competitor's lower price. Most Robinson-Patman Act cases are brought by private parties, who may sue for three times the amount of damage sustained because of price discrimination. Enforcement is under the jurisdiction of the U.S. Department of Justice and the Federal Trade Commission. The act was cosponsored by Sen. Joseph T. Robinson and Rep. Wright Patman.   WILLARD F. MUELLER

robot

A robot may be defined as a completely self-controlled device consisting of electronic, electrical, or mechanical units; more generally, it is a machine devised to function in place of a living agent. The word *robot* comes from a story and play produced in 1921 called *R.U.R.* (for Rossum's Universal Robots), by Karel Capek. In Czech the word *robot* means "worker," but the English translation (1923) retained the original term. The sense of a possible, capable, and willing worker makes the concept of robots so important.

As far back as the days of Homer, who described "handmaids of gold resembling living young damsels" (*Iliad*, book 18), the fictional robot has traditionally been a mobile device, humanoid in appearance. Today the majority of robots are not humanoid, but instead are properly engineered machines designed for a particular function.

Most robots sit alongside assembly lines and perform such tasks as welding, painting, and inspection. Japan is both the leading maker and user of robots, with a majority of them employed on automobile assembly lines. In general, such robots do not have the ability to learn new tasks; instead they perform carefully orchestrated procedures, guided by a computer program (see AUTOMATION).

Robots have ventured into other areas. In medicine, a robotic arm equipped with surgical tools has assisted doctors in a delicate brain operation; in the field of COMPUTER-AIDED DESIGN AND COMPUTER-AIDED MANUFACTURING (CAD/CAM), robotic structures have been used to manufacture such things as integrated circuits and solid models.   RUTH V. BUCKLEY

Bibliography: Baranson, Jack, *Robots in Manufacturing* (1983); Chen, Wayne, *The Year of the Robot—1981* (1981); Coiffet, Philippe, *Robot Technology*, 2 vols. (1983); Logsdon, Tom, *The Robot Revolution* (1984); Owen, Tony, *Assembly with Robots* (1985); Reichardt, Jasia, *Robots: Facts, Fiction and Prediction* (1978).

Roca, Julio A.   [roh'-kah]

Julio Argentino Roca, b. July 17, 1843, d. Oct. 19, 1914, was an Argentine general and statesman who was twice president of Argentina (1880–86, 1898–1904). As President Nicolás Avellaneda's minister of war, Roca drove (1878–79) the Patagonian Indians south, opening vast areas of the Pampas for colonization. During Roca's first term as president, the Argentine economy expanded rapidly, but inflation, graft, and corruption were persistent problems. During his second administration, Roca stabilized the currency and settled boundary disputes with Chile and Brazil. After leaving office, he continued to dominate Argentine politics.

Bibliography: Ferns, Henry S., *Argentina* (1969).

Rocafuerte, Vicente   [roh-kah-fwayr'-tay]

Vicente Rocafuerte, b. May 3, 1783, d. May 16, 1847, a general in the Ecuadorian wars of independence, was president of Ecuador (1835–39) and the longtime political rival of Gen. Juan José FLORES. Rocafuerte led (1834) an unsuccessful revolt against Flores's government. He and Flores settled their differences, and Rocafuerte succeeded Flores as president. The coalition of conservatives (Flores's faction) and liberals (Rocafuerte's faction) soon broke up, and Flores resumed the presidency. A long period of political rivalry ensued.

Bibliography: Rodriguez, J., *Emergence of Spanish America* (1976).

Rochambeau, Jean Baptiste Donatien de Vimeur, Comte de   [roh-shahm-boh', doh-nah-see-an' duh vee-mur']

The comte de Rochambeau, b. July 1, 1725, d. May 12, 1807, was a career general who, during the American Revolution, commanded the French forces that helped defeat the British army in the YORKTOWN CAMPAIGN. As a young officer, Rochambeau served ably in the War of the Austrian Succession (1740–48) and Seven Years' War (1756–63).

Dispatched by King Louis XVI to help the American revolutionists, he landed in Newport, R.I., with about 5,500 troops in 1780 but remained inactive for a year because the French fleet was blockaded off Narragansett Bay. On May 21, 1781, he persuaded George Washington to join forces with the marquis de LAFAYETTE's besiegers and the comte de GRASSE's blockading French fleet against Gen. Charles CORNWALLIS at Yorktown.

In the early months of the French Revolution, Rochambeau commanded France's northern army; he was made marshal of France in 1791. Imprisoned during the Reign of Terror, he was later awarded a pension and membership in the Legion of Honor by Napoleon.   A. LLOYD MOOTE

Bibliography: Weelen, Jean-Edmond, *Rochambeau, Father and Son* (1936); Whitridge, Arnold, *Rochambeau* (1965; repr. 1974).

Roche, Kevin   [rohch]

The architect Kevin Roche, b. Dublin, June 14, 1922, is a leading designer for business and industry in the United States. His structures, with their elegant, taut glass skins, resemble mammoth, shimmering greenhouses or crystal palaces—for example, the Power Center for the Performing Arts, University of Michigan, Ann Arbor (1965–71), One United Nations Plaza in New York City (1969–76), and Union Carbide Headquarters, Danbury, Conn. (1980). Roche went to the United States in 1948 to study (1948–49) with Ludwig Mies van der Rohe at the Illinois Institute of Technology in Chicago. There he was profoundly influenced by Eero SAARINEN, whose firm he joined in 1950. After Saarinen's death in 1961, Roche and John Dinkeloo completed the existing Saarinen projects; in 1966 the firm became Kevin Roche, John Dinkeloo and Associates. Its work has shown, primarily, a vastness of scale that makes each project look like a first model of the original idea—as in the Ford Foundation, New York City (1963–68), or the Knights of Columbus, New Haven, Conn. (1965–69). Some of the projects show an ingenious progression of scale within a single building. In some cases the architects have attempted to enfold nature, as in the Ford Foundation's interior garden and the Oakland Museum in California (1961–68), which is designed as an underground, landscaped series of terraces.

C. RAY SMITH

Bibliography: *Kevin Roche, John Dinkeloo and Associates* (1975).

Roche's limit   [rohsh]

The French mathematician Édouard Roche (1820–83) calculated that if a satellite were to approach a planet within a certain distance, called the Roche limit, then the tidal forces exerted by the planet would overcome the gravitational forces holding the satellite together, and the satellite would disintegrate. For a satellite having the same average density as the planet, the critical distance is 2.44 times the radius of the planet. The rings of Jupiter, Saturn, and Uranus lie entirely within the Roche limit for each planet and may be the remains of a satellite. This reasoning takes no account of the cohesiveness of the material of the satellite and does not apply to artificial satellites.

J. M. A. DANBY

Rochester   (Minnesota)   [rah'-ches-tur]

Rochester is a city in southeastern Minnesota. The seat of Olmsted County, it has a population of 57,855 (1980). An important electronics center, Rochester is also the home of the MAYO CLINIC and the commercial and cultural center of the large, surrounding dairying region. Originally a wagon-train campground, the site was settled in 1854 and named for Rochester, N.Y. The clinic was established in 1889 by Dr. William W. Mayo and his sons.

Rochester   (New York)

Rochester, the seat of Monroe County, N.Y., is a city and port on the Genesee River and Lake Ontario. The city's population is 241,741 (1980); that of the 5-county metropolitan area is 971,879. Once the home of photography pioneer George Eastman, abolitionist Frederick Douglass, and women's rights leader Susan B. Anthony, Rochester is a major industrial city with several specialized industries, a cultural and educational center, and a port of entry on the St. Lawrence Seaway.

Since the late 19th century, medical instruments, optical equipment, and photographic industries have been the mainstays of the Rochester economy, along with office machinery, clothing, shoes, and foods. Surrounding the city is rich farmland producing fruit and vegetables.

Rochester's many educational institutions include the University of Rochester (1850), with its prestigious EASTMAN SCHOOL OF MUSIC, and the Rochester Institute of Technology (1829). Cultural facilities include the Rochester Museum and Science Center, the International Museum of Photography, and the Rochester Philharmonic Orchestra. Durand-Eastman Park on Lake Ontario, the botanic gardens in Highland Park, and the Seneca Park zoo are the main park attractions.

Rochester's first white settler was Ebenezer Allen, who built a mill for the local Seneca Indians on a 40-ha (100-acre) parcel; his land was purchased by Col. Nathaniel Rochester and two partners, and their settlement was incorporated as the village of Rochesterville in 1817. The village grew quickly, with the construction of the Erie Canal (1822) improving transportation for the local farmers and for an active flour industry. Rochester's role as Flour City ended with the country's westward expansion and the coming of the railroad, but a flourishing nursery industry took its place. The city's modern industrial development began in the second half of the 19th century.

Rochester Institute of Technology

Established in 1829 as the Rochester Athenaeum and given its present name in 1944, the Rochester Institute of Technology (enrollment: 12,670; library: 351,000 volumes) is a private coeducational school in Rochester, N.Y. Students are able to earn bachelor's and master's degrees in business administration and all fields of technology, including applied arts and sciences, photography, and printing.

rock

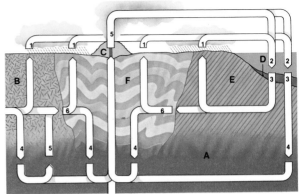

Igneous, sedimentary, and metamorphic rocks gradually and continuously change into one another. Cooling of molten magma (A) forms intrusive igneous rocks (B) below the Earth's surface and extrusive igneous rocks (C) above the surface. Surface rocks eventually erode (1) into particles, which are washed into the seas and deposited (2) as sediment (D). Compaction and cementation (3) of accumulated sediment form sedimentary rocks (E). Accumulation of more sediment forces these rocks into the hot plastic mantle, where they melt (4), mix with other materials, rise, and solidify again (5). Combined heat and pressure (6) may change igneous and sedimentary rocks into metamorphic rocks (F).

Rock is the solid substance that forms the Earth's crust. Most geologists exclude SOIL from this category and further restrict the term to materials formed by natural processes.

Rocks are classified as igneous, sedimentary, or metamorphic according to how they formed. Those which solidified from molten or partly molten material are called IGNEOUS ROCKS. SEDIMENTARY ROCKS form by the accumulation of sediment, mineral particles that have either settled from a state of suspension in air or water or have been precipitated from a state of solution. METAMORPHIC ROCKS are those which have undergone marked transformation, in response to heat, pressure, or chemical alteration.

The molten material (MAGMA) from which all igneous rocks form may issue as LAVA from volcanoes; such rock is said to be extrusive. Intrusive igneous rocks are those which form from consolidation of magma underground.

Sedimentary rocks are said to be clastic if they consist of particles of older rock (gravel, for example), chemical if precipitated from solution (rock salt, for example), or organic if formed from the remains or secretions of plants or animals (coal, for example). Particles of lava exploded into the air during volcanic eruption may settle to the ground and form deposits of volcanic ash. Such rocks are called pyroclastics.

As a result of metamorphism, solidified accumulations of mud (SHALE) or volcanic ash (TUFF) may alter to SLATE. In the heated depths of the Earth's crust, slate may recrystallize into an aggregate of platy (MICA) or elongated minerals called SCHIST. The addition of new ingredients supplied by migrating fluids may convert schist to GRANITE. If, as a result of crystal uplift combined with erosion, the granite is exposed at the surface, it will eventually decompose and provide the ingredients for new deposits of sedimentary rock.

Bibliography: Bailey, D. K., and MacDonald, R., eds., *The Evolution of Crystalline Rocks* (1976); Ernst, W. G., *Earth Materials* (1969); Harker, Alfred, *Metamorphism*, 2d ed. (1939); Jackson, K. C., *Textbook of Lithology* (1970); Pettijohn, Francis J., *Sedimentary Rocks*, 3d ed. (1975); Prinz, Martin, et al., eds., *Simon and Schuster's Guide to Rocks and Minerals* (1978); Ramsay, John G., *Folding and Fracturing of Rocks* (1967); Wyckoff, Jerome, *Rock, Time and Landforms* (1966).

See also: PETROGRAPHY; PETROLOGY.

rock music

Rock music emerged during the mid-1950s to become the major popular musical form of young audiences in the United

States and Western Europe. Its stylistic scope is too broad to be encompassed by any single definition; the only feature common to all rock music is a heavy emphasis on the beat.

Rock 'n' Roll, 1950-62. The primary source of rock 'n' roll was RHYTHM AND BLUES, an idiom popular among black audiences that combined elements of urban BLUES (in the structure, vocal style, and use of amplified guitar), GOSPEL MUSIC (in the piano accompaniments and vocal harmonizing), and JAZZ (in the saxophone solos). Rhythm and blues began to gain a wider audience during the late 1940s, and in 1951 the disc jockey Alan Freed, who played an important role in attracting white teenagers to the music, substituted the term "rock 'n' roll," previously used as a sexual reference in lyrics. Major record producers, observing the success of rhythm and blues and rock 'n' roll songs distributed on "race records" (i.e., record labels marketed to black audiences), issued "covers"—competing, "sanitized" versions of the same songs, but recorded by white artists. Covers—whatever their artistic quality—brought new stylistic influences to rock 'n' roll (white COUNTRY AND WESTERN and popular music) and eased the transition for white audiences. This audience, still hesitant at accepting black music, made Bill Haley's "Rock Around the Clock" (1955) the first important breakthrough for white rock 'n' roll. What appealed to this new audience, accustomed to the relatively bland TIN PAN ALLEY brand of popular music, was rock 'n' roll's driving dance rhythms, its direct, adolescent-level message, and its suggestion of youthful rebellion.

Rock 'n' roll's first superstar was Elvis PRESLEY. With his country-and-western background, Presley led the way for other "rockabilly" (*rock* plus *hillbilly*) artists; with his spasmodic hip gyrations, he introduced a sexual suggestiveness that outraged conservative adults; with his legions of teenage fans, he brought to rock 'n' roll the cult of personality and became the archetype of the rock star as cultural hero.

Other popular figures, while commanding a smaller audience, also made significant contributions to the style; among them, Chuck BERRY nourished the music's basic roots, Jerry Lee Lewis expanded its country branch, and Little Richard provided frantic showmanship. Despite the dynamism of such figures, by the late 1950s a malaise had set in; the music had become formula ridden, sentimental, and often—as in love-death ballads like "Teen Angel"—distinctly maudlin. Seeking a more honest expression, a significant segment of the adolescent and young adult audiences transferred their allegiance to FOLK MUSIC, as sung by such groups as Peter, Paul, and Mary, a folk trio; to traditional balladeers like the Kingston Trio; and to the prophets of modern folk/social commentary, Joan BAEZ and Bob DYLAN.

Rock, 1963-69. The renewal of rock 'n' roll came from the unlikely locale of Liverpool, England. Here, The BEATLES made their start in 1960, at first imitating American styles and then weaving from the various strands of American rock 'n' roll an individual style marked—in both music and lyrics—by wit and a sense of fun. Their successes came quickly during 1963 and '64, and their domination of the record market was complete and unprecedented. Then, rather than repeat the formulas of their initial triumphs, they chose the more precarious route of experimentation and growth. From 1965 to 1969 they introduced new sonorities, textures, forms, rhythms, melodic designs, and lyric conceptions, and were at the forefront of a revolutionary epoch in popular music. Rock 'n' roll had evolved into an expression of greater sophistication, complexity, and breadth. It had become a new idiom: rock.

Other English groups also came into prominence around 1964, taking their places as equals with American artists in the development of rock. The ROLLING STONES, the most prominent and durable of these groups, presented yet another image of rock—one of anger, alienation, and sensuality.

Other trends of the 1960s included the merging of rhythm and blues with black gospel styles to create SOUL MUSIC; the beginnings of jazz-rock, as originally synthesized by the band Blood, Sweat and Tears; folk-rock, a blending of folk with rock; and the emergence of the "California sound." The folk-rock style, first suggested by Bob Dylan at the 1965 Newport Folk Festival, brought to folk music a hard beat and amplification, and to rock a new poetic sensibility and social consciousness. A deeper significance of the blending was its demonstration of rock's tendency to absorb all challenging idioms.

Chuck Berry displays his flamboyant technique during a typically energetic performance. Berry became one of the formative figures of rock 'n' roll, recording such classics of the genre as "Maybelline" (1955) and "Johnny B. Goode" (1958). Berry's powerfully rhythmic blues style greatly influenced the British groups who revitalized rock 'n' roll during the 1960s.

(Above) The Beatles, a phenomenally successful English quartet from Liverpool, became the major innovative force in rock 'n' roll during the 1960s.

(Left) Elvis Presley shocked conservative audiences and delighted youthful fans with the uninhibited hip gyrations that became a hallmark of his early performances. A charismatic entertainer, Presley emerged as the dominant male vocalist of the early years of rock 'n' roll, blending elements of rhythm and blues, gospel, and country and western music.

The "California sound," despite its name, was not a uniform style, but a term that reflected the rise of California as a major center of rock activity and experimentation. In the early 1960s, California was the scene of "surfing music" (popularized by the BEACH BOYS), but over the course of the decade the music changed to parallel the trends of hippies (the Mamas and the Papas), student protest (Country Joe and the Fish), and a countercultural affair with drugs.

Widespread popularity of hallucinogenic drugs (particularly LSD, or "acid") produced psychedelic Acid Rock, whose apostles included JEFFERSON AIRPLANE and the GRATEFUL DEAD.

Rock's first major effort in musical theater was the hippie revue *Hair* (1967), a spectacularly successful pageant celebrating youth, love, and drugs. Closely following were such rock-opera successes as *Tommy* and *Jesus Christ Superstar*.

By the end of the 1960s the distinctions between rock 'n' roll and rock were evident. The earlier instrumentation of saxophone, piano, amplified guitar, and drums had been replaced by several amplified guitars, drums, and an ever-increasing reliance on electronic technology. To the standard patterns of 12-bar blues and 32-bar song form were added extended, unique forms, sometimes encompassing the entire side of a record album; to the lyrics of teenage love and adolescent concerns were added social commentary, glorification of drugs, and free-association poetry. Descriptive group names (Crew Cuts, Everly Brothers, Beach Boys) were replaced by nondescriptive, enigmatic names (The WHO, Jefferson Airplane, Big Brother and the Holding Company). Finally, the separation between performer and composer seemed to vanish as the two merged in a single performer-composer. As

demonstrated by the WOODSTOCK FESTIVAL in August 1969, rock music was by this time an intrinsic element in the life of American youth and a powerful articulation of their moods, hopes, and fears.

Rock, 1970–79. This decade saw the fragmentation of rock into subdivisions beyond the general categories of hard rock (extremely loud and electronically amplified) and mellow rock (softer, sometimes with acoustic instruments). The terms identifying these subdivisions were not firm definitions but merely guides to styles that were tenuous, fluid, and often overlapping.

Some styles were blendings of rock with other established idioms, the rock contribution invariably being a heavy beat and electronic technology. Thus, folk-rock and country-rock each retained the character of folk and country music. REGGAE, which emerged from Jamaica around 1972, is still a vital style. It is an integration of rock, soul, calypso, and other Latin rhythms. Jazz-rock fusion, or simply fusion, was a meeting between rock instrumentalists, attracted to the broad creative opportunities and musicianship of jazz, and jazz musicians, attracted to rock's electronics and commercial potential.

Other styles, more clearly based on rock principles and precedents, ranged from the benign bubble-gum rock of the Osmond Brothers, directed toward the youngest popular music fans, to the intentionally vile punk rock, which punctuated its strident denunciations with vulgarity. Heavy metal rock continued the hallucinogenic approach of acid rock, but within a narrower musical dimension, relying upon the hypnotic power of repetitiveness, loud volume, and electronic distortion. Glitter rock was more a theatrical approach than a musical style; it offered glittering costumes and bizarre, sometimes androgynous, exhibitions (Alice Cooper, David Bowie, Kiss). New wave rock, which made its debut as the 1970s drew to a close, appeared to be something of an old wave, with its return to a more basic, unadorned metric emphasis and a greater lyricism.

Most rock music of the period was intended almost solely for listening, not for dancing. The inevitable reaction was DISCO, a music first and foremost for dancing. With its thumping regularity of accented beats divided into minibeats, disco was decried by hardline rock fans as mechanical, commercial, and unlyrical. Nevertheless, its following increased and, after the BEE GEES composed and recorded their disco-beat soundtrack for the film *Saturday Night Fever* (1977), disco became for a while a major sector of rock music.

The Eclectic 1980s. Rock music, by the mid-1980s, had presented no clear-cut new musical direction. Bands became more production oriented, in part because of the sudden explosion of "videos" on TV screens. Ranging from televised

(Above) *Led Zeppelin, one of the most successful "heavy metal" rock groups, features the powerful voice of Robert Plant and the instrumentation of Jimmy Page, John Paul Jones, and John Bonham. Their hard, blues-derived rock has earned the group four gold albums.*

(Left) *An estimated 500,000 people attended the Woodstock Festival, held Aug. 15–17, 1969, near Bethel, N.Y. This musical celebration, featuring some of the most famous rock and folk musicians of the 1960s, was the most publicized countercultural event of the decade.*

Jamaican composer Bob Marley was the great popularizer of reggae. With his group, The Wailers, he brought his rock-influenced island music to worldwide audiences in the 1970s. Marley's songs reflected his Rastafarian beliefs. Even when he sang about the "rude boys" of the Jamaican slums or composed love ballads, the basic message of his work was political: an end to racial oppression, and a turning toward a black-centered Christianity that would make all blacks free.

concerts to minutes-long acted-out versions of rock songs, videos proved to be a powerful tool for introducing new groups (the Australian Men at Work, for example). With their emphasis on the visual, though, they encouraged the use of bizarre, grotesque "stories" and staging, while the music remained secondary. Although fading musically, punk remained a strong visual style. It was outshone, however, by the glittery, androgynous look of such immensely popular performers as Michael JACKSON and Boy George, of the British group Culture Club.

The influence of British bands on the U.S. rock scene remained strong. Their music was as eclectic as the work of their predecessors, the Beatles, but it drew from a far narrower range: punk, disco, pop-rock, reggae.

At the same time, there was a nostalgic return to older, simpler rock idioms and even to the romantic, melodic pop music of the prerock era. Singer Linda Ronstadt worked in these earlier modes, and sang the contemporary compositions of British musician Elvis Costello, whose songs harked back to rhythm-and-blues and country-western styles. Ex-MOTOWN singer-composer Lionel Richie wrote popular ballads that lacked any reference to soul music or rhythm-and-blues.

Despite what appeared to be a loss of momentum in the first years of the 1980s, the scope and significance of rock remains without precedent in the history of popular music. Beginning as a minority expression on the fringe of American society, it developed into a distinct counterculture during the 1960s, and a decade later had become a dominant cultural force, affecting and reflecting the mores and moods of American youth and weaving itself into the very fabric of society.

EDWARD A. BERLIN

Bibliography: Baker, Glenn, and Cope, Stuart, *The New Music* (1981); Clark, Al, *The Rock Yearbook* (1984); Clark, Dick, and Robinson, Richard, *Rock, Roll and Remember* (1976); Marcus, Greil, *Mystery Train: Images of America in Rock and Roll Music* (1982); Naha, Ed, comp., *Lillian Roxon's Rock Encyclopedia*, rev. ed. (1978); Nite, Norm N., *Rock On: The Illustrated Encyclopedia of Rock 'n Roll*, 2 vols. (1974, 1978); Rolling Stone Press, *The Rolling Stone Illustrated History of Rock and Roll*, rev. ed. (1980); Shaw, Arnold, *The Rockin' 50's* (1974) and *A Dictionary of American Pop-Rock* (1982).

rock salt: see HALITE.

Rockefeller   (family)

American industrialist and philanthropist **John Davison Rockefeller**, b. Richford, N.Y., July 8, 1839, d. May 23, 1937, began his career in Cleveland, Ohio, before the Civil War. In 1863 he and his partners formed an oil business that eventually absorbed many Cleveland refineries and expanded into Pennsylvania oil fields to become the world's largest refining concern. Rockefeller founded (1870) the Standard Oil Compa-

John D. Rockefeller took the first step toward establishing his industrial empire during the 1860s, when he and his partners founded the business that became Standard Oil.

ny of Ohio; the Standard Oil Trust, which he formed in order to avoid state controls, was dissolved (1892) by the Ohio Supreme Court. The division of his operations into 18 companies—later to include more than 30 corporations—under the umbrella of Standard Oil of New Jersey (1899) helped him to accumulate a personal fortune of over $1 billion. In 1911 this venture, however, was interpreted by the U.S. Supreme Court as "a monopoly in restraint of trade" and thus illegal according to the Sherman Anti-Trust Act; Standard Oil was broken up into 39 separate companies. Rockefeller retired the same year but expanded his efforts in philanthropy, which claimed about one-half of his vast fortune. He created such institutions as the Rockefeller Foundation, the General Education Board, and the Rockefeller Institute for Medical Research; founded the University of Chicago; and presented many gifts to colleges and churches. His son, **John D. Rockefeller, Jr.**, b. Cleveland, Jan. 29, 1874, d. May 11, 1960, continued and expanded his father's philanthropic interests. Together they were also large shareholders in Standard Oil of New Jersey. This helped to sustain that part of their still enormous wealth that was not invested in new enterprises, such as the construction of Rockefeller Center and Riverside Church in New York City. John D., Jr., also donated the land on which the United Nations headquarters were built. His children benefited from trusts established by their grandfather, who was known for most of his life as J. D. Rockefeller. **John D. Rockefeller III**, b. New York City, Mar. 21, 1906, d. July 10, 1978, operated family businesses and philanthropies. The second son, **Nelson**, is covered in a separate article below. **Laurance**, b. New York City, May 26, 1910, a third son, is a conservationist. A fourth son, **Winthrop**, b. New York City, May 1, 1912, d. Feb. 22, 1973, was governor of Arkansas (1966–70). **David**, b. New York City, June 12, 1915, headed New York's Chase Manhattan Bank (1961–81). Among more than 20 present-day Rockefeller offspring, the most prominent, **John (Jay) D. Rockefeller IV**, b. New York City, June 18, 1937, was elected governor of West Virginia in 1976 and reelected in 1980. In 1984 he was elected to the U.S. Senate.

JOHN F. STACKS

Bibliography: Abels, Jules, *The Rockefeller Billions* (1965); Collier, Peter, and Horowitz, David, *The Rockefellers: An American Dynasty* (1976); Fosdick, Raymond B., *John D. Rockefeller, Jr.* (1956); Hawke, David D., *John D., the Founding Father of the Rockefellers* (1980); Manchester, William, *A Rockefeller Family Portrait* (1959).

Rockefeller, Nelson A.

Nelson A. Rockefeller, U.S. public official, served as vice-président (1974–77) under Gerald Ford and as governor (1959–73) of New York, where his administration was notable for programs in education and social welfare and increased taxes. He was one of the heirs to the political, financial, and philanthropic dynasty begun by his grandfather, John D. Rockefeller, during the late 19th century.

Nelson Aldrich Rockefeller, b. Bar Harbor, Maine, July 8, 1908, d. Jan. 26, 1979, served (1959–73) as Republican governor of New York for four terms and was appointed vice-president (1974–77) by President Gerald R. Ford under the provisions of the 25th Amendment. A grandson of the industrialist John D. Rockefeller, Nelson Rockefeller was graduated (1930) from Dartmouth College and worked in family enterprises until his appointment by President Franklin D. Roosevelt as coordinator (1940–44) of inter-American affairs. He then became assistant secretary of state (1944–45) for Latin American affairs, head (1950–51) of the International Development Advisory Board, undersecretary of health, education, and welfare (1953–54), and special assistant (1954–55) to President Dwight D. Eisenhower. He also chaired (1952–58) the President's Advisory Committee on Government Organization. In 1958, Rockefeller defeated W. Averell Harriman in the New York gubernatorial race. As governor he greatly increased the size and scope of the state government; in 1971 he was criticized for his role in the ATTICA PRISON RIOT. He ran unsuccessfully for the Republican nomination for president in 1960, 1964, and 1968, and in 1973 he resigned as governor to establish and chair the National Commission on Critical Choices for America. As vice-president he chaired an investigatory commission on the Central Intelligence Agency.

Bibliography: Connery, Robert H., and Benjamin, Gerald, *Rockefeller of New York: Executive Power in the Statehouse* (1979); Desmond, James, *Nelson Rockefeller: A Political Biography* (1964); Underwood, James E., *Governor Rockefeller of New York* (1982).

Rockefeller Center

In the official, corporate sense, the designation *Rockefeller Center* refers to a group of 21 office buildings and a theater under single ownership that are distributed over an area of midtown Manhattan fronting on Fifth and Sixth avenues between 48th and 52d streets. According to historical usage and the popular view, however, the term applies only to the original 14 buildings standing entirely between Fifth and Sixth avenues and constructed between 1931 and 1939 under the financial sponsorship of John D. Rockefeller, Jr.

The 14 buildings of the 1939 group, designed by a consortium of architects, are arranged in what might be called a rectilinear pinwheel form. The anchor and central focus of this plan is the 70-story RCA (Radio Corporation of America) Building. The smaller buildings, of which three are skyscrapers in their own right, are sited so that their long horizontal axes lie either parallel to that of the RCA or at right angles thereto. The dynamic molding of space created by the way the buildings are sited can be clearly comprehended from the observation deck of the RCA Building. All the office towers and other structures are steel-framed, and the high, narrow, slablike form of the RCA Building had to be specially braced because of its vulnerability to wind loads. In addition to office space, Rockefeller Center includes restaurants, shops, originally two theaters—the Center Theater was demolished in 1954—including RADIO CITY MUSIC HALL, an ice-skating rink, exhibit rooms, broadcasting studios, a network of underground streets and walkways, and numerous murals, statuary, and sculptural decoration.   CARL W. CONDIT

Bibliography: Balfour, Alan, *Rockefeller Center* (1978); Giedion, Siegfried, *Space, Time and Architecture*, 3d ed. (1959); Karp, Walter, *The Center* (1983); Krinsky, Carol, *Rockefeller Center* (1978); Scully, Vincent, *American Architecture and Urbanism* (1969).

Rockefeller Foundation

The Rockefeller Foundation, a private foundation with a mandate "to promote the well-being of mankind throughout the world," was founded in 1913 by John D. Rockefeller. It not only makes grants to individuals and institutions, but also operates its own programs and maintains a field staff of specialists in agriculture, health, and social sciences to work where needed throughout the world. Since its inception it has allocated over $1.7 billion to grant recipients working in fields of interest to the foundation. It currently supports programs in agricultural science, equal opportunity, international relations, population and health, and the arts and humanities. Its total endowment is approximately $1 billion.

Rockefeller University

One of the world's leading medical research centers, Rockefeller University was founded by John D. Rockefeller in 1901

as the Rockefeller Institute for Medical Research. Located in New York City, it became a graduate-level educational institution in 1954 and assumed its present name in 1965.

Rocket

George and Robert Stephenson's Rocket, winner of the 1829 time trials conducted by the Liverpool & Manchester Railway, demonstrated the practicality of steam locomotion. The Rocket's speed and performance were due to its multitube boiler and an improved exhaust system.

The *Rocket* was the early English LOCOMOTIVE, built by George and Robert STEPHENSON, that won the Rainhill trials, a competition sponsored by the Liverpool & Manchester Railway in 1829. By winning the *Rocket* proved its reliability and convinced the railway of the practicality of steam motive power. The *Rocket* had a multitube boiler and an efficient method of exhausting the steam and creating a draft in the firebox. It completed the trials with an average speed of 24 km/h (15 mph) and a maximum of 47 km/h (29 mph).   JOHN F. STOVER

Bibliography: Nock, O. S., ed., *Encyclopedia of Railroads* (1977).

rockets and missiles

A rocket, in its conventional form, is an internal combustion engine that needs no outside air to operate. It carries both fuel and oxidizer, which are burned together in a combustion chamber and produce hot gases that are discharged through a nozzle. Inside the combustion chamber the burning gases exert pressure in all directions. If the chamber were sealed, all these pressures would be balanced and the rocket would not move. The gases are allowed to escape at high speed through the nozzle, however, causing an imbalance in the chamber. Because the pressure exerted on the rocket in the forward direction is much greater than in the backward direction, the rocket shoots forward. It obeys Newton's third law of motion: for every action there is an equal and opposite reaction. In the rocket the escaping exhaust gases are the action, and the forward pressure, or thrust, is the reaction.

Because a rocket carries its own fuel and oxidizer, and because Newton's law is valid everywhere, the rocket can operate both within the Earth's atmosphere and in the vacuum of space. Rockets can thus be used to launch artificial satellites (see SATELLITE, ARTIFICIAL), probes, or manned spacecraft for SPACE EXPLORATION, or to power a variety of short- or long-range missiles for military purposes.

Although since World War II almost all of the costly research and development in rocketry has been accomplished by governments, in the early 1980s U.S. business began to investigate the profit potential in operating private launch facilities for satellite-carrying rockets, many of which could be bought from the military's outmoded rocket stocks.

EARLY HISTORY

The first rockets were probably made in China. When Mongol hordes besieged the town of Kai-feng-fu in AD 1232, the townsfolk repulsed them with "arrows of flying fire." Tied to

A Chinese warrior prepares to ignite the fuse of an early military rocket, to which a long stick was attached to give the missile stability in flight. The use of gunpowder-propelled rockets probably originated in China around the 13th century and quickly spread through Asia and into Europe.

The test-firing of a Congreve rocket at Woolwich, London, is depicted in an English engraving from 1846. Invented by Sir William Congreve, this variety of artillery rocket was used by British and American armies during the first half of the 19th century.

the shafts were tubes containing an early form of gunpowder, which produced a fiery exhaust. That these rockets were not purely incendiary devices is implied in an ancient manuscript that describes them as "making a noise like thunder" and "travelling a great distance."

In the Middle East, and Europe, the art of rocketry appeared soon afterward. In 1242 the English Franciscan monk Roger Bacon produced a secret formula for gunpowder, specifying 41.2 parts saltpeter, 29.4 parts charcoal, and 29.4 parts sulfur. He also succeeded in distilling saltpeter—an oxygen-producing ingredient—to achieve the faster rates of burning that would make rockets more practicable.

In *The Book of Fighting on Horseback and With War Engines*, composed about 1280, the Syrian scholar al-Hassan-al-Rammah gave instructions for making gunpowder and rockets, which he called "Chinese arrows." Rockets are also mentioned in a German chronicle of 1258, and the Italian historian Muraroti describes how, during the siege of Chiozzia (near Venice) in 1379, a defending tower was set ablaze by a black powder rocket, thereby eliminating the last pocket of resistance.

The British first encountered rocket warfare in India, to which the secret of rocket manufacture had probably been brought during the 17th century by Arab traders. Manuscripts suggest that the 18th-century Indian ruler HYDER ALI employed thousands of men for throwing rockets during warfare. Constructed of a thick stalk of bamboo 2.5 to 3 m (8 to 10 ft) long attached to a tube of iron weighing from 2.5 to 5.5 kg (6 to 12 lb) containing the fuse and powder, these rockets were said to be able to reach a distance of 2.5 km (1.5 mi).

When the first examples of the Indian rockets reached England around 1770, Captain Thomas Desaguliers examined their structure at the Royal Laboratory at Woolwich, but he failed to reproduce their range or accuracy. The matter rested there until 1804, when William Congreve took up the challenge and asked Woolwich to have several large rockets made to his specifications. Because a rocket has no recoil, Congreve thought that they might find application both at sea and on land. Within a year he had produced a 24-pounder with a range of about 1,800 m (6,000 ft). Congreve rockets were first used in battle during the Napoleonic Wars on the night of Oct. 8, 1806, when 18 rocket boats were quietly slipped from mother ships and rowed into Boulogne harbor (France) to enable officers and men of the Royal Marine Artillery to attack the French invasion fleet. The rockets—32-pounders measuring 1.06 m (3.5 ft) long by 10 cm (4 in) in diameter—had balancing sticks 4.5 m (15 ft) long and a range of about 2,700 m (9,000 ft). Some of the warheads contained ball-shot to create a shrapnel effect; others had a liquid incendiary compound that squeezed out a flame from holes in the pointed nosecap and impaled wooden ships and buildings. The year 1810 saw the publication in London of W. Moore's treatise *On the Motion of Rockets*, which contained a mathematical study of rocket motors and trajectories.

By 1844, William Hale, an Englishman, had invented spin-stabilized rockets, which eliminated the cumbersome guide sticks. These rockets were set into rotation by deflecting the

exhaust through offset nozzles drilled in the baseplate, and, later, by restricting the expanding exhaust gases on one side of the nozzles by the use of semicircular vanes.

DEVELOPMENT OF MODERN ROCKETRY

Rocketry had to wait half a century before further big advances were made, and these were of a theoretical nature.
Tsiolkovsky. A Russian schoolteacher, Konstantin E. TSIOLKOVSKY, established in 1883 that a rocket would work in the vacuum of space; in 1903 he published his first treatise on space travel, advocating the use of liquid propellants. His notebooks of the first quarter of the 20th century contain sketches of spaceships fueled with liquid oxygen and liquid hydrogen, or liquid oxygen and kerosene. The sketches showed valves for controlling the flow of liquids to the combustion chamber and vanes in the exhaust for steering. The occupants were depicted in a supine position to withstand the full force of acceleration, and the pressurized cabin had double-wall protection against meteoroids.

Tsiolkovsky also advocated step rockets—rocket stages arranged in tandem that dropped off as soon as the next rocket fired, thus reducing deadweight. In this way, he suggested, the high speeds necessary to place satellites in orbit could be

Left) Konstantin Tsiolkovsky, a Russian scientist and educator, was the first to set forth the theory of rocket motion and to suggest the possibility of space travel in reaction propulsion vessels.

(Below) Tsiolkovsky's design for a rocket called for the mixing (A) of liquid-hydrogen (H) and liquid-oxygen (O) fuels, producing the heated gases that escape (B) and propel the craft.

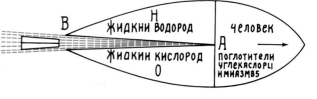

Hermann Oberth (foreground) and Wernher von Braun (fourth from left) pose before models of rockets that they helped to develop. These German scientists came to work for the United States after World War II and contributed greatly to the American space program.

Robert Goddard (left), who conducted the first successful launch of a liquid-fueled rocket, works with assistants at his laboratory in Roswell, N. Mex. Goddard's pioneering rocket flight on Mar. 16, 1926, achieved an altitude of 12.5 m (41 ft) and lasted less than 3 seconds.

attained. He advocated the use of gyroscopes and stabilizing rockets and even went so far as to describe spinning habitats in which people could live under artificial gravity, obtaining food and oxygen from closed-cycle biological systems.

Goddard. A long road still had to be traveled before rockets could be applied so ambitiously. Robert H. GODDARD, the founder of U.S. rocketry, had invented a bazooka-type solid-fuel rocket during World War I and in 1919 published *A Method of Reaching Extreme Altitudes*. Two years later he began the experiments with liquid fuels that Tsiolkovsky had never attempted. On Mar. 16, 1926, at Auburn, Mass., Goddard became the first to launch a liquid-propellant rocket. Fueled by gasoline and liquid oxygen, it rose to a height of 12.5 m (41 ft), reached a top speed of 100 km/h (60 mph), and landed 56 m (184 ft) from the launch stand. Although few people recognized it as such at the time, it was a turning point in history. Later, at his lonely test station at Roswell, N.M., Goddard succeeded in launching (May 1935) a rocket with gyro-controlled exhaust vanes to an altitude of 2,300 m (7,500 ft) at a top speed of about 1,100 km/h (700 mph).

Germany. Meanwhile, in Germany, Hermann OBERTH had published, in 1923, *Die Rakete zu den Planetenräumen* (The Rocket into Planetary Space). Like Goddard, he favored liquid fuels because they were more energetic and controllable. Inspired by Oberth's enthusiasm, German rocket enthusiasts in July 1927 founded the Verein für Raumschiffahrt (VfR, or Society for Space Travel). Its members included Willy Ley, Johannes Winkler, Hermann Oberth, Max Valier, Walter Hohmann, Guido von Pirquet, Klaus Riedel, Kurt Heinish, and Rudolf Nebel, all of whom passionately desired to improve the performance of the often-erratic liquid-fueled rockets.

On Feb. 21, 1931, Winkler became the second person to launch a liquid-fuel rocket. Powered by liquid methane and liquid oxygen, the rocket made a disappointingly brief hop of just 3 m (9 ft); three weeks later, however, it ascended to more than 600 m (2,000 ft). The entire VfR built a series of small test models known as Mirak and Repulsor. A young enthusiast who joined the group at this time was the 18-year-old Wernher VON BRAUN. The group tested its rockets at the Raketenflugplatz (Rocket Flying Field), in a suburb of Berlin, and soon came into conflict with the city authorities. Late-model Repulsors, although not fueled to capacity, could reach altitudes of 1.6 km (1 mi); they did not, however, always fly true.

The economic depression of the early 1930s took its toll; money ran low, and it became obvious that further useful work would be impossible without additional funds. Nebel,

Riedel, and von Braun therefore approached the German army and demonstrated one of their Repulsors at the army proving grounds at Kummersdorf, about 100 km (60 mi) south of Berlin. The artillery experts were interested but unconvinced. They wanted measured thrusts and other data.

Von Braun gathered what data he could find and returned to Kummersdorf with results that were to change the course of history. The army realized that the rocket fell outside the scope of the Versailles Treaty—which barred the Germans from building aircraft—and in 1933, the same year in which Adolf Hitler came to power, a special section of the Army Weapons Department was established at Kummersdorf with Captain (later General) Walter Dornberger at its head. The young von Braun was placed in charge of rocket development while he was still studying for his doctoral degree, and work began on a series of experimental liquid-fuel rockets. Within a few years highly improved rockets were being fired in secret by von Braun's small team at the North Sea island of Borkum, near Emden. In December 1934 two A-2 rockets, called Max and Moritz, ascended approximately 2.5 km (1.5 mi). The VfR, meanwhile, finally disbanded because of financial problems, and the Raketenflugplatz returned to its original use as an army ammunition depot.

American technicians ready a captured German V-2 rocket for launching at the U.S. Army Missile Range in White Sands, N. Mex. The V-2, a liquid-fueled rocket used as a ballistic missile, measured 14 m (46 ft) in height and had an effective range of 322 km (200 mi).

In April 1937 a major rocket research station was completed near the village of PEENEMÜNDE on the Baltic coast. Former VfR stalwarts Klaus Riedel, Hans Hueter, Kurt Heinish, and Helmut Zoike were now able to resume their work in rocketry alongside von Braun. At Peenemünde the large A-4 rocket was developed as an artillery weapon. This rocket was later used to bombard London, Antwerp, and other targets in 1944-45. The German High Command called it the V-2 (for Weapon of Vengeance No. 2; see V-2). The first such weapon, the V-1 (see V-1), had been the Fieseler Fi 103 flying bomb, a small, pilotless aircraft powered by a simple pulse-jet engine, and it was also directed against London and southeastern England. After the war the V-2 was used as a SOUNDING ROCKET for upper-atmosphere research; other sounding rockets such as Viking and AEROBEE were built using the same technology.

USSR. The Soviets, too, had not been idle. On Aug. 17, 1933, a group of Soviet researchers led by Mikhail K. Tikhonravov launched the GIRD 09 rocket, which flew to a height of about 400 m (1,310 ft). The 09 was fueled with liquid oxygen and a mixture of gasoline and colophony, a dark-colored rosin obtained from turpentine. Its builders included a young man, Sergei P. KOROLEV, who many years later would develop the rocket that launched *Sputnik 1,* the world's first artificial satellite.

A more conventional Soviet rocket, the GIRD X, designed by Friedrich A. Tsander, was powered by gasoline and liquid oxygen. On Nov. 25, 1933, it soared nearly 4,900 m (16,000 ft). The Soviets had also test-flown a rocket-propelled flying bomb (Project 212) in 1939, but it never went into production. Designed by Korolev, it had a small nitric acid–kerosene engine designed by Valentin Glushko. Glushko also developed a series of pump-fed nitric acid–kerosene engines for the auxiliary propulsion of Soviet military aircraft.

MILITARY MISSILES

From these beginnings grew the immense challenge of the postwar era; as tension developed between the USSR and the Western Allies, the demand for weapons of even greater power increased. In little more than a decade missiles that at best could carry chemical explosives a few hundred kilometers were superseded by multistage ballistic missiles capable of lobbing thermonuclear warheads into the heart of another continent. These gave rise to the ANTIBALLISTIC MISSILE and also focused attention on the merits of short-range tactical missiles.

Ballistic missiles (the name is derived from the ballistic path they follow after the initial propulsion phase) usually make use of the multistage principle, a major breakthrough in rocket technology. The multistage rocket consists of two or more rockets mounted parallel or in tandem. The first rocket carries the upper stages to a certain altitude and separates when its propellants are exhausted. The next stage fires and lifts the remaining stage or stages still higher. The final speed attained by the last stage is equal to the sum of the net changes in velocity (Δv) accomplished by each stage. In this way unnecessary structure is discarded as soon as it is no longer accelerating the vehicle, and the payload can attain the high speeds necessary to reach a distant target.

Any long- or short-range missile equipped with a GUIDANCE AND CONTROL SYSTEM is called a guided missile. To achieve accuracy ballistic missiles usually depend on inertial guidance systems using precision GYROSCOPES and other devices that sense deviations from a preset flight path and restore the vehicle to that path, usually by swiveling the engines to produce offset thrust. Because this type of guidance system does not give out a signal, it cannot be jammed by radio waves. Once engine thrust is terminated by the guidance system, the vehicle follows a ballistic path like an artillery shell, usually without further power or guidance. The guidance systems of tactical missiles may be either external or internal. External guidance, which is effective only over short ranges, makes use of a homing system or of a light beam or radar beam, aimed at the target, that the missile follows. Internal guidance, however, does not permit control of the trajectory after the missile has been launched. Such a guidance system may consist, for example, of an electronic memory storing a pre-programmed course.

Ballistic missiles that are launched from land include the intercontinental ballistic missile (ICBM), with a range exceeding 8,000 km (5,000 mi); the intermediate-range ballistic missile (IRBM), with a range between 2,500 and 8,000 km (1,500 and 5,000 mi); the medium-range ballistic missile (MRBM), with a range between 800 and 2,500 km (500 and 1,500 mi);

(Left) A U.S. Minuteman ICBM is poised for launching in its protective silo. Most recent versions of this three-stage, solid-fuel missile have a range of 13,000 km (8,000 mi) and attain a maximum speed of 24,000 km/h (15,000 mph). The Minuteman missiles, along with Trident submarines and B-52 bombers, constitute the U.S. strategic nuclear force.

(Above) Surface-to-Air Missiles (SAMs) are important in modern warfare for their ability to intercept supersonic aircraft. This was proved during the Yom Kippur War of 1973, when Egyptian troops used Russian SAMs to inflict severe losses on Israel's air force.

(Left) The missile-launching tubes of an American submarine are opened for maintenance. The Polaris missiles fired from this submarine are launched while the vessel is submerged.

(Left) *American-built Nike-Hercules missiles lie at varying states of launch readiness at an air base on Taiwan. These missiles, which became operational in 1958, have a range of 140 km (87 mi). Despite its antiaircraft function, the Nike-Hercules can accommodate a nuclear warhead.* (Right) *A pair of U.S. Army specialists test-fire a TOW (tube-launched optically tracked wireguided) missile in the California desert. This antitank weapon, developed by the Hughes Aircraft Co., is targeted by electronic signals transmitted from a tracking telescope.*

and the short-range ballistic missile (SRBM), with a range up to 800 km (500 mi).

ICBM development was spurred in 1954 by the development of the hydrogen bomb and by reductions in the dimensions of atomic bombs, which made possible the design of warheads that could be carried by missiles. The first ICBMs successfully launched in the United States were the ATLAS (1958), the TITAN (1959), and the MINUTEMAN I (1961). These were followed by Minuteman II (1965) and Minuteman III (1970), which together with the Titan make up the land-based U.S. strategic nuclear force. Development of the MX MISSILE, a 10-warhead ICBM, began in 1979. After a prolonged debate over a basing mode for the MX, a presidential commission recommended in 1983 that 100 MX missiles be deployed in modified Minuteman silos. The commission also recommended deployment of a new smaller missile, dubbed midgetman.

The United States began to develop the submarine-launched ballistic missile (SLBM) in 1954, the same year that the first nuclear submarine, the *Nautilus*, was launched. Under the Fleet Ballistic Missile (FBM) Program, 41 submarines had been built by 1968, each armed with 16 POLARIS missiles. The latest version is the Polaris A3, which has a range of 4,600 km (2,800 mi). The POSEIDON SLBM, the development of which was begun in 1964, is twice as heavy as the Polaris A3, has twice its payload capacity, and is armed with ten 50-kiloton bombs. The approaching end of the Poseidon development program and the strategic demand for an SLBM with a much longer range led to the initiation of the TRIDENT program in 1975. A Soviet submarine, armed with 16 missiles comparable in range to the Polaris A1, became operational only in 1966. An effort comparable to the FBM Program began in the USSR in 1970. The military significance of the SLBMs lies in their near-invulnerability when the submarines carrying them are submerged (see NUCLEAR STRATEGY).

A system for the use of multiple warheads on a single missile first became operational in 1964. At the end of 1967 the multiple independently targeted reentry vehicle (MIRV) concept was originated, whereby multiple warheads are independently targeted near the end of the ballistic missile flight (see MIRV MISSILE). A further refinement was the installation of a homing system in the MIRV warhead for navigation and target recognition. A maneuvering reentry vehicle (MARV), utilizing radar scanning devices and a computerized guidance system, has been developed to deliver multiple nuclear warheads with pinpoint accuracy. The MIRV has the advantage of increasing the possibility of penetrating an antiballistic missile system and therefore is more lethal. A disadvantage is the reduced possibility of ARMS CONTROL, because spy satellites can verify the number of strategic weapons but not the number and type of bombs with which they are armed. Both the United States and the USSR deploy MIRV-equipped ICBMs.

Tactical missiles are intended for battlefield use rather than against distant targets. They include surface-to-surface missiles, surface-to-air missiles (SAMs), air-to-surface missiles, and air-to-air missiles. Surface-to-surface missiles were first used on a large scale in World War II and were still being developed during the 1960s. The best-known types are the American Honest John, which has a range of more than 35 km (22 mi) and a conventional or nuclear warhead, and its Soviet counterpart, known by the NATO code name *Frog*. A few guided missiles with ranges comparable to those of the V-1 (220 km/137 mi) and the V-2 (3,200 km/2,000 mi) have been developed. Examples are the American Lance (48-km/30-mi range), which superseded the Honest John; the smaller Little John (16-km/10-mi range); the Sergeant (150-km/93-mi range); and the Pershing (200-to-800-km/125-to-500-mi range).

SURFACE-TO-AIR MISSILES, used primarily against enemy aircraft and rockets, had been developed during World War II by both the Allies and Germany. After the war the Americans developed the Nike Ajax and Nike Hercules; the Talos, Tartar, and Terrier; the Hawk; and the Redeye, which can be fired from the shoulder. The USSR has also developed a large number of SAMs. The range of SAMs is usually no more than 50 km (30 mi). Some can intercept targets at a distance of 100 km (62 mi); others, especially shoulder-fired missiles, have a considerably shorter range.

Air-to-surface rockets are fired by aircraft against ground targets and were used during World War II by many nations. The Germans were the first to use successfully rockets fired from aircraft against other planes, notably with the Messerschmitt fighter. Many such air-to-air missiles were developed after World War II, some equipped with radar or infrared

A Sparrow III missile appears moments after being launched from the underside of Phantom F-4H fighter. This radar-homing air-to-air missile (AAM) is tipped with a 27-kg (60-lb) explosive warhead and is designed to intercept enemy aircraft at distances up to 9 km (5.59 mi).

guidance systems. These missiles can generally be used against both air and surface targets. The American SIDEWINDER, Sparrow Super Falcon, and Phoenix, and the Soviet Ash and Atoll, are important examples. All are guided missiles, with ranges of up to 20 km (12 mi).

The CRUISE MISSILE is more accurately classified as an unmanned airplane rather than a rocket, because it is propelled by a jet engine and travels over a flat, nonballistic path. Early cruise missiles developed by the United States during the 1950s were superseded by faster and less-vulnerable ballistic missiles. The development of more efficient engines and better guidance systems, however, has recently made possible the development of medium- to long-range cruise missiles capable of carrying conventional or nuclear warheads.

SPACE ROCKETS

Many of the rockets that opened the space age were straightforward adaptations of ballistic missiles to which upper stages were added to give the higher speeds necessary to achieve

Soviet and U.S. programs to develop modern rockets, both for military and civilian purposes, owe much to the V-2 ballistic missile developed by Germany during World War II. Testing of captured V-2s directed scientists in their early efforts to construct a launch vehicle. The first artificial satellite, Sputnik 1, was launched into orbit on Oct. 4, 1957, by a Soviet A rocket. The United States soon responded, and its second satellite, Vanguard 1, was boosted by a Vanguard rocket, which had a lift-off thrust of 12,250 kg (27,000 lb). Research continued with the Jupiter C, developed to test nose-cone materials for reentry into the Earth's atmosphere. The Juno II, modified from a Jupiter IRBM, served as a satellite booster. The Soviet Union boosted the first manned capsule, bearing Yuri Gagarin, into orbit on Apr. 12, 1961, with an A-1 rocket, a modification of that used in the Sputnik launch. On May 5, 1961, the United States successfully accomplished a nonorbital manned spaceflight, utilizing a Redstone booster to lift Alan Shepard's Mercury capsule. The Delta was used to place Pioneer, Intelsat, TIROS, and Telstar satellites in orbit. The first U.S. manned orbital spacecraft, bearing John Glenn, was launched using an Atlas rocket on Feb. 20, 1962. Using an A-2 booster, the Soviet Union launched Voskhod 1, the first three-man capsule, into orbit on Oct. 12, 1964. The Titan II, a converted ICBM generating 193,500 kg (430,000 lb) of lift-off thrust, boosted the Gemini capsules into orbit. The addition of two solid-fuel tanks gave its successor, the Titan III, a lift-off thrust of 1,000,000 kg (2,400,000 lb). The Soviet Union embarked on its Soyuz manned space program during the late 1960s and early 1970s using an uprated A-2 rocket that can place up to 7,500 kg (16,500 lb) into low Earth orbit. (Opposite page) The need to loft larger, heavier payloads led U.S. aerospace engineers to develop the Saturn 1B, which was used for several Apollo missions and Skylab crew launchings. Larger still, the Saturn V, which became operational in 1967, developed 3,442,500 kg (7,650,000 lb) of lift-off thrust. This rocket boosted the Apollo 11 spacecraft on its historic voyage to the Moon. The Soviet Union upgraded the size and power of its rockets in 1965 with the development of the D-1 rocket, which, in various configurations, has been used in the Proton, Zond, Luna, and Salyut programs. The U.S. Space Shuttle, a reusable vehicle that became operational in the early 1980s, reduces the excessive cost of spaceflight. The shuttle is boosted by two reusable solid-fuel rockets attached to a detachable fuel tank.

V-2   Soviet A   Vanguard   Jupiter C   Juno II

Soviet A-1   Redstone   Delta   Atlas   Soviet A-2   Titan II   Titan III   Soviet A-2 (uprated)

Earth orbit or to project payloads on lunar and interplanetary missions. The first Sputniks, as well as the Soviet manned spacecraft, were launched by rockets adapted from a Soviet ICBM with the NATO code name *Sapwood*. Even the powerful Soviet PROTON rocket, first introduced in 1965 and ultimately used to launch the Salyut space station, embodied a good deal of military technology. In the United States the JUNO I rocket that launched *Explorer 1* was developed from the army's JUPITER C rocket, which in turn was a successor of the REDSTONE. The THOR IRBM was used in combination with Able, AGENA, and DELTA stages. A modified Atlas ICBM was used to launch the four manned Mercury orbital flights and was later combined with Agena and CENTAUR stages for heavier payloads. The Titan ICBM was developed for use in the manned Gemini program and a variety of other missions.

In addition, the National Aeronautics and Space Administration (NASA) developed or contracted for new launch vehicles, including the Delta, SCOUT, and SATURN rockets. Delta, the first rocket to be built specifically for NASA, was developed by the Douglas Aircraft Company and grew into a large family of vehicles that has provided launch reliability since 1960. Scout, the first rocket developed by NASA itself, also became operational in 1960 and was a low-cost means of launching lighter payloads. The Saturn I rocket, conceived by Wernher von Braun in 1958, was first launched with all stages operational in January 1964. After a number of interim im-

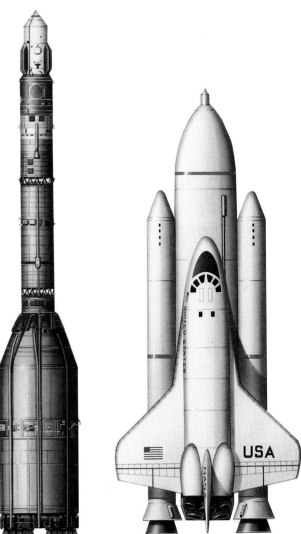

Saturn IB   Saturn V   Soviet D-1   Space Shuttle

provements in the Saturn I, the Saturn V rocket was developed. Test-launched in 1967 and 1968, it performed flawlessly in the Apollo program.

With the growth of space exploration and its commercial applications, a number of countries have developed their own launch capability. The EUROPEAN SPACE AGENCY'S ARIANE became a leader in the 1980s in the international competition for launching satellites; other such rockets include France's Diamant and Japan's H-1, the latter being planned for service in the late 1980s. Private firms such as Space Services, Inc., of the United States and OTRAG of West Germany are also developing their own rocket fleets—for example, Space Service's Conestoga booster for small payloads. The concept of employing reusable rockets instead of expendables such as the above was explored in the early 1980s by the U.S. SPACE SHUTTLE program, with its recoverable solid-propellant boosters and craft. The craft demonstrated its abilities in satellite launch and repair, but even before the 1986 *Challenger* disaster the concept of reusable rockets—as designed thus far—had been found far less economical in fact than that of expendables. Nevertheless, West Germany, France, Great Britain, the Soviet Union, and Japan were all pursuing shuttle-type plans in addition to their other programs.

KENNETH GATLAND

PRINCIPLES OF ROCKET PROPULSION

A rocket propulsion system produces a force, known as the thrust, that acts (according to Newton's third law) in the direction exactly opposite to the flow of ejected propellants. According to Newton's second law, this thrust force is equal to the rate of change of momentum of the ejected matter, which depends on both the rate at which the propellants are burned in the engine and the effective exhaust velocity at which the resulting gases are expelled. The effective exhaust velocity for chemical propellants is usually between 1,500 and 4,500 m/sec (4,900 and 14,700 ft/sec). Its value increases with the square root of the combustion temperature (hotter flames are better) and inversely as the square root of the average molecular weight of the exhaust gas (low-molecular-weight elements such as hydrogen are best).

The Saturn space-launch vehicle has a takeoff thrust of about 3.45 million kg (7.6 million lb) and consumes about 12,700 kg (28,600 lb) of propellant per second at an effective exhaust velocity of 2,600 m/sec (8,600 ft/sec) for about 2½ minutes. In contrast, a small attitude-control rocket engine may produce only 0.045 kg (0.1 lb) of thrust with a very small propellant flow for short, pulsed durations of 0.02 to 0.2 seconds.

The impulse, or total impulse, of a rocket is the product of thrust and the effective firing duration. A typical shoulder-launched short-range rocket may have an average thrust of 300 kg (660 lb) for an effective duration of 0.2 seconds, giving a total impulse of 60 kg-sec (132 lb-sec). In contrast, the Saturn rocket has a total impulse of 510 million kg-sec (1,140 million lb-sec).

Specific impulse is the amount of thrust derived from each pound of propellant in one second of engine operation. It is equal to the exhaust velocity (in ft/sec) divided by the accel-

eration of gravity (32.2 ft/sec^2). Specific impulse is the common measure of propellant and propulsion-system performance, and is somewhat analogous to the reciprocal of the specific fuel consumption used with conventional automobile or aircraft engines. The larger the value of this specific impulse, the better a rocket's performance. Improving specific impulse by using propellants of higher energy means that more thrust will be obtained for each pound of propellant consumed. Specific impulse is often expressed in terms of the number of seconds for which 1 pound mass of propellant will produce a thrust of 1 pound force.

The most important parameter affecting the ultimate maximum flight velocity is a rocket's mass ratio, the relationship between a rocket vehicle and the amount of propellant it can carry. The mass ratio is obtained by dividing the total mass at lift-off by the total mass remaining after the propellants have burned. In general, a high mass ratio means that a maximum amount of propellant is pushing a minimum amount of inert vehicle mass, resulting in a high vehicle velocity. High values of specific impulse (high-energy propellants and low-molecular-weight exhaust gases) and mass ratio are necessary for difficult missions.

ROCKET PROPULSION SYSTEMS

Rocket propulsion systems can be classified according to their energy source (chemical combustion, nuclear, solar), the types of vehicles they are used on (missiles, spacecraft, sounding rockets), the amount of thrust produced, or the type of propellant (see PROPELLANT, ROCKET).

TABLE 1: USES OF CHEMICAL ROCKETS

Type (Thrust)	Application
High-thrust liquid propellant (22,700 to 794,500 kg/ 50,000 to 1,750,000 lb)	Space-launch vehicle and large ballistic missile first-, second-, or third-stage propulsion; rocket-propelled research test sled
Medium-thrust liquid propellant (90 to 13,600 kg/ 200 to 30,000 lb)	Moon or planet landing and takeoff; major orbit or space-trajectory adjustment; separation of stages; short-range ground-launched missiles
Low-thrust liquid propellant (0.0004 to 70 kg/ 0.001 to 150 lb)	Attitude control; precise rendezvous maneuvers; minor orbit adjustments; station-keeping
High-thrust solid propellant (31,800 to 1,134,000 kg/ 70,000 to 2,500,000 lb)	Space-launch vehicle boosters and second stages; ballistic missiles
Medium-thrust solid propellant (460 to 22,700 kg/ 1,000 to 50,000 lb)	Weather sounding rockets; upper stages for missiles or space launch vehicles; attainment of special orbits; airplane-assisted takeoff; retrorockets; larger air-launched missiles; infantry support weapons
Low-thrust solid propellant (50 to 910 kg/ 100 to 2,000 lb)	Antitank rockets; small missiles; Fourth-of-July rockets; shoulder-launched antiaircraft weapons

TABLE 2: CHARACTERISTICS OF ROCKET PROPULSION SYSTEMS

Engine Type	Specific Impulse (sec)	Duration of Operation	Typical Working Fluid	Status of Technology
Chemical: liquid bipropellant	200 to 460	Seconds to minutes	Liquid oxygen and hydrogen	In production
Chemical: liquid monopropellant	150 to 235	Seconds to minutes	Hydrazine	In production
Chemical: solid propellant	180 to 300	Seconds to minutes	Nitroglycerin in nitrocellulose, or powdered metal and oxidizer	In production
Nuclear fission	300 to 1,100	Seconds to minutes	Hydrogen	Development stopped
Electrothermal: arc heating	300 to 2,000	Days	Hydrogen	Development essentially stopped
Electromagnetic: magnetoplasma	300 to 15,000	Weeks	Hydrogen	Several have flown
Electrostatic: ion	1,000 to 25,000	Months	Cesium	Several have flown
Solar heating	300 to 700	Days	Hydrogen	Not yet developed

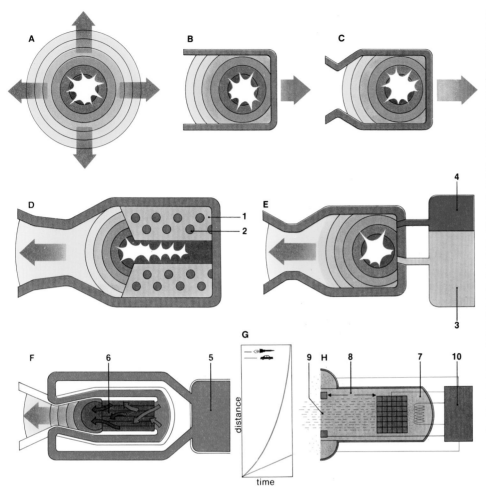

The force of an explosion in an unrestricted space (A) is evenly distributed. Should that explosion occur in a semienclosed chamber (B), its force escapes through the one possible exit, providing an equal and opposite reaction that impels it in the opposite direction. The chamber of a rocket engine (C) is designed to maximize thrust as its fuel undergoes a sustained explosion. Most rockets require an oxidant for combustion. In the solid-propellant rocket (D), fuel (1) and oxidant (2) are packed together in the combustion chamber. In the liquid-propellant rocket (E), fuel (3) and oxidant (4) are pumped into the chamber, where they are burned. The nuclear rocket (F) is fueled by liquid hydrogen (5), which is vaporized, rather than burned, in its reactor (6). The outwardly expanding gases thus created provide its propulsive force. Unlike the automobile, rockets accelerate constantly while their engines are in operation (G). An ion rocket (H), because of its extended period of operation, could therefore possibly approach the speed of light. A propellant, such as cesium or mercury, is ionized in a vaporizer (7) and accelerated through an electrostatic field (8)—both powered by a nuclear reactor (10)—before exiting (9), providing the rocket's propulsive force. If the ionized particles are not neutralized, however, they will eventually cause the rocket to cease functioning.

Liquid-Propellant Rockets. A liquid-propellant rocket engine system consists of one or more thrust chambers, one or more vehicle tanks that contain the propellants, a feed mechanism to force the liquids into the thrust chamber, a power source to furnish the energy required by the feed mechanism, suitable valves and piping to transfer the liquids, a structure to transmit the thrust forces, and control devices to start and regulate propellant flow rates.

The thrust chamber, consisting of an injector, a combustion chamber, and a nozzle, is the device where the liquid propellants are metered, injected, atomized, mixed, and burned to form hot, gaseous reaction products, which in turn are accelerated and ejected at a high velocity to impart thrust. The injector is usually an intricate assembly of pipes and accurately oriented injection holes that introduce the propellants into the combustion chamber, atomizing and mixing them in such a way as to create a relatively uniform mixture of fuel and oxidizer in droplets that will readily evaporate and burn in the combustion chamber. The chamber may be cooled by circulating one of the propellants (usually the fuel) through cooling jackets or passages. Heat may also be absorbed by ablative materials, ceramics, or special metals. Alternatively, certain special high-temperature materials, such as molybdenum metal, can be used to radiate away excess heat. The exhaust nozzle allows the hot gas to expand and accelerate to supersonic velocities. A convergent-divergent nozzle with smooth internal contours is commonly used. In some applications the nozzle axis is moved (by hinging or gimballing the thrust chamber, or sometimes the complete engine) so as to steer the vehicle by changing the direction of the thrust vector.

Two principal types of feed systems are used for liquid-

propellant rocket engines: those which use pumps for moving the propellants from their tanks to the thrust chamber (this type is usually found in high-thrust booster applications), and those which use high-pressure gas for expelling or displacing the propellants from their tanks (usually used in spacecraft attitude-control and maneuvering applications). Because liquid propellants float in the zero-gravity environment of space, special devices are necessary to ensure that the outlet pipe will always be filled with liquid.

For low-thrust attitude-control applications, rocket engines are usually mounted in pairs at the perimeter of a spacecraft; two thrust chambers pointing in opposite directions are fired simultaneously to give a true turning moment to the vehicle. A minimum of 12 thrust chambers is needed to allow rotational control in each of two directions about three perpendicular axes. For precise angular position control in space, only a small impulse need be applied at one time; position-control rockets typically operate for pulsed durations of from 20 to 100 milliseconds.

Solid-Propellant Rockets. Solid-propellant rocket engines, commonly called rocket motors, come in many different types and sizes. The solid propellant to be burned is contained within the combustion chamber, or case. The propellant charge is called the grain and contains the chemical elements for complete burning. Once ignited, it usually burns smoothly on all of its exposed surfaces.

By changing the design of the internal exposed grain surfaces, it is possible to vary the amount of propellant exposed and thus the amount of propellant that will burn. The burning rate of the solid propellant—usually between 0.3 and 3.3 cm/sec (0.1 and 1.3 in/sec) in a direction perpendicular to the burning surface—depends on the propellant ingredients.

The rate increases with chamber pressure (which in turn is determined by the nozzle design and the grain configuration) and the ambient temperature of the propellant grain prior to ignition.

The objective of a good design is to pack as much solid propellant as possible into a given chamber volume. The ideal unit is an end-burning grain, where the grain burns in cigarettelike fashion from one end to the other. This grain type has been used in past jet-assisted takeoff rockets for aircraft. For higher thrust and shorter duration a more complex initial internal surface is chosen, such as a two-dimensional internal star grain (used in air-launched missiles).

Nuclear and Electric Rockets. The nuclear rocket generates its power not by chemical combustion, but by heating a propellant such as hydrogen in a fission reactor and expelling that propellant at a high velocity. In this way, exhaust velocities twice those of the best chemical rockets can be reached. Although extensive efforts have been directed toward nuclear-fission-reactor rocket propulsion, notably the now-abandoned NERVA project in the United States, none of the different concepts and approaches has as yet been selected for a practical propulsion system, and prospects for developing one in the future do not look promising.

Among the ideas for electric propulsion, there exist three basic types: electrothermal, electrostatic, and electromagnetic. In an electrothermal system the propellant is heated or vaporized by electric resistance heaters or electric arcs, and the heated gas is expanded through a nozzle as in a chemical rocket. The electrostatic system achieves acceleration through the interaction of electrostatic fields on charged propellant particles such as ions or small, charged liquid droplets or colloidal particles. Rockets that make use of ions such as cesium or mercury are known as ion rockets. The electromagnetic system achieves acceleration through the interaction of electric and magnetic fields on a propellant plasma, which is a high-temperature, electrically neutral gas that contains electrons, ions, and neutral molecular species.

All types of electric propulsion depend on a relatively large, heavy, high-output, vehicle-borne power source—usually employing solar radiation, chemical, or nuclear energy—and heavy power conversion and conditioning equipment to transform the power into the proper voltage and frequency. The weight of the electrical generating or conversion equipment, even when solar energy is employed, can become excessive, particularly if the efficiency in converting electricity to thrust is low.

Electric propulsion systems can be used for changing the orbits or overcoming perturbations of artificial satellites, for correcting spaceflight trajectories, for space-vehicle attitude control, and for achieving interplanetary transfers or solar-system escape. A small number of electrical propulsion systems have been flown in spacecraft. Electromagnetic thrusters operated successfully for about five years in a communications satellite launched in 1968, producing a total of about 12 million pulses. Electrostatic and electromagnetic propulsion systems give very good performance. They have high values of specific impulse but are limited to a very low thrust (0.45 g to 0.9 kg/0.001 to 2.0 lb) and a very low vehicle acceleration.

Future Trends. Certain types of novel rocket engines are currently being developed. Several of the rocket propulsion units for the space shuttle vehicle have required new technology: the reuse capability and automatic self-check features of the liquid-propellant main engine have not been built into prior rocket engines, and the specific impulse of this engine is slightly better than that of any previous hydrogen-oxygen rocket.

It is unlikely that further major performance improvements can be achieved with conventional chemical propellants. For certain deep-space flight missions, electrical rockets have good potential, but the number of these built will probably be small. Several other advanced and imaginative concepts have been and are being studied, but none has yet shown sufficient promise to warrant intensive development. These concepts include laser beams that interact with propellant in a spacecraft, solar sails, the photon rocket, fusion nuclear

rockets, and metastable chemical propellants. While these ideas are speculative and will require major new inventions, they enhance the prospect of high-speed, long-distance space travel.   GEORGE P. SUTTON

Bibliography: Baker, David, *The Rocket* (1978); Gatland, Kenneth, *Missiles and Rockets* (1975); Hosny, Ahmed Nabil, *Propulsion Systems* (1974); Ley, Willy, *Rockets, Missiles, and Men in Space* (1968); Ordway, Frederick I., III, and Sharpe, Mitchell, *The Rocket Team* (1979); Sutton, George P., and Ross, Donald M., *Rocket Propulsion Elements* (1976); von Braun, Wernher, and Ordway, Frederick I., III, *History of Rocketry and Space Travel,* rev. ed. (1975), and *The Rockets' Red Glare* (1976).

Rockford   [rahk'-furd]

Rockford is a city straddling the Rock River in northern Illinois near the Wisconsin border. The seat of Winnebago County and the state's second largest city, it has a population of 139,712 (1980). It is an important commercial and industrial city and a leading producer of machine tools, fasteners, supplies, and furniture. Much of Rockford's present population is of Swedish descent, and a Scandinavian Midsummer Festival is held annually.

Rockford was founded in 1834 and originally named Midway for a stagecoach stop between Chicago and Galena. The earliest settlers were from New England, but in 1852, Swedish immigrants began arriving, establishing a thriving furniture industry.

rockfowl

The two species of rockfowl, sometimes called bald crows because of the lack of feathers on the head, are ground-feeding birds native to West Africa. Usually classified in the babbler family, Timaliidae, both the gray-necked, or red-headed, rockfowl, *Picathartes oreas,* and the white-necked, or yellow-headed, rockfowl, *P. gymnocephalus,* are endangered species.

Rockingham, Charles Watson-Wentworth, 2d Marquess of   [rahk'-ing-uhm]

Charles Watson-Wentworth, 2d marquess of Rockingham, b. May 13, 1730, was prime minister of Great Britain from July 1765 to July 1766 and from March 1782 until his death on July 1, 1782. He and his followers in Parliament, dubbed Rockingham Whigs, advocated a conciliatory policy toward the North American colonists. During his first ministry Rockingham secured repeal of the STAMP ACT of 1765 but passed (1766) the only slightly less objectionable Declaratory Act, asserting Parliament's right to legislate for—and tax—the colonies. After George III replaced him with William PITT the Elder, Rockingham spent 16 years as opposition leader. A poor orator, he relied on Edmund BURKE to press the case against the war (1775–83) with the American rebels. During his brief second ministry Rockingham opened peace negotiations with the Americans.

Bibliography: Guttridge, G. H., *The Early Career of Lord Rockingham, 1730-1765* (1952) and *English Whiggism and the American Revolution* (1963).

Rockne, Knute   [rahk'-nee, noot]

Knute Kenneth Rockne, b. Voss, Norway, Mar. 4, 1888, d. Mar. 31, 1931, was an American college football player and coach at the University of Notre Dame, South Bend, Ind. Although he is remembered primarily as a coach, he made his biggest impact on the sport as a player. In 1913, as a receiver, he and quarterback Gus Dorias made the forward pass an offensive weapon. As a coach (1918–30), Rockne tallied 105 wins, 12 losses, and 5 ties, an 89.7 percent winning average, the best record of any college coach. His inspirational half-time speeches have become part of the Rockne legend. Rockne died in a plane crash shortly after his 43d birthday. He was elected to the College Football Hall of Fame in 1951.

Bibliography: Brondfield, Jerry, *Rockne: The Coach, the Man, the Legend* (1976); Daley, Arthur, *Knute Rockne: Football Wizard of Notre Dame* (1960).

Rockwell, Norman

The Dugout, *an oil painting by the American illustrator Norman Rockwell done for the Sept. 4, 1948, cover of the* Saturday Evening Post, *captures the spirit and flavor of American life with witty insight. (The Brooklyn Museum, New York City.)*

Norman Rockwell, b. New York City, Feb. 3, 1894, d. Nov. 8, 1978, was America's most famous and popular illustrator. His name became synonymous with his colorful, realistically detailed, and frequently humorous views of Middle America. As Rockwell's reputation grew, his range extended to include the major events and personalities of the period. He did many of his major illustrations for the *Saturday Evening Post*, whose more than 300 covers by Rockwell became its trademark. His best-known work was the series the *Four Freedoms*, which were reproduced as posters during World War II. In addition, Rockwell did numerous illustrations for the Boy Scouts of America, including the official Scout calendar (1926–76), and contributed work to such periodicals as *Boys' Life*, *Life*, and *Look*. Since his death Rockwell's paintings, many of them originals for magazine covers, have become highly prized. His autobiography, *My Adventures as an Illustrator*, was published in 1960.

Bibliography: Finch, Christopher, *Norman Rockwell's America* (1975); Guptill, Arthur L., *Norman Rockwell: Illustrator*, 3d ed. (1970); Rockwell, Norman, *Norman Rockwell: Artist and Illustrator*, ed. by T. S. Buechner (1970); Walton, Donald, *A Rockwell Portrait* (1978).

Rocky Mountain goat: see MOUNTAIN GOAT.

Rocky Mountain spotted fever

Rocky Mountain spotted fever, or tick fever, is a severe rickettsial infection transmitted to humans by tick bites. It occurs throughout the Rocky Mountain region, the eastern seaboard of the United States from Delaware to Florida, and Central and South America.

Initial symptoms—headache, high fever, chills, painful bones, joints, and muscles, and growing weakness—appear 2 to 14 days after contact with infected ticks. During the first few days of sickness, a generalized skin rash develops and in severe cases becomes hemorrhagic, reflecting damage to the circulatory system. Central nervous system effects, appearing after about a week of fever, range from agitation and insomnia to delirium and coma. The fever usually disappears after about two weeks, but full recovery may require several weeks or months in untreated individuals. Individuals treated late in their illness or not at all may suffer brain or heart damage.

Treatment with antibiotics is effective if started early. Preventive measures include the wearing of protective clothing in tick-infested country, spraying of campgrounds and other recreational areas with insecticides, and inspecting for ticks on the skin.   PETER L. PETRAKIS

Rocky Mountains

The Rocky Mountains, the major mountain system of North America, are part of the great cordillera extending through the western regions of both North and South America. They extend for about 4,890 km (3,000 mi) in a north-south orientation from northern Alberta, Canada, to central New Mexico. The width of this region varies from 120 to 645 km (75 to 400 mi). Elevation varies from approximately 1,525 m (5,000 ft) to 4,399 m (14,432 ft) at Mount Elbert, Colo. The Rockies received their name from explorers during the early 19th century because of the mountains' rugged topography. The mountains have long been a barrier to transportation, and settlements initially emerged in a linear pattern in the adjacent plains. The discovery (1858) of gold, and later of other minerals, was the major catalyst to economic development in the area. Miners' needs provided economic opportunities for farmers and businessmen, many of whom became the first permanent residents. Today thousands of people visit the area's many national parks, monuments, and summer and winter sports resorts.

Topography and Geology. The Rockies are high, rugged, young mountains. The present landscape is the product of regional uplift during the late Cretaceous Period (100 million–65 million years ago) and subsequent etching by weathering and erosion. These mountains may be divided into four provinces: the southern Rockies, Wyoming Basin, middle Rockies, and northern Rockies.

The major mountain groups making up the southern Rockies are the Elk, Front, Gore, Jemez, Laramie, Park, Sangre de Cristo, and Sawatch ranges and the San Juan and Wet mountains. The southern Rockies extend from western New Mexico up through west central Colorado and into southern Wyoming. These ranges are the highest of the Rockies; Mount EL- BERT (4,399 m/14,432 ft) in the Sawatch Range of Colorado is the entire system's highest peak. The southern Rockies are made up of parallel uplifts trending generally north to south. Precambrian (3,980 million–600 million years ago) igneous and metamorphic rocks compose the core of these uplifts, and younger sedimentary rocks lie along the margins. The San Juan Mountains, made up primarily of volcanic rocks from the Tertiary Period (65 million–12 million years ago), are the exception to this pattern.

The Wyoming Basin, with topography similar to that of the GREAT PLAINS, is located mostly in southwestern Wyoming and northwestern Colorado. Mountains are buried beneath the relatively flat terrain, probably representing severe erosion and filling of intermontane basins. The rocks are layered within a Precambrian core and include Paleozoic, Mesozoic (70 million–35 million years ago), and Tertiary formation.

The middle Rockies divide into eastern and western segments. The eastern part includes the Beartooth, Bighorn, Laramie, and Wind River mountains, located in western Wyoming. These mountains are structural upwarps, with Precambrian rock cores and Paleozoic and Mesozoic rocks along the flanks. The western part of the middle Rockies includes the TETON, WASATCH, Gros Ventre, Owl Creed, Snake, and Vinta ranges in northern Utah, southwestern Wyoming,

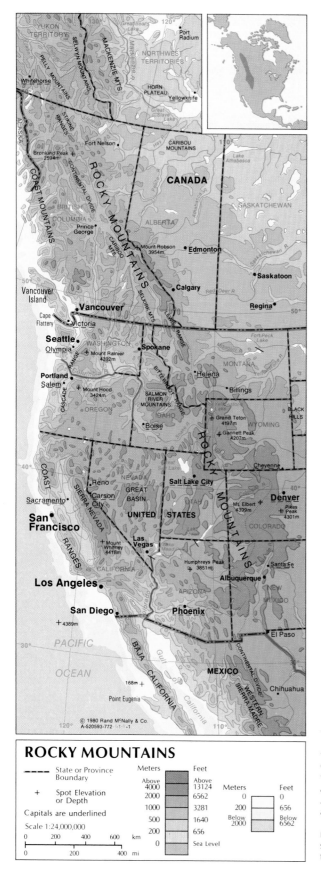

ROCKY MOUNTAINS

	Meters	Feet		
- - - - State or Province Boundary	Above 4000	Above 13124		
+ Spot Elevation or Depth	2000	6562	Meters	Feet
	1000	3281	0	0
Capitals are underlined	500	1640	200	656
Scale 1:24,000,000	200	656	Below 2000	Below 6562
0 200 400 600 km	0	Sea Level		
0 200 400 mi				

© 1980 Rand McNally & Co.
A-520593-772- -1-1-1

and southeastern Idaho. They are composed of folded and faulted rocks of Paleozoic and Mesozoic age with an occasional granitic intrusion.

The northern Rockies are located in Canada (in British Columbia and western Alberta) and in the United States (in northwestern Montana and the northern tip of Idaho). The Canadian part of the northern Rockies, usually called the Canadian Rockies, includes the Cariboo and Selkirk mountains; the Bitterroot, Clearwater, and Salmon River mountains lie mostly south of the border, in the United States. The northern Rockies are composed of Precambrian, Paleozoic, and Mesozoic sedimentary rocks with large areas of granitic intrusions and lava flows. Thrust faulting of the sedimentary rocks is a major mountain-forming process in this province.

Glaciation during the Pleistocene Epoch (2.5 million–70,000 years ago) played a major role in producing the present Rocky Mountain landscape. The peaks of all provinces illustrate classic examples of glacial erosion and deposition features. In addition, steep hillslopes, intense thunderstorms accompanied by copious precipitation, and recently exploitive activities of clear-cut lumbering and livestock overgrazing have subjected the geologic structures to intense soil erosion.

Environment. The Rockies are an oasis between the desert to the west and the plains to the east. Vegetation and soils are affected by the cooling of air masses as the elevation increases, and precipitation also increases with elevation. Latitude also influences the climate. In most of the Rockies five vegetation zones are often recognized. At elevations below 1,645 m (5,400 ft), plains with associated grasses are common. On the foothills (elevations to 2,135 m/7,000 ft), sagebrush, juniper, and piñon grow. Montane vegetation—ponderosa pine, Douglas fir, lodgepole pine, and aspen—prevails up to 2,750 m (9,000 ft). In the subalpine zone (to 3,500 m/11,500 ft), englemann spruce, lodgepole pine, and aspen grow. Above 3,500 m (11,500 ft) alpine flowers and grasses are found. Soils range from desert types to poorly developed, rocky soils at higher elevations and on steep slopes. Fauna includes ROCKY MOUNTAIN GOATS; bighorn sheep; black, brown, and grizzly bear; coyotes; lynx; and wolverines.

The CONTINENTAL DIVIDE winds through the Rockies, bifurcating drainage; to the east of the divide rivers flow to the Gulf of Mexico, and the rivers of the western slopes drain toward the Pacific Ocean. The Colorado, Columbia, Green, Salmon, San Juan, and Snake rivers flow westward; the Arkansas, Missouri, North and South Platte, and Yellowstone rivers flow eastward. Runoff and meltwater from the snow-covered peaks supplying these rivers and lakes provide the water supply for one-quarter of the United States and support the economic development of the region. The lakes and reservoirs of the Rockies store water for municipal supplies, irrigation, flood control, recreation, and hydroelectric power generation.

ECONOMIC AND CULTURAL GEOGRAPHY

Economic development centers on mining, forestry, agriculture, recreation, and the service industries that support the other economic activity. A wide variety of metallic minerals is found in the Rockies, including significant deposits of copper, gold, lead, molybdenum, silver, tungsten, and zinc. The Wyoming basin and several smaller areas contain significant reserves of coal, natural gas, oil-shale, and petroleum. Forestry is a major industry in the Rocky Mountain region. Agriculture includes dry-land and irrigated farming, plus livestock grazing. Cool temperatures and poor soils limit farming at the higher elevations, and livestock are frequently moved between summer and winter pastures. The scenic splendor and recreational opportunities draw hundreds of thousands of tourists to the Rockies annually. National parks (including GLACIER, GRAND TETON, YELLOWSTONE, and Rocky Mountain national parks in the United States and Jasper, Waterton Lakes, and Yoho national parks in Canada), forests, resorts (such as ASPEN, Colo., and BANFF, Alberta), and vacation ranches attract an international clientele.

The Rockies are sparsely populated; probably less than a million permanent residents live there. There are two types of settlements: isolated, dispersed farmsteads or ranches, and towns and villages. The latter category includes resort towns

Rugged Ypsilon Mountain (center) reaches 4,116 m (13,504 ft) in the Mummy Range, a spur of the Front Range of the Rockies. These lofty peaks are located in the northeastern corner of Rocky Mountain National Park, in Colorado. Rowe Glacier is at the northern tip of the range.

and mining towns, both of which have been characterized by rapid growth during recent years.   TERRENCE J. TOY

Bibliography: American West Staff, *The Magnificent Rockies* (1973); Athearn, Robert G., *High Country Empire: The High Plains and Rockies* (1965); Eberhart, Perry, and Schmuck, Philip, *The Fourteeners: Colorado's Great Mountains* (1970); Johnston, T. Edgar, *Fauna of the Rockies,* ed. by Elizabeth Anderson (1977); Lavender, David S., *The Rockies,* rev. ed. (1975); Sprague, Marshall, *The Great Gates: The Story of the Rocky Mountain Passes* (1964); Walker, Bryce S., *The Great Divide* (1973).

rococo music   [roh-koh′-koh]

The musical manifestations of the rococo style (early and mid-18th century) developed most conspicuously in France and Germany but differed markedly according to the artistic predilections of those two countries.

The *style galant* (gallant style) was the French musical reaction to the formality and complex counterpoint of the baroque era; it emphasized highly ornamented melody in short, regular phrases supported by simple harmonies. It was an instrumental style that was best adapted to the harpsichord (*clavecin*) but was also used in ensemble music. Important during the regency and reign of Louis XV (1715–74), the *style galant* appealed particularly to the aristocracy, enchanted by its light, elegant superficialities. It appeared typically in the smaller forms, emphasizing charm and grace rather than serious expression. The leading composers were Françqis Couperin (see COUPERIN family) and Jean Philippe RAMEAU.

The *empfindsamer Stil* (sensitive style) was the German reaction to the baroque style. Avoiding the lavishly ornamented *style galant* of the French, the Germans infused music with shifting moods in which every phrase was laden with expressive feeling. Composers sought contrasts through a wide range of tempos and dynamics, harmonies and modulations, chromaticism, and contrasting themes. Works by C. P. E. BACH, Johann STAMITZ, J. J. Quantz (1697–1773), and Christian Cannabich (1731–98) are typical. The musical rococo was overshadowed by the rise of the Viennese classical style of Beethoven, Haydn, and Mozart.   ELWYN A. WIENANDT

Bibliography: Grout, Donald Jay, *A History of Western Music,* rev. ed. (1973); Lang, Paul Henry, *Music in Western Civilization* (1941).

rococo style

The term *rococo style,* or *the rococo,* refers to a style of decoration current in Europe, particularly France, during the 18th century. It applies both to interior decoration and to ornaments. By extension it may also be applied to some sculpture, paintings, furniture, and architectural details, although hardly to architecture as such. It was a style of high fashion and had few popular forms.

Rococo is derived from the French word *rocaille,* originally meaning the bits of rocky decoration sometimes found in 16th-century architectural schemes. It was first used in its modern sense around 1800, at about the same time as ba-

roque, and, like baroque, was initially a pejorative term (see BAROQUE ART AND ARCHITECTURE). The revival of the rococo occurred gradually during the 19th century, beginning as a vogue for collecting French 18th-century pictures and furniture and for imitation rococo interiors.

The earliest rococo forms appeared around 1700 at Versailles (see VERSAILLES, PALACE OF) and its surrounding *châteaux* as a reaction against the oppressive formality of French classical-baroque in those buildings. In 1701 a suite of rooms at Versailles, including the king's bedroom, was redecorated in a new, lighter, and more graceful style by the royal designer, Pierre Lepautre (1648–1716). Versailles remained the creative center of the rococo until Louis XIV's death, in 1715, after which the initiative passed to Paris. Successive waves of the style during the Regency (1715–23) and the long reign of Louis XV (1723–74) may be seen in such Parisian interiors as the Hôtel de Toulouse—*Galerie dorée,* 1718-19, by François Antoine Vassé (1681–1736); the Hôtel de Lassay—late 1720s, by Jean Aubert (d. 1741); and the Hôtel de Soubise—1736-39, by Germain BOFFRAND (1667–1754).

The essence of rococo interior decoration is twofold; first, the forms are almost flat instead of being, as in baroque schemes, in high relief; second, architectural and sculptural features are eliminated so that the designer is confronted with a smooth surface, interrupted only by the window recesses and the chimneypiece. In a typical rococo decorative scheme, series of tall wooden panels (including the doors), decorated with brilliantly inventive carved and gilded motifs in low relief, are arranged around the room. After 1720 the panels were usually painted ivory white and the motifs tended to be concentrated at the tops, bottoms, and centers with straight moldings down the sides. Further motifs appeared on the dadoes and along the coving, which replaced the cornice, at the tops of the walls. The forms were fine and were originally based on ribbons; later forms consisted mainly of elongated C- and S-shapes; plant tendrils, leaves, blossoms, and sometimes shells and small birds were also introduced.

In later schemes the forms were often mildly asymmetrical in arrangement, but asymmetry was more the province of three-dimensional objects, such as wall brackets, candlesticks, and table ornaments, the master designer of which was Juste Aurèle MEISSONNIER. Mirrors were an important part of the ensemble, and paintings were sometimes set into the paneling over the doors. The overall effect is glittering and lively, a fitting background to 18th-century aristocratic social life, with its emphasis on privacy and its cult of human relationships.

In rococo painting, the powerful rhythms, dark colors, and heroic subjects characteristic of baroque painting gave way to quick, delicate movements, pale colors, and subjects illustrating the varieties of love: romantic love, as in Antoine WATTEAU's *Pilgrimage to Cythera* (1717; Louvre, Paris); erotic love, as in François BOUCHER's *Cupid a Captive* (1754; Wallace Collection, London); or mother love, as in Jean Baptiste CHARDIN's *The Morning Toilet* (c.1740; Nationalmuseum, Stock-

(Left)*This rococo Meissen-ware rhinoceros (c.1745), created by Johann Joachim Kaendler and Peter Reinicke, reflects the influence of Chinese decoration and manufacturing techniques on European ware. (Antique Porcelain Company, New York City.)*

(Below)*The delicate colors and courtly subjects typical of the French rococo style are exemplified in Antoine Watteau's Pilgrimage to Cythera (1717; Louvre, Paris.)*

(Left) *The Amalienburg (1734-40), a hunting lodge in the park of Nymphenburg Palace, was designed by François Cuvilliés, one of the earliest and most inventive exponents of French rococo in Bavaria. The Amalienburg is considered the finest example of secular German rococo.*

(Below) *The Abbey Church of Ottobeuren (1748-67), completed by Johann Michael Fischer, typifies south German church rococo. This style, retaining some elements of baroque architecture, features a profusion of playful and richly polychromatic decorative elements.*

holm). Sculpture was equally lively and unheroic, but its most typical manifestation was portrait busts, the outstanding quality of which was realism, as is evident in Jean Baptiste LEMOYNE's *Réaumur* (1751; Louvre).

During the second quarter of the century the rococo style spread from France to other countries, and above all to Germany. Francophile German princes eagerly adopted the latest fashions from Paris and often employed French-trained architects and designers. Transplanted to Germany, the rococo took a more fanciful and wayward turn, with greater emphasis on forms derived from nature. The supreme example of German rococo style is François CUVILLIÉS's Hall of Mirrors in his AMALIENBURG PAVILION (1734-40), a hunting lodge in the park of NYMPHENBURG PALACE, near Munich. Germany, however—like Austria and Italy to some extent—also produced an indigenous form of rococo, a style evolved out of, rather than in reaction against, the baroque. Because the baroque style in Austria, Germany, and Italy was already much freer than in France, it needed only a fairly small adjustment in scale, pace, and mood to turn baroque decorative forms into rococo ones. This type of rococo found a home both in churches and in palaces. Its most beautiful manifestation is the interior of the pilgrimage church of Die Wies (1745-54) in southern Bavaria, executed by the brothers Johann Baptist and Dominikus ZIMMERMANN.

Germany's other great contribution to the rococo style was the rediscovery (1709-10) of the Chinese art of porcelain

manufacture (see POTTERY AND PORCELAIN) at Meissen, near Dresden. MEISSEN WARE achieved enormous popularity, and soon every major court in continental Europe had its own porcelain factory. Small porcelain figures such as those made by Franz Anton Bustelli (1723-63) at Nymphenburg (see NYMPHENBURG WARE) are perhaps the quintessence of the rococo, fusing all its qualities into a single miniature art.

The rococo style began to decline in the 1760s, denounced by critics who condemned it as tasteless, frivolous, and symbolic of a corrupt society. Within 20 years it was supplanted, together with the baroque, by NEOCLASSICISM.

MICHAEL KITSON

Bibliography: Goncourt, Edmond and Jules de, *L'Art au dixhuitième siècle* (1880-82; trans. as *French XVIII Century Painters,* 1948); Hempel, Eberhard, *Baroque Art and Architecture in Central Europe* (1965); Kal-

Jean Honoré Fragonard's The Swing (c.1767) epitomizes the frivolous and erotic "gallant scenes" at which he excelled. Influenced by the luxurious work of Boucher, Fragonard descended to sentimentality in his later works in this genre. (Wallace Collection, London.)

nein, W. G., and Levey, Michael, *Art and Architecture of the Eighteenth Century in France* (1972); Kimball, Fiske, *The Creation of the Rococo* (1943; repr. 1965); Kitson, Michael, *The Age of Baroque* (3d ed., 1976); Levey, Michael, *Rococo to Revolution* (1966); Wittkower, Rudolf, *Art and Architecture in Italy 1600–1750* (3d ed., 1973).

Rodchenko, Aleksandr Mikhailovich [rawt'-chink-uh]

Alexander Mikhailovich Rodchenko, b. Nov. 23 (N.S.), 1891, d. Sept. 3, 1956, was the founder of Russian nonobjectivism, a style related to suprematism but less pure in color and texture. He began his career under the influence of Kasimir Malevich. At an exhibition in 1919, Rodchenko showed *Black on Black* (1918; Tretyakov Gallery, Moscow), painted in reaction to Malevich's *White on White* (1918; Museum of Modern Art, New York City). In 1919, with the constructivist Vladimir Tatlin, Rodchenko made three-dimensional constructions in wood, metal, and cardboard. Soon after, he turned to more practical arts to serve the USSR.   TANIA MARIE BAYARD

Bibliography: Barr, Alfred, Jr., *Cubism and Abstract Art* (1936); Gray, Camilla, *The Russian Experiment in Art, 1863–1922* (1971).

rodent

Rodents are mammals of the order Rodentia and are characterized by an upper and lower pair of front teeth (incisors) specialized for gnawing. Most rodents are small, enabling them to occupy habitats that could not support larger mammals. Rodents are found in nearly every terrestrial habitat, including higher in the mountains than any other mammals. Some, such as the house mouse, *Mus*, and house rat, *Rattus*, have been accidentally transported by humans to all parts of the world; others, like the muskrat, *Ondatra*, and nutria, *Myocastor*, have been deliberately released in new areas to provide a source of fur.

Rodents are of considerable value to humans. Some, such as the beaver, *Castor*, muskrat, and nutria, are important fur animals; others, such as the squirrels, *Sciurus*, of North America, the hutias, *Capromys*, of Cuba, and the pacas, *Cuniculus*, of Central and South America, are used as human food. Rodents are also beneficial in destroying large quantities of insects and weeds, and many of the significant achievements in biological research were made possible only through the use of laboratory rats and mice. Several rodents, including the golden hamster, *Mesocricetus*, and the guinea pig, *Cavia*, make fine pets. Rodents are herbivorous or omnivorous, omnivorous rodents adding insects and other small organisms to their plant diet. Because of their usually large numbers and

the consequent effects of these numbers on food sources, as well as because they are all preyed upon by other animals, rodents are a vital element in the ecology of most regions.

Rodents also have detrimental aspects, one of the most critical being the transmission of disease. Rat-borne plague, for example, has caused innumerable human deaths (and the deaths of the rats as well) throughout the centuries and has inexorably affected human history. Rodents also cause serious economic damage by feeding on crops and stored foods.

Characteristics. The number of rodent species is estimated at between 1,700 and 5,000; the more modern classifications tend toward the lower number. These species are grouped into roughly 100 to more than 350 genera and into 34 or 35 families, including 8 extinct families. Rodents range in size from the North and Central American pygmy mice, *Baiomys*, which range from 50 to 80 mm (2 to 3 in) long, plus a 35- to 55-mm (1.4- to 2.2-in) tail, and weigh about 7 g (¼ oz), to the Central and South American capybara, *Hydrochoerus*, which may reach 1.3 m (4 ft) long, plus a very short tail, 53 cm (21 in) high at the shoulders, and over 50 kg (110 lb) in weight. The extinct North American beaver *Castoroides*, which lived during the Pleistocene, about a million years ago, was 2.3 m (7.5 ft) long, including the tail, and about the height of a small bear. Most rodents are the familiar mouse or squirrel types, but some, like the Eurasian mole rats, *Spalax*, resemble moles, and the South American maras, *Dolichotis*, suggest nonhopping rabbits. Most rodents are fully haired, except possibly for the tail, with some, like the chinchilla, *Chinchilla*, having especially thick coats, whereas the East African naked mole rat, *Heterocephalus*, is practically hairless. Some rodents, like the beaver, have webbed hind feet or are otherwise modified for swimming; the North and Central American flying squirrels, *Glaucomys*, have a flap of skin along each side of the body between the front and hind legs and use these flaps for gliding through the air.

Internally, all rodents are similar. The upper and lower jaws each have a pair of ever-growing incisor teeth (never forming closed roots) whose bases extend far back into the upper and lower jaws. The front face of each incisor consists of hard enamel, but the rest of the tooth is of softer dentine; this results in differential wear, always leaving a sharp cutting edge on the tooth. There are no other incisors or a canine tooth, and the first and (in the lower jaw) the second premolars are also lacking, leaving a gap, called the diastema, between the incisors and the cheek teeth. The cheek teeth (premolars and molars) may be short (low-crowned) and rooted, or tall (high-crowned) and ever growing. The front teeth and the cheek teeth are offset in relation to each other, so that when the upper and lower incisors are together in gnawing, the cheek teeth do not meet and wear uselessly, and vice versa. The skull depression (glenoid fossa) at the rear of the skull that acts as a socket for the rearward projecting hinge (articular condyle) of the lower jaw is shallow and elongated from front to rear, permitting the lower jaw to move back and forth as well as from side to side.

In rodents, the masseter muscle—which runs from the skull to the lower jaw and in many mammals serves in the closing of the jaws—is principally involved in moving the lower jaw back and forth and from side to side. The masseter muscle on each side of the head is divided into three parts; the outermost part is essentially similar in all rodents, but the remaining two parts, referred to as outer and inner (or deeper), vary in their attachments on the lower jaw and skull.

Rodent Classification. These variations in the attachment of the masseter muscle were originally used to divide the rodent

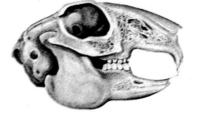

Jaws of rodents have continuously growing, chiselike incisors, adapted for gnawing, in the front; cheek teeth on each side for grinding vegetation; and a gap between the two types of teeth.

order into three suborders. Some rodents, however, do not fit readily into any of them. Consequently, four groups are often recognized—protogomorphs, sciuromorphs, hystricomorphs, and myomorphs—but whether three or four groups are designated as suborders, they are now more generally thought of as convenience groups for dealing with the many species.

The most primitive type of attachments is found in the protogomorph group and was present in the earliest-known fossil rodent. It still exists in a generally similar form in the living North American mountain beavers, *Aplodontia*, usually considered the most primitive of all living rodents. Broadly simplified, in the protogomorph type, the outer portion of the masseter muscle runs from the front of the cheekbone (a bony bar technically called the zygomatic arch) to the rear of the lower jaw, and the inner portion runs from the middle of the cheekbone to the middle of the lower jaw.

In the squirrellike sciuromorphs the inner portion remains essentially the same, but the outer portion has shifted its attachment forward from the cheekbone and onto the front side of the skull, where it lies in a groove formed to hold it. Shifting the muscle attachment farther to the front increases the length of the muscle and its efficiency in moving the jaw forward, as when gnawing. In the guinea-piglike hystricomorphs (sometimes called caviomorphs), the outer portion of the muscle remains essentially the same, while the inner portion has shifted its attachment to the front of the skull, passing through an enlarged opening (the infraorbital canal) below the front of the cheekbone to do so. In the ratlike myomorphs, considered the most advanced of the rodents, both portions of the masseter muscle have shifted their attachments forward from the cheekbone onto the front side of the skull, the inner portion passing through an enlarged opening beneath the cheekbone.

Reproduction. Rodents are generally nocturnal and are usually social animals; some, however, are solitary. Breeding cycles vary considerably. Females have a duplex type of uterus, in which the two uteri remain separated but are joined to a single vagina. Males commonly have a penis bone (os penis, or baculum). Gestation varies from about 16 days in the golden hamster to 4½ months in the capybara. Litter size varies from one to more than 18. Usually only the female raises the young, but in the pygmy mice, for example, the male parent also contributes to their care. Reproductive age may be attained at 60 days or earlier, as in the Eurasian steppe lemming, *Lagurus*, and reproductive life may continue into old age, but most rodents are short-lived, rarely surviving naturally beyond 2 or 3 years. Old World porcupines, *Hystrix* and *Acanthion*, however, may live over 20 years.

Evolution. The earliest-known rodent, *Paramys*, lived in North America from the late Paleocene to the middle Eocene, about 56 million to 45 million years ago. It was unquestionably a rodent and not a transitional form and provided no definite information as to its origins. Indeed, no other fossil has yet been found that links the rodents to any other mammal group. It is believed, however, that the rodents evolved from early insectivores, as did the primates, and that the ancestors of the rodents and of the primates were themselves closely related.   EDWIN E. ROSENBLUM

Bibliography: Delany, M. J., *The Ecology of Small Mammals* (1974); Ellerman, J. R., *Families and Genera of Living Rodents*, 2 vols. (1940; repr. 1966); Hanney, Peter W., *Rodents: Their Lives and Habits* (1975); Vinogradov, B. S., and Argiropulo, A. I., *Key to Rodents*, trans. by Jean Salkind (1968); Wray, J. D., *Small Mammals* (1974).

rodeo

A rodeo is a festival consisting of a set of competitive sports based on the traditional working skills of cowhands—riding and roping cattle and horses. *Rodeo* is a Spanish word that denotes a gathering place of cattle—literally, a roundup. The modern rodeo is a colorful event that flourishes in the western United States, Florida, several eastern cities, and most of Canada. Most major rodeos are held under the auspices of the Rodeo Cowboys Association (RCA), founded in 1945. The most important rodeos are the Frontier Days Celebration in Cheyenne, Wyo., the Roundup in Pendleton, Oreg., the Cali-

A contestant attempts to keep his seat for a full 10 seconds during the bull-riding competition of the Calgary Exhibition and Stampede, the oldest and one of the most celebrated rodeos of the Canadian west. Today rodeos feature 5 standard events and often include additional specialty contests and shows.

fornia Rodeo in Salinas, Calif., the Stampede in Calgary, Alberta, Canada, and the National Finals Rodeo in Oklahoma City, Okla. The rodeo has its origins in the development of the cattle industry. Once or twice each year the cattle were rounded up and driven to various market towns. After the hard work of the roundup the cowboys were paid off, and they usually celebrated the occasion. Informal competitions were held in which the cowboys bet their wages on their individual skills. The first rodeo with an admission charge for spectators was held in Prescott, Ariz., in 1888. Then, as now, the rodeo consisted of five standard events—bareback bronc-riding, saddle bronc-riding, bull-riding, calf-roping, and steer-wrestling, sometimes called bull-dogging. In bareback bronc-riding, an untamed horse, called a bronco, tries to buck the rider off its back. Using only one hand, the rider tries to hold on to a special rigging for a specified time period of 8 to 10 seconds. If the rider falls, or if his or her free hand touches any part of his or her own body or that of the horse, the rider is disqualified. Saddle bronc-riding is similar to bareback riding, except that a special lightweight saddle is used and the rider holds on to a single piece of rope. Again, the free hand must not be used. Bull-riding, because of the ferocity of the Brahma bull, is the most dangerous event in the rodeo. The rider holds on to a bull-rope that circles the trunk of the bull and, using just one hand, must stay on for a 10-second period. In all three events the spirit and strength of the animals are factors in the judging. Calf-roping and steer-wrestling are events in which the contestant tries to accomplish a set of maneuvers in the shortest possible time. In calf-roping, a calf is released into the arena through a chute and the cowhand, mounted on horseback, pursues. The rider must throw the lariat, or rope, over the calf's neck, dismount, throw the calf to the ground, and tie its feet while the horse keeps the rope taut. In steer-wrestling, a steer is released from the chute, and the mounted cowhand rides alongside it and then leaps from the saddle, grabbing the steer by the horns in midflight. By digging in with the heels, the cowhand first must halt the steer then flip it over onto its back as quickly as possible. Rodeo cowhands receive no regular fee. They compete solely for the prize money. Some contestants, such as six-time world champion Larry Mahan, may annually collect up to $50,000 in prize money. The average winnings, however, amount to around $15,000.   GORDON STANG

Bibliography: Porter, W., *Roping and Riding* (1975); St. John, Bob, *On Down the Road* (1977); Schnell, Fred, *Rodeo* (1971).

Rodgers   (family)

The Rodgers were a family of distinguished American naval officers. **John Rodgers**, b. near Havre de Grace, Md., 1773, d. Aug. 1, 1838, helped capture the French frigate *Insurgente* in 1799 and was promoted to captain that year. In 1805, Rodgers imposed a peace treaty on Tripoli, ending the TRIPOLITAN WAR. As commanding officer of the frigate *President*, he engaged the British warship *Little Belt* on May 16, 1811, an act contributing to the onset of the War of 1812. Rodgers was a highly successful commerce raider during the war, and after peace was restored he served until 1837 as president of the

Board of Navy Commissioners (the ranking commissioned post in the navy), except for the years 1824–27, when he was commander of the Mediterranean squadron.

His son, **John Rodgers**, b. near Havre de Grace, Md., Aug. 8, 1812, d. May 5, 1882, served in the navy during the U.S. Civil War and led the punitive Rodgers-Low expedition to Korea in 1871. As the ranking rear admiral on active duty, he headed the first Naval Advisory Board, which in 1881 laid the foundations for creation of a revamped navy of steam-driven, steel-hulled warships. **John Rodgers**, b. Washington, D.C., Jan. 15, 1881, d. Aug. 27, 1926, the second officer to be designated a naval aviator, was the great-grandson of the founder of the dynasty. Numerous other officers of the army and navy bore the Rodgers surname.   KENNETH J. HAGAN

Bibliography: Johnson, R., *Rear Admiral John Rodgers, 1812–1882* (1967); Paullin, C., *Commodore John Rodgers* (1910; repr. 1967).

Rodgers, Bill

William Henry Rodgers, b. Hartford, Conn., Dec. 23, 1947, became the dominant figure in long-distance running after winning the 26-mi 385-yd (42.2-km) Boston Marathon in 1975 in the then-record time of 2 hr 9 min 55 sec. He had run track while attending Wesleyan University but after graduating stopped running; Frank Shorter's 1972 Olympic Games Marathon victory inspired him to resume. Rodgers, who is 1 m 74 cm (5 ft 8.5 in) tall and weighs 57 kg (128 lb), has run more sub-2 hr 11 min marathons than any other runner; he also holds the world record in the 25-km (15.5-mi) and the American record in the 30-km (18.6-mi) track races and the one-hour run. Rodgers has won the New York Marathon 4 consecutive times (1976–79) and the Boston Marathon 3 times.

Rodgers, Richard

Richard Rodgers, b. Hammels Station, N.Y., June 28, 1902, d. Dec. 30, 1979, was the American musical theater's most successful and influential composer. His work with the lyricist Lorenz HART between 1925 and 1942 produced a series of innovative works, including *A Connecticut Yankee* (1927), *On Your Toes* (1936), and *Pal Joey* (1940). After Hart's death, Rodgers began an equally successful collaboration with Oscar HAMMERSTEIN II, a 16-year partnership that began with *Oklahoma!* in 1943. The Rodgers-Hart shows were unique amalgams of story and music. The Rodgers-Hammerstein collaboration in effect created a new form, the American music-drama, and produced such notable works as *Carousel* (1945), *South Pacific* (1948), and *The King and I* (1951). After Hammerstein's death in 1960, Rodgers wrote his own lyrics for the musical *No Strings* (1962) and worked with the lyricist Stephen SONDHEIM on *Do I Hear a Waltz?* (1965).   DAVID EWEN

Bibliography: Ewen, David, *Richard Rodgers* (1957); Rodgers, Richard, *Many Stages* (1975).

Rodin, Auguste   [roh-dan']

One of the greatest and most prolific sculptors of the 19th century, Auguste Rodin, b. Nov. 12, 1840, d. Nov. 17, 1917, succeeded, often contentiously, in bringing new life and direction to a dying art. Today major collections of his work on permanent display are at the Musée Rodin (Hôtel Biron, Paris), the Rodin Museum (Philadelphia), and the California Palace of the Legion of Honor (San Francisco).

The son of a minor employee of the Parisian police department, Rodin enrolled at the age of 14 in the École Impériale Spéciale de Dessin et de Mathématiques, a school that trained craftsmen and decorative artists. Rodin began (1857) earning his living as a studio helper on ornamental detail for other sculptors. At the same time he found time to work at home on his own projects and to continue studies in anatomy and, with Antoine Louis BARYE, in sculpture.

In 1875–76, after an exhilarating trip to Italy and firsthand knowledge of the sculptures of Michelangelo, Rodin completed his first masterwork, a young male nude (later called *The Age of Bronze*). This sculpture led to the first of numerous public controversies that were to beset Rodin throughout his

The Age of Bronze (1875–76), an unidealized study of a male figure, displays Rodin's characteristic interest in the accurate portrayal of anatomical detail. Rodin, who rejected the academic standards of his time in favor of a more direct approach to nature, often scandalized his contemporaries, who accused him of casting his work from models. (Musée du Luxembourg, Paris.)

career. Accustomed to the highly artificial appearance of most 19th-century academic sculpture, the critics of the day refused to believe that Rodin was able to model a figure so realistically without using plaster casts of a live model. In 1880 he received a commission from the French government for *The Gates of Hell*, a work that preoccupied him for the rest of his life. His starting point was Dante's *Inferno*, but the images of torment and despair depicted on the *Gates* rapidly became more generalized.

During the 1880s, Rodin became one of the most successful French artists. He received many commissions for public monuments, including *The Burghers of Calais* (1884–95), the *Monument to Victor Hugo* (1889–1909), and the *Monument to Balzac* (1891–98). Although Rodin regarded this last work—a dramatic portrayal of Balzac's spirit—to be one of his greatest, the society that commissioned it rejected the piece as an unfinished and grotesque botch. This led to one of the most bitter public debates in the history of 19th-century art.

Rodin was not only a sculptor of public monuments but a tireless artist who produced numerous small and intimate sculptures. These works range from highly developed pieces such as *Eternal Spring* (1884) and *The Kiss* (1886; first marble version, Musée Rodin), two of his most popular studies of youthful passion, to fragmentary studies of limbs and heads. He was also much in demand as a portrait sculptor and produced memorable images of many of the most famous men and women of his time, ranging from Victor Hugo (1883) to George Bernard Shaw (1906) and Pope Benedict XV (1915), and of many society figures on both sides of the Atlantic.

After 1900, Rodin worked mostly on a smaller scale, for example, on studies of ballet dancers (c.1910–12) and on drawings. The outbreak of World War I in 1914 brought him considerable hardship; his health and mental stability gave way rapidly before his death in 1917.   JOHN L. TANCOCK

Bibliography: Cladel, Judith, *Rodin*, trans. by James Whitall (1938); Descharnes, Robert, and Chabrun, Jean François, *Auguste Rodin*, trans. by Edita Lausanne (1967); Elsen, Albert E., *Auguste Rodin: Readings on His Life and Work* (1965), *Rodin* (1963), and *Rodin's Gates of Hell* (1960); Elsen, Albert E., and Varnedoe, J. Kirk T., *The Drawings of Rodin* (1971); Gsell, Paul, *On Art and Artists* (1957); Hale, William H., *The World of Rodin* (1969); Rilke, Rainer Maria, *Auguste Rodin*, trans. by Jessie Lemont and Hans Trausil (1945); Sutton, Denys, *Triumphant Satyr: The World of Auguste Rodin* (1966); Tancock, John L., *The Sculpture of Auguste Rodin* (1969; rev. ed. 1976).

Roe v. Wade and Doe v. Bolton

The cases of *Roe* v. *Wade* and *Doe* v. *Bolton* (1973) were companion cases in which the U.S. Supreme Court held, with some qualification, that state laws prohibiting abortions were unconstitutional. *Roe* involved a Texas statute making it a felony for anyone to destroy a fetus except on "medical advice for the purpose of saving the mother's life." *Doe* dealt with a Georgia statute allowing an abortion when the woman's life was endangered, when the child would be born with a severe defect, or when pregnancy had resulted from rape.

Invalidating both statutes in 7–2 rulings, the Court, speaking through Justice Harry Blackmun, held that the constitutional right of privacy—whether based on the 14TH AMENDMENT's concept of personal liberty or on the 9TH AMENDMENT's reservation of rights to the people—"includes the right of a woman to decide whether or not to terminate her pregnancy." Blackmun went on to say that the right to an abortion is not unqualified and must be balanced against the state's interest in regulation. He outlined what the states might and might not do. During the first trimester of pregnancy the states might not proscribe abortions at all but could regulate abortion procedures in order to protect maternal health. After that stage the states might regulate or even prohibit abortions subject to appropriate medical judgment. The decision aroused nationwide controversy, and a movement arose to overrule the Court through constitutional amendment.

ROBERT J. STEAMER

Bibliography: Krason, Stephen M., *Abortion: Politics, Morality, and the Constitution* (1984); Rubin, Eva, *Abortion, Politics, and the Courts: Roe vs. Wade and Its Aftermath* (1982).

Roebling, John A. and Washington Augustus
[rohb'-ling]

Roebling is the family name of two American engineers, father and son, who were pioneers in the development of suspension bridges and wire cable. They are best known as the designers and builders of the Brooklyn Bridge.

John Augustus Roebling, b. Mühlhausen, Germany, June 12, 1806, immigrated to the United States in 1831. In 1841 he produced the first wire cable in the United States and built a railroad suspension bridge (1851–55) over Niagara Falls. He designed the Brooklyn Bridge but, while supervising preliminary construction operations, was injured and died on July 22, 1869.

Washington Augustus Roebling, b. Saxonburg, Pa., May 26, 1837, was made chief engineer of the Brooklyn Bridge after his father's death. He completed the bridge in 1883. In his later years he managed the family firm in Trenton, N.J., where he died on July 21, 1926.

Bibliography: McCullough, David, *The Great Bridge* (1972; repr. 1983); Schuyler, Hamilton, *The Roeblings: A Century of Engineers, Bridgebuilders, and Industrialists* (1931; repr. 1978); Steinman, David B., *Builders of the Bridge: The Story of John Roebling and His Son* (1945; repr. 1972).

Roehm, Ernst   [rurm]

The German army officer Ernst Roehm (or Röhm), b. Nov. 28, 1887, d. June 30, 1934, was the leader of the Nazi storm troops (SA, or *Sturmabteilung*). Roehm was wounded in World War I and afterward helped set up the National Socialist (Nazi) party. The SA (also called the Brownshirts) was formed from his private army in 1921. After coming into conflict with Nazi leader Adolf Hitler over the role of the SA, Roehm went to Bolivia, where he remained from 1925 to 1930, returning to reorganize the SA. When Hitler took power in 1933, Roehm became a minister in Germany. Fearing him as a rival, Hitler had him shot in the 1934 blood purge.   ROBIN BUSS

Roentgen, Wilhelm Conrad   [ruhnt'-gen]

The German physicist Wilhelm Conrad Roentgen, b. Mar. 27, 1845, d. Feb. 10, 1923, discovered X rays, for which he received (1901) the first Nobel Prize for physics. He observed (1895) that barium platinocyanide crystals across the room fluoresced whenever he turned on a Crooke's, or cathode-ray discharge, tube, even when the tube, an electron emitter, was shielded by black cardboard or thin metal sheets. Roentgen

correctly hypothesized that a previously unknown form of radiation of very short wavelength was involved, and that these *X rays* (a term he coined) caused the crystals to glow. He later demonstrated the metallurgical and medical use of X rays.

Bibliography: Grey, Vivian, *Roentgen's Revolution: The Discovery of the X-Ray* (1973); Nitske, W. Robert, *The Life of Wilhelm Conrad Roentgen, Discoverer of the X-Ray* (1971).

Roethke, Theodore   [ret'-ke]

One of the most distinguished poets in the United States in the mid-20th century, Theodore Roethke, b. Saginaw, Mich., May 25, 1908, d. Aug. 1, 1963, won the 1954 Pulitzer Prize for poetry with *The Waking* (1953) and both the National Book Award and the Bollingen Prize for the collection *Words for the Wind* (1957).

Educated at the University of Michigan (B.A., 1929; M.A., 1936) and at Harvard University (1929–31), Roethke became an influential teacher and maintained a lively correspondence with many of his contemporaries (published in *Selected Letters*, 1968). His first book, *Open House* (1941), showed the strong influence of Robert Frost.

In *The Lost Son and Other Poems* (1948), Roethke opened up a poetic language and territory that dazzled his peers. Using an associative linking of images rather than a logical exposition of balanced argument, he created a series of poem-sequences that explored his own subconscious. Although poets had used Sigmund Freud and Carl Jung as sources for imagery and metaphor for some time, Roethke was the first American to translate the psychology of the subconscious into poetic expression. Always in some sense a nature poet, he also became a poet who described the anxieties and difficulties of self-knowledge.

In *Words for the Wind* Roethke extended poetry beyond the range of such modern masters as Ezra POUND and T. S. ELIOT. Roethke was always troubled by the problem of influence, and he dreaded sounding like an echo of some earlier, more forceful poet. When a posthumous volume, *The Far Field* (1964), appeared, some critics felt that it contained too many echoes of Walt Whitman, William Butler Yeats, and others. Subsequent critical judgment has, however, affirmed how singular Roethke's achievement was, and his own influence has continued to be felt among younger poets.

His notebooks, published as *Straw for the Fire* (1972), are filled with evidence of a thoroughly poetic mind, constantly at work on its own insights and constantly recognizing the wonder of the natural world.   CHARLES MOLESWORTH

Bibliography: Blessing, R. A., *Theodore Roethke's Dynamic Vision* (1974); Chaney, N., *Theodore Roethke: The Poetics of Wonder* (1982); Foster, A. T., *Theodore Roethke's Meditative Sequences* (1985); Parini, J., *Theodore Roethke: An American Romantic* (1979); Sullivan, R., *Theodore Roethke: The Garden Master* (1975); Williams, H., *The Edge Is What I Have* (1976); Wolff, G., *Theodore Roethke* (1981).

Roger II, King of Sicily

Roger II, b. Dec. 22, 1095, d. Feb. 26, 1154, founder of the kingdom of Sicily, built on the strong political foundation laid by his father, Roger I (1031–1101), count of Sicily, and gained control of Calabria and Apulia, Norman possessions on the mainland. In return for Roger's support, the antipope Anacletus II crowned him king of Sicily in 1130. Pope Innocent II was forced to recognize Roger's sovereignty after Roger defeated Innocent's army in 1139. Roger widened his kingdom by raiding Byzantine states and conquering the North African coastal areas from Tunis to Tripoli. He ruled wisely and prosperously, establishing a centralized administrative structure. His civil service system was admired throughout Europe, and his court was an important center for cultural interchange with the East. Roger sent many travelers abroad, prompting the Arabian geographer al-Idrisi to dedicate a famous geography work to him. Roger was succeeded by his son William I (r. 1154–66).

JAMES M. POWELL

Bibliography: Curtis, Edmund, *Roger of Sicily and the Normans in Lower Italy, 1016–1154* (1912); Norwich, John J., *The Kingdom in the Sun* (1970).

Rogers, Carl

Carl Ransom Rogers, b. Oak Park, Ill., Jan. 8, 1902, d. Feb. 4, 1987, founded client-centered psychotherapy (earlier called nondirective psychotherapy) and in the development of scientific methods for studying psychotherapeutic outcomes and processes. Rogers's CLIENT-CENTERED THERAPY is among the most influential and widely employed techniques in modern U.S. clinical psychology.

Rogers was educated at the University of Wisconsin (B.A., 1924), Union Theological Seminary, and Teachers College, Columbia University (Ph.D., 1931). After spending 12 years in Rochester, N.Y., as psychologist and as director in the Child Study Department of the Society for the Prevention of Cruelty to Children, Rogers moved in 1940 to Ohio State University; in 1945 to the University of Chicago, where he became director of the Counseling Center; and in 1957 to the University of Wisconsin, where he studied client-centered therapy with schizophrenic patients. From 1963 until his death he was a resident fellow at the Center for Studies of the Person in La Jolla, Calif., of which he was a cofounder.

Learning to be a psychotherapist is the central theme in Rogers's theory—that is, the psychotherapist's learning how he or she can create a relationship that the client may use for his or her own personal growth. Rogers regards it as an empirical fact, buttressed by research, that if this relationship can be created, the person can use it. The characteristics of a helping relationship are that the therapist is (1) genuine, not maintaining a facade or acting a role, (2) accepting of both his or her own experience and that of the client, and (3) empathetic and understanding. Provided with the emotional climate of client-centered therapy, the troubled person is likely to trust his or her experience, to find new meaning within it, to base choices on more complete evidence, and to find life more lively and satisfying.

Rogers was a leader in the scientific study of psychotherapy, transcribing his therapy protocols for study, using William Stephenson's Q-sort method for studying self and ideal concepts before and after therapy, and utilizing both direct observation and psychological tests to measure psychotherapeutic growth. In discussions with B. F. Skinner, Rogers explored the philosophical assumptions and the models of human nature inherent in humanistic and behavioristic conceptions. Later, he was concerned with the implications of therapeutic understanding for broader areas of life—education, group relations, and marriage.

Among Rogers's works are *Counseling and Psychotherapy* (1942), *Client-Centered Therapy* (1951), *On Becoming a Person* (1961), *Freedom to Learn for the Eighties* (1983), and the autobiographical *On Becoming Carl Rogers* (1980).

DAVID F. RICKS

Bibliography: Evans, Richard I., *Carl Rogers: The Man and His Ideas* (1975) and *Dialogue with Carl Rogers* (1981); Kovel, Joel, *A Complete Guide to Psychotherapy* (1976); Nye, Robert D., *Three Views of Man: Perspectives from Sigmund Freud, B. F. Skinner and Carl Rogers*, 2d ed. (1981).

See also: HUMANISTIC PSYCHOLOGY.

Rogers, Ginger

Singer, actress, and dancer Ginger Rogers, b. Virginia McMath, in Independence, Mo., July 16, 1911, is best known for the movie musicals she made with Fred ASTAIRE. After playing vaudeville as a teenager, she made her debut on Broadway in 1929 and entered feature films in 1930.

The famous Rogers and Astaire dance team first starred in *Flying Down to Rio* (1933) and developed their now classic routines in *The Gay Divorcée* (1934), *Top Hat* (1935), and *Swing Time* (1936). Rogers, who also appeared in dramatic roles, won an Academy Award for *Kitty Foyle* (1940). She made numerous films during the next two decades and returned to the musical comedy stage in *Hello, Dolly* (1965) and *Mame* (1969).

Bibliography: Croce, Arlene, *The Fred Astaire and Ginger Rogers Book* (1978); Dickens, H. C., *The Films of Ginger Rogers* (1975; repr. 1984).

Rogers, John   (clergyman)

John Rogers, b. *c.*1500, d. Feb. 4, 1555, was an English Protestant reformer, the editor of Matthew's Bible, who was martyred under Queen Mary I. Educated at Cambridge, he became (1534) chaplain to English merchants in Antwerp, where he met William TYNDALE and converted to Protestantism. After Tyndale's death (1536), Rogers used the translations prepared by Tyndale with those of Miles COVERDALE to produce the first complete English Bible, published (1537) under the pseudonym Thomas Matthew.

Returning to London (1548), Rogers was given preferments and appointed lecturer at Saint Paul's Cathedral. After Mary's succession to the throne he was imprisoned, sentenced to death, and burned at Smithfield. He was the first Protestant to be martyred under Mary.

Bibliography: Haller, William, *Foxe's Book of Martyrs and the Elect Nation* (1963); Hughes, Philip, *The Reformation in England*, 4 vols. (1950–54).

Rogers, Randolph

Randolph Rogers, b. Waterloo, N.Y., July 6, 1825, d. July 29, 1892, was a late-neoclassical sculptor who worked in Italy. Although the pose of his celebrated *Nydia, the Blind Girl of Pompeii* (1853; Metropolitan Museum of Art, New York City) resembles the Hellenistic work *Old Market Woman* (Vatican Museum), his bronze doors (1855–59) illustrating Columbus's adventures for the Capitol Rotunda in Washington, D.C., are early examples of Renaissance inspiration in American art. The strong, simple bronze *Meriwether Lewis* (1861) for the Washington Monument in Richmond, Va., is Rogers's finest portrait.

JOAN SIEGFRIED

Bibliography: Rogers, Millard, *Randolph Rogers: American Sculptor in Rome* (1971).

Rogers, Robert

Robert Rogers, b. Methuen, Mass., Nov. 7, 1731, d. May 8, 1795, achieved fame in the French and Indian War of 1754–63 as a commander of colonial rangers. Rogers grew up in New Hampshire and soon after joining the army in 1755 he was given command of an independent company of rangers. By 1758 he was in charge of ranger companies for the British army. He established his reputation the next year when his troops burned the village of the Saint Francis Indians, killing about 200 people.

After the French and Indian War, Rogers went to London, where he became known as a writer, publishing his *Journals, A Concise Account of North America* (both 1765), and a play, *Ponteach* (1766). He returned to America to serve (1766–67) as commander at Mackinac. His hopes of leading an expedition in search of a Northwest Passage were frustrated, and after accusations of corruption his career became engulfed in scandal. In the American Revolution he fought briefly—and ineffectively—for the British.

REGINALD HORSMAN

Bibliography: Cuneo, John R., *Robert Rogers of the Rangers* (1959).

Rogers, Will

Will Rogers, b. Oologah, Indian Territory (now Claremore, Okla.), Nov. 4, 1879, d. Aug. 15, 1935, was an American humorist and actor famous for his witty, homespun commentaries on contemporary events. He grew up on a ranch and began his career as an entertainer in rodeos and Wild West shows. Shortly after making his New York City debut in 1905, he began exchanging banter with the audience, and by 1915 he had developed the stage persona of a rough, straight-talking cowboy who debunked pretension and fashionable attitudes. He began to write a syndicated newspaper column in 1922 and made a series of films between 1929 and his death in a plane crash in 1935. Rogers's books include *Rogerisms—the Cowboy Philosopher on Prohibition* (1919), *Illiterate Digest* (1924), and *Autobiography* (1949; repr. 1977).

Bibliography: Alworth, E. P., *Will Rogers* (1974); Rogers, Betty, *Will Rogers* (1979; repr. 1982).

Rogers, William P.

The American lawyer and government official William Pierce Rogers, b. Norfolk, N.Y., June 23, 1913, served (1969–73) as President Richard Nixon's secretary of state. He received (1937) his law degree from Cornell University and served in the navy in World War II. He was (1953–57) deputy attorney general of the United States and attorney general (1957–61). As attorney general he was a strong advocate of civil rights. As secretary of state he was overshadowed by the assistant for national security affairs, Henry Kissinger, who succeeded him. In 1986, Rogers headed the commission that investigated the destruction of the SPACE SHUTTLE *Challenger.*

Roget's Thesaurus: see THESAURUS.

Rohlfs, Christian   [rohlfs]

The German painter and graphic artist Christian Rohlfs, b. Dec. 22, 1848, d. Jan. 8, 1938, produced an enormous body of works—more than 400 were destroyed by the Nazis—ranging in style from impressionist to muted expressionist. Criticism of his avant-garde work forced Rohlfs to leave (*c.*1900) the Weimar Art School after a 30-year career to teach at the Folkwang School at Hagen, where his friendship with the expressionist painter Emil Nolde completely changed his style; he abandoned oil painting for tempera, watercolor, and woodcuts. Rohlfs spent his last decade (1927–38) in Switzerland, producing the exquisite flower paintings for which he is best known.

Bibliography: Roh, Franz, *German Art in the 20th Century* (1968); Selz, Peter, *German Expressionist Painting* (1957); Wilson, David, trans., *Christian Rohlfs: Watercolors, Drawings, and Prints* (1968).

Röhm, Ernst: see ROEHM, ERNST.

Rohmer, Eric   [roh'-mer]

Editor of the influential film journal *Cahiers du Cinéma* from 1958 to 1963, French filmmaker Eric Rohmer, b. Jean Maurice Schérer, Dec. 1, 1920, is known for the epigrammatic quality of his writing and the moral and psychological insights conveyed by his films. His first highly successful film cycle, which he labeled "moral tales for the bourgeoisie," included such controlled and sensitive films as *My Night at Maud's* (1969), *Claire's Knee* (1970), and *Chloe in the Afternoon* (1972)—each a lighthearted investigation into the nature of temptation. *The Marquise of O* (1976), adapted from the 19th-century short story by the German writer Heinrich von Kleist, was a departure, but Rohmer returned to his contemporary sketches with a new cycle—among the films: *Le Beau Mariage,* 1982; *Pauline at the Beach,* 1983; *Full Moon in Paris,* 1984—all characterized by slight plots where conversation is more revealing than action. He won top prize at the Venice Film Festival for *Summer* (1986). Rohmer writes as well as directs all of his films.   GAUTAM DASGUPTA

Rohmer, Sax

Sax Rohmer was the pseudonym of Arthur Sarsfield Ward, b. 1883?, d. June 1, 1959, an English novelist who is best known for his exotic, well-researched mysteries. He had a lifelong interest in Egyptology and occult literature. After brief careers in finance and journalism, Rohmer achieved a literary reputation with *Dr. Fu Manchu* (1913). Rohmer subsequently pitted his Chinese master criminal against Nayland Smith, a suave English hero, in many popular adventure books, movies, and a radio series.

Bibliography: Van Ash, Cay, and Rohmer, Elizabeth S., *Master of Villainy: A Biography of Sax Rohmer* (1972).

Rojas Zorrilla, Francisco de   [roh'-hahs thohr-eel'-yah]

Francisco de Rojas Zorrilla, b. Oct. 4, 1607, d. Jan. 23, 1648, was a Spanish playwright of the school of Calderón. Two of his plays, *Del rey abajo ninguno* (Below the King All Men Are Peers, 1650) and *Entre bobos anda el juego* (Merry Sport with Fools, 1637), are considered masterpieces of the Spanish theater of the Golden Age. Like several of his tragedies, *Del rey abajo ninguno* deals with honor, a popular theme of the time. Don García, the protagonist, kills the man who has attempted to seduce his wife after making sure that the culprit is not the king. *Entre bobos anda el juego,* a comedy, is based on the stock situation of the old man who wants to marry a young woman, here resolved by a happy ending. Either extremely comic or intensely tragic and dramatic, Rojas's plots influenced a number of French playwrights of the 17th century.

ROBERTO GONZÁLEZ-ECHEVARRÍA

Bibliography: MacCurdy, R. R., *Francisco de Rojas Zorrilla and the Tragedy* (1968).

Rolamite   [rohl'-uh-myt]

The first elemental mechanism to be discovered in a century, the Rolamite is a simple, flexible suspension system for rollers that is used in a variety of mechanical devices. It was developed in 1966 by Donald Wilkes as a result of his search for a reliable miniature mechanical switch. The switch that Wilkes designed was one-eighth the size of the previous switch and had about half the number of parts.

In its simplest form the Rolamite consists of a rectangular frame, two rollers, and a flexible band. The rollers are suspended within the S-shaped loops of the metallic band. When the band is tightened the rollers are in pure rolling contact with the band and there is no slippage. This configuration allows the rollers to roll within the guide rails with as low as $1/10$ the friction of the best ball and roller bearings in a similar application. In this rudimentary form the Rolamite functions as a near-frictionless suspension system for the rollers.

By using bands with varying widths or cutouts, the rollers can be made to seek preferred positions between the guide rails. This effect is caused by the tendency of each band loop to straighten itself out; as long as the band width is constant, the straightening forces are equal and the rollers move freely. If the band widths on the rollers are different, the roller with the wider band will dominate, the band will try to unwind, and a driving force proportional to the difference in band widths will be created. By varying the shapes of the cutouts and the diameters of the rollers, Rolamites with a wide variety of springlike characteristics can be obtained.

Recent applications of the Rolamite range over a wide field of mechanical and electromechanical devices. A bathroom scale employing Rolamites would have fewer parts and be more accurate than an ordinary scale, and the claim has been made that if Rolamites were used on a piano, several hundred component parts would be eliminated.   ALEXANDER COWIE

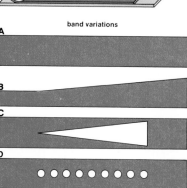

band variations

Varying widths or cutouts on the band loop in a Rolamite mechanism provide different springlike responses. (A) A band of uniform width produces zero force. (B) A band of varying width acts like a spring with negative-force constant. (C) A triangular slot in the band yields a positive-spring constant. (D) Circular holes lead to a detenting mechanism with a sinusoidal variation in force.

Roland

The hero of the medieval French epic the CHANSON DE RO-LAND (c.1100), Roland is left by his uncle Charlemagne in command of the rear guard at Roncesvalles, where he comes under Saracen attack. Asked by his friend Oliver to blow the horn that will summon aid, Roland refuses the request until too late—probably out of chivalric pride—and he and Oliver are killed in the ensuing battle.

Roland de la Platière, Jeanne Manon Phlipon

[roh-lahn' duh lah plah-tee-air']

Jeanne Manon Phlipon Roland de la Platière, known as Madame Roland, b., Paris, Mar. 17, 1754, d. Nov. 8, 1793, is usually regarded as the animating spirit of the GIRONDIST faction in the FRENCH REVOLUTION. The daughter of an engraver, she was greatly influenced by her reading of Plutarch and Jean Jacques Rousseau. By prolific correspondence and by the establishment of a salon in Paris in 1791, she helped to create a coterie of deputies sympathetic to her rather unrealistic republicanism. In 1792, Jean Marie Roland de Platière (b. 1734), the conscientious public servant whom she had married in 1780, became minister of the interior. Madame Roland was held responsible for the anti-Parisian policy pursued by her husband and her friends after the September Massacres. Although Roland resigned in January 1793, Madame Roland was arrested at the end of May. Going to the guillotine, she spoke the immortal words: "Liberty, what crimes are committed in thy name!" On learning of her death, Roland killed himself.
M. J. SYDENHAM

Bibliography: May, Gita, *Madame Roland and the Age of Revolution* (1970).

Roldán (family) [rohl-dahn']

Pedro Roldán, 1624–c.1700, and his daughter Luisa Roldán, 1656–1704, were late baroque sculptors in Seville, Spain. **Pedro,** who had studied in Granada with Alonso de Mena, was also influenced by the style of Martínez Montañés. Pedro's most significant works are polychromed wood altarpieces (*retablos*) such as the *Descent from the Cross* (1666; Church of San Francisco, Seville) and single images of religious figures. The *Descent*'s vibrant movement, bright color, and subject matter foreshadow his greatest achievement, the sculpture for the main altar of the Hospital de la Caridad, Seville (1670–72). Among Pedro's many followers was his daughter **Luisa.** Her early career developed in Seville, but in 1695 she became sculptor to the king in Madrid. She is most noted for her small terra-cotta groups, such as the *Mystical Marriage of Saint Catherine* (Hispanic Society, New York City).
EDWARD J. SULLIVAN

Bibliography: Brown, Jonathan, "Hieroglyphs of Death and Salvation: The Decoration of the Church of the Hermandad de la Caridad," *The Art Bulletin* 52 (1970).

role

Role is a term drawn from the language of theater to describe the set of expectations associated with a person's position in a social organization. All social organizations are characterized by differentiation of function. A status is a particular location within such a structure. For every status there is an associated role—a set of expectations about behavior.

For example, a modern corporation may be characterized as a social structure that is roughly represented by an organization chart, which shows relationships of dominance, subordination, and differentiation. Vice-president for public relations may be a status within the organization. The job description for that position would be part of the specification for that particular role. Stable role definitions enable social organizations to function effectively. When parts are well known, well practiced, and agreed on by everyone in the cast, smooth performances result.

The language of role theory lends itself well to the discussion of a variety of forms of social conflict. For example, the

traditional status of women in Western society has for hundreds of years included role expectations about performances of home maintenance, food preparation, and child-rearing, but no major professional or leadership functions. Consequently, when women achieve advancement in social structures outside the home, role conflict is created. This conflict in turn creates pressure for the redefinition of traditional role expectations associated with sex.

In modern role theory, occupancy of any status is seen to be partly ascribed and partly attained, with the contribution of these two factors varying from role to role. Any particular individual's social identity is describable as a set of validated social roles, some relatively more ascribed, such as age and sex, and some relatively more achieved, such as professional affiliation. Role involvement is consistently high for ascribed roles and is variable for attained roles. The way any individual is evaluated socially is a complex result of the number and character of validated social roles and the degree of involvement with those roles.

The most important role theory pioneer in the social sciences was George Herbert MEAD. J. L. Moreno, Robert MERTON, and Theodore R. Sarbin have each provided major application of role theory.
KARL E. SCHEIBE

Bibliography: Biddle, B. J., and Thomas, E. J., *Role Theory: Concepts and Research* (1966); Jackson, John A., *Role* (1971); Merton, Robert K., *Social Theory and Social Structure*, 3d. ed. (1968); Perlman, Helen, *Persona: Social Role and Personality* (1968).

See also: CLASS, SOCIAL; NORM, SOCIAL; SOCIAL STRUCTURE AND ORGANIZATION; STATUS.

Rolfe, John [rawlf]

John Rolfe, b. 1585, was one of the first English settlers in Virginia. He went to the colony of JAMESTOWN around 1610 and is credited with developing the strain of tobacco that became Virginia's staple crop. In 1614 he married the Indian princess POCAHONTAS, whom he later took to England. After her death (1617), Rolfe returned to America, where he was killed in a war with the POWHATAN Indians in 1622.

Rolland, Romain [roh-lahn']

Romain Rolland, b. Jan. 29, 1866, d. Dec. 29, 1944, was a French novelist, dramatist, and essayist who received the Nobel prize for literature in 1916. His best-known work, the 10-volume novel cycle *Jean-Christophe* (1906–12; Eng. trans., 1910–13), recounting the stormy career of a German musician, reflected his lifelong commitment to humanism. Rolland's wide cultural interests are illustrated not only by his studies of music and art (he wrote a history of opera in 1895 and earned a doctorate in art) but by his work toward a popular theater and his plays on historical themes. He also wrote biographies of Beethoven (1903), Michelangelo (1908), and Tolstoy (1911). His pacifist stand during World War I aroused some hostility but made him a hero within the European intellectual community. He was subsequently influenced by both Marxism and Indian thought. A second novel cycle, *The Soul Enchanted* (Eng. trans., 1925–34), appeared between 1922 and 1933.

Bibliography: Starr, William T., *Romain Rolland: One Against All, A Biography* (1971); Zweig, Stefan, *Romain Rolland* (1921; repr. 1970).

roller

Rollers, birds named for their trait of performing aerial acrobatics during display flights, are members of two genera, *Coracias* and *Eurystomus*, of the family Coraciidae. Members of other genera related to the true rollers are known as ground rollers and cuckoo rollers. True rollers range from 25 to 45 cm (10 to 18 in) in length and have vivid plumages of blue, green, violet, or reddish brown. The sexes do not differ much in appearance. Their strong, wide bills curve downward, having a slight hook. Rollers inhabit Africa, Eurasia, the Philippines, the Indo-Malaysian region, and Australia. The birds are accomplished fliers, frequently tumbling or somersaulting in the air. Many species capture insects in midair, and others swoop down on prey from tree perches. They use holes in trees, banks, or rocks for nests, adding little or no nest lining, and lay 3 to 6 eggs. The young, which are naked and helpless when hatched, are cared for by both sexes.

The Indian roller, *Coracias benghalensis*, which ranges throughout southeastern Asia, is brown with greenish blue cap and wing feathers and has a bluish white throat. The common roller, *C. garrulus*, a migratory species of southern Europe, is also blue and brown.   ROBERT J. RAIKOW

Roller Derby

Roller Derby is the competitive and sometimes violent sport of high-speed roller-skating on banked indoor tracks. Matches are between two teams that consist of 5 men and 5 women. The men skate against the opposing men and the women against the opposing women in alternating 12-minute heats. Each squad has 2 blockers, 2 jammers, and 1 pivotman. The pack begins to skate at the referee's signal. Blocking and body checking are allowed. When a jammer pulls away from the pack for a jam (scoring play) he or she has 60 seconds in which to score; one point is earned for each opposing player passed after skating a full lap ahead of the pack. Roller Derby grew out of dance roller-skating marathons in 1935 and was organized and promoted by Leo Seltzer.

Bibliography: Deford, Frank, *Five Strides on the Banked Track: The Life and Times of the Roller Derby* (1971).

roller-skating

Roller-skating, which involves moving on special shoes or attachments to shoes that have wooden, metal, or, recently, plastic-composite wheels, is popular around the world as both a form of recreation and an organized sport for both children and adults. Children often roller-skate on the sidewalks of cities; most teenagers and adults skate in indoor rinks. Amateur athletes compete in speed- and figure-skating under the auspices of the Fédération Internationale de Roller-skating.

Men compete in national and international championships over 1,000, 5,000, 10,000, and 20,000 m; women race over 500, 3,000, and 5,000 m. Other competitive activities on roller skates include figure-skating and roller-dancing, which are both similar to their ice-skating counterparts, and roller hockey, which is similar to ice hockey in its rules and can be played on almost any smooth, sufficiently large surface.

The first roller skates were made in Holland early in the 18th century. By the mid-20th century roller-skating was a popular recreation in the United States and western Europe. The invention of the ball-bearing wheel in 1884 further encouraged roller-skating and led to the use of hard maple floors. In the first decades of the 20th century competitive skating grew in popularity in the United States and elsewhere. In the late 1970s the development of improved types of roller skates made the sport one of the most popular in the United States. In 1979 about 28 million roller skaters were practicing on more than 6,000 roller rinks nationwide.

Bibliography: Boorstin, Sharon, *Keep on Rolling* (1978); O'Neill, E. R., *Roller Skating* (1960).

Rolling Stones, The

The British rock band The Rolling Stones emerged from the British rock music scene of the early 1960s at about the same time as the Beatles. In contrast to the relatively clean-cut Beatles, however, the Stones adopted an aggressively sexual and defiant stance that helped make them one of the most successful of all rock groups. Formed in 1963 as a rhythm and blues band playing their interpretation of black-American urban blues, the Stones soon developed their own distinctive style and by the late '60s were playing what many consider to be the finest rock music of its time. They were also notorious—for their frequent arrests for drug possession, for the rioting that often occurred at their concerts, and for their disastrous concert (1969) at Altamont, Calif., where a spectator was killed by members of a motorcycle gang. Guitarist Brian

Jones, b. Feb. 28, 1944, died mysteriously in his swimming pool on July 3, 1969. Current band members include singer Mick Jagger, b. July 26, 1944, whose extraordinary style and voice have dominated the group; guitarist Keith Richard, b. Dec. 18, 1943, with whom Jagger has composed much of the band's material; bassist Bill Wyman, b. Oct. 24, 1941; drummer Charlie Watts, b. June 2, 1941; and guitarist Ron Wood, b. Oct. 24, 1941.

Bibliography: Elman, Richard M., *Uptight with the Stones—A Novelist's Report* (1973); Greenfield, Robert, *STP* (1974); Sanchez, Tony, *Up and Down with the Rolling Stones* (1979).

Discography: *Between the Buttons; Exile on Main Street; High Tide and Green Grass*, vols. 1 and 2; *Hot Rocks; Let it Bleed; Some Girls; Sticky Fingers.*

Rolls-Royce

Rolls-Royce is the manufacturer of some of the finest passenger automobiles and aircraft engines in the world. The company was founded in 1903 in Manchester, England, by Henry (later Sir Henry) Royce (1863–1933), a manufacturer of electrical equipment, and Charles S. Rolls (1877–1910), a wealthy sportsman who ran an automobile sales firm in partnership with Claude Johnson (1864–1926). As the business grew, new quarters were needed, and in 1906 the company moved to Derby. After Rolls was killed in an airplane crash in 1910 and Royce's health deteriorated, Johnson assumed control. The Silver Ghost, introduced in 1906, established the distinctive Rolls-Royce style and quality.

Rolls-Royce was drawn into aircraft-engine manufacturing during World War I and promptly acquired a reputation for high quality in this field also. At the outbreak of World War II the Rolls-Royce Merlin, which powered the British SPITFIRE fighter plane, was the best liquid-cooled aircraft engine in the world. During World War II the Rolls-Royce was chosen to develop the Whittle jet engine, the ancestor of all modern jet engines. Rolls-Royce became one of the world's leading designers and builders of jet engines.

After World War II, aircraft engines became by far the largest part of the firm's business. Maintaining leadership in a highly sophisticated technology, however, involves risks, because of the high costs of research and development. In the early 1970s a combination of technical mistakes and other adverse circumstances threatened Rolls-Royce with bankruptcy. Because of the company's vital place in the economy, the British government took control of the aircraft-engine segment of the business. The manufacture of Rolls-Royce automobiles remained profitable and continues as a private enterprise.   JOHN B. RAE

Bibliography: Bennett, Martin, *Rolls Royce* (1974); Harker, Ronald W., *The Engines Were Rolls-Royce* (1979); Lloyd, Ian, *Rolls Royce*, 3 vols. (1978); Nockolds, Harold, *The Magic of a Name* (1932); Schlaifer, Robert, *The Development of Aircraft Engines* (1950).

Rölvaag, Ole Edvart [rurl'-vawk oh'-le ed'-vahrt]

The Norwegian-American novelist and educator Ole Rölvaag, b. Norway, Apr. 22, 1876, d. Nov. 5, 1931, is among the greatest of American immigrant novelists. His triology, made up of *Giants in the Earth* (1924–25; Eng. trans., 1927), *Peder Victorious* (1928; Eng. trans., 1929), and *Their Father's God* (1931; Eng. trans., 1931), conveys a starkly realistic portrait of the hardships of immigrant life on the Dakota prairies in the late 19th century. Rölvaag also taught Norwegian at Saint Olaf's College, in Minnesota.   F. M. PAULSEN

Bibliography: Reigstad, Paul, *Rölvaag: His Life and Art* (1972).

Romains, Jules [roh-man']

Jules Romains was the pseudonym of the French playwright and novelist Louis Farigoule, b. Aug. 26, 1885, d. Aug. 14, 1972, who delighted French audiences between the wars with such farcical comedies as *Doctor Knock* (1923; Eng. trans., 1925). His serious intellectual interest, however, was unanimism, or the psychology of the group. In his 27-volume novel cycle,

Men of Good Will (1932-46; Eng. trans., 1933-46), he sought to portray every aspect of French life during 25 years of the 20th century. Romains also wrote poetry and essays and was elected to the Académie Française in 1946.

Bibliography: Boak, Denis, *Jules Romains* (1974); Norrish, P. J., *Drama of the Group* (1958).

Roman art and architecture

During the period of the kingdom (753–509 BC) and in the first two centuries of the Republic (509–31 BC), Roman art and architecture, which developed in a very small area of west central Italy, was heavily influenced by ETRUSCAN and other Italic traditions and only incidentally by Greek art. As Rome grew in power to become the political center of an already Hellenized Mediterranean world, a truly Roman art began to emerge in the later 3d and especially during the 2d century BC. Under the growing influence of GREEK ART and GREEK ARCHITECTURE, Rome began to modernize its traditional forms of architecture, sculpture, and painting.

The outcome was a highly complex art. Temple architecture, for example, never entirely disavowed its Italic origins, whereas many works of sculpture were entirely Greek in appearance. In addition, such completely new creations as monumental vaulted buildings emerged (see ARCH AND VAULT). Roman art progressed along no single, easily discernible course. A number of disparate artistic currents and traditions coexisted and influenced one another, not infrequently within the same genre, as in portraiture. Spurts of great inventiveness occasionally enlivened a generally retrospective trend. The art of the provinces from Britain to Mesopotamia, from the Balkans to Morocco, exhibited an almost boundless variety of forms.

ARCHITECTURE
Building Materials, Techniques, and Forms. By far the most popular building material, from the beginnings down to the early Empire, was mud brick strengthened by timbers (half-timbered construction), used in the superstructures of domestic, sacral, and public buildings.

For terraces, fortifications, and foundations, as well as for some superstructures, the early Romans used many types of local stone. Hard limestone was generally cut irregularly (*opus siliceum*), whereas softer varieties such as volcanic tufa were sawed into blocks (*opus quadratum*). In the 2d century BC the stronger travertine began to displace tufa and other masonry in the superstructures of buildings. Increasing quantities and different varieties of marble were used in the late Republic and throughout the Empire (31 BC–AD 324).

From Etruscan times terra-cotta had been the prevalent material for roof tiles and for protective coverings of the wooden parts of buildings. The use of terra-cotta to cover wood declined as stone temples became predominant in the 3d century BC. From the early Empire on, baked bricks began to be manufactured in great quantities, mainly for the facings of cement walls (*opus testaceum*).

In the 2d century BC an unusually strong cement (*opus caementicium*) that included a volcanic dust called *pozzolana* began to supersede the more traditional materials. Building could now be accomplished more rapidly and economically, and a great change took place in architecture. Cement could be formed within and over timber frameworks and so be used for such difficult construction as vaulting. The facing of cement walls usually consisted of smooth, irregularly shaped stones (*opus incertum*), of squared stones set on edge to form a neat network pattern (*opus reticulatum*, shortly after 100 BC), or of baked bricks (*opus testaceum*, from *c*.30 BC). These facings frequently provided the base for stucco or marble incrustation. Complex sequences of interior spaces with increasingly daring vaults and domes were constructed in the 1st and 2d centuries in baths, market buildings, and palaces; more and more of the traditional building types, such as temples and basilicas, were reshaped under the influence of the cement vault. The best-preserved example is the Hadrianic PANTHEON (*c*.118–28; Rome), the temple to all the gods, with its huge, coffered-concrete dome spanning 43.3 m (142 ft).

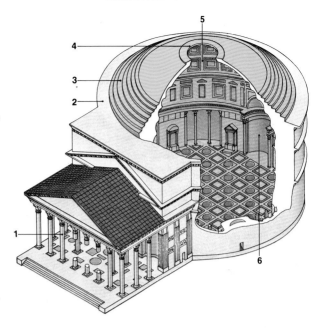

The Pantheon (c.118–28) in Rome was built by Hadrian on the site of an earlier temple by Agrippa. This cutaway model, showing the portico (1), rotunda (2), hemispherical stepped dome (3), oculus (4), coffered ceiling (5), and semicircular apse (6), illustrates the innovative Roman use of concrete to span vast interior spaces.

The conventional forms of Etruscan and Greek architecture still continued to be used for many purposes. Originally prevalent in temples until the later Republic, the Tuscan order began to absorb some elements of the Greek Doric order and became Roman Doric.

The Greek Ionic order, and more so the Corinthian order, was widely used in Italy from the 2d century BC on. Probably in Augustan times elements of the Ionic and Corinthian capitals were fused.

A late-Republican development destined to have great success was the framing of the round arch with a superposed and generally engaged order, as on the outside of the COLOSSEUM (AD 72–82). With the ever-increasing use of concrete in the structure of buildings, the orders, originally structural, were gradually relegated to a purely decorative function.

Local materials, techniques, and building forms more or less dominated architecture in the provinces. The eastern Mediterranean continued in the established local and Greek Hellenistic building conventions, but imperial Rome succeeded in exporting to the East such building types as monumental baths, aqueducts, and, to some extent, amphitheaters, not previously found there.

Types of Civic Buildings. In the early Republic the TEMPLE was still basically Etruscan—top-heavy with wide eaves and bulky terra-cotta decorations. In the 2d century BC, however, local traditions and Greek forms merged to create a more graceful structure: the podium and deep front porch of the Etruscan temple were retained and Greek proportions and forms adopted. This type of temple, generally employing the Corinthian order, gained ground rapidly in Italy and the West.

The BASILICA, a multipurpose rectangular hall that may have originated in Greece, first appeared in Rome in the 2d century BC. Usually situated in the town forum, it generally had a spacious and lofty central hall covered with a flat ceiling and surrounded on all sides by a single- or double-colonnaded aisle, usually with a gallery.

The monumental honorary or TRIUMPHAL ARCH began its history about 200 BC but received its standard form in the early Empire. Supported by stout piers, a centrally vaulted passageway carried an upper story, the *attica*, on which gilded bronze statues were placed. An engaged or partially freestanding order framed the piers and passage. Some arches had smaller passageways flanking the central vault.

Contrary to Greek practice, the stage and semicircular orchestra and seating arrangement (*cavea*) were joined in the Roman theater to form one structure, often built on level ground with the cavea resting on a complex of vaulted substructures that doubled as access passageways. An intricately articulated columnar facade provided an elegant backdrop for the low stage. Similar substructures were built for the seating areas of the oval amphitheater, as in the Colosseum, and in the hairpin-shaped circus used for chariot races.

As early as 19 BC (Baths of Agrippa, Rome), huge, symmetrically planned imperial baths (*thermae*), which had large, sunken tubs and pools for crowds of people, were constructed. Some idea of the enormous, ingeniously vaulted halls can be seen today in the ruins of the Baths of Caracalla (AD 212–16; Rome; see CARACALLA, BATHS OF) and in the central hall of the Baths of Diocletian, (AD c.298–305 or 306, Rome; see DIOCLETIAN, BATHS OF), which is now the church of Santa Maria degli Angeli. In an official register of AD 354, no fewer than 952 baths were listed in the city of Rome.

Types of Domestic Buildings. The simple Etrusco-Italic town house (*domus*), with rooms grouped axially around a dark central hall (ATRIUM), took on Greek forms in the 2d century BC, especially with the addition of a range of single-column colonnades (*peristyle*) around a rear garden. By the early Empire, the central atrium had become no more than an elegant entrance hall. Surrounding the garden peristyle were grand dining halls and sitting rooms modeled on and named after Eastern prototypes (see HOUSE, in Western architecture).

Country villas were built to serve well-to-do persons either as working farms or as retreats for relaxation (see MYSTERIES, VILLA OF THE). Although some villas display a rigorous symmetry, others are less coherently arranged, with long sequences of peristyles, colonnaded or vaulted ambulatories, and subsidiary buildings reaching into the landscape and incorporating it. HADRIAN'S VILLA (AD 118–34), an immense complex near Tivoli outside Rome, typifies this arrangement.

By the late 1st century AD an imperial PALACE occupied most of the Palatine Hill in Rome. This ostentatious residence of the ruler contained some of the largest concrete vaults attempted until then. Following the age of Nero, vaulted architecture was also changing the aspect of domestic architecture in the city, and by the mid-2d century whole quarters of large, brick-faced concrete tenement houses (*insulae*) dominated the cities of Rome and Ostia, where several are still preserved to a height of two stories.

Few remains exist of early Roman tombs, but from late Republican times on a profusion of sepulchral structures, ranging from modest funerary altars to pretentious and complex structures, survive. Some tombs were rock-cut with carved facades; others were freestanding structures of one or more stories. The archaic Etruscan *tumulus* was revived in the 1st century BC, but the cylindrical portion tended to rise tower-like, as in the well-preserved tomb of Hadrian (AD 135–39;

(Left) *The Arch of Trajan (AD c.114–17), Benevento, is a fine example of the balance between Roman architecture and sculptural decoration, here consisting of composite columns and marble reliefs.*

(Below) *In the Basilica of Maxentius, or Constantine (c.306–13), Rome, a series of huge groin vaults supported on barrel-vaulted side aisles roofed the enormous central hall.*

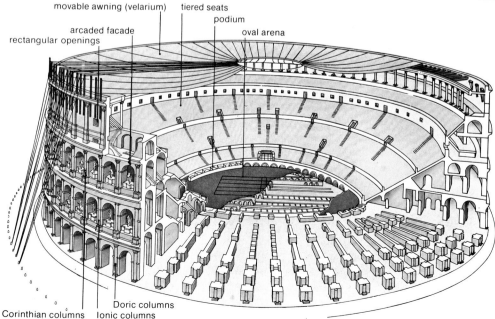

movable awning (velarium)   tiered seats
podium
arcaded facade
oval arena
rectangular openings

Corinthian columns
Doric columns
Ionic columns

The largest Roman amphitheater, the Colosseum (AD 72–82), Rome, was a 4-story, elliptical structure seating about 50,000 spectators. The exterior facade was embellished with superimposed Doric, Ionic, and Corinthian columns and with Corinthian pilasters at the top.

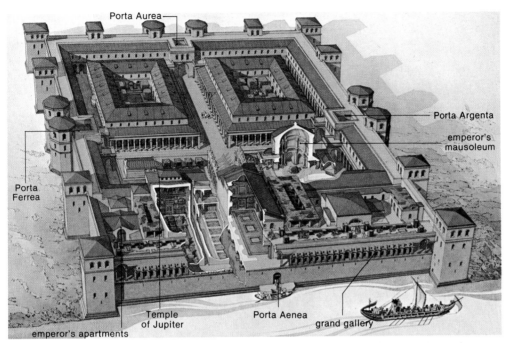

Porta Aurea

Porta Argenta

emperor's
mausoleum

Porta
Ferrea

Temple
of Jupiter

Porta Aenea

grand gallery

emperor's apartments

Diocletian's Palace, built (c.300) at Spalato (modern Split), in Yugoslavia, combined an imperial palace with the high walls, large towers, heavy fortifications, and barracks of a fortress. Intended as a retirement retreat for the emperor, the complex also included a temple, a library, and his mausoleum.

now Castel Sant' Angelo, Rome). In the age of Augustus the *columbarium,* a collective tomb containing many niches for ash urns, appeared. During the later Empire, the brick-faced cement tomb became the most popular form in Italy.

SCULPTURE
Monumental sculpture in stone, bronze, or terra-cotta was employed both in and out of architectural contexts. Terracotta sculpture is found primarily on early temples, either as figural or ornamental relief on covering plaques, or as large statues along the roof edges and in the gables.

Bronze Sculpture. The more expensive bronze, sometimes gilded, was used widely for honorary statues of civic leaders and private citizens, who are usually depicted wearing the toga but occasionally appear in military armor, on horseback, or nude or seminude in the Greek style (see BRONZES). Cult images of the gods in the temples were often in bronze, and bronze copies of famous works of Greek sculpture were also prized. Because of their material value, however, most bronzes were melted down in late antiquity and few exist today, but large numbers of marble copies have survived.

Marble Sculpture. Sculpture in stone had its beginnings in the Etrusco-Italic funerary tradition of tombstones and grave statues. As interest in Greek art increased, marble copies of Greek masterpieces, as well as eclectic works in the Greek manner, were commissioned by wealthy Romans to decorate their residences. Both in the Greek East and in Italy, there developed a thriving copying industry that was to a large extent in the hands of Greek artisans, who also made many marble ornamental works of a purely decorative nature.

Portrait Sculpture. One of the great Roman contributions is portrait sculpture. Its roots lie both in the Roman custom of keeping ancestor masks (*imagines maiorum*) in the home and in the practice of erecting honorary statues in public places. Etruscan and Greek Hellenistic portrait art also contributed substantially to the development of Roman portrait sculpture. Surviving examples are mainly marble copies, especially busts, a typically Roman, abbreviated portrait form that flourished from the late Republic onward. Other materials such as bronze and terra-cotta were also used. The 1st century BC was a period of great creativity in which the images of patricians became so realistic they seem veristic. This tradition persisted into the imperial age but with diminished strength, for in the reign of Augustus (31 BC–AD 14) a more subdued, idealized portrait style, based on Greek forms, was developed. A somewhat more uniform style with classicizing overtones emerged

(Left) The bronze equestrian statue of Marcus Aurelius (AD c.161–80) was placed in the Piazza dei Campidoglio in Rome by Michelangelo when he laid out the square in 1538. Preserved only because early Christians mistakenly believed that it represented Constantine, the statue inspired all subsequent equestrian portraits.

(Left) This statue (c.50 BC–AD 15) of a Roman patrician with the busts of his ancestors exemplifies the intense realism and individualism of Roman portrait sculpture. (Museo Capitolino, Rome.)

(Below) The Gemma Augustea (1st century AD) is a large Roman onyx cameo, engraved with an allegorical scene honoring Augustus. (Kunsthistorisches Museum, Vienna.)

(AD c.100–150), but in the later decades of the 2d century a new element gradually emerged and fully blossomed in portraits executed between 200 and 250, making these years the second great inventive period in the art: for the first time in antiquity portraits display an emotional expressiveness, often capturing complex emotions. This trend, however, was quickly dispersed in the latter half of the century, which saw a development toward a highly formal portrait art, with rigid features and aloof expressions announcing the Late Antique period, which achieved full expression in the next century.

Relief Sculpture. During the Republic, figural relief sculpture was largely a feature of private funerary art, and the overwhelming majority of imperial reliefs, both in Rome and the provinces, belong to this category. They range from a wide spectrum of local styles, some markedly primitive, to a very refined manner following Greek forms. Friezes or panels on tombs were also used, showing, perhaps, the deceased at work in his profession or as a benefactor of the community. Extremely popular sources of funerary art were the Greek myths, depicted on small grave altars as well as on large mausoleums. Beginning in the reign of Hadrian, more and more sculpted marble sarcophagi with mythological subjects were produced, but stock scenes of the life of the deceased and battle scenes were also used (see SARCOPHAGUS).

In the late Republic relief sculpture began to commemorate historical events, but the great period of the historical relief commenced with the reign of Augustus and continued for more than two centuries. This new and typically Roman art form became an effective vehicle of imperial propaganda: tangible achievements of the rulers as well as abstract notions of ideology were expressed in narrative or allegorical fashion in reliefs adorning large monuments such as arches, altars (*Ara Pacis Augustae*, 13–9 BC; Rome), and statue bases. The compositions in these reliefs are sometimes crowded and spatial, reminiscent of those in painting, but at other times figures stand statuelike and isolated.

WALL PAINTING

If real polychrome marble paneling was unattainable, painting and stucco were the major means of decorating interior wall surfaces, evidence for which comes almost exclusively from HERCULANEUM and POMPEII, the towns destroyed by the eruption of Mount Vesuvius in AD 79. The technique of imitating an articulated marble-encrusted wall in painted stucco, called the first, or incrustation, style, was widespread in Hellenistic Greece as well as in Italy during the Republic. Such walls were divided into a base, a main zone, and an upper zone. Early in the 1st century BC the second, or architectural, style was developed. In this form the impression of a first-style wall, with the beveled edges of its blocks and the shadows cast by them, was retained. Above the lowest zone a vertical architectural framework bracketed views of a city, a countryside, a seascape, or even a mythological scene. The third style, beginning c.20 BC, returned to the two-dimensional wall surface. Although the vertical division continued in the form of large panels, the architectural elements of the second style

This frieze from the Ara Pacis, or Altar of Peace, depicts a group of senators bearing tributes in a procession celebrating the dedication of the altar to the emperor Augustus in 13 BC.

This representation (AD c.60–79) of a young couple from Pompeii is one of the few surviving examples of Roman portrait painting. The fresco is remarkable for its expressive realism and for such individualized details as the woman's elaborate coiffure and her writing tablet and stylus. (Museo Nazionale, Naples.)

now became a delicate surface decoration, and the views beyond the wall disappeared. Finally, in the sixties of the 1st century AD the fourth style made its appearance; deep vistas again appear, this time through narrow facsimile windows arrayed in the upper zone; however, some of the two-dimensionality of the third style remains. Little evidence exists of any further development of wall decoration after AD 79.

Primary evidence is almost entirely lacking for monumental painting. The wall decorations of Campanian towns and a few other sites offer only a dim reflection of what was certainly a major Roman art form. Most present knowledge is derived at second hand from literary sources. An old and apparently long-lasting tradition in Rome was that of triumphal painting. By means of a sequence of posterlike, temporary illustrations, the progress of military campaigns in remote lands was documented in Rome during the triumphal procession with maplike bird's-eye views of enemy cities, of detailed battle scenes, and the like. This was art with an immediate political purpose: It aimed to cultivate popular support for the returning general who might seek public office in forthcoming elections. Poster art lived on in the Empire, the spiral frieze on the Column of Trajan (AD 106–13) being, to some extent, a permanent relief version of this type of art.

As a consequence of the conquests of the 2d century BC, Greek artists flocked to Rome, and masses of original paintings found their way, as war booty, into private and public collections. These have all disappeared. Just as was true of originals of sculpture, however, they also were copied more or less faithfully; thus, the figural panels forming part of preserved wall decorations are either true copies of lost Greek originals or draw on a number of motifs from various sources; the second is more probable.

PAVING, MOSAIC, AND STUCCOWORK

Floor paving took various forms. *Opus signinum* consisted of bits of crushed travertine and terra-cotta mixed with mortar; other styles included *opus sectile*, limestone and, later, marble slabs of various shapes (usually geometric) and colors. When baked bricks were manufactured in great quantities, these, too, were much used for flooring, set on edge and placed in a herringbone pattern (*opus spicatum*).

The tradition of MOSAIC floor pavements reached Rome from Greece, where it began with black-and-white pebble compositions. In Hellenistic times, however, they were made with tesserae, small, specially cut stone cubes of various colors. This art experienced great popularity, the prime example being the large *Alexander Mosaic* (c.100 BC; Museo Nazionale, Naples), a copy of an early Hellenistic painting, found in Pompeii. In early imperial Italy, mosaics, at this time often made with tesserae of glass paste, spread to the wall surfaces, and, occasionally, to the ceiling, in subtly toned polychromy. At the same time, floor mosaics became for the most part sketchily rendered black figures and ornaments on a white ground. During the late 2d and increasingly in the 3d century,

The Battle of Issus, *a mosaic from the House of the Faun, Pompeii, is a Roman copy of an original late-4th-century BC Hellenistic painting attributed to Philoxenus of Eretria. (Museo Nazionale, Naples.)*

the provinces surpassed the homeland in making excellent polychrome pavement mosaics.

In the early centuries the raw surfaces of mud brick, rubble, and cement walls were covered with a thick layer of lime-and-sand plaster over which a thin coating of smoothed stucco made of limestone or marble dust was applied. In the early 1st century BC, as vaulted architecture gained ground throughout the Empire, stucco became, and remained, the most practical material for covering and adorning surfaces that were often curved. Stucco relief, a typically Roman decorative art form, followed the development of wall painting, borrowing from it ornamental and figural motifs. The stucco master either formed the relief design out of the still-workable material with a spatula as he was applying it, or he applied finished, mold-formed pieces.

DECORATIVE ARTS

In addition to architecture and its allied arts, numerous decorative arts flourished in ancient Rome. Small gems were engraved mainly for seal rings; intricate cameos were made of layered onyx, sardonyx, or agate, some large with multifigured relief scenes; and elegant vessels of silver and bronze were cast with or without engraved or relief decoration. The more common bronze was also used for a wide variety of small objects ranging from simple household fixtures and utensils to fine statuettes. By far the most common material, however, was terra-cotta, which was used for countless objects—for figurines of all kinds, for decorative plaques and lamps, and, above all, for a type of molded ceramic ware called *terra sigillata* that was glazed red to imitate metal. After glassblowing was invented in the 1st century BC, this material also became relatively low in cost; a thriving industry developed in the later Empire. Coins, first minted in the 3d century BC, were made of gold, silver, and bronze. Many subjects appeared on both sides during the Republic, but in the Empire, the obverse usually bore the profile effigy of the emperor; the reverse were historical scenes, buildings, or figures, abstract concepts of imperial ideology.   GERHARD M. KOEPPEL

Bibliography: Boethius, Axel, and Ward-Perkins, J. B., *Etruscan and Roman Architecture* (1970); Brilliant, Richard, *Roman Art from the Republic to Constantine* (1974); Heintze, Helga Von, *Roman Art* (1972); Kähler, Heintz, *Art of Rome and Her Empire* (1963); MacDonald, William L., *Roman Architecture* (1965); Strong, Donald E., *Roman Art* (1976); Toynbee, Jocelyn M. C., *The Art of the Romans* (1965); Ward-Perkins, J. B., *Roman Art* (1977) and *Roman Architecture* (1977); Wheeler, Mortimer, *Roman Art and Architecture* (1964).

Roman Catholic church

The Roman Catholic church, the largest of the Christian churches, although present in all parts of the world, is identified as Roman because of its historical roots in Rome and because of the importance it attaches to the worldwide ministry of the bishop of Rome, the pope (see PAPACY). Several EASTERN RITE CHURCHES, whose roots are in regional churches of the Eastern Mediterranean, are in full communion with the Roman Catholic church.

In 1980 there were some 783 million Roman Catholics, approximately 18% of the world's population. The 51 million Roman Catholics in the United States (1982) constitute 22% of that country's population. These statistics are based on baptisms, usually conferred on infants, and do not necessarily imply active participation in the church's life nor full assent to its beliefs.

A growing estrangement between the Catholic church in the West and the Orthodox church of the East in the first millennium led to a break between them in the 11th century, and the two regions diverged in matters of theology, liturgy, and disciplinary practices. Within Western Christianity beginning with the 16th-century REFORMATION, the Roman Catholic church came to be identified by its differences with the Protestant churches.

Roman Catholic Beliefs. The basic religious beliefs of Roman Catholics are those shared by other Christians as derived from the New Testament and formulated in the ancient CREEDS of the early ecumenical councils (see COUNCIL, ECUMENICAL), such as Nicaea (325) and Constantinople (381). The central belief is that God entered the world through the Incarnation of his Son, the Christ or Messiah, Jesus of Nazareth. The founding of the church is traced to the life and teachings of Jesus, whose death is followed by resurrection from the dead after which he sends the Holy Spirit to assist believers. This triple mission within the Godhead is described doctrinally as the divine Trinity, God one in nature but consisting in three divine persons.

Roman Catholics attach special significance to the rites of BAPTISM and EUCHARIST. Baptism is sacramental entry into Christian life, and the Eucharist is a memorial of Christ's death and resurrection in which he is believed to be sacramentally present. The Eucharist is celebrated daily in the Roman Catholic church. Catholics also regard as SACRAMENTS the forgiveness of sins in reconciliation with the church (CONFESSION), ordination to ministry (HOLY ORDERS), marriage of Christians, postbaptismal anointing (CONFIRMATION), and the ANOINTING OF THE SICK.

Catholic ethical doctrines are based ultimately on the New Testament teachings but also on the conclusions reached by the church, especially by the popes and other teachers. In recent times the pope and bishops have formulated guidelines regarding social justice, racial equality, disarmament, human rights, contraception, and abortion. The official opposition to artificial contraception is not accepted by a large number of practicing Catholics. The Roman Catholic church's prohibition of remarriage after divorce is the strictest of the Christian churches, although the church does admit the possibility of annulments for marriages judged to be invalid.

The Worship of the Church. The public worship of the Roman Catholic church is its liturgy, principally the Eucharist, which is also called the MASS. After the recitation of prayers and readings from the Bible, the presiding priest invites the faithful to receive communion, understood as sharing in the sacramental presence of Christ. At the Sunday liturgy the priest preaches a sermon or homily, applying the day's biblical texts to the present lives of believers. The church observes a liturgical calendar similar to that of other Christians, following a cycle of ADVENT, CHRISTMAS, EPIPHANY, LENT, EASTER, and PENTECOST. It also follows a distinctive cycle of commemoration of the saints. The worship of the church is expressed as well in rites of baptism, confirmation, weddings, ordinations, penitential rites, burial rites or funerals, and the singing of the DIVINE OFFICE. A distinguishing mark of Catholic worship is prayer for the dead.

The Roman Catholic church also fosters devotional practices, both public and private, including Benediction of the Blessed Sacrament (a ceremony of homage to Christ in the Eucharist), the ROSARY, novenas (nine days of prayer for some special intention), pilgrimages to shrines, and veneration of saints' relics or statues. The devotional importance attached to the SAINTS (especially the Virgin MARY) distinguishes Roman

Catholicism and Eastern Orthodoxy from the churches of the Reformation. In the last two centuries the Roman Catholic church has taught as official doctrine that Mary from her conception was kept free of original sin (the IMMACULATE CONCEPTION) and that at the completion of her life was taken up body and soul into heaven (the ASSUMPTION). Catholics are also encouraged to practice private prayer through meditation, contemplation, or spiritual reading. Such prayer is sometimes done in a retreat house with the assistance of a director.

The Organization of the Church. The Roman Catholic church is structured locally into neighborhood parishes and regional dioceses administered by bishops. In recent times national episcopal conferences of bishops have assumed some importance. Catholic church polity is characterized, however, by a centralized government under the pope, who is regarded as the successor to the apostle Peter, entrusted with a ministry of unity and encouragement. The First VATICAN COUNCIL (1869–70) further enhanced the role of the papacy by declaring that the church's INFALLIBILITY (or inability to err on central issues of the Christian faith) can be exercised personally by the pope in extraordinary circumstances. This teaching of the pope's primacy and infallibility is a major stumbling block to the unification of the Christian churches.

The pope is elected for life by the College of CARDINALS (about 130). He is assisted in the governance of the church by the bishops, especially through the World Synod of Bishops that meets every three years. More immediately in the VATICAN CITY, the papal city-state within Rome, the pope is aided by the cardinals and a bureaucracy known as the Roman CURIA. The Vatican is represented in many countries by a papal nuncio or apostolic delegate and at the United Nations by a permanent observer.

By tradition the all-male ordained clergy (bishops, priests, and deacons) are distinguished from the laity, who assist in the ministry of the church. In the Western (Latin) rite of the Catholic church, bishops and priests are ordinarily celibate. In many of the Eastern Rite churches, priests are allowed to marry. Some Catholics live together in RELIGIOUS ORDERS, serving the church and the world under vows of poverty, chastity, and obedience. Members of these orders or congregations include sisters (or NUNS), brothers, and priests. Priests who belong to religious orders are sometimes called regular clergy, because they live according to a rule (Latin *regula*). Most priests, however, are ordained for ministry in a diocese under a bishop and are called diocesan or secular priests.

Church discipline is regulated by a code of CANON LAW. A revised code for the Latin rite went into effect in 1983. A code for the Eastern Rite churches is in preparation.

The Church in a Time of Change. To initiate renewal in the Roman Catholic church, the late Pope John XXIII convoked a general council, the Second VATICAN COUNCIL (1962–65). This meeting of bishops and their advisors from around the world was also attended by Orthodox, Anglican, and Protestant observers. The council initiated changes that are still being carried out in the postconciliar era. The chief reforms in church practices were: changes in liturgical language (from Latin to the vernacular) and reformulation of sacramental rituals; a new ecumenical openness toward other Christian churches; increased stress on the collective responsibility of bishops in the church's mission (collegiality); more acute concern for political and social issues, especially where moral questions are involved; attempts to adapt the Gospel to diverse cultural traditions; reform of priestly education; and partial acceptance of diversity in theology and local practices. These changes led to uneasiness and concern in some who felt that innovation had gone too far. For others the changes were seen as insufficient and painfully slow. Church leaders now recognize that implementation of the conciliar program will involve a long process of ongoing renewal.   MICHAEL A. FAHEY

Bibliography: Bühlmann, Wilbert, *The Coming of the Third Church* (1977); Dulles, Avery, *Models of the Church* (1974); Haughton, Rosemary, *The Catholic Thing* (1979); Hebblethwaite, Peter, *The Runaway Church* (1978); McBrien, Richard, *Catholicism* (1980); Noel, Gerard, *The Anatomy of the Catholic Church* (1980); Rahner, Karl, *The Shape of the Chruch to Come* (1974).

Roman de la Rose, Le   [roh-mahn' duh lah rohz, luh]

Le Roman de la Rose (*Romance of the Rose*), one of the most influential of medieval poems, is a long (22,000 lines) French dream ALLEGORY. The first part of the poem (*c*.1225), by GUILLAUME DE LORRIS, is an idealistic narration of the adventures of a lover seeking to pluck the rose of love. The second part (*c*.1275), by Jean de Meun, is a cynical satire against love, women, and the church. CHAUCER translated part of the *Roman* into English early in his career, and the poem's conflicting attitudes toward love reappear throughout his works.
                                        DAVID M. ZESMER

Bibliography: Lewis, C. S., *The Allegory of Love* (1936; repr. 1968).

Roman Empire: see ROME, ANCIENT.

Roman law

Roman law refers to the legal system that originated in ancient Rome and that later became the basis of law in Western Europe and in countries influenced by European legal codes.
Origins. Roman law had its origins, long before there was a Roman state, in family customs handed down from one generation to another and in judgments (*leges regiae*) of chieftains or kings. By the time of the establishment of the Roman Republic (509 BC) a considerable amount of this customary law existed. It was not written but oral law, however, in the keeping of the most ancient patrician families (gentes), and this meant that the common people (plebeians) were at a disadvantage in disputes. Years of agitation ended with the appointment of a commission (*decemviri legibus scribundis*, or twelve legal experts) that collected and published the oral customs in Rome's first codification, *The Twelve Tables* (451–450 BC). These dealt mainly with problems related to property and to the procedures for obtaining redress for wrongs.

The Twelve Tables were enacted as statutes by one of the Roman governmental assemblies (the COMITIA CENTURIATA), and occasionally thereafter statutes were enacted by other legislative bodies. But the great expansion of law under the republic came from two other sources: jurisconsults and praetors. The jurisconsults were prominent citizens who found the study and interpretation of the law a satisfying and respected pursuit. Since early statutes coincided with the very beginning of writing in Rome, the language was sparing and often needed elaboration. The jurisconsults had great prestige, and they were regularly consulted by officials and laymen alike. Indeed, with the establishment of the principate (27 BC) the first emperor, Augustus, gave certain jurisconsults the authority to issue responses to legal queries as though he himself had been asked, a practice that continued under later emperors.

The praetors were annually elected magistrates whose duties included the administration of the law courts. They too were faced with uncertainties or omissions in statutory law, and thus each made it a practice to publish before entering office an edict that stated under what circumstances he would grant a suit. This edict was good only for his year of office, but successors regularly consulted the previous edict and kept of it what had proved equitable and popular, discarding portions that had been less so. By this method a vast amount of practical and equitable law accumulated, introduced experimentally and tested on the increasingly complicated problems of an expanding commercial state. As the powers of the emperors and bureaucratic officials increased and those of elected officials declined, however, praetors showed less initiative; in the early 2d century AD, Emperor Hadrian had praetorian edicts drawn up by a jurist and codified. This standardized edict then became the subject of study and commentary by jurists, whose writing furnished much of later Roman law.

The emperor, as a magistrate, also had the right to issue edicts on legal affairs. But unlike that of the republican magistrates his power was lifelong, so that his edicts were effective for a considerable time. Further, succeeding emperors usually observed the enactments of their predecessors. The emperors depended a good deal on the advice of eminent jurists and, especially in the early principate, asked for the concurrence of the Senate, a body of elder statesmen who advised the magistrates. The concurrence of the Senate eventually became a matter of course; enactments by the emperors became the only source of law. Under the authority of the Eastern Roman (Byzantine) emperor JUSTINIAN I, select committees directed by the jurist Tribonian collected, edited, and organized (AD 528–34) the scattered and sometimes contradictory legal materials from all these sources and published them as the *Corpus Juris Civilis* (Body of Civil Law), which is the form in which most Roman law has come down to us (see JUSTINIAN'S CODE).

Branches of the Law. Traditionally, the study of Roman law is divided into five parts. The law of persons dealt with the legal status of individuals and groups—free or slave, citizen or alien, male or female, parent or child, and so on. It also established the juristic person or corporation, a fictitious person endowed by the state with the rights of a natural person. The law of property dealt with rights of ownership. The law of succession or inheritance governed the transfer of property to heirs whose rights depended on their relationship to the deceased, and also regulated the making of wills. The law of obligations concerned rights and obligations arising from contracts and also from illegal acts—torts or delicts—that obliged the offender to recompense the injured person. The law of actions contained the procedures to be followed in disputes. It evolved from a considerable dependence on self-help by the plaintiff in the earliest days to an almost complete dependence, from summons to execution, on the state.

Influence of Roman Law. By the time of Justinian most of western Europe was in the hands of barbarian kings who administered a mixture of their own GERMANIC LAW and earlier Roman law. But in the 11th century Italian scholars rediscov-

ered and began to study and teach the *Corpus Juris Civilis*. This happened at the very time that expanding trade and commercial activity made the law of a universal state more appropriate than any other. Thus Roman law became the basis of the law of all western Europe, with the exception of England (see CIVIL LAW; COMMON LAW). It spread to the New World and is basic in South and Central America, Louisiana, and Quebec; it was adopted in South Africa and Sri Lanka and plays a role in the codes of emerging states. Through Byzantium it reached Russia, and it still furnishes parts of the law in the USSR. The Roman *jus gentium* (law of the peoples), developed in the republic to govern relations with non-Romans, became the basis of much of modern commercial law.

FRANK BOURNE

Bibliography: Buckland, W. W., *A Text-Book of Roman Law from Augustus to Justinian*, 3d ed. (1964); Crook, John, *Law and Life of Rome* (1977); Honore, Anthony M., *Tribonian* (1978) and *Ulpian* (1982); Jolowicz, H. F., *Historical Introduction to the Study of Roman Law*, 4th ed. (1978); Jones, A. H. M., *Studies in Roman Government and Law* (1960); Kunkel, Wolfgang, *An Introduction to Roman Legal and Constitutional History*, trans. by J. M. Kelly, 2d ed. (1973); Nicholas, Barry, *Introduction to Roman Law* (1962); Schulz, Fritz, *History of Roman Legal Science* (1946); Watson, Alan, *The Law of the Ancient Romans* (1970); Wolff, H. J., *Roman Law: A Historical Introduction* (1951; repr. 1976).

Roman mythology: see MYTHOLOGY.

Roman numerals: see NUMERAL.

Roman roads

An intricate transportation network, the Roman road system gave citizens of the ancient empire access to the most distant

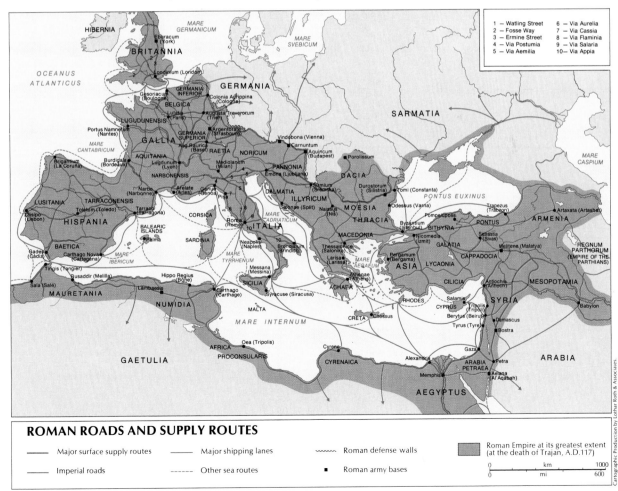

1 — Watling Street	6 — Via Aurelia
2 — Fosse Way	7 — Via Cassia
3 — Ermine Street	8 — Via Flaminia
4 — Via Postumia	9 — Via Salaria
5 — Via Aemilia	10 — Via Appia

ROMAN ROADS AND SUPPLY ROUTES

——— Major surface supply routes ——— Major shipping lanes ～～～ Roman defense walls ▨ Roman Empire at its greatest extent (at the death of Trajan, A.D.117)

——— Imperial roads - - - - Other sea routes ■ Roman army bases

0   km   1000
0   mi   600

Cartographic Production by Lothar Roth & Associates.

provinces. The first all-weather roads connected the capital and those Italian towns which had been recently subdued or colonized by the Romans. The Via Appia (Appian Way; begun in 312 BC), for example, joined Rome with Capua, which had just been crushed in the Samnite War; the Via Flaminia connected Rome with the Latin colony of Ariminum in former Celtic territory. These paved roads and others—usually constructed of stones, rubble, and concrete—were of great strategic importance, facilitating the administration and control of conquered lands. By the end of the republic (1st century BC), roads had been constructed in some of the provinces—such as southern Gaul and Illyria—but the great period of construction outside of Italy came under the emperors. In Britain and North Africa, as in Italy, the progress of Roman expansion may be traced by charting the development of the Roman road network.

The first of the great roads were begun by the censors and special curatores, who awarded contracts and supervised construction schedules. As the roads were extended into the provinces, however, this responsibility passed to individual governors, who were expected to meet the costs of construction and repair. Often the emperor subsidized construction; he was invariably given the lion's share of credit in the inscriptions on the provincial milestones. For the emperor, road construction was a means of advertising his benevolence and authority.

Initially, Roman authorities constructed roads to accommodate military movements and transport—communication between towns and camps being an essential precondition of control—but the roads were also used by merchants (who paid duties on goods at regular intervals), couriers, and ordinary citizens or subjects.

Although traffic was carefully monitored by Roman officials, the road network facilitated the exchange of ideas, styles, and goods; it was a vital link between the central authority and the inhabitants of the provinces.

The Romans constructed a total of about 80,000 km (50,000 mi) of highways through more than 30 modern nations. The network remained in use during the Middle Ages, and remnants of it are still in existence.   JOHN W. EADIE

Bibliography: Ashby, Thomas, *The Roman Campagna in Classical Times* (1927; repr. 1979); Margary, I. D., *Roman Roads in Britain*, 2 vols., rev. ed. (1967); Sitwell, Nigel, *The Roman Roads of Europe* (1981); Von Hagen, V. W., *The Roads That Led to Rome* (1967).

Roman Senate: see SENATE, ROMAN.

romance

In the Middle Ages the term *romance* signified a narrative written in a vernacular, or "romance" language, derived from Latin, such as French. The term then became associated with the content of these works—which were usually tales of love and chivalry involving a heroic quest. Medieval romances, including *Sir Gawain and the Green Knight*, influenced many Elizabethan writers (see ELIZABETHAN AGE) but were later treated dismissively by neoclassical critics who disdained their obviously fictional appeal. By the 19th century, however, greater respect was granted to imaginative projections of the real world. Nathaniel HAWTHORNE argued that the writer of romance was free to pursue psychological truths denied to the realism of the novel. Hawthorne's novels and tales, especially *The Marble Faun* (1860), contain elements of GOTHIC ROMANCE. The traditional objection to the romance—that it is escapist and immoral—is given further validity by contemporary examples of the form: the sentimental erotic adventures produced for the mass market.

Bibliography: Beer, Gillian, *The Romance* (1970); Johnston, Arthur, *Enchanted Ground* (1964); Lincoln, E. T., ed., *Pastoral and Romance* (1969); Pettet, E. H., *Shakespeare and the Romance Tradition* (1949); Ramsey, L. C., *Chivalric Romances* (1983).

Romance languages

The Romance languages are a group of closely related vernaculars descended from the LATIN LANGUAGE, a member of the Italic branch of INDO-EUROPEAN LANGUAGES. The designation *Romance* is derived from the Latin phrase *romanica loqui*, "to speak in Roman fashion," which attests to the popular, rather than literary, origins of the languages.

The Romance languages that have acquired national standing as the official tongues of modern nations are: Spanish—the most widely used Romance language—spoken in Spain, Latin America, and some of the Caribbean islands; Portuguese, spoken in Portugal, Brazil, and in parts of Africa formerly under Portuguese rule; French, spoken in France, Belgium, Switzerland, Canada, parts of the Caribbean, and many of the African countries that were formerly under French or Belgian rule; Italian, spoken primarily in Italy and Switzerland; and Romanian, spoken principally in Romania.

In strict geographical terms, these languages are even more widespread, for there are large pockets of Spanish speakers in the United States, Italian speakers in Argentina, Romanian speakers in Yugoslavia, and so on.

Nonnational Languages.   Several distinct Romance languages function as nonnational, regional vernaculars. Among these are Rheto-Romance, or Rhaetian, which consists of a group of related languages spoken in Switzerland, where they are called Romansch, and in northern Italy, where they are called Ladin or Friulian. In southern France, Provençal, or Occitan, is spoken by about 12 million people. Formerly more unified as a literary language, Provençal now consists of a series of local dialects.

Catalan, with about 5 million speakers, is used alongside Spanish as the language of Catalonia on the Spanish Mediterranean coast from the French border to Valencia. It is also spoken in Alghero, Sardinia, in the Balearic Islands, and in the Pyrenean valley of Aran, the French region of Roussillon, and the principality of Andorra. During the Middle Ages, Catalan was closely related to the southern French dialects.

Sardinian is the collective name for a group of Romance languages spoken on the island of Sardinia by nearly 1 million people. It is of particular interest to Romance scholars because of the archaic features of its dialects, such as the retention of the Latin sound k that other Romance languages have palatalized (compare Sardinian *kelu* with French *ciel*, Italian and Spanish *cielo*, and Romanian *cer*).

Ladino, also called Judaeo-Romance or Sephardic, is spoken by Sephardic Jews in Istanbul, Salonika, and elsewhere around the Mediterranean. It is based on 15th-century Spanish, reflecting the time when the Jews were expelled from Spain by royal edict. The language also contains Turkish, Greek, and Hebrew elements.

Romance creoles, whose origins are found in PIDGINS or simplified trade languages, have also sprung up around the world. Haitian and Louisiana French are such languages, as are the varieties of Portuguese found in Macao and Goa.

At least one recorded Romance language, Dalmatian, has become extinct. Formerly spoken along the eastern coast of the Adriatic, Dalmatian consisted of at least two dialects: Ragusan, known only from a few medieval documents, and Veglian, which disappeared in 1898 when its last speaker was blown up by a land mine.

Vulgar Latin.   From the evidence of Latin grammarians, popular playwrights, and inscriptions, it is apparent that in Republican Rome the spoken language of the lower classes was undergoing modifications in pronunciation and grammar that ultimately were to differentiate it from the written language and the language of the privileged. During the period of empire and Roman expansion, it was this Latin of the people, so-called Vulgar Latin, that was carried to the far-flung provinces by soldiers, merchants, and colonists.

Not all provinces were Romanized at the same time, however. Sicily and Sardinia were colonized as early as 238 BC, while Dacia—modern Romania—did not come under Roman occupation until about AD 100. In the provinces, Vulgar Latin underwent further modification by the subjugated peoples, who brought to it their own speech habits and pronunciation influenced by their own indigenous languages. The Iberians, for example, pronounced Latin one way, whereas the Gauls pronounced it another.

The collapse of the empire's frontiers during the 5th century under the thrust of Germanic tribes left Rome cut off from the provinces, and the outer regions drifted apart as each modified its form of spoken Latin in unique ways. In every region of the former Latin-speaking world, the emerging Romance languages then in turn began to break up among themselves.

French and Provençal. In Gallo-Roman France, a split occurred between north and south, assisted by incursions of Germanic-speaking Franks—whence the name "France"—into the north. Here, too, further dialectalization occurred throughout the Middle Ages, resulting in a multitude of speech forms such as Francien, Picard, Norman, Lorrain, and Walloon. Southern French, or Provencal, split into Languedocien, Auvergnat, and many other dialects. The dialect of Paris gradually became the national language, however, because of the political prestige of the capital and today is accepted as the model for the French language.

Italian. Dialectal varieties of the emerging Italian language revolved around Gallo-Italian in the northwest; a northeastern or Venetian group; a central dialectal group that included the speech of Tuscany, Umbria, northern Latium (the province of Rome), and Corsica; and clusters of dialects to the south, including Abruzzese-Neapolitan and Calabrian-Sicilian. The ultimate predominance of Tuscan as the standard was a result more of the cultural than of any political prestige of Florence. Although the speech of Tuscany has long been considered the most prestigious form of Italian, however, that of Rome is fast becoming the standard language.

Spanish and Portuguese. On the Iberian peninsula, two languages developed, each with its own dialects. Galician-Portuguese broke into northwestern, central, and southern dialects; Spanish came to embrace Leonese and Castilian in the center of the peninsula, Aragonese further to the east, and Andalusian in the south. The dialect of Lisbon vies with that of Rio de Janeiro in Brazil as the standard form of Portuguese taught in North American schools and as the model for the language.

Castilian Spanish, spoken in central Spain, including the capital Madrid, is generally thought of as the most prestigious form of Spanish, although Mexican Spanish is often taught in North American classrooms.

Romanian. Romanian has broken into several dialects, such as Macedo-Romanian, spoken in southern Macedonia, and Isto-Romanian, the language of a few thousand people in northeastern Yugoslavia. The dialect of Bucharest serves as the standard language.

LINGUISTIC FEATURES

Similarities and differences among the Romance languages and their relation to Latin may be seen in the following sentences, which mean "The poet loves the girl":

Latin	Poeta puellam amat
French	Le poète aime la jeune fille
Italian	Il poeta ama la ragazza
Portuguese	O poeta ama a menina
Spanish	El poeta ama a la muchacha
Romanian	Poetul iube fata

The word *poet* was borrowed from Greek by Latin, underscoring the fact that not all Romance words, even when derived from Latin, were originally Italic. Some vocabulary may differ from one Romance language to another because words were taken from different Latin forms with similar meanings, or were borrowed from the local native languages. Sometimes words were incorporated into one or the other of the Romance languages from neighboring tongues; Spanish *izquierdo*, "left," for example, comes from Basque, and Romanian *sticlă*, "drinking glass," comes from Slavic. It was also often the case that new words entered Romance languages from the vocabulary of conquering peoples: Spanish *aceite* and Portuguese *azeite*, "oil," come from Arabic, and French *danser*, "to dance," and *gagner*, "to harvest," were borrowed from Germanic.

The Case System. Broadly speaking, the trend or direction of change in the Romance languages has been to reduce the Latin case system through elimination of the distinctive endings. The Latin word *porta*, "door," for instance, had four singular forms: nominative and vocative *porta*; accusative *portam*; genitive and dative *portae*; and ablative *portá*. Modern Romance languages, however, use only one singular form: French *porte*, Italian and Portuguese *porta*, and Spanish *puerta*. Other modern Romance linguistic features include the elimination of neuter gender, the development of the definite article, greater use of prepositions, stricter word order, and the emergence of auxiliary verbs to express tense.

Verb Paradigms. French leveled the verb paradigms to such an extent that subject pronouns became mandatory (contrast French *je chante*, "I sing," with Italian *canto*); but in general the Latin paradigm has remained intact. Compare the Latin and Romance present tense, singular indicative forms of the verb "to sing":

	Latin	French	Spanish	Portuguese	Italian	Romanian
1st person	canto	je chante	canto	canto	canto	cînt
2d person	cantas	tu chantes	cantas	cantas	canti	cînti
3rd person	canta	il chante	canta	canta	canta	cîntă

Notable in phonology was the loss of opposition between Latin long and short vowels, the voicing of intervocalic voiceless consonants, and in some languages the loss of syllable- and word-final *s*. The emergence of accentual patterns led to the reduction or loss of many unstressed vowels in the more heavily accented languages such as Gallo-Roman and Old French, and to the diphthongization of some stressed vowels in most of the Romance languages. Only in French and Portuguese, however, did vowels before a nasal consonant undergo nasalization—compare French *main*, "hand," with Portuguese *mão* and Spanish and Italian *mano*.

HISTORICAL IMPORTANCE

Latin continued to be the only medium of written expression during the early Middle Ages, and the first extant text of substantial length in Romance—the so-called Oaths of Strasbourg, a treaty of alliance sworn by two of Charlemagne's descendants—dates as late as 842. No other group of languages, however, provides such extensive documentation of both the mother tongue, Latin, and the descendant Romance languages. This invaluable legacy has allowed greater insight into the causes and effects of language change, and offers a unique opportunity for historical linguists to test many of their hypotheses.

James M. Anderson

Bibliography: Anderson, J. M., and Rochet, B., *Historical Romance Morphology* (1978); Auerbach, Erich, *Introduction to Romance Languages and Literature* (1961); Elcock, W. D., *The Romance Languages* (1960); Grandgent, C. H., *An Introduction to Vulgar Latin* (1907); Hall, R. A., Jr., *External History of the Romance Languages* (1974); Iordan, Iorgu, and Orr, John, *An Introduction to Romance Linguistics, Its Schools and Scholars*, 2d ed. (1970); Posner, Rebecca, *The Romance Languages: A Linguistic Introduction* (1970); Pountain, C. J., *Structures and Transformations: The Romance Verb* (1983).

Romanenko, Yury Viktorovich [roh-mahn-eng'-koh]

The Soviet cosmonaut Yury Viktorovich Romanenko, b. Aug. 1, 1944, was an air force engineering school graduate and an instructor-pilot before becoming a cosmonaut in 1970. He made his first flight, as commander of Soyuz 26, with Georgy Grechko. Launched on Dec. 10, 1977, they docked with the Salyut 6 space station and carried out many experiments before returning to Earth on Mar. 16, 1978, aboard Soyuz 28, which had been left by other cosmonauts. His second mission was made with Cuban cosmonaut Arnaldo Tamayo Mendez aboard Soyuz 38. Launched on Sept. 20, 1980, the men joined Leonid Popov and Valery Ryumin aboard Salyut 6 and returned to Earth six days later. His third mission began on Feb. 6, 1987, when he and Aleksandr Laveikin entered space aboard Soyuz TM-2 and docked with the Mir space station for an extended stay.

James Oberg

Romanesque art and architecture

Romanesque art and architecture flourished throughout western Europe from about 1050 to about 1200, although its first manifestations occurred before the year 1000, and its influence remained strong in some areas of Europe well into the 13th century. Unlike CAROLINGIAN ART AND ARCHITECTURE and OTTONIAN ART AND ARCHITECTURE, from which it drew many forms and elements, Romanesque was a truly pan-European movement.

By the beginning of the 11th century, European civilization had become stable and prosperous under the aegis of the Christian church, through whose network of abbeys the new artistic order was established and spread. An unprecedented building activity stimulated the development of innovative architectural techniques and styles, which in turn demanded new forms of pictorial and sculptural decoration.

The resultant flowering of Romanesque art, once thought of merely as a transitional phase between EARLY CHRISTIAN ART AND ARCHITECTURE and GOTHIC ART AND ARCHITECTURE, is now considered to be a distinct and important phase of European art.

ARCHITECTURE

The word *Romanesque* originally meant "in the Roman manner." This description is at least partly applicable to Romanesque ecclesiastical architecture, not only in the use of the Roman round arch, but also in the adoption of the major forms of antique Roman vaulting (see ARCH AND VAULT). The simplest and most widely employed type of vault was the barrel vault, which is nothing more than the prolongation of the soffit, or undersurface, of an arch. More complex was the so-called groin vault, a structure formed by the intersection at a right angle of two barrel vaults.

Most Romanesque churches retained the basic plan of the Early Christian BASILICA: a long, three-aisled NAVE intercepted by a TRANSEPT and terminating in a semicircular APSE crowned by a conch, or half-dome. Whereas Early Christian structures employed thin, flat walls to support thin roofs and wooden ceilings, however, the masonry structure of Romanesque churches assumed far more complicated configurations, in which heavy piers and arched openings divide the interior into well-defined spatial areas, while large masses of clearly separated geometric forms impart to the exterior an aura of grandeur and power. The greatest breakthrough of Romanesque architecture, however, occurred in interior vaulting. Groin vaults had long been used in the lower side-aisles of the nave, but the thin walls of pre-Romanesque churches could support only wooden ceilings and roofs. By redesigning and reinforcing the walls, Romanesque builders were able to span the wide and often lofty nave with a solid barrel vault and thus create completely vaulted structures.

France. Fully vaulted churches eventually became standard in France, the most creative center of Romanesque architecture and the birthplace of one of the most beautiful features of medieval architecture, the ambulatory with radiating chapels. An ambulatory is a semicircular aisle curving around the apse that opens out onto small chapels, generally five in number. With the invention of the ambulatory, the previously solid rear wall of the main apse gave way to a gracefully curving open ARCADE. On the exterior these various elements resulted in an imposing pyramidal grouping. This whole complex of architectural forms at the east end of medieval churches is known as the chevet.

The first use of a chevet occurred during the rebuilding of the abbey church of Saint Martin in Tours shortly before 1000. In its final form Saint Martin's established the model for the so-called pilgrimage churches erected (c.1000–c.1150) along the roads that took medieval pilgrims to the tomb of Saint James at Santiago de Compostela in northern Spain. As an architectural type, the pilgrimage church features a well-developed chevet, such as that of Saint Sernin (c.1080–1120) in Toulouse, along with an extremely tall two-story nave crowned by a barrel vault. Above the lofty ground-story arcade, twin arches open out into an upper gallery situated above the groin vaults of the side aisles, and thin colonnettes, or shafts, rising from the pavement to the main barrel vault divide the nave into a series of separate sections, or bays. At the interior's east end, the gaps between the slender columns of the apsidal arcade offer intriguing vistas opening out into the ambulatory and the lighted chapels beyond.

Complementing the striking interiors of these churches are imposing exteriors in which towers play an important role. In Italy, bell towers, or CAMPANILES, were almost always built as independent structures, as exemplified by the Leaning Tower

Santiago de Compostela (c.1075–1128), in Galicia, represents the culmination of Romanesque architecture in Spain. Erected by Bishop Diego Pelaez on the site of previous shrines housing the relics of Spain's patron saint, Santiago de Compostela became one of the most important pilgrimage sites in Europe. Built on a cruciform plan similar to a contemporary pilgrimage church, Saint Sernin in Toulouse, Santiago de Compostela, at the time of its construction, was the only church in Spain to incorporate the French chevet.

The cruciform plan of Saint Sernin (c.1050–1120), Toulouse, epitomizes that of the Romanesque pilgrimage church, featuring a double-aisled nave, aisled transepts, and a chevet with five radiating chapels.

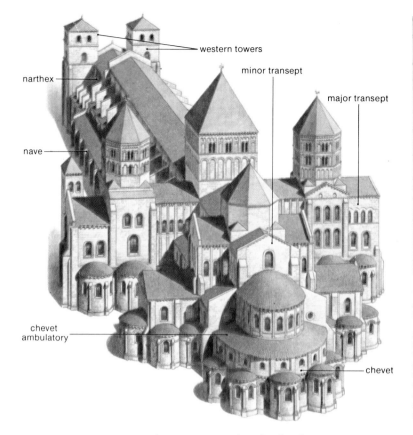

narthex

western towers

nave

minor transept

major transept

chevet
ambulatory

chevet

The monastic churches of Burgundy, France, are among the finest examples of Romanesque style. (Left) The third abbey church of Cluny (completed 1130), known as Cluny III, featured a barrel-vaulted nave with double aisles, pointed arches, double transepts, and a chevet. The enclosed narthex at the west end made Cluny III the longest church in France. (Above) The enclosed narthex was also a feature of the 11th-century Benedictine abbey church of Saint Philibert, Tournus, near Cluny. Saint Philibert's nave is distinguished by transverse arches supporting lateral, or transverse, barrel vaults that span the width of the nave between the piers.

of Pisa (1174–1272). In northern Europe, on the other hand, towers had been integrated with the main body of the church since pre-Romanesque times. Along with bell towers and stair towers, northern churches often incorporated towers built over the crossing, that area where the nave and the transept intersect. Some of these crossing towers, such as that at the smaller pilgrimage church of Sainte Foy (1050–1120) in Conques, are called lanterns because their windows illuminate the area in front of the sanctuary with a pool of light.

All of these architectural elements were brought together and magnified in one of Europe's most magnificent structures, the third church built for the Burgundian abbey of Cluny. Generally referred to as Cluny III (completed in 1130), this church was largely destroyed in the early 19th century, but its appearance can be accurately reconstructed from early views. Cluny III's nave consisted of five, rather than the traditional three, aisles, and the central, barrel-vaulted aisle rose to a dizzying height of 29.29 m (96 ft). Intercepting the nave were two equally lofty transepts, and towers crowned both crossings and each arm of the main transept. In direct anticipation of Gothic practice, pointed arches were used throughout the ground-story arcade and the side aisles. Above the blind arcade of the second story rose a third story, known as a CLERE-STORY; each of its bays was pierced by three round-headed windows. Aside from providing ample light for the interior, these windows signaled a daring innovation in medieval construction, because before Cluny III the security of the barrel vaults depended on the solid masonry of the upper walls or on the abutment of a gallery. So daring was this technique that some of the vaults in Cluny III fell in 1120, although they were repaired in time for the general consecration of the church in 1130.

Normandy and England. Among the many and diverse regional styles of Romanesque that flourished throughout western Europe during the 11th and 12th centuries, the most significant in terms of structural innovation was NORMAN ARCHITECTURE. Working mainly in Normandy and (after 1066) England, Norman architects solved the problem, posed by

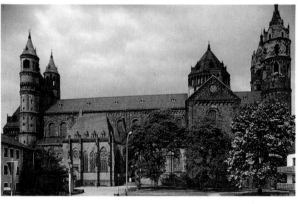

Flanked by two round towers at each end, the red sandstone cathedral of Worms is a characteristic example of the German Romanesque style.

Cluny III, of sustaining a high vault atop a windowed clerestory. The Norman architects discovered that by supporting the vault with a grid of thin diagonal arches, or ribs, they could lessen the outward pressure of the vault's masonry and thus balance heavy vaults on lighter walls. Rib vaulting was first employed (c.1104) consistently in the Norman DURHAM CATHEDRAL in England, and from then on, rib vaulting became standard in Normandy. Because most of the other Anglo-Norman structures were built on too vast a scale to permit high vaults, Durham remained an anomaly in England; in France, however, the introduction of rib vaulting marked a crucial step in the development of Gothic architecture.

Germany. German builders had been in the forefront in the early development of towers and in the elaboration of the immense western entrance facades known as westworks. The culminating monuments of German Romanesque architecture

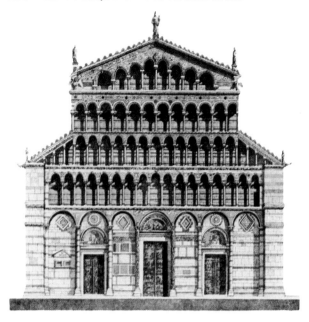

The four-story arcaded facade of the west end (1250–70) of the Cathedral of Pisa (1053–1272) is continued around the exterior of the church and repeated on the campanile, or Leaning Tower (1174–1350). The cathedral, the largest Tuscan Romanesque church, was designed on a basilican plan; each arm of the transept ends in an apse, creating two smaller basilicas within the cathedral. The campanile, cathedral, and baptistery (1152–1278) are located on the Piazza del Duomo.

are the Rhineland cathedrals of Mainz (12th–13th centuries), Speyer (begun 1030), and Worms (1150–81). When the nave of Speyer Cathedral was finally vaulted (c.1125), its height surpassed even that of Cluny III.

Italy. The profuse external embellishment of German Romanesque churches, as well as their retention of "old-style" apses, link them with contemporary structures of northern Italy, and particularly with the products of Lombard architecture. With few exceptions, however, the main internal areas of the larger churches throughout Italy continued to be covered by wooden ceilings or open rafters—in most instances, the present high vaults date from a later period. A distinguishing feature of Tuscan Romanesque architecture is the surprisingly classical character of its architectural details. For example, in the noble interior of the largest Tuscan Romanesque church, the Cathedral of Pisa (1063–1121), the marble columns are all crowned with capitals of antique Roman form.

SCULPTURE

After the fall (AD 476) of the Roman Empire the practice of decorating buildings with large reliefs ceased for almost 600 years. The revival of monumental relief sculpture as a major form of art is one of the outstanding achievements of the Romanesque period. Often highly stylized and at times verging on the abstract, Romanesque reliefs were used chiefly to embellish the church portals.

France. The first sculptured doorway of truly monumental size was the now-destroyed entranceway of Cluny III, whose style and magnitude are reflected in the still-extant portal of the Burgundian church of Sainte Madeleine at Vézelay (1120–32). In the Vézelay reliefs, the variety in subject matter that characterizes the decorative art of Romanesque churches is apparent in the wide range of secular as well as religious themes. Above the two openings of the doorway, within the TYMPANUM, a huge seated Christ erupts through the inner arch of small boxes, and energizing rays descend from his outstretched hands onto the apostles below. Even though this central motif follows an established convention in Christian art for representing the descent of the Holy Spirit at Pentecost, there is little that is conventional in the surrounding re-

liefs. The keen interest in far-off countries engendered by the First Crusade (1095–99) is reflected in the lintels over the doors and the boxes surrounding the tympanum, whose reliefs depict the fabulous races with which medieval writers peopled distant lands. Among the exotic foreigners displayed are dog-headed men of India, porcine-faced Ethiopians, and at the extreme outer end of the right lintel a family of big-eared Panotii comprised of a mother in a topless gown, a father clothed in leaves, and a child who has shut himself up in his huge ears like a clam.

The Apocalypse from Revelations, the mystical last book of the New Testament, supplied many of the images found on French Romanesque portals. Particularly vivid in execution are the sweeping panoramas of the Last Judgment found at Sainte Foy in Conques and Saint Lazare in Autun, which include graphic depictions of the tortures of the damned. On the other hand, the sculptors of west central France often omitted the tympana and distributed sculptured areas over the upper parts of the facade; at the Cathedral of Angoulême, for example, the whole of the towering west facade above the doorway is covered with saints and dancing angels surrounding an ascending Christ. Throughout France, human figures and fantastic animals of every sort were used to decorate the interior capitals of churches and cloisters. One of the few French Romanesque sculptors known by name, the famous GISLEBERTUS, carved (c.1130–35) such figures for almost all the

The tympanum of the central portal of the church of Sainte Madeleine (1120–32), Vézelay, France, portrays Christ inspiring the Apostles to spread the gospel throughout the world. In addition to the imaginative representations of foreign peoples, the tympanum is framed by astrological symbols and depictions of seasonal occupations.

A fragment of the lintel of the north portal of the Cathedral of Saint Lazare, Autun (c.1120–35), France, shows Eve plucking the forbidden fruit of Eden. This relief may be the work of Gislebertus, who executed much of Saint Lazare's sculptural decoration. The flattened relief and the long, sinuous lines of the figure and the vegetation are characteristic of Burgundian decoration. (Musée Rolin, Autun.)

interior capitals of Saint Lazare in Autun. Although his figures are even flatter and more linear in style than those at Vézelay, Gislebertus feelingly conveyed in his *Flight into Egypt* the tender care with which Mary places a protective arm over the little Christ Child. On either side of this scene, lush vegetation supplants the usual conventionalized leaves of the Corinthian type of capital.

Italy. Sculpture in the Romanesque period was confined largely to reliefs. No freestanding, life-size human figures were created, and only a few smaller figures executed in the round are extant.

Striking examples of the latter figural type appear on the bishop's throne (c.1150) in the southern Italian church of San Nicola of Bari, which probably was carved to commemorate an Italian victory over the Saracens. The victorious Christian soldier in the center of this group lends only token support to the seat of the chair, whose main weight rests on the shoulders of two half-naked Saracens who are loudly protesting the burden they have to bear. The strongly plastic qualities of the figures' sturdy, squat bodies is a recurring characteristic in Italian Romanesque sculpture.

The most important and prolific sculptural centers in Italy, however, were those of the northern Italian region known as Lombardy. In contrast to French Romanesque sculptures the Lombard Romanesque school was dominated by three well-known personalities: Wiligelmo da Modena (fl. early 12th century), the founder of the school; Nicolò of Verona (fl. 12th century); and Benedetto ANTELAMI (fl. late 12th–early 13th centuries).

Although all three were influenced somewhat by contemporary French sculpture, their work expresses a distinctly Lombardic quality of heaviness and earthiness that is immediately apparent in the powerfully bovine figures of Adam and Eve in Wiligelmo's *Genesis* reliefs (1107–1110) at Modena. Wiligelmo's sturdy style was refined further in Nicolò's sculptures (c.1138) for the portal of San Zeno in Verona, where the civic pride of the independent northern Italian communes is reflected in the local cavalry represented on the tympanum. Antelami, whose career extended into the early years of the 13th century, was the most forward looking of the three Lombard sculptors. His masterpieces, the figures (c.1190) of David and Ezekiel set into niches on the facade of the cathedral of Fidenza, are actually carved in relief, although they give the impression of being freestanding statues. Their ponderous forms and noble monumentality clearly presage the sculptural works of Michelangelo.

Meuse Valley. Very little stone sculpture was produced in Belgium and Germany during the Romanesque period, but

This bronze baptismal font (1107–12) in the Church of Saint Barthélemy, Liège, exemplifies the superior metalwork produced by the Mosan school of the Meuse Valley region. Created by Renier de Huy for the abbot Hellin, the font, originally supported by 12 oxen representing the Apostles, portrays 3 baptismal scenes from the New Testament in addition to the central scene of Christ's baptism.

both countries excelled in metalwork. In the Meuse Valley region of Belgium and northern France, the so-called Mosan school of metalwork produced (1107–12) an early masterpiece in the bronze baptismal font executed by Renier de Huy (fl. 12th century) for a church in Liège. In contrast to Burgundian expressionism and Lombardic ponderousness, Renier's figures are tinged with the graceful naturalism usually associated with classical art. Whether or not Renier had actually studied Hellenistic reliefs, as some experts have argued, his work demonstrates the wide range of styles represented in Romanesque sculpture, which excluded neither naturalism nor idealized beauty.

The Maiestas Christi *fresco (c.1123), from the church of San Clemente in Tahull, Spain, is one of the finest surviving examples of Spanish Romanesque mural painting. Executed by the Master of Tahull, the work retains Byzantine stylization but infuses it with bold colors and simplified decoration. (Museo de Bellas Artes de Cataluña, Barcelona.)*

Benedetto Antelami's earliest known work, the Deposition *(1178), a marble relief in the right transept of the Cathedral of Parma, Italy, displays his imaginative synthesis of Provençal and Byzantine styles. Antelami—whose name was derived from the Magistri Antelami, the guild in which he received his training—was a leading influence in the transition of sculptural styles from Romanesque to Gothic.*

The War of the Angels, *a miniature from a copy of the* Commentary on the Apocalypse *of Beatus of Liebana, was produced (1028–72) at the abbey of Saint-Sever-sur-Ardour in southern France. These illuminations reflect the compound influences of Spanish and Byzantine manuscript traditions in the dark, rich colors, the vivid representations, and the interlaced and overlapping forms, as in the scaly tentacle of the Beast of the Apocalypse. (Bibliothèque Nationale, Paris.)*

PAINTING

Frescoes. The interiors of nearly all Romanesque churches originally were decorated, either entirely or in part, with frescoes (see FRESCO PAINTING). Among the pictorial subjects chosen for the walls and vaults, the most important and most frequently occurring theme is the so-called *Maiestas Christi*, a conventional representation of the transcendental deity that was reserved for the half-dome of the apse. The *Maiestas* fresco (c.1123), on the apsidal vault of the Catalan church of San Clemente de Tahull, is the best-preserved Romanesque representation of this theme and follows a long-established convention in portraying Christ seated on a rainbow with his right hand raised in blessing. Also traditional is the enclosure of the scene within an oval frame known as a mandorla, the symbol of divine glory. But the artist of Tahull has wholly transformed this time-honored image into highly schematized patterns, almost caricaturing the features of Christ. In the subdued light of the sanctuary, however, it is precisely this totally unrealistic interpretation of the deity that best expresses the all-pervading presence of the Lord. At Tahull, as in many other Romanesque pictorial works, the discarding of any reference to the actual appearance of things enabled the artist to achieve the maximum spiritual intensity.

Manuscript Illumination. Because time and climate have destroyed or badly damaged most Romanesque frescoes, ILLUMINATED MANUSCRIPTS provide the principal source of present-day knowledge of Romanesque painting. Romanesque illuminators, like the sculptors of the Last Judgment portals, made use of the vivid imagery of the Apocalypse. A collection of commentaries (Bibliothèque Nationale, Paris) on the Apocalypse, illuminated (1028–72) at the abbey of Saint-Sever-sur-Ardour, in southern France, includes a highly original illustration of the passage that describes how winged locusts with human faces torment humankind with the poisonous stings of their scorpion tails. In a memorable representation of this scene, the Saint-Sever artist depicted six screeching creatures on a checkerboard background who, urged on by Satan, angrily lash out at their victims.

The powerful expressionism of these Apocalypse scenes gives way to a more elegant beauty in the large ornamental initials with which Romanesque manuscripts abound. Like the sculptured capitals in the Romanesque churches, these fantastically ornate letters often include human figures, as well as dragons and other creatures. Often the figures assume the very shape of the initials, as in a copy of Pope Gregory I, the Great's *Moralia* (Bibliothèque Municipale, Dijon), made (1111) at the abbey of Citeaux in France.

HISTORICAL IMPORTANCE

The international scope of Romanesque art is apparent in the broad range of influences it assimilated and transformed. Echoes of Carolingian and Ottonian illumination can be detected in many Romanesque manuscripts, and the sophisticated art of the Byzantine Empire had a widespread impact on all forms of Romanesque painting. In architecture, the dome and the horseshoe arch were introduced from the Near East and from Islamic art and architecture, and in the south of France, Roman triumphal arches provided the inspiration for the triple portals of the church of Saint-Gilles-du-Gard (c.1140–c.1150).

In 12th-century Sicily a mélange of Saracenic, Byzantine, and Norman Romanesque styles resulted in a series of extraordinarily exotic monuments, whereas at the opposite end of Europe, the wooden stave churches of Norway preserved in their carved decorations the ancient animal art of the barbarian era.

Romanesque art bore within it the seeds of succeeding artistic trends. Rib vaulting was only one of several Norman Romanesque elements that played important roles in the evolution of Gothic architecture. In Italy, Romanesque sculpture laid the groundwork for the first monument of the dawning Renaissance, Nicola PISANO's pulpit (1260) for the Pisa Baptistery. Finally, the classical spirit of Renier's Liège reliefs was splendidly revived (c.1181) by the Mosan goldsmith NICHOLAS OF VERDUN. His later works, however, bear so many similarities to the contemporaneous Gothic sculpture of the Cathedral of Chartres that they can no longer be considered truly Romanesque.   WILLIAM M. HINKLE

Bibliography: Atroshenko, V. I., and Collins, Judith, *The Origins of the Romanesque* (1986); Conant, K. J., *Carolingian and Romanesque Architecture: 800 to 1200*, 4th ed. (1978); Decker, Hans, *Romanesque Art in Italy* (1959); Dodwell, C. R., *Painting in Europe: 800–1200* (1971); Gantner, Joseph, and Pobé, Marcel, *The Glory of Romanesque Art* (1956); Grabar, A., and Nordenfalk, C., *Romanesque Painting from the 11th to the 13th Century* (1957); Künstler, Gustav, ed., *Romanesque Art in Europe: Architecture and Sculpture* (1973); Palol Salellas, Pedro de, *Early Medieval Art in Spain* (1967); Schapiro, Meyer, *Romanesque Art* (1977); Stoddard, W. S., *Monastery and Cathedral in France* (1966); Swarzenski, Hans, *Monuments of Romanesque Art: The Art of Church Treasures in North-Western Europe*, 2d rev. ed. (1967); Webb, Geoffrey, *Architecture in Britain: The Middle Ages* (1956).

Romania   [roh-mayn'-ee-ah]

Romania, a socialist republic on the lower Danube River in southeastern Europe, borders the USSR on the north and northeast, Hungary and Yugoslavia on the west, and Bulgaria on the south. To the southeast is a 245-km-long (152-mi) shoreline on the BLACK SEA, the main attraction of an important tourist industry. The nation's economy, less developed than those of most other European nations, is growing rapidly under the direction of a series of 5-year plans that emphasize industrialization. The name *Romania* came into being in 1861, following the unification of the Turkish-controlled principalities of MOLDAVIA and WALACHIA in 1859, and refers to Romania's Latin heritage as the Roman province of Dacia during the 2d and 3d centuries AD. Romania achieved full independence from the Ottoman Empire in 1877. The monarchy, established in 1881, was ended in 1947 when Communists gained control and proclaimed Romania a people's republic. Officially redesignated a socialist republic in 1965, Romania maintains a position of relative independence from the USSR in foreign affairs while upholding an orthodox socialist regime at home.

LAND AND RESOURCES

Romania is divided into three regions. In the center is the Transylvanian basin, an area of hilly, fertile farmlands developed on beds of sand, marl, and clay overlain by deposits of loess and alluvium. Elevations within the basin range from 300 to 600 m (1,000 to 2,000 ft). Surrounding the basin is the second region, the CARPATHIAN MOUNTAINS. The Eastern Carpathians, stretching from the Soviet border to cover most of western Romania, average 1,200 m (3,900 ft) in elevation. The Southern Carpathians, or Transylvanian Alps, are higher; rising to their highest point in Mount Moldoveanu, they extend from the Prahova Valley in the east to the Timas-Cerna corridor in the west. The Western Carpathians, between the Danube and Somes rivers, have an average elevation of 645 m (2,115 ft). Romania's third region is one of plains that ring the entire country except in the north and are separated from the

Peles Castle in Sinais, Romania, a health resort in the Transylvanian Alps, was formerly a summer residence of the Romanian royal family. The 160-room structure is now a museum, containing an internationally known collection of art and furnishings.

SOCIALIST REPUBLIC OF ROMANIA

LAND. Area: 237,500 km² (91,699 mi²). Capital and largest city: Bucharest (1985 est. pop., 1,961,000).
PEOPLE. Population (1987 est.): 22,900,000; density (1987 est.): 96.4 persons per km² (249.7 per mi²). Distribution (1987 est.): 53% urban, 47% rural. Annual growth (1987): 0.5%. Official language: Romanian. Major religions: Orthodoxy, Roman Catholicism, Protestantism.
EDUCATION AND HEALTH. Literacy (1986): 98% of adult population. Universities (1987, including polytechnic institutes) 11. Hospital beds (1985): 212,670. Physicians (1985): 47,400. Life expectancy (1984): women—72.6; men—67.0. Infant mortality (1985): 25.6 per 1,000 live births.
ECONOMY. GNP (1984): $45.5 billion; $2,020 per capita. Labor distribution (1984): agriculture—29.2%; mining, manufacturing, and public utilities—36.8%; construction—7.4%; transportation and communication—6.8%; trade—5.9%; services—11.9%. Foreign trade (1984): imports—$10.3 billion; exports—$12.6 billion; principal trade partners—USSR, West Germany, East Germany, Iran, Egypt, Italy. Currency: 1 leu = 100 bani.
GOVERNMENT. Type: Communist one-party state. Legislature: Grand National Assembly. Political subdivisions: 40 districts, municipality of Bucharest.
COMMUNICATIONS. Railroads (1985): 11,269 km (7,002 mi) total. Roads (1985): 72,799 km (45,235 mi) total. Major ports: 5. Major airfields: 4.

mountains by hilly piedmonts. The western plain, reaching to the Hungarian and Yugoslavian borders, is an extension of Europe's mid-Danubian plain. In the south is the Walachian plain, a gently sloping area that descends southward from 300 m (1,000 ft) near the southern piedmont to 30 m (100 ft) in the marshes, lakes, and wet meadowlands near the Danube River. In the northeast, extending from the piedmont to the Prut River border with the USSR, lies the Moldavian plain, an area of undulating lowlands and tablelands between 200 and 500 m (650 and 1,650 ft) in elevation. The marshy Danube Delta expands downstream from Galaţi, and lying to the south, between the Danube and the Black Sea, is the DOBRUJA, a low plateau. The highest elevation in the country is Moldoveanul (2,543 m/8,343 ft).
Soils. True black chernozem soil, well suited to agriculture, is found in the Moldavian plain; degraded or modified chernozem varieties occur in the other plains as well as in the Transylvanian basin. Along the Danube and its tributaries are belts of fertile, alluvial soil. Brown forest soils occur on the lower mountain slopes.
Climate. Romania's warm summers and cold winters define a transitional temperate-continental type of climate. Average annual precipitation is about 635 mm (25 in) and ranges from more than 1,270 mm (50 in) in the mountainous areas to less than 400 mm (15 in) in Dobruja and the Danube Delta. Most rain falls in late spring and early summer; late autumn and winter are the driest periods. The average temperature is between −3° and −5° C (27° and 23° F) in January and 22° to 24° C (72° to 75° F) in July. Significantly cooler temperatures

prevail at all seasons in the mountains; the warmest areas in summer are the Walachian plain and Dobruja in the south.
Drainage. Except for eastern Dobruja, which drains directly to the Black Sea, all of Romania is drained by the DANUBE RIVER and its tributaries. The major tributaries are the Prut, Siret, Ialomiţa, Argeş, Olt, Jiul Mures, Somes, and Timas rivers. Spring flooding of the rivers is a serious and recurring problem, and in the Danube Delta and along the northern bank of the Danube in the Walachian plain are extensive marshlands. Romania has about 2,500 small lakes.
Vegetation and Animal Life. Forests cover about one-quarter of Romania and most of the lower mountain slopes. Coniferous forests, with fir and spruce predominating, supply most of the commercial timber cut at higher elevations in the Carpathian Mountains. Beech and other deciduous trees predominate on the lower slopes. Alpine pastures occur above the treeline between 1,525 and 1,830 m (5,000 and 6,000 ft), and tundra occurs at higher elevations. Large animals include deer, bears, foxes, wolves, and boars. Numerous species of predatory birds and waterfowl frequent the Danube Delta and marshes.
Resources. Romania's major natural resources are its fertile soils and its rapidly descending waters ideally suited for hydroelectric exploitation. Although several petroleum and natural gas deposits are rapidly approaching exhaustion, new petroleum deposits were located in the Black Sea in 1979. Lead, zinc, sulfur, salt, and lignite also occur in considerable quantities. Approximately two-thirds of the land is suitable for farming; of this, just under half is used for crops.
PEOPLE
About 87% of the population are ethnically Romanian; 8% are Hungarian; 2%, German; and 1%, Gypsy. The remainder is made up of small groups of Jews (listed as an ethnic group), Ukrainians, Serbs and other Yugoslavs, Russians, Bulgarians, Czechs and Slovaks, and others. The Hungarian minority is concentrated in the Transylvanian basin and western plains; the German population is centered between Braşov and Sibiu in southern Transylvania and in the Banat. Most other minorities live close to the border regions.
Language and Religion. Romanian, an eastern ROMANCE LANGUAGE, is the official language. Magyar is used by the Hungarian minority, and German and other languages by the relevant minorities. Most minorities have resisted assimilation.

Most Romanians belong to the Romanian Orthodox church, an independent Eastern ORTHODOX CHURCH headed by a patriarch in Bucharest. About half of Romania's Hungarians are Roman Catholics, and the remainder either Calvinists or Unitarians. Lutheranism, the second largest Protestant denomination, draws most of its adherents from the German minority.
Demography. Romania has one of the least urbanized populations in Europe, with nearly half of its inhabitants living in rural areas. The capital, BUCHAREST, is the largest city. Other

ROMANIA

Meters	Feet
4000	13124
2000	6562
1000	3281
500	1640
200	656
0	0
200	656
2000	6562

┼┼┼┼ Canal
——— Railroad
•⬦•⬦ Oil Pipeline
▲ Major Oil Field
+ Spot Elevation

Scale 1:5,000,000

© 1980 Rand McNally & Co.
A-552700-772

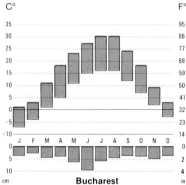

Bars indicate monthly ranges of temperatures (red) and precipitation (blue) of Bucharest, the capital of Romania. Bucharest's location in southeast Romania gives it a continental humid climate with moderate rainfall and considerable temperature variation.

A construction crew makes repairs in front of the contemporary Parliament Building in Bucharest, the capital of Romania. Bucharest, situated in the southeastern portion of the nation, is the easternmost capital of a European country outside of the USSR.

large cities, with more than 200,000 inhabitants, are BRĂILA, BRAȘOV, CLUJ-NAPOCA, CONSTANȚA, CRAIOVA, GALAȚI, IAȘI, Oradea, PLOIEȘTI, and TIMIȘOARA.

The most densely populated areas are central Walachia in and around Bucharest and Ploiești; southwestern Walachia, along the Siret River valley in Moldavia; and the lowlands of Transylvania. The most sparsely settled areas are the Carpathian uplands, Dobruja, and the marshlands along the Danube flood plain and delta.

Education and Health. The literacy rate is very high, and education is compulsory and free for 10 years between the ages of 6 and 16. Eight years are spent in junior, and 2 years in senior general schools. In addition, general or special high schools offer 4- and 5-year courses, and preschool facilities and specialized vocational schools are also provided. Romanian is the primary language of instruction; Hungarian and German are used in the schools of the relevant minority

groups. Numerous institutions offer higher education, including seven universities located at Brașov, Bucharest, Cluj-Napoca, Craiova, Galați, Iași, and Timișoara. Romania also has a technological university and three polytechnic institutes. Health care is free in a system that includes hospitals, clinics, and sanatoriums.

The Arts. Contemporary arts in Romania draw inspiration from European folk traditions and from the prevailing cultural doctrine of socialist realism. The decorative folk medium, with its colorful geometric motifs expressed in wood carvings, textiles, pottery, and architecture, is favored by the government. Renowned artists include Nicolae Grigorescu and Teodor Aman in the 19th century; and Constantin BRANCUSI, Stefan Luchian, and Nicolae Tonitza in the 20th century. Brancusi, who lived most of his life abroad, was an outstanding modern sculptor, and is probably the best-known Romanian artist outside his own country. Georges ENESCO is the founder of the modern school of Romanian music, although the lilting folk melodies remain popular. Important literary figures are discussed in the article ROMANIAN LITERATURE. The government, pursuing a policy of making culture accessible to the people, maintains more than 8,000 culture houses and clubs, in addition to numerous theaters, museums, and libraries.

ECONOMIC ACTIVITY

The Romanian economy is highly centralized and functions within a framework of official plans aimed at transforming Romania from an underdeveloped, agricultural nation into an industrial nation. The country made spectacular advances in the postwar era, achieving growth rates of about 11% annually in some years, the highest in Europe. Rapid industrialization and pressure to increase export earnings, however, have led to severe shortages of consumer items and the imposition of rationing.

Manufacturing. Industry is nationalized, and heavy industry has had the most impressive growth in recent decades. Steel is produced at Galaţi, Oraviţa, Reşiţa, and Steierdorf-Anina. Metallurgy is also important at Hunedoara and Baia-Mare, steel and other metals forming the basis for a rapidly expanding machine-building industry. Further development of the chemical, petroleum, and natural-gas industries is also stressed. Food processing and textile manufacture are the leading light industries.

Power. About 20% of all Romania's electricity is derived from the huge IRON GATE hydroelectric complex, which opened in 1972 and was jointly constructed by Romania and Yugoslavia. The remainder is derived mainly from thermal-electric plants that are fueled by Romania's coal, petroleum, and natural gas. Nuclear power plants are under construction, and as petroleum reserves become exhausted Romania is expected to harness more of its largely undeveloped hydroelectric-power resources. In the 1980s the country did not produce enough energy to meet its needs and therefore experienced frequent power shortages.

Agriculture. More than 90% of agriculture is socialized in cooperative and state farms, and agriculture employs a little more than one-quarter of the total labor force. Agricultural productivity is low, and production quotas are rarely met. Among the factors contributing to this low productivity are underinvestment, inconsistent policies of mechanization, inclement weather conditions, and inefficient administration. The principal crops are corn, wheat, rye, sugar beets, potatoes, vegetables, oils, and fruit. Dairy products, wines and spirits, and prepared meats are also produced in significant amounts.

Forestry and Fishing. Careful harvesting of once-overexploited timber reserves is the basis for important lumber, paper, and furniture industries. Fishing is a minor but expanding economic activity, most of the 127,000-metric-ton (140,000-U.S.-ton) catch coming from the lakes and rivers of the Danube Delta.

Transportation. Long-haul tasks are primarily handled by the railroads; trucks are increasingly used for short-distance hauling. Nearly two-thirds of all roads are unpaved. The oceangoing merchant marine consists of about 100 ships. The leading ports are Constanţa, Brăila, Mangalia, Galaţi, and Tulcea. The Danube is one of the most important inland waterways of Europe. The Danube–Black Sea Canal, begun in 1949 and then abandoned, was finally completed in 1984. The 64-km (40-mi) channel, 7 m (24 ft) deep, flows southeast from Cernavoda, a new port on the Danube, to the recently expanded port of Constanţa.

Trade. Romanian foreign trade has grown and diversified dramatically since the early 1960s. Trade with the USSR and other Communist countries has increased in absolute terms but accounts for a decreasing proportion of total foreign

(Left) *Timber from the forests of the Carpathian Mountains provides the raw material for one of Romania's key industries, the manufacture of paper, pulp, and other wood products for export.* (Below) *This dam on the Danube River, which forms the boundary between Romania and Yugoslavia, was constructed as a joint project by the two nations. Iron Gates 1, the hydroelectric plant served by the dam, generates 2,300 MW of power that is shared equally between the two countries.*

trade. West Germany is a major trading partner, and Romanian trade with Third World countries, especially in the Middle East, is increasing; these developing countries serve as markets for Romania's manufactured goods and as suppliers of needed raw materials. The leading exports are foodstuffs, lumber, fuel, textiles, transportation equipment, machine tools, and pharmaceuticals. The leading imports are machinery, industrial equipment, rolled steel, iron ore, and coke and coking coal. The eighth 5-year plan (1986–90) called for a 52.7% increase in the volume of foreign trade over the period 1981–85.

GOVERNMENT

Political power resides in the Romanian Communist party (RCP), especially its central committee, secretariat, political executive committee, and standing presidium. The highly personalized regime is focused on RCP General Secretary Nicolae CEAUŞESCU and his wife, Elena, who holds the position of first deputy premier. According to the constitution of 1965, legislative power is vested in the Grand National Assembly of 349 deputies, elected for terms of 5 years. Between the assembly's infrequent sessions, the State Council, elected by the assembly, exercises legislative powers. Ordinary administrative powers are vested in the Council of Ministers. The judicial system consists of a supreme court and county, local, and military courts, all of which are elected. People's councils elect local administrative officials at the county and lower levels.

HISTORY

Dacian tribes living in what is now Romania were defeated by Roman Emperor TRAJAN in AD 106, and for the next 165 years the country was the Roman province of Dacia. During that time the native population was Romanized, and the Romanian language developed from spoken Latin. The Romans abandoned the region toward the end of the 3d century, and in subsequent centuries Romania was invaded by Goths, Slavs, and Bulgars. Hungarians occupied TRANSYLVANIA from the 11th century on, and the area maintained essential independence of both the Turks and the Austrians until the end of the 17th century. In 1711, however, Austria secured effective control. The nuclei of modern Romania, the two Danubian states of Walachia and Moldavia, emerged in the 13th and 14th centuries, respectively. Turks established suzerainty in the 15th century, and, despite fierce resistance, the Romanian feudal lords became vassals of the OTTOMAN EMPIRE while maintaining considerable autonomy. Some of these princes, such as MICHAEL THE BRAVE, attempted to defy the Ottomans and to extend the sphere of their control. From 1711 to 1821 governors were appointed by the sultan, with local authority resting with the boyars, the landlords of large estates. During the RUSSO-TURKISH WAR of 1828, Russia occupied Walachia and Moldavia, and although they nominally remained Ottoman possessions, they actually became Russian protectorates.

In 1848 a Romanian rebellion against both foreign and boyar control was suppressed. Following the CRIMEAN WAR, Russian troops vacated Moldavia and Walachia, which were recognized as autonomous principalities under Ottoman suzerainty. In 1859, Alexandru CUZA was elected prince of both principalities, and they were officially united as Romania in 1861–62. Bold sociopolitical reforms took place during Cuza's reign. In 1866, however, he was forced to abdicate and was replaced by Prince Charles of Hohenzollern-Sigmaringen, who led Romania in its War of Independence (1877–78; see BERLIN, CONGRESS OF) from the Ottoman Empire and was crowned (1881) as King CAROL I.

During the next 35 years the state was gradually modernized, and foreign policy was directed toward regaining Transylvania and BESSARABIA, leading to Romania's participation (1913) in the second BALKAN WAR. Carol I was succeeded by his nephew FERDINAND in 1914, and Romania joined World War I against the Central Powers in 1916. With the Allied victory in 1918, postwar Romania's area doubled to 296,400 km² (114,000 mi²) and included the regained territories of Transylvania, Bessarabia, the Banat, and BUCOVINA.

In the years immediately following World War I, extensive land reform and limited democratization of the political process took place. Romania became an active participant in international affairs and was a founding member of the League of Nations and of the LITTLE ENTENTE (1921) and Balkan Entente (1934). In 1938, King CAROL II established a royal dictatorship, but he abdicated when opposition to his rule by groups such as the fascist IRON GUARD led to violence on both sides; Carol II was replaced by his son Michael. The same year Romania was forced to cede Bessarabia to the USSR, northern Transylvania to Hungary, and southern Dobruja to Bulgaria. In 1940 the government passed into the hands of Gen. Ion ANTONESCU, who assumed dictatorial powers, and Romania became allied with the Axis. Romanian forces, joining Adolf Hitler's invasion of the USSR, were defeated, and the USSR invaded Romania. Antonescu was overthrown on Aug. 23, 1944, and Romania reentered World War II on the side of the Allies. Communist groups forced King Michael to accept a pro-USSR government in 1945.

After the war Communist strength increased, and in December 1947, King Michael was forced to abdicate and Romania was proclaimed a people's republic, with Gheorghe GHEORGHIU-DEJ, leader of the Romanian Communist party, as the nation's new leader. He was a loyal follower of the USSR until it became clear during the early 1960s that the USSR wanted to relegate Romania to the status of a perpetually underdeveloped supplier state. In response, Gheorghiu-Dej steered Romania on an increasingly independent course, and in a statement of April 1964 the Romanian leadership declared its economic and political independence from the USSR. Nicolae Ceauşescu, who succeeded Gheorghiu-Dej on

his death in 1965, implemented a policy of independent multilateral socioeconomic development. Although a member of both the COUNCIL FOR MUTUAL ECONOMIC ASSISTANCE (COMECON) and the WARSAW TREATY ORGANIZATION, Romania pursues an active foreign policy independent of the USSR while upholding an orthodox socialist regime in domestic affairs.

WALTER M. BACON, JR.

Bibliography: American University, *Area Handbook for Romania* (1972); Fischer-Galaţi, Stephen A., *New Rumania: From People's Democracy to Socialist Republic* (1967) and *Twentieth Century Rumania* (1970); Gilberg, Trond, *Modernization in Romania since World War II* (1975); Hale, Julian, *Ceauşescu's Romania* (1971) and *The Land and People of Romania* (1972); Ionescu, Ghiţa, *Communism in Romania, 1944-1962* (1964); Jowitt, Kenneth, *Revolutionary Breakthroughs and National Development: The Case of Romania, 1944-1965* (1971); Riker, Thad W., *The Making of Roumania* (1931; repr. 1970); Seton-Watson, Robert W., *History of the Roumanians from Roman Times to the Completion of Unity* (1934; repr. 1963); Thompson, Juliet, *Old Romania* (1977); Turnock, David, *An Economic Geography of Romania* (1971).

Romanian language: see ROMANCE LANGUAGES.

Romanian literature

Romanian literature as the expression of national life in poetry, fiction, and the theater—all in the vernacular of the people—has been in full bloom for only about 150 years. A literary language began to develop before the end of the 16th century with translations of the Bible and other religious works, and during the 17th and 18th centuries this language was used in historical chronicles. For much of the 18th and well into the 19th century, however, high society spoke and wrote Greek, and Romanian literature stagnated.

The expulsion of the Greeks from Romania in 1821 led to a resurgence in national feeling. A modern idiom was developed both for translations, mainly from French, and original writings. Vasile ALECSANDRI supplied the stage with plays, and his collection of folktales helped mold a language capable of poetic expression. The first novels appeared during the 1850s, but the genre did not come of age until publication of Duiliu Zamfirescu's *Viaţa le tară* (Country Life, 1894).

Zamfirescu was among those influenced by the literary critic Titu Maiorescu, who deplored imitations of foreign models. In 1863, Maiorescu had founded the literary circle *Junimea* (Youth) and its journal, *Convorbiri literare* (Literary Conversations), in which, among other writers, the poet EMINESCU and the dramatist CARAGIALE found encouragement and publication.

The standard set by Eminescu for lyric poetry continued into the 20th century, particularly in the works of Tudor Arghezi, Ion Barbu, and Lucian Blaga. Eminent 20th-century novelists include Camil and Cezar Petrescu, Liviu Rebreanu, Mihail Sadoveanu, and, since World War II, Marin Preda. Although written outside of Romania, the fantastic tales of Mircea ELIADE are a part of the now well-established national literature.

ERIC TAPPE

Bibliography: Steinberg, Jacob, ed., *Introduction to Rumanian Literature* (1966); Tappe, Eric Ditmar, ed., *Rumanian Prose and Verse* (1956).

Romanov (dynasty) [roh'-muh-nawf or ruh-mahn'-uhf]

The Romanov dynasty ruled Russia from 1613 until the February Revolution of 1917 (see RUSSIAN REVOLUTIONS OF 1917). The family was descended from Andrei Ivanovich Kobyla, a Muscovite boyar who lived in the first half of the 14th century. The name *Romanov* was taken from Roman Yuriev (d. 1543), the father of Anastasia Romanova (d. 1560), who was the first wife of Tsar IVAN IV.

MICHAEL Romanov, grandnephew of Anastasia, was elected tsar by a National Assembly in 1613; he was the first of the dynasty to rule Russia. Important Romanov rulers included PETER I, whose reign marks the beginning of imperial Russia; CATHERINE II, actually a German who married into the family; ALEXANDER I, who defeated Napoleon in 1812; and ALEXANDER II, who emancipated the serfs in 1861. The last Romanov tsar,

NICHOLAS II, abdicated in March 1917. He and his immediate family were executed (July 1918) at Ekaterinburg (modern Sverdlovsk).   DONALD L. LAYTON

Bibliography: Bergamini, John, *The Tragic Dynasty: The History of the Romanovs* (1969); Cowles, Virginia, *The Romanovs* (1971); Mazour, Anatole G., *Rise and Fall of the Romanovs* (1960).

Romans, Epistle to the

The Epistle to the Romans is the longest of Saint PAUL's letters and is therefore placed first among the letters in the New Testament of the BIBLE. It is the only Pauline letter written to a community not founded by the apostle and is more of an essay presenting some of Paul's ideas on salvation than a response to particular problems. It was probably written about AD 57–58 before Paul departed from Corinth for Jerusalem to deliver the collection he had taken for the church there.

Chapters 1–4 develop in greater detail the theme of justification by faith, which appears in polemical form in GALATIANS. Chapters 5–8 show the effect of salvation on humans. In chapters 9–11, Paul tries to fathom God's plan for the Jews, his chosen people, who have not followed Jesus. The implications for Christian life of Jesus, faith, and salvation are drawn out in chapters 12–15. Chapter 16 is a letter of introduction for the deaconess Phoebe and is thought by many to have been originally a separate letter.

The exact nature and purpose of Romans is controversial, and it is difficult to determine whether it is a theological letter-essay, a last testament, an introduction of Paul to the Roman Christians, or a response to particular problems in Rome that Paul had heard about. Romans is a particularly rich and complex epistle; its teachings on justification, the Jews, and attitudes toward civil government have been debated from the Reformation to the present.   ANTHONY J. SALDARINI

Bibliography: Barrett, Charles K., *A Commentary on the Epistle to the Romans* (1957); Barth, Karl, *The Epistle to the Romans* (1933; repr. 1965); Minear, Paul S., *The Obedience of Faith* (1971).

romanticism   (art)

Romanticism in the visual arts, as in literature and music, is full of disparate and contradictory ideas and is thus difficult to define. Romanticism is not a style but a movement, an attitude of mind, or, as Charles Baudelaire expressed it, "a mode of feeling." Starting in the 1750s, it became a potent force at the turn of the century and lasted until about the 1850s. Romanticism's exact date of death is undetermined, but some historians argue that it has survived into our own century as SURREALISM.

The seeds of romanticism are to be found in an obsessive interest in the art of the past, including the energetic figures in Michelangelo's frescoes, the exuberant colors of Peter Paul Rubens's canvases, the golden idylls of Claude Lorrain's landscapes, and the threatening presence of Salvator Rosa's craggy rocks. In literature, Edmund Burke's *Philosophical Enquiry into the Sublime and Beautiful* (1757) was particularly important for its discussion of the sublime, the frightening and awesome element in nature that produces the aesthetic response of terror, just as the beautiful induces love in the beholder. Critics of the mid-18th century also reevaluated Dante's *Divine Comedy* and Milton's *Paradise Lost* as embodying the sublime as Burke defined it. These two poems, which had previously been undervalued, became two of the most important texts used by romantic artists. Literature, both past and present, was a major source of inspiration for them. If classical texts were chosen, they were often those that included elements of the supernatural, such as the plays of Aeschylus. If Shakespeare was selected, the most likely plays were not the histories, but *The Tempest, Hamlet,* or *A Midsummer Night's Dream.* The epic songs of the Celtic bard Ossian, a largely mythic creation of the Scottish writer James Macpherson, were also popular; they told of heroism and love in a misty and ancient past in the Scottish Highlands. Contemporary literature that inspired romantic artists included the poetry of Lord Byron, Samuel Taylor Coleridge, and Goethe and the novels of Sir Walter Scott.

William Blake derived the subject matter of his visionary paintings and writings from the Bible and other mystical sources. Jacob's Dream (c.1820), a delicate watercolor, one of his characteristic mediums, is Blake's visualization of a biblical passage (Gen. 28:12–18). Although generally unrecognized during most of his lifetime, Blake exerted a powerful influence on later romantic authors and painters. (British Museum, London.)

Romantic artists often wished to break the accepted, rational rules of academic art, allowing a greater role for the uncontrolled, the limitless, the irrational. One of the clearest statements is to be found in William BLAKE's annotations to Sir Joshua REYNOLDS's *Discourses,* which had been delivered at the Royal Academy: "What has Reasoning," Blake demanded, "to do with the Art of Painting? Knowledge of Ideal Beauty is Not to be Acquired. It is Born with us."

The stress on an inner vision as fundamental to romantic artists was expressed by them in a great variety of ways. In Germany, for example, the ethereal beings in the art of Philipp Otto RUNGE are as romantic as the landscapes of Caspar David FRIEDRICH, behind whose trees and mountains lies an elaborate religious symbolism. The reaction of the artist as an individual to his own ideas and to his surroundings was of paramount importance for the romantic artist. If single, characteristic threads can be disentangled from the complex web of romanticism and labeled as valid for all artists, they are those of individualism and introspection.

Exotic subject matter—in place and in time—also appealed to the romantics. The excitement of the people, horses, and lions of North Africa and the barbaric splendor of *The Death of Sardanapalus* (1827–28; Louvre, Paris), the last Assyrian king (Ashurbanipal, 668–626 BC, called Sardanapalus by the Greeks), were all painted by Eugène DELACROIX, that "volcano artistically concealed," according to Baudelaire, "beneath a

The mood of pensive melancholy expressed in Moonrise over the Sea (1823) is frequently found in the work of Caspar David Friedrich. Friedrich typically adopted a reverential approach to the portrayal of nature's grandeur. (Staatliche Museen, West Berlin.)

J. M. W. Turner celebrated the beauty and vigor of nature in such works as Rain, Steam, and Speed—the Great Western Railway *(1844). Turner's treatment of light, color, mass, and atmosphere anticipated that of the later impressionists. (National Gallery, London.)*

bouquet of flowers." Artists and architects alike became fascinated with the primitive, such as Stonehenge, with its circle of stone monoliths, which was associated with the Druids.

The supremacy of neoclassical architecture, as inspired by the achievements of the ancient Greeks, was increasingly questioned. Egyptian, Hindu, Moorish, and Gothic buildings were seen as admirable architectural wonders to be emulated. The absorption of romantic artists in the past and in exotic cultures is reflected in the diversity of architectural styles used in buildings. There was also a great love of ruins, old, or freshly made—as in the Désert de Retz (c.1785), a four-story French mansion constructed in the form of a single fluted column, broken, cracked, and lush with vegetation on its fragmented top. Alongside a taste for the sublime, there was a taste for the picturesque (that which was worthy of a picture) in landscape gardening.

About other themes in romantic art, it becomes increasingly difficult to generalize because opposites may often be set side by side as equally true. Pastoral scenes in morning mist or by moonlight (C. D. FRIEDRICH, Samuel PALMER) were as prized as scenes of storms, avalanches, and disastrous fires (J. M. W. TURNER). Napoleon's campaigns could be com-

Eugène Delacroix's The Death of Sardanapalus *(1827-28) displays romanticism's exotic element. For Delacroix, the representation of historical or imaginary events took precedence over the landscapes and mystical visions favored by some contemporaries. (Louvre, Paris.)*

memorated in superb battle scenes (Baron GROS) or their savagery excoriated (Francisco de GOYA). All these artists may be called romantic, sharing as they do a passion for every aspect of nature and its moods and a fascination with man's potential for violence, which can lead either to glory or to disaster.

DAVID IRWIN

Bibliography: Andrews, Keith, *The Nazarenes* (1964); Brion, Marcel, *Art of the Romantic Era* (1966); Clark, Kenneth M., *The Romantic Rebellion* (1973); Eitner, Lorenz, *Neo-Classicism and Romanticism*, 2 vols. (1970); Honour, Hugh, *Romanticism* (1979); Rosenblum, Robert, *Transformations in Late Eighteenth-Century Art* (1967).

romanticism　(literature)

In European and American literature, romanticism is an aesthetic movement that attained its peak during the first third of the 19th century. Its expression in art and music as well as in literature brought major innovations in attitude and style that proved of far-reaching significance.

The term is derived from medieval romances, which were fanciful tales of larger-than-life adventure and highly colored sentiment. This association with a world of fantasy is fundamental to romanticism. In contrast to REALISM, which aims at a faithful reproduction of reality as perceived by the senses, romanticism attempts to capture the play of the imagination.

The romantic approach is perhaps best illustrated by William BLAKE's response to the question "When the sun rises, do you not see a round disc of fire somewhat like a guinea?" He answered, "Oh no, no. I see an Innumerable company of the Heavenly host crying, 'Holy, Holy, Holy is the Lord God Almighty!'" The physical phenomenon—"a round disc of fire"—is less important to the romantic than the imaginative vision. In this reliance on what Samuel Taylor COLERIDGE in the "Dejection: An Ode" called the "shaping spirit of imagination," romanticism is subjective and intensely idealistic.

Many of the cardinal features of romanticism stem from the primacy of the imagination: irrationalism; exaltation of the exceptional—and creative—individual; religious fervor; fascination with the mysterious and inaccessible (in the historical past or geographically distant and exotic, or in the supernatural); exuberant outpouring of personal feeling; empathy with nature; abundance of imagery; rebellion against traditional social and literary norms; and the longing to break out of the confines of the here-and-now.

English Romanticism. William WORDSWORTH's and Coleridge's *Lyrical Ballads* (1798) are generally thought to mark the formal beginning of English romanticism. In the preface, Wordsworth outlined the "new poetry" that came from "the spontaneous overflow of powerful feelings." English romanticism is distinguished for its lyric poetry: Wordsworth's "The Daffodil" and "Ode on Intimations of Immortality," Coleridge's "Kubla Khan" and "The Rime of the Ancient Mariner," Percy Bysshe SHELLEY's "Ode to the West Wind" and "To a Skylark," and the sonnets of John KEATS. Lord BYRON's epics, *Childe Harold's Pilgrimage* and *Don Juan*, are more satirical in tone. English romanticism is also responsible for important contributions to aesthetic theory, in Coleridge's *Biographia Literaria* (1817) and Shelley's *Defence of Poetry* (1821).

Germany. In Germany aesthetic theory was predominant, particularly with the first generation of romantics, known as the *Frühromantiker* ("early romantics"), who gathered in Berlin and later in Jena during the closing years of the 18th century. The brothers August Wilhelm von SCHLEGEL and Friedrich von SCHLEGEL formulated innovative aesthetic concepts, often presented in paradoxical terms, in their journal *Athenäum*. Under the influence of the philosopher Johann Gottlieb FICHTE, the *Frühromantiker* were metaphysical and mystical in inclination. Their major poets were NOVALIS and Wilhelm Heinrich Wackenroder (1773-98), both of whom died young, and Ludwig TIECK.

The second generation of German romantics, the *Hochromantiker* ("high romantics"), centered in Heidelberg between 1802 and 1815, were more practical and creative. Their work includes the folk songs and lyrics of Achim von ARNIM, Clemens BRENTANO, Heinrich HEINE, Eduard MÖRIKE, and Johann

Ludwig UHLAND, and the tales of Adelbert von CHAMISSO, Joseph EICHENDORFF, Ernst Theodor Amadeus HOFFMANN, and Heinrich August de La Motte-Fouqué (1777–1843).

France. Romanticism flowered later in France (as it did in Spain and Italy), not reaching its height until the end of the 1820s, the '30s, and even the '40s, when its force had weakened in England and Germany. The advent of romanticism in the southern European countries was delayed primarily by an established classical tradition that resisted the new modes of romanticism, and secondarily by the political turmoil following the French Revolution and the Napoleonic Wars.

Bitter controversies involving political and religious loyalties accompanied the emergence of romanticism in France, the main strife taking place in the theater and culminating in the notorious battle between the warring factions on the opening night of Victor HUGO's *Hernani* (1830). Hugo, Alexandre DUMAS *père,* and Alfred de MUSSET all used William Shakespeare as a model to effect the departure from accepted classical practices. The lyric poetry of Alphonse de LAMARTINE, Musset, and Hugo was romantic in its pronounced personal emotionality.

The United States. Romanticism was never as recognizably a movement in the United States as it was in Europe. The closest approximation to European romanticism was the New England TRANSCENDENTALISM of Ralph Waldo EMERSON and Henry David THOREAU. Other American writers, however, shared the belief in the importance of the creative imagination, among them Nathaniel HAWTHORNE, Henry Wadsworth LONGFELLOW, Herman MELVILLE, Edgar Allan POE, and Walt WHITMAN.

Other Movements. Although romanticism was superseded by realism as the dominant literary mode by the middle of the 19th century, it keeps resurfacing in varying forms. SYMBOLISM is clearly a direct descendant of romanticism in its advocacy of the imagination and in the central role it assigns to the symbolic image. AESTHETICISM is another descendant, as are, somewhat more distantly, such movements as SURREALISM, IMPRESSIONISM, and DADA. All spring from a belief in the imagination as the highest creative faculty, however bizarre the outcome.

In this sense, romanticism is more than a 19th-century movement; in emphasizing the primacy of the imagination over the intellect, it is a term for an artistic tendency that, in opposition to CLASSICISM, will probably continue to ebb and flow throughout the history of literature.   LILIAN R. FURST

Bibliography: Barzun, Jacques, *Romanticism and the Modern Ego* (1944); Bowra, Maurice, *The Romantic Imagination* (1950); Furst, Lilian

Joseph Severn painted Shelley near the Baths of Caracalla (1819) during Shelley's sojourn in Rome. During that visit Shelley wrote acts 2 and 3 of Prometheus Unbound (1820), one of the great lyrical dramas of the romantic period. (Keats-Shelley Memorial House, Rome.)

Josef Danhauser's portrayal of some of the leading figures of the romantic movement includes (left to right): *Alexandre Dumas père, Victor Hugo, George Sand, Niccolò Paganini, Gioacchino Rossini, Franz Liszt, Marie d'Agoult, Byron, and Beethoven.*

R., *Romanticism,* 2d ed. (1976); Gleckner, R. F., and Enscoe, G. E., eds., *Romanticism: Points of View,* 2d ed. (1970); Halsted, John B., *Romanticism: Definition, Explanation, and Evaluation* (1965) and, as ed., *Romanticism: A Collection of Documents* (1968); Jones, Howard M., *Revolution and Romanticism* (1974); Peyre, Henri, *What Is Romanticism?,* trans. by Roda P. Roberts (1976); Quennell, Peter, *Romantic England: Writing and Painting, 1717–1851* (1970); Thorlby, A. K., *The Romantic Movement* (1966); Wellek, René, *Concepts of Criticism* (1963).

romanticism   (music)

Although the romantic musical style was anticipated by some composers as early as the mid-18th century, romanticism in music usually is thought to have begun in the early 19th century and to have continued until about 1890. It thus followed the classical period and preceded postromanticism, which extends to about 1920.

Some critics have objected to the application of the term *romanticism* to music. Nevertheless, the deep interest that 19th-century composers took in setting romantic poems to music and using romantic novels and dramas as the subject matter for operas and symphonic poems gives validity to the idea of the interpenetration of the arts as a characteristic of romantic expression. Many themes of romanticism—the cult of youth, individualism, emphasis on becoming rather than being, intensity and extremes of feeling, love of nature, alienation, nationalism, idealism—find their expression also in the music of the time.

The Austrian composer Franz Schubert was a pivotal figure in the transition from classicism to romanticism in musical composition during the early 1800s. Working out of the classical tradition, Schubert developed the expressive melodies and emotionalism that became identified with romantic music. Romanticism was most fully expressed in Schubert's lieder, songs based on the verses of such German romantic poets as Goethe and Heine.

Frédéric Chopin, the most prominent composer of romantic piano music, masterfully exploited the tonal and expressive range of the piano, fully establishing it as an instrument for solo performance. Chopin used subtle chromatic progressions and lyrical melodies in a vast number of compositions ranging from lively mazurkas to melancholy nocturnes. Chopin was a member of the second generation of romantic composers writing during the mid-19th century.

The operatic works of the German composer Richard Wagner marked the culmination of romanticism, fusing music and drama in an expressive unity unsurpassed in musical history. By using such techniques as the leitmotiv, a germinal musical passage associated with a particular person or situation that recurs throughout the opera, Wagner brought his subject and the music into close dramatic rapport. Wagner drew on Germanic legend, as in The Ring of the Nibelungs *(1853–74).*

Certain characteristics distinguish romantic music from its classical forebears and from its modern successors: long, expressive melodies, usually with wide leaps and based on consonant intervals; emphasis on colorful harmony and instrumentation, often for their own sake; freedom and flexibility in rhythm and treatment of musical form; expansion of the resources of musical nuance; a sense of historicism that led many composers to revive earlier technical musical devices; and the pervasiveness of tonality, though treated with increasing flexibility, as the basic organizing principle of music.

Romantic musical styles were anticipated in the mid-18th century in the music of Carl Philipp Emanuel BACH, who influenced the classical composers Haydn and Mozart. This is most notable in their compositions in the minor mode. Such works as Mozart's D minor and C minor piano concertos exhibited in turn some of the devices of the romantic music to come. Beethoven, who dominated the musical world of the early 19th century, has been considered too seminal a composer to be classified as either classical or romantic. Contemporaries such as SCHUBERT, SPOHR, and WEBER, however, may with more justification be considered the first generation of romantic composers, although many of their earlier works remain in the classical tradition.

The succeeding generation of musical romantics included such composers as BERLIOZ, BERWALD, CHOPIN, GLINKA, LISZT, MENDELSSOHN, SCHUMANN, VERDI, and WAGNER, some of whom lived well into the second half of the 19th century. Whereas most cultural historians consider the movement known as romanticism to have ended with the failure of the revolutions of 1848–49, musical romanticism continued to flourish for many years. Within that broad grouping, however, many distinct developmental trends could be discerned. The major romantic composers all exhibited self-expressive traits, but some tended to work more within the Western mainstream of classically derived forms and harmonic systems. Schumann and later romantics such as BRAHMS, DVOŘÁK, FRANCK, SAINT-SAËNS, and TCHAIKOVSKY may be included in their number. Other composers were more interested in expanding the structural, orchestral, and harmonic resources of music. Wagner and Liszt both were major innovators who influenced the course of music for generations, counting among their followers such late romantic figures as BRUCKNER, MAHLER, RIMSKY-KORSAKOV, SCRIABIN, and Richard STRAUSS. Musical nationalism making use of folk-music idioms was concurrently developing among the late romantics, as exhibited in the music of composers such as GRIEG, MUSSORGSKY, and SMETANA.

No clear line can be drawn between figures such as Wagner and Mahler and the development of various postromantic styles, including the impressionism of DEBUSSY and the serialism of SCHOENBERG. Romanticism itself has remained one of many musical resources for 20th-century composers such as

PROKOFIEV, SHOSTAKOVICH, SIBELIUS, and, more recently, some of the composers who have reacted against serialism and sought a more eclectic musical language.   R. M. LONGYEAR

Bibliography: Abraham, Gerald, *A Hundred Years of Music*, 3d ed. (1964); Blume, Friedrich, *Classic and Romantic Music* (1970); Donakowski, Conrad L., *A Muse for the Masses: Ritual and Music in an Age of Democratic Revolution, 1770–1870* (1977); Einstein, Alfred, *Music in the Romantic Era* (1947); Grout, Donald, *A History of Western Music*, 2d ed. (1979); Kirby, F. E., ed., *Music in the Romantic Period: An Anthology* (1986); Klaus, Kenneth, *The Romantic Period in Music* (1970); Longyear, R. M., *Nineteenth-Century Romanticism in Music*, 2d ed. (1973); Newman, William, *The Sonata since Beethoven* (1969); Plantinga, Leon, *Romantic Music* (1985); Tovey, Donald, *Essays in Musical Analysis* (1935–45).

Romany language: see INDO-IRANIAN LANGUAGES.

Romberg, Sigmund [rahm'-berg]

One of the most popular American composers of light music, Hungarian-born Sigmund Romberg, b. July 29, 1887, d. Nov. 10, 1951, brought the traditions of European operetta to the American theater. He wrote the music for many of Broadway's best-known operettas, including *Maytime* (1917), *Blossom Time* (1921), *The Student Prince* (1924), *The Desert Song* (1926), and *The New Moon* (1928). Romberg later turned to musical comedy with *Up in Central Park* (1945), and, from 1929, he also wrote music for films.   DAVID EWEN

Bibliography: Arnold, Elliott, *Deep in My Heart* (1949); Green, Stanley, *World of Musical Comedy*, 2d ed. (1974); Traubner, Richard, *Operetta: A Theatrical History* (1983).

Rome (Italy)

Rome (Italian: Roma), once the seat of a vast empire, is now the capital of Italy and the seat of the supreme pontiff of the Roman Catholic church (at VATICAN CITY, a sovereign state within Rome). The city is also the capital of Italy's Rome province and LATIUM region. Located in central Italy on both sides of the Tiber River between the Apennine Mountains and the Tyrrhenian Sea (27 km/17 mi to the west), the city was originally situated there because it is the first easy crossing of the Tiber upstream from the sea. The city of Rome has a population of 2,830,650 (1984 est.), and 3,115,000 persons (1980) live in the metropolitan area. The city covers an area of 1,507 km² (582 mi²).

CONTEMPORARY CITY

The Tiber, flowing through Rome from north to south, divides the city. On the east bank, the most visible and plentiful remains of classical Rome are located south of Piazza Venezia. To the northwest and along the Tiber, medieval Rome centers on the area between the Via del Corso and the Corso Vittorio

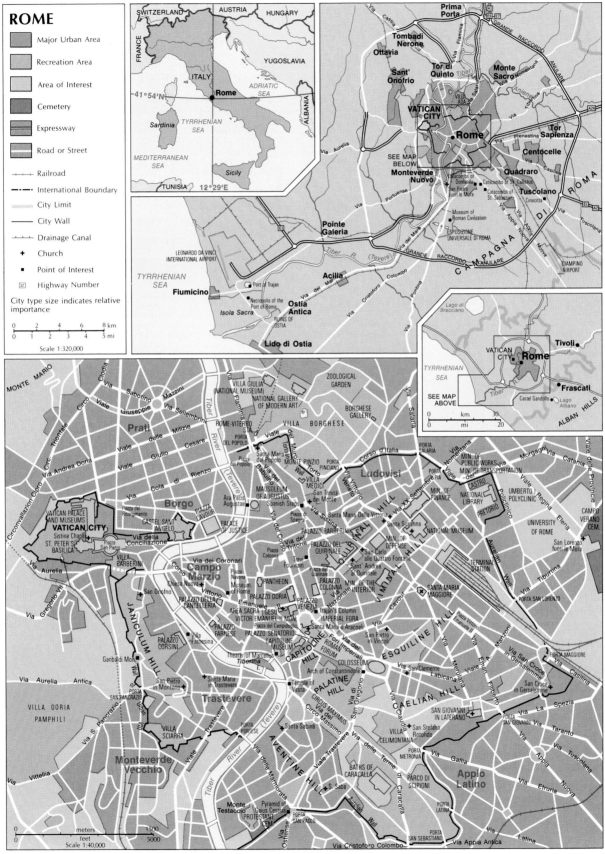

ROME

▨	Major Urban Area
▨	Recreation Area
▨	Area of Interest
▨	Cemetery
▨	Expressway
▨	Road or Street

┼┼┼┼	Railroad
─·─·─	International Boundary
▬▬	City Limit
───	City Wall
┼┼┼┼	Drainage Canal
✚	Church
■	Point of Interest
32	Highway Number

City type size indicates relative importance

0   2   4   6   8 km
0   1   2   3   4   5 mi
Scale 1:320,000

Inset map (Italy):
SWITZERLAND AUSTRIA HUNGARY
FRANCE
ITALY YUGOSLAVIA
41°54'N
ADRIATIC SEA
Rome
Sardinia TYRRHENIAN SEA ALBANIA
MEDITERRANEAN SEA
Sicily
TUNISIA 12°29'E

Rome metropolitan inset:
Prima Porta
Tombadi Nerone
Ottavia
Sant' Onofrio
Tor di Quinto
Monte Sacro
VATICAN CITY
Rome
Tor Sapienza
Centocelle
SEE MAP BELOW
Monteverde Nuovo
Quadraro
Tuscolano
Catacombs of Domitilla
San Pietro fuori le Mura
Catacombs of St. Callistus
Catacombs of St. Sebastian
Cinecittà
Museum of Roman Civilization
ESPOSIZIONE UNIVERSALE DI ROMA
Pointe Galeria
GRANDE RACCORDO ANULARE
CAMPAGNA DI ROMA
CIAMPINO AIRPORT
GRANDE RACCORDO ANULARE

Coastal inset:
TYRRHENIAN SEA
LEONARDO DA VINCI INTERNATIONAL AIRPORT
Tiber R. (Tevere)
Fiumicino
Port of Trajan
Necropolis of the Port of Rome
Isola Sacra
RUINS OF OSTIA
Acilia
Ostia Antica
Lido di Ostia
Cristoforo Colombo

Region inset:
Lago di Bracciano
VATICAN CITY
Rome
Tivoli
TYRRHENIAN SEA
SEE MAP ABOVE
Castel Gandolfo
Lago Albano
Frascati
ALBAN HILLS
0   km   30
0   mi   20

Main city map labels:
MONTE MARIO
Prati
Borgo
VATICAN PALACE AND MUSEUMS
VATICAN CITY
Sistine Chapel
ST. PETER'S BASILICA
VILLA BARBERINI
JANICULUM HILL
VILLA DORIA PAMPHILI
Monteverde Vecchio
VILLA GIULIA (NATIONAL MUSEUM)
NATIONAL GALLERY OF MODERN ART
ZOOLOGICAL GARDEN
BORGHESE GALLERY
VILLA BORGHESE
ROME-VITERBO STA.
PORTA DEL POPOLO
Piazza del Popolo
Santa Maria del Popolo
MONTE PINZIO
VILLA MEDICI
Spanish Steps
MAUSOLEUM OF AUGUSTUS
Ara Pacis Augustae
CASTEL SANT' ANGELO
PALACE OF JUSTICE
PIAZZA CAVOUR
Campo Marzio
PANTHEON
Museum of Rome
Chiesa Nuova
San Onofrio
PALAZZO DELLA CANCELLERIA
PALAZZO FARNESE
PALAZZO CORSINI
Villa Farnesina
Theater of Marcellus
Tiberina I.
Garibaldi Mon.
San Pietro in Montorio
Santa Maria in Trastevere
Trastevere
PORTA SAN PANCRAZIO
VILLA SCIARRA
Monte Testaccio
Pyramid of Caius Cestius
PROTESTANT CEM.
PORTA SAN PAOLO
Santa Sabina
S. Saba
AVENTINE HILL
CIRCUS MAXIMUS (Circo Massimo)
BATHS OF CARACALLA
PALATINE HILL
CAPITOLINE HILL
CAPITOLINE MUSEUM
PALAZZO SENATORIO
Santa Maria d'Aracoeli
Fori Imperiali
IMPERIAL FORA
Trajan's Column
VICTOR EMANUEL II MON.
Piazza del Campidoglio
ROMAN FORUM
Arch of Constantinople
COLOSSEUM
Temple of Vesta
PALAZZO VENEZIA
PALAZZO DORIA
PALAZZO COLONNA
Piazza Navona
Trevi Fountain
Piazza di Spagna
San Trinità dei Monti
Santa Susanna
QUIRINAL HILL
PALAZZO DEL QUIRINALE
PALAZZO BARBERINI
MIN. OF DEFENSE
Sant' Andrea al Quirinale
San Carlo alle Quattro Fontane
MIN. OF THE INTERIOR
Ludovisi
CASTRO PRETORIO
NATIONAL LIBRARY
MIN. OF FINANCE
MIN. OF PUBLIC WORKS
MIN. OF TRANSPORTATION
PORTA SALARIA
PORTA PIA
NATIONAL MUSEUM
SANTA MARIA MAGGIORE
VIMINAL HILL
TERMINAL STATION
UMBERTO I POLYCLINIC
UNIVERSITY OF ROME
CAMPO VERANO CEM.
San Lorenzo fuori le Mura
PORTA SAN LORENZO
ESQUILINE HILL
San Pietro in Vincoli
Piazza Vittorio Emanuele II
PORTA MAGGIORE
Santa Croce in Gerusalemme
CAELIAN HILL
SAN GIOVANNI IN LATERANO
San Stefano Rotondo
VILLA CELIMONTANA
PORTA METRONIA
PARCO DI SCIPIONI
Baths of Caracalla
PORTA LATINA
Appio Latino
PORTA SAN SEBASTIANO
Via Appia Antica
Via Cristoforo Colombo

0   meters   1500
0   feet   5000
Scale 1:40,000

Compilation and Design by Lothar Roth & Associates

Rome, the capital of Italy and one of the world's richest cultural centers, blends modern development with ancient and Renaissance monuments. The baroque Piazza de Spagna (foreground) and Saint Peter's Basilica (background) are among the city's famous sights.

Ruins of the Appian Way, one of the first great highways built (312 BC) by the Romans, are found in the vicinity of the catacombs outside Rome. Used principally for military purposes, the highway linked Rome with conquered territories in southern Italy.

Emmanuele. During the 16th century Pope SIXTUS V began the modern transformation in the area east of the Via del Corso. Here were built the Vatican and Lateran palaces; new, wide streets; and the many squares, fountains, statues, and palaces for which Rome is famous. On the west bank of the Tiber are Vatican City and Trastevere, which has maintained much of its medieval charm.

Economic Activity and Transportation. The economy of Rome depends heavily on tourism. Industry includes metallurgy, electronics, and glass, cement, and furniture manufacturing. Rome is the financial, cultural, transportation, and administrative center of Italy. The banking, insurance, printing, publishing, and fashion industries are quite important. The thriving Italian movie industry is centered at Cinecittà (Cinema City), located a few miles outside of Rome.

Rome is an important transportation center, with four major railway stations (including the main Termini station) and two international airports—Ciampino (an older airport, southeast of the city) and Leonardo da Vinci (the newer facility, to the southwest) at Fiumicino. The city's subway system, Metropolitana, was opened in 1952; a second line was begun in 1975.

Government and Communications. The city's government consists of a mayor (*sindaco*), an 80-member legislative city council, and a 14-member city advisory board (selected from the city council membership to implement the council's legislation). All these officials are popularly elected every 4 years.

Fourteen daily newspapers are published in Rome (the leading paper is the conservative *Il Messaggero*), and the two state-owned television channels and three radio channels operate there. The Vatican publishes its own newspaper, *L'Osservatore Romano,* and operates its own radio station, Radio Vatican.

Educational, Cultural, and Historic Landmarks. The state-run University of Rome (1303; see ROME, UNIVERSITY OF) has an enrollment of 150,000 students. In addition, Rome has several church-run colleges; academies of fine arts; and the Conservatorio di Musica Santa Cecilia (1570), the oldest music academy in the world.

Many of Rome's museums are among the world's greatest. The VATICAN MUSEUMS AND GALLERIES contain the richest collections. Other great classical collections are housed in the National and Capitoline museums; magnificent paintings are in the Borghese, Corsini, Doria, and Colonna collections. Rome's

opera house is one of Europe's finest. Rome has more than 30 km² (12 mi²) of public gardens and parks.

The city's ancient ruins include the COLOSSEUM, the CATACOMBS, the FORUM, the Arch of Constantine, the Baths of Caracalla, the Circus Maximus, the Capitol, and the Pantheon. The many palaces include CASTEL SANT'ANGELO, the VATICAN PALACE (in which is the SISTINE CHAPEL), Villa Farnesina, Villa Borghese, Palazzo Doria, Palazzo Barberini, and Palazzo Corsini.

Rome is well known for its many piazzas (squares), including the Popolo, Spagna, Colonna, Quirinale, and Campidoglio. The numerous churches include SAINT PETER'S BASILICA, San Giovanni in Laterano, San Paolo Fuori le Mura, and Santa Maria Maggiore. The monument to Victor Emmanuel II commemorates the unification of Italy in the 19th century.

HISTORY

Continuous settlements probably began about 1000 BC on Rome's future site—around the fording point of the Tiber and in the surrounding hills that (unlike other low-lying areas of Latium) were free of malaria. Probably by the 6th century BC several separate tribal settlements, including those of the LATINS and SABINES, had coalesced to form a single city. This early city was built on seven hills; CAPITOLINE HILL and the Palatine Hill (nearest the east bank of the Tiber) were the first site of the city, and between them was the Roman Forum. Farther out, the Aventine, Caelian, Esquiline, Viminal, and Quirinal hills provided vital protection to the city. The city eventually became the capital of the Roman Empire (see ROME, ANCIENT).

During the 5th century AD the city entered a decline and was sacked (410) by the Visigoths under ALARIC I and by the Vandals (455). Temporal political and social authority in the city of Rome gradually devolved upon the pope, or bishop of Rome, who began to claim primacy among western bishops.

During the 6th to early 8th century the city was the center of the duchy of Rome, a Byzantine fief. In 754 the popes, with Frankish aid, were able to assert their independence and hegemony over a large portion of central Italy called the PAPAL STATES, with Rome as their capital. Rome suffered, nevertheless, a severe decline during the Middle Ages. The city became the scene of power struggles between Rome's leading families, especially the Orsini and Colonna, the papacy, and secular rulers. During the 12th century ARNOLD OF BRESCIA challenged papal authority, and his movement successfully exiled Pope EUGENE III and established a commune (1144-45) until Holy Roman Emperor FREDERICK I intervened. Factional struggles such as that between the GUELPHS AND GHIBELLINES continued during the 13th century. When the papacy was removed to Avignon, France, during the 14th century, Rome experienced one of its most serious declines.

Rome began its great recovery under papal guidance during the second half of the 15th century. By the mid-16th century the city saw numerous new and splendid buildings constructed and ancient monuments rebuilt as art and architecture enjoyed a renaissance. Growth continued in the later 16th century as population steadily increased, and Rome again became a premier world city. In 1870, when the Papal States joined the newly created Kingdom of Italy, Rome, the capital, had a population exceeding 225,000 inhabitants. The LATERAN TREATY created (1929) the separate state of Vatican City within the city, and, being the papal city, Rome escaped damage during World War II.   DANIEL R. LESNICK

Bibliography: Chamberlain, Russell, *Rome* (1976); Elling, Christian, *Rome: The Biography of Its Architecture from Bernini to Thorvaldsen* (1975; repr. 1976); Simon, Kate, *Rome: Places and Pleasures* (1972).

Rome (New York)

Rome is an industrial city in central New York on the Mohawk River and the New York State Barge Canal. It has a population of 43,826 (1980). The city is an agricultural distribution center and manufactures machinery, metal products, and paint. It was laid out as Lynchville in 1786 when Dominick Lynch purchased land on the site of Fort Stanwix (1758), now a national monument. In 1768, Sir William Johnson concluded an important treaty with the Iroquois Nations at the fort. During the American Revolution Fort Stanwix was besieged (1777) by a British force under Barry St. Leger. An American relief force led by Nicolas HERKIMER was ambushed at nearby Oriskany and forced to retreat, but rumors that Benedict Arnold was approaching with a large Revolutionary force caused the British to abandon the siege (see SARATOGA, BATTLES OF). Rome flourished as a result of construction of the Erie Canal, begun there in 1817.

Rome, ancient

Ancient Rome grew from a small prehistoric settlement on the Tiber River in Latium in central Italy into an empire that encompassed all of the Mediterranean world. The Romans developed a civilization that formed the basis for modern Western civilization. The history of Rome comprises three major epochs: the kingship from the legendary foundation of Rome to 509 BC; the republic from 509 BC to 31 BC; and the empire, which survived until Rome finally fell to the German chieftain Odoacer in AD 476.

The genius of the Romans lay in the military, in government administration, and in the law. Decisive but cautious imperialists, they valued crafty diplomacy as much as military discipline. The Romans conquered Greece, adopting Greek culture and transmitting it to the medieval world. Unlike the Greeks, they did not develop a philosophical theory of state and society; they were the practitioners of power and law. Roman civil law, which reached its peak under the emperors, excelled in precision of formulation and logic of thought; but it was a law of inequality and social prejudice, and that also became part of the Roman heritage.

EARLY ROME: THE KINGSHIP

According to legend, Rome was founded by descendants of AENEAS, a Trojan who fled to Italy after the fall of Troy. Two of those descendants were ROMULUS AND REMUS, twin brothers who were abandoned at birth and suckled by a bitch wolf. The brothers founded a town on the Palatine, one of the seven hills of Rome, and ruled it jointly for a while. They eventually quarreled, and Romulus killed his brother, becoming the sole ruler. According to tradition, Rome was founded on Apr. 21, 753 BC; the ancient Romans celebrated the anniversary of that day, and it is still a national holiday in Italy.

The earliest traces of human habitation in the territory of the city of Rome date from the Bronze Age (c.1500 BC), but archaeological evidence for continuity of settlement dates

This bronze sculpture group portrays a she-wolf suckling the twins Romulus and Remus, who were the children of Rhea Silvia and the god Mars. According to legend, Romulus founded (753 BC) Rome after killing his brother, Remus, and became the first of seven legendary kings who ruled Rome before the founding (509 BC) of the republic. (Palazzo dei Conservatori, Rome.)

only from the 8th century. That evidence indicates the coexistence of LATINS and SABINES, two different but closely related peoples. Although the Sabines spoke Oscan, Latin appears to have been the language of Rome from its earliest beginnings.

In the 7th century the Latin and Sabine villages coalesced to form a unified city on the eastern, or left, bank of the Tiber, about 24 km (15 mi) from its mouth. It was protected by strongholds on its hills, and it controlled the Tiber ford and the trade route to the central uplands. Rome soon outstripped other towns in Latium in wealth and power.

The Latin Kings. According to later historians, who often freely mixed facts with legend, Romulus was succeeded as king by Numa Pompilius (c.715–673 BC). Numa's reign was long and peaceful, and the foundations of Roman law and religious practices are credited to him. The fourth king, according to tradition, was Ancus Marcius (r. 641–616), who is credited with founding the plebeian class and with building the first bridge across the Tiber; the latter feat allowed the Romans to extend their dominions westward toward the sea.

The Etruscan Kings. In the late 7th century the ETRUSCANS, an advanced people from Etruria, to the northwest of Latium, placed members of their royal family, the Tarquins, on the Roman throne. The Etruscan kings were Lucius TARQUINIUS PRISCUS (Tarquin the Elder), Servius Tullius (r. c.578–535), and Lucius TARQUINIUS SUPERBUS (Tarquin the Proud). The Etruscans are generally credited with expanding the power and influence of Rome. Under their rule the marshes were drained, a large part of Latium was brought under Rome, and the Capitoline temple, the Circus Maximus, and the ancient Forum were built.

According to tradition, it was Sextus Tarquinius, the son of Tarquinius Superbus, who brought down the dynasty. His rape of LUCRETIA, a virtuous matron, supposedly turned the Romans against the Etruscan rulers. For whatever reason, the father, Tarquinius Superbus, was expelled in 510 BC. The Roman Senate (see SENATE, ROMAN), which had originated as an advisory body to the monarch, decreed that Rome should have no more kings.

THE REPUBLIC

The Roman republic, founded, according to tradition, in 509 BC, had an aristocratic form of government. It was headed by the Senate and by magistrates, later called CONSULS—usually two in number—who were elected annually by the Senate.

The Patricians versus the Plebeians. The Senate was made up of the PATRICIANS—the upper class; the general body of citizens—the PLEBEIANS—were effectively frozen out of government. In the early 5th century the plebeians revolted and forced the Senate to accept their representatives, the TRIBUNES, into the government.

In 445 BC the ban on intermarriage between the patricians and plebeians was removed. Gradually the plebeians gained admission to virtually all state offices, winning the consulship in 366. The struggle between the orders lasted for 200 years; it came to an end in 287 when the plebiscites—the laws voted by the assembly of the plebeians—became binding on all people, plebeians and patricians alike. The main benefactors of that development were the few plebeian families that gained riches and offices and mixed with the patricians to form a new governing class, called the nobility.

The Conquest of Italy. Despite internal political conflict, Rome under the early republic continued to expand. The Romans warred with the Latin League (made up of other cities in Latium), but in 493, Rome concluded an alliance with the league. In time Rome dominated all Latium. With the help of the Latins the republic defeated various mountain tribes that pressed in on Latium. In 396 they destroyed the Etruscan city of Veii. A foreign calamity soon overtook Rome, however: tribes from GAUL crossed the Alps, shattered the Etruscan defenses, and sacked Rome in 390. Through perseverance and luck, combined with military prowess and cunning diplomacy, the Romans were able to reestablish their position. When the other Latin cities tried to assert their independence, Rome defeated them in the Latin War (340–338) and dissolved their league. The Romans fought intermittent wars (343–290) with the SAMNITES.

The Romans profited from the disunity among their adversaries. Although the Samnites, the Umbrians, the Etruscans, and even the Gauls belatedly united forces, they were crushed (295) at Sentinum (present Sassoferrato). Conflicts with Tarentum (modern Taranto), a Greek city in southern Italy, followed (282–272). PYRRHUS, the Greek king of Epirus, came to the aid of the Tarentines, scoring two victories against Rome but suffering heavy losses. He finally departed

This detail from a frieze (c.330–310 BC) in the Tomb of the Warrior at Porta Aurea, Paestum, depicts Samnite warriors returning from battle. The Samnite Wars (343–290 BC) extended Roman territorial control into Campania and central Italy. (Museo Nazionale, Naples.)

from Italy in 275. With the capture of Tarentum in 272 the Roman conquest of Italy was nearly completed.

To consolidate their hold on southern and central Italy, the Romans perfected two methods; first, they planted Roman and Latin military colonies on lands that they confiscated. Second, they awarded complete Roman citizenship only to some cities and tribes—as a reward for speedy romanization and faithfulness to Rome. Other cities and tribes had limited citizenship imposed on them; they were forced to conclude a perpetual alliance with Rome and to provide soldiers for Roman wars, and they were deprived of an independent foreign policy. In 264, Roman Italy comprised about 135,000 km² (52,000 mi²), inhabited by 292,000 Roman (male) citizens, and about 700,000 Roman allies.

The First and Second Punic Wars. After the conquest of Italy, Rome encountered new rivals abroad. CARTHAGE, a wealthy Phoenician, or Punic, city in North Africa, had built up a maritime empire that extended to Sardinia, Corsica, and part of Sicily. Competition between Rome and Carthage over the island of Sicily, the great producer of grain for the Mediterranean area, led to the PUNIC WARS.

The First Punic War (264–241) arose from a conflict over the Sicilian cities of Messana (modern Messina) and Syracuse.

The Romans invaded Sicily, but Carthage controlled the seas around it. Although they were not a seafaring people, the Romans built a fleet and defeated the Carthaginians in several battles. Time and again, however, the Roman fleets were wrecked by the elements. In 241 the Romans finally routed the Carthaginians, off the Aegates (now Egadi) Islands near the western tip of Sicily. Carthage was forced to surrender Sicily and agreed to pay a huge indemnity. Rome became a world power, but the price was high: about 20 percent of its citizens were killed in the war.

Nevertheless, the Romans continued to expand; they seized Sardinia and Corsica in 238. Carthage protested but was forced to pay an additional indemnity. In 237 the Carthaginian general HAMILCAR BARCA was sent to Spain, where he conquered large areas. The Romans regarded that conquest as a challenge and decided to invade Spain and Africa, but another Carthaginian general, HANNIBAL, forestalled their scheme. The Second Punic War (218–201) had begun. In a daring march from Spain, Hannibal crossed the Pyrenees, southern Gaul, and the Alps and in the autumn of 218 moved down into Italy. The Romans were routed at Trebia (218), at Lake Trasimene (217), and at Cannae in southern Italy (216), where the Romans sustained especially heavy losses. The Gauls in northern Italy—only recently conquered by the Romans (225–220)—had now rallied to Hannibal, and now the Samnites and many other peoples of southern Italy also abandoned Rome.

The Romans refused to accept defeat, however. They never again risked a pitched battle; instead the Roman general Quintus Fabius Maximus (see FABIUS family) devised a brilliant strategy of delay and harassment that eventually wore down the Carthaginians. The Romans also sent an army to Spain and managed to cut Hannibal off from any reinforcements. The tide of war turned in 210, when the command in

The Roman general Scipio Africanus Major assumed command (216 BC) of the Roman forces in Spain during the Second Punic War. The three Punic Wars were fought against Carthage. In the first war (264–241 BC) Rome seized Sicily from Carthaginian control. During the second war (218–201 BC) the Romans withstood an invasion of Italy by the Carthaginian general Hannibal and, under Scipio's command, expelled the Carthaginians from Spain and invaded Africa to defeat Hannibal. In the third war (149–146 BC) Carthage was razed.

Spain was assumed by Publius Cornelius Scipio, later called SCIPIO AFRICANUS MAJOR. He twice defeated the Carthaginians and terminated their rule in Spain; in 204 he led the Roman invasion of Africa. The Carthaginian government recalled Hannibal, who left behind him a ravaged Italy and the memory of splendid but futile victories. The Carthaginians were finally beaten at Zama in 202, when, at the hands of Scipio, Hannibal suffered his only defeat. The walls of Carthage were impregnable, and Scipio advocated leniency. Carthage surrendered its fleet, paid an enormous indemnity, and became a dependent ally of Rome.

The Macedonian and Syrian Wars. In addition to Carthage, Rome had to contend with another foreign enemy—Macedo-

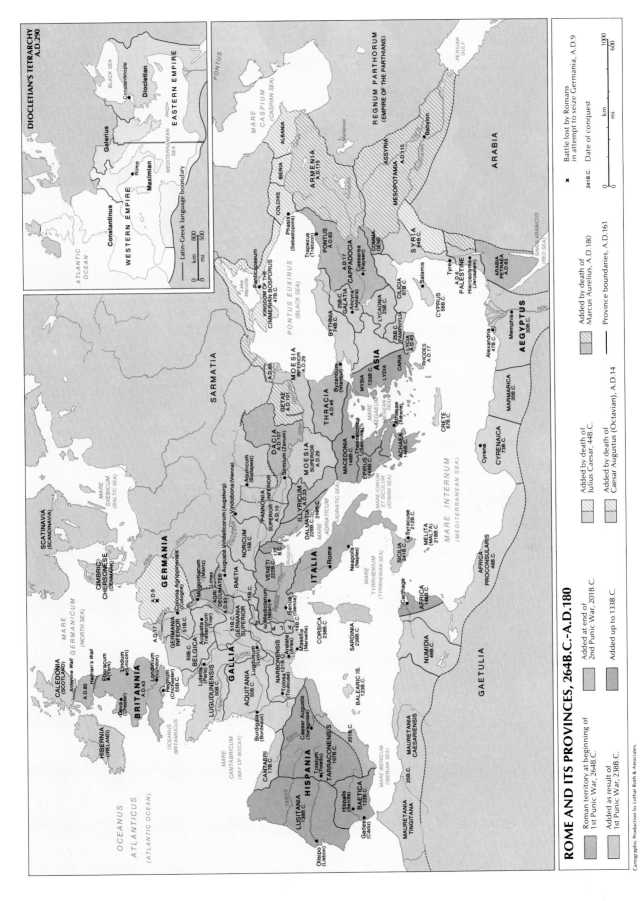

ROME AND ITS PROVINCES, 264B.C.-A.D.180

Roman territory at beginning of 1st Punic War, 264B.C.

Added as result of 1st Punic War, 238B.C.

Added at end of 2nd Punic War, 201B.C.

Added up to 133B.C.

Added by death of Julius Caesar, 44B.C.

Added by death of Caesar Augustus (Octavian), A.D.14

Added by death of Marcus Aurelius, A.D.180

Province boundaries, A.D.161

Latin-Greek language boundary

× Battle lost by Romans in attempt to seize Germania, A.D.9

241B.C. Date of conquest

DIOCLETIAN'S TETRARCHY A.D.290

WESTERN EMPIRE — Constantinus, Maximian
EASTERN EMPIRE — Diocletian, Galerius

Cartographic Production by Lothar Roth & Associates.

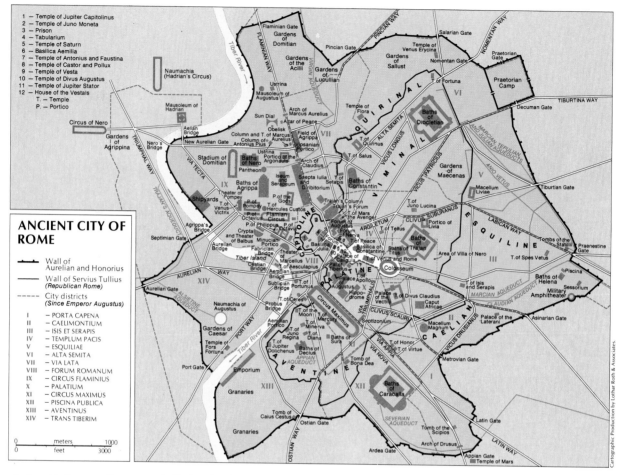

ANCIENT CITY OF ROME

1 – Temple of Jupiter Capitolinus
2 – Temple of Juno Moneta
3 – Prison
4 – Tabularium
5 – Temple of Saturn
6 – Basilica Aemilia
7 – Temple of Antonius and Faustina
8 – Temple of Castor and Pollux
9 – Temple of Vesta
10 – Temple of Divus Augustus
11 – Temple of Jupiter Stator
12 – House of the Vestals
T. – Temple
P. – Portico

Wall of
Aurelian and Honorius
Wall of Servius Tullius
(Republican Rome)
City districts
(Since Emperor Augustus)

I – PORTA CAPENA
II – CAELIMONTIUM
III – ISIS ET SERAPIS
IV – TEMPLUM PACIS
V – ESQUILIAE
VI – ALTA SEMITA
VII – VIA LATA
VIII – FORUM ROMANUM
IX – CIRCUS FLAMINIUS
X – PALATIUM
XI – CIRCUS MAXIMUS
XII – PISCINA PUBLICA
XIII – AVENTINUS
XIV – TRANS TIBERIM

nia (see MACEDONIA, KINGDOM OF). During the Second Punic War, PHILIP V of Macedonia had been an ally of Hannibal. Roman diplomats had enlisted the help of the Aetolian League, and, during the First Macedonian War (214–205), Philip was contained in Greece. The Roman Senate was alarmed, however, by the news (or rumors) of an alliance between Philip and the Seleucid king ANTIOCHUS III of Syria. When Philip began to expand his territory eastward, Rhodes and Pergamum urged Rome to intervene. By the end of the Second Punic War, however, the citizen population of Rome had shrunk to about 214,000. Seemingly it was not the moment for a new war. The leaders in the Senate knew better: Rome had to act while it had a veteran army and proven commanders. Confronted with a Roman ultimatum, Philip refused to yield. The Second Macedonian War (200–196) was decided by a single battle (197) at Cynoscephalae in Thessaly, where the Roman legions routed the Macedonian phalanx. A political masterstroke followed. At Corinth the Roman commander Titus Quinctius FLAMININUS proclaimed (196) the Greek cities free from Macedonia. In reality Rome assumed the protectorate of the Greek states. When Antiochus III invaded Greece (in the Syrian War, 192–188), the Romans defeated his army at Thermopylae and destroyed it (190) at Magnesia in Anatolia. Syria had to surrender its fleet; it also had to leave the whole of Anatolia as a Roman sphere of influence. The Macedonian king PERSEUS, the son of Philip V, also tried his luck against Rome (Third Macedonian War, 171–168). His army was slaughtered (168) at Pydna in Greece. After an uprising Macedonia was annexed (148) as a Roman province; in 146 the Achaean League was crushed and Corinth was destroyed. All the Greek world was under Roman hegemony.

The Third Punic War and the Iberian Campaigns. Rome's conflict with Carthage was not finished, however. Fearful of that

African power's economic recovery, Rome declared war when Carthage became embroiled in hostilities with NUMIDIA, Rome's ally. In this Third Punic War (149–146), the Romans won a quick victory, and the Carthaginians accepted all Roman demands and surrendered their arms. Then they were told to abandon their city and settle inland as farmers, for Carthage was to be destroyed. The Carthaginians rescinded their surrender and defended themselves heroically for almost 3 years. When Carthage was finally captured, it was razed (146) under the supervision of Scipio Aemilianus (later known as SCIPIO AFRICANUS MINOR).

Rome's campaigns in Spain against the warlike Iberians were protracted, unprofitable, and costly in Roman casualties. They were concluded only in 133, when Scipio Aemilianus destroyed Numantia, a center of the Celtiberians.

Political and Economic Change. Rome's foreign wars brought great new wealth to the senatorial landed aristocracy and to a newly emerging class, the equestrians, or equites, who were largely financiers and publicans, or tax gatherers. The importation of inexpensive raw materials from the colonies undermined Rome's peasant economy, and the influx of thousands of slaves made possible the organization of latifundia, or large landed estates. As a result of economic dislocation, a large portion of the population of Rome became unemployed and dependent on the public dole. Mobs of the unemployed roamed the streets, ready to be swayed by demagogues.

Economic changes also brought forth genuine reformers. The best known were two brothers, Tiberius Sempronius and Caius Sempronius Gracchus (see GRACCHUS family). In 133, Tiberius was elected tribune on a platform of redistribution of the land to the poor. Predictably, the large landholders in the Senate opposed him. When the Senate declared his reelection illegal his followers rioted, and Tiberius was killed in the

This model of imperial Rome by Italo Gismondi includes the Circus Maximus and emperor's palaces in the foreground. Of Rome, Cicero wrote, "I believe, Romulus foresaw that this city would provide a visiting place and a home for a world empire. . . ."

(Left) *Julius Caesar, a military hero as a result of his victories in the Gallic Wars, defeated his rivals to secure absolute power in Rome by 48 BC. Caesar's period of rule ended with his murder by republican conspirators in 44 BC.*

(Below) *This relief from Ostia portrays trade activity in one of the town's marketplaces. Located at the mouth of the Tiber River, Ostia, which dates from the 4th century BC, served as Rome's harbor, naval base, and primary commercial center.*

violence that erupted. Caius then took over his elder brother's reforms. He became tribune in 123 and extended reform to the tax system and the judiciary. By then, a conservative reaction had set in; Caius was killed by a mob in 121.

Anarchy and Civil War. The deaths of the Gracchi opened a century of anarchy and civil wars. Their attempts at reform also marked the beginning of two political groupings in the Senate: the *Optimates,* the conservative "good men," and the *Populares,* who pressed for reforms, represented trends, or tendencies, rather than political parties. War (112–105) with King JUGURTHA of Numidia and an invasion of Italy by the Cimbri and Teutons, two Germanic tribes, demonstrated the inadequacy of Rome's conscript army. Gaius MARIUS, an equestrian, distinguished himself as a general. He introduced a volunteer, semiprofessional army and threw its ranks open to the proletarians or common people. The German invaders were wiped out (102–101), but the proletarian soldiers clamored for land. The ruling oligarchy refused to recognize their demands. As a result repeated coalitions were formed between destitute veterans and ambitious generals.

In 91, Rome's allies in Italy rose in a great revolt called the Social War. Under this pressure the Romans granted the franchise to all Italians and mercilessly crushed those who did not submit. Civil war followed (88–82). Marius, the great popular hero, died in 86. The opposing forces were led by Lucius Cornelius SULLA, who had the support of the aristocrats. Sulla, with his private proletarian army, marched on Rome and dispersed the legal government. He routed his populist enemies and ruled as dictator (82–81). Sulla ordered thousands of his enemies assassinated and their property confiscated. His goal was to restore the rule of the oligarchs, but he failed to remedy socioeconomic conditions that had undermined their rule, and they proved unfit to govern.

Pompey and Caesar. The next two great rivals for power in Rome were POMPEY THE GREAT and Julius CAESAR. Both had made their reputations in the army, and both were highly ambitious. In 60 BC, Pompey and Caesar joined Marcus Licinius CRASSUS, the richest man in Rome, forming an unofficial compact, sometimes called the First Triumvirate (see TRIUMVIRATE); they were able to rule despite the opposition of the Senate. Caesar spent much of the next years in the north, successfully fighting the GALLIC WARS. In his absence Pompey consolidated his power, primarily by concluding an alliance with the Senate. Crassus died in 53, thereby dissolving the triumvirate.

In 52 the Senate made Pompey sole consul and 2 years later ordered Caesar to disband his army (his campaign against the Gauls was now successfully completed). Instead, Caesar crossed the Rubicon into Italy proper early in 49 and marched against Rome, precipitating yet another civil war. In a series of battles he defeated Pompey, who fled to the east. Caesar secured Spain, then pursued Pompey to Greece, defeating him at Pharsalus (48). Pompey escaped —with remnants of

his army—to Egypt, where he was murdered. Caesar followed Pompey to Egypt and was soon drawn into the civil war there. He made CLEOPATRA his mistress and established her as queen of Egypt.

Caesar conducted a series of campaigns, winning victories at Zela (modern Zile) in Anatolia (47), at Thapsus in North Africa (46), and at Munda in Spain (45). Back in Rome, he was now firmly in control of the government. He set about reforming the laws and reorganizing the administration of the colonies. Under Caesar, Rome controlled all of Italy, Gaul, Spain, Numidia, Macedonia, Greece, Palestine, Egypt, and virtually all of the Mediterranean islands. Greek art and philosophy had permeated Roman culture, and Rome perceived itself as the civilizer of the barbarians.

Caesar, made dictator for life in 44, seemed to be moving toward a monarchical system. On March 15 his autocratic rule was cut short; republican conspirators, led by Marcus Junius BRUTUS and Gaius CASSIUS LONGINUS, stabbed Caesar to death in the Senate.

The Fall of the Republic. Caesar's opponents had underestimated the allegiance of Caesar's partisans; they were now

(Top) *In commemoration of the murder (44 BC) of Julius Caesar, a silver denarius of Brutus, one of his assassins, was minted in the east in 43–42 BC.*

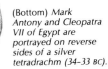

(Bottom) *Mark Antony and Cleopatra VII of Egypt are portrayed on reverse sides of a silver tetradrachm (34–33 BC).*

galvanized into action by Mark ANTONY and by Octavian (later AUGUSTUS), Caesar's grandnephew and heir. Antony, Octavian, and Marcus Aemilius LEPIDUS formed a triumvirate—sometimes called the Second Triumvirate—and forced the Senate to accept their rule. They instituted a reign of terror, and at the Battle of PHILIPPI (42) they defeated the forces of Brutus and Cassius, both of whom committed suicide.

By 31, Octavian had defeated Antony and had successfully established himself as princeps, or first citizen. The Senate conferred numerous honors upon him, among them the military command (imperium), hence the modern term *emperor*. The republic was dead.

THE EMPIRE

Octavian established a system of government called the principate that endured for two centuries. The principate, "rule by the first citizen," was a monarchy disguised as a republic. The princeps (the emperor) ostensibly ruled by commission from the Senate and the people. There was no automatic system of succession. Normally an emperor succeeded to the throne by virtue of connection—by blood, adoption, or affinity—with a predecessor, or one could seize power by force and inaugurate a new dynasty.

The Age of Augustus. Octavian, assuming (27 BC) the title and name Imperator Caesar Augustus, carried forth many of the reforms of Julius Caesar. He established his government in 27 BC, rebuilt the city of Rome, and became a great patron of the arts. During his reign the Roman Empire was at its height; it had no rivals—thus began the 200 years of peace known as the Pax Romana. The system of ROMAN ROADS and a sophisticated postal system helped unify the empire. Commerce and trade boomed among the far-flung possessions. Augustus reformed the Senate, made the system of taxation more equitable, and revived the census. He died in AD 14 and was succeeded by his stepson Tiberius.

The Julio-Claudian Dynasty. TIBERIUS, the son of LIVIA DRUSILLA, second wife of Augustus, continued the policies of Augustus. Highly frugal in his expenditures, he left the empire in healthy financial condition. The later years of his reign, however, were marked by court intrigue, mostly concerning the succession.

Tiberius was succeeded (AD 37) by his great-nephew CALIGULA. The latter's reign was noted for cruelty, torture, and licentiousness. Almost certainly insane during much of his reign, he was assassinated in AD 41 by a cabal of the PRAETORIAN GUARD, an elite body of the emperor's personal bodyguards that constituted an increasingly powerful institution. The officers of the guard named Caligula's uncle, CLAUDIUS I, as emperor. Claudius was generally an efficient administrator, although historians have blamed him for being too much under the control of his civil servants and his wives, MESSALINA and AGRIPPINA II. Claudius passed over his own son, Britannicus (41–55), for the succession in favor of Agrippina's son, Nero. Agrippina is believed to have poisoned Claudius once she was assured that Nero would succeed him.

NERO, the last emperor in the Julio-Claudian dynasty, assumed the throne in 54. He governed well in his early years when he was under the influence of Lucius Annaeus SENECA and Sextus Afranius Burrus (d. 62), chief of the Praetorian guard. Gradually, however, the influence of his mother and of his second wife, Poppaea Sabina (d. 65), triumphed, and Nero's reign turned bloodthirsty. He poisoned Britannicus, his mother, and Burrus, and legend says that he kicked Poppaea to death. Nero was accused of burning Rome in 64; he in turn blamed a new sect, the Christians, for the fire and began the first Roman persecution of them; Saint Peter and Saint Paul were among its victims. Nero committed suicide in 68 when he saw that a revolution against him was succeeding. He was followed by GALBA and, in 69 (the year of the four

(Left) *The Forum Romanum, situated in a valley between the Palatine and Capitoline hills, flourished as a religious and administrative center during imperial times.*

(Right) *This Roman sculpture group portrays members of the Praetorian guard. Emperor Augustus organized (27 BC) the Praetorians as the official bodyguards of the emperor, and they remained an integral part of Roman politics until disbanded in AD 312. (Louvre, Paris.)*

(Left) *This relief from the Ara Pacis (Altar of Peace; 13–9 BC) portrays the emperor Augustus (Octavian) with his family. Augustus, who assumed formal control of Rome in 27 BC, established the foundations of the Roman Empire through a consolidation of legal and administrative reforms. His reign began the 200-year Pax Romana, during which Rome was unchallenged in its domination of the Mediterranean world.*

A Roman mosaic depicts gladiators bearing characteristic arms for combat. Introduced in Rome during the 3d century BC as part of funeral ceremonies, gladiatorial games became one of the most popular and brutal forms of entertainment in ancient Rome.

emperors), by Otho (32–69), Vitellius (15–69), and Vespasian.

The Flavian Dynasty. VESPASIAN (r. 69–79), founder of the Flavian dynasty, declared emperor by his soldiers in the East, brought order and efficiency to the administration of Rome's affairs. He built the COLOSSEUM and other important public works. He was succeeded by two sons, TITUS (r. 79–81), a popular and generous ruler, and DOMITIAN (r. 81–96), who began his reign by following his brother's policies, but whose rule (despite his generally efficient administration) became progressively more despotic. His wife had him murdered.

The Antonines. The next six emperors are generally classified as the Antonines, although they do not belong to a single family or dynasty. They ruled for nearly a century; the period is sometimes called the Golden Age of the Roman Empire. The first Antonine, Nerva (c.30–98; r. 96–98), was elected by the Senate in an effort to assert its power over the military. An elderly, well-respected statesman, he was opposed by the Praetorian guard. He adopted as his successor the great soldier TRAJAN (a Spaniard, the first non-Italian to serve as emperor). Trajan (r. 98–117), one of Rome's greatest emperors, expanded the empire into modern Romania and into Armenia and Mesopotamia and built impressive aqueducts, roads, theaters, and basilicas. His successor, HADRIAN (r. 117–38), was another soldier. He was more cautious in his foreign relations than Trajan, although he put down a Jewish revolt in Jerusalem (AD 132–35) with great brutality. ANTONINUS PIUS had a long and prosperous reign (138–61) and was succeeded by joint emperors, the philosopher MARCUS AURELIUS (r. 161–80) and Lucius Verus (130–69; r. 161–69). After Verus died Marcus ruled alone.

Marcus Aurelius was a benevolent and humane emperor—with one notable exception: he brutally persecuted the Christians. His reign also saw an increasing number of interior rebellions and attacks on the empire's borders. The reign (180–92) of his son COMMODUS is generally regarded as the beginning of Rome's long decline. Commodus was thor-

Roman columns, paying tribute to the achievements of emperors and sometimes housing their remains, were richly decorated with sculpture. This frieze from the column of Antoninus Pius, erected by Marcus Aurelius, shows captives being led to work. (Vatican Museums.)

oughly unfit to rule, and his reign was marked by despotism, licentiousness, and brutality. He was strangled in 192; a long period of short, violent reigns, marked by constant court intrigues, followed.

The Crisis of the 3d Century. In the 3d century the Roman world plunged into a prolonged and nearly fatal crisis. The reasons were manifold. Sharp divisions between the opulent notables in the cities and the poor and hardly civilized peasants created tensions. The wars that began under Marcus Aurelius continued, and increased taxation destroyed the prosperity of the empire. To meet rising military costs and to pay the bureaucracy, the emperors, including CARACALLA (r.

The Column of Trajan (AD 106–13), one of the greatest monuments of ancient Rome, stands in the Forum of Trajan. Decorated with a continuous spiral of relief sculptures, the column commemorates Emperor Trajan's Dacian victory (105). Under Trajan, during the period known as the Golden Age of the Roman Empire, great territorial expansion occurred and extensive building took place within Rome and the provinces.

This 2d-century marble relief portrays Emperor Marcus Aurelius (r. 161–80) making a sacrificial libation. Marcus, a Stoic philosopher, reigned with Lucius Aurelius Verrus as his coemperor until Verrus's death in 169. As sole emperor, Marcus was engaged primarily in defending Rome's Danube frontier against the barbarian invasions. Before his death at Vindobonda (Vienna), he succeeded in restoring temporary Roman rule at the northern borders. (Palazzo dei Conservatori, Rome.)

EMPERORS OF ROME

Ruler*	Reign	Ruler	Reign	Ruler*	Reign	Ruler	Reign
Augustus	27 BC–AD 14	Heliogabalus	218-22	Maximian	286-305	Maximus (emperor in the West)	383-88
Tiberius	14-37	Alexander Severus	222-35	Constantius I	305-06	Eugenius (emperor in the West)	392-94
Caligula	37-41	Maximinus Thrax	235-38	Galerius	305-11	**Emperors in the West**	
Claudius I	41-54	Gordian I	238	Constantine I	306-37	Honorius	395-423
Nero	54-68	Gordian II	238	Maximian	306-08	Constantius III	421
Galba	68-69	Balbinus	238	Maxentius	306-12	Valentinian III	425-55
Otho	69	Pupienus	238	Severus	306-07	Petronius Maximus	455
Vitellius	69	Gordian III	238-44	Licinius	308-24	Avitus	455-56
Vespasian	69-79	Philip	244-49	Maximinus	308-13	Majorian	457-61
Titus	79-81	Decius	249-51	Constantius II	337-61	Libius Severus	461-65
Domitian	81-96	Gallus	251-53	Constans	337-50	Anthemius	467-72
Nerva	96-98	Hostilian	251	Constantine II	337-340	Olybrius	472
Trajan	98-117	Aemilianus	253	Magnentius	350-53	Glycerius	473
Hadrian	117-38	Valerian	253-60	Julian	361-63	Julius Nepos	473-75
Antoninus Pius	138-61	Gallienus	253-68	Jovian	363-64	Romulus Augustulus	475-76
Marcus Aurelius	161-80	Claudius II	268-70	Valentinian I (emperor in the West)	364-75	**Emperors in the East**	
Lucius Aurelius Verus	161-69	Aurelian	270-75	Valens (emperor in the East)	364-78	Arcadius	395-408
Commodus	180-92	Tacitus	275-76	Gratian (emperor in the West)	367-83	Theodosius II	408-50
Pertinax	193	Florian	276	Valentinian II (emperor in the West)	375-92	Marcian	450-57
Didius Julian	193	Probus	276-82	Theodosius I	379-95	Leo I	457-74
Septimius Severus	193-211	Carus	282-83			Leo II	473-74
Caracalla	211-17	Carinus	283-85			Zeno	474-91
Geta	211-12	Numerianus	283-84				
Macrinus	217-18	Diocletian	284-305				

* At various times, but especially after 283, the Roman imperial title was shared by two or more rulers. In 395 the empire was divided permanently into eastern and western portions. The year 476 marks the traditional end of the empire in the West; the empire in the East (the Byzantine Empire) continued to exist for nearly 1,000 years.

211-17), debased the coinage; the resulting inflation proved pernicious. The defenses of the empire on the Rhine and Danube collapsed under the attack of various Germanic and other tribes, and the eastern provinces were invaded by the Persians. Finally, the discipline of the army—in which half-Romanized provincials and totally non-Romanized barbarians were now serving—broke down. In the 50 years from 235 to 284 more than 2 dozen emperors ruled, all but one of whom suffered a violent death.

The Reforms of Diocletian and Constantine. Out of the turmoil of the 3d century a new totalitarian Rome emerged. The emperor DIOCLETIAN (r. 284-305) adopted the title dominus (master) and transformed the principate into the dominate and citizens into subjects. He adopted an elaborate court ceremonial with many oriental elements. The requisitions and forced labor to which the emperors of the 3d century had resorted in order to save the state were transformed into a lasting system. Peasants·were gradually deprived of their personal freedom and tied to the soil. The artisan corporations, and even the higher civil servants, were organized as hereditary castes, and a crushing burden of taxation was imposed on them. Two social groups were preeminent: the rich landowners, who in their fortified villas foreshadowed the medieval feudal lords, and the imperial bureaucracy.

CONSTANTINE I (r. 306-37) may be regarded as the second founder of the empire. He successfully fought off his numerous opponents and, once firmly in power, reorganized the entire system of local government (into prefectures, dioceses, and provinces). He legalized Christianity (and was himself converted), thereby enlisting the church in service of the state. He moved the capital to BYZANTIUM, which he had rebuilt and renamed Constantinople (330). Constantine's reforms were not enough, however, to halt the slide of the empire into impotence.

Division of the Empire. From 395 the empire was permanently divided into the Latin Western and the Greek Eastern or BYZANTINE EMPIRE, with its capital at Constantinople. The Eastern Empire lived on until 1453, when the Turks conquered Constantinople. The Western Empire was overrun and gradually dismembered by various Germanic tribes. In 410 the Visigoths (see GOTHS) and in 455 the VANDALS plundered the city of Rome. Finally in 476 the German ODOACER deposed the last emperor of the west, the child Romulus Augustulus. And so the history of ancient Rome ended ingloriously. The idea of

Rome and of the Roman Empire, however, survived its fall, and from the symbiosis of Roman and Germanic elements arose the new states and societies of medieval Europe.

J. LINDERSKI

Bibliography: Bloch, Raymond, *The Origins of Rome* (1960); Carcopino, Jerome, *Daily Life in Ancient Rome,* trans. by E. O. Lorimer (1940); Cary, Max, and Scullard, H. H., *A History of Rome; Down to the Reign of Constantine,* 3d ed. (1956); Cunliffe, Barry, *Rome and the Barbarians* (1975); Grant, Michael, *The Climax of Rome* (1968), *The Decline and Fall of the Roman Empire: A Reappraisal* (1976), and *History of Rome* (1978); Hadas, Moses, ed. and trans., *History of Rome, from Its Origins to 529 A.D., as Told by the Roman Historians* (1956); Haywood, Richard M., *The Myth of Rome's Fall* (1958); Jones, A. H. M., *The Later Roman Empire,* 3 vols. (1968), and *The Roman Economy* (1974); Lewis, Naphtali, and Reinhold, Meyer, *Roman Civilization,* 2 vols. (1966); Mattingly, Harold, *Roman Imperial Civilization* (1957; repr. 1971); Scullard, Howard H., *From the Gracchi to Nero: A History of Rome from 133 B.C. to A.D. 68,* 3d ed. (1970); Sinnigen, William G., and Boak, Arthur E. R., *A History of Rome to A.D. 565,* 6th ed. (1977).

See also: EUROPE, HISTORY OF; ITALY, HISTORY OF; LATIN LITERATURE; ROMAN ART AND ARCHITECTURE; ROMAN LAW.

Rome, University of

Founded in 1303 by Pope Boniface VIII and made a state school in 1870, the University of Rome (enrollment: 150,000; library: 1,000,000 volumes) is a coeducational state institution in Rome, Italy. It grants undergraduate and graduate degrees. Museums of mineralogy, medicine, and Greek and Roman sculpture are associated with the university.

Romeo and Juliet

In *The Tragedy of Romeo and Juliet* (c.1595), William SHAKESPEARE experiments with stock comic materials—the hyperbole of romantic love, brawling servants, fussy old fathers, garrulous and bawdy nurses—but transforms them into tragedy. After the slaying of Mercutio by the belligerent Tybalt (act 3, scene 1), all comedy is dispelled by a sense of impending disaster. The tragedy of Romeo and Juliet's love is set in the larger context of the feud between the Capulets and the Montagues, which poisons all possibility of happiness. The play has an extraordinary lyric grace not found in the source, Arthur Brooke's *The Tragicall Historye of Romeus and Juliet* (1562).

MAURICE CHARNEY

Bibliography: Brooke, Nicholas, *Shakespeare's Early Tragedies* (1968); Colie, Rosalie L., *Shakespeare's Living Art* (1974).

Rømer, Ole   [rurm'-ur, ohl-e]

The Danish astronomer Ole Christensen Rømer, b. Sept. 25, 1644, d. Sept. 19, 1710, made the first determination of the velocity of LIGHT and was the inventor of the astronomical TRANSIT CIRCLE. Rømer worked at the Paris Observatory under G. D. Cassini (see CASSINI family) and Jean PICARD. He demonstrated (1676) the velocity of light by observing that the precisely predicted times of the eclipses of one of Jupiter's moons were dependent upon the distance from Jupiter to Earth. Rømer became professor of mathematics at the University of Copenhagen in 1681 and became mayor of Copenhagen in 1705.   STEVEN J. DICK

Rommel, Erwin   [ruhm'-ul]

German field marshal Erwin Rommel (left) inspects defenses along the French coast in February 1944, preparatory to the expected Allied invasion. Rommel's shrewd leadership of the German Africa Corps in Libya won him the nickname the Desert Fox.

Erwin Rommel, b. Nov. 15, 1891, d. Oct. 14, 1944, was a German field marshal in World War II. Commissioned in 1912, he served with distinction in World War I. A war college instructor and a liaison officer between the army and the Hitler Youth organization during the 1930s, he was promoted to brigadier general in 1939 and was subsequently assigned to Hitler's headquarters during the Polish campaign. The following spring he commanded an armored division during the Battle of France, and in 1941 he went to North Africa to lead the German Africa Corps. There he came to be known as the Desert Fox and attained the rank of field marshal. He was decisively defeated (November 1942) at El ALAMEIN, 240 km (150 miles) west of Cairo. In December 1943 he was transferred to France to defend the northwestern coast against the expected Allied invasion. Once the landing (June 1944) had succeeded, Rommel realized that the war was hopelessly lost and that to condone Hitler's senseless continuation of it would be irresponsible. Injured in a strafing attack on July 17, 1944, Rommel could not personally participate in the attempt to overthrow Hitler three days later, but he was gravely implicated. Because of his popularity, his opposition was kept secret; he was given the choice of suicide, to be reported as death from his wounds, as an alternative to execution as a traitor, which would have placed his family and close associates in grave danger. Thus he died by his own hand.   DONALD S. DETWILER

Bibliography: Irving, David, *The Trial of the Fox: The Search for the True Field Marshal Rommel* (1977); Mitcham, Samuel, *Rommel's Desert War* (1984); Young, Desmond, *Rommel: The Desert Fox* (1950).

Romney, George   [rahm'-nee]

The British portrait and history painter George Romney, b. Dec. 15, 1734, d. Nov. 15, 1802, was the leading rival of Thomas Gainsborough and Sir Joshua Reynolds in the late 18th century; his romantic pictures of Lady Hamilton (1782–86) are especially well known. Romney had little formal education before being apprenticed (1755–57) to the traveling portrait painter Christopher Steele and then spending 5 years as an itinerant portraitist. In 1762 he exhibited portraits and subject pictures in London; there he won a prize (1763) for *The Death of Wolfe*, which enabled him to visit Paris briefly in 1764. Subsequently, after the public success of his group portrait of the Warren family (1769), he returned to Europe, this time to spend 2 years in Italy, mainly in Rome (1773–75). There he drew from life and studied the antique. Returning to London, he painted numerous churchmen and aristocrats in a simplified and tranquil neoclassical style; he also spent much time doing many studies of his friend Emma Hart, later Lady Hamilton. Encouraged by the poet William Hayley and others, he illustrated classical and modern authors, particularly William Shakespeare and John Milton. He became obsessed with schemes for subjects in a grand, historical style but in the end had no enduring success as a history painter.
                                   MALCOLM CORMACK

Bibliography: Chamberlain, A. B., *George Romney* (1910; repr. 1971); Jaffé, P., *Drawings by George Romney from the Fitzwilliam Museum, Cambridge* (1977); Ward, Humphrey, and Roberts, W., *Romney*, 2 vols. (1904); Waterhouse, E. K., *Painting in Britain, 1530–1790* (1953).

Romulus and Remus   [rahm'-yoo-luhs, ree'-muhs]

In Roman mythology, Romulus and Remus are regarded as the founders of Rome. Livy and Eutropius called them sons of the god Mars and Rhea Silvia, a vestal virgin and the daughter of Numitor, king of Alba Longa, who had been driven from his throne by Amulius. After birth the twins were placed in a container and cast upon the Tiber by the usurper, but they floated ashore and were nursed by a shewolf until found and brought up by shepherds. When grown, they restored Numitor to his throne and founded Rome. Romulus killed Remus in a quarrel and became the first of Rome's seven kings. According to the legend, he established an asylum for fugitives on the Capitoline Hill, organized the rape of the Sabine women, founded the Senate, and divided the people into tribal units. Romulus was venerated by the Romans as QUIRINUS, god of the winter solstice.

Bibliography: Grant, Michael, *Roman Myths* (1972).

rondo   [rohn'-doh]

A musical form especially favored by composers of the classical era for the final movements of their sonatas, symphonies, and concertos, the rondo derives from a form widely used by French keyboard composers of the 17th century. The early instrumental *rondeau*—of uncertain relation to a medieval poetic form of the same name—consisted of a fixed refrain alternating with a succession of couplets, usually in different keys (as in the pattern ABACADA). In what may be regarded as the standard version of the later rondo, the number of couplets, known as episodes, is usually held to three: the first and third episodes are similar, while the second is enlarged in the manner of a development section in SONATA form (ABACABA). This schema was very freely handled by Mozart and Beethoven, in whose rondos the recurring refrain—itself sometimes called the rondo—is often varied or abbreviated after its initial appearance. The form offers great scope for ingenuity, and most examples are exuberant or playful.

Rono, Henry

The Kenyan runner Henry Rono, b. Feb. 12, 1952, emerged in 1978 as one of track history's greatest performers. In that year he set four world records: at 3,000 m (7 min 32.1 sec), the steeplechase (8:05.4), 5,000 m (13:08.4; lowered by Rono himself to 13:06.20 in 1981), and 10,000 m (27:22.4). Kenya's boycott of the 1980 Olympics in Moscow prevented Rono's competing there. He retired from track in 1983.

Ronsard, Pierre de   [rohn-sahr']

Pierre de Ronsard, b. Sept. 11, 1524, d. Dec. 27, 1585, once called the "Prince of Poets," is considered the greatest poet of the French Renaissance. He was leader of the Pléiade poets, followers of Joachim DU BELLAY, who, in 1549, called on French poets to cultivate the resources of their native language. His assimilation of classical and native idiom and verse forms expanded the range of French poetry. He was equally skilled at writing love poems, pastorals, sonnets, philosophical poems, and political verse. Ronsard's verse collections include *Odes* (1550) and *Sonnets pour Hélène* (1574).

Bibliography: Armstrong, Elizabeth, *Ronsard and the Age of Gold* (1968); Cave, Terence, ed., *Ronsard the Poet* (1973).

roof and roofing

The covering of the top of a building, or roof, consists of three major components: the structural framing members; a stiff membrane, or roof deck, spanning structural members; and a waterproof outer layer of roofing. The earliest roofing materials were probably mud and sod supported by logs and woven reeds. The early Greeks and Romans manufactured kiln-dried clay tile to cover their public buildings and dwellings; clay tile is still popular. Bundles of straw or reeds tied to horizontal framing timbers formed the roofing for the thatched cottages in medieval Europe, and slate was used throughout

Conventional roof coverings are fixed to a timber framework. Straw bundles are tied to the frame to make a thatched roof (1). Thatch, first used in ancient Egypt, is still seen in rural areas of Europe. Stone flags (2) are usually hung on the supporting lath with pegs. Baked ceramic tiles (3) have been used in Mediterranean countries since ancient times. A lipped variation called the pantile (4) overlaps in two directions. The fire-resistance and impermeability of slate (5) has made it for centuries a sought-after roof covering. Modern dwellings are frequently roofed with asphalt-impregnated felt shingles (6), sometimes reinforced by an underlayer of hot asphalt.

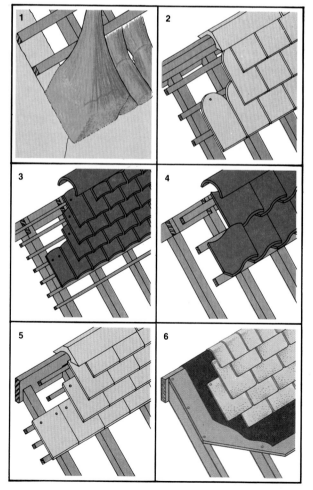

the Middle Ages as a covering for the great cathedrals. By the 1500s copper sheets were pounded out by hand and used in limited quantities; in 1750 the first copper sheets were rolled. After that time much of the slate and tile roofing was replaced by copper, which is still widely used. Sheet lead has been used as a roofing material for centuries: a lead roof on the HAGIA SOPHIA is still in good condition after 1,400 years.

Roofing shakes, split from straight-grained woods such as Western red cedar, or uniform, sawed wooden shingles have been popular roof coverings, particularly on houses in North America. Steel, aluminum, copper, lead, various alloys, and clad metals are also used as modern roof coverings. The metal used may be in either flat or corrugated sheets, joined together with specially designed joints that allow for expansion and contraction during temperature change.

Asphalt and coal-tar pitch came into general use as roofing materials after 1892, when a chemist developed an asphalt-impregnated paper for that purpose. Roll roofing and asphalt tiles are made of heavy felt saturated with asphalt or coal-tar pitch. Mineral granules are rolled into the upper surface while the asphalt is still soft. Roll roofing is nailed or fastened to the roof deck with hot asphalt, coal-tar pitch, or an adhesive in order to form a finished roof. Asphalt shingles are nailed or stapled to a wooden roof deck. A built-up roof is produced by applying alternate layers of roofing felt and hot asphalt or coal-tar pitch. The top layer is given a hot flood coat of asphalt or coal-tar pitch into which granules of rock, gravel, slag, or ceramic particles may be imbedded while the flood coat is hot.

The latest development in roof covering is the roofing membrane; by applying synthetic rubber or plastic with a brush, roller, or spray gun, a monolithic membrane that follows any roof contour can be formed.   DON A. WATSON

Bibliography: Brann, Donald R., *Roofing Simplified,* rev. ed. (1977); Geary, Donald, *Roofs and Siding* (1977).

rook

The rook, *Corvus frugilegus,* is a large crowlike bird belonging to the family Corvidae. It measures about 46 cm (18 in) in length and has a glossy black plumage with a purplish sheen. Rooks range throughout Eurasia, from Britain southward to Spain in the west and eastward to China. They feed mainly in open fields, eating insects, earthworms, and other small animals, as well as nuts, fruits, and seeds—especially cultivated grains. Rooks nest in colonies, or rookeries, usually located in the tops of trees.   ROBERT J. RAIKOW

Rookwood ware   [ruk'-wud]

Originating in the 19th-century hobby of painting on china, Rookwood ware was one of the earliest and most prominent of American art potteries. The pottery works was founded in 1880 in Cincinnati by Maria Longworth Nichols. Typical Rookwood ware was based on the barbotine technique of painted slip decoration under a thick transparent glaze, producing deep tones of olive, brown, and amber. The firm won awards at the Paris exhibitions of 1889 and 1900 and at the World's Columbian Exposition of 1893 in Chicago. By about 1930 the firm had declined, and it finally closed in 1967.

BETTY ELZEA

Bibliography: Peck, Herbert, *The Book of Rookwood Pottery* (1968).

Rooney, Mickey

The actor Mickey Rooney, b. Joe Yule, Jr., in Brooklyn, N.Y., Sept. 24, 1920, began his career as a child film star in a series (1927–33) of some 50 silent comedies in which he played Mickey McGuire, a comic-strip character. He later gave memorable performances in the Andy Hardy series (1937–46), *Huckleberry Finn* (1939), and *National Velvet* (1944). He also worked in television (1950s) and in nightclubs (1960s), and he starred in the Broadway musical *Sugar Babies* (1979). He has continued a motion picture career with such films as *The Black Stallion* (1980). In 1983, Rooney received a special Academy Award honoring his versatility as a performer.

Roosa, Stuart A.   [roo'-suh]

The American astronaut Stuart Allen Roosa, b. Durango, Colo., Aug. 16, 1933, flew on the third manned mission to the Moon. Roosa became an Air Force pilot in 1953 and graduated from the Aerospace Research Pilot School in 1965, the year he was selected as an astronaut. On his only mission in space, he was command module pilot of *Apollo 14* (Jan. 31–Feb. 9, 1971), staying in lunar orbit while commander Alan Shepard and lunar-module pilot Edgar D. Mitchell explored the lunar surface (see APOLLO PROGRAM). Roosa retired (1976) from NASA and from the Air Force with the rank of colonel. Since 1977 he has been president of Jet Industries in Austin, Tex.   DAVID DOOLING

Bibliography: Lewis, Richard S., *The Voyages of Apollo* (1974).

Roosevelt, Eleanor   [rohz'-uh-velt]

Eleanor Roosevelt, one of the most active women on the American political scene during the mid-20th century, was an admired and influential advocate of humanitarian causes. The wife of President Franklin D. Roosevelt, she expanded the role of First Lady into a highly regarded and effective position. While serving (1945–52, 1961–62) as a member of the U.S. delegation to the United Nations, Eleanor Roosevelt helped draft the UN Declaration of Human Rights.

The wife of a popular U.S. president, Anna Eleanor Roosevelt, b. New York City, Oct. 11, 1884, d. Nov. 7, 1962, was a tireless worker for social causes. A niece of President Theodore Roosevelt, she was raised by her maternal grandmother after the premature death of her parents. In 1905 she married her cousin Franklin Delano Roosevelt; they had six children, one of whom died in infancy. Although extremely shy, she became active in politics after her husband was stricken with polio in 1921.

When Franklin became president in 1933, Eleanor Roosevelt made herself a powerful voice on behalf of a wide range of social causes, including youth employment and civil rights for blacks and women. She conducted press conferences, had her own radio program, and wrote a daily newspaper column, "My Day," which was nationally syndicated. After her husband's death, she continued in public life. She served (1945–52, 1961–62) as a U.S. delegate to the United Nations and helped draft the UN Declaration of Human Rights. Her books include *The Autobiography of Eleanor Roosevelt* (1961) and *This I Remember* (1949).

Bibliography: Faber, Doris, *The Life of Lorena Hickok, E. R.'s Friend* (1980); Hareven, Tamara, *Eleanor Roosevelt: An American Conscience* (1968; repr. 1975); Hershan, Stella, *A Woman of Quality* (1970); Lash, Joseph P., *Eleanor and Franklin* (1971) and *Eleanor: The Years Alone* (1972); MacLeish, Archibald, *The Eleanor Roosevelt Story* (1965).

Roosevelt, Franklin Delano

Franklin Delano Roosevelt, 32d president of the United States (1933–45), greatly expanded the role of the federal government with a wide-ranging economic and social program, the New Deal, designed to counter the Great Depression of the 1930s. He also led the nation through most of its participation in the global struggle of World War II.

Early Life. Of Dutch and English ancestry, Roosevelt was born on Jan. 30, 1882, at Hyde Park, N.Y., to James Roosevelt, scion of a noted, wealthy family, and his second wife, Sara Delano Roosevelt. Franklin led a sheltered youth, educated by governesses, his life revolving about the Hyde Park family estate in rural Dutchess County, trips to Europe, athletics (especially swimming and boating), and hobbies, such as stamp and bird collecting. Although he cherished fun and companionship, he rarely confided his innermost thoughts, perhaps as a device for evading his mother's attempts at domination.

At the exclusive Groton School (Groton, Mass.), Franklin was imbued with a sense of social responsibility. He was an average student at Harvard University, edited the *Harvard Crimson* in his senior year, and after graduation (1904) attended (1904–07) Columbia Law School. He dropped out of law school upon admission to the New York bar and worked (1907–10) for a Wall Street law firm.

Tall, handsome, athletic, and outgoing, Franklin married a distant cousin, a shy young woman, Anna Eleanor Roosevelt, on Mar. 17, 1905. Her uncle, President Theodore Roosevelt, gave the bride away. Their children were Anna Eleanor, James, Elliott, Franklin Delano, Jr., and John; a sixth child died in infancy. The Roosevelts were active in New York social circles but at the same time devoted considerable energy to the plight of the less fortunate. Franklin's handling of small-claims cases in the municipal court system deepened his concern for the common people. Although a Democrat, he admired the progressivism of Uncle Teddy and decided early upon a political career. His opportunity came in 1910 when Dutchess County Republicans split between old guard conservatives and progressives. A colorful, dynamic campaigner, Roosevelt toured dirt roads in an open red Maxwell automobile, soliciting the votes of normally Republican farmers, and won a seat as a Democrat in the New York state senate.

Rise to National Prominence. Roosevelt gained quick recognition by his leadership of upstate New York Democrats in a fight against Tammany Hall's nominee for the U.S. Senate. At the 1912 Democratic National Convention he backed Woodrow Wilson in a bitter contest for the party's presidential nomination and was subsequently awarded the post of assistant secretary of the navy (serving 1913–20). He gained considerable administrative experience under his superior, Josephus DANIELS, a progressive North Carolina newspaper editor, and made a reputation as a jingoist and an advocate of navy interests. Some of the Wilsonians, however, viewed Roosevelt as dandified and superficial, a characterization that plagued him in later years.

The Roosevelt name and his progressive image won him the party's vice-presidential nomination in 1920 on the ticket with the conservative newspaper publisher Gov. James M. Cox of Ohio. The Democrats had little hope of victory. Americans, tired of war and Europe's problems, opted for Warren G. Harding's promise of a "return to normalcy." Roosevelt's campaign, regarded as a sacrificial gesture, was highlighted by a vigorous defense of Wilson's advocacy of U.S. membership in the League of Nations.

In the summer of 1921, while vacationing at his summer home on Campobello Island (New Brunswick, Canada), Roosevelt was stricken with poliomyelitis. Recovery was slow, and the family's wealth appeared adequate to allow him a genteel retirement to the Hyde Park estate, a course urged by his mother. Instead, encouraged by Eleanor and by advisor Louis McHenry Howe, Roosevelt slowly regained his aspirations for public office, although he permanently lost the use of his legs. Intensive therapy, including swimming, hastened partial physical recovery. At the Democratic National Convention of 1924, Roosevelt signaled his return to politics with the Happy Warrior speech that placed Gov. Alfred E. SMITH of New York in nomination for the presidency. When Smith finally secured the nomination in 1928, he persuaded Roosevelt to run for the New York governorship. Smith's identification with New York City's Tammany Hall was a liability. He hoped that Roosevelt's appeal to Protestant, rural upstate voters would swing the Empire State to him in the presidential contest with the Republican Herbert C. Hoover.

FRANKLIN DELANO ROOSEVELT
32d President of the United States (1933–45)

Nickname: "FDR"
Born: Jan. 30, 1882, Hyde Park, N.Y.
Education: Harvard College (graduated 1904); Columbia Law School
Profession: Public Official, Lawyer
Religious Affiliation: Episcopalian
Marriage: Mar. 17, 1905, to Anna Eleanor Roosevelt (1884–1962)
Children: Anna Eleanor Roosevelt (1906–75); James Roosevelt (1907–   ); Elliott Roosevelt (1910–   ); Franklin Delano Roosevelt (1914–   ); John Aspinwall Roosevelt (1916–81)
Political Affiliation: Democrat
Writings: *The Happy Warrior, Alfred E. Smith* (1928); *F.D.R.: His Personal Letters* (4 vols., 1947–50), ed. by Elliott Roosevelt
Died: Apr. 12, 1945, Warm Springs, Ga.
Buried: Hyde Park, N.Y. (family plot)

Vice-President and Cabinet Members
Vice-President: John N. Garner (1933–41); Henry A. Wallace (1941–45); Harry S. Truman (1945)
Secretary of State: Cordell Hull (1933–44); Edward R. Stettinius (1944–45)
Secretary of the Treasury: William H. Woodin (1933–34); Henry Morgenthau, Jr. (1934–45)
Secretary of War: George H. Dern (1933–36); Harry H. Woodring (1937–40); Henry L. Stimson (1940–45)
Attorney General: Homer S. Cummings (1933–39); Frank Murphy (1939–40); Robert H. Jackson (1940–41); Francis B. Biddle (1941–45)
Postmaster General: James A. Farley (1933–40); Frank C. Walker (1940–45)
Secretary of the Navy: Claude A. Swanson (1933–39); Charles Edison (1940); Frank Knox (1940–44); James V. Forrestal (1944–45)
Secretary of the Interior: Harold L. Ickes
Secretary of Agriculture: Henry A. Wallace (1933–40); Claude R. Wickard (1940–45)
Secretary of Commerce: Daniel C. Roper (1933–38); Harry L. Hopkins (1939–40); Jesse H. Jones (1940–45); Henry A. Wallace (1945)
Secretary of Labor: Frances Perkins

Although Smith lost his own state and the traditionally Democratic South in the 1928 contest, Roosevelt, proving his mobility in a strenuous campaign, managed a narrow victory. His governorship was molded in the progressive tradition. Its accomplishments included the development of public power, civil-service reform, and social-welfare measures. In addition, Roosevelt cultivated a presidential image with the help of a loyal group of advisors: Howe was his principal political manager; James A. FARLEY, a Catholic, was assigned the task of winning delegates to the 1932 presidential convention; Henry Morgenthau, Jr. (see MORGENTHAU family), Roosevelt's Hudson Valley neighbor, was an agriculture advisor; Frances PERKINS, industrial commissioner of New York, advised on labor questions and social security; and Samuel I. Rosenman was a speechwriter and confidant. A smashing victory in the 1930 gubernatorial election, the growing appeal of the Roosevelt name as the Great Depression (see DEPRESSION OF THE 1930S) made Hoover politically vulnerable, and identification with both Southern and progressive party elements won Roosevelt the party's 1932 presidential nomination, despite fierce opposition by a conservative coalition headed by Smith.

Presidency. Roosevelt's opponents claimed that he was intellectually and physically unfit for the presidency. Anxious to belie such charges, he chartered a Ford trimotor airplane and, as a dramatic gesture, flew to Chicago; there, at the Democratic National Convention, he pledged to the American people a NEW DEAL. That expression, symbol of an era in American history, represented a cluster of ideas formulated by the candidate and his BRAIN TRUST, a group of advisors recruited from New York's Columbia University. Faced with the prospect of governing the nation in the worst economic crisis in its history, Roosevelt desired an examination of causes and remedies free from the pressures of a political campaign. The advisory group, organized a few months before the July convention, was unofficially headed by Raymond Moley, a professor of public law, and included Rexford G. TUGWELL, an agricultural economist, and A. A. BERLE, Jr., a specialist in corporate structure and finance. They concluded that the United States had become an interdependent society (a "concert of interests") and that the agricultural depression of the 1920s had brought down the rest of the nation's economic structure. In the Forgotten Man speech drafted by Moley, Roosevelt presented the group's theory that productivity had outpaced the capacity of farmers and laborers to consume. During the campaign he also argued that big business should be accountable to society ("an economic constitutional order") and spoke in favor of conservation, relief, social insurance, and cheaper electricity. The Depression helped give Roosevelt an overwhelming victory in November.

On the eve of the March 1933 inauguration, the nation's banking system collapsed as millions of panicky depositors tried to withdraw savings that the banks had tied up in long-term loans. Approximately 12 to 14 million Americans were unemployed, and business nearly ground to a halt. In ringing tones, Roosevelt told the nation that "the only thing we have to fear is fear itself" and promised effective leadership in the crisis. That same day he closed the banks by proclamation, summoned a special session of Congress for the passage of emergency banking legislation, and began the process that within a week provided the liquidity that banks needed in order to reopen. The banks also had to regain public confidence, and in his first "fireside chat" radio broadcast the new president urged the American people to stop hoarding cash. Millions obliged as the self-assured new chief executive offered a vigorous contrast to his dour, embattled predecessor.

The New Deal. Although Roosevelt's New Deal is frequently described as an improvisation, much of it was planned in advance. His domestic program consistently accorded priority to agricultural recovery, with provision for crop restriction in the Agricultural Adjustment Act (AAA) of 1933 (see AGRICULTURAL ADJUSTMENT ADMINISTRATION); passage of the Soil Conservation Act of 1935, later expanded in response to the Supreme Court's ruling (1936) against AAA; and the second AAA Act in 1938, which pledged to the nation the maintenance of a large grain reserve. The New Deal also sought to rationalize the business system by temporarily ending bitter economic warfare (the National Industrial Recovery Act and its fair practice codes; see NATIONAL RECOVERY ADMINISTRATION). Unemployment insurance was introduced, and the new social security program guaranteed income for retired Americans. The New Deal also encouraged the growth of industrial unionism, the end of child labor, and maximum hours and minimum wages legislation on a national basis.

The credit of the United States was used to salvage millions of urban home mortgages (Home Owners Loan Corporation) and farms (FARM CREDIT ADMINISTRATION) and to encourage private business by expanding the Reconstruction Finance Corporation that had been established under the Hoover administration. Steps were also taken to promote public construction projects. Roosevelt's attempts at reflation of the currency to 1927-29 price levels led to abandonment of the gold standard in 1933 and reduction of the gold content of the dollar. Although in the 1932 campaign he had promised a balanced budget, Roosevelt showed a greater commitment to his pledge that no American should go hungry. Emergency expenditures for relief, also designed to "prime the economic pump," poured into the economy through the Federal Emergency Relief Administration, later the WORKS PROGRESS ADMINISTRATION, leading to record federal deficits.

The TENNESSEE VALLEY AUTHORITY, a major New Deal creation that was uniquely Roosevelt's, provided for public development of cheap electrical power. Roosevelt conceived the project in terms of broad regional planning, including scientific farming, development of water transportation, energy, soil conservation, public health and educational facilities, and recreation. He had hoped to extend the concept to other areas of the country but was thwarted by charges of socialism and the declining popularity of the New Deal in the late 1930s. Roosevelt was also deeply committed to the conservation movement and youth employment, both of which found expression through the CIVILIAN CONSERVATION CORPS.

In the 1930s, Roosevelt's foreign policy was subordinated to the needs of internal economic recovery. Despite passage in 1934 of the Trade Agreements Act, which authorized reciprocal tariff reductions, the decade was characterized by international economic warfare. Congress enacted neutrality legislation intended to prevent U.S. involvement in the event of another world war. The president sought to improve relations with Latin America through his GOOD NEIGHBOR POLICY.

As president, Roosevelt pioneered the political use of radio, frequently addressing the American people in a relaxed, homey manner. His unique political style, charm, and charisma brought him a record four terms. He beat Hoover in 1932, secured an overwhelming landslide victory over Alfred M. Landon in 1936, defeated Wendell L. Willkie for an unprecedented third term, and won against Thomas E. Dewey in 1944.

As an administrator, Roosevelt frequently bypassed his cabinet, relying on informal advisors who held minor posts in government. While he enlarged the role of government through his New Deal, he usually created emergency agencies to implement new programs for fear they would be stifled by the bureaucracy. He met his greatest defeat at the hands of the U.S. Supreme Court, which declared much of the early New Deal legislation unconstitutional. When he attempted to increase the size of the court and pack it with younger, more liberal justices in 1937, conservative opponents of the New Deal—and many liberals—summoned sufficient public and congressional opposition to stop the plan.

Commander in Chief. Roosevelt had hoped to keep the United States out of World War II, which began in September 1939, although he urged preparedness and advocated that the nation should serve as an arsenal for the democracies. Adolf Hitler's stunning victories that culminated in the fall of France prompted his decision to seek a third term in 1940. Gradually, Roosevelt moved the United States toward belligerency by the exchange of overage destroyers for the right to use British bases in the West Indies; through the LEND-LEASE program, which provided arms for Britain and later the USSR; and by the convoying of supply ships to England. The Japanese at-

tack on PEARL HARBOR on Dec. 7, 1941, and Germany's declaration of war gave him a new sense of mission after months of indecision caused by divided U.S. public opinion about involvement in the war.

During World War II, Roosevelt and Winston Churchill, Great Britain's prime minister, personally determined Allied military and naval strategy in the West. They gave priority to Germany's defeat and, in view of Hitler's claim that Germany was never defeated, only betrayed, in the first war, insisted on unconditional surrender. Although Roosevelt had joined with Churchill in the pre-Pearl Harbor ATLANTIC CHARTER (1941), a broad and idealistic statement of peacetime aims, he insisted during the war on limiting the Allied effort to military victory. He had great faith in his personal powers of persuasion, and, despite indications that Stalin's ambitions in Eastern Europe might violate the Atlantic Charter, Roosevelt foresaw Soviet-U.S. cooperation through a United Nations.

Under the pressures of wartime leadership, Roosevelt's health deteriorated. After the YALTA CONFERENCE, Roosevelt, exhausted from overwork, traveled to his Warm Springs, Ga., spa for a vacation in the spring of 1945. He died there on April 12 of a cerebral hemorrhage.

The Roosevelt presidency proved one of the most eventful in U.S. history. In the face of the potential collapse of the capitalist system, Roosevelt ushered in the interventionist state, which managed the economy in order to achieve publicly determined ends. In coming to the aid of Britain in World War II he determined that the preservation of Western liberal democratic institutions was a legitimate concern of the United States. In the process he converted the Democratic party to majority status through its appeal to urban, minority-group, and laboring-class voters and made it the vehicle of liberal reform in the 20th century.   ELLIOT A. ROSEN

Bibliography: Burns, James M., *Roosevelt: The Lion and the Fox* (1956) and *Roosevelt: The Soldier of Freedom* (1970); Dallek, Robert, *Franklin D. Roosevelt and American Foreign Policy, 1932-1945* (1979); Freidel, Frank, *Franklin D. Roosevelt*, 4 vols. (1952-73); Jones, Alfred H., *Roosevelt's Image Brokers* (1974); Lash, Joseph P., *Eleanor and Franklin* (1971) and *Roosevelt and Churchill, 1939-1941* (1976); Leuchtenburg, William E., *Franklin D. Roosevelt and the New Deal* (1963); Rosen, Elliot A., *Hoover, Roosevelt, and the Brains Trust* (1977); Schlesinger, Arthur, *The Age of Roosevelt*, 3 vols. (1957-60); Tugwell, Rexford G., *Roosevelt's Revolution* (1977).

Roosevelt, Theodore

Theodore Roosevelt became the 26th president of the United States after the death by assassination of William McKinley, on Sept. 14, 1901; he was elected to the office in his own right in 1904, serving until 1909. As president and political leader, Roosevelt was an articulate spokesman for the aspirations and values of progressivism, the reform movement that flourished in the United States from 1900 to World War I. He dominated that era in the nation's history.

Early Life and Career. Roosevelt was born into an old, prosperous Dutch family in New York City on Oct. 27, 1858. His father, a glass importer, wielded enormous influence over the boy, instilling in him a determination to strengthen his frail, asthmatic body; to follow a stern Christian moral code; and to enjoy the life of the mind. Young Roosevelt was educated at Harvard, where he graduated in 1880, still unsure of his life's work. In that year he married Alice H. Lee, a woman from Massachusetts. Her death (1884), only hours after his mother had died, left him bereaved, but in just less than three years he married Edith Kermit Carow.

During the 1880s, Roosevelt divided his life between politics and writing. He served three one-year terms in the New York Assembly (1882-84), where he became known as an independent Republican. He supported civil service reform, legislation to benefit working people, and bills designed to improve the government of New York City. He proved himself a party regular, however, with his support, in 1884, of James G. Blaine against Democrat Grover Cleveland for the presidency. After living as a rancher in the Dakota Territory for two years, he returned (1886) and ran for mayor of New York City, finishing last in a three-way race. His literary and

THEODORE ROOSEVELT
26th President of the United States (1901–09)

Nickname: "TR"; "Trust-Buster"; "Teddy"
Born: Oct. 27, 1858, New York City
Education: Harvard College (graduated 1880)
Profession: Author, Public Official
Religious Affiliation: Dutch Reformed
Marriage: Oct. 27, 1880, to Alice Hathaway Lee
  (1861–84); Dec. 2, 1886, to Edith Kermit Carow
  (1861–1948)
Children: Alice Lee Roosevelt (1884–1980); Theodore
  Roosevelt (1887–1944); Kermit Roosevelt
  (1889–1943); Ethel Carow Roosevelt (1891–1977); Ar-
  chibald Bulloch Roosevelt (1894–1979); Quentin
  Roosevelt (1897–1918)
Political Affiliation: Republican
Writings: *The Naval War of 1812* (1882); *The Winning
  of the West* (1889–96); *African Game Trails* (1910);
  Autobiography (1913); *America and the World War*
  (1915)
Died: Jan. 6, 1919, Oyster Bay, N.Y.
Buried: Young's Memorial Cemetery, Oyster Bay, N.Y.

Vice-President and Cabinet Members
Vice-President: Charles Warren Fairbanks (1905–09)
Secretary of State: John M. Hay (1901–05); Elihu Root
  (1905–09); Robert Bacon (1909)
Secretary of the Treasury: Lyman J. Gage (1901–02);
  Leslie M. Shaw (1902–07); George B. Cortelyou
  (1907–09)
Secretary of War: Elihu Root (1901–04); William H.
  Taft (1904–08); Luke E. Wright (1908–09)
Attorney General: Philander C. Knox (1901–04); Wil-
  liam H. Moody (1904–06); Charles J. Bonaparte
  (1906–09)
Postmaster General: Charles Emory Smith (1901–02);
  Henry C. Payne (1902–04); Robert J. Wynne
  (1904–05); George B. Cortelyou (1905–07); George
  von L. Meyer (1907–09)
Secretary of the Navy: James D. Long (1901–02); Wil-
  liam H. Moody (1902–04); Paul Morton (1904–05);
  Charles J. Bonaparte (1905–06); Victor H. Metcalf
  (1906–08); Truman H. Newberry (1908–09)
Secretary of the Interior: Ethan A. Hitchcock
  (1901–07); James R. Garfield (1907–09)
Secretary of Agriculture: James Wilson
Secretary of Commerce and Labor: George B. Cortel-
  you (1903–04); Victor H. Metcalf (1904–06); Oscar
  S. Straus (1906–09)

historical writing, which began early in the decade, gained
momentum late in the 1880s when he wrote, among other
works, biographies of Thomas Hart Benton (1886) and Gou-
verneur Morris (1888) and published the first two volumes of
his well-researched *Winning of the West* (1889). This work
was completed in 1896 with an additional two volumes.

Roosevelt's political career blossomed in the next 10 years.
Named a civil-service commissioner in 1889 by President Benjamin Harrison, he battled successfully to increase the number of positions that were based on merit and to improve the
commission's administrative procedures. He resigned this office in 1895 to become president of New York City's Board of
Police Commissioners in the reform administration of William
L. Strong. After 2 years he was back in Washington, this time
as assistant secretary of the navy under President William Mc-
Kinley. A nationalist and an expansionist, Roosevelt used his
office in whatever way he could to prepare the nation for war
with Spain. Once the SPANISH-AMERICAN WAR came (1898), he
helped organize the ROUGH RIDERS, saw considerable action
in Cuba, and returned to the United States a colonel with
fond remembrances of his regiment's bravery. Roosevelt's
sudden fame and his reputation as an independent moved
Thomas Collier PLATT, boss of New York's Republican party,
to nominate him for governor in 1898. He won in a close
election that fall.

Roosevelt's governorship (1899–1900) prepared him well for
high office in Washington. He steered a middle course between subservience to the political machine and independent reformism. He championed civil service, backed a measure to tax corporation franchises, and approved several bills
supportive of labor and social reform. In general, he had developed the concept of a positive, active state government by
the time "Boss" Platt decided to "kick him upstairs." Working
with others, Platt engineered Roosevelt's nomination as President McKinley's vice-presidential running mate in 1900. In
November the Republican ticket was easily elected.

Presidency. McKinley's assassination in September 1901 cata-
pulted Roosevelt to the presidency, much to the dismay of
Republican conservatives. He assured his party that he would
continue McKinley's policies, and until 1904 he moved cautiously while working to gain control of the national Republican organization. Even so, these years witnessed certain new
directions in Washington as Roosevelt sought to accommodate the developing reform movement. Disturbed, as were
others, by the growing power of the large corporations, Roosevelt ordered (1902) the Justice Department to bring suit under the SHERMAN ANTI-TRUST ACT (1890) against the Northern
Securities Company, a railroad monopoly in the northwest.
This suit launched a "trust-busting" crusade against big business that would carry over into Roosevelt's second administration. In 1903 he persuaded Congress to establish the Bureau of Corporations, an investigative agency of interstate
corporations, lodged in the newly created Department of
Commerce and Labor. He also supported the Elkins Bill
(1903), which prohibited the use of the rebate by railroads.

Roosevelt departed from past practice in another way.
When, in 1902, the anthracite coal miners struck, he became
the first president to intervene in a labor-management dispute, threatening to seize the mines in order to persuade the
recalcitrant owners to accept mediation. An arbitration commission subsequently awarded the miners a favorable settlement. Finally, Roosevelt advanced the cause of conservation.
An enthusiastic supporter of the Newlands Bill (1902) on rec-
lamation and irrigation, Roosevelt also backed Chief Forester
Gifford PINCHOT in expanding the nation's forest reserve, setting aside waterpower sites and millions of acres of coal
lands, and encouraging conservation on the state level.

His record together with his firm control of the Republican
party won Roosevelt the presidential nomination, then the
1904 election against Democrat Alton B. Parker. His second
administration reflected the quickened pace of the progressive movement, and he assumed an increasingly radical posture. In 1906, Congress enacted moderate reformist legislation: the Hepburn Act, which strengthened the authority of
the Interstate Commerce Commission over railroads; the

Meat Inspection and the Pure Food and Drug bills, which, respectively, provided for federal inspection of packing plants and prohibited the interstate transportation of adulterated drugs or mislabeled foods; and an employer's liability law (subsequently declared unconstitutional).

During his remaining White House years, Roosevelt combined assaults on the "malefactors of wealth" with the presentation of reform proposals to Congress, including federal supervision of all interstate business. Many of his detractors charged that his radical policies had precipitated the Banker's Panic of 1907. As right-wing criticism mounted, Roosevelt's relations with Congress soured, and many of his initiatives were frustrated during his last year in office.

Roosevelt's conduct of foreign relations was even bolder and more vigorous than his domestic program. After Colombia's rejection (1903) of a treaty giving the United States rights to a canal across the isthmus of Panama, he supported a Panamanian revolt and then negotiated a similar treaty with the new nation. He subsequently supervised the construction of the Panama Canal and in 1904 promulgated the Roosevelt Corollary to the MONROE DOCTRINE, justifying U.S. intervention in the affairs of Latin American nations if their weakness or wrongdoing warranted such action. In 1905 he mediated the Russo-Japanese War, for which he won the Nobel Peace Prize, and in general he worked to maintain the balance of power in Asia and the Pacific. In the Atlantic he also played a role in smoothing over a 1905 crisis among the European powers on the Moroccan question. A staunch imperialist, Roosevelt used his office to streamline the army and enlarge the navy in order to protect U.S. acquisitions abroad. Overall he labored effectively to prepare the United States for a larger role in world affairs.

Postpresidential Years. By the time Roosevelt stepped down from the presidency in 1909, the Republican party was badly divided between the conservatives and the progressives. In the next two years, under his chosen successor, William Howard TAFT, the rift widened, essentially because of Taft's inept leadership. When Roosevelt returned from an African safari and a grand tour of Europe in June 1910, he intervened in Republican party affairs hoping to conciliate the warring factions. His efforts unsuccessful, he went into retirement at his Oyster Bay, N.Y., home but was drawn into politics once again after a series of disputes with Taft. Roosevelt, now the leader of the Republican's progressive wing, challenged his former friend for the party's presidential nomination in 1912 but was crushed by the Taft "steamroller" in Chicago and subsequently established the National PROGRESSIVE PARTY (popularly known as the BULL MOOSE PARTY). His campaign theme, the New Nationalism, represented the most ambitious and comprehensive reform program of the day, excepting socialism. His platform called for increases in economic regulation and new social reforms. The ensuing campaign centered on Roosevelt and the Democratic candidate, Woodrow WILSON, whose New Freedom was developed as an alternative to Bull Moose formulas. Roosevelt divided the Republican vote with Taft, and Wilson was elected.

In the years after 1912, Roosevelt gradually returned to his former Republicanism. He became a critic of Wilson's foreign policy and moved ever closer to advocating war with Germany. Still a prolific writer, he wrote his acclaimed autobiography (1913) during this period. He aspired to the Republican presidential nomination in 1916 but was disappointed when the party turned to Charles Evans Hughes for its standard-bearer. Roosevelt fell ill in 1918 and died at Sagamore Hill, his Oyster Bay home, on Jan. 6, 1919.

The significance of Roosevelt's leadership lay in his use of high office to curb private greed and power in a day when Americans were disturbed by the abuses of big business, the waste of the nation's natural resources, and the threatened loss of traditional values. He elevated the presidency to a level it had not reached since the time of Abraham Lincoln. Some have labeled Roosevelt a rank opportunist for his shifting of position on key issues, but as a democratic politician he prided himself in responding to the changing needs of the citizenry. A master publicist for the reform movement in the

early 20th century, he commanded widespread popular support as much because of his remarkable personality as anything else: he was colorful, witty, robust, outspoken, and humane.   ROBERT F. WESSER

Bibliography: Blum, John M., *The Republican Roosevelt,* 2d ed. (1954); Burton, David H., *Theodore Roosevelt* (1973); Chessman, G. Wallace, *Theodore Roosevelt and the Politics of Power* (1969); Harbaugh, William H., *The Life and Times of Theodore Roosevelt,* new rev. ed. (1975); McCullough, David, *Mornings on Horseback* (1981); Morris, Edmund, *The Rise of Theodore Roosevelt* (1979); Mowry, George E., *The Era of Theodore Roosevelt: 1900-1912* (1958); Norton, A. A., *Theodore Roosevelt* (1980); Pringle, Henry F., *Theodore Roosevelt: A Biography,* rev. ed. (1956).

root   (botany):   see PLANT.

root   (mathematics)

A root, or solution, of an EQUATION is a real or complex number that satisfies the equation. A root of a number a is a solution of the equation $x^n = a$. For $n = 2$, the equation is $x^2 = a$, and the solutions $x = \pm \sqrt{a}$ are called the square roots of a. Similarly, $x = \sqrt[3]{a}$ is called the cube root of a, and so on. The equation $x^n = a$ is a special case of a POLYNOMIAL equation $a_n x^n + a_{n-1} x^{n-1} + \ldots + a_0 = 0$, which, by the fundamental theorem of algebra, always has n (real or complex) roots. The square root of -1 is of particular interest in algebra, for there is no number that multiplied by itself yields -1 as a result. Therefore, the square root of -1 is called an imaginary number; its symbol is i.   JAMES M. ORTEGA

Root, Elihu

An American statesman, Elihu Root, b. Clinton, N.Y., Feb. 15, 1845, d. Feb. 7, 1937, won the Nobel Peace Prize in 1912 for his efforts on behalf of world peace. Admitted to the bar shortly after the Civil War, Root, a Republican, was U.S. attorney for the southern district of New York from 1883 to 1885. As secretary of war (1899–1904) in the cabinets of William McKinley and Theodore Roosevelt, he reorganized the army and established (1901) the Army War College. He was Roosevelt's secretary of state (1905–09), reforming the consular service, improving U.S. relations with Latin America, and sponsoring (1908) a series of arbitration treaties—that now bear his name—with most European nations. Root convinced Latin American leaders to participate in the Second Hague Conference; as chief U.S. counsel before the Hague Tribunal he settled a dispute with Great Britain regarding North Atlantic coastal fisheries. A staunch supporter of the League of Nations, Root helped draft (1920–21) the constitution of the INTERNATIONAL COURT OF JUSTICE.   ROBERT H. FERRELL

Bibliography: Jessup, Philip C., *Elihu Root,* 2 vols. (1938); Leopold, R. W., *Elihu Root and the Conservative Tradition* (1954; repr. 1965).

Root, John Wellborn

The American architect John Wellborn Root, b. Lumpkin, Ga., Jan. 10, 1850, d. Jan. 15, 1891, played a leading role in the development of the SKYSCRAPER and in the CHICAGO SCHOOL OF ARCHITECTURE. He received much of his education in England but returned to the United States to graduate (1869) from New York University as a civil engineer. Root moved to Chicago in 1871, where he and Daniel H. BURNHAM formed their celebrated partnership in 1873, with Root as the designer. Root's plans for the Montauk Block (1881–82) reveal his skill in uniting functionally expressive architecture and new technology with the needs of the occupants. Such subsequent buildings as The Rookery (1885–86) and the Rand-McNally Building (1888–90) continued this fusion of function and innovation. Root's masterpiece is the Monadnock Building (1889–91), a 16-story masonry slab with elegantly tapered walls ending in a simple flared parapet.   J. MEREDITH NEIL

Bibliography: Hoffman, Donald, *The Architecture of John Wellborn Root* (1973); Monroe, Harriet, *John Wellborn Root: A Study of His Life and Work* (1869; repr. 1966).

Roots

Alex HALEY wrote his family's fictionalized history, *Roots* (1976), after tracing his ancestors back seven generations to a small village in Gambia. Haley's history begins with the abduction of ancestor Kunta Kinte into slavery in the American South. Kinte's descendants live through the entire black American experience. Televised in two sections (1977, 1979), *Roots* was among the most popular programs ever shown on U.S. television.   CHARLOTTE D. SOLOMON

Rops, Félicien   [rohps]

The Belgian etcher and painter Félicien Rops, b. July 7, 1833, d. Aug. 23, 1898, is known for the always imaginative and often erotic and sacrilegious imagery of his prints. A talented printmaker, he exploited all the nuances of the DRYPOINT, AQUATINT, and soft-ground ETCHING techniques. Rops was largely self-taught. As a youth he contributed illustrations to student magazines. In 1856 he founded the satirical magazine *Uylenspiegel,* for which he produced some of his best lithographs (1859–60). After 1862 he became known as a book illustrator, working with such authors as Charles Baudelaire and Stéphane Mallarmé.   STEPHANIE WINKELBAUER

roquette   [roh-ket']

Roquette, or arugula, *Eruca sativa,* of the mustard family, Cruciferae, is a coarse annual herb whose strong-flavored leaves are used in salads. The plant's leaves closely resemble those of the turnip and radish. When used as a vegetable, roquette must be grown in cool temperatures, because it goes to seed quickly in hot weather. Leaves are cut six to eight weeks after planting. The flowers are white or creamy yellow and have an orange-blossom odor. In India and the Mediterranean region, the seeds are pressed for their oil.   O. A. LORENZ

Rorem, Ned   [rohr'-uhm]

Composer Ned Rorem, b. Richmond, Ind., Oct. 23, 1923, is best known for the several hundred art songs he has written. During the time he lived in Morocco and Paris (1949–57), his song texts came from several languages. His settings since returning to the United States, however, have been drawn primarily from the work of Walt Whitman and from 20th-century American poets. Rorem has also composed several song cycles, five operas, and many instrumental works. Since writing his *Paris Diary* (1966), he has published a series of diaries, as well as essays on music and literature.   EDWARD A. BERLIN

Rorschach test: see PROJECTIVE TESTS.

Rosa, João Guimarães

A major force in modern Brazilian literature, João Guimarães Rosa, b. June 27, 1908, d. Nov. 19, 1967, practiced medicine in the *sertão,* the sparsely populated hinterland where he had been born, before becoming a diplomat in the Brazilian foreign service. The *sertão,* however, remained the background for his fiction, which includes several volumes of short stories—notably *Sagarana* (1946; Eng. trans., 1966) and *The Third Bank of the River* (1962; Eng. trans., 1968). It was his monumental novel *The Devil to Pay in the Backlands* (1956; Eng. trans., 1963), however, that brought him international fame and that sustains his reputation today.

Bibliography: Harss, L., and Dohmann, B., *Into the Mainstream: Conversations with Latin American Writers* (1969); Vincent, J. S., *João Guimarães Rosa* (1978).

Rosa, Salvator

Although an accomplished Italian poet and musician, and famous in his time for his talents as a comic actor and satirist, Salvator Rosa, b. 1615, d. Mar. 15, 1673, is best known today for his brooding landscape paintings that prefigure the romantic painters of a later era. Rosa was born and trained in Naples, and his nature studies in the Neapolitan countryside had

an important influence on his later work. For nine years (1640–49) Rosa lived under the patronage of the Medicis in Florence, where most of his quasi-romantic landscapes—characterized by their dark skies, looming crags, and picturesque ruins—were painted, as well as the seascapes and battle scenes for which he was also noted.   ELEANOR TUFTS

Bibliography: Rowarth, Wendy W., *Pictor Successor: A Study of Salvator Rosa as Satirist, Cynic, and Painter* (1978).

Rosario   [roh-sahr'-ee-oh]

Rosario, a major port city and transportation center of Argentina, lies on the Paraná River, 300 km (190 mi) northwest of Buenos Aires. It has a population of 875,623 (1980). Food processing, petroleum refining, and brick making are economically important. Two of Argentina's six rail systems link the city to the port of Buenos Aires. The National University of Rosario (1968) is located there.

Rosario was founded in 1725, and by the end of the 19th century it had become the principal shipping point for produce from the interior.   RICHARD W. WILKIE

rosary

A rosary is a circular string of beads used by Roman Catholics for counting prayers. The term is also applied to the prayer beads used by Buddhists, Hindus, and Muslims. In the Western church, the rosary commonly consists of 5 (originally 15) decades, or sets of 10 beads, for the recitation of the Hail Mary (*Ave Maria*), separated by a single bead for the recitation of the Our Father (*Paternoster,* or Lord's Prayer). The Glory Be to the Father (*Gloria Patri*) is generally said after each decade. During the recitation of the prayers, meditation on a series of biblical themes, called the joyous, sorrowful, and glorious mysteries, is recommended. A feast of the Rosary is kept on October 7, the anniversary of the Christian victory over the Muslim Turks at Lepanto (1571).

Bibliography: Ward, J. N., ed., *Five for Sorrow, Ten for Joy* (1974).

Rosas, Juan Manuel de   [roh'-sahs]

Juan Manuel de Rosas, b. Mar. 30, 1793, d. Mar. 14, 1877, twice governor of Buenos Aires (1829–32 and 1835–52), ruled Argentina as virtual dictator during his second term of office. A ruthless tyrant, he is nevertheless credited with unifying the country when it was seriously threatened with disintegration.

Born to a wealthy family that owned vast cattle ranches on the Argentine coast, the young Rosas led the life of a gaucho (cowboy) until he was appointed (1820) head of the provincial army. After the conservative provincial government of Manuel Dorrego was overthrown (1828), Rosas emerged as the advocate for federalism, the autonomy of the constituent states of the Argentine federation. With his gaucho militia, he fought the insurgent centralist unitarians. He began to consolidate his power in 1835. Under his guidance, the province of Buenos Aires came to dominate even more than before the political and economic affairs of the inland provinces. The Mazorca—a personal police organization answerable only to Rosas—dealt with opponents of his dictatorship. Rosas's tenure was sustained not only by his considerable manipulative talents but also by an expanding economy. Markets for Argentine goods, particularly in Great Britain, created prosperity; immigration contributed to agricultural and industrial expansion; the public debt was reduced. Disputes with Britain and France, however, led to at least two blockades of Buenos Aires. Also, the commercial monopoly enjoyed by Buenos Aires caused the interior provinces to revolt in 1852. Rosas was defeated by Gen. Justo José de URQUIZA at Monte Caseros and went into permanent exile in Great Britain.

Bibliography: Burgin, Miron, *Economic Aspects of Argentine Federalism* (1946); Cady, John F., *Foreign Intervention in the Rio de La Plata 1838–50* (1929; repr. 1969).

Roscellin   [rahs'-uh-lin]

Roscellin (or Roscelin), c.1045–1120, was a French philosopher credited with originating NOMINALISM, the doctrine that only real things are individuals and that species or universals are mere words. He taught at Compiègne, Loches, Besançon, and Tours. Virtually none of his writing survives, and thus his views can only be imperfectly reconstructed from the testimony of his opponents. He was severely criticized by Saint Anselm and also by Peter ABELARD, who, however, studied under Roscellin and shows his influence. The Synod of Soissons charged Roscellin with heresy (1092) for teaching that the three persons of the Trinity are three separate individuals. He apparently recanted or satisfactorily explained his views because he escaped condemnation.

Bibliography: Gilson, Étienne, *History of Christian Philosophy in the Middle Ages* (1955).

Roscommon   [rahs-kahm'-uhn]

Roscommon is a county in Connacht province in north central Ireland. Situated on Ireland's fertile central plain, the county has an area of 2,463 km² (951 mi²) and a population of 54,543 (1981). The county town is Roscommon. Livestock raising and agriculture are economically important. Sheep are raised in the highlands, oats and potatoes are grown, and coal is mined in the hills. Most of Roscommon belonged to the O'Kelly family before the English invasion of the area in the 17th century. It continued to remain isolated from England after the occupation.

rose

The rose has been celebrated in the art, music, literature, and religions of numerous civilizations since ancient times, and garden roses were cultivated by Egyptians as early as 4000 BC. Today roses are grown commercially and in home gardens, and hybrids are developed with much planning and great care. The genus *Rosa*, comprising 150 species as well as numerous hybrids and cultivars, belongs to the family Rosaceae and is related to the apple, the strawberry, the cherry, and the almond. Indigenous to the Northern Hemisphere, rose species are distributed from China to Europe and temperate North America. A few occur north of the Arctic Circle and at high elevations in the tropics.

Roses grow on erect, climbing, or trailing shrubs, the stems of which are covered with thorns. The leaves, which alternate along a branch, have 3 to 11 toothed leaflets. Solitary flowers or loose clusters bloom at the tips of stems. The ovary of the flower, known as the hip, turns bright red, yellow, or black at maturity. At the rim of a hip grow five sepals, which alternate with five petals, a trait common to ancient species and elaborate modern varieties. At the center of the petals, stamens are arranged in several concentric whorls; in many rose cultivars, the stamens have become petallike, giving rise to the full double flowers prized by gardeners. Most species impart a distinctive fragrance.

Most roses that are cultivated today are hybrids of early species. Classic old roses include the French rose, *R. gallica;* the tea rose, *R. odorata;* the cabbage rose, *R. centifolia;* and the richly fragrant damask rose, *R. damascena,* which yields attar of roses, an essential oil used in perfumes. Other important parents of modern rose cultivars include the climbing Cathay rose, *R. cathayensis;* the trailing memorial rose, *R. wichuraiana;* the China rose, *R. chinensis;* and a Japanese rose, *R. multiflora.*

Hundreds of cultivars have been developed by selection and hybridization of Old World species; the breeding of New World species in creating new cultivars has as yet been unexplored. The most popular group consists of the hybrid tea roses, having a wide color range, a unique fragrance, and continuous bloom throughout the growing season. Other commonly grown types include: floribundas, with numerous petals; polyanthas, having large clusters of flowers; miniatures, the entire plant of which ranges from 7 to 30 cm (3 to 12 in) in height; and rambling or climbing roses.

Other popular rose species include the prairie rose, *R. setigera,* a rambler native to North America; the Burnet or Scottish rose, *R. spinosissima,* an extremely hardy plant having many thorns; and the rugosa rose, *R. rugosa,* a Japanese species that is planted in hedges and produces rose hips that are a commercial source of a tea and a syrup rich in vitamin C. The Cherokee rose, *R. laevigata,* and the Lady Banks rose, *R. banksiae,* are climbers that frequently are grown against garden walls.

Bibliography: Edwards, Gordon, *Wild and Old Garden Roses* (1975); Gault, S. M., and Synge, P. M., *The Dictionary of Roses in Color* (1971); Gore, Catherine F., *The Book of Roses* (1978); Shepherd, Roy E., *History of the Rose* (1954; repr. 1978); Taylor, N., and Wolff, G. P., *Taylor's Guide to Roses* (1985).

hybrid tea rose · hybrid rugosa · French rose · miniature rose · grandiflora

Roses, genus Rosa, *are prized for their rich colors, fragrance, and elegant forms. The hybrid tea rose is a modern type noted for its long blooming period and spicy fragrance. The hybrid rugosa is a hardy type of East Asian origin; it bears reddish orange fruit, or rose hips, in the fall. Grandifloras, derived from hybrid tea roses and floribundas, bear many-petaled flowers. Miniature roses, some producing blooms no larger than a fingernail, have become popular houseplants. The French rose,* R. gallica, *is an old garden type.*

Rose, Pete

Peter Edward Rose, b. Cincinnati, Ohio, Apr. 14, 1941, is one of the most versatile, aggressive baseball players in history. Nicknamed ''Charlie Hustle,'' this switch-hitter has played both infield and outfield. Rose joined the Cincinnati Reds in 1963 and was voted Rookie of the Year. Starting in 1965 he batted over .300 for 9 straight seasons, winning consecutive batting crowns (1968–69) with averages of .335 and .348. In 1973, Rose again won the batting title (.338), earning National League (NL) Most Valuable Player honors. In 1978 he achieved his 3,000th hit and that year set an NL record by hitting safely in 44 consecutive games. Traded to the Phillies after the 1978 season, he became (1979) the only player ever to collect 200 or more hits in 10 different years. During the 1984 season Rose surpassed Carl Yastrzemski's all-time record (3,308) for games played and returned to the Reds as player-manager. On Sept. 11, 1985, he broke Ty Cobb's record (4,191) for most career hits, a mark once considered unapproachable. Rose's lifetime batting average through 1985 was .304.

Bibliography: Libby, Bill, *Pete Rose: They Call Him Charlie Hustle* (1972); Rose, Pete, *Pete Rose: My Life in Baseball* (1979).

rose of Jericho

The rose of Jericho, common name for *Anastatica hierochuntica*, is a small rounded herb in the mustard family, Cruciferae. Native to deserts from Arabia to Syria and Algeria, its leaves are oval, and white flowers are borne in spikes, followed by short, wide fruit with two seeds. After fruiting, the plant sheds its leaves and rolls up into a dry ball, which is blown across the desert. When it reaches a moist area, the seeds are dropped and immediately start to germinate—thus the frequently used name, resurrection plant.

Rose of Lima, Saint

The first canonized saint of the Americas, Saint Rose, b. 1586, d. Aug. 24 or 30, 1617, was a recluse and mystic who lived her whole life in Lima. A Dominican tertiary, she is remembered for her dedication to prayer, rigorous ascetic practices, and works of charity. She was canonized in 1671. Feast day: Aug. 23 (formerly Aug. 30).

rose window

Rose windows derive their name from their shape, which is round and made up of petallike forms radiating from a central point. Adorned with stained glass, they first appeared in Gothic cathedrals of the 12th century, such as the Cathedral of Notre Dame in Paris (begun 1163). Large windows ranging from 9 to 12 m (30 to 40 ft) in diameter were placed on the western facades of the buildings; smaller windows were used at the ends of the north and south transepts. The windows symbolize the Virgin Mary, whose flower is a rose.

In early rose windows the glass was supported by plate tracery with the design pierced in the stone. Later, more flexible bar tracery was used, with bars built up on the arch principle and thus not wholly dependent on the walls for support. The glass in nearly all rose windows is arranged in a nonrepresentational design, with colors arranged for the sake of a unified decorative effect. An interesting exception is the rose window in the Cathedral at León, Spain (13th to 14th century), in which the figures of the apostles radiate about the center, those below the center being upside down. By the late 1300s, rose windows in the flamboyant style (with flamelike tracery) began to appear, as in the north rose (late 1400s) of the Cathedral of Saint Étienne at Sens, France.   MARION B. WILSON

Bibliography: Lee, Lawrence, et al., *Stained Glass* (1976); Nervo, Joanne, comp., *Stained Glass Window Patterns* (1972).

Rosebery, Archibald Philip Primrose, 5th Earl of [rohz'-bur-ee]

Britain's prime minister from Mar. 3, 1894, to June 21, 1895, Archibald Philip Primrose, 5th earl of Rosebery, b. May 7,

1847, d. May 21, 1929, led a divided and ineffectual ministry. Rosebery, a Liberal imperialist, served (1886, 1892–94) as foreign secretary under William Ewart GLADSTONE. During Rosebery's 15-month tenure as prime minister, a factionalized Liberal party was unable to push any legislation past the united Conservatives, and Rosebery resigned when Commons rejected a minor Liberal measure. His establishment (1894) of a protectorate over Uganda and his support of the SOUTH AFRICAN WAR (1899–1902) estranged him from his party. The breach was completed in 1905 when Rosebery declared his opposition to Irish Home Rule. Rosebery wrote several books, including biographies of the William Pitts (1891, 1910).

Bibliography: James, Robert R., *Rosebery* (1963).

Rosecrans, William S. [rohz'-kranz]

William Starke Rosecrans, b. Kingston, Ohio, Sept. 6, 1819, d. Mar. 11, 1898, was a moderately successful Union general in the U.S. Civil War. He graduated (1842) from West Point and after 12 years in the army resigned to enter the kerosene business in Cincinnati. Returning to the army in 1861, Rosecrans— a talented strategist who often argued with his superiors— served ably under Gen. George B. MCCLELLAN and Gen. John POPE. As an army commander he won the battles of Iuka and Corinth in 1862 and in 1863 brilliantly maneuvered the Confederates out of Chattanooga without a battle. He was relieved of his command, however, after his forces were routed by Gen. Braxton BRAGG at nearby CHICKAMAUGA in September 1863. After the war, Rosecrans served as minister to Mexico (1867–69) and as a U.S. congressman from California (1881–85).   WARREN W. HASSLER, JR.

Bibliography: Lamers, William M., *The Edge of Glory: A Biography of General William S. Rosecrans* (1961).

rosemary

Rosemary, R. officinalis, a perennial evergreen shrub, is used as an herbal seasoning. Its leaves add flavor to meat dishes, soups, and potatoes, and its flowers yield an aromatic oil that is used in perfumes.

Rosemary is an evergreen shrub, *Rosmarinus officinalis*, of the mint family, Labiatae, native to the Mediterranean and adjoining areas. It grows to about 1.8 m (6 ft) high and is cultivated for its aromatic leaves and its usually blue flower clusters. The dried leaves are used as food seasoning; the flower clusters are the source of rosemary oil, which is used in inexpensive perfumes. Rosemary has long been a symbol of fidelity and remembrance. The name *rosemary* is also applied to a North American evergreen shrub, *Ceratiola ericoides*, of the crowberry family, Empetraceae. Wild rosemary is *Ledum palustre*, an Asiatic evergreen shrub of the heath family, Ericaceae.

Rosenberg, Alfred [roh'-zen-bairk]

Alfred Rosenberg, b. Jan. 12, 1893, d. Oct. 16, 1946, was an ideologist of German Nazism. Russian–born, he studied architecture before joining (1919) the National Socialist (Nazi) party in Munich. As editor of the party newspaper, *Völkischer Beobachter*, he developed anti-Christian and anti-Semitic theories. His book *Der Mythus des 20. Jahrhunderts* (The Myth of the 20th Century, 1934), an exposition of German racial purity, provided a theoretical framework for Adolf Hitler's policies. Minister for the occupied eastern territories during World War II, Rosenberg was hanged as a war criminal after he was found guilty at the Nuremberg Trials. English translations of his memoirs (1949) and selected writings (1970) have been published.

Bibliography: Cecil, Robert, *The Myth of the Master Race: Alfred Rosenberg and Nazi Ideology* (1972); Chandler, Albert R., *Rosenberg's Nazi Myth* (1945; repr. 1969).

Rosenberg, Harold [roh'-zen-burg]

The American art critic Harold Rosenberg, b. New York City, Feb. 2, 1906, d. July 11, 1978, was one of the major writers (along with Clement GREENBERG) on first-generation American abstract expressionism (1940s and '50s) and the originator of the term *action painting*. His publications include numerous essays for periodicals and many books devoted to the analysis of contemporary art, such as *The Tradition of the New* (1959), *The Anxious Object: Art Today and Its Audience* (1966), *The De-definition of Art: Action Art to Pop to Earthworks* (1972), and *Art On the Edge: Creators and Situations* (1975).

BARBARA CAVALIERE

Bibliography: Krim, S., "Remembering Harold Rosenberg," *Commentary*, November 1978; Kuspit, D. B., "Two Critics: Thomas B. Hess and Harold Rosenberg," *Artforum*, December 1978.

Rosenberg, Isaac

Isaac Rosenberg, b. Nov. 25, 1890, is among the most admired of a group of British poets whose work describes the experience of World War I trench warfare. Of Russian-Jewish origin, he wrote early poems interpreting Hebrew myth, but is better known for his haunting, elegiac war poems, such as "Break of Day in the Trenches." He died in battle on Apr. 1, 1918.

Bibliography: Parsons, Ian, *The Collected Works of Isaac Rosenberg* (1979).

Rosenberg, Julius and Ethel

Julius Rosenberg, b. New York City, May 12, 1918, and Ethel Greenglass Rosenberg, b. New York City, Sept. 28, 1915, were the first U.S. civilians executed for espionage. Julius Rosenberg, a member of the Communist party, was an engineer employed by the U.S. Army Signal Corps during World War II. He and his wife, Ethel, were accused of furnishing vital information about the atomic bomb to Soviet agents in 1944 and 1945. The major witness against them was Ethel's brother, David Greenglass, an employee at the Los Alamos atomic bomb

Julius and Ethel Rosenberg were convicted of giving information on U.S. nuclear weapons to the USSR. Although they steadfastly denied the charges, they were executed. Their trial spurred public debate on capital punishment, Communism, and the U.S. judicial process.

project. Greenglass, who testifed that he fed top-secret data about nuclear weapons to the Rosenbergs, was later sentenced to 15 years in prison. The Rosenbergs were convicted under the Espionage Act of 1917, and on Apr. 5, 1951, they were sentenced to death, which sparked worldwide protests. Despite the many and varied pleas that their lives be spared, President Dwight D. Eisenhower refused to commute their sentences, and they were executed on June 19, 1953.

Bibliography: Goldstein, Alvin H., *The Unquiet Death of Julius and Ethel Rosenberg* (1975); Meeropol, Michael and Robert, *We Are Your Sons: The Legacy of Ethel and Julius Rosenberg* (1975); Nizer, Louis, *The Implosion Conspiracy* (1973); Schneir, Walter and Miriam, *Invitation to an Inquest* (1965); Wexley, John, *The Judgment of Julius and Ethel Rosenberg* (1977).

Rosenbusch, Harry [roh'-zen-bush]

The German geologist Karl Heinrich Ferdinand "Harry" Rosenbusch, b. June 24, 1836, d. June 20, 1914, made important contributions to the geology of his time with a system for classifying rocks by their mineral content and their geological positioning in the Earth. He earned (1869) a Ph.D. from the University of Freiburg and taught at Freiburg (1870–73), the University of Strasbourg (1873–78), and the University of Heidelberg (1878–1908). Rosenbusch's research centered on the nature of rocks—particularly igneous rocks, which he divided into three classes: plutonic rocks situated deep within the Earth, dike rocks injected into neighboring rock masses, and volcanic rocks erupted from the surface of the Earth. His texts on the microscopic physiography of minerals (1873) and of bulky materials (1877) became standards, and his emphasis on field studies and microscopic studies did much to help advance the then-new science of mineralogy.

Rosenkavalier, Der [roh'-zen-kah-vahl-eer, dur]

The preeminence of Richard Strauss's *Der Rosenkavalier* (*The Rose-Bearer*) among operatic comedies is due not only to the beauty and liveliness of its music, but also to the sensitivity of the libretto by Hugo von Hofmannsthal. After the work's successful premiere in Dresden on Jan. 26, 1911, it won international acclaim. Although the opera is named for the young cavalier, Octavian, its central figure is the poignant Marschallin.

Field Marshal von Werdenberg is a commanding figure in the Vienna of the Empress Maria Theresa. But he is out of the city much of the time, and his wife, the Marschallin, is given to dalliances with younger men. Her most fervent love has been the teenage Octavian. Early one morning their dalliance is interrupted by the arrival of the Marschallin's boorish cousin, Baron Ochs von Lerchenau, a rustic nobleman who has come to town seeking the hand of Sophie von Faninal as his bride. Octavian makes his escape disguised as a servant girl, Mariandel, but not before the lecherous Baron has shown interest in him. Ochs has come to ask the Marschallin to designate a suitable bearer of the silver rose (token of betrothal among the aristocracy) to Sophie. The Marschallin, as a private joke, suggests Octavian.

The jest turns to sober reality. The Marschallin has realized that Octavian will some day meet a younger woman, and Octavian does indeed fall in love at first sight with Sophie. The Baron is soon eliminated, trapped by Octavian—disguised once again as Mariandel—into a humiliating assignation at a local inn. The Marschallin, hastily summoned, demands that Ochs disqualify himself as bridegroom, and he retires. Now Octavian, faced with the choice between his last and newest love, turns to Sophie. The Marschallin gracefully withdraws.

ROBERT LAWRENCE

Bibliography: Lehmann, Lotte, *Five Operas and Richard Strauss*, trans. by Ernest Pawel (1964); Mann, William, *Richard Strauss: A Critical Study of the Operas* (1966).

Rosenquist, James [roh'-zen-kwist]

The American artist James Rosenquist, b. Grand Forks, N.Dak., Nov. 29, 1933, has assimilated the techniques he learned as a billboard painter to the close-up, fragmented compositions he has produced since the 1960s, when he became associated with the POP ART movement. His paintings and assemblages of the '60s were enormous, garishly colored montages that focused on American popular culture (Coca-Cola, Marilyn Monroe, space technology). Rosenquist's major work of this period, the huge *F-111* (1965; Scull Collection, New York City), reflects his negative feelings about this experimental bomber in particular and American society in general. His paintings of the 1970s maintain the same "billboard" style, but the images and juxtapositions are more obscure, making his meaning more difficult to decipher. Rosenquist has experimented with other media, including film and environments. His earlier paintings have inspired a later series of lithographs.

LISA M. MESSINGER

Bibliography: Tucker, Marcia, *James Rosenquist* (1972).

Rosenwald, Julius   [roh'-zen-wahld]

Julius Rosenwald, b. Springfield, Ill., Aug. 12, 1862, d. Jan. 6, 1932, businessman and philanthropist, contributed millions of dollars to the welfare and education of blacks and Jews, food for German children after World War I, and gifts to the University of Chicago. As a young man Rosenwald was modestly successful in the clothing business. In 1895 he purchased one-fourth of Sears, Roebuck and Company, a retail and mail-order department store. He served as president of this firm (1910–25) and became (1925) chairman of the board. Rosenwald established (1917) the Julius Rosenwald Fund, which has provided gifts for education, including part of the costs for the construction of more than 4,500 schools for blacks in 15 southern states. He also established (1929) the Museum of Science and Industry in Chicago.

Bibliography: Jarrette, Alfred Q., *Julius Rosenwald* (1975); Werner, M. R., *Julius Rosenwald: The Life of a Practical Humanitarian* (1939).

Rosenzweig, Franz   [roh'-zen-tsvyk]

Franz Rosenzweig, b. Kassel, Germany, Dec. 25, 1886, d. Dec. 9, 1929, was a major figure in early-20th-century Jewish philosophy. From a culturally assimilated German-Jewish family, Rosenzweig decided to convert to Christianity, but he set himself first the task of finding a sense of what it meant to be a Jew so that his way to Christianity could be like that of the first Christians. This endeavor led (1913) him to a religious experience in which he rediscovered Judaism in its full depth. During his military service on the eastern front in World War I, he began to write—on postcards mailed home—his chief philosophic work, *The Star of Redemption* (1921; Eng. trans., 1971). This book has influenced Jews in both Europe and the United States who, like Rosenzweig, have sought to rediscover their Jewish identity.

After the war, Rosenzweig joined with other gifted German-Jewish intellectuals in developing an educational institution—the Jewish Lehrhaus (adult study center) in Frankfurt am Main—which embodied his pedagogical program for revitalizing Jewish culture. His active involvement lasted only until 1921, when he developed progressive paralysis. Despite this handicap he wrote several important essays and, with Martin Buber, produced a new translation of the Bible into German.

JOSEPH L. BLAU

Bibliography: Glatzer, Nahum N., ed., *Franz Rosenzweig: His Life and Thought*, 2d rev. ed. (1976).

Roses, Wars of the

The Wars of the Roses (1455–85) is the name given to a series of armed clashes between the houses of LANCASTER and YORK, rival claimants to the English crown. The name was first used long after the wars took place; it refers to the white rose of York and the red rose of Lancaster—badges supposedly used by the contenders. The Lancastrian king HENRY VI, an ineffectual ruler subject to periods of insanity, was challenged by Richard, duke of York, who claimed the throne through descent from Edward III. After the Battle of Saint Albans (1455), York became protector of the kingdom, but Henry's wife, MARGARET OF ANJOU, and the BEAUFORT family, along with oth-

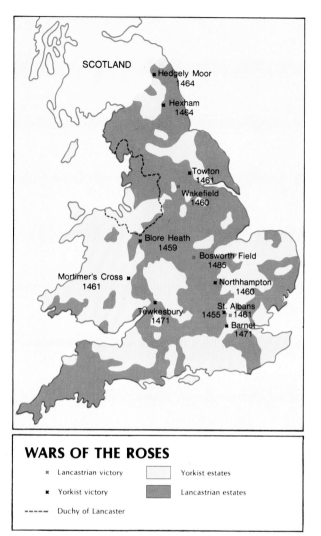

WARS OF THE ROSES

✳	Lancastrian victory		Yorkist estates
✴	Yorkist victory	▓	Lancastrian estates
-----	Duchy of Lancaster		

ers of her followers, recovered control. The war resumed in 1459, and in June 1460, York, allied with Richard Neville, earl of WARWICK, invaded England and defeated (July 10, 1460) a royal army at Northampton. York claimed the throne, but instead he was designated Henry's successor. Margaret, whose son was effectively disinherited, sent her army against the Yorkists at Wakefield, where York was killed (1460). The next year, York's son fought the decisive Battle of Towton and was crowned EDWARD IV. Henry, Margaret, and their son fled to Scotland.

War broke out again in 1469 when Warwick, estranged from Edward and allied with the king's brother George, duke of Clarence, invaded from Calais, defeated the king's forces at Edgecote, and briefly held Edward prisoner. After Edward regained control, Warwick invaded again, joining forces with Henry VI, who was restored to the throne. Edward fled to the Netherlands, but he returned (1471) and defeated Warwick and the Lancastrians at Barnet and Tewkesbury. Henry was imprisoned in the Tower of London, where he died.

The third phase of the wars began in 1483 when RICHARD III usurped the throne from his nephew, Edward IV's son EDWARD V. The Lancastrian claimant, Henry Tudor, aided by the French and by disaffected Yorkist nobles, invaded England and defeated Richard at Bosworth (1485). The new king was crowned HENRY VII.

GEORGE HOLMES

Bibliography: Chrimes, S. M., *Lancastrians, Yorkists, and Henry VII* (1964); Lander, J. R., *The Wars of the Roses* (1965); Ross, Charles, *Wars of the Roses* (1976).

Rosetta Stone   [roh-zet'-uh]

The Rosetta Stone is a block of black basalt bearing inscriptions that eventually supplied the key to the decipherment of the Egyptian hieroglyphic script. The stone was found accidentally in August 1799 by a group of soldiers in Napoleon's army while they were conducting engineering works at Fort Julien, near Rosetta (Arabic: Rashid), approximately 56 km (35 mi) northeast of Alexandria. Under the Treaty of Capitulation, signed in 1801, the stone was ceded to the British military authorities and taken to England for preservation in the British Museum. Its inscriptions, which record a decree issued in 196 BC under Ptolemy V Epiphanes, are written in two languages, Egyptian and Greek. The Egyptian version is written twice, once in hieroglyphics and once in demotic, a cursive development of the hieroglyphic script.

At the time of its discovery, it was accurately conjectured that the contents of the three different texts were identical; only the Greek, however, could be understood, as all knowledge of hieroglyphic writing had been lost since the 4th century AD, and of demotic shortly afterward. Two distinct, but interrelated, problems confronted the many scholars who worked on the inscriptions: the first was to discover whether the hieroglyphic signs represented phonetic sounds or were

The Rosetta Stone, a basalt slab inscribed by the priests of the Egyptian pharaoh Ptolemy V (r. 205–180 BC), became the key to the decipherment of Egyptian hieroglyphic writings. The script was deciphered (1822) by the French scholar Jean François Champollion, who discovered that the stone was inscribed in two languages— Egyptian and Greek— and three alphabets— hieroglyphic, demotic, and Greek.

merely pictorial symbols; the second was to determine the meanings of the individual words. Only Thomas YOUNG, a British physicist and medical practitioner, made any substantial progress in 20 years, but his achievement fell short of true decipherment. The distinction of making the final breakthrough in 1822 belongs to the French scholar Jean François CHAMPOLLION.   I. E. S. EDWARDS

Bibliography: Andrews, C., *The British Museum Book of the Rosetta Stone* (1985); Budge, E. A. W., *The Rosetta Stone* (1904).

rosewood

Rosewood is the popular name for a group of tropical woods that are noted for their beauty and are highly prized as veneers in making fine furniture, paneling, and decorative pieces. The four most important species are the Brazilian *Dalbergia nigra* (a JACARANDA), an almost black, oily, fragrant wood; *D. latifolia*, from India and Pakistan, a dark purple wood sometimes streaked with yellow; *D. Stevensoni*, from Honduras, which is used to make percussion instruments such as the xylophone; and *D. melanosylon*, an African wood that resembles ebony.

Rosh Hashanah   [rohsh huh-shah'-nah]

Rosh Hashanah (Hebrew for "head of the year") is the Jewish New Year, commemorating the creation of the world. It is celebrated in early fall, Tishri 1 by the Jewish calendar. Rosh Hashanah is a solemn occasion, the Day of Judgment, usher-

ing in the penitential season that culminates ten days later on YOM KIPPUR.

The distinctive feature of the synagogue service is the blowing of a ram's horn (SHOFAR). The liturgy of the day stresses the sovereignty of God and the hope that all humans will at last recognize him as Father and King.

The festival is celebrated for two days by the traditionally observant, whereas Reform Jews keep it for one day, in accord with biblical law. On the afternoon of the first day it is customary to go to a river or pond and recite tashlich, scriptural verses on repentance and forgiveness of sin.

BERNARD J. BAMBERGER

Bibliography: Schauss, Hayyim, *Jewish Festivals*, rev. ed. (1969).

Rosicrucians   [roh-zi-kroo'-shuhnz]

Rosicrucians are members of a worldwide esoteric society whose official emblem combines a rose and a cross. The society was apparently founded in Europe in medieval times and was given impetus by the publication of *Fama fraternitatis* (Account of the Brotherhood, 1614) and the *Confessio fraternitatis* (Confession of the Brotherhood, 1615). These pamphlets were probably written by the Lutheran pastor Johan Valentin Andrea (1586–1654). They describe the initiation into the mysteries of the east (particularly of ancient Egypt) of Christian Rosenkreuz, who was allegedly born in 1378 but is presumed to be an allegorical figure. In the 18th century several Rosicrucian groups were active in Russia, Poland, and Germany. The movement has close links with Freemasonry.

The first Rosicrucian society in the United States was founded in Pennsylvania in 1694. The Ancient Mystical Order Rosae Crucis has headquarters in San Jose, Calif. Founded in 1909 by H. Spencer Lewis, AMORC is an international fraternal order that operates through a system of lodges and fosters the Rosicrucian philosophy of developing humankind's highest potentialities and psychic powers.

Bibliography: Lewis, H. Spencer, *Rosicrucian Questions and Answers with a Complete History*, 16th ed. (1984); Lewis, Ralph, *Mental Alchemy*, 3d ed. (1984); Waite, Arthur E., *The Brotherhood of the Rosy Cross* (1924); Yates, Frances A., *The Rosicrucian Enlightenment* (1972; repr. 1986).

rosin   [rahz'-in]

Rosin, also called colophony, is a translucent, brittle RESIN used in varnish and many other products. It is produced as a residue when crude turpentine is distilled to make the essential oil, spirit of turpentine. Rosin and its derivatives are employed in paper and textile sizing, in lubricants, insulation, linoleum, adhesives, soaps, sealing wax, polishes, printing inks, and pitch. Rosin is also rubbed on the bows of stringed instruments and on the shoes of dancers to increase friction.

FRANCES GIES

rosinweed   [rahz'-in-weed]

Rosinweed is the common name of about 20 species of wildflowers, genus *Silphium*, in the daisy family, Compositae. The plants are tall perennials and produce sunflowerlike blooms. Also called the compass plant, *S. laciniatum* bears leaves that often point north and south. All species are native to North America.

Roskilde   [raws'-kil-de]

Roskilde is a city in northeastern Denmark on the Roskilde Fjord. The seat of Roskilde county and a residential suburb of Copenhagen, about 32 km (20 mi) to the east, Roskilde has a population of 39,747 (1983 est.). The city produces foodstuffs and has a meat-research institute; a nuclear power research station is nearby. Dominating Roskilde is its enormous cathedral, consecrated in the 15th century, which is the burial place of many of the country's kings and queens. A museum of Viking artifacts opened in 1969. Named for Hroar (Ro), its legendary founder, and for springs (*kilde*) of the region, Roskilde served as the capital of Denmark from the early 10th century until 1443 and was a bishopric from the mid-1000s until 1536 and again after 1923. In 1658 the Treaty of Roskilde, settling a war between Denmark and Sweden, was drawn up and signed there.

Rosmini-Serbati, Antonio [rohz-mee'-nee-sahr-bah'-tee]

A 19th-century Italian churchman, Antonio Rosmini-Serbati, b. Mar. 24, 1797, d. July 1, 1855, is best known as a philosopher, patriot, and founder of a religious congregation. Born into a wealthy, noble family, he spent many years as canon and then dean of Milan cathedral. In 1828 he founded the Institute of Charity, often called the Rosminians, devoted to charitable and missionary activities. He was a prolific philosophic writer whose work was influenced by Hegel and Kant as well as by Plato, Augustine, and Aquinas. Rosmini was also an active Italian nationalist, serving in the effort to promote Italian unity. He also attempted to reconcile Catholicism and political liberalism.   T. TACKETT

Bibliography: Cleary, D., *The Principles of Rosmini's Moral Philosophy* (1961); Leetham, Claude R., *Rosmini* (1957).

Ross, Alexander

A fur trader and author, Alexander Ross, b. Scotland, May 9, 1783, d. Oct. 23, 1856, emigrated to Upper Canada (Ontario) about 1805. With John Jacob Astor's Pacific Fur Company (see ASTOR family), he took part (1811) in the founding of ASTORIA, a fur-trading post in Oregon. He joined the NORTH WEST COMPANY in 1813, after it acquired Astoria, and when the North West merged (1821) with the HUDSON'S BAY COMPANY, he worked for the latter for 4 years. Ross subsequently moved to the RED RIVER SETTLEMENT, where he served as sheriff and a member of the council. His several books include *The Fur Hunters of the Far West* (2 vols.; 1855) and *The Red River Settlement* (1856), a useful, somewhat exaggerated account of the history of the colony.   GEORGE F. G. STANLEY

Ross, Betsy

Elizabeth Ross, b. Philadelphia, Jan. 1, 1752, d. Jan. 30, 1836, was a Philadelphia seamstress and upholsterer who, according to popular legend, made the first American flag at the request of George Washington. Some details of the legend are of doubtful authenticity, but records show that she did supply flags to the Pennsylvania navy in 1777.

Bibliography: Morris, R., *The Truth about the American Flag* (1976).

Ross, Diana

Pop singer and film actress Diana Ross, b. Detroit, Mar. 26, 1944, was the lead singer of the Supremes, originally comprising Ross, Florence Ballard, and Mary Wilson. After joining MOTOWN in 1961, the group went on to record 12 number-one hits—more than anyone in rock history except Elvis Presley and the Beatles. After Ross left (1969) the group to solo, she had 6 more number-one records. Her performance in the film *Lady Sings the Blues* (1972) won her an Oscar nomination for best actress.

Ross, Harold

The founder of *The New Yorker* magazine, Harold Wallace Ross, b. Aspen, Colo., Nov. 16, 1892, also served as its editor from its formation in 1925 until his death on Dec. 6, 1951. After starting the magazine he saw it through several years of financial crisis and formed its editorial policy. His colleagues agreed that Ross, a high school dropout, had a rare genius for editing. Ross fashioned *The New Yorker* into one of the foremost U.S. literary magazines. He helped to form its local focus, unique style, and reputation for literary merit.

Bibliography: Grant, Jane, *Ross, the New Yorker and Me* (1968); Thurber, James, *The Years with Ross* (1959).

Ross, Sir James Clark

Sir James Clark Ross, b. Apr. 15, 1800, d. Apr. 3, 1862, was a British naval officer and explorer who discovered the north magnetic pole on June 1, 1831, while on an expedition to the Arctic led by his uncle, Sir John Ross. From 1839 to 1843 he commanded an expedition to the Antarctic where he discovered the Ross Sea (1841) and Victoria Land region and named Mount Erebus. He published *A Voyage of Discovery and Research in the Southern and Antarctic Regions* (1847).

Ross, John

John Ross, or Coowescoowe, b. Oct. 3, 1790, d. Aug. 1, 1866, of Scottish and CHEROKEE Indian ancestry, was a distinguished and dedicated tribal leader. In the War of 1812 he led the Cherokee against the CREEK confederacy. He was president of the Cherokee Council (1819–26), an associate chief (1827), and principal chief (1828–39). During those years Ross warred with Georgia, when it sought to remove the Cherokee from their ancestral lands, especially after President Jackson signed the Indian Removal Act in 1830. Ross led a delegation to Washington (1832–33) to plead the Cherokee cause, but to no avail. In 1838–39, when the Cherokee were forced west over what the Indians called the "trail of tears" to INDIAN TERRITORY, Ross led them on the terrible march. He later served as chief of the United Cherokee Nation.   DANIEL JACOBSON

Bibliography: Moulton, Gary E., *John Ross, Cherokee Chief* (1978).

Ross, Sinclair

The Canadian novelist and short-story writer Sinclair Ross, b. Saskatchewan, Jan. 22, 1908, described the isolation and severity of the Canadian prairie in his first novel, *As For Me and My House* (1941). His other publications include *The Lamp at Noon and Other Stories* (1968).

Ross and Cromarty [krahm'-ur-tee]

Ross and Cromarty is a former county in the HIGHLANDS of northern Scotland. It included part of the Outer HEBRIDES island of Lewis. The county town was Dingwall.

The earliest known inhabitants, the Picts, were converted to Christianity during the 6th and 7th centuries. Norse pirates plagued the area until the 12th century. Clashes between local clans continued there long after other areas of Scotland had been subdued. In 1889, Ross County (1661) and Cromarty County (1685) were merged into one. During the reorganization of local government in 1975, Ross and Cromarty was divided between the HIGHLAND and Western Isles regions.

Ross Dependency

The Ross Dependency, an area composed of both land and ice shelf and covering 751,000 km^2 (290,000 mi^2), is an overseas territory under the jurisdiction of New Zealand. Located in Antarctica between 160° east and 150° west longitude and south of 60° south latitude, it includes the Ross Sea and its islands, parts of Victoria Land and King Edward VII Peninsula, and the Queen Maud Range.

The Ross Dependency was established in 1923. Sir Edmund HILLARY established a base there in 1957 from which he and others explored and mapped the dependency during the INTERNATIONAL GEOPHYSICAL YEAR (1957–58). The region continues to be explored by the nations who cooperatively maintain stations in Antarctica to collect and analyze geophysical data.

Ross Ice Shelf

The Ross Ice Shelf, the world's largest body of floating ice, is situated along the Ross Sea—an arm of the Pacific Ocean—in Antarctica. Its highly variable area is about 530,000 km^2 (205,000 mi^2). Eight valley glaciers drain into the shelf. Sir James Clark Ross discovered and explored the shelf in 1841. Richard E. BYRD established Little America at the seaward edge in 1928. Extensively charted since World War II, the ice shelf has an airfield and several research stations.

Rossby waves [raws'-bee]

Rossby waves are the long, sinusoidal, horizontal meanders in the JET STREAM that separate tropical air from polar air. These waves are named for Carl Gustaf Rossby, who first identified them and explained their role in transferring heat from the low latitudes to the poles.

Rossby waves are produced as a result of the differences in the deflecting effect of the Coriolis force at different latitudes. They have a wavelength of about 10,000 km (6,000 mi). Rossby waves with great amplitude cause warm and cold air masses within to detach, producing the low- and high-pressure systems of the mid-latitudes.

Rossellini, Roberto   [rohs-sel-lee'-nee]

One of the principal founders of Italian neorealism, film director Roberto Rossellini, b. May 8, 1906, d. June 3, 1977, first achieved prominence with *Open City* (1945), filmed during and after the German evacuation of Rome and portraying Italian resistance groups and Gestapo reprisals. The film had an unprecedented immediacy, owing in large part to Rossellini's use of authentic settings and of the physical presences of such fine performers as Anna Magnani and Aldo Fabrizzi. Rossellini's success continued with the anecdotal *Paisan* (1946), the stark *Germany Year Zero* (1947), and the controversial *The Miracle* (1948). After *Stromboli* (1949), which carried his reliance on realistic settings to excess, Rossellini made only one film of note during the next decade—*Saint Francis* (1950). He returned to his former brilliance with *General della Rovere* (1959). Since 1962, Rossellini worked exclusively in theater and television.   GAUTAM DASGUPTA

Bibliography: Guarner, José L., *Roberto Rossellini*, trans. by Elisabeth Cameron (1970).

Rossellino   (family)   [rohs-sel-lee'-noh]

The Rossellino family was a group of Florentine artists, the most important members of which were Bernardo Rossellino and his brother Antonio.

A noted architect, **Bernardo Rossellino**, b. 1409, d. Sept. 23, 1464, worked with Leon Battista Alberti on the Palazzo Rucellai (1446-51) in Florence. He also worked on the Florence Duomo (1441-94), where he later became Capomaestro (1461-64), and on the Palazzo Piccolomini (1460-63) in Pienza. As a sculptor Bernardo revealed a clarity of form visible in his major work, the tomb of Leonardo Bruni in Santa Croce, Florence (1444-47), for which he created a new type of sepulchral monument using a triumphal arch.

Antonio Rossellino, 1427-79, created outstanding portrait busts, including those of Giovanni Chellini (1456; Victoria and Albert Museum, London), a remarkable characterization based on a life mask, and Matteo Palmieri (1468; Museo Nazionale, Florence). His most innovative work, the tomb of the Cardinal of Portugal in San Miniato al Monte, Florence (1461-66), reveals the artist's characteristic combination of elegance, sensitivity, and freedom of handling.   GIULIA BARTRUM

Bibliography: Avery, Charles, *Florentine Renaissance Sculpture* (1970); Pope-Hennessy, John, *Italian Renaissance Sculpture* (1971); Seymour, Charles, Jr., *Sculpture in Italy 1400-1500* (1966).

Rossetti, Christina G.   [roh-zet'-ee]

The English poet Christina Georgina Rossetti, b. Dec. 5, 1830, d. Dec. 29, 1894, was the sister of Pre-Raphaelite painter-poet Dante Gabriel Rossetti. Born into a family of intense literary, artistic, and religious interests, she wrote childhood verses that were printed on a private family press and published several poems under the pseudonym Ellen Alleyne in *The Germ*, a short-lived periodical begun in 1850 by her brother William and his friends. In *Goblin Market* (1862), her first published volume of poetry, she displayed a taste for the fantastic, a brooding melancholy, and a lyric gift that would characterize much of her work. Along with later volumes of poetry, such as *The Prince's Progress* (1866) and *A Pageant* (1881), she wrote nursery rhymes and tales for children, including *Sing Song* (1872) and *Speaking Likenesses* (1874). Rossetti's deep religious feelings made her a devout Anglican and inspired her to write a wide variety of religious works.   PHILIP FLYNN

Bibliography: Bellas, Ralph A., *Christina Rossetti* (1977); Packer, Lona, *Christina Rossetti* (1963); Sawtell, Margaret, *Christina Rossetti: Her Life and Religion* (1955).

Rossetti, Dante Gabriel

The sinuous, subtly erotic women in Dante Gabriel Rossetti's The Bower Meadow *(1872) are the hallmark of this English Pre-Raphaelite poet and painter's style. The work also shows Rossetti's characteristic blend of romanticized realism and conscious archaism. (City Art Galleries, Manchester, England.)*

The poet, painter, and designer Dante Gabriel Rossetti, b. Gabriel Charles Dante Rossetti, May 12, 1828, d. Apr. 9, 1882, was a cofounder of the PRE-RAPHAELITES, a group of English painters and poets who hoped to bring to their art the richness and purity of the medieval period. The son of the exiled Italian patriot and scholar Gabriele Rossetti and a brother of the poet Christina Rossetti, Dante showed literary talent early, winning acclaim for his poem "The Blessed Damozel" (1847) before he was 20 years old. As a student at the Royal Academy Antique School (1845-47), he met William Holman Hunt and John Millais, with whom he launched the Pre-Raphaelite Brotherhood in 1848. Rossetti's first Pre-Raphaelite paintings in oils, based on religious themes and with elements of mystical symbolism, were *The Girlhood of Mary Virgin* (1849) and *Ecce Ancilla Domini* (1850), both in the Tate Gallery, London. Although he won support from John Ruskin, criticism of his paintings caused him to withdraw from public exhibitions and turn to watercolors, which could be sold privately. Subjects taken from Dante Alighieri's *Vita Nuova* (which Rossetti had translated into English) and Sir Thomas Malory's *Morte Darthur* inspired his art in the 1850s. His visions of Arthurian romance and medieval design also inspired his new friends of this time, William Morris and Edward Burne-Jones.

Romantic love was Rossetti's main theme in both poetry and painting. Elizabeth Siddal, whom he married in 1860, was the subject of many fine drawings, and his memory of her after she died (1862) is implicit in the *Beata Beatrix* (1863; Tate Gallery, London). Toward the end of his life, Rossetti sank into a morbid state, possibly induced by his disinterment (1869) of the manuscript poems he had buried with his wife and by savage critical attacks on his poetry. He spent his last years as an invalid recluse.   WILLIAM GAUNT

Bibliography: Doughty, Oswald, *Dante Gabriel Rossetti, A Victorian Romantic*, 2d ed. (1960); Fleming, Gordon H., *Rossetti and the Pre-Raphaelite Brotherhood* (1967); Gaunt, William, *The Pre-Raphaelite Dream* (1966); Rossetti, Dante Gabriel, *Letters*, ed. by Oswald Doughty and J. R. Wahl, 4 vols. (1965-67); Rossetti, William Michael, *Ruskin, Rossetti, Pre-Raphaelitism* (1899; repr. 1971); Surtees, Virginia, *The Paintings and Drawings of Dante Gabriel Rossetti: A Catalogue Raisonné*, 2 vols. (1971).

Rossini, Gioacchino   [rohs-see'-nee]

Gioacchino Rossini, b. Feb. 29, 1792, d. Nov. 13, 1868, was one of the most significant and influential composers of opera in

Gioacchino Rossini, portrayed in his old age by the photographer Nadar, was one of the most acclaimed Italian composers of the early 19th century. Among his most famous works are the comic operas The Barber of Seville *(1816) and* Cinderella *(1817) and the influential grand opera* William Tell *(1829). After 1829, Rossini abandoned the opera and composed only church music and a few secular works.*

the 19th century. His parents were both musical and intermittently pursued careers as professional musicians. His mother sang opera in Ferrara, Bologna, and Trieste; his father was a town trumpeter in Pesaro and played the horn in various operatic orchestras.

After receiving some harpsichord lessons Rossini was instructed in voice and harmony, and by the age of ten he was already accomplished enough as a singer and accompanist to begin earning money in churches and theaters. In 1806 he entered the Liceo Musicale of Bologna, where he studied music theory and the cello. Four years later he left the Liceo to pursue his career as a composer of operas.

Rossini's first opera to be performed publicly, the one-act comedy *La Cambiale di matrimonio* (The Bill of Marriage), was given in Venice in 1810. Between 1811 and 1814, 12 new operas by Rossini appeared in Venice, Milan, Rome, and Bologna. The most popular of these were *La Pietra del paragone* (The Touchstone; Milan, 1812), *Tancredi* (Venice, 1813), and *L'Italiana in Algeri* (The Italian Girl in Algiers; Venice, 1813), works that established Rossini's fame not only in Italy but throughout Europe.

In 1815, Rossini became musical director of the Teatro San Carlo and Teatro del Fondo in Naples. The following year he composed his best-known opera, *Il Barbiere di Siviglia* (THE BARBER OF SEVILLE; Rome). Other significant operas followed in the next few years: *Otello* (Naples, 1816), *La Cenerentola* (Cinderella; Rome, 1817), *La Gazza ladra* (The Thieving Magpie; Milan, 1817), and *La Donna del lago* (The Lady of the Lake; Naples, 1819). The last opera he composed for Italy was *Semiramide* (Venice, 1823).

In 1824, Rossini assumed the directorship of the Théâtre Italien in Paris. His first two operas to French texts, *Le Siège de Corinthe* (The Siege of Corinth; 1826) and *Moïse* (Moses; 1827), were revisions of earlier Italian works. He went on to produce a sparkling opéra comique, *Le Comte Ory* (Count Ory, 1828), and the grand opera *Guillaume Tell* (William Tell, 1829), a landmark in the history of romantic opera.

Guillaume Tell, the composer's 39th opera, was also his last, although he lived for another 39 years. He produced two significant religious works, the *Stabat Mater* (1842) and the *Petite Messe solennelle* (Short Solemn Mass, 1864), and numerous piano pieces and songs grouped under the title *Pèches de vieillesse* (Sins of Old Age), but no further stage works. From 1837 to 1855 he lived in Italy, then moved to Paris, where he spent the remainder of his life.

CHARLOTTE GREENSPAN

Bibliography: Stendhal (Marie Henri Beyle), *Life of Rossini*, trans. and annotated by Richard N. Coe, rev. ed. (1970); Toye, Francis, *Rossini* (1934; repr. 1963); Weinstock, Herbert, *Rossini: A Biography* (1968).

Rosso, Medardo   [rohs'-soh]

The Italian artist Medardo Rosso, b. June 20, 1858, d. Mar. 31, 1928, was one of the most important impressionist sculptors.

On visits to Paris during the 1880s and '90s, he was greatly struck by the impressionists' preoccupation with the effects of light. Using plaster and wax, he modeled his forms softly, as though they had been dissolved and highlighted by the transient play of light across their surfaces. One of his most important works, *Conversation in the Garden* (1893; Galleria Nazionale d'Arte Contemporanea, Rome), aptly illustrates this quality. Rosso's sculptures won the admiration of Auguste Rodin.

HARRY RAND

Bibliography: Barr, M. S., *Medardo Rosso* (1963).

Rosso Fiorentino   [rohs'-soh fee-ohr-en-tee'-noh]

Giovanni Battista di Jacopo di Guasparre Rosso, b. Mar. 8, 1495, a leader of central Italian MANNERISM, became known as Il Rosso Fiorentino. He had a temperamental, individualistic nature and, as a youth, was unable to find any master who suited him for long; nonetheless, he did experience the stylistic influence of Andrea del Sarto and Fra Bartolommeo. Giorgio Vasari, his biographer, cites an early collaboration with Jacopo Carucci Pontormo on a predella (now lost) for Sarto's *Annunciation* (c.1512-13). Rosso's *Assumption* fresco (1516-17; Santissima Annunziata, Florence) is his earliest extant work. Here, the abstract patterning, erratic turbulence of the figures, and unexpected, violent colors—which were to become a hallmark of his art—are first seen. His mature works, such as the famous *Deposition* (1521; Galleria Pittorica, Volterra), make clear his break with the classical style of the High Renaissance for the sake of an expressive, highly personal "anticlassicism." Here, unusual figural proportions, sharply stylized gestures, perspectival distortions, and coloristic abnormalities lend to the scene a quality of a mystical apparition rather than a recording of actual events. In 1524 he went to Rome, where he encountered the achievements of Michelangelo, and became somewhat more reconciled to classicism. His work thereafter tended to combine a sculpturesque solidity with an expressive Mannerist aesthetic to create the *Dead Christ with Angels* (1525-26; Museum of Fine Arts, Boston). The sack of Rome (1527) forced him to leave for the north of Italy; in 1530 he was called to France by François I to participate in the decoration of the château at Fontainebleau (see FONTAINEBLEAU, SCHOOL OF). There Rosso, along with Francesco Primaticcio, created a new idiom of painting, sculpture, and the decorative arts that was to have far-reaching consequences. He died, probably by his own hand, in Paris on Nov. 14, 1540.

EDWARD J. SULLIVAN

Bibliography: Friedlaender, Walter, *Mannerism and Anti-Mannerism in Italian Painting* (1965); Haraszti-Takacs, Marianne, and Racz, Eva, *The Masters of Mannerism*, 2d rev. ed. (1977); Hauser, Arnold, *Mannerism*, 2 vols. (1965); Shearman, John, *Mannerism* (1967).

Rostand, Edmond   [raws-tahn']

Edmond Rostand, b. Apr. 1, 1868, d. Dec. 2, 1918, was a French dramatist whose plays represent the final flowering of the 19th-century romantic tradition. His greatest work, CYRANO DE BERGERAC (1897; Eng. trans., 1898), was a dazzling popular success and remains a worldwide favorite to this day. Its hero, marred by an enormous nose, rises heroically above his bodily defect in scenes of unparalleled verve, wit, and pathos. One of Rostand's earlier works, *The Romancers* (1894; Eng. trans., 1899), has been adapted as the highly successful musical comedy *The Fantasticks*. His other plays include *L'Aiglon* (The Eaglet, 1900), a sentimental account of the life of Napoleon I's ill-starred son, and *Chantecler* (1910), in which all the characters are animals. In 1910, Rostand became the youngest writer to be elected to the Académie Française. He died a victim of the widespread influenza epidemic of 1918.

Bibliography: Amoia, Alba, *Edmond Rostand* (1978).

Rostock   [rohs'-tohk]

Rostock, the principal port of East Germany, lies about 190 km (120 mi) northwest of Berlin. Located 13 km (8 mi) inland, it is connected with Warnemünde, its advance port on the Baltic, by the Warnow River. The population is 239,422 (1983 est.). Rostock has large storage tanks for petroleum and modern port facilities. Industries include shipbuilding, fish processing, and the manufacturing of chemicals and machinery. The town hall and the churches of Saint Mary, Saint Nicholas, and Saint Peter date from the 14th and 15th centuries. The University of Rostock (1419) was important in the spread of Lutheranism.

Slavic (Wendish) settlements, first established on the site in the 12th century, were superseded by three German towns that were united later in the 12th century. Rostock was a powerful member of the Hanseatic League. The city later declined, to recover only after World War II.

Rostov-on-Don [rahs'-tawv]

Rostov-on-Don is the capital of Rostov oblast of the Russian Soviet Federated Socialist Republic in the USSR. It is situated on the high right bank of the Don River, about 45 km (30 mi) east of the Sea of Azov. The city's population is 983,000 (1984 est.). Rostov-on-Don is an important transport center at the gateway to the Caucasus and is one of the USSR's leading producers of agricultural machines. The city's hinterland provides tobacco, grapes, and vegetables for processing. The city is the educational center of the northern Caucasus. Rostov State University was founded in 1915.

Rostov-on-Don arose as a garrison town in 1749 after the Russians had gained control of the region from the Turks. Its industrial development dates from the 19th century. The city changed hands several times in 1941–43 as the Germans attempted to drive into the Caucasus. THEODORE SHABAD

Rostropovich, Mstislav [raws-traw-poh'-vich]

Mstislav Rostropovich, b. Mar. 27, 1927, is one of the world's finest cellists and a leading conductor. He was a highly honored artist in his native Soviet Union in the 1950s and '60s but fell into official disfavor when he demonstrated his political unorthodoxy by openly befriending the dissident writer Alexander Solzhenitzyn. Thereafter, his professional career was severely curtailed, and as a consequence he fled to the West, followed shortly by his wife, the noted soprano Galina Visnevskaya, and children. In 1974 he was appointed music director of the National Symphony Orchestra in Washington, D.C. The following year he and his wife were denounced by the Soviet government and divested of their Soviet citizenship.

Bibliography: Ewen, David, ed., *Musicians since 1900* (1978).

Roswitha von Gandersheim: see HROSWITHA VON GANDERSHEIM.

Roszak, Theodore [raw'-shahk]

The American sculptor Theodore Roszak, b. Poland, May 1, 1907, d. Sept. 3, 1981, was best known for his primitivistic, rough-textured sculptural forms. Executed in welded steel brazed with copper, nickel, and silver, such works represent a style he developed after 1945. Roszak began his career as a painter of cubist-romantic works. During the late 1930s and early '40s he turned to constructivist experiments in brass, steel, wood, and plastic. BARBARA CAVALIERE

Bibliography: Arnason, H. H., *Theodore Roszak* (1956); Roszak, Theodore, *In Pursuit of an Image* (1955); Selz, Peter, *New Images of Man* (1959).

rotary engine: see WANKEL ENGINE.

Rotary International

Rotary International is an association of business and professional men and women, founded in 1905. Now an international organization with nearly 993,000 members in 159 countries, it functions as a fellowship and as a service organization that sponsors community projects and funds student exchange programs and university scholarships. The name Rotary came from the early practice of rotating weekly meetings among members' offices. Although the clubs were long exclusively male, a 1987 Supreme Court decision required that in the United States they begin to admit women.

rotary press

A rotary press is a method of PRINTING in which a cylindrical printing surface and a cylindrical impression surface rotate toward each other. Paper passes between the cylinders to receive the print. For rotary-offset printing, a third cylinder is used: a rubber-covered offset cylinder coming between the impression and plate cylinders. Because only cylinders are involved in a rotary press, speeds are much faster. The restricting factor is the ability to control the paper at speed. By combining rotary printing units and passing the paper from one unit to another, two, three, four, or even more colors may be printed during a single pass through the machinery. Multicolor rotary machines can be constructed by grouping a number of plate cylinders, with their inking systems, around one large common-impression cylinder. This produces a more compact machine with improved paper transport. Important features of rotary printing are that it allows great variations in machine design—cylinders may be positioned horizontally, vertically, or angled—and permits in-line operations other than printing to be performed. These include folding, slitting, perforating, and numbering. Rotary machines can also combine different printing processes, for example, letterpress and web-offset. The original application of rotary printing was for newspapers; it is now used for book, magazine, and general work as well as for specialized forms of printing. M. C. FAIRLEY

Bibliography: Durrant, W. R., et al., *Machine Printing* (1973).

ROTC: see RESERVE OFFICERS TRAINING CORPS.

Roth, Philip

The novelist Philip Milton Roth, b. Newark, N.J., Mar. 19, 1933, began his literary career by caricaturing the various clichés of American Jewish life. His later work still features Jewish protagonists, but Roth is now considered a major American writer, along with Saul Bellow and Bernard Malamud, both Jewish writers whose works, like Roth's, transcend their ethnicity. Roth gained immediate literary recognition when his first book, *Goodbye Columbus* (1959), a novella and five short stories about urban and suburban Jews, won the 1960 National Book Award. His first novel, *Letting Go* (1962), takes aim at the idiosyncrasies of university faculties. The widely read *Portnoy's Complaint* (1969) describes, often hilariously, the sexual anxieties of a Jewish neurotic with an overpowering mother. Roth has also written perceptively about midwestern Protestantism (*When She Was Good*, 1967) and sex and psychoanalysis (*The Professor of Desire*, 1977), among several other satiric, comic novels. His most important work, however, may be the Zuckerman tetralogy—*The Ghost Writer* (1979), *Zuckerman Unbound* (1981), *The Anatomy Lesson* (1983), and *The Counterlife* (1986)—four novels in which Nathan Zuckerman becomes a famous writer whose works and life somewhat resemble those of his creator, Roth. *The Counterlife*, by relating alternative possibilities in that life, attempts to deny the resemblance. MELVIN J. FRIEDMAN

Bibliography: Bloom, Harold, ed., *Philip Roth* (1986); Jones, J., and Nance, G., *Philip Roth* (1981); Pinsker, S., ed., *Critical Essays on Philip Roth* (1982); Roth, P., *Reading Myself and Others* (1975).

Roth v. United States

In the case of *Roth* v. *United States* (1957) and the companion case of *Alberts* v. *California*, the U.S. Supreme Court held that obscenity is not protected expression under the 1st and 14th Amendments to the Constitution. Samuel Roth had been convicted under a federal statute making it a crime to send "obscene, lascivious, or filthy" matter through the mail. Specifically, he had advertised and sold a quarterly publication,

American Aphrodite, that dealt in literary erotica. Donald Alberts had been convicted under California's obscenity law for disseminating pictures of nude and scantily clad women sometimes depicted in bizarre poses and without any artistic pretension.

Although upholding the convictions of Roth and Alberts and declaring unequivocally that "obscenity is not within the area of constitutionally protected speech and press," the court fashioned a doctrine so difficult to apply that it opened up a new era of permissible obscenity and a torrential flood of litigation. The test for obscenity in Justice William Brennan's words was "whether to the average person, applying contemporary community standards, the dominant theme of the material taken as a whole appeals to the prurient interest."

ROBERT J. STEAMER

See also: MILLER V. CALIFORNIA; PORNOGRAPHY.

Rothko, Mark [rahth'-koh]

Blue, Orange and Red *(1961) is typical of the later, abstract expressionist style of Mark Rothko, in which irregular shapes of color appear to float on large canvases. (Private collection.)*

The American artist Mark Rothko, b. Dvinsk, Russia, Sept. 25, 1903, was the most transcendental painter associated with ABSTRACT EXPRESSIONISM. His early paintings of the 1940s are luminously pale scenes made up of indistinct shapes that often suggest primitive life forms floating over a background of banded colors. By 1947, Rothko had concluded that his earlier works, with their reference to figures and objects, were too restrictive.

Attempting to universalize his art, Rothko began to work with various arrangements of hovering, rectangular areas of color. Over the next 3 years, this format was reduced and solidified into Rothko's mature style: 2 to 5 rectangles of glowing color suspended one above another against a luminous field. *Number 10* (1950; Museum of Modern Art, New York City) is an example. The emptiness of Rothko's paintings symbolizes humanity's spiritual yearnings; like religious icons, these pictures are intended to evoke humility and exaltation in the viewer. From 1958 on, his works became increasingly austere and more transcendental.

Rothko felt that his paintings were best viewed in a light similar to that in his studio—that is, a dim, changing light within a relatively small exhibition area, so that the canvases

might glow and pulsate. He was uninterested in relationships of form and color but sought to convey basic human emotions—fear, ecstasy, dread,—by isolating the viewer before an amorphous image conducive to meditation. The viewer is made to feel singular, yet part of a greater scheme.

One of Rothko's last projects was the completion of a set of large canvases for a nondenominational chapel in Houston, Tex. He died, a suicide, on Feb. 25, 1970.

HARRY RAND

Bibliography: O'Doherty, Brian, *American Masters: The Voice and the Myth* (1973); Rosenberg, Harold, *The De-definition of Art* (1972); Sandler, Irving, *The Triumph of American Painting* (1970); Seldes, Lee, *The Legacy of Mark Rothko* (1978); Waldman, Diane, *Mark Rothko* (1978).

Rothschild (family) [rawth'-chyld]

The Rothschilds, a family of bankers who control an international consortium of banks (the House of Rothschild), have had an enormous impact on European economic history since the late 18th century. The founder of the House of Rothschild, **Mayer Amschel Rothschild**, b. Feb. 23, 1744, d. Sept. 19, 1812, grew up in the Jewish ghetto of Frankfurt am Main and entered a banking house as a young man. With his five sons—**Amschel Mayer**, b. June 12, 1773, d. Dec. 6, 1855; **Salomon Mayer**, b. Sept. 9, 1774, d. July 27, 1855; **Nathan Mayer**, b. Sept. 16, 1777, d. July 28, 1836; **Karl Mayer**, b. Apr. 24, 1788, d. Mar. 10, 1855; and **Jacob Mayer**, b. May 15, 1792, d. Nov. 15, 1868—he started a business that dealt in luxury items, coins, and commercial papers. Spurred by the investment opportunities presented by the French Revolutionary and Napoleonic wars, the firm turned to banking; and by the early years of the 19th century, the five brothers had established branches in Frankfurt, London, Paris, Vienna, and Naples. This enormously strengthened the ability of the firm to maneuver, and its preeminence in banking circles dates from this period.

After the death of Mayer Amschel, the House of Rothschild became dealers in government securities and in the stocks of insurance companies and industrial firms. During the 1840s the sons of the five Rothschild brothers took their places in the firm. In France, loans were made (1871, 1872) to the government after it lost the war with Prussia, while, in England, funds were advanced (1875) to Prime Minister Benjamin Disraeli for the purchase of the Suez Canal. By the middle of the 19th century, in spite of anti-Semitic prejudice, Rothschilds had been elected to Parliament in England and elevated to the nobility in that country and in France. The Neapolitan and Viennese branches of the firm were dissolved with the advent of fascism in Italy and Germany, but the House of Rothschild continues to wield substantial power to this day. Family members who did not enter the family business have been active in philanthropy, finance, and science.

Bibliography: Corti, E. C., *The Reign of the House of Rothschild, 1830–1871* (1928; repr. 1974) and *The Rise of the House of Rothschild* (1972); Cowles, Virginia S., *The Rothschilds: A Family of Fortune* (1973); Morton, Frederic, *The Rothschilds* (1961).

Baron Nathan Mayer Rothschild succeeded his father, Lionel Nathan, as head of the London branch of the international Rothschild banking firm in 1879 and became known for both nonpartisan policies and generous philanthropy. Elected to the House of Commons at the age of 25, Rothschild became the first Jewish member of the House of Lords when he was raised to the peerage in 1885.

rotifer   [roht'-i-fur]

The freshwater rotifer, Trichotria tetractis, resembles a short, hollow, food grinder. The mouth (left) is rimmed by cilia, which move like a wheel.

A rotifer, or wheel animalcule, is a minute, multicellular, free-living aquatic animal in the phylum Rotifera. It possesses a conspicuous circlet of cilia around the anterior end and mouth. The cilia beat in a swirling action, suggesting a wheel; the term *rotifer* means wheel carrier. By creating a current, the beating cilia draw food and water into the mouth. Food consists of small protozoans and algae. An internal grinding organ that breaks up hard particles of food may be seen through the transparent body. The grinding organ, in a muscular pharynx, or mastax, is lined with several hard, projecting, jawlike structures. About 1,500 species of rotifers exist.

LORUS J. AND MARGERY MILNE

rotogravure   [roh-toh-gruh–vuer']

Rotogravure is printing produced on a web-fed rotary photogravure machine using an intaglio image etched below the surface of a copper- or chromium-plated cylinder. It is used mainly for long-run production of magazines and for the printing of packaging foils and plastics and wall and floor

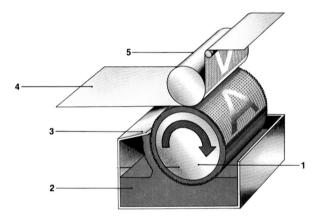

Rotogravure printing involves the use of a rotating printing cylinder (1) in which an image is etched as tiny cells. The cylinder turns in a trough (2) from which ink is deposited in the cells and on the roll surface. A doctor blade, or metal scraper (3), wipes off the surface ink. The image cells are then pressed against the paper (4) by an impression roll (5), and the ink is transferred to the paper.

coverings. The printing area consists of minute cells of varying depths; the deeper the cell, the more ink is carried and transferred to the paper, thus producing the light as well as dark parts of an illustration. In the ROTARY PRESS the printing cylinder is immersed in a fluid (low-viscosity), volatile ink that, after the printing process, dries rapidly by evaporation and absorption into the paper. Before the impression is made on the paper, excess ink is removed with a flexible steel "doctor blade." The paper web then passes between the printing cylinder and a rubber-covered impression cylinder to draw the ink out of the cells for printing.   M. C. FAIRLEY

Bibliography: Durrant, W. R., *Machine Printing* (1973).

Rotterdam   [raht'-ur-dam]

Rotterdam, in the province of South Holland, has a population of 568,167 (1982 est.), making it the second largest city in the Netherlands. Its urban agglomeration has a population of 1,023,918 (1981 est.), exceeding even that of Amsterdam. The

Delfshaven, a district of Rotterdam, contains several older sections that were relatively undamaged by the intense bombing to which the city was subjected during World War II. Rotterdam, which developed as a medieval fishing village, is today the world's busiest port.

focus of the region's activity is Rotterdam's harbor as well as the many industries that have been developed since World War II.

Contemporary City. Rotterdam-Europoort is the world's busiest port, handling 250.3 million metric tons (275.9 million U.S. tons) of shipping in 1981. Located at the mouths of the Rhine and Meuse (or Maas) rivers, it is the gateway to the inland industrial centers of northern Europe. The cargo carried by the river-barge traffic is transferred to oceangoing vessels at the Dutch harbor. Rotterdam's status as a free port further stimulates its transshipment activities. Shipping to the Mediterranean and Scandinavia is also important. The original harbor, several kilometers inland from the North Sea, has undergone frequent, major expansion since 1947. Facilities to accommodate large container ships and supertankers have been added. The construction of new districts such as Europoort and Maasvlakte has extended the world's largest artificial harbor into the sea.

In recent decades city leaders have stimulated industrial expansion to provide economic diversity. The most significant development has been in the field of petrochemicals. Pipeline systems have been constructed, and five refineries are now in operation. Fertilizers, plastics, and margarine are the major manufactures; metallurgy, shipbuilding, and machine-tool, textile, and distillery production are growing.

Innovative modern planning and architecture were involved in the city's reconstruction following the bombardments of World War II. Most of the city center, part of the quays, and a large area of slums were destroyed, but huge buildings such as the Wholesale Center, broad avenues, and efforts to provide some green space have given Rotterdam a new and pleasant aspect. The key to this development was the founding in 1948 of the International Building Center. Congested surface transportation remains a problem despite the construction of the Maas Tunnel (1937–42), new bridges and beltways, and a developing subway system. Fine collections of Dutch and Flemish art are displayed at the Boymans–van Beuningen Museum.

History. At the close of the 17th century Rotterdam emerged as a shipping center, engulfing the harbor of DELFT and profiting from the East Indies trade. Rotterdam's competition with Antwerp for European trade in the 19th century was aided by the construction of the New Waterway canal to the sea (1866–72).   JONATHAN E. HELMREICH

Rottweiler [raht'-wy-lur]

The Rottweiler's name comes from the German town of Rottweil, long a principal site for cattle dealers and meat packers. Originally a cattle-driving breed, the Rottweiler declined in the mid-19th century but later regained favor as a formidable guard dog.

The Rottweiler is a breed of dog similar to the Doberman pinscher in outline, but much more massive and with comparatively small ears set high, carried flat, and hung over to the side of the head. The short, smooth, glossy coat is black with clear tan to rust markings. The breed, developed from Roman cattle dogs and named for the town of Rottweil in Württemberg in southern Germany, was developed into a police dog in the early 20th century. It was officially recognized by the American Kennel Club in 1955. JOHN MANDEVILLE

Bibliography: American Kennel Club, *The Complete Dog Book*, 17th ed. (1985).

Rouault, Georges [roo-oh']

The French artist Georges Rouault, b. May 27, 1871, d. Feb. 13, 1958, stands almost alone among the important painters of the 20th century in having dedicated much of his work to religious themes. Trained as a maker of stained-glass windows (1885–90), he helped to restore the windows at Chartres Cathedral; his later work—with its jewellike colors and black outlines—was to reflect this experience. At the École des Beaux-Arts in Paris, Rouault studied under Gustave Moreau (1891–98), who recognized the young artist's talent and encouraged him.

It was after his conversion to Roman Catholicism in 1895

In The Old King *(1937), by 20th-century French painter Georges Rouault, the glowing compartments of color with heavy, black outlines reveal the artist's interest in Gothic stained-glass windows. (The Carnegie Institute, Pittsburgh, Pa.)*

that Rouault began to concentrate on biblical subjects, both in his paintings and his numerous etchings and lithographs. His best-known work is the series of prints published in 1948 under the title *Miserere*; included in it are etchings that were prepared much earlier (1914–18) and completed in 1927. Although he exhibited with the Fauves in 1905, Rouault was not actually influenced by them. He belongs, rather, to the much broader movement of expressionism, with its focus on intensely felt human emotions. His closest artistic ties are with Chaim Soutine in France; Edvard Munch in Norway; and, in Germany, Emil Nolde and other German expressionists.

Apart from his religious works, Rouault painted judges, prostitutes, and tragic clowns as well as occasional still lifes. His art was essentially melancholy, depicting the tragedy of the human condition but seeing hope in the teachings of Christ. DAVID IRWIN

Bibliography: Courthion, Pierre, *Rouault* (1977); Dyrness, William A., *Rouault: A Vision of Suffering and Salvation* (1971); Kaplan, E., *Prints* (1983); Soby, James, T., *Georges Rouault*, 3d ed. (1947); Wolfsy, Alan, *Georges Rouault: The Graphic Work* (1975).

Roubiliac, Louis François [roo-beel-yahk']

A native of France, Louis François Roubiliac, b. *c.*1705, d. Jan. 11, 1762, became the leading sculptor of his time in England, where he settled about 1731. Having won renown with his statue of Handel for the Vauxhall Gardens (1738), he went on to produce lively monuments such as *Lady Elizabeth Nightingale* (1761; Westminster Abbey, London) as well as works of great dignity and insight such as *Sir Isaac Newton* (1755; Trinity College, Cambridge). MALCOLM CORMACK

Bibliography: Esdaile, K. A., *Life and Work of Louis François Roubiliac* (1928); Whinney, M., *Sculpture in Britain 1530–1830* (1964).

Rouen [roo-ahn']

Rouen is a city in northwestern France on the Seine River, about 115 km (70 mi) northwest of Paris. The city population is 101,945 (1982) and that of the conurbation, 400,000 (1982). Rouen serves as a major port for Paris and as a transshipment point for imported bulk products such as petroleum, coal, phosphates, wood products, and wines, as well as manufactured goods from Paris. Rouen's industries manufacture textiles, fertilizer chemicals, perfumes, foundry products, paper, and processed food. Ship repairing and petroleum refining are also economically important. Despite severe destruction during World War II, the city has saved much of its past and is known as the Museum City. Historical and architectural treasures make Rouen a tourist center. The restored 13th-century Cathedral of Notre Dame is but one of several important churches. The city is now part of the future planning region for Greater Paris. The university was established in 1966. Several museums exhibit the work of French masters.

The site of Rouen was originally settled by Celts and later by the Romans as Rotumagus. Its name was changed to Rouen during the Middle Ages. The city was held by the English from 1066 to 1204 and from 1419 to 1449. The trial and execution of Joan of Arc occurred there in 1431. It was taken by the Germans in 1870 and again in 1940 but recaptured by the Allies in 1944. LAWRENCE M. SOMMERS

Rough Riders

The Rough Riders were a regiment of U.S. cavalry volunteers who fought in the Spanish-American War. Theodore ROOSEVELT, their chief organizer, served as lieutenant colonel under commander Leonard WOOD. Because of transportation problems their horses had to be abandoned in Florida; thus the Rough Riders fought mostly on foot when they reached Cuba.

Bibliography: Roosevelt, Theodore, *The Rough Riders* (1899; repr. 1961).

roulette

Roulette is a game in which one or more players gamble against the bank, or house, playing on a rectangular table in

Henri Rousseau received no formal training as a painter, and his style had no precedent. Like many of his works, The Sleeping Gypsy (1897) has a visionary, surreal quality that is both comic and foreboding. (Museum of Modern Art, New York City.)

the center of which is a wheel whose perimeter is nonconsecutively numbered 1 through 36 and zero and double zero. Half the numbers are in red and half in black, except for the zero and double zero, which are in green. Each number has a corresponding slot. A croupier spins a small ball in one direction inside the wheel, which spins in the opposite direction. When the ball comes to rest, that slot designates the winning number. On either side of the wheel is a layout on which bets are placed. Betting and winning on any single number pays 35-to-1. A bet on two numbers, one of which wins, pays 17-to-1. Betting on three numbers, with one winning, pays 11-to-1; four numbers pays 8-to-1; six pays 5-to-1. Several bets with payoffs of 2-to-1 are possible, including bets on the separated horizontal groups of numbers (1-12, 13-24, and 25-36), and on the three vertical columns of numbers. Although the payoff on a single number bet is 35-to-1, the odds against winning are actually 38-to-1, giving the bank an average yield of 5.26 percent—higher than almost any other casino game. Roulette probably originated in the late 18th century, and has become a fixture in most gambling houses.

Bibliography: Adams, W. W., *The Wheel Segment Method of Playing Roulette*, rev. ed. (1976); Leigh, Norman, *Thirteen Against the Bank* (1976); Nolan, Walter I., *The Facts of Roulette* (1970).

Roundheads

The Roundheads were the parliamentarian opponents of King CHARLES I in the ENGLISH CIVIL WAR (1642–48). They were so-called because many of them were Puritans (see PURITANISM) who wore their hair close-cropped, in contrast with the shoulder-length wigs of the royalist CAVALIERS.

roundworm: see ASCARIASIS; NEMATODE.

Rous, Francis Peyton   [roos]

The work of physician Francis Peyton Rous, b. Baltimore, Oct. 5, 1879, d. Feb. 16, 1970, gave rise to the virus theory of cancer causation. In 1960, Rous found that he could transmit a sarcoma (cancerous tumor) from one Plymouth rock hen to another by using an injection of tumor filtrate. Although Rous did not state that a virus was the agent, the Rous chicken sarcoma virus was the first tumor virus identified, and it opened up a whole new area of cancer research. Rous shared the 1966 Nobel Prize for physiology or medicine for his work.

Rousseau, Henri   [roo-soh']

The Frenchman Henri (Le Douanier) Rousseau, b. May 21, 1844, d. Sept. 2, 1910, having spent most of his life as a customs inspector (or *douanier*), devoted himself to painting upon his retirement and became the most distinguished primitive artist of the modern era. His gifts included an exceptional sense of design and feeling for color, but it was his exotic and sometimes bizarre vision of a purely imaginary tropical world that made his works unique and unforgettable.

Born into a family of modest means, Rousseau served twice in the army in his youth. He was then employed as a minor inspector at a toll station near Paris. Rousseau took up his chosen career in 1885 and retired on a small pension in 1893.

Rousseau's earliest works display the formal characteristics of all primitive art: flat surfaces, minute detail, stiff and frontally posed figures of arbitrary proportions, as in *Carnival Evening* (1886; Philadelphia Museum of Art). The paintings he sent to the Salon des Indépendants from 1886 to 1910 generally met with derision. Such artists, however, as Henri de Toulouse-Lautrec and Edgar Degas began to recognize a new aesthetic direction in Rousseau's work, pointing away from the naturalism of the impressionists. His paintings from this period include *The Sleeping Gypsy* (1897) and *The Dream* (1910; Museum of Modern Art, New York City). In these later works, Rousseau simplified his compositions with larger forms and made a bolder use of color.   PHILIP GOULD

Bibliography: Alley, Ronald, *Portrait of a Primitive: The Art of Henri Rousseau* (1978); Bouret, Jean, *Henri Rousseau*, trans. by Martin Leake (1961); Rich, D. C., *Henri Rousseau*, 2d rev. ed. (1946, 1970); Uhde, Wilhelm, *Five Primitive Masters*, trans. by Ralph Thompson (1949); Vallier, Dora, *Henri Rousseau* (1964); Werner, Alfred, *Henri Rousseau* (1957); Wilenski, R. H., *Modern French Painters*, 2d ed. (1944-45).

Rousseau, Jean Jacques

A philosopher and social critic, Jean Jacques Rousseau exerted profound influence on the political thought of the late 18th century, particularly that of the French Revolution, and on the romantic movement.

Life. Rousseau was born in Geneva, Switzerland, on June 28, 1712. His mother died in childbirth, and he was raised as a Calvinist by an aunt. Leaving Geneva in 1728, he led an unsettled life but came under the protection of Madame de Warens at Chambéry; she influenced his conversion to Catholicism. After serving briefly as a tutor at Lyon, he set out

Jean Jacques Rousseau, one of the great French philosophers of the 18th century, emphasized the primacy of individual liberty in such writings as his major political treatise, The Social Contract (1762), and his work on education, Émile (1762). This emphasis and his introspective autobiographical works anticipated the focus of later romantic writings.

for Paris in 1742, where a new system of musical notation he had developed attracted the attention of Denis DIDEROT. Diderot invited him to contribute articles on music to the *Encyclopédie*. In 1745, Rousseau met an uneducated servant girl, Thérèse Le Vasseur, with whom he had a number of illegitimate children. In 1754 he reconverted to Protestantism.

In his first publication, *Discourse on the Arts and Sciences* (1750), Rousseau articulated the fundamental theme that runs through his social philosophy: the conflict between present societies and the nature of man. Relying upon the Platonic contrast of appearance and reality, he showed how politeness conceals a ruthless and calculating egoism. He held that neither science nor art expresses fundamental human needs; instead, both are expressions of pride and vanity. (Despite these views, in 1752 he composed an opera, *Le Devin du village*, which was performed before Louis XV.) Finally, he concluded that material progress had actually undermined the possibility of genuine human relationships.

In 1762 he published his best-known and most-influential works, *Émile*, a treatise on education, and *The Social Contract*, a major work of political philosophy. At this point Rousseau's personality difficulties became more acute. Always an emotional and temperamental man, he quarreled with Diderot and the other philosophes. In 1766 he moved to England at the invitation of the great Scottish philosopher David Hume, with whom he subsequently had a falling out that became a scandal. Increasingly, Rousseau displayed all of the classic symptoms of paranoia. His last years were spent on works such as his *Confessions*, in which he attempted to come to terms with himself. He died on July 2, 1778, in Paris.

Philosophical Position. Rousseau must be understood in terms of his relationship to both the 18th-century ENLIGHTENMENT and to his influence on 19th-century romanticism. To begin with, he shared the Enlightenment view that society had perverted natural man, the "noble savage" who lived harmoniously with nature, free from selfishness, want, possessiveness, and jealousy. He argued that the restoration of the arts and sciences had not contributed to the purification of humankind but to its corruption. Rousseau also believed that social relationships of all kinds were based on an inequality that resulted from an unnatural distribution of power and wealth. All similarity to the other philosophes of the Enlightenment, however, stops at this point. Rousseau's view of the nature of humankind contrasts sharply with those of the other encyclopedists. Rousseau was utterly opposed to the materialism and determinism of Diderot as well as to the belief of Claude Adrien HELVÉTIUS that human motivation could be explained by the desire to maximize pleasure and to minimize pain. In opposition to Diderot, Rousseau stressed the inner life of feeling and sentiment. In opposition to Jean Le Rond d'ALEMBERT, in the *Letter to d'Alembert* (1758), he contrasts self-love, which is naturally good, to pride, which requires an invidious comparison with another. Finally, Rous-

seau's denial that science and art lead automatically to progress stands in opposition to the Marquis de CONDORCET's notion of progress as leading to the ultimate perfection of humankind.

The basic philosophical distinction between Rousseau and the other philosophes is nowhere clearer than in methodology. Whereas the other philosophes pursued the nature of humankind empirically in physiological and psychological studies or in historical and anthropological researches, Rousseau sought the nature of humans in the wholly private realm of intuition and conscience. Superficially, all of his works appear to have a historical character much like the works of other writers of the Enlightenment. By his own admission, however, Rousseau's historical format is purely rhetorical, with no concern for actual details. Whereas the Baron de MONTESQUIEU studied past and present societies to discover the historical origins of political obligation, Rousseau looked inward for the fundamental source of moral obligation. For Montesquieu, the determination of the right was a matter of empirical fact that could be discovered in the structure of actual social and political institutions. For Rousseau, however, the moral realm served as an absolute and independent standard external to any actual society by which it could be assessed.

In departing from the Enlightenment faith in reason, understood as abstraction from external experience, and in emphasizing the inner life as a source of truth, Rousseau has more in common with the romanticists of the 19th century. His influence on the romantic movement was enormous. His true philosophical successor, however, was another late-18th-century philosopher, Immanuel KANT, who also had rejected the external empiricism of the philosophes. Rousseau is credited by Kant with having introduced a great discovery about the nature of freedom.

Major Works. Rousseau's method is clearly visible in *Émile*, where the narrative of development and education is a vehicle for a theory of humans derived from reflection on moral intuitions. The most important of these intuitions is that humans are basically good and, if proper development is fostered, the natural goodness of the individual can be protected from the corrupting influences of society. The child Émile must therefore be raised in a rural rather than an urban environment, so that he may develop in continuity with nature rather than in opposition to it. The earliest impulses of the child are allowed to develop but are channeled into a genuine respect for persons, a respect growing out of self-love rather than pride. Brought into community by an instinctual pity, or sympathy for those around him, Émile develops a moral sense, and an urge toward perfection and inner growth allows him to rise above the passions and achieve virtue. Interestingly, the only book allowed Émile in his education is Daniel Defoe's *Robinson Crusoe*, which in itself displays the way in which character matures in harmony with nature if natural ingenuity is allowed to work unhindered by the corruptions of society.

Nevertheless, society must be dealt with, and this Rousseau does in his most influential work, *The Social Contract*. The individual, progressing in the development of a moral sense, can, for Rousseau, find genuine happiness and fulfillment only in a social situation. Thus one of the first principles of Rousseau's political philosophy is that politics and morality never be separated. The second important principle is freedom, which the state is created to preserve. The state is a unity and as such expresses the general will. This is contrasted to the will of all, which is merely the aggregate will, the accidentally mutual desires of the majority. John LOCKE and others had assumed that what the majority wants must be correct. Rousseau questioned this assumption, arguing that the individuals who make up the majority may, in fact, wish something that is contrary to the goals or needs of the state, to the common good. The general will is to secure freedom, equality, and justice within the state, regardless of the will of the majority, and in the SOCIAL CONTRACT (for Rousseau a theoretical construct rather than a historical event, as Enlightenment thinkers had frequently assumed) individual sovereignty is given up to the state in order that these goals might be achieved. When a state fails to act in a moral fashion, it ceases to function in the proper manner and ceases to exert genuine authority over the individual.

An important factor in insuring the cohesion of the state and in insuring its proper functioning is a sound civil religion. It is, for Rousseau, necessary that all citizens subscribe to beliefs in (1) a supreme being, (2) personal immortality, (3) the ultimate reward of virtue and punishment of vice, and (4) the principle of toleration. The assumption should not be made, however, that Rousseau conceived of this as an external imposition of religion by the state, for to him these appeared to be clear and self-evident principles that could and should be adopted by any rational and moral agent. The specific content of these beliefs will vary, however, as will the content of the laws of any particular state. They will reflect the peculiar historical and geographical factors of a region, as Rousseau makes clear in his constitutions for Corsica (1765) and Poland (1770–71). Only by keeping all of these factors in mind is it possible to constitute a state that fulfills, rather than corrupts, the natural goodness of humanity.

Rousseau's name was invoked by the Jacobins during the French Revolution to justify the Terror and the feast of the Supreme Being. Rousseau himself would have been appalled by such use of his ideas, which ignored the essential balance of factors in his philosophy. Nevertheless, his failure to deal directly with the practical problem of how the general will is determined leaves the concept open to a totalitarian interpretation. This is a one-sided view, however. Rousseau offered a unique and many-faceted interpretation of the nature of man and society.   NICHOLAS CAPALDI

Bibliography: Cassirer, Ernst, *The Question of Jean-Jacques Rousseau* (1932; Eng. trans., 1954); Green, F. C., *Jean-Jacques Rousseau: A Critical Study of his Life and Writings* (1955); Grimsley, Ronald, *Jean-Jacques Rousseau: A Study in Self-Awareness*, 2d. ed. (1969), and *The Philosophy of Rousseau* (1973); Hendel, C. W., *Jean-Jacques Rousseau*, 2d ed. (1962); Huizinga, J. H., *Rousseau, the Self-Made Man* (1976); Noone, J., *Rousseau's Social Contract: A Conceptual Analysis* (1980); Shklar, J. N., *Men and Citizens: A Study of Rousseau's Social Theory* (1969).

Rousseau, Théodore

The French painter Pierre Étienne Théodore Rousseau, b. Apr. 15, 1812, d. Dec. 22, 1867, was the leader of the BARBIZON SCHOOL of landscapists and a major precursor of IMPRESSIONISM. He began his formal training as a painter at the age of 14 and was one of the earliest to work *en plein air*—outdoors, painting directly from the landscape. In his earlier work Rousseau favored wild, unspoiled scenery, such as the Auvergne Mountains, which he rendered in free-flowing brush strokes and vibrant colors. Although he exhibited successfully at the 1836 Salon—the official annual Paris showing—he was refused consistently between 1837 and 1847. His paintings were, however, collected by a discriminating group that included Charles Baudelaire, Honoré Daumier, Eugène Delacroix, and George Sand.

In about 1837, Rousseau settled in the rural village of Barbizon, at the edge of the Forest of Fontainebleau near Paris, and turned from the romantic scenes of the previous decade to serene pastorals, always painted directly from nature with unwavering fidelity. His house became the center for all the painters of the Barbizon school. His close friend Jean François Millet moved to Barbizon in 1849 and painted its laborers and farmers for the rest of his life. Rousseau finally achieved public success in the 1850s and was recognized as one of the leading French landscape artists of the century.   EDWARD T. MCCLELLAN

Bibliography: Bouret, J., *The Barbizon School and 19th Century French Landscape Painting* (1973); Hoeber, A., *Barbizon Painters* (1969).

Roussel, Albert   [roo-sel']

Albert Roussel, b. Apr. 5, 1869, d. Aug. 23, 1937, was an outstanding French neoclassical composer. Before commencing serious music studies, he joined the navy and spent a considerable amount of time in the Orient. He studied (1898–1907)

at the Schola Cantorum in Paris and also taught (1902–14) there.

Roussel's music was initially impressionistic, an example being his Indian-influenced opera-ballet *Padmâvatî* (1918); it later tended toward neoclassicism, illustrated by the orchestral *Suite in F* (1927) and the ballet *Bacchus et Ariane* (1931). His best-known works include the last two of his four symphonies and the ballet *The Spiker's Feast*.   KAREN MONSON

Bibliography: Deane, Basil, *Albert Roussel* (1961).

Roussillon   [roo-see-yohn']

Roussillon, a historic province on France's southwestern Mediterranean coast, corresponds to the present department of Pyrénées-Orientales. Wine grapes and peaches grow in the valleys of the area. The main city is PERPIGNAN. Settled by Iberians in the 7th century BC, the region became a Roman colony in the 2d century BC. It was occupied by the Visigoths in AD 462 and the Arabs about AD 720. It became a part of the Frankish realm in the mid-8th century. In 1172 the region was united with Aragon. Louis XIV of France acquired it under the Treaty of the Pyrenees in 1659.

Roux, Pierre Paul Émile   [roo]

Pierre Paul Émile Roux, b. Dec. 17, 1853, d. Nov. 3, 1933, a French physician and bacteriologist, contributed to an understanding of DIPHTHERIA and other diseases. With Swiss bacteriologist Alexandre Yersin, he showed that a toxin is the active agent in producing diphtheria—work that made possible the development of diphtheria immunization therapy.

Rowe, Nicholas   [roh]

Nicholas Rowe, b. June 30, 1674, d. Dec. 6, 1718, was an English dramatist of the Restoration period whose lasting contribution to literature was his edition (1709) of Shakespeare's works. Rowe divided the plays into acts and scenes, modifications that are still in use. His own dramas, among them *The Fair Penitent* (1703), differ markedly from most dramas of the period in their high moral tone. Rowe was named poet laureate of England in 1715.

Rowell, Newton Wesley   [row'-ul]

A Canadian political leader, Newton Wesley Rowell, b. Nov. 1, 1867, d. Nov. 22, 1941, served (1911–17) in the Ontario legislature as Liberal party leader. A member of the Canadian House of Commons from 1917 to 1921, he was president of the council (1917–20) in Sir Robert BORDEN's Unionist cabinet. In 1920 he represented Canada at the first session of the League of Nations. Appointed (1936) chief justice of Ontario, Rowell was also chairman (1937–38) of the Royal Commission on Dominion-Provincial Relations until ill health forced his resignation.

rowing

Rowing is the action of moving a vessel through the water by using bladed sticks called oars. Rowing was originally the only reliable source of propulsion for a boat, but it has lost most of its practical and economic functions and is now practiced primarily as a recreation and sport throughout the world. Rowing dates back to antiquity when galley slaves were used to provide locomotion for warships. The earliest account of sport rowing in literature may be found in Vergil's *Aeneid;* a race is described at the funeral games held in honor of the father of Aeneas. Rowing in its modern form developed on the Thames River in England. By the early 1700s a favorite pastime of the upper class was to wager on rowing races held on the river. In the United States the first race was held in 1811 in New York City. As in England, ferrymen rowed their barges in competition. Professional and amateur rowing flourished in the 19th century, especially in the United States, England, Canada, and Australia. With the changes in the definition of professionalism in the late-19th century, amateur

Spectators crowd the banks of the Millstone River near Princeton, New Jersey to watch an 8-oared shell regatta. Rowing competitions are conducted over still stretches of water, usually on a course measuring 2,000 m (6,560 ft) in length. The coxswain, who determines tactics during the race, sits in the stern, steering the lightweight shell and helping oarsmen maintain the rhythm of their rowing.

rowing acquired more prestige, and the 1-mi, 550-yd (2.5-km) Diamond Sculls at the Henley Royal Regatta (founded 1839) became the world's top amateur race. In modern rowing events, boats compete in two categories, either sculling or sweep events. In sweep events a rower holds one oar and is part of a crew of 2, 4, or 8. In sculling, a rower holds two oars and competes in boats that have 1, 2, or 4 scullers. Racing boats are called shells and vary in size according to the number of crew members. A modern 8-man shell weighs about 110 kg (242 lb), is 18.3 m (60 ft) long, and has a very narrow beam of about 61 cm (24 in). Crew members sit on sliding seats mounted on rollers that permit leg muscles to be brought into use with each stroke. Rowing technique must be precise and repeated in unison by each boat member. Any mistake will reduce speed. Rowing was adopted as an Olympic Games event in 1900, and international amateur championships are held annually. In the United States two important regattas are held annually, the Harvard-Yale race and the Intercollegiate Rowing Association regatta.

GERALD S. COUZENS

Bibliography: Chant, Christopher, *Rowing for Everyone* (1977); Howard, Ronnie, and Hunt, Nigel, *Knowing Rowing* (1978); Langfield, John, *Better Rowing* (1974); Scott, A. C., and Williams, J. P., eds., *Rowing: A Scientific Approach* (1967).

Rowland, Henry Augustus [roh'-luhnd]

Henry Augustus Rowland, b. Honesdale, Pa., Nov. 27, 1848, d. Apr. 16, 1901, was an American experimental physicist who invented the concave DIFFRACTION GRATING, revolutionizing spectrum analysis. Using his gratings, Rowland identified 39 chemical elements in the solar atmosphere and published (1888) a highly accurate map of the solar spectrum. His experiments in electricity proved that a moving electrostatic charge has the same magnetic effect as an electric current. Rowland also improved thermometric methods and redetermined the values of important physical constants.

RICHARD HIRSH

Rowlandson, Thomas

The English artist, caricaturist, and illustrator Thomas Rowlandson, b. July 14, 1756, d. Apr. 21, 1827, was a brilliant draftsman whose lively, wash-colored pen-and-ink sketches primarily consist of witty observations of life in England during the Regency period.

Rowlandson studied at the Royal Academy of Arts in London, where his drawings of the nude were greatly admired;

he also spent some time in Paris. He won the Academy's silver medal in 1777, 2 years after his first exhibition there, and, in the late '70s, set out on travels through the Continent and the English provinces, making copious sketchbook studies. In 1789, Rowlandson, the son of a tradesman, came into a sizable legacy from a widowed aunt. Led into dissolute habits, especially gambling, he lost his inheritance and survived by making and selling more drawings; his output was vast.

Rowlandson was above all a master of line. His caricatures are often coarse and deliberately ugly; their content is more ephemeral than that of his watercolors, perhaps because they were composed and executed in great haste. His masterly book illustrations are best exemplified by those for William Combe's *Tour of Dr. Syntax in Search of the Picturesque* (1812), but some of his most pleasing work is topographical: views of the English countryside and of London, some of which also became book illustrations, as in *Microcosm of London* (1808).

RAYMOND LISTER

Bibliography: Hayes, J., *Rowlandson Watercolours and Drawings* (1972); Paulson, R., *Rowlandson: A New Interpretation* (1972).

Roxana [rahk-san'-uh]

Roxana, or Roxane, daughter of a Bactrian baron, married ALEXANDER THE GREAT in 327 BC. Her son, later Alexander IV, was born after his father's death (323). Four years later, Roxana joined forces with OLYMPIAS, Alexander's mother, but was captured and imprisoned by CASSANDER, king of Macedonia, who had her put to death (c.310).

ROBIN BUSS

Roxas y Acuna, Manuel [roh'-hahs ee ah-koo'-noh]

Manuel Roxas y Acuna, b. Jan. 1, 1892, d. Apr. 15, 1948, was the first president of the Philippine republic. A member (1921–33) of the House of Representatives, he was a rival of Manuel QUEZON, the leading nationalist of the 1930s, who had him ousted as Speaker of the House. During Japan's World War II occupation of the Philippines, Roxas cooperated with the pro-Japanese government, but he was subsequently cleared of charges of collaborating after Gen. Douglas MacArthur testified in his behalf. Elected president of the Senate when the Philippine Congress was reconvened in 1945, Roxas became (1946) the first president of an independent Philippines. He died in office 2 years later.

RICHARD BUTWELL

Bibliography: Lichauco, Marcial P., *Roxas* (1952).

Roxburgh   [rahks'-bur-uh]

Roxburgh is a former county in southeastern Scotland located on the border with England. The principal town is Jedburgh. The economy is based on livestock grazing, fishing, and the cultivation of grains and fruits as well as the manufacturing of textiles and agricultural and fishing equipment. Abbotsford, home of Sir Walter Scott, is located there.

Occupied by the Romans in the early centuries AD, Roxburgh was later part of the Anglo-Saxon kingdom of Northumbria. It was incorporated into Scotland in 1011 but was the scene of numerous border conflicts with the English. During the reorganization of Scotland's local government in 1975, Roxburgh became part of the BORDERS administrative region.

Roy, Gabrielle   [rwah]

A French-Canadian novelist, Gabrielle Roy, b. St. Boniface, Manitoba, Mar. 22, 1909, d. July 13, 1983, was the first Canadian to win a major French literary prize. Her winning novel, *Bonheur d'occasion* (1945; trans. as *The Tin Flute*, 1947), like much of her work, describes life in the isolated regions of Manitoba. Her other novels include *Alexandre Chenevert, caissier* (1954; trans. as *The Cashier*, 1955), *The Hidden Mountain* (1961; Eng. trans., 1962) and *Ces Enfants de ma vie* (1977; trans. as *Children of My Heart*, 1979).

Roy, Rammohun   [rahm-moh'-huhn]

Rammohun Roy, b. 1774, d. Sept. 27, 1833, was a noted statesman and religious leader in British-ruled India. He mastered many languages and worked for the British East India Company until 1815, when he began to write—his translation of the Upanishads is especially famous, and he was a pioneer in Indian journalism. Roy tried to purify Hindu teachings and practices and to eliminate from Hinduism such illiberal elements as the caste system and discrimination against women. He founded (1828) the BRAHMO SAMAJ, a religious society that greatly influenced 19th-century Hinduism. Turning to secular education, he asked the British to improve teaching of the sciences in India. Because of his efforts to plot a new course of self-determination for his people, he has been called the father of modern India.

Bibliography: Collet, Sophia D., *The Life and Letters of Raja Rammohun Roy* (1900; repr. 1962); Singh, Iqbal, *Rammohun Roy: A Biographical Inquiry into the Making of Modern India* (1958).

Royal Academy of Dramatic Art

The Royal Academy of Dramatic Art in London trains its students in acting, directing, lighting, makeup, and set and costume design. Founded (1904) by Sir Herbert Beerbohm TREE, it received a royal charter in 1920, and under the direction of Kenneth Barnes gained a reputation as one of the world's most prestigious schools for theatrical training.

Royal Astronomical Society

One of the world's leading professional astronomical organizations, the Royal Astronomical Society began as the Astronomical Society of London in 1820 and was incorporated under its present name in 1831. Its headquarters are in Burlington House, London. The society publishes the Quarterly Journal, *Geophysical Journal*, *Memoirs*, and *Monthly Notices*.

Royal Ballet, The

The Royal Ballet, so named by royal charter in 1956, began its existence as the Vic-Wells Ballet, whose first performance was at Old Vic's, London, May 5, 1931. Its first director and choreographer was Dame Ninette de VALOIS, a former soloist with the Ballets Russes de Serge Diaghilev; her students formed the new company's nucleus. De Valois built her company on the solid triple foundation of a school, a theater, and a carefully planned repertoire of both classic and new British ballets, the latter supplied by herself and Sir Frederick ASHTON, whom she engaged as dancer and resident choreographer in 1935. When Dame Alicia MARKOVA, the company's ballerina from 1932 to 1935, decided to leave, de Valois was ready with a home-trained successor in Dame Margot FONTEYN.

Such ballets as de Valois's *Checkmate* (1937) and Ashton's *Les Patineurs* (1937) formed the basis for the national style of ballet—strong, clear characterization and lyrical, elegant dancing. During World War II the company—then known as Sadler's Wells Ballet—undertook long provincial tours, interspersed with London seasons, and thus became firmly established as the British national ballet. With the coming of peace the company took up residence at the Royal Opera House, Covent Garden, which reopened on Feb. 20, 1946, with a new production of *The Sleeping Beauty*. This production also opened the company's first New York season in 1949, giving it international status. Since then the company has made regular tours throughout the world.

The Royal Ballet produced two more important choreographers in Kenneth MACMILLAN and John CRANKO. De Valois retired as director in 1963, to be succeeded by Ashton; in 1970, Ashton was in turn succeeded by MacMillan, who resigned as director in 1978, although remaining as resident choreographer, with Norman Morrice taking over as director. The company and its school have produced several generations of leading dancers.   DAVID VAUGHAN

Bibliography: Clarke, Mary, *The Sadler's Wells Ballet* (1955; repr. 1977); Vaughan, David, *The Royal Ballet at Covent Garden* (1975).

Royal Canadian Mounted Police

The Royal Canadian Mounted Police (RCMP) is Canada's federal police force. At the request of eight provinces (all but Ontario and Quebec) the RCMP also does provincial policing; in addition, it performs municipal police functions in about 170 municipalities. It is the only police force in the Yukon Territory and the Northwest Territories, including the Arctic islands. As Canada's security service it investigates espionage and subversion.

The RCMP operates the National Police Services for the benefit of all Canadian police forces. These services include the Crime Detection Laboratories; the National Fingerprint Identification Bureau; the Crime Index; the Fraudulent Cheques Research, Commercial Fraud, and Firearms Registration sections; the National Police College; and the Canadian Police Information Centre (linked with a U.S. Federal Bureau of Investigation computer).

The federal minister of justice is responsible to Parliament for the administration of the RCMP. In 1980 the RCMP's total force numbered over 19,000. Twelve operational divisions, most of which have jurisdiction over specific provinces or geographical areas, include about 40 subdivisions and almost 700 detachments. The force has about 20 liaison and visa control offices throughout the world. It also acts as the Canadian representative of Interpol.

History. The force was established as the North-West Mounted Police (NWMP) in 1873, 6 years after Canadian confederation. Its mission was to police on horseback the vast western plains known then as the North-West Territories (now Manitoba, Saskatchewan and Alberta). On July 8, 1874, 275 scarlet-tunicked NWMP set out from Dufferin, Manitoba, on their famous march to the foothills of the Rocky Mountains. By 1877 they had brought law and order to the western plains. In 1885, when the building of the Canadian Pacific Railway caused unrest among the Indian tribes, the NWMP helped to suppress the rebellion.

Anticipating the Klondike gold rush of the late 1890s, some of the NWMP moved north to the Yukon. In 1904 the NWMP became the Royal North-West Mounted Police. In 1905 it began provincial police work for Alberta and Saskatchewan (assuming provincial duties for Manitoba, Nova Scotia, New Brunswick, and Prince Edward Island in 1932 and for Newfoundland and British Columbia in 1950). In 1920 the force absorbed the Dominion Police and assumed the federal policing of all Canada. As the Royal Canadian Mounted Police, it moved its headquarters from Regina, Saskatchewan, to Ottawa. Over the years the RCMP, also known as "Mounties," acquired a legendary reputation for persistence and bravery.

NORA HICKSON KELLY

Bibliography: Dempsey, Hugh A., *Men in Scarlet* (1974); Horrall, S. W., *The Pictorial History of the Royal Canadian Mounted Police* (1973); Kelly, Nora and William, *The Royal Canadian Mounted Police* (1973) and *Horses of the Royal Canadian Mounted Police* (1984).

Royal Copenhagen ware

Denmark's oldest porcelain factory was founded in 1775 in Copenhagen by Franz Heinrich Müller. In 1779 the factory was taken over by the state and designated the Royal Danish Porcelain Manufactory, a name retained today although the factory has been in private hands since 1867. The factory's best-known tableware pattern—stylized flower forms painted in underglaze-blue—originated in this early period. The factory created (1789–1803) the immense *Flora Danica* service, decorated with flower paintings by J. C. Bayer and originally intended as a gift to Catherine II of Russia. After the factory again changed hands in 1883, a period of reorganization and experimentation occurred under Philip Schou and art director Arnold Krog, who evolved a new style of underglaze painting in muted blues and grays that won a Grand Prix at the Paris Exposition of 1889. In the 20th century, besides well-designed porcelain tablewares, Royal Copenhagen has produced distinguished works in stoneware by Patrick Nordström and Axel Salto.

BETTY ELZEA

Bibliography: Hayden, Arthur, *Royal Copenhagen Porcelain* (1911); Owen, Pat, *The Story of Royal Copenhagen Christmas Plates* (1978); Penkala, Maria, *European Porcelain* (1985).

Royal Danish Ballet

The Royal Danish Ballet has been in existence since the opening of the first Royal Theatre in Copenhagen, Dec. 18, 1748; earlier there had been court ballets. The first important ballet master was Vincenzo Galeotti (1775–1812), whose *The Whims of Cupid and the Ballet-Master* (1786) is still performed. His successor was the French dancer Antoine Bournonville, whose Danish-born son August, after studying and dancing abroad, took over the company in 1829 and remained its director for nearly 50 years (see BOURNONVILLE, AUGUST). He created the Danish national style, with its precise footwork and light, floating jumps. After his death, Danish ballet went into a decline until Harald Lander became ballet master (1932–51). While preserving the Bournonville heritage, he created new ballets, such as *Qarrtsiluni* (1942), in a more contemporary vein—a pattern followed by Flemming FLINDT from 1966 to 1977.

It was only after World War II that Danish ballet became known abroad. Thus, dancers like Margot Lander and Børge Ralov never gained an international reputation, unlike Margrethe Schanne, Mona Vangsaae, and Henning Kronstam, who succeeded Flindt as director in 1978. Others, like Erik BRUHN, Toni Lander, Peter MARTINS, and Peter SCHAUFUSS, left Denmark to seek fame abroad.

DAVID VAUGHAN

Bibliography: Fog, Dan, *The Royal Danish Ballet 1760–1958 and August Bournonville* (1961).

Royal Gorge

Royal Gorge in the Grand Canyon of the Arkansas River is located in south central Colorado. About 16 km (10 mi) in length, it has spectacular brownish red granite walls that rise straight up more than 305 m (1,000 ft) above the water. A suspension bridge near Canon City, completed in 1929, crosses the gorge about 321 m (1,053 ft) above the river, as does an aerial tramway completed in 1969. A cable railroad descends into the canyon on the north side, and a scenic railroad at the base of the canyon runs along the river.

Royal Greenwich Observatory

Royal Greenwich Observatory, one of the oldest extant observatories, was established by Charles II in 1675 at Greenwich and transferred to Herstmonceux Castle, near Halisham,

Sussex, England, after World War II. Its first two directors were John FLAMSTEED and Edmond HALLEY; the third director, James BRADLEY, discovered (1784) the nutation of the Earth. In 1884 the meridian (0° longitude) at Greenwich was chosen the world's PRIME MERIDIAN, from which east-west longitude and time zones are calculated (see also GREENWICH MEAN TIME). Instruments at the site include a photographic zenith tube (1955), a 36-in (91-cm) Yapp reflecting telescope (1932), and a 38-in (96-cm) Hargreaves reflector (1972). The observatory's 98-in (2.5-m) Isaac Newton telescope, completed in 1967, was moved to the island of La Palma in the Canary Islands and began operating there in 1984; the observatory is also constructing its 165-in (4.2-m) William Herschel telescope at this site. In 1986 the decision was made to transfer the remaining facilities and all operations of the Royal Greenwich Observatory to Cambridge University.

Bibliography: Forbes, Eric G., Meadows, A. J., and Howse, Derek, *Greenwich Observatory*, 3 vols. (1975); McCrea, William H., *Royal Greenwich Observatory: An Historical Review Issued on the Occasion of Its Tercentenary* (1975).

Royal Institution of Great Britain

The Royal Institution of Great Britain, in London, England, was founded in 1799 by Benjamin Thompson to promote science and the extension of useful knowledge. It sponsors both research in its Davy-Faraday Laboratory and lectures for institution members and for schools. In the mid-1980s the institution had 2,500 members.

Royal Ontario Museum

The Royal Ontario Museum, in the city of Toronto, is the largest and most diversified museum complex in Canada. It was established in 1912 as a loose federation of five museums dedicated, respectively, to archaeology, geology, mineralogy, paleontology, and zoology. In addition to these the museum's collections cover ethnology, textiles, entomology, mammalogy, ornithology, and astronomy, and contain decorative arts and historic art objects from all over the world. Its collections of Chinese, Japanese, Islamic, and Indian art are among the finest anywhere. Included in the museum complex are the McLaughlin Planetarium and the Canadiana Building; the latter houses exhibitions of 19th-century glass, as well as the art and artifacts of Canada's pioneers.

The museum has a library of research collections and a Far Eastern library; together these contain 92,000 volumes. The museum's activities include formally organized programs for children, college students, and adults; professional museum workers' training programs; lectures, films, concerts, arts festivals, dance recitals, and study clubs for the general public; and permanent, traveling, and temporary exhibitions. The museum publishes *The Rotunda* (a quarterly magazine), an annual report, and scholarly writings in the fields of art, archaeology, and science.

BARBARA CAVALIERE

Bibliography: Heinreich, Theodore, *Art Treasures in the Royal Ontario Museum* (1963).

Royal Pavilion at Brighton

An oriental pleasure palace set in an English seaside resort, the Royal Pavilion at Brighton was originally a large 18th-century farmhouse. Henry HOLLAND transformed it (1787), at the behest of King George IV (then prince regent), into a Palladian villa. In 1815 the prince commissioned John NASH, his favorite architect, to realize a more exotic vision. By 1822, Nash, in collaboration with the prince and a number of decorators, had created the extraordinary but harmonious Royal Pavilion.

Beneath its many bulbous domes and a forest of minaret-shaped chimneys are two stories: on the second floor are a number of comparatively small but elegant bedrooms; the ground floor is filled with a suite of enormous rooms decorated and furnished in a wildly exuberant Chinese-Mogul style. They include a gallery, two drawing rooms, the central domed saloon, and, at the building's north and south ends respectively, the huge Banqueting Room and Music Room.

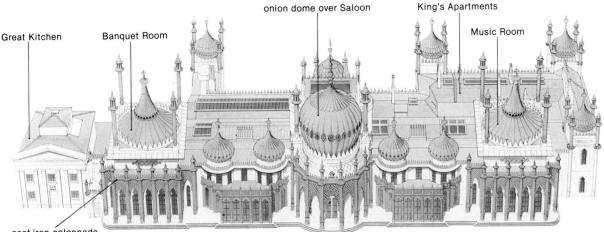

Great Kitchen Banquet Room onion dome over Saloon King's Apartments Music Room

cast-iron colonnade

The Royal Pavilion at Brighton, a seaside villa redesigned (1815-22) by John Nash for the prince regent, expresses the fascination with the exotic that accompanied 19th-century romanticism. Its unrestrained ornamentation includes elaborate lacework, a large onion dome over the Saloon, minarets, and pagodalike spires over the Banquet Room and Music Room. Formerly a royal residence, the structure is today open to the public.

Bibliography: Davis, Terence, *John Nash, the Prince Regent's Architect*, rev. ed. (1973); Musgrave, Clifford, *Royal Pavilion: An Episode in the Romantic* (1959); *The Royal Pavilion, Brighton*, catalogue (1975).

Royal Shakespeare Company

World tours and inventive interpretations of Shakespeare's plays, other classics, and modern works have made the Royal Shakespeare Company a renowned repertory company. Formed in 1961, its roots go back to David Garrick's Stratford-upon-Avon Jubilee (1769) and to the Shakespeare Memorial Theatre, opened in 1879. Its two member companies are based in Stratford and London. It has had such noteworthy directors as Barry Jackson, Anthony Quayle, Peter Hall, and Trevor Nunn.   GLENN LONEY

Royal Society

Founded in 1660 as a club of learned men and granted charters from Charles II in 1662 and 1663, the Royal Society of London "for Natural Knowledge" is one of the world's oldest and most prestigious scientific societies. The society, which has always conducted and supported scientific research and projects, advises the British government in scientific matters in a semiofficial capacity. In 1977-78, the society received £2,172,000 in Parliamentary grant-in-aid for its various projects. The society, whose headquarters is in London, has more than 900 fellows and foreign members. It holds annual meetings, publishes *Philosophical Transactions* (1666), *Proceedings* (1880), and *Notes and Records* (1938), and awards medals, such as the Copley Medal, which dates from 1731, and the Royal Medals, dating from 1825 and 1965.

Bibliography: Andrade, Edward N. da C., *A Brief History of the Royal Society* (1960); Hartley, Harold, ed., *The Royal Society: Its Origins and Founders* (1960); Purver, Margery, *The Beginning of the Royal Society* (1960) and *The Royal Society: Concept and Creation* (1967).

See also: SCIENTIFIC ASSOCIATIONS.

Royal Swedish Ballet

Ballet in Sweden began with court performances in the 17th century. The first professional troupe was organized by the French ballet master Louis Gallodier in 1773 at the newly built Royal Opera. Some of the dancers were Swedish, but choreographers, such as Antoine Bournonville, his famous son August, and Filippo Taglioni (see TAGLIONI family), were imported from abroad. The first Swedish choreographer was Anders Selinder (1806-74), appointed in 1833, who used native folk material in his ballets.

Ballet declined in Sweden as elsewhere in the second half of the 19th century and only regained vitality when Mikhail Fokine was engaged as choreographer (1913-14), an association cut short by World War I. Little work of any significance was produced by the Royal Swedish Ballet until Antony Tudor was appointed director in 1949, followed by Mary Skeaping (1953-62), under whom the repertory was strengthened by both classic and contemporary works. The most important contemporary Swedish choreographers have come out of modern dance rather than ballet: Birgit Cullberg, Birgit Åkesson, and Ivo Cramer, all of whom have created works for the Royal Swedish Ballet.   DAVID VAUGHAN

Royce, Josiah   [roys, juh-zy'-uh]

Josiah Royce, b. Grass Valley, Calif., Nov. 20, 1855, d. Sept. 14, 1916, was a leading proponent of philosophical IDEALISM whose thought dominated American philosophy until World War I. He studied at the University of California and, for a time, in Germany. After receiving his doctorate from Johns Hopkins University (1878), he returned to the University of California as an instructor of English. Four years later he was invited to teach at Harvard on a temporary basis. In 1885 he became a regular member of the philosophy department at Harvard, where he taught until his death.

Royce's idealism combined the rationalism of system building and proof of the absolute with traits of American philosophy: the appeal to experience, voluntarism, and the focus on ideas as plans of action, not as purely cognitive entities. This combination led to the characterization of his position as a voluntaristic idealism. According to Royce, God is not just all-knower but is also cosmic purpose. To be an individual, then, is to embody purpose. The infinity of mutually interpreting and intercommunicating selves constitutes the absolute self, the absolute community, which is, as the whole, a conscious unity of all the parts.

Royce's idealism gave rise to important ideas for the philosophy of religion and ethics. He also exhibited a profound interest in logic, and his work in this area greatly influenced his overall philosophical position.   SANDRA B. ROSENTHAL

Bibliography: Buranelli, Vincent, *Josiah Royce* (1964); Fuss, Peter L., *The Moral Philosophy of Josiah Royce* (1965); Kuklick, Bruce, *Josiah Royce: An Intellectual Biography* (1972); Powell, Thomas F., *Josiah Royce* (1967); Robinson, Daniel S., *Royce's Logical Essays* (1971).

Rozelle, Pete   [roh-zel']

Alvin Ray Rozelle, b. South Gate, Calif., Mar. 1, 1926, commissioner of the National Football League (NFL), presided over the development of professional football into the most popular big-money sport in the United States. He became commissioner in 1960 at the age of 33 and the next year designed federal legislation that permitted selling television broadcast rights to a single network for the entire league. In 1966,

Rozelle negotiated the merger agreement with the rival American Football League (AFL) that made possible the Super Bowl championship game and led to the inclusion of 10 AFL teams in the NFL in 1970.

Różewicz, Tadeusz   [roo-zhev'-eech]

One of Poland's leading poets and playwrights, Tadeusz Różewicz, b. Oct. 9, 1921, writes about the horrors of war and postwar civilization. Rejecting traditional notions of artistic beauty, he creates poetry from the less attractive aspects of modern civilization. Among his better-known works are *The Card Index* (1960; Eng. trans., 1969), whose hero lies in bed answering questions about life, and *The Old Woman Broods* (1968; Eng. trans., 1969), which depicts the world as a rubbish heap.

Rozhdestvensky, Valery   [ruhzh-dyest-vyen'-skee]

The Soviet cosmonaut Valery Il'ich Rozhdestvensky, b. Feb. 13, 1939, was the engineer on the aborted *Soyuz 23* space-flight (Oct. 14-16, 1976), which accidentally made the USSR's first space splashdown. A failure in the SOYUZ automatic approach system prevented the linkup of *Soyuz 23* with the SALYUT 5 space station. Rozhdestvensky and commander Vyacheslav Zudov made an emergency night landing; their capsule fell by accident into Lake Tengiz, the only large body of water in the desert recovery zone. Landing in the midst of a blizzard, they nearly died of exposure. A graduate of the Soviet Naval Engineering School, Rozhdestvensky was a navy engineer specializing in underwater rescue and diving prior to his recruitment (1965) into the cosmonaut program, where he specialized in space walking and spacesuit designing. His other spaceflight duties included backup crew for *Salyut 3* (1974) and communications officer for *Salyut 6* (1977-79).

JAMES OBERG

Bibliography: Hooper, Gordon R., "Missions to Salyut 5," *Spaceflight*, April 1977.

RR Lyrae stars   [ly'-ray]

RR Lyrae stars, named for their prototype star, RR Lyrae, are pulsating VARIABLE STARS that have periods between 1 hour and 1 day. Because they occur in globular clusters as well as in the Galaxy, they are sometimes known as cluster CEPHEIDS, or cluster variables. Their brightness varies by about one magnitude during the pulsation cycle. All RR Lyrae stars have very nearly the same mean absolute magnitude, slightly fainter than magnitude zero. Thus, a measurement of the mean apparent magnitude of any RR Lyrae star immediately yields the distance of the star. The distances of many clusters have been obtained by studying the apparent magnitudes of the RR Lyrae stars that they contain. In 1952, A. D. Thackeray and A. J. Wesselink revised the distances of the Magellanic clouds when they detected the presence of RR Lyrae stars at apparent magnitudes in agreement with those expected on the basis of the revised PERIOD-LUMINOSITY RELATION for classical Cepheids.

R. H. GARSTANG

Ruanda: see RWANDA.

Ruanda-Urundi   [roo-ahn'-dah-oo-roon'-dee]

The former Belgian mandate of Ruanda-Urundi covered about 54,994 km² (21,234 mi²) in central Africa, between the present nations of Tanzania, Uganda, and Zaire. The area was inhabited by TUTSI when Sir Richard Burton and John Hanning Speke first explored it in 1858. In 1899, Germany made Ruanda-Urundi part of GERMAN EAST AFRICA. Control of the area was given to Belgium in 1923, and in 1962 the independent nations of BURUNDI and RWANDA were proclaimed.

Rubaiyat of Omar Khayyam   [roo'-by-yaht]

Best known to English readers in the translation (1859) of Edward FITZGERALD, the *Rubaiyat of Omar Khayyam* is a long, early-12th-century Persian poem attributed to OMAR KHAYYAM.

Rubai is Persian for "quatrain," and *rubaiyat* is the plural; thus the poem is a collection of quatrains celebrating sensual pleasure, as in the famous lines, "A jug of wine, a loaf of bread—and thou/Beside me singing in the wilderness." there have been many later attempts to translate the poem, but none has excelled FitzGerald's poignant paraphrase of Omar's hedonistic philosophy.

rubber

Rubber was originally a natural, elastic product obtained from the secretion of certain plants. Today there is not just one substance called rubber, but a class, made up of a number of materials that have the unique property of high elasticity. A strip of rubber can be stretched to several times its original length without breaking and will return instantly to that length when released. Arising from this, rubber is relatively soft—several thousand times less stiff than steel—and possesses in high degree the property of resilience or bounciness.

These unique properties are a result of the chemical structure of the rubber molecule, which is very large compared with simple chemicals. The rubber molecule is an example of a polymer (see POLYMERIZATION), a long chain made up of tens of thousands of smaller units, or monomers, strung together, each monomer unit having a molecular size comparable with that of a simple substance such as sugar. The long molecules of rubber are very flexible, and tying the molecules together with *crosslinks* makes rubber elastic. The process that creates the crosslinks is called vulcanization. Some polymers other than rubber are slightly elastic, such as polyvinyl chloride (PVC), but rubbers have an unusually wide spacing between crosslinks, giving them their extraordinary elasticity. The term *elastomer* is sometimes used to cover all "rubbery" polymers.

HISTORY

Natural rubber has been used for trivial purposes for many centuries. Its "discovery" is generally attributed to Christopher Columbus, who observed the inhabitants of Haiti using rubber to make playballs; it was probably also used by them in various religious rites. Europeans later discovered that rubber could be extracted from many different kinds of trees and shrubs, mostly native to the tropics.

Toward the end of the 18th century European scientists started to look at the properties of this curious material. The British scientist Joseph Priestley, observing its ability to rub out pencil marks, gave rubber its English name. Its name in French, *caoutchouc*, is more apt, however, coming from the Indian-American word *cachuchu*, "the wood that weeps."

By the start of the 19th century rubber was an expensive curiosity with no serious uses. Thomas Hancock devised methods for mechanically working rubber so it could be shaped, and he built England's first rubber factory in 1820. In

The rubber tree, Hevea brasiliensis, is the most important source of natural rubber, which is made from the tree's sap, a milky-white liquid called latex.

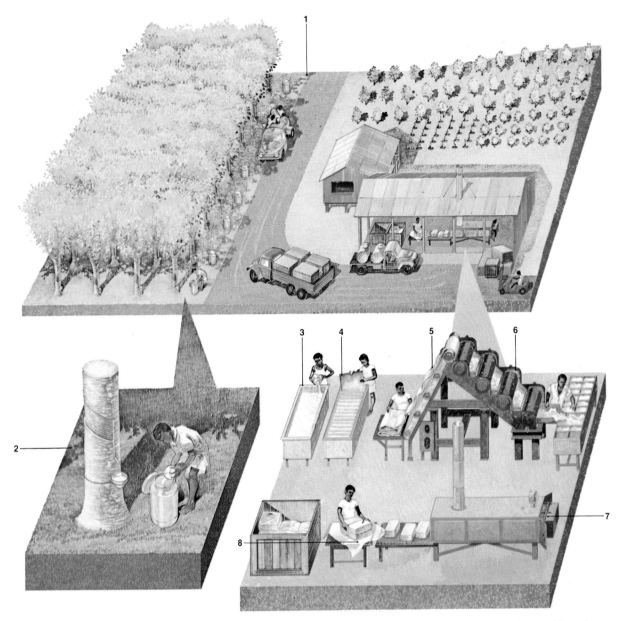

The rubber plantations (1) of Southeast Asia are the source of most of the world's natural rubber. The watery latex, or sap, is tapped from the tree (2) by scoring the bark with a knife to a depth of 1 mm (0.04 in) and slanting the cut downward to channel the sap into a cup. The latex is strained into aluminum tanks (3) to remove impurities. Acid is added to coagulate the rubber particles, which are deposited on aluminum partitions (4), rolled into sheets (5), and shredded (6). The rubber is dried and compressed into bales (7) and is wrapped for shipment (8).

1823, Charles MACINTOSH devised a practical method of waterproofing fabric with rubber. Natural rubber, however, contains virtually no crosslinks, so it becomes soft and sticky when hot and stiff when cold. Vulcanization, accidentally discovered by Charles GOODYEAR in 1839, overcame this problem, yielding a tough, elastic material suitable for manufactured products. Goodyear heated rubber with sulfur, which causes the crosslinking. The same vulcanization process, with elaborations, is used today.

Until the late 19th century all rubber was natural rubber extracted haphazardly from trees scattered in the jungles of South America. It was expensive and the supply was uncertain. During the 1860s the British government conceived the idea of transporting rubber trees to the British colonies in Asia so that the trees could be grown on a large scale on organized plantations. The most promising rubber source was the Brazilian Pará rubber tree, *Hevea brasiliensis*. Because of

Brazil's legal restrictions the British government hired Henry Wickham, then in Brazil, to transport some seeds of the tree to England. This he did in 1876; the seeds were germinated in England, and the young seedlings were shipped to Ceylon, Malaysia, and Singapore. All the natural rubber produced today in Asia—90% of the world's total production—comes from trees that are descendants of Wickham's seeds.

This establishment of substantial, controlled production of natural rubber coincided with the establishment of the automotive industry. The pneumatic tire had already been invented in 1845 by Robert William Thomson of Scotland for horse-drawn carriages and was "reinvented" in 1888 by John Boyd Dunlop of Ireland. The sudden demand for large quantities of rubber for tires accelerated the young rubber industry. Today 60% of all rubber produced is used to make tires.

NATURAL-RUBBER PRODUCTION

Natural rubber is secreted by the tree as latex, a milky white liquid that contains about 30% rubber as very small particles suspended in water. South American Indians extracted the latex by simply slashing the trees with axes, but with the arrival of trees in Asia the tapping method was devised. It involves removing a thin sliver of bark with a knife. The latex flows out from just under the cut bark; after about two hours flow ceases. The latex is collected in cups and is coagulated with an acid to make solid rubber. The wet solid rubber is dried either by exposing thin sheets to hot smoke or, more recently, by mechanically chopping the block into small particles for fast drying in an oil-fired dryer. The dried rubber is then compacted into bales for export. A small proportion is exported as liquid latex from which, for economy and transport, part of the water has been removed in a centrifuge.

Because of improvements resulting from plant–breeding research, trees of several commercial varieties now exist that yield as much as six times more rubber than the wild tree (see GUAYULE). In addition, special chemicals, or yield stimulants, are used to boost production. Surprisingly little natural rubber comes today from South America; 90% is from Asia, and nearly half the world total comes from Malaysia. Other leading Asian producers include Indonesia, Thailand, Sri Lanka, and India; substantial amounts of rubber are produced in Africa, mainly Liberia, and much of this rubber is produced on large estates—one in Liberia is 30,750 ha (76,000 acres). The majority of rubber produced worldwide, however, comes from small holdings of a few hectares.

SYNTHETIC-RUBBER PRODUCTION

In 1826, Michael Faraday—although he was not aware of the class of molecules known as polymers—discovered that natural rubber is composed of units of a chemical compound, ISOPRENE. Later 19th-century French and German chemists showed how isoprene could be converted into rubber. No practical means of producing synthetic rubber, however, was devised until Germany, deprived of access to Asian rubber during World War I, undertook limited production of a synthetic rubber. Interest in synthetic rubber, however, evaporated after the war, and subsequent economic depression discouraged most further effort. In 1941–42 the United States, similarly faced with the loss of Asian rubber, undertook a program—second in scale only to the nuclear-bomb project—to develop a supply of this vital strategic material. By 1945, U.S. plants were producing 1 million U.S. tons of synthetic rubber a year. During the 1950s and '60s many other countries started production, and synthetic rubber has now become a universally available commodity.

Synthetic rubber developed during World War II was not a replica of natural rubber but was synthesized from two monomers—styrene and butadiene—that were more readily available than isoprene. These and all other monomers used for synthetic rubber are currently obtained from petroleum (see PETROCHEMICALS). Addition of suitable catalysts to the monomers causes them to polymerize, or join together, to form the necessary long molecules. Polymerization often occurs in soapy water, and the rubber is formed as a latex, like natural rubber in the tree. It is coagulated and baled like natural rubber, and vulcanization is similarly achieved.

Styrene-butadiene rubber (SBR) remains the most important synthetic rubber manufactured. Techniques for direct imitation of natural rubber (polyisoprene) by polymerizing the isoprene monomer eluded chemists until the 1950s. Synthetic polyisoprene, however, is more expensive to make than is styrene-butadiene rubber and is of greatest interest to those countries, such as the USSR, which aim to be independent of imported rubber; some is also produced in the United States and Europe.

Other than these two, a wide range of synthetic rubbers is now produced from various monomers. Styrene-butadiene, polyisoprene, and a third, polybutadiene, are general-purpose types, especially used in tires. The other types are specialty materials that are expensive and not suitable for general use. Two examples are polychloroprene, or neoprene, used for high chemical resistance, and nitrile, or Buna N, a copolymer of butadiene and acrylonitrile silicone rubbers, used for very high temperatures.

Production of Natural and Synthetic Rubbers
(thousands of metric tons)

Year	Natural	Synthetic	% Synthetic
1900	45	—	0
1925	535	—	0
1950	1,890	534	22
1975	3,315	6,855	67
2000	8,000 (est.)	18,000 (est.)	69

RUBBER PRODUCTS

Neither natural nor synthetic rubber is used in pure form. Vulcanizing chemicals must be added, primarily sulfur. A filler, such as carbon black (hence, black tires), is often added to provide extra strength and stiffness, and usually some oil is included to help processing and reduce cost. The typical rubber mix contains 60% or less rubber.

No major differences exist in the processes for making products from natural and synthetic rubbers. In the simplest process the mix is shaped by placing it in a heated mold, and the heat simultaneously effects shaping and vulcanization. For more complex products, such as tires, a number of components are made, some with fiber or steel-cord reinforcement; these are then joined to form the product.

Tires, the main product of the rubber industry for decades, accounts for 60% to 70% of all rubber used, natural and synthetic. Other uses include footwear, industrial conveyor belts and car fan belts, hose, flooring, and cables. Some products are made directly from latex. Surgical and domestic gloves, for example, are made by dipping a ceramic former into latex, withdrawing the former, and then drying. Latex foam is made by beating air into the latex before coagulating it.

NATURAL VERSUS SYNTHETIC

Neither natural nor synthetic rubber can be considered better in quality than the other; each has its own properties and prices, and the manufacturer chooses according to the needs of the product. In the treads of car tires, for example, the standard synthetic rubber, styrene-butadiene, is used for good wear and grip. In larger tires, in which heat generation is a problem, natural rubber is used. The larger the tire and the tougher the use, the higher the content of natural rubber: aircraft tires are 100% natural rubber.

Natural rubber is not good under extreme environmental conditions, however; it would not be used, for example, to make a jet engine gasket to withstand very hot oil. Also, when it is stretched, the high concentrations of ozone that are found in some climates can cause it to crack. Conversely, it is basically much stronger than any synthetic and is less liable to fail under repeated stressing, so it is widely used in engineering applications such as engine mountings.

Both kinds of rubber are needed in the modern world. In fact, production of natural rubber since 1945 has failed to

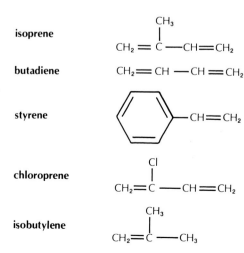

match the growing demand for rubber, with the result that natural rubber has seen its share of the rubber business steadily decline, and today two-thirds of the world's rubber is synthetic. This trend may be halted by improved productivity and developments such as the invention of epoxidized natural rubber (ENR), which is produced by chemically treating natural rubber.   P. W. ALLEN

Bibliography: Allen, P. W., *Natural Rubber and the Synthetics* (1972); Blackley, D. C., *Synthetic Rubbers* (1983); Eirich, F. R., ed., *Science and Technology of Rubber* (1978); Goering, T. J., and D'Silva, E. H., *Natural Rubber* (1982); Grilli, E. R., et al., *The World Rubber Economy* (1981); Morton, Maurice, *Rubber Technology*, 2d ed. (1973; repr. 1981); Stinson, Stephen C., "Rubber Chemicals Face Smaller Market," *Chemical & Engineering News*, Apr. 15, 1985.

Rubbia, Carlo

The Italian physicist Carlo Rubbia, b. Mar. 31, 1934, was awarded, along with Simon VAN DER MEER, the 1984 Nobel Prize for physics for their work leading to the discoveries of the W and Z FUNDAMENTAL PARTICLES. Rubbia studied physics in Italy and the United States before accepting (1961) a position at the EUROPEAN ORGANIZATION FOR NUCLEAR RESEARCH (CERN) near Geneva. There he concentrated on studies of high-energy particle collisions, using the large CERN accelerator. By the mid-1970s he had conceived of a plan to use colliding beams of accelerated protons and antiprotons to produce the W and Z particles that had been predicted by the ELECTROWEAK THEORY. In 1983, Rubbia and his coworkers at CERN announced their discovery of these particles, and in 1984 they further discovered evidence for the top QUARK.

Rubbra, Edmund [ruhb'-ruh]

Edmund Rubbra, b. May 23, 1901, d. Feb. 13, 1986, was an English composer of a modern-romantic disposition. Resisting formal schooling, he worked in factories and was largely self-taught in music until 1918, when he commenced study with Cyril Scott and continued with Gustave Holst and Vaughan Williams. Rubbra's compositions, frequently polyphonic, include an opera and 11 symphonies in addition to concertos, choral works, songs, and piano and chamber pieces. He taught at Oxford University (1947–68) and at the Guildhall School of Music in London (1961–74). His writings include *Holst* (1947) and *Counterpoint* (1960).   KAREN MONSON

Bibliography: Schafer, R. M., *British Composers in Interview* (1963).

rubella: see GERMAN MEASLES.

Rubens, Peter Paul   [roo'-bens]

The Flemish baroque painter Peter Paul Rubens, b. June 28, 1577, d. May 30, 1640, was the most renowned northern European artist of his day, and is now widely recognized as one of the foremost painters in Western art history. By completing the fusion of the realistic tradition of Flemish painting with the imaginative freedom and classical themes of Italian Renaissance painting, he fundamentally revitalized and redirected northern European painting.

Rubens's upbringing mirrored the intense religious strife of his age—a fact that was to be of crucial importance in his artistic career. His father, an ardently Calvinist Antwerp lawyer, fled in 1568 to Germany to escape religious persecution, but after his death (1587) the family moved back to Antwerp, where Peter Paul was raised a Roman Catholic and received his early training as an artist and a courtier. By the age of 21 he was a master painter whose aesthetic and religious outlook led him to look to Italy as the place to complete his education. Upon arriving (1600) in Venice, he fell under the spell of the radiant color and majestic forms of Titian, whose work had a formative influence on Rubens's mature style. During Rubens's 8 years (1600–08) as court painter to the duke of Mantua, he assimilated the lessons of the other Italian Renaissance masters and made (1603) a journey to Spain that had a profound impact on the development of Spanish baroque art. The artist also spent a considerable amount of time in Rome, where he painted altarpieces for the church of Santa Croce in Gerusalemme (1602; now in Hôpital du Petit-Paris, Grasse) and the Chiesa Nuova (1607–08; first version in Musée

In The Judgment of Paris (1625), Peter Paul Rubens, the most influential Flemish painter of the 17th century, draws on themes from classical mythology. The painting illustrates Rubens's synthesis of Northern and Italian artistic styles. (National Gallery, London.)

Peter Paul Rubens painted The Artist and his Wife, Isabella Brant *(1609) shortly after returning to his native city of Antwerp and marrying. During the next decade he reached the height of his fame as the leading European master. (Alte Pinakothek, Munich.)*

de Peinture et Sculpture, Grenoble, France), his first widely acknowledged masterpieces. His reputation established, Rubens returned (1608) to Antwerp following the death of his mother and quickly became the dominant artistic figure in the Spanish Netherlands.

In the mature phase of his career, Rubens either executed personally or supervised the execution of an enormous body of works that spanned all areas of painting and drawing. A devout Roman Catholic, he imbued his many religious paintings with the emotional tenor of the Counter-Reformation. This aggressively religious stance, along with his deep involvement in public affairs, lent Rubens's work a conservative and public cast that contrasts sharply with the more private and secular paintings of his great Dutch contemporary, Rembrandt. But if his roots lay in Italian classical art and in Roman Catholic dogma, Rubens avoided sterile repetition of academic forms by injecting into his works a lusty exuberance and almost frenetic energy. Glowing color and light that flickers across limbs and draperies infuse spiraling compositions such as *The Descent from the Cross* (1611; Antwerp Cathedral) with a characteristically baroque sense of movement and tactile strength.

A love of monumental forms and dynamic effects is most readily apparent in the vast decorative schemes he executed in the 1620s, including the famous 21-painting cycle (1622–25; Louvre, Paris), chronicling the life of Marie de Médicis, originally painted for the Luxembourg Palace. In order to complete these huge commissions, Rubens set up a studio along the lines of Italian painters' workshops, in which fully qualified artists executed paintings from the master's sketches. Rubens's personal contribution to the over 2,000 works produced by this studio varied considerably from work to work. Among his most famous assistants were Anthony VAN DYCK and Frans SNYDERS.

Rubens's phenomenal productivity was interrupted from time to time by diplomatic duties given him by his royal patrons, Archduke Ferdinand and Archduchess Isabella, for whom he conducted (1625) negotiations aimed at ending the war between the Spanish Netherlands and the Dutch Republic and helped conclude (1629–30) a peace treaty between England and Spain. Charles I of England was so impressed with Rubens's efforts that he knighted the Flemish painter and commissioned his only surviving ceiling painting, *The Allegory of War and Peace* (1629; Banqueting House, Whitehall Palace, London).

During the final decade of his life, Rubens turned more and more to portraits, genre scenes, and landscapes. These later works, such as *Landscape with the Château of Steen* (1636; National Gallery, London), lack the turbulent drama of his earlier paintings but reflect a masterful command of detail and an unflagging technical skill. Despite recurring attacks of arthritis, he remained an unusually prolific artist throughout his last years, which were spent largely at his estate, Château de Steen.   ROWLAND ELZEA

Bibliography: Burchard, Ludwig, and d'Hulst, R.-A., *Rubens' Drawings*, 2 vols. (1963); Gerson, Noel B., *Peter Paul Rubens: A Biography of a Giant* (1973); Jaffé, Michael, *Rubens and Italy* (1977); Rooses, Max, *Rubens*, trans. by Harold Child, 2 vols. (1904); Rubens, Peter Paul, *Letters*, trans. by Ruth S. Magurn (1971); Stechow, Wolfgang, *Rubens and the Classical Tradition* (1968); Wedgwood, C. V., *The World of Rubens, 1577–1640* (1967); White, Christopher, *Rubens and His World* (1968).

Rubicon River   [roo'-bi-kahn]

The Rubicon is a historical name for a short, small river in north central Italy that formed the ancient boundary between Italy and Cisalpine Gaul. The present streams of Fiumicino and Uso have each been identified as the Rubicon. Both flow from the Apennines to the Adriatic Sea between Cesenatico and Rimini. In 49 BC, Julius CAESAR defied a senatorial order to lay down his command and marched his army across the Rubicon into Italy, thus provoking civil war. "Crossing the Rubicon" has come to mean the taking of an irrevocable step.

rubidium

Rubidium is a silvery white radioactive chemical element and a member of the ALKALI METALS, a group that includes sodium, potassium, and cesium. Its symbol is Rb; its atomic number, 37; and its atomic weight, 85.4678. Its name is derived from the Latin *rubidius*, meaning "deepest red." Rubidium is relatively abundant and is considered to rank 16th in the Earth's crust. It was discovered in 1861 by Robert Bunsen and Gustav Kirchhoff in a spectroscopic examination of the mineral lepidolite. The pure metal is usually prepared by reducing the chloride with calcium. Like other members of the alkali metal group, rubidium ignites spontaneously in air and reacts violently with water, setting fire to the liberated hydrogen. The refined metal must consequently be kept under dry mineral oil, in a vacuum, or in an inert atmosphere.

Rubidium is a soft metal that can be liquid at room temperature, although the pure element melts at 38.89° C (102° F) and boils at 688° C (1,270° F). Of the 17 known isotopes of rubidium, only ^{85}Rb and ^{87}Rb occur naturally. Rubidium-87 is a beta emitter with a half-life of 5 x 10^{11} years.

Rubidium has oxidation states of +1, +2, +3, and +4. It is one of the most reactive metals, resembling potassium in its chemical properties. The compound $RbAg_4I_5$ has the highest room-temperature conductivity of any known ionic crystal. The element is used as a getter in vacuum tubes, as a component in photocells, and in the making of special glasses.

                                                J. ALISTAIR KERR

Bibliography: Perelman, F. M., *Rubidium and Caesarium* (1965); Sneed, Cannon M., and Breasted, Robert C., *Comprehensive Inorganic Chemistry*, vol. 6, in *The Alkali Metals* (1960).

rubidium-strontium dating: see RADIOMETRIC AGE-DATING.

Rubinstein, Anton [roo'-bin-styn]

The Russian pianist Anton Rubinstein, b. Nov. 28 (N.S.), 1829, d. Nov. 20 (N.S.), 1894, had a reputation as a virtuoso second only to that of Franz Liszt. Rubinstein first performed in public at age 9, and at age 10 he made his first of many tours, one of which (1872–73) took him to the United States for 215 triumphant concerts in 239 days. His compositions—ranging from short piano pieces to operas—were also successful during his lifetime, but few are performed today. He was a cofounder of the Saint Petersburg Conservatory, serving as director during 1862–67 and 1887–91. His brother Nicolai, b. June 14 (N.S.), 1835, d. Mar. 23 (N.S.), 1881, was reputedly Anton's equal as a pianist, but rarely played in public, concentrating instead on conducting and education. He was director of the Moscow Conservatory from 1866 to 1881.

Bibliography: Bowen, Catherine D., "Free Artist": The Story of Anton and Nicholas Rubinstein (1939); Rubinstein, Anton, Autobiography of Anton Rubinstein (1890; repr. 1970); Schonberg, Harold C., The Great Pianists (1963).

Rubinstein, Arthur

The celebrated pianist Arthur Rubinstein, b. Łódź, Poland, Jan. 28, 1887, d. Dec. 20, 1982, enjoyed one of the longest active performing careers in musical history and was admired particularly for his interpretations of the romantic repertoire, especially such composers as Chopin, Brahms, and Grieg. He first performed in concert at the age of 7; he made his formal debut in Berlin in 1899 playing a Mozart concerto. He was then engaged in other German cities and in Warsaw and also toured Russia. After studying for a brief time with Paderewski, he gave recitals in Paris (1905), and in the following year he made his U.S. debut in New York City. He gave recitals with the violinist Eugene Ysaye in London (1916), after which he toured Spain and South America, becoming an ardent champion of Spanish music. He became a U.S. citizen in 1946. Rubinstein frequently toured internationally—as far as China and Japan—both in recital and as a soloist with major symphony orchestras. Having appeared as himself in several Hollywood movies, he was the subject of a television special, The Life and Art of Arthur Rubinstein (1968), and a full-length film documentary, Arthur Rubinstein—Love of Life (1975). One of the most frequently recorded classical artists, he published two volumes of autobiography, My Young Years (1973) and My Many Years (1980).

Discography: Beethoven, L. v., Concertos nos. 1–5; Brahms, J., Concertos nos. 1 and 2; Chopin, F., Ballades (4), Mazurkas (complete), Nocturnes (19), Preludes, Op. 28, and Waltzes (14); Falla, M. de, Nights in the Gardens of Spain; Grieg, E., Concerto in A minor and Favorite Encores; Mozart, W. A., Concertos nos. 17, 20, 21, 23, 24; Schubert, F., Sonata in B Flat; Schumann, R., Carnaval.

Rubinstein, Ida Lvovna

The Russian-born actress and would-be dancer Ida Lvovna Rubinstein, b. c.1885, d. Sept. 20, 1960, studied privately with Mikhail Fokine and made her debut in Salomé (1909), which he had choreographed. Because of her great beauty, Serge Diaghilev cast her in the leading roles of Cléopâtre (1909) and Schéhérazade (1910) in his first two Paris seasons. Her wealth enabled her to commission (1911) Le Martyre de Saint Sebastien from composer Claude Debussy and poet Gabriele D'Annunzio, with herself in the title role, and to form her own ballet company in 1928, presenting ballets by such choreographers as Fokine, Léonid Massine, Bronislava Nijinska, and Kurt Jooss, with scores by Maurice Ravel, Igor Stravinsky, Arthur Honegger, and others. She retired in 1935.

DAVID VAUGHAN

Rublev, Andrei [roo-blyawf']

Regarded as the most notable icon painter Russia has produced and the first truly Russian painter, Andrei Rublev, c.1370–c.1430, was a monk at the Trinity-Saint Sergius Monastery. His career as a painter began under the influence of Theophanes the Greek, and it developed during a time of growing confidence and optimism in Muscovy. Rublev's style, with its characteristically flowing outline and pure, deep color, is graceful and elegant; his figures seem to convey the essence of spirituality. These qualities can be seen in his most famous icon, The Old Testament Trinity (c.1411; Tretyakov Gallery, Moscow): three angels, rendered in delicate curves, appear against a simple gold background.   ALAN C. BIRNHOLZ

Bibliography: Hamilton, George H., The Art and Architecture of Russia (1954; repr. 1975); Onasch, Konrad, Icons (1963).

ruby

Ruby is one of the most highly prized gems (see GEMS). A transparent variety of the aluminum oxide mineral CORUNDUM, it owes its red to pale rose color to minute amounts of chromium. The most valuable stones have a deep pigeon's-blood red color. Although a brilliant stone, it lacks the fire of a diamond and is often cut to enhance the color, even at the expense of weight. For more than 500 years the finest rubies have come from a small area near Mogok, Burma, where they are washed and sieved from limestone gravels. Rubies also occur in the gem gravels of Thailand, Cambodia, Ceylon, and North Carolina. The stone often referred to as a ruby in the Old Testament and other ancient texts may actually have been a garnet or a spinel. The confusion between these stones has been perpetuated in the names of less valuable gems. The Black Prince's Ruby of the British crown jewels is in fact a spinel. Since 1902, when Auguste Verneuil developed the flame-fusion process, artificial rubies have been produced from ammonia alum and chrome alum. In 1960 an artificial ruby was used in the first working laser (see LASER AND MASER).

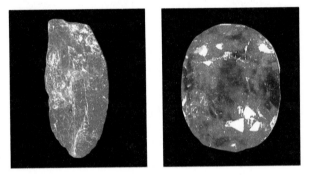

(Left) Ruby, a highly prized gemstone, is a transparent deep red form of corundum. The color results from traces of chromic oxide. (Right) Rubies are usually step cut with a series of rectangular facets. Star rubies are cut with a rounded cabochon top.

Bibliography: Desautels, Paul E., The Gem Kingdom (1977); Kraus, Edward H., and Slawson, Chester B., Gems and Gem Materials, 5th ed. (1947); MacFall, Russell P., Minerals and Gems (1975); Weinstein, Michael, The World of Jewel Stones (1958).

Rudaki, Abu Abdollah Jafar [roo-dah-kee']

Generally regarded as the first major poet of the Islamic period, Abu Abdollah Jafar Rudaki was born near the Asian capital of Samarkand AD c.859, and died there c.940. He was panegyrist to the Samanid ruler Nasr I ebn Ahmad until 937 and a figure of importance at court. Of Rudaki's prodigious output of lyrics, panegyrics, and narrative poems, about 1,000 lines survive.   JEROME W. CLINTON

Bibliography: Arberry, A. J., Classical Persian Literature (1958); Rypka, Jan, History of Iranian Literature, rev. ed., trans. by P. Van Popta-Hope (1968).

See also: PERSIAN LITERATURE.

rudder

A rudder is a movable blade, attached at or near the rear of a vessel, that is used to steer it. The first rudders were crude paddles held aft over the sides of log canoes. These crude paddles evolved into long steering oars that were tied to the sides of the vessel and were controlled by levers called tillers attached to their upper ends. Viking long ships and medieval trading vessels were steered with a single large steering oar. This oar was on the helmsman's right as he faced forward—the steerboard (starboard) side of the vessel. (The left side, which was always brought against a dock, was the port side.) In 12th-century Europe, a board hung on hinges attached to a vessel's sternpost replaced the steering oar and was controlled by a large tiller. This tiller was needed to increase leverage on the rudder, especially on vessels with large sail areas rigged to sail into the wind. As ships got bigger and more powerful, various mechanical arrangements were used to provide the even greater leverage required to turn the rudder. Rudders of modern ships may be moved by cables, gears, or hydraulic lines, which are controlled by automatic electronic devices. Rudders controlled by rudder bars or pedals are also used to provide directional control of many aircraft.

Rude, François [rood]

The French sculptor François Rude, b. Jan. 4, 1784, d. Nov. 3, 1855, is known for his many public monuments in the city of Paris. Rude won the Prix de Rome in 1812 but, because of political events, was forced to spend over a decade in Belgium instead of visiting Rome. Shortly after his return to Paris, he won the commission for *The Departure of the Volunteers of 1792* (1833–35), also known as the *Marseillaise*. This monumental group in high relief on the base of the ARC DE TRIOMPHE DE L'ÉTOILE won the public's admiration for its expression of patriotic fervor. His native city of Dijon honored Rude with a commission in 1850; the results, his *Hébé* (completed by a pupil after his death) and *L'Amour*, reflect the unique combination in Rude's work of the classic and romantic traditions.   PHILIP GOULD

Bibliography: Novotny, Fritz, *Painting and Sculpture in Europe 1780–1880* (1960).

Rudolf, Lake

Lake Rudolf, or Lake Turkana, lies in the Great Rift Valley in northern Kenya, East Africa. Its northern end extends into Ethiopia. The lake has an area of about 9,100 km² (3,500 mi²) but is shrinking because of evaporation. It is relatively shallow, with a maximum depth of 73 m (240 ft) and is becoming increasingly saline. The Omo and Turkwell rivers are the main tributaries, but there is no outlet. Small volcanic islands in the south indicate a volcanic origin. Located at an altitude of 375 m (1,230 ft), the lake, although remote, is a tourist attraction. Count Teleki explored it in 1888 and named it after the crown prince of Austria.   G. N. UZOIWGE

Rudolf, Austrian Archduke

Crown Prince Rudolf of Austria, b. Aug. 21, 1858, was the only son of Emperor FRANCIS JOSEPH. Rudolf's death (Jan. 30, 1889) in a hunting lodge at Mayerling, near Vienna, was officially ruled the result of a suicide pact with his mistress. According to some rumors, however, he was murdered because of his sympathies with Hungarian nationalism.

Bibliography: Judtmann, Fritz, *Mayerling: The Facts behind the Legend* (1971); Lonyay, Karoly, *Rudolf: The Tragedy of Mayerling* (1941).

Rudolf I, King of Germany

The first German king after the chaotic Interregnum (1254–73), Rudolf I, b. May 1, 1218, d. July 15, 1291, established the HABSBURG dynasty in Austria, where it ruled until 1918. A son of Albert IV, count of Habsburg, Rudolf held scattered lands in the Upper Rhineland and Switzerland. After the HOHENSTAUFEN king Conradin died (1268), Rudolf was elected his successor. Crowned at Aachen (1273), he launched a campaign to revive the monarchy's prestige and to recover alienated fiefs. King OTTOKAR II of Bohemia, who had sought to succeed Conradin, refused to surrender the duchies of Aus-

The German king Rudolf I regained by force the eastern lands usurped by Ottokar II of Bohemia during the Great Interregnum. His marriage to Isabella of Burgundy helped to contain expansionist pressures from the French in the west, although the French were able to prevent his coronation as Holy Roman emperor.

tria, Styria, Carinthia, and Carniola, prompting Rudolf to declare war in 1276. Ottokar quickly came to terms with Rudolf, but two years later he rebelled and was killed in the Battle of the Marchfeld near Dürnkrut, Aug. 26, 1278. Rudolf gave most of the new territory to his own sons in 1282, thus raising the Habsburg family to the rank of a major German dynasty.

In Germany, Rudolf is credited with quelling internal unrest as he strove to spark urban prosperity. He had difficulty checking French expansionism on his western frontier, and he lacked a firm policy toward Italy and the papacy. Unable to arrange for his own imperial coronation, Rudolf also failed to persuade German electors to pass the crown to his son, who finally succeeded to the German throne (as ALBERT I) in 1298.   RAYMOND H. SCHMANDT

Bibliography: Barraclough, Geoffrey, *The Origins of Modern Germany*, rev. ed. (1966); Heer, Friedrich, *The Holy Roman Empire* (1969); Wandruska, Adam, *The House of Hapsburg* (1969).

Rudolf II, Holy Roman Emperor

Holy Roman emperor during the late Renaissance, Rudolf II, b. July 18, 1552, d. Jan. 20, 1612, was an avid patron of the arts and sciences. On his accession (1576), Rudolf moved the imperial court from Vienna to Hradčany Palace in Prague, where he lived in increasing seclusion. The first two decades of his reign were marred by Catholic-Protestant enmity. Rudolf's intolerance of Protestants caused widespread discontent. Nevertheless, he attracted painters, sculptors, jewelers, writers, and scientists to Prague, including the astronomers Tycho Brahe and Johannes Kepler and the English mathematician John Dee. Melancholic and eccentric, Rudolf suffered intense bouts of depression. Between 1605 and 1611 he was forced to cede major portions of his realm to his brother MATTHIAS, who succeeded him.   H. G. KOENIGSBERGER

Bibliography: Evans, R. J. W., *Rudolf II and his World* (1973); Holzer, Hans, *The Alchemist: The Secret, Magical Life of Rudolf von Habsburg* (1974).

Rudolph, Paul

The American architect Paul Rudolph, b. Elkton, Ky., Oct. 23, 1918, established his reputation through the design of several ingenious beach houses in Florida. His first large-scale commission, the Jewett Arts Center (1955) at Wellesley College, attempted to blend in style with the neighboring Gothic buildings. His later projects became more sculptural and vigorous. His School of Architecture building (1964) at Yale University generated a great deal of comment. It was first praised for its bold, aggressive forms and spatial ingenuity, but it was later criticized for insensitivity toward the needs of its occupants. The project for a Government Services Center (1962) in Boston is perhaps the best application of his sculptural vocabulary to an urban site. Rudolph's appeal owes much to an evocative, linear technique of drawing unbuilt projects; his completed buildings, however, are often less convincing.

LEON SATKOWSKI

Bibliography: Rudolph, Paul, *Paul Rudolph* (1974).

Rudolph, Wilma

Wilma Glodean Rudolph, b. Clarksville, Tenn., June 23, 1940, was an American Olympic Games track and field star. She was handicapped with a lame, brace-supported leg as a child but through rehabilitation became a champion sprinter. Her career culminated in the 1960 Olympics, where she was the single most successful track and field competitor, winning both the 100-m and 200-m dashes. Rudolph was also on the first-place 4 × 100-m relay team. Prior to her Olympic appearance she set a 200-m-dash world record, and although her record-breaking 100-m-dash time in the Olympics was invalidated by wind assistance, she did gain the record the following year.

Bibliography: Hollander, Phyllis, *American Women in Sports* (1972).

rue

The rue, R. graveolens, is an aromatic herb grown for its bitter-tasting leaves. Also known as herb of grace, rue was once considered to be an antidote against poisons and a protection against witches' spells.

Rue, the common name of the genus *Ruta* of perennial herbs, comprises 40 species of plants that originate in southern Europe. The rue family, Rutaceae, also includes such citruses as orange and lemon trees and such trees as satinwood, which yields timber used in cabinetry.

Common rue, or herb of grace, *R. graveolens*, a shrublike herb, has a woody base and aromatic blue green leaves that are evergreen in warmer climates. It bears yellow flowers and fruit consisting of capsules divided into four or five lobes. During earlier centuries, it was believed to cure such maladies as poisoning and gout; today it is used to flavor an alcoholic beverage of northern Italy known as grappa.

Goat's rue, *Galega officinales*, a perennial herb of the legume family, Leguminosae, is grown as an ornamental shrub and is also cultivated for animal feed. Meadow rue is the common name for the genus *Thalictrum*, also perennial herbs.

Rueda, Lope de   [roo-ay′-dah]

Lope de Rueda, *c*.1505–1565, was a Spanish playwright and actor-manager who, according to Miguel de Cervantes, was the first in Spain to stage comedies with any degree of professionalism. He is known principally for his *pasos,* or one-act comedies, which, following the conventions of the Italian commedia dell'arte, delighted audiences with their raucous humor. The best known of his 24 extant farces is *Las aceitunas* (Olives, 1548).

ROBERTO GONZÁLEZ-ECHEVARRÍA

Bibliography: Crawford, J. P. Wickersham, *Spanish Drama Lefore Lope de Vega* (1937; repr. 1975); Shergold, N. D., *A History of the Spanish Stage: From Medieval Times until the End of the Seventeenth Century* (1967).

rugby

Rugby is a kicking, passing, and tackling game that originated in England and is the direct ancestor of American football. The game is popular in Great Britain, France, Australia, New Zealand, and South Africa and exists in two forms: rugby union and rugby league. Rugby union, an exclusively amateur game, is played on a grass field 110 yd (100 m) long and 75 yd (69 m) wide by 2 teams of 15 players. The rugby ball resembles an American football but is approximately 24 in (61 cm) at its widest circumference and thus easier to kick and more difficult to pass. Because blocking and interference are illegal, no heavy padding is required, and a uniform consists of shorts, jersey, and cleated shoes.

Play starts with a kickoff, and the aim of each team is to carry the ball across the opponent's goal line or kick the ball over the crossbar of the goalposts centered on each goal line. Players advance the ball by running with the ball, passing it, or kicking it. Forward passes are not permitted, and passes are made behind the ballcarrier using a two-handed underarm motion. In rugby union, when a player is tackled the ball must be released immediately and may then be played by any player of either team. Play is continuous except when interrupted for a rule infraction or when the ball is in "touch," that is, out of bounds. When the ball goes out of bounds it is returned to play in a "line-out," in which the eight forwards from each team form two parallel lines about 0.6 m (2 ft) apart. A player from the team that last touched the ball tosses it between the two lines, and the teams then struggle for possession. If play is interrupted by a rule infraction, or if possession of the ball is unclear, a "scrum" is called by the referee. In a scrum, 8 players from each team mass together in two 3–2–3 formations, each facing the opponent's goal. The ball is dropped between the two front trios, who try to "heel" it back to waiting teammates. Points are scored when a ballcarrier crosses the goal line to score a try (4 points), when a kick for a conversion after a try goes over the goal crossbar (2 points), or when a dropkick or penalty kick passes over the crossbar (3 points).

Rugby league, first played in 1895 and now dominated by professional teams from the Midlands and north of England and from Australia, differs from rugby union in several respects. Teams consist of 13 players; scrums are formed of 6 players on each side; and a tackled player retains possession of the ball, "heeling" it to a teammate after regaining his feet. These variations from the older game of rugby union, devised (*c*.1840) at Rugby School, are designed to encourage pass-

Forwards of both teams struggle for possession of the ball during a scrum in a rugby union match. The task of the forwards is to "heel" the ball to the scrum half, who then passes to the running backs who advance the ball. Rugby union, which is played only by amateurs, originated in England during the 1840s.

Rugby union, a sport that originated in England in the 1840s, is played by 2 teams of 15 players on a 75 × 110 yd field called a pitch. Points are scored by advancing the ball over the opposite team's goal line, or drop-kicking it over the crossbar of the goalpost.

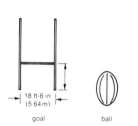

goal   ball

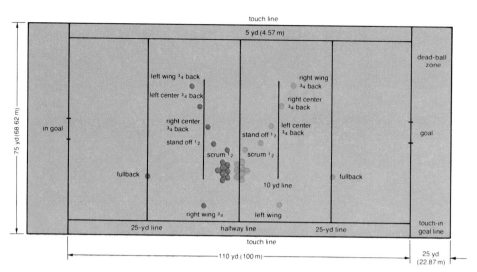

ing and running and make the game more attractive to spectators.

Bibliography: Creek, F. N., and Rutherford, Don, *Rugby* (1975); Powell, John T., *Inside Rugby—the Team Game* (1976); Thornett, John, *How to Play Rugby Union* (1976) and *This World of Rugby* (1967).

Rugby School

Founded in 1567, Rugby School is a private preparatory school for boys in Rugby, Warwickshire, England. The school became celebrated in the 19th century during the headmastership of Dr. Thomas ARNOLD, whose son, the poet Matthew Arnold, wrote about the school. Another alumnus, Thomas Hughes, described it in *Tom Brown's Schooldays* (1857).

Ruggles, Carl   [ruhg'-ulz]

The American composer Carl Ruggles, b. Marion, Mass., Mar. 11, 1876, d. Oct. 24, 1971, exemplified New England independence and individualism no less than did his friend Charles Ives. After studies at Harvard, Ruggles stubbornly went his own way, shunning the musical mainstream. Active in major musical societies, he supported himself in minor conducting and teaching jobs. From 1937 until 1946 he taught at the University of Florida in Miami. Highly self-critical, he deliberately limited his production to a small number of works, variously exploring piano, vocal, chamber, and orchestral idioms in terse, densely compressed, but boldly sonorous and vigorous forms. Ruggles's music has not been widely heard, although his orchestral works *Men and Mountains* (1924) and *Sun Treader* (1933) have won success in performances and recordings.   JOHN W. BARKER

rugs and carpets

Rugs and carpets are a form of decorative art; as such, they are as representative of a culture as its painting or architecture. People have made them and used them in their living quarters for thousands of years. The earliest rugs were crudely woven; they were tacked to walls to provide insulation from winds and sun and laid on the bare ground for the sake of warmth and comfort. Throughout history, rugs have served a surprising variety of purposes. The nomads of Central Asia sewed pieces of woven work into the saddle and tent bags that were used to transport household paraphernalia. In Scandinavia pile weavings served as cloaks and sleigh robes by day and blankets or bed coverings by night. In 16th- and 17th-century England and also in the Netherlands, imported Oriental rugs were draped over tables, offering a warm, decorative touch in an often chilly climate. In Spain the Alpujarra peasant rugs were first made as bed coverings. In many countries rugs were used to pay taxes; they were also included in dowries and given as imperial gifts. Navajo weavings traditionally functioned as blankets that the Indians wore, slept under, and hung on their walls for protection against the

weather. In Muslim countries worshipers perform their five daily prayers on prayer rugs that are laid on the ground. Today rugs of uncommon beauty are often displayed as wall hangings, and thick-pile carpets are used to upholster raised platforms for seating.

In current usage the word *carpet* refers to any heavy fabric that is tacked down on a floor and covers it completely. Carpeting of this sort is usually woven in wide strips that are joined together when the carpet is laid. A rug, on the other hand, is generally woven as a single piece, covers only part of the floor, and is not tacked down. The terms *rug* and *carpet* are interchangeable in the context of Oriental rugs and carpets.

WOVEN RUGS

Techniques of Manufacture. The basic techniques of rug making were first developed in the East. Traditional Oriental rugs are made on vertical looms strung with 3 to 24 warp (vertical) threads per cm (8 to 60 per in) of width. Working from bottom to top, the rug maker either weaves the rug with a flat surface or knots it for a pile texture. Pile rugs use 5- to 7.5-cm (2- to 3-in) lengths of yarn tied in Turkish (Ghiordes) or Persian (Sehna) knots with rows of horizontal weft yarn laced over and under the vertical warp threads for strength. After the carpet is completely knotted, its pile is sheared, and the warp threads at each end are tied into a fringe. The finer the yarn and the closer the warp threads are strung together, the denser the weave and, usually, the finer the quality. Fine-textured and valuable rugs have 62 or more knots per cm² (400 per in²); coarse-textured rugs may have less than 8 per cm² (50 per in²). In traditional Scandinavian weaving (rya) the knot is actually tied like the Turkish knot, but the pile alone is 5 to 7.5 cm (2 to 3 in) long, and the rows of knots are separated by 10 to 20 weft rows.

Flat-woven rugs are lighter in weight and less bulky than pile rugs. The best-known and earliest type is the kilim, which has a plain weave made by shooting the weft yarn over and under the warp threads in one row, then alternating the weft in the next row. The soumak type is woven in a herringbone pattern by wrapping a continuous weft around pairs of warp threads.

Materials and Motifs. The same materials are used in flat-woven and pile rugs. Warp and weft yarns are either wool or cotton. In pile rugs, the knots are usually wool, sometimes goat's or camel's hair, depending on the region. Silk, traditionally a costly material, is found principally in fine Persian carpets and some Chinese rugs. Yarns have been used in their natural colors or colored with dyes extracted from flowers, roots, and insects. Colors, available in a wide spectrum, often have had symbolic as well as decorative importance, especially in Oriental rugs.

Despite the existence of distinctive regional styles and motifs, many designs are common to diverse regions in the East and even in the West. These designs may be rectilinear or curvilinear, naturalistic or abstract; they may be based on motifs such as the sun wheel, the tree of life, the cloud band of China, the pear-shaped figure (*boteh*) that heralds the Islamic paisley design, flowers of all kinds, animals, birds, and insects. Muslim prayer rugs are always distinguished by the prayer niche (mihrab) woven into the pattern; this represents the actual prayer niche in the Great Mosque at Mecca, toward which the rug must point during use.

OTHER TYPES OF RUGS
In the West, rugs have been made by several other techniques as well. For hooked rugs, thin strips of outworn woolen goods traditionally were drawn through a linen, cotton, or burlap backing with a metal hook to form slightly raised loops on the surface. Later on, yarn was also used for hooking. Favorite designs of early-American hooked rugs included flowers, geometrical and abstract patterns, and pictorial scenes with landscapes and animals. For traditional braided rugs, strips of outworn cloth were plaited together and then wound flat in a circle or oval. In patchwork rugs, snippets of cloth were sewed on homespun woolen material. In Shaker rugs, cloth scraps were threaded together like a necklace and then sewed onto a strong backing material. In needlepoint rugs, each intersection of a mesh canvas backing is covered with individual stitches of wool yarn.

RUGS AROUND THE WORLD
Rugs are mentioned in the Old Testament and in Homer; they were known to the ancient Chinese, the Egyptians, and the Greeks. The earliest-known hand-knotted carpet, dating from about 500 BC, was discovered well preserved in ice in a tomb at PAZYRYK, in southern Siberia. Rugs were made in Persia during the reign of Cyrus (549–530 BC), whose tomb was said to have been covered with precious carpets. By the 16th century, traditions of rug making were highly developed in Persia and Turkey. Rug making then spread north to the Caucasus and east to India, Turkestan, and China; finally, it reached Europe and the West. The American Indians developed weaving traditions independently.

Persia and India. A graceful, curvilinear style and a masterful use of color is typical of Persian rugs. The great tradition of rug making culminated in the 16th and 17th centuries in densely woven court carpets of the Safavid period. Usually classified according to the particular type of design displayed in each, they include medallion carpets, whose large central medallion patterns are embellished with flowers; garden carpets, incorporating flowerbeds, paths, and often even canals and pools; flower carpets; vase carpets, in which an ornamental vase holds flowers and vines; animal carpets; and hunting carpets, portraying a favorite royal sport.

Regional and village carpets of Persia most often use the central medallion design or all-over pattern of flowers or other flowing forms; they are usually but not always more coarsely woven than court carpets. Regional carpets are usually designated by their place of origin, such as Bakhtiari, Bijar, Feraghan, Hamadan, Herez, Isfahan, Kashan, Kerman, Khorassan, Kurdistan, Sarouk, Sehna, Shiraz, and Tabriz.

The golden age of Indian rug making occurred under the Mogul emperors who ruled from the mid-16th to the mid-17th century and who imported not only designs and traditions from Persia but weavers as well. The greatest Indian examples were the finely woven florals and the hunting carpets, with their remarkably naturalistic designs.

The Caucasus. Caucasian rugs are made by various tribes in the mountainous district between the Black and Caspian seas. The designs are often dense all-over patterns of geometric elements—squares, diamonds, stars, and frets—or motifs drawn with angular lines in bold, clear colors. The rugs are generally small, with wide multiple borders. The best known include the Baku, Chichi, Daghestan, Kabistan, Kazak, Kuba, Shirvan, the flat-woven Soumak, and the Karabagh, with an unusual floral design of Persian influence. The Armenian dragon carpet, combining an ancient dragon motif with Persian flowers, was made during the 15th and 16th centuries

(Above) *This detail of a 17th-century Caucasian carpet, found in a mosque in Niğde, Anatolia (modern Turkey), exhibits a bold, geometric arrangement of stylized floral motifs. Its vivid colors and angular forms are characteristic of Caucasian carpets. (Metropolitan Museum of Art, New York City.)*

(Left) *An Indian hunting carpet, dating from the period of the Mogul emperor Jahangir (r. 1605–28), features naturalistic floral and animal motifs. The carpets of the Mogul courts are renowned for their extremely fine weaving and their detailed pictorial designs. (J. Paul Getty Museum, Malibu, Calif.)*

(Left) *A magnificent 16th-century Persian carpet, believed to have been crafted at court workshops at Tabriz, combines intricate arabesque and Chinese cloud patterns with a complex central medallion. The rich colors and curvilinear designs of the finest Persian carpets are unsurpassed in the history of the art. (Metropolitan Museum of Art, New York City.)*

and was much more opulent than the better-known yet simpler Caucasian rugs.

Turkey. Turkish carpets were the first Orientals to be imported into Europe and often appeared in late-Renaissance paintings; Hans Holbein the Younger painted a particular type so often that it came to be called a Holbein. Most were woven in villages in Anatolia (the part of Turkey that lies in Asia Minor) in bright, rich colors with geometric forms such as the star and diamond as well as linear floral forms. In the mid-16th century, elegant court rugs woven on royal looms in Constantinople incorporated the more graceful curvilinear style of Persia. One well-known type was the Star Ushak, with its distinctive star-shaped medallions.

Turkish prayer rugs are of particular interest. The mihrabs usually have pointed arches and stepped sides, and the field is sometimes ornamented with a hanging lamp or candlesticks. The best known are the Ghiordes, with freestanding columns supporting the mihrab; Ladik, with its stylized tulips; Kula; Konya; and Mudjur. Regional carpets with primarily geometric designs include the Bergama and Yuruk.

Central Asia and Turkestan. Carpets made by the nomads of central Asia are collectively designated as Turkoman carpets. These carry a number of names including Afghan, Baluchi, and Bokhara, the last comprising Royal (Tekke), Pendeh, Yomud, and Beshir carpets. The geographic and cultural isolation of the region accounts for the distinctive character of the rugs. Most are reddish and have a geometric design that incorporates, in an all-over pattern, the coat of arms (*gul*) of the individual tribe.

Samarkand, although actually a collection and marketing center rather than a rug-producing center, is the name applied to the rugs produced more than 300 km (about 200 mi) away in Kashgar, Khotan, and Yarkand in what is now far western China. The Samarkand style is less angular than the Turkoman style and not as graceful as that of Chinese rugs. The principal design motifs are medallions in the shape of flattened circles, a pomegranate tree growing out of a vase, and such Chinese figures as bats, butterflies, and frets.

China. Simplicity of design, serenity of composition, a limited

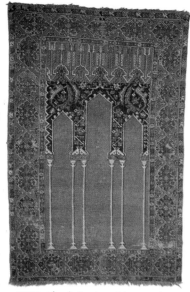

This Turkish prayer rug from Anatolia, dating from the 17th to early 18th centuries, depicts a columned prayer niche, or mihrab, surrounded by geometric and floral borders. (Textile Museum, Washington, D.C.)

range of subdued and harmonious colors, and symbolic motifs characterize Chinese carpets. The earliest surviving examples date from the late Ming dynasty in the mid-17th century; they are decorated with simple arrangements of geometric forms, typically a medallion, sometimes with a dragon, and repeat patterns. Rugs of the K'ang-hsi period (1662–1722) continued Ming forms with greater naturalism and more ornamentation. From the late 17th century onward, the Chinese have woven the unique pillar rugs designed to encircle the columns of palaces and temples during festivals. During the latter half of the 18th century ornate and opulent palace rugs, the design of which was greatly influenced by the floral patterns of Persia, were woven. Rugs for export followed, favoring a central dragon motif or ornate floral designs. At the end

(Left) A late-19th-century Chinese pillar carpet, decorated with animal masks, Buddhist symbols, and stylized natural forms, creates a unified dragon design when wrapped about a column. The pillar carpet is unique to Chinese carpet design. (Textile Museum, Washington, D.C.)

(Above right) A French Savonnerie carpet, crafted during the 17th century, blends architectural and floral motifs in an illusionistic style typical of both the pictorial and decorative arts of the period. (Metropolitan Museum of Art, New York City.)

(Below right) A woven Navajo rug (c.1940), combining abstract and geometric forms, features a central motif of mythic female figures and an angular border design.

of the 19th century, anilines replaced natural dyes and introduced an often harsh and garish quality to the once-harmonious color schemes.

Frequently recurring designs in Chinese rugs include geometrics such as the familiar meander or key border and fret; animals, including various dragon forms, the Fu dog, storks, cranes, butterflies, and bats; realistic and identifiable flowers, each with its symbolic meaning; Taoist and Buddhist symbols; natural forms including clouds, water, and mountains; the Chinese character *shou*, the symbol for long life; and the many permutations of round medallions.

Spain. Rug making was introduced (AD 711) to Spain by the invading Moors. Their rugs first incorporated the geometric forms of Islamic art; later, combined Muslim and Christian motifs were used, particularly heraldic motifs, as in the well-known Admiral carpets woven for the heirs of Spanish admirals. After the 18th century the best Spanish rugs were the low-looped, folk-art Alpujarras made by the peasants in the mountain district of southern Spain.

France. The best-known French rugs are the AUBUSSON, a flat tapestry weave, and the Savonnerie, a knotted pile or tufted weave. Aubusson rugs had been woven for 9 centuries when, in the early 17th century, Henry IV established court looms in the Louvre to produce Oriental-type pile carpets. These rugs came to be called Savonnerie for the soap factory (*savonnerie*) that housed the looms for a time. The designs of both types reflected contemporaneous French art styles.

England. The English rug industry, developed in the 16th century, was invigorated by the French Protestants, many of them weavers, who fled to England for religious asylum after the Edict of Nantes was revoked. Early carpet works at Wilton and Axminster wove pile carpets in which bright floral patterns predominated. The great industrial advances of the 18th century—the spinning jenny, power looms, Jacquard weaving—revolutionized carpet making and affected design as well as production. Reacting against the machine technology and Victorian taste, the 19th-century ARTS AND CRAFTS MOVEMENT, led by William Morris, emphasized handcrafts and original design in the decorative arts.

Scandinavia. Scandinavia's unique shaggy pile weavings, called rya, were first woven as a defense against the harsh northern climate. Early designs were simple geometrics; later ones included ecclesiastical and folk motifs such as stars, wheels, flowers, and trees. Although folk rya declined in the 19th century, it is currently flourishing as an art form, especially in Finland.

Navajo Rugs. Typical Navajo weavings repeat a few simple geometric shapes—stripes, rectangles, zigzag lines, diamonds—in minimal designs using primarily natural-colored wools (usually black, gray, tan, or brown) in a flat tapestry weave. The westward expansion of the railroad in the 1880s introduced commercial yarn and aniline dyes (replacing vegetable dyes). Among notable contemporary Navajo designs are those produced at Chinle, Ariz., and at Two Gray Hills and Ganado, N.Mex.

Contemporary Trends. More than 97 percent of all machine-made carpets are now made of synthetic fibers, principally nylon. Area rugs are also fashionable; these, in both contemporary and period designs, are often made of natural fibers like sisal or of hand-tufted wool in natural colors. Various textures are used, among them surfaces that are sculptured or cut to different levels and areas of both cut and uncut loops. Many contemporary artists design pile or flat-weave rugs and wall hangings. Durable synthetic fibers are also used outdoors on patios, on boats, and around pools. JOAN SCOBEY

Bibliography: Erdmann, Kurt, *Seven Hundred Years of Oriental Carpets* (1970); Fogg Art Museum, *Turkoman Rugs* (1966); Kahlenberg, M. H., and Berlant, Anthony, *The Navajo Blanket* (1972); Landreau, A. N., and Pickering, W. R., *From the Bosporus to Samarkand: Flat-Woven Rugs* (1969); Lorentz, H. A., *A View of Chinese Rugs* (1973); McMullen, Joseph V., *Islamic Carpets* (1965); Scobey, Joan, *Rugs & Wall Hangings* (1974); Weeks, J. G., and Treganowan, D., *Rugs and Carpets of Europe and the Western World* (1969).

See also: CARPET INDUSTRY; LOOM; TAPESTRY; WEAVING.

Ruhr Valley [roor]

The Ruhr Valley, one of the world's most vital industrial regions, is in West Germany. The 235-km-long (145-mi) Ruhr River and its tributaries—the Mohne and Lenne—water the region. Overlying one of the world's most extensive coal deposits, the region's industries produce steel, iron, and other metals, and chemicals. The major industrial cities within the Ruhr area are DORTMUND, DUISBURG, ESSEN, MÜLHEIM AN DER RUHR, Oberhausen, and Witten. Duisburg, the great RHINE RIVER port, serves as the entrepôt for the Ruhr Valley. Although the region's settlement dates to the Stone Age, its industrial development did not begin until the early 19th century. The Ruhr endured heavy Allied bombing during World War II when 75% of its facilities were destroyed.

Ruisdael, Jacob van [roys'-dahl]

Jacob van Ruisdael's The Mill at Wijk *(c.1665) exhibits the dramatic intensity and precise realism characteristic of the Dutch artist's work. Ruisdael's carefully balanced compositions, among the finest landscapes of 17th-century Holland, often emphasize the subtle play of light from a melancholy, clouded sky. (Rijksmuseum, Amsterdam.)*

Jacob van Ruisdael, c.1628–1682, the most celebrated landscapist of the Dutch school, is known for his generally accurate and atmospheric representations of the Dutch countryside. Ruisdael, the son of an art dealer, entered the Guild of Haarlem in 1648 and went to Amsterdam in 1691. Although he showed unusual artistic ability, he did not intend to make art his career. On the advice of his friend Nicolaes Berchem, however, he took up painting in earnest and met with popular success almost at once because his work was calculated to appeal to the Dutch taste for pictures that closely imitate nature.

Ruisdael's skies are especially well executed, depicting bright light and great floating clouds such as may be seen to advantage in flat landscapes. Other works depict the wilder aspects of nature, as well as hinting at decay and transience. These aspects of Ruisdael's work have been seen as prophetic of 19th-century German romanticism.

In one of his most famous paintings, *The Mill at Wijk* (c.1665; Rijksmuseum, Amsterdam), many of the characteristic elements of his work are combined: a cloud-laden sky, a somewhat somber landscape containing a few diminutive human figures, and a group of buildings dominated by a large windmill. The foreground in particular, with its disturbed water and reeds, invites comparison with the works of such German romantics as Caspar David Friedrich and Karl Friedrich Schinkel. Meindert Hobbema was among his pupils.

RAYMOND LISTER

Bibliography: Levey, Michael, *Ruisdael: Jacob van Ruisdael and Other Painters of His Family* (1977); Stechow, Wolfgang, *Dutch Landscape Painting of the Seventeenth Century* (1966).

Ruisdael, Salomon van

The Dutch landscape painter Salomon van Ruisdael (or Ruysdael), c.1602–1670, lived and worked in Haarlem for most of his life. He settled there in 1616 with his brother Izaack, who was the father of the great Dutch landscapist Jacob van Ruisdael. Salomon van Ruisdael's work was first influenced by the art of the Dutch painters Esaias van de Velde and Pieter de Molyn. Ruisdael evolved a tonal atmospheric quality similar to that of his contemporary Jan van GOYEN, but his feathery trees and studies of reflections in river and lake scenes were individual traits of his work, as in *River Landscape* (c.1630; Rijksmuseum, Amsterdam). Ruisdael also painted still-life subjects, usually with game or fish. His son Jacob (not to be confused with his famous cousin) was also a landscape painter. Ruisdael was buried in Saint Bavo's church in Haarlem on Nov. 2, 1670.   CHARLES I. MINOTT

Bibliography: Levey, Michael, *Ruisdael: Jacob van Ruisdael and Other Painters of His Family* (1977); Rosenberg, Jakob, et al., *Dutch Art and Architecture 1600–1800*, 2d ed. (1972); Stechow, Wolfgang, *Dutch Landscape Painting of the Seventeenth Century* (1966).

Ruiz, José Martínez   [roo-eeth, mar-teen'-eth]

José Martínez Ruiz, b. June 8, 1874, d. Mar. 2, 1967, was a prolific Spanish writer whose work, characterized by terse style and subtle attention to detail, includes more than 100 volumes of novels, essays, and dramas. He often used the pseudonym Azorin. His most distinguished works are *El alma Castellana* (The Castilian Soul, 1900), a collection of essays; *Las confesiones de un pequeño filósofo* (Confessions of a Little Philosopher, 1904); and *An Hour of Spain* (1924; Eng. trans., 1930). He was an important figure in a politically liberal literary circle, whom he called the generation of '98. The group was devoted to the cultural rebirth of Spain after that country's defeat (1898) in the Spanish-American war. He wrote several studies of classical Spanish literature, and his style was widely imitated by the succeeding generation of writers.

Bibliography: Krause, Anne, *Azorin, The Little Philosopher* (1948).

Ruiz de Alarcón y Mendoza, Juan   [roo-eeth' day ahl-ar-kohn' ee mayn-doh'-thah]

Juan Ruiz de Alarcón y Mendoza, b. c.1581, d. Aug. 4, 1639, was one of the most important playwrights of Spain's 17th-century Golden Age. His drama is unique in its period in that it concentrates on social mores and individual conduct instead of broad philosophical issues. Alarcón's protagonists are liars, schemers, and egotists whose weaknesses are humorous but intolerable to virtuous men and women. His most famous play, *La verdad sospechosa* (The Suspected Truth, c.1610), concerns a liar who is ultimately punished for his vice. It was adapted as *Le Menteur* (1643) by the French playwright Corneille, who gave it a happier ending.

Alarcón was afflicted with a hunchback. Born in Mexico, he lived there for many years, but emigrated to Madrid to pursue his literary career. His views on morality and society were far ahead of their time, and he was the subject of much ridicule by his contemporaries.   ROBERTO GONZÁLEZ-ECHEVARRÍA

See also: SPANISH LITERATURE.

Rukavishnikov, Nikolay   [roo-kah-vish'-ni-kuhf]

The Soviet cosmonaut Nikolay Nikolayevich Rukavishnikov, b. Sept. 18, 1932, made preparatory SOYUZ space test flights for the SALYUT program and the APOLLO-SOYUZ TEST PROJECT. After graduation (1957) from the Moscow Engineering and Physics Institute, he became an engineer in the space design bureau and later (1967) a cosmonaut. Rukavishnikov was test engineer on the three-man *Soyuz 10* spacecraft, which on Apr. 23, 1971, became the first spacecraft to dock with the *Salyut 1* space station. Surprisingly, the cosmonauts returned to Earth immediately; Western observers have assumed that a planned 30-day stay was thwarted by technical problems.

With Cmdr. Anatoly Filipchenko, Rukavishnikov made a 6-day dry run (Dec. 2–8, 1974) for the Apollo-Soyuz Test Project

aboard *Soyuz 16*. He made a third space flight (Apr. 10–12, 1979) aboard *Soyuz 33*. A propulsion failure prevented Rukavishnikov and Bulgarian cosmonaut Georgy Ivanov from reaching the *Salyut 6* space station; an emergency landing profile forced the cosmonauts to experience an 8g (twice normal) deceleration on reentry.   JAMES OBERG

Rukeyser, Muriel   [roo'-ky-sur]

The American poet Muriel Rukeyser, b. New York City, Dec. 15, 1913, d. Feb. 12, 1980, is best known for her passionate concern with social issues. A comprehensive selection of her earlier poetry is collected in *Waterlily Fire* (1962), and her more recent work appears in *Gates* (1976) and *Collected Poems* (1978). The poetry in these volumes reveals a style of great flexibility ranging from lyric and symbolic to satiric, according to her subject. She has translated poetry from several languages. The scope of her intellectual interests is further indicated by two highly regarded biographies, one of an American physicist, *Willard Gibbs* (1942), the other of an Elizabethan astronomer, *The Traces of Thomas Hariot* (1971).

rum

Rum is an alcoholic beverage distilled from sugarcane byproducts that are produced in the process of manufacturing sugar. MOLASSES, the thick syrup remaining after sugarcane juice has been crystallized by boiling, is usually used as the basis for rum, although the juice itself, or other sugarcane residues, is also used. The molasses is allowed to ferment, and the ferment is then distilled to produce a clear liquid that is aged in oaken casks. The golden color of some rums results from the absorption of substances from the oak. The darker, heavier Jamaican rums—made for the most part in Jamaica, Barbados, and Guyana—are produced from a combination of molasses and skimmings from the sugar boiling vats; the darkest, Guyana's Demarara, is produced by very rapid fermentation and is not particularly heavy bodied. The fermentation of other substances in the molasses enhances the liquid's flavor and aroma. After distilling, the rum is darkened by the addition of caramel and is aged from 5 to 7 years. Lighter, dryer rums from Puerto Rico and the Virgin Islands are more rapidly fermented with cultured yeasts and are aged from 1 to 4 years. Rum from imported molasses is also produced in New England and other regions of the world.

The rum industry developed in conjunction with the growth of sugar plantations in the West Indies. The English were the first to adopt the drink (its name may be derived from a Devonshire word, *Rumbullion*, meaning "a great tumult"). Beginning in the 17th century, distilleries operating in New York and New England produced rum from West Indian molasses. Traders used the rum to buy slaves in Africa; the slaves were sold in the West Indies for cargoes of molasses that became New England rum. The attempt by the British to levy heavy duties on molasses imported from the French and Spanish West Indies (see NAVIGATION ACTS) was an important factor in pre-Revolutionary colonial unrest in America.

Bibliography: Alderman, Clifford L., *Rum, Slaves and Molasses: The Story of New England's Triangular Trade* (1972); Tritton, S. M., *Spirits, Aperitifs and Liqueurs: Their Production* (1975); Waugh, Alec, *Wines and Spirits* (1968).

Rumania: see ROMANIA.

Rumford, Benjamin Thompson, Count

Benjamin Thompson, also known as Count Rumford, b. Woburn, Mass., Mar. 26, 1753, d. France, Aug. 21, 1814, was an American-born British scientist noted for his research on heat. A loyalist during the American Revolution, Thompson moved to London in 1776, where he worked in the British Colonial Office and conducted experiments on gunpowder. He was knighted in 1784 and then became aide-de-camp to the elector of Bavaria. During his 11 years in Bavaria, Thompson reorganized the Bavarian army, abolished mendicancy in Munich, and established workhouses for the poor. In 1791 the elector made Thompson a count of the Holy Roman Empire.

While in Munich, Thompson investigated the nature of heat and demonstrated that, contrary to the prevailing belief that heat was a fluid, it was in fact a form of mechanical motion. His research also led to improvements in heating and cooking equipment. Thompson was a founder of the Royal Institution; he endowed the Rumford medals of the Royal Society and the American Academy of Arts and Sciences and also endowed a professorship at Harvard University.

Bibliography: Brown, Sanborn, *Count Rumford: Physicist Extraordinary* (1962; repr. 1979); Larsen, Egon, *An American in Europe* (1953); Sparrow, W. J., *Knight of the White Eagle* (1964); Thompson, James A., *Count Rumford of Massachusetts* (1935).

Rumi, Jalal al-Din al-

The founder of the Sufi order known as the "Whirling Dervishes," Jalal al-Din al-Rumi, called Maulavi, 1207–73, was a Persian mystic and poet revered both for his spiritual teachings and his poetic innovations. In 1231, Rumi began to teach his mystical doctrine, and in 1244 he came under the influence of Shams Tabrizi, an itinerant Sufi. The earliest of his poetical works is a collection of lyrical odes named for Tabriz. The second is called the *Masnavi,* or *Mathnavi* (c.1246–73; Eng. trans., 1925–40), a long poem in six books consisting of fables and anecdotes describing the soul's quest for union with God. Rumi's poetic style is characterized by a depth of feeling and wealth of images drawn from daily life, often in disregard of the rigid rules of Persian rhetoric.

Bibliography: Nicholson, Reynold A., trans., *Rumi: Poet and Mystic* (1950; repr. 1978); Schimmel, Annemarie, *The Triumphal Sun: A Study of the Works of the Jaloloddin Rumi* (1978); Whinfield, E. H., ed. and trans., *Teachings of Rumi, The Masnavi* (1975).

See also: SUFISM.

ruminant

Ruminant means cud-chewer and refers to even-toed (split-hoofed), cud-chewing mammals, including the cattle, sheep, goats, deer, antelope, and chevrotains and the camels and llamas—the camels and llamas, however, are not zoologically classified with the others in the suborder Ruminantia.

Rumination is one of the methods evolved by mammals to utilize cellulose, which no mammal can digest on its own. All cellulose digestion, usually referred to as fermentation, is done by microbes within the mammal's digestive tract.

The ruminant stomach is divided into four compartments (camels have three). The first of these, called the rumen, is where most fermentation occurs. The rumen contains both bacteria and protozoans that use their cellulose-digesting enzymes to break down the cellulose into mostly short-chain fatty acids, such as acetic acid, and into other compounds, including ammonia. The fatty acids and other nutrients enter the bloodstream through the rumen and, in the case of the cow, may provide up to 70% of the animal's energy supply.

The fermentation process also creates a great deal of gas in the form of carbon dioxide and methane, which must be released through the mouth (by eructation, or belching). Ruminants produce large amounts of slightly alkaline saliva, both to provide a sufficient liquid medium for the fermentation of the bulky food material and to buffer and neutralize the resulting acids to the microbes' requirements (pH 6.0–7.5). The pH of the rumen fluid, however, varies with the seasons (especially in wild ruminants) and with the diet and may drop to normal lows of about pH 5.25.

After partial fermentation, some of the remaining coarse, fibrous material is formed into small masses called boli (singular, bolus), or cuds, and brought back to the mouth where they are chewed and then reswallowed. This time the food passes into the second chamber, the reticulum, where some additional fermentation takes place, and then into the third chamber, or omasum, where most of the water is reabsorbed. From the omasum the food passes into the fourth chamber, the abomasum, or true stomach, where ordinary digestion occurs. EDWIN E. ROSENBLUM

rummy

Rummy, known in some localities as rum, rhum, or romme, is among the most popular of all card games. It requires a standard 52-card deck and may be played by two to six players. The king is the highest-ranking card, although for scoring purposes the king, queen, jack, and 10 are each worth 10 points; all other cards are worth their face value. To start play, 7-card hands are dealt face down if three or four play; 6-card hands are dealt when five or six play; and in two-handed rummy, 10 cards are dealt to each player. The remaining cards are turned face down to form the stock. Then, through a process of drawing and discarding cards, each player attempts to meld, that is, to develop a hand containing only sets of 3 or 4 cards of the same rank or sequences of three or more cards in the same suit. Rummy is achieved when a player melds his or her hand in a single turn; if more than one turn is needed to meld all cards then a player "goes out." Each player has a second objective: to hold the lowest-valued total of unmelded cards. Such cards count against the player when an opponent achieves rummy or goes out.

The most notable offshoot of rummy is gin rummy, a game for two. Each player is dealt 10 cards face down, the remainder forming the stock, and each tries to form melds so that the unmelded cards—called deadwood—in the hand total 10 or less. A player with such a holding may "knock," that is, knock on the table and lay a card on the discard pile, leaving 10 in the hand. He or she lays down the remaining cards, segregating them into melded and unmelded cards, and announces the remaining point count of 10 or less. The opponent then shows his or her hand and, before taking a count of unmelded cards, lays off wherever possible unmatched cards from his or her hand to the melds in the knocker's hand. If the opponent has a count equal to or less than the knocker's, or can reduce the count to the knocker's count or less, then the opponent is awarded a score determined by the difference between their deadwood counts. Gin occurs when one player has melded all cards and holds no deadwood. A player who goes gin gets a bonus of 25 points, plus the point-value of the opponent's unmelded cards. Games are played to 100 points.

Rummy developed from the Spanish game of *Con quien?* (literally, "with whom?"), pronounced Coon Can by American players. Various games have developed from *Con quien?*, including canasta, but two-handed gin rummy is the most commonly played form in the United States.

Bibliography: Jacoby, Oswald, *How to Win at Gin Rummy* (1959).

Runcie, Robert Alexander Kennedy

The English churchman Robert Alexander Kennedy Runcie, b. Oct. 2, 1921, became archbishop of Canterbury in January 1980. He served with distinction as a tank commander in World War II, earning the Military Cross for bravery. He was educated at Oxford and was ordained in 1951. Runcie served as principal of Cuddeston Theological College from 1960 to 1969 and was bishop of Saint Albans from 1970 to 1980.

Rundstedt, Karl Rudolf Gerd von   [runt'-shtet]

Gerd von Rundstedt, b. Dec. 12, 1875, d. Feb. 24, 1953, was a German field marshal during World War II. He played a role in the secret rearmament of Germany before the war and held major commands in the invasions of Poland (1939), France (1940), and Russia (1941). Despite disagreements with Adolf Hitler on strategy for the Russian campaign, he became supreme commander in the west for most of the period from 1942 to 1945 and directed the 1944 Ardennes offensive (see BULGE, BATTLE OF THE).

Bibliography: Blumentritt, Guenter von, *Von Rundstedt: The Soldier and the Man*, trans. by Cuthbert Reavely (1952).

Runeberg, Johan Ludvig   [roo'-nuh-bairg]

A Finnish poet who wrote in Swedish, Johan Ludvig Runeberg, b. Feb. 5, 1804, d. May 6, 1877, laid the foundation of an idealist-heroic tradition that subsequently had far-reaching effects on Scandinavian literature. Serbian folksongs were an important influence in the evolution of Runeberg's own simple style of love and nature poetry. *Songs of Ensign Stål* (1848, 1860; Eng. trans., 1925), dealing with the war that led to Finland's annexation by Russia, exemplifies his national idealism and admiration of military heroism. Other works by Runeberg include *Nadeschda* (1841; Eng. trans., 1879) and *King Fjalar* (1844; Eng. trans., 1904).

runes

Runes are the 24 letters (later 16 in Scandinavia and 30 or more in Anglo-Saxon England) of an ancient Germanic alphabet used from the 2d or 3d to the 16th century. Perhaps derived ultimately from the Etruscan alphabet (see WRITING SYSTEMS, EVOLUTION OF), the runic alphabet—called the *fuþark* from its first six letters, *f*, *u*, *þ* ("th"), *a*, *r*, and *k*—was used mainly for charms and inscriptions, on stone, wood, metal, or bone. Each letter had a name, which was itself a meaningful word. The rune *f*, for instance, could stand for either the sound "f" or the *fehu*, "cattle," which was the name given to the rune.   DAVID YERKES

Bibliography: Elliott, Ralph W. V., *Runes: An Introduction* (1959; repr. 1981); Page, Raymond I., *An Introduction to English Runes* (1973).

Runge, Philipp Otto   [rung'-ge]

One of the most curious and tragic figures of the romantic era, the German painter Philipp Otto Runge, b. July 23, 1777, d. Dec. 2, 1810, sought to rejuvenate religious art through mystical landscape paintings replete with flower symbolism and hieroglyphs. Runge studied in Copenhagen (1799–1801) and Dresden (1801–04) before returning to his native Hamburg. He was deeply distressed by the Napoleonic Wars and had little time in which to execute his grand ideas before his early death at age 33. The unfinished allegorical cycle called *The Four Phases of the Day* was to be displayed in a cathedrallike setting to the accompaniment of poems by Ludwig Tieck and music by Ludwig Berger; only *Morning* (1808–09; Kunsthalle, Hamburg) was completed. Runge also executed several compelling portraits, including *The Hülsenbeck Children* (1805–06; Kunsthalle, Hamburg).

Bibliography: Bisanz, Rudolph M., *German Romanticism and Philipp Otto Runge* (1970).

running and jogging

Running or jogging, because of its basic simplicity, is probably the oldest sport. In prehistoric times running was both a means of hunting food and of escaping danger, and thus it contributed to the survival of the human species. Today running or jogging is one of the world's most popular recreational and competitive sports. Running or jogging (no precise distinction is made between the two; jogging is merely slow running for either training or fitness) is now practiced by more than 25 million Americans, primarily adults, who are interested in improving their general physical fitness levels, increasing energy levels, losing weight, lowering blood pressure, and looking and feeling better.

The Marathon. For the ancient and modern Olympic history of this 26-mi 385-yd (42.2-km) race, see MARATHON. Whereas the Olympic marathon is contested only once every four years, the famous Boston Marathon has been staged annually since 1897. Until the early 1960s only 200–300 runners competed. Thereafter, however, the number of runners increased steadily, finally forcing the organizers of the race to impose stiff qualifying standards that limited the field. This procedure is now applied in several long-distance races. Even with such restrictions in effect, the Boston Marathon's starting field numbered 7,623 in 1982. The New York Marathon, run through that city's five boroughs, began in 1970 with 126 runners; in 1981 more than 16,000 competed. The 1982 London Marathon accommodated 16,350 runners.

The Running Boom. The extraordinary increase in the popularity of running and jogging in the 1970s occurred not only in marathons but in all running events. Most of the new converts to running chose to pursue the sport in isolation, but many others decided to participate in occasional road races in order to test themselves against other runners. For example, the 7-mi (11.3-km) Bay to Breakers race, in San Francisco, the second oldest and now the biggest U.S. race, had 35,000 official entrants in 1982, with estimates for all competitors ranging up to 60,000.

The jogging population has been augmented by two significant groups: (1) women in general and (2) runners, primarily men, 40 years of age and over (in competition they are placed in a special Master's category). Before the 1970s few women ran, and amateur regulations barred them from races longer than 2.5 mi (4 km). Up until 1972 women were not officially permitted to compete in the Boston Marathon. By 1980 women made up nearly 40 percent of all joggers, and the figure continues to grow. Several for-women-only races have drawn more than 5,000 starters; the women's world record in the marathon dropped nearly 35 minutes between 1970 and 1980, whereas the men's record was not improved on substantially. Running by individuals 40 years of age and older has signaled this group's interest in long-term fitness. Many large corporations in the United States urge their employees, especially their older ones, to run to counter the physical degeneration brought on by sedentary desk jobs. Studies of the effects of running programs have shown that a healthy and fit work force is usually more productive.

Training to Run. As running or jogging becomes more publicized, growing numbers of people are likely to take up the sport. It is recommended that beginners past age 35, especially those who are overweight or who smoke, have a complete physical examination before embarking on a running regimen. Supervised jogging programs, also recommended, are available at local YMCAs, community centers, or health clubs.

A good pair of running shoes is essential. Running can be practiced almost anywhere; in a backyard, on a local high school track, in public parks, or along the roadside. One of the great advantages of running is that it is usually easy to practice year-round. The key to undertaking a running program is to begin slowly and cautiously. Many beginners, especially those who run alone, make the mistake of overexerting themselves. The human body grows stronger and more fit when subjected to gradual increases of physical stress. When this stress is applied too early or too forcefully, however, it creates fatigue, irritability, and injury. Most accomplished runners also perform warm-up exercises that include stretching of the major leg muscles. Almost anyone who does not have a severe physical handicap can learn to run and enjoy running provided he or she is willing to proceed with patience.

AMBY BURFOOT

Bibliography: Cooper, Kenneth H., *The New Aerobics* (1970); Fixx, James F., *The Complete Book of Running* (1977); Glover, Bob, and Shepherd, Jack, *The Runner's Handbook: A Complete Fitness Guide for Men and Women on the Run* (1978); *Runner's World* editors, *Beginning Running* (1972) and *Running after Forty*, rev. ed. (1979); Sheehan, George, *Dr. Sheehan on Running* (1975) and *Running and Being* (1978); Ulloyot, Joan, *Women's Running* (1976).

Runyon, Damon   [ruhn'-yuhn, day'-muhn]

American journalist and short-story writer Alfred Damon Runyon, b. Manhattan, Kans., Oct. 4, 1880, d. Dec. 10, 1946, became famous for his colorful stories about the New York underworld, which carefully recorded its slang and dialect. His best-known work, *Guys and Dolls* (1931), was turned into a Broadway hit in 1950. It has since become a staple of the American musical theater.   CHARLOTTE D. SOLOMON

Bibliography: Mosedale, J., *The Men Who Invented Broadway* (1981).

Rupert, Prince

Prince Rupert of the Rhine, b. Prague, Dec. 17, 1619, d. Nov. 29, 1682, served both CHARLES I and CHARLES II of England as a soldier and a sailor. He was the third son of FREDERICK V, elector palatine, who by claiming the throne of Bohemia started the Thirty Years' War. Having gained military experience in Europe, Rupert joined his uncle Charles I in the ENGLISH CIVIL WAR and, following spectacular success as a cavalry officer, became commander in chief in 1644. A year later, however, a series of defeats, resentment of his harsh and imperious manner, and unjustified suspicion of treachery led to his dismissal. He and Charles I were partly reconciled, and he served the royalist cause as a naval commander until 1653. When Charles II was restored to the throne in 1660, Rupert returned to England and was later appointed admiral in both of the Anglo–Dutch Wars.   MAURICE ASHLEY

Bibliography: Morrah, Patrick, *Prince Rupert of the Rhine* (1976).

Rupert's Land

Rupert's Land was the name given to a tract of Canadian territory granted to the HUDSON'S BAY COMPANY by King Charles II of England in 1670. Named after Prince Rupert, first governor of the company, it originally comprised only the land that drained into Hudson Bay. Later, however, it came to include most of western Canada. In 1869 control of the territory passed to Canada.

Rupp, Adolph

Adolph Frederick "The Baron" Rupp, b. Halstead, Kans., Sept. 1, 1901, d. Dec. 10, 1977, was one of U.S. college basketball's most successful coaches. He won a record 874 games (of 1,064) and produced 25 All-Americans during his 42-year career at the University of Kentucky. His teams won 27 Southeast Conference titles and 4 NCAA championships. Rupp also coached the U.S. team to a gold medal at the 1948 Olympics.

Rurik (dynasty) [roo'-rik]

The Rurik family was the first dynasty to rule Russia. According to Russian tradition, its founder was a Varangian (VIKING) adventurer named **Rurik**, d. c.879, who established himself in Novgorod about 862. **Igor**, b. c.877, supposedly Rurik's son, ruled from 912 until his death in 945; he moved his capital to Kiev and assumed the title of grand prince (or grand duke). Early Rurik rulers included VLADIMIR I, who brought Christianity to Russia in 989, and his son, YAROSLAV the Wise (r. 1019–54), who beautified Kiev and codified Russian law.

With the decline of Kiev in the 12th century, the title of grand prince passed to towns lying to the northeast, where descendants of the Rurik line had established themselves. Over time, the rulers of Moscow strengthened their claim to the title. Important Muscovite rulers included **Ivan I**, b. c.1304, d. Mar. 31, 1341 (r. 1328–41), who added new territory to Muscovy; IVAN III; and IVAN IV. The last of the Rurik rulers was **Fyodor I**, b. May 31, 1557, d. Jan. 7, 1598 (r. 1584–98), the son of Ivan IV. Following a period of chaos and war (the TIME OF TROUBLES), the Romanov family succeeded to the Russian throne in 1613.   DONALD L. LAYTON

Bibliography: Paszkiewicz, Henryk, *The Making of the Russian Nation* (1963; repr. 1977); Vernadsky, George, *The Origins of Russia* (1959; repr. 1975).

Ruse [rus'-e]

Ruse is a river port city on the Danube in northeastern Bulgaria. The population is 178,920 (1983 est.). A growing manufacturing city, Ruse produces sugar, flour, beer, textiles, and machinery. The harbor and the bridge to Giurgiu, Romania, across the Danube, make Ruse an important commercial and transportation center.

The Romans fortified the city in the 2d century AD and stationed their Danubian fleet there. In the 7th century Ruse was destroyed by barbarians, and in the 14th century it came under Turkish rule. Since 1877 it has been a part of Bulgaria.

rush

Rushes, genus *Juncus,* are about 240 species of perennial herbs belonging to the rush family, Juncaceae. These plants, which have unbranched stems and grasslike leaves, grow in dense clumps. They bear clusters of green or brown flowers. The leaves and stems of rushes are used to weave baskets, mats, and chair seats. They grow in boggy areas of temperate regions throughout the world. The species *J. effusus* grows from .3 to 1.8 m (1 to 6 ft) tall. Widely distributed in northern temperate zones, it is grown commercially in Japan, where it is woven into tatami. A variety of this species, *J. effusus spiralis,* has stems that twist spirally.

Rush, Benjamin

The American physician and political and social reformer Benjamin Rush, b. Philadelphia, Jan. 4, 1746, d. Apr. 19, 1813, challenged many established theories and sought new ways of combating illness. He pioneered in military hygiene and the treatment of mental illness, writing the first American text on the subject, entitled *Medical Inquiries and Observations upon the Diseases of the Mind* (1812). As a social reformer, he fought for better education for women and the abolition of both slavery and capital punishment. A political activist, he was a signer of the Declaration of Independence and served on the ratifying convention in Pennsylvania for the new federal constitution. From 1797 on, Rush was treasurer of the U.S. Mint.

Bibliography: Hawke, David F., *Benjamin Rush: Revolutionary Gadfly* (1971); Riedman, Sarah, and Creen, Clarence, *Benjamin Rush* (1964); Rush, Benjamin, *The Autobiography of Benjamin Rush*, ed. by George W. Corner (1948; repr. 1970).

Rush, Richard

Richard Rush, b. Philadelphia, Aug. 29, 1780, d. July 30, 1859, the son of physician Benjamin Rush, was an American statesman. He served as U.S. attorney general from 1814 to 1817. In 1817, as acting secretary of state, he concluded the Rush-Bagot convention with Charles Bagot, British ambassador to Washington; this agreement limited naval armaments on the Great Lakes. While American minister to Great Britain (1817–25), Rush negotiated the Convention of 1818, which provided for joint Anglo-American occupation of the Oregon Territory and established the boundary between the United States and British North America east of the Rockies. Rush was secretary of the treasury (1825–29) and was an unsuccessful candidate for the vice-presidency in 1828; he later helped establish the Smithsonian Institution. He was ambassador to France from 1847 to 1849.

Bibliography: Powell, J. H., *Richard Rush, Republican Diplomat, 1780–1859* (1942).

Rush, William

The first native sculptor of the United States, William Rush, b. Philadelphia, July 4, 1756, d. Jan. 17, 1833, learned wood carving from his father, a ship carpenter, before being apprenticed (1771) to Edward Cutbush, an English figurehead carver. After the Revolution, Rush's shop produced ships' ornaments and figureheads that earned him an international reputation. A surviving figurehead, the robed female *Virtue* (1810; Masonic Lodge, Philadelphia), demonstrates the allegorical subject he preferred and the animation he introduced into the tradition. After studying gestures and details in art books, engravings, and antique casts, Rush attempted freestanding figures. His *Water Nymph and Bittern* (1809; bronze copy, Fairmount Park, Philadelphia), originally the carved centerpiece for the fountain in front of the Center Square Water Works, personifies the Schuylkill River. Although unclassical in proportion, the statue's ponderated pose, organic appearance, and form-defining drapery are truly sculptural. Rush's full-length wooden portrait *George Washington* (1814; Independence Hall, Philadelphia) has more vitality and force than any other sculptured image of the first president.

JOAN SIEGFRIED

Bibliography: Graven, Wayne, *Sculpture in America* (1968); Marceau, Henri, *William Rush 1756–1833: The First Native American Sculptor* (1937).

Rushmore, Mount

Gutzon Borglum's 18-m-high (60-ft) heads of Presidents Washington, Jefferson, Lincoln, and Theodore Roosevelt, carved into the face of Mount Rushmore—a granite outcropping in the Black Hills of South Dakota—are sometimes visible from as far as 100 km (62 mi) away.

Mount Rushmore National Memorial is located in the Black Hills of southwestern South Dakota. Sculptures approximately 18 m (60 ft) high of the heads of U.S. presidents George Washington, Thomas Jefferson, Abraham Lincoln, and Theodore Roosevelt have been carved from Mount Rushmore's granite outcropping. The four presidents were chosen to represent, respectively, the nation's founding, philosophy, unity, and expansion. Gutzon BORGLUM designed and oversaw construction (1927–41) of the monument. The project was funded primarily by the federal government.

Rusk, Dean

A U.S. secretary of state (1961–69), David Dean Rusk, b. Cherokee County, Ga., Feb. 9, 1909, helped to shape U.S. foreign policy, advocating involvement in both the Korean and the Vietnam wars. Prior to becoming secretary of state Rusk had an extensive diplomatic career and served as president of the Rockefeller Foundation (1952–60). Since leaving government, Rusk, a former Rhodes scholar (1933–34), has taught at University of Georgia Law School.

Bibliography: Halberstam, David, *The Best and The Brightest* (1972); Rusk, Dean, *Vietnam: Four Steps to Peace* (1965).

Ruska, Ernst August Friedrich [rus'-kah]

The German physicist and electrical engineer Ernst August Friedrich Ruska, b. Dec. 25, 1906, is best known for his development of the ELECTRON MICROSCOPE. Ruska constructed (1931) a magnetic lens and designed (1932) the first practical electron microscope while he was a student at the Technical University of Berlin. Subsequently, he improved and simplified the instrument.   KENNETH THIBODEAU

Ruskin, John [ruhs'-kin]

The English writer John Ruskin, b. Feb. 18, 1819, d. Jan. 20, 1900, was prominent as an art and literary critic and as a social reformer. The only child of a prosperous middle-class couple, he traveled abroad as a boy and developed an interest in art and architecture. While at Oxford he began the serious study of art, which later bore fruit in *Modern Painters*, a five-volume work that appeared between 1843 and 1860.

His aesthetic theory was based on "truth to nature," but this was truth as apprehended by the imagination and not by the eye. Such truth he found most forcefully presented by the paintings of J. M. W. Turner. Affection for Gothic architecture and the principles on which it was based moved Ruskin to write *The Seven Lamps of Architecture* (1849) and *The Stones of Venice* (1851-53). Accepted as an authority on art, he was a regular and unsparing critic of Victorian painting and a champion of the Pre-Raphaelites.

Ruskin applied similar aesthetic principles to literature, condemning what he called mere realism and praising the vivid imaginative representations of Dante and Spenser. He coined the term *pathetic fallacy* to characterize an anthropomorphism in literature that he considered false to nature.

Ruskin's personal life was not happy. His marriage (1848) to his cousin Effie Gray was apparently never consummated and was annulled in 1854. Another romantic episode resulted in rejection by a 10-year-old girl with whom he became infatuated.

Ruskin's belief that art reflects the morality of society and his total distaste for the forces of industrialism led him to the second great concern of his life—social reform. To this end he lectured widely and wrote numerous essays, the latter collected in such books as *Unto This Last* (1862) and *Fors Clavigera* (1871-84). In the latter his ferocious attack on James McNeill WHISTLER's paintings led to a libel action in 1878, which was decided against Ruskin and brought his public career to an end. *Praeterita* (1886-89), a delightful fragment of autobiography written during his retirement, was his final book.

Ruskin's reputation as a writer and thinker declined after his death. Modern judgment, however, has recognized his influence as a social reformer, his contribution to the assessment of Turner's genius, and the brilliant flashes of perception in his prose works. Ruskin's drawings are now admired as an important aspect of his career.

Bibliography: Ball, A. H. R., *Ruskin as Literary Critic* (1928); Bell, Quentin, *Ruskin* (1963; repr. 1978); Clark, Kenneth, ed., *Ruskin Today* (1964); Conner, Patrick, *Savage Ruskin* (1979); Cook, Edward T., *Studies in Ruskin* (1890; repr. 1978); Evans, Joan, *John Ruskin* (1952; repr. 1970); Rosenberg, John D., *The Darkening Glass: A Portrait of Ruskin's Genius* (1961); Whitehouse, J. Howard, *John Ruskin* (1974).

John Ruskin, one of the most influential critics of the Victorian era, explored the relationship between aesthetic values and society in his major writings. Ruskin's multivolume Modern Painters (1846-60) championed the art of J. M. W. Turner, and The Stones of Venice (1851-53) gave added impetus to the English Gothic revival of the late 19th century.

Russel, Benjamin

An important publisher and staunch Federalist, Benjamin Russel, b. Boston, Sept. 13, 1761, d. Jan. 4, 1845, cofounded *The Massachusetts Centinel and the Republican Journal* (1784), which was to become the *Columbian Centinel* (1790) under his sole ownership. An able journalist, he used vigorous writing and cartoons to further the Federalist cause. His paper encouraged ratification of the Constitution.

Russel has been credited with coining the term *gerrymander* and labeling the Monroe administration as the "era of good feelings." He retired from journalism in 1828 and was elected to state and local offices.   ROBERT V. HUDSON

Russell, Bertrand

Bertrand Russell, a seminal figure in the development of 20th-century philosophical thought, made major contributions in the areas of mathematics, logic, education, and social reform. Russell, who received the 1950 Nobel Prize for literature, endorsed the application of rationality to all aspects of thought and language. His early pacifism, which led to his imprisonment in 1918, evolved into a dedicated activism against nuclear armament, for which he was again briefly incarcerated in 1961.

One of the most influential philosophical thinkers of the 20th century, Bertrand Arthur William Russell, 3d Earl Russell, b. Trelleck, Wales, May 18, 1872, d. Feb. 2, 1970, was a grandson of the 1st Earl Russell, who had twice been prime minister of Great Britain.

Life. Orphaned at three, Bertrand was reared by his puritanically religious but politically liberal paternal grandmother. He rebelled early against her rigid moral views, but her otherwise progressive beliefs influenced his later social thinking.

Russell was educated (1890-94) at Trinity College, Cambridge University, and remained there as a fellow (1895-1901) and lecturer (1910-16) until he was dismissed because of his active defense of unpopular causes such as socialism and his opposition to World War I. In 1918 he was imprisoned for his radical pacifism. Russell traveled, wrote, and lectured widely in Great Britain and the United States in the interwar period. On the death (1931) of his older brother he succeeded to the earldom. During the 1930s he modified his commitment to pacifism to acknowledge the necessity to oppose Nazi Germany. Reelected a fellow at Trinity in 1944, he resumed his pacifist stance in the postwar years and was especially vigorous in his denunciation of nuclear weapons. Russell founded the Campaign for Nuclear Disarmament (1958) and the Committee of 100 (1960) as his advocacy of civil disobedience became progressively stronger in the antinuclear movement. As a further outlet for his political views he participated (1964) in the organization of the Who Killed Kennedy Committee, questioning the findings of the Warren Commission concerning the assassination of U.S. president John F. Kennedy. Together with Jean Paul Sartre, he organized (1967) the Vietnam War Crimes Tribunal in Stockholm, which was directed against the U.S. military effort in Vietnam.

In addition to his political involvements, Russell took an active interest in moral, educational, and religious issues. His religious views, as set forth in his book *Why I Am Not a Christian* (1927), were considered controversial by many. In 1931, Russell and his second wife (he married four times) founded the experimental Beacon Hill School, which influenced the founding of similarly progressive schools in England and the United States.

Throughout his life Russell was a prolific and highly regarded writer in many fields, ranging from logic and mathematics to politics to short works of fiction. In 1950 he was awarded the Nobel Prize for literature. His private life was characterized by many disappointments and unsuccessful personal relationships, however. He scorned easy popularity with either right or left and exhibited an unbreakable faith in the power of human reason. Russell remained active and wrote extensively until his death at the age of 97. The most interesting account of his life is contained in his autobiography (3 vols., 1967-69).

Philosophical Views. Although he had many preoccupations, Russell's primary contribution lay in philosophy, most particularly in LOGIC and the theory of knowledge. His early philosophical views grew out of a concern to establish a vigorous logical foundation for mathematics, a concern that produced *Principles of Mathematics* (1903). Building on the work of Gottlob FREGE, Giuseppe PEANO, and others, Russell argued that arithmetic could be constructed from purely logical notions and the concepts of "class" and "successor." In *Principia Mathematica* (3 vols., 1910-13), written with Alfred North WHITEHEAD, this program was carried out in detail. Even when disagreeing with Russell, contemporary logicians and philosophers of mathematics acknowledge *Principia* to be the most important treatise on logic of the 20th century.

Russell used the rigorous methods of formal logic for a wide variety of problems. His "theory of descriptions" in particular has been called a model of philosophical reasoning. The argument concerns the meaning of referring to nonexistent objects, such as "the present king of France." Russell's solution is to say that the logical form of the statement is obscured by its grammatical form, and that analysis displays a description coupled with a false assertion of existence.

Russell was seriously concerned with the application of logical analysis to epistemological questions and attacked this problem by trying to break down human knowledge into minimum statements that were verifiable by empirical observation, reason, and logic. He was deeply convinced that all facts, objects, and relations were logically independent, both of one another and of our ability to know them, and that all knowledge is dependent on sense experience. With G. E. MOORE, his former pupil Ludwig WITTGENSTEIN, and others, Russell helped guide postwar British philosophy in a more positivist direction, focusing on the logical analysis of philosophical propositions and on the language of everyday life. Russell's basic position, which he first formulated in *Our Knowledge of the External World* (1914), is referred to as logical atomism, by which he meant that all propositions (statements about experienced reality) can be broken down into the logically irreducible subpropositions and terms that constitute them. By combining and recombining these logically independent and discrete terms, we can describe reality as something that occurs at the point of such combinations, called the point event. Another aspect of this argument showed that the logical and grammatical meaning of sentences do not always coincide; Russell insisted that the logical meaning should take precedence.

Difficulties of analysis led Russell to give up many of the characteristic theses of logical atomism, and with his *Analysis of Mind* (1921) and *Analysis of Matter* (1926) he shifted to what has been called neutral monism. In this phase Russell combines a stringent empiricism with an optimistic view of the progress of science that leads to the conception of philosophy as a piecemeal analysis of the findings of science. His examination of the bases of scientific method culminated in *Human Knowledge, Its Scope and Limits* (1948).

Throughout his life Russell acknowledged difficulties in his positions and was ready to admit criticisms and modify his views. While ranging over an immense field, Russell demonstrated an openness to ideas, an aversion to dogma, and a rigor in analysis that more than justify his position, with Moore and Wittgenstein, as a fountainhead of 20th-century English and American philosophy.   BRUCE O. BOSTON

Bibliography: Ayer, A. J., *Russell* (1972); Clark, R. W., *The Life of Bertrand Russell* (1975); Jager, Ronald, *The Development of Bertrand Rus-*

sell's *Philosophy* (1972); Pears, D. F., *Bertrand Russell and the British Tradition in Philosophy* (1967) and, as ed., *Bertrand Russell* (1972); Russell, Bertrand, *My Philosophical Development* (1959); Schilpp, Paul, ed., *The Philosophy of Bertrand Russell*, rev. ed. (1963); Schoenman, Ralph, ed., *Bertrand Russell, Philosopher of the Century* (1967); Urmson, J. O., *Philosophical Analysis: Its Development Between the Two World Wars* (1956); Watling, John, *Bertrand Russell* (1970).

Russell, Bill

William Felton Russell, b. Monroe, La., Feb. 12, 1934, an American college and professional basketball player, is considered the finest defensive center in the history of the game. He first received national attention as a member of the University of San Francisco team that won National Collegiate Athletic Association (NCAA) championships in 1955 and 1956. Russell was selected as an all-American for his performance during those years. After graduation he led the U.S. basketball team to a gold medal in the 1956 Olympic Games. The now-defunct St. Louis Hawks, of the professional National Basketball Association (NBA), owned draft rights to Russell, but they traded him to the Boston Celtics. In Russell's 13 years with the Celtics the team won 11 NBA titles. He was named to the NBA all-star team 11 times and won the Most Valuable Player award 5 times (1958, 1961, 1962, 1963, and 1965). In his career Russell had 21,721 rebounds and scored 14,522 points. After leaving the Celtics, he became a part-time broadcaster, and from 1973 to 1977 he was coach and general manager of the Seattle SuperSonics.   HOWARD LISS

Bibliography: Russell, Bill, and McSweeney, William, *Go Up for Glory* (1966); Russell, Bill, with Taylor Branch, *Second Wind* (1979).

Russell, Charles M.

The artist Charles Marion Russell, b. St. Louis, Mo., Mar. 19, 1864, d. Oct. 24, 1926, dealt exclusively with a single subject: the American West. At the age of 15 he set out for Montana, where he worked as a herder, hunter, trapper, and cowboy while developing as an artist. At the age of 29 he began painting seriously, devoting himself to scenes of range and mountain life. His vivid, dramatic, and sometimes humorous illustrations of cowboys, Indians, and animals, such as *Lost in a Snowstorm—We Are Friends* (1888; Amon Carter Museum, Fort Worth, Tex.), are spirited and truthful records of the Wild West.   DAVID TATHAM

Bibliography: Renner, Frederick, *Charles M. Russell*, rev. ed. (1974).

The vigor and authentic detail of Charles M. Russell's A Bronc to Breakfast (1908) are characteristic of the artist's style. A former cowboy intimately acquainted with range life, Russell realistically portrayed the incidents and characters common to the American West of the late 19th century. (MacKay Collection, Montana Historical Society.)

Russell, Charles Taze

The American religious leader Charles Taze Russell, the founder of a millenarian sect now known as the Jehovah's Witnesses, taught the imminence of the Second Coming of Christ. Although Russell's reputation was later somewhat tarnished by scandal, the Jehovah's Witnesses have continued to flourish.

Charles Taze Russell, b. Pittsburgh, Pa., Feb. 16, 1852, d. Oct. 31, 1916, called Pastor Russell, was the first president of the Watch Tower Bible and Tract Society of Pennsylvania, the legal agency of JEHOVAH'S WITNESSES. In 1870, at the age of 18, Russell began a systematic study of the Bible with a small group of associates. Becoming convinced of the imminence of Christ's millennial reign, he began to preach and spread his teachings, and in 1879 he founded the *Watch Tower* journal. In 1884 he established the Watch Tower Bible and Tract Society, of which he was president until his death. Notable among Russell's writings is a 6-volume collection, *Millennial Dawn* (1886-1904).   FREDERICK W. FRANZ

Russell, George W.

George William Russell, b. Apr. 10, 1867, d. July 17, 1935, was an Irish poet and journalist who wrote under the pen name Æon, shortened inadvertently by his printer to Æ. A painter in his youth, he subsequently became active in the political, social, and literary movements of his day. Russell's importance in literature is a result of the role he played as friend and counselor to Yeats and other leading figures of the IRISH LITERARY RENAISSANCE. He supported the cause of Irish nationalism as editor (1904-30) of the weekly *Irish Homestead* and its successor, *Irish Statesman*. His first volume of poetry, *Homeward: Songs by the Way* (1894), is considered his finest.

Bibliography: Davis, Robert B., *George Russell* (1977); O'Brien, James, and Kain, Richard, *George Russell-Æ* (1976).

Russell, Henry Norris

The American astrophysicist Henry Norris Russell, b. Oyster Bay, N.Y., Oct. 25, 1877, d. Feb. 18, 1957, is known for his pioneering work in the field of STELLAR EVOLUTION. Russell received a doctorate (1899) from Princeton University and spent most of his life teaching there. The work for which he is primarily remembered, known as the HERTZSPRUNG-RUSSELL DIAGRAM, provided a relationship between the brightness and spectral class of stars. Published in 1914, this work was the foundation for all subsequent investigations of the evolution of stars.   STEVEN J. DICK

Russell, John Russell, 1st Earl

The 1st Earl Russell, b. Aug. 18, 1792, d. May 28, 1878, known for most of his life as Lord John Russell, was a leading British Liberal statesman. The younger son of the 6th duke of Bedford, he was elected to the House of Commons as a Whig in 1813. True to the liberal traditions of his wealthy family, he espoused the causes of CATHOLIC EMANCIPATION (largely achieved in 1828-29) and electoral reform. As paymaster general in the 2d Earl GREY's government he introduced the 1832 parliamentary reform bill (see REFORM ACTS), and as home secretary (1835-39) he liberalized the government of Ireland. In this period he coined the name of the emerging Liberal party, of which he was the leading spokesman.

Lord John Russell (later 1st Earl Russell) helped to found Great Britain's Liberal party and served twice as prime minister. During his long political career he was a strong advocate of parliamentary reforms and reforms in public health, education, religious equality, labor, trade, and capital punishment.

Russell served as minority prime minister from 1846 to 1852. He championed free trade following the 1846 repeal of the CORN LAWS, and he advocated university reform; but despite considerable expenditure on public works and other relief measures, he was largely unable to help victims of the Irish potato famine (1846-51). His Durham letter (1850) against Roman and Anglican Catholicism was a deviation from his usual tolerance. Russell's government was largely ineffective, and in 1851 he was forced to dismiss his foreign minister, Lord PALMERSTON, who had endorsed Napoleon III's coup in France.

Toppled from power in 1852, Russell served in the ministry of Lord ABERDEEN (1852-55) and briefly, in 1855, as colonial secretary under Lord Palmerston; in the latter office, Russell represented Britain at Vienna in an unsuccessful attempt to end the Crimean War. He later served (1859-65) as foreign secretary in Palmerston's second ministry, assisting in the unification of Italy. He was made an earl in 1861. After Palmerston's death (1865), Russell again became prime minister, but he resigned (1866) after failing to secure passage of a second parliamentary reform bill.   DONALD SOUTHGATE

Bibliography: Prest, John, *Lord John Russell* (1972); Walpole, Spencer, *Life of Lord John Russell*, 2 vols., 2d ed. (1899; repr. 1968).

Russell, Lillian

An actress and singer celebrated for her remarkable beauty, Lillian Russell, stage name of Helen Louise Leonard, b. Clinton, Iowa, Dec. 4, 1861, d. June 6, 1922, was probably the most photographed woman in the United States during her heyday. Her 33-year career, which spanned burlesque and light opera, was launched with her appearance (1878) in the chorus of Edward Rice's *Pinafore* company in New York. Vivacious and extroverted, she married four times and always attracted crowds of admirers.

Russell, Sir William Howard

A British journalist, William Howard Russell, b. Mar. 28, 1820, d. Feb. 10, 1907, was one of the first war correspondents. Born near Dublin, he attended Trinity College and then worked for the *Times* of London in 1841, reporting from Ireland until 1849. He later joined the paper's London staff as a parliamentary correspondent. He is best known, however, for his letters from the Crimea, subsequently published as *The War 1855-56*, in which he criticized the management of the Crimean War. In addition to reporting from many other trouble spots of the world, Russell founded the *Army and Navy Gazette*. By 1865 he had become its owner as well as editor. Knighted in 1895, Russell also served as a member of Parliament.

R. W. DESMOND

Bibliography: Atkins, J. B., *The Life of William Howard Russell*, 2 vols. (1911); Fleming, Alice, *Reporters at War* (1970); Furneaux, Rupert, *The First War Correspondent: William Howard Russell of "The Times"* (1944).

Russell Sage College

Established in 1916, Russell Sage College (enrollment: 1,430; library: 175,000 volumes) is a private liberal arts school for women in Troy, N.Y. Master's degrees are offered in some fields. The college operates the Junior College of Albany (1957; enrollment: 900) and an evening division.

Russell Sage Foundation

The Russell Sage Foundation was established in 1907 by Margaret Slocum Sage in memory of her husband, Russell SAGE, to improve social and living conditions in the United States. It conducts research in culture, citizenship, institutions, and policy analysis and publishes the results of this research. Its assets in 1978 were more than $41 million.

Russell's paradox

Russell's paradox refers to an inconsistency in SET THEORY discovered by Bertrand RUSSELL. Let *S* be the set of all sets, and only those sets, which do not contain themselves as an element. For instance, the set of potatoes belongs to *S* because the set of potatoes is not a potato. Consider the statement "*S* is an element of itself." Is this statement true or false? If it were true, *S* would be an element of itself, and therefore not in *S*—by the definition of *S*. Thus the statement must be false. But in this case, *S* is not an element of itself, and therefore is in *S*, by definition. Thus, in either case, a contradiction is reached. In modern logic and set theory, the paradox is removed by adopting restrictive axioms that prevent *S* from being a set.   AVNER ASH

See also: PARADOX (mathematics).

Russia/Union of Soviet Socialist Republics, history of

European Russia was occupied by Indo-European and Ural-Altaic peoples from about the 2d millennium BC. Among the peoples present in the steppe north of the Black Sea were the CIMMERIANS. They were conquered by the SCYTHIANS in the 7th century BC. The Scythians in turn were largely displaced by the SARMATIANS in the 3d century BC. In the early centuries AD a succession of tribes, the GOTHS, the HUNS, and the AVARS, ruled the area. The KHAZARS (7th century) and the Bulgars (8th century) established substantial states. Slavic settlements in the area are documented from the 6th century on.
MEDIEVAL RUSSIA
The SLAVS probably came from southern Poland and the Baltic shore and settled in the region of mixed forest and meadowlands north of the fertile but unprotected steppe lands of the south. The Slavs engaged in agriculture, hunting, and fishing and gathered products of the forest. They settled beside the rivers and lakes along the water route that was used by VIKING warrior-traders (the Varangians) to reach Constantinople. Using their superior military and organizational skills, the Varangians exacted tribute from the Slavs and to this end consolidated their rule in key points on the route to Constantinople. About 862 a group of Varangians led by RURIK took control of NOVGOROD. From there Rurik moved south and established (879) his authority in KIEV, strategically located above the Dnepr rapids where the open steppe met with the belt of Slavic settlements in the forest-meadow region.
Kievan Rus'. Under Rurik's successor, Oleg (d. *c.*912), Kiev became the center of a federation of strong points controlled by Varangian "dukes" who soon became Slavicized in language and culture. Attempts by Duke SVYATOSLAV I (r. 945-72) to create an "empire" in the region between the Dnepr and Danube failed, but Kiev was effectively protected from nomads in the east by the Khazar state on the Volga. With the conversion (*c.*988) of Duke VLADIMIR I to Eastern Christianity, Kiev developed into a major cultural center, with splendid architecture, richly adorned churches, and monasteries that spread Byzantine civilization.

The Kievan Rus' political and cultural apogee was reached under YAROSLAV the Wise, who ruled from 1019 to 1054. Po-

MEDIEVAL RUSSIA

—— Kievan boundary in 1237

—— Western boundary of the Mongol Empire

▨ Principality of Moscow in 1462

0 ___ km ___ 1000
0 ___ mi ___ 600

Cartographic Production by Lothar Roth & Associates

Mongol Rule. The overlordship of the Mongols (see also TA-TARS) proved costly in economic terms, because the initial conquest and subsequent raids to maintain the Russians in obedience were destructive of urban life and severely depleted the population. Equally costly—even to cities that escaped conquest, such as Novgorod—were the tribute payments in silver. Politically the yoke was not burdensome, for the Mongols ruled indirectly through local princes, and the church was even shown respect and exempted from tribute (enabling it to assume a cultural and national leadership role). The most deleterious long-lasting effect of Mongol rule was isolation from Byzantium and western Europe, which led to a turning inward that produced an aggressive inferiority complex. The exceptions were the free cities of Novgorod and Pskov, ruled by oligarchies of merchants (the princes, such as ALEXANDER NEVSKY, were merely hired military leaders) in active contact with the HANSEATIC LEAGUE.

Rise of Moscow. In the shadow of Mongol overlordship and in the harsh environment of central Russia, to which the population had fled from the south, the society and polity of MOSCOW, or Muscovy, developed. Members of the ruling family of Kievan Rus' had seized free lands in the northeast and colonized them with peasants to whom they offered protection in return for payments in money and kind. Each one of these princes was full master of his domain, which he administered and defended with the help of his retainers (BO-YARS). A semblance of family unity was maintained by the claim of common descent from Rurik and of a "national" consciousness based on the Kievan cultural heritage.

Taking advantage of genealogy, Mongol favor, church support, geographic situation, and wealth, some of the local princes—for example, those of VLADIMIR, YAROSLAVL, Moscow, Suzdal, and Tver—became dominant in their region and gradually forced the weaker rulers (along with their boyars) into their own service. Of these principalities Moscow gradually emerged as the most powerful. Its ruler Ivan I (Ivan Kalita; r. 1328–41) was granted the title grand duke of Vladimir by the khanate as well as the right to collect tribute for the Mongols from neighboring principalities. His grandson DIMITRY DONSKOI won the first major Russian victory over the Mongols at Kulikovo (1380). Finally, after victory in a fierce civil war, the elimination of a main rival at Tver (1485), and the winning over of most small independent princes, IVAN III, grand duke of Moscow (r. 1462–1505), emerged as the sole ruler in central Russia. The Golden Horde had regained control after Kulikovo, but a century later it was seriously weakened by internal strife. In 1480, therefore, Ivan III successfully challenged Mongol overlordship by refusing the tribute.

Moscow's triumph was not complete, however, because another putative heir to Kiev remained—the Grand Duchy of Lithuania, to whose rule many of the independent princes of the southwest and the large boyar retainers of Belorussia had gravitated. To the south and east the Muslim successors of the Golden Horde, the khanates of Kazan, Astrakhan, and the Crimea, were serious threats to Muscovy's security.

Although Moscow's annexation of Novgorod (1478) and Pskov (1510) gave it access to the profitable Baltic trade and control over the far-flung colonial lands of the northeast, it also opened the gates to religious and cultural challenges to the spiritual and artistic self-sufficiency and provincialism of central Russia. A conflict arose between church and state as well as between cultural nativism and innovation; it ended, in the second quarter of the 16th century, in a compromise that reaffirmed and strengthened the political values of Moscow (autocracy) while respecting the economic power and position of the church and liberalizing its cultural life to admit the influences from the Balkans and western Europe. Yet the strain between those who wanted a spiritualistic church, divested of worldly wealth (the nonpossessors, or Volga Elders), and the possessors, followers of Joseph of Volokolamsk (d. 1515), who wished to retain the church's wealth and institutional power, continued to affect Muscovite cultural life.

Organization of the Muscovite State. The main political task of the grand dukes of Moscow was the absorption of formerly independent princes and their servitors into the service

litically, Kiev was the center of a federation of principalities tied together by their rulers who claimed to be descendants of Rurik. The unity of Kievan Rus' was more of an ideal than a reality (many internal feuds existed), but it served as an inspiration to later generations. The socioeconomic base of this polity has been a subject of controversy; liberal historians have singled out the trading role of the princes and their retinues (*druzhina*), whereas the Soviets have insisted on the primacy of agriculture and artisanal production. Probably trade was the mainstay of political power, and agriculture (complemented by hunting and fishing) was the major occupation of the population. Culturally, Kiev served as the agent of transmission for Byzantine civilization—Orthodox Christianity and its art (music, architecture, and mosaics); it also developed, however, into the creative center of a high-level indigenous culture represented, in literature, by the sermons of Hilarion (d. after 1055) and Vladimir Monomakh (d. 1125); in historiography, by the early-12th-century *Primary Chronicle;* in law, by Yaroslav's codification, *Pravda;* and in monastic life, by Kiev's 11th-century cave monastery (Lavra). This culture served as the common foundation for the later Ukrainian, Belorussian, and Great Russian civilizations.

The decline of Kievan Rus' (starting in the late 11th century) was brought about by internecine feuds, by a change in Byzantine trade patterns—which made the old river route obsolete—and by the depopulation resulting from slaughter by nomadic invaders from the east. The end, however, came swiftly when the MONGOLS, surging forth from Central Asia, overran the South Russian plain. Kiev was sacked in 1240, and the Mongol khans of the GOLDEN HORDE at Sarai on the Volga established their control over most of European Russia for about two centuries.

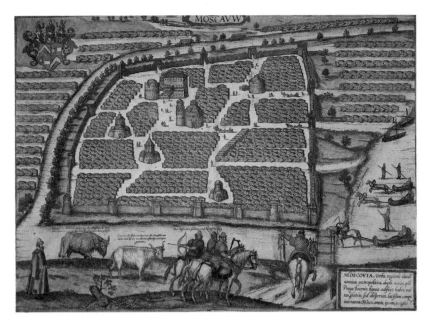

(Below) A 16th-century icon bears the portrait of Ivan IV (the Terrible), the first Russian ruler to assume the title of tsar ("caesar"). During his 50-year reign (1533–84) he conquered the Tatar khanate of Kazan and forced the khanate of Astrakan to accept Muscovite supremacy. Ivan shattered the power of his boyars (nobles), set aside half of his state as his personal domain, and ruled by terror from 1565 on. (Nationalmuseet, Copenhagen.)

(Above) A plan of medieval Moscow, published in Germany in 1572, shows a walled city built of wood. Moscow was founded in 1156 when Yury Dolgoruky, prince of Suzdal, fortified his estate on the Moskva River. The site is now occupied by the Kremlin ("fortress").

hierarchy of Moscow. This absorption was achieved by expanding the membership of the boyar council (duma) to include the newcomers. A system of precedence (mestnichestvo) based on both family status and service position kept the boyar class divided. In addition, from the late 15th century on, the grand duke created a class of military servitors (dvorianstvo) entirely subordinated to him by grants of land on a temporary basis, subject to performance of service. The peasantry remained outside this system, with village communes taking care of local fiscal and police matters. Towns were under the direct rule of the grand duke's representatives and enjoyed no municipal freedoms.

The culmination of absolutism was dramatically symbolized by the grandson of Ivan III, IVAN IV (r. 1533–84). Assuming (1547) the title of tsar, he underlined his claim to the succession of both Byzantium and the Golden Horde. The conquests of the khanates of Kazan (1552) and Astrakhan (1556) followed, putting the entire course of the Volga under Russian control. These conquests initiated further expansion (1581) into Siberia, whose western regions were conquered by the Cossack leader YERMAK TIMOFEYEVICH, sponsored by the Novgorod family of salt merchants, the Stroganovs.

Relying on his absolute power and increased military potential, Ivan IV attempted to eliminate the competition of Lithuania and gain a port on the Baltic. The 25-year war (1558–83) against Poland-Lithuania, Livonia, and Sweden—accompanied by several devastating raids of Crimean Tatars against Moscow (for example, in 1571)—ended in failure and seriously debilitated the country. To mobilize all resources

and cope with internal opposition, Ivan IV set up his own personal guard and territorial administration (oprichnina, 1565–72), whose exactions and oppression did great damage to both the economy and the social stability of the realm. The combined needs of the military servitor class for labor and of the government for tax-paying peasants led to legislation limiting the mobility of peasants. The edicts of Ivan's successors (Fyodor I, r. 1584–98, and BORIS GODUNOV, r. 1598–1605) initiated a process that culminated in the complete enserfment of the Russian peasantry (Code of 1649).

THE 17TH AND 18TH CENTURIES

The Muscovite dynasty ended in 1598 with the death of Ivan IV's son Fyodor I. Real power during Fyodor's reign had been exercised by his brother-in-law Boris Godunov, who was chosen to succeed him. Although Boris was a strong ruler, he was regarded by many as a usurper. The exhausted country was, therefore, precipitated into turmoil marked by the appearance of a series of pretenders to the throne and provoking invasions by Poland, Sweden, and the Crimean Tatars (see TIME OF TROUBLES; 1598–1613). Disgruntled boyar families, enserfed peasants, COSSACKS, and lower clergy tried in turn to take advantage of the anarchy, but none succeeded. Eventually, a militia of noble servitors (dvoriane) and townspeople of the northeast, based in Nizhni Novgorod, expelled the Poles from Moscow, drove back the Swedes and Cossacks, and elected young MICHAEL Romanov as tsar in 1613. The ROMANOV dynasty was to rule Russia until 1917.

An Era of Conflict. Beneath a veneer of traditional forms and static structures profound changes took place in the course of

Ivan the Terrible's capture of the Tatar khanate of Kazan in 1552, portrayed in this 16th-century painting, opened the way for Russian expansion into the Volga region. The Cathedral of Saint Basil the Blessed in Moscow was built in honor of the Kazan victory.

the 17th century, changes that resulted in religious, cultural, political, and socioeconomic disarray. Efforts at reforming the church structure and at modernizing the ritual along Byzantine and Ukrainian lines, led by NIKON (patriarch from 1652 to 1666), were resisted in the name of earlier spiritualist traditions by large segments of the population (led by monks and parish priests). These OLD BELIEVERS, about 25 percent of the population, were persecuted by the state and virtually split away from official culture and civil society. In suppressing the Old Believers the church lost much of its moral authority and autonomy vis-à-vis the state.

The religious crisis exacerbated the cultural conflict over the extent and character of Westernization. Trade contacts, especially with England and the Dutch, brought foreigners to Russia, and diplomatic exchanges grew more frequent as Russia became involved in European military and diplomatic events. Technological innovations for military purposes brought in their wake Western (especially Polish) fashions and cultural goods, leading to new trends in art (the so-called Moscow baroque in architecture, literature, and icon painting). The cultural gap between the elites and the people was deepened by political, social, and economic conflicts: urban strife at times threatened the stability of the regime itself (for example, the salt riots of Moscow, 1648, and revolts in Pskov and Novgorod, 1650). The military servitors' struggle to establish full control (legalized by the Code of 1649) over their peasants led to numerous revolts. In 1670–71 dissatisfied Cossacks, persecuted Old Believers, escaped serfs, and disgruntled urban elements joined forces under Stenka RAZIN in a revolt that swept the entire Volga valley and threatened Moscow itself.

The government, especially under Tsar ALEXIS (r. 1645–76), tried to cope with the difficulties by centralizing the local administrations (*prikazy,* or departments) under direct supervision of the boyar duma and the tsar, assisted by professional hereditary clerks (*diaki*). Naturally, the fiscal burden grew in proportion to centralization. To ensure domestic control and to carry on an active foreign policy (for example, the annexation of the Ukraine in 1654 and wars with Poland leading to a "perpetual peace" in 1686), a professional army of *streltsy* (musketeers) and foreign mercenaries and modernized technology were introduced. Although absolutism was retained intact, factionalism and palace coups became more frequent and made pursuing coherent policies difficult. When Tsar Fyodor III died in 1682 the situation was ripe for the energetic intervention of a genuine leader. After the brief but tumultuous regency of SOPHIA, 1682–89, Fyodor's half brother Peter grasped the opportunity.

The Reforms of Peter the Great. By dint of his driving energy and ruthlessness, PETER I (r. 1682–1725) transformed Russia and brought it into the concert of European nations. A struggle of almost 20 years with CHARLES XII of Sweden (1700–21; see NORTHERN WAR, GREAT) and wars with Ottoman Turkey (1710–11) and Persia (1722–23) radically changed Russia's in-

The Cossack rebel leader Stenka Razin is drawn by cart to his execution in 1671. Stenka and his band of propertyless Don Cossacks spearheaded a peasant revolt in southern Russia in 1670. They were finally defeated by tsarist troops at Simbirsk (modern Ulyanovsk).

Peter the Great (r. 1682–1725) was the first Russian monarch to journey beyond the boundaries of Russia. Traveling incognito, he worked as a shipbuilder in England and the Netherlands, where this portrait was painted. He later embarked on a complete reorganization of Russian society, based on his own observations of Western government, education, economics, and culture.

ternational position (symbolized by Peter's assumption of the new title *emperor* in 1721). By the Treaty of Nystad (1721) with Sweden, Russia acquired the Baltic province of Livonia (including Estonia and most of Latvia), giving it a firm foothold on the Baltic Sea and a direct relationship with western Europe. In the south gains were modest, but they marked the beginning of a Russian imperial offensive on the Black and Caspian seas.

These territorial gains, requiring much effort and great expenditures of labor and resources, forced Peter to transform the institutional framework of the state and to attempt a restructuring of society as well. The central administration was streamlined along functional lines: a set of colleges on the European model displaced the *prikazy,* and a senate of appointed officials replaced the boyar duma; the church was put under direct state administration with the abolition of the patriarchate and the establishment of a Holy Synod (1721) of appointed ecclesiastical members supervised by a lay official. A navy was created, and the army was reorganized along professional Western lines, the peasantry furnishing the recruits and nobility the officers. The local administration, however, remained a weak link in the institutional chain, although it maintained the vast empire in obedience. The peasantry was subjected to compulsory labor (as in the building of the new capital, Saint Petersburg, now LENINGRAD, begun in 1703) and to military service, and every individual adult male peasant was assessed with a head, or poll, tax. By these measures the state severed the last legal ties of the peasants to the land and transformed them into personal serfs, virtually chattel, who could be moved and sold at will.

Other classes of society were not immune from state service either. Compulsory, lifelong service was imposed on the nobility, and their status was made dependent on ranks earned in military or administrative office (the Table of Ranks of 1722 also provided for automatic ennoblement of commoners through service). State service required education, and Peter introduced compulsory secular, Westernized schooling for the Russian nobleman. While resistance to compulsory service gradually forced its relaxation, education became an internalized value for most nobles who were culturally Westernized by the mid-18th century.

Peter failed to reshape the merchants into a Western bourgeoisie, however, and his efforts at modernizing the economy had mixed results. The clergy turned into a closed castelike estate, losing its spiritual and cultural influence. The limitations of Peter's reforming drive were due to the inherent paradox of his policy and approach: he aimed at liberating the creative forces of Russian society, but he expected to accomplish this liberation only at his command and through compulsion, at a pace that precluded an adaptation of traditional patterns and values. He succeeded in transforming the upper class but failed to change the common people; the deep cultural gulf in the long run undermined the regime.

Public celebrations are held in Saint Petersburg (above) to commemorate the centennial anniversary of the city's founding by Peter the Great in 1703. The city is now called Leningrad, and it is the center of Russian culture, education, and science.

The Imperial Succession. Peter's impetuousness did not allow the new structure and patterns to congeal, and after his death (1725) instability plagued the new institutional setup. Having had his son, Alexis, tortured to death for alleged treason, Peter abolished the traditional practice of succession, declaring (1722) that the emperor could choose his successor. For the next half-century the throne was exposed to a series of palace coups instigated by cliques of favorites and dignitaries with the support of the Guards regiments. After the reign (1725–27) of Peter's widow, CATHERINE I, Peter II (r. 1727–30), ANNA (r. 1730–40), Ivan VI (r. 1740–41), ELIZABETH (r. 1741–62),

(Left) The efforts of Peter I (the Great) to recast Russia in a Western mold are satirized in this cartoon, which shows the emperor, in Western dress, cutting off the beard of a nobleman.

(Below) Empress Catherine II (the Great) meets with Joseph II of Austria during her tour (1787) of the Crimea. Russia's annexation of the Crimea was part of Catherine's program of strategic territorial expansion.

and CATHERINE II (r. 1762–96), who supplanted her husband, PETER III, all came to the throne in this manner. The only serious attempt at limiting the power of the throne (1730), however, failed because of divisions among the nobility and their continued dependence on state service. The autocracy managed to keep the nobility in subordination by promoting the economic status of that class through salaries, gifts, and the extension of its legal rights over the serfs, particularly following the traumatic experience of the great peasant uprising (1773–75) under Yemelian PUGACHEV.

The government proved unable to regularize its structure and practices through a code of laws because it was feared that such a code would delegate power to impersonal institutions. Personalized authority was favored by most subjects, however, as a protection against abuses of officials and as a source of rewards.

The tension between a rational and automatic rule of law and a personalized authority was never resolved in imperial Russia.

Expansion and Westernization. Two important processes dominated the 18th century. The first was imperial expansion southward and westward. The southern steppe lands were gradually settled by Russians, and the autonomous local social groupings—especially the Cossacks (whose hetmanate in the Ukraine was abolished in 1764)—lost their status and were assimilated into Russian serf society. The process was formally completed by the Treaty of Küçük Kainarji (1774), ending the first major RUSSO-TURKISH WAR, by which Russia secured the northern shore of the Black Sea, and by the annexation (1783) of the Crimea, which put an end to the nomadic threats from the southeast. By extending (1783) serfdom to the Ukraine the economic integration of that area with Russia was achieved, and its large, prosperous estates were soon able to feed a growing urban population and to export grain abroad.

The empire's expansion westward was the result of the Partitions of Poland (1772, 1792, 1795; see POLAND, PARTITIONS OF), which awarded Russia most of the eastern and central regions of the Polish-Lithuanian Commonwealth. This expansion enhanced Russia's economic potential and brought it closer to western Europe, but it also burdened the empire with insolvable national and religious problems and saddled it with onerous diplomatic, military, and police tasks.

The second process shaping 18th-century Russia is best characterized as the cultural Westernization of the Russian elites. It was furthered by the establishment of new educational institutions (the Academy of Sciences, 1725; the University of Moscow, 1755; and military and private schools), the creation of a modern national literature along Western lines (exemplified in the work of Mikhail LOMONOSOV and Aleksandr SUMAROKOV), and the beginnings of scientific research and discoveries (Lomonosov). Increased sophistication heightened yearnings for free expression and implementation

RUSSIAN EXPANSION WESTWARD (IN EUROPE)

Moscow in 1462		Acquisitions by 1801	
Acquisitions by 1505		Acquisitions by 1914	
Acquisitions by 1689		Dividing line between European and Asian Russia	
Acquisitions by 1725			

0   km   1000
0   mi   600

Cartographic Production by Lothar Roth & Associates

of enlightened Western moral and social values. It led to a conflict between state control and educated society's demand for creative freedom and to the emergence of an oppositionist intelligentsia. In 1790, for example, Aleksandr RADISHCHEV denounced the moral evils of serfdom in *A Journey from Saint Petersburg to Moscow.*

Imperial expansion and cultural Westernization were accompanied by economic modernization. Russia became a notable producer of iron, lumber, and naval stores (pine products) and witnessed the expansion of urbanization and social amenities. Catherine II intensified these developments and reaped their benefits. She decided that Russian society should contribute more directly to economic activity. To this end she fostered security of property and person, at least for members of the upper classes. The nobility were freed from compulsory state service (1762) and guaranteed their property rights. The Statute on the Provinces (1775) and the Charters to the Nobility and the Towns (1785) involved noble and urban elites in local administration through elected officials.

THE 19TH CENTURY

Alexander I. Catherine's grandson ALEXANDER I, who succeeded to the throne after the brief reign (1796–1801) of his unbalanced father, PAUL I, intended to give regular institutional form to the results of the social and cultural evolution of the 18th century. The first years of Alexander's reign were marked by intensive efforts at reforming the administration and at expanding the educational facilities. Although the reforms did not bring about constitutionalism or limit the autocracy, they did inaugurate rapid bureaucratization with better trained officials.

Russia's involvement in the NAPOLEONIC WARS proved a major impediment to the normal evolution of the country. NAPOLEON I's invasion of Russia in 1812, although ending in his own defeat, was hardly a victory for Russia. The wars proved costly, and the ultimate political gains (Finland, penetration into the Caucasus) were rather slim despite Alexander's diplomatic role after 1815 (notably in the HOLY ALLIANCE).

During the wars the younger generation of educated society had acquired self-confidence and a desire to be of use to their country and people; upon the return of peace they tried to put their ideals into practice. Unavoidably, this led to a clash with a government that was loath to give society genuine freedom and that, after 1815, became more restrictive and obscurantist. Secret societies were organized under the leadership of progressive officers, and, on the sudden death of Alexander I in December 1825, they tried to take over the gov-

Napoleon, on horseback, surveys Russian soldiers taken prisoner in the Battle of Eylau (1807) in this painting by Antoine Gros. The Peace of Tilsit (1807) followed a second Russian defeat, at Friedland. In 1812 the French army invaded Russia and occupied Moscow. Lack of supplies and the severe winter forced the French to retreat, harried by Russian forces. Russia emerged from the Napoleonic Wars as a major military power.

ernment. This abortive insurrection of the DECEMBRISTS traumatized Alexander's successor, his brother NICHOLAS I, into a policy of reaction and repression.

Nicholas I. Nicholas I's reign, however, was by no means static, and it proved seminal in many respects. In spite of strict censorship, the golden age of Russian literature occurred with the work of Aleksandr PUSHKIN, Nikolai GOGOL, the young Fyodor DOSTOYEVSKY, Leo TOLSTOI, and Ivan TURGENEV. Stimulated by this literary flowering, discussion circles sprang up in Moscow and Saint Petersburg in which the intelligentsia debated Russia's identity, its historical path and role, and its relationship to western Europe (the SLAVOPHILES AND WESTERNIZERS represented the two main lines of interpretation that emerged).

Nicholas was unfavorably disposed to the humanities and limited admissions to the universities, but he promoted technical and professional training. During his reign a number of technical institutions of higher learning were founded, and state support for needy students in professional schools was expanded. By the end of the reign a cadre of well-trained professionals and officials had been prepared to carry out reforms. Nicholas's government also brought to a successful conclusion the codification of laws (1833; the achievement of Mikhail SPERANSKY), which enabled an orderly and systematic economic development of the country. The building of railroads was initiated, the currency was stabilized, and protective tariffs were introduced. As a result private enterprise was activated, especially in consumer goods (textiles), in which even peasant capital and skill participated. These developments only served to underscore the backward nature of an agrarian economy based on serf labor. Nicholas was well aware of this, but, fearing political and social disturbances, he did not go beyond discussions in secret committees and the improvement of the administration of state peasants.

The government's timidity was conditioned not only by fear of a peasant uprising and a distrust of the nobility but also by its international policies. Nicholas's reign was for the most part peaceful, although Russia did participate in securing Greek independence (1828–29) and in curtailing Turkish power in the Black Sea. Nicholas also acted as the "gendarme of Europe" when he crushed the Polish insurrection of 1831–33 and helped Austria subdue the Hungarians in 1849. The empire further expanded in the Far East (in the Amur River valley). At the end of his reign Nicholas embroiled Russia in the CRIMEAN WAR (1853–56). Although the immediate cause of the war was a dispute over the guardianship of the

Holy Places in Palestine, underlying the conflict was the EASTERN QUESTION, the prolonged dispute over the disposition of the territories of the fast-declining Ottoman Empire. The Russians fought on home ground against British and French troops assisted by Sardinian and Austrian forces. The course of the war revealed the regime's weaknesses, and the death (1855) of Nicholas allowed his son, ALEXANDER II, to conclude a peace (the Treaty of Paris, 1856) that debarred Russian warships from the Black Sea and Straits.

Alexander II and Emancipation of the Serfs. Russian society now expected and demanded far-reaching reforms, and Alexander acted accordingly. The crucial reform was the abolition of serfdom on Mar. 3 (N.S.), 1861. In spite of many shortcomings it was a great accomplishment that set Russia on the way to becoming a full-fledged modern society. The main defects of the emancipation settlement were that cancellation of labor obligations took place gradually, the peasants were charged for the land they received in allotment (through a redemption tax), and the allotments proved inadequate in the long run. The last was a consequence of demographic pressures due to the administrative provisions of the act that restricted the mobility of the peasants and tied them to their village commune, which was held responsible for the payment of taxes; the former serfs remained second-class citizens and were denied full access to regular courts. Nevertheless, 20 million peasants became their own masters, they received land allotments that preserved them from immediate proletarization, and the emancipation process was accomplished peacefully.

Three other major reforms followed emancipation. The first was the introduction (1864) of elected institutions of local government, zemstvos, which were responsible for matters of education, health, and welfare; however, the zemstvos had limited powers of taxation, and they were subjected to close bureaucratic controls. Secondly, reform of the judiciary introduced jury trials, independent judges, and a professional class of lawyers. The courts, however, had no jurisdiction over "political" cases, and the emperor remained judge of the last resort. Finally, in 1874, the old-fashioned military recruiting system gave way to universal, compulsory 6-year military service.

The impetus for reform was thwarted and arrested by external and domestic events. Externally, the Polish rebellion of 1863–64 gave pause to the government and, by exacerbating nationalistic feelings, strengthened the conservative opposition to further reforms. The Russo-Turkish War of 1877–78 un-

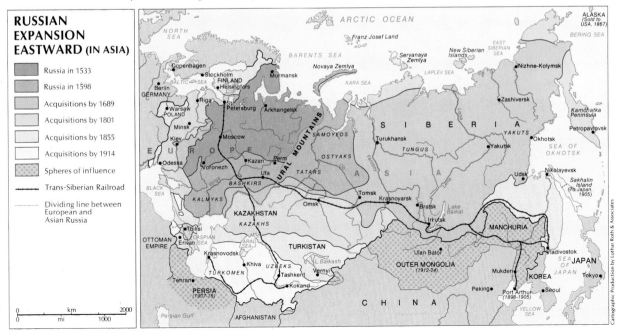

RUSSIAN EXPANSION EASTWARD (IN ASIA)

- Russia in 1533
- Russia in 1598
- Acquisitions by 1689
- Acquisitions by 1801
- Acquisitions by 1855
- Acquisitions by 1914
- Spheres of influence
- Trans-Siberian Railroad
- Dividing line between European and Asian Russia

The assassination of Tsar Alexander II by bomb-throwing revolutionaries in 1881 is depicted in this wood engraving. Alexander, who had emancipated the serfs and was ready to enact further reforms, was succeeded by his conservative son Alexander III.

dermined the financial equilibrium, and chauvinistic passions were aroused when the Treaty of San Stefano, which greatly increased Russian influence in the Balkans, was substantially revised by the Congress of Berlin (see BERLIN, CONGRESS OF). At home in the 1860s radical university students and nihilist (see NIHILISM) critics such as Nikolai CHERNYSHEVSKY voiced dissatisfaction with the pace and direction of the reforms. Radical associations were formed to propagandize socialist ideas, and student youth "went to the people" in 1874–76 to enlighten and revolutionize the peasantry. Repressed by the government, the young radicals turned to terrorism. Eventually a group of NARODNIKI (populists) called the People's Will condemned the emperor to death, and after several dramatic but unsuccessful attempts they killed him on Mar. 13 (N.S.), 1881.

Alexander III. Alexander II's violent death inaugurated the conservative and restrictive reign of his son ALEXANDER III. Nonetheless, the process of social and economic change released by the reforms could not be arrested. Now society proved more dynamic and took the lead in the drive for modernization and liberalization; the government, on the other hand, incapable of giving up its autocratic traditions, acted as a barrier. The deepening agrarian crisis—dramatized by the famine of 1891—turned the active elements from criticism to overt opposition. At the same time, industrialization

energetically pushed by Sergei WITTE, minister of finance (1892–1903), brought in its wake labor conflict, urban poverty, and business cycles.

Nicholas II. Alexander was succeeded by his son NICHOLAS II in 1894. The new emperor soon dashed society's hopes for political and social reform. To deflect attention from the worsening social situation and to neutralize the revitalized revolutionary movement, especially among the workers, the government embarked on imperialist adventures in the Far East, provoking a war with Japan (1904–05; see RUSSO-JAPANESE WAR). Russia suffered a humiliating defeat, although the peace terms (Treaty of Portsmouth, 1905) were less onerous thanks to U.S. president Theodore Roosevelt's mediation and Japan's exhaustion.

The war triggered widespread disturbances within Russia, including rural violence, labor unrest (in Saint Petersburg troops fired on a large crowd of demonstrating workers; Bloody Sunday, Jan. 22, 1905), and naval mutinies (most notably, that led by sailors of the battleship *Potemkin* in Odessa, June 1905). The turmoil of the RUSSIAN REVOLUTION OF 1905 culminated in the general strike of October, which forced Nicholas II to grant a constitution. Russia received a representative legislative assembly, the DUMA, elected by indirect suffrage. The executive, however, remained accountable only to the emperor. Limited as its powers were (the suffrage was further restricted in 1907), the Duma made the government more responsive to public opinion. From 1906 to 1911 the government was directed by Pyotr STOLYPIN, who combined repressive action with land reforms to improve the position of the peasants.

The new political activity contributed to the remarkable upsurge of Russia's artistic and intellectual creativity (called the Silver Age) that lasted until the outbreak of World War I in 1914. Russia became a major contributor to modern Western culture, through the work, most notably, of painter Wassily KANDINSKY, composer Igor STRAVINSKY, the symbolist writers (see SYMBOLISM, literature), and impresario Serge DIAGHILEV.

Thus the years 1905–14 were a period of great complexity and ferment. To many this feverish intellectual creativity, which had its social and political counterpart in rural unrest, industrial discontent, revolutionary agitation, and nationalist excesses (for example, the POGROMS against the Jews), proved that the imperial regime was nearing its inevitable end, which the outbreak of war only served to delay. On the other side, liberals and moderate progressives saw in these phenomena harbingers of Russia's decisive turn to political democracy and social and economic progress, which was abruptly stopped in 1914.

In any event Russia went to war in August 1914. Determined to prevent further Austro-Hungarian encroachment in the Balkans, the Russian government rallied to the support of Serbia when Austria-Hungary declared war on that Balkan nation. Russia's alliance with France and Britain (see TRIPLE EN-

The Russian flagship Petropavlovsk, hit by a Japanese torpedo, sinks with a loss of 600 men early in the Russo-Japanese War (1904-05). Russia's humiliating defeat in that war contributed to the mounting internal unrest, which flared up in the Revolution of 1905.

RULERS OF THE RUSSIAN EMPIRE

Rurik Dynasty		Romanov Dynasty	
1462–1505	Ivan III	1682–89	Sophia (regent)
1505–33	Vasily III	1682–96	Ivan V (co-tsar)
1533–84	Ivan IV	1682–1725	Peter I
	(Ivan the Terrible)		(Peter the Great)
1584–98	Fyodor I	1725–27	Catherine I
		1727–30	Peter II
Time of Troubles		1730–40	Anna
1598–1605	Boris Godunov	1740–41	Ivan VI
1605	Fyodor II	1741–62	Elizabeth
1605–06	False Dmitri	1762	Peter III
1606–10	Vasily Shuisky	1762–96	Catherine II
1610–13	Interregnum	1796–1801	Paul I
		1801–25	Alexander I
Romanov Dynasty		1825–55	Nicholas I
1613–45	Michael Romanov	1855–81	Alexander II
1645–76	Alexis I	1881–94	Alexander III
1676–82	Fyodor III	1894–1917	Nicholas II

Russian soldiers and sailors, dissatisfied with the conduct of World War I, played a major role in forcing the abdication (March 1917) of the emperor and later rallied to support the Bolsheviks in overthrowing the provisional government in November 1917.

TENTE) and Austria-Hungary's with Germany helped transform the local Balkan conflict into WORLD WAR I. The strains of that bloody and disastrous conflict produced a breakdown of both the political system and the social fabric in Russia. Food riots in Petrograd (formerly Saint Petersburg) and other cities toppled the monarchy in March (N.S.; February, O.S.) 1917.

THE UNION OF SOVIET SOCIALIST REPUBLICS

Following the abdication of the emperor the Duma established a provisional government, headed first by Prince Georgy Lvov (1861–1925) and later by Aleksandr KERENSKY. The government's authority was challenged, however, by an increasingly radical Soviet (council) of Soldiers' and Workers' Deputies, and it could not stem the tide of disintegration. Eventually agrarian unrest, mass desertions at the front, turmoil in the cities, and disaffection of the non-Russian nationalities gave the Bolsheviks (see BOLSHEVIKS AND MENSHEVIKS) under Vladimir Ilich LENIN an opening to seize power in November (N.S.; October, O.S.) 1917. Thus the second of the two RUSSIAN REVOLUTIONS OF 1917 occurred.

Lenin's Regime. The Bolsheviks (soon renamed the Communist party of the USSR) immediately announced sweeping reforms: the abolition of private property and redistribution of land, the establishment of workers' control of industry, the replacement of the old system of justice with revolutionary tribunals, and many more. Elections to a Constituent Assembly were held in November, but the Bolsheviks, although they had a majority in the industrial centers, won only 25 percent of the seats. The assembly was dissolved after one day, and one-party Communist rule was established.

The breakdown of society continued, however, even after the USSR left the war (by the humiliating terms of the Treaty of BREST-LITOVSK, March 1918). The end of World War I marked only the beginning of a civil war that lasted until 1921 and in the course of which the country underwent an orgy of violence and suffered famine, epidemics, and total economic collapse. The Bolsheviks managed to retain control of the center of Russia and eventually defeated the White Russian armies and their foreign supporters.

During the civil war the Bolsheviks attempted to carry out sweeping nationalization of the economy under tight centralized control. The policies of War Communism caused further disruption, however. In 1921, with his party still in power but the country prostrate, Lenin inaugurated the NEW ECONOMIC POLICY, which allowed society to regain coherence and strength by permitting some private enterprise, especially in the agrarian sector. At the same time, foreign help and trade enabled the Soviet government to reconstruct the basic industrial plant.

Stalin's Regime. When Lenin died in January 1924, a prolonged succession struggle ensued. The chief contenders were Joseph STALIN and Leon TROTSKY, between whom other powerful figures such as Nikolai BUKHARIN, Lev KAMENEV, and Grigory ZINOVIEV shifted their allegiances. By 1928, however, Stalin had effectively broken all his rivals and was the clear leader of the country.

In 1928, Stalin ended the New Economic Policy, and, with the help of new social elements (homeless youths, young workers, semiintellectuals), which he mobilized, he embarked on what has been called the second revolution. In fact it was the first revolution that the Bolsheviks were able to carry out successfully: agriculture was collectivized (at tremendous human cost; see KULAKS), and a fast pace of industrialization was initiated. By the mid-1930s an impressive industrial plant was in operation, although it had been erected at the price of several million lives.

To eliminate all potential opposition and to secure his personal power Stalin purged the ranks of the party. The GREAT PURGE, launched in 1934, developed a momentum of its own. In addition to the political and military leadership, it engulfed technicians, scholars, artists, and members of the scientific and scholarly elite. Realizing that the effectiveness of fear had reached a limit in 1939, Stalin halted the purge, and the country regained a degree of normalcy even though most purge victims remained in labor camps (see GULAG).

During the 1930s the USSR sought to move out of diplomatic isolation, joining the League of Nations in 1934 and seeking improved relations with the Western democracies in the face of the rising threat from Nazi Germany. By 1939, however, Stalin was convinced that the Western powers would tolerate unlimited German expansion in the east. In August 1939, therefore, he concluded a pact with Adolf Hitler (see NAZI-SOVIET PACT), in which the two powers agreed to divide Poland between them. The German invasion of Poland began WORLD WAR II.

(Left) This photograph of Lenin (left) and Stalin was taken in 1922. It was later used by Stalin's supporters to suggest that the two leaders were close associates. Lenin, however, actually distrusted Stalin.

(Right) The German-Soviet Nonaggression Pact of 1939 is lampooned in this cartoon as a misbegotten marriage between Hitler and Stalin.

An aerial photograph shows Stalingrad burning during a German attack in 1942. A Russian counterattack trapped the German 6th Army. Its surrender marked a turning point in World War II.

Despite his efforts Stalin failed to keep peace with Hitler, who invaded the USSR on June 22, 1941. The war was extraordinarily difficult and bloody. The Germans came within 30 km (about 20 mi) of Moscow, cut off Leningrad completely, and occupied some parts of the Caucasus. The Red Army, however, managed to hold fast. In the prolonged Battle of Stalingrad (1942–43; see STALINGRAD, BATTLE OF) the tide was finally turned, and the Red Army began to advance westward. At the end of the war Soviet troops occupied Eastern and parts of Central Europe, and within the next few years Soviet-type regimes were imposed on Bulgaria, Czechoslovakia, Hungary, Poland, Romania, and East Germany. Stalin also proceeded to launch an aggressive campaign of ideological conformity both within the USSR and in the Communist world at large, contributing to the development of COLD WAR with the West. He died in March 1953 on the eve of what seemed about to become a second purge wave.

The Post-Stalin Period. Nikita KHRUSHCHEV and his successors managed to keep the Soviet system intact. The international position of the USSR has waxed stronger as many countries (especially of the Third World) have become dominated by Marxist and pro-Soviet leaders. At the same time, a powerful rival for leadership of the Communist world arose in China. Under Leonid BREZHNEV, who came to power in 1964, the Soviets pursued a policy of détente with Western nations, allowing cultural exchanges with the West and greater opportunities for tourism. They also changed somewhat the industrial priorities to increase consumer goods and housing, although the military establishment and the space program still account for a high percentage of the gross national product and agriculture developed beginning in 1979. To cope with external pressures and internal dissent, the government resorted to tighter ideological surveillance, forcible expulsion, and preventive arrests. After Brezhnev's death in November 1982, the Soviet leadership passed to Yuri V. ANDROPOV, and when he died (February 1984) to Konstantin U. CHERNENKO. Chernenko was succeeded in March 1985 by the charismatic Mikhail S. GORBACHEV, who quickly consolidated his power and promoted a new, younger generation of leaders. Gorbachev's policy of *Glasnost* ("openness") raised hopes that conditions under his rule might be more relaxed than those under his predecessors. (For further information on Soviet history, see COMMUNISM.)

MARC RAEFF

Bibliography: Auty, R., and Obolensky, D., eds., *An Introduction to Russian History*, vol. 1 in *Companion to Russian Studies* (1976); Blum, J., *Lord and Peasant in Russia from the Ninth to the Nineteenth Century* (1981); Carr, E. H., *A History of Soviet Russia*, 7 vols. (1951–60); Cohen, S. F., *Rethinking the Soviet Experience: Politics and History since 1917* (1985); Dmytryshyn, B., *A History of Russia* (1977); Fennell, John, *The Crisis of Medieval Russia* (1983); Florinsky, M. T., *Russia: A History and an Interpretation*, 2 vols. (1953); Halperin, Charles, *Russia and the Golden Horde* (1985); Lyashchenko, P. I., *History of the National Economy of Russia to the 1917 Revolution*, trans. by L. M. Herman (1949; repr. 1970); McCauley, M., *The Soviet Union since 1917* (1980); Parker, W. H., *A Historical Geography of Russia* (1969); Pipes, R., *Russia under the Old Regime* (1975); Raeff, M., ed., *Russian Intellectual History* (1966) and *Understanding Imperial Russia* (1985); Salisbury, H. E., *Black Night, White Snow: Russia's Revolutions, 1905–1917* (1978); Seton-Watson, H., *The Russian Empire, 1801–1917* (1967); Treadgold, D. W., *Twentieth Century Russia*, 5th ed. (1981); Vernadsky, G., and Fisher, R. T., eds., *Dictionary of Russian Historical Terms from the Eleventh Century to 1917* (1980).

Russian-American Company

The Russian-American Company was a Russian trading company chartered in 1799 to administer the fur-trading settle-

The USSR displays its military might to both its own people and the world at large in the annual May Day parade through Moscow. As a result of the cold war and arms race with the United States since World War II, the USSR has built up an enormous nuclear arsenal.

ments established in Alaska and the Aleutian Islands by Gregory SHELEKHOV. It was originally given exclusive trading privileges in the area north of latitude 55° N. In 1821, Tsar Alexander I extended its jurisdiction south to latitude 51° N, but U.S. protests resulted in accords in 1824 with the United States, Spain, and Great Britain that set the southern boundary of Russian America at 54° 40′ N.

Under the administration of Aleksandr BARANOV, the company had headquarters first on Kodiak Island and then at Sitka. Outposts were established as far south as Fort Ross, Calif. Its fur trade flourished, but it was unable to attract permanent Russian settlers. Disputes with the British and declining profits caused the Russian government to lose interest in the company; its charter was allowed to lapse in 1862. In 1867 all the Russian possessions in America were sold to the United States.

Bibliography: Gibson, James R., *Imperial Russia in Frontier America* (1976); Okun, S. B., *The Russian-American Company* (1951).

Russian art and architecture

The course of Russian art and architecture reflects Russia's contacts with, and isolation from, other traditions. Initially, BYZANTINE ART AND ARCHITECTURE provided the norms, but this tie was interrupted by the Mongol (Tatar) occupation (c.1240–1480). Liberation from the Tatars by the theocratic and semi-Asiatic rulers established in the KREMLIN palace of Moscow did not end the isolation, and Russia never experienced the influence of the Italian Renaissance. Beginning with enforced Westernization under PETER I (r. 1682–1725), however, Russian art was strongly influenced by the European mainstream. Among the distinctive traits of Russian artistic expression have been exuberant color, rich ornamentation, asymmetry of form, and a taste for literal representation as well as abstraction. Religious art, which reached its peak during the 1400s, predominated until the late 17th century. The 19th-century realist movement developed into the Russian nationalist school, which remains the style approved by Soviet official culture. In the early 20th century, Russian avant-garde artists made pioneering contributions to modern art and architecture.

Beginnings of Russian Art. Russian art began with the conversion of the people to Christianity about 989; because the new Orthodox faith came from Constantinople (now Istanbul), the capital of Eastern Christianity, the distinctive art of Byzantium served as a model. The Cathedral of Saint Sophia (1018–37) in Kiev illustrates the initial pervasive influence. The original 5-aisled rectangular brick church was topped by 13 squat domes. The cathedral was enormously enlarged in the 17th century to a 9-aisled church, with the exterior in Ukrainian baroque. The interior of the original church, however, is decorated by artists from Constantinople with superb mosaics that follow the customary Byzantine iconographic scheme. The most venerated painting in Russia, predating the Tatar invasion, was the icon *The Virgin of Vladimir* (late 11th–early 12th centuries; Tretyakov Gallery, Moscow), painted in Constantinople. The tender pose of the Madonna and Child set the model for countless Russian versions of the subject.

Emergence of Russian Styles. Distinct national traits evolved in centers that were farther removed from Byzantine influence. The Cathedral of Saint Sophia (c.1045–62) in Novgorod is notable for the marked perpendicular elevation of its white stucco walls and the elongation of the five dome drums. Inside, less costly frescoes replaced mosaic decoration. Height became even more pronounced in the cubicular stone churches of the city of Vladimir, such as the Assumption (or Dormition) Cathedral (1158–61; enlarged 1185–89) and the Cathedral of Saint Dmitri (1193–97), the white stone facade of which is covered with rich floral and animal carvings.

In time, the wooden architecture of the north contributed multifaceted surfaces and a multiplicity of gables and drums, as well as conical towers and characteristic onion-shaped domes; both of these forms were disseminated to Eastern and Central Europe, as far west as Bavaria. Exuberance of form and decoration, culminating in the fantastical multitowered

The archangel Michael is depicted in this fragment of an icon by Andrei Rublev, painted about 1400 for Zvenigorod Cathedral. Rublev, a monk and the greatest of all Russian icon painters, purified and simplified the ornate Byzantine style. His work was the model for future ecclesiastical Russian art. (Tretyakov Gallery, Moscow.)

and polychromed Cathedral of Saint Basil in Moscow (1555–60), replaced the severity typical of earlier structures and predominated in Muscovite architecture through the 17th century.

The ICONOSTASIS—a tall altar screen composed of hierarchically ranged rows of icons—appeared in the 15th century. These screens added great splendor to church interiors, as did the large jeweled frames, developed in the 16th century,

Saint Basil's Cathedral in Red Square, Moscow, was built during the reign of Ivan the Terrible. Designed in an ornate style derived from native church architecture, the central sanctuary is surrounded by eight chapels, each crowned with an onion dome.

The Summer Palace at Peterhof, Peter the Great's Russian Versailles on the Gulf of Finland, was originally designed by the French rococo architect J. B. A. Le Blond; it was enlarged and completed in 1752 by Bartolommeo Rastrelli, who also laid out the enormous gardens and designed its numerous fountains and pavilions.

which often covered all but the faces in the icons. In painting, the somber hues and static poses of the original Byzantine models evolved into luminous colors and graceful poses. These features distinguish the work of three medieval masters: THEOPHANES THE GREEK, Andrei RUBLEV, and Dionysius (c.1440–c.1505). Icon painting declined after 1551, when a church council banned free composition and prescribed adherence to consecrated models. The 17th century is known for the mannered icons of Simon Ushakov (1626–86) and the intricate works of the Stroganov school, elaborately decorated icons for private worship.

Westernization of Russian Culture. The forceful elimination of traditional Muscovite forms in art and architecture under Peter the Great marked a decline in traditional Russian culture until the 19th century. With the help of foreign masters and teachers and through state patronage, Western art and architecture were transplanted first to the new capital of Saint Petersburg (begun 1703; now Leningrad), a grandiose city with an elaborate, carefully designed plan that contrasts sharply with the chaotic and spontaneous sprawl of Moscow.

Vladimir Borovikovsky's Portrait of M. Lopukhina, painted in 1797, shows the strong influence of Western portraiture and the decline of native iconographic styles. Peter the Great's European sojourn resulted in the founding of the Academy of Fine Arts to train Russian painters in Western techniques. (Tretyakov Gallery, Moscow.)

Under ELIZABETH, EMPRESS OF RUSSIA (r. 1741–62), the exuberant Russian late baroque flourished; the Italian architect Bartolommeo RASTRELLI was its primary proponent as designer of Saint Petersburg's WINTER PALACE (1754–62), Tsarskoe Selo (now Pushkino) Palace (1749–56), and the Smolny Cathedral in Saint Petersburg (1748–55). Neoclassicism in the style of Robert ADAM came to dominate under CATHERINE II, the Great (r. 1762–96), after being introduced by the Scottish architect Charles CAMERON, in remodelings at Tsarskoe Selo (1780–85) and in the country palace (1782–86) at Pavlovsk. The huge ensembles planned by Karl Rossi (1775–1849), the Winter Palace Square (1819–29) and the Alexander Theatre (1827–32), gave Saint Petersburg a neoclassical homogeneity. From the mid-18th century onward, Russian architects became prominent: Matvei Kazakov (1733–1812) in his designs for the Kremlin Senate (1776–87) and Moscow University (1786–93); Vasili Bazhenov (1737–99) for the Pashkov House (1784–86) in Moscow; Ivan Starov (c.1743–1808) for the Tauride Palace (1783–88) in Saint Petersburg; and Andrei Voronikhin (1760–1814) for that city's Kazan Cathedral (1801–11).

In painting, national talent also emerged in the mid-18th century. The work of Dmitri Levitsky (1735–1822) and Vladimir Borovikovsky (1757–1825), whose portraits mark the first achievements of Russia's new art, shows full mastery of Western technique and conventions yet retains a local flavor. Whether they painted royalty, as in Borovikovsky's *Portrait of Catherine the Great Walking in the Park at Tsarskoe Selo* (1794; Russian State Museum, Leningrad), or young girls, as in Levitsky's famous series of seven paintings (1773–76) of students at the Smolny Institute, their works radiate freshness and informality.

19th-Century Painting and Architecture. The high quality of Russian portraiture was maintained in the first half of the 19th century by two romantic painters: Orest Kiprensky (1782–1836) and Karl Briullov (1799–1852). Other genres also began to develop: Alexei Venetsianov (1780–1847) started a school that specialized in idyllic peasant scenes; Pavel Fedotov (1815–52) pioneered in social satire; and Aleksandr Ivanov (1806–58) was an important religious painter.

Realism gave Russian painting a national idiom. Its development was spurred by the secession of 13 painters and a sculptor from the Academy of Arts (established 1757) in 1863 and the formation (1870) of an independent Association of Traveling Art Exhibits, whose members were called the Wanderers, or the Peredvizhniki. Middle-class collectors and an independent professional status freed painters from court patronage and the bureaucratic supervision of the academy. Ivan KRAMSKOI, Ilya REPIN, and Vasili Perov (1833–82) excelled in the critical social genre that reflected the intellectuals' quest for reform. Aleksei Savrasov (1830–97), Ivan Shishkin (1832–98), and Arkhip Kuindzhi (1842–1910) depicted the beauties of the Russian landscape; Vasily VERESHCHAGIN specialized in battle scenes; and Vasili Surikov (1848–1916) devoted himself to historical painting. Mikhail Nesterov (1862–1942) and Viktor Vasnetsov (1848–1926) added a religious and epic strain.

The development of a national style occurred earlier in architecture. Konstantin Ton (1794–1881) introduced 17th-century Moscovite ornamentation in civic structures and designed neo-Byzantine churches under Nicholas I (r. 1825–55). By the end of the century many private residences and public buildings, such as the Historical Museum (1878–83) in Moscow, were built in pseudo-Muscovite style, and churches were patterned on Russian medieval architecture, as is the Saint Vladimir Cathedral, Kiev (1876–82).

The Art of Fabergé. The work of the jeweler Peter Carl FABERGÉ has become synonymous with late Tsarist art, because his most famous creations were for the imperial family and its court—the fantastical Easter eggs fashioned of precious metals and gems. The three Fabergé ateliers—in Saint Petersburg, Kiev, and London—also produced an enormous variety of everyday objects, such as desk accessories, cigarette cases, and umbrella handles, in luxurious materials. Fabergé designs were invariably eclectic, and the workmanship was of the highest order. The firm ceased operations in 1918.

Léon Bakst designed the sets for the Ballets Russes' 1910 production of Schéhérazade (above). Bakst's sumptuous decor contributed much to the near-legendary status of Serge Diaghilev's company. (Musée des Arts Décoratifs, Paris.) Michael Perchin's enamel, gold, diamond, and rock-crystal egg (right), presented by Nicholas II to Czarina Alexandra Feodorovna in 1896, conceals miniatures of the royal residences that are revealed by pressing the emerald at the apex. (Pratt Collection, New York City.)

Influence of New European Movements. About 1890 a reaction against the realists' obsession with nationalist subjects and socially useful art brought a resurgence of new painting that lasted into the 1920s. Isaak Levitan (1861–1900) turned to the outdoor (*en plein air*) painting of landscapes; Konstantin Korovin (1861–1939) and Valentin Serov (1865–1911) used the color discoveries of the impressionists; and Mikhail VRUBEL experimented with new decorative forms. Aleksandr BENOIS and Serge DIAGHILEV familiarized the Russian public with leading trends abroad through their magazine, *Mir iskusstva* (World of Art, 1898–1904), and their art exhibitions. They also showed Russian art (1906) in Paris and staged seasons of Russian ballet (beginning 1909) with exotic costume designs by Léon BAKST and other Russian painters.

The decade preceding World War I was one of a rapid succession of diverse movements. The symbolist Blue Rose movement, started in 1907, and the Cézannist Knave of Diamonds movement, started in 1910, opened the way for a new

vanguard that was crucial for the development of modernism in both Russia and the West. Natalia GONCHAROVA and Mikhail LARIONOV started as primitivists, relying on medieval icons and peasant prints (*lubki*), but by 1912 their work had evolved into the semiabstract rayonism, which was related to the CUBISM and FUTURISM of the West. Wassily KANDINSKY painted his first nonrepresentational works about 1910; in

Wassily Kandinsky's Couple on Horseback *was painted in 1907, three years before he abandoned representational art for pure abstraction. In this scene from Russian folklore, Kandinsky achieves a fairy-tale atmosphere by using dots of glowing color to shape the forms. (Städtische Galerie, Munich.)*

Vladimir Tatlin's 1919 model for Monument to the 3d International *was an iron spiral enclosing three rotating glass chambers. The actual structure, never built, would have been 394 m (1,300 ft) tall, making it the largest sculpture ever conceived. Tatlin founded the Russian constructivist movement.*

Suprematist Composition was painted sometime after 1920 by Kasimir Malevich. Suprematism, inspired by cubism and other innovations in Western art, sought to combine pure colors and geometric shapes into abstract patterns. It was eventually suppressed, along with other avant-garde art movements, by the Soviet government. (Stedelijk Museum, Amsterdam.)

1913, Vladimir TATLIN created his first three-dimensional abstract structures; and Kasimir MALEVICH, who was a founder of SUPREMATISM, exhibited his rigorously abstract groupings of colors and shapes in 1915.

Effects of the 1917 Revolution. The Bolshevik Revolution found support among the advocates of radical art forms, who played a prominent role in the administration of culture from 1917 to 1921. Art was no longer confined to the easel and the studio but moved into the streets. Painters designed posters, other propaganda, and outdoor decorations for political events. Architects also worked on creating a new environment. Inspired by the search for pure forms inaugurated by Malevich, Tatlin, and El LISSITZKY, others—including Moisei Ginzburg (1892-1946), Ivan Leonidov (1902-59), and Konstantin Melnikov (1890-1974)—pioneered the constructivist style (see CONSTRUCTIVISM) with their theoretical tracts and functional projects. Many of their designs for large housing developments—combining living quarters with communal and service buildings—and for cities with flexible zones and garden belts were never realized; however, they revolutionized urban planning in the USSR.

Dominance of Official Art. After 1921 many painters continued to innovate in the mass media and in practical arts such as photography, cinema, industrial and theater design, and typography. Others returned to easel painting, and various neorealist groups flourished under government patronage for the rest of the decade. Kuzma Petrov-Vodkin (1878-1939) and Aleksandr Deineka (1899-1969) were the outstanding painters. This diversity came to an end in 1932, however, when the Communist party imposed single nationwide unions of painters and architects. In 1934 socialist realism was promulgated as the official style: in the pictorial field, it took 19th-century Russian realists as the model; in architecture, it advocated a pastiche of quasi-classical styles. Political dictates and cultural isolationism prevailed for the next 25 years. Since the 1960s there has been a timid liberalization: socialist realism is no longer restricted to purposive representation of topical subjects and may encompass personal, lyrical statements as well. Dissident painters, however, insist on full freedom of expression; they experiment widely in various styles and forms, but must remain outside the state system of patronage and display.

ELIZABETH KRIDL VALKENIER

Bibliography: Bowlt, John, *Russian Art of the Avant-Garde: Theory and Criticism 1902-1934* (1976); Golomshtok, Igor, and Glezer, Alexander, *Soviet Art in Exile* (1977); Gray, Camilla, *The Russian Experiment in Art, 1863-1922* (1970); Hamilton, George Heard, *The Art and Architecture of Russia*, 2d ed. (1976); Hare, Richard, *The Art and Artists of Russia* (1965); Kaganovich, Kira and Abraam, *Arts of Russia*, 2 vols. (1967); Kennett, Audrey, *The Palaces of Leningrad* (1973); Lazarev, Viktor, *Old Russian Murals and Mosaics from the XI to the XVI Century*, trans. by Boris Roniger, rev. by Nancy Dunn (1966); Rice, Tamara Talbot, *A Concise History of Russian Art*, rev. ed. (1974); Shvidkovsky, O. A., ed., *Building in the U.S.S.R., 1917-1932* (1971); Valkenier, Elizabeth, *Russian Realist Art, the State and Society* (1977); Voyce, Arthur, *The Art and Architecture of Medieval Russia* (1967).

Russian Blue

The Russian Blue has a double coat of short blue hair with a silvery sheen. Lighter shades—or lavender—are preferred in competition.

The Russian Blue cat, once known as the Archangel Blue, is noted for its coat of remarkable quality: soft, thick, and silky like sealskin, and in varying shades of blue including lavender. The body is long and slender, the head broad with wide-set vivid green eyes. The ears are large and pointed. The Russian Blue was brought to Great Britain about 1860 by sailors trading from Baltic ports.

EVERETT SENTMAN

Russian language: see SLAVIC LANGUAGES.

Russian literature

Russian literature rivals other national literatures in critical esteem, a position it has achieved primarily through works written since 1820. Russians honor the poet Aleksandr PUSHKIN, who died in 1837, above all other writers; but it was through the great mid-19th-century masters of prose fiction—especially Fyodor DOSTOYEVSKY, Leo TOLSTOI, and Ivan TURGENEV—that Russian literature first gained the attention of foreign readers. Among later authors the short-story writer and dramatist Anton CHEKHOV is the most admired. Of writers since the 1917 Revolution, the most widely read are Boris PASTERNAK—important for both his fiction and his poetry—and the novelists Mikhail SHOLOKHOV and Aleksandr SOLZHENITSYN.

Origins. Russian literature began with the conversion of Russia to Christianity in the late 10th century. As Kiev at this time was the capital and most important city of Russia, early literature is said to belong to the Kievan period. Most of the early literature was religious and was written in Old Church Slavonic (see SLAVIC LANGUAGES)—a language of the Balkan Slavs, akin to the Russian vernacular, that the Russians adopted for use in the church. Written literature consisted at first of biblical and liturgical texts, as well as some medieval romances translated from the Greek. Original Kievan writings include the sermons of Hilarion, lives of the saints, and the historical works known as the chronicles, of which the best known is the *Primary Chronicle* (c.1112). Written in the vernacular and compiled by monks, the chronicles form a valuable historical record and are also the most significant early Russian literary genre. The most famous work of the period, however, is the short epic *The Lay of Igor's Campaign* (1187), evoking conditions in Russia at the time.

In the Kievan period, Russia also possessed a rich oral literature. The *byliny*, or folk chants, were heroic lays in which the 10th-century Grand Prince Vladimir of Kiev figures in a role comparable to that of King Arthur in Arthurian legend. Retold and reworked over the centuries, the *byliny* survived in oral form into the 19th century, when they, as well as traditional folktales and religious lays, were finally transcribed.

Muscovite Period. From about 1240 to 1480, Russia's princes ruled as vassals of the Tatars. During this period, in which the ascendancy of Moscow occurred, literature remained largely religious, didactic, and historical, with continuing emphasis on lives of the saints and on chronicles. One well-known work of the time, the *Zadonshchina*, is a 15th-century account of the Russians' first major victory over the Tatars at Kulikovo in 1380.

The two most celebrated monuments of 16th-century Russian literature are a handbook of domestic etiquette, the *Domostroy*, and the acrimonious *Correspondence between Prince A. M. Kurbsky and Tsar Ivan IV* (1564–79; Eng. trans., 1955). During the 17th century a schism occurred in the church, from which arose the polemical autobiography *Life of the Archpriest Avvakum* (1672–75; Eng. trans., 1924) by the leader of the Old Believers. Russian drama also first appeared during the 17th century, in the works translated and staged for the tsar by the German monk Johann Gottfried Gregori and in the original works of Simeon Polotsky (1629–80).

The 18th Century. With the advent of the 18th century, led by Tsar Peter the Great (r. 1682–1725), Russia came under the influence of the culturally as well as economically more advanced civilization of Western Europe. Russian writers, struggling to create a literature comparable to that found abroad, felt hampered by the undeveloped condition of their language. A burst of literary activity ensued, involving literary imitation and linguistic experiments.

Antioch Kantemir (1709–44) was the first poet to write in the vernacular; his "On the Detractors of Learning, to My Mind" (1729; Eng. trans., 1749) brought him to the attention of influential social reformers. Poet, scholar, and scientist Mikhail LOMONOSOV played a particularly prominent part in standardizing the colloquial language, proposing three distinct literary styles. Gavrila DERZHAVIN, the most important poetic predecessor of Pushkin, wrote vital yet majestic poetry, characterized by baroque imagery.

Nikolai KARAMZIN helped forge the modern cultural language with his sentimental *Letters of a Russian Traveler* (1790; Eng. trans., 1803) and with his chief work, the 11-volume *Istoriya gosudarstva rossiyskogo* (History of the Russian State, 1804–27). Ivan KRYLOV, Russia's greatest fablist, also wrote at this time. For the stage, Aleksandr SUMAROKOV produced the tragedy *Demetrius the Impostor* (1781; Eng. trans., 1806) and several minor comedies; and Denis FONVIZIN is noted for two comedies of manners, *The Brigadier* (1766; Eng. trans., 1916) and *The Young Hopeful* (1782; Eng. trans., 1933). By now Russia had acquired a new literary center, Saint Petersburg, the imperial capital since 1712.

Pushkin and His Immediate Successors. In the 19th century, Russia's greatest literary genius, Aleksandr Pushkin, completed the process of adapting the language as a literary vehicle. His greatest poems include the verse novel *Eugene One-*

Aleksandr Pushkin, portrayed (1827) by Orest Kiprensky, is considered Russia's greatest poet and the founder of modern Russian literature. Pushkin's work represents the culmination of earlier Russian folk and literary traditions. The neoclassicism and romanticism characteristic of his earlier work developed into an accomplished realism influencing all later 19th-century Russian literature. (Tretyakov Gallery, Moscow.)

gin (1823–31; Eng. trans., 1881); *The Bronze Horseman* (1832; Eng. trans., 1931), a collection of folktales; the verse play BORIS GODUNOV; and a wealth of lyrics notable for their precise, imagistic style. His best-known prose works are the novel *A Captain's Daughter* (1836; Eng. trans., 1846), the tale *The Queen of Spades* (1833; Eng. trans., 1850), and a collection of five short stories, *The Tales of Belkin* (1830; Eng. trans., 1894). Pushkin's prolific career ended early when he died in a duel at the age of 38.

Another significant writer at the time of Pushkin was the playwright Aleksandr GRIBOYEDOV, whose fame rests on the comedy *Woe from Wit* (1823; Eng. trans., 1857). Two successors of Pushkin were the nature poet Fyodor Tyutchev and the romantic Mikhail LERMONTOV, whose works deal with frustration and isolation. When Lermontov died, also in a duel, at the age of 26, he left an impressive collection of lyrics and longer poems, as well as A HERO OF OUR TIME, Russia's first psychological novel.

After Pushkin, emphasis began to shift from poetry to prose. Nikolai GOGOL, who moved from romanticism to realism, was an inspired and eccentric talent. He is best known for such historical short stories as "Taras Bulba" (1835; Eng. trans., 1860), about Cossack life; for the satire The INSPECTOR GENERAL; for the remarkable novel DEAD SOULS; and for his Saint Petersburg tales, among which "The Overcoat" (1842; Eng. trans., 1922) is preeminent.

Realism. Although it had produced several powerful original talents, Russia in the 1840s still lacked a general literary move-

Three of Russia's greatest 19th-century prose writers—Ivan Turgenev (left); Fyodor Dostoyevsky (center), portrayed (1872) by V. G. Perov; and Leo Tolstoi (right), photographed (1910) with his wife, Sophia, shortly before his death—are shown. These writers, the leading exponents of realism in mid-19th-century literature, explored the human condition and the philosophical concerns of their time in works that focused on character development, psychological motivation, factual detail, and the current social and political climate.

ment. The extremely influential literary critic Vissarion BELIN-SKY sought to remedy the deficiency, insisting that art had a duty to society, that it must reflect reality, and that it must have a message. Under his tutelage a movement satisfying these criteria began in the mid-1840s. At first termed the natural school, after Belinsky's death the movement developed into the so-called realist school.

The general characteristics of 19th-century Russian realism include the urge to explore the human condition in a spirit of serious enquiry, although without excluding humor and satire; the tendency to set works of fiction in the Russia of the writer's own day; the cultivation of a straightforward style, but one also involving factual detail; an emphasis on character and atmosphere rather than on plot and action; and an underlying tolerance of human weakness and wickedness. The leading realists began to be published in the late 1840s—the novelists Ivan Turgenev, Fyodor Dostoyevsky, and Count Leo Tolstoi; the playwright Aleksandr Ostrovsky; the poet Nikolai NEKRASOV; and the novelist and political thinker Aleksandr HERZEN.

Turgenev, Dostoyevsky, and Tolstoi. Turgenev is renowned for his *Sportsman's Sketches* (1847–52; Eng. trans., 1855), sympathetically describing serf life; for his short love stories; and above all for a sequence of six novels, including FATHERS AND SONS, in which he ventilated all the major political, social, and philosophical controversies of his day. Dostoyevsky's major works are four long novels—The BROTHERS KARAMOZOV, CRIME AND PUNISHMENT, The IDIOT, and The POSSESSED—which present a clash between the mind and the heart, or between rationality, which Dostoyevsky detested, and intuitiveness, in which he discerned (especially in its religious manifestations) the only hope of rescuing Russia and the world from their self-inflicted troubles. Tolstoi's masterpieces, the long novels ANNA KARENINA and WAR AND PEACE, also weave religious and philosophical problems into the fabric of the fiction.

Chekhov and Gorky. A reformer of the theater, and author of short stories and plays, Anton Chekhov wrote toward the end of the Russian realist movement. He was perhaps Russia's greatest dramatist; his plays of human isolation and despair continue to be performed throughout the world. Best known are his UNCLE VANYA, The THREE SISTERS, and The CHERRY ORCHARD. A contemporary of Chekhov, the playwright, novelist, and story writer Maksim GORKY wrote his most famous play, The LOWER DEPTHS, at the turn of the century. Gorky's communist sympathies enabled him to enjoy certain privileges after the revolution.

Symbolism and Other, Competing Movements. From the mid-1890s, symbolism began to supersede realism as the dominant literary movement. The symbolists advocated creative experiment with poetic language and helped restore both craftsmanship and mystery to literature. The most famous of the Russian symbolist poets was Aleksandr BLOK, who survived the revolution to write descriptions of it in the well-known poems published under the title *The Twelve* (1917; Eng.

Anton Chekhov and Maksim Gorky, two of Russia's finest dramatists, were photographed (1900) in Yalta. Chekhov, whose work is a high point in Russian literary realism, greatly influenced Gorky, the first to practice socialist realism in the Soviet era.

trans., 1920). Other leading symbolist poets were Valery BRYUSOV, Konstantin BALMONT, and Andrei BELY.

Meanwhile other movements arose in opposition to symbolism. The futurist poets Vladimir MAYAKOVSKY and Velimir Khlebnikov (1885–1922) sought to invent new poetic forms and scorned the art of the past. The acmeists valued the classical and European tradition, leading representatives of the movement being Nikolai GUMILEV, Osip MANDELSTAM, and Anna AKHMATOVA. Another group, the imagists, stressed the supreme importance of poetic imagery; this movement produced only one major poet, Sergei YESENIN.

The Soviet Period and Socialist Realism. The Bolshevik Revolution of 1917 marked the beginning of the Soviet period in literature. Literature became subordinated to politics. For about a decade writers were prevented from publishing any so-called counterrevolutionary material, but they were not instructed by politicians what and how to write. By the time Joseph Stalin had come to power, however, the situation had changed.

From about 1930 on, authors were required to idealize the new Soviet industrialization program and the collectivization of agriculture. In order to intensify the regimentation of literature, the many competing literary groups of the 1920s were amalgamated into a single association, the Union of Writers of the USSR, established in 1934 under the sponsorship of literature's best-known survivor from the prerevolutionary era, Maksim Gorky. At the same time, the newly evolved aesthetic method, socialist realism, was imposed as the only permissible literary technique. According to the government, socialist realism demanded from the artist "a truthful, historically concrete depiction of reality in its revolutionary development." In practice, socialist realism imposed on literature a simple, uniform style and an abstention from stylistic or structural experiment, together with the insistence that authors show only positive aspects of the Soviet system and the beneficence of the Communist party.

But several important writers had begun publishing before the crackdown of 1934 and continued to enjoy some immunity from the strictures of socialist realism. Valentin KATAYEV's *Time Forward* (1932; Eng. trans., 1933) is a carefully written account of the work of Russian technicians at Magnitogorsk; the three-volume *And Quiet Flows the Don* (1928–33; Eng. trans., 1934), along with its sequel, *The Don Flows Home to the Sea* (1940; Eng. trans., 1940), by the Nobel Prize winner Mikhail Sholokhov, is a regional novel set in Cossack lands; and Leonid LEONOV's six novels on industrialization include the internationally acclaimed *Sot* (1930; trans. as *Soviet River*, 1932) and *The Russian Forest* (1954; Eng. trans., 1966). Such leading 20th-century exponents as Konstantin FEDIN and Aleksei N. TOLSTOI have also helped keep the long novel an established genre in Russia.

Émigré and Post-Stalinist Literature. The foremost expatriate prose writers of the Soviet period were Vladimir NABOKOV and Ivan BUNIN. After 1940, Nabokov wrote primarily in English, developing into an American rather than a Russian writer. Bunin, however, who had emigrated in 1919, continued to write in his native language and on Russian themes. In 1933 he became the first Russian to receive the Nobel Prize for literature.

Following Stalin's death in 1953, restrictions on literature were somewhat relaxed. For a few years Ilya EHRENBERG's short novel *The Thaw* (1953; Eng. trans., 1966) epitomized this new official liberality. Aleksandr Solzhenitsyn's novel ONE DAY IN THE LIFE OF IVAN DENISOVICH, about the Soviet labor camps under Stalin, was published during a thaw, but his slightly later novels *Cancer Ward* (1968; Eng. trans., 1968–69), *The First Circle* (1968; Eng. trans., 1968), *August 1914* (1971; Eng. trans., 1972), and *The GULAG ARCHIPELAGO* had to be published abroad.

Solzhenitsyn was awarded the 1970 Nobel Prize for literature. Boris Pasternak, offered the 1958 Prize for his works, including DOCTOR ZHIVAGO, published outside the USSR, was forced by his government to decline the award.

Poetry, Drama, and Criticism. Verse is in many ways a more important branch of the modern literature than prose, largely

Aleksandr Solzhenitsyn, the most celebrated contemporary Russian writer, was awarded the 1970 Nobel Prize for literature, which he was unable to accept until 1974, following his deportation from the USSR to the West. Solzhenitsyn, whose works were repressed by the Soviet state after 1966, fuses the traditions and humanitarian concerns of earlier Russian literature with a modern politicization.

KOV—sought to legitimize the goals and achievements of nationalistic music and to oppose the dominance of Western musical influences. Although linked by common propagandistic aims and by the characteristic absence of formal musical education, the composers wrote in differing styles. The most lasting musical achievements were made by Borodin, Mussorgsky, and Rimsky-Korsakov. Borodin is noted for his use of Russian orientalisms in works such as *In the Steppes of Central Asia* (1880) and his opera *Prince Igor*. In his numerous operas on historical and fairy-tale subjects, as well as in the well-known symphonic suite *Scheherezade* (1891), Rimsky-Korsakov exploited the unusual modal tendencies of Russian folk music, and his orchestration was colorful and effective.

Mussorgsky was undoubtedly the most original composer of the Five. Continuing Dargomyzhsky's search for musical realism, he combined an instinctive flair for the nuances of folk music with flexible, textually motivated rhythmic practices and unusual harmonic juxtapositions in his many songs, his operatic masterpiece *Boris Godunov* (1869–72), and his suite for piano *Pictures at an Exhibition* (1874). Although he was misunderstood by many of his contemporaries, Mussorgsky's legacy has been profoundly important for music in the 20th century.

owing to leading poets who survived the revolution and continued writing either in Russia or abroad. Such poets include Mayakovsky, Mandelstam, Akhmatova, Pasternak, and Marina Tsvetayeva (1892–1941). Of these only Pasternak and Akhmatova survived World War II. Some of the best-known writers of the 1960s include the poets Andrei VOZNESENSKY; Yevgeny YEVTUSHENKO, noted for his "Babi Yar" (1961), an attack on anti-Semitism in the USSR; and Joseph BRODSKY, who has recently emigrated.

Drama of the Soviet period has seen some original producers and designers, but no significant playwrights. After the formalists of the 1920s, literary criticism was overtaken by socialist realism, becoming substantially a branch of politics and acquiring a heavily censorious sociological bias.

RONALD HINGLEY

Bibliography: Auty, Robert, and Obolensky, Dimitri, eds., *An Introduction to Russian Language and Literature* (1976); Brown, Edward J., *Russian Literature since the Revolution*, 2d ed. (1969); Fennell, John, and Stokes, Antony, *Early Russian Literature* (1974); Freeborn, Richard, *The Rise of the Russian Novel* (1973); Harkins, William E., *Dictionary of Russian Literature* (1957); Hingley, Ronald, *Russian Writers and Society in the Nineteenth Century*, rev. ed. (1977), and *Russian Writers and Soviet Society, 1917–1978* (1979); Markov, Vladimir, *Russian Futurism: A History* (1968); Mathewson, Rufus W., *The Positive Hero in Russian Literature* (1975); Mirsky, Dimitrii S., *A History of Russian Literature* (1949); Slonin, Marc, *The Epic of Russian Literature from its Origins through Tolstoy* (1950) and *Soviet Russian Literature*, 2d ed. (1978); Struve, Gleb, *Russian Literature under Lenin and Stalin* (1972).

Russian music

The beginnings of a distinctively national art music in Russia date from the first half of the 19th century. Until this time musical activity was concentrated in the Russian Orthodox church and in traditional folk genres.

NATIONALISM

The performance of Mikhail GLINKA's opera *A Life for the Tsar* (1836) is usually cited as the turning point for Russian music. In this historical opera, as well as in his subsequent opera *Ruslan and Ludmila* (1842), the orchestral fantasy *Kamarinskaya* (1848), and numerous songs, Glinka fused the typical melodies, harmonies, and rhythms of Russian folk music with the forms and techniques of Italian opera—creating an eclectic, but distinctly national, idiom. Glinka's younger contemporary, Aleksandr DARGOMYZHSKY, is best known for his influence on subsequent nationalist composers through his posthumously produced opera *The Stone Guest* (1872), a radical attempt to promote musical realism by abandoning the forms and conventions of traditional opera in favor of continuous recitative.

Nationalists Versus the West. The FIVE (or the Mighty Five) is the label given to a group of Russian composers that formed during the 1860s. Supported by the influential critic Vladimir Stasov (1824–1906), the Five—Mily BALAKIREV, Aleksandr BORODIN, César CUI, Modest MUSSORGSKY, Nikolai RIMSKY-KORSA-

This 19th-century engraving shows the last scene of Mikhail Glinka's *Ruslan and Ludmila* (1842), an opera based on Pushkin's romantic poem of the same name. Glinka was one of the first composers to work in a distinctly Russian idiom. (Leningrad Theater Museum.)

Nikolai Rimsky-Korsakov is considered one of the foremost members of The Five, a group of nationalist composers who broke with conservative tradition by assimilating Russian folk melodies to their music.

(Above) *The exoticism typical of the nationalists is evident in this scene from Aleksandr Borodin's masterpiece,* Prince Igor *(1890). This work, an opera in four acts reflecting Russian folk and Oriental traditions, was partially revised and orchestrated by Rimsky-Korsakov and Glazunov. Borodin, a highly respected professor of chemistry who composed only in his spare time, was, as were all members of The Five, untutored in musical composition.*

(Below) *Modest Mussorgsky, another member of The Five, is considered the most original composer of the group. Much of his work, most notably the opera Boris Godunov (1869-72), based on Pushkin's play, was altered after his death by Rimsky-Korsakov. Mussorgsky's own arrangements were revived during the 20th century.*

The conspicuous targets of the nationalists were Aleksandr Serov (1820–71), a prominent music critic, Wagnerite, and opera composer, and Anton RUBINSTEIN, a legendary piano virtuoso as well as a prolific composer. Rubinstein and his brother Nicholas (1835–81) were responsible for establishing the first music conservatories in Russia, founded on German models, in Saint Petersburg (1862) and Moscow (1866). Peter Ilich TCHAIKOVSKY was one of the first graduates of the former and subsequently taught at the latter. Without rejecting his national heritage, Tchaikovsky evolved a more cosmopolitan, romantic, yet highly personal style in his operas, ballets, symphonies, concertos, and chamber music.

In Saint Petersburg, under the tutelage of Rimsky-Korsakov, a new generation of nationalists gained recognition. The most prominent of these were Aleksandr GLAZUNOV, noted particularly for his ballets and other orchestral works and chamber music, and Anatol LIADOV, the author of exquisite symphonic miniatures. In Moscow, Tchaikovsky's heirs included Anton ARENSKY and Sergei TANEYEV. Sergei RACHMANINOFF and Aleksandr SCRIABIN were classmates at the Moscow Conservatory; both pursued careers as pianists, conductors, and composers. Though active rivalry continued to exist—most notably between the schools of Saint Petersburg and Moscow—the distinctions between the nationalists and their Western-oriented opponents became blurred.

Early 20th Century. Beginning in the first decade of the 20th century, the exotic and colorful qualities of Russian music were fully revealed to the West through the endeavors of the entrepreneur Serge DIAGHILEV. With lavish productions he staged the Western premiere (1908) of *Boris Godunov* and

(Above) *Tchaikovsky's* Swan Lake, *shown as first presented (1877) in Moscow, was initially not well received. Today it is one of the classic works found in the repertoires of all major dance companies. Tchaikovsky's poignant, highly melodic works are composed in a romantic style reflecting Western traditions yet with a strong undercurrent of Russian nationalism.*

(Below) *Sergei Rachmaninoff, greatly influenced by Tchaikovsky, became one of the leading romantic composers of the Moscow school and one of the most celebrated piano virtuosos of the 20th century. Rachmaninoff's second piano concerto (1901), in C minor, is among his most acclaimed works.*

Igor Stravinsky's ballet Petrushka *was first presented (1911) by Serge Diaghilev's Ballets Russes, with Vaslav Nijinsky in the title role. The early work of Stravinsky, who was discovered by Diaghilev and was closely associated with the impresario for many years, reflects the exotic style of Rimsky-Korsakov, Stravinsky's first teacher.*

Dmitry Shostakovich, one of the foremost Soviet composers of the 20th century, was alternately praised and condemned during Stalin's regime by authorities who sought to use his music for political ends. Shostakovich continued to experiment with style, extending the form and structure of the symphony.

other Russian classics in Paris, and with his newly formed *Ballets Russes* he introduced the ballets *Firebird* (1910), *Petrushka* (1911), and *The Rite of Spring* (1913) by Igor STRAVINSKY. The "barbaric" rhythmic and harmonic novelties of *The Rite* were considered revolutionary and exerted a powerful influence on the future course of music. Stravinsky's successful collaborations with Diaghilev continued until the latter's death. Diaghilev's commissions and controversial productions helped launch the careers of many other composers, including that of Sergei PROKOFIEV. Like many of his contemporaries, Prokofiev was dissatisfied with the oppressive academicism of the Saint Petersburg Conservatory, and while still a student he was branded a musical rebel for his percussive piano writing and satirical miniatures.

The period before the revolution also witnessed the rise of virtuoso performers. In addition to the pianists already mentioned, the violin students of Leopold AUER—including Mischa ELMAN, Jascha HEIFETZ, and Nathan MILSTEIN—as well as the bass singer Fyodor CHALIAPIN, gained international prestige.

SOVIET MUSIC

After the October revolution in 1917, many composers and performers chose to leave Russia. Among those who pursued successful careers in the West were Stravinsky, Rachmaninoff, Nikolai Medtner (1880–1951), Nicolai (1873–1945) and Alexander TCHEREPNIN, and Serge KOUSSEVITZKY. Prokofiev spent nearly 20 years concertizing and composing in the United States and Europe, but in the mid-1930s he elected to return to the Soviet Union.

The early years after the Bolshevik revolution were marked by a spirit of artistic innovation. The creation (1922) of a conductorless orchestra, the demonstration (1920) of the prototype of the first electronic instrument (see THEREMIN) by Leon Theremin (1896–   ), and the ballet *Iron Foundry* (1927) by Alexander Mossolov (1900–73)—illustrating with realistic sound effects a contemporary industrial theme—were among the many attempts to find creative means suited to the revolutionary ideology. Older composers who maintained a continuity with prerevolutionary culture included Reinhold GLIÈRE and Nikolai Miaskovsky (1881–1950).

The Association of Contemporary Music (ACM), established in 1923, actively supported the modernistic experiments as well as the performance of new works by the European avant-garde. In opposition, the Russian Association for Proletarian Music (RAPM), which won increasing authority, advocated the creation of a simple, folk-oriented "mass" music. The abolition (1932) of the RAPM, the establishment of the government-sponsored Union of Soviet Composers, and the concom-

itant rise of the doctrine of socialist realism signaled the end of the permissive period in Soviet music.

The unexpected official denunciation (1936) of Dmitry SHOSTAKOVICH's highly successful opera *Lady Macbeth of the Mtsensk District* (1934) was the first explicit application of socialist realism to music. Recognizing music to be a powerful weapon in the ideological struggle, this ambiguous doctrine called for music "founded on the truthful, historically concrete representation of reality in its revolutionary development." The formula effectively banned the modernistic directions characteristic of contemporary Western music and fostered conservative and readily accessible styles. Shostakovich, one of the first generation of Soviet composers, had achieved early success with his First Symphony (1925) and subsequent works and was able to reestablish himself spectacularly with his Fifth Symphony (1937). Mildly dissonant counterpoint, march rhythms, and sensitive orchestration became the hallmarks not only of Shostakovich's style but that of many other Soviet composers as well. Composers who reached artistic maturity during the 1930s and '40s included Aram KHATCHATURIAN, Dmitri Kabalevsky, Yuri Shaporin (1887–63), and Vissarion Shebalin (1902–63).

In 1948, Soviet composers and musicians were again found to be ideologically deficient. In contrast to 1936, when the attack was aimed at a single composer, this time it was broadly based, focusing in particular on the most prominent composers—Prokofiev, Shostakovich, Miaskovsky, and Khachaturian. The rehabilitation of the country's leading composers and the resurrection of many suppressed compositions was accomplished only after Stalin's death, in 1953. Soviet composers then began to show a renewed interest in the modern compositional techniques of the West, and many, including Shostakovich, began to incorporate these techniques into their compositions.

A new generation of composers emerged in the 1960s and '70s—including Edison Denisov (1929–   ), Sergei Slonimsky (1932–   ), Andrei Volkonsky (1933–   ), Alfred Schnittke (1934–   ), Leonid Hrabovsky (1935–   ), Arvo Pärt (1935–   ), Boris Tishchenko (1939–   ), and Valentin Silvestrov (1937–   )—who demonstrated mastery of aleatoric, serial, electronic, and other avant-garde techniques. During the entire Soviet period Russia continued to produce outstanding virtuoso instrumentalists, including the pianists Vladimir ASHKENAZI, Lazar BERMAN, Emil GILELS, and Sviatoslav RICHTER, the violinists David OISTRAKH and Leonid Kogan (1924–82), and the cellist Mstislav ROSTROPOVICH.　　　　　LAUREL E. FAY

Bibliography: Asafiev, Boris, *Russian Music from the Beginning of the Nineteenth Century*, trans. by Alfred Swan (1953); Calvocoressi, Michel, and Abraham, Gerald, *Masters of Russian Music* (1963; repr. 1971); Krebs, Stanley, *Soviet Composers and the Development of Soviet Music* (1970); Schwarz, Boris, *Music and Musical Life in Soviet Russia: 1917–1970* (1972); Seaman, Gerald, *History of Russian Music*, vol. 1 (1967); Stasov, Vladimir, *Selected Essays on Music*, trans. by Florence Jonas (1968; repr. 1980).

Russian Orthodox church: see ORTHODOX CHURCH.

Russian Revolution of 1905

The Russian Revolution of 1905 broke out at a time when the imperial Russian forces were suffering humiliating defeats in the Far East at the hands of the Japanese (1904–05; see RUSSO-JAPANESE WAR), although revolutionary movements had been simmering in the tsarist empire for at least five decades. The fighting began on Jan. 22 (N.S.), 1905, when an estimated 1,000 workers were killed by Cossacks who fired on peaceful demonstrators, led by a priest, Father Gapon, in Saint Petersburg. This incident—dubbed Bloody Sunday—resulted in an alliance of liberal and radical groups against the government. During the spring and summer, peasant uprisings became increasingly commonplace, and a series of strikes and mutinies (including that aboard the battleship *Potemkin* in Odessa) spread throughout European Russia, Poland, and Finland, becoming a general strike in October. Unwillingly, Emperor NICHOLAS II agreed on Oct. 30 (N.S.) to issue a manifesto prepared by Count Sergei WITTE, his chief minister. This October Manifesto extended suffrage, promised freedom from arbitrary arrest without a hearing, and provided for an elected legislature, or DUMA, instead of the constituent assembly that the revolutionaries had demanded.   K. M. SMOGORZEWSKI

Bibliography: Floyd, David, *Russia in Revolt: 1905: The First Crack in Tsarist Power* (1969); Sablinsky, Walter, *The Road to Bloody Sunday: Father Gapon and the St. Petersburg Massacre of 1905* (1976); Salisbury, Harrison, *Black Night, White Snow: Russia's Revolution, 1905–1917* (1978); Trotsky, Leon, *1905*, trans. by Anya Bostock (1971).

Russian Revolutions of 1917

The abdication of Emperor NICHOLAS II in March (N.S.; February, O.S.) 1917, in conjunction with the establishment of a provisional government based on Western principles of constitutional liberalism, and the seizure of power by the Bolsheviks in November (N.S.; October, O.S.) are the political focal points of the Russian Revolutions of 1917. The events of that momentous year must also be viewed more broadly, however: as an explosion of social tensions associated with rapid industrialization; as a crisis of political modernization, in terms of the strains placed on traditional institutions by the demands of Westernization and of World War I; and as a social upheaval in the broadest sense, involving a massive, spontaneous expropriation of gentry land by angry peasants, the destruction of traditional social patterns and values, and the struggle for a new, egalitarian society. Looking at the revolutionary process broadly, one must also include the Bolsheviks' fight to keep the world's first "proletarian dictatorship" in power after November, first against the Germans, and then in the civil war against dissident socialists, anti-Bolshevik "White Guards," foreign intervention, and anarchist

Demonstrators attempting to present the tsar with a petition of grievances in Saint Petersburg were fired on by imperial troops on Jan. 22, 1905. The event touched off the Revolution of 1905, during which the nation was paralyzed by strikes, arson, and terrorist acts.

peasant bands. Finally, one must see the psychological aspects of revolutionary change: elation and hope, fear and discouragement, and ultimately the prolonged agony of bloodshed and privation, both from war and repression, and the "bony hand of Tsar Hunger," who strangled tens of thousands and, in the end, brought the revolutionary period to a close after the civil war by forcing the Bolsheviks to abandon the radical measures of War Communism in favor of a New Economic Policy (NEP). Throughout, the events in Russia were of worldwide importance. Western nations saw "immutable" values and institutions successfully challenged, COMMUNISM emerged as a viable social and political system, and Third World peoples saw the power of organized workers' and peasants' movements as a means of "liberating" themselves from "bourgeois" exploitation. As such, the Revolutions of 1917 ushered in the great social, political, and ideological divisions of the contemporary world.

Historical Background. Historians differ over whether the Revolutions of 1917 were inevitable, but all agree on the importance of three related causal factors: massive discontent, the revolutionary movement, and World War I, each operating in the context of the ineptitude of a rigid, absolutist state.

The emancipation of the serfs in 1861 left the countryside in deep poverty. The newly freed peasants received inadequate land allotments, particularly in areas of fertile soil, and even these had to be purchased with "redemption payments." Class antagonisms sharpened, particularly since government-promoted industrialization sent impoverished peasants flocking to jobs in urban areas for low wages under oppressive conditions. Government efforts to industrialize also required huge tax revenues, which intensified pressures on workers and peasants alike. Meanwhile, the rising business and professional classes expressed unhappiness with tsarist rule and yearned for a Western-style parliamentary system.

By 1905 discontent among the bourgeoisie, peasantry, and proletariat had spurred Russian intellectuals to create the major political organizations of 1917. Populist groups, organized in the countryside by the 1890s, joined radical socialist workers' groups in the founding of the Socialist Revolutionary party in 1901. The Marxist Social Democratic Labor party was established in 1898. Five years later it divided into two factions: the Mensheviks, who favored a decentralized, mass party; and the Bolsheviks of Vladimir Ilich LENIN, who wanted a tightly organized, hierarchical party (see BOLSHEVIKS AND MENSHEVIKS). Middle-class liberals formed the Constitutional Democratic party (Cadets) in 1905.

Russian losses in the RUSSO-JAPANESE WAR precipitated the RUSSIAN REVOLUTION OF 1905. The massive urban strikes, rural rioting, and almost total liberal disaffection from the tsarist

Russian gentry wager their serfs in lieu of money during a card game in this satirical engraving (1854) by Gustave Doré. Although Tsar Alexander II abolished serfdom in 1861, the conditions under which most Russian peasants existed were not significantly improved.

Emperor Nicholas II appears in a photograph, taken about 1911, of the Russian imperial family. To his right sits Empress Alexandra and, at her feet, their hemophiliac son, Aleksei. Flanking the emperor are his daughters (left to right), Anastasia, Tatyana, Olga, and Marie.

regime in 1905 have been called a "dress rehearsal" for 1917. Reluctantly, Nicholas II granted a range of civil liberties, established limited parliamentary government through a DUMA, abolished peasant redemption payments, and under Pyotr STOLYPIN began an agrarian reform program to promote the growth of a rural middle class. These measures momentarily quieted the populace, but they also raised new expectations; many concessions were later withdrawn, thus exacerbating tensions. Furthermore, the social stability that some thought the tsar's promises offered required time to develop, and this Russia did not have.

The March Revolution. In 1914, Russia was again at war (see WORLD WAR I). Land reform was suspended, and new political restrictions were imposed. Disastrous military defeats sapped public morale, and ineffective organization on the home front made the government's incompetence obvious to all. The emperor, assuming command of the army in 1915, became identified with its weakness. The sinister influence of Empress ALEXANDRA's favorite, Grigory RASPUTIN, increased. By the winter of 1916–17, disaffection again rent all sectors of society—including liberals, peasants, and industrial workers.

When food shortages provoked street demonstrations in Petrograd on Mar. 8 (N.S.; Feb. 23, O.S.), 1917, and garrison soldiers refused to suppress them, Duma leaders demanded that Nicholas transfer power to a parliamentary government. With the Petrograd Soviet of Workers' and Soldiers' Deputies, a special Duma committee on March 15 (N.S.; March 2, O.S.) established a provisional government headed by Prince Georgi Lvov, a liberal. On the same day, the emperor abdicated. He attempted to give the crown to his brother Michael, but Michael refused to accept it. The 300-year-old Romanov dynasty came to an end.

The new provisional government was almost universally welcomed. Civil liberties were proclaimed, new wage agreements and an 8-hour day were negotiated in Petrograd, discipline was relaxed in the army, and elections were promised for a Constituent Assembly that would organize a permanent democratic order. The existence of two seats of power, however—the provisional government and the Petrograd Soviet—not only represented a potential political rivalry but also reflected the different aspirations of different sectors of Russian society.

For most Russians of privilege—members of the bourgeoisie, the gentry, and many professionals—the March Revolution meant clearing the decks for victory over Germany and for the establishment of Russia as a leading European liberal democracy. They regarded the provisional government as the sole legitimate authority. For most workers and peasants, however, revolution meant an end to an imperialist war, ma-

jor economic reforms, and the development of an egalitarian social order. They looked to the Petrograd Soviet and other soviets springing up around the country to represent their interests, and they supported the government only insofar as it met their needs.

Political Polarization. Differing conceptions of the revolution quickly led to a series of crises. Widespread popular opposition to the war caused the Petrograd Soviet on April 9 (N.S.; March 27, O.S.) to repudiate annexationist ambitions and to establish in May a coalition government including several moderate socialists in addition to Aleksandr KERENSKY, who had been in the cabinet from the beginning. The participation of such socialists in a government that continued to prosecute the war and that failed to implement basic reforms, however, only served to identify their parties—the Socialist Revolutionaries, Mensheviks, and others—with government failures. On July 16–17 (N.S.; July 3–4, O.S.), following a disastrous military offensive, Petrograd soldiers, instigated by local Bolshevik agitators, demonstrated against the government in what became known as the "July Days."

The demonstrations soon subsided, and on July 20 (N.S.; July 7, O.S.), Kerensky replaced Lvov as premier. Soon, however, the provisional government was threatened by the right, which had lost confidence in the regime's ability to maintain order. In early September (N.S.; late August, O.S.), General Lavr KORNILOV was thwarted in an apparent effort to establish a right-wing military dictatorship. Ominously, his effort was backed by the Cadets, traditionally the party of liberal constitutionalism. The crises faced by the provisional government reflected a growing polarization of Russian politics toward the extreme left and extreme right.

Meanwhile, another revolution was taking place that, in the view of many, was more profound and ultimately more consequential than were the political events in Petrograd. All over Russia, peasants were expropriating land from the gentry. Peasant-soldiers fled the trenches so as not to be left out, and the government could not stem the tide. New shortages consequently appeared in urban areas, causing scores of factories to close. Angry workers formed their own factory committees, sequestering plants to keep them running and to gain new material benefits. By the summer of 1917 a social upheaval of vast proportions was sweeping over Russia.

The November Revolution. Sensing that the time was ripe, Lenin and the Bolsheviks rapidly mobilized for power. From the moment he returned from exile on Apr. 16 (N.S.; Apr. 3, O.S.), 1917, Lenin, pressing for a Bolshevik-led seizure of power by the soviets, categorically disassociated his party from both the government and the "accommodationist" socialists. "Liberals support the war and the interests of the bourgeoisie!" he insisted, adding that "socialist lackeys" aided the liberals by agreeing to postpone reforms and continue fighting. With appealing slogans such as "Peace, Land, and Bread!" the Bolsheviks identified themselves with Russia's broad social revolution rather than with political liberty or

Aleksandr Kerensky assumed control of the provisional government formed after the tsar's abdication in March 1917. Kerensky's government, unable to stabilize the nation, fell before the Bolshevik-led uprising that took place in November (N.S.) 1917.

(Below) *Vladimir Ilich Lenin, revolutionary leader, delivers a vitriolic address before a Russian crowd. Lenin returned from Swiss exile following the tsar's abdication to assume control of the revolutionary movement that eventually seized power from the provisional government.*

(Above) *The Bolshevik Revolution began on Nov. 6–7, 1917, when Red Guards stormed the Winter Palace, headquarters of the provisional government, in Petrograd. Although this painting stresses martial heroism, the seizure was virtually unopposed.*

the political revolution of March. Better organized than their rivals, the Bolsheviks worked tirelessly in local election campaigns. In factories they quickly came to dominate major committees; they also secured growing support in local soviets. A Bolshevik-inspired military uprising was suppressed in July. The next month, however, after Kornilov's attempted coup, Bolshevik popularity soared, and Lenin's supporters secured majorities in both the Petrograd and Moscow soviets, winning 51 percent of the vote in Moscow city government elections. Reacting to the momentum of events, Lenin, from hiding, ordered preparations for an armed insurrection. Fully aware of what was about to transpire, the provisional regime proved helpless.

On the night of November 6–7 (N.S.; October 24–25, O.S.) the Bolsheviks seized power in Petrograd in the name of the soviets, meeting little armed resistance. An All-Russian Congress of Soviets of Workers' and Soldiers' Deputies, meeting in Petrograd at the time, ratified the Bolsheviks' actions on November 8. The congress also declared the establishment of a soviet government headed by a Council of People's Commissars chaired by Lenin, with Leon TROTSKY in charge of foreign affairs.

The Civil War and Its Aftermath. Few, however, expected Lenin's "proletarian dictatorship" to survive. Bolsheviks now faced the same range of economic, social, and political problems as did the governments they had replaced. In addition, anti-Bolsheviks began almost at once to organize armed resistance. Some placed hope in the Constituent Assembly, elected November 25 (N.S.; November 12, O.S.); others hoped for foreign intervention. Few appreciated Lenin's political boldness, his audacity, and his commitment to shaping a Communist Russia.

These traits soon became apparent. The November Constituent Assembly elections returned an absolute majority for the Socialist Revolutionaries, but Lenin simply dispersed the Assembly when it met in January 1918. He also issued a decree on land in November 1917, sanctifying the peasants' land seizures, proclaiming the Bolsheviks to be a party of poor peasants as well as workers and broadening his own base of support. He sued the Germans for peace, but under terms of the Treaty of BREST-LITOVSK (March 1918) he was forced to surrender huge portions of traditionally Russian territory. Shortly afterward, implementing policies called War Communism, Lenin ordered the requisition of grain from the countryside to feed the cities and pressed a program to nationalize virtually all Russian industry. Centralized planning began, and private trade was strictly forbidden. These measures, together with class-oriented rationing policies, prompted tens of thousands to flee abroad.

Not surprisingly, Lenin's policies provoked anti-Bolshevik resistance, and civil war erupted in 1918. Constituent Assembly delegates fled to western Siberia and formed their own "All-Russian" government, which was soon suppressed by a reactionary "White" dictatorship under Admiral Aleksandr Kolchak. Army officers in southern Russia organized a "Volunteer Army" under Generals Lavr Kornilov and Anton Denikin and gained support from Britain and France; both in the Volga region and the eastern Ukraine, peasants began to organize against Bolshevik requisitioning and mobilization. Soon anarchist "Greens" were fighting the "Reds" (Bolsheviks) and Whites alike in guerrilla-type warfare. Even in Moscow and Petrograd, leftist Socialist Revolutionaries took up arms against the Bolsheviks, whom they accused of betraying revolutionary ideals.

In response, the Bolsheviks unleashed their own Red Terror under the Cheka (political police force) and mobilized a Red Army commanded by Trotsky. The Bolsheviks defeated Admiral Kolchak's troops in late 1919, and in 1920 they suppressed the armies of Baron Pyotr N. WRANGEL and General Denikin in the south. Foreign troops withdrew, and after briefly marching into Poland the Red Army concentrated on subduing peasant uprisings.

Тов. Ленин ОЧИЩАЕТ
землю от нечисти.

An early Soviet cartoon pictures "Comrade Lenin sweeping the land of its rubbish." The "rubbish" refers to capitalists and monarchists. The new Bolshevik regime was quick to grasp the applications of propaganda in consolidating and legitimizing Soviet authority.

Some Western historians attribute ultimate Bolshevik victory in this war to White disorganization, half-hearted support from war-weary Allies, Cheka ruthlessness, and the inability of Greens to establish a viable alternative government. Most important, however, was the fact that even while Bolshevik popularity declined, Lenin and his followers were still identified with what the majority of workers and peasants wanted most: radical social change rather than political freedom, which had never been deeply rooted in Russian tradition. In contrast, the Whites represented the old, oppressive order.

Nevertheless, with the counterrevolution defeated, leftist anti-Bolshevik sentiment erupted. The naval garrison at Kronshtadt, long a Bolshevik stronghold, rebelled in March 1921 along with Petrograd workers in favor of "Soviet Communism without the Bolsheviks!" This protest was brutally suppressed. The Menshevik and Socialist Revolutionary parties, harassed but not abolished during the civil war, gained support as the conflict ended. The Bolsheviks outlawed these parties, signaling their intention to rule alone. Lenin, however, was astute enough to realize that a strategic retreat was required. At the Tenth Party Congress, in 1921, the NEW ECONOMIC POLICY was introduced, restoring some private property, ending restrictions on private trade, and terminating forced grain requisitions. The foundations had been laid for building Bolshevik socialism, but the revolutionary period proper had come to an end.   WILLIAM G. ROSENBERG

Bibliography: Carr, E. H., *The Bolshevik Revolution, 1917-1923*, 3 vols. (1951-53) and *The Russian Revolution: From Lenin to Stalin* (1979); Chamberlin, William H., *The Russian Revolution* (1935); Kenez, Peter, *Civil War in South Russia*, 2 vols. (1971, 1977); Medvedev, Roy A., *The October Revolution*, trans. by George Saunders (1979); Pares, Bernard, *The Fall of the Russian Monarchy* (1939); Pipes, Richard, *The Formation of the Soviet Union*, rev. ed. (1964); Rabinowitch, Alexander, *The Bolsheviks Come to Power* (1976); Rosenberg, William G., *Liberals in the Russian Revolution* (1974); Salisbury, Harrison, *Black Night, White Snow: Russia's Revolution, 1905-1917* (1978); Shapiro, Leonard B., *The Communist Party of the Soviet Union* (1960); Trotsky, Leon, *The History of the Russian Revolution*, trans. by Max Eastman (1932; repr. 1957).

Russian Soviet Federated Socialist Republic

The Russian Soviet Federated Socialist Republic (RSFSR) is the largest and most populous of the 15 constituent republics of the USSR. Its area is 17,074,723 km² (6,592,812 mi²), or 76% of the total Soviet area, and its population is 137,552,000 (1979), or 52% of the USSR's population. The republic's capital is Moscow. The RSFSR, also known as the Russian Federation, is the historical homeland of the ethnic Russians and the dominant political and economic entity of the USSR.

The topography is composed of four clearly defined regions: the Russian plain of European Russia, extending from the Arctic Ocean in the north to the CAUCASUS MOUNTAINS in the south; the URAL MOUNTAINS; the vast swampy and forested West Siberian plain; and the uplands of East Siberia and the Soviet Far East extending to the Pacific.

The climate is continental, with cold winters and warm summers. The annual temperature range increases from west to east, with the coldest spot in the Northern Hemisphere in northeast Siberia. The January average temperature varies from 3° C (37° F) in the southwest to −22° C (−8° F) in the northeast, and July temperatures average 9° C (48° F) in the north and 25° C (77° F) in the southeast. Annual rainfall varies from 610 mm (24 in) in the west to 127 mm (5 in) in the southeast. Precipitation is abundant along the Pacific coast.

The ethnic Russians, who account for 83% of the republic's population, are a Slavic people of the Eastern Orthodox religion. About 83% of all the ethnic Russians in the USSR live in the RSFSR. In addition to Moscow, the largest cities are GORKY, KUIBYSHEV, and LENINGRAD in European Russia; CHELYABINSK and SVERDLOVSK in the Urals; and NOVOSIBIRSK and OMSK in SIBERIA.

The RSFSR has important mineral resources, including coal, petroleum, natural gas, iron ore, and other metals. Some of the USSR's largest manufacturing complexes are centered in the republic's major cities. Agriculture—primarily grain growing (especially wheat) and cattle raising—is concentrated in the steppes. Transportation is oriented toward railroads. Water transport during the warm season takes place on the AMUR, LENA, OB, VOLGA, and YENISEI rivers.

The Russian republic was the first to be formed following the Bolshevik Revolution of 1917. It became known as a federation because it includes many smaller entities for ethnic minorities—16 autonomous republics, 5 autonomous oblasts, and 10 autonomous okrugs.   THEODORE SHABAD

Russian wolfhound: see BORZOI.

Russo-Finnish War

The Russo-Finnish War, also called the Winter War, was waged by the USSR against Finland from Nov. 30, 1939, to Mar. 12, 1940. Following the German invasion of Poland (September 1939), the Kremlin made several far-reaching demands on Finland, including demilitarization of the Mannerheim Line and the cession of islands and a naval base in the Gulf of Finland, part of the Karelian Isthmus, and Petsamo, the Finns' only ice-free port on the Arctic Sea. The Finns refused, and the Russians invaded Finland. Using highly mobile ski troops, the Finns put up an unexpectedly fierce defense. World sympathy went to the Finns; volunteers came from Sweden and Norway; but after two months of bitter fighting, the Russians won supremacy and came to terms with Finland.

By the Treaty of Moscow (Mar. 12, 1940), the Finns ceded to Soviet Russia an area of more than 41,000 km² (16,000 mi²) with a population of about 450,000, territory that included the city of Viipuri (Vyborg) and a naval base at Hanke (Hangö). The Russians also received the right to construct a railroad across Finland to Sweden. In June 1941 hostilities between the USSR and Finland resumed and became part of the general world war.   LOUIS L. SNYDER

Bibliography: Chew, Allen F., *The White Death: The Epic of the Soviet-Finnish Winter War* (1971); Engle, Eloise, and Paananen, Lauri, *The Winter War: The Russo-Finnish Conflict, 1939-1940* (1973); Jakobson, M., *The Diplomacy of the Winter War* (1961); Krosby, P. H., *Finland, Germany and the USSR, 1940-1941* (1968); Paley, A. L., *The Russo-Finnish War* (1973); Tanner, Vaino, *The Winter War: Finland Against Russia, 1939-1940* (1957).

Russo-Japanese War

The Russo-Japanese War (1904-05) was the first conflict in modern times in which an Asian power defeated a European country. The war resulted from the conflicting ambitions of Russia and Japan to control Manchuria and Korea. Fighting began on Feb. 8, 1904, when the Japanese attacked and bottled up the Russian fleet at Port Arthur (now Lü-shun) after Russia, which had occupied Manchuria during the BOXER UPRISING in China, refused to withdraw its troops. Despite the recent construction of the Trans-Siberian Railroad, the Russians were unable to transport adequate troops and supplies to the east and suffered a series of defeats, including the loss of Port Arthur (January 1905) and the Battle of Mukden (February-March 1905).

Finally, in May 1905, a Russian fleet that had sailed from the Baltic was annihilated in the Battle of TSUSHIMA by a Japanese fleet under the command of Adm. TOGO HEIHACHIRO. The belligerents accepted the mediation of U.S. president Theodore Roosevelt, and a peace treaty was signed at Portsmouth, N.H., on Sept. 5, 1905.

Russia acknowledged Japanese predominance in Korea, transferred to Japan its lease of Port Arthur and the Liaotung Peninsula, and ceded the southern half of Sakhalin. Russia's humiliation in the war revealed the weaknesses of the tsarist government and thus helped precipitate the RUSSIAN REVOLUTION OF 1905.

Bibliography: Hoyt, H. P., *The Russo-Japanese War* (1967); Warner, Denis and Peggy, *The Tide at Sunrise: A History of the Russo-Japanese War, 1904-1905* (1975); White, J. A., *The Diplomacy of the Russo-Japanese War* (1964).

Russo-Turkish Wars

Minor Russo-Turkish conflicts date from the mid-16th century, but it was not until the end of the following century that anti-Turkish policy became a constant in Russia's foreign relations. By the beginning of the 18th century, the OTTOMAN EMPIRE was in decline, while Russia was embarking on an ambitious program of territorial expansion. Over the next two centuries Russian leaders, motivated by such ideologies as Orthodox Christianity and PAN-SLAVISM as well as by strategic and economic factors, sought to expand their influence in southeastern Europe and to acquire the Ukraine, Crimea, and the Caucasus region. These goals, and the ambition to control the Black Sea and the Dardanelles, directly threatened Turkish interests and territory and resulted in frequent wars.

Eighteenth-Century Conflicts. PETER I, seeking to end Russia's landlocked isolation, made several assaults on the Ottoman Empire's port of Azov before gaining it by the Treaty of Karlowitz (1699). The Turks, however, with the assistance of the Crimean Tatars, became involved in the Great Northern War (1700–21; see NORTHERN WAR, GREAT) and defeated the armies of Peter in 1711, regaining Azov by the Treaty of Pruth (1711).

The campaigns of 1736–39 marked Russia's first deliberate effort to reach the Black Sea. By the Nissa Treaty (1739), Russia reacquired Azov (but without the right to fortify it) and received trading rights in the Sea of Azov and the Black Sea.

The War of 1768–74 was the first of CATHERINE II's assaults on the Ottoman Empire. Russia's victorious campaign ended with the signing of the Treaty of Kucuk Kainarji (1774), which ultimately became a major source of controversy in Russo-Turkish relations. Russia gained strategic enclaves on the northern Black Sea coast, important commercial and navigation privileges in the Ottoman Empire and Black Sea, and the vaguely defined right to intervene and speak on behalf of the Christian population of the Ottoman Empire.

During the 1780s, Catherine's Oriental Project, designed to expel the Turks from Constantinople, put constant pressure on the Ottoman Empire and led to a Turkish declaration of war in 1787. Russia and Austria fought successfully as allies until the latter signed a separate peace in 1791. The Treaty of Jassy (1792) reaffirmed Russian control of the Crimea (annexed in 1783) and gave Russia lands between the Bug and Dnestr rivers. Russia thus replaced the Ottoman Empire as the dominant power in the Black Sea region.

Turkish forces surrender (December 1877) at Pleven after holding the Bulgarian city against Russian siege for 4½ months. The controversial settlement following the Russian victory, the Treaty of San Stefano, prompted European diplomatic intervention at the Congress of Berlin.

Nineteenth-Century Conflicts. The Russo-Turkish War of 1806–12 erupted during the NAPOLEONIC WARS. Turkey had already made pro-French moves by November 1806, when Russian troops moved into the Danubian principalities of Moldavia and Walachia (in present-day Romania). Encouraged by French victories, Turkey declared war the next month. Fighting continued in an inconclusive fashion until Russia, anticipating Napoleon's invasion, signed the Treaty of Bucharest (1812) with Turkey. The settlement granted Bessarabia to Russia.

Additional fighting grew out of a series of disputes involving Russia's professed rights to protect the Christians in the Balkans and out of issues associated with the Greek revolution against Turkey (1821–29). War began in 1828 and ended with the Treaty of Adrianople (see ADRIANOPLE, TREATY OF; 1829). Acknowledging that Britain, France, and Austria would resist an extensive increase in Russian power, Saint Petersburg relinquished its Balkan conquests but acquired a protectorship in Moldavia and Walachia, domination of the mouth of the Danube River, and control of Georgia, eastern Armenia, and territories in the Caucasus.

British concern about the stability of the Ottoman Empire, quarreling between French-backed Catholics and Russian Orthodox clergy over church rights in the Holy Places of Turkish-ruled Palestine, and Turkish resistance to attempted Russian interference in southeastern Europe led to the outbreak (1853) of the CRIMEAN WAR between Russia and Turkey. Britain and France joined the Turks in 1854. By the Treaty of Paris (1856) Russia was forced to abandon its post-1774 territorial acquisitions, with the exception of the Crimea and most of the eastern conquests.

Turkish efforts to suppress nationalist agitation in the Balkans, particularly in Bulgaria, Serbia, and Bosnia-Hercegovina, led to the Russo-Turkish War of 1877–78. After a difficult military campaign, Russia compelled the Ottoman Empire to sign (1878) the harsh Treaty of San Stefano. Because the extensive rights and territories surrendered by Constantinople greatly augmented Saint Petersburg's strength and thus threatened the European balance of power, the other great powers pressured Russia to attend the Congress of Berlin (see BERLIN, CONGRESS OF). The resulting Treaty of Berlin (1878) reversed some Russian gains but also brought extensive changes to the Balkan peninsula and recognized Russia's acquisition of Batum, Kars, and Ardahan in the Caucasus region and southern Bessarabia.

World War I. Turkey entered WORLD WAR I on the side of Germany and Austria-Hungary with a naval bombardment of Russian Black Sea fortifications on Oct. 29, 1914. Turkish and Russian armies fought each other in the area of the Caucasus Mountains and Armenia. In late 1917, after the Bolshevik Revolution, an armistice was concluded. By the Treaty of BREST-LITOVSK (1918), Russia left the war, and Turkey regained Kars and Ardahan. Batum, also recovered by Turkey in 1918, was returned to Russia in 1921.   S. VICTOR PAPACOSMA

Bibliography: Medlicott, W. N., *The Congress of Berlin and After* (1963); Seton-Watson, Hugh, *The Russian Empire, 1801–1917* (1967); Stavrianos, L. S., *The Balkans Since 1453* (1958).

See also: EASTERN QUESTION.

rust: see DISEASES, PLANT.

rust, metallic: see CORROSION.

rutabaga   [root'-uh-bay-guh]

Rutabaga, *Brassica napus,* a biennial herb of the mustard family, Cruciferae, is harvested annually for its smooth, thick, yellow or white root. The plant is believed to be a cross between the white turnip and the cabbage and to have originated in Europe during the Middle Ages. Rutabaga requires a cool growing climate. It is especially popular in northern Europe, as evidenced by its other common names:

The rutabaga, B. napus, is a large edible root that grows best in cool climates. It is a major crop in northern Europe and Canada, and it is also cultivated in the northern United States.

Swede, Swedish turnip, and Russian turnip. Its culture is similar to that of the TURNIP, although rutabaga takes 4 to 6 weeks longer to mature. The roots have a sweet flavor and store well; if kept cool and at high humidity, they may be used for several months. They are often treated with wax to prevent water loss during storage.

O. A. LORENZ

Ruth, Babe

Babe Ruth remains perhaps the most famous baseball player in history despite the fact that most of his batting records have been eclipsed. Before joining the New York Yankees, Ruth had been an outstanding pitcher for the Boston Red Sox. The Yankees converted him into an outfielder, and Ruth led the team to four world championships (1923, 1927-28, 1932).

George Herman "Babe" Ruth, b. Baltimore, Md., Feb. 6, 1895, d. Aug. 16, 1948, was one of professional baseball's greatest sluggers and probably the best-known player of the 1920s and early 1930s. As a New York Yankee, Ruth took the game out of the dead-ball era, saved it from the Black Sox scandal of 1919, and single-handedly revitalized the sport as the country's national pastime. He teamed with Lou Gehrig to form what became the greatest one-two hitting punch in baseball and was the heart of the 1927 Yankees, a team regarded by some baseball experts as the best in baseball history. Nicknamed the Sultan of Swat, Ruth started his major league career as a left-handed pitcher with the Boston Red Sox in 1914. In 158 games for Boston he compiled a pitching record of 89 victories and 46 losses, including two 20-win seasons—23 wins in 1916 and 24 wins in 1917. He eventually added 5 more wins as a Yankee hurler and ended his pitching career with a 2.28 earned run average; he also had 3 wins against no losses in World Series competition, including one stretch of 29⅔ consecutive scoreless innings. It is for his prowess at bat, not at the mound, however, that Ruth is remembered today. He was sold to New York by Boston following the 1919 season and after a permanent shift to the outfield responded by smashing a record 54 home runs while compiling a .376 bat-

ting average. In 22 seasons with the Red Sox, Yankees, and Boston Braves, Ruth led the league in home runs a record 12 times—including 59 in 1921 and a then-record 60 in 1927. He retired in 1935 with 714 career home runs, a record not surpassed until Hank Aaron's performance in 1974. Ruth was elected to the Baseball Hall of Fame in 1936 as one of the first five charter members.

Bibliography: Creamer, Robert, Babe (1974); Ruth, Claire M., with Bill Slocum, The Babe and I (1959); Ruth, George H., with Bob Considine, The Babe Ruth Story (1948); Smelser, Marshall, The Life That Ruth Built: A Biography (1975); Wagenheim, Kal, Babe Ruth (1974).

Ruth, Book Of

The Book of Ruth is the eighth book of the Old Testament of the BIBLE. A short story, it tells how Ruth, the Moabite widow of a Bethlehemite, with her mother-in-law Naomi's assistance, married an older kinsman Boaz, thereby preserving her deceased husband's posterity and becoming an ancestor of King David. The plot is artfully constructed and exhibits a pronounced belief in the comprehensive but hidden providence of God that works quietly in ordinary events. The legal customs concerning levirate marriage, redemption of property, and gleaning in the fields are relatively ancient, and the vocabulary and style are consistent with a date between 950 and 750 BC. The Davidic genealogy is a secondary appendix, written between 500 and 350 BC, which served to increase the importance of the book for postexilic Jews.

NORMAN K. GOTTWALD

Bibliography: Broch, Yitzhak I., The Book of Ruth (1975); Campbell, Edward F., Ruth (1975); Hals, Ronald M., The Theology of the Book of Ruth (1969).

Ruthenia [roo-thee'-nee-uh]

Ruthenia is a historic name for a region of Eastern Europe, also known as the Carpatho-Ukraine, and now known as the Transcarpathian Oblast in the Ukrainian Soviet Socialist Republic of the USSR. The region is bordered by Romania, Hungary, Czechoslovakia, and Poland. Its main city is Uzhgorod.

The area was part of the Slavic Kievan state in the 10th and 11th centuries but came under Hungarian rule in the 13th century. The inhabitants, Ruthenes, who are ethnically and linguistically related to Ukrainians, attempted to gain a partial autonomy in the 19th century, but their efforts were thwarted by forced Magyarization. Ruthenia was assigned by the Trianon Treaty (1920) to Czechoslovakia. It was occupied by Hungary in 1939 and then was ceded to the USSR in 1945.

ruthenium [roo-thee'-nee-uhm]

Ruthenium is a hard, lustrous, silver gray metal resembling platinum. A chemical element, its symbol is Ru; its atomic number, 44; and its atomic weight, 101.07. Ruthenium was discovered in 1828 by Gottfried Wilhelm Osann, but credit is generally given to Karl Klaus, who was the first to obtain (1844) the pure metal. Ruthenium is not attacked by strong acids, even aqua regia. Its major use is in alloys with platinum and palladium, in which it is an effective hardener. These alloys are mainly used to make jewelry and electrical contacts with a high wear resistance.

Rutherford, Sir Ernest [ruhth'-ur-furd]

Sir Ernest Rutherford, b. near Nelson, New Zealand, Aug. 30, 1871, d. Oct. 19, 1937, perhaps more than any other scientist, formed modern-day views concerning the nature of matter. After distinguishing himself in his undergraduate work in his native New Zealand, Rutherford matriculated to Cambridge University's Cavendish Laboratory, which was at that time under the directorship of Sir Joseph John Thomson, the leading authority on electromagnetic phenomena. Rutherford's early work with Thomson led to investigations of electricity and radiation and eventually to a detailed study of radioactivity.

In 1898, Rutherford obtained the physics professorship at McGill University, Montreal, and soon demonstrated his talents by discovering several radioactive elements. Although

Sir Ernest Rutherford profoundly influenced modern physics by formulating the first explanation of radioactivity. He discovered two basic forms of radioactivity and in 1908 received the Nobel Prize for chemistry for this work. He announced his greatest discovery—the nuclear structure of the atom—in 1911.

others had pioneered the earliest developments in RADIOACTIVITY, Rutherford soon achieved dominance in this field. He found that at least two kinds of radiation, which he labeled alpha and beta, existed. Working with Frederick Soddy in 1902–03, Rutherford identified the phenomenon of radioactive half-life and formulated the still-accepted explanation of radioactivity: each decay of the atoms of radioactive materials signifies the transmutation of a parent element into a daughter, with each type of atom having its own transformation period. This theory stimulated many other scientists, including Rutherford, to order all known radioactive elements into their decay series and to search for any missing members. Rutherford was awarded the 1908 Nobel Prize for chemistry for his work in radioactivity. Moving to the University of Manchester in 1907, Rutherford almost immediately began to examine alpha particles because, since they were relatively massive and of atomic dimensions, he felt that they were the key to understanding the nature of matter. Indeed, Rutherford and Hans Geiger showed (1908) conclusively that alpha particles were doubly charged helium ions.

Rutherford made his greatest discovery in 1909. Shortly after his move to Manchester, he found that a few alpha particles, when bombarding thin metal foils, were deflected from their incident beam through more than 90°. "It was almost as incredible," Rutherford later responded in a now-classic statement, "as if you fired a fifteen-inch shell at a piece of tissue paper and it came back and hit you." Early in 1911 he finally announced his version of the structure of the atom: a very small, tightly packed, charged nucleus sprinkled with opposite charges in the mostly empty surrounding void. The deflected alpha particles were those which had come into close proximity with the nucleus and had rebounded in various oblique directions.

About the time that Rutherford moved (1919) to Cambridge to succeed Thomson as director of the Cavendish Laboratory, he discovered artificial disintegration—the artificial splitting of the atom—a signal discovery that presaged his entry into the field of nuclear physics. Members of his Cavendish team discovered the neutron and the disintegration phenomena produced by artificially accelerated particles.

Rutherford was president (1925–30) of the Royal Society, which had given him its highest award, the Copley Medal, in 1922. Rutherford was knighted in 1914, raised to the peerage in 1931, and awarded the Order of Merit in 1921.

ERICH ROBERT PAUL

Bibliography: Andrade, E. N., *Rutherford and the Nature of the Atom* (1964); Bunge, M., and Shea, W. R., eds., *Rutherford and Physics at the Turn of the Century* (1979); Kelman, Peter, and Stone, A. H., *Ernest Rutherford: Architect of the Atom* (1968).

Rutherford, Joseph Franklin

The second leader of the JEHOVAH'S WITNESSES, Joseph Franklin Rutherford, b. Missouri, Nov. 8, 1869, d. Jan. 8, 1942, was an effective organizer and propagandist. A lawyer by profes-

sion, "Judge" Rutherford wrote about 22 books that further developed the movement's doctrine and attacked other denominations as pious frauds. He led the Jehovah's Witnesses in their attempt to withdraw from political and social entanglements and was imprisoned for a year (1918) for obstructing the war effort by counseling his followers to refuse the draft and not to salute the flag.

rutherfordium: see ELEMENT 104.

rutile   [roo'-teel]

Rutile, a minor ore mineral of titanium, is the most stable of three naturally occurring forms of titanium oxide (TiO_2; see OXIDE MINERALS). Rutile forms prismatic or needlelike crystals (tetragonal system), most commonly red brown in color. Hardness is 6 to $6\frac{1}{2}$, streak is pale brown, luster is adamantine to metallic, and specific gravity is 4.2 to 4.3. Widespread in small amounts, rutile occurs in intermediate basic igneous rocks as a high-temperature accessory mineral, in gneiss and schist, and in high-temperature veins and pegmatite dikes. Because it is highly resistant to chemical and physical weathering, it is common in placer deposits.

Rutile, a widespread titanium dioxide mineral, is commonly found with feldspar, hematite, and quartz. Crystals are generally prismatic. Knee-shaped twin crystals are often observed. Colors vary from red to brown to black, depending on the amount of iron impurities that are usually present. Rutile is a source of titanium metal and of white titanium-dioxide pigments for use in paints and fibers.

Rutland   [ruht'-luhnd]

Rutland is a city in western Vermont, on Otter Creek, between the Green and Taconic mountains. The seat of Rutland County, it is Vermont's second largest city, with a population (1980) of 18,436. In addition to its important tourist industry, Rutland's economy is based on diversified manufacturing. Nearby marble quarries are also important. Rutland is the headquarters of the Green Mountain National Forest. Settled by New Englanders in 1770, the city was named for Rutland, Mass. During the American Revolution two forts, Rutland and Ranger, were built in the area. From 1784 to 1804, Rutland was Vermont's capital. Quarrying and the arrival of the railroad resulted in Rutland's becoming the largest city in the state by 1880.

Rutledge, Ann   [ruht'-luhj]

According to Abraham Lincoln's biographer William Henry HERNDON, Lincoln fell in love with Ann Rutledge, b. c.1813, d. Aug. 25, 1835, the daughter of the innkeeper at New Salem, Ill. She was engaged to Lincoln's friend John McNamar, who was mysteriously absent from 1832 until after Ann's sudden death from brain fever. Herndon interpreted Lincoln's subsequent grief as proof of a romance, an assessment that historians find unsubstantiated.

Rutledge, John

A signer of the U.S. Constitution, John Rutledge, b. Charleston, S.C., September 1739, d. July 18, 1800, was a leading southern aristocrat who supported the colonies' struggle for independence. He served (1765) as a delegate to the Stamp Act Congress from South Carolina, where during the American Revolution he was governor, and represented that state at the Continental Congress (1774–75, 1782–83). He was designated (1787) as South Carolina's delegate to the Constitutional Convention. Rutledge was appointed (1789) to the U.S. Supreme Court by President George Washington but resigned (1791) to become chief justice of the South Carolina Supreme Court. Washington appointed (1795) Rutledge chief justice of the U.S. Supreme Court—a post at which he presided for 1 month—but Rutledge was so vehemently opposed to the recently approved Jay's Treaty that the Senate refused to confirm him.

Bibliography: Barry, Richard H., *Mr. Rutledge of South Carolina* (1942; repr. 1971).

Ruusbroec, Jan van: see RUYSBROECK, JOHN.

Ruwenzori [roo-wuhn-zohr'-ee]

The Ruwenzori Range lies north of the equator in east central Africa, along the border between Uganda and Zaire. About 130 km (80 mi) long and up to about 50 km (30 mi) wide, it rises to its maximum height of 5,119 m (16,795 ft) at Mount Stanley's Margherita Peak. The range, a huge faulted block, consists of ancient metamorphic rocks. Abundant rainfall contributes to the growth of forests, grasslands, and cultivated crops. The mountaintops are always snow-covered. The Ruwenzori Range is thought to be the legendary "Mountains of the Moon," erroneously described by Ptolemy as the source of the Nile River.

Ruysbroeck, John [roys'-brook]

The Flemish devotional writer John Ruysbroeck, or Jan van Ruusbroec, b. 1293, d. Dec. 2, 1381, was one of the forerunners of the religious movement called the *devotio moderna* or "modern devotion," within the Roman Catholic church. His treatises *The Seven Steps of the Ladder of Spiritual Love* (n.d.; Eng. trans., 1944) and *The Spiritual Espousals* (1350; Eng. trans., 1952) exerted a strong influence on such mystics as Groote and on later Dutch, German, and English mysticism.
R. P. MEIJER

Bibliography: Mommaers, Paul, *The Land Within*, trans. by N. D. Smith (1976); Wautier d'Aygalliers, Alfred, *Ruysbroeck the Admirable* (1925; repr. 1969).

Ruysch, Rachel [roys]

A leading still-life painter of the baroque period, Rachel Ruysch, 1664–1750, was noted for her brilliantly colored pictures of flower arrangements. She often varied these compositions with butterflies or, in outdoor settings, with other insects, reptiles, or small mammals. After studying with the Dutch flower painter Willem van Aelst, Ruysch developed into a successful professional artist who combined marriage and children with a career. In 1708 she became court painter to the elector palatine Johann Wilhelm van Pfalz, working until 1716 at his court in Düsseldorf.
ELEANOR TUFTS

Bibliography: Grant, Maurice H., *Rachel Ruysch 1664–1750* (1956).

Ruyter, Michiel Adriaanszoon de [royt'-ur]

One of the greatest naval commanders in Dutch history, Michiel Adriaanszoon de Ruyter, b. Mar. 24, 1607, d. Apr. 29, 1676, brought the United Provinces repeated and crucial victories during the second and third ANGLO-DUTCH WARS. He received much of his early experience in the merchant marine and fought under Maarten Tromp (see TROMP family) in the first Anglo-Dutch war (1652–54), becoming vice-admiral in 1653. In the second war (1665–67), his triumphs enabled the United Provinces to achieve an advantageous peace with England. His repeated victories over the larger combined forces

of England and France in the third war (1672–74) saved his country from invasion. He died at Syracuse, Sicily, of wounds suffered in battle.
HERBERT H. ROWEN

Bibliography: Blok, Petrus J., *Life of Admiral de Ruyter*, trans. by G. J. Renier (1933; repr. 1975); Rogers, P. G., *The Dutch in the Medway* (1970).

Ružička, Leopold [roo'-zheech-kah]

Leopold Ružička, b. Sept. 13, 1887, d. Sept. 26, 1976, was a Croatian-born Swiss organic chemist who synthesized many-membered ring compounds and sex hormones, for which he shared the 1939 Nobel Prize for chemistry with Adolf Butenandt. Ružička found that civetone, an odorous substance from the civet cat, is a 17-membered ring ketone, and muscone, from the musk deer, is a 15-membered ring ketone (see CYCLIC COMPOUNDS). These studies were important because, until that time, rings higher than 8 members were theorized to be too unstable to exist. Ružička also did extensive work on TERPENES and synthesized the male sex hormones androsterone and testosterone. His patent for the preparation of testosterone from cholesterol earned him a fortune.
ROBERT J. PARADOWSKI

Rwanda [ru-ahn'-dah]

The landlocked republic of Rwanda, in east central Africa, is bounded on the north by Uganda, on the east by Tanzania, on the south by Burundi, and on the west by Zaire. Principally an agricultural and pastoral society, Rwanda achieved independence from Belgium in 1962.

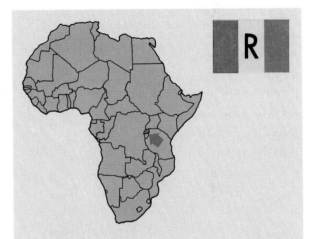

REPUBLIC OF RWANDA

LAND. Area: 26,338 km² (10,169 mi²). Capital and largest city: Kigali (1981 est. pop., 156,650).
PEOPLE. Population (1986 est.): 6,489,000; density (1986 est.): 246 persons per km² (638 per mi²). Distribution (1985): 5% urban, 95% rural. Annual growth (1983): 3.3%. Official languages: French, Kinyarwanda. Major religions: Roman Catholicism, traditional religions, Protestantism, Islam.
EDUCATION AND HEALTH. Literacy (1980): 50% of adult population. Universities (1987): 1. Hospital beds (1983): 9,015. Physicians (1983): 258. Life expectancy (1983): women—48.0; men—45.0. Infant mortality (1985): 102 per 1,000 live births.
ECONOMY. GDP (1984): $1.6 billion; $257 per capita. Labor distribution (1985): agriculture—91%; government and services—7%; industry and commerce—2%. Foreign trade (1984 est.): imports—$204.9 million; exports—$147.9 million; principal trade partners—Belgium-Luxembourg, Kenya, Japan, West Germany. Currency: 1 Rwanda franc = 100 centimes.
GOVERNMENT. Type: one-party state. Legislature: National Development Council. Political subdivisions: 10 prefectures.
COMMUNICATIONS. Railroads (1987): none. Roads (1983): 7,900 km (4,910 miles) total. Major ports: none. Major airfields: 2.

The plains surrounding Lake Bulera rise abruptly to form the slopes of Muhavura (background). This peak is the third highest (4,127 m/13,541 ft) of the inactive volcanoes of the Virunga range, part of the East African Rift system in the northwestern part of the country.

LAND, PEOPLE, AND ECONOMY

Rwanda lies on the great East African plateau, and the average elevation is more than 1,525 m (5,000 ft). The highest point in the country, Mount Karlsimbi, rises to 4,507 m (14,787 ft). The rich soil is especially fertile in the alluvial valleys and volcanic northwest. The average temperature is about 19° C (66° F), and rainfall averages about 1,143 mm (45 in) per year. Lake Kivu in the northwest drains into Lake TANGANYIKA, and the Kagera River drains much of the eastern border. The Savanna highlands, which make up most of the Central plateau, are mostly badly eroded and deforested grassland. Wildlife is preserved in Kagera National Park and in Volcano National Park, known for its rare mountain gorillas. Rwanda has small amounts of tin, beryl, and tungsten.

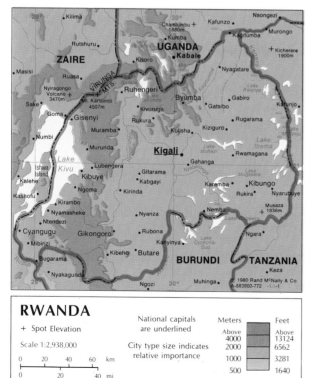

RWANDA

+ Spot Elevation
National capitals are underlined
Scale 1:2,938,000
City type size indicates relative importance

Meters	Feet
Above 4000	Above 13124
2000	6562
1000	3281
500	1640

0 20 40 60 km
0   20   40 mi

Three ethnic groups—Hutu (90%), TUTSI, and Twa (see PYGMY)—make up Rwanda's indigenous population. The official languages are Kinyarwanda and French. Nearly 70% of the inhabitants are Christian, mostly Roman Catholics. The remainder of the population practice traditional religions and Islam. KIGALI, the capital, is the major city.

Education is free for children aged 7 to 15. About 80% of the primary schools and most of the secondary schools are run by Christian missions. The National University of Rwanda was founded at Butare in 1963.

More than 85% of Rwandese engage in subsistence agriculture (bananas, sweet potatoes, cassava, and livestock) or cash-crop agriculture (coffee, tea, and pyrethrum); about 40% of the land is under cultivation. Although the country is generally able to feed itself except in years of drought, rapid population growth is placing increasing pressure on the land. Manufacturing employs only a small percentage of the labor force and accounts for about 20% of the GDP. Industries include coffee, tea, flour, cigar, beer, and soft-drink production and the manufacture of light consumer goods. Mining of tin and tungsten ores accounts for less than 1% of the GDP. Imports exceed exports in most years.

GOVERNMENT AND HISTORY

According to the constitution of 1978, Rwanda is a republic with a presidential system. The ruling military junta, however, holds all key positions. Maj. Gen. Juvenal Habyarimana has been president since 1973. The sole legal political party is the National Revolutionary Movement for Development.

Rwanda developed from modest beginnings into a highly centralized kingdom, with the pastoral Tutsi minority dominating the agricultural Hutu majority. The area was a German protectorate (1899–1916) and subsequently was part of Belgian-controlled RUANDA-URUNDI.

In 1959 the Hutus revolted against the Tutsi aristocracy, driving many Tutsis out of the country. In 1961, Rwanda declared its independence, which was not internationally recognized until July 1, 1962. Since independence Rwanda's history has been marked by severe ethnic conflicts. Habyarimana took power in a bloodless coup on July 5, 1973, during such a crisis. He has since been elected, running unopposed, to successive five-year terms.   G. N. UZOIGWE

Bibliography: American University, *Area Handbook for Rwanda* (1969); Best, Alan C., and Blij, Harm, *African Survey* (1977); Lemarchand, René, *Rwanda and Burundi* (1970).

Ryan, Cornelius

The Irish-American journalist and historian Cornelius Ryan, b. Dublin, June 5, 1920, d. Nov. 23, 1974, wrote three best-selling chronicles of World War II—*The Longest Day: June 6, 1944* (1959; film, 1962), *The Last Battle* (1966), and *A Bridge Too Far* (1974; film, 1977). With Kelley Frank Raymond, he wrote the biography *MacArthur: Man of Action* (1950) and *Star-Spangled Mikado* (1947), a history of Japan during the occupation.   CHARLOTTE D. SOLOMON

Bibliography: Ryan, Cornelius and Kathryn, *A Private Battle* (1979).

Ryan, Nolan

The right-handed baseball pitcher Lynn Nolan Ryan, b. Refugio, Tex., Jan. 31, 1947, is known primarily for his blazing fastball and his ability to strike out batters. Ryan's major league records include the following: most strikeouts in a season (383); most games pitched with 10 or more strikeouts, both for a season (23) and career (174); and most career no-hit games thrown (5). He also has, through 1987, 4,547 career strikeouts, the most in baseball history, and a won-lost record of 261–242. Ryan has played his long career for 3 teams—the New York Mets (1966–71), California Angels (1972–78), and Houston Astros (1979–   ).

Bibliography: Ryan, Nolan, with Bill Libby, *The Other Game* (1977).

Ryazan   [ree-ah-zahn']

Ryazan is the capital of Ryazan oblast in the Russian Soviet Federated Socialist Republic of the USSR. It is situated on the right bank of the Oka River, 185 km (115 mi) southeast of Moscow. The city has a population of 453,000 (1979). Ryazan was largely bypassed by the Soviet industrialization drive during the 1930s but expanded greatly after the 1950s with the building of large new industrial facilities. One of central Russia's largest petroleum refineries and a chemical fiber manufacturing plant, producing viscose rayon, are located there.

Ryazan is one of the oldest of Russian cities, first mentioned in historical chronicles dating from 1095. In the winter of 1237–38, Mongols sacked the city while attempting to reach Novgorod. Ryazan was the center of an early Russian principality in the 14th century and was absorbed into the Moscow-dominated Russian state in 1520. The 14th-century Uspensky Cathedral and the late-15th-century Archangel Cathedral have been preserved within the city's former kremlin, or fortress.   THEODORE SHABAD

Rydberg, Abraham Viktor   [rood'-bairg]

A Swedish poet, novelist, and scholar, Abraham Viktor Rydberg, b. Dec. 18, 1828, d. Sept. 21, 1895, began his career by writing short stories for a small-town newspaper. His historical novels owed a debt to Sir Walter Scott, but he also used them as vehicles to express his opposition to the dogmatism of the church. *Bibelns Lära Om Kristus* (The Bible's Teaching on Christ, 1862) introduced Swedish readers to modern biblical criticism. His philosophical lyrics are collected in *Dikter* (Poems, 1882) and *Nya Dikter* (New Poems, 1891).

Rydberg, Johannes Robert

A Swedist physicist and mathematician Johannes Robert Rydberg, b. Nov. 8, 1854, d. Dec. 28, 1919, derived quantitative relationships for the vast amount of spectroscopic data that had accumulated in the late 19th century. In the process, he introduced clarifying terminology and suggested that chemical elements be organized in the periodic table by atomic number rather than atomic weight. Rydberg's faith that spectral studies could assist in a theoretical understanding of the atom and its chemical properties was justified in 1913 by the work of Niel Bohr (see HYDROGEN SPECTRUM). An important spectroscopic constant based on a hypothetical atom of infinite mass is called the Rydberg (R) in his honor (see QUANTUM MECHANICS; SPECTRUM).   RICHARD HIRSH

Ryder, Albert Pinkham   [ry'-dur]

Albert Pinkham Ryder, b. New Bedford, Mass., Mar. 19, 1848, d. Mar. 28, 1917, was the foremost American visionary painter. He spent most of his life in New York City, where he settled about 1870. Until 1880 his subjects were bucolic and seemingly innocent—sheep in a meadow, a cow at pasture, horses in a stable—but even in these scenes Ryder generates a sense of the haunted. After 1880 the impasto is heavier—applied, sometimes over several years, in layer upon layer of paint; the forms are at once simplified and distorted; the aura of unreality is heightened.

Ryder frequently based his pictures on themes from the Old and New Testaments as well as from the works of Geoffrey Chaucer, William Shakespeare, and Richard Wagner. All nature is energized, reflecting the human condition. In *Jonah* (c.1890; National Collection, Washington, D.C.) most of the canvas is given over to a depiction of the churning sea; this mirrors the turmoil within Jonah, who is flailing about at the bottom of the picture. During this period several versions appeared of the lone boat set upon the boundless sea, an image probably suggested by memories of the whalers of New Bedford.

Ryder selected broad shapes and luminous colors that would serve to express his deepest feelings. His late works reflect his increasing isolation and eccentricity, as is evident in *Death on a Pale Horse* or *The Race Track* (c.1910; Cleveland Museum of Art).   ABRAHAM A. DAVIDSON

Bibliography: Davidson, Abraham A., *The Eccentrics and Other American Visionary Painters* (1978); Goodrich, Lloyd, *Albert P. Ryder* (1959).

The American romantic visionary Albert Pinkham Ryder began Siegfried and the Rhine Maidens *(1888-91) after seeing a performance of Wagner's opera* Götterdämmerung. *(Andrew Mellon Collection, National Gallery of Art, Washington, D.C.)*

rye

The cereal grain rye, *Secale cereale* of the grass family, Gramineae, is closely related to wheat and is grown as a bread grain, as a livestock feed, and for distillation into grain alcohol spirits. The plant is also useful as a green manure and for hay, straw, and pasturage. The most winter-hardy of the cereals, rye does well on poor soils and in cool climates that are not hospitable to wheat cultivation. It is grown primarily in northern and eastern Europe, including the USSR. The crop is of minor importance in the United States, where it is grown principally in South Dakota and Minnesota.

The cultivation of rye began long after that of wheat and barley, perhaps as late as the first millennium BC. Although rye flour lacks the glutenous proteins that make wheat dough

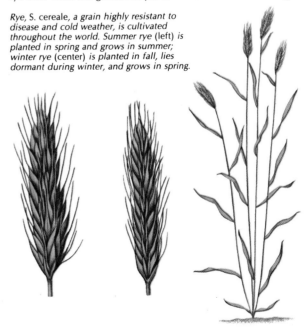

Rye, S. cereale, *a grain highly resistant to disease and cold weather, is cultivated throughout the world. Summer rye (left) is planted in spring and grows in summer; winter rye (center) is planted in fall, lies dormant during winter, and grows in spring.*

elastic enough for leavening, bread made from rye was once the principal type eaten in wheat-poor areas of Europe, and rye still is used, either by itself or in a wheat blend, for over half the bread made in Germany and for a large proportion of the bread in other European countries. Bread made from rye is heavier, denser, and usually darker than wheat bread.

The rye plant has slim seed spikes and long beards and produces dark grains. Rye flowers, unlike those of wheat, barley, and oats, are self-sterile and must be cross-pollinated by the wind. The methods for sowing, harvesting, and milling rye are similar to those used for the other cereals. In the United States approximately 60 percent of rye production is used for feed, 25 percent for food, and 15 percent for seed and industrial products.

ERGOT, a toxic fungus (*Claviceps purpures*), frequently infects rye kernels. When eaten by livestock or humans the fungus can cause hallucinations and various, sometimes deadly, illnesses. Epidemics of ergot-caused disease were frequent in Europe during medieval times. Modern cylinder or disc separators remove most infected kernels.   J. A. SHELLENBERGER

Bibliography: Kent, N. L., *Technology of Cereals*, 3d ed. (1983); Leonard, Warren H., and Martin, John H., *Cereal Crops* (1963); Matz, Samuel A., ed., *Cereal Science* (1969).

rye whiskey: see WHISKEY.

Ryle, Gilbert [ryl]

The philosopher Gilbert Ryle, b. Aug. 19, 1900, d. Oct. 6, 1976, is one of the better-known figures of the British "ordinary language" movement (see ANALYTIC AND LINGUISTIC PHILOSOPHY). He was educated at Queen's College, Oxford, later became a tutor in philosophy at Christ Church, and was eventually given the post of Waynflete professor of metaphysics and philosophy at Oxford. He was also a fellow of Magdalen College, Oxford, and served (1947–71) as the editor of the periodical *Mind*. Ryle's most important book, *The Concept of Mind* (1949), has been widely read and discussed. In it he analyzes "mental concepts." These work well in everyday life, but can be puzzling when an individual reflects upon them philosophically. Ryle argues that the individual must "map" various mental concepts and determine their position in relation to other concepts. He challenges the Cartesian distinction between body and mind, claiming instead that the mind is the form or organizing principle of the body. In *Dilemmas* (1954), Ryle considers seemingly irreconcilable propositions (for example, free will versus fatalism) and attempts to show that in each case the only conflict is conceptual-linguistic, not genuine.   E. D. KLEMKE

Bibliography: Addis, Laird, and Lewis, Douglas, *Moore and Ryle: Two Ontologies* (1965); Lyons, William, *Gilbert Ryle* (1980); Wood, O. P., and Pitcher, G., eds., *Ryle: A Collection of Critical Essays* (1970).

Ryle, Sir Martin

The English astronomer Sir Martin Ryle, b. Sept. 27, 1918, d. Oct. 14, 1984, received the 1974 Nobel Prize for physics, with Antony HEWISH, for his work on the technique of aperture synthesis in RADIO ASTRONOMY. A graduate of Oxford (1942), Ryle served as professor of radio astronomy at the University of Cambridge from 1959 to 1982, and from 1972 to 1982 he bore the title of Astronomer Royal.

Rymer, Thomas [ry'-mur]

Thomas Rymer, b. c.1641, d. Dec. 14, 1713, was an English historian and literary critic. Appointed historiographer royal in 1692, he started an immense collection of public documents—under the title *Foedera* (1704–35)—dealing with England's foreign relations from the early 12th century to the mid-17th. As a critic, Rymer followed the French classical tradition, attacking Shakespeare's *Othello* in *A Short View of Tragedy* (1692). He also wrote a play of his own, the unsuccessful tragedy *Edgar* (1678).

Rysbrack, Michael [ris'-brak]

A native of Belgium, John Michael Rysbrack, b. June 1694, d. Jan. 8, 1770, became one of England's leading sculptors during the first half of the 18th century. Having been trained in the classical tradition, he went to England in 1720 and worked under the architect James Gibbs. Rysbrack produced a large number of monuments, the most famous being his statue *Hercules* (1747; Stourhead, Wiltshire, England). He also executed portrait busts, always showing a strong feeling for his sitter's character.   MALCOLM CORMACK

Bibliography: Webb, Marjorie Isabel, *Michael Rysbrack Sculptor* (1954); Whinney, Margaret, *Sculpture in Britain 1530–1830* (1964).

Ryukyu Islands [ree-oo'-kue]

The Japanese Ryukyu Islands (also known as the Luchu Islands) comprise an archipelago extending from Kyushu, southernmost of the Japanese main islands, south for about 1,050 km (650 mi) to Taiwan. The islands compose Okinawa prefecture. The 143 islands and islets, separating the East China Sea from the Pacific Ocean, are divided into three main groups: the Amami Islands in the north, the Okinawa Islands in the center, and the Sakishima Islands in the south. The islands have a population of 1,118,000 (1981 est.). OKINAWA is the largest and most populous island of the Ryukyus and contains the capital and largest city, Naha, a major seaport. The economy is basically agricultural; sugar and pineapples are exported.

Originally an independent kingdom, the Ryukyus were conquered by the Chinese in the 14th century and by the Japanese in the 17th century; they were finally incorporated into Japan in 1879. The scene of one of the bloodiest campaigns of World War II, Okinawa was captured by U.S. troops in 1945. The islands were returned (1972) to Japan, although the United States retained the right to operate military facilities on Okinawa.

Ryumin, Valery [ri-oo'-min]

The Soviet civilian cosmonaut Valery Viktorovich Ryumin, b. Aug. 16, 1939, together with his fellow crew member Leonid Popov, set (1980) a new space endurance record of 185 days, only one year after Ryumin had set a record of 175 days with fellow cosmonaut Vladimir LYAKHOV. Ryumin graduated from the Moscow forestry school's electronics department and served as a Soviet army tank commander before becoming an aerospace engineer and then (1973) a cosmonaut. He was the flight engineer for the *Soyuz 25* spacecraft (Oct. 9–11, 1977), which failed to dock with the *Salyut 6* space station.

Ryumin substituted for the ailing cosmonaut Valentin Lebedev in the 1980 endurance mission. Launched aboard *Soyuz 35* on Apr. 9, 1980, he and Popov docked with *Salyut 6* and the automated *Progress 8* cargo craft the following day. During their residence in *Salyut 6*, the cosmonauts were resupplied by Progress crafts 9, 10, and 11. They also were visited by several teams of cosmonauts, one of which used their *Soyuz 35* to return to earth. They made their own descent on Oct. 11, 1980, in the *Soyuz 37* left behind by Viktor Gorbatko and Vietnamese cosmonaut Pham Tuan.   JAMES OBERG

Bibliography: Baker, D., *The History of Manned Space Flight* (1982).

Ryun, Jim [ry'-uhn]

James Ronald Ryun, b. Wichita, Kans., Apr. 29, 1947, was an American track star known for his record-breaking runs. Ryun, the first high school student to run a mile in less than 4 min, reached the semifinals in the 1,500-m race in the 1964 Olympics. In 1965, as a sophomore at the University of Kansas, he set a world record by running a mile in 3 min 55.3 sec. The following year Ryun received the Sullivan Award as the outstanding athlete in the United States. In 1967 he set two new world records: he lowered his mile time to 3 min 51.1 sec, and he set a 1,500-m record at 3 min 33.1 sec. In the 1968 Olympic Games, Ryun was beaten by Kip Keino in the 1,500-m competition.